THIRD EDITION

STRATEGY
Process, Content, Context

AN INTERNATIONAL PERSPECTIVE

BOB DE WIT Maastricht School of Management, The Netherlands

RON MEYER Rotterdam School of Management, Erasmus University, The Netherlands

THOMSON
™

Australia • Canada • Mexico • Singapore • Spain • United Kingdom • United States

THOMSON

Strategy: Process, Content, Context – 3rd Edition

Copyright © 2004 Bob de Wit and Ron Meyer

The Thomson logo is a registered trademark used herein under licence.

For more information, contact Thomson Learning, High Holborn House, 50–51 Bedford Row, London, WC1R 4LR or visit us on the World Wide Web at: http://www.thomsonlearning.co.uk

British Library Cataloguing-in-Publication Data
A catalogue record for this book is available from the British Library

ISBN 1-86152-964-3

First edition published by West Publishing Company
Second edition published 1998 by International Thomson Publishing Business Press
Reprinted 1998 and 1999
Reprinted 2001 and 2002 by Thomson Learning
Third Edition published 2004 by Thomson Learning

Typeset by J&L Composition, Filey, North Yorkshire

Printed in Italy by G. Canale & C.

BRIEF CONTENTS

CONTENTS

SECTION i

STRATEGY   1

SECTION ii

STRATEGY PROCESS   49

SECTION

iv

STRATEGY CONTEXT   419

8 THE INDUSTRY CONTEXT   421

9 THE ORGANIZATIONAL CONTEXT   477

SECTION

V

PURPOSE 589

SECTION vi

CASES 645

LIST OF EXHIBITS

ACKNOWLEDGEMENTS

It could be said of me that in this book I have only made up a bunch of other men's flowers, providing of my own only the string that ties them together.
Montaigne (1533–1592); French moralist and essayist

As Montaigne, we have created a book that is a 'bouquet of other people's flowers' – we have brought together many of the leading ideas, concepts, frameworks and theories in the field of strategic management and have arranged them in a way that each complements the 'beauty' and 'fragrance' of the others. While we are proud of the job we have done in selecting the most attractive flowers and arranging them into a lush bouquet, we are aware that we are much indebted to the hundreds of authors whose contribution to the topic of strategy we have used to compose this book. In particular, we are very grateful to the writers whose work we have been allowed to reprint here – without their cooperation, and the permission of their publishers, we would not have been able to create the structure of the book as we had envisioned.

Even when it comes to the string tying the flowers together, we have received considerable support, which should not go unmentioned. During the ten years since the publication of the first edition, many colleagues and readers from around the world have provided valuable feedback, leading to considerable changes in the book. We have also benefited from the comments and suggestions received from our students and executive program participants, as we have had the opportunity to present our ideas at universities and companies in dozens of countries around the world. To all of these people, we would like to express our gratitude – and we would like to encourage all to keep on contributing towards the next edition.

We started the process of creating this new edition in the autumn of 2002, by organizing a Strategic Management Society mini-conference in Rotterdam entitled 'Plurality, Perspectives and Paradoxes in Strategy', at which a number of topics were explored that are central to our approach to strategy. We would like to thank the participants of this conference, and in particular Charles Hampden-Turner, Anne Huff, Barry Johnson, Marianne Lewis, John McGee, Jane McKenzie, Andrew Pettigrew, Rob van Tulder and Richard Whittington for their inputs and inspiration.

Following the conference, we were able to find a number of colleagues willing to participate in reviewing chapter rewrites and in supplying material for short cases. We greatly appreciate the contribution of the following team:

Ard Pieter de Man

Peer Ederer

Wolter Lemstra

Marc Padberg

Martin Rademakers

Winfried Ruigrok

Rob van Tulder

Leonard Zijlstra

Special mention is due for Martin Rademakers, who was also our key support in selecting the 22 long cases in this book. We would also like to highlight the essential role of our two research assistants, Casper van der Veen and Geert van Deth, who spent months doing anything and everything needed to ensure that the third edition would be completed on time. And in the background, of course, always our office manager, Karin Feteris, making sure the place didn't fall apart in the meantime.

Finally, we also want to thank the team at Thomson Learning and Southwestern for working so hard with us at creating a truly global book. While many books are written for a national audience and then exported to other countries, Thomson/Southwestern has shared our ambition to create a book suited to readers all around the world. In particular we would like to thank our former editor, Anna Faherty, who pleasantly, but unrelentingly, hounded us to start on the third edition, and our current co-editors, Geraldine Lyons in London and John Szilagyi in Mason, Ohio, who have successfully taken up the challenge of coordinating this book project across so many national borders. And last, but not least, we would like to thank the man who got us started as 'flower arrangers' ten years ago, our first editor, David Godden, who has now retired to a life of growing real flowers in New Zealand.

PREFACE

Not only is there an art in knowing a thing, but also a certain art in teaching it.
Cicero (106–43 BC); Roman orator and statesman

What is a good strategy for teaching and learning about the topic of strategy? Judging by the similarity of the strategic management textbooks currently available, there seems to be a general consensus among business professors on the best approach to this task. It is not an exaggeration to say that strategic management education is dominated by a strong *industry recipe* (Spender, 1989). Almost all textbooks share the following characteristics:

- Few differing perspectives. Only a limited number of perspectives and theories are presented, often as accepted knowledge, from which prescriptions can easily be derived.

- Step-by-step structure. A step-by-step strategic planning approach is used as the books' basic structure, to decompose strategy-making into a number of simple sequential activities.

- No primary material. The key academic articles and books on strategy are reworked into the textbook authors' own words to create consistent and easily digestible pieces of text.

- Domestic orientation. Despite fancy subtitles referring to globalization, the choice of perspectives, theories, examples and cases are heavily biased towards the textbook authors' own domestic context.

It is interesting to speculate on the causes of this isomorphism in the 'strategic management education' industry. Institutionalists would probably point to the need for legitimacy, which leads textbook authors to conform to widely accepted practices and to avoid major innovations (e.g. Abrahamson, 1996; Powell and DiMaggio, 1991). Social psychologists would likely suggest that over the years shared cognitive structures have developed within the strategic management community, which makes the prevailing educational paradigm difficult to challenge (e.g. Smircich and Stubbart, 1985; Walsh, 1995). Theorists taking a new institutional economics perspective would probably interpret the uniformity of strategic management textbooks as a form of lock-in, caused by the large investments already made by publishers and business professors based on a shared educational 'standard' (e.g. Arthur, 1996; David, 1994). Whatever the reason, it is striking that the character of strategic management textbooks has not significantly changed since the founding of the field.

But what would strategy education look like if educational orthodoxy would be actively challenged and the industry rules were broken? How might strategy be taught if the current constraints were thrown aside and the teaching process was boldly reinvented? In short, what would happen if some strategic thinking were applied to the teaching of strategy?

During the last 15 years, we have continuously asked ourselves these questions. Our conclusion is that all four of the above features of current strategic management textbooks greatly inhibit the development of independent strategic thinkers and therefore urgently need to be changed. It is for this reason that we decided to create a book ourselves, with the following characteristics:

- Multiple strategy perspectives. A broad range of differing, and often conflicting, perspectives and theories are presented, reflecting the richness of current debate among academics and practitioners in the field of strategic management.

- Issue-based structure. An issue-based book structure is used, with each chapter focusing on a key strategic issue, which is discussed from a variety of angles, leaving readers to draw their own conclusions.

- Original readings. A large number of original articles and book chapters are included, to offer readers a first-hand account of the ideas and theories of influential strategy thinkers.

- International orientation. A strong international orientation is at the core of this book, as reflected in the choice of topics, theories, readings, examples and cases.

In the following paragraphs the rationale behind the choice for these characteristics will be explained. Following this discussion, the structure of the book and the ways in which it can be employed will be further clarified.

USING MULTIPLE STRATEGY PERSPECTIVES

Education, n. That which discloses to the wise and disguises from the foolish their lack of understanding.
The Devil's Dictionary, Ambrose Bierce (1842–1914); American columnist

What should students learn in a strategic management or business policy course? It seems an obvious question to start with, especially for professors who teach about objective setting. Yet, in practice, the large majority of strategic management textbooks do not make their teaching objectives explicit. These books implicitly assume that the type of teaching objectives and teaching methods needed for a strategic management course do not radically differ from any other subject – basically, strategy can be taught in the same way as accounting or baking cookies. Their approach is based on the following teaching objectives:

- Knowledge. To get the student to clearly understand and memorize all of the major 'ingredients'.

- Skills. To develop the student's ability to follow the detailed 'recipes'.

- Attitude. To instill a disciplined frame of mind, whereby the student automatically attempts to approach all issues by following established procedures.

This is an important way of teaching – it is how all of us were taught to read and write, do arithmetic and drive a car. This type of teaching can be referred to as *instructional*, because students are told what to know and do. The instructor is the authority who has all of the necessary knowledge and skills, and it is his/her role to transfer these to the students. Thus the educational emphasis is on communicating know-how and ensuring that students are able to repeat what they have heard. Students are not encouraged to question the knowledge they receive – on the contrary, it is the intention of instructional teaching to get students to absorb an accepted body of knowledge and to follow established recipes. The student should *accept*, *absorb* and *apply*.

However, while instructing students on a subject and programming their behavior might be useful in such areas as mathematics, cooking and karate, we believe it is not a very good way of teaching strategy. In our opinion, a strategic management professor should have a different set of teaching objectives:

- Knowledge. To encourage the understanding of the many, often conflicting, schools of thought and to facilitate the gaining of insight into the assumptions, possibilities and limitations of each set of theories.

- Skills. To develop the student's ability to define strategic issues, to critically reflect on existing theories, to creatively combine or develop conceptual models where necessary and to flexibly employ theories where useful.

- Attitude. To instill a critical, analytical, flexible and creative mindset, which challenges organizational, industry and national paradigms and problem-solving recipes.

In other words, strategy professors should want to achieve the opposite of instructors – not to instill recipes, but rather to encourage students to dissect and challenge recipes. Strategic thinking is in its very essence questioning, challenging, unconventional and innovative. These aspects of strategic thinking cannot be transferred through instruction. A critical, analytical, flexible and creative state of mind must be developed by practicing these very qualities. Hence, a learning situation must encourage students to be critical, must challenge them to be analytical, must force them to be mentally flexible and must demand creativity and unconventional thinking. Students cannot be instructed to be strategists, but must learn the art of strategy by thinking and acting themselves – they must *discuss*, *deliberate* and *do*. The role of the professor is to create the circumstances for this learning. We therefore refer to this type of teaching as *facilitative*.

This teaching philosophy has led to a radical departure from traditional textbooks that focus on knowledge transfer and application skills, and that have often been written from the perspective of just one paradigm. In this book the fundamental differences of opinion within strategic management are not ignored or smoothed over. On the contrary, it is the mission of this book to expose students to the many, often conflicting, perspectives in the field of strategy. It is our experience that the challenge of comparing and reconciling rivaling strategy perspectives sharpens the mind of the 'apprentice' strategists. Throwing students into the midst of the central strategy debates, while simultaneously demanding that they apply their thinking to practical strategic problems, is the most likely way to enhance the qualities of creativity, flexibility, independence and analytical depth that students will need to become true strategic thinkers.

FOCUSING ON STRATEGY ISSUES

Some people are so good at learning the tricks of the trade that they never get to learn the trade.
Sam Levenson (1911–1980); American teacher and comedian

While it is the objective of this book to increase students' strategic thinking abilities by exposing them to a wide range of theories and perspectives, it is not the intention to confuse and disorient. Yet in a subject area like strategic management, in which there is a broad spectrum of different views, there is a realistic threat that students might go deaf listening to the cacophony of different opinions. The variety of ideas can easily become overwhelming and difficult to integrate.

For this reason, the many theories, models, approaches and perspectives have been clustered around ten central strategy issues, each of which is discussed in a separate chapter. These ten strategy issues represent the key questions with which strategists must deal in practice. Only the theorists whose ideas have a direct bearing on the issue at hand are discussed in each chapter.

The advantage of this issue-based book structure is that it is *decision-oriented* – each chapter is about a key type of strategic decision that needs to be made. Students are challenged to look at a strategic issue holistically, taking various aspects and perspectives into account, and to arrive at a proposed course of action. This type of decision-focus closely reflects what strategizing managers need to do in practice. Step-by-step books are much more *tool-oriented*, teaching students how to go through each phase of a strategic planning process and how to use each analysis framework – useful, especially for junior analysts, but unlikely to stimulate real strategic thinking and to provide insight into difficult strategic choices.

Within each chapter, the conflicting perspectives on how the strategic issue should be approached are contrasted with one another by staging a virtual 'debate'. Two opposite perspectives are presented to kick off the debate and highlight areas of disagreement, after which the students (and their professors) are invited to further debate the issue and decide on the value and limitations of each point of view. While the chapter text offers a general introduction to the nature of the strategic issue and gives an overview of the hotly debated questions, no attempt is made to present the 'right answer' or provide a 'grand unifying theory' – students must make up their own minds based on the arguments placed before them.

The advantage of this debate-based chapter structure is that it encourages the students' engagement and that it provokes critical thinking. As students need to determine the strengths and weaknesses of each strategy perspective, they also become more adept at combining different 'lenses' to gain a fuller understanding of a problem, while becoming more skilled at balancing and mixing prescriptions to find innovative solutions to these problems. Some students will feel ill at ease not being presented the 'right approach' or the 'best practice', as they are used to getting in many other books, but this is all the more reason to avoid giving them one – as strategizing managers the security of one truth won't get them far, so it is preferable to learn to deal with (and benefit from) a variety of opinions as soon as possible.

USING ORIGINAL READINGS

Education is not filling a bucket but lighting a fire.
William Butler Yeats (1865–1939); Irish poet and dramatist

There are no better and livelier debates than when rivals put forward their own ideas as forcefully as they can. For this reason, we have chosen to structure the strategy debates by letting influential theorists speak for themselves. Instead of translating the important ideas of key writers into our own words, each chapter contains four original readings in which the theorists state their own case. These four readings can be viewed as the discussants in the debate, while our role is that of chairmen – we set the stage for the debate and introduce the various perspectives and 'speakers', but as conscientious chairmen we avoid taking a position in the debate ourselves.

The four readings in each chapter have been selected with a number of criteria in mind. As a starting point, we were looking for the articles or books that are widely judged to be classics in the field of strategy. However, to ensure the broad representation of different perspectives, we occasionally looked beyond established classics to find a challenging minority point of view. Finally, discussants are only as good as their ability to communicate to the non-initiated, and therefore we have sometimes excluded certain classics as too technical.

To keep the size of the book within acceptable limits, most readings have had to be reduced in length, while extensive footnotes and references have had to be dropped. At all times this editing has been guided by the principle that the author's key ideas and arguments must be preserved intact. To compensate for the loss of references in each article, a combined list of the most important references has been added to the end of each chapter.

TAKING AN INTERNATIONAL PERSPECTIVE

He who knows only his side of the case, knows little of that.
John Stuart Mill (1806–1873); English philosopher

While almost all strategic management textbooks have been mainly produced for their author's domestic market and are later exported overseas, this book has been explicitly developed with an international audience in mind. For students the international orientation of this book has a number of distinct advantages:

- Cross-cultural differences. Although there has been relatively little cross-cultural research in the field of strategy, results so far indicate that there are significant differences in strategy styles between companies from different countries. This calls into question the habit among strategy researchers to present universal theories, without indicating the cultural assumptions on which their ideas have been based. It is not unlikely that strategy theories have a strong cultural bias and therefore cannot be simply transferred from one national setting to another. Much of the debate going on between strategy theorists might actually be based on such divergent cultural assumptions. In this book the issue of cross-cultural differences in strategy style is raised in each chapter, to debate whether strategists need to adapt their theories, perspectives and approaches to the country in which they are operating.

- International context. Besides adapting to a specific country, many companies are operating in a variety of countries at the same time. In this international arena they are confronted with a distinct set of issues, ranging from global integration and coordination, to localization and transnationalization. This set of issues presented by the international context is debated in depth in Chapter 10.

- International cases and illustrations. To explore how the various strategy perspectives can be applied to different national contexts, it is imperative to have cases and illustrations from a wide variety of countries, spread around the world. In this book the 33 cases (22 long and 11 short cases) cover more than 20 countries and most of the cases have an international orientation. The 20 main illustrations have also been drawn from around the world. It must be noted, however, that we have had a bias towards well-known firms from developed economies, as these examples are more recognizable to most audiences around the world.

IMPROVEMENTS TO THE THIRD EDITION

Change is not made without inconvenience, even from worse to better.
Samuel Johnson (1709–1784); English lexicographer

While high-fashion designers launch their new collections on an annual basis, we have taken the automotive industry as our inspiration, bringing out a new 'model' every four to six years. This long 'cycle time' has allowed us to thoroughly test new ideas and to distinguish which of the developments in the field of strategic management are important innovations and which are short-lived fashions. It has also given us the opportunity to do a major 'overhaul', instead of a more superficial 'make over'.

The result is a third edition that contains a number of significant improvements when compared to the previous edition. While the basic approach and structure have remained largely the same, major revisions have been implemented. These alterations are partially due to new advances in the field of strategic management, but also reflect the continual learning that has taken place as this new teaching format has developed emergently. In particular, the book has benefited greatly from the comments and suggestions given by hundreds of professors and students from around the world. The main improvements over the previous edition are the following:

- New structure within chapters. All chapters have been thoroughly restructured to enhance readability. In the previous edition, each chapter started with a central debate, highlighting points of disagreement between strategists. This left some students confused, as they had difficulty understanding the key issues being debated. Therefore, in the new edition, each chapter begins with a review of the key strategy issues, explaining important strategy concepts and frameworks, after which the central debate is introduced. This revised order should greatly improve students' ability to gain an overview over the debate, before moving on to the readings at the end of each chapter.

- New topics. Besides a new structure, all chapters have also been significantly expanded, to give a more comprehensive coverage of the main topics in the area of strategic management. A number of new topics have been added, including strategic renewal, business models, alliance capabilities, business ecosystems, disruptive technologies and co-evolution, while others have been given much more space, such as sources of competitive advantage, market segmentation, value chain analysis, corporate integration mechanisms, multi-business synergy, post-acquisition integration, strategic alliances, industry development, strategic leadership, corporate governance and strategy implementation.

- New illustration boxes. A new feature is the addition of two extensive illustrations per chapter (20 in total). For each strategy perspectives described in the book, an exhibit has been included, giving a well-known company that employs this strategy perspective. These examples make it much easier for students to see how a particular strategy perspective leads to concrete organizational behavior in practice. As with all of the examples and cases in the book, these illustrations have been taken from a broad range of industries and countries, to stretch students' horizons and to emphasize that the concepts being discussed are widely applicable.

- New short cases. In addition to the two illustrations per chapter, this edition will again include 11 short cases that provide a good example of the debate at hand. As before, these short cases can be used if there is insufficient time to prepare one of the longer cases. The short cases have proven to be particularly valuable in executive programs and in-company courses, where managers can read and discuss them on the spot. All of these short cases are new or revised.

- New long cases. Despite the beauty of some 'classic' cases, students are generally not enthusiastic when confronted with old material. Therefore, the majority of the cases have been replaced by new ones. What remains unchanged is that a good spread across countries and industries has been achieved, and that there are at least two cases per chapter that provide an excellent fit.

- New readings. Approximately a third of the readings are new, in particular to represent some new developments in the field of strategic management. To ensure that this book did not become too heavy, we have also reduced the total number of readings to four per chapter. The selection procedure has been greatly influenced by the feedback received from the book's current adopters.

- New website materials. Naturally, to complement the new text and cases, new teaching notes and supplementary materials have been developed and posted on our website (www.strategy-academy.org or www.thomsonlearning.co.uk). This website currently features two entirely new services. One is a 'tools section', where various strategy frameworks and methodologies are available for professors and students. This section will be under continuous development, with new tools added on a regular basis. The other addition is a 'test section', which includes a multiple-choice exam database for professors and practice questions for students.

- New executive edition. For some purposes a book of more than thousand pages is less suitable – some students have even suggested that the book is so heavy that it should be labeled as a potential health risk. So for those preferring a lighter version, a slimmed down edition is available, without the 22 long cases and the 44 readings. This edition, titled *Strategy Synthesis*, is particularly suited to short courses and executive education programs, or as a complementary text.

We are aware that these changes might bring some inconvenience, even though in Samuel Johnson's words they are 'from worse to better'. As every strategist knows, 'software upgrades' require users to invest time and energy to acquaint themselves with the new version. However, we trust that previous 'users' will find the 3.0 version of our book well worth the additional investment.

CONTACT US

A stand can be made against invasion by an army; no stand can be made against invasion by an idea.
Victor Hugo (1802–1885); French poet, novelist and playwright

Books are old-fashioned, but based on a proven technology that is still the most appropriate under most circumstances. One drawback, however, is that a book is unidirectional, allowing us to send a message to you, but not capable of transmitting your comments, questions and suggestions back to us. This is unfortunate, as we are keen on communicating with our audience and enjoy hearing what works and doesn't work 'in the field'.

Therefore, we would like to encourage both students and professors to establish contact with us. You can dø this by visiting our website (www.strategy-academy.org or www.thomsonlearning.co.uk) to check out the extra features we have for you and to leave your comments and suggestions. But you can also contact us directly by email at b.dewit@strategy-academy.org or r.meyer@strategy-academy.org.

REFERENCES

Abrahamson, E. (1996) 'Management Fashion', *Academy of Management Review*, Vol. 21, pp. 254–285.

Arthur, W.B. (1996) 'Increasing Returns and the New World of Business', *Harvard Business Review*, July/August, pp. 100–109.

David, P.A. (1994) 'Why are Institutions the "Carriers of History"?: Path Dependence and the Evolution of Conventions, Organizations and Institutions', *Structural Change and Economic Dynamics*, Vol. 10, No. 3, pp. 205–220.

Powell, W.W., and DiMaggio, P.J. (eds) (1991) *The New Institutionalism in Organization Analysis*, University of Chicago Press, Chicago, IL.

Smircich, L., and Stubbart, C. (1985) 'Strategic Management in an Enacted World', *Academy of Management Review*, Vol. 10, pp. 724–736.

Spender, J.-C. (1989) *Industry Recipes: The Nature and Sources of Managerial Judgement*, Basil Blackwell, Oxford.

Walsh, J. (1995) 'Managerial and Organizational Cognition: Notes from a Trip Down Memory Lane', *Organization Science*, Vol. 6, pp. 280–321.

STRATEGY

CHAPTER

1

INTRODUCTION

Men like the opinions to which they have become accustomed from youth; this prevents them from finding the truth, for they cling to the opinions of habit.

Moses Maimonides (1135–1204);
Egyptian physician and philosopher

Where there is much desire to learn, there of necessity will be much arguing, much writing, many opinions; for opinion in good men is but knowledge in the making.

John Milton (1608–1674); English poet

THE NATURE OF STRATEGY

In a book entitled *Strategy*, it seems reasonable to expect Chapter 1 to begin with a clear definition of strategy that would be employed with consistency in all subsequent chapters. An early and precise definition would help to avoid conflicting interpretations of what should be considered strategy and, by extension, what should be understood by the term 'strategic management'. However, any such sharp definition of strategy here would actually be misleading. It would suggest that there is widespread agreement among practitioners, researchers and theorists as to what strategy is. The impression would be given that the fundamental concepts in the area of strategy are generally accepted and hardly questioned. Yet, even a quick glance through current strategy literature indicates otherwise. There are strongly differing opinions on most of the key issues and the disagreements run so deep that even a common definition of the term strategy is illusive.

This is bad news for those who prefer simplicity and certainty. It means that the topic of strategy cannot be explained as a set of straightforward definitions and rules to be memorized and applied. The strongly conflicting views mean that strategy cannot be summarized into broadly agreed on definitions, rules, matrices and flow diagrams that one must simply absorb and learn to use. If the fundamental differences of opinion are not swept aside, the consequence is that a book on strategy cannot be like an instruction manual that takes you through the steps of how something should be done. On the contrary, a strategy book should acknowledge the disagreements and encourage thinking about the value of each of the different points of view. That is the intention of this book.

The philosophy embraced here is that an understanding of the topic of strategy can only be gained by grappling with the diversity of insights presented by so many prominent thinkers and by coming to terms with the fact that there is no simple answer to the question of what strategy is. Readers who prefer the certainty of reading only one opinion, as opposed to the intellectual stimulation of being confronted with a wide variety, should read no further – there are plenty of alternatives available. Those who wish to proceed should lay aside their 'opinions of habit', and open their minds to the many other opinions presented, for in these pages there is 'knowledge in the making'.

IDENTIFYING THE STRATEGY ISSUES

If the only tool you have is a hammer, you treat everything like a nail.
Abraham Maslow (1908–1970); American psychologist

The approach taken in this book is in line with the moral of Maslow's remark. To avoid hammering strategy issues with only one theory, a variety of ways of viewing strategic questions will be presented. But there are two different ways of presenting a broad spectrum of theoretical lenses. This point can be made clear by extending Maslow's hammer-and-nail analogy. To become a good carpenter, who wisely uses a variety of tools depending on what is being crafted, an apprentice carpenter will need to learn about these different instruments. One way is for the apprentice to study the characteristics and functioning of all tools individually, and only then to apply each where appropriate. However, another possibility is for the apprentice to first learn about what must be crafted, getting a feel for the materials and the problems that must be solved, and only then to turn to the study of the necessary tools. The first approach to learning can be called 'tools-driven' – understanding each tool comes first, while combining them to solve real problems comes later. The second approach to learning can be termed 'problem-driven' – understanding problems comes first, while searching for the appropriate tools is based on the type of problem.

Both options can also be used for the apprentice strategist. In a tools-driven approach to learning about strategy, all major theories would first be understood separately, to be compared or combined later when using them in practice. A logical structure for a book aiming at this mode of learning would be to allot one chapter to each of the major theories or schools of thought. The advantage of such a theory-based book structure would be that each chapter would focus on giving the reader a clear and cohesive overview of one major theory within the field of strategy. For readers with an interest in grasping the essence of each theory individually, this would probably be the ideal book format. However, the principal disadvantage of a theory-by-theory summary of the field of strategy would be that the reader would not have a clear picture of how the various theories relate to one another. The apprentice strategist would be left with important questions such as: 'Where do the theories agree and where do they differ? Which strategy phenomena does each theory claim to explain and which phenomena are left unaccounted for? Can various theories be successfully combined or are they based on mutually exclusive assumptions? And which strategy is right, or at least most appropriate under particular circumstances? Not knowing the answers to these questions, how could the apprentice strategist try to apply these new theoretical tools to practice?

This book is based on the assumption that the reader wants to be able to actively solve strategic problems. Understanding the broad spectrum of theories is not an end in itself, but a means for more effective strategizing. Therefore, the problem-driven approach to learning about strategy has been adopted. In this approach, key strategy issues are first identified and then each is looked at from the perspective of the most appropriate theories. This has resulted in an issue-based book structure, in which each chapter deals with a particular set of strategy issues. In each chapter, only the theories that shed some light on the issues under discussion are brought forward and compared to one another. Of course, some theories are relevant to more than one set of issues and therefore appear in various chapters.

In total, ten sets of strategy issues have been identified that together largely cover the entire field of strategic management. These ten will be the subjects of the remaining ten chapters of this book. How the various strategy issues have been divided into these ten sets will be explained in the following paragraphs.

Strategy dimensions: Process, content and context

The most fundamental distinction made in this book is between strategy process, strategy content and strategy context (see Figure 1.1). These are the three dimensions of strategy that can be recognized in every real-life strategic problem situation. They can be generally defined as follows:

- Strategy process. The manner in which strategies come about is referred to as the strategy process. Stated in terms of a number of questions, strategy process is concerned with the *how*, *who* and *when* of strategy: how is, and should, strategy be made, analyzed, dreamt-up, formulated, implemented, changed and controlled; who is involved; and when do the necessary activities take place?

- Strategy content. The product of a strategy process is referred to as the strategy content. Stated in terms of a question, strategy content is concerned with the *what* of strategy: what is, and should be, the strategy for the company and each of its constituent units?

- Strategy context. The set of circumstances under which both the strategy process and the strategy content are determined is referred to as the strategy context. Stated in terms of a question, strategy context is concerned with the *where* of strategy: where (that is in which firm and which environment) are the strategy process and strategy content embedded.

It cannot be emphasized enough that strategy process, content and context are not different parts of strategy, but are distinguishable dimensions. Just as it is silly to speak of the length, width and height parts of a box, one cannot speak of the three parts of strategy either. Each strategic problem situation is by its nature three dimensional, possessing process, content and context characteristics, and only the understanding of all three dimensions will give the strategist real depth of comprehension. In particular, it must be acknowledged that the three dimensions interact (Pettigrew and Whipp, 1991; Ketchen, Thomas and McDaniel, 1996). For instance, the manner in which the strategy process is organized will have a significant impact on the resulting strategy content, while likewise, the content of the current strategy will strongly influence the way in which the strategy process will be conducted in future. If these linkages are ignored, the strategist will have a flat view instead of a three-dimensional view of strategy. A useful analytical distinction for temporarily unraveling a strategic problem situation will have turned into permanent means for fragmenting reality.

FIGURE 1.1   Dimensions of strategy and the organizational purpose

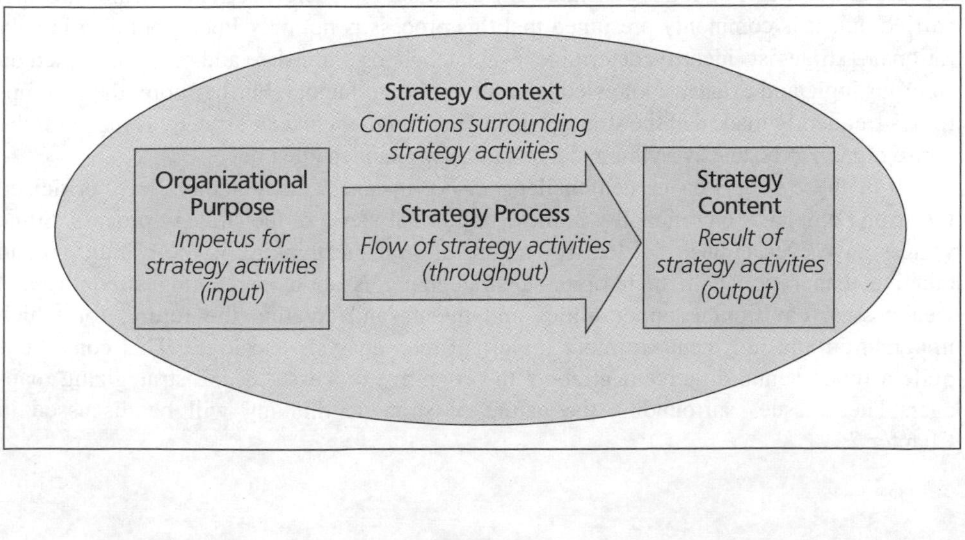

However, it is possible to concentrate on one of the strategy dimensions if the other two are kept in mind. In fact, to have a focused discussion it is even necessary to look at one dimension at a time. The alternative is a debate in which all topics on all three dimensions would be discussed simultaneously: such a cacophony of opinions would be lively, but most likely less than fruitful. Therefore, the process–content–context distinction will cautiously be used as the main structuring principle of this book, splitting the text into three major sections.

A fourth section has been added to these three, although strictly speaking it is not about strategy. In the above list, the questions of how, who, when, what and where were mentioned, but not yet the question of *why* – why do organizations exist and why do their strategies move them in a certain direction? This is the issue of organizational purpose – the impetus to strategy activities. Making strategy is not an end in itself, but a means for reaching particular objectives. Organizations exist to fulfill a purpose and strategies are employed to ensure that the organizational purpose is realized. Given the importance of this topic to the understanding of strategy, purpose has been given an equal position next to process, content and context as a separate section of this book.

This four-fold structure fits closely with the situation within the academic field of strategic management. To a large extent, strategy literature is divided along these lines. Most strategy research, by its very nature, is more atomistic than holistic, focusing on just a few variables at once. Consequently, most writings on strategy, including most of the theories discussed in this book, tend to favor just one, or at most two, strategy dimensions, which is usually complex enough given the need to remain comprehensible. In particular, the divide between strategy process and strategy content has been quite pronounced, to the extent of worrying some scholars about whether the connections between the two are being sufficiently recognized (Pettigrew, 1992). Although sharing this concern, use of the process–content–context–purpose distinction here reflects the reality of the current state of debate within the field of strategic management.

Strategy process: Thinking, forming and changing

Section II of this book will deal with the strategy process. Traditionally, most textbooks have portrayed the strategy process as a basically linear progression through a number of distinct steps. Usually a split is made between the strategy analysis stage, the strategy formulation stage and the strategy implementation stage. In the analysis stage, strategists identify the opportunities and threats in the environment, as well as the strengths and weaknesses of the organization. Next, in the formulation stage, strategists determine which strategic options are available to them, evaluate each and choose one. Finally, in the implementation stage, the selected strategic option is translated into a number of concrete activities, which are then carried out. It is commonly presumed that this process is not only linear, but also largely rational – strategists identify, determine, evaluate, choose, translate and carry out based on rigorous logic and extensive knowledge of all important factors. Furthermore, the assumption is frequently made that the strategy process is comprehensive – strategy is made for the entire organization and everything can be radically changed all at once.

All of these beliefs have been challenged. For instance, many authors have criticized the strong emphasis on rationality in these traditional views of the strategy process. Some writers have even argued that the true nature of strategic thinking is more intuitive and creative than rational. In their opinion, strategizing is about perceiving strengths and weaknesses, envisioning opportunities and threats and creating the future, for which imagination and judgment are more important than analysis and logic. This constitutes quite a fundamental disagreement about the cognitive processes of the strategizing manager. These issues surrounding the nature of strategic thinking will be discussed in Chapter 2.

The division of the strategy process into a number of sequential phases has also drawn heavy criticism from authors who believe that in reality no such identifiable stages exist. They dismiss the linear analysis–formulation–implementation distinction as an unwarranted simplification, arguing that the strategy process is messier, with analysis, formulation and implementation activities going on all the time, thoroughly intertwined with one another. In their view, organizations do not first make strategic plans and then execute them as intended. Rather, strategies are usually formed incrementally, as organizations think and act in small iterative steps, letting strategies emerge as they go along. This represents quite a difference of opinion on how strategies are formed within organizations. These issues surrounding the nature of strategy formation will be discussed in Chapter 3.

The third major assumption of the traditional view, comprehensiveness, has also been challenged. Many authors have pointed out that it is unrealistic to suppose that a company can be boldly redesigned. They argue that it is terribly difficult to orchestrate an overarching strategy for the entire organization that is a significant departure from the current course of action. It is virtually impossible to get various aspects of an organization all lined up to go through a change at the same time, certainly if a radical change is intended. In practice, different aspects of an organization will be under different pressures, on different timetables and have different abilities to change, leading to a differentiated approach to change. Moreover, the rate and direction of change will be seriously limited by the cultural, political and cognitive inheritance of the firm. Hence, it is argued, strategic change is usually more gradual and fragmented than radical and coordinated. The issues surrounding this difference of opinion on the nature of strategic change will be discussed in Chapter 4.

These three chapter topics – strategic thinking, strategy formation and strategic change – do not constitute entirely separate subjects. Let it be clear that they are not phases, stages or elements of the strategy process that can be understood in isolation. Strategic thinking, strategy formation and strategic change are different aspects of the strategy process, which are strongly linked and partially overlapping (see Figure 1.2). They have been selected because they are sets of issues on which there is significant debate within the field of strategy. As will become clear, having a particular opinion on one of these aspects will have a consequence for views held on all other aspects as well.

FIGURE 1.2   Aspects of the strategy process

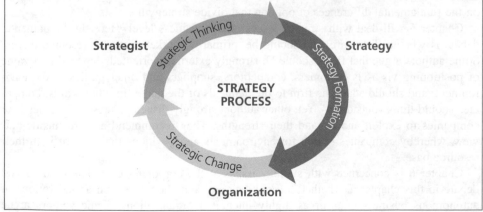

Strategy content: Business, corporate and network levels

Section III of this book will deal with the strategy content. Strategies come in all shapes and sizes, and almost all strategy writers, researchers and practitioners agree that each strategy is essentially unique. There is widespread disagreement, however, about the principles to which strategies should adhere. The debates are numerous, but there are three fundamental sets of issues around which most conflicts generally center. These three topics can be clarified by distinguishing the level of strategy at which each is most relevant.

Strategies can be made for different groups of people and/or activities within an organization. The lowest level of aggregation is one person or task, while the highest level of aggregation encompasses all people and/or activities within an organization. The most common distinction between levels of aggregation made in the strategic management literature is between the functional, business and corporate levels (see Figure 1.3). Strategy issues at the *functional level* refer to questions regarding specific functional aspects of a company (operations strategy, marketing strategy, financial strategy, etc.). Strategy at the *business level* requires the integration of functional level strategies for a distinct set of products and/or services intended for a specific group of customers. Often companies only operate in one such business, so that this is the highest level of aggregation within the firm. However, there are also many companies that are in two or more businesses. In such companies, a multi-business or *corporate level* strategy is required, which aligns the various business level strategies.

A logical extension of the functional–business–corporate distinction is to explicitly recognize the level of aggregation higher than the individual organization. Firms often cluster together into groups of two or more collaborating organizations. This level is referred to as the multi-company or *network level*. Most multi-company groups consist of only a few parties, as is the case in strategic alliances, joint ventures and value-adding partnerships. However, networks can also have dozens, even hundreds, of participants. In some circumstances, the corporation as a whole might be a member of a group, while in other situations only a part of the firm joins forces with other organizations. In all cases, when a strategy is developed for a group of firms, this is called a network level strategy.

In line with the generally accepted boundaries of the strategic management field, this book will focus on the business, corporate and network levels of strategy, although this will often demand consideration of strategy issues at the functional level as well. In Section II, on the strategy process, this level distinction will not be emphasized yet, but in Section III, on the strategy content, the different strategy issues encountered at the different levels of strategy will be explored. And at each level of strategy, the focus will be on the fundamental differences of opinion that divide strategy theorists.

Chapter 5 will deal with strategy issues at the business level. Here the fundamental debate is whether firms are, and should be, primarily market-driven or resource-driven. Some authors argue that firms should be strongly externally oriented, engaged in a game of positioning vis-à-vis customers, competitors, suppliers and other parties in the environment, and should adapt the firm to the demands of the game. In other words, companies should think 'outside-in'. Yet, other authors strongly disagree, stressing the need for companies to exploit and expand their strengths. They recommend a more 'inside-out' view, whereby companies search for environments and positions that best fit with their resource base.

Chapter 6 is concerned with strategy issues at the corporate level. The fundamental debate in this chapter is whether corporations are, and should be, run as federations of autonomous business units or as highly integrated organizations. Some authors argue that corporate strategists should view themselves as investors, with financial stakes in a portfolio of business units. As a shrewd investor, the corporate center should buy up cheap companies, divest underperforming business units, and put money into its business

FIGURE 1.3 Levels of strategy

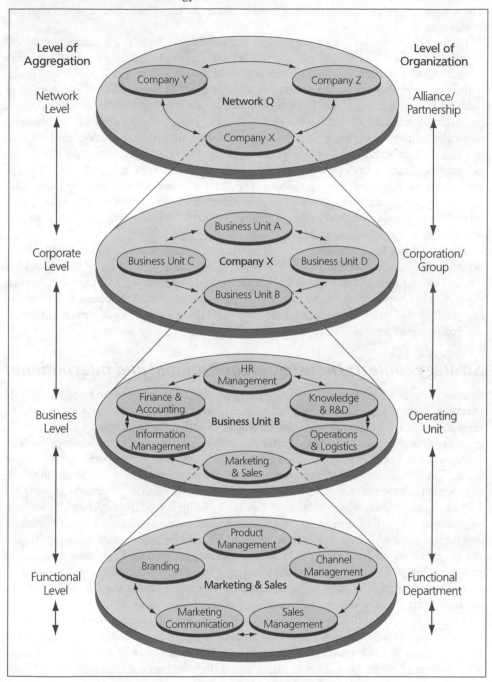

units with the highest profit potential, independent of what industry they are in. Each business unit should be judged on its merits and given a large measure of autonomy, to be optimally responsive to the specific conditions in its industry. However, other authors are at odds with this view, pointing to the enormous potential for synergy that is left untapped. They argue that corporations should be tightly knit groupings of closely related business units that share resources and align their strategies with one another. The ensuing synergies, it is forecast, will provide an important source of competitive advantage.

Chapter 7 focuses on the strategy issues at the network level. The fundamental debate in this chapter revolves around the question whether firms should develop long-term collaborative relationships with other firms or should remain essentially independent. Some authors believe that competition between organizations is sometimes more destructive than beneficial, and argue that building up durable partnerships with other organizations can often be mutually advantageous. Participation in joint ventures, alliances and broader networks requires a higher level of inter-organizational trust and interdependence, but can pay off handsomely. It is therefore recommended to selectively engage in joint – that is, multi-company – strategy development. Other authors, however, are thoroughly skeptical about the virtues of interdependence. They prefer independence, pointing to the dangers of opportunistic partners and creeping dependence on the other. Therefore, it is recommended to avoid multi-company level strategy development and only to use alliances as a temporary measure.

Again, it must be emphasized that the analytical distinction employed here should not be interpreted as an absolute means for isolating issues. In reality, these three levels of strategy do not exist as tidy categories, but are strongly interrelated and partially overlapping. As a consequence, the three sets of strategy issues identified above are also linked to one another. In Section III it will become clear that taking a stand in one debate will affect the position that one can take in others.

Strategy context: Industry, organizational and international

Section IV in this book is devoted to the strategy context. Strategy researchers, writers and practitioners largely agree that every strategy context is unique. Moreover, they are almost unanimous that it is usually wise for managers to strive for a fit between the strategy process, strategy content and the specific circumstances prevalent in the strategy context. However, disagreement arises as soon as the discussion turns to the details of the alignments. Does the context determine what the strategizing manager must do, or can the manager actually shape the context? Some people argue or assume that the strategy context has a dynamic all its own, which strategists can hardly influence, and therefore that the strategy context sets strict confines on the freedom to maneuver. The context is not malleable and hence the motto for the strategist is 'adapt or die'. Others believe that strategists should not be driven by the context, but have a large measure of freedom to set their own course of action. Frequently it is argued that strategizing managers can, and should, create their own circumstances, instead of being enslaved by the circumstances they find. In short, the strategy context can be determined, instead of letting it determine.

In Section iv, the difference of opinion on the power of the context to determine strategy surfaces when discussing the various aspects of the strategy context. The section has been split into three chapters, each focusing on a different aspect of the strategy context. Two distinctions have been used to arrive at the division into three chapters (see Figure 1.4). The first dichotomy employed is that between the organization and its industry environment. The *industry context* will be the subject of Chapter 8. In this chapter, the strategic issues revolve around the question whether the industry circumstances set the rules to which companies must comply, or whether companies have the freedom to choose their own strategy and even change the industry conditions. The *organizational context* will be dealt with in Chapter 9. Here, the key strategic issues have to do with the question of whether the organizational circumstances largely determine the strategy process and strategy content followed, or whether the strategist has a significant amount of control over the course of action adopted.

FIGURE 1.4   Aspects of the strategy context

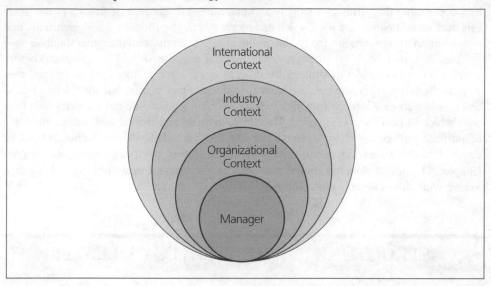

The second dichotomy employed is that between the domestic and the international strategy context. The domestic context does not raise any additional strategic issues, but the *international context* clearly does. Strategists must deal with the question of whether adaptation to the diversity of the international context is strictly required or whether companies have considerable freedom to choose their strategy process and content irrespective of the international context. The difference of opinion between writers on the international context actually goes one step further. Some authors predict that the diversity of the international context will decline over time and that companies can encourage this process. If global convergence takes place, it is argued, adaptation to the international context will become a non-issue. Other authors, however, disagree that international diversity is declining and therefore argue that the international context will remain an issue that strategists must attempt to deal with. This debate on the future of the international context is conducted in Chapter 10.

Organizational purpose

Oddly enough, most authors write about strategy without any reference to the organizational purpose being pursued. It is generally assumed that all organizations exist for the same basic reasons, and that this purpose is self-evident. However, in reality, there is extensive disagreement about what the current purposes of organizations are, and especially about what their purpose should be. Some people argue that it is the business of business to make money. In their view, firms are owned by shareholders and therefore should pursue shareholders' interests. And it is the primary interest of shareholders to see the value of their stocks increase. On the other hand, others believe that companies exist to serve the interests of multiple stakeholders. In their opinion, having a financial stake in a firm should not give shareholders a dominant position vis-à-vis other groups that also have an interest in what the organization does. Other stakeholders usually include employees, customers, suppliers and bankers, but could also include the local community, the broader industry and even the natural environment.

This is a very fundamental debate, with broader societal implications than any of the other strategy issues. Given the important role played by business organizations in modern times, the purposes they attempt to fulfill will have a significant impact on the functioning of society. It is not surprising, therefore, to see that organizational purpose is also discussed by people other than strategy theorists and practitioners. The role of firms and the interests they should pursue are widely debated by members of political parties, environmental conservation groups, unions, the media, political action groups and the general public.

Arguably, in a book on strategy, organizational purpose should be discussed before moving on to the subject of strategy itself – as Figure 1.1 visualizes, organizational purpose is the impetus for strategy activities. In principle this is true, but the 'issue of existence' is not an easy topic with which to start a book – it would be quite a hefty appetizer with which to begin a strategy meal. Therefore, to avoid intellectual indigestion, the topic of purpose will be saved for dessert. The last text part of the book, Section v, will be devoted to the issues surrounding purpose. This section comprises only one chapter, Chapter 11 entitled 'Organizational purpose', as the discussion will be staged broadly, asking what drives organizations forward.

STRUCTURING THE STRATEGY DEBATES

For every complex problem there is a simple solution that is wrong.
George Bernard Shaw (1856–1950); Irish playwright and critic

Every real-life strategic problem is complex. Most of the strategic issues outlined earlier in this chapter will be present in every strategic problem, making the prospect of a simple solution an illusion. Yet, even if each set of strategy issues is looked at independently, it seems that strategy theorists cannot agree on the right way to approach them. On each of the topics, there is widespread disagreement, indicating that no simple solution can be expected here either.

Why is it that theorists cannot agree on how to solve strategic problems? Might it be that some theorists are right, while others are just plain wrong? In that case, it would be wise for problem-solvers to select the valid theory and discard the false ones. While this might be true in some cases, it seems unlikely that false theories would stay around long enough to keep a lively debate going. Eventually, the right (i.e. unfalsified) theory would prevail and disagreements would disappear. Yet, this does not seem to be happening in the field of strategic management.

Could it be that each theorist only emphasizes one aspect of an issue – only takes one cut of a multi-faceted reality? In that case, it would be wise for problem-solvers to combine the various theories that each look at the problem from a different angle. However, if this were true, one would expect the different theories to be largely complementary. Each theory would simply be a piece in the bigger puzzle of strategic management. Yet, this does not explain why there is so much disagreement, and even contradiction, within the field of strategy.

It could also be that strategy theorists start from divergent assumptions about the nature of each strategy issue and therefore logically arrive at a different perspective on how to solve strategic problems. In that case, it would be wise for problem-solvers to combine the various theories, in order to look at the problem from a number of different angles.

All three possibilities for explaining the existing theoretical disagreements should be kept open. However, entertaining the thought that divergent positions are rooted in fundamentally different assumptions about strategy issues is by far the most fruitful to the strategist confronted with complex problems. It is too simple to hope that one can deal with the contradictory opinions within the field of strategy by discovering which strategy theories are right and which are wrong. But it is also not particularly practical to accept all divergent theories as valid depictions of different aspects of reality – if two theories suggest a different approach to the same problem, the strategist will have to sort out this contradiction. Therefore, in this book the emphasis will be on surfacing the basic assumptions underlying the major theoretical perspectives on strategy, and to debate whether, or under which circumstances, these assumptions are appropriate.

Assumptions about strategy tensions

At the heart of every set of strategic issues, a fundamental tension between apparent opposites can be identified. For instance, in Chapter 7 on network level strategy, the issues revolve around the fundamental tension between competition and cooperation. In Chapter 8 on the industry context, the fundamental tension between the opposites of compliance and choice lies at the center of the subject (see Figure 1.5). Each pair of opposites creates a tension, as they seem to be inconsistent, or even incompatible, with one another; it seems as if both elements cannot be fully true at the same time. If firms are competing, they are not cooperating. If firms must comply with the industry context, they have no choice. Yet, although these opposites confront strategizing managers with conflicting pressures, somehow they must be dealt with simultaneously. Strategists are caught in a bind, trying to cope with contradictory forces at the same time.

The challenge of strategic management is to wrestle with these tricky strategy tensions. All strategy theories make assumptions, explicitly or implicitly, about the nature of these tensions and devise ways in which to deal with them. However, every theorist's assumptions differ, giving rise to a wide variety of positions. In fact, many of the major disagreements within the field of strategic management are rooted in the different assumptions made about coping with these strategy tensions. For this reason, the theoretical debate in each chapter will be centered around the different perspectives on dealing with a particular strategy tension.

FIGURE 1.5   Chapter topics and strategy tensions

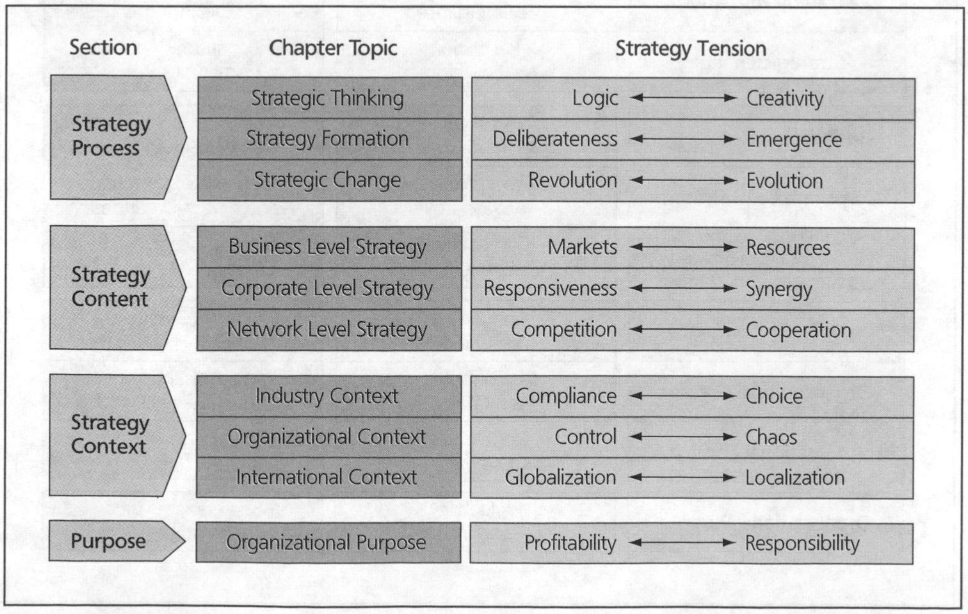

Section	Chapter Topic	Strategy Tension	
Strategy Process	Strategic Thinking	Logic ← →	Creativity
	Strategy Formation	Deliberateness ← →	Emergence
	Strategic Change	Revolution ← →	Evolution
Strategy Content	Business Level Strategy	Markets ← →	Resources
	Corporate Level Strategy	Responsiveness ← →	Synergy
	Network Level Strategy	Competition ← →	Cooperation
Strategy Context	Industry Context	Compliance ← →	Choice
	Organizational Context	Control ← →	Chaos
	International Context	Globalization ← →	Localization
Purpose	Organizational Purpose	Profitability ← →	Responsibility

Identifying strategy perspectives

The strategy issues in each chapter can be viewed from many perspectives. On each topic there are many different theories and hundreds of books and articles. While very interesting, a comparison or debate between all of these would probably be very chaotic, unfocused and incomprehensible. Therefore, in each chapter the debate has been condensed into its most powerful form – two diametrically opposed perspectives are confronted with one another. These two poles of each debate are not always the most widely held perspectives on the particular set of strategy issues, but they do expose the major points of contention within the topic area.

In every chapter, the two strategy perspectives selected for the debate each emphasize one side of a strategy tension over the other (see Figure 1.6). For instance, in Chapter 7 the discrete organization perspective stresses competition over cooperation, while the embedded organization perspective does the opposite. In Chapter 8, the industry dynamics perspective accentuates compliance over choice, while the industry leadership perspective does the opposite. In other words, the two perspectives represent the two extreme ways of dealing with a strategy tension, emphasizing one side or emphasizing the other.

In the first part of each chapter, the core strategic issue and the underlying strategy tension will be explained. Also, the two strategy perspectives will be outlined and compared. However, such a measured overview of the perspectives lacks color, depth and vigor. Reading the summary of a debate does not do it justice – just like reading the summary of a sports match is nothing like watching a game live. Therefore, to give readers a first-hand impression of the debate, theorists representing both sides will be given an opportunity to state their own case by means of a reading. Readers will be part of a virtual debate in which the authors of four readings will participate. The first two readings

FIGURE 1.6   Strategy topics, paradoxes and perspectives

Strategy Topics	Strategy Paradoxes	Strategy Perspectives
Strategic Thinking	Logic vs. Creativity	Rational Reasoning vs. Generative Reasoning
Strategy Formation	Deliberateness vs. Emergence	Strategic Planning vs. Strategic Incrementalism
Strategic Change	Revolution vs. Evolution	Discontinuous Renewal vs. Continuous Renewal
Business Level Strategy	Markets vs. Resources	Outside-in vs. Inside-out
Corporate Level Strategy	Responsiveness vs. Synergy	Portfolio Organization vs. Integrated Organization
Network Level Strategy	Competition vs. Cooperation	Discrete Organization vs. Embedded Organization
Industry Context	Compliance vs. Choice	Industry Dynamics vs. Industry Leadership
Organizational Context	Control vs. Chaos	Organizational Leadership vs. Organizational Dynamics
International Context	Globalization vs. Localization	Global Convergence vs. International Diversity
Organizational Purpose	Profitability vs. Responsibility	Shareholder Value vs. Stakeholder Values

in each chapter will speak on behalf of the two pole perspectives. The second set of two readings is intended to bring in additional issues and arguments not fully covered in the two lead contributions. All of the readings will receive a short introduction, to assist in understanding their pertinence to the debate at hand. The only thing that will not be done – and cannot be done – is to give readers the outcome of the debate. This readers will have to decide for themselves.

Viewing strategy tensions as strategy paradoxes

So, what should readers be getting out of each debate? With both strategy perspectives emphasizing the importance of one side of a strategy tension over the other, how should readers deal with these opposites? Of course, after hearing the arguments, it is up to readers to judge for themselves how the strategy tensions should be handled. However, there are four general ways of approaching them:

■ As a puzzle. A puzzle is a challenging problem with an optimal solution. Think of a crossword puzzle as an example. Puzzles can be quite complex and extremely difficult to analyze, but there is a best way of solving them. Some of the most devious puzzles are those with seemingly contradictory premises. Strategy tensions can also be viewed as puzzles. While the pair of opposites seems to be incompatible with one another, this is only because the puzzle is not well understood yet. In reality, there is one best way of relieving the tension, but the strategist must unravel the problem first. Some writers seem to suggest that there are optimal ways of dealing with strategy tensions under all circumstances, but others argue that the optimal solution is situation dependent.

■ As a dilemma. A dilemma is a vexing problem with two possible solutions, neither of which is logically the best. Think of the famous prisoner's dilemma as an example. Dilemmas confront problem-solvers with difficult either-or choices, each with its own advantages and disadvantages, but neither clearly superior to the other. The uneasy feeling this gives the decision-maker is reflected in the often-used expression 'horns of a dilemma' – neither choice is particularly comfortable. Strategy tensions can also be viewed as dilemmas. If this approach is taken, the incompatibility of the opposites is accepted, and the strategist is forced to make a choice in favour of either one or the other. For instance, the strategist must choose either to compete or cooperate. Which of the two the strategist judges to be most appropriate will usually depend on the specific circumstances.

■ As a trade-off. A trade-off is a problem situation in which there are many possible solutions, each striking a different balance between two conflicting pressures. Think of the trade-off between work and leisure time as an example – more of one will necessarily mean less of the other. In a trade-off, many different combinations between the two opposites can be found, each with its own pros and cons, but none of the many solutions is inherently superior to the others. Strategy tensions can also be viewed as trade-offs. If this approach is taken, the conflict between the two opposites is accepted, and the strategist will constantly strive to find the most appropriate balance between them. For instance, the strategist will attempt to balance the pressures for competition and cooperation, depending on the circumstances encountered.

■ As a paradox. A paradox is a situation in which two seeming contradictory, or even mutually exclusive, factors appear to be true at the same time (e.g. Poole and Van de Ven, 1989, Reading 1.3; Quinn and Cameron, 1988). A problem that is a paradox has no real solution, as there is no way to logically integrate the two opposites into an internally consistent understanding of the problem. As opposed to the either-or nature of the dilemma, the paradox can be characterized as a 'both-and' problem – one factor is true and a contradictory factor is simultaneously true (e.g. Collins and Porras, 1994; Lewis, 2000). Hence, a paradox presents the problem-solver with the difficult task of wrestling with the problem, without ever arriving at a definitive solution. At best, the problem-solver can find a workable reconciliation to temporarily cope with the unsolvable paradox. Strategy tensions can also be viewed as paradoxes. If this approach is taken, the conflict between the two opposites is accepted, but the strategist will strive to accommodate both factors at the same time. The strategist will search for new ways of reconciling the opposites as best as possible. To take the same example as above, the strategist faced with the tension between competition and cooperation will attempt to do both as much as possible at the same time, with the intention of reaping the 'best of both worlds'.

Most people are used to solving puzzles, resolving dilemmas and making trade-offs. These ways of understanding and solving problems are common in daily life. They are based on the assumption that, by analysis, one or a number of logical solutions can be identified. It might require a sharp mind and considerable effort, but the answers can be found.

However, most people are not used to, or inclined to, think of a problem as a paradox. A paradox has no answer or set of answers – it can only be coped with as best as possible. Faced with a paradox, one can try to find novel ways of combining opposites, but one will know that none of these creative reconciliations will ever be *the* answer. Paradoxes will always remain surrounded by uncertainty and disagreements on how best to cope.

So, should strategy tensions be seen as puzzles, dilemmas, trade-offs or paradoxes (see Figure 1.7)? Arguments can be made for all, but viewing strategy tensions as strategy

FIGURE 1.7   Strategy tensions as puzzles, dilemmas, trade-offs and paradoxes

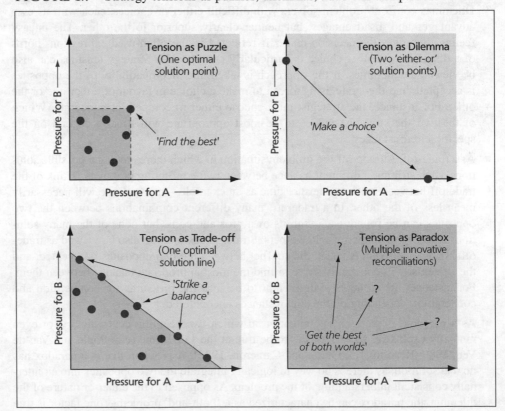

paradoxes is the ultimate intellectual challenge. Looking at the tensions as paradoxes will help readers to avoid 'jumping to solutions' and will encourage the use of creativity to find ways of benefiting from both sides of a tension at the same time. Hence, throughout this book, the strategy tensions will be presented as strategy paradoxes, and readers will be invited to view them as such.

Taking a dialectical approach

As stated earlier, the debate in each chapter has been condensed into its most powerful form – two diametrically opposed perspectives are confronted with one another, each emphasizing one pole of the paradox. These two opposite positions are in fact the thesis and the antithesis of the debate, challenging the reader to search for an appropriate synthesis somewhere between the two extremes. This form of debate is called 'dialectical inquiry' – by using two opposite points of view, the problem-solver attempts to arrive at a better understanding of the issue and a 'higher level resolution' that integrates elements of both the thesis and the antithesis. This approach has a number of advantages:

- Range of ideas. By presenting the two opposite poles in each debate, readers can quickly acquire an understanding of the full range of ideas on the strategy issue. While these two extreme positions do not represent the most widely held views, they do clarify for the reader how diverse the thinking actually is on each strategy issue. This is the *book-end function* of presenting the two opposite perspectives – they 'frame' the full set of views that exist on the topic.

- Points of contention. Usually there is not across-the-board disagreement between the various approaches to each strategy issue, but opinions tend to diverge on a number of critical points. By presenting the two opposite poles in each debate, readers can rapidly gain insight into these major points of contention. This is the *contrast function* of presenting the two opposite perspectives – they bring the key points of contention into sharper focus.

- Stimulus for bridging. As the two opposite poles in each debate are presented, readers will be struck by the fact that neither position can be easily dismissed. Both extreme strategy perspectives make a strong case for a particular approach and readers will experience difficulty in simply choosing one over the other. With each extreme position offering certain advantages, readers will feel challenged to incorporate aspects of both into a more sophisticated synthesis. This is the *integrative function* of presenting the two opposite perspectives – they stimulate readers to seek a way of getting the best of both worlds.

- Stimulus for creativity. Nothing is more creativity evoking than a challenging paradox whereby two opposites seem to be true at the same time. By presenting the two opposite poles of each debate, which both make a realistic claim to being valid, readers are challenged to creatively resolve this paradoxical situation. This is the *generative function* of presenting the two opposite perspectives – they stimulate readers to generate innovative ways of 'transcending' the strategic paradox.

Each chapter starts with the most traditional pole as the thesis, which is then contrasted with the less-established opposite pole as the antithesis. As for the synthesis, that is up to each strategist to find (see Figure 1.8).

FIGURE 1.8   Strategy synthesis

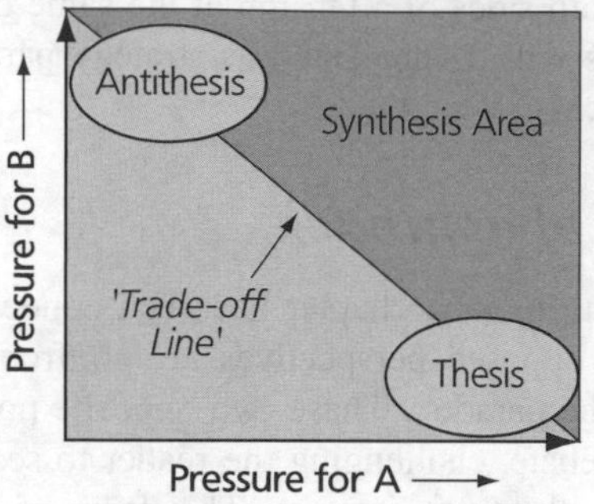

DEVELOPING AN INTERNATIONAL PERSPECTIVE

Every man takes the limits of his own field of vision for the limits of the world.
Arthur Schopenhauer (1788–1860); German philosopher

In a highly integrated world economy, in which many firms operate across national boundaries, strategy is by nature an international affair. Some theorists ignore the international arena as irrelevant, uninteresting or too complex, but most theorists, particularly those interested in strategy content, acknowledge the importance of the international context and write extensively on international competition and global strategy. In this book there has been a strong preference to include those authors, who explicitly place their arguments within an international setting. Gaining an international perspective is greatly enhanced by reading works that do not take a domestic arena as their default assumption.

To further accentuate the international angle in this book, the international context has been singled out for a closer look in Chapter 10. In this chapter, the conflicting views about developments in the international context will be debated. This, too, should challenge readers to take an international perspective.

However, despite all this attention paid to the international competitive arena, internationalizing companies, cross-border strategies and global products, few authors explicitly question whether their own strategy theories can be globally standardized. Most fail to wonder whether their theories are equally applicable in a variety of national settings. It is seldom asked whether they base themselves on universally valid assumptions, or if they have been severely limited by their domestic 'field of vision'. Yet, there is a very real danger that theories are based on local assumptions that are not true or appropriate in other nations – a threat that could be called 'think local, generalize global'.

Developing an international perspective requires strategists to guard against the indiscriminate export of domestically generated strategy theories across international borders. For international strategists it is important to question whether theories 'travel' as well as the companies they describe. Unfortunately, at the moment, strategizing managers have little to base themselves on. There has been only a modest amount of international comparative research carried out in the field of strategy. National differences in strategic management practices and preferences have occasionally been identified, but in general the topic has received little attention. In practice, the international validity of locally formulated strategy theories has gone largely unquestioned in international journals and forums.

Although there is still so little published material to go on, in this book readers will be encouraged to question the international limitations of strategy theories. Furthermore, they will be challenged to question whether certain strategy perspectives are more popular and/or appropriate in some countries than in others. To point readers in the right direction, at the end of each chapter a sub-section will be presented that places the strategy topic being debated in an international perspective. In these sub-sections, it will be argued that the strategy paradoxes identified in this book are fundamentally the same around the world, but that there might be international differences in how each paradox is coped with. Strategy perspectives and theories might be more predominant in particular countries because they are based on certain assumptions about dealing with the strategy paradoxes that are more suitable to the national context. In each 'international perspective' sub-section, a number of factors will be discussed that might cause national differences in strategy styles.

Using the cases

An additional way of gaining an international perspective is by trying to employ the strategy perspectives in a variety of national settings. It is especially when trying to deal with concrete strategic problems on an international stage that the limitations of each theory will become more apparent. For this reason, a large number of cases have been included in this book, from many different countries. In each case, readers are encouraged to evaluate the specific national circumstances in which the problem situation is embedded, and to question whether the national context will have an influence on the validity or appropriateness of the various strategy theories and perspectives.

The cases have been selected to cover a wide variety of countries and industries. Furthermore, they have been chosen for their fit with a particular chapter. Each of the following ten chapters in this book has three corresponding cases, in which the paradox under discussion is prominently present. Two of the three cases per chapter are relatively lengthy, and have been grouped together in Section vi of this book. The short case for each chapter has been inserted as an exhibit into the main text. In each case readers will encounter the fact that grappling with strategy paradoxes in 'practice' is just as difficult as dealing with them in 'theory'.

EXHIBIT 1.1 SHORT CASE

DISNEY: ANY MAGIC LEFT IN THE MOUSE HOUSE?

It is little known that the world's most famous mouse, who goes by such names as Topolino in Italy, Musse Pigg in Sweden and Mi Lao Shu in China, actually used to be a bunny. The main character in Walt Disney's first cartoon was a creature named Oswald the Lucky Rabbit, but after Disney was cheated out of his copyrights, he modified the ears and renamed him Mickey Mouse. What is more widely known is that Walt, and his brother Roy, subsequently captured the attention of audiences around the world with Mickey as *Steamboat Willie* (1928), in the first cartoon with synchronized sound. After some modest successes with such new characters as Goofy and Donald Duck, the business of Disney Brothers Studios really started to accelerate when they moved into full-length animated films, releasing blockbusters such as *Snow White and the Seven Dwarfs* (1937), *Pinocchio* (1940) and *Bambi* (1942). Soon Disney discovered the lucrative merchandising business, licensing the use of Disney characters for such things as clothing, pencils and soda-cans. On the basis of this success, Disney branched out into TV programs, film music and live-action movie productions. In 1955, Walt's dream of creating a 'Magical Kingdom' was realized when Disneyland was opened in Anaheim, California. After Walt's death in 1966, Roy carried on to build Disney World in Orlando, Florida, which was completed just before he passed away in 1971.

While the empire the brothers left behind carried on to entertain billions of children and adults the world over, the creative pipeline dried up completely. After the release of Walt's last project, *Jungle Book*, in 1967, the Disney studios spent the 1970s looking for ways to emulate the founder's magic, but without result. By 1983, only 4% of US movie-goers went to a Disney picture, and the 15-year drought of hit movies was being severely felt in the sales of Disney merchandise and licensing income. In the same year, the Disney Channel was launched in the United States, but did not get off to a flying start. Making things worse, the hordes that initially swamped the theme parks were getting bored with Disney's dingy image and visitor numbers began to shrink, while at the same time Disney was incurring heavy costs to finish the Epcot Center at Disney World. To stem the tide, a new management team was hired in 1984, consisting of a brash young executive from Paramount Studios, Michael Eisner, who became CEO, and a level-headed operational man from Warner Brothers, Frank Wells, who became COO.

At Paramount, Eisner had produced hit movies such as *Raiders of the Lost Ark* and *Grease*, as well as the successful television shows *Happy Days* and *Cheers*. He was known as passionate, creative and hands-on, with a fanatical attention to detail, to the extent of getting involved in reading scripts and selecting costumes. Wells, on the other hand, was known for his operational planning and people skills. Together they quickly set out to rejuvenate Disney, beginning with the business they knew best – movies. In the live-action movie business, they redirected Disney towards lower budget films, using promising scripts from less-established writers and actors who seemed at the end of their careers. Through a new subsidiary, Touchstone Pictures, Disney also entered the attractive market for films for the teen and young adult audience. With hits such as *Good Morning Vietnam* and *Down and Out in Beverly Hills,* Disney reached a 19% US box office share by 1988, causing Eisner to comment that 'nearly overnight, Disney went from nerdy outcast to leader of the popular crowd'. Later Disney was responsible for successes such as *Pretty Woman* (1990) and *Pulp Fiction* (1994) – the latter made by Miramax, an avant-garde movie studio Disney had acquired a year before.

The animation part of the business was also revitalized, with major investments made in new animation technology and new people – in particular a new creative producer, Jeffrey Katzenberg. Eventually, this resulted in a series of very successful films: *The Little Mermaid* (1989), *Beauty and the Beast* (1991), *Aladdin* (1992) and *The Lion King*

(1994). To keep the new movies in the limelight, alliances were formed with McDonald's and Coca-Cola involving promotional tie-ins. And to get spin-off merchandise flowing in greater volumes, Eisner moved beyond mere licensing, building up a global chain of Disney stores. Helped by a little luck, Disney also profited from the new home video trend that was sweeping the world. Not only could Disney release its new movies twice – first in the theatres and then on video – it could also re-release a steady stream of classic pictures for home audiences.

In the theme park business, the major innovation spearheaded by Eisner and Wells was to make Disneyland and Disney World more appealing to adults. In 1989 the Disney-MGM Studios theme park was opened near Disney World, as well as the Pleasure Island nightlife complex. Based on the success of Tokyo Disneyland, which was opened in 1983, Disney also built a theme park outside of Paris, called Euro Disney, which opened in 1992. It turned out that while the Japanese visitors appreciated an almost replica of Disney World in Tokyo, European tastes were very different, requiring a long period of adaptation to the local market conditions and causing Euro Disney (later renamed Disneyland Paris) to suffer significant losses over a number of years.

Then, in 1994, Frank Wells was killed in a helicopter crash, Eisner had bypass heart surgery, and a period of boardroom infighting commenced, leading to the high profile departure of the studio head, Katzenberg (who later received US$250 million in compensation and teamed up with Steven Spielberg and David Geffen to found a new independent film company, DreamWorks SKG). Other executives also left, pointing to Eisner's overbearing presence. 'People get tired of being second guessed and beaten down,' a former studio executive remarked. 'When people came out of Michael's office wounded, Frank was the emergency room,' another Disney insider reported to *Fortune*, but with Wells gone, no one was there to repair damaged egos and sooth hurt feelings. However, Eisner viewed the situation differently: 'I've never had a problem with anybody who was truly talented . . . This autonomy crap? That means you're off working alone. If you want autonomy, be a poet.'

During this period, Eisner made his biggest move yet, acquiring Capital Cities/ABC for US$19.6 billion. This deal included the ABC Television Network (distributing to 224 affiliated stations), the ABC

Radio Networks (with 3400 radio outlets) and an 80% share of ESPN, a sport-oriented network, which includes various cable channels and radio stations. Ironically, Eisner had previously worked for ABC as daytime programmer, and felt that he had a lot to add to ABC: 'I would love, every morning, to go over and spend two hours at ABC. Even though my children tell me that I am in the wrong generation and I don't get it anymore, I am totally convinced that I could sit with our guys and make ABC No. 1 in two years.' To help him manage during this period, Eisner hired Michael Ovitz as second man, but this ended in divorce within 16 months, and a US$100 million severance package.

Soon after this episode, Disney's artistic and financial performance began to deteriorate. Between 1984 and 1997, operating income grew more than 20% per year, reaching US$4.5 billion, but between 1998 and 2003 the company got nowhere near this level. Eisner's major headache was ABC, which was the top-rated network at the time of the acquisition, but quickly fell to third place in the ratings. The network had a short-lived success in 2000 with one blockbuster show, *Who Wants to be a Millionaire?*, but once this fad had ebbed away, ABC sunk back into last place. In an attempt to turn around fortunes, Eisner fired the head of ABC Entertainment, Stu Bloomberg, in 2002, and installed Susan Lyne. She immediately indicated that she was reconsidering Disney's vertical integration strategy, whereby Disney subsidiary, Touchstone Television, provides the majority of programs for ABC. This strategy is beneficial when shows turn out to be hits, because Touchstone can then supply reruns and related materials to other parts of the Disney family. The downside of wanting to do everything itself is that Disney runs all risks alone and that ABC cannot tap into multiple talent pools.

At the same time, Disney's animation track record has been wobbly since Katzenberg left – movies such as *Pocahontas* (1995) and *Tarzan* (1999) did not do too badly, although soaring costs made them only mildly profitable. Other features, such as *Atlantis* (2001) and *Treasure Island* (2002) were box office fiascos. Disney's real animation successes have come from the organization's deal with Pixar, an independent studio specializing in computer-generated animations, run by former Apple CEO, Steve Jobs. Such co-productions as *Toy Story* (1995), *Monsters Inc.* (2000) and *Lilo and Stitch* (2002) have been hits in the cinemas and on DVD. Yet, this makes Disney all the more dependent on Pixar, raising the question whether Disney should develop these capabilities in-house instead of sticking to current animation competences.

In the area of live-action films, Disney's approach changed dramatically after Joe Roth took over in 1994. Instead of Katzenberg's policy of setting a 'financial box' within which the creatives had to operate, Roth moved to bigger budgets, big names and big special effects – and just a few too many big disasters. Illustrative were *Pearl Harbor* (2001) and *Gangs of New York* (2002), both with immense production budgets, yet unable to live up to their promise. The result has been a high market share for Disney films, but profitability hovering just above zero, so Roth too has exited the company. Add to this that Disney seriously over-built the number of Disney Stores, necessitating the closing of about a quarter of the 550 US outlets, while in the mature theme park business, tight consumer spending and a general fear of traveling have plagued operations. The head of this division, Paul Pressler, also left the company in 2002, further thinning the ranks of long-term senior managers.

All these developments have led analysts to raise some big question marks. For instance, in *The Economist* the question was asked whether Eisner had upset the balance between the suits and the ponytails – the logic-oriented managers and the creative types – placing too much emphasis on rationalistic management systems. Moreover, it was wondered whether Eisner had gone overboard in his micro-management of all aspects of the business, trying to influence everything from the program schedule of ABC to the furniture at the new Animal Kingdom Lodge, not allowing for enough individual autonomy. Another question was whether Eisner had just basically run out of good ideas to challenge the rules of the game in the entertainment industry and had become too settled. Could it also be that striving for synergy within Disney had led to insufficient responsiveness to the specific characteristics of each separate business?

Eisner's response to these questions has been characteristically upbeat: 'Maybe I'm crazy, but I don't consider this a crisis,' Eisner told *Fortune*. 'We're being buried a little prematurely here . . . I spend my life being Odysseus. I tie myself to the mast, and don't listen to the Sirens. The Sirens in my business are agents, investment bankers, the media, people saying that your testosterone level is gone because you haven't made an acquisition in

▶

the last ten minutes.' He points out that major turn-around initiatives have been introduced, chopping thousands of jobs. And Disney is well positioned to gain from the accelerating sales of DVDs and the commercial downloading of songs, games and characters into a wide variety of new gadgets, such as personal digital assistants and cell phones. In Anaheim, Downtown Disney and Disney's California Adventure were opened in 2001, while overseas the new Tokyo Disney Sea Park was opened in 2000, Disneyland Paris is being expanded and a new park is set to open in Hong Kong in 2006.

As Eisner says: 'We've solidified our company . . . when the economy turns, and when the fear of flying goes away, when we get a couple of hits on ABC – and because of how lean we've made the company – I believe it becomes a gusher. I want to be here to take advantage of all the work we've done and all the crap we took . . . we'll be the premier growth company in the business.' But then again, the clock might strike 12 and the magic might be over.

Sources: Disney *Annual Report 2002*; *The Economist*, September 28 2002 and January 16 2003; *Fortune*, December 23 2001; *Harvard Business Review*, January–February 2000; *Business Week*, June 24 2002; http://disney.go.com.

READINGS

Unless a variety of opinions are laid before us, we have no opportunity of selection, but are bound of necessity to adopt the particular view which may have been brought forward. The purity of gold cannot be ascertained by a single specimen; but when we have carefully compared it with others, we are able to fix upon the finest ore.
Herodotus (5th century BC); Greek historian

In the following ten chapters the readings will represent the different points of view in the debate. The readings will 'lay the variety of opinions before us'. However, in this opening chapter there is no central debate. Therefore, four readings have been selected that provide a stimulating introduction to the topic of strategy, or reinforce some of the arguments made in the preceding pages. Here, each of the readings will be briefly introduced and its relevance for the discussion will be highlighted.

The opening reading, 'The First Strategists' by Stephen Cummings, places the central question of this book – What is strategy? – in a historical perspective. Cummings takes the reader back to the ancient Greeks, to whom we owe the term strategy, in a quest to uncover some fundamental characteristics of military strategy and strategists, which he believes are still important for business strategists today. The charm of this extract lies not only in its clear and concise rendition of Hellenic thought, but also in its ability to place the current state of the art of strategic thinking in the humbling context of history. This reading convincingly points out that many seemingly modern strategy issues are actually millennia old. The development of the business strategy field may be a recent academic trend, stretching no further back than the 1960s, but outside commerce many of the great minds throughout history have occupied themselves with the topic of strategy, especially in the fields of war (see, for instance, the famous Chinese theorist Sun Tzu's *The Art of War* and Karl von Clausewitz's *On War*) and politics (for example, Niccolo Machiavelli's *The Prince and the Discourses*). The debate, which Cummings opens with this reading, is to what extent the principles of military strategy can be applied to the business context. Can business strategists learn from military strategists, and vice versa? Stated even more broadly, to what measure are there parallels between strategy in such diverse fields as war, politics, sports, biology and business? Are there universal principles of strategy? The extent to which the strategy principles of one area are valid in another is a recurrent theme in strategy literature.

Reading 1.2, 'Complexity: The Nature of Real World Problems', is the first chapter of Richard Mason and Ian Mitroff's classic book, *Challenging Strategic Planning Assumptions*. This thought-provoking extract has been selected for this chapter to serve as an introduction to the complex nature of the strategic problems addressed in this book. Mason and Mitroff's main argument is that most strategic problems facing organizations are not 'tame' – that is, they are not simple problems that can be separated and reduced to a few variables and relationships, and then quickly solved. Strategic problems are usually 'wicked': strategists are faced with situations of organized complexity in which problems are complicated and interconnected, there is much uncertainty and ambiguity, and they must deal with conflicting views and interests. Therefore, strategic problems have no clearly identifiable correct solutions, but must be tackled by debating the alternatives and selecting the most promising option. Mason and Mitroff call on strategists to systematically doubt the value of all available solutions and to employ dialectics – which is exactly the approach taken in this book. In the context of this chapter, the most important message that Mason and Mitroff have is that the variety of opinions might make things more complex, but are also a useful resource for finding better quality solutions.

While Mason and Mitroff describe how *problem-solving* strategists can deal with complexity and differing perspectives, the authors of Reading 1.3 take a look at the same subjects from a *theory-building* point of view. In this reading, 'Using Paradox to Build Management and Organization Theories', Marshall Scott Poole and Andrew Van de Ven also explore what to do with contrary or contradictory assumptions, explanations and conclusions, but as management theorists rather than as strategizing managers. This well-known article has been selected for this chapter because it provides further insight into why it is valuable for 'strategic thinkers' in general to embrace opposing theories and 'to play them off against one another'. In particular, this article explains the value of paradoxes for advancing our understanding of how organizations and management work. According to Poole and Van de Ven, paradoxes are especially interesting because 'they present opportunities to discover different assumptions, shift perspectives, pose problems in fundamentally different ways, and focus on different research questions'. Besides encouraging theorists to give up 'the pursuit of an elusive consistency' and to 'work with inconsistencies, contradictions and tensions', Poole and Van de Ven also propose four 'methods for resolving or capitalizing on paradoxes'. While all four approaches are useful, for the problem-solving strategist the fourth option is of particular interest – synthesis. Similar to the discussion earlier in this chapter, Poole and Van de Ven argue that a new conception can be developed, that creatively integrates the opposing phenomena without 'eliminating' the tension. The authors conclude by speculating that the world is inherently paradoxical, which suggests that management thinkers would do well to get used to viewing reality in terms of paradoxes.

The last reading, 'Cultural Constraints in Management Theories' by Geert Hofstede, has been selected to sow further doubt about the universal validity of strategic management theories. Hofstede is one of the most prominent cross-cultural researchers in the field of management and is known, in particular, for his five dimensions for measuring cultural traits. In this reading he briefly describes the major characteristics of management in Germany, Japan, France, Holland, South-East Asia, Africa, Russia and China, contrasting them all to the United States, to drive home his point that management practices differ from country to country depending on the local culture. Each national style is based on cultural characteristics that differ sharply around the world. Hofstede argues that theories are formulated within these national cultural contexts, and thus reflect the local demands and predispositions. Therefore, he concludes that universal management theories do not exist – each theory is culturally constrained. If Hofstede is right, this re-emphasizes the necessity to view strategic management and strategy theories from an international perspective. Readers must judge which strategy approach is best suited to the national circumstances with which they are confronted.

READING

1.1

The first strategists

By Stephen Cummings[1]

Origin of strategy

The word *strategy* derives from the ancient Athenian position of *strategos*. The title was coined in conjunction with the democratic reforms of Kleisthenes (508–7 BC), who developed a new sociopolitical structure in Athens after leading a popular revolution against a Spartan-supported oligarchy. Kleisthenes instituted 10 new tribal divisions, which acted as both military and political subunits of the district of Athens. At the head of each tribe was elected a strategos. Collectively, the 10 incumbent *strategoi* formed the Athenian war council. This council and its individual members, by virtue of the kudos granted them, also largely controlled nonmilitary politics.

Strategos was a compound of *stratos*, which meant 'army,' or more properly an encamped army *spread out* over ground (in this way *stratos* is also allied to *stratum*) and *agein*, 'to lead.' The emergence of the term paralleled increasing military decision-making complexity. Warfare had evolved to a point where winning sides no longer relied on the deeds of heroic individuals, but on the coordination of many units of men each fighting in close formation. Also, the increasing significance of naval forces in this period multiplied the variables a commander must consider in planning action. Consequently, questions of coordination and synergy among the various emergent units of their organizations became imperative considerations for successful commanders.

Of what interest are the origins of strategy to those engaging in strategic activities and decision making in organizations today? In the words of Adlai Stevenson, we can see our future clearly and wisely only when we know the path that leads to the present. Most involved in corporate strategy have little knowledge of where that path began. A great deal of insight into strategy can be gained from examining those from whom we inherit the term. The first strategists, the Greek strategoi, perhaps practiced strategy in its purest sense.

Strategy and strategist as defined by ancient theorists

Aineias the Tactician, who wrote the earliest surviving Western volume on military strategy, *How to Survive under Siege*, in the mid fourth century BC, was primarily concerned with how to deploy available manpower and other resources to best advantage. The term strategy is defined in more detail by Frontinus in the first century AD, as 'everything achieved by a commander, be it characterized by foresight, advantage, enterprise, or resolution.'

Ancient Athenian theorists also had clear ideas about the characteristics that were necessary in an effective strategos. According to Xenophon, a commander 'must be ingenious, energetic, careful, full of stamina and presence of mind, loving and tough, straightforward and crafty, alert and deceptive, ready to gamble everything and wishing to have everything, generous and greedy, trusting and suspicious.' These criteria for identifying an excellent strategist still ring true.

Xenophon goes on to describe the most important attribute for an aspiring strategos/statement as 'knowing the business which you propose to carry out.' The Athenians in this period were very concerned that their leaders had an awareness of how things worked at the 'coal-face.' Strategoi were publicly elected by their fellow members of the Athenian organization; and to be considered a credible candidate, one had to have worked one's way into this position by demonstrating prowess at both individual combat and hands-on military leadership. Wisdom was considered to be a citizen's ability to combine political acumen and practical intelligence, and strategoi should be the wisest of citizens. The organization's future lay in the hands of these men and, ipso facto, the strategic leadership of the Athenian organization was not to consider itself immune from hardship when times were tough: 'No man was fitted to give fair and honest advice in council if he has not, like his fellows, a family at stake in the hour of the city's danger.'

[1]Source: This article was reprinted from *Long Range Planning*, Vol. 26, No. 3, S. Cummings, 'Brief Case: The First Strategists', pp. 133–135, © 1993. With permission from Elsevier.

To the ancient Athenians strategy was very much a line of function. The formulation of strategy was a leadership task. The Athenian organization developed by Kleisthenes was extremely recursive. The new tribes, and the local communities that these tribes comprised, formed the units and subunits of the army, and were, in their sociopolitical structures, tantamount to the city-state in microcosm. Decision makers at all levels of the corporation were expected to think strategically, in accordance with the behavior exhibited by those in leadership roles at higher levels of the Athenian system. Strategoi were expected both to direct and take part in the thick of battle, leading their troops into action. For a strategos not to play an active combat role would have resulted in a significant diminution in the morale of those fighting for his tribe.

Practical lessons from the strategoi

If military practice is identified as a metaphor for business competition, the strategic principles of the great strategoi still provide useful guides for those in the business of strategy formulation today. For Pericles, perhaps the greatest of the Athenian strategoi, the goal of military strategies was 'to limit risk while holding fast to essential points and principles.' His often quoted maxims of 'Opportunity waits for no man' and 'Do not make any new conquests during the war' are still applicable advice in a modern business environment.

Epaminondas of Thebes was said to have brought the two arms of his military corporation, infantry and cavalry, together in a 'fruitful organizational blend.' The Theban's strategic principles included economy of force coupled with overwhelming strength at the decisive point; close coordination between units and meticulous staff planning combined with speed of attack; and as the quickest and most economical way of winning a decision, defeat of the competition not at his weakest point but at his strongest. Epaminondas was Philip of Macedon's mentor, and it was largely due to the application of the Theban's innovations that the Macedonian army grew to an extent where it was able to realize Alexander the Great's (Philip's son) vast ambitions. The close integration of all its individual units became the major strength of the Macedonian army organization.

Alexander himself is perhaps the most famous ancient exponent of a contingency approach to strategy. It is often told that as a young man he was asked by his tutor Aristotle what he would do in a given situation. Alexander replied that his answer would depend on the circumstances. Aristotle described a hypothetical set of circumstances and asked his original question again. To this the student answered, 'I cannot tell until the circumstances arise.' In practice Alexander was not often caught without a 'plan B.' An example is related by Frontinus: 'At Arbela, Alexander, fearing the numbers of the enemy, yet confident in the valour of his own troops, drew up a line of battle facing in all directions, in order that the men, if surrounded, might be able to fight from any side.'

Ancient approaches to the learning of strategy

The ancient Greeks took great interest in both the practical and theoretical aspects of strategic leadership. They favored the case method as the best means of passing this knowledge from one generation of strategists to the next. Frontinus argued that 'in this way commanders will be furnished with specimens of wisdom and foresight, which will serve to foster their own power of conceiving and executing like deeds.' Aineias and Xenophon also used and championed such methods in ways that would please any Harvardophile. The best-crafted exposition of the case method, however, belongs to Plutarch, biographer to the ancient world's greatest leaders:

It is true, of course, that our outward sense cannot avoid apprehending the various objects it encounters, merely by virtue of their impact and regardless of whether they are useful or not: but a man's conscious intellect is something which he may bring to bear or avert as he chooses, and can very easily transfer . . . to another object as he sees fit. For this reason, we ought to seek out virtue not merely to contemplate it, but to derive benefit from doing so. A colour, for example, is well suited to the eye if its bright and agreeable tones stimulate and refresh the vision, and in the same way we ought to apply our intellectual vision to those models which can inspire it to attain its own proper virtue through the sense of delight they arouse . . . [Such a model is] no sooner seen than it rouses the spectator into action, and yet it does not form his character by mere imitation, but by promoting the understanding of virtuous deeds it provides him with a dominating purpose.

Now, as then, our strategic vision can be refreshed and stimulated through studying the character and deeds of the great strategic leaders of the past.

READING
1.2

Complexity: The nature of real world problems

By Richard Mason and Ian Mitroff[1]

Try a little experiment. Make a short list of the major problems or issues facing policymakers in the world today. Now take your list and arrange it as a matrix like the one in Figure 1.2.1. For each element in the matrix ask yourself the following question: Is the solution to one problem (the row problem) in any way related to the solution of the other problem (the column problem)? If the answer is yes, place a check mark at the point where the row and column intersect; otherwise leave it blank. When you have completed the process, review the matrix and count the number of blanks. Are there any?

'Not fair!' you may say. 'There were a lot of check marks in my matrix because many of these world problems are linked together.' World problems involve all nations. One would not expect to get the same result if the focus was, say, on one's company, city, family, or personal life. Really? Try it and see. Recently, several managers at a major corporation tried this little experiment as part of a strategic planning effort. Among the issues and problem areas they identified were the following:

- Satisfy stockholder dividend and risk requirements.
- Acquire adequate funds for expansion from the capital markets.
- Insure a stable supply of energy at reasonable prices.
- Train a corps of middle managers to assume more responsibility.
- Develop a marketing force capable of handling new product lines.

The managers found that all of these problems and issues were related to each other. Some were only related weakly, but most were related quite strongly. Repeated attempts in other contexts give the same result: *basically, every real world policy problem is related to every other real world problem.* This is an important finding. It means that every time a policymaker attempts to solve a particular policy problem he or she must consider its potential relationship with all other problems. To do this one must have both a comprehensive set of concepts for dealing with any policy and a rich set of tools for acquiring the holistic information needed to guide policy making.

FIGURE 1.2.1   Problem interaction matrix

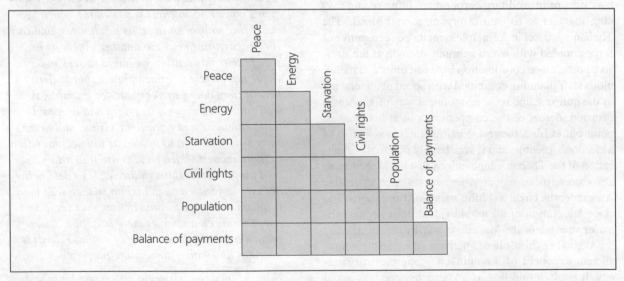

[1]Source: This article was adapted from Chapter 1 of R. Mason and I. Mitroff, *Challenging Strategic Planning Assumptions*, © John Wiley & Sons, Inc. 1981. This material is used by permission of John Wiley & Sons, Inc.

Characteristics of complexity

There are several characteristics of policy making that the foregoing little experiment is intended to illustrate:

- Any policy-making situation comprises many problems and issues.

- These problems and issues tend to be highly interrelated. Consequently, the solution to one problem requires a solution to all the other problems. At the same time, each solution creates additional dimensions to be incorporated in the solutions to other problems.

- Few, if any, problems can be isolated effectively for separate treatment.

These are the characteristics of complexity. Complexity literally means the condition of being tightly woven or twined together. Most policymakers find that the problems they face today are complex in this sense. Moreover, almost all of today's problems seem to be getting more plentiful and complex.

There is an especially vexing aspect of complexity as it presents itself to policymakers. It is organized. As we have seen in the little experiment, there tends to be an illusive structure underlying problems that gives pattern and organization to the whole. Organization is usually considered the route to the solution of a complex problem. In reality, however, organization in complexity can become an insurmountable barrier to the solution of a problem. This is the major challenge to real world problem solving because we have very few intellectual tools for coping with 'organized complexity.'

The tools we have available seem to work best on simple problems, those that can be separated and reduced to relatively few variables and relationships. These problems of simplicity usually have a one-dimensional value system or goal structure that guides the solution. Three factors – separability, reducibility, and one-dimensional goal structure – mean that simple problems can be bounded, managed, and, as Horst Rittel (1972) puts it, 'tamed.'

Ironically, problems of the utmost complexity can also be tamed as long as the complexity is 'disorganized.' That is, whenever the number of variables is very large and the variables are relatively disconnected, the problem can be tamed with the elegant simplicity of statistical mechanics. For example, there is no known way of predicting how a given individual will vote on a political candidate. However, using polling procedures and statistical techniques it is possible to predict with a fair degree of confidence how an entire population of voters will vote. Similarly, it is difficult to predict whether a given customer will purchase a new product or not. However, using market research methods, a fairly good estimate can be made of a new product's potential market share.

Perhaps one of the greatest insights of the twentieth century is the discovery that when a problem situation meets the condition for random sampling – many individual elements exhibiting independent, probabilistic behavior – there is a potential statistical solution to the problem. In short, disorganized complexity can generally be tamed by statistical means.

One place where the assumption of disorganized complexity has proven invaluable in the past is in the actuarial sciences. Today, however, the insurance industry is discovering that many of the risks once assumed to be reasonably independent and hence analyzable according to standard actuarial methods are no longer so. People, organizations, and facilities have become more tightly woven together over wider geographical areas. Consequently, the probabilities of death, accident, fire, or disaster on which the risks and premiums are based are no longer as straightforward as they once were. The result is that the statistical methods that applied under conditions of disorganized complexity have become less reliable as the system has become more organized.

The great difficulty with connected systems of organized complexity is that deviations in one element can be transmitted to other elements. In turn, these deviations can be magnified, modified, and reverberated so that the system takes on a kind of unpredictable life of its own. Emery and Trist (1965) refer to this condition as 'environmental connectedness' and have labeled this type of environment the 'turbulent' environment.

Emery and Trist cite an interesting case to illustrate the nature of environmental connectedness and the great difficulties it presents to policy makers. In Great Britain after World War II, a large food canning company began to expand. Its main product was a canned vegetable – a staple in the English diet. As part of the expansion plan, the company decided to build a new, automated factory, requiring an investment of several million pounds sterling. For over a decade the company had enjoyed a 65 percent market share for their product line and saw no reason for this strong market position to deteriorate. Given this large volume, the new plant offered the 'experience curve' advantages of economies to scale and made possible the long production runs required to meet the demand from the traditional market.

After ground was broken, but well before the factory was completed, a series of seemingly detached and isolated socioeconomic events occurred. These relatively insignificant events were to change the destiny of the company. Taken collectively, they rendered the factory economically obsolete and threw the corporate board of directors into a state of turmoil. The scenario of events went something like this. Due to the release of wartime controls on steel strip and tin, a number of new small firms that could economically can imported fruit sprang up. Initially, they in no way competed directly with the large vegetable canner. However, since their business was seasonal, they began to look for ways to keep their machinery and labor employed during the winter. Their answer came from a surprising source – the US quick-frozen food industry. The quick-freezing process requires a substantial degree of consistency in the crop. This consistency is very difficult to achieve. However, it turned out that large crops of the vegetable were grown in the United States and a substantial portion of US crops was unsuitable for quick freezing (a big industry in the United States) but quite suitable for canning. Furthermore, American farmers had been selling this surplus crop at a very low price for animal feed and were only too happy to make it available at an attractive price to the small canners in the United Kingdom. The canners jumped at the opportunity and imported the crop. Using off-season production capacity they began to offer a low-cost product in the large canner's market. The small canners' position was further strengthened as underdeveloped countries began to vie with the United States in an effort to become the cheapest source of supply for the crop.

These untimely events in the large canner's supply market were compounded by events in its product market. Prior to the introduction of quick-freezing, the company featured a high quality, higher price premier brand that dominated the market. This market advantage, however, was diminished by the cascading effect of several more unpredictable events. As the scenario unfolded the quick-frozen product captured the high quality strata of the market, a growing dimension due to increased affluence. The smaller canners stripped off the lower price layers of the market, aided in part by another seemingly unrelated development in retailing – the advent of supermarkets. As supermarkets and large grocery chains developed, they sought to improve their position by establishing their own in-house brand names and by buying in bulk. The small canner filled this need for the supermarket chains. Small canners could undercut the price of the manufacturer's brand product because they had low production costs and almost no marketing expenses. Soon supermarket house brands (which had accounted for less than 1 percent of the market prior to the war) became the source of 50 percent of the market sales. The smaller canners were the benefactors of almost all of this growth.

As a result, the company's fancy new automated factory was totally inappropriate for the current market situation. The company's management had failed to appreciate that a number of outside events were becoming connected with each other in a way that was leading up to an inevitable general change. They tried desperately to defend their traditional product lines, but, in the end, this was to no avail. After a series of financial setbacks, the company had to change its mission. It reemerged several years later with a new product mix and a new identity. Management had learned the hard way that their strategy problems were neither problems of simplicity nor problems of disorganized complexity. They were problems of organized complexity.

Many corporate policy planning and strategy issues exhibit this property of organized complexity. The vegetable canning company's automated plant decision clearly was made under conditions of organized complexity. Pricing problems also frequently display this characteristic. Recently, a large pharmaceutical firm addressed the seemingly simple problem of setting a price for its primary drug line. The company's management soon learned, however, that there was an intricate web of corporate relationships woven around this one decision. Below the surface there was a structure of complex relationships between the firm's drug pricing policy and physicians, pharmacists, patients, competitors, suppliers, the FDA, and other parties. These relationships organized the complexity of the firm's pricing decision problem. Purely analytical or statistical methods were rendered inappropriate.

'Wicked' problems

Today, few of the pressing problems are truly problems of simplicity or of disorganized complexity. They are more like the problems described in the illustrative cases above and the ones we uncovered in our little experiment – problems of organized complexity. These problems simply cannot be tamed in the same way that other problems can. For this reason Rittel refers to these problems of organized complexity as 'wicked' problems. Wicked problems are not necessarily wicked in the perverse sense of being evil. Rather, they are wicked like the head of a hydra. They are an ensnarled web of tentacles. The more you attempt to tame them, the more complicated they become.

Rittel (1972) has identified several characteristic properties of wicked problems that distinguish them from tame problems. These properties are:

1 *Ability to formulate the problem*

   a Tame problems can be exhaustively formulated and written down on a piece of paper.

   b Wicked problems have no definitive formulation.

2 *Relationship between problem and solution*

   a Tame problems can be formulated separately from any notion of what their solution might be.

   b Every formulation of a wicked problem corresponds to a statement of solution and vice versa. Understanding the problem is synonymous with solving it.

3 *Testability*

   a The solution to a tame problem can be tested. Either it is correct or it is false. Mistakes and errors can be pinpointed.

   b There is no single criteria system or rule that determines whether the solution to a wicked problem is correct or false. Solutions can only be good or bad relative to one another.

4 *Finality*

   a Tame problems have closure – a clear solution and ending point. The end can be determined by means of a test.

   b There is no stopping rule for wicked problems. Like a Faustian bargain, they require eternal vigilance. There is always room for improvement. Moreover, since there is neither an immediate nor ultimate test for the solution to the problem, one never knows when one's work is done. As a result, the potential consequences of the problem are played out indefinitely.

5 *Tractability*

   a There is an exhaustive list of permissible operations that can be used to solve a tame problem.

   b There is no exhaustive, enumerable list of permissible operations to be used for solving a wicked problem.

6 *Explanatory characteristics*

   a A tame problem may be stated as a 'gap' between what 'is' and what 'ought' to be and there is a clear explanation for every gap.

   b Wicked problems have many possible explanations for the same discrepancy. Depending on which explanation one chooses, the solution takes on a different form.

7 *Level of analysis*

   a Every tame problem has an identifiable, certain, natural form; there is no need to argue about the level of the problem. The proper level of generality can be found for bounding the problem and identifying its root cause.

   b Every wicked problem can be considered as a symptom of another problem. It has no identifiable root cause; since curing symptoms does not cure problems, one is never sure the problem is being attacked at the proper level.

8 *Reproducibility*

   a A tame problem can be abstracted from the real world, and attempts can be made to solve it over and over again until the correct solution is found.

   b Each wicked problem is a one-shot operation. Once a solution is attempted, you can never undo what you have already done. There is no trial and error.

9 *Replicability*

   a The same tame problem may repeat itself many times.

   b Every wicked problem is essentially unique.

10 *Responsibility*

   a No one can be blamed for failing to solve a tame problem, although solving a tame problem may bring someone acclaim.

   b The wicked problem solver has 'no right to be wrong.' He is morally responsible for what he is doing and must share the blame when things go wrong. However, since there is no way of knowing when a wicked problem is solved, very few people are praised for grappling with them.

Characteristics of wicked problems. Most policy planning and strategy problems are wicked problems of organized complexity. These complex wicked problems also exhibit the following characteristics:

1 Interconnectedness. Strong connections link each problem to other problems. As a result, these connections sometimes circle back to form feedback loops. 'Solutions' aimed at the problem seem inevitably to have important opportunity costs and side effects. How they work out depends on events beyond the scope of any one problem.

2 Complicatedness. Wicked problems have numerous important elements with relationships among them,

including important 'feedback loops' through which a change tends to multiply itself or perhaps even cancel itself out. Generally, there are various leverage points where analysis and ideas for intervention might focus, as well as many possible approaches and plausible programs of action. There is also a likelihood that different programs should be combined to deal with a given problem.

3 Uncertainty. Wicked problems exist in a dynamic and largely uncertain environment, which creates a need to accept risk, perhaps incalculable risk. Contingency planning and also the flexibility to respond to unimagined and perhaps unimaginable contingencies are both necessary.

4 Ambiguity. The problem can be seen in quite different ways, depending on the viewer's personal characteristics, loyalties, past experiences, and even on accidental circumstances of involvement. There is no single 'correct view' of the problem.

5 Conflict. Because of competing claims, there is often a need to trade off 'goods' against 'bads' within the same value system. Conflicts of interest among persons or organizations with different or even antagonistic value systems are to be expected. How things will work out may depend on interaction among powerful interests that are unlikely to enter into fully cooperative arrangements.

6 Societal constraints. Social, organizational, and political constraints and capabilities, as well as technological ones, are central both to the feasibility and the desirability of solutions.

These characteristics spell difficulty for the policymaker who seeks to serve a social system by changing it for the better. Policymakers must choose the means for securing improvement for the people they serve. They must design, steer, and maintain a stable social system in the context of a complex environment. To do this, they require new methods of real world problem solving to guide their policy-making activities. Otherwise, they run the risk of setting their social systems adrift.

Implications for policy making.
The wicked problems of organized complexity have two major implications for designing processes for making policy:

1 There must be a broader participation of affected parties, directly and indirectly, in the policy-making process.

2 Policy making must be based on a wider spectrum of information gathered from a larger number of diverse sources.

Let us consider each of these implications in turn. The first implication indicates that policy making is increasingly becoming a political process, political in the sense that it involves individuals forming into groups to pursue common interests. Turn again to the results of the little experiment conducted at the outset of this chapter. You will find that in almost every case there are a variety of individual interests at stake in each problem area cited. Furthermore, one of the major factors creating the linkages between problem areas – organizing their complexity – is the number of diverse individual interests that cut across problem areas. Individuals are part of the problem and hence must be part of the solution.

This means that the raw material for forging solutions to wicked problems is not concentrated in a single head, but rather is widely dispersed among the various parties at stake. For any given wicked problem there is a variety of classes of expertise. Every affected party is an expert on some aspect of the problem and its solution. Furthermore, the disparate parties are bound together in a common venture. Thus some form of collective risk sharing is needed in order to deal effectively with the consequences of wicked problems. This suggests the need for a substantial degree of involvement in the policy-making process by those potentially affected by a policy in its formulation process. Effective policy is made *with*, or if adequate representation is present, *for*, but *not at* people. At least those involved should be able to voice their opinion on the relative goodness or badness of proposed solutions.

The diversity of parties at stake is related to the second implication. Since much of the necessary information for coping with wicked problems resides in the heads of several individuals, methods are needed to obtain this information from them and to communicate it to others. This means that as many of the different sources of information as possible must be identified. The relevant information must be obtained from each and stated in an explicit manner.

Contained in the minds of each participant in a wicked problem are powerful notions as to what is, what ought to be, why things are the way they are, how they can be changed, and how to think about their complexity. This represents a much broader class of information than is commonly used to solve problems of simplicity or of disorganized complexity. Also, this participant-based information is less likely to have been stated and recorded in a communicable form. Consequently, this information must be 'objectified' – explicitly, articulated – so that the basis for each party's judgments may be exchanged with others. Objectification has the advantages of being explicit, providing a memory, controlling the delegation of judgments, and raising pertinent issues that might have been ignored otherwise. It also stimulates *doubt*.

To be in doubt about a piece of information is to withhold assent to it. Given the range of diverse information that characterizes a wicked problem, participants in the policy-making process are well advised to develop a healthy respect for the method of doubt. In dealing with problems of organized complexity one should start with Descartes' rule: 'The first precept was never to accept a thing as true until I knew it was such without a single doubt.' This does not mean that one should be a 'nay sayer' or a permanent skeptic. To do so would impede responsible action that must be taken. What it does imply is that one should withhold judgment on things until they have been tested.

All problem-solving methods presuppose some form of guarantor for the correctness of their solutions. Problems of simplicity can be tested and solutions guaranteed by means of repeated solving, just as a theorem is proven in mathematics. This is because simple problems can be stated in closed form. The solutions to problems of disorganized complexity can be guaranteed within some stated confidence interval or degree of risk because the problems are statistical in nature. However, since there are no clearly identifiable correct solutions to problems of organized complexity, neither analytic nor statistical proofs can guarantee results. For solutions to wicked problems, the method of doubt is the best guarantor available.

Dialectics and argumentation are methods of *systematizing* doubt. They entail the processes of

1 making information and its underlying assumptions explicit;
2 raising questions and issues toward which different positions can be taken;
3 gathering evidence and building arguments for and against each position;
4 attempting to arrive at some final conclusion.

Being fundamentally an argumentative process, these four processes are inherent to policy making. For every policy decision there are always at least two alternative choices that can be made. There is an argument for and against each alternative. It is by weighing the pros and cons of each argument that an informed decision can be reached. In policy making these processes of dialectics and argumentation are inescapable.

In addition to the need for participation by a variety of parties and the existence of diverse information sources, two other characteristics of wicked problems should be noted. One is that they must be dealt with in a holistic or synthetic way as well as in an analytic way. Two processes are necessary: to subdivide a complex problem into its elements and to determine the nature of the linkages that give organization to its complexity – the task of analysis; and to understand the problem as a *whole* – the task of synthesis. A critical dimension of wicked problems of organized complexity is that they must ultimately be dealt with in their totality. This calls for holistic thinking. Analysis is only an aid toward reaching a synthesis.

A second characteristic of these problems is that there is some form of latent structure within them. They are organized to some extent. Organization is not an all or nothing phenomenon. Consequently, systems thinking and methods can be used to gain better insight into the structural aspects of wicked problems.

Quest for new methods. The nature and implications of organized complexity suggest some new criteria for the design of real world problem-solving methods. These criteria are:

1 Participative. Since the relevant knowledge necessary to solve a complex problem and also the relevant resources necessary to implement the solution are distributed among many individuals, the methods must incorporate the active involvement of groups of people.
2 Adversarial. We believe that the best judgment on the assumptions in a complex problem is rendered in the context of opposition. Doubt is the guarantor.
3 Integrative. A unified set of assumptions and a coherent plan of action are needed to guide effective policy planning and strategy making. Participation and the adversarial process tend to differentiate and expand the knowledge base. Something else is needed to bring this diverse but relevant knowledge together in the form of a total picture.
4 Managerial mind supporting. Most problem-solving methods and computer aids focus on 'decision support systems,' that is, on systems that provide guidance for choosing a particular course of action to solve a particular decision problem. Problems of organized complexity, as we have seen, are ongoing, ill structured, and generally 'wicked.' The choice of individual courses of action is only a part of the manager's or policymaker's need. More important is the need to achieve insight into the nature of the complexity and to formulate concepts and world views for coping with it. It is the policymaker's thinking process and his or her mind that needs to be supported.

READING

1.3

Using paradox to build management and organization theories

by Marshall Scott Poole and Andrew H. Van de Ven[1]

Like most social scientists, organization and management theorists are socialized to develop internally consistent theories. The presence of contrary or contradictory assumptions, explanations, or conclusions is often viewed as an indicator of poor theory building, and theorists are encouraged to devote their efforts to carefully defined and delimited analyses. The value of rigor and coherence cannot be denied. However, these qualities are not sufficient to guarantee good theories. Ralph Waldo Emerson's dictum, 'A foolish consistency is the hobgoblin of little minds' must also be kept in mind. Social science loses an important resource for theory development if the incompatible or inconsistent theses which inevitably arise in the study of organizations are ignored or are eliminated. There is growing recognition that significant advances in management and organization theory will require ways to address paradoxes inherent in human beings and their social organizations (Quinn & Cameron, 1988).

Because organizational theories attempt to capture a multifaceted reality with a finite, internally consistent statement, they are essentially incomplete. A good theory is, by definition, a limited and fairly precise picture. It does not attempt to cover everything and would fail to meet the parsimony criterion if it did. Scope conditions are one means of expressing the limitations of theories. Less evident, but as effective, is reliance on a limited, carefully prescribed set of assumptions and explanatory principles. These assumptions and explanations implicitly state what is relevant and what is not. They determine the operative scope of a theory by specifying what can be explained or understood and what must be regarded as 'not of interest for this theory,' or as irrelevant. Theories always constrain the theorist's field of vision; one of the canons of good theory construction is to recognize these limitations.

Additionally, researchers are adjured to perfect their theories and to test them. As they do this, there is a tendency for the theory to dominate researchers' thinking. The researcher must focus on the theory, iron out its problems, work out measurement techniques, test the

theory and revise it, and defend tests against criticism. As a result, the theory tends to bind the researcher's judgment. The researcher develops a 'trained incapacity' to appreciate aspects not mentioned in her or his theory. As this progression toward consistency continues, the theory becomes more and more 'perfect,' with less and less correspondence to the multifaceted reality it seeks to portray.

An alternative strategy for theory building can be proposed: *Look for theoretical tensions or oppositions and use them to stimulate the development of more encompassing theories*. This strategy requires an exploration of the tradition of theoretical debate surrounding important issues, an identification of alternative or opposing theories or explanations, and discovery of ways of relating, contraposing, or integrating them. The result will be theories less susceptible to the limitations of perspective which attend many middle range theories.

This strategy is not a replacement for traditional, univocal theory building, but rather an additional arrow for the theorist's quiver. The researcher consciously and tenaciously pursues theoretical inconsistencies, rather than dismissing them or resigning them to the 'theoretical disagreements' category. Rather than regarding each theory as a self-encapsulating whole, the theorist can play theories off against one another, gaining insights from multiple perspectives and comparative analysis. In this view, theories are not statements of some ultimate 'truth' but rather are alternative cuts of a multifaceted reality. Alternative theories give partial views, and the theorist's task is to sort them out and work out their relationships.

Contemporary theory construction methods are biased toward consistency. Relatively little attention has been paid to the resolution of tensions or oppositions. This set of theory-building strategies is proposed to help researchers come to terms with theoretical tensions.

Paradox – a term with a long history in philosophical and rhetorical studies – is one key to understanding

[1]Source: This article was adapted from M.S. Poole and A.H. Van de Ven, 'Using Paradox to Build Management and Organization Theories', *Academy of Management Review*, Vol. 14, No. 4, pp. 562–578, © 1989 by Academy of Management. Reproduced with permission of Academy of Management via Copyright Clearance Center.

how to work with theoretical contradictions and oppositions embedded in complex traditions. This term has several layers of meaning, each of which captures some of the features which make theoretical paradoxes so interesting and thought provoking.

In general parlance, many writers use the term loosely, as an informal umbrella for interesting and thought-provoking contradictions of all sorts. In this sense, a paradox is something which grabs our attention, a puzzle needing a solution.

In rhetorical studies *paradox* designates a trope which presents an opposition between two accepted theses. For example, the Elizabethan rhetorician Sherry wrote, 'He always is an enemy to his own plans, yet he claims to be a friend to other men's.' Sherry thus questioned the trustworthiness of this man by showing a contradiction in his behaviors. The rhetorical paradox is intended to cause the audience to reconsider set opinions or to throw into contrast taken-for-granted presumptions. Its impact stems from its shock value.

In logic, *paradox* has a narrower, specialized meaning. A logical paradox 'consists of two contrary or even contradictory propositions to which we are led by apparently sound arguments' (Van Heigenoort, 1972, p.45). Taken singly, each proposition is incontestable, but taken together they seem to be inconsistent or incompatible. One famous logical paradox is the Liar, first studied by the Megaric philosophers around 400 B.C. If someone says, 'I always lie,' how are we to understand this statement? It seems both true and false. Such great and diverse thinkers as Aristotle, Chrysippus, Russell, and Wittgenstein have proposed resolutions for the Liar's Paradox. Much effort has been devoted to resolving or understanding paradoxes, because they divulge inconsistencies in our logic or assumptions. They present opportunities to discover different assumptions, shift perspectives, pose problems in fundamentally different ways, and focus on different research questions.

All three levels of meaning inform this analysis. We are interested in paradox in the lay sense – in the interesting tensions, oppositions, and contradictions between theories which create conceptual difficulties. Because theory building is a discursive enterprise, rhetorical strategies of handling paradox effectively are a central concern. Communication and rhetorical studies have a long tradition of thought concerned with the creation of knowledge through discourse and with effective expression. Four discursive strategies, which will be discussed, are open to theorists interested in paradox. The paradoxes in management are not, strictly speaking, logical paradoxes. However, an understanding of paradoxes and ways to work with them is greatly enriched by the philosophical tradition. By far the largest body of work on paradoxes can be attributed to logicians, and the philosophical treatment of paradoxes will be used as a touchstone for this analysis.

Four general methods to address paradox in management and organization theories are suggested. These four methods for addressing paradox are illustrated by applying them to the action–structure paradox in organizational theory.

Four ways to address paradox in organization and management theories

Organizational and management theories involve a special type of paradox – social paradoxes. Many such paradoxes have been identified. These paradoxes include: the difficulty in reconciling the explanation of behavior as a function of structural determination with the equally strong claim that it is the product of purposive action (Burrell & Morgan, 1979; Van de Ven & Poole, 1988); good arguments for two incompatible conceptualizations or organizational climate – as an aggregation of individual climate perceptions or as a macrolevel system property (Glick, 1985, 1988; James, Joyce, & Slocum, 1988); the question of whether social organizations are fundamentally stable orders or continuously changing emergents (Burrell & Morgan, 1979; Pfeffer, 1982; Weick, 1979); and the trade-off between the need to establish individual identity in groups and the collective nature of group action (Smith & Berg, 1987). Each 'side' of these tensions has been advocated or emphasized by different theorists, but together they form a tradition of theoretical discourse which is potentially richer than either theory by itself. The problem is how best to mine this rich vein of insight.

This is not a trivial problem, as the example of the stability–change tension illustrates. It is evident that organizations are admixtures of stability and change: Organizations are relatively stable, enduring features of life, yet when we look closely they do not appear stable at all. They are continuously changing, continuously being produced and renewed by member activities. Nevertheless, an argument can be made that stability is primary; any change is observable only in contrast to some stable state. Organizational change also can be explained as aberrations from the stable state, as sudden upheavals which disrupt organizational stability. The incorporation of stability and continuous change in the same theory poses a paradox, because each is defined as the opposite of the other. Hernes (1976) argued that adequate theories must explain stability and change in the same terms. Generally, however, organizational theories have emphasized either stability or change, slighting the other term. As Van de Ven and Poole (1988) showed, most organizational theorists have attempted to incorporate both stability and change, but as specific theories develop and are refined, there seems to be pressure to take one as the primary term and to subordinate the other. How can both faces of organizations be encompassed in the same framework?

Theorists can attempt to use these and other tensions in several ways. They can identify in which side of a tension their current work is anchored and then expand their perspective by addressing criticisms lodged by the other side. For example, researchers who assume a relatively stable organizational backdrop for their work might attempt to enlarge their theories by taking into account the criticisms implied by Weick's (1979) perspective. Alternatively, theorists can start at the concrete level, identify anomalies in their object of study, and locate tensions that could account for these anomalies. The organizational climate literature, for example, is replete with inconsistent findings, which may be traceable to inconsistent definitions of climate as a psychological or organizational construct, respectively. Once the tension has been identified, it might be possible to move toward some synthesis, or theorists can start with abstract oppositions themselves and carry them into a problem area. This is a case of theoretical interests generating particular applications. A good example is Allison's (1971) *Essence of Decision*, which contrasted three decision models applied to the Cuban missile crisis (see Reading 3.3 in this book).

Some examples of nonparadoxical situations in theory building are also useful, because not all inconsistencies are paradoxes. The tension between empirical observation and theoretical propositions is not a paradox, because valid empirical observations can correct a theory. Nor are most contradictions within a single theory paradoxes; most often, these stem from faulty reasoning and can be eliminated by correcting it. The types of paradoxes concerned with here are tensions and oppositions between well-founded, well-reasoned, and well-supported alternative explanations of the same phenomenon. When juxtaposed, they present a puzzle for the theorist, because each side seems valid, yet they are in some sense incompatible or hard to reconcile.

As these examples show, paradoxes in social theories are not strictly logical paradoxes. Social scientific paradoxes tend to be looser: The opposing terms are often somewhat vague, and instead of logical contradictions, tensions and oppositions between incompatible positions must be considered. Further, whereas logical paradoxes exist in timeless, abstract thought, social paradoxes are about a real world, subject to its temporal and spatial constraints. This opens the possibility of dealing with social paradoxes not only through logical resolutions, but through taking into account the temporal or spatial nature of the social world. Thus, methods of coping with logical paradox must be transformed when social scientific paradoxes are considered.

Four methods for working with paradox

We propose four generic ways in which two opposing theses, A and B, might be related: (1) We can keep A and B separate and their contrasts appreciated; (2) We can situate A and B at two different levels or locations in the social world (e.g., micro and macro levels, respectively); (3) We can separate A and B temporally in the same location; or (4) We can find some new perspective which eliminates the opposition between A and B. Stated schematically, the four relations correspond to opposition, spatial separation, temporal separation, and synthesis, respectively. They represent a logically exhaustive set of relationships opposing terms can take in the social world. Each of the four methods represents a different way of transforming our theories and ways of thinking.

Opposition: Accept the paradox and use it constructively

The first response is to accept the paradox and learn to live with it. This response does not mean that the paradox is ignored. Rather, the implications of the paradox are pursued actively and used to stimulate theory development. A great deal can be learned from juxtaposing contradictory propositions and assumptions, even if they are incompatible. Theorists may feel a strain toward cognitive consistency, but that does not mean that their theories must fit together neatly. Paradoxes remind theorists of this inconsistency and enable them to study the dialectic between opposing levels and forces which are captured in different theories.

However, living with paradox has its costs as well. Usually, contrary perspectives are embraced by different researchers. This may produce specialized versions of the two theories which retard the recognition of relationships and generate diatribes between proponents of the 'correct' horn of a dilemma. Nor is it always clear just what sort of relationship 'tensions between opposing positions' constitute. This ambiguity can result in sloppy analysis. Notwithstanding, to accept a paradox is a positive stance. It is to acknowledge that theorists need not be completely consistent; that seemingly opposed viewpoints can inform one another; that models are, after all, just models, incapable of fully capturing the 'buzzing, booming confusion,' no matter how strongly logical arrogance tries to convince theorists otherwise.

The remaining three strategies attempt to resolve paradox by spelling out the nature of the tensions between contrary positions.

Spatial separation: Clarify levels of analysis

The second response resolves paradoxes by clarifying levels of reference and the connections among them. Level distinctions such as part-whole, micro-macro, or individual-society have proven extremely useful for social research. This approach assumes that one horn of the paradox operates at one level of analysis (e.g., macro), while the other horn operates at a different level (micro). To utilize this strategy successfully, it is necessary to specify as precisely as possible how the levels interrelate.

Researchers who take this approach must grapple with difficult and important theoretical problems. Despite much research on the aggregation of individual acts, attitudes, and preferences into social actions, climates, and choices there is still no completely satisfactory solution. The same can be said for other level distinctions. Given the difficulty of spelling out interlevel relations, many researchers have let them stand, while advancing only partial and tentative solutions. However, many insights have resulted from attempts to sort out levels and their relationships.

Of the same general type as the level distinction is spatial separation of paradoxical explanations. One horn of the paradox is assumed to operate in one physical or social locus, while the other operates in a different locus. For example, Explanation A might hold for the upper echelons of an organization, while Explanation B holds for line workers. Some treatments of motivation, for instance, implicitly assume that top executives must be understood in different terms than workers or lower-level management.

Temporal separation: Take time into account

A third approach takes into account the role of time. In this resolution, one horn of the paradox is assumed to hold during one time period and the other during a different time period. The two contrary assumptions or processes exert separate influence, and each may influence the other through its prior action. Several types of temporal relationships may exist among contrary forces:

- one side of the paradox may influence the conditions under which the other will operate, as in Reese and Overton's (1973) formulation of cognitive development, in which behavioral learning sets the stage for cognitive acquisitions;
- one side may create the conditions necessary for the existence of the other, as in Smelser's (1962) theory of collective action, in which individual activities may be the 'precipitating event' for collective beliefs to develop; and
- there may also be mutual influence over time, with swings between one side and the other, as in Buckley's (1968) morphogenetic theory of social systems.

The difficulty of achieving a clear temporal separation of contrary assumptions, theories, or processes remains to be solved. When does behavioral theory stop holding and cognitive theory begin? At what point does individual motivation leave off and collective action begin? Most attempts at temporal resolution have glossed over the issue of transition points and focused instead on the periods of relatively pure action on either side of the paradox.

Synthesis: Introduce new terms to resolve the paradox

The resolution of paradoxes by level distinctions or temporal analysis leaves each set of assumptions or processes basically intact. Both sides of the paradox are assumed to be fundamentally sound, and the paradox is resolved by separating them and specifying how one side influences the other. However, it is also possible that the paradox may stem from conceptual limitations or flaws in theory or assumptions. To overcome these limitations it is necessary to introduce new concepts or a new perspective.

However, such advances are hard-won, and many apparent resolutions may lead to dead ends. When perspectives radically shift, theorists may lose as well as gain. The new perspective may oversimplify some issues or ignore the problems that originally gave rise to previous positions. These risks are the price theorists pay for theoretical advances.

Combinations and reflections

Although analytically distinct, the four approaches can be combined in practice. For example, paradoxical terms may be related both temporally and by level. Moreover, the first approach, which accepts paradox and tries to work out its implications, can serve as a preliminary step to the other three. By accepting paradoxes, the researcher undertakes to examine his or her theories for hidden tensions and to search for opposing or contrary positions. Once identified, relationships among the positions can be explored with the three remaining methods.

No matter which of the four responses are chosen, working with paradoxes is challenging. It is difficult to manage the dialectic between positions if theorists choose to live with paradoxes. If theorists attempt to resolve paradoxes, they face formidable obstacles. Nevertheless, the recognition of paradoxes forces theorists to ask different questions and to come up with answers that stretch the bounds of current thinking. The resulting formulations are likely to be of interest not just to organizational scholars, but more widely as well.

Discussion

The complexity of organizations guarantees that theories cannot give a complete representation. Nevertheless, in pursuit of an elusive consistency, researchers may create self-encapsulating theories which may freeze thinking. There is great potential to enliven current theory and to develop new insights if theorists search for and work with inconsistencies, contradictions, and tensions in their theories, and in the relationships between them.

Much of the contemporary organizational theory is still struggling to live with paradoxes. A constructive approach to living with paradox is to adopt the first method, that is, to juxtapose and compare how contrasting theories deal with the same organizational problems. This strategy requires theorists to engage in comparative analysis of theories cast on both sides of the paradox and at different levels of analysis. In addi-

tion to generating insights from divergent perspectives, this approach helps the researcher become aware of tensions and oppositions which can be addressed by the other three methods.

If theorists attack a paradox by clarifying levels of analysis, they are led to formulations which specify how theories operating at different levels or in different sectors of the organization or society interrelate. The hallmark of this approach is careful specification of levels and of the way one level maps onto another, and vice versa.

If temporal sequence is used to resolve a paradox, researchers must work out a formulation with alternating cycles of two or more theoretical explanations. It is especially important to discuss, as does Buckley (1968), how the transitions between the various phases are accomplished.

Finally, if paradoxes are addressed by advancing new concepts or distinctions, a new conception must be developed. In this approach, any distinction is for analytical purposes only; retaining it as an assumption about the nature of organizations unnecessarily bifurcates a holistic phenomenon. The theory tries to provide an analytical vocabulary that would enable researchers to study in a fundamentally new way.

There is no single best way to address paradox, and each of the four methods suggested here has both benefits and costs. The objective has been to advance and advocate an additional level of theoretical reflection. Rather than simply recognizing incompatible positions and stopping, theorists should attempt to specify the relationships among them. Sometimes this specification can lead to a creative integration that greatly enhances understanding.

The four modes of paradox resolution can be regarded as a set of *topoi* for theory development. *Topoi* was the term used by classical Greek thinkers to designate standard forms of argument that served as models for the invention of arguments for specific cases. These four modes of paradox resolution can serve as *topoi* for the generation of organizational and management theories; they give us a range of theoretical possibilities to work with.

Although the focus has been on methods for resolving or capitalizing on paradoxes, paradoxes should not be 'eliminated.' Indeed, rather than using paradoxes to build theory, researchers can build theories about paradoxes, which is what Smith and Berg (1987) have done.

Nor is it clear that researchers can ever avoid paradoxes. One challenge is the possibility that the resolution of one paradox may inadvertently create another.

The complexity and interdependence of individuals and organizations typically exceed researchers' capabilities to describe or explain them with coherent and consistent theories. Resolutions of paradox in one aspect of a theory often create inconsistencies in another part of the theory. Thus, it seems unlikely that theorists can ever escape or resolve theoretical paradoxes completely. It has been suggested that at the heart of any theory that solves a paradox is another, different paradox, waiting to be discovered. If this is true, there is one consolation: Tackling the same old, well-known paradoxes, researchers may uncover as yet unknown ones that can move social inquiry in new directions. This also raises the issue of whether the world is consistent or whether it is actually inherently paradoxical.

READING 1.4 Cultural constraints in management theories

By Geert Hofstede[1]

Lewis Carroll's *Alice in Wonderland* contains the famous story of Alice's croquet game with the Queen of Hearts. Alice thought she had never seen such a curious croquet-ground in all her life; it was all ridges and furrows; the balls were live hedgehogs, the mallets live flamingoes, and the soldiers had to double themselves up and to stand on their hands and feet to make the arches. You probably know how the story goes: Alice's flamingo mallet turns its head whenever she wants to strike with it; her hedgehog ball runs away; and the doubled-up soldier arches walk around all the time. The only rule seems to be that the Queen of Hearts always wins.

Alice's croquet playing problems are good analogies to attempts to build culture-free theories of management. Concepts available for this purpose are themselves alive with culture, having been developed within a particular cultural context. They have a tendency to guide our thinking toward our desired conclusion. As the same reasoning may also be applied to the arguments in this reading, I better tell you my conclusion before I continue – so that the rules of my game are understood. In this reading we take a trip around the world to demonstrate that there are no such things as universal management theories.

Diversity in management *practices* as we go around the world has been recognized in US management literature for more than 30 years. The term 'comparative management' has been used since the 1960s. However, it has taken much longer for the US academic community to accept that not only practices but also the validity of theories may stop at national borders, and I wonder whether even today everybody would agree with this statement.

The idea that the validity of a theory is constrained by national borders is more obvious in Europe, with all its borders, than in a huge borderless country like the US. Already in the sixteenth century Michel de Montaigne, a Frenchman, wrote a statement which was made famous by Blaise Pascal about a century later; *'Vérite en-deça des Pyrenées, erreur au-delà'* – 'There are truths on this side of the Pyrenées which are falsehoods on the other.'

From Don Armado's love to Taylor's science

According to the comprehensive ten-volume Oxford English Dictionary, the words 'manage,' 'management,' and 'manager' appeared in the English language in the 16th century. The oldest recorded use of the word 'manager' is in Shakespeare's *Love's Labour's Lost*, dating from 1588, in which Don Adriano de Armado, 'a fantastical Spaniard,' exclaims (Act I scene ii. 188): 'Adieu, valour! rust, rapier! be still, drum! for your manager is in love; yea, he loveth.'

The linguistic origin of the word is from Latin

munus, hand, via the Italian *maneggiare*, which is the training of horses in the manege; subsequently its meaning was extended to skillful handling in general, like of arms and musical instruments, as Don Armado illustrates. However, the word also became associated with the French *menage*, household, as an equivalent of 'husbandry' in its sense of the art of running a household. The theater of present-day management contains elements of both *manege* and *menage* and different managers and cultures may use different accents.

The founder of the science of economics, the Scot Adam Smith, in his 1776 book *The Wealth of Nations*, used 'manage,' 'management' (even 'bad management') and 'manager' when dealing with the process and the persons involved in operating joint stock companies. British economist John Stuart Mill (1806–1873) followed Smith in this use and clearly expressed his distrust of such hired people who were not driven by ownership. Since the 1880s the word 'management' appeared occasionally in writings by American engineers, until it was canonized as a modern science by Frederick W. Taylor in *Shop Management* in 1903 and in *The Principles of Scientific Management* in 1911.

While Smith and Mill used 'management' to describe a process and 'managers' for the persons involved, 'management' in the American sense – which has since been taken back by the British – refers not only to the process but also to the managers as a class of people. This class (1) does not own a business but sells its skills to act on behalf of the owners and (2) does not produce personally but is indispensable for making others produce, through motivation. Members of this class carry a high status and many American boys and girls aspire to the role. In the US, the manager is a cultural hero.

Let us now turn to other parts of the world. We will look at management in its context in other successful modern economies: Germany, Japan, France, Holland, and among the overseas Chinese. Then we will examine management in the much larger part of the world that is still poor, especially South-East Asia and Africa, and in the new political configurations of Eastern Europe, and Russia in particular. We will then return to the US via mainland China.

Germany

The manager is not a cultural hero in Germany. If anybody, it is the engineer who fills the hero role. Frederick Taylor's scientific management was conceived in a society of immigrants – where a large number of workers with diverse backgrounds and skills had to work together. In Germany this heterogeneity never existed.

Elements of the medieval guild system have survived in historical continuity in Germany until the present day. In particular, a very effective apprenticeship system exists both on the shop floor and in the office, which alternates practical work and classroom courses. At the end of the apprenticeship the worker receives a certificate, the *Facharbeiterbrief*, which is recognized throughout the country. About two thirds of the German worker population holds such a certificate and a corresponding occupational pride. In fact, quite a few German company presidents have worked their way up from the ranks through an apprenticeship. In comparison, two thirds of the worker population in Britain have no occupational qualification at all.

The highly skilled and responsible German workers do not necessarily need a manager, American-style, to 'motivate' them. They expect their boss or *Meister* to assign their tasks and to be the expert in resolving technical problems. Comparisons of similar German, British, and French organizations show the Germans as having the highest rate of personnel in productive roles and the lowest both in leadership and staff roles.

Japan

The American type of manager is also missing in Japan. In the United States, the core of the enterprise is the managerial class. The core of the Japanese enterprise is the permanent worker group; workers who for all practical purposes are tenured and who aspire at life-long employment. They are distinct from the non-permanent employees – most women and subcontracted teams led by gang bosses, to be laid off in slack periods. University graduates in Japan first join the permanent worker group and subsequently fill various positions, moving from line to staff as the need occurs while paid according to seniority rather than position. They take part in Japanese-style group consultation sessions for important decisions, which extend the decision-making period but guarantee fast implementation afterwards. Japanese are to a large extent controlled by their peer group rather than by their manager.

American theories of leadership are ill-suited for the Japanese group-controlled situation. During the past two decades, the Japanese have developed their own 'PM' theory of leadership, in which P stands for performance and M for maintenance. The latter is less a concern for individual employees than for maintaining social stability. In view of the amazing success of the Japanese economy in the past 30 years, many

Americans have sought for the secrets of Japanese management hoping to copy them.

France

The manager, US style, does not exist in France either. The French researcher Philippe d'Iribarne (1990) identifies three kinds of basic principles (*logiques*) of management. In the USA, the principle is the *fair contract* between employer and employee, which gives the manager considerable prerogatives, but within its limits. This is really a labor market in which the worker sells his or her labor for a price. In France, the principle is the *honor* of each class in a society which has always been and remains extremely stratified, in which superiors behave as superior beings and subordinates accept and expect this, conscious of their own lower level in the national hierarchy but also of the honor of their own class. The French do not think in terms of managers versus nonmanagers but in terms of *cadres* versus *non-cadres*; one becomes cadre by attending the proper schools and one remains it forever; regardless of their actual task, cadres have the privileges of a higher social class, and it is very rare for a non-cadre to cross the ranks.

The conflict between French and American theories of management became apparent in the beginning of the twentieth century, in a criticism by the great French management pioneer Henri Fayol (1841–1925) on his US colleague and contemporary Frederick W. Taylor (1856–1915). Fayol was a French engineer whose career as a *cadre supérieur* culminated in the position of *Président-Directeur-Général* of a mining company. After his retirement he formulated his experiences in a pathbreaking text on organization: *Administration industrielle et générale*, in which he focused on the sources of authority. Taylor was an American engineer who started his career in industry as a worker and attained his academic qualifications through evening studies. From chief engineer in a steel company he became one of the first management consultants. Taylor was not really concerned with the issue of authority at all; his focus was on efficiency. He proposed to split the task of the first-line boss into eight specialisms, each exercised by a different person; an idea which eventually led to the idea of a matrix organization.

Taylor's work appeared in a French translation in 1913, and Fayol read it and showed himself generally impressed but shocked by Taylor's 'denial of the principle of the Unity of Command' in the case of the eight-boss-system. Seventy years later André Laurent, another of Fayol's compatriots, found that French managers in a survey reacted very strongly against a suggestion that one employee could report to two different bosses, while US managers in the same survey showed fewer misgivings. Matrix organization has never become popular in France as it has in the United States.

Holland

In my own country, Holland or as it is officially called, the Netherlands, the study by Philippe d'Iribarne found the management principle to be a need for consensus among all parties, neither predetermined by a contractual relationship nor by class distinctions, but based on an open-ended exchange of views and a balancing of interests. In terms of the different origins of the word 'manager,' the organization in Holland is more *menage* (household) while in the United States it is more *manege* (horse drill).

At my university, the University of Limburg at Maastricht, we asked both the Americans and a matched group of Dutch students to describe their ideal job after graduation, using a list of 22 job characteristics. The Americans attached significantly more importance than the Dutch to earnings, advancement, benefits, a good working relationship with their boss, and security of employment. The Dutch attached more importance to freedom to adopt their own approach to the job, being consulted by their boss in his or her decisions, training opportunities, contributing to the success of their organization, fully using their skills and abilities, and helping others. This list confirms d'Iribarne's findings of a contractual employment relationship in the United States, based on earnings and career opportunities, against a consensual relationship in Holland. The latter has centuries-old roots, the Netherlands were the first republic in Western Europe (1609–1810), and a model for the American republic. The country has been and still is governed by a careful balancing of interests in a multi-party system.

In terms of management theories, both motivation and leadership in Holland are different from what they are in the United States. Leadership in Holland presupposes modesty, as opposed to assertiveness in the United States. No US leadership theory has room for that. Working in Holland is not a constant feast, however. There is a built-in premium on mediocrity and jealousy, as well as time-consuming ritual consultations to maintain the appearance of consensus and the pretense of modesty. There is unfortunately another side to every coin.

The overseas Chinese

Among the champions of economic development in the past 30 years we find three countries mainly populated by Chinese living outside the Chinese mainland: Taiwan, Hong Kong and Singapore. Moreover, overseas Chinese play a very important role in the economies of Indonesia, Malaysia, the Philippines and Thailand, where they form an ethnic minority. If anything, the little dragons – Taiwan, Hong Kong and Singapore – have been more economically successful than Japan, moving from rags to riches and now counted among the world's wealthy industrial countries. Yet very little attention has been paid to the way in which their enterprises have been managed.

Overseas Chinese enterprises lack almost all characteristics of modern management. They tend to be small, cooperating for essential functions with other small organizations through networks based on personal relations. They are family-owned, without the separation between ownership and management typical in the West, or even in Japan and Korea. They normally focus on one product or market, with growth by opportunistic diversification; in this, they are extremely flexible. Decision making is centralized in the hands of one dominant family member, but other family members may be given new ventures to try their skills on. They are low-profile and extremely cost-conscious, applying Confucian virtues of thrift and persistence. Their size is kept small by the assumed lack of loyalty of non-family employees, who, if they are any good, will just wait and save until they can start their own family business.

Overseas Chinese prefer economic activities in which great gains can be made with little manpower, like commodity trading and real estate. They employ few professional managers, except their sons and sometimes daughters who have been sent to prestigious business schools abroad, but who upon return continue to run the family business the Chinese way.

The origin of this system, or – in the Western view – this lack of system, is found in the history of Chinese society, in which there were no formal laws, only formal networks of powerful people guided by general principles of Confucian virtue. The favors of the authorities could change daily, so nobody could be trusted except one's kinfolk – of whom, fortunately, there used to be many, in an extended family structure. The overseas Chinese way of doing business is also very well adapted to their position in the countries in which they form ethnic minorities, often envied and threatened by ethnic violence.

Overseas Chinese businesses following this unprofessional approach command a collective gross national product of some 200 to 300 billion US dollars, exceeding the GNP of Australia. There is no denying that it works.

Management transfer to poor countries

Four-fifths of the world population live in countries that are not rich but poor. After World War II and decolonization, the stated purpose of the United Nations and the World Bank has been to promote the development of all the world's countries in a war on poverty. After 40 years it looks very much like we are losing this war. If one thing has become clear, it is that the export of Western – mostly American – management practices and theories to poor countries has contributed little to nothing to their development. There has been no lack of effort and money spent for this purpose: students from poor countries have been trained in this country, and teachers and Peace Corps workers have been sent to the poor countries. If nothing else, the general lack of success in economic development of other countries should be sufficient argument to doubt the validity of Western management theories in non-Western environments.

If we examine different parts of the world, the development picture is not equally bleak, and history is often a better predictor than economic factors for what happens today. There is a broad regional pecking order with East Asia leading. The little dragons have passed into the camp of the wealthy: then follow South-East Asia (with its overseas Chinese minorities), Latin America (in spite of the debt crisis), South Asia, and Africa always trails behind. Several African countries have only become poorer since decolonization.

Russia and China

The crumbling of the former Eastern bloc has left us with a scattering of states and would-be states of which the political and economic future is extremely uncertain. The best predictions are those based on a knowledge of history, because historical trends have taken revenge on the arrogance of the Soviet rulers who believed they could turn them around by brute power. One obvious fact is that the former bloc is extremely heterogeneous, including countries traditionally closely linked with the West by trade and travel, like the Czech

Republic, Hungary, Slovenia, and the Baltic states, as well as others with a Byzantine or Turkish past: some having been prosperous, others always extremely poor.

Let me limit myself to the Russian republic, a huge territory with some 140 million inhabitants, mainly Russians. We know quite a bit about the Russians as their country was a world power for several hundreds of years before communism, and in the nineteenth century it has produced some of the greatest writers in world literature. If I want to understand the Russians – including how they could so long support the Soviet regime – I tend to re-read Lev Nikolayevich Tolstoy. In his most famous novel *Anna Karenina* one of the main characters is a landowner, Levin, whom Tolstoy uses to express his own views and convictions about his people. Russian peasants used to be serfs; serfdom had been abolished in 1861, but the peasants, now tenants, remained as passive as before. Levin wanted to break this passivity by dividing the land among his peasants in exchange for a share of the crops; but the peasants only let the land deteriorate further. Here follows a quote:

> [Levin] read political economy and socialistic works . . . but, as he had expected, found nothing in them related to his undertaking. In the political economy books – in [John Stuart] Mill, for instance, whom he studied first and with great ardour, hoping every minute to find an answer to the questions that were engrossing him – he found only certain laws deduced from the state of agriculture in Europe; but he could not for the life of him see why these laws, which did not apply to Russia, should be considered universal. . . . Political economy told him that the laws by which Europe had developed and was developing her wealth were universal and absolute. Socialist teaching told him that development along those lines leads to ruin. And neither of them offered the smallest enlightenment as to what he, Levin, and all the Russian peasants and landowners were to do with their millions of hands and millions of acres, to make them as productive as possible for the common good.

In the summer of 1991, the Russian lands yielded a record harvest, but a large share of it rotted in the fields because no people were to be found for harvesting. The passivity is still there, and not only among the peasants. And the heirs of John Stuart Mill (whom we met before as one of the early analysts of 'management') again present their universal recipes which simply do not apply.

Citing Tolstoy, I implicitly suggest that management theorists cannot neglect the great literature of the countries they want their ideas to apply to. The greatest novel in Chinese literature is considered Cao Xueqin's *The Story of the Stone*, also known as *The Dream of the Red Chamber* which appeared around 1760. It describes the rise and fall of two branches of an aristocratic family in Beijing, who live in adjacent plots in the capital. Their plots are joined by a magnificent garden with several pavilions in it, and the young, mostly female members of both families are allowed to live in them. One day the management of the garden is taken over by a young woman, Tan-Chun, who states:

> I think we ought to pick out a few experienced trust-worthy old women from among the ones who work in the Garden – women who know something about gardening already – and put the upkeep of the Garden into their hands. We needn't ask them to pay us rent; all we need ask them for is an annual share of the produce. There would be four advantages in this arrangement. In the first place, if we have people whose sole occupation is to look after trees and flowers and so on, the condition of the Garden will improve gradually year after year and there will be no more of those long periods of neglect followed by bursts of feverish activity when things have been allowed to get out of hand. Secondly there won't be the spoiling and wastage we get at present. Thirdly the women themselves will gain a little extra to add to their incomes which will compensate them for the hard work they put in throughout the year. And fourthly, there's no reason why we shouldn't use the money we should otherwise have spent on nurserymen, rockery specialists, horticultural cleaners and so on for other purposes.

As the story goes on, the capitalist privatization – because that is what it is – of the Garden is carried through, and it works. When in the 1980s Deng Xiaoping allowed privatization in the Chinese villages, it also worked. If we remember what Chinese entrepreneurs are able to do once they have become overseas Chinese, we shouldn't be too surprised. But what works in China – and worked two centuries ago – does not have to work in Russia, not in Tolstoy's days and not today. I am not offering a solution: I only protest against a naive universalism that knows only one recipe for development, the one supposed to have worked in the United States.

A theory of culture in management

There is something in all countries called 'management,' but its meaning differs to a larger or smaller extent from one country to the other, and it takes considerable historical and cultural insight into local conditions to understand its processes, philosophies, and problems. If already the word may mean so many different things, how can we expect one country's theories of management to apply abroad? One should be extremely careful in making this assumption, and test it before considering it proven. Management is not a phenomenon that can be isolated from other processes taking place in a society. It interacts with what happens in the family, at school, in politics, and government. It is obviously also related to religion and to beliefs about science. Theories of management always had to be interdisciplinary, but if we cross national borders they should become more interdisciplinary than ever.

As the word culture plays such an important role in my theory, let me give you my definition, which differs from some other very respectable definitions. Culture to me is *the collective programming of the mind which distinguishes one group or category of people from another*. In the part of my work I am referring to now, the category of people is the nation.

Cultural differences between nations can be, to some extent, described using five bipolar dimensions. The position of a country on these dimensions allows us to make some predictions on the way their society operates, including their management processes and the kind of theories applicable to their management.

The first dimension is labeled *power distance*, and it can be defined as the degree of inequality among people which the population of a country considers as normal: from relatively equal (that is, small power distance) to extremely unequal (large power distance). All societies are unequal, but some are more unequal than others.

The second dimension is labeled *individualism*, and it is the degree to which people in a country prefer to act as individuals rather than as members of groups. The opposite of individualism can be called *collectivism*, so collectivism is low individualism. The way I use the word it has no political connotations. In collectivist societies a child learns to respect the group to which it belongs, usually the family, and to differentiate between in-group members and out-group members (that is, all other people). When children grow up they remain members of their group, and they expect the group to protect them when they are in trouble. In

return, they have to remain loyal to their group throughout life. In individualist societies, a child learns very early to think of itself as 'I' instead of a part of 'we.' It expects one day to have to stand on its own feet and not to get protection from its group any more; and therefore it also does not feel a need for strong loyalty.

The third dimension is called *masculinity* and its opposite pole *femininity*. It is the degree to which tough values like assertiveness, performance, success and competition, which in nearly all societies are associated with the role of men, prevail over tender values like the quality of life, maintaining warm personal relationships, service, care for the weak, and solidarity, which in nearly all societies are more associated with women's roles. Women's roles differ from men's roles in all countries; but in tough societies, the differences are larger than in tender ones.

The fourth dimension is labeled *uncertainty avoidance*, and it can be defined as the degree to which people in a country prefer structured over unstructured situations. Structured situations are those in which there are clear rules as to how one should behave. These rules can be written down, but they can also be unwritten and imposed by tradition. In countries that score high on uncertainty avoidance, people tend to show more nervous energy, while in countries that score low, people are more easy-going. A (national) society with strong uncertainty avoidance can be called rigid; one with weak uncertainty avoidance, flexible. In countries where uncertainty avoidance is strong a feeling prevails of 'what is different, is dangerous.' In weak uncertainty avoidance societies, the feeling would rather be 'what is different, is curious.'

The fifth dimension is labeled *long-term versus short-term orientation*. On the long-term side one finds values oriented towards the future, like thrift (saving) and persistence. On the short-term side one finds values rather oriented towards the past and present, like respect for tradition and fulfilling social obligations.

Table 1.4.1 lists the scores on all five dimensions for the United States and for the other countries we just discussed. The table shows that each country has its own configuration on the five dimensions. Some of the values in the table have been estimated based on imperfect replications or personal impressions. The different dimension scores do not 'explain' all the differences in management I described earlier. To understand management in a country, one should have both knowledge of and empathy with the entire local scene. However, the scores should make us aware that people in other countries may think, feel, and act very differently from us when confronted with basic problems of society.

TABLE 1.4.1 Culture dimension scores for 10 countries

	Power Distance	Individualism	Masculinity	Uncertainty Avoidance	Long-Term Orientation
USA	40 L	91 H	62 H	46 L	29 L
Germany	35 L	67 H	66 H	65 M	31 M
Japan	54 M	46 M	95 H	92 H	80 H
France	68 H	71 H	43 M	86 H	30*L
Netherlands	38 L	80 H	14 L	53 M	44 M
Hong Kong	68 H	25 L	57 H	29 L	96 H
Indonesia	78 H	14 L	46 M	48 L	25*L
West Africa	77 H	20 L	46 M	54 M	16 L
Russia	95*H	50*M	40*L	90*H	10*L
China	80*H	20*L	50*M	60*M	118 H

* Estimated.

H = top third, M = medium third, L = bottom third (among 53 countries and regions for the first four dimensions; among 23 countries for the fifth).

Idiosyncrasies of American management theories

In comparison to other countries, the US culture profile presents itself as below average on power distance and uncertainty avoidance, highly individualistic, fairly masculine, and short-term oriented. The Germans show a stronger uncertainty avoidance and less extreme individualism; the Japanese are different on all dimensions, least on power distance; the French show larger power distance and uncertainty avoidance, but are less individualistic and somewhat feminine; the Dutch resemble the Americans on the first three dimensions, but score extremely feminine and relatively long-term oriented; Hong Kong Chinese combine large power distance with weak uncertainty avoidance, collectivism, and are very long-term oriented; and so on.

The American culture profile is reflected in American management theories. I will just mention three elements not necessarily present in other countries: the stress on market processes, the stress on the individual, and the focus on managers rather than on workers.

The stress on market processes

During the 1970s and 1980s it has become fashionable in the United States to look at organizations from a 'transaction costs' viewpoint. Economist Oliver Williamson has opposed 'hierarchies' to 'markets.' The reasoning is that human social life consists of economic transactions between individuals. We found the same in d'Iribarne's description of the US principle of the contract between employer and employee, the labor market in which the worker sells his or her labor for a price. These individuals will form hierarchical organizations when the cost of the economic transactions (such as getting information, finding out whom to trust etc.) is lower in a hierarchy than when all transactions would take place on a free market.

From a cultural perspective the important point is that the 'market' is the point of departure or base model, and the organization is explained from market failure. A culture that produces such a theory is likely to prefer organizations that internally resemble markets to organizations that internally resemble more structured models, like those in Germany or France. The ideal principle of control in organizations in the market philosophy is competition between individuals. This philosophy fits a society that combines a not-too-large power distance with a not-too-strong uncertainty avoidance and individualism; besides the USA, it will fit all other Anglo countries.

The stress on the individual

I find this constantly in the design of research projects and hypotheses; also in the fact that in the US psychology is clearly a more respectable discipline in management circles than sociology. Culture however is a collective phenomenon. Although we may get our information about culture from individuals, we have to interpret it at the level of collectivities. There are snags here known as the 'ecological fallacy' and the 'reverse ecological fallacy.' None of the US college textbooks on methodology I know deals sufficiently with the problem of multilevel analysis.

A striking example is found in the otherwise excellent book *Organizational Culture and Leadership* by Edgar H. Schein (1985). On the basis of his consulting experience he compares two large companies, nicknamed 'Action' and 'Multi.' He explains the difference in cultures between these companies by the group dynamics in their respective boardrooms. Nowhere in the book are any conclusions drawn from the fact that the first company is an American-based computer firm, and the second a Swiss-based pharmaceutics firm. This information is not even mentioned. A stress on interactions among individuals obviously fits a culture identified as the most individualistic in the world, but it will not be so well understood by the four-fifths of the world population for whom the group prevails over the individual.

One of the conclusions of my own multilevel research has been that culture at the national level and culture at the organizational level – corporate culture – are two very different phenomena and that the use of a common term for both is confusing. If we do use the common term, we should also pay attention to the occupational and the gender level of culture. National cultures differ primarily in the fundamental, invisible values held by a majority of their members, acquired in early childhood, whereas organization cultures are a much more superficial phenomenon residing mainly in the visible practices of the organization, acquired by socialization of the new members who join as young adults. National cultures change only very slowly if at all; organizational cultures may be consciously changed, although this isn't necessarily easy. This difference between the two types of culture is the secret of the existence of multinational corporations that employ employees with extremely different national cultural values. What keeps them together is a corporate culture based on common practices.

The stress on managers rather than workers

The core element of a work organization around the world is the people who do the work. All the rest is superstructure, and I hope to have demonstrated to you that it may take many different shapes. In the US literature on work organization, however, the core element, if not explicitly then implicitly, is considered the manager. This may well be the result of the combination of extreme individualism with fairly strong masculinity, which has turned the manager into a cultural hero of almost mythical proportions. For example, he – not really she – is supposed to make decisions all the time. Those of you who are or have been managers must know that this is a fable. Very few management decisions are just 'made' as the myth suggests it. Managers are much more involved in maintaining networks; if anything, it is the rank-and-file worker who can really make decisions on his or her own, albeit on a relatively simple level.

Conclusion

This article started with Alice in Wonderland. In fact, the management theorist who ventures outside his or her own country into other parts of the world is like Alice in Wonderland. He or she will meet strange beings, customs, ways of organizing or disorganizing and theories that are clearly stupid, old-fashioned or even immoral – yet they may work, or at least they may not fail more frequently than corresponding theories do at home. Then, after the first culture shock, the traveler to Wonderland will feel enlightened, and may be able to take his or her experiences home and use them advantageously. All great ideas in science, politics and management have traveled from one country to another, and been enriched by foreign influences. The roots of American management theories are mainly in Europe: with Adam Smith, John Stuart Mill, Lev Tolstoy, Max Weber, Henri Fayol, Sigmund Freud, Kurt Lewin and many others. These theories were replanted here and they developed and bore fruit. The same may happen again. The last thing we need is a Monroe doctrine for management.

FURTHER READING

Woe be to him who reads but one book.
George Herbert (1593–1632); English poet

At the end of each chapter, a number of follow-up books and articles will be suggested for readers who wish to delve deeper into a particular topic and avoid the dangers of reading only one book. These lists of recommended readings will be selective, instead of exhaustive, to assist readers in finding a few key works that can provide a stimulating introduction to the subject and a good starting point for further exploration.

As a follow up to this chapter, readers interested in tensions and paradoxes have a number of stimulating sources to examine. A recent article by Marianne Lewis in the *Academy of Management Review*, entitled 'Exploring Paradox: Toward a More Comprehensive Guide', is very good, as is an older book by Robert Quinn, *Beyond Rational Management*. A very valuable hands-on approach to dealing with paradoxes is provided by Barry Johnson in his book *Polarity Management*. Another highly recommended work is *Building Cross-Cultural Competence: How to Create Wealth from Conflicting Values* by Charles Hampden-Turner and Fons Trompenaars, which looks at cross-cultural management paradoxes.

An older book by Charles Hampden-Turner, *Charting the Corporate Mind: From Dilemma to Strategy*, is also thought provoking in its account of how dialectics can be employed as a problem-solving approach. In the same way, Richard Mason and Ian Mitroff's book *Challenging Strategic Planning Assumptions* makes for very good reading. For a more detailed account of 'wicked' problems, readers should actually go back to Horst Rittel, who coined the term. His article, together with Melvin Webber, entitled 'Dilemmas in a General Theory of Planning', is a particularly readable essay.

On the topic of international cultural differences, Geert Hofstede's original book, *Culture's Consequences*, and its more popular follow-up, *Cultures and Organizations: Software of the Mind*, are highly recommended. For a broader discussion of international differences in management and business systems, readers are advised to turn to *The Seven Cultures of Capitalism*, by Charles Hampden-Turner and Fons Trompenaars, *European Management Systems*, by Ronnie Lessem and Fred Neubauer, and *A European Management Model: Beyond Diversity*, by Roland Calori and Philippe de Woot.

REFERENCES

Allison, G. (1971) *Essence of Decision*, Little Brown, Boston.

Astley, W.G., and Van de Ven, A.H. (1983) 'Central Perspectives and Debates in Organization Theory', *Administrative Science Quarterly*, Vol. 28, pp. 245–273.

Barrett, D. (1998) *The Paradox Process: Creative Business Solutions Where You Least Expect to Find Them*, Amacom, New York.

Berger, P.L., and Luckmann, T. (1966) *The Social Construction of Reality*, Doubleday, New York.

Buckley, W.S. (1968) *Sociology and Modern Systems Theory*, Prentice Hall, Englewood Cliffs, NJ.

Burrell, B., and Morgan, G. (1979) *Sociological Paradigms and Organizational Analysis*, Heinemann Educational Books, London.

Calori, R., and de Woot, P. (eds.) (1994) *A European Management Model: Beyond Diversity*, Prentice Hall, London.

Cannon, T. (1997) *Welcome to the Revolution: Managing Paradox in the 21st Century*, Pitman, London.

Cicourel, A.V. (1971) *Cognitive Sociology*, Free Press, New York.

Clarke, T., and Clegg, S. (1998) *Changing Paradigms: The Transformation of Management Knowledge for the 21st Century*, HarperCollins, London.

Coleman, J.S. (1986) 'Social Theory, Social Research, and a Theory of Action', *American Journal of Sociology*, Vol. 16, pp. 1309–1335.

Collins, J.C., and Porras, J.I. (1994) *Built to Last: Successful Habits of Visionary Companies*, Harper Business, New York.

Conklin, E.J., and Weil, W. (2002) 'Wicked Problems: Naming the Pain in Organizations', *GPSS Working Paper*.

Cummings, S. (1993) 'Brief Case: The First Strategists', *Long Range Planning*, Vol. 26, No. 3, June, pp. 133–135.

D'Iribarne, P. (1990) *La Logique d'Honneur*, Editions du Seuil, Paris.

Eisenhardt, K.M. (2000) 'Paradox, Spirals, Ambivalence: The New Language of Change and Pluralism', *Academy of Management Review*, Vol. 25, No. 4, pp. 703–705.

Emery, F.E., and Trist, E.L. (1965) 'The Causal Texture of Organizational Environments', *Human Relations*, Vol. 18, pp. 21–32.

Fayol, H. (1916/1949) *General and Industrial Management*, Pitman, London.

Fletcher, J.L., and Olwyler, K. (1997) *Paradoxical Thinking: How to Profit from Your Contradictions*, Berrett-Koehler, San Fransisco.

Giddens, A. (1979) *Central Problems in Social Theory*, University of California Press, Berkely, CA.

Glick, W. (1985) 'Conceptualizing and Measuring Organizational and Psychological Climate: Pitfall in Multilevel Research', *Academy of Management Review*, Vol. 10, pp. 601–616.

Glick, W. (1988) 'Response: Organizations are not Central Tendencies: Shadow Boxing in the Dark, Round 2', *Academy of Management Review*, Vol. 13, pp. 133–137.

Hampden-Turner, C. (1990) *Charting the Corporate Mind: From Dilemma to Strategy*, Basil Blackwell, Oxford.

Hampden-Turner, C., and Trompenaars, F. (1990) *The Seven Cultures of Capitalism*, Doubleday, New York.

Hampden-Turner, C., and Trompenaars, F. (2000) *Building Cross-Cultural Competence: How to Create Wealth from Conflicting Values*, Yale University Press, New Haven.

Handy, C. (1994) *The Age of Paradox*, Harvard Business School Press, Boston.

Hernes, G. (1976) 'Structural Change in Social Processes', *American Journal of Sociology*, Vol. 82, pp. 513–545.

Hinterhuber, H.H., and Popp, W. (1992) 'Are You a Strategist or Just a Manager?', *Harvard Business Review*, January–February, pp. 105–113.

Hofstede, G. (1980) *Culture's Consequences*, Sage, London.

Hofstede, G. (1991) *Cultures and Organizations: Software of the Mind*, McGraw-Hill, London.

Hofstede, G. (1993) 'Cultural Constraints in Management Theories', *Academy of Management Executive*, Vol. 7, No. 1, pp. 8–21.

James, L., Joyce, W., and Slocum Jr., J.W. (1988) 'Comment: Organizations Do Not Cognize', *Academy of Management Review*, Vol. 13, pp. 129–132.

Johnson, B. (1996) *Polarity Management*, HRD Press Inc, Amherst, MA.

Ketchen, D.J., Thomas, J.B., and McDaniel, R.R (1996) 'Process, Content and Context: Synergistic Effects on Organizational Performance', *Journal of Management*, Vol. 22, pp. 231–257.

Lessem, R., and Neubauer, F.F. (1994) *European Management Systems*, McGraw-Hill, London.

Lewis, M. (2000) 'Exploring Paradox: Toward a More Comprehensive Guide', *Academy of Management Review*, Vol. 25, No. 4, pp. 760–776.

Machiavelli, N. (1950) *The Prince and the Discourses*, Modern Library, New York.

Mason, R.O., and Mitroff, I.I. (1981) *Challenging Strategic Planning Assumptions*, Wiley, New York.

Merton, R.K. (1948) *Social Theory and Social Structure*, Free Press, New York.

Mintzberg, H. (1990) 'Strategy Formation: Schools of Thought', in: J.W. Frederickson (ed.), *Perspectives on Strategic Management*, Harper & Row, New York.

Mintzberg, H., and Lampel, J. (1999) 'Reflecting on the Strategy Process', *Sloan Management Review*, Vol. 40, No. 3, Spring, pp. 21–30.

Nielsen, H.A. (1967) 'Antinomies', *New Catholic Encyclopedia*, McGraw-Hill, New York, pp. 621–623.

Pettigrew, A. (1992) 'The Character and Significance of Strategy Process Research', *Strategic Management Journal*, Vol. 13, pp. 5–16.

Pettigrew, A., and Whipp, R. (1991) *Managing Change for Competitive Success*, Basil Blackwell, Oxford.

Pfeffer, J. (1982) *Organizations and Organization Theory*, Pitman, Marshfield, MA.

Poole, M.S., and Van de Ven, A.H. (1989) 'Using Paradox to Build Management and Organization Theories', *Academy of Management Review*, Vol. 14, No. 4, pp. 562–578.

Quinn, R.E. (1988) *Beyond Rational Management: Mastering the Paradoxes and Competing Demands of High Performance*, Jossey-Bass, San Francisco.

Quinn, R.E., and Cameron, K.S. (1988) *Paradox and Transformation: Toward a Theory of Change in Organization and Management*, Ballinger Publishing, Cambridge, MA.

Reese, H., and Overton, W.F. (1973) 'Models of Development and Theories of Development', in: J.R. Nessleroade and H.W. Reese (eds.), *Life-span Developmental Psychology: Methodological Issues*, Academic Press, New York.

Rescher, N. (2001) *Paradoxes: Their Roots, Range and Resolution*, Open Court Publishing, Chicago.

Rittel, H. (1972) 'On the Planning Crisis: Systems Analysis of the "First and Second Generations"', *Bedriftsokonomen*, No. 8, pp. 390–396.

Rittel, H., and Webber, M. (1973) 'Dilemmas in a General Theory of Planning', *Policy Sciences*, Vol. 4, pp. 155–169.

Ropo, A., and Hunt, J.G. (1995) 'Entrepreneurial Processes as Virtuous and Vicious Spirals in a Changing Opportunity Structure: A Paradoxical Perspective', *Entrepreneurship, Theory and Practice*, Spring, pp. 91–111.

Rumelt, R.P. (1980) 'The Evaluation of Business Strategy', in: W.F. Glueck (ed.), *Business Policy and Strategic Management*, Third Edition, McGraw-Hill, New York.

Schein, E.H. (1985) *Organizational Culture and Leadership*, Jossey-Bass, San Francisco.

Smelser, N. (1962) *Theory of Collective Behavior*, Free Press, New York.

Smith, A. (1776/1986) *The Wealth of Nations*, Penguin Books, Harmondsworth.

Smith, K.K., and Berg, D.N. (1987) *Paradoxes of Group Life*, Jossey-Bass, San Francisco.

Sun Tzu (1983) *The Art of War*, Delacorte Press, New York.

Taylor, F.W. (1903) *Shop Management*, Harper, New York.

Taylor, F.W. (1911) *The Principles of Scientific Management*, Harper, New York.

Thurbin, P.J. (1998) *The Influential Strategist: Using the Power of Paradox in Strategic Thinking*, Financial Times, London.

Trompenaars, F., and Hampden-Turner, C. (2001) *21 Leaders for the 21st Century*, Capstone Publishing Ltd, Oxford.

Van de Ven, A.H., and Astley, W.G. (1981) 'Mapping the Field to Create a Dynamic Perspective on Organization Design and Behavior', in: A. Van de Ven and W. Joyce (eds.), *Perspectives on Organization Design and Behavior*, Wiley, New York, pp. 427–468.

Van de Ven, A.H., and Poole, M.S. (1988) 'Paradoxical Requirements for a Theory of Organizational Change', in: R. Quinn and K. Cameron (eds.), *Paradox and Transformation: Toward a Theory of Change in Organization and Management*, Ballinger, Cambridge, MA, pp. 19–63.

Van Heigenoort, J. (1958) 'Social Behavior as Exchange', *American Journal of Sociology*, Vol. 63, pp. 597–606.

Van Heigenoort, J. (1972) 'Logical Paradoxes', in: P. Edwards (ed.), *Encyclopedia of Philosophy*, Macmillan, New York, pp. 45–51.

Von Clausewitz, K. (1982) *On War*, Penguin, Harmondsworth.

Wacker, W. and Taylor, J. (2000) *The Visionary's Handbook: Nine Paradoxes That Will Shape the Future of Your Business*, HarperCollins, New York.

Weick, K. (1979) *The Social Psychology or Oganizing*, Second Edition, Addison-Wesley, Reading, MA.

Wing, R.L. (1988) *The Art of Strategy: A New Translation of Sun Tzu's Classic 'The Art of War'*, Doubleday, New York.

Whittington, R. (1993) *What Is Strategy and Does It Matter?*, Routledge, London.

STRATEGY PROCESS

Follow the course opposite to custom and you will almost always do well.

Jean Jacques Rousseau (1712–1778); French philosopher

Given the variety of perspectives on strategy, finding a precise definition with which all people agree is probably impossible. Therefore, in this book we will proceed with a very broad conception of strategy as 'a course of action for achieving an organization's purpose'. In this section, it is the intention to gain a better insight into how such a course of action comes about – how is, and should, strategy be made, analyzed, dreamt-up, formulated, implemented, changed and controlled; who is involved; and when do the necessary activities take place?

The process by which strategy comes about can be dissected in many ways. Here, the strategy process has been unraveled into three partially overlapping issues, each of which requires managers to make choices, and each of which is (therefore) controversial (see Figure II.1):

- Strategic thinking. This issue focuses on the *strategist*. The question is how managers should organize their thinking to achieve a successful strategic reasoning process.

- Strategy formation. This issue focuses on the *strategy*. The question is how managers should organize their strategizing activities to achieve a successful strategy formation process.

- Strategic change. This issue focuses on the *organization*. The question is how managers should organize changes to achieve a successful strategic renewal process.

The most important term to remember throughout this section is *process*. In each chapter the discussion is not about one-off activities or outcomes – a strategic thought, a formed strategy or a strategic change – but about the ongoing processes of thinking, forming and changing. These processes need to be organized, structured, stimulated, nurtured and/or facilitated over a prolonged period of time and the question concerns which approach will be successful in the long term, as well as in the short term.

FIGURE II.1 The strategy process chapters

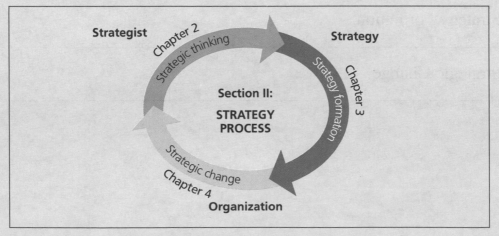

STRATEGIC THINKING

Rational, adj. Devoid of all delusions save those of observation, experience and reflection.

The Devil's Dictionary, Ambrose Bierce (1842–1914); American columnist

INTRODUCTION

What goes on in the mind of the strategist? A fascinating question that is easy to ask, but difficult to answer. Yet, it is a question that is important in two ways – generally and personally. Generally, knowing what goes on in the minds of managers during strategy processes is essential for understanding their choices and behaviors. Opening up the 'black box' of the strategist's mind to see how decisions are made can help to anticipate or influence this thinking. Grasping how managers shape their strategic views and select their preferred actions can be used to develop more effective strategy processes. It is due to this importance of strategic thinking that a separate chapter in this book is devoted to the subject. Yet, for each reader personally, the topic of strategic thinking is also of key importance, as it automatically raises the questions 'what is going on in *my* mind?' and 'how strategic is *my* thinking?'. Exploring the subject of strategic thinking triggers each person to explore their own thought processes and critically reflect on their own strategy preferences. Ideally, wondering about the mind of the strategist should inspire readers to constantly question their own assumptions, thoughts, beliefs and ideas, and to sharpen their strategic thinking, as they move through the following chapters. For this reason, it seems only appropriate to start the book with this topic.

So, what goes on in the mind of the strategist? Well, a lot, but if reduced to its bare essentials it can be said that strategists are engaged in the process of dealing with *strategic problems*. Not problems in the negative sense of troublesome conditions that need to be avoided, but in the neutral sense of challenging situations that need to be resolved – a strategic problem is a set of circumstances requiring a reconsideration of the current course of action, either to profit from observed opportunities or to respond to perceived threats. To deal with these strategic problems, managers must not simply think, but they must go through a *strategic reasoning process*, searching for ways to define and resolve the challenges at hand. Managers must structure their individual thinking steps into a reasoning process that will result in effective strategic behavior. The question is how managers actually go about defining strategic problems (how do they identify and diagnose what is going on?) and how they go about solving strategic problems (how do they generate, evaluate and decide on potential answers?). It is this issue of strategic reasoning, as a string of strategic thinking activities directed at defining and resolving strategic problems, that will be examined in further detail below.

THE ISSUE OF STRATEGIC REASONING

The mind of the strategist is a complex and fascinating apparatus that never fails to astonish and dazzle on the one hand, and disappoint and frustrate on the other. We are often surprised by the power of the human mind, but equally often stunned by its limitations. For the discussion here it is not necessary to unravel all of the mysteries surrounding the functioning of the human brain, but a short overview of the capabilities and limitations of the human mind will help us to understand the issue of strategic reasoning.

The human ability to know is referred to as 'cognition'. As strategists want to know about the strategic problems facing their organizations, they need to engage in *cognitive activities*. These cognitive activities (or strategic thinking activities) need to be structured into a strategic reasoning process. Hence, the first step towards a better understanding of what goes on in the mind of the strategist is to examine the various cognitive activities making up a strategic reasoning process. The four main cognitive activities will be discussed in the first sub-section below. To be able to perform these cognitive activities, people need to command certain mental faculties. While very sophisticated, the human brain is still physically strictly limited in what it can do. These limitations to people's *cognitive abilities* will be reviewed in the second sub-section. To deal with its inherent physical shortcomings, the human brain copes by building simplified models of the world, referred to as *cognitive maps*. The functioning of cognitive maps will be addressed in the third sub-section.

In Figure 2.1 the relationship between these three topics is visualized, using the metaphor of a computer. The cognitive abilities of our brains can be seen as a hardware level question – what are the physical limits on our mental faculties? The cognitive maps used by our brains can be seen as an operating system level question – what type of platform/language is 'running' on our brain? The cognitive activities carried out by our brains can be seen as an application level question – what type of program is strategic reasoning?

Cognitive activities

The strategic reasoning process consists of a number of strategic thinking elements or cognitive activities – mental tasks intended to increase the strategist's knowing. A general distinction can be made between cognitive activities directed towards *defining* a strategic

FIGURE 2.1   Cognitive activities, maps and abilities

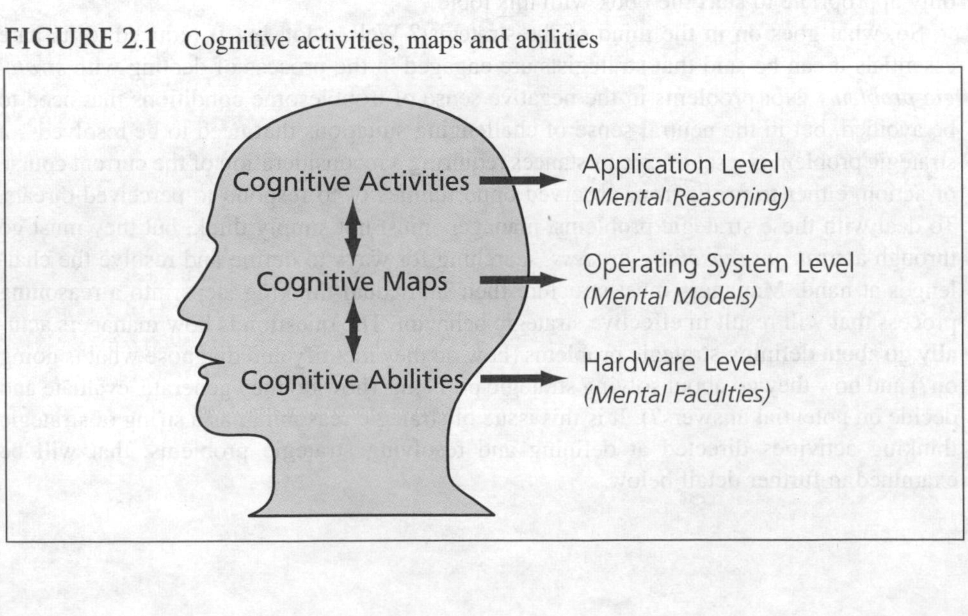

problem, and cognitive activities directed at *solving* a strategic problem. Each of these two major categories can be further split in two (see Figure 2.2), leading to the following general elements of a strategic reasoning process:

- **Identifying.** Before strategists can move to benefit from opportunities or to counter threats, they must be aware of these challenges and acknowledge their importance. This part of the reasoning process is variably referred to as identifying, recognizing or sense-making.
- **Diagnosing.** To come to grips with a problem, strategists must try to understand the structure of the problem and its underlying causes. This part of the reasoning process is variably referred to as diagnosing, analyzing or reflecting.
- **Conceiving.** To deal with a strategic problem, strategists must come up with a potential solution. If more than one solution is available, strategists must select the most promising one. This part of the reasoning process is variably referred to as conceiving, formulating or imagining.
- **Realizing.** A strategic problem is only really solved once concrete actions are undertaken that achieve results. Strategists must therefore carry out problem-solving activities and evaluate whether the consequences are positive. This part of the reasoning process is variably referred to as realizing, implementing or acting.

A structured approach to these four cognitive activities is to carry them out in the above order, starting with problem identification and then moving through diagnosis to conceiving solutions and finally realizing them (i.e. clockwise movement in Figure 2.2). In this approach the first step, identifying strategic problems, would require extensive external and internal scanning, thorough sifting of incoming information and the selection of priority issues. In the next reasoning step, the strategic problems recognized would have to be diagnosed by gathering more detailed data, and by further analyzing and refining this information. Once the problem had been properly defined, a strategy could be formulated by evaluating the available options and deciding which solution would be best. In the final phase, realization, the strategist would need to ensure execution of the proposed solution by consciously planning and controlling implementation activities. In this case, the four

FIGURE 2.2   Elements of a strategic reasoning process

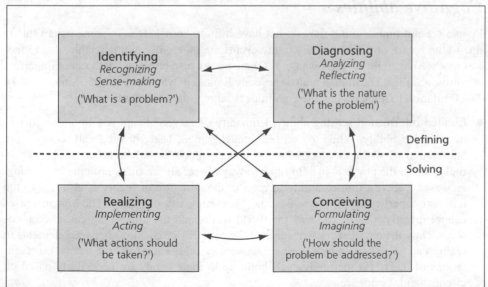

elements of the strategic reasoning process could actually be labeled recognizing, analyzing, formulating and implementing.

However, strategists do not always reason in this step-by-step fashion. Their thinking is often less orderly, with identifying, diagnosing, conceiving and realizing intermingled with one another – even going on at the same time. Nor are the cognitive activities as straightforward as portrayed above. The identification of strategic problems is often not about objective observation, but rather subjective interpretation – by looking at the world from a particular angle, strategists see and value particular strengths, weaknesses, opportunities and threats. Such sense-making activities (Weick, 1979; Gioia and Chittipeddi, 1991) lead to attention being paid to some issues, while others do not make the strategic agenda (Dutton, 1988; Ocasio, 1997). Likewise, diagnosing strategic problems is not always a structured analytical process. Gaining a deeper understanding of strategic problems may involve explicit analysis, but also intuitive reflecting – by employing unconscious reasoning rules strategists often quickly form a general picture of how key aspects of a strategic problem are interrelated.

Conceiving strategic solutions can be equally 'messy' and subjective. Often, strategic options are not chosen from an available repertoire of potential solutions, but they are invented. In other words, new options are often not selected, discovered or figured out, but are envisioned – strategists imagine how things could be done. Such idea generation can involve reasoning by analogy or metaphor, brainstorming or pure fantasizing. New potential solutions may come to the strategist in a flash (eureka!) or emerge over time, but usually require a period of incubation beforehand and a period of nurturing afterwards. Furthermore, strategists often find it impossible to objectively prove which new idea would be the best solution. Therefore, the process of deciding on the solution to be pursued may involve more judgment than calculation.

Finally, it must be emphasized that action does not always come last, in the form of solution implementation. Often, strategists do not wait for a problem to be precisely defined and for a solution to be fully conceived before starting to act. On the contrary, strategists often feel they must first act – they must have experience with a problem and know that the current strategy will not be able to overcome the problem. To find a suitable solution it is often also necessary to test certain assumptions in practice and to experiment. Hence, acting regularly precedes, or goes hand in hand with, all other cognitive activities.

Cognitive abilities

People are not omniscient – they do not have infinite knowledge. To some extent this is due to the nature of reality – many future events are inherently unpredictable, due to factors that are uncertain or unknowable. Yet, humans are also burdened with rather imperfect cognitive abilities. The human brain is severely limited in what it can know (Simon, 1957). The limitation to human's cognitive abilities is largely due to three factors:

- Limited information sensing ability. Humanity's first 'handicap' is a limited information-sensing ability. While the senses – touch, smell, taste, hearing and seeing – are bombarded with stimuli, much of reality remains unobservable to humans. This is partially due to the physical inability to be everywhere, all the time, noticing everything. However, people's limited ability to register the structure of reality is also due to the inherent superficiality of the senses and the complexity of reality. The human senses cannot directly identify the way the world works and the underlying causal relationships. Only the physical consequences of the complex interactions between elements in reality can be picked up by a person's sensory system. Therefore, the mental representations of the world that individuals build up in their minds are necessarily based on circumstantial evidence.

- Limited information processing capacity. Unfortunately, a second drawback is that humans do not have unlimited data processing abilities. Thinking through problems with many variables, complex relationships and huge amounts of data is a task that people find extremely difficult to perform. Approaching every activity in this way would totally overload a person's brain. For this reason, humans hardly ever think through a problem with full use of all available data, but necessarily make extensive use of mental shortcuts, referred to as 'cognitive heuristics' (Janis, 1989). Cognitive heuristics are mental 'rules of thumb' that simplify a problem, so that it can be more quickly understood and solved. Cognitive heuristics focus a person's attention on a number of key variables that are believed to be most important, and present a number of simple decision rules to rapidly resolve an issue. The set of possible solutions to be considered is also limited in advance.

- Limited information storage capacity. Another human cognitive shortcoming is poor memory. People have only a limited capacity for storing information. Remembering all individuals, events, dates, places and circumstances is beyond the ability of the human brain. Therefore, people must store information very selectively and organize this information in a way that it can be easily retrieved when necessary. Here again, cognitive heuristics are at play – 'rules of thumb' make the memorization process manageable in the face of severe capacity limitations. Such heuristics help to simplify complex clusters of data into manageable chunks and help to categorize, label and store this information so that it can be recalled at a later time.

To deal with these severe physical limitations, the brain has come up with more than only simple cognitive heuristics. The human mind has come to work with more holistic cognitive maps.

Cognitive maps

Knowledge that people have is stored in their minds in the form of 'cognitive maps' (e.g. McCaskey, 1982; Weick and Bourgnon, 1986), also referred to as 'cognitive schemata' (e.g. Anderson, 1983; Schwenk, 1988), 'mental models' (e.g. Day and Lord, 1992; Knight et al., 1999), 'knowledge structures' (e.g. Lyles and Schwenk, 1992; Walsh, 1995) and 'construed reality' (Finkelstein and Hambrick, 1996). These cognitive maps are representations in a person's mind of how the world works. A cognitive map of a certain situation reflects a person's beliefs about the importance of the issues and about the cause and effect relationships between them.

Cognitive maps are formed over time through education, experience and interaction with others. Based on the inputs of their senses, people will infer causal relationships between phenomena, making guesses about unobservable factors and resolving inconsistencies between the bits of information received. In turn, people's cognitive maps steer their senses; while cognitive maps are built on past sensory data, they will consequently direct which new information will be sought and perceived. A person's cognitive map will focus attention on particular phenomena, while blocking out other data as noise, and will quickly make clear how a situation should be perceived. In this way, a cognitive map provides an interpretive filter or perceptual screen, aiding the senses in selecting and understanding external stimuli (Starbuck and Milliken, 1988). Furthermore, cognitive maps help to direct behavior, by providing an existing repertoire of 'problem-solving' responses (also referred to as 'scripts' or 'recipes') from which an appropriate action can be derived.

In building their cognitive maps, people acquire a lot of their knowledge by means of direct experience. They learn to communicate, play an instrument, drive a vehicle and solve problems by doing. This knowledge is added to people's cognitive maps without being explicitly articulated. In other words, knowledge gained through experiential learning is usually not codified into formal rules, principles, models or theories, but remains tacit (Polanyi, 1966; Nonaka, 1991). People formulate implicit models and draw conclusions, but do so largely unconsciously. In this way, cognitive maps evolve without people themselves being entirely aware of their own cognitive map. Hence, when people use their 'intuition', this is not a mystical or irrational way of reasoning, but thinking guided by the tacit knowledge they have acquired in the past (Behling and Eckel, 1991). Intuitive thinking is the opposite of analytical thinking – informal and holistic (Von Winterfeldt and Edwards, 1986). Informal means that the thinking is largely unconscious and based on assumptions, variables and causal relationships not explicitly identifiable by those doing the thinking. Holistic means that the thinker does not aim at unraveling phenomena into their constituent parts, but rather maintains a more integrated view of reality.

Yet, people's cognitive maps are not developed independently, but rather in interaction with one another. People tend to construct a shared understanding of the world by interacting with each other within a group over an extended period of time. By exchanging interpretations of what they see, it is said that they *enact* a shared reality (Daft and Weick, 1984; Smircich and Stubbart, 1985). The resulting shared cognitive map is variably referred to as the group's dominant logic (Prahalad and Bettis, 1986), common paradigm (Kuhn, 1970) or belief system (Noorderhaven, 1995). Such a shared worldview can exist within small social units, such as a firm or a family, but also within larger units, such as an industry or a nation.

As individuals can belong to different groups, they can be influenced by different belief systems simultaneously. As members of a national culture, their cognitive maps will to a certain extent be influenced by the beliefs dominant within the nation. As employees of a company, their cognitive maps will be affected by the beliefs common within the firm and the industry as well. In the same manner, people can be impacted by the professional community to which they belong, their religious affiliation, their political party and any other groups in which they interact with others (Hambrick et al., 1993; Sutcliffe and Huber, 1998). Due to the mutually inclusive nature of group membership, an individual's cognitive map will be a complex combination of elements taken from different group-level dominant logics. While these paradigms on which an individual draws can be complementary, or overlapping yet consistent, it is quite possible that inconsistencies arise (Schein, 1985; Trice and Beyer, 1993).

As shared beliefs develop over time through interaction and are passed on through socialization, they remain largely tacit. The shared cognitive map of a group is literally 'common sense' – sense shared by a common group of people. However, where members of different groups come into conflict with one another, or where an individual needs to deal with the inconsistencies brought on by multiple group memberships, beliefs can become more articulated. Different behaviors, based on different cognitive maps, will often lead to the identification and codification of beliefs, either to protect them or to engage in debate with people with other views. As paradigms become more articulated, they also become more mobile, making it possible to transfer ideas to people without direct interaction.

The downside of cognitive maps is that they exhibit a high level of rigidity. People are generally not inclined to change their minds. Once people's cognitive maps have formed, and they have a grip on reality, they become resistant to signals that challenge their conceptions. As McCaskey (1982) remarks, the mind 'strives mightily to bring order, simplicity, consistency, and stability to the world it encounters', and is therefore reluctant to welcome the ambiguity presented by contradicting data. People tend to significantly overestimate the value of information that confirms their cognitive map, underestimate disconfirming information, and they actively seek out evidence that supports their current beliefs (Schwenk, 1984). Once an interpretive filter is in place, seeing is not believing, but believing is seeing. People might have the impression that they are constantly learning, but they are largely learning within the bounds of a paradigm. When an individual's map is supported by similar beliefs shared within a firm, industry or country, the ability to question key aspects of a paradigm will usually be rather limited. Not only does the individual have no 'intellectual sounding board' for teasing out new ideas, but deviation from the dominant logic might also have adverse social and political ramifications within the group (e.g. DiMaggio and Powell, 1983; Aldrich and Fiol, 1994). Not for nothing the old proverb is: 'old ideas never change; they eventually die out' (Kuhn, 1970).

For strategists, cognitive rigidity is particularly worrying. Strategists should be at the forefront of market developments, identifying changing circumstances and new opportunities before their competitors. Strategic thinking is by its very nature focused on understanding and shaping the future, and therefore strategists must have the ability to challenge current beliefs and change their own mind. They must be able to come up with innovative, but feasible, new strategies that will fit with the unfolding reality. This places extraordinary cognitive demands on strategists – they must be able to overcome the limitations of their own cognitive maps and develop a new understanding.

THE PARADOX OF LOGIC AND CREATIVITY

Information's pretty thin stuff, unless mixed with experience.
Clarence Day (1874–1935); American essayist

Many management theorists have noted that the opposites of intuition and analysis create a tension for managers (e.g. Langley, 1989, 1995; Pondy, 1983). While some researchers make a strong case for more formal analysis (e.g. Isenberg, 1984; Schoemaker and Russo, 1993), there is a broad understanding that managers need to employ both intuitive and analytical thinking, even if they are each other's opposites.

The extensive use of intuitive judgment among managers is understood by most as necessary and beneficial. A manager's intuition is built up through years of experience and contains a vast quantity of tacit knowledge that can only superficially be tapped by formal analysis. Intuition can also give a 'richer' assessment, by blending in all types of qualitative information. Moreover, intuitive thinking is often better at capturing the big picture than analytical thinking. And very practically, intuition is needed to cut corners: without the widespread use of cognitive heuristics, management would grind to a halt, overloaded by the sheer complexity of the analyses that would need to be carried out. Such a situation of rationality gone rampant is referred to as 'paralysis by analysis' (Lenz and Lyles, 1985; Langley, 1995).

However, it is equally clear to most that human intuition is often unreliable. Cognitive heuristics are 'quick and dirty' – efficient, but imprecise. They help people to intuitively jump to conclusions without thorough analysis, which increases speed, but also increases the risk of drawing faulty conclusions. The main danger of cognitive heuristics is that they are inherently biased, as they focus attention on only a few variables and interpret them in a particular way, even when this is not appropriate (e.g. Tversky and Kahneman, 1986; Bazerman, 1990). For this reason, many academics urge practitioners to bolster their intuitive judgments with more explicit rational analysis. Especially in the case of strategic decisions, more time and energy should be made available to avoid falling prey to common cognitive biases. Otherwise the ultimate result might be a 'corporate gravestone' with the epitaph *'extinct by instinct'* (Langley, 1995).

While the tension between intuition and analysis is important, it does not go to the heart of the strategic reasoning issue. For strategists the more fundamental question is how they can escape getting stuck with an outdated cognitive map. How can they avoid the danger of building up a flawed picture of their industry, their markets and themselves? As strategists must be acutely aware of the unfolding opportunities and threats in the environment, and the evolving strengths and weaknesses of the organization, they must be able to constantly re-evaluate their views.

On the one hand, this requires rigorous *logical thinking*. All the key assumptions on which a strategist's cognitive map has been based need to be reviewed and tested against developments in the firm and its environment. On the other hand, strategists must have the ability to engage in *creative thinking*. To be able to see new opportunities and strengths, strategists must be able to think beyond current models of reality. Both demands on strategists will now be reviewed in more detail.

The demand for logical thinking

It is clear that if managers only base their strategic decisions on heavily biased cognitive maps, unconsciously built up through past experience, this will lead to very poor results. Managers need to have the ability to critically reflect on the assumptions they hold, to check whether they are based on actual fact, or on organizational folklore and industry recipes. They must be capable of making their tacit beliefs more explicit, so that the validity of these mental models can be evaluated and they can be further refined. In short, to be successful strategists, managers need to escape the confines of their own cognitive maps – and those of other stakeholders engaged in the strategy process.

Assessing the validity of a cognitive map requires strong logical thinking. Logical thinking is a disciplined and rigorous way of thinking, on the basis of formal rules. When employing logic, each step in an argumentation follows from the previous, based on valid principles. In other words, a logical thinker will only draw a conclusion if it is arrived at by a sound succession of arguments.

Logical thinking can be applied to all four cognitive activities outlined in Figure 2.2. When identifying and diagnosing a strategic problem, logical thinking can help to avoid the emotional interpretations that so often color people's understanding of environmental opportunities and threats, and organizational strengths and weaknesses. Logical thinking can also expose a person's bullish or bearish bias and can be instrumental in discarding old 'theories' of how the firm and its environment function. By analyzing the empirical facts and rigorously testing the hypotheses on which the firm's shared cognitive map has been built, the strategist can prevent building a false model of reality.

When conceiving and realizing a strategic solution, logical thinking can help to avoid the danger of following outdated habits and routines. Routines are programed courses of action that originally were deliberately conceived, but have been subsequently internalized and are used automatically (March and Simon, 1993). Habits are programed courses of action that have developed unconsciously. By explicitly formulating strategic options and subjecting them to formal evaluation, the strategist can break away from such established behavior and develop new approaches to gaining and retaining competitive advantage. Moreover, logical thinking can aid in making a distinction between fantasy and feasibility. Sound logic can serve to weed out strategic options that are flights of fancy, by analyzing the factors that will determine success or failure.

The demand for creative thinking

Creative thinking is the opposite of logical thinking. As described above, when employing logic, a thinker bases each step in a train of thought on the previous steps, following formal rules of valid thinking. De Bono (1970) refers to this pattern of thought as 'vertical thinking'. However, when creativity is used, the thinker does not take a valid step, but takes a leap of imagination, without being able to support the validity of the mental jump. In creative thinking a person abandons the rules governing sound argumentation and draws a conclusion that is not justified based on the previous arguments. In this way the thinker generates a new understanding, but without objective proof that the new idea 'makes sense'. De Bono refers to this pattern of thought as 'lateral thinking'.

In essence, creative thinking takes liberty in following thinking rules. One idea might lead to another idea, without formal logic interfering. One variable might be linked by the thinker to another, without a sound explanation of why a correlation is assumed. Creativity in effect creates a new understanding, with little attention paid to supporting evidence. Often logic is used afterwards to justify an idea that was actually generated by creative means.

When identifying and diagnosing strategic problems, creative thinking is often needed. Old cognitive maps usually have a very compelling logic, locking people into old patterns of thinking. These old cognitive maps are usually tried and tested, and have become immune to external signals that they are no longer fitting. Thinking within the boundaries of a shared cognitive map is generally accepted and people tend to proceed rationally – that is, they try to avoid logical inconsistencies. Challenging a cognitive map's fundamental assumptions, however, cannot be done in a way that is logically consistent with the map itself. Contradicting a paradigm is illogical from the point of view of those who accept the paradigm. Therefore, changing a rigid and subjective cognitive map, rooted in a shared paradigm, requires strategists to imagine new ways of understanding the world that do not logically follow from past beliefs. Strategic thinkers need to be willing and able to break with orthodoxy and make leaps of imagination, that are not logically justified, but needed to generate novel ways of looking at old problems.

The same is true when conceiving and realizing strategic solutions. New strategies often do not follow from the facts, but need to be invented – they are not analyzed into existence, but need to be generated, if they are to be innovative and distinctive. Creative solutions do not follow from the dominant logic, but are the unexpected answers that emerge when the grip of the dominant logic is loosened.

Unfortunately, the conclusion must be that logical thinking and creative thinking are not only opposites, but that they are partially incompatible as well. They are based on methods that are at odds with one another. Strategizing managers would probably love to be fully logical and fully creative at the same time, but both require such a different mindset and range of cognitive skills that in practice it is very difficult to achieve both simultaneously. The demand for logic and creativity is not only contradictory for each individual, but also within teams, departments and the overall firm: while strategizing groups would like to be fully capable of logical and creative thinking, finding ways of incorporating both forms of strategic thinking into a workable strategy process is extremely challenging. Commonly, conflicting styles lead to conflicting people, and therefore a blend between the two is not that simple. It is for this reason that we speak of the 'paradox of logic and creativity' – the two demands on managers seem to be contradictory, yet both are required at the same time.

EXHIBIT 2.1 SHORT CASE

SMIT: SALVAGING STRATEGY?

When in 2001 Russian president Vladimir Putin promised his nation to raise the sunken nuclear submarine *Kursk* and to give its crew an honorable land burial, few believed that it would be possible to sal-

vage such a dangerous wreck, at such a depth, in the cold and stormy arctic waters before the onset of winter. The company that was able to pull off this amazing feat was Smit, the world's leading provider of maritime services, working together with the heavy transport company, Mammoet. Besides its headline-grabbing salvage business, Smit is involved in a broad range of 'ship-based' services, such as harbor towage (getting an ocean-faring boat into and out of dock), heavy lift and transport (getting big objects like oil rigs and bridge parts to the right destination) and offshore terminal support (operational services and getting supplies to offshore oil platforms). With its base in the world's largest harbor, Rotterdam, and regional headquarters in Singapore, Cape Town and Houston, Smit operates on a worldwide basis, employing approximately 2900 people. In 2002 the company's revenues totaled €319 million, earning an operating result of €13 million.

The company, founded in 1842 by Fop Smit, has a history filled with many remarkable achievements, inspired by the company's long-time slogan 'any job, any sea'. For example, in 1896, Smit was the first company in the world to tow a ship dock overseas, from Rotterdam to Angola, even though there were no suitable ocean-going tugboats available. The company has also been involved in many complex salvage operations: for instance, it recently raised the Japanese training vessel, Ehime Maru, which had sunk in deep water near Hawaii after colliding with a US submarine. Typical for all these operations has been the company's 'can do' attitude and the improvisation skills of its crews. More than 100 years ago a senior Smit manager was famously quoted as saying 'experience or not, we'll do it and we'll go there!', and this attitude has remained central to the Smit culture ever since.

This entrepreneurial 'get up and go' has been the major factor driving the growth of Smit throughout most of the 20th century, leading the company to enter many new foreign markets and new lines of business. From 1921 to 1980, the company was run by two members of the Smit family, first Murk Lels and then Piet Kleyn van Willigen, both with a strong entrepreneurial streak, yet with little interest in doing extensive strategic analyses. Their decision to enter a new country or to offer a new service was largely dependent on two criteria: it needed to be maritime and it needed to be lucrative. In their view, a business was potentially lucrative if it promised significant sales opportunities – with little regard to the question whether a market was structurally attractive or not. This mode of thinking brought the company into many new areas. For instance, in the 1960s Smit was asked to start towing oil rigs and terminal platforms for the emerging off-shore oil

industry, which triggered the company's jump into terminal provisioning services, sea-going firefighting and terminal maintenance, requiring various specialized ships to be built. In the 1970s, Smit saw growing opportunities to tow ultra-heavy objects across the ocean (e.g. icebergs from Antarctica to the Persian Gulf) and therefore had three giant tugboats built. Within the company the joke circulated that a new business was actually only interesting if new ships were necessary – growth was driven by 'new toys for the boys'.

When in 1980 the last family member of the board of directors decided to retire, it was determined that an emotionally detached outsider should take the helm and restructure the extensive portfolio of businesses that Lels and Kleyn van Willigen had built up. From 1980 to 1988, Koos Groenendijk, a former shipping company manager, worked at trimming the corporate portfolio, while from 1988 to 1998 Fred Busker, a former Royal Dutch Shell manager, attempted to achieve more focus. 'We threw sentiments overboard and took a rational look at things', said Mr Busker, leading to the closing down and selling off of many unprofitable business units. But while 'sinking leaky businesses' went relatively well, the difficulty faced by Groenendijk and Busker was that they did not have the intimate industry knowledge to find new growth opportunities. Both missed the experienced-based intuition and sense of entrepreneurial risk-taking that their predecessors had long been able to tap. Moreover, while there were still many 'can-do' people in the organization, few had the capability to develop a good business case to justify the huge investments needed to launch a new type of service. After some failed attempts to try something new, both CEOs retreated to optimizing the existing businesses within the current rules of the game.

Yet, at the same time, other companies were nibbling at Smit's core businesses. In the Rotterdam harbor a new towing competitor emerged, without the high costs of an overengineered and overstaffed fleet. In heavy transport and lifting the company was being challenged by low cost 'Mom and Pop' outfits on the one hand, and new entrants from the shipping and construction industries on the other. All of this had an increasingly negative impact on the company's growth and profitability.

In 1997 the Smit family decided to float 100% of the company's shares on the Amsterdam Stock Exchange, after which a new CEO was installed,

Nico Buis, a highly regarded former navy officer and director of the Dutch intelligence and security service. Although Buis was very well connected in the maritime sector and did an excellent job representing the company to the outside world, he too did not know how to revive the slipping business fortunes. In 2000, despite the buoyant global economy, Smit was forced to issue its first profit warning, while also being reprimanded by the stock exchange for providing the warning too late. The company was doubly punished by shareholders, who felt that the company did not have a clear strategic direction, while also not having its financial reporting systems adequately organized.

Anticipating the retirement of Buis in 2002, a search was started in 2000 to find a successor with the capability to reinvigorate the company and set a clear strategic course for the Smit fleet of companies. Within the organization many competent managers were identified, but it was felt that they excelled at operational management, not strategic leadership: most talented managers had worked hard at developing their ability to solve challenging client problems, not at building new businesses and strengthening the competitive advantage of existing ones. Within the company, improvisation skills and 'technical inventiveness' were qualities in abundance, but strategizing skills and 'business innovativeness' were insufficiently developed. For this reason, once more an outsider was sought, resulting in the hiring of Ben Vree in November 2000.

Vree was headhunted from Van Ommeren / Vopak, a large international company in the tank storage business (e.g. storing oil and chemicals in tanks in harbors). With his background in business-to-business marketing in the oil and maritime industries, Vree was seen as someone who could bring marketing and strategic thinking into the operationally minded Smit company. Vree was also a charismatic leader, with a forceful presence, yet a listening ear and a warm personality, making him the right person, it was felt, to lead the needed change process within the company.

Vree was given a year and a half, until June 2002, to get to know the business and to prepare himself for taking over as CEO. His very first task was to lead the strategy review process that Buis had started in response to the profit warning. What Vree found was a technically competent company, with an excellent reputation, strategically adrift and under competitive pressure from all sides. He also saw that the lack of central direction, coupled with entrepreneurial drive, had led foreign subsidiaries to 'do their own thing', with little regard to synergy with the rest of the company. Even more worrying was the impending brain drain – many of the key operational people storing the tacit knowledge on which Smit depended for its competitive advantage would be retiring within a few years. And at the root of all of these problems Vree found that the strategic thinking capability at Smit was woefully inadequate, which had led to the dominance of operational thinking.

Vree and Buis quickly took measures to redirect the company and improve the operating results. The sprawling portfolio of localized business units was reorganized into four global divisions: Harbor Towage, Terminals, Salvage and Transport & Heavy Lift. In these new divisions the autonomy of the foreign subsidiaries was strongly restrained, to start building consistent business strategies for Smit's international customers (e.g. shipping companies, oil firms and international ship insurers). Various non-performing businesses were sold or closed. Much emphasis was also placed on fortifying the company's current position and increasing profitability, to fend off the threat of operating losses.

But a month after taking over the helm in June 2002, Vree was forced to issue the second profit warning in the company's history. In particular, the results in the economically volatile Transport & Heavy Lift division had deteriorated quickly. For Vree it was clear that Smit could not downsize itself out of this difficult strategic position. Besides the necessary cost cutting and restructuring that he had already initiated, the company needed to find its way back to growth. New opportunities had to be identified and diagnosed, and new strategies conceived and realized. But how to get Smit to do this successfully was the question on Vree's mind. How could he improve the strategic thinking capability of his organization to achieve the necessary strategic reorientation? For Vree there was no doubt that getting his crew to set the right course was much more preferable than letting others salvage his business once it had run aground.

Sources: www.smit-international.com; company interviews.

PERSPECTIVES ON STRATEGIC THINKING

Irrationally held truths may be more harmful than reasoned errors.

T.H. Huxley (1825–1895); English biologist

While the need for both logical and creative thinking is clear, this does place strategists in a rather awkward position of needing to bring two partially contradictory forms of thinking together in one strategic reasoning process. Logical thinking helps to make the strategic reasoning process more *rational* – rigorous, comprehensive and consistent, instead of haphazard, fragmentary and ad hoc. Creative thinking, on the other hand, helps to make the strategic reasoning process more *generative* – producing more unorthodox insights, imaginative ideas and innovative solutions, instead of having a bland, conformist and conservative output. In finding a balance between these opposite forms of thinking, the main question is whether the strategic reasoning process should actually be a predominantly rational affair, or a much more generative process. Is strategizing largely a rational activity, requiring logical thinking to be the dominant modus operandi, with occasional bits of creativity needed here and there to generate new ideas? Or is strategizing largely a generative activity, requiring creative thinking to be the standard operating procedure, with occasional bits of logical analysis needed here and there to weed out unfeasible ideas?

The answer to this question should be found in the strategic management literature. Yet, upon closer inspection, the opinions outlined in both the academic and popular literature show that views vary widely among researchers and managers alike. A wide spectrum of differing perspectives can be recognized, each giving their own angle on how strategic thinking should use logic and creativity – sometimes explicitly mentioning the need for both, but more commonly making implicit assumptions about the role of logic and creativity in strategy processes.

As was outlined in Chapter 1, it is not the intention here to summarize all of the 'schools of thought' on the topic of strategic thinking. Instead, only the two most opposite points of view will be presented in this section. These two poles in the debate are not necessarily the most popular points of view and at times they might seem somewhat extreme, arguing in terms of 'black-and-white' instead of shades of gray. Yet, as the two pure 'archetypes' they do form the ultimate pair for a good debate – a clear-cut thesis and antithesis in a process of dialectical inquiry.

At the one end of the spectrum, there are those who argue that strategic reasoning should be a predominantly rational process, requiring logic to be the main form of thinking in use. This point of view is referred to as the 'rational reasoning perspective'. At the other pole, there are those who argue that the essence of strategic reasoning is the ability to break through orthodox beliefs and generate new insights and behaviors, requiring the extensive use of creativity. This point of view will be referred to as the 'generative reasoning perspective'.

The rational reasoning perspective

 Strategists employing the rational reasoning perspective argue that strategic reasoning is predominantly a 'logical activity' (Andrews, 1987, Reading 2.1 in this book). To deal with strategic problems the strategist must first consciously and thoroughly analyze the problem situation. Data must be gathered on all developments external to the organization, and this data must be processed to pinpoint the opportunities and threats in the organization's environment. Furthermore, the organization itself must be appraised, to uncover its strengths and weaknesses and to establish which resources are available. Once the problem has been defined, a number of alternative strategies can be identified by matching external opportunities to internal strengths. Then, the strategic options must be extensively screened, by evaluating them on a number of criteria, such as internal consistency, external consonance, competitive advantage, organizational feasibility, potential return and risks. The best strategy can be selected by comparing the scores of all options and determining the level of risk the strategist is willing to take. The chosen strategy can subsequently be implemented.

This type of intellectual effort requires well-developed analytical skills. Strategists must be able to rigorously, consistently and objectively comb through huge amounts of data, interpreting and combining findings to arrive at a rich picture of the current problem situation. Possible solutions require critical appraisal and all possible contingencies must be logically thought through. Advocates of the rational reasoning perspective argue that such reasoning strongly resembles the problem-solving approach of chess grand masters (Simon, 1987). They also thoroughly assess their competitive position, sift through a variety of options and calculate which course of action brings the best chances of success. Therefore, the reasoning processes of chess grand masters can be used as an analogy for what goes on in the mind of the strategist.

While depicted here as a purely step-by-step process of recognition, analysis, formulation and implementation, proponents of the rational reasoning perspective note that in reality strategists often have to backtrack and redo some of these steps, as new information becomes available or chosen strategies do not work out. Strategists attempt to be as comprehensive, consistent and rigorous as possible in their analyses and calculations, but of course they cannot know everything and their conclusions are not always perfect: even with the most advanced forecasting techniques, not all developments can be foreseen; even with state of the art market research, some trends can be missed; even with cutting edge test marketing, scenario analyses, competitive simulations and net present value calculations, some selected strategies can turn out to be failures. Strategists are not all knowing, and do make mistakes – their rationality is limited by incomplete information and imperfect cognitive abilities. Yet, strategists try to be as rational as possible. Simon (1957) refers to this as 'bounded rationality' – 'people act intentionally rational, but only limitedly so'. This coincides with Ambrose Bierce's famous sarcastic definition of logic as 'the art of thinking and reasoning in strict accordance with the limitations and incapacities of the human misunderstanding'.

The (boundedly) rational strategist must sometimes improvise to make up for a lack of information, but will try to do this as logically as possible. Inferences and speculation will always be based on the facts as known. By articulating assumptions and explicitly stating the facts and arguments on which conclusions have been based, problem definitions and solutions can be debated within the firm to confirm that they have been arrived at using sound reasoning. This strongly resembles the scientific method, in that hypotheses are formulated and tested as a means for obtaining new knowledge. Only by this consistent alignment of mental models with empirical reality can the strategist avoid the danger of becoming stuck with an outdated cognitive map.

The alternative to this rational approach, it is often pointed out, is to be irrational and illogical, which surely cannot be a desirable alternative for the strategist. Non-rational reasoning comes in a variety of forms. For instance, people's thinking can be guided by their emotions. Feelings such as love, hate, guilt, regret, pride, anxiety, frustration and embarrassment can all cloud the strategist's understanding of a problem situation and the possible solutions. Adherents of the rational reasoning perspective do not dispute the importance of emotions – the purpose of an organization is often based on 'personal values, aspirations and ideals', while the motivation to implement strategies is also rooted in human emotions. However, the actual determination of the optimal strategy is a 'rational undertaking' par excellence (Andrews, 1987: 32).

Neither is intuitive thinking an appealing alternative for strategists. Of course, intuition can often be useful: decision rules based on extensive experience (cognitive heuristics) are often correct (even if they have been arrived at unconsciously) and they save time and effort. For example, Simon argues that even chess grand masters make many decisions intuitively, based on tacit rules of thumb, formulated through years of experience. Yet, intuitive judgments must be viewed with great suspicion, as they are difficult to verify and infamously unreliable (e.g. Hogarth, 1980; Schwenk, 1984). Where possible, intuitive thinking should be made explicit – the strategist's cognitive map should be captured on paper (e.g. Anthony et al., 1993; Eden, 1989), so that the reasoning of the strategist can be checked for logical inconsistencies.

Creative thinking is equally suspicious. Of course, creativity techniques can be beneficial for triggering some unexpected ideas. Whether it is by means of brainstorming, six thinking caps or action art, creative thinking can spark some unconventional thoughts. Even a rational scientist like Newton has remarked that 'no great discovery was ever made without a bold guess'. But this is usually where the usefulness of creativity ends, and to which it should be limited. In creative thinking anything goes and that can lead to anything between odd and ludicrous. To be able to sift the sane from the zany, logic is needed. To make sense of the multitude of new ideas the logical thinker must analyze and evaluate them. A more serious drawback is that in practice many 'creative ideas' are just someone's unsupported beliefs, dressed up to sound fashionable. 'Creative thinking' is often just an excuse for intellectual laziness.

In conclusion, advocates of the rational reasoning perspective argue that emotions, intuition and creativity have a small place in the strategic reasoning process, but that logical thinking should be the dominant ingredient. It could be said that the rational reasoning process of the strategist strongly resembles that of the scientist. The scientific methods of research, analysis, theorizing and falsification are all directly applicable to the process of strategic reasoning – so much so, that the scientific method can be used as the benchmark for strategy development processes. Consequently, the best preparation for effective strategic reasoning would be to be trained in the scientific tradition.

EXHIBIT 2.2 THE RATIONAL REASONING PERSPECTIVE

BERKSHIRE HATHAWAY: CONTROL YOUR EXCITEMENT

At the peak of the 'new economy', few people were derided as much as Warren Buffett, chairman of the insurance and investment conglomerate Berkshire Hathaway. Buffett – admiringly nicknamed the 'Sage of Omaha' – had gained a phenomenal reputation as an investor during the 1980s and 1990s, but to most it was clear that he had not grasped the opportunities presented by the internet. The grand old man might have been the guru of the old economy, but he simply did not understand the new rules of the information economy. He was considered a pitiful example of a once brilliant mind that had not been able to make the leap beyond conventional beliefs and comprehend the 'new paradigm'. The investment strategy of Berkshire Hathaway was deemed hopelessly outdated. At the peak of the dot.com boom, in September 1999, when almost all funds were rushing into new economy shares, the investment portfolio of Berkshire consisted of companies like Coca-Cola, Walt Disney, Gillette and *The Washington Post*. The shares of Berkshire traded at their lowest level in years.

The person least perturbed by this new, dubious status was Buffett himself. In his 1999 annual 'Letter to the Berkshire Hathaway Shareholders', he displayed an untouched faith in the fundamentals that had created an empire worth US$51 billion: 'If we have a strength, it is in recognizing when we are operating well within our circle of competence and when we are approaching the perimeter. . . . we just stick with what we understand. If we stray, we will have done so inadvertently, not because we got restless and substituted hope for rationality'. He refused to invest in internet stocks, which he considered 'chain letters', in which early participants get rich at the expense of later ones.

When valuing companies, Buffett's approach was based on a solid analysis of company fundamentals, 'to separate investment from speculation'. In his view, ultimately, share prices reflect a company's fundamentals and therefore nothing can substitute for a thorough diagnosis of these fundamentals. Another part of Buffett's approach was focus, concentrating the bulk of the investments in a limited number of stocks, and sticking to this. Furthermore, he avoided investing in ill-understood businesses and in fast-changing industries, 'in which the long-term winners are hard to identify'. Conscientious and consistent application of these principles had led to an exceptional track record – between 1965 and 1998 Berkshire shares outper-

formed the S&P 500 in all but three years. The compounded annual return over this period of Berkshire was 24.7%, against 10.5% for the S&P 500.

By 2001 the dot.com boom was history and Buffett was proven right – again. From the moment the stock market started to plunge, Berkshire shares were on the rise. Buffett had resisted the irrational emotions by emphasizing the need for rational reasoning, even when the conclusions were not fashionable. Nothing was more characteristic of this attitude than his 2000 'Letter to the Berkshire Shareholders', in which he wrote: 'We have embraced the 21st century by entering such cutting-edge industries as brick, carpet, insulation and paint. Try to control your excitement.'

Sources: www.berkshirehathaway.com; www.economist.com; *The Economist*, March 15 2001.

The generative reasoning perspective

Strategists taking a generative reasoning perspective are strongly at odds with the unassailable position given to logic in the rational reasoning perspective. They agree that logic is important, but stress that it is often more a hindrance than a help. The heavy emphasis placed on rationality can actually frustrate the main objective of strategic reasoning – to generate novel insights, new ways of defining problems and innovative solutions. Analysis can be a useful tool, but as the aim of strategic reasoning is to tear up outdated cognitive maps and to reinvent the future, creative thinking should be the driving force, and logical thinking a supporting means. For this reason, proponents of the generative reasoning perspective argue that strategists should avoid the false certainty projected by rational approaches to strategic reasoning, but should nurture creativity as their primary cognitive asset.

In the generative reasoning perspective, emphasis is placed on the 'wicked' nature of strategic problems (Rittel, 1972; Mason and Mitroff, 1981). It is argued that strategic problems cannot be easily and objectively defined, but that they are open to interpretation from a limitless variety of angles. The same is true for the possible solutions – there is no fixed set of problem solutions from which the strategist must select the best one. Defining and solving strategic problems, it is believed, is fundamentally a creative activity. As such, strategic reasoning has very little in common with the thought processes of the aforementioned chess grand master, as was presumed by the rationalists. Playing chess is a 'tame' problem. The problem definition is clear and all options are known. In the average game of chess, consisting of 40 moves, 10 120 possibilities have to be considered (Simon, 1972). This makes it a difficult game for humans to play, because of their limited computational capacities. Chess grand masters are better at making these calculations than other people and are particularly good at computational short cuts – recognizing which things to figure out and which not. However, even the best chess grand masters have been beaten at the game by highly logical computers with a superior number crunching capability. For the poor chess grand master, the rules of the game are fixed and there is little room for redefining the problem or introducing innovative approaches.

Engaging in business strategy is an entirely different matter. Strategic problems are wicked. Problem definitions are highly subjective and there are no fixed sets of solutions. It is therefore impossible to 'identify' the problem and 'calculate' an optimal solution. Opportunities and threats do not exist, waiting for the analyst to discover them. A strategist understands that a situation can be 'viewed' as an opportunity and 'believes' that certain factors can be threatening if not approached properly. Neither can strengths and weaknesses be objectively determined – a strategist can employ a company characteristic as a strength, but can also turn a unique company quality into a weakness by a lack of vision. Hence, doing a SWOT analysis (strengths, weaknesses, opportunities and threats) actually has little to do with logical analysis, but in reality is nothing less than a creative interpretation of a problem situation. Likewise, it is a fallacy to believe that strategic options follow more or less logically from the characteristics of the firm and its environment. Strategic options are not 'deduced from the facts' or selected from a 2×2 matrix, but are dreamt up. Strategists must be able to use their imaginations to generate previously unknown solutions. If more than one strategic option emerges from the mind of the strategist, these cannot be simply scored and ranked to choose the optimal one. Some analyses can be done, but ultimately the strategist will have to intuitively judge which vision for the future has the best chance of being created in reality.

Hence, a generative reasoning process is more than just brainstorming or having a wild idea every once in a while. In a generative reasoning process all strategic thinking activities are oriented towards creating, instead of calculating – 'inventing' instead of 'finding' (Liedtka, 2000). This type of creative thinking is very hard work, as strategists must leave the intellectual safety of generally accepted concepts to explore new ideas, guided by little else than their intuition. They must be willing to operate without the security of a dominant logic; experimenting, testing, arguing, challenging, doubting and living amongst the rubble of demolished certainties, without having new certainties to give them shelter. To proponents of the generative reasoning perspective, it is essential for strategists to have a slightly contrarian (Hurst, Rush and White, 1989), revolutionary predisposition (Hamel, 1996). Strategists must enjoy the challenge of thinking 'out of the box', even when this disrupts the status quo and is not much appreciated by those with their two feet (stuck) on the ground. As Picasso once remarked, 'every act of creation is first of all an act of destruction' – strategists must enjoy the task of eroding old paradigms and confronting the defenders of those beliefs. And if some analyses can be done to support this effort, then they can serve a valuable purpose in the overall strategy process.

In conclusion, advocates of the generative reasoning perspective argue that the essence of strategic reasoning is the ability to creatively challenge 'the tyranny of the given' (Kao, 1996) and to generate new and unique ways of understanding and doing things. As such, strategic reasoning closely resembles the frame-breaking behavior common in the arts. In fields such as painting, music, motion pictures, dancing and architecture, artists are propelled by the drive to challenge convention and to seek out innovative approaches. Many of their methods, such as brainstorming, experimentation, openness to intuition, and the use of metaphors, contradictions and paradoxes, are directly applicable to developing strategy. Consequently, the best preparation for strategic reasoning might actually be to be trained in the artistic tradition of iconoclastic creativity and mental flexibility.

EXHIBIT 2.3 THE GENERATIVE REASONING PERSPECTIVE

3M: KISSING FROGS

When Bill Hewlett of Hewlett Packard was asked which company he most admired for its innovative capability, his response was immediate: '3M! . . . You don't know what they're going to come up with next. The beauty of it is that they probably don't know what they're going to come up with either!'

For almost 100 years, 3M (Minnesota Mining and Manufacturing) has been known for its ability to come up with surprising new products and frame-breaking approaches to business. The US$16 billion company continually reinvents itself – as a rule, 30% of the company revenues come from products that are less than four years old. Examples of successful 3M product innovations are the sticky Post-it Notes, Thinsulate thermal insulation material and Scotch cellophane tape. Many of these innovative products created new markets, while others have fundamentally changed the rules of the game in existing markets. While the company started as a mining and abrasive manufacturing firm, today 3M has leading positions in areas such as office products, display and graphics materials, electronics and telecommunications, healthcare, safety, security and protection services, and transportation.

With such a track record in new product development, one might expect 3M to have an enormous R&D department, which is half true – the entire firm is one big R&D organization. Instead of limiting creative thinking to a few people in white coats, 3M's approach has been to get everyone in the organization involved in innovation. Technical employees can spend up to 15% of their time 'bootlegging' – freely working on their individual pet ideas that they hope will one day become useful innovations for the company. They have access to additional financial and material resources to support them in this. An inter-disciplinary venture team then tries to push the idea further or sends it back to the drawing board. These innovations can be product ideas, but process innovations are equally welcome. And innovation is not limited to the techies – employees in marketing, sales and administrative functions are also stimulated to come up with innovative practices.

An inherent part of the 3M culture is the belief that developing winning ideas is a process requiring enormous perseverance: 'You have to kiss a lot of frogs to find the prince,' according to a 3M researcher. Critical in finding the new prince is encouraging the organization to take risks and not to be afraid of making mistakes. Within 3M, the corporate hero is the one who has continued against all odds to create a successful innovation from something everyone thought frivolous. The top manage-ment wants no boundaries to its people's imagination and allows them to have a 'healthy disrespect for the rules' – it's better to ask forgiveness than ask permission. Very often, a venture team rejection motivates developers to work even harder on an idea. As one 3M manager remarked: 'It takes six to seven years to kill an idea in 3M.'

3M acknowledges the inspirational value of stories about innovations and the story of Post-it Notes is a classic example. In 1968, a 3M scientist trying to improve acrylate adhesives for tapes discovered an adhesive that did not permanently stick. After fruitless efforts to sell the idea internally, a new company recruit in 1973 was directly convinced of the potential and developed products as tiles and tapes for bulletin boards. The ultimate niche application was found later in the 1970s when Art Fry, a new-product development researcher, while singing in church suddenly realized that the adhesive would be the solution to the scrap paper bookmarks that kept falling out of his church choir hymn book. In the company many remained skeptical, pointing to processing difficulties and extreme waste production, to which Fry responded: 'Really, that is great news! If it were easy, then anyone could do it. If it really is as tough as you say, then 3M is the company that can do it.' Market analysis also did not reveal any customer demand for the product, so Fry suggested giving away sales samples to create demand.

Typical for the lateral thinking used by 3M is taking a technology from one business area and using it somewhere else. This is how the medical division started – automotive masking tape was adapted to the needs of surgeons to have a better way of attaching surgical drapes. Over the last ten years 3M has worked on improving the efficiency and speed of the new product development process. This has led to tension with the slack and mind-set required to come up with out-of-the box ideas. Conscious of this, the company has worked hard to structure the right conditions for spontaneity and creativity, and remains committed to nurturing a generative culture. And for good reason, as pointed out by one 3M researcher: 'Remember, one prince can pay for a lot of frogs.'

Sources: www.3M.com; Insead, case nr. 802–002–1; *The Economist*, February 18 1999.

INTRODUCTION TO THE DEBATE AND READINGS

When you have eliminated the impossible, whatever remains, however improbable, must be the truth.

'Sherlock Holmes', Arthur Conan Doyle (1859–1930);
English novelist

Imagination is more important than knowledge.

Albert Einstein (1879–1955);
German-American physicist

So, how should managers engage in strategic reasoning processes and how should they encourage fruitful strategic reasoning within their organizations? Should managers view strategic reasoning primarily as a rational and deductive activity or as a more imaginative and generative process? Should strategists train themselves to follow procedural rationality – rigorously analyzing problems using scientific methods and calculating the optimal course of action? Or should strategists practice to 'boldly go where no one has gone before' – redefining problems and inventing new courses of action?

As mentioned earlier, the strategic management literature does not offer a clear-cut answer to the question of which strategic reasoning approach is the optimal one. On the contrary, the variety of opinions among strategy theorists is dauntingly large, with many incompatible prescriptions being given. At the center of the debate on strategic reasoning is the paradox of logic and creativity. Many points of view have been put forward on how to reconcile these opposing demands, but no common perspective has yet emerged. Therefore, it is up to individual strategists to form their own opinion on how best to deal with the topic of strategic thinking.

To help strategists to come to grips with the variety of perspectives on this issue, four readings have been selected that each shed their own light on the debate. As outlined in Chapter 1, the first two readings will be representative of the two poles in this debate (see Table 2.1), while the second set of two readings will bring in extra arguments to add further flavor to the discussion.

Selecting the first reading to represent the rational reasoning perspective was not easy, as few authors make a point of arguing their rational leanings. The position of logical thinking is so entrenched in much of the management literature, that most writers adopt

TABLE 2.1   Rational reasoning versus generative reasoning perspective

	Rational reasoning perspective	*Generative reasoning perspective*
Emphasis on	Logic over creativity	Creativity over logic
Dominant cognitive style	Analytical	Intuitive
Thinking follows	Formal, fixed rules	Informal, variable rules
Nature of thinking	Deductive and computational	Inductive and imaginative
Direction of thinking	Vertical	Lateral
Problem defining seen as	Recognizing and analyzing activities	Reflecting and sense-making activities
Problem solving seen as	Formulation and implementation activities	Imagining and doing activities
Value placed on	Consistency and rigor	Unorthodoxy and innovativeness
Assumption about reality	Objective, (partially) knowable	Subjective, (partially) creatable
Thinking hindered by	Incomplete information	Adherence to current cognitive map
Decisions based on	Calculation	Judgment
Metaphor	Strategy as science	Strategy as art

the rational reasoning perspective without making this choice explicit. Hence, it has not proved possible to present a vocal defender of this perspective to get a nicely polarized debate going. Instead, as the first debate reading in this chapter, a classic work has been selected that is a good example of the rational approach to strategic thinking. This reading, 'The Concept of Corporate Strategy', by Kenneth Andrews, has been drawn from one of the most influential textbooks in the field of strategy, *Business Policy: Text and Cases* (Christensen, Andrews, et al., 1987). Andrews is arguably one of the godfathers of strategic management and this chapter from his book has had considerable impact on theorists and practitioners alike. True to the rational reasoning perspective, Andrews argues that strategy analysis and formulation should be conducted consciously, explicitly and rationally. In his view, strategic reasoning is a 'logical activity', while subsequent strategy implementation 'comprises a series of subactivities that are primarily administrative'. It should be noted that in this article Andrews is positioning himself in opposition to strategic incrementalists (see Chapter 3), not vis-à-vis proponents of the generative reasoning perspective. Therefore, he does not counter any of the major arguments raised by advocates of this perspective.

The second reading in this chapter, highlighting the views of the generative reasoning perspective, is 'The Mind of the Strategist', by Kenichi Ohmae. Ohmae, formerly head of McKinsey's Tokyo office, is one of Japan's most well-known strategy authors. In this reading, taken from the book of the same name, Ohmae argues that the mind of the strategist is not dominated by linear, logical thinking. On the contrary, a strategist's thought processes are 'basically creative and intuitive rather than rational'. In his view, 'great strategies. . .originate in insights that are beyond the reach of conscious analysis'. He does not dismiss logic as unnecessary, but notes that it is insufficient for arriving at innovative strategies. Yet, he observes that in most large companies creative strategists 'are being pushed to the sidelines in favor of rational, by-the-numbers strategic and financial planners', leading to a withering of strategic thinking ability.

In Reading 2.3, Jeanne Liedtka suggests an alternative metaphor to the rational reasoning's 'strategy as science' and the generative reasoning's 'strategy as art'. Her article is entitled 'Strategy as Design', and her argument is that the process of designing offers a rich metaphor for understanding the process of strategizing – somewhere between the processes of science and art. In describing what designers do, Liedtka points out that there is a fundamental distinction between design and science: designers invent something new, while science investigates that which exists. Designers 'conjure an image of a future reality', which cannot be determined logically, and as such designers resemble artists. Yet, designers are different to artists in that they do not create in a free-flow 'trial-and-error' type of way. Designers, like scientists, formulate hypotheses for testing, build models and check for the internal consistency of the design. Liedtka goes on to describe a number of characteristics of successful 'design thinking' that she believes are also true for effective strategic thinking. Towards the end of her article she responds to concerns about design thinking voiced by Henry Mintzberg (1990, 1991) in a well-known exchange with Igor Ansoff (1991). In subsequent works (1994; 1998, Mintzberg et al.), Mintzberg has used the label 'Design School' to refer to people such as Kenneth Andrews, which Liedtka believes does not do justice to the design metaphor. Many of the points made by Liedtka about using design thinking as part of the overall strategy formation process will be examined in more detail in Chapter 3.

The fourth reading, 'Decision-Making: It's Not What You Think', is by Henry Mintzberg and Frances Westley. Mintzberg, in particular, is well known for his critical stabs at the rational reasoning perspective and for challenging managers to move beyond a mechanistic view of strategizing. Yet, in this reading Mintzberg and Westley are more even-handed in looking at different styles of strategizing. This reading has been selected because it neatly summarizes the strengths and weaknesses of starting the strategic reasoning process at different points in Figure 2.2 – either starting with problem identification and diagnosis (which the authors call 'thinking first'), or with solution conception (called 'seeing first'), or with solution realization (called 'doing first'). Mintzberg and Westley argue that the rational approach of starting with identification and diagnosis, and then moving to conception and realization is actually uncommon and only works best for certain types of problems (ones that Mason and Mitroff would call 'tame'). They do not dismiss 'thinking first' outright, but strongly suggest that the other two forms of decision-making should be accorded at least equal prominence. In 'seeing first' the strategic reasoning process is started with conception (new ideas incubate before extensive analysis), after which outcomes are diagnosed and realized. In 'doing first' people start by acting and reflect on what they are doing along the way – putting realization in the lead, with conception, diagnosis and identification trailing behind. In both 'seeing first' and 'doing first' logic plays a much less dominant role, providing space for creativity to blossom and for new solutions to be generated. The authors conclude that 'no organization can do without any one approach', and therefore that the three forms should be combined. Yet, despite Mintzberg and Westley's advice to blend 'thinking first', 'seeing first' and 'doing first', the question remains how this can be achieved in one and the same organization, while the conditions fostering the one approach are so different than the conditions enabling the other.

The concept of corporate strateg

By Kenneth Andrews[1]

What strategy is

Corporate strategy is the pattern of decisions in a company that determines and reveals its objectives, purposes, or goals, produces the principal policies and plans for achieving those goals, and defines the range of business the company is to pursue, the kind of economic and human organization it is or intends to be, and the nature of the economic and noneconomic contribution it intends to make to its shareholders, employees, customers, and communities. In an organization of any size or diversity, *corporate strategy* usually applies to the whole enterprise, while *business strategy*, less comprehensive, defines the choice of product or service and market of individual businesses within the firm. Business strategy is the determination of how a company will compete in a given business and position itself among its competitors. Corporate strategy defines the businesses in which a company will compete, preferably in a way that focuses resources to convert distinctive competence into competitive advantage. Both are outcomes of a continuous process of strategic management that we will later analyze in detail.

The strategic decision contributing to this pattern is one that is effective over long periods of time, affects the company in many different ways, and focuses and commits a significant portion of its resources to the expected outcomes. The pattern resulting from a series of such decisions will probably define the central character and image of a company, the individuality it has for its members and various publics, and the position it will occupy in its industry and markets. It will permit the specification of particular objectives to be attained through a timed sequence of investment and implementation decisions and will govern directly the deployment or redeployment of resources to make these decisions effective.

Some aspects of such a pattern of decisions may be in an established corporation unchanging over long periods of time, like a commitment to quality, or high technology, or certain raw materials, or good labor relations. Other aspects of a strategy must change as or before the world changes, such as a product line, manufacturing process, or merchandising and styling practices. The basic determinants of company character, if purposefully institutionalized, are likely to persist through and shape the nature of substantial changes in product-market choices and allocation of resources.

It would be possible to extend the definition of strategy for a given company to separate a central character and the core of its special accomplishment from the manifestations of such characteristics in changing product lines, markets, and policies designed to make activities profitable from year to year. *The New York Times*, for example, after many years of being shaped by the values of its owners and staff, is now so self-conscious and respected an institution that its nature is likely to remain unchanged, even if the services it offers are altered drastically in the direction of other outlets for its news-processing capacity.

It is important, however, not to take the idea apart in another way, that is, to separate goals from the policies designed to achieve those goals. The essence of the definition of strategy I have just recorded is pattern. The interdependence of purposes, policies, and organized action is crucial to the particularity of an individual strategy and its opportunity to identify competitive advantage. It is the unity, coherence, and internal consistency of a company's strategic decisions that position the company in its environment and give the firm its identity, its power to mobilize its strengths, and its likelihood of success in the marketplace. It is the interrelationship of a set of goals and policies that crystallizes from the formless reality of a company's environment a set of problems an organization can seize upon and solve.

What you are doing, in short, is never meaningful unless you can say or imply what you are doing it for: the quality of administrative action and the motivation lending it power cannot be appraised without knowing its relationship to purpose. Breaking up the system of corporate goals and the character-determining major

[1]Source: This article was adapted with permission from Chapter 2 of *The Concept of Corporate Strategy*, 1987, McGraw-Hill Companies Inc.

attainment leads to narrow and mechanical ptions of strategic management and endless logic pping.

We should get on to understanding the need for strategic decisions and for determining the most satisfactory pattern of goals in concrete instances. Refinement of definition can wait, for you will wish to develop definition in practice in directions useful to you.

Summary statements of strategy

Before we proceed to clarification of this concept by application, we should specify the terms in which strategy is usually expressed. A summary statement of strategy will characterize the product line and services offered or planned by the company, the markets and market segments for which products and services are now or will be designed, and the channels through which these markets will be reached. The means by which the operation is to be financed will be specified, as will the profit objectives and the emphasis to be placed on the safety of capital versus level of return. Major policy in central functions such as marketing, manufacturing, procurement, research and development, labor relations, and personnel, will be stated where they distinguish the company from others, and usually the intended size, form, and climate of the organization will be included.

Each company, if it were to construct a summary strategy from what it understands itself to be aiming at, would have a different statement with different categories of decision emphasized to indicate what it wanted to be or do.

Reasons for not articulating strategy

For a number of reasons companies seldom formulate and publish a complete strategy statement. Conscious planning of the long-term development of companies has been until recently less common than individual executive responses to environmental pressure, competitive threat, or entrepreneurial opportunity. In the latter mode of development, the unity or coherence of corporate effort is unplanned, natural, intuitive, or even nonexistent. Incrementalism in practice sometimes gives the appearance of consciously formulated strategy, but may be the natural result of compromise among coalitions backing contrary policy proposals or

skillful improvisatory adaptation to external forces. Practicing managers who prefer muddling through to the strategic process would never commit themselves to an articulate strategy.

Other reasons for the scarcity of concrete statements of strategy include the desirability of keeping strategic plans confidential for security reasons and ambiguous to avoid internal conflict or even final decision. Skillful incrementalists may have plans in their heads that they do not reveal, to avoid resistance and other trouble in their own organization. A company with a large division in an obsolescent business that it intends to drain of cash until operations are discontinued could not expect high morale and cooperation to follow publication of this intent. In a dynamic company, moreover, where strategy is continually evolving, the official statement of strategy, unless couched in very general terms, would be as hard to keep up to date as an organization chart. Finally, a firm that has internalized its strategy does not feel the need to keep saying what it is, valuable as that information might be to new members.

Deducing strategy from behavior

In your own company you can do what most managements have not done. In the absence of explicit statements and on the basis of your experience, you may deduce from decisions observed what the pattern is and what the company's goals and policies are, on the assumption that some perhaps unspoken consensus lies behind them. Careful examination of the behavior of competitors will reveal what their strategy must be. At the same time none of us should mistake apparent strategy visible in a pattern of past incremental decisions for conscious planning for the future. What will pass as the current strategy of a company may almost always be deduced from its behavior, but a strategy for a future of changed circumstances may not always be distinguishable from performance in the present. Strategists who do not look beyond present behavior to the future are vulnerable to surprise.

Formulation of strategy

Corporate strategy is an organization process, in many ways inseparable from the structure, behavior, and culture of the company in which it takes place. Nevertheless, we may abstract from the process two important aspects, interrelated in real life but separable for the purposes of analysis. The first of these we may call formulation, the second implementation. Deciding what strategy should be may be approached as a rational undertaking, even if, as in life, emotional attachments (to metal skis or investigative reporting) may complicate choice among future alternatives (for ski manufacturers or alternative newspapers). The principle subactivities of strategy formulation as a logical activity include indentifying opportunities and threats in the company's environment and attaching some estimate of risk to the discernible alternatives. Before a choice can be made, the company's strengths and weaknesses should be appraised together with the resources on hand and available. Its actual or potential capacity to take advantage of perceived market needs or to cope with attendant risks should be estimated as objectively as possible. The strategic alternative that results from matching opportunity and corporate capability at an acceptable level of risk is what we may call an *economic strategy*.

The process described thus far assumes that strategists are analytically objective in estimating the relative capacity of their company and the opportunity they see or anticipate in developing markets. The extent to which they wish to undertake low or high risk presumably depends on their profit objectives. The higher they set the latter, the more willing they must be to assume a correspondingly high risk that the market opportunity they see will not develop or that the corporate competence required to excel competition will not be forthcoming.

So far we have described the intellectual processes of ascertaining what a company *might do* in terms of environmental opportunity, of deciding what it *can do* in terms of ability and power, and of bringing these two considerations together in optimal equilibrium. The determination of strategy also requires consideration of what alternatives are preferred by the chief executive and perhaps by his or her immediate associates as well, quite apart from economic considerations. Personal values, aspirations and ideals do, and in our judgment quite properly should, influence the final choice of purposes. Thus what the executives of a company *want to do* must be brought into the strategic decision.

Finally strategic choice has an ethical aspect – a fact much more dramatically illustrated in some industries than in others. Just as alternatives may be ordered in terms of the degree of risk they entail, so may they be examined against the standards of responsiveness to the expectations of society the strategist elects. Some alternatives may seem to the executive considering them more attractive than others when the public good

or service to society is considered. What a company *should do* thus appears as a fourth element of the strategic decision.

The ability to identify the four components of strategy – (a) market opportunity, (b) corporate competence and resources, (c) personal values and aspirations, and (d) acknowledged obligations to segments of society other than stockholders – is easier to exercise than the art of reconciling their implications in a final choice of purpose. Taken by itself each consideration might lead in a different direction.

If you put the various aspirations of individuals in your own organization against this statement you will see what I mean. Even in a single mind contradictory aspirations can survive a long time before the need to calculate trade-offs and integrate divergent inclinations becomes clear. Growth opportunity attracted many companies to the computer business after World War II. The decision to diversify out of typewriters and calculators was encouraged by growth opportunity and excitement that captivated the managements of RCA, General Electric, and Xerox, among others. But the financial, technical, and marketing requirements of this business exceeded the capacity of most of the competitors of IBM. The magnet of opportunity and the incentive of desire obscured the calculations of what resources and competence were required to succeed. Most crucially, where corporate capability leads, executives do not always want to go. Of all the components of strategic choice, the combination of resources and competence is most crucial to success.

The implementation of strategy

Since effective implementation can make a sound strategic decision ineffective or a debatable choice successful, it is as important to examine the processes of implementation as to weigh the advantages of available strategic alternatives. The implementation of strategy comprises a series of subactivities that are primarily administrative. If purpose is determined, then the resources of a company can be mobilized to accomplish it. An organizational structure appropriate for the efficient performance of the required tasks must be made effective by information systems and relationships permitting coordination of subdivided activities. The organizational processes of performance measurement, compensation, management development – all of them enmeshed in systems of incentives and controls – must be directed toward the kind of behavior required by organizational purpose. The role of personal leadership is important and sometimes decisive in the accomplishment of strategy. Although we know that organizational structure and processes of compensation, incentives, control, and management development influence and constrain the formulation of strategy, we should look first at the logical proposition that structure should follow strategy in order to cope later with the organizational reality that strategy also follows structure. When we have examined both tendencies, we will understand and to some extent be prepared to deal with the interdependence of the formulation and implementation of corporate purpose. Figure 2.1.1 may be useful in understanding the analysis of strategy as a pattern of interrelated decisions.

Criteria for evaluation

How is the actual or proposed strategy to be judged? How are we to know that one strategy is better than another? A number of important questions can regularly be asked. As is already evident, no infallible indicators are available. With practice they will lead to reliable intuitive discriminations.

- Is the strategy indentifiable and has it been made clear either in words or in practice? The degree to which attention has been given to the strategic alternatives available to a company is likely to be basic to the soundness of its strategic decision. To cover in empty phrases ('Our policy is planned profitable growth in any market we can serve well') an absence of analysis of opportunity or actual determination of corporate strength is worse than to remain silent, for it conveys the illusion of a commitment when none has been made. The unstated strategy cannot be tested or contested and is likely therefore to be weak. If it is implicit in the intuition of a strong leader, the organization is likely to be weak and the demands the strategy makes upon it are likely to remain unmet. A strategy must be explicit to be effective and specific enough to require some actions and exclude others.

- Does the strategy exploit fully domestic and international environmental opportunity? The relation between market opportunity and organizational development is a critical one in the design of future plans. Unless growth is incompatible with the resources of an organization or the aspirations of its

FIGURE 2.1.1 The strategy process

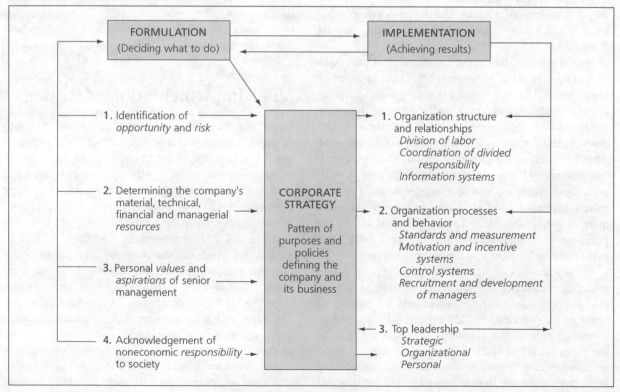

management, it is likely that a strategy that does not purport to make full use of market opportunity will be weak also in other aspects. Vulnerability to competition is increased by lack of interest in market share.

- Is the strategy consistent with corporate competence and resources, both present and projected? Although additional resources, both financial and managerial, are available to companies with genuine opportunity, the availability of each must be finally determined and programmed along a practicable time scale. This may be the most difficult question in this series.
- Are the major provisions of the strategy and the program of major policies of which it is comprised internally consistent? One advantage of making as specific a statement of strategy as is practicable is the resultant availability of a careful check on fit, unity, coherence, compatibility, and synergy – the state in which the whole of anything can be viewed as greater than the sum of its parts.
- Is the chosen level of risk feasible in economic and personal terms? The riskiness of any future plan should be compatible with the economic resources of the organization and the temperament of the managers concerned.
- Is the strategy appropriate to the personal values and aspirations of the key managers? Conflict between personal preferences, aspirations, and goals of the key members of an organization and the plan for its future is a sign of danger and a harbinger of mediocre performance or failure.

- Is the strategy appropriate to the desired level of contribution to society? To the extent that the chosen economic opportunity of the firm has social costs, such as air or water pollution, a statement of intention to deal with these is desirable and prudent.
- Does the strategy constitute a clear stimulus to organizational effort and commitment? Generally speaking, the bolder the choice of goals and the wider range of human needs they reflect, the more successfully they will appeal to the capable membership of a healthy and energetic organization.
- Are there early indications of the responsiveness of markets and market segments to the strategy? A strategy may pass with flying colors all the tests so far proposed, and may be in internal consistency and uniqueness an admirable work of art. But if within a time period made reasonable by the company's resources and the original plan the strategy does not work, then it must be weak in some way that has escaped attention.

A business enterprise guided by a clear sense of purpose rationally arrived at and emotionally ratified by commitment is more likely to have a successful outcome, in terms of profit and social good, than a company whose future is left to guesswork and chance. Conscious strategy does not preclude brilliance of improvisation or the welcome consequences of good fortune. Its cost is principally thought and work for which it is hard but not impossible to find time.

READING 2.2 The mind of the strategist
By Kenichi Ohmae[1]

As a consultant I have had the opportunity to work with many large Japanese companies. Among them are many companies whose success you would say must be the result of superb strategies. But when you look more closely, you discover a paradox. They have no big planning staffs, no elaborate, gold-plated strategic planning processes.

Some of them are painfully handicapped by lack of the resources – people, money, and technology – that seemingly would be needed to implement an ambitious strategy. Yet despite all these handicaps, they are outstanding performers in the marketplace. Year after year, they manage to build share and create wealth.

[1]Source: This article was adapted with permission from the Introduction, and Chapters 1 and 17 of *The Mind of the Strategist: The Art of Japanese Business*, McGraw-Hill, New York, 1982.

How do they do it? The answer is easy. They may not have a strategic planning staff, but they do have a strategist of great natural talent: usually the founder or chief executive. Often – especially in Japan, where there is no business school – these outstanding strategists have had little or no formal business education, at least at the college level. They may never have taken a course or read a book on strategy. But they have an intuitive grasp of the basic elements of strategy. They have an idiosyncratic mode of thinking in which company, customers, and competition merge in a dynamic interaction out of which a comprehensive set of objectives and plans for action eventually crystallizes.

Insight is the key to this process. Because it is creative, partly intuitive, and often disruptive of the status quo, the resulting plans might not even hold water from the analyst's point of view. It is the creative element in these plans and the drive and will of the mind that conceived them that give these strategies their extraordinary competitive impact.

Both in Japan and in the West, this breed of natural or instinctive strategist is dying out or at least being pushed to the sidelines in favor of rational, by-the-numbers strategic and financial planners. Today's giant institutions, both public and private, are by and large not organized for innovation. Their systems and processes are all oriented toward incremental improvement – doing better what they are doing already. In the United States, the pressure of innumerable social and governmental constraints on corporate activities – most notably, perhaps, the proliferation of government regulations during the 1960s and 1970s – has put a premium on the talent for adaptation and reduced still further the incentive to innovate. Advocates of bold and ambitious strategies too often find themselves on the sidelines, labeled as losers, while the rewards go to those more skilled at working within the system. This is especially true in mature industries, where actions and ideas often move in narrow grooves, forcing out innovators. Conversely, venture capital groups tend to attract the flexible, adaptive minds.

In all times and places, large institutions develop cultures of their own, and success is often closely tied to the ability to conform. In our day, the culture of most business corporations exalts logic and rationality; hence, it is analysts rather than innovators who tend to get ahead. It is not unreasonable to say that many large US corporations today are run like the Soviet economy. In order to survive, they must plan ahead comprehensively, controlling an array of critical functions in every detail. They specify policies and procedures in meticulous detail, spelling out for practically everyone what can and what cannot be done in particular circumstances. They establish hurdle rates, analyze risks, and anticipate contingencies. As strategic planning processes have burgeoned in these companies, strategic thinking has gradually withered away.

My message, as you will have guessed by now, is that successful business strategies result not from rigorous analysis but from a particular state of mind. In what I call the mind of the strategist, insight and a consequent drive for achievement, often amounting to a sense of mission, fuel a thought process which is basically creative and intuitive rather than rational. Strategists do not reject analysis. Indeed they can hardly do without it. But they use it only to stimulate the creative process, to test the ideas that emerge, to work out their strategic implications, or to ensure successful execution of high potential 'wild' ideas that might otherwise never be implemented properly. Great strategies, like great works of art or great scientific discoveries, call for technical mastery in the working out but originate in insights that are beyond the reach of conscious analysis.

If this is so – if the mind of the strategist is so deeply at odds with the culture of the corporation – how can an already institutionalized company recover the capacity to conceive and execute creative business strategies? In a book entitled *The Corporate Strategist* that was published in Japan in 1975, I attempted to answer that question in a specifically Japanese context.

In Japan, a different set of conditions from those in the West inhibits the creation of bold and innovative strategies. In the large Japanese company, promotion is based on tenure; there is no fast track for brilliant performers. No one reaches a senior management post before their mid-fifties, and chief executives are typically over 60 – well past the age when they are likely to be able to generate dynamic strategic ideas. At the same time, the inventive, often aggressive younger people have no means of contributing in a significant way to the strategy of the corporation. The result: strategic stagnation or the strong probability of it.

How, I asked myself, could the mind of the strategist, with its inventive élan, be reproduced in this kind of corporate culture? What were the ingredients of an excellent strategist, and how could they be reproduced in the Japanese context? These were the questions I addressed in my book. The answer I came up with involved the formation within the corporation of a group of young 'samurais' who would play a dual role. On the one hand they would function as real strategists, giving free rein to their imagination and entrepreneurial flair in order to come up with bold and innovative strategic ideas. On the other hand they would serve as staff analysts, testing out, digesting, and assigning priorities to the ideas, and providing staff assistance to line managers in implementing the approved strategies. This 'samurai' concept has since been adopted in several Japanese firms with great success.

Such a solution would not fit the circumstances of the typical American or European company. Yet it seems to me that the central notion of my book and of a sequel published in Japan 18 months later is relevant to the problem of strategic stagnation in any organization. There are ways in which the mind of the strategist can be reproduced, or simulated, by people who may lack a natural talent for strategy. Putting it another way, although there is no secret formula for inventing a successful strategy, there are some specific concepts and approaches that can help anyone develop the kind of mentality that comes up with superior strategic ideas. Thus the reader will find in this reading no formulas for successful business strategy. What I will try to supply in their place is a series of hints that may help him or her develop the capacity for and the habit of strategic thinking.

Analysis: The starting point

Analysis is the critical starting point of strategic thinking. Faced with problems, trends, events, or situations that appear to constitute a harmonious whole or come packaged as a whole by the common sense of the day, the strategic thinker dissects them into their constituent parts. Then, having discovered the significance of these constituents, he reassembles them in a way calculated to maximize his advantage.

In business as on the battlefield, the object of strategy is to bring about the conditions most favorable to one's own side, judging precisely the right moment to attack or withdraw and always assessing the limits of compromise correctly. Besides the habit of analysis, what marks the mind of the strategist is an intellectual elasticity or flexibility that enables him to come up with realistic responses to changing situations, not simply to discriminate with great precision among different shades of gray.

In strategic thinking, one first seeks a clear understanding of the particular character of each element of a situation and then makes the fullest possible use of human brainpower to restructure the elements in the most advantageous way. Phenomena and events in the real world do not always fit a linear model. Hence the most reliable means of dissecting a situation into its constituent parts and reassembling them in the desired

pattern is not a step-by-step methodology such as systems analysis. Rather, it is that ultimate nonlinear thinking tool, the human brain. True strategic thinking thus contrasts sharply with the conventional mechanical systems approach based on linear thinking. But it also contrasts with the approach that stakes everything on intuition, reaching conclusions without any real breakdown or analysis (Figure 2.2.1).

No matter how difficult or unprecedented the problem, a breakthrough to the best possible solution can come only from a combination of rational analysis, based on the real nature of things, and imaginative reintegration of all the different items into a new pattern, using nonlinear brainpower. This is always the most effective approach to devising strategies for dealing successfully with challenges and opportunities, in the market arena as on the battlefield.

Determining the critical issue

The first stage in strategic thinking is to pinpoint the critical issue in the situation. Everyone facing a problem naturally tries in his or her own way to penetrate to the key issue. Some may think that one way is as good as another and that whether their efforts hit the mark is largely a matter of luck. I believe it is not a question of luck at all but of attitude and method. In problem solving, it is vital at the start to formulate the question in a way that will facilitate the discovery of a solution.

Suppose, for example, that overtime work has become chronic in a company, dragging down profitability. If we frame the question as What should be done to reduce overtime?, many answers will suggest themselves:

- work harder during the regular working hours;
- shorten the lunch period and coffee breaks;
- forbid long private telephone conversations.

Such questioning is often employed by companies trying to lower costs and improve product quality by using zero defect campaigns and quality control (QC) circles that involve the participation of all employees. Ideas are gathered, screened, and later incorporated in the improvement program. But this approach has an intrinsic limitation. *The questions are not framed to point toward a solution; rather, they are directed toward finding remedies to symptoms.*

Returning to our overtime problem, suppose we frame the question in a more solution-oriented way: Is this company's work force large enough to do all the work required? To this question there can be only one

FIGURE 2.2.1 Three kinds of thinking process

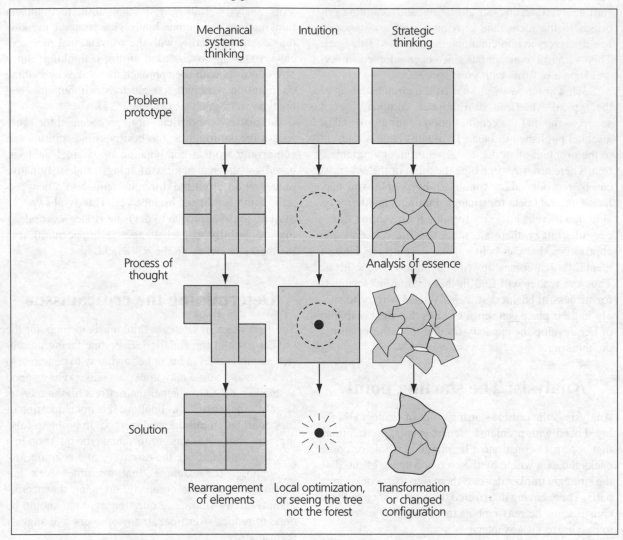

of two answers – yes or no. To arrive at the answer yes, a great deal of analysis would be needed, probably including a comparison with other companies in the same industries, the historical trend of workload per employee, and the degree of automation and computerization and their economic effectiveness. On the other hand, if – after careful perusal of the sales record, profit per employee, ratio between direct and indirect labor, comparison with other companies, and so on – the answer should turn out to be no (i.e. the company is currently understaffed), this in itself would be tantamount to a solution of the original problem. This solution – an increase in personnel – will be validated by all the usual management indicators. And if the company adopts this solution, the probability increases that the desired outcome will

actually follow. This way, objective analysis can supplant emotional discussions.

That is not the only way the question could have been formulated, however. We might have asked it this way: Do the capabilities of the employees match the nature of the work? This formulation, like the previous one, is oriented toward deriving a possible solution. Here too, a negative answer would imply a shortage of suitable personnel, which would in turn suggest that the solution should be sought either in staff training or in recruiting capable staff from elsewhere. On the other hand, if the answer is yes, this indicates that the problem of chronic overtime lies not in the nature of the work but in the amount of the workload. Thus, not training but adding to the work force would then be the crucial factor in the solution.

If the right questions are asked in a solution-oriented manner, and if the proper analyses are carried out, the final answer is likely to be the same, even though it may have started from a differently phrased question and may have been arrived at by a different route. In either case, a question concerning the nature and amount of work brings the real issue into focus and makes it easy to arrive at a clear-cut verdict.

It is hard to overstate the importance of formulating the question correctly. People who are trained and motivated to formulate the right questions will not offer vague proposals for 'improvements', as are seen in many suggestion boxes. They will come up with concrete, practical ideas.

By failing to grasp the critical issues, too many senior managers today impose great anxiety on themselves and their subordinates, whose efforts end in failure and frustration. Solution-oriented questions can be formulated only if the critical issue is localized and grasped accurately in the first place. A clear common understanding of the nature of a problem that has already been localized provides a critical pressure to come up with creative solutions. When problems are poorly defined or vaguely comprehended, one's creative mind does not work sharply. The greater one's

tolerance for lukewarm solutions, half measures and what the British used to call muddling through, the more loosely the issue is likely to be defined. For this reason, isolating the crucial points of the problem – in other words, determining the critical issue – is most important to the discovery of a solution. The key at this initial stage is to *narrow down the issue by studying the observed phenomena closely*.

Figure 2.2.2 illustrates one method often used by strategists in the process of abstraction, showing how it might work in the case of a large, established company faced with the problem of declining competitive vigor.

The first step in the abstraction process is to use such means as brainstorming and opinion polls to assemble and itemize the respects in which the company is at a disadvantage vis-à-vis its competitors. These points can then be classified under a smaller number of headings (shown in Figure 2.2.2 as Concrete Phenomena) according to their common factors.

Next, phenomena sharing some common denominator are themselves combined into groups. Having done this, we look once again at each group as a unit and ask ourselves what crucial issue each unit poses. The source of the problem must be understood before any real solution can be found, and the process of

FIGURE 2.2.2   Narrowing down the issue

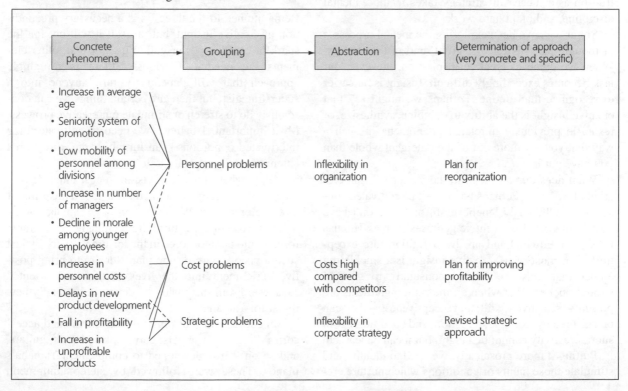

abstraction enables us to bring the crucial issues to light without the risk of overlooking anything important.

Once the abstraction process has been completed, we must next decide on the right approach to finding a solution. Once we have determined the solution in principle, there remains the task of working out implementation programs and then compiling detailed action plans. No solution, however perfectly it may address the critical issue, can be of the slightest use until it is implemented. Too many companies try to short-circuit the necessary steps between identification of critical issues and line implementation of solutions by skipping the intermediate steps: planning for operational improvement and organizing for concrete actions. Even the most brilliant line manager cannot translate an abstract plan into action in a single step.

The art of strategic thinking

Most of us are familiar with Thomas Alva Edison's recipe for inventive genius: '1 percent inspiration, 99 percent perspiration.' The same ratio holds true for creativity in any endeavor, including the development of business strategy. Don't be misled by the ratio. That spark of insight *is* essential. Without it, strategies disintegrate into stereotypes. But to bring insight to fruition as a successful strategy takes method, mental discipline, and plain hard work.

So far we have been exploring the mental processes or thought patterns for the 'grunt' part of the strategy. When we come to creative inspiration, however, our task becomes exceedingly difficult. Insight is far easier to recognize than define. Perhaps we might say that creative insight is the ability to combine, synthesize, or reshuffle previously unrelated phenomena in such a way that you get more out of the emergent whole than you have put in.

What does this all mean to the strategist? Can creativity be taught? Perhaps not. Can it be cultivated consciously? Obviously I believe so, or I wouldn't have written this article. Inventive geniuses such as Thomas Edison or Edwin Land are by definition rare exceptions. For most of us, creative insight is a smoldering ember that must be fanned constantly to glow. I strongly believe that when all the right ingredients are present – sensitivity, will, and receptiveness – they can be nurtured by example, direction, and conditioning. In short, creativity cannot be taught, but it can be learned.

Putting it more prosaically, we need to identify and stimulate those habits or conditions which nurture cre-

ativity and at the same time to crystallize the constraints or boundaries defining our probability of success. In my experience, there are at least three major constraints to which the business strategist needs to be sensitive. I think of them as the essential Rs: reality, ripeness, and resources.

Let's begin with *reality*. Unlike scientific conceptualizers or creative artists, business strategists must always be aware of the customer, the competition, and the company's field of competence. *Ripeness*, or timing, is the second key consideration that the business strategist must address. Unless the time is ripe for the proposed strategy, it is virtually certain to fail. *Resources*, my third R, constitute such an obvious constraint that it is amazing that they should be ignored or neglected by strategists. Yet examples abound of strategies that failed because their authors were not sensitive to their own resource limitations. Take diversification as a case in point. Few food companies trying to move into pharmaceuticals, chemical companies moving into foods, or electronic component manufacturers moving into final assembly have succeeded. The basic reason in most cases has been that the companies involved were not sensitive to the limitations of their own internal resources and skills.

Conditions of creativity

Being attuned to the three Rs is a necessary precondition of creative insight, but in itself it will not fan the spark of creative power within us. For that, other elements are needed. Obviously, there is no single approach that will dependably turn anyone into a superstrategist, but there are certain things we can consciously do to stretch or stimulate our creative prowess. Most important, I believe, we need to cultivate three interrelated conditions – an initial charge, directional antennae, and a capacity to tolerate static.

Call it what you will – vision, focus, inner drive – the initial charge must be there. It is the mainspring of intuitive creativity. We have seen how Yamaha, originally a wood-based furniture company, was transformed into a major force in the leisure industry by just such a vision, born of one man's desire to bring positive enrichment into the lives of the work-oriented Japanese. From this vision he developed a totally new thrust for Yamaha.

An entire family of musical instruments and accessories – organs, trumpets, cornets, trombones, guitars, and so on – was developed to complement Yamaha's pianos. These were followed by stereo equipment, sporting goods, motorcycles and pleasure boats. Music schools were established. Then came the Yamaha Music Camp, complete with a resort lodge complex, a game reserve, an archery range, and other leisure-oriented pursuits. Today, Yamaha plans concerts and is involved with concert hall management as well, reaping profits while enriching the lives of millions of Japanese.

If the initial charge provides the creative impetus, directional antennae are required to recognize phenomena which, as the saying goes, are in the air. These antennae are the component in the creative process that uncovers and selects, among a welter of facts and existing conditions, potentially profitable ideas that were always there but were visible only to eyes not blinded by habit.

Consider how these directional antennae work for Dr Kazuma Tateishi, founder and chairman of Omron Tateishi Electronics. Tateishi has an uncanny flair for sensing phenomena to which the concept of flow can be applied. He perceived the banking business as a flow of cash, traffic jams and congested train stations as blocked flows of cars and people, and production lines as a physical flow of parts. From these perceptions evolved the development of Japan's first automated banking system, the introduction of sequence controllers that automatically regulate traffic according to road conditions and volume, and the evolution of the world's first unmanned railroad station based on a completely automatic system that can exchange bills for coins, issue tickets and season passes, and adjust fares and operate turnstiles. Today, Omron's automated systems are used in many industrial operations from production to distribution. Dr Tateishi is a remarkable example of a man whose directional antennae have enabled him to implement his youthful creed: 'Man should do only what only man can do.'

Creative concepts often have a disruptive as well as a constructive aspect. They can shatter set patterns of thinking, threaten the status quo, or at the very least stir up people's anxieties. Often when people set out to sell or implement a creative idea, they are taking a big risk of failing, losing money, or simply making fools of themselves. That is why the will to cope with criticism, hostility, and even derision, while not necessarily a condition of creative thinking, does seem to be an important characteristic of successful innovative strategists. To squeeze the last drop out of my original metaphor, I call this the static-tolerance component of creativity.

Witness the static that Soichiro Honda had to tolerate in order to bring his clean-engine car to market. Only corporate insiders can tell how much intracompany interference he had to cope with. That the government vainly brought severe pressure on him to stay out of the auto market is no secret, however. Neither is the public ridicule he bore when industry experts scoffed at his concept.

Dr Koji Kobayashi of NEC tolerated static of a rather different kind. Despite prevailing industry trends, he clung fast to his intuitive belief (some 20 years ahead of its time) that computers and telecommunications would one day be linked. To do so, he had to bear heavy financial burdens, internal dissension, and scorn. All this leads me to a final observation. Strategic success cannot be reduced to a formula, nor can anyone become a strategic thinker merely by reading a book. Nevertheless, there are habits of mind and modes of thinking that can be acquired through practice to help you free the creative power of your subconscious and improve your odds of coming up with winning strategic concepts.

The main purpose of this contribution is to encourage you to do so and to point out the directions you should pursue. The use of Japanese examples to illustrate points and reinforce assertions may at times have given it an exotic flavor, but that is ultimately of no importance. Creativity, mental productivity and the power of strategic insight know no national boundaries. Fortunately for all of us, they are universal.

READING

2.3

Strategy as design

By Jeanne Liedtka[1]

The field of business strategy is in need of new metaphors. We need new metaphors that better capture the challenges of making strategies both real and realizable, metaphors that bring life to the human dimension of creating new futures for institutions. In that spirit, I attempt here to interest the reader in the resuscitation of an old metaphor that I see as offering new possibilities – the metaphor of strategy as a process of design. The metaphor of design offers rich possibilities for helping us to think more deeply about the formation of business strategy, and it is time to liberate the idea of design from its association with outmoded approaches to strategy.

Such liberation would allow us to see one more important goal of strategy formulation as the design of a 'purposeful space' – virtual rather than physical – in which particular activities, capabilities, and relationships are encouraged. These, in turn, produce a particular set of associated behaviors and hence, outcomes in the marketplace. Theories of design have much to teach us about the creation of such spaces.

The idea of design

As we move into the literature of the design field, a set of themes and issues emerges over time in the discussion of the design process. The notion of synthesis – the creation of a coherent harmonious whole emerging with integrity from a collection of specific design choices – constitutes the earliest and most fundamental notion of what constitutes 'good' design, in architecture as well as in business strategy. More recent views, have tended to emphasize the concept of the 'best' solution to a stated problem. Perhaps most emblematic of this shift in focus was the emergence of the 'Bauhaus' School in Germany in the 1920s, with its emphasis on flexibility, function, and connecting design to what Walter Gropius called 'the stuff of life'. Together, these themes of beauty and utility illustrate modern design's interest in serving two functions – utilitarian and symbolic.

Models of the design process

Within this context of the goals and principles of design, serious attention to the process of design is a fairly recent phenomena (Bazjanac, 1964) occurring in the middle of this century and in tandem with developments in the fields of mathematics and systems science, which had a major impact on design thinking.

All early models of the design process have one thing in common: they all view the design process as a sequence of well defined activities and are all based on the assumption that the ideas and principles of the scientific method can be applied to it. Design theorists of this era generally describe the design process as consisting of two phases: analysis and synthesis. In the analytical phase, the problem is decomposed into a hierarchy of problem subsets, which in turn produce a set of requirements. In the ensuing stage of synthesis, these individual requirements are grouped and realized in a complete design.

Unlike in business, however, these early models with their emphasis on 'systematic procedures and prescribed techniques' met with immediate criticism for the linearity of their processes and their lack of appreciation for the complexity of design problems. Hörst Rittel (1972) first called attention to what he described as the 'wicked nature' of design problems. Such problems, he asserted, have a unique set of properties. Most importantly, they have no definitive formulation or solution. The definition of the 'problem' itself is open to multiple interpretations (dependent upon the *Weltanschauung*, or worldview, of the observer) and potential solutions are many, with none of them able to be proven to be correct. Writers in the field of business strategy have argued that many issues in strategy formulation are 'wicked' as well, and that traditional approaches to dealing with them are similarly incapable of producing intelligent solutions (Mason and Mitroff, 1981).

Rittel asserted that these 'first generation models' were ill-suited for dealing with wicked problems. Instead, he saw design as a process of argumentation, rather than merely analysis and synthesis. Through

[1]Source: Originally published as 'In Defense of Strategy as Design', in *California Management Review*, Vol. 42, No. 3, pp. 8–30. Permission applied for.

argumentation, whether as part of a group or solely within the designer's own mind, the designer gained insights, broadened his or her *Weltanschauung*, and continually refined the definition of the problem and its attendant solution. Thus, the design process came to be seen as one of negotiation rather than optimization, fundamentally concerned with learning and the search for emergent opportunities. Rittel's arguments are consistent with recent calls in the strategy literature for more attention to 'strategic conversations' (Liedtka and Rosenblum, 1996), in which a broad group of organizational stakeholders engage in dialogue-based processes out of which shared understanding and, ultimately, shared choices emerge.

The role of hypotheses in the design process

More recently design theorists have explored a number of these issues in greater depth. The issue of the role of the scientific method in the design process has been an on-going focus of discussion. In general, studies of design processes frequently suggest a hypothesis-driven approach similar to the traditional scientific method. Nigel Cross (1995) in reviewing a wide range of studies of design processes in action, notes, 'It becomes clear from these studies that architects, engineers, and other designers adopt a problem-solving strategy based on generating and testing potential solutions.' Donald Schon (1983) after studying architects in action, described design as 'a shaping process' in which the situation 'talks back' continually and 'each move is a local experiment which contributes to the global experiment of reframing the problem'. Schon's designer begins by generating a series of creative 'what if' hypotheses, selecting the most promising one for further inquiry. This inquiry takes the form of a more evaluative 'if then' sequence, in which the logical implications of that particular hypothesis are more fully explored and tested. The scientific method then – with its emphasis on cycles of hypothesis generating and testing and the acquisition of new information to continually open up new possibilities – remains central to design thinking.

However, the nature of 'wicked problems' makes such trial and error learning problematic. Rittel makes this point from the perspective of architecture – a building, once constructed, cannot be easily changed, and so learning through experimentation in practice is undesirable. This is the ultimate source of 'wickedness' in such problems: their indeterminacy places a premium on experimentation, while the high cost of change makes such experimentation problematic. As in business, we know that we might be able or be forced to change our strategies as we go along – but we'd rather not. This apparent paradox is what gives the design process – with its use of constructive forethought – its utility. The designer substitutes mental experiments for physical ones. In this view, design becomes a process of hypothesis generating and testing, whose aim is to provide the builder with a plan that tries to anticipate the general nature of impending changes.

A concern of the design process, however, is the risk of 'entrapment', in which a designer's investment in early hypotheses make them difficult to give up as the design progresses, despite the presence of disconfirming data. Design is most successful, then, when it creates a virtual world, a 'learning laboratory', where mental experiments can be conducted risk-free and where investments in early choices can be minimized. As Schon (1983) points out:

Virtual worlds are contexts for experiment within which practitioners can suspend or control some of the everyday impediments to rigorous reflection-in-action. They are representative worlds of practice in the double sense of 'practice'. And practice in the construction, maintenance, and use of virtual worlds develops the capacity for reflection-in-action which we call artistry.

Design's value lies in creating a 'virtual' world in which experiments (mental rather than physical) can be conducted on a less costly basis. This offers a very different perspective from which to think about the creation of business strategies. Traditional approaches to strategy have shared the perspective of early design theorists and assumed that planning creates value primarily through a process of controlling, integrating, and coordinating – that the power of planning is in the creation of a systematic approach to problem-solving – de-composing a complex problem into sub-problems to be solved and later integrated back into a whole. While integration, coordination, and control are all potentially important tasks, a focus on these dramatically underestimates the value of planning in a time of change. The metaphor of design calls attention to planning's ability to create a virtual world in which hypotheses can be generated and tested in low cost ways.

Invention versus discovery

Contemporary design theorists have been especially attentive to the areas in which design and science diverge, however, as well as converge. The most fundamental difference between the two, they argue, is that design thinking deals primarily with what does not yet exist; while scientists deal with explaining what is. A common theme is that scientists discover the laws that govern today's reality, while designers invent a different future. Designers are, of course, interested in explanations of current reality to the extent that such understanding reveals patterns in the underlying relationships essential to the process of formulating and executing the new design successfully, but the emphasis remains on the future. Thus, while both methods of thinking are hypothesis-driven, the design hypothesis differs from the scientific hypothesis. Rather than using traditional reasoning modes of induction or deduction, March (1976) argues that design thinking is adductive: 'Science investigates extant forms. Design initiates novel forms. A scientific hypothesis is not the same thing as a design hypothesis . . . A speculative design cannot be determined logically, because the mode of reasoning involved is essentially adductive.'

Adductive reasoning uses the logic of conjecture. Cross borrows from Philosopher C.S. Peirce this elaboration of the differences among the modes: 'Deduction proves that something must be; induction shows that something actually is operative; adduction merely suggests that something may be.' Thus, a capacity for creative visualization – the ability to 'conjure' an image of a future reality that does not exist today, an image so vivid that it appears to be real already – is central to design. Successful designers – in business or the arts – are great conjurers, and the design metaphor reminds us of this.

Underlying this emphasis on conjectural thinking and visualization is an on-going inquiry into the relationship between verbal and non-verbal mediums. Design theorists accord a major role to the use of graphic and spatial modeling media – not merely for the purpose of communicating design ideas, but for the generation of ideas as well. 'Designers think with their pencils' is a common refrain. Some theorists have argued that verbalization may in fact, 'obstruct intuitive creation', noting that the right side of the brain is mute. Arnheim (1992) asserts that the image 'unfolds' in the mind of the designer as the design process progresses; and that it is, in fact, the unfolding nature of the image that makes creative design possible: As long as the guiding image is still developing it remains tentative, generic, vague. This vagueness, however, is by no means a negative quality. Rather it has the positive quality of a topological shape. As distinguished from geometric shapes, a topological shape stands for a whole range of possibilities without being tangibly committed to any one of them. Being undefined in its specifics, it admits distortions and deviations. Its pregnancy is what the designer requires in the search for a final shape. Thus, the designer begins with what Arnheim calls 'a center, an axis, a direction', from which the design takes on increasing levels of detail and sophistication as it unfolds.

Architect Frank Gehry's description of the Guggenheim Bilbao Museum captures these themes of experimentation in virtual worlds, and the role of sketches and models in the unfolding process (see Exhibit 2.3.1). In the story of Gehry's creation, we witness the designer bringing his or her own previous experiences to the new site and, through a process of iteration that moves back and forth between the general idea and the specific design of its subcomponents, the design evolves, gaining clarity and definition.

EXHIBIT 2.3.1 CASE STUDY

THE DESIGN OF THE GUGGENHEIM BILBAO: AN UNFOLDING PROCESS

In describing this century's 100 'greatest design hits', *New York Times* Architecture Critic Herbert Muschamp included ten buildings, among them Antoni Gaudi's Casa Mila (1906), Mies van der Rohe's Barcelona Pavilion (1929), Frank Lloyd Wright's Fallingwater (1936), Le Corbusier's Chapel at Ronchamp (1950), and I.M. Pei's Bank of China tower in Hong Kong (1982). Number 100, and the only building listed designed in the last decade, was Frank Gehry's Guggenheim Museum in Bilbao. Writing in the *Los Angeles Times*, Architecture Critic Nicolai Ouroussoff effuses:

Gehry has achieved what not so long ago seemed impossible for most architects: the invention of radically new architectural forms that nonetheless speak to the man on the street. Bilbao has become a pilgrimage point for those who, until now, had little interest in architecture. Working class Basque couples arrive toting children on weekends. The cultural elite veer off their regular flight paths so they can tell friends that they, too, have seen the building in the flesh. Gehry has become, in the eyes of a world attuned to celebrity, the great American architect, and, in the process, he has brought hope to an entire profession.

Van Bruggen chronicles the story of the design of the Bilbao Museum, tracing, through a series of interviews with Gehry, the unfolding nature of the design process, with its emphasis on experimentation and iteration, and its comfort with ambiguity. Gehry explains how the design process begins: 'You bring to the table certain things. What's exciting, you tweak them based on the context and the people . . . Krens (Guggenheim Foundation Director), Juan Ignacio (future director of the Bilbao museum site), the Basques, their desire to use culture, to bring the city to the river. And the industrial feeling . . . I knew all of that when I started sketching.'

Gehry's first sketches are on pieces of hotel stationery they are 'fast scrawls and mere annotations . . . the hand functions as an immediate tool of the mind'. Later, on an airplane, as the design evolves, the sketches begin to capture the basics of his scheme for the site. As Van Bruggen notes, he has

begun to take hold of the complexities of the site . . . Allowing the pen to take possession of the space helps him to clarify the program requirements and re-imagine the problem. . . . Elements shift and are regrouped to contribute to a different kind of understanding, a leap from the conditional, technical aspects of building into unrestrained, intuitive sense perception, into sculptural architecture. From here on, a delicate process of cutting apart while holding together takes place, a going back and forth from sketches into models in order to solve problems and refine the plastic shapes of the building.

Gehry explains 'I start drawing sometimes, not knowing where it is going . . . It's like feeling your way along in the dark, anticipating that something will come out usually. I become a voyeur of my own thoughts as they develop, and wander about them.

Sometimes I say "boy here it is, it's coming". I understand it, I get all excited and from there I'll move to the models, and the models drain all of the energy, and need information on scale and relationships that you can't conceive in totality in drawings. The drawings are ephemeral. The models are specific; they then become like the sketches in the next phase.' The models change scale and materials as the project progresses, becoming increasingly detailed, and moving from paper to plastic to wood to industrial foam. In total, six different models were developed over the course of the Bilbao project.

Computer modeling plays a critical role as the physical models evolve. 'The Guggenheim Museum Bilbao would not have stayed within the construction budget allotted by the Basque Administration had it not been for Catia, a computer program originally developed for the French aerospace industry,' Van Bruggen observes. Gehry's staff customized the software to model the sculptural shapes, accelerating the layout process and devising more economically buildable designs. These computer models were always translated back into physical models.

Throughout, the process remains iterative. Gehry observes that 'often the models take me down a blind alley, and I go back to sketches again. They become the vehicle for propelling the project forward when I get stuck.' In the end, the process from first sketch into final building remains one of 'unfolding':

In the first sketch, I put a bunch of principles down. Then I become self critical of those images and those principles, and they evoke the next set of responses. And as each piece unfolds, I make the models bigger and bigger, bringing into focus more elements and more pieces of the puzzle: And once I have the beginning, a toehold into where I'm going, I then want to examine the parts in more detail. And those evolve, and at some point I stop, because that's it. I don't come to a conclusion, but I think there's a certain reality of pressure to get the thing done that I accept.

Sources: See H. Muschamp, 'Blueprint: The Shock of the Familiar', *New York Times*, December 13 1998, section 6, p. 61, col. I; N. Ouroussoff, 'I'm Frank Gehry', *Los Angeles Times*, October 25 1998, home edition, p. 17; C. Van Bruggen, Frank O. Gehry: *Guggenheim Museum Bilbao* (New York, NY: Guggenheim Museum Publications, 1997, pp. 33, 31, 71, 03, 135, 104, 130).

The general versus the particular

In addition to the prominent role played by conjecture and experimentation in design thinking, there is also a fundamental divergence between the concern of science for generalizable laws and design's interest in the particulars of individual cases. Buchanan and Margolis (1995) argue that there can be no 'science' of design:

> *Designers conceive their subject matter on two levels: general and particular. On a general level, a designer forms an idea or a working hypothesis about the nature of products or the nature of the human-made in the world . . . But such philosophies do not and cannot constitute sciences of design in the sense of the natural, social, or humanistic science. The reason for this is simple: design is fundamentally concerned with the particular, and there is no science of the particular . . . Out of the specific possibilities of a concrete situation, the designer must conceive a design that will lead to this or that particular product . . . (The designer does not begin with) an indeterminate subject waiting to be made determinate. It is an indeterminate subject waiting to be made specific and concrete.*

This quality of indeterminacy has profound implications for the design process. First, the tendency to project determinacy onto past choices – 'prediction after the fact' – is ever present and must be avoided, or it undermines and distorts the true nature of the design process. Second, creative designs do not passively await discovery – designers must actively seek them out. Third, the indeterminacy of the process suggests the possibility for both exceptional diversity and continual evolution in the outcomes produced (even within similar processes). Finally, because design solutions are always matters of invented choice, rather than discovered truth, the judgment of designers is always open to question by the broader public.

Each of these implications resonates with business experiences. Richard Pascale's (1984) contrasting stories of Honda's entry into the US motorcycle market chronicles the kind of retrospective rationalization that can accompany well known business success stories. Similarly the need to seek out the future is one of the most common prescriptions in today's writings on strategy. Similarly, the search for and belief in the ideal of the one right strategy can stifle creativity cause myopia that misses opportunity and paralyze organizational decision processes.

However, the final implication – this notion of the inevitable need to justify to others the 'rightness' of the design choices made – is perhaps the most significant implication for the design of strategy processes in business organizations. Because strategic choices can never be 'proven' to be right, they remain always contestable and must be made compelling to others in order to be realized. This calls into play Rittel's role of argumentation and focuses attention on others, and the role of rhetoric in bringing them into the design conversation. Participation becomes key to producing a collective learning that both educates individuals and shapes the evolving choices simultaneously. Thus, design becomes a shared process, no longer the province of a single designer.

The role of values in design

Participation is critical, in part, because of the role that values, both individual and institutional, play in the design process. Values drive both the creation of the design and its acceptance.

Successful designs must embody both existing and new values simultaneously. 'Designers persuade', Williamson (1983) argues, 'by referencing accepted values and attributing these to a new subject'. It is the linkage to values already present in the *Weltanschauung* of the observer that allows the new design to find acceptance. The ability to establish and communicate these links is essential to achieving a successfully implemented design. Designs that embody values and purpose that are not shared – however innovative – fail to persuade.

Given the indeterminacy of the choices made, the ability to work with competing interests and values is inevitable in the process of designing. Buchanan and Margolis (1995) note that the question of whose values matter has changed over time, evolving from 1950s beliefs about the 'ability of experts to engineer socially acceptable results' for audiences that were seen as 'passive recipients of preformed messages', towards a view of audiences as 'active participants in reaching conclusions'.

The 'charette' plays a fundamental role in making design processes participative and making collective learning possible. Charettes are intensive brainstorming sessions in which groups of stakeholders come together. Their intention is to share, critique, and invent in a way that accelerates the development of large-scale projects. The charette at the Guggenheim Bilbao, for example, lasted for two months. One of the most well-known users of charettes is the architectural firm Duaney Plater-Zyberg, who specialize in the design of new 'traditional towns' like Seaside, Florida, or Disney's Celebration. In their charette for the design of a new town outside of Washington, DC, Duaney Plater-Zyberg brought together architects, builders, engineers, local officials, traffic consultants, utility company representatives, computer experts, architecture professors, shopping mall developers, and townspeople for a discussion/critique that lasted seven days. The more complex the design process, the more critical a role the charette plays.

Design as dialectical

In the design literature, there is clear recognition of the fundamentally paradoxical nature of the design process and its need to mediate between diverging forces. Findeli (1990) notes: 'The discipline of design has got to be considered as paradoxical in essence and an attempt to eliminate one pole to the benefit of the other inevitably distorts its fundamental nature. [The goal becomes] to perceive this dualism as a dialectic, to transform this antagonism into a constructive dynamic.'

Echoing a similar theme, Buchanan and Margolis (1995) situate design as a dialectic at the intersection of constraint, contingency, and possibility. Successful design remains ever mindful of the constraints imposed by the materials and situation at hand, as well as the changing, and contingent, preferences of the audience that it serves. Simultaneously however, it holds open the promise of the creation of new possibilities – available by challenging the status quo, reframing the problem, connecting the pieces, synthesizing the learning, and improvising as opportunities emerge.

The design of New York's Central Park by Frederick Law Olmsted and Calvert Vaux in the 1850s offers a look at the way in which successful design mediates the tension between constraint, contingency, and possibility. In the competition held to award the contract for the design of the park, only Olmsted and Vaux were able to envision a design that succeeded in meeting all of the requirements set forth – that the Park must allow carriages to transverse it, rather than go around it, while retaining a park-like feel – requirements that other designers had seen as impossible to satisfy. They did this by envisioning the park space as three dimensional, rather than two, and proposing the construction of buried roadways that would allow cross-town vehicular traffic, but would be out of site to those enjoying the park.

This tension created by the often diverging pulls of necessity, uncertainty, and possibility define design's terrain. It is a landscape where a mindset that embraces traditional dichotomies – art versus science, intuition versus analysis, the abstract versus the particular, ambiguity versus precision – find little comfort.

Implied characteristics of design thinking

To summarize, despite the avowed plurality that design theorists use to describe the field more precisely, a set of commonalties does emerge from the recent work on the attributes of design thinking.

First, design thinking is synthetic. Out of the often disparate demands presented by sub-units' requirements, a coherent overall design must be made to emerge. The process through which and the order in which the overall design and its sub-unit designs unfold remains a source of debate. What is clear is that the order in which they are given attention matters, as it determines the givens of subsequent designs, but ultimately successful designs can be expected to exhibit considerable diversity in their specifics.

Second, design thinking is adductive in nature. It is primarily concerned with the process of visualizing what might be, some desired future state, and creating a blueprint for realizing that intention.

Third, design thinking is hypothesis-driven. As such, it is both analytic in its use of data for hypothesis testing and creative in the generation of hypotheses to be tested. The hypotheses are of two types. Primary is the design hypothesis. The design hypothesis is conjectural and, as such, cannot be tested directly. Embedded in the selection of a particular promising design hypothesis, however, are a series of assumptions about a set of cause–effect relationships in today's environment that will support a set of actions aimed at transforming a situation from its current reality to its desired future state. These explanatory hypotheses must be identified and tested directly. Cycles of hypothesis generation and testing are iterative. As successive loops of 'what if' and 'if then' questions are explored, the hypotheses become more sophisticated and the design unfolds.

Fourth, design thinking is opportunistic. As the above cycles iterate, the designer seeks new and emergent possibilities. The power of the design lies in the particular. Thus, it is in the translation from the abstract/global to the particular/local that unforeseen opportunities are most likely to emerge. Sketching and modeling are important tools in the unfolding process, as Gehry's description of the Guggenheim Bilbao design illustrates.

Fifth, design thinking is dialectical. The designer lives at the intersection of often conflicting demands – recognizing the constraints of today's materials and the uncertainties that cannot be defined away, while envisioning tomorrow's possibilities. Olmsted's Central Park testifies to the ability of innovative design to both satisfy and transcend today's constraints to realize new possibilities.

Finally, design thinking is inquiring and value-driven – open to scrutiny, welcoming of inquiry, willing to make its reasoning explicit to a broader audience, and cognizant of the values embedded within the conversation. It recognizes the primacy of the *Weltanschauung* of its audience. The architect imbues the design with his or her own values, as reflected in Gehry's design of the Guggenheim Bilbao. Successful designs, in practice, educate and persuade by connecting with the values of the audience, as well.

Implications for strategy-making as a design process

Having developed a clearer sense of the process of design itself, we can begin to describe the possibilities that the use of such a metaphor might hold for thinking about business strategy, in general, and the design of strategy-making processes, in particular:

■ Strategic thinking is synthetic. It seeks internal alignment and understands interdependencies. It is systemic in its focus. It requires the ability to understand and integrate across levels and elements, both horizontal and vertical, and to align strategies across those levels. Strategic thinking is built on the foundation of a systems perspective. A strategic thinker has a mental model of the complete end-to-end system of value creation, and understands the interdependencies within it. The synthesizing process creates value not only in aligning the components, but also in creatively re-arranging them. The creative solutions produced by many of today's entrepreneurs often rest more with the redesign of aspects of traditional strategies rather than with dramatic breakthroughs.

■ Strategic thinking is adductive. It is future-focused and inventive, as Hamel and Prahalad's (1994) popular concept of strategic intent illustrates. Strategic

intent provides the focus that allows individuals within an organization to marshal and leverage their energy, to focus attention, to resist distraction, and to concentrate for as long as it takes to achieve a goal. The creation of a compelling intent, with the sense of 'discovery, direction, and destiny' of which Hamel and Prahalad speak, relies heavily on the skill of alternative generation. As Simon (1993) has noted, alternative generation has received far less attention in the strategic decision-making literature than has alternative evaluation, but is more important in an environment of change. Yet, it is not merely the creation of the intent itself, but the identification of the gap between current reality and the imagined future that drives strategy-making. The ability to link past, present, and future in a process that Neustadt and May (1986) have called 'thinking in time':

> *Thinking in time [has] three components. One is recognition that the future has no place to come from but the past, hence the past has predictive value. Another element is recognition that what matters for the future in the present is departures from the past, alterations, changes, which prospectively or actually divert familiar flows from accustomed channels. . . . A third component is continuous comparison, an almost constant oscillation from the present to future to past and back, heedful of prospective change, concerned to expedite, limit, guide, counter, or accept it as the fruits of such comparison suggest.*

■ Strategic thinking is hypothesis-driven. In an environment of ever-increasing information availability and decreasing time to think, the ability to develop good hypotheses and to test them efficiently is critical. Because it is hypothesis-driven, strategic thinking avoids the analytic–intuitive dichotomy that has characterized much of the debate about strategic thinking. Strategic thinking is both creative and critical, in nature. Figuring out how to accomplish both types of thinking simultaneously has long troubled cognitive psychologists, since it is necessary to suspend critical judgment in order to think more creatively. Strategic thinking accommodates both creative and analytical thinking sequentially in its use of iterative cycles of hypothesis generating and testing. Hypothesis generation asks the creative question 'what if . . .?' Hypothesis testing follows with the critical question 'if . . . , then . . .?' and brings relevant data to bear on the analysis, including an analysis of a hypothetical set of financial flows associated with the idea. Taken together, and repeated over time, this sequence allows us to pose ever-improving hypotheses, without forfeiting the ability to explore new ideas. Such experimentation allows an organization to move beyond simplistic notions of cause and effect to provide on-going learning.

■ Strategic thinking is opportunistic. Within this intent-driven focus, there must be room for opportunism that not only furthers intended strategy, but that also leaves open the possibility of new strategies emerging. In writing about the role of 'strategic dissonance' in the strategy-making process at Intel, Robert Burgelman (1991) has highlighted the dilemma involved in using a well-articulated strategy to channel organizational efforts effectively and efficiently against the risks of losing sight of alternative strategies better suited to a changing environment. This requires that an organization be capable of practicing 'intelligent opportunism' at lower levels. He concludes: 'One important manifestation of corporate capability is a company's ability to adapt without having to rely on extraordinary top management foresight.'

■ Strategic thinking is dialectical. In the process of inventing the image of the future, the strategist must mediate the tension between constraint, contingency, and possibility. The underlying emphasis of strategic intent is stretch – to reach explicitly for potentially unattainable goals. At the same time, all elements of the firm's environment are not shapeable and those constraints that are real must be acknowledged in designing strategy. Similarly, the 'unknowables' must be recognized and the flexibility to deal with the range of outcomes that they represent must be designed in.

■ Strategic thinking is inquiring and, inevitably, value-driven. Because any particular strategy is invented, rather than discovered – chosen from among a larger set of plausible alternatives – it is contestable and reflective of the values of those making the choice. Its acceptance requires both connection with and movement beyond the existing mindset and value system of the rest of the organization. Such movement relies on inviting the broader community into the argumentation process – the strategic conversation. It is through participation in this dialogue that the strategy itself unfolds,

both in the mind of the strategist and in that of the larger community that must come together to make the strategy happen. The conversation is what allows the strategist to pull his or her colleagues 'through the keyhole' into a new *Weltanschauung*.

Taken together, these characteristics borrowed from the field of design – synthetic, adductive, dialectical, hypothesis-driven, opportunistic, inquiring, and value-driven – describe strategic thinking.

Concerns with the design metaphor

Having delineated the characteristics of design thinking, I will now discuss Mintzberg's (1990, 1994) concerns with the design metaphor. The most prominent of these include:

1 Design suggests that strategy is a process of thought, decoupled from action.
2 Design gives too much emphasis to creativity and uniqueness.
3 In design, implementation must wait for formulation to be completed.
4 Design gives too central a role to the designer – the CEO in the business application of the term.
5 Design is overwhelmingly concerned with fit and focus.

Design as decoupling thought from action

Mintzberg is concerned that the design process is primarily a process of reflection – of cognition rather than action – and that, as such, it precludes learning: 'Our critique of the design school revolves around one central theme: its promotion of thought independent of action, strategy formation above all as a process of conception, rather than as one of learning.'

Mintzberg's preference for action appears to be rooted in a belief that in environments characterized by complexity, change, and uncertainty, learning can only occur in action. The process of constructive forethought that this article suggests, however, is not 'independent of action'. Much of the forethought in the design process is directed specifically at iterative cycles of hypothesis generating and testing whose very purpose is to examine the likely consequences in action of the hypotheses being tested. In support of Mintzberg's point, however, these 'experiments' are conducted mentally rather than physically. Rather than a liability, this is, for design theorists, one of the key benefits of design – the ability to create a virtual environment for risk-reduced, entrapment-minimizing decision-making. Who would choose to construct a building 'as you go along', rather than laying out the design in advance? The likely efficiency, quality coherence, and integrity of the result using the latter process would appear to be far superior to the former. Similarly, to use Mintzberg's own example of the potter at her craft (Mintzberg 1987), do we want to suggest that it is preferable for the potter to think of her creation only while sitting at the wheel, and never beforehand? The mistakes made at the wheel are clearly more expensive and difficult to undo. The same logic would appear to be compelling for business, especially to the extent to which we accept strategic problems as 'wicked'. Given the ability to do either, would we actively choose to experiment on our customers in the marketplace instead of on 'virtual' customers living in a virtual world? At times, of course, new possibilities may only present themselves at the potter's wheel, necessitating the conduct of actual experiments in the 'real' versus the virtual world. An important aspect of the design process lies with identifying those areas of uncertainty and potential opportunism. The challenge is not to choose correctly between planning and opportunism – an either/or – it is how to develop capabilities to do both in productive ways.

One hypothesizes that it is Mintzberg's assumption that strategists lack, and cannot reasonably be expected to develop, the ability to conduct high-quality thought experiments – those that truly model reality. This is an assumption on which disagreement exists. It is one generally not shared by a group of influential learning theorists (Senge 1990) who have devoted significant attention to the ways in which skills in systems thinking and mental modeling can improve the capability for more effective action. Further, the contention that managers are, in fact, clearly more capable of 'learning from their mistakes' after the fact, rather than at thinking their way to successful choices before the fact, remains unsubstantiated. A review of the design literature suggests that rather than abandoning the process of design, we could more fruitfully turn our attention to enhancing strategists' capabilities to be better designers.

Emphasis on creativity and uniqueness

Here, Mintzberg has two concerns about using the design metaphor: first, design's insistence that the resulting design be 'unique', second that the 'best' designs emerge from a creative process. There can be no disagreement that a shared emphasis on creative process exists between Mintzberg's design school and the larger design literature, and that this process occurs for both within the context of an emphasis on the particular rather than the generalizable. Where there is less clarity is around what constitutes 'unique' and 'best'. The design literature argues strongly for the possibility of diversity in design, even in the case of similar purpose and circumstance; it does not, however, insist that such diversity, or 'uniqueness', will inevitably be the result of good design. Similarly, 'best' in the design world is strongly linked with purpose – both utilitarian and symbolic – rather than with uniqueness, as it might be in a purely creative process. Thus, we might expect that the 'best' design in situations sharing a common purpose and experiences and in similar circumstances might look a lot alike. Achieving uniqueness might require reducing the emphasis on achieving purpose. While the world of fine arts might view this as a worthy trade-off, the world of design would not.

Formulation precedes implementation

As above, it is literally true in the design field that the act of creation precedes the act of implementation. However, the generative cycle described here is ultimately always repeated and is issue, rather than calendar, driven. For some issues, the loop is continually in motion – a movement back and forth between mental designing and physical implementation that may appear almost simultaneously. Where major new commitments are required, the cycle operates in a more visible, episodic way. It does not insist that the world stand still while lengthy planning cycles operate. Again, though the process of design separates thinking and action, it does not separate 'thinking' from 'thinking about the consequences of action' – these are, in fact, one and the same for design theorists.

What is also clear, however, is that while design theorists talk very little about implementation as an explicit topic, in practice, designers such as Frank Gehry devote tremendous attention to the ultimate reality that their designs represent and what it will take to realize them. In fact, the distinction between formulation and implementation becomes wholly artificial in the practice of designing. What part of design thinking is not fundamentally about implementation – making reality of an image of some future state? The question is not whether implementation precedes, succeeds, or occurs simultaneously with formulation. Within the design process itself, the distinction simply does not make sense. The important issue behind the formulation/implementation dichotomy is the separation of who is involved in each.

The prominence of the Architect/CEO in the design process

Mintzberg equates 'the CEO' with 'the Architect' and objects to the extent to which this devalues the role of other organizational members. This is understandable, given the recent history of the architecture field, which has had as much, or perhaps even more, of a 'great man' tenor than the management field. However, the 'great man' obsession of the architecture field should not be confused with the nature of the design process.

In the recent practice of architecture, the roles of designer and builder have, in fact, been made distinct. However, today's notion that architects have the overwhelmingly dominant role in the design process and that builders are mere executors of completed designs only emerged within the last century. In the building of the great cathedrals of Europe, the architects' role was seen as the communication of the general direction, and builders had great latitude in interpreting these design prescriptions, using their knowledge base.

The question of whether design suffers when created by someone who does not understand building as a process, is an important one. Leading architects like Frank Lloyd Wright and Frank Gehry would have answered an emphatic yes. What remains lost, despite an understanding of building, is the opportunity to continually reshape the original design, while under construction, to take advantage of emergent opportunities or to deal with unanticipated constraints. No mental experiments, however carefully conceived and repeated, can anticipate all relevant future developments. Conversely, there is nothing in the idea or process of design itself that suggests that designers ought not to be builders, or vice-versa. While this distinction has emerged in practice in the field of architecture, it is not necessarily an aspect of design practice that we would want to incorporate into business practice, for many of the reasons that Mintzberg reviews. In exploring the transition of the design metaphor to business in a more complete way, the opportunity is to see all managers as designers (and builders as well), each with responsibility for the design of a different piece of the system, within the context of a shared sense of overall purpose.

Design as primarily concerned with focus and fit

Mintzberg's last concern is that design is primarily concerned with the fit between current competencies and external opportunities, that a well-articulated design's likelihood of providing focus impedes change, and that flexibility rather than focus, should be the dominant criteria.

The concept of fit carries with it the same two connotations in the design world that it does in the strategy literature. One is fit as internal cohesion and alignment among sub-systems. The second is fit as what Wright called 'kinship', or harmony, with the surrounding environment. Both are seen as critically important aspects of design. Interestingly, however, both are considered as 'constraints' in the design process. That is, they are important aspects of current reality that must be attended to. The way that they are attended to, however, is in the context of an ever-present tension between them and some different view of a new future. Constraints are not allowed to drive the design process; nor can they be ignored. Instead, they are an important part of the dialectic always underway which the designer tries to mediate through a process of invention. This is a much more powerful view of the natural antagonism between constraint and possibility than has existed in the business strategy field. In business strategy we have tended to capture this tension as a dichotomy that firms must choose between – labeling them the 'strategic fit' and 'strategic intent' perspectives. The design field sets the bar far higher: designers are expected to find creative higher level solutions that honor both the current reality and some different future. Perhaps we should expect the same of business strategists at whatever position they occupy in the organization.

Mintzberg's second point argues that a well-articulated strategy impedes change and that on the focus–flexibility continuum, a design approach locates itself too close to the focus end, forfeiting necessary flexibility to deal with change. Mintzberg's contention that the more articulated the strategy, the harder it is to change and its corollary – the 'fuzzier' the strategy, the more it welcomes change – must be seriously questioned. For several decades, change theorists have argued the opposite – that a clear picture of the desired future state is an essential ingredient in achieving change. In the views of these theorists, the enemy of change is more likely to be the lethargy and lack of action introduced by confusion and 'fuzziness', rather than active resistance mobilized by clarity. In twenty years of work with managers of companies attempting to implement new strategies, I have yet to hear a manager lament, 'if only the strategy was less clear, I would have more freedom to act'. The refrain is universally the opposite – 'if only they would lay out where they think we're headed, I would be happy to do my part!' The goal of achieving clarity in the ultimate design does not imply that such clarity is present throughout the design process. Clearly things start 'fuzzy' and get clearer. They get clearer through a process of iteration, as needed for implementation. Once implemented, things get fuzzy again as the design evolves in a process similar to the cycles of 'chaos' and 'single-minded focus' that Andy Grove describes at Intel (Grove, 1996).

The focus/flexibility conundrum remains one of the central strategic questions of this decade, but the issue here is not primarily one of design versus opportunism. Design, by its nature, is open to emergent opportunity if viewed as an on-going process. Flexibility can, in fact, be designed into systems. In fact, it must be designed into systems in order to be achieved. The mere lack of constructive forethought offers no guarantee of openness to opportunity – quite the opposite, if we believe in the old dictum that 'luck finds the prepared mind.' The trade-off between focused commitment to a particular strategy and an alternative strategy that maximizes flexibility is, instead, often reflected in the former strategy's superior ability to deliver efficiently against a particular purpose and the latter's ability to change purpose. That difference in performance is not a choice made by choosing design, it is a choice made in the process of designing.

Leveraging the design metaphor

The metaphor of design offers a window into a deeper understanding of the process of strategy making. It does this by calling attention to the process of creating a purposeful space. Such spaces 'work' because of much more than the structures visible to the eye. They work because they create an environment that fuses form and function; that builds relationships and capabilities and targets specific outcomes; that inspires, at an emotional and aesthetic level, those who work towards a shared purpose. Values play a vital role here, as do hypothesis generating and testing, and the ability to conjure a vivid picture of a set of possibilities that do not yet exist.

What would we do differently in organizations today, if we took seriously the design metaphor? A lot, I believe. It would call for significant changes in the way that strategic planning is approached today, especially in large organizations. The problems with traditional approaches to planning have long been recognized. They include: the attempt to make a science of planning with its subsequent loss of creativity, the excessive emphasis on numbers, the drive for administrative efficiency that standardized inputs and formats at the expense of substance, and the dominance of single techniques, inappropriately applied. Decades later, strategists continue to struggle to propose clear alternatives to traditional processes. Design offers a different approach and would suggest processes that are more widely participative, more dialogue-based, issue-driven rather than calendar-driven, conflict-using rather than conflict-avoiding, all aimed at invention and learning, rather than control. In short, we should involve more members of the organization in two-way strategic conversations. We should view the process as one of iteration and experimentation, and pay sequential attention to idea generation and evaluation in a way that attends first to possibilities before moving onto constraints. Finally and perhaps most importantly, we would recognize that good designs succeed by persuading, and great designs by inspiring.

Decision-making: It's not what you think

By Henry Mintzberg and Frances Westley[1]

How should decisions be made? Easy, we figured that out long ago. First define the problem, then diagnose its causes, next design possible solutions, and finally decide which is best. And, of course, implement the choice.

But do people always make decisions that way? We propose that this rational, or 'thinking first', model of decision-making should be supplemented with two very different models – a 'seeing first' and a 'doing first' model. When practicing managers use all three models, they can improve the quality of their decisions. Healthy organizations, like healthy people, have the capacity for all three.

Consider how a real decision was made, a personal one in this case. It begins with a call from an aunt:

> 'Hi, kiddo. I want to buy you a housewarming present. What's the color scheme in your new apartment?'
> 'Color scheme? Betty, you've got to be kidding. I'll have to ask Lisa. Lisa, Betty wants to know the color scheme of the apartment.'
> 'Black,' daughter Lisa says.
> 'Black? Lisa, I've got to live there.'
> 'Black,' she repeats.

A few days later, father and daughter find themselves in a furniture store. They try every desk, every chair: Nothing works. Shopper's lethargy sets in. Then Lisa spots a black stool: 'Wouldn't that look great against the white counter?' And they're off. Within an hour, they have picked out everything – in black, white and steel gray.

The extraordinary thing about this ordinary story is that our conventional theories of decision-making can't explain it. It is not even clear what the final decision was: to buy the stool; to get on with furnishing an apartment; to do so in black and white; to create a new lifestyle? Decision-making can be mysterious.

The limits of 'thinking first'

Rational decision-making has a clearly identified process: define → diagnose → design → decide.

However, the rational approach turns out to be uncommon.

Years ago, one of us studied a host of decisions, delineating the steps and then laying them out. A decision process for building a new plant was typical. The process kept cycling back, interrupted by new events, diverted by opportunities and so on, going round and round until finally a solution emerged. The final action was as clear as a wave breaking on the shore, but explaining how it came to be is as hard as tracing the origin of that wave back into the ocean.

Often decisions do not so much emerge as erupt. Here is how Alexander Kotov, the chess master, has described a sudden insight that followed lengthy analysis:

> So, I mustn't move the knight. Try the rook move again. . . . At this point you glance at the clock. 'My goodness! Already 30 minutes gone on thinking about whether to move the rook or the knight. It if goes on like this you'll really be in time trouble.' And then suddenly you are struck by the happy idea – why move rook or knight? What about B-QN1? And without any more ado, without analysis at all, you move the bishop. Just like that.

Perhaps, then, decision-making means periods of groping followed by sudden sharp insights that lead to crystallization, as A. Langley and co-authors suggested in a 1995 *Organizational Science* article (see Figure 2.4.1). Or perhaps it is a form of 'organized anarchy', as Stanford professor James March and colleagues have written. They characterize decision-making as 'collections of choices looking for problems, issues and feelings looking for decision situations in which they may be aired, solutions looking for issues to which they might be an answer, and decision-makers looking for work' (see Figure 2.4.2). But is the confusion, as described by those authors, in the process, or is it in the observers? Maybe messy, real-life decision-making makes more sense than we think, precisely because so much of it is beyond conscious thought.

[1]Source: This article was adapted with permission from MIT *Sloan Management Review*, Vol. 42, No. 3, Spring 2001, pp. 89–93.

FIGURE 2.4.1   Groping precedes zeroing in

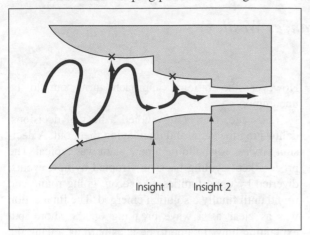

Insight 1   Insight 2

FIGURE 2.4.2   Choices looking for problems

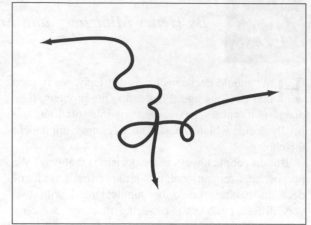

'Seeing first'

Insight – 'seeing into' – suggests that decisions, or at least actions, may be driven as much by what is seen as by what is thought. As Mozart said, the best part about creating a symphony was being able to 'see the whole of it at a single glance in my mind'. So, understanding can be visual as well as conceptual.

In W. Koehler's well-known 1920s experiment, an ape struggled to reach a banana placed high in its cage. Then it *saw* the box in the corner – not just noticed it, but realized what could be done with it – and its problem was solved. Likewise after Alexander Fleming really *saw* the mold that had killed the bacteria in some of his research samples (in other words, when he realized how that mold could be used), he and his colleagues were able to give us penicillin. The same can be true for strategic vision. Vision requires the courage to see what others do not – and that means having both the confidence and the experience to recognize the sudden insight for what it is.

A theory in Gestalt psychology developed by G. Wallas in the 1920s identifies four steps in creative discovery: preparation → incubation → illumination → verification. Preparation must come first. As Louis Pasteur put it, 'Chance favors only the prepared mind.' Deep knowledge, usually developed over years, is followed by incubation, during which the unconscious mind mulls over the issue. Then with luck (as with Archimedes in the bathtub), there is that flash of illumination. That eureka moment often comes after sleep – because in sleep, rational thinking is turned off, and the unconscious has greater freedom. The conscious mind returns later to make the logical argument. But that verification (reasoning it all out in linear order for

purposes of elaboration and proof) takes time. There is a story of a mathematician who solved a formula in his sleep. Holding it in his mind's eye, he was in no rush to write it down. When he did, it took him four months!

Great insights may be rare, but what industry cannot trace its origins to one or more of them? Moreover, little insights occur to all of us all the time. No one should accept any theory of decision-making that ignores insight.

'Doing first'

But what happens when you don't see it and can't think it up? Just do it. That is how pragmatic people function when stymied: They get on with it, believing that if they do 'something', the necessary thinking could follow. It's experimentation – trying something so that you can learn.

A theory for 'doing first', popularized in academia by organizational-behavior professor Karl Weick, goes like this: enactment → selection → retention. That means doing various things, finding out which among them works, making sense of that and repeating the successful behaviors while discarding the rest. Successful people know that when they are stuck, they must experiment. Thinking may drive doing, but doing just as surely drives thinking. We don't just think in order to act, we act in order to think.

Show us almost any company that has diversified successfully, and we will show you a company that has learned by doing, one whose diversification strategy emerged through experience. Such a company at the outset may have laid out a tidy strategy on the basis of assessing its weaknesses and strengths (or, if after

1990, its 'core competencies'), which it almost certainly got wrong. How can you tell a strength from a weakness when you are entering a new sphere? You have no choice but to try things out. Then you can identify the competencies that are really core. Action is important; if you insist on 'thinking first' and, for example, doing formalized strategic planning (which is really part of the same thing), you may in fact discourage learning.

Making decisions through discussion, collage and improvisation

Thus the three major approaches to decision-making are 'thinking first', 'seeing first' and 'doing first'. They correlate with conventional views of science, art and craft. The first is mainly verbal (comprising words in linear order), the second is visual, the third is visceral. Those who favor thinking are people who cherish facts, those who favor seeing cherish ideas and those who favor doing cherish experiences (see Table 2.4.1).

We have for some years conducted workshops on the three approaches with midcareer managers sent by Asian, European and North American companies to our International Masters Program in Practicing Management (www.impm.org). We begin with a general discussion about the relationship between analysis, ideas and action. It soon becomes evident that practicing managers recognize the iterative and connected nature of those elements. We then ask small groups first to discuss an issue for about an hour (one of their own or else what we call a 'provocative question'. For example: 'How do you manage customer service when you never see a customer?' or 'How do you organize without structure?'), summarize their conclusions on a flip chart and report back to the full group. Next we give the groups colored paper, pens, scissors and glue. Each small group must create a collage about the issue they discussed in the thinking-first session. At the end of that second workshop, the groups view one another's images and compare 'seeing first' with 'thinking first' – in terms of both process and results. Finally, each group, with only a few minutes of preparation time permitted, improvises a skit to act out its issue. Again, the groups consider the results.

Reactions to the approaches are revealing. Participants note that in the thinking-first workshop, the initial discussions start off easily enough, no matter what the mix of nationalities or work backgrounds. Participants list comments on flip charts and spontaneously use bulleted items and numbers – with the occasional graph thrown in. Almost no time is spent in discussing *how* to go about analyzing the problem. Groups quickly converge on one of several conventional analytic frameworks: cause and effect, problem and solution, pros and cons, and so on.

Many participants observe that such frameworks, particularly when adopted early, blunt exploration. Quality and depth of analysis may be sacrificed for process efficiency. Thinking-first workshops encourage linear, rational and rather categorical arguments. All too often, the result is a wish list, with disagreements hidden in the different points. In other words, there may be less discipline in thinking first than we believe. Thinking comes too easily to most of us.

But when a group must make a picture, members have to reach consensus. That requires deeper integration of the ideas. 'We had to think more to do this', a participant reported. The artistic exercise 'really forces you to capture the essence of an issue', another added. People ask more questions in the seeing-first exercise; they become more playful and creative.

'In "thinking first", we focused on the problems; in "seeing first", we focused on the solutions', one person said. One group believed it had agreement on the issue

TABLE 2.4.1   Characteristics of the three approaches to making decisions

'Thinking first' features the qualities of	'Seeing first' features the qualities of	'Doing first' features the qualities of
Science	Art	Craft
Planning, programming	Visioning, imagining	Venturing, learning
The verbal	The visual	The visceral
Facts	Ideas	Experiences

after the thinking-first workshop. Only when the picture making began did its members realize how superficial that agreement was – more of a compromise. In contrast, when you really do see, as someone said, 'The message jumps out at you.' But to achieve that, the group members have to find out more about one another's capabilities and collaborate more closely. 'I felt it became a group project, not just my project', said a participant who had chosen the topic for his group. The seeing-first exercise also draws out more emotions; there is more laughter and a higher energy level. This suggests that being able to see a trajectory – having a vision about what you are doing – energizes people and so stimulates action. In comparing the seeing-first exercise with the thinking-first discussion, a participant remarked, 'We felt more liberated.' The pictures may be more ambiguous than the words, but they are also more involving. A frequent comment: 'They invite interpretation.'

One particularly interesting observation about the pictures was that 'the impression lasts longer'. Studies indicate that we remember pictures much longer and more accurately than words. As R. Haber demonstrated in *Scientific American* in 1970, recall of images, even as many as 10,000 shown at one-second intervals, is nearly 98% – a capability that may be linked to evolution. Humans survived by learning to register danger and safety signals first. Emotion, memory, recall and stimulation are powerfully bundled in 'seeing first'. Contrast that with one comment after the thinking-first workshop: 'Twenty-four hours later, we won't remember what this meant.'

In fact, although many participants have not made a picture since grade school, the art produced in the seeing-first workshops is often remarkable. Creativity flows freely among the managers, suggesting that they could come up with more creative ideas in their home organizations if they more often used symbols beyond words or numbers.

Our multicultural groups may like the art workshop for overcoming language barriers, but groups of managers from the same company, country or language group have responded equally well. One British participant who was working on a joint venture with an American partner found that out. He met with his US counterpart a few days after the workshops. 'We talked past each other for two hours', he reported. When he suggested they create a picture of their common concerns, they finally were able to connect.

The improvisation skits – 'doing first' – generate more spontaneity. Participants respond to one another intuitively and viscerally, letting out concerns held back in conversation and even in artwork. For example, turf battles become evident in the way people stand and talk. Humor, power, fear and anger surface. (M. Crossen and M. Sorrenti discuss improvisation at length in a helpful article published in 1997 in *Advances in Strategic Management*.)

Weick has suggested that a key aspect of effective action in organizations is the ability to remain open to signals from others, even under extreme pressure. He believes that such heedfulness, as he calls it, is a finely honed skill among group improvisers such as jazz musicians. Organizations that recognize opportunities for improvisation – and hone the skills required – increase their capacity for learning. In improvisation, people have to respond with a speed that eliminates many inhibitions. 'Having to just act gets rid of the fears', a participant said. Another added, after watching a colleague play the role of a frustrated bank customer, 'The output can be scarily real.'

Mere words, in contrast, feel more abstract and disconnected – numbers, even more so – just as the aggregations of marketing are more abstract than the experience of selling. The skits bring out what the words and numbers do not say – indeed, what problems they cause. 'Not everything is unsayable in words', claimed playwright Eugène Ionesco, 'only the living truth.' Or as Isadora Duncan, the modern-dance pioneer, insisted, 'If I could say it, I wouldn't have to dance it.' Thus 'doing first' facilitates the dancing that is so lacking in many of today's organizations.

Enough thinking?

The implications for our large, formalized, thinking-obsessed organizations are clear enough: not to suspend thinking so much as put it in its place, alongside seeing and doing. Isn't it time we got past our obsession with planning and programming, and opened the doors more widely to venturing and visioning? A glance at corporate reports, e-mail and meetings reveals that art is usually something reserved for report covers – or company walls. And when organizations separate the thinking from the doing, with the former coming from the heads of powerful formulators and the latter assigned to the hands of ostensibly docile implementers, those formulators lose the benefits of experimenting – and learning.

Each approach has its own strengths and weaknesses (see Table 2.4.2). 'Thinking first' works best when the issue is clear, the data reliable and the world structured; when thoughts can be pinned down and

TABLE 2.4.2 When each decision-making approach works best

Approach	Works best when	Example
'Thinking first'	■ The issue is clear ■ The data is reliable ■ The context is structured ■ Thoughts can be pinned down ■ Discipline can be applied	As in an established production process
'Seeing first'	■ Many elements have to be combined into creative solutions ■ Commitment to those solutions is key ■ Communication across boundaries is essential	As in new-product development
'Doing first'	■ The situation is novel and confusing ■ Complicated specifications would get in the way ■ A few simple relationship rules can help people move forward	When companies face a disruptive technology

discipline applied, as in an established production process. 'Seeing first' is necessary when many elements have to be combined into creative solutions and when commitment to those solutions is key, as in much new-product development. The organization has to break away from the conventional, encourage communication across boundaries, bust up cerebral logjams and engage the heart as well as the head. 'Doing first' is preferred when the situation is novel and confusing, and things need to be worked out. That is often the case in a new industry – or in an old industry thrown into turmoil by a new technology. Under such circumstances, complicated specifications get in the way, and a few simple relationship rules can help people move forward in a coordinated yet spontaneous manner.

That suggests the advantages of combining all three approaches. In order to learn, a company group might tackle a new issue first by craft, which is tied to doing; then, in order to imagine, by art, which is tied to seeing; finally, in order to program, by science, which is tied to thinking. In ongoing situations, art provides the overview, or vision; science specifies the structure, or plan; and craft produces the action, or energy. In other words, science keeps you straight, art keeps you interested, and craft keeps you going. No organization can do without any one approach. Isn't it time, then, to move beyond our narrow thinking about decision-making: to get in *touch*, to *see* another point of view?

STRATEGIC THINKING IN INTERNATIONAL PERSPECTIVE

Those who judge by their feelings do not understand reasoning, for they wish to get an insight into a matter at a glance, and are not accustomed to look for principles. Contrarily, others, who are accustomed to argue from principles, do not understand the things of the heart, seeking for principles and not being able to see at a glance.

Blaise Pascal (1623–1662); French scientist and philosopher

From the preceding articles it has become clear that opinions differ sharply about what goes on, and should go on, in the mind of the strategist. There are strongly conflicting views on how managers deal with the paradox of logic and creativity. It is up to each reader to judge whether the rational or the generative reasoning perspective is more valuable for understanding strategic thinking. Yet, we hope that readers will feel challenged to consider the possibility that both perspectives may be useful at the same time. Although they are opposites, and partially contradictory, both perspectives might reveal crucial aspects of strategic thinking that need to be combined to achieve superior results. Blending logic and creativity in ingenious ways might allow strategists to get 'the best of both worlds'. What such mixes of logic and creativity in the mind of the strategist could be like will remain a matter for debate – with strategists using their own logical and/or creative thinking to come up with answers.

Hence, this last part of the chapter is not intended to present a grand synthesis. Readers will have to grapple with the paradox of logic and creativity themselves, by contrasting the thesis (the rational reasoning perspective) and the antithesis (the generative reasoning perspective). In this final part of the chapter it is the intention to view the topic of strategic thinking from an international perspective. The explicit question that must be added to the debate on the mind of the strategist is whether there are discernible national differences in approaches to strategic thinking. Are there specific national preferences for the rational or the generative reasoning perspective, or are the differing views spread randomly across the globe? Are each of the perspectives rooted in a particular national context, making it difficult to extend them to other countries, or are they universally applicable? In short, are views on strategic thinking the same all around the world?

Unfortunately, this question is easier asked than answered. Little cross-cultural research has been done in the field of strategic management and hardly any on this specific topic. This may be partially due to the difficulty of international comparative research, but it probably also reflects the implicit assumption by most that theories on strategic thinking are universally applicable. Few of the authors cited in this chapter suggest that there are international differences or note that their theories might be culturally biased and of limited validity in other national settings.

Yet, the assumption that strategic thinking is viewed in the same way around the world should be questioned. The human inclination to suppose that all others are the same as us is well known – it is a common cognitive bias. In international affairs, however, such an assumption must always be challenged. Strategists operating internationally cannot afford the luxury of assuming that their views are universally accepted and applicable. Therefore, the thought must be entertained that strategists in some countries are more attracted to the rational reasoning perspective, while in other countries the generative reasoning perspective is more pervasive.

As a stimulus to the debate whether there are such national preferences in perspective on strategic thinking, we would like to bring forward a number of factors that might be of influence on how the paradox of logic and creativity is tackled in different countries. It goes almost without saying that more concrete international comparative research is needed to give this debate a firmer footing.

Position of science

Science and the scientific method do not play the same role, and are not accorded the same value, in all societies. In some countries, science and scientists are held in high esteem, and scientific inquiry is believed to be the most fruitful way for obtaining new knowledge. Typical for these nations is that the scientific method has come to pervade almost all aspects of life. Objective knowledge and skill in analytical reasoning are widely believed to be the critical success factors in most professions – even to become a nurse, a journalist, a sports instructor, an actor or a musician requires a university education. Managers, too, are assumed to be scientifically trained, often specializing in management studies. Much of this education strongly promotes formal, explicit, analytical thinking, and pays little attention to creativity, imagination and intuition. In these nations a more pronounced preference for the rational reasoning perspective might be expected.

In other countries, science holds a less predominant position (Redding, 1980). Scientific methods might shed some light on issues, but other ways of obtaining new insights – such as through experience, intuition, philosophizing, fantasizing, and drawing analogies – are also valued (Keegan, 1983; Kagono et al., 1985). The bounds of socially acceptable reasoning are less constrictive than in more rationalist nations. Leaps of imagination and logical inconsistencies are tolerated, as normal aspects in the messy process of sense-making (Pascale, 1984). In general, thinking is viewed as an art and therefore science has not made deep inroads into most of the professions. Managers, in particular, do not require a specific scientific training, but need to be broadly developed generalists with flexible minds (Nonaka and Johanson, 1985). In these countries, a stronger preference for the generative thinking perspective can be expected.

Level of uncertainty avoidance

National cultures also differ with regard to their tolerance for ambiguity. As Hofstede points out in Reading 1.4 in this book, some societies feel uncomfortable with uncertain situations and strive for security. Countries that score high on Hofstede's 'uncertainty avoidance dimension' typically try to suppress deviant ideas and behaviors, and institute rules that everyone must follow. People in these countries exhibit a strong intellectual need to believe in absolute truths and they place great trust in experts (Schneider, 1989). They have a low tolerance for the ambiguity brought on by creative insights, novel interpretations and 'wild ideas' that are not analytically sound. Therefore, it can be expected that strategists in high uncertainty avoidance cultures will be more inclined towards the rational reasoning perspective than in nations with a low score.

Level of individualism

As stated at the beginning of this chapter, strategists with a generative inclination are slightly rebellious. They show little reverence for the status quo, by continuously questioning existing cognitive maps and launching creative reinterpretations. As the dissenting voice, they often stand alone, and are heavily criticized by the more orthodox. This lonely position is difficult to maintain under the best of circumstances, but is especially taxing in highly collectivist cultures. If strategists wish to be accepted within their group, organization and community, they cannot afford to stick out too much. There will be a strong pressure on the strategist to conform. In more individualist cultures, however, there is usually a higher tolerance for individual variety. People find it easier to have their own ideas, independent of their group, organization and community (see Hofstede's individualism dimension, in Reading 1.4). This gives strategists more intellectual and emotional freedom to be the 'odd man out'. Therefore, it can be expected that strategists in more individualist cultures will be more inclined towards the generative reasoning perspective than those in collectivist cultures.

Position of strategists

Countries also differ sharply with regard to the hierarchical position of the managers engaged in strategy. In many countries strategic problems are largely defined and solved by the upper echelons of management. To reach this hierarchical position requires many years of hands-on experience and climbing through the ranks. Therefore, by the time managers are in the position of being a strategist they are middle-aged and thoroughly familiar with their business – with the danger of being set in their ways. They will also have been promoted several times by senior managers who believe that they will function well within the organization. In general, the effect is that the competent and conformist managers are promoted to strategy positions, while innovative dissidents are selected out along the way. In such countries, creative strategic reasoning often does not take place within large organizations, but within small start-ups, to which the creatively inclined flee.

In cultures that score lower on Hofstede's power distance dimension, managers throughout the organization are often involved in strategy discussions. The responsibility for strategy is spread more widely among the ranks. Younger, less experienced managers are expected to participate in strategy formation processes, together with their senior colleagues. In general, this leads to a more open, messy and lively debate about the organization's strategy and provokes more creative strategic thinking. Therefore, it can be expected that in less hierarchical cultures the generative reasoning perspective will be more popular than in cultures with stronger hierarchical relations.

FURTHER READING

Anyone interested in the topic of strategic thinking will sooner or later run into the work of Herbert Simon. His concept of bounded rationality was originally explored in the book *Models of Man*, which is still interesting reading, but *Organizations*, written together with James March, is a more comprehensive and up-to-date source with which to start. Also, a good introduction to (bounded) rationality is given by Niels Noorderhaven, in his book *Strategic Decision Making*, which additionally covers the topics of emotions, intuition and cognition in relationship to the strategy process. Another excellent book exploring the role of emotions in economic decision-making behavior and engaging in a debate with rational choice theorists is *Alchemies of the Mind: Rationality and the Emotions*, by Jon Elster.

For a more in-depth discussion on the interplay between cognition and strategic decision-making, a stimulating book is R. Hogarth's *Judgement and Choice: The Psychology of Decision*. Also an excellent book is *The Essence of Strategic Decision Making*, by Charles Schwenk, in particular with regard to the discussion of cognitive biases. A good research article summarizing the role of cognition in (strategic) management is James Walsh's (1995) 'Managerial and Organizational Cognition: Notes from a Trip Down Memory Lane'. On the topic of the social construction of reality, Karl Weick's *The Social Psychology of Organizing* is still the classic that should be read. A shorter article on the same topic is 'Strategic Management in an Enacted World' by Linda Smircich and Charles Stubbart (1985).

Readers interested in the link between creativity and strategic thinking might want to start with *Creative Management*, an excellent reader edited by John Henry, which contains many classic articles on creativity from a variety of different disciplines. A second step would be to read Gareth Morgan's imaginative book, *Imaginization: The Art of Creative Management*, or John Kao's *Jamming: The Art and Discipline of Business Creativity*, both of which make challenging proposals for improving an organization's creative thinking. Also stimulating is the book *Strategic Innovation*, by Charles Baden-Fuller and Martyn Pitt, which contains a large number of cases on companies exhibiting creative thinking. For a practical guide to creative thinking Stephen Reid's recent book, *How to Think: Building Your Mental Muscle*, is quite useful.

REFERENCES

Aldrich, H.E., and Fiol, C.M. (1994) 'Fools Rush In? The Institutional Context of Industry Creation', *Academy of Management Review*, Vol. 19, No. 4, pp. 645–670.

Anderson, J.R. (1983) *The Architecture of Cognition*, Harvard University Press, Cambridge, MA.

Andrews, K. (1987) *The Concept of Corporate Strategy*, Irvin, Homewood.

Ansoff, H.I. (1965) *Corporate Strategy: An Analytic Approach to Business Policy for Growth and Expansion*, McGraw-Hill, New York.

Ansoff, H.I. (1991) 'Critique of Henry Mintzberg's The "Design School": Reconsidering the Basic Premises of Strategic Management', *Strategic Management Journal*, September, pp. 449–461.

Anthony, W.P., Bennett, R.H., Maddox, E.N., and Wheatley, W.J. (1993) 'Picturing the Future: Using Mental Imagery to Enrich Strategic Environmental Assessment', *Academy of Management Executive*, Vol. 7, No. 2, pp. 43–56.

Archer, L., (1963) 'Systemation Method for Designers', *Design*, pp. 172–188.

Arnheim, R. (1992) 'Sketching and the Psychology of Design', in: V. Margolis and R. Buchanan (eds), *The Idea of Design*, MIT Press, Cambridge, MA.

Baden-Fuller, C., and Pitt, M. (1996) *Strategic Innovation*, Routledge, London.

Bazerman, M.H. (1990) *Judgment in Managerial Decision Making*, Second Edition, Wiley, New York.

Bazjanac, V., 'Architectural Design Theory: Models of the Design Process', in: W. Spillers (ed.), *Basic Questions of Design Theory*, American Elsevier, New York, pp. 3–20.

Bazjanac, V. (1964) *The Writings of C. Alexander: Notes on the Synthesis of Form*, Harvard University Press, Boston, MA.

Behling, O., and Eckel, N.L. (1991) 'Making Sense Out of Intuition', *Academy of Management Executive*, Vol. 5, No. 1, pp. 46–54.

Buchanan, R., and Margolis, V. (eds.) (1995) *Discovering Design*, University of Chicago Press, Chicago, IL.

Burgelman, R. (1991) 'Intraorganizational Ecology of Strategy Making and Organizational Adaptation', *Organizational Science*, 213, p. 208, and pp. 239–262.

Calori, R., Johnson, G., and Sarnin, P. (1994) 'CEO's Cognitive Maps and the Scope of the Organization', *Strategic Management Journal*, Vol. 15, No. 6, July, pp. 437–457.

Christensen, C.R., Andrews, K.R., Bower, J.L., Hamermesh, R.G., and Porter, M.E. (1982) *Business Policy: Text and Cases*, Fifth Edition, Irwin, Homewood, IL.

Christensen, C.R., Andrews, K.R., Bower, J.L., Hamermesh, R.G., and Porter, M.E. (1987) *Business Policy: Text and Cases*, Sixth Edition, Irwin, Homewood, IL.

Cross, N. (1995) 'Discovering Design Ability', in: R. Buchanan and V. Margolis (eds.), *Discovering Design*, University of Chicago Press, Chicago, IL.

Daft, R., and Weick, K. (1984) 'Toward a Model of Organizations as Interpretation Systems', *Academy of Management Review*, Vol. 9, pp. 284–295.

Day, D.V. and Lord, R.G. (1992) 'Expertise and Problem Categorization: The Role of Expert Processing in Organizational Sense-Making', *Journal of Management Studies*, Vol. 29, pp. 35–47.

De Bono, E. (1970) *Lateral Thinking*, Harper & Row, New York.

DiMaggio, P., and Powell, W.W. (1983) 'The Iron Cage Revisited: Institutional Isomorphism and Collective Rationality in Organizational Fields', *American Sociological Review*, Vol. 48, pp. 147–160.

Dutton, J.E. (1988) 'Understanding Strategies Agenda Building and its Implications for Managing Change', in: L.R. Pondy, R.J. Boland, Jr., and H. Thomas (eds.), *Managing Ambiguity and Change*, Wiley, Chichester.

Eden, C. (1989) 'Using Cognitive Mapping for Strategic Options Development and Analysis (SODA)', in: J. Rosenhead (ed.), *Rational Analysis in a Problematic World*, Wiley, London.

Elster, J. (1999) *Alchemies of the Mind: Rationality and the Emotions*, Cambridge University Press, Cambridge.

Emery, F.E., and Trist, E.L. (1965) 'The Causal Texture of Organizational Environments', *Human Relations*, Vol. 18, pp. 21–32.

Findeli, A. (1990) 'The Methodological and Philosophical Foundations of Moholy-Nagy's Design Pedagogy in Chicago (1927–1946)', *Design Issues*, 711, pp. 4–19, and pp. 32–33.

Finkelstein, S., and Hambrick, D.C. (1996) *Strategic Leadership: Top Executives and Their Effects on Organizations*, West, St. Paul.

Gioia, D.A., and Chittipeddi, K. (1991) 'Sensemaking and Sensegiving in Strategic Change Intuition', *Strategic Management Journal*, Vol. 12, pp. 433–448.

Grove, A. (1996) *Only the Paranoid Survive*, Doubleday, New York.

Hambrick, D.C., Geletkanycz, M.A., and Fredrickson, J.W. (1993) 'Top Executive Commitment to the Status Quo: Some Tests of Its Determinants', *Strategic Management Journal*, Vol. 14, No. 6, pp. 401–418.

Hamel, G. (1996) 'Strategy as Revolution', *Harvard Business Review*, July–August, Vol. 74, No. 4, pp. 69–82.

Hamel, G., and Prahalad, C.K. (1994) *Competing for the Future*, Harvard Business School Press, Boston, MA.

Henry, J. (ed.) (1991) *Creative Management*, Sage in association with the Open University, London.

Hofstede, G. (1980) *Culture's Consequences*, Sage, London.

Hogarth, R.M. (1980) *Judgement and Choice: The Psychology of Decision*, Wiley, Chichester.

Huff, A.S. (ed.) (1990) *Mapping Strategic Thought,* Wiley, Chichester.

Hurst, D.K., Rush, J.C. and White, R.E. (1989) 'Top Management Teams and Organizational Renewal', *Strategic Management Journal*, Vol. 10, No. 1, pp. 87–105.

Isenberg, D.J. (1984) 'How Senior Managers Think', *Harvard Business Review*, November–December, Vol. 63, No. 6, pp. 81–90.

Janis, I.L. (1989) *Crucial Decisions: Leadership in Policymaking and Crisis Management*, Free Press, New York.

Kagono, T.I., Nonaka, K., Sakakibira, K., and Okumara, A. (1985) *Strategic vs. Evolutionary Management*, Amsterdam, North-Holland.

Kao, J. (1996) *Jamming: The Art and Discipline of Business Creativity*, HarperBusiness, New York.

Keegan, W.J. (1983) 'Strategic Market Planning: The Japanese Approach', *International Marketing Review*, Vol. 1, pp. 5–15.

Knight, D., Pearce, C.L., Smith, K.G., Olian, J.D., Sims, H.P., Smith, K.A., and Flood, P. (1999) 'Top Management Team Diversity, Group Process, and Strategic Consensus', *Strategic Management Journal*, Vol. 20, pp. 445–465.

Kuhn, T.S. (1970) *The Structure of Scientific Revolutions*, University of Chicago Press, Chicago.

Langley, A. (1989) 'In Search of Rationality: The Purposes Behind the Use of Formal Analysis in Organizations', *Administrative Science Quarterly*, Vol. 34, No. 4, pp. 598–631.

Langley, A. (1995) 'Between "Paralysis by Analysis" and "Extinction by Instinct"', *Sloan Management Review*, Vol. 36, No. 3, Spring, pp. 63–76.

Lenz, R.T., and Lyles, M. (1985) 'Paralysis by Analysis: Is Your Planning System Becoming Too Rational?', *Long Range Planning*, Vol. 18, No. 4, pp. 64–72.

Liedtka, J. (2000) 'In defense of strategy as design', *California Management Review*, Vol. 42, No. 3, Spring, pp. 8–30.

Liedtka, J., and Rosenblum, J. (1996) 'Shaping Conversations: Making Strategy, Managing Change', *California Management Review*, Vol. 39, No. 1, Fall, pp. 141–157.

Lyles, M.A., and Schwenk, C.R. (1992) 'Top Management, Strategy and Organizational Knowledge Structures', *Journal of Management Studies*, Vol. 29, pp. 155–174.

March, J.G., and Simon, H.A. (1993) *Organizations*, Second Edition, Blackwell, Cambridge, MA.

March, L. (1976) 'The Logic of Design', in: L. March, (ed.), *The Architecture of Form*, Cambridge University Press, Cambridge, MA.

Mason, R.O., and Mitroff, I.I. (1981) *Challenging Strategic Planning Assumptions*, Wiley, New York.

McCaskey, M.B. (1982) *The Executive Challenge: Managing Change and Ambiguity*, Pitman, Boston.

Mintzberg, H. (1987) 'Crafting Strategy', *Harvard Business Review*, July–August, pp. 66–75.

Mintzberg, H. (1990) 'The Design School: Reconsidering the Basic Premises of Strategic Management', *Strategic Management Journal*, Vol. 11, No. 3, pp. 171–195.

Mintzberg, H. (1991) 'Learning 1, Planning 0: Reply to Igor Ansoff', *Strategic Management Journal*, September, pp. 463–466.

Mintzberg, H. (1994) *The Rise and Fall of Strategic Planning*, The Free Press, New York.

Mintzberg, H. Ahlstrand, B., and Lampel, J. (1998) *Strategy Safari: A Guided Tour through the Wilds of Strategic Management*, The Free Press, New York.

Mintzberg, H. and Westley, F. (2001) 'Decision Making: It's Not What You Think', *Sloan Management Review*, Vol. 42, No. 3, pp. 89–93.

Morgan, G. (1993) *Imaginization: The Art of Creative Management*, Sage, Newbury Park, CA.

Neustadt, R., and May, E. (1986) *Thinking in Time: The Uses of History for Decision-Makers*, The Free Press, New York.

Nonaka, I. (1991) 'The Knowledge-Creating Company', *Harvard Business Review*, Vol. 69, No. 6, November–December, pp. 96–104.

Nonaka, I., and Johanson, J.K. (1985) 'Japanese Management: What about "Hard" Skills?', *Academy of Management Review*, Vol. 10, No. 2, pp. 181–191.

Noorderhaven, N.G. (1995) *Strategic Decision Making*, Addison-Wesley, Wokingham.

Ocasio, W. (1997) 'Towards an Attention-Based View of the Firm', *Strategic Management Journal*, Vol. 18, Special Issue, July, pp. 187–206.

Ohmae, K. (1975) *The Corporate Strategist*, President Inc., New York.

Ohmae, K. (1982) *The Mind of the Strategist*, McGraw-Hill, New York.

Pascale, R.T. (1984) 'Perspectives on Strategy: The Real Story Behind Honda's Success', *California Management Review*, Vol. 26, No. 3, Spring, pp. 47–72.

Pond, L. (1918) *The Meaning of Architecture: An Essay in Constructive Criticism*, Marshall Jones Company, Boston, MA.

Pondy, L.R. (1983) 'Union of Rationality and Intuition in Management Action', in: S. Srivastava (ed.), *The Executive Mind*, Jossey-Bass, San Francisco.

Polanyi, M. (1966) *The Tacit Dimension*, Routledge & Kegan Paul, London.

Prahalad, C.K., and Bettis, R.A. (1986) 'The Dominant Logic: A New Linkage between Diversity and Performance', *Strategic Management Journal*, Vol. 7, No. 6, November–December, pp. 485–601.

Redding, S.G. (1980) 'Cognition as an Aspect of Culture and its Relationship to Management Processes: An Exploratory View of the Chinese Case', *Journal of Management Studies*, Vol. 17, May, pp. 127–148.

Reid, S. (2002) *How to Think: Building Your Mental Muscle*, Prentice Hall, London.

Rittel, H. (1972) 'On the Planning Crisis: Systems Analysis of the "First and Second Generations"', *Bedriftsokonomen*, No. 8, pp. 390–396.

Rittel, H., and Webber, M. (1973) 'Dilemmas in a General Theory of Planning', *Policy Sciences*, Vol. 4, pp. 155–169.

Roos, J., and Victor, B. (1999) 'Towards a New Model of Strategy-making as Serious Play', *European Management Journal*, Vol. 17, No. 4, April, pp. 348–355.

Schein, E.H. (1985) *Organizational Culture and Leadership*, Jossey-Bass, San Francisco.

Schneider, S.C. (1989) 'Strategy Formulation: The Impact of National Culture', *Organization Studies*, Vol. 10, No. 2, pp. 149–168.

Schoemaker, P.J.H., and Russo, J.E. (1993) 'A Pyramid of Decision Approaches', *California Management Review*, Vol. 36, No. 1, Fall, pp. 9–32.

Schon, D. (1983) *The Reflective Practitioner: How Professionals Think in Action*, Basic Books, New York.

Schwenk, C.R. (1984) 'Cognitive Simplification Processes in Strategic Decision-Making', *Strategic Management Journal*, Vol. 5, No. 2, April–June, pp. 111–128.

Schwenk, C.R. (1988) *The Essence of Strategic Decision Making*, Lexington Books, Lexington, MA.

Senge, P. (1990) *The Fifth Discipline*, Doubleday, New York.

Simon, H.A. (1957) *Models of Man*, Wiley, New York.

Simon, H.A. (1969) *The Sciences of the Artificial*, MIT Press, Cambridge, MA.

Simon, H.A. (1972) 'Theories of Bounded Rationality', in: C. McGuire, and R. Radner (eds.), *Decision and Organization*, Amsterdam, pp. 161–176.

Simon, H.A. (1987) 'Making Management Decisions: The Role of Intuition and Emotion', *Academy of Management Executive*, Vol. 1, No. 1, pp. 57–64.

Simon, H.A. (1993) 'Strategy and Organizational Evolution', *Strategic Management Journal*, Vol. 14, pp. 131–142.

Smircich, L., and Stubbart, C. (1985) 'Strategic Management in an Enacted World', *Academy of Management Review*, Vol. 10, No. 4, pp. 724–736.

Sutcliffe, K.M., and Huber, G.P. (1998) 'Firm and Industry Determinants of Executive Perceptions of the Environment', *Strategic Management Journal*, Vol. 19, pp. 793–807.

Starbuck, W., and Milliken, F. (1988) 'Challenger: Fine-Tuning the Odds Until Something Breaks', *Journal of Management Studies*, Vol. 25, No. 4, July.

Trice, H.M., and Beyer, J.M. (1993) *The Cultures of Work Organizations*, Prentice Hall, Englewood Cliffs.

Tversky, A., and Kahneman, D. (1986) 'Rational Choice and the Framing of Decisions', *Journal of Business*, Vol. 59, No. 4, pp. 251–278.

Von Ghyczy, T., Von Oetinger, B., and Bassford, C. (2001) *Clausewitz on Strategy*, Wiley, New York.

Von Winterfeldt, D., and Edwards, W. (1986) *Decision Analysis and Behavioural Research*, Cambridge University Press, Cambridge.

Walsh, J. (1995) 'Managerial and Organizational Cognition: Notes from a Trip Down Memory Lane', *Organization Science*, Vol. 6, pp. 280–321.

Weick, K.E. (1979) *The Social Psychology of Organizing*, Random House, New York.

Weick, K.E., and Bourgnon, M.G. (1986) 'Organizations as Cognitive Maps', in: H.P. Sims Jr. and D.A. Gioia (eds.), *The Thinking Organization*, Jossey-Bass, San Francisco.

Williamson, J. (1983) *Decoding Advertisements*, Marion Bryars Publishers, New York.

STRATEGY FORMATION

To plan, v. To bother about the best method of accomplishing an accidental result.

The Devil's Dictionary, Ambrose Bierce (1842–1914); American columnist

INTRODUCTION

There are many definitions of strategy and many ideas of how strategies should be made. In the introduction to section ii of this book on 'Strategy process', our definition of strategy was kept basic to encompass the large majority of these different views – 'strategy is a course of action for achieving an organization's purpose'. Taking this definition as a starting point, a major distinction can be observed between people who see strategy as an *intended* course of action and those who regard strategy as a *realized* course of action. Mintzberg and Waters (1985) have remarked that these two views of strategy are not contradictory, but complementary. Intended strategy is what individuals or organizations formulate prior to action (a *pattern of decisions*), while realized strategy refers to the strategic behavior exhibited in practice (a *pattern of actions*). Of course, not all behavior is necessarily strategic – if the actions do not follow a pattern directed at achieving the organization's purpose, it does not qualify as strategy.

The process by which an intended strategy is created is called 'strategy formulation'. Normally strategy formulation is followed by strategy implementation. However, intentions sometimes end up not being put into practice – plans can be changed or canceled along the way. The process by which a realized strategy is formed is called 'strategy formation'. What is realized might be based on an intended strategy, but it can also be the result of unplanned actions as time goes by. In other words, the process of strategy formation encompasses both formulation and action. Strategy formation is the entire process leading to strategic behavior in practice.

For managers with the responsibility for getting results, it would be too limited to only look at the process of strategy formulation and to worry about implementation later. Managers must ask themselves how the entire process of strategy formation should be managed to get their organizations to act strategically. Who should be involved, which activities need to be undertaken and to what extent can strategy be formulated in advance? In short, for managers finding a way to realize a strategic pattern of actions is the key issue.

THE ISSUE OF REALIZED STRATEGY

Getting an organization to exhibit strategic behavior is what all strategists aim to achieve. Preparing detailed analyses, drawing up plans, making extensive slide presentations and holding long meetings might all be necessary means to achieve this end, but ultimately it is the organization's actions directed at the market-place that count. The key issue facing managers is, therefore, how this strategic behavior can be attained. How can a successful course of action be realized in practice?

To answer these questions, it is first necessary to gain a deeper understanding of the 'who' and 'what' of strategy formation – 'what type of strategy formation activities need to be carried out?' and 'what type of strategy formation roles need to be filled by whom?'. Both questions will be examined in the following sections.

Strategy formation activities

In Chapter 2 it was argued that the process of strategic reasoning could be divided into four general categories of activities – identifying, diagnosing, conceiving and realizing. These strategic problem-solving activities, taking place in the mind of the strategist, are in essence the same as those encountered in organizations at large. Organizations also need to 'solve strategic problems' and achieve a successful pattern of actions. The difference is that the organizational context – involving many more people, with different experiences, perspectives, personalities, interests and values – leads to different requirements for structuring the process. Getting people within an organization to exhibit strategic behavior necessitates the exchange of information and ideas, decision-making procedures, communication channels, the allocation of resources and the coordination of actions.

When translated to an organizational environment, the four general elements of the strategic reasoning process can be further divided into the eight basic building blocks of the strategy formation process, as illustrated in Figure 3.1.

FIGURE 3.1   The main strategy formation activities

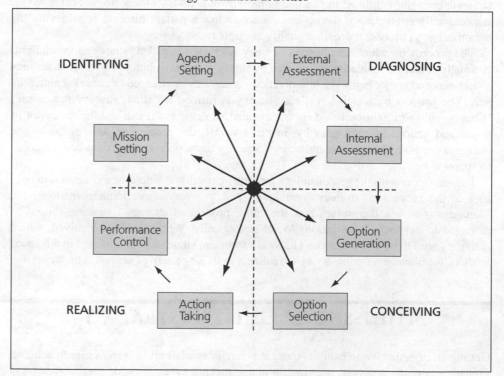

Strategic issue identification activities. If a strategy is seen as an answer to a perceived 'problem' or 'issue', managers must have some idea of what the problem is. 'Identifying' refers to all activities contributing to a better understanding of what should be viewed as problematic – what constitutes an important opportunity or threat that must be attended to if the organization's purpose is to be met. The key activities here are:

- Mission setting. What the organization sees as an issue will in part depend on its mission – the enduring set of fundamental principles outlining what purpose the organization wishes to serve, in what domain and under which conditions. A company's mission, encompassing its core values, beliefs, business definition and purpose, forms the basis of the organization's identity and sets the basic conditions under which the organization wishes to function. Where a company has a clearly developed mission, shared by all key players in the organization, this will strongly color its filtering of strategic issues. The mission does not necessarily have to be formally captured in a mission statement, but can be informally internalized as a part of the company culture. The topic of mission is discussed at more length in Chapter 11.

- Agenda setting. Besides the organizational mission as screening mechanism, many other factors can contribute to the focusing of organizational attention on specific strategic issues. For instance, the cognitive map of each strategist will influence which environmental and organizational developments are identified as issues. Furthermore, group culture will have an impact on which issues are discussible, which are off-limits to open debate, and under what conditions discussions should take place. Getting people to sit up and take notice will also depend on each actor's communication and political skills, as well as their sources of power, both formal and informal. Together these attention-focusing factors determine which issues are picked up on the 'organizational radar screen', discussed and looked into further. It is said that these issues make it on to the 'organizational agenda', while all other potential problems receive less or no attention. Many of these organizational factors are discussed more extensively in Chapters 4 and 9.

Strategic issue diagnosis activities. To come to grips with a 'problem' or 'issue', managers must try to comprehend its structure and its underlying causes. Especially since most strategic issues are not simple and straightforward, but complex and messy, it is very important to gain a deeper understanding of 'what is going on' – which 'variables' are there and how are they interrelated? This part of the strategy formation processes can be divided into the following activities:

- External assessment. The activity of investigating the structure and dynamics of the environment surrounding the organization is commonly referred to as an external assessment or analysis. Typically such a diagnosis of the outside world includes both a scan of the direct (market) environment and the broader (contextual) environment. In both cases the analyst wants to move beyond observed behavior, to understand 'what makes the system tick'. What is the underlying structure of the industry and the market that is conditioning each party's behavior? And what are the characteristics and strategies of each important actor, including customers, competitors, suppliers, distributors, unions, governments and financiers? Furthermore, only understanding the current state of affairs is generally insufficient; it is also necessary to analyze in which direction external circumstances are developing. Which trends can be discerned, which factors seem to be driving the industry and market dynamics, and can these be used to forecast or estimate future developments? In Chapters 5, 7 and 8, these questions surrounding external assessment are discussed in more detail.

- Internal assessment. The activity of investigating the capabilities and functioning of the organization is commonly referred to as an internal assessment or analysis. Typically such a diagnosis of the inner workings of the organization includes an assessment of the *business system* with which the firm creates value and the *organizational system* that has been developed to facilitate the business system. When dissecting the business system, attention is directed at understanding the resources and chain of value-adding activities that enable the firm to offer a set of products and services. To gain insight into the functioning of the organizational system, it is necessary to determine the structure of the organization, the processes used to control and coordinate the various people and units, and the organizational culture. In all these analyses a mere snapshot of the firm is generally insufficient – the direction in which the organization is developing must also be examined, including a consideration of the main change drivers and change inhibitors. Furthermore, for strategy making it is important to compare how the organization scores on all aforementioned factors compared to rival firms. In Chapters 4 and 5 these topics are investigated in more depth.

Strategy conception activities. To deal with a strategic 'problem' or 'issue', managers must come up with a potential solution. A course of action must be found that will allow the organization to relate itself to the environment in such a way that it will be able to achieve its purpose. 'Conceiving' refers to all activities that contribute to determining which course of action should be pursued. In this part of the strategy formation process, the following categories of activities can be discerned:

- Option generation. Creating potential strategies is what option generation is about. Sometimes managers will immediately jump at one specific course of action, limiting their strategic option generation activities to only one prime candidate. However, many managers will be inclined to explore a number of different avenues for approaching a specific strategic issue, thereby generating multiple strategic options. Each option can range in detail from a general outline of actions to be taken, up to a full-blown strategic plan, specifying goals, actions, tasks, responsibilities, resource allocation, milestones and performance measures. Which questions each strategic option should address is the main focus of discussion in the strategy content section of this book.

- Option selection. The potential 'solutions' formulated by managers must be evaluated to decide whether they should be acted upon. It must be weighed whether the strategic option generated will actually lead to the results required and then it must be concluded whether to act accordingly. Especially where two or more strategic options have come forward, managers need to judge which one of them is most attractive to act on. This screening of strategic options is done on the basis of evaluation criteria, for instance perceived risk, anticipated benefits, the organization's capacity to execute, expected competitor reactions and follow-up possibilities. Sometimes a number of the evaluation criteria used are formally articulated, but generally the evaluation will at least be partially based on the experience and judgment of the decision-makers involved. Together, these activities of assessing strategic options and arriving at a selected course of action are also referred to as 'strategic decision-making'.

Strategy realization activities. A strategic 'problem' or 'issue' can only be resolved if concrete actions are undertaken that achieve results. Managers must make adjustments to their business or organizational system, or initiate actions in the market – they must not only think, talk and decide, but also do, to have a tangible impact. 'Realizing' refers to all these practical actions performed by the organization. If there is a clear pattern to these actions, it can be said that there is a realized strategy. In this part of the strategy formation process, the following activities can be distinguished:

- Action taking. A potential problem solution must be carried out – intended actions must be implemented to become realized actions. This performing of tangible actions encompasses all aspects of a firm's functioning. All hands-on activities, more commonly referred to as 'work', fall into this category – everything from setting up and operating the business system to getting the organizational system to function on a day-to-day basis.

- Performance control. Managers must also measure whether the actions being taken in the organization are in line with the option selected and whether the results are in line with what was anticipated. This reflection on the actions being undertaken can be informal, and even unconscious, but it can be formally structured into a performance monitoring and measuring system as well. Such performance measurement can be employed to assess how well certain people and organizational units are doing vis-à-vis set objectives. Incentives can be linked to achieving targets, and corrective steps can be taken to ensure conformance to an intended course of action. However, deviation from the intended strategy can also be a signal to re-evaluate the original solution or even to re-evaluate the problem definition itself. An important issue when engaging in performance control is the determination of which performance indicators will be used – micro-measuring all aspects of the organization's functioning is generally much too unwieldy and time-consuming. Some managers prefer a few simple measures, sometimes quantitative (e.g. financial indicators), sometimes qualitative (e.g. are clients satisfied?), while others prefer more extensive and varied measures, such as a balanced scorecard (Kaplan and Norton, 2001; Simons, 1995).

Note that these strategy formation activities have not been labeled 'steps' or 'phases'. While these eight activities have been presented in an order that seems to suggest a logical sequence of steps, it remains to be seen in which order they should be carried out in practice. In Figure 3.1 the outer arrows represent the logical clockwise sequence, similar to the rational reasoning process discussed in Chapter 2. The inner arrows represent the possibility to jump back and forth between the strategy formation activities, similar to the irregular pattern exhibited in the generative reasoning process in Chapter 2.

Strategy formation roles

In all strategy formation processes the activities discussed above need to be carried out. However, there can be significant differences in who carries out which activities. Roles in the strategy formation process can vary as tasks and responsibilities are divided in alternative ways. The main variations are due to a different division of labor along the following dimensions:

- Top vs. middle vs. bottom roles. Strategy formation activities are rarely the exclusive domain of the CEO. Only in the most extreme cases will a CEO run a 'one-man show', carrying out all activities except realization. Usually some activities will be divided among members of the top management team, while other activities will be pushed further down to divisional managers, business unit managers, and department managers (e.g. Bourgeois and Brodwin, 1983; Floyd and Wooldridge, 2000). Some activities might be delegated or carried out together with people even further down the hierarchy, including employees on the work floor. For activities such as external and internal assessment and option generation it is more common to see participation by people lower in the organization, while top management generally retains the responsibility for selecting, or at least deciding on, which strategic option to follow. The recurrent theme in this question of the vertical division of activities is how far down activities can and should be pushed – how much *empowerment* of middle and lower levels is beneficial for the organization?

- Line vs. staff roles. By definition line managers are responsible for realization of strategic options pertaining to the primary process of the organization. Because they are responsible for achieving results, they are often also given the responsibility to participate in conceiving the strategies they will have to realize. Potentially, line managers can carry out all strategy formation activities without staff support. However, many organizations do have staff members involved in the strategy formation process. Important staff input can come from all existing departments, while some organizations institute special strategy departments to take care of strategy formation activities. The responsibilities of such strategy departments can vary from general process facilitation, to process ownership to full responsibility for strategy formulation.

- Internal vs. external roles. Strategy formation activities are generally seen as an important part of every manager's portfolio of tasks. Yet, not all activities need to be carried out by members of the organization, but can be 'outsourced' to outsiders (e.g. Robinson, 1982). It is not uncommon for firms to hire external agencies to perform diagnosis activities or to facilitate the strategy formation process in general. Some organizations have external consultants engaged in all aspects of the process, even to the extent that the outside agency has the final responsibility for drawing up the strategic options.

In organizing the strategy formation process, a key question is how formalized the assignment of activities to the various potential process participants should be. The advantage of formalization is that it structures and disciplines the strategy formation process (e.g. Chakravarthy and Lorange, 1991, Reading 3.1 in this book; Hax and Maljuf, 1984). Especially in large organizations, where many people are involved, it can be valuable to keep the process tightly organized. Formalization can be achieved by the establishment of a strategic planning system. In such a system, strategy formation steps can be scheduled, tasks can be specified, responsibilities can be assigned, decision-making authority can be clarified, budgets can be allocated and evaluation mechanisms can be put in place. Generally, having unambiguous responsibilities, clearer accountability and stricter review of performance will lead to a better functioning organization. The added benefit of formalization is that it gives top management more control over the organization, as all major changes must be part of approved plans and the implementation of plans is checked.

Yet, there is a potential danger in using formal planning systems as a means to make strategy. Formalization strongly emphasizes those aspects that can be neatly organized such as meetings, writing reports, giving presentations, making decisions, allocating resources and reviewing progress, while having difficulty with essential strategy-making activities that are difficult to capture in procedures. Important aspects such as creating new insights, learning, innovation, building political support and entrepreneurship can be sidelined or crushed if rote bureaucratic mechanisms are used to produce strategy. Moreover, planning bureaucracies, once established, can come to live a life of their own, creating rules, regulations, procedures, checks, paperwork, schedules, deadlines and double-checks, making the system inflexible, unresponsive, ineffective and demotivating (e.g. Marx, 1991; Mintzberg, 1994a).

THE PARADOX OF DELIBERATENESS AND EMERGENCE

The ability to foretell what is going to happen tomorrow, next week, next month and next year. And to have the ability afterwards to explain why it didn't happen.

Winston Churchill (1874–1965); British prime minister and writer

Strategy has to do with the future. And the future is unknown. This makes strategy a fascinating, yet frustrating, topic. Fascinating because the future can still be shaped and strategy can be used to achieve this aim. Frustrating because the future is unpredictable, undermining the best of intentions, thus demanding flexibility and adaptability. To managers, the idea of creating the future is highly appealing, yet the prospect of sailing for *terra incognita* without a compass is unsettling at best.

This duality of wanting to intentionally design the future, while needing to gradually explore, learn and adapt to an unfolding reality, is the tension central to the topic of strategy formation. It is the conflicting need to figure things out in advance, versus the need to find things out along the way. On the one hand, managers would like to forecast the future and to orchestrate plans to prepare for it. Yet, on the other hand, managers understand that experimentation, learning and flexibility are needed to deal with the fundamental unpredictability of future events.

In their influential article, 'Of Strategies: Deliberate and Emergent', Mintzberg and Waters (1985) were one of the first to explicitly focus on this tension. They argued that a distinction should be made between deliberate and emergent strategy (see Figure 3.2). Where realized strategies were fully intended, one can speak of 'deliberate strategy'. However, realized strategies can also come about 'despite, or in the absence of, intentions', which Mintzberg and Waters labeled 'emergent strategy'. In their view, few strategies were purely deliberate or emergent, but usually a mix between the two.

Hence, in realizing strategic behavior managers need to blend the conflicting demands for deliberate strategizing and strategy emergence. In the following paragraphs both sides of this paradox of deliberateness and emergence will be examined further.

FIGURE 3.2   Deliberate and emergent strategy

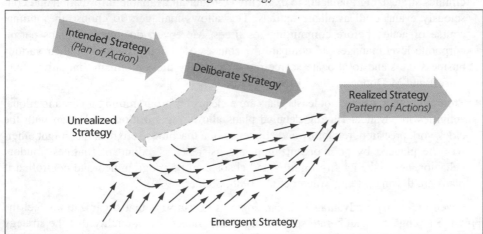

Source: Mintzberg and Waters, 1985; reprinted with permission from *Strategic Management Journal*, © 1985 John Wiley and Sons Ltd.

The demand for deliberate strategizing

Deliberateness refers to the quality of acting intentionally. When people act deliberately, they 'think' before they 'do'. They make a plan and then implement the plan. A plan is an intended course of action, stipulating which measures a person or organization proposes to take. In common usage, plans are assumed to be articulated (made explicit) and documented (written down), although strictly speaking this is not necessary to qualify as a plan.

As an intended course of action, a plan is a means towards an end. A plan details which actions will be undertaken to reach a particular objective. In practice, however, plans can exist without explicit objectives. In such cases, the objectives are implicitly wrapped up in the plan – the plan incorporates both ends and means.

All organizations need to plan. At the operational level, most firms will have some degree of production planning, resource planning, manpower planning and financial planning, to name just a few. When it comes to strategic behavior, there are also a number of prominent advantages that strongly pressure organizations to engage in deliberate strategizing:

- Direction. Plans give organizations a sense of direction. Without objectives and plans, organizations would be adrift. If organizations did not decide where they wanted to go, any direction and any activity would be fine. People in organizations would not know what they were working towards and therefore would not be able to judge what constitutes effective behavior (e.g. Ansoff, 1965; Chakravarthy and Lorange, 1991, Reading 3.1).

- Commitment. Plans enable early commitment to a course of action. By setting objectives and drawing up a plan to accomplish these, organizations can invest resources, train people, build up production capacity and take a clear position within their environment. Plans allow organizations to mobilize themselves and to dare to take actions that are difficult to reverse and have a long payback period (e.g. Ghemawat, 1991; Marx, 1991).

- Coordination. Plans have the benefit of coordinating all strategic initiatives within an organization into a single cohesive pattern. An organization-wide master plan can ensure that differences of opinion are ironed out and one consistent course of action is followed throughout the entire organization, avoiding overlapping, conflicting and contradictory behavior (e.g. Ackoff, 1980; Andrews, 1987).

- Optimization. Plans also facilitate optimal resource allocation. Drawing up a plan disciplines strategizing managers to explicitly consider all available information and consciously evaluate all available options. This allows managers to choose the optimal course of action before committing resources. Moreover, documented plans permit corporate level managers to compare the courses of action proposed by their various business units and to allocate scarce resources to the most promising initiatives (e.g. Ansoff and McDonnell, 1990; Bower, 1970).

- Programming. Last, but not least, plans are a means for programming all organizational activities in advance. Having detailed plans allows organizations to be run with the clockwork precision, reliability and efficiency of a machine. Activities that might otherwise be plagued by poor organization, inconsistencies, redundant routines, random behavior, helter-skelter fire fighting and chaos, can be programmed and controlled if plans are drawn up (e.g. Grinyer et al., 1986; Steiner, 1979).

Given these major advantages, it can come as no surprise that organizations feel the pressure to engage in deliberate strategizing. Deliberateness is a quality that the strategy formation process cannot do without.

The demand for strategy emergence

Emergence is the process of becoming apparent. A strategy emerges when it comes into being along the way. Where there are no plans, or people divert from their plans but their behavior is still strategic, it can be said that the strategy is emergent – gradually shaped during an iterative process of 'thinking' and 'doing'.

Emergent strategy differs from ad hoc behavior in that a coherent pattern of action does evolve. While managers may have no prior intentions, they can explore, learn and piece together a consistent set of behaviors over time. Such an approach of letting strategy emerge has a number of major advantages that organizations also need to consider:

- Opportunism. As the future is unknown and therefore unpredictable, organizations must retain enough mental freedom to grab unforeseen opportunities as they emerge. Organizations must keep an open mind to sense where positive and negative circumstances are unfolding, so that they can respond rapidly to these new conditions – proactively riding the wave of opportunity, using the momentum in the environment and/or the organization to their advantage. This ability to 'play the field' is an important factor in effective strategy formation (e.g. Quinn, 2002; Stacey, 2001).

- Flexibility. Not only must managers keep an open mind, they must keep their options open as well, by not unnecessarily committing themselves to irreversible actions and investments. Letting strategy emerge means not prematurely locking the organization in to a preset course of action, but keeping alternatives open for as long as practically possible. And where commitments must to be made, managers need to select 'robust' options, which permit a lot of leeway to shift along with unfolding events. This pressure to remain flexible is also an important demand on strategizing managers (e.g. Beinhocker, 1999; Evans, 1991).

- Learning. Often, the best way to find out what works is to give it a try – to act before you know. Letting strategy emerge is based on the same principle, that to learn what will be successful in the market must be discovered by experimentation, pilot projects, trial runs and gradual steps. Through the feedback obtained by hands-on 'doing', a rich insight can grow into what really works. As Thomas Alva Edison is well known for remarking, invention is 5% inspiration and 95% perspiration, and this is probably equally true for 'inventing the corporate future'. Learning is hard work, but it is an essential part of strategy formation (e.g. Pascale, 1984; Mintzberg, 1994d).

- Entrepreneurship. Building on the previous point, often the best way to find out what works is to let various people give it a try – to tap into the entrepreneurial spirits within the organization. Different people in the organization will have different strategic ideas and many of them will feel passionately about proving that their idea 'can fly'. By providing individuals, teams and/or entire units with a measure of autonomy to pursue innovative initiatives, firms can use the energy of 'intrapreneurs' within the organization, instead of forcing them to conform or start on their own (e.g. Amabile, 1998; Pinchot, 1985). As true incubators, firms can facilitate various divergent projects simultaneously, increasing commitment or closing them down as their potential unfolds (e.g. Burgelman, 1983, 1991; Lyon, Lumpkin and Dess, 2000).

- Support. A major shift in strategy generally requires a major shift in the political and cultural landscape of an organization – careers will be affected, vested departmental interests will be impacted and cultural values and beliefs will be challenged. Rarely can such shifts be imposed top-down by decree. Getting things done in organizations includes building coalitions, blocking rivals, convincing wavering parties, confronting opposing ideas and letting things 'sink in', all with the intention of gradually building enough support to move forward. Yet, finding out where enough support can be mustered to move forward, and where side steps or even reversals are needed, is an ongoing process and cannot be predicted in advance. Hence, strategizing managers must understand the internal political and cultural dynamics of their organizations and pragmatically shape strategy depending on what is feasible, not on what is ideal (e.g. Allison, 1971; Quinn, 1980).

Each of these points seems to be the opposite counterpart of the advantages of deliberate strategizing – while deliberateness creates commitment, emergence allows for flexibility; while deliberateness gives direction, emergence allows for opportunism; while deliberateness facilitates fixed programming, emergence allows for ongoing learning. This places managers in a paradoxical position. While both deliberate strategizing and strategy emergence seem to have advantageous characteristics, they are each other's opposites and are to a certain extent contradictory – a firm cannot be fully committed to detailed and co-ordinated long-term plans, while simultaneously adapting itself flexibly and opportunistically to unfolding circumstances, ongoing learning and unpredictable political and cultural processes. With two conflicting demands placed on the strategy formation process at the same time, managers need to choose one at the expense of the other, trying to strike the best possible balance between deliberateness and emergence.

EXHIBIT 3.1 SHORT CASE

AIRBUS: PLANNING BEYOND PLANES?

When aviation pioneers Orville and Wilbur Wright flew their first aircraft more than a century ago, they probably never imagined that some successors of their Flyer would carry a price tag of over US$200 million per aircraft and require R&D investments in excess of US$10 billion per model. Yet, this is the current reality facing the two remaining makers of large passenger aircraft in the world – Boeing in Seattle, USA, and Airbus, headquartered in Toulouse, France. Other large manufacturers such as McDonnell Douglas and Lockheed have had to bow out of this high stakes game, as they were not capable of realizing the economies of scale in production and R&D needed to survive in this industry. Only the long-time market leader Boeing and the upstart challenger Airbus have had an attractive enough range of aircraft models to achieve the volume needed to survive the shakeout.

While Boeing is a straightforward company, with a traditional structure, Airbus is a somewhat odd firm, with an odd history. Back in 1969, a consortium of French and German firms was formed with the intention of jointly developing an aircraft that could compete with the American giants. This consortium was later expanded to include Spanish and British companies as well. The consortium was often derided as a mere job-creation program and a less-than-subtle vehicle for funneling state aid into a 'strategic industry'. The consortium also had many teething problems, as it needed to develop cross-border decision-making processes involving many parties, many interested local and national governments and without strong central leadership. Yet, despite the internal difficulties and the external criticisms, Airbus was able to create the successful A300B passenger jet. Within ten years of its inception, Airbus captured a strong foothold in the market for large passenger jets, having 256 orders from 32 customers. This encouraged the consortium partners to turn their loose alliance into a more structured federation and to conceive a long-term vision to develop a complete family of large aircraft, ranging from 100-seat to 400-seat passenger jets. Underpinning this vision was the assumption that a broad choice of aircraft types would enable airlines to switch more easily to Airbus.

So by the early 1980s Airbus was looking for a second type to add to its line up. Given the economic downturn and increased fuel prices at that time, airlines indicated that they were interested in a new type of aircraft with the ability to carry the same number of passengers over the same distance as the well-established Boeing 727–200, while burning just half as much fuel. Airbus's answer was the A320, which was launched in 1984. In 1987 the product range was further extended with two larger aircraft, the four-engine A340 and twin-engine A330. In 1993, in the midst of the worst financial crisis suffered by the airline industry until then, Airbus launched a relatively small passenger jet, the A319. This move ensured that adequate numbers of this type of plane were available to meet a recovery of demand that, according to Airbus planners, would occur in 1996. They were right – from 1995 onwards, US air carriers started to replace part of their fleets, as 25% of their planes were over 20 years old. Moreover, new anti-noise regulations came into effect in many markets, which favored the relatively quiet Airbus jets.

Despite a strongly expanded market share, the Airbus consortium members were still not convinced that they would be able to compete with Boeing in the long run, especially as Boeing had been able to entice McDonnell Douglas, into a merger in 1996, even though Airbus had been courting McDonnell Douglas for years. Three worries were foremost in the minds of the Airbus executives. First, the consortium structure was proving to be a severe burden on strategic decision-making. Every decision required the consent of all participating companies and negotiations on 'who would get what' could be long and bitter. There was a growing feeling that if the 'parents' had so many 'children' together, it was about time they got around to marrying. Secondly, after deregulation of the airline industry, the boom and bust cycles in the aircraft industry had become more severe. In the past, the state-owned flag carriers could plan their fleet expansion and renewal without much concern for the swings in demand among air passengers. The privatized carriers and new commercial airlines, however, were much more vulnerable to swings in demand, leading them to order aircraft in good times and to cancel orders *en masse* as soon as the market declined. The Airbus companies felt that something would need to be done to make Airbus less vulnerable to such cyclicality, especially since Boeing had a lot of stable military business in its portfolio to offset swings in the commercial aircraft business. Thirdly, it worried Airbus that Boeing still had a monopoly at the top end of the market with its 747 jumbo jet. The resulting revenues gave Boeing the advantage of having higher investment power than Airbus. Therefore, it was felt that the only way to keep up with Boeing would be to attack it directly in the heart of its empire.

Finding an answer to these worries took the Airbus partners several years, but in 2000 major steps were taken to address all three. It was announced that from January 1 2001 the consortium would be transformed into a single corporate entity. Furthermore, to ensure that the company would

have a balanced portfolio of businesses, Airbus was made part of a larger, newly established company, the European Aeronautic Defense and Space Corporation (EADS), which brings together a broad range of companies with airborne activities (i.e. commercial and defense airplanes and helicopters, missiles, satellites and rocket launchers). Moreover, it was announced that Airbus would start to develop a 555-seat double-decker mega jet, the A380, to overtake the Boeing 747 at the high end of the market.

With a long history of complex and prolonged negotiations between partner organizations, no one was surprised that the CEO of the unified Airbus, Noël Forgeard, made centralization of strategic decision-making one of his top priorities. He wanted to make use of the momentum to create an effective and efficient strategy formation process that fits well with the challenges faced by the company. It was clear to him that strong strategic planning would be required, given the inevitability of deciding on new aircraft types far in advance. With R&D investments for a new aircraft type surpassing US$10 billion and years of development time, strategists did not have the luxury of test marketing a few different product types and keeping the best one – they had to get it right first time. The payback period of the average aircraft is in excess of ten years and aircraft designs can last up to 50 years, placing a premium on forecasting which product will fit the needs for many years to come. For instance, the Boeing 747 jumbo jet has been in production for more than 30 years and is still being sold, which has netted Boeing more than US$20 billion in profits. On the other hand, getting it wrong can mean billions down the drain and years of delay in developing an alternative.

Yet, planning in the aircraft industry has never been more difficult. It used to be easier to calculate when airlines would need to replace old planes and to project market growth. But the old airlines have been in turmoil since deregulation – new competitors are entering and the traditional business model of a 'hub-and-spoke' airline network is being challenged by low cost 'point-to-point' carriers. This difficulty in forecasting industry developments has led to sharp contrasts between the future expectations of Boeing and Airbus. In deciding to pursue the 555-seat A380, Airbus based itself on the projection that air traffic would grow by 5% per year and that crowded airport hubs, with limited starting and landing capacity, would need bigger aircraft. Its forecasts showed that over the next 20 years there would be an attractive US$300 billion market for 1400 mega carriers that could carry up to 600 passengers. Boeing, on the contrary, believed that air travel was going to fragment, and most growth would not come from routes connecting crowded hub airports, but from long-haul point-to-point services such as Singapore–Los Angeles. Therefore, smaller and faster planes would have a bright future, and Boeing decided to unfold plans to develop a new aircraft, the Sonic Cruiser, which would be smaller than the 747, but would travel at 95% of the speed of sound.

Since then, the market for aircraft has proven to be even more unpredictable than anticipated. The post-internet bubble economic downturn, followed by the events of September 11 2001, the Second Gulf War and the SARS scare of 2003 have sent the airline industry into a tailspin. Airlines have delayed or canceled orders, sending prices plunging down to earth and leading to huge overcapacity at Airbus and Boeing. With the future unclear and little market enthusiasm for its Sonic Cruiser, Boeing has quietly shelved its grand plans and instead has come up with relatively low-cost plans for a super-stretched version of the 747 jumbo jet. Airbus, however, has already committed itself to multi-billion investments for its A380 program and can hardly reduce its engineering resources as the project is in full swing.

To Forgeard the challenge of making strategy in an unpredictable environment is not restricted to the big 'aircraft type' decisions taken every eight to ten years. More and more, Airbus wants to make its money on options added to an aircraft and the services surrounding the aircraft, instead of only on the basic product itself. Forgeard is thinking of services such as fleet planning, maintenance, financing and refurbishing, plus extra options such as in-flight internet. Yet, the difficulty is that his organization is used to making long-term product strategies, based on market forecasts and a strong measure of technology-push. It is not used to identifying potential service needs and developing innovative offerings to fulfill them. A different approach to strategy formation might be required.

Hence, the question facing Forgeard and Airbus is how they should go about shaping their strategy in future. Is it a matter of making even better forecasts or are there other ways of dealing with the unpredictability and unknowability of industry developments? And can Airbus use the same approach to strategy formation for the task of developing new options and services as it has used to develop new aircraft? The answer is vital, since Forgeard has pledged that Airbus will become bigger than Boeing before 2007 – which means adding a few billion to its current sales of US$17 billion, while not crash landing in the meantime.

Sources: *Airfinance Journal*, September 2002; *Aviation Week*, July 2 2000; *Aviation Week and Space Technology*, December 24 2001; *Business Week*, January 21 2002; *Financial Times*, September 8 2000; *Fortune*, August 2 1999 and March 5 2001; *Industry Week*, June 11 2001.

PERSPECTIVES ON STRATEGY FORMATION

It is impossible for a man to learn what he thinks he already knows.
Epictetus (c. 60–120); Roman philosopher

In Hollywood, most directors do not start shooting a movie until the script and storyboard are entirely completed – the script details each actor's words, expression and gestures, while the storyboard graphically depicts how each scene will look in terms of camera angles, lighting, backgrounds and stage props. Together they form a master plan, representing the initial intentions of the director. However, it frequently happens that a director has a new insight, and changes are made to the script or storyboard 'on the fly'. Yet, on the whole, most 'realized movies' are fairly close to directors' initial intentions.

For some directors this is madness. They might have a movie idea, but in their mind's eye they cannot yet picture it in its final form. Some elements might have already crystallized in their thoughts, but other parts of the film can only be worked out once the cameras are rolling and the actors start playing their roles. In this way, directors can let movies emerge without having a detailed script or storyboard in advance to guide them. It can be said that such movies are shaped by gradually blending together a number of small intentional steps over a long period of time, instead of taking one big step of making a master plan and implementing it. This approach of taking many small steps is called 'incrementalism'.

The question is how this works for managers making strategy. Is it best to deliberately draw up a storyboard for the film and trust that the 'actors' are flexible enough to adapt to minor changes in the script as time goes by? Or is the idea of a master plan misplaced, and are the best results achieved by developing a strategy incrementally, emergently responding to opportunities and threats as they unfold along the way? In short, how should strategizing managers strike a balance between deliberateness and emergence?

Unfortunately, the strategic management literature does not offer a clear-cut answer to this question. In both the academic journals and the practitioner-oriented literature, a wide spectrum of views can be observed on how managers should engage in strategy formation. While some writers suggest that there might be different styles in balancing deliberateness and emergence (e.g. Chaffee, 1985; Hart, 1992), most seem intent on offering 'the best way' to approach the issue of strategy formation – which often differs significantly from 'the best way' advised by others.

To come to grips with this variety of views, here the two diametrically opposed pole positions will be identified and discussed. On the basis of these two 'points of departure' the debate on how to deal with the paradox of deliberateness and emergence can be further explored. At one pole we find those managers and theorists who strongly emphasize deliberateness over emergence. They argue that organizations should strive to make strategy in a highly deliberate manner, by first explicitly formulating comprehensive plans, and only then implementing them. In accordance with common usage, this point of view will be referred to as the 'strategic planning perspective'. At the other pole are those who strongly emphasize emergence over deliberateness, arguing that in reality most new strategies emerge over time and that organizations should facilitate this messy, fragmented, piecemeal strategy formation process. This point of view will be referred to as the 'strategic incrementalism perspective'.

The strategic planning perspective

 Advocates of the strategic planning perspective argue that strategies should be deliberately planned and executed. In their view, anything that emerges unplanned is not really strategy. A successful pattern of action that was not intended cannot be called strategy, but should be seen for what it is – brilliant improvisation or just plain luck (Andrews, 1987). However, managers cannot afford to count on their good fortune or skill at muddling through. They must put time and effort into consciously formulating an explicit plan, making use of all available information and weighing all of the strategic alternatives. Tough decisions need to be made and priorities need to be set, before action is taken. 'Think before you act' is the strategic planning perspective's motto. But once a strategic plan has been adopted, action should be swift, efficient and controlled. Implementation must be secured by detailing the activities to be undertaken, assigning responsibilities to managers and holding them accountable for achieving results (e.g. Ansoff and McDonnell, 1990; Chakravarthy and Lorange, 1991, Reading 3.1).

Hence, in the strategic planning perspective, strategies are intentionally designed, much as an engineer designs a bridge. Building a bridge requires a long formulation phase, including extensive analysis of the situation, the drawing up of a number of rough designs, evaluation of these alternatives, choice of a preferred design, and further detailing in the form of a blueprint. Only after the design phase has been completed do the construction companies take over and build according to plan. Characteristic of such a planning approach to producing bridges and strategies is that the entire process can be disassembled into a number of distinct steps that need to be carried out in a sequential and orderly way. Only by going through these steps in a conscious and structured manner will the best results be obtained (e.g. Armstrong, 1982; Powell, 1992).

For advocates of the strategic planning perspective, the whole purpose of strategizing is to give organizations direction, instead of letting them drift. Organizations cannot act rationally without intentions – if you do not know where you are going, any behavior is fine, which soon degenerates into 'muddling through' (e.g. Ansoff, 1991; Steiner, 1979). By first setting a goal and then choosing a strategy to get there, organizations can get 'organized'. Managers can select actions that are efficient and effective within the context of the strategy. A structure can be chosen, tasks can be assigned, responsibilities can be divided, budgets can be allotted and targets can be set. Not unimportantly, a control system can be created to measure results in comparison to the plan, so that corrective action can be taken.

Another advantage of the planning approach to strategy formation is that it allows for the *formalization* and *differentiation* of strategy tasks. Because of its highly structured and sequential nature, strategic planning lends itself well to formalization. The steps of the strategic planning approach can be captured in planning systems (e.g. Kukalis, 1991; Lorange and Vancil, 1977), and procedures can be developed to further enhance and organize the strategy formation process. In such strategic planning systems, not all elements of strategy formation need to be carried out by one and the same person, but can be divided among a number of people. The most important division of labor is often between those formulating the plans and those implementing them. In many large companies the managers proposing the plans are also the ones implementing them, but deciding on the plans is passed up to a higher level. Often other tasks are spun off as well, or shared with others, such as diagnosis (strategy department or external consultants), implementation (staff departments) and evaluation (corporate planner and controller). Such task differentiation and specialization, it is argued, can lead to a better use of management talent, much as the division of labor has improved the field of production. At the same, having a formalized system allows for sufficient coordination and mutual adjustment, to ensure that all specialized elements are integrated back into a consistent organization-wide strategy (e.g. Grinyer et al., 1986; Jelinek, 1979).

Last, but not least, an advantage of strategic planning is that it encourages long-term thinking and commitment. 'Muddling through' is short-term oriented, dealing with issues of strategic importance as they come up or as a crisis develops. Strategic planning, on the other hand, directs attention to the future. Managers making strategic plans have to take a more long-term view and are stimulated to prepare for, or even create, the future (Ackoff, 1980). Instead of just focusing on small steps, planning challenges managers to define a desirable future and to work towards it. Instead of wavering and opportunism, strategic planning commits the organization to a course of action and allows for investments to be made at the present that may only pay off in the long run (e.g. Ansoff, 1991; Miller and Cardinal, 1994).

One of the difficulties of strategic planning, advocates of this perspective will readily admit, is that plans will always be based on assumptions about how future events will unfold. Plans require forecasts. And as the Danish physicist Niels Bohr once joked, 'prediction is very difficult, especially about the future'. Even enthusiastic planners acknowledge that forecasts will be inaccurate. As Makridakis, the most prolific writer on the topic of forecasting, writes (1990: 66), 'the future can be predicted only by extrapolating from the past, yet it is fairly certain that the future will be different from the past'. Consequently, it is clear that rigid long-range plans based on such unreliable forecasts would amount to nothing less than

Russian roulette. Most proponents of the strategic planning perspective therefore caution for overly deterministic plans. Some argue in favor of 'contingency planning', whereby a number of alternative plans are held in reserve in case key variables in the environment suddenly change. These contingency plans are commonly based on different future 'scenarios' (Van der Heijden, 1996; Wilson, 2000, Reading 3.4 in this book). Others argue that organizations should stage regular reviews, and realign strategic plans to match the altered circumstances. This is usually accomplished by going through the planning cycle every year, and adapting strategic plans to fit with the new forecasts.

The strategic planning perspective shares many of the assumptions underlying the rational reasoning perspective discussed in Chapter 2. Both perspectives value systematic, orderly, consistent, logical reasoning and assume that humans are capable of forming a fairly good understanding of reality. And both are based on a calculative and optimizing view of strategy-making. It is, therefore, not surprising that many managers who are rationally inclined also exhibit a distinct preference for the strategic planning perspective.

EXHIBIT 3.2 THE STRATEGIC PLANNING PERSPECTIVE

SAMSUNG ELECTRONICS: SHOOTING FOR THE STARS

At the end of the 1960s, Byung-Chull Lee was chairman of the Samsung Group, one of the major South Korean *chaebol* – a conglomerate manufacturing a wide array of products, ranging from clothing to ships. Samsung had worked hard to overcome the devastation of the Korean War (1951–1954), but Lee had even more ambitious plans. He wanted to move beyond traditional low value-added industries, into a more attractive industrial sector – electronics. So, in 1969 he launched Samsung Electronics, initially oriented towards the manufacturing of 'white goods' (home appliances), such as refrigerators, stoves and vacuum cleaners. The founding of Samsung Electronics fitted perfectly in the South Korean government's 'Eight-Year Development Plan for Electronics Industries', which provided the firm with significant government support in R&D, the establishment of new plants and access to cheap loans.

Once Samsung Electronics had established a position in white goods by the start of the 1980s, Lee went to Japan to personally investigate where further growth opportunities could be found. Here he observed how the developments in semiconductors were speedily opening up enormous opportunities for new high-tech products. He became convinced that Samsung should not move cautiously in this area, following Sony and Matsushita, but should try to boldly grab a leadership role for itself – becoming an innovative industry shaper instead of remaining a reactive copycat. But for this

to be successful, Samsung could not allow its strategy to slowly emerge, but rather would need to set extremely ambitious long-term goals and commit the organization to a disciplined roadmap to go from being a 'nobody' to becoming 'number one'.

Based on Lee's vision, a business project team for semiconductors was secretly formed in 1982. The team ran a study to find out what the most attractive semiconductor product would be, which resulted in forecasts and strategic options for a range of different electronic components. In 1983, after thorough evaluations, Samsung decided to enter the DRAM (dynamic random access memory) chip industry. A long-term strategic plan was drawn up which would take the company from acquiring relatively simple technologies, to modifying imported technology, to designing new products through reverse engineering, to eventually developing advanced products. Finally, Samsung would become a 'black-belt master' in product and process innovation. To further refine this broad, long-term strategic plan, Samsung hired a group of US-educated South Korean engineers and sent them with a team of managers to the United States to work on the DRAM business project. Their assignment was to write a more detailed business plan and to recruit more engineers. Once the 'blueprint' was finished and approved by Lee, Samsung started DRAM assembly activities for the US-based Micron Technologies.

Over the next ten years, Samsung followed its strategy largely as planned and by the early 1990s had become the industry leader in DRAMs. Its approach of setting extremely ambitious goals and

▶

then developing detailed plans to be implemented with a relentless discipline, also paid off in the subsequent years. During 1997 and 1998 the industry was hit by a dramatic dip in demand and prices for memory chips. But while some competitors became nervous about short-term profitability and 'adapted' themselves to the unfolding circumstances, slashing capital spending and production capacity, Samsung remained committed to its long-term plans and continued to invest and strengthen its memory chip production operations. When the bust cycle turned into boom again, Samsung was one of the few companies with sufficient DRAM manufacturing capacity to reap the benefit.

Since then, Samsung Electronics has gone from strength to strength, building on its DRAM knowhow. By 2003, it had become world market leader in TFT-LCD screens, computer monitors, VCRs and microwave ovens, and number two in many more areas. The company employs approximately 55 000 people and generates more than US$23 billion in revenues, accounting for about 18% of South Korea's exports. In 1999 the company was spun off from the Samsung conglomerate, with new ambitious plans, targeting yet other chip-based product categories as areas where it wanted to become number one or two, such as cellular telephones and notebook computers. So far, its strategic planning approach has made huge steps in this direction. Samsung has clearly lived up to its name, meaning 'three stars' in Korean, and written with the characters that translate as 'large, strong and lasting forever'.

Sources: *Far Eastern Economic Review,* September 14 2002; Yu, 1999; Haour and Cho, 2000; www.samsung.com.

The strategic incrementalism perspective

To advocates of the strategic incrementalism perspective, the planners' faith in deliberateness is misplaced and counter-productive. In reality, incrementalists argue, new strategies largely emerge over time, as managers proactively piece together a viable course of action or reactively adapt to unfolding circumstances. The strategy formation process is not about rigidly *setting* the course of action in advance, but about flexibly *shaping* the course of action by gradually blending together initiatives into a coherent pattern of actions. Making strategy involves sense-making, reflecting, learning, envisioning, experimenting and changing the organization, which cannot be neatly organized and programmed. Strategy formation is messy, fragmented, and piecemeal – much more like the unstructured and unpredictable processes of exploration and invention than like the orderly processes of design and production (e.g. Mintzberg, 1990a; Quinn, 1978, Reading 3.2).

Yet proponents of the strategic planning perspective prefer to press strategy formation into an orderly, mechanistic straightjacket. Strategies must be intentionally designed and executed. According to strategic incrementalists, this excessive emphasis on deliberateness is due to planners' obsession with rationality and control (e.g. Wildavsky, 1979; Mintzberg, 1993). Planners are often compulsive in their desire for order, predictability and efficiency. It is the intention of strategic planning to predict, analyze, optimize and program – to deliberately fine-tune and control the organization's future behavior. For them, 'to manage' is 'to control' and therefore only deliberate patterns of action constitute good strategic management.

Incrementalists do not question the value of planning and control as a means for managing some organizational processes, but point out that strategy formation is not one of them. In general, planning and control are valuable for routine activities that need to be efficiently organized (e.g. production or finance). But planning is less suitable for nonroutine activities – that is, for doing new things. Planning is not appropriate for innovation (e.g. Hamel, 1996; Kanter, 2002). Just as R&D departments cannot plan the invention of new products, managers cannot plan the development of new strategies. Innovation, whether in products or strategies, is not a process that can be neatly structured and controlled. Novel insights and creative ideas cannot be generated on demand, but surface at unexpected moments, often in unexpected places. Nor are new ideas born full-grown, ready to be evaluated and implemented. In reality, innovation requires brooding, tinkering, experimentation, testing and patience, as new ideas grow and take shape. Throughout the innovation process it remains unclear which ideas might evolve into blockbuster strategies and which will turn out to be miserable disappointments. No one can objectively determine ahead of time which strategic initiatives will 'fly' and which will 'crash'. Therefore, managers engaged in the formation of new strategies must move incrementally, letting novel ideas crystallize over time, and increasing commitment as ideas gradually prove their viability in practice. This demands that managers behave not as planners, but as 'inventors' – searching, experimenting, learning, doubting, and avoiding premature closure and lock-in to one course of action (e.g. Stacey, 1993, Reading 9.2 in this book; Beinhocker, 1999).

Recognizing that strategy formation is essentially an innovation process has more consequences. Innovation is inherently subversive, rebeling against the status quo and challenging those who are emotionally, intellectually or politically wedded to the current state of affairs. Creating new strategies involves confronting people's cognitive maps, questioning the organizational culture, threatening individuals' current interests and disrupting the distribution of power within the organization (e.g. Hamel, 1996; Johnson, 1988). None of these processes can be conducted in an orderly fashion, let alone be incorporated into a planning system. Changing people's cognitive maps requires complex processes of unlearning and learning. Cultural and political changes are also difficult processes to program. Even for the most powerful CEO, managing cognitive, cultural and political changes is not a matter of deliberate control, but of incremental shaping. Less powerful managers will have an even weaker grip on the unfolding cognitive, cultural and political reality in their organization, and therefore will be even less able to plan. In short, managers who understand that strategy formation is essentially a disruptive process of organizational change will move incrementally, gradually molding the organization into a satisfactory form. This demands that managers behave not as commanders, but as 'organizational developers' – questioning assumptions, challenging ideas, getting points on the strategic agenda, encouraging learning, championing new initiatives, supporting change and building political support.

Incrementalists point out that planning is particularly inappropriate when dealing with wicked problems. While solving tame problems can often be planned and controlled, strategizing managers rarely have the luxury of using generic solutions to fix clearly recognizable strategic problems. Strategic problems are inherently wicked – they are essentially unique, highly complex, linked to other problems, can be defined and interpreted in many ways, have no correct answer, nor a delimited set of possible solutions. The planning approach of recognizing the problem, fully analyzing the situation, formulating a comprehensive plan and then implementing the solution, is sure to choke on a wicked problem. A number of weaknesses of planning show up when confronted with a wicked problem:

- Problems cannot be simply recognized and analyzed, but can be interpreted and defined in many ways, depending on how the manager looks at it. Therefore, half the work of the strategizing manager is *making sense* out of complex problems. Or, as Rittel and Webber (1973) put it, the definition of a wicked problem is the problem! Managers must search for new ways for understanding old problems and must be aware of how others are reinterpreting what they see (e.g. Liedtka, 2000; Smircich and Stubbart, 1985). This inhibits strategic planning and encourages strategic incrementalism.

- A full analysis of a wicked problem is impossible. Due to a wicked problem's complexity and links to other problems, a full analysis would take, literally, forever. And there would always be more ways of interpreting the problem, requiring more analysis. Strategic planning based on the complete understanding of a problem in advance there-fore necessarily leads to paralysis by analysis (e.g. Langley, 1995; Lenz and Lyles, 1985). In reality, however, managers move proactively despite their incomplete understanding of a wicked problem, learning as they go along. By acting and thinking at the same time, strategizing managers can focus their analyses on what seems to be important and realistic in practice, gradually shaping their understanding along the way.

- Developing a comprehensive plan to tackle a wicked problem is asking for trouble. Wicked problems are very complex, consisting of many sub-problems. Formulating a master plan to solve all sub-problems in one blow would require a very high level of planning sophistication and an organization with the ability to implement plans in a highly coordinated manner – much like the circus performers who can keep ten plates twirling at the ends of poles at the same time. Such organizations are rare at best, and the risk of a grand strategy failing is huge – once one plate falls, the rest usually come crashing down. This is also known as Knagg's law: the more complex a plan, the larger the chance of failure. Incrementalists therefore argue that it is wiser to tackle sub-problems individually, and gradually blend these solutions into a cohesive pattern of action.

- Planners who believe that formulation and implementation can be separated under-estimate the extent to which wicked problems are interactive. As soon as an organization starts to implement a plan, its actions will induce counteractions. Customers will react, competitors will change behavior, suppliers will take a different stance, regulatory agen-cies might come into action, unions will respond, the stock markets will take notice and company employees will draw conclusions. Hence, action by the organization will change the nature of the problem. And since the many counterparties are intelligent players, capable of acting strategically, their responses will not be entirely predictable. Planners will not be able to forecast and incorporate other parties' reactions into the plans. Therefore, plans will be outdated as soon as implementation starts. For this rea-son, incrementalists argue that action must always be swiftly followed by redefinition of the problem and reconsideration the course of action being pursued. Over time, this iterative process of action–reaction–reconsideration will lead to the emergence of a pattern of action, which is the best possible result given the interactive nature of wicked problems.

- This last point, on the unpredictability of external and internal reactions to a plan, leads up to a weakness of strategic planning that is possibly its most obvious one – strategy has to do with the future and the future is inherently *unknown*. Developments cannot be clearly forecast, future opportunities and threats cannot be predicted, nor can future strengths and weaknesses be accurately foreseen. In such unknown terrain, it is fool-hardy to commit oneself to a preset course of action unless absolutely necessary. It makes much more sense in new and unpredictable circumstances to remain flexible and adaptive, postponing fixed commitments for as long as possible. An unknown future requires not the mentality of a train conductor, but of an explorer – curious, probing, venturesome and entrepreneurial, yet moving cautiously, step-by-step, ready to shift course when needed.

To proponents of the strategic incrementalism perspective, it is a caricature to call such behavior ad hoc or muddling through. Rather, it is behavior that acknowledges the fact that strategy formation is a process of innovation and organizational development in the face of wicked problems in an unknown future. Under these circumstances, strategies must be allowed to emerge and 'strategic planning' must be seen for what it is – a contradiction in terms.

EXHIBIT 3.3 THE STRATEGIC INCREMENTALISM PERSPECTIVE

YOSHINOYA: ONE STORE AT A TIME

Yoshinoya's first east coast outlet opened on Times Square in 2002. Yoshinoya is Japan's answer to McDonald's – fast food Japanese-style. With its 845 outlets across Japan and 171 outlets overseas, mainly in the United States, Yoshinoya may not be as big as McDonald's yet, but its growth is phenomenal and its profitability enough to make Ronald McDonald jealous. In 2001 the company recorded a ¥16.7 billion pre-tax profit. And Yoshinoya still has enormous ambitions. Shuji Abe, president of Yoshinoya, has indicated that he believes that it should be possible to grow to 1200 outlets in Japan and 1000 restaurants abroad by 2006. But, Abe emphasizes, this growth must be realized 'one store at a time' and not on the basis of some pre-set strategic plan.

Yoshinoya was founded in Tokyo in 1899 and became the first fast-food chain in Japan in the 1960s, serving only *gyudon* – a bowl of rice topped with thin-sliced braised beef. The company's slogan has been 'fast, delicious and cheap', and its positioning has been one of stressing the importance of the customer, personal service and quality. But instead of standardizing the fast-food formula and then rolling it out across Japan, Yoshinoya's philosophy has been to avoid a 'cookie-cutter' approach and a rigid expansion blueprint. In Abe's view, such a 'copy-paste' program of expansion would be dangerous, and would make insufficient use of the company's ability to learn, improve and adapt along the way. In the Japanese food service industry, with its many local characteristics and unfolding rules of the game, much still remains to be discovered en route. Hence, Yoshinoya considers ongoing experimentation and innovation crucial, making extensive use of

pilot projects, which are flexibly and rapidly exploited whenever they prove viable. The company has also established a corporate university, Yoshinoya College, partially to secure high operational standards via training, but as a platform for bottom-up innovation and continuous improvement as well. The company slogan of 'one store at a time' is a reflection of Yoshinoya's dedication to grow organically and in a sure-footed manner, building on its emerging insights into where the fast-food business is headed and can be shaped.

Yoshinoya's approach of strategic incrementalism has also worked well for its expansion abroad. Again, Yoshinoya sees internationalization as an ongoing learning process, requiring a pioneering mentality, instead of that of a conqueror, imposing itself on its environment. Yoshinoya gained its first foothold in the US market in Los Angeles in 1979 and gradually expanded towards 96 outlets in California. Along the way, Yoshinoya gradually reshaped its formula to fit the US market circumstances better. For instance, it deviated from the franchise method used in Japan, finding out that fully owned restaurants worked better. Management systems were changed and the company found out what type of local items to add to its menu. Given its success in California, in 2002 Yoshinoya decided that it was time to look for opportunities in the rest of the United States, starting along the east coast.

What Yoshinoya will look like in the coming years might not be entirely certain, but the company has at least determined one clear long-term intention: 'We are reshaping the fast-food experience.' It might be time for the competition to consider a McRice-Bowl as a response.

Sources: *Nation's Restaurant News*, November 8 2002; *The Nikkei Weekly*, November 13 2000; *Financial Times*, December 21 1992; www.yoshinoyausa.com; www.yoshinoya.com/eng.

INTRODUCTION TO THE DEBATE AND READINGS

Those who triumph compute at their headquarters a great number of factors prior to a challenge. Little computation brings defeat. How much more so with no computation at all!

Sun Tzu (5th century BC);
Chinese military strategist

It is a mistake to look too far ahead. Only one link of the chain of destiny can be handled at a time.

Winston Churchill (1874–1965);
British prime minister and writer

So, how should strategies be formed in practice? Should managers strive to formulate and implement strategic plans, supported by a formalized planning and control system? Or should managers move incrementally, behaving as inventors, organizational developers and explorers? As no consensus has yet developed within the field of strategic management on how to balance deliberateness and emergence, it is up to each individual to assess the arguments put forward in the ongoing debate and to form their own opinion.

As an input to the process of assessing the variety of perspectives on this issue, four readings have been selected that each shed their own light on the debate. As in the previous chapter, the first two readings will be representative of the two poles in this debate (see Table 3.1), while the second set of two readings will bring in extra arguments to add further flavor to the discussion.

As opening reading in this debate, 'Managing the Strategy Process', by Balaji Chakravarthy and Peter Lorange, has been selected to represent the strategic planning perspective. Lorange is one of the most well-known writers on the topic of formal planning systems (Lorange, 1980; Lorange and Vancil, 1977) and this reading is taken from the

TABLE 3.1 Strategic planning versus strategic incrementalism perspective

	Strategic planning perspective	*Strategic incrementalism perspective*
Emphasis on	Deliberateness over emergence	Emergence over deliberateness
Nature of strategy	Intentionally designed	Gradually shaped
Nature of formation	Figuring out	Finding out
View of future	Forecast and anticipate	Partially unknown and unpredictable
Posture towards the future	Make commitments, prepare	Postpone commitments, remain flexible
Formation process	Formally structured and comprehensive	Unstructured and fragmented
Formation process steps	First think, then act	Thinking and acting intertwined
Decision-making	Hierarchical	Dispersed
Decision-making focus	Optimal resource allocation and coordination	Experimentation and parallel initiatives
Implementation focused on	Programming (organizational efficiency)	Learning (organizational development)
Strategic change	Implemented top-down	Requires broad cultural and cognitive shifts

1991 textbook he co-authored with Chakravarthy, entitled *Managing the Strategy Process: A Framework for a Multibusiness Firm*. As most proponents of the strategic planning perspective, Chakravarthy and Lorange do not actively defend their assumption that formal planning is beneficial. Rather, basing themselves on this supposition, they concentrate on outlining a framework for effectively structuring strategic planning activities. Their ideal is an extensive strategic planning system, comprised of a number of distinct steps, procedures, mechanisms and roles. However, they go further than only structuring strategic planning. In their view, a formal planning system will not lead to effective strategy formation if it is not linked to other organizational systems. In particular, the strategic planning system needs to interact with the monitoring, control and learning system the incentives system and the staffing system. As such, Chakravarthy and Lorange champion a highly comprehensive and structured approach to strategic planning.

As spokesman for the strategic incrementalism perspective, James Brian Quinn has been chosen. Together with Henry Mintzberg, Quinn has been one of the most influential pioneers on the topic of emergent strategy. Quinn's article, 'Logical Incrementalism', which is reprinted here as Reading 3.2, and his subsequent book *Strategies for Change* (1980), are widely accepted as having been instrumental in developing the strategic incrementalism perspective. In his reading, Quinn explains some of the key shortcomings of formal strategic planning and goes on to make a case for strategic incrementalism. Important in his argumentation is that strategic incrementalism is distinguished from muddling through. Incrementalism is a proactive approach to strategy formation – managers can intentionally choose to let unintended strategies emerge. Muddling through is also incremental in nature, but reactive and ad hoc – improvised decisions are made to deal with unplanned and poorly controllable circumstances. To make this distinction more explicit, Quinn refers to the proactive strain of incremental behavior as 'logical incrementalism'. By 'logical' he means 'reasonable and well-considered'. However, logical incrementalism is not always logical by the definition used in Chapter 2 – incremental behavior is not necessarily 'dictated by formal logic'. Therefore, for the sake of accuracy and clarity, the term strategic incrementalism will be used in this book instead of logical incrementalism.

To complement the arguments brought forward by the first authors, a classic study of strategy formation by Graham Allison has been selected, entitled 'Conceptual Models and Decision-Making' (Reading 3.3). In this article and in his famous 1971 book *The Essence of Decision: Explaining the Cuban Missile Crisis*, Allison examines the organizational decision-making surrounding the Cuban missile crisis in 1962 and comes up with three opposing models for explaining the behavior of the parties involved. His base hypothesis is that people behave rationally and therefore that decision-making is focused on selecting the optimal course of action after a comprehensive analysis. This *rational actor model* largely fits with the rational reasoning and strategic planning perspectives. He carries on to present two other models that explain why suboptimal policies are often pursued. On the one hand, the *organizational process model* suggests that ingrained organizational routines often inhibit rational behavior. On the other hand, the *bureaucratic politics model* describes how conflicting interests and objectives can result in processes of political maneuvering and positioning within an organization. In the context of this chapter, Allison's contribution is to highlight the importance of these behavioral dynamics on strategy formation. These are the sources of inertia and muddling through with which strategists, both planners and incrementalists, have to struggle.

Reading 3.4 is 'From Scenario Thinking to Strategic Action' by Ian Wilson. This article has been selected to bring the important tool of scenario development into the discussion. Both strategic planners and strategic incrementalists agree that strategizing requires managers to think about the future, and scenario development is one of the most often mentioned methods to take a structured approach to such forward thinking. Scenarios are 'plausible descriptions of alternative futures', requiring managers to envision different directions in which the environment and the firm might develop. Much has been written about scenario use in strategy formation processes, although most of the literature comes from business professionals with experience in its application (e.g. Wack, 1985a; Van der Heijden, 1996). Wilson, too, is a scenario veteran, having spent years as strategic planner at General Electric. In this reading, Wilson does not go into all of the technical details of scenario development, but highlights how scenarios can be used to strengthen strategy formation. He argues that scenarios can be used at four levels of sophistication, ranging from a simple strategy evaluation technique to a full-blown method for developing strategic plans. In his view, scenarios are a valuable means for creating strategic plans that avoid the pitfall of trying to predict the future. Working with various scenarios challenges managers to formulate strategies that are *resilient* (i.e. 'robust') – that fit a variety of future conditions. For proponents of the strategic planning perspective this probably sounds like an excellent refinement of their approach. To strategic incrementalists, however, scenario thinking sounds more like a useful way to assist in mental experimentation and for uncovering cognitive maps (e.g. De Geus, 1988) than as a convincing argument to plan.

Managing the strategy process

By Balaji Chakravarthy and Peter Lorange[1]

There are five distinct steps in the strategy process (see Figure 3.1.1). The first three steps involve the strategic planning system; the final two steps cover the role of the monitoring, control, and learning system and the incentives and staffing systems, respectively.

The strategic planning system

The purpose of the first step in the planning system, *objectives setting*, is to determine a strategic direction for the firm and each of its divisions and business units. Objectives setting calls for an open-ended reassessment of the firm's business environments and its strengths in dealing with these environments. At the conclusion of this step, there should be agreement at all levels of the organization on the goals that should be pursued and the strategies that will be needed to meet them. It is worth differentiating here between objectives and goals. Objectives refer to the strategic intent of the firm in the long run. Goals, on the other hand, are more specific statements of the achievements targeted for certain deadlines – goals can be accomplished, and when that happens the firm moves closer to meeting its objectives. Objectives represent a more enduring challenge.

FIGURE 3.1.1 The strategy process

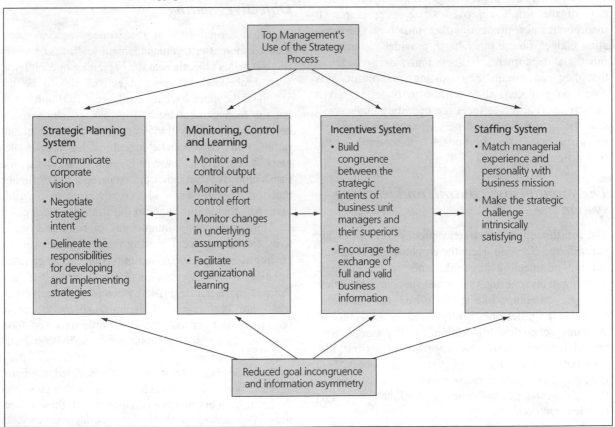

[1]Source: This article was adapted from Chapter 1 of B.S. Chakravarty and P. Lorange, *Managing the Strategy Process: A Framework for a Multibusiness Firm,* © 1991, reprinted by permission of Pearson Education, Inc., Upper Saddle River, NJ.

The second step, *strategic programming*, develops the strategies identified in the first step and defines the cross-functional programs that will be needed to implement the chosen strategies. Cross-functional cooperation is essential to this step. At the end of the strategic programming step a long-term financial plan is drawn up for the firm as a whole and each of its divisions, business units, and functions. On top of the financial projections from existing operations, the long-term financial plan overlays both the expenditures and revenues associated with the approved strategic programs of an organizational unit. The time horizon for these financial plans is chosen to cover the typical lead times that are required to implement the firm's strategic programs. A five-year financial plan is, however, very common. The purpose of the five-year financial plan is to ensure that the approved strategic programs can be funded through either the firm's internally generated resources or externally financed resources.

The third step, *budgeting*, defines both the strategic and operating budgets of the firm. The strategic budget helps identify the contributions that the firm's functional departments, business units, and divisions will be expected to make in a given fiscal year in support of the firm's approved strategic programs. It incorporates new product/market initiatives. The operating budget, on the other hand, provides resources to functional departments, business units, and divisions so that they can sustain their existing momentum. It is based on projected short-term activity levels, given past trends. Failure to meet the operating budget will hurt the firm's short-term performance, whereas failure to meet the strategic budget will compromise the firm's future.

The monitoring, control, and learning system

The fourth step in the strategy process is *monitoring, control, and learning*. Here the emphasis is not on output but on meeting key milestones in the strategic budget and on adhering to planned spending schedules. Strategic programs, like strategic budgets, are monitored for the milestones reached and for adherence to spending schedules. In addition, the key assumptions underlying these programs are validated periodically. As a natural extension to this validation process, even the agreed-on goals at various levels are reassessed in the light of changes to the resources of the firm and its business environment.

The incentives and staffing systems

The fifth and final step in the strategy process is *incentives and staffing*. One part of this is the award of incentives as contracted to the firm's managers. If the incentives system is perceived to have failed in inducing the desired performance, redesigning the incentives system and reassessing the staffing of key managerial positions are considered at this step.

Linking organizational levels and steps in strategic planning

An effective strategy process must allow for interactions between the organizational levels and iterations between the process steps. Figure 3.1.2 describes some of the interactions and iterations in the strategic planning steps. The formal interactions in the process are shown in the figure by the solid line that weaves up and down through the organizational levels and across the three steps. The informal interactions that complement the formal interactions are shown by dotted loops.

Objectives setting

The first formal step of the strategy process commences soon after top management reaffirms or modifies the firm's objectives at the beginning of each fiscal year. Embedded in these objectives should be the vision of the chief executive officer (CEO) and his or her top management team. Top management's vision helps specify what will make the firm great. An elaboration of this vision can be done through a formal statement of objectives. However, it is not the formality of a firm's objectives but rather the excitement and challenge that top management's vision can bring to a firm's managers that is important to the strategy process.

Along with its communication of corporate objectives, top management must provide a forecast on key environmental factors. Assumptions on exchange rates, inflation, and other economic factors – as well as projections on the political risks associated with each country – are best compiled centrally so as to ensure objectivity and consistency. These objectives and forecasts are then discussed with a firm's divisional and business unit managers.

Once the corporate objectives are decided, top management negotiates, for each division and business unit in the firm, goals that are consistent with these objectives. The nature of these negotiations can vary. In some firms, top management may wish to set goals in a top-down fashion; in others, it may invite subordinate

FIGURE 3.1.2   Steps in the strategy process

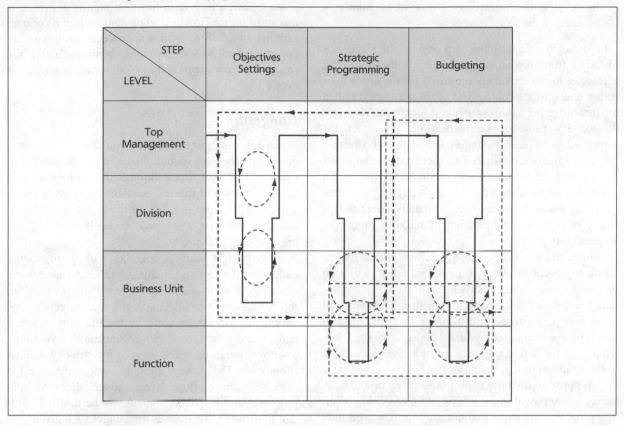

managers to participate in the goal-setting process. Managers are encouraged to examine new strategies and modify existing ones in order to accomplish their goals. The proposed strategies are approved at each higher level in the organizational hierarchy, then eventually by top management. Top management tries to make certain that the strategies as proposed are consistent with the firm's objectives and can be supported with the resources available to the firm. Modifications, where necessary, are made to the objectives, goals, and strategies in order to bring them in alignment. Another important outcome of the objectives-setting step is to build a common understanding across the firm's managerial hierarchy of the goals and strategies that are intended for each organizational unit.

The objectives-setting step in Figure 3.1.2 does not include the functional departments. As we observed earlier, the primary role of these departments is a supporting one. They do not have a profit or growth responsibility, and their goals cannot be decided until the second step, when strategic programs in support of approved business unit goals begin to be formed. It is not uncommon, however, for key functional managers to be invited to participate in the objectives-setting step

either as experts in a corporate task force or, more informally, as participants in the deliberations that are held at the business unit level.

It is important that divisional proposals be evaluated on an overall basis as elements of a corporate portfolio and not reviewed in a sequential mode. In the latter case, the resulting overall balance in the corporate portfolio would be more or less incidental, representing the accumulated sum of individual approvals. It makes little sense to attempt to judge in isolation whether a particular business family or business strategy is attractive to the corporate portfolio. That will depend on a strategy's fit with the rest of the portfolio and on the competing investment opportunities available to the firm in its business portfolio.

Strategic programming

The second step in the process has two purposes:

1 To forge an agreement between divisional, business unit, and functional managers on the strategic programs that have to be implemented over the next few years.

2 To deepen the involvement of functional managers in developing the strategies that were tentatively selected in the first step.

The strategic programming step begins with a communication from top management about the goals and strategies that were finally approved for the firm's divisions and business units. The divisonal manager then invites his or her business unit and functional managers to identify program alternatives in support of the approved goals and strategies. Examples of strategic programs include increasing market share for an existing product, introducing a new product, and launching a joint marketing campaign for a family of divisional products. As in these examples, a strategic program typically requires the cooperation of multiple functional departments.

However, the functional specialties within a firm often represent different professional cultures that do not necessarily blend easily. Further, day-to-day operating tasks can be so demanding that the functional managers may simply find it difficult to participate in the time-consuming cross-functional teamwork. A key challenge for both divisional and business managers is to bring about this interaction.

The proposed strategic programs travel up the hierarchy for approval at each level. At the division level, the programs are evaluated not only for how well they support the approved strategies but also for how they promote synergies within the firm. Synergies can come from two sources: through economies of scale and/or economies of scope. The creation of synergies based on economies of scale calls for a sharing of common functional activities – such as research and development (R&D), raw materials procurement, production, and distribution – so as to spread over a larger volume the overhead costs associated with these functions. The creation of economies of scope, on the other hand, requires a common approach to the market. Examples of such an approach include the development of a common trademark, the development of products/services that have a complementary appeal to a customer group, and the ability to offer a common regional service organization for the firm's diverse businesses.

At the corporate level, the proposed strategic programs provide an estimate of the resources that will be required to support the divisional and business unit goals. These goals, as well as their supporting strategies, are once again reassessed; and where needed, modifica-tions are sought in the proposed strategic programs. As noted earlier, a long-term financial plan is drawn up at this stage for the firm as a whole and each of its organizational units. The approved strategic programs are communicated to the divisions, business units, and functional departments at the beginning of the budgeting cycle.

Budgeting

When top management decides on the strategic programs that the firm should pursue, it has de facto allocated all of the firm's human, technological, and financial resources that are available for internal development. This allocation influences the strategic budgets that may be requested at each level in the organizational hierarchy.

The strategic budgets, together with the operating budgets of the various organizational units, are consolidated and sent up for top management approval. When top management finally approves the budgets of the various organizational units, before the start of a new budget year, it brings to a close what can be a year-long journey through the three steps of the strategy-making subprocess. The strategy implementation subprocess is then set into motion. Even though the two subprocesses are described sequentially here, it is important to mention that even as the budget for a given year is being formed, the one for the prior year will be under implementation. Midcourse corrections to the prior year's budget can have an impact on the formulation of the current budget.

If the actual accomplishments fall short of the strategic budget, in particular, the negative variance may suggest that the firm's managers failed to implement its chosen strategy efficiently. But it can also suggest that the strategic programs that drive this budget may have been ill conceived or even that the goals underlying these programs may have been specified incorrectly. The monitoring, control, and learning system provides continuous information on both the appropriateness of a strategic budget and the efficiency with which the budget is implemented. This information, based on the implementation of the prior year's strategic budget, can trigger another set of iterations between the three strategy-making steps, calling into question the goals and strategies on which the current year's budget are based. These iterations are shown by the dotted rectangles in Figure 3.1.2.

Logical incrementalism

By James Quinn[1]

When I was younger I always conceived of a room where all these [strategic] concepts were worked out for the whole company. Later I didn't find any such room . . . . The strategy [of the company] may not even exist in the mind of one man. I certainly don't know where it is written down. It is simply transmitted in the series of decisions made.

Interview quote

Introduction

When well-managed major organizations make significant changes in strategy, the approaches they use frequently bear little resemblance to the rational-analytical systems so often touted in the planning literature. The full strategy is rarely written down in any one place. The processes used to arrive at the total strategy are typically fragmented, evolutionary, and largely intuitive. Although one can usually find embedded in these fragments some very refined pieces of formal strategic analysis, the real strategy tends to evolve as internal decisions and external events flow together to create a new, widely shared consensus for action among key members of the top management team. Far from being an abrogation of good management practice, the rationale behind this kind of strategy formulation is so powerful that it perhaps provides the normative model for strategic decision making, rather than the step-by-step 'formal systems planning' approach so often espoused.

The formal systems planning approach

A strong normative literature states what factors should be included in a systematically planned strategy and how to analyze and relate these factors step-by-step. The main elements of this 'formal' planning approach include:

- analyzing one's own internal situation: strengths, weaknesses, competencies, problems;
- projecting current product lines, profits, sales, investment needs into the future;
- analyzing selected external environments and opponents' actions for opportunities and threats;
- establishing broad goals as targets for subordinate groups' plans;
- identifying the gap between expected and desired results;
- communicating planning assumptions to the divisions;
- requesting proposed plans from subordinate groups with more specific target goals, resource needs, and supporting action plans;
- occasionally asking for special studies of alternatives, contingencies, or longer-term opportunities;
- reviewing and approving divisional plans and summing these for corporate needs;
- developing long-term budgets presumably related to plans;
- implementing plans;
- monitoring and evaluating performance (presumably against plans, but usually against budgets).

While this approach is excellent for some purposes, it tends to focus unduly on measurable quantitative factors and to underemphasize the vital qualitative, organizational, and power-behavioral factors that so often determine strategic success in one situation versus another. In practice, such planning is just one building block in a continuous stream of events that really determine corporate strategy.

The power-behavioral approach

Other investigators have provided important insights on the crucial psychological, power, and behavioral relationships in strategy formulation. Among other

[1] Source: This article was originally published as 'Strategic Change: Logical Incrementalism' in *Sloan Management Review*, Fall, 1978, pp. 7–21. Reproduced by permission.

things, these have enhanced understanding about: the multiple goal structures of organizations, the politics of strategic decisions, executive bargaining and negotiation processes, 'satisficing' (as opposed to maximizing) in decision making, the role of coalitions in strategic management, and the practice of 'muddling' in the public sphere. Unfortunately, however, many power-behavioral studies have been conducted in settings far removed from the realities of strategy formulation. Others have concentrated solely on human dynamics, power relationships, and organizational processes and ignored the ways in which systematic data analysis shapes and often dominates crucial aspects of strategic decisions. Finally, a few have offered much normative guidance for the strategist.

The study

Recognizing the contributions and limitations of both approaches, I attempted to document the dynamics of actual strategic change processes in some 10 major companies as perceived by those most knowledgeably and intimately involved in them. Several important findings have begun to emerge from these investigations:

- Neither the power-behavioral nor the formal systems planning paradigm adequately characterizes the way successful strategic processes operate.
- Effective strategies tend to emerge from a series of 'strategic subsystems,' each of which attacks a specific class of strategic issue (e.g. acquisitions, divestitures, or major reorganizations) in a disciplined way, but which blends incrementally and opportunistically into a cohesive pattern that becomes the company's strategy.
- The logic behind each subsystem is so powerful that to some extent it may serve as a normative approach for formulating these key elements of strategy in large companies.
- Because of cognitive and process limits, almost all of these subsystems – and the formal planning activity itself – must be managed and linked together by an approach best described as logical incrementalism.
- Such incrementalism is not muddling. It is a purposeful, effective, proactive management technique for improving and integrating both the analytical and behavioral aspects of strategy formulation.

This article will document these findings, suggest the logic behind several important subsystems for strat-

egy formulation, and outline some of the management and thought processes executives in large organizations use to synthesize them into effective corporate strategies. Such strategies embrace those patterns of high-leverage decisions (on major goals, policies, and action sequences) that affect the viability and direction of the entire enterprise or determine its competitive posture for an extended time period.

Critical strategic issues

Although certain 'hard data' decisions (e.g. on product-market position or resource allocations) tend to dominate the analytical literature, executives identified other 'soft' changes that have at least as much importance in shaping their concern's strategic posture. Most often cited were changes in the company's

- overall organizational structure or its basic management style;
- relationships with the government or other external interest groups;
- acquisition, divestiture, or divisional control practices;
- international posture and relationships;
- innovative capabilities or personnel motivations as affected by growth;
- worker and professional relationships reflecting changed social expectations and values;
- past or anticipated technological environments.

When executives were asked to 'describe the processes through which their company arrived at its new posture' *vis-à-vis* each of these critical domains, several important points emerged. First, a few of these issues lent themselves to quantitative modeling techniques or perhaps even formal financial analyses. Second, successful companies used a different subsystem to formulate strategy for each major class of strategic issues, yet these subsystems were quite similar among companies even in very different industries. Finally, no single formal analytical process could handle all strategic variables simultaneously on a planned basis. Why?

Precipitating events

Often external or internal events over which managements had essentially no control would precipitate urgent, piecemeal, interim decisions that inexorably shaped the company's future strategic posture. One clearly observes this phenomenon in the decisions forced on General Motors by the 1973–74 oil crisis; the shift in posture pressed upon Exxon by sudden nationalizations; or the dramatic opportunities allowed for Haloid Corporation and Pilkington Brothers Ltd by the unexpected inventions of xerography and float glass.

In these cases, analyses from earlier formal planning cycles did contribute greatly, as long as the general nature of the contingency had been anticiapted. They broadened the information base available (as in Exxon's case), extended the options considered (Haloid-Xerox), created shared values to guide decisions about precipitating events in consistent directions (Pilkington), or built up resource bases, management flexibilities, or active search routines for opportunities whose specific nature could not be defined in advance (General Mills, Pillsbury). But no organization – no matter how brilliant, rational, or imaginative – could possibly foresee the timing, severity, or even the nature of all such precipitating events. Further, when these events did occur there might be neither time, resources, nor information enough to undertake a full formal strategic analysis of all possible options and their consequences. Yet early decisions made under stress conditions often meant new thrusts, precedents, or lost opportunities that were difficult to reverse later.

An incremental logic

Recognizing this, top executives usually consciously tried to deal with precipitating events in an incremental fashion. Early commitments were kept broadly formative, tentative, and subject to later review. In some cases neither the company nor the external players could understand the full implications of alternative actions. All parties wanted to test assumptions and have an opportunity to learn from and adapt to the others' responses. For example: Neither the potential producer nor user of a completely new product or process (like xerography or float glass) could fully conceptualize its ramifications without interactive testing. All parties benefited from procedures that purposely delayed decisions and allowed mutual feedback. Some companies, like IBM or Xerox, have formalized this concept into 'phase program planning' systems. They make concrete decisions only on individual phases (or stages) of new product developments, establish interactive testing procedures with customers, and postpone final configuration commitments until the latest possible moment.

Similarly, even under pressure, most top executives were extremely sensitive to organizational and power relationships and consciously mananged decision processes to improve these dynamics. They often purposely delayed initial decisions, or kept such decisions vague, in order to encourage lower-level participation, to gain more information from specialists, or to build commitment to solutions. Even when a crisis atmosphere tended to shorten time horizons and make decisions more goal oriented than political, perceptive executives consciously tried to keep their options open until they understood how the crisis would affect the power bases and needs of their key constituents.

Incrementalism in strategic subsystems

One also finds that an incremental logic applies in attacking many of the critical subsystems of corporate strategy. Those subsystems for considering diversification moves, divestitures, major reorganizations, or government-external relations are typical and will be described here. In each case conscious incrementalism helps to

1   cope with both the cognitive and process limits on each major decision;
2   build the logical-analytical framework these decisions require;
3   create the personal and organizational awareness, understanding, acceptance, and commitment needed to implement the strategies effectively.

The diversification subsystem

Strategies for diversification, either through research and development (R&D) or acquisitions, provide excellent examples. The formal analytical steps needed for successful diversification are well documented. However, the precise directions that R&D may project the company can only be understood step-by-step as scientists uncover new phenomena, make and amplify discoveries, build prototypes, reduce concepts to practice, and interact with users during product introductions. Similarly, only as each acquisition is sequentially identified, investigated, negotiatcd for, and integrated into the organization can one predict its ultimate impact on the total enterprise.

A step-by-step approach is clearly necessary to guide and assess the strategic fit of each internal or external diversification candidate. Incremental processes are also required to manage the crucial psychological and power shifts that ultimately determine the program's overall direction and consequences. These processes help unify both the analytical and behavioral aspects of diversification decisions. They create the broad conceptual consensus, the risk-taking attitudes, the organizational and resource flexibilities, and the adaptive dynamism that determine both the timing and direction of diversification strategies. Most important among these processes are:

- Generating a genuine, top-level psychological commitment to diversification. General Mills, Pillsbury, and Xerox all started their major diversification programs with broad analytical studies and goal-setting exercises designed both to build top-level consensus around the need to diversify and to establish the general directions for diversification. Without such action, top-level bargaining for resources would have continued to support only more familiar (and hence apparently less risky) old lines, and this could delay or undermine the entire diversification endeavor.

- Consciously preparing to move opportunistically. Organizational and fiscal resources must be built up in advance to exploit candidates as they randomly appear. And a 'credible activist' for ventures must be developed and backed by someone with commitment power. All successful acquirers created the potential for profit centered divisions within their organizational structures, strengthened their financial-controllership capabilities, took action to create low-cost capital access, and maintained the shortest possible communication lines from the acquisitions activist to the resource-committing authority. All these actions integrally determined which diversifications actually could be made, the timing of their accession, and the pace at which they could be absorbed.

- Building a 'comfort factor' for risk taking. Perceived risk is largely a function of one's knowledge about a field. Hence well-conceived diversification programs should anticipate a trial-and-error period during which top managers reject early proposed fields or opportunities until they have analyzed enough trial candidates to 'become comfortable' with an initial selection. Early successes tend to be 'sure things' close to the companies' past (real or supposed) expertise. After a few successful diversifications, managements tend to become more confident and accept other candidates – farther from traditional lines – at a faster rate. Again, the way this process is handled affects both the direction and pace of the actual program.

- Developing a new ethos. If new divisions are more successful than the old – as they should be – they attract relatively more resources and their political power grows. Their most effective line managers move into corporate positions, and slowly the company's special competency and ethos change. Finally, the concepts and products that once dominated the company's culture may decline in importance or even disappear. Acknowledging these ultimate consequences to the organization at the beginning of a diversification program would clearly be impolitic, even if the manager both desired and could predict the probable new ethos. These factors must be handled adaptively, as opportunities present themselves and as individual leaders and power centers develop.

Each of the above processes interacts with all others (and with the random appearance of diversification candidates) to affect action sequences, elapsed time, and ultimate results in unexpected ways. Complexities are so great that few diversification programs end up as initially envisioned. Consequently, wise managers recognize the limits to systematic analysis in diversification, and use formal planning to build the 'comfort levels' executives need for risk taking and to guide the program's early directions and priorities. They then modify these flexibly, step-by-step, as new opportunities, power centers, and developed competencies merge to create new potentials.

The divestiture subsystem

Similar practices govern the handling of divestitures. Divisions often drag along in a less-than-desired condition for years before they can be strategically divested. In some cases, ailing divisions might have just enough yield or potential to offer hoped-for viability. In others, they might represent the company's vital core from earlier years, the creations of a powerful person nearing retirement, or the psychological touchstones of the company's past traditions.

Again, in designing divestiture strategies, top executives had to reinforce vaguely felt concerns with detailed data, build up managers' comfort levels about issues, achieve participation in and commitment to decisions, and move opportunistically to make actual changes. In many cases, the precise nature of the decision was not clear at the outset. Executives often made seemingly unrelated personnel shifts or appointments that changed the value set of critical groups, or started a series of staff studies that generated awareness or acceptance of a potential problem. They might then instigate goal assessment, business review, or 'planning' programs to provide broader forums for discussion and a wider consensus for action. Even then they might wait for a crisis, a crucial retirement, or an attractive sale opportunity to determine the timing and conditions of divestiture. In some cases, decisions could be direct and analytical. But when divestitures involved the psychological centers of the organization, the process had to be much more oblique and carefully orchestrated.

The major reorganization subsystem

It is well recognized that major organizational changes are an integral part of strategy. Sometimes they constitute a strategy themselves, sometimes they precede and/or precipitate a new strategy, and sometimes they help to implement a strategy. However, like many other important strategic decisions, macro-organizational moves are typically handled incrementally and outside of formal planning processes. Their effects on personal or power relationships preclude discussion in open forums and reports of such processes.

In addition, major organizational changes have timing imperatives (or 'process limits') all their own. In making any significant shifts, executives must think through the new roles, capabilities, and probable individual reactions of the many principals affected. They may have to wait for the promotion or retirement of a valued colleague before consummating any change. They then frequently have to bring in, train, or test new people for substantial periods before they can staff key posts with confidence. During this testing period they may substantially modify their original concept of the reorganization, as they evaluate individuals' potentials, their performance in specific roles, their personal drives, and their relationships with other team members.

Because this chain of decisions affects the career development, power, affluence, and self-image of so many, executives tend to keep close counsel in their discussions, negotiate individually with key people, and make final commitments as late as possible in order to obtain the best matches between people's capabilities, personalities, and aspirations and their new roles. Typically, all these events do not come together at one convenient time, particularly the moment annual plans are due. Instead executives move opportunistically, step-by-step, selectively moving people toward a broadly conceived organizational goal, which is constantly modified and rarely articulated in detail until the last pieces fit together.

The government-external relations subsystem

Almost all companies cited government and other external activist groups as among the most important forces causing significant changes in their strategic postures during the periods examined. However, when asked 'How did your company arrive at its own strategy vis-à-vis these forces?' it became clear that few companies had cohesive strategies (integrated sets of goals, policies, and programs) for government-external relations, other than lobbying for or against specific legislative actions. To the extent that other strategies did exist, they were piecemeal, *ad hoc* and had been derived in a very evolutionary manner. Yet there seemed to be very good reasons for such incrementalism. The following are two of the best short explanations of the way these practices develop:

> We are a very large company, and we understand that any massive overt action on our part could easily create more public antagonism than support for our viewpoint. It is also hard to say in advance exactly what public response any particular action might create. So we tend to test a number of different approaches on a small scale with only limited or local company identification. If one approach works, we'll test it further and amplify its use. If another bombs, we try to keep it from being used again. Slowly we find a series of advertising, public relations, community relations actions that seem to help. Then along comes another issue and we start all over again. Gradually the successful approaches merge into a pattern of actions that becomes our strategy.

> I [the president] start conversations with a number of knowledgeable people . . . I collect articles and talk to people about how things get done in Washington in this particular field. I collect data from any reasonable source. I begin wide-ranging discussions with people inside and outside the corporation. From these a pattern eventually emerges. It's like fitting together a jigsaw puzzle. At first the vague outline of an approach appears like the sail of a ship in a puzzle. Then suddenly the rest of the puzzle becomes quite clear. You wonder why you didn't see it all along. And once it's crystallized, it's not difficult to explain to others.

In this realm, uncontrollable forces dominate. Data are very soft, often can be only subjectively sensed, and may be costly to quantify. The possible responses of individuals and groups to different stimuli are difficult to determine in advance. The number of potential opponents with power is very high, and the diversity in their viewpoints and possible modes of attack is so substantial that it is physically impossible to lay out probabilistic decision diagrams that would have much meaning. Results are unpredictable and error costs extreme. Even the best intended and most rational-seeming strategies can be converted into disasters unless they are thoroughly and interactively tested.

Formal planning in corporate strategy

What role do classical formal planning techniques play in strategy formulation? All companies in the sample do have formal planning procedures embedded in their management direction and control systems. These serve certain essential functions. In a process sense, they

- provide a discipline forcing managers to take a careful look ahead periodically;
- require rigorous communications about goals, strategic issues, and resource allocations;
- stimulate longer-term analyses than would otherwise be made;
- generate a basis for evaluating and integrating short-term plans;
- lengthen time horizons and protect long-term investments such as R&D;
- create a psychological backdrop and an information framework about the future against which managers can calibrate short-term or interim decisions.

In a decision-making sense, they

- fine-tune annual commitments;
- formalize cost-reduction programs;
- help implement strategic changes once decided on (for example, coordinating all elements of Exxon's decision to change its corporate name).

Formal plans also 'increment'

Although individual staff planners were often effective in identifying potential problems and bringing them to top management's attention, the annual planning process itself was rarely (if ever) the initiating source of really new key issues or radical departures into new product/market realms. These almost always came from precipitating events, special studies, or conceptions implanted through the kinds of 'logical incremental' processes described above.

In fact, formal planning practices actually institutionalize incrementalism. There are two reasons for this. First, in order to utilize specialized expertise and to obtain executive involvement and commitment, most planning occurs from the bottom up in response to broadly defined assumptions or goals, many of which are longstanding or negotiated well in advance. Of necessity, lower-level groups have only a partial view of the corporation's total strategy, and command only a fragment of its resources. Their power bases, identity, expertise, and rewards also usually depend on their existing products or processes. Hence, these products or processes, rather than entirely new departures, should and do receive their primary attention. Second, most managements purposely design their plans to be 'living' or 'evergreen.' They are intended only as frameworks to guide and provide consistency for future decisions made incrementally. To act otherwise would be to deny that further information could have a value. Thus, properly formulated formal plans are also a part of an incremental logic.

Special studies

Formal planning was most successful in stimulating significant change when it was set up as a special study on some important aspect of corporate strategy. For example, when it became apparent that Pilkington's new float glass process would work, the company formed a Directors' Float Glass Committee consisting of all internal directors associated with float glass 'to consider the broad issues of float glass [strategy] in both the present and the future.' The committee did not attempt detailed plans. Instead, it tried to deal in broad concepts, identify alternate routes, and think through the potential consequences of each route some 10 years ahead. Of some of the key strategic decisions it was later remarked, 'It would be difficult to identify an exact moment when the decision was made... Nevertheless, over a period of time a consensus crystallized with great clarity.'

Such special strategic studies represent a subsystem of strategy formulation distinct from both annual planning activities and the other subsystems exemplified above. Each of these develops some important aspect of strategy, incrementally blending its conclusions with those of other subsystems, and it would be virtually impossible to force all these together to crystallize a completely articulated corporate strategy at any one instant.

Total posture planning

Occasionally, however, managements do attempt very broad assessments of their companies' total posture. Shortly after becoming CEO of General Mills, James McFarland decided that his job was 'to take a very good company and move it to greatness,' but that it was up to his management group, not himself alone, to decide what a great company was and how to get there. Consequently he took some 35 of the company's topmost managers away for a three-day management retreat. On the first day, after agreeing to broad financial goals, the group broke up into units of six to eight people. Each unit was to answer the question 'What is a great company?' from the viewpoints of stockholders, employees, suppliers, the public, and society. Each unit reported back at the end of the day, and the whole group tried to reach a consensus through discussion.

On the second day the groups, in the same format, assessed the company's strengths and weaknesses relative to the defined posture of 'greatness.' The third day focused on how to overcome the company's weaknesses and move it toward a great company. This broad consensus led, over the next several years, to the surveys of fields for acquisition, the building of management's initial comfort levels with certain fields, and the acquisition-divestiture strategy that characterized the McFarland era at General Mills.

Yet even such a major endeavor is only a portion of a total strategic process. Values that had been built up over decades stimulated or constrained alternatives. Precipitating events, acquisitions, divestitures, external relations, and organizational changes developed important segments of each strategy incrementally. Even the strategies articulated left key elements to be defined as new information became available, polities permitted, or particular opportunities appeared. Major product thrusts proved unsuccessful. Actual strategies therefore evolved as each company overextended, consolidated, made errors, and rebalanced various thrusts over time. And it was both logical and expected that this would be the case.

Logical incrementalism

All of the above suggest that strategic decisions do not lend themselves to aggregation into a single massive decision matrix where all factors can be treated relatively simultaneously in order to arrive at a holistic optimum. Many have spoken of the cognitive limits that prevent this. Of equal importance are the process limits – that is, the timing and sequencing imperatives necessary to create awareness, build comfort levels, develop consensus, select and train people, and so forth – that constrain the system yet ultimately determine the decision itself. Unlike the preparation of a fine banquet, it is virtually impossible for the manager to orchestrate all internal decisions, external environmental events, behavioral and power relationships, technical and informational needs, and actions of intelligent opponents so that they come together at any precise moment.

Can the process be managed?

Instead, executives usually deal with the logic of each subsystem of strategy formulation largely on its own merits and usually with a different subset of people. They try to develop or maintain in their own minds a consistent pattern among the decisions made in each subsystem. Knowing their own limitations and the unknowability of the events they face, they consciously try to tap the minds and psychic drives of others. They often purposely keep questions broad and decisions vague in early stages to avoid creating undue rigidities and to stimulate others' creativity. Logic, of course, dictates that they make final commitments *as late as possible* consistent with the information they have.

Consequently, many successful executives will initially set only broad goals and policies that can accommodate a variety of specific proposals from below, yet give a sense of guidance to the proposers. As they come forward the proposals automatically and beneficially attract the support and identity of their sponsors. Being only proposals, the executives can treat these at less politically charged levels, as specific projects rather than as larger goal or policy precedents. Therefore, they can encourage, discourage, or kill alternatives with considerably less political exposure. As events and opportunities emerge, they can incrementally guide the pattern of escalated or accepted proposals to suit their own purposes without getting prematurely committed to a rigid solution set that unpredictable events might prove wrong or that opponents find sufficiently threatening to coalesce against.

A strategy emerges

Successful executives link together and bring order to a series of strategic processes and decisions spanning years. At the beginning of the process it is literally impossible to predict all the events and forces that will shape the future of the company. The best executives can do is to forecast the forces most likely to impinge on the company's affairs and the ranges of their possible impact. They then attempt to build a resource base and a corporate posture so strong in selected areas that the enterprise can survive and prosper despite all but the most devastating events. They consciously select market/technological/product segments the concern can dominate given its resource limits, and place some side bets in order to decrease the risk of catastrophic failure or to increase the company's flexibility for future options.

They then proceed incrementally to handle urgent matters, start longer-term sequences whose specific future branches and consequences are perhaps murky, respond to unforeseen events as they occur, build on successes, and brace up or cut losses on failures. They constantly reassess the future, find new congruencies as events unfurl, and blend the organization's skills and resources into new balances of dominance and risk aversion as various forces intersect to suggest better – but never perfect – alignments. The process is dynamic, with neither a real beginning nor end.

Strategy deals with the unknowable, not the uncertain. It involves forces of such great number, strength, and combinatory powers that one cannot predict events in a probabilistic sense. Hence logic dictates that one proceed flexibly and experimentally from broad concepts toward specific commitments, making the latter concrete as late as possible in order to narrow the bands of uncertainty and to benefit from the best available information. This is the process of logical incrementalism.

READING 3.3

Conceptual models and decision-making

By Graham Allison[1]

This study proceeds from the premise that marked improvement in our understanding of such events depends critically on more self-consciousness about what observers bring to the analysis. What each analyst sees and judges to be important is a function not only of the evidence about what happened but also of the 'conceptual lenses' through which he looks at the evidence. The principal purpose of this paper is to explore some of the fundamental assumptions and categories employed by analysts in thinking about problems of governmental behavior, especially in foreign and military affairs. The general argument can be summarized in three propositions:

1 Analysts think about problems of foreign and military policy in terms of largely implicit conceptual models that have significant consequences for the content of their thought. Clusters of related assumptions constitute basic frames of reference or conceptual models in terms of which analysts both ask and answer the questions: What happened? Why did the event happen? What will happen? Such assumptions are central to the activities of explanation and prediction, for in attempting to explain a particular event, the analyst cannot simply describe the full state of the world leading up to that event. The logic explanation requires that he single out the relevant, important determinants of the occurrence. Moreover, as the logic of prediction underscores, the analyst must summarize the various determinants as they bear on the event in question. Conceptual models both fix the mesh of the nets that the analyst drags through the material in order to explain a particular action of decision and direct him to cast his net in select ponds, at certain depths, in order to catch the fish he is after.

2 Most analysts explain (and predict) the behavior of national governments in terms of various forms of one basic conceptual model, here entitled the Rational Policy Model (Model I). In terms of this conceptual model, analysts attempt to understand happenings as the more or less purposive acts of unified national governments. For these analysts,

[1] Source: This article was adapted from 'Conceptual Models and the Cuban Missile Crisis', *The American Political Science Review*, No. 3, September 1969, pp. 689–718. Permission applied for.

the point of an explanation is to show how the nation or government could have chosen the action in question, given the strategic problem that it faced.

3 Two 'alternative' conceptual models, here labeled an Organizational Process Model (Model II) and a Bureaucratic Politics Model (Model III) provide a base for improved explanation and prediction. Although the standard frame of reference has proved useful for many purposes, there is powerful evidence that it must be supplemented, if not supplanted, by frames of reference which focus upon the large organizations and political actors involved in the policy process. Model I's implication that important events have important causes, i.e. that monoliths perform large actions for big reasons, must be balanced by an appreciation of the facts (a) that monoliths are black boxes covering several gears and levers in a highly differentiated decision-making structure, and (b) that large acts are the consequences of innumerable and often conflicting smaller actions by individuals at various levels of bureaucratic organizations in the service of a variety of only partially compatible conceptions of national goals, organizational goals, and political objectives. Recent developments in the field of organization theory provide the foundation for the second model, what Model I categorizes as 'acts' and 'choices' are instead outputs of large organizations functioning according to certain regular patterns of behavior. The third model focuses on the internal politics of a government. Happenings in foreign affairs are understood, according to the bureaucratic politics model, neither as choices nor as outputs. Instead, what happens is categorized as outcomes of various overlapping bargaining games among players arranged hierarchically in the national government. A Model III analyst displays the perceptions, motivations, positions, power, and maneuvers of principal players from which the outcome emerged.

A central metaphor illuminates differences among these models. Foreign policy has often been compared to moves, sequences of moves, and games of chess. If one were limited to observations on a screen upon which moves in the chess game were projected without information as to how the pieces came to be moved, one would assume – as Model I does – that an individual chess player was moving the pieces with reference to plans and maneuvers toward the goal of winning the game. But a pattern of moves can be imagined that would lead the serious observer, after watching several games, to consider the hypothesis that the chess player was not a single individual but rather a loose alliance of semi-independent organizations, each of which moved its set of pieces according to standard operating procedures. For example, movement of separate sets of pieces might proceed in turn, each according to a routine, the king's rook, bishop, and their pawns repeatedly attacking the opponent according to a fixed plan. Furthermore, it is conceivable that the pattern of play would suggest to an observer that a number of distinct players, with distinct objectives but shared power over the pieces, were determining the moves as the resultant of collegial bargaining. For example, the black rook's move might contribute to the loss of a black knight with no comparable gain for the black team, but with the black rook becoming the principal guardian of the 'palace' on that side of the board.

The space available does not permit full development and support of such a general argument. Rather, the sections that follow simply sketch each conceptual model, articulate it as an analytic paradigm, and apply it to produce an explanation.

Model I: Rational policy

How do analysts account for the coming of the First World War? According to Hans Morgenthau (1960), 'the First World War had its origin exclusively in the fear of a disturbance of the European balance of power.' In the period preceding World War I, the Triple Alliance precariously balanced the Triple Entente. If either power combination could gain a decisive advantage in the Balkans, it would achieve a decisive advantage in the balance of power. 'It was this fear,' Morgenthau asserts, 'that motivated Austria in July 1914 to settle its accounts with Serbia once and for all, and that induced Germany to support Austria unconditionally. It was the same fear that brought Russia to the support of Serbia, and France to the support of Russia.' How is Morgenthau able to resolve this problem so confidently? By imposing on the data a 'rational outline.' The value of this method, according to Morgenthau, is that 'it provides for rational discipline in action and creates astounding continuity in foreign policy which makes American, British, or Russian foreign policy appear as an intelligent, rational continuum . . . regardless of the different motives, preferences, and intellectual and moral qualities of successive statesmen.'

Deterrence is the cardinal problem of the contemporary strategic literature. Thomas Schelling's *Strategy of Conflict* (1960) formulates a number of propositions focused upon the dynamics of deterrence in the nuclear age. One of the major propositions concerns the stability of the balance of terror: in a situation of mutual deterrence, the probability of nuclear war is reduced not by the 'balance' (the sheer equality of the situation) but rather by the *stability* of the balance, i.e. the fact that neither opponent in striking first can destroy the other's ability to strike back. How does Schelling support this proposition? Confidence in the contention stems not from an inductive canvass of a large number of previous cases, but rather from two calculations. In a situation of 'balance' but vulnerability, there are values for which a rational opponent could choose to strike first, e.g. to destroy enemy capabilities to retaliate. In a 'stable balance' where no matter who strikes first, each has an assured capability to retaliate with unacceptable damage, no rational agent could choose such a course of action (since that choice is effectively equivalent to choosing mutual homicide). Whereas most contemporary strategic thinking is driven *implicitly* by the motor upon which this calculation depends, Schelling explicitly recognizes that strategic theory does assume a model. The foundation of a theory of strategy is, he asserts, 'the assumption of rational behavior – not just of intelligent behavior, but of behavior motivated by conscious calculation of advantages, calculation that in turn is based on an explicit and internally consistent value system.'

What is striking about these examples from the literature of foreign policy and international relations are the similarities among analysts of various styles when they are called upon to produce explanations. Each assumes that what must be explained is an action, i.e. the realization of some purpose or intention. Each assumes that the actor is the national government. Each assumes that the action is chosen as a calculated response to a strategic problem. For each, explanation consists of showing what goal the government was pursuing in committing the act and how this action was a reasonable choice, given the nation's objectives. This set of assumptions characterizes the rational policy model. The assertion that Model I is the standard frame of reference implies no denial of highly visible differences among the interests of Sovietologists, diplomatic historians, international relations theorists, and strategists. Indeed, in most respects, differences among the work of Hans Morgenthau and Thomas Schelling could not be more pointed. Appreciation of the extent to which each relies predominantly on Model I, however, reveals basic similarities among Morgenthau's method of 'rational reenactment,' and Schelling's 'vicarious problem solving;' family resemblances among

Morgenthau's 'rational statesman' and Schelling's 'game theorist.'

Most contemporary analysts (as well as laymen) proceed predominantly – albeit most often implicitly – in terms of this model when attempting to explain happenings in foreign affairs. Indeed, that occurrences in foreign affairs are the *acts of nations* seems so fundamental to thinking about such problems that this underlying model has rarely been recognized: to explain an occurrence in foreign policy simply means to show how the government could have rationally chosen that action. To prove that most analysts think largely in terms of the rational policy model is not possible. In this limited space it is not even possible to illustrate the range of employment of the framework. Rather, my purpose is to convey to the reader a grasp of the model and a challenge: let the readers examine the literature with which they are most familiar and make their judgment.

The general characterization can be sharpened by articulating the rational policy model as an 'analytic paradigm.' Systematic statement of basic assumptions, concepts, and propositions employed by Model I analysts highlights the distinctive thrust of this style of analysis. To articulate a largely implicit framework is of necessity to caricature. But caricature can be instructive.

Model I: Basic unit of analysis: Policy as national choice

Happenings in foreign affairs are conceived as actions chosen by the nation or national government. Governments select the action that will maximize strategic goals and objectives. These 'solutions' to strategic problems are the fundamental categories in terms of which the analyst perceives what is to be explained.

Model I: Organizing concepts

National actor. The nation or government, conceived as a rational, unitary decisionmaker, is the agent. This actor has one set of specified goals (the equivalent of a consistent utility function), one set of perceived options, and a single estimate of the consequences that follow from each alternative.

The problem. Action is chosen in response to the strategic problem which the nation faces. Threats and opportunities arising in the 'international strategic market place' move the nation to act.

Static selection. The sum of activity of representatives of the government relevant to a problem constitutes what the nation has chosen as its 'solution.' Thus the action is conceived as a steady-state choice among alternative outcomes (rather than, for example, a large number of partial choices in a dynamic stream).

Action as rational choice. The components include:

- Goals and objectives. National security and national interests are the principal categories in which strategic goals are conceived. Nations seek security and a range of further objectives. (Analysts rarely translate strategic goals and objectives into an explicit utility function; nevertheless, analysts do focus on major goals and objectives and trade off side effects in an intuitive fashion.)

- Options. Various courses of action relevant to a strategic problem provide the spectrum of options.

- Consequences. Enactment of each alternative course of action will produce a series of consequences. The relevant consequences constitute benefits and costs in terms of strategic goals and objectives.

- Choice. Rational choice is value-maximizing. The rational agent selects the alternative whose consequences rank highest in terms of his goals and objectives.

Model I: Dominant inference pattern and general propositions

This paradigm leads analysts to rely on the following pattern of inference: if a nation performed a particular action, that nation must have had ends towards which the action constituted an optimal means. The rational policy model's explanatory power stems from this inference pattern. Puzzlement is relieved by revealing the purposive pattern within which the occurrence can be located as a value-maximizing means.

The disgrace of political science is the infrequency with which propositions of any generality are formulated and tested. 'Paradigmatic analysis' argues for explicitness about the terms in which analysis proceeds, and seriousness about the logic of explanation. Simply to illustrate the kind of propositions on which analysts who employ this model rely, the formulation includes several.

The basic assumption of value-maximizing behavior produces propositions central to most explanations. The general principle can be formulated as follows: the likelihood of any particular action results from a com-

bination of the nation's (1) relevant values and objectives, (2) perceived alternative courses of action, (3) estimates of various sets of consequences (which will follow from each alternative), and (4) net valuation of each set of consequences. This yields two propositions.

- An increase in the cost of an alternative, i.e. a reduction in the value of the set of consequences which will follow from that action, or a reduction in the probability of attaining fixed consequences, reduces the likelihood of that alternative being chosen.

- A decrease in the costs of an alternative, i.e. an increase in the value of the set of consequences which will follow from that alternative or an increase in the probability of attaining fixed consequences, increases the likelihood of that action being chosen.

Model II: Organizational process

For some purposes, governmental behavior can be usefully summarized as action chosen by a unitary, rational decisionmaker: centrally controlled, completely informed, and value maximizing. But this simplification must not be allowed to conceal the fact that a 'government' consists of a conglomerate of semi-feudal, loosely allied organizations, each with a substantial life of its own. Government leaders do sit formally, and to some extent in fact, on top of this conglomerate. But governments perceive problems through organizational sensors. Governments define alternatives and estimate consequences as organizations process information. Governments act as these organizations enact routines. Government behavior can therefore be understood according to a second conceptual model, less as deliberate choices of leaders and more as *outputs* of large organizations functioning according to standard patterns of behavior.

To be responsive to a broad spectrum of problems, governments consist of large organizations among which primary responsibility for particular areas is divided. Each organization attends to a special set of problems and acts in quasi-independence on these problems. But few important problems fall exclusively within the domain of a single organization. Thus government behavior relevant to any important problem reflects the independent output of several organizations, partially coordinated by government leaders. Government leaders can substantially disturb, but not substantially control, the behavior of these organizations.

To perform complex routines, the behavior of large numbers of individuals must be coordinated. Coordination requires standard operating procedures: rules according to which things are done. Assured capability for reliable performance of action that depends upon the behavior of hundreds of persons requires established 'programs.' Indeed, if the 11 members of a football team are to perform adequately on any particular down, each player must not 'do what he thinks needs to be done' or 'do what the quarterback tells him to do.' Rather, each player must perform the maneuvers specified by a previously established play which the quarterback has simply called in this situation.

At any given time, a government consists of *existing* organizations, each with a *fixed* set of standard operating procedures and programs. The behavior of these organizations – and consequently of the government – relevant to an issue in any particular instance is therefore determined primarily by routines established in these organizations prior to that instance. But organizations do change. Learning occurs gradually, over time. Dramatic organizational change occurs in response to major crises. Both learning and change are influenced by existing organizational capabilities.

These loosely formulated propositions amount simply to *tendencies*. Each must be hedged by modifiers like 'other things being equal' and 'under certain conditions.' In particular instances, tendencies hold – more or less. In specific situations the relevant question is: more or less? But this is as it should be. For, on the one hand, 'organizations' are no more homogeneous a class than 'solids.' When scientists tried to generalize about 'solids,' they achieved similar results. Solids tend to expand when heated, but some do and some don't. More adequate categorization of the various elements now lumped under the rubric 'organizations' is thus required. On the other hand, the behavior of particular organizations seems considerably more complex than the behavior of solids. Additional information about a particular organization is required for further specification of the tendency statements. In spite of these two caveats, the characterization of government action as organizational output differs distinctly from Model I. Attempts to understand problems of foreign affairs in terms of this frame of reference should produce quite different explanations.

Model II: Basic unit of analysis: Policy as organizational output

The happenings of international politics are, in three critical senses, outputs of organizational processes. First, the actual occurrences are organizational outputs. Government leaders' decisions trigger organizational routines. Government leaders can trim the edges of this output and exercise some choice in combining outputs. But the mass of behavior is determined by previously established procedures. Second, existing organizational routines for employing present physical capabilities constitute the effective options open to government leaders confronted with any problem. The fact that fixed programs (equipment, men, and routines which exist at the particular time) exhaust the range of buttons that leaders can push is not always perceived by these leaders. But in every case it is critical for an understanding of what is actually done. Third, organizational outputs structure the situation within the narrow constraints of which leaders must contribute their 'decision' concerning an issue. Outputs raise the problem, provide the information, and make the initial moves that color the face of the issue that is turned to the leaders. As Theodore Sorensen has observed: 'Presidents rarely, if ever, make decisions – particularly in foreign affairs – in the sense of writing their conclusions on a clean slate . . . The basic decisions, which confine their choices, have all too often been previously made.' If one understands the structure of the situation and the face of the issue – which are determined by the organizational outputs – the formal choice of the leaders is frequently anti-climatic.

Model II: Organizing concepts

Organizational actors.   The actor is not a monolithic 'nation' or 'government' but rather a constellation of loosely allied organizations on top of which government leaders sit. This constellation acts only as component organizations perform routines.

Factored problems and fractionated power. Surveillance of the multiple facets of foreign affairs requires that problems be cut up and parcelled out to various organizations. To avoid paralysis, primary power must accompany primary responsibility. But if organizations are permitted to do anything, a large part of what they do will be determined within the organization. Thus each organization perceives problems, processes information, and performs a range of actions in quasi-independence (within broad guidelines of national policy). Factored problems and fractionated power are two edges of the same sword. Factoring permits more specialized attention to particular facets of problems than would be possible if government leaders tried to cope with these problems by themselves. But this additional attention must be paid for in the coin of discretion for what an organization attends to, and how organizational responses are programmed.

Parochial priorities, perceptions, and issues. Primary responsibility for a narrow set of problems encourages organizational parochialism. These tendencies are enhanced by a number of additional factors: (1) selective information available to the organization, (2) recruitment of personnel into the organization, (3) tenure of individuals in the organization, (4) small group pressures within the organization, and (5) distribution of rewards by the organization. Clients, government allies, and extra-national counterparts galvanize this parochialism. Thus organizations develop relatively stable propensities concerning operational priorities, perceptions, and issues.

Action as organizational output. The preeminent feature of organizational activity is its programmed character: the extent to which behavior in any particular case is an enactment of preestablished routines. In producing outputs, the activity of each organization is characterized by:

- Goals: Constraints defining acceptable performance. The operational goals of an organization are seldom revealed by formal mandates. Rather, each organization's operational goals emerge as a set of constraints defining acceptable performance. Central among these constraints is organizational health, defined usually in terms of bodies assigned and dollars appropriated. The set of constraints emerges from a mix of expectations and demands of other organizations in the government, statutory authority, demands from citizens and special interest groups, and bargaining within the organization. These constraints represent a quasi-resolution of conflict – the constraints are relatively stable, so there is some resolution. But conflict among alternative goals is always latent; hence, it is a quasi-resolution. Typically, the constraints are formulated as imperatives to avoid roughly specified discomforts and disasters.

- Sequential attention to goals. The existence of conflict among operational constraints is resolved by the device of sequential attention. As a problem arises, the subunits of the organization most concerned with that problem deal with it in terms of the constraints they take to be most important. When the next problem arises, another cluster of subunits deals with it, focusing on a different set of constraints.

- Standard operating procedures. Organizations perform their 'higher' functions, such as attending to problem areas, monitoring information, and preparing relevant responses for likely contingencies, by doing 'lower' tasks, for example, preparing budgets, producing reports, and developing hardware. Reliable performance of these tasks requires standard operating procedures (hereafter SOPs). Since procedures are 'standard' they do not change quickly or easily. Without these standard procedures, it would not be possible to perform certain concerted tasks. But because of standard procedures, organizational behavior in particular instances often appears unduly formalized, sluggish, or inappropriate.

- Programs and repertoires. Organizations must be capable of performing actions in which the behavior of large numbers of individuals is carefully coordinated. Assured performance requires clusters of rehearsed SOPs for producing specific actions, e.g. fighting enemy units or answering an embassy's cable. Each cluster comprises a 'program' (in the terms both of drama and computers) which the organization has available for dealing with a situation. The list of programs relevant to a type of activity, e.g. fighting, constitutes an organizational repertoire. The number of programs in a repertoire is always quite limited. When properly triggered, organizations execute programs; programs cannot be substantially changed in a particular situation. The more complex the action and the greater the number of individuals involved, the more important are programs and repertoires as determinants of organizational behavior.

- Uncertainty avoidance. Organizations do not attempt to estimate the probability distribution of future occurrences. Rather, organizations avoid uncertainty. By arranging a *negotiated environment*, organizations regularize the reactions of other actors with whom they have to deal. The primary environment, relations with other organizations that comprise the government, is stabilized by such arrangements as agreed budgetary splits, accepted areas of responsibility, and established conventional practices. The secondary environment, relations with the international world, is stabilized between allies by the establishment of contracts (alliances) and 'club relations' (US State and UK Foreign Office or US Treasury and UK Treasury). Between enemies, contracts and accepted conventional practices perform a similar function, for example, the rules of the 'precarious status quo' which President Kennedy referred to in the missile crisis. Where the international environment cannot be negotiated, organizations deal with remaining uncertainties by establishing a set of *standard scenarios* that constitute the contingencies for which they prepare.

- Problem-directed search. Where situations cannot be construed as standard, organizations engage in search. The style of search and the solution are largely determined by existing routines. Organizational search for alternative courses of action is problem-oriented: it focuses on the atypical discomfort that must be avoided. It is simple-minded: the neighborhood of the symptom is searched first; then, the neighborhood of the current alternative. Patterns of search reveal biases which in turn reflect such factors as specialized training or experience and patterns of communication.

- Organizational learning and change. The parameters of organizational behavior mostly persist. In response to non-standard problems, organizations search and routines evolve, assimilating new situations. Thus learning and change follow in large part from existing procedures. But marked changes in organizations do sometimes occur. Conditions in which dramatic changes are more likely include: (1) Periods of budgetary feast. Typically, organizations devour budgetary feasts by purchasing additional items on the existing shopping list. Nevertheless, if committed to change, leaders who control the budget can use extra funds to effect changes. (2) Periods of prolonged budgetary famine. Though a single year's famine typically results in few changes in organizational structure but a loss of effectiveness in performing some programs, prolonged famine forces major retrenchment. (3) Dramatic performance failures. Dramatic change occurs (mostly) in response to major disasters. Confronted with an undeniable failure of procedures and repertoires, authorities outside the organization demand change, existing personnel are less resistant to change, and critical members of the organization are replaced by individuals committed to change.

Central coordination and control. Action requires decentralization of responsibility and power. But problems lap over the jurisdictions of several organizations. Thus the necessity for decentralization runs headlong into the requirement for coordination. Both the necessity for coordination and the centrality of foreign policy to national welfare guarantee the involvement of government leaders in the procedures of the organizations among which problems are divided and power shared. Each organization's propensities and routines can be disturbed by government leaders' intervention. Central direction and persistent control of organizational activity, however, is not possible. The relation among organizations, and between organizations and the government leaders depends critically on a number of structural variables including: (1) the nature of the job; (2) the measures and information available to government leaders; (3) the system of rewards and punishments for organizational members; and (4) the procedures by which human and material resources get committed. For example, to the extent that rewards and punishments for the members of an organization are distributed by higher authorities, these authorities can exercise some control by specifying criteria in terms of which organizational output is to be evaluated. These criteria become constraints within which organizational activity proceeds. But constraint is a crude instrument of control. Intervention by government leaders does sometimes change the activity of an organization in an intended direction. But instances are fewer than might be expected. As Franklin Roosevelt, the master manipulator of government organizations, remarked:

> *The Treasury is so large and far-flung and ingrained in its practices that I find it is almost impossible to get the action and results I want . . . But the Treasury is not to be compared with the State Department. You should go through the experience of trying to get any changes in the thinking, policy, and action of the career diplomats and then you'd know what a real problem was. But the Treasury and the State Department put together are nothing compared with the Na-a-vy . . . To change anything in the Na-a-vy is like punching a feather bed. You punch it with your right and you punch it with your left until you are finally exhausted, and then you find the damn bed just as it was before you started punching.*

(Eccles, 1951: 336).

Decisions of government leaders. Organizational persistence does not exclude shifts in governmental behavior. For government leaders sit atop the conglomerate of organizations. Many important issues of governmental action require that these leaders decide what organizations will play out which programs where. Thus stability in the parochialisms and SOPs of individual organizations is consistent with some important shifts in the behavior of governments. The range of these shifts is defined by existing organizational programs.

Model II: Dominant inference pattern and general propositions

If a nation performs an action of this type today, its organizational components must yesterday have been performing (or have had established routines for performing) an action only marginally different from this action. At any specific point in time, a government consists of an established conglomerate of organizations, each with existing goals, programs, and repertoires. The characteristics of a government's action in any instance follows from those established routines, and from the choice of government leaders – on the basis of information and estimates provided by existing routines – among existing programs. The best explanation of an organization's behavior at t is $t - 1$; the prediction of $t + 1$ is t. Model II's explanatory power is achieved by uncovering the organizational routines and repertoires that produced the outputs that comprise the puzzling occurrence.

A number of general propositions have been stated above. In order to illustrate clearly the type of proposition employed by Model II analysts, this section formulates several more precisely.

Organizational action. Activity according to SOPs and programs does not constitute far-sighted, flexible adaptation to 'the issue' (as it is conceived by the analyst). Detail and nuance of actions by organizations are determined predominantly by organizational routines, not government leaders' directions.

- SOPs constitute routines for dealing with standard situations. Routines allow large numbers of ordinary individuals to deal with numerous instances, day after day, without considerable thought, by responding to basic stimuli. But this regularized capability for adequate performance is purchased at the price of standardization. If the SOPs are appropriate, average performance, i.e. performance aver-

aged over the range of cases, is better than it would be if each instance were approached individually (given fixed talent, timing, and resource constraints). But specific instances, particularly critical instances that typically do not have 'standard' characteristics, are often handled sluggishly or inappropriately.

- A program, i.e. a complex action chosen from a short list of programs in a repertoire, is rarely tailored to the specific situation in which it is executed. Rather, the program is (at best) the most appropriate of the programs in a previously developed repertoire.

- Since repertoires are developed by parochial organizations for standard scenarios defined by that organization, programs available for dealing with a particular situation are often ill-suited.

Limited flexibility and incremental change. Major lines of organizational action are straight, i.e. behavior at one time is marginally different from that behavior at $t - 1$. Simpleminded predictions work best: Behavior at $t + 1$ will be marginally different from behavior at the present time.

- Organizational budgets change incrementally – both with respect to totals and with respect to intra-organizational splits. Though organizations could divide the money available each year by carving up the pie anew (in the light of changes in objectives or environment), in practice, organizations take last year's budget as a base and adjust incrementally. Predictions that require large budgetary shifts in a single year between organizations or between units within an organization should be hedged.

- Once undertaken, an organizational investment is not dropped at the point where 'objective' costs outweigh benefits. Organizational stakes in adopted projects carry them quite beyond the loss point.

Administrative feasibility. Adequate explanation, analysis, and prediction must include administrative feasibility as a major dimension. A considerable gap separates what leaders choose (or might rationally have chosen) and what organizations implement.

- Organizations are blunt instruments. Projects that require several organizations to act with high degrees of precision and coordination are not likely to succeed.

- Projects that demand that existing organizational units depart from their accustomed functions and perform previously unprogrammed tasks are rarely accomplished in their designed form.

- Government leaders can expect that each organization will do its 'part' in terms of what the organization knows how to do.

- Government leaders can expect incomplete and distorted information from each organization concerning its part of the problem.

- Where an assigned piece of a problem is contrary to the existing goals of an organization, resistance to implementation of that piece will be encountered.

Model III: Bureaucratic politics

The leaders who sit on top of organizations are not a monolithic group. Rather, each is, in his own right, a player in a central, competitive game. The name of the game is bureaucratic politics: bargaining along regularized channels among players positioned hierarchically within the government. Government behavior can thus be understood according to a third conceptual model not as organizational outputs, but as outcomes of bargaining games. In contrast with Model I, the bureaucratic politics model sees no unitary actor but rather many actors as players, who focus not on a single strategic issue but on many diverse intra-national problems as well, in terms of no consistent set of strategic objectives but rather according to various conceptions of national, organizational, and personal goals, making government decisions not by rational choice but by the pulling and hauling that is politics.

The apparatus of each national government constitutes a complex arena for the intra-national game. Political leaders at the top of this apparatus plus the men who occupy positions on top of the critical organizations form the circle of central players. Ascendancy to this circle assures some independent standing. The necessary decentralization of decisions required for action on the broad range of foreign policy problems guarantees that each player has considerable discretion. Thus power is shared.

The nature of problems of foreign policy permits fundamental disagreement among reasonable men concerning what ought to be done. Analyses yield conflicting recommendations. Separate responsibilities laid on the shoulders of individual personalities encourage differences in perceptions and priorities. But the issues are of first order importance. What the nation does really matters. A wrong choice could mean irreparable damage. Thus responsible men are obliged to fight for what they are convinced is right.

Men share power. Men differ concerning what must be done. The differences matter. This milieu necessitates that policy be resolved by politics. What the nation does is sometimes the result of the triumph of one group over others. More often, however, different groups pulling in different directions yield a resultant distinct from what anyone intended. What moves the chess pieces is not simply the reasons which support a course of action, nor the routines of organizations which enact an alternative, but the power and skill of proponents and opponents of the action in question.

This characterization captures the thrust of the bureaucratic politics orientation. If problems of foreign policy arose as discreet issues, and decisions were determined one game at a time, this account would suffice. But most 'issues' emerge piecemeal, over time, one lump in one context, a second in another. Hundreds of issues compete for players' attention every day. Each player is forced to fix upon his issues for that day, fight them on their own terms, and rush on to the next. Thus the character of emerging issues and the pace at which the game is played converge to yield government 'decisions' and 'actions' as collages. Choices by one player, outcomes of minor games, outcomes of central games, and 'foul-ups' – these pieces, when stuck to the same canvas, constitute government behavior relevant to an issue.

Model III: Basic unit of analysis: Policy as political outcome

The decisions and actions of governments are essentially intra-national political outcomes: outcomes in the sense that what happens is not chosen as a solution to a problem but rather results from compromise, coalition, competition, and confusion among government officials who see different faces of an issue; political in the sense that the activity from which the outcomes emerge is best characterized as bargaining. Following Wittgenstein's use of the concept of a 'game,' national behavior in international affairs can be conceived as outcomes of intricate and subtle, simultaneous, overlapping games among players located in positions, the hierarchical arrangement of which constitutes the government. These games proceed neither at random nor at leisure. Regular channels structure the game. Deadlines force issues to the attention of busy players. The moves in the chess game are thus to be explained in terms of the bargaining among players with separate and unequal power over particular pieces and with separable objectives in distinguishable subgames.

Model III: Organizing concepts

Players in positions.   The actor is neither a unitary nation, nor a conglomerate of organizations, but rather a number of individual players. Groups of these players constitute the agent for particular government decisions and actions. Players are men in jobs.

Individuals become players in the national security policy game by occupying a critical position in an administration. For example, in the US government the players include 'Chiefs': The President, Secretaries of State, Defense, and Treasury, Director of the CIA, Joint Chiefs of Staff and, since 1961, the Special Assistant for National Security Affairs; 'Staffers': the immediate staff of each Chief; 'Indians': the political appointees and permanent government officials within each of the departments and agencies; and '*Ad Hoc* Players': actors in the wider government game (especially 'Congressional Influentials'), members of the press, spokesmen for important interest groups (especially the 'bipartisan foreign policy establishment' in and out of Congress), and surrogates for each of these groups. Other members of the Congress, press, interest groups, and public form concentric circles around the central arena – circles which demarcate the permissive limits within which the game is played.

Positions define what players both may and must do. The advantages and handicaps with which each player can enter and play in various games stems from his position. So does a cluster of obligations for the performance of certain tasks.

All of these obligations are his simultaneously. His performance in one affects his credit and power in the others. The perspective stemming from the daily work which he must oversee – the cable traffic by which his department maintains relations with other foreign offices – conflicts with the President's requirement that he serve as a generalist and coordinator of contrasting perspectives. The necessity that he be close to the President restricts the extent to which, and the force with which, he can front for his department. When he defers to the Secretary of Defense rather than fighting for his department's position – as he often must – he strains the loyalty of his officialdom. The Secretary's resolution of these conflicts depends not only upon the position but also upon the player who occupies the position.

For players are also people. Men's metabolisms differ. The core of the bureaucratic politics mix is personality. How each man manages to stand the heat in his kitchen, each player's basic operating style, and the complementarity or contradiction among personalities and styles in the inner circles are irreducible pieces of the policy blend. Moreover, each person comes to his position with baggage in tow, including sensitivities to certain issues, commitments to various programs, and personal standing and debts with groups in the society.

Parochial priorities, perceptions and issues. Answers to the questions: 'What is the issue?' and 'What must be done?' are colored by the position from which the questions are considered. For the factors which encourage organizational parochialism also influence the players who occupy positions on top of (or within) these organizations. To motivate members of his organization, a player must be sensitive to the organization's orientation. The games into which the player can enter and the advantages with which he plays enhance these pressures. Thus propensities of perception stemming from position permit reliable prediction about a player's stances in many cases. But these propensities are filtered through the baggage which players bring to positions. Sensitivity to both the pressures and the baggage is thus required for many predictions.

Interests, stakes, and power.   Games are played to determine outcomes. But outcomes advance and impede each player's conception of the national interest, specific programs to which he is committed, the welfare of his friends, and his personal interests. These overlapping interests constitute the stakes for which games are played. Each player's ability to play successfully depends upon his power. Power, i.e. effective influence on policy outcomes, is an elusive blend of at least three elements: bargaining advantages (drawn from formal authority and obligations, institutional backing, constituents, expertise, and status), skill and will in using bargaining advantages, and other players' perceptions of the first two ingredients. Power wisely invested yields an enhanced reputation for effectiveness. Unsuccessful investment depletes both the stock of capital and the reputation. Thus each player must pick the issues on which he can play with a reasonable probability of success. But no player's power is sufficient to guarantee satisfactory outcomes. Each player's needs and fears run to many other players. What ensues is the most intricate and subtle of games known to man.

The problem and the problems.   'Solutions' to strategic problems are not derived by detached analysts focusing coolly on the problem. Instead, deadlines and events raise issues in games, and demand decisions of busy players in contexts that influence the face the issue wears. The problems for the players are both narrower and broader than the strategic problem. For each player focuses not on the total strategic problem but rather on the decision that must be made now. But each decision has critical consequences not only for the strategic problem but for each player's organizational, reputational, and personal stakes. Thus the gap between the problems the player was solving and the problem upon which the analyst focuses is often very wide.

Action-channels. Bargaining games do not proceed randomly. Action-channels, i.e. regularized ways of producing action concerning types of issues, structure the game by pre-selecting the major players, determining their points of entrance into the game, and distributing particular advantages and disadvantages for each game. Most critically, channels determine 'who's got the action,' that is, which department's Indians actually do whatever is chosen.

Action as politics. Government decisions are made and government actions emerge neither as the calculated choice of a unified group, nor as a formal summary of leaders' preferences. Rather the context of shared power but separate judgments concerning important choices, determines that politics is the mechanism of choice. Note the environment in which the game is played: inordinate uncertainty about what must be done, the necessity that something be done, and crucial consequences of whatever is done. These features force responsible men to become active players. The *pace of the game* – hundreds of issues, numerous games, and multiple channels – compels players to fight to 'get other's attention,' to make them 'see the facts,' to assure that they 'take the time to think seriously about the broader issue.' The *structure of the game* – power shared by individuals with separate responsibilities – validates each player's feeling that 'others don't see my problem,' and 'others must be persuaded to look at the issue from a less parochial perspective.' The *rules of the game* – he who hesitates loses his chance to play at that point, and he who is uncertain about his recommendation is overpowered by others who are sure – pressures players to come down on one side of a 51–49 issue and play. The rewards of the game – effectiveness, i.e. impact on outcomes, as the immediate measure of performance – encourages hard play. Thus, most players come to fight to 'make the government do what is right.'

Streams of outcomes. Important government decisions or actions emerge as collages composed of individual acts, outcomes of minor and major games, and foul-ups. Outcomes which could never have been chosen by an actor and would never have emerged from bargaining in a single game over the issue are fabricated piece by piece. Understanding of the outcome requires that it be disaggregated.

Model III: Dominant inference pattern and general propositions

If a nation performed an action, that action was the *outcome* of bargaining among individuals and groups within the government. That outcome included *results* achieved by groups committed to a decision or action, *resultants* which emerged from bargaining among groups with quite different positions and *foul-ups*. Model III's explanatory power is achieved by revealing the pulling and hauling of various players, with different perceptions and priorities, focusing on separate problems, which yielded the outcomes that constitute the action in question.

- Action and intention. Action does not presuppose intention. The sum of behavior of representatives of a government relevant to an issue was rarely intended by any individual or group. Rather separate individuals with different intentions contributed pieces which compose an outcome distinct from what anyone would have chosen.

- Where you stand depends on where you sit. Horizontally, the diverse demands upon each player shape his priorities, perceptions, and issues. For large classes of issues, e.g. budgets and procurement decisions, the stance of a particular player can be predicted with high reliability from information concerning his seat.

- Chiefs and Indians. The aphorism 'where you stand depends on where you sit' has vertical as well as horizontal application. Vertically, the demands upon the President, Chiefs, Staffers, and Indians are quite distinct.

The foreign policy issues with which the President can deal are limited primarily by his crowded schedule: the necessity of dealing first with what comes next. His problem is to probe the special face worn by issues that come to his attention, to preserve his leeway until time has clarified the uncertainties, and to assess the relevant risks.

Foreign policy chiefs deal most often with the hottest issue *de jour*, though they can get the attention of the President and other members of the government for other issues which they judge important. What they cannot guarantee is that 'the President will pay the price' or that 'the others will get on board.' They must build a coalition of the relevant powers that be. They must 'give the President confidence' in the right course of action.

Most problems are framed, alternatives specified, and proposals pushed, however, by Indians. Indians fight with Indians of other departments; for example, struggles between International Security Affairs of the Department of Defense and Political-Military of the State Department are a microcosm of the action at higher levels. But the Indian's major problem is how to get the attention of chiefs, how to get an issue decided, how to get the government 'to do what is right.'

In policy making then, the issue looking *down* is options: how to preserve my leeway until time clarifies uncertainties. The issue looking *sideways* is commitment: how to get others committed to my coalition. The issue looking *upwards* is confidence: how to give the boss confidence in doing what must be done. To paraphrase one of Neustadt's assertions which can be applied down the length of the ladder, the essence of a responsible official's task is to induce others to see that what needs to be done is what their own appraisal of their own responsibilities requires them to do in their own interests.

Conclusion

At a minimum, the intended implications of the argument presented here are four. First, formulation of alternative frames of reference and demonstration that different analysts, relying predominantly on different models, produce quite different explanations should encourage the analyst's self-consciousness about the nets he employs. The effect of these 'spectacles' in sensitizing him to particular aspects of what is going on – framing the puzzle in one way rather than another, encouraging him to examine the problem in terms of certain categories rather than others, directing him to particular kinds of evidence, and relieving puzzlement by one procedure rather than another – must be recognized and explored.

Second, the argument implies a position on the problem of 'the state of the art.' While accepting the commonplace characterization of the present condition of foreign policy analysis – personalistic, non-cumulative,

and sometimes insightful – this article rejects both the counsel of despair's justification of this condition as a consequence of the character of the enterprise, and the 'new frontiersmen's' demand for *a priori* theorizing on the frontiers and *ad hoc* appropriation of 'new techniques.' What is required as a first step is non-casual examination of the present product: inspection of existing explanations, articulation of the conceptual models employed in producing them, formulation of the propositions relied upon, specification of the logic of the various intellectual enterprises, and reflection on the questions being asked. Though it is difficult to overemphasize the need for more systematic processing of more data, these preliminary matters of formulating questions with clarity and sensitivity to categories and assumptions so that fruitful acquisition of large quantities of data is possible are still a major hurdle in considering most important problems.

Third, the preliminary, partial paradigms presented here provide a basis for serious reexamination of many problems of foreign and military policy. Model II and Model III cuts at problems typically treated in Model I terms can permit significant improvements in explanation and prediction. Full Model II and III analyses require large amounts of information. But even in cases where the information base is severely limited, improvements are possible.

Fourth, the present formulation of paradigms is simply an initial step. As such it leaves a long list of critical questions unanswered. Given any action, an imaginative analyst should always be able to construct some rationale for the government's choice. By imposing, and relaxing, constraints on the parameters of rational choice (as in variants of Model I) analysts can construct a large number of accounts of any act as a rational choice. But does a statement of reasons why a rational actor would choose an action constitute an explanation of the *occurrence* of that action? How can Model I analysis be forced to make more systematic contributions to the question of the determinants of occurrences? Model II's explanation of t in terms of $t - 1$ is explanation. The world is contiguous. But governments sometimes make sharp departures. Can an organizational process model be modified to suggest where change is likely? Attention to organizational change should afford greater understanding of why particular programs and SOPs are maintained by identifiable types of organizations and also how a manager can improve organizational performance. Model III tells a fascinating 'story.' But its complexity is enormous, the information requirements are often overwhelming, and many of the details of the bargaining may be superfluous. How can such a model be made parsimonious? The three models are obviously not exclusive alternatives. Indeed, the paradigms highlight the partial emphasis of the framework – what each emphasizes and what it leaves out. Each concentrates on one class of variables, in effect, relegating other important factors to a *ceteris paribus* clause. Model I concentrates on 'market factors:' pressures and incentives created by the 'international strategic marketplace.' Models II and III focus on the internal mechanism of the government that chooses in this environment. But can these relations be more fully specified? Adequate synthesis would require a typology of decisions and actions, some of which are more amenable to treatment in terms of one model and some to another. Government behavior is but one cluster of factors relevant to occurrences in foreign affairs. Most students of foreign policy adopt this focus (at least when explaining and predicting). Nevertheless, the dimensions of the chess board, the character of the pieces, and the rules of the game – factors considered by international systems theorists – constitute the context in which the pieces are moved.

READING

3.4

From scenario thinking to strategic action

By Ian Wilson[1]

Introduction

One day in the fall of 1976 I arranged a meeting between Pierre Wack, who at that time headed Royal Dutch/Shell's Business Environment component, and some of my colleagues in General Electric's strategic planning staff. The focus of our discussion was to be the role of scenarios in corporate planning.

At that time, GE had, arguably, the most elaborate and sophisticated strategic planning system in the corporate world, and Shell was enjoying an international reputation for its pioneering scenarios work. Yet in each case something was missing. Wack was convinced that his scenarios needed a tighter linkage to strategic planning and decision-making if they were ever to engage operations managers seriously and continuously. And GE, still shaken and puzzled by the fallout from the first 'oil shock', needed to ground its strategy in an assessment of the future that acknowledged, more explicitly, the inherent uncertainties that then marked the future business environment. The two parties thus came to this discussion from differing points of view, but focused on the same central need: linking perceptions about the future to current decisions.

This meeting marked a turning point in my recognition of the critical importance of strengthening the connection between scenario development and strategic action. From this point forward I recognized that, although developing coherent, imaginative and useful scenarios is certainly important, translating the implications of the scenarios into executive decisions and, ultimately, into strategic action was the ultimate reason and justification for the exercise.

Cultural barriers to implementation

Scenarios are not an end in themselves. They are a management tool to improve the quality of executive decision making. Yet experience shows that actually using scenarios for this purpose turns out to be a more perplexing problem than the scenario development process itself. As in the larger domain of strategy, implementation – execution – turns out to be the crucial issue.

The causes of this implementation problem, in part practical and procedural, are still largely cultural and

[1] Source: This article was reprinted from *Technological Forecasting and Social Change*, Vol. 65, I. Wilson, 'From Scenario Thinking to Strategic Action', pp. 23–29, © 2000. With permission from Elsevier.

psychological. The planning culture in most corporations is still heavily biased toward single-point forecasting. In such a context, the managers' premise is, 'Tell me what the future will be; then I can make my decision.' So their initial reaction, when confronted with the apparent emphasis in scenarios on 'multipoint forecasting', is likely to be one of confusion and disbelief, complaining that three (or four) 'forecasts' are more confusing, and less helpful, than one. The fact that this is a misperception of the nature and role of scenarios does not in any way lessen the implementation problem.

However, the major cultural barrier to scenario implementation stems from the way we define managerial competence. Good managers, we say, *know* where they are, where they're going, and how they'll get there. *We equate managerial competence with 'knowing'*, and assume that decisions depend on facts about the present and about the future. Of course, the reality is that *we have no facts about the future*. In a 1975 presentation to the American Association for the Advancement of Science (AAAS), I highlighted this problem in the following way: 'However good our futures research may be, we shall never be able to escape from the ultimate dilemma that all our knowledge is about the past, and all our decisions are about the future.'

Scenarios face up to this dilemma, confronting us with the need to acknowledge that we do not, and cannot, know the future. In the most fundamental way, scenarios seek, as Pierre Wack put it, to change our 'mental maps' of the future. But, in doing so, scenarios also may seem to challenge the way we define managerial competence. That is, by acknowledging uncertainty, scenarios underscore the fact that we cannot know the future, and so we perceive them as challenges to our presumptions of 'knowing', and thus of managerial competence. And because few, if any, corporate cultures reward incompetence, managers have a vested interest in not acknowledging their ignorance, and so in resisting the intrusion of scenario planning into traditional forms of executive decision-making.

Dealing with the dilemma

A starting point for dealing with this dilemma is to establish a clear-cut 'decision focus' for every set of scenarios. The first step in the scenario process is *not* a review of the changing forces affecting the business environment, but rather agreement on the strategic decision(s) that the scenarios should be designed to

illuminate. While it is true that scenarios can also be used as a learning tool to explore general areas of risk and opportunity, this use normally leads to the development of more focused scenarios before decisions are taken. This crucial step establishes, at the outset, that the ultimate purpose of the scenarios is not just to develop plausible descriptions of alternative futures – not even to redraw our mental maps of the future, important as that is – but rather to help executives make better, more resilient strategic decisions. By tying scenarios to needed decisions, we effectively link them to specific planning needs, and prevent the process from straying off into overly broad generalizations about the future of society or the global economy.

Usually, the right decisions on which to focus decisions are strategic rather than tactical. This is because scenarios normally deal more with longer term trends and uncertainties, often with a 5- to 10-year time horizon, rather than short-term developments. Virtually any decision or area of strategic concern in which external factors are complex, changing, and uncertain is a suitable target for the scenario process. However, I have found that the narrower the scope of the decision or strategy (a specific investment or market entry decision, for example), the easier the scenario construction – and interpretation – will be. Developing scenarios for broad strategic concerns – the long-range positioning of a diversified business portfolio, for example – is more difficult.

A word of caution is needed at this point. While clarifying the strategic focus of the scenarios is a critical first step, it is equally important to note that this is not the time for strategizing. Decision-makers, particularly senior executives, have a natural impatience with analysis and a tendency to want to 'cut to the chase'. On many occasions I have had to check this otherwise praiseworthy tendency toward action so that the context for action – the scenarios themselves – can first be established. Once executives see that the process *both begins and ends* with an emphasis on action, they are more easily persuaded of the true value of scenario planning.

What *not* to do

Agreeing that the usefulness of scenarios depends upon their ability to influence executive action is a good first step because at least it focuses attention on what would otherwise be a potential problem. However, it leaves unanswered the questions: What do we do with scenarios once we have developed them?

How do we translate what we learn from them into action? Before attempting to answer these questions, there are two things that we should *not* do.

First, we do *not* develop a complete strategy for each of the scenarios, and then by some means – maybe by applying the test of discounted cash value – select the one that appears to give the greatest promise of success and profitability. I know of no management team that would willingly undertake to go through a full-blown strategy development exercise two or three or four times (however, many scenarios have been developed). Such a course would more likely lead to 'paralysis by analysis' than to constructive action. And, in any case, it would be based on a further misunderstanding of scenario planning: the real aim is to develop a resilient strategy within the framework of alternative futures provided by the scenarios.

Before proceeding, a word of explanation – and caution – is needed at this point. In a number of places in this article I refer to the objective of scenario planning as being the development of a resilient strategy. Now, it should be obvious that resilience is not the only quality to be sought in a strategy; and, taken to an extreme, resilience could mean little more than the lowest common denominator of scenario-specific strategies. At a time that calls for bold, even radical, action in many markets, such an interpretation would be a prescription for mediocrity at best, extinction at worst. My point is, rather, that, before taking bold steps, the strategy should be tested against a variety of scenarios so that the management team is forewarned of potential vulnerabilities. Resilience can then be built into the strategy, *not* by reducing its force or boldness, but rather by 'hedging' or contingency planning.

The second thing that we do not do is assign probabilities to the scenarios and then develop a strategy for the 'most probable' one. Of course, in saying this, I am taking a controversial position. Probability has more to do with forecasts than with scenarios; and scenarios are not forecasts, for one cannot, reasonably and at the same time, 'forecast' three or four quite different futures. Scenarios, as a collection of futures, are intended to establish the boundaries of our uncertainty and the limits to plausible futures.

However, I recognize that there is a very powerful human tendency, born of past experience and culture, to assign probabilities at the end of the scenario process. Every individual ends up with his or her own private assessment of probability; and it is almost certainly better to bring these assessments out into the open for group discussion than to leave them suppressed in indi-

vidual minds. Indeed, doing this usually serves to underscore the wide diversity of opinions – and the consequent foolishness of trying to reach some sort of consensus on this matter. However, whichever course of action one elects – to engage in this group assessment or not – the critical point is to avoid playing the probabilities game to the point of focusing on one 'most probable' scenario to the exclusion of the others. To do so would negate the whole value of the scenario planning exercise.

What to do

Using scenarios to make strategic decisions requires considerable skill and sophistication: and these qualities take time to acquire. Initially, therefore, any organization experimenting with scenario planning needs some sort of a template, a primer, or step-by-step approach to moving from scenarios to strategy. Some critics will protest that this approach trivializes strategy development, substituting analytical structure for intuitive insight. However, in defense of this utilitarian approach, consider the analogy of learning to play the piano. The beginner has to learn the notes, practice scales, and play rhythmically, paced by a metronome. Only after mastering technique can the piano player perform with feeling and insight. So, too, the beginning scenario player needs to learn some basic techniques that will help to bridge the gap between scenarios and strategy before graduating to a more sophisticated approach.

In this spirit, I offer the following primer of four approaches to this problem, ranging from the most elemental to the more sophisticated.

Sensitivity/risk assessment

This approach can be used to evaluate a specific strategic decision such as a major plant investment or a new business development drive. Here, the need for the decision is known beforehand: the question, therefore, is simply whether or not to proceed, after assessing the strategy's resilience or vulnerability in different business conditions.

A step-by-step approach first identifies the key conditions (such as market growth rate, changes in regulatory climate, technological developments) that the future market or industry environment would have to meet to justify a 'go' decision, and then assesses the state of these conditions in each scenario. It is then possible to compare the scenario conditions with the desired future conditions, and to assess how successful and how resilient or vulnerable, a 'go' decision would be in each scenario. Finally, it is possible to assess the overall resilience of a decision to proceed with the proposed strategy, and to consider the need or desirability of 'hedging' or modifying the original decision in some way in order to increase its resilience.

This approach provides a relatively straightforward application of scenarios to decision-making, using a series of descriptive and judgmental steps. However, it depends on having a very clear and specific decision focus, one which lends itself to a 'go/no go' decision.

An illustration of this approach was provided by a paper company confronted with a decision on whether or not to invest $600 million in a new paper-making facility. The company did not normally use scenarios in its strategic planning, but decided that they would be useful here, given the long life span (30–35 years) of the plant and the corresponding range of uncertainties regarding future electronic technology development, consumer values and time use, prospects for advertising, and general economic conditions.

The scenarios showed, as one might expect, vastly different levels of demand growth, but similar patterns of eventual decline, with the timing of key threats remaining a critical uncertainty. Playing out the investment decision in these different environments suggested that only in the most optimistic conditions would the company meet its 'hurdle rate' for return on investment. As a result, the executives decided on a more incremental approach to the investment, significantly scaling down the initial plant size.

Strategy evaluation

Another relatively straightforward role for scenarios is to act as 'test beds' to evaluate the viability of an existing strategy, usually one that derives from traditional single-point forecasting. By playing a company wide or business unit strategy against the scenarios it is possible to gain some insight into the strategy's effectiveness in a range of business conditions, and so to identify modifications and/or contingency planning that require attention.

First, it is necessary to disaggregate the strategy into its specific thrusts (e.g., 'Focus on upscale consumer market segments,' 'Diversify into related services areas') and spell out its goals and objectives. Then it is possible to assess the relevance and likely success (in terms of meeting the desired objectives) of these thrusts in the diverse conditions of the scenarios. Assessing the results of this impact analysis should

then enable the management team to identify: (a) opportunities that the strategy addresses and those that it misses; (b) threats/risks that the analysis has foreseen or overlooked; and (c) comparative competitive success or failure.

At this point, it is possible to identify options for changes in strategy and the need for contingency planning.

This approach offers a natural and relatively simple first use of scenarios in a corporate strategic planning system. Assessing an existing strategy requires less sophistication than developing a new strategy; nevertheless, assessment provides a quick demonstration of the utility of scenarios in executive decision-making by identifying important 'bottom-line' issues that require immediate attention.

A large department-store chain introduced scenarios this way into its strategic exploration of future patterns of change in the economy, consumer values, life styles, and the structure and operations of the retail industry. The company used these scenarios in three distinct ways: (1) evaluate the likely payoff from its current strategy; (2) assess and compare the strategies of key competitors (note: this was an interesting – and useful – application of scenario planning, assessing the competitors' as well as one's own strategy); and (3) analyze retail strategy options to identify the most resilient ones for possible inclusion in the company's strategy (the company did, in fact, expand greatly into specialty stores as a result of this exercise).

Strategy development (using a 'planning-focus' scenario)

This approach is an attempt to bridge the 'culture gap' between traditional planning that relies on single-point forecasting and scenario planning. Basically, it consists of selecting one of the scenarios as a starting point and focus for strategy development, and then using the other scenarios to test the strategy's resilience and assess the need for modification, 'hedging' or contingency planning.

The steps involved in this approach are as follows: (a) review the scenarios to identify the key opportunities and threats for the business, looking at each scenario in turn and then looking across all scenarios (to identify common opportunities and threats); (b) determine, based on this review, what the company should do, and should not do, in any case; (c) select a 'planning focus' scenario (usually the 'most probable' one); (d) integrate the strategic elements identified in step b into a coherent strategy for the 'planning focus' scenario; (e) test this strategy against the remaining scenarios to assess its resilience or vulnerability; and (f) review the results of this test to determine the need for strategy modification, 'hedging', and contingency planning.

It should be obvious that this approach flies in the face of my earlier assertion that scenarios should not deal in probabilities. And, while the other scenarios are not discarded, there is still the danger that this approach may close executives' minds to 'unlikely' (which often means 'unpleasant') scenarios and so limits their search for strategy options. However, the approach can be justified as a useful intermediate step (between traditional and scenario planning) in weaning executives away from their reliance on single-point forecasting. It does not commit the ultimate sin of disregarding the other scenarios entirely; and, in its step-by-step process, it does address many of the key questions that scenario-based strategy should ask.

Shell Canada used this approach when it introduced scenarios into its strategic planning system in the early 1980s. As a member of the Royal Dutch/Shell Group, its executives were well aware of the strict interpretation of scenario-based planning, but felt that this modified approach would help the company ease into the new process by making this concession to traditional thinking. In fact, the discussion of probabilities revealed so much uncertainty in executive opinion about future trends, that two scenarios – each with dramatically different drivers – were selected as the 'planning focus'. The company then proceeded to structure its strategic positioning in answer to three questions: (1) What strategies should we pursue no matter which scenario materializes? (2) What strategies should we pursue if either of the 'planning focus' scenarios materializes? (3) How sensitive are base strategies to variations in assumptions under contingent conditions?

In fact, in the end, Shell Canada did succeed, both in bridging the gap between the old and new approaches to strategy development and in preserving the value of considering, and planning for, different business conditions.

Strategy development (without using a 'planning-focus' scenario)

In this approach, executives take all scenarios at face value without judging probabilities, and aim for the development of a resilient strategy that can deal with wide variations in business conditions. The step-by-step process in this approach considers: (1) identifying the key elements of a successful strategy (such as geographic scope, market focus, product range, basis of competition); (2) analyzing each scenario to determine the optimal setting for each strategy element (e.g., what would be the best marketing strategy for Scenario A? for Scenario B?); (3) reviewing these scenario-specific settings to determine the most resilient option for each strategy element; and (4) integrating these strategy options into an overall, coordinated business strategy.

Without doubt, this is the most sophisticated – and demanding – approach, one that most closely approximates the goal of stategizing within the scenarios framework, and that makes optimal use of the scenarios in strategy development. It provides management with the maximum feasible range of choice, and forces careful evaluation of these options against differing assumptions about the future. It does, however, demand effort, patience, and sophistication, and works best when the decision-makers participate directly throughout the process.

This was the case with a large European financial-services company in which the senior management team was, in effect, both the scenario- and the strategy-development team. After structuring scenarios around their perceptions of the critical uncertainties facing the business, they first identified the strategic opportunities and threats arising from these scenarios. They then used this framework to assess the company's current competitive position and prospective vulnerability. Their approach to strategy development then led them to the following steps: (1) first, to single out 11 key elements of a well-rounded strategy (e.g., product scope, alliances, distribution/delivery, technology); (2) second, to identify the optimal strategic option for each of these 11 elements in each of the four scenarios; and (3) finally, to select the most resilient option for each element, and to integrate the options into a coherent strategy for the company.

Conclusion

I have chosen to emphasize this one aspect of scenario planning – moving from the scenarios themselves to strategy development to action – because, in my experience, it is perhaps the most critical phase of the scenario process. More scenario projects fail because they have no impact on strategy and management decisions rather than because they were unimaginative or poorly constructed.

Moving from traditional planning to scenario-based strategic planning requires a transformation of corporate culture. Scenario planning is not merely a new planning tool, but rather a new way of thinking. Using scenarios on a one-shot basis requires much less investment than instituting them as an integral part of corporate planning. Many, perhaps most, of the problems in introducing scenario planning into an organization stem from a failure to recognize the magnitude and duration of the implementation effort that is required to use this technology to change the prevailing management assumptions.

Like scenarios themselves, this effort has to be tailored to the needs of the organization, but some requirements are constant: senior management commitment, communications, education and guidance, and practice, practice, practice. Like the piano player, the scenarios user will be able to progress from beginning exercises, as outlined here, to intuitive and insightful action only with time, patience, and practice.

STRATEGY FORMATION IN INTERNATIONAL PERSPECTIVE

What we anticipate seldom occurs; what we least expect generally happens.
Benjamin Disraeli (1804–1881); British prime minister and novelist

From the preceding readings it has become evident that views differ sharply as to whether strategies should be formed by means of planning or incrementalism. It is clear that a wide variety of approaches exists to deal with the paradox of deliberateness and emergence. None of the authors, however, suggest that their views may be more appropriate in some countries than in others. Nor do any of them mention the possibility that an organization's choice of approach may be influenced by national circumstances. In other words, so far the international angle has been conspicuously absent. It has generally been assumed that international differences are a non-issue.

Yet, the question whether there are specific national preferences for the strategic planning or the strategic incrementalism perspective seems quite legitimate. In the past, a few international comparative studies have been carried out that show significantly different levels of formal planning across various industrialized countries. For instance, Steiner and Schollhammer (1975) reported that planning was found to be most common and most formalized in the United States, with other English-speaking countries (Britain, Canada and Australia) also exhibiting a high score. At the other extreme were Italy and Japan, where very little formal planning was witnessed. The low propensity to engage in formal planning in Japan has been noted by a number of other authors as well (e.g. Kagono et al., 1985). Hayashi (1978: 221) remarks that Japanese firms 'distrust corporate planning in general', while Ohmae (1982: 225) characterizes Japanese companies as 'less planned, less rigid, but more vision- and mission-driven' than Western companies. Unfortunately, there are no cross-cultural studies of a more recent date to confirm that these international dissimilarities still exist. However, many observers have suggested that there remain discernible national differences in approaches to strategy formation (e.g. Gilbert and Lorange, 1995; Mintzberg, 1994a; Schneider, 1989).

Although it is difficult to generalize at the national level, since there can be quite a bit of variance within a country, it is challenging to pursue these observed international dissimilarities. Are there really national strategy formation styles and what factors might influence their existence? As a stimulus to the international dimension of this debate, we put forward the following country characteristics as possible influences on how the paradox of deliberateness and emergence is dealt with in different national settings. As we noted at the end of Chapter 2, these propositions are intended to encourage discussion, but more concrete international comparative research is needed to give this debate a firmer footing.

Level of professionalization

The high incidence of formal planning systems in Australia, Britain, Canada, New Zealand and the United States seems odd, given their high level of individualism and their strong preference for a market economy. One might expect that the English-speaking countries' fondness of unplanned markets would be a reflection of a general dislike of planning. Yet, strangely, 'most large US corporations are run like the Soviet economy' of yesteryear, with strong central plans and top-down control, Ohmae concludes (1982: 224).

One explanation might be that formalized planning and control systems are a logical consequence of having professional management (e.g. Mintzberg, 1994a). Nowhere in the industrialized world, with the exception of France, has there been a stronger development of a distinct managerial class than in the English-speaking countries (Hampden-Turner and Trompenaars, 1993; Lessem and Neubauer, 1994). These professional managers run companies on behalf of the owners, who are usually distant from the operations (i.e. often minority shareholders). In the division of labor, the managers perform the 'thinking' tasks – analyzing, planning, coordinating, leading, budgeting, motivating, controlling – while the workforce concentrates on performing the primary activities. This makes it possible for large, complex production processes to be controlled by a hierarchy of professional managers. It is commonly believed that these managers possess general skills that allow them to run a wide variety of different businesses.

In companies with professional management, the split between thinking and doing is made more explicit than in other organizations. The managers are the officers who formulate the strategies and the personnel on the work floor are the troops that must implement them – 'management' has intentions that the 'employees' must realize. This requires formal planning to guide workers' actions and a tight control system to ensure compliance. This mechanism is usually employed all the way up the hierarchy, as higher level managers use a planning and control system to steer and coordinate the behavior of lower level managers. All the way at the top, senior management must also make plans to win the approval of the shareholders.

This stratified organizational model, that Mintzberg dubs the machine bureaucracy (1979), is also prevalent in France, where the distinction between *cadre* employees and *non-cadre* personnel is also very strong (Hofstede, 1993, Reading 1.4 in this book). In many other countries, however, the split between managerial and non-managerial tasks is not as radical. For instance, in Germany and Japan, senior employees are expected to be involved in operational matters, while junior employees are expected to contribute to strategy formation, by coming up with ideas and passing on information to seniors. In such countries, there is less need to use formal planning and control mechanisms to manage employees, since the 'managers' have direct and informal links with those 'managed'. Usually these managers have risen through the ranks, giving them the richness of information and contacts needed to manage without highly formalized systems. In these nations, consensus-building and personal control are the important management skills, and these are not readily transferable to another industry or even another organization.

In yet other countries, the dominant form of organization is that of direct control by one person or a family. This usually means that organizations remain relatively small, although they can compensate by linking up into networks based on personal connections between the top bosses. This organizational model, common in Italy and among the overseas Chinese (see Hofstede, 1993, Reading 1.4; Weidenbaum and Hughes, 1996) will be further discussed in Chapter 7. Here it is sufficient to conclude that in such organizations there is also little need for formalized planning and control systems to manage employees. The top boss, who is usually also the owner, steers the firm personally, with little regard for 'professional' methods.

The conclusion is that the national propensity to engage in formal planning is probably influenced by the level of professionalization of management within the country. In nations where the machine bureaucracy is the predominant organizational model, a stronger inclination towards formal planning systems can be expected.

Preference for internal control

While the previous section discussed different *types* of internal control, and the related organizational models, it should be noted that countries can also differ with regard to the *level* of internal control their citizens prefer. In some cultures, people have a strong desire for order and structure – clear tasks, responsibilities, powers, rules and procedures. Ambiguous situations and uncertain outcomes are disliked and therefore management strives to control organizational processes. Management can reduce uncertainty in a number of ways. Structure can be offered by strictly following traditions or by imposing top-down paternalistic rule. However, uncertainty can also be reduced by planning (Kagono et al., 1985; Schneider, 1989). By setting direction, coordinating initiatives, committing resources, and programming activities, structure can be brought to the organization. In this way, planning can help to alleviate people's anxiety about 'disorganization'. In cultures that are more tolerant towards ambiguity and uncertainty, one can expect a weaker preference for planning.

The importance of planning as a means for structuring and controlling is particularly important in cultures where there is little confidence in self-organization. This is especially true in individualistic cultures, where organizational members cannot always be counted on to work towards the common good (Hofstede, 1993, Reading 1.4). In these countries, extensive planning and control systems are often used as a formal means for getting people to cooperate, coordinate and serve the organization's interests. Strategic plans function as internal contracts, to limit dysfunctional opportunistic behavior (Allaire and Firsirotu, 1990; Bungay and Goold, 1991). In cultures with a stronger group-orientation, there is usually more trust that individuals will be team players, making formal control mechanisms redundant (Nonaka and Johansson, 1985). Therefore, in general, one can expect a weaker preference for planning in collectivist cultures.

Preference for external control

Cultures also differ with regard to the level of control that organizational members prefer to have over their environment. At the one extreme are cultures in which people strive to manage or even dominate their surroundings. In these countries, there is a strong desire to create the future and a fear of losing control of one's destiny. George Bernard Shaw's famous remark that 'to be in hell is to drift, to be in heaven is to steer', neatly summarizes these feelings. The consequence is that organizations in these nations are strongly drawn to proactive and deliberate strategy-making, under the motto 'plan or be planned for' (Ackoff, 1980). Drawing up plans to actively engage the outside world meets people's need to determine their own fate. This cultural characteristic is particularly pronounced in Western countries (Trompenaars, 1993).

At the other extreme are cultures in which most people passively accept their destiny. They believe that most external events are out of their hands and that they exert no control over the future. In such fatalistic cultures people tend to approach opportunities and threats reactively, on a day-to-day basis. Such muddling through behavior rarely leads to emergent strategy, but more often to disjointed, unpatterned action.

In the middle are cultures in which people believe neither in domination of, or submission to, external circumstances. In these cultures people accept that events are unpredictable and that the environment cannot be tightly controlled, yet trust that individuals and organizations can proactively seek their own path among these uncertainties. The environment and the firm, it is thought, co-evolve through interaction and mutual adjustment, often in unforeseen ways. This requires firms to 'develop an attitude of receptivity and high adaptability to changing conditions' (Maruyama, 1984). This way of thinking is particularly pronounced in South-East Asia, and leads to a stronger inclination towards the strategic incrementalism perspective (Kagono et al., 1985; Schneider, 1989).

Time orientation

A culture's time orientation can also be expected to influence national preferences for dealing with the paradox of deliberateness and emergence. There are a number of dimensions along which cultures' perception of time can differ. Cultures can be more involved with the past, the present or the future, whereby some make a strong linear separation between these phases, while others emphasize the continuity of time or even its cyclical nature. With regard to the future, a distinction can also be made between cultures with a more short-term or long-term orientation (Hofstede, 1993, Reading 1.4).

In general, it can be expected that people in cultures that heavily accentuate the past, or the present, over the future, will be less inclined to think and act strategically. In cultures that emphasize the near future, however, it is likely that individuals and organizations will exhibit a preference for planning. A focus on the not-too-distant future, which is more predictable than the long-term future, fits well with a strategic planning approach. In these countries, intentions are formulated, courses of action are determined and resources are committed, but with a relatively short planning horizon. Plans will only be adopted if results can be expected in the 'foreseeable' future. As Hofstede (1993) reports, the English-speaking countries belong to this category of short-term oriented cultures (see also Calori, Valla and de Woot, 1994; Kagono et al., 1985).

In cultures with a stronger long-term orientation, strategic incrementalism can be expected to be a more predominant perspective. Since the long-term future is inherently unknown, planning for the future is seen as an inappropriate response. In these countries, it is generally believed that the unpredictability of the long-term future must be accepted and accommodated. This requires an attitude of caution and flexibility, linked to curiosity, learning and persistence. Actions are often taken that are not optimal in the short run, but point in the right long-term direction. As Hofstede (1993) reports, many South-East Asian countries fall into this category, as do some European countries.

FURTHER READING

For readers interested in an overview of the strategy formation literature, the best place to start is with *Strategy Safari: A Guided Tour Through the Wilds of Strategic Management*, by Henry Mintzberg, B. Ahlstrand and Joseph Lampel. Two other interesting overviews are 'How Strategies Develop in Organizations', by Andy Bailey and Gerry Johnson, and 'An Integrative Framework for Strategy-Making Processes', by Stuart Hart.

There are many books that give a detailed rendition of how strategic planning should be conducted within organizations. Igor Ansoff's and E. McDonnell's well-known textbook, *Implanting Strategic Management*, is an excellent, yet taxing, description of strategy-making from a planning perspective, while George Steiner's *Strategic Planning: What Every Manager Must Know* is a more down to earth prescription. Between these two extremes is a whole range of widely sold planning-oriented textbooks, such as Arthur Thompson and A.J. Strickland's *Strategic Management: Concepts and Cases*, and Thomas Wheelen and David Hunger's *Strategic Management and Business Policy*. For further reading on formal planning systems, Balaji Chakravarthy and Peter Lorange's book *Managing the Strategy Process: A Framework for a Multibusiness Firm* is a good place to start. On the link between planning and forecasting, the book *Forecasting, Planning and Strategy for the 21st Century*, by Spiro Makridakis, provides a useful introduction. A good book on scenarios is by Kees van der Heyden, entitled *Scenarios: The Art of Strategic Conversation*.

The most articulate critic of planning is probably Henry Mintzberg, whose book *The Rise and Fall of Strategic Planning* makes for thought-provoking reading. David Hurst's article 'Why Strategic Management is Bankrupt' also provides many interesting arguments against strategic planning. For a more extensive description of the strategic incrementalism perspective, James Brian Quinn's book *Strategies for Change* is still a good starting point. The fascinating book *Competing on the Edge: Strategy as Structured Chaos*, by Kathleen Eisenhardt and Shona Brown, also incorporates incrementalist approaches, as does Ralph Stacey's excellent textbook *Strategic Management and Organizational Dynamics*. Also highly recommended are Ikujiro Nonaka's article 'Toward Middle-Up-Down Management: Accelerating Information Creation' and Robert Burgelman's article 'Corporate Entrepreneurship and Strategic Management: Insights from a Process Study'.

For a better understanding of the political processes involved in strategy formation the reader might want to turn to Andrew Pettigrew's article 'Strategy Formulation as a Political Process', or to Jeffrey Pfeffer's book *Power in Organizations*. Graham Allison's classic book *The Essence of Decision: Explaining the Cuban Missile Crisis* is also highly recommended. The cultural processes are vividly described in Gerry Johnson's *Strategic Change and the Management Process*, and more popularly in Rosabeth Moss Kanter's *The Change Masters*. Further articles and books that explore the link between strategy formation and strategic change are presented at the end of Chapter 4.

REFERENCES

Ackoff, R.L. (1980) *Creating the Corporate Future*, Wiley, Chichester.
Allaire, Y., and Firsirotu, M. (1990) 'Strategic Plans as Contracts', *Long Range Planning*, Vol. 23, No. 1, pp. 102–115.
Allison, G.T. (1969) 'Conceptual Models and The Cuban Missile Crisis', *The American Political Science Review*, No. 3, September, pp. 689–718.
Allison, G.T. (1971) *The Essence of Decision: Explaining the Cuban Missile Crisis*, Little Brown, Boston.
Amabile, T.M. (1998) 'How to Kill Creativity', *Harvard Business Review*, Vol. 76, No. 5, September–October, pp. 76–87.
Andrews, K.R. (1987) *The Concept of Corporate Strategy*, Third Edition, Irwin, Homewood, IL.
Ansoff, H.I. (1965) *Corporate Strategy: An Analytic Approach to Business Policy for Growth and Expansion*, McGraw-Hill, New York.
Ansoff, H.I. (1991) 'Critique of Henry Mintzberg's The "Design School": Reconsidering the Basic Premises of Strategic Management', *Strategic Management Journal*, September, pp. 449–461.
Ansoff, H.I., and McDonnell, E. (1990) *Implanting Strategic Management*, Second Edition, Prentice Hall, New York.
Armstrong, J.S. (1982) 'The Value of Formal Planning for Strategic Decisions: Review of Empirical Research', *Strategic Management Journal*, Vol. 3, pp. 197–211.
Bailey, A., and Johnson, G. (1992) 'How Strategies Develop in Organizations', in: D. Faulkner and G. Johnson (eds.), *The Challenge of Strategic Management*, Kogan Page, London.
Beinhocker, E.D. (1999) 'Robust Adaptive Strategies', *Sloan Management Review*, Vol. 40, No. 3, Spring, pp. 95–106.
Bourgeois, L.J., and Brodwin, D.R. (1983) 'Putting Your Strategy into Action', *Strategic Management Planning*, March–May.

Bower, J.L. (1970) *Managing the Resource Allocation Process*, Harvard Business School Press, Boston.

Bungay, S., and Goold, M. (1991) 'Creating a Strategic Control System', *Long Range Planning*, Vol. 24, No. 6, pp. 32–39.

Burgelman, R.A. (1983) 'Corporate Entrepreneurship and Strategic Management: Insights from a Process Study', *Management Science*, Vol. 29, No. 12, pp. 1349–1364.

Burgelman, R.A. (1991) 'Intraorganizational Ecology of Strategy Making and Organizational Adaptation: Theory and Field Research', *Organization Science*, Vol. 2, No. 3, pp. 239–262.

Calori, R., Valla, J.-P., and De Woot, P. (1994) 'Common Characteristics: The Ingredients of European Management', in: R. Calori and P. De Woot (eds.), *A European Management Model: Beyond Diversity*, Prentice Hall, Hemel Hempstead.

Campbell, A., Goold, M., and Alexander M. (1994) *Corporate-Level Strategy: Creating Value in the Multibusiness Company*, Wiley, New York.

Chaffee, E.E. (1985) 'Three Models of Strategy', *Academy of Management Review*, Vol. 10, No. 1, January, pp. 89–98.

Chakravarthy, B.S., and Lorange, P. (1991) *Managing the Strategy Process: A Framework for a Multibusiness Firm*, Prentice Hall, Englewood Cliffs, NJ.

Cohen, M.D., March, J.G., and Olsen, J.P. (1972) 'A Garbage Can Model of Organization Choice', *Administrative Science Quarterly*, March, pp. 1–25.

De Geus, A. (1988) 'Planning as Learning', *Harvard Business Review*, March–April, pp. 70–74.

Eccles, M. (1951) *Beckoning Frontiers*, Knopf, New York.

Eisenhardt, K.M., and Brown, S.L. (1998) *Competing on the Edge: Strategy as Structured Chaos*, Harvard Business School Press, Boston.

Evans, J.S. (1991) 'Strategic Flexibility for High Technology Manoeuvres: A Conceptual Framework', *Journal of Management Studies*, Vol. 28, January, pp. 69–89.

Floyd, S.W., and Wooldridge, B. (2000) *Building Strategy from the Middle Reconceptualizing Strategy Process*, Sage, Thousand Oaks.

Ghemawat, P. (1991). *Commitment: The Dynamic of Strategies*, Free Press, New York.

Gilbert, X., and Lorange, P. (1995) 'National Approaches to Strategic Management: A Resource-based Perspective', *International Business Review*, Vol. 3, No. 4, pp. 411–423.

Gluck, F.W., Kaufman, S.P., and Walleck, A.S. (1982) 'The Four Phases of Strategic Management', *Journal of Business Strategy*, Winter, pp. 9–21.

Godet, M. (1987) *Scenarios and Strategic Management*, Butterworths, London.

Grinyer, P.H., Al-Bazzaz, S., and Yasai-Ardekani, M. (1986) 'Towards a Contingency Theory of Corporate Planning: Findings in 48 U.K. Companies', *Strategic Management Journal*, Vol. 7, pp. 3–28.

Hamel, G. (1996) 'Strategy as Revolution', *Harvard Business Review*, Vol. 74, No. 4, July–August, pp. 69–82.

Hampden-Turner, C., and Trompenaars, A. (1993) *The Seven Cultures of Capitalism: Value Systems for Creating Wealth in the United States, Japan, Germany, France, Britain, Sweden and the Netherlands*, Doubleday, New York.

Haour, G., and Cho, H.J. (2000) 'Samsung Electronics Co. Ltd in the 1990s: Sustaining Competitiveness', *IMD Business Case*.

Hart, S.L. (1992) 'An Integrative Framework for Strategy-Making Processes', *Academy of Management Review*, Vol. 17, No. 2, pp. 327–351.

Hax, A.C., and Majluf, N.S. (1984) *Strategic Management: An Integrative Approach*, Prentice Hall, Englewood Cliffs, NJ.

Hayashi, K. (1978) 'Corporate Planning Practices in Japanese Multinationals', *Academy of Management Journal*, Vol. 21, No. 2, pp. 211–226.

Hayes, R.H. (1985) 'Strategic Planning: Forward in Reverse?', *Harvard Business Review*, November–December, pp. 111–119.

Hofstede, G. (1993) 'Cultural Constraints in Management Theories', *Academy of Management Executive*, Vol. 7, No. 1, pp. 81–94.

Hurst, D.K. (1986) 'Why Strategic Management is Bankrupt', *Organizational Dynamics*, Vol. 15, Autumn, pp. 4–27.

Jelinek, M. (1979) *Institutionalizing Innovation*, Praeger, New York.

Johnson, G. (1987) *Strategic Change and the Management Process*, Basil Blackwell, Oxford.

Johnson, G. (1988) 'Rethinking Incrementalism', *Strategic Management Journal*, Vol. 9, No. 1, January–February, pp. 75–91.

Kagono, T., Nonaka, I., Sakakibara, K., and Okumara, A. (1985) *Strategic vs. Evolutionary Management*, Amsterdam, North-Holland.

Kanter, R. (1983) *The Change Masters: Innovation for Productivity in the American Corporation*, Basic Books, New York.

Kanter, R.M. (2002) 'Strategy as Improvisational Theater', *Sloan Management Review*, Vol. 43, No. 2, pp. 76–81.

Kaplan, R.S., and Norton, D.P. (2001) *The Strategy-Focused Organization: How Balanced Scorecard Thrive in the New Business Environment*, Harvard Business School Press, Boston, MA.

Kiechel, W., III. (1984) 'Sniping at Strategic Planning', *Planning Review*, May, pp. 8–11.

Kukalis, S. (1991) 'Determinants of Strategic Planning Systems in Large Organizations: A Contingency Approach', *Journal of Management Studies*, Vol. 28, pp. 143–160.

Langley, A. (1995) 'Between "Paralysis and Analysis" and "Extinction by Instinct"', *Sloan Management Review*, Vol. 36, No. 3, Spring, pp. 63–76.

Lenz, R.T., and Lyles, M. (1985) 'Paralysis by Analysis: Is Your Planning System Becoming Too Rational?', *Long Range Planning*, Vol. 18, No. 4, pp. 64–72.

Lessem, R., and Neubauer, F.F. (1994) *European Management Systems*, McGraw-Hill, London.

Liedtka, J. (2000) 'In Defense of Strategy as Design', *California Management Review*, Vol. 42, No. 3, pp. 8–30.

Lindblom, C.E. (1959) 'The Science of Muddling Through', *Public Administration Review*, Spring, pp. 79–88.

Lorange, P. (1980) *Corporate Planning: An Executive Viewpoint*, Prentice Hall, Englewood Cliffs, NJ.

Lorange, P., and R.F. Vancil (1977) *Strategic Planning Systems*, Prentice Hall, Englewood Cliffs, NJ.

Lyon, D.W., Lumpkin, G.T., and Dess, G.G. (2000) 'Enhancing Entrepreneurial Orientation Research: Operationalizing and Measuring a Key Strategic Decision Making Process', *Journal of Management*, Vol. 26, pp. 1055–1085.

Makridakis, S. (1990) *Forecasting, Planning and Strategy for the 21st Century*, Free Press, New York.

Maruyama, M. (1984) 'Alternative Concepts of Management: Insights from Asia and Africa', *Asia Pacific Journal of Management*, Vol. 1, January, pp. 100–111.

Marx, T.G. (1991) 'Removing the Obstacles to Effective Strategic Planning', *Long Range Planning*, Vol. 24, No. 4, August, pp. 21–28.

Miles, R., Snow, C., Meyer, A., and Coleman, H. (1978) 'Organizational Strategy, Structure, and Process', *Academy of Management Review*, Vol. 3, No. 3, July, pp. 546–562.

Miller, C.C., and Cardinal, L.B. (1994) 'Strategic Planning and Firm Performance: A Synthesis of more than Two Decades of Research', *Academy of Management Journal*, Vol. 37, No. 6, pp. 1649–1665.

Mintzberg, H. (1979) *The Structuring of Organizations: A Synthesis of the Research*, Prentice Hall, Englewood Cliffs, NJ.

Mintzberg, H. (1990a) 'The Design School: Reconsidering the Basic Premises of Strategic Management', *Strategic Management Journal*, Vol. 11, pp. 171–195.

Mintzberg, H. (1990b) 'Strategy Formation: Schools of Thought', in: J. Frederickson (ed.), *Perspectives on Strategic Management*, Ballinger, Boston.

Mintzberg, H. (1991) 'Learning 1. Planning 0: Reply to Igor Ansoff', *Strategic Management Journal*, September, pp. 463–466.

Mintzberg, H. (1993) 'The Pitfalls of Strategic Planning', *California Management Review*, Vol. 36, No. 1, Fall, pp. 32–45.

Mintzberg, H. (1994a) 'The Fall and Rise of Strategic Planning', *Harvard Business Review*, Vol. 73, No. 1, January–February.

Mintzberg, H. (1994b) 'Rethinking Strategic Planning Part I: Pitfalls and Fallacies', *Long Range Planning*, Vol. 27, No. 3, pp. 12–21.

Mintzberg, H. (1994c) 'Rethinking Strategic Planning Part II: New Roles for Planners', *Long Range Planning*, Vol. 27, No. 3, pp. 22–30.

Mintzberg, H. (1994d) *The Rise and Fall of Strategic Planning*, Prentice Hall, Englewood Cliffs, NJ.

Mintzberg, H., Ahlstrand, B., and Lampel, J. (1998) *Strategy Safari: A Guided Tour Through the Wilds of Strategic Management*, The Free Press, New York.

Mintzberg, H., and Waters, J.A. (1985) 'Of Strategy: Deliberate and Emergent', *Strategic Management Journal*, Vol. 6, No. 3, July–September, pp. 257–272.

Morgenthau, H. (1960) *Politics Among Nations*, Third Edition, Knopf, New York.

Nonaka, I. (1988) 'Toward Middle-Up-Down Management: Accelerating Information Creation', *Sloan Management Review*, Vol. 29, No. 3, Spring, pp. 9–18.

Nonaka, I., and Johansson, J.K. (1985) 'Japanese Management: What about "Hard" Skills?', *Academy of Management Review*, Vol. 10, No. 2, pp. 181–191.

Ohmae, K. (1982) *The Mind of the Strategist*, McGraw-Hill, New York.

Pascale, R.T. (1984) 'Perspectives on Strategy: The Real Story Behind Honda's Success', *California Management Review*, Vol. 26, No. 3, pp. 47–72.

Pettigrew, A.M. (1977) 'Strategy Formulation as a Political Process', *International Studies of Management and Organization*, Vol. 7, Summer, pp. 47–72.

Pfeffer, J. (1981) *Power in Organizations*, Pitman, Marshfield, MA.

Pinchot, G., III, (1985) *Intrapreneuring: Why You Don't Have to Leave the Company to Become an Entrepreneur*, Harper & Row, New York.

Porter, M.E. (1987) 'The State of Strategic Thinking', *Economist*, May 23, pp. 21.

Powell, T.C. (1992) 'Strategic Planning as Competitive Advantage', *Strategic Management Journal*, Vol. 13, pp. 551–558.

Quinn, J.B. (1978) 'Strategic Change: "Logical Incrementalism"', *Sloan Management Review*, Fall, pp. 7–21.

Quinn, J.B. (1980) *Strategies for Change*, Irwin, Homewood, IL.

Quinn, J.B. (1985) 'Managing Innovation: Controlled Chaos', *Harvard Business Review*, Vol. 63, No. 3, May–June, pp. 73–84.

Quinn, J.B. (2002) 'Strategy, Science and Management', *Sloan Management Review*, Vol. 43, No. 4.

Rittel, H.W., and Webber, M.M. (1973) 'Dilemmas in a General Theory of Planning', *Policy Sciences*, Vol. 4, pp. 155–169.

Robinson, R.B. (1982) 'The Importance of Outsiders in Small Firm Strategic Planning', *Academy of Management Journal*, Vol. 25, pp. 80–93.

Schein, E.H. (1985) *Organizational Culture and Leadership*, Jossey-Bass, San Francisco.

Schelling, T. (1960) *The Strategy of Conflict*, Harvard University Press, Cambridge, MA.

Schneider, S.C. (1989) 'Strategy Formulation: The Impact of National Culture', *Organization Studies*, Vol. 10, No. 2, pp. 149–168.

Shrivastava, P., and Grant, J. (1985) 'Empirically Derived Models of Strategic Decision-Making Processes', *Strategic Management Journal*, Vol. 6, pp. 97–113.

Simons, R. (1995) *Levers of Control: How Managers Use Innovative Control Systems to Drive Strategic Renewal*, HBS Press, Boston, MA.

Smircich, L., and Stubbart, C. (1985) 'Strategic Management in an Enacted World', *Academy of Management Review*, Vol. 10, No. 4, pp. 724–736.

Stacey, R.D. (1993) 'Strategy as Order Emerging from Chaos', *Long Range Planning*, Vol. 26, No. 1, pp. 10–17.

Stacey, R.D. (1996) *Strategic Management and Organizational Dynamics*, Second Edition, Pitman, London.

Stacey, R.D. (2001) *Complex Responsive Processes in Organizations: Learning and Knowledge Creation*, Routledge, London.

Steiner, G.A. (1979) *Strategic Planning: What Every Manager Must Know*, Free Press, New York.

Steiner, G.A., and Schollhammer, H. (1975) 'Pitfalls in Multi-National Long-Range Planning', *Long Range Planning*, Vol. 8, No. 2, April, pp. 2–12.

Thompson, A.A., and Strickland III, A.J. (1995) *Strategic Management: Concepts and Cases*, Eighth Edition, Irwin, Chicago.

Trompenaars, A. (1993) *Riding the Waves of Culture: Understanding Cultural Diversity in Business*, The Economist Books, London.

Van der Heyden, K. (1996) *Scenarios: The Art of Strategic Conversation*, Wiley, New York.

Wack, P. (1985a) 'Scenarios: Unchartered Waters Ahead', *Harvard Business Review*, Vol. 64, No. 5, September–October, pp. 73–89.

Wack, P. (1985b) 'Scenarios: Shooting the Rapids', *Harvard Business Review*, Vol. 64, No. 6, November–December, pp. 139–150.

Weidenbaum, M., and Hughes, S. (1996) *The Bamboo Network: How Expatriate Chinese Entrepreneurs Are Creating a New Economic Superpower in Asia*, Free Press, New York.

Wheelen, T.L., and Hunger, J.D. (1992) *Strategic Management and Business Policy*, Fourth Edition, Addison-Wesley, Boston.

Wildavsky, A. (1979) *Speaking Truth to Power: The Art and Craft of Policy Analysis*, Little, Brown & Co., Toronto.

Wilson, I. (2000) 'From Scenario Thinking to Strategic Action', *Technological Forecasting and Social Change*, Vol. 65, No. 1, September, pp. 23–29.

Yu, S. (1999) 'The Growth Pattern of Samsung Electronics: A Strategy Perspective', *International Studies of Management Organization*, Vol. 28, No. 4, pp. 57–72.

STRATEGIC CHANGE

There is nothing more difficult to take in hand, more perilous to conduct, or more uncertain in its success, than to take the lead in the introduction of a new order of things. Because the innovator has for enemies all those who have done well under the old conditions, and lukewarm defenders in those who may do well under the new.

Niccolo Machiavelli (1469–1527); Florentine statesman and political philosopher

INTRODUCTION

In a world of new technologies, transforming economies, shifting demographics, reforming governments, fluctuating consumer preferences and dynamic competition, it is not a question of whether firms *should* change, but of where, how and in what direction they *must* change. For 'living' organizations, change is a given. Firms must constantly be aligned with their environments, either by reacting to external events, or by proactively shaping the businesses in which they operate.

While change is pervasive, not all change in firms is strategic in nature. Much of the change witnessed is actually the ongoing operational kind. To remain efficient and effective, firms constantly make 'fine-tuning' alterations, whereby existing procedures are upgraded, activities are improved and people are reassigned. Such operational changes are directed at increasing the performance of the firm within the confines of the existing system – within the current basic set-up used to align the firm with the environment. Strategic changes, on the contrary, are directed at creating a new type of alignment – a new fit between the basic set-up of the firm and the characteristics of the environment. Strategic changes have an impact on the way the firm does business (its 'business system') and on the way the organization has been configured (its 'organizational system'). In short, while operational changes are necessary to maintain the business and organizational systems, strategic changes are directed at renewing them.

For managers the challenge is to implement strategic changes on time, to keep the firm in step with the shifting opportunities and threats in the environment. Some parts of the firm's business system and organizational system can be preserved, while others need to be transformed for the firm to stay up-to-date and competitive. This process of constantly enacting strategic changes to remain in harmony with external conditions is called 'strategic renewal'. This chapter examines the issue of the series of strategic change steps required in order to bring about a process of ongoing strategic renewal.

THE ISSUE OF STRATEGIC RENEWAL

There are many actions that constitute a strategic change – a reorganization, a diversification move, a shift in core technology, a business process redesign and a product portfolio reshuffle, to name a few. Each one of these changes is fascinating in itself. Yet, here the discussion will be broader than just a single strategic change, looking instead at the process of how a series of strategic changes can be used to keep the firm in sync with its surroundings (see Figure 4.1). How can 'a path of strategic changes' be followed to constantly renew the firm and avoid a situation whereby the firm 'drifts' too far away from the demands of the environment (Johnson, 1988).

To come to a deeper understanding of the issue of strategic renewal, the first step that must be taken is to examine what is actually being renewed during a process of strategic renewal. The areas of strategic renewal will be explored in the next section. After this initial analysis of 'what' is being changed, a distinction will be made between the magnitude and the pace of change. The magnitude of change refers to the size of the steps being undertaken, whereby the question is whether managers should move in bold and dramatic strides, or in moderate and undramatic ones. The pace of change refers to the relative speed at which the steps are being taken, whereby the question is whether managers should move quickly in a short period of time, or more gradually over a longer time span.

Areas of strategic renewal

Firms are complex systems, consisting of many different elements, each of which can be changed. Therefore, to gain more insight into the various areas of potential change, firms need to be analytically disassembled into a number of component parts. The most fundamental distinction that can be made within a firm, is between the business system and the organizational system:

- Business system. The term business system refers to the way a firm conducts its business. A simple definition would be 'how a firm makes money'. A more formal defini-

FIGURE 4.1 Example of an ongoing strategic renewal process

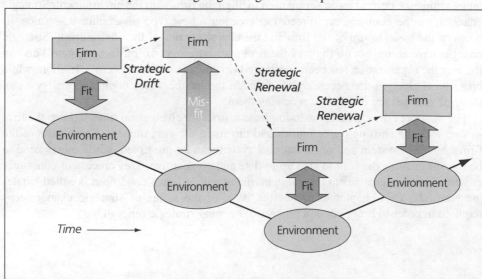

tion of business system is 'the specific configuration of resources, value-adding activities and product/service offerings directed at creating value for customers'. Each firm has its own specific system for taking certain resources as inputs (e.g. materials and know-how), adding value to them in some type of manner (e.g. production and branding) and then selling a particular package of products and/or services as output. As such, a firm's business system (or 'value creation system') is particular to the type of business that the firm is in – an airplane manufacturer conducts its business differently to an airline.

- Organizational system. The term organizational system refers to the way a firm gets its people to work together to carry out the business. A simple definition would be 'how a firm is organized'. A more formal definition of the organizational system would be 'how the individuals populating a firm have been configured, and relate to one another, with the intention of facilitating the business system'. Every firm needs to determine some type of organizational structure, dividing the tasks and responsibilities among the organizational members, thereby instituting differing functions and units. Firms also require numerous organizational processes to link individual members to each other, to ensure that their separate tasks are coordinated into an integrated whole. And firms necessarily have organizational cultures, and sub-cultures, as organizational members interact with one another and build up joint beliefs, values and norms.

In Figure 4.2 the relationship between the business system and the major components of the organizational system is depicted. As this figure illustrates, the business system is 'supported' by the organizational system, with the organizational members 'at its base'. While each firm's business and organizational systems are essentially unique, their general configuration can be fairly similar to that of other firms. Where firms have a comparable business 'formula', it is said that they share the same business model. Likewise, where firms have a similar organizational 'form', they are said to subscribe to the same organizational model.

Both the business system and the organizational system can be further disaggregated into component parts and examined in more detail. With this aim in mind, the business system will be at the center of attention in Chapter 5. Here the organizational system will be further dissected. Actually, the term dissection conjures up images of the organizational system as 'corporate body', which is a useful metaphor for distinguishing the various

FIGURE 4.2 General view of the business system and the organizational system

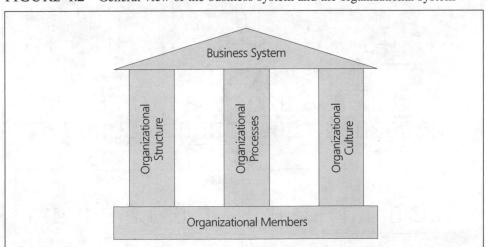

components of an organizational system (Morgan, 1986). Following Bartlett and Ghoshal (1995) the organizational system can be divided into its anatomy (structure), physiology (processes) and psychology (culture). Each of these components, summarized in Figure 4.3, will be examined in the following sub-section.

Organizational structure. Organizational structure refers to the clustering of tasks and people into smaller groups. All organizations need at least some division of labor in order to function efficiently and effectively, requiring them to structure the organization into smaller parts. The main question when determining the organizational structure is which criteria will be used to differentiate tasks and to cluster people into particular units. While there are numerous structuring (or decomposition) criteria, the most common ones are summarized in Figure 4.4. In a simple organization tasks might be divided according to just one criterion, but in most organizations multiple criteria are used (either sequentially or simultaneously).

To balance this horizontal differentiation of tasks and responsibilities, all organizations also have integration mechanisms, intended to get the parts to function well within the organizational whole (Lawrence and Lorsch, 1967). While some of these integration mechanisms are found in the categories of organizational processes and culture, the most fundamental mechanism is usually built into the organizational structure – formal authority. In organizations, managers are appointed with the specific task of supervising the activities of various people or units and to report to managers higher up in the hierarchy.

FIGURE 4.3 Detailed view of the components of the organizational system

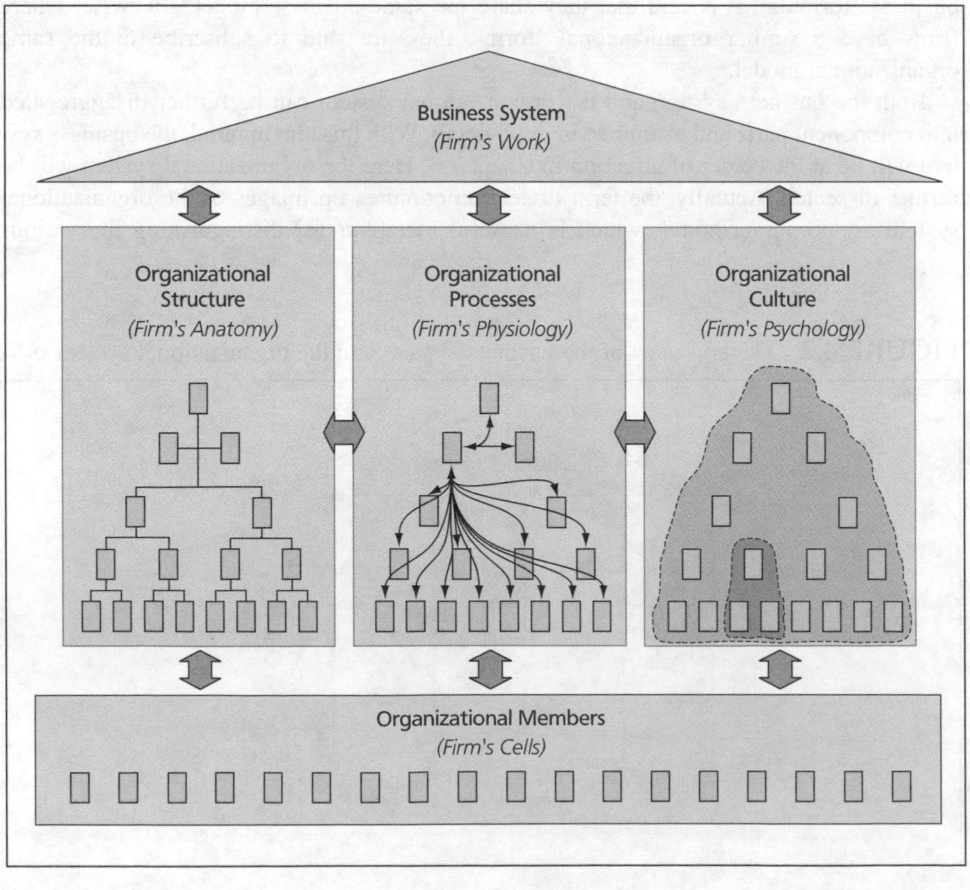

Depending on the span of control of each manager (the number of people or units reporting to him/her) an organizational structure will consist of one or more layers of management. At the apex of this vertical structure is the board of directors, with the ultimate authority to make decisions or ratify decisions made at lower levels in the hierarchy. The most important questions in this context are the number of management layers needed and the amount of authority delegated to lower levels of management. It should be noted that the organizational charts used to represent the formal structure of an organization (see Figure 4.3) need not be an accurate reflection of the informal organizational structure as it operates in reality.

Organizational processes. Organizational processes refer to the arrangements, procedures and routines used to control and coordinate the various people and units within the organization. Some formalized processes span the entire organization, such as business planning and control procedures, and financial budgeting and reporting processes. Other control and coordination processes have a more limited scope, such as new product development meetings, yearly sales conferences, weekly quality circles, web-based expert panels and quarterly meetings with the board of directors. But not all organizational processes

FIGURE 4.4 Organizational structuring criteria

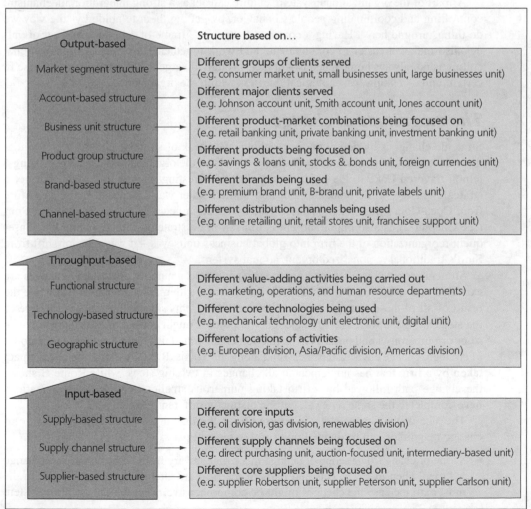

are institutionalized as ongoing integration mechanisms. Often, integration across units and departments is needed for a short period, making it useful to employ task forces, committees, working groups, project teams and even joint lunches as means for ensuring coordination.

While all of these processes are formalized to a certain degree, many more informal organizational processes exist, such as communicating via hallway gossip, building support through personal networking, influencing decision-making through informal negotiations and solving conflicts by means of impromptu meetings.

Organizational culture. Organizational culture refers to the worldview and behavioral patterns shared by the members of the same organization (e.g. Schein, 1985; Trice and Beyer, 1993). As people within a group interact and share experiences with one another over an extended period of time, they construct a joint understanding of the world around them. This shared belief system will be emotionally charged, as it encompasses the values and norms of the organizational members and offers them an interpretive filter with which to make sense of the constant stream of uncertain and ambiguous events around them. As this common ideology grows stronger and becomes more engrained, it will channel members' actions into more narrowly defined patterns of behavior. As such, the organizational culture can strongly influence everything, from how to behave during meetings to what is viewed as ethical behavior.

As part of the organizational system, culture can act as a strong integration mechanism, controlling and coordinating people's behavior, by getting them to abide by 'the way we do things around here'. Having a common 'language', frame of reference and set of values also makes it easier to communicate and work together. However, an organizational culture is not always homogeneous – in fact, strongly divergent sub-cultures might arise in certain units, creating 'psychological' barriers within the organization.

The magnitude of change

Strategic change is by definition far-reaching. We speak of strategic change when fundamental alterations are made to the business system or the organizational system. Adding a lemon-flavored Coke to the product portfolio is interesting, maybe important, but not a strategic change, while branching out into bottled water was – it was a major departure from Coca-Cola's traditional business system. Hiring a new CEO, like Ben Vree at Smit (see Chapter 2), is also important, but is in itself not a strategic change, while his consequent reorganization of the firm into global business units was – it was a major shift from Smit's traditional regionalized organizational system.

Strategic renewal is often even more far-reaching, as a number of strategic changes are executed in a variety of areas to keep the firm aligned with market demands. But while the result of all of these strategic changes is far-reaching, this says nothing about the size of the steps along the way. The strategic renewal process might consist of a few large change steps or numerous small ones. This distinction is illustrated in Figure 4.5. The total amount of strategic change envisaged is measured along the Y-axis. Route A shows the change path taken by a firm that has implemented all changes in two big steps, while Route B shows the change path followed by a firm taking numerous smaller steps. Both organizations have completed the same renewal, but via distinctly different routes.

The size of the change steps is referred to as the magnitude of change. This issue of change magnitude can be divided into two component parts:

- Scope of change. The scope of change in a firm can vary from broad to narrow. Change is broad when many aspects and parts of the firm are altered at the same time. In the most extreme case the changes might be comprehensive, whereby the business system is entirely revised, and the organizational structure, processes, culture and people are changed in unison. However, change can also be much more narrowly focused on a specific organizational aspect (e.g. new product development processes) or department (e.g. marketing). If many changes are narrowly targeted, the total result will be a more piecemeal change process.

■ Amplitude of organizational changes. The amplitude of change in firms can vary from high to low. The amplitude of change is high when the new business system, organizational culture, structure, processes or people are a radical departure from the previous situation. The amplitude of change is low when the step proposed is a moderate adjustment to the previous circumstances.

Where a change is comprehensive and radical, the magnitude of the change step is large. In Figure 4.5 this is represented as a large jump along the Y-axis. Where a change is narrow and moderate, the magnitude of the step is small. However, the above distinction also clarifies that there are two rather different types of medium-sized change steps – a focused radical change (narrow scope, high amplitude) and a comprehensive moderate change (broad scope, low amplitude). Both changes are 'mid-sized', yet significantly different to manage in practice.

The pace of change

Strategic renewal takes time. Yet, there is a variety of ways by which the strategic renewal process can take place over time. Strategic change measures can be evenly spread out over an extended period, allowing the organization to follow a relatively steady pace of strategic renewal. However, it is also possible to cluster all changes into a few short irregular bursts, giving the renewal process an unsteady, stop-and-go pace.

This distinction is seen in Figure 4.5 as well. The total time period needed for achieving a strategic change is measured along the X-axis. Route A shows the change path taken by a firm that has had an unsteady pace of change, while Route B tracks the path taken by a firm on a more steady change trajectory. Both organizations have completed the same strategic renewal process by T^3 and by T^6, but have distributed their change activities differently during the period.

In Figure 4.5 it can also be seen that the pace of organizational changes can be decomposed into two related parts:

FIGURE 4.5 Example of two alternative change paths

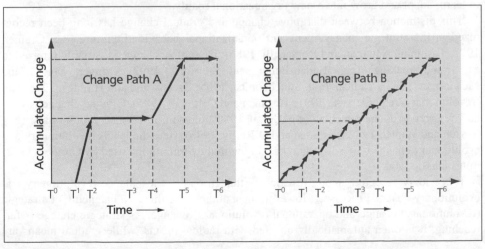

- Timing of change. First, the pace of change depends on the moment at which changes are initiated. The timing of change can vary from intermittent to constant. Where change is intermittent, it is important for a firm to determine the right moment for launching a new initiative (for example, T^1 and T^4 in change path A). The need to 'wait for the right timing' is often a reason for spreading change activities unevenly over time. On the other hand, change can be constant, so that the exact moment for kicking off any new set of measures is less important, as long as there is no peak at any one moment in time (see change path B).

- Speed of change. The pace of change also depends on the time span within which changes take place. The speed of change can vary from high to low. Where a major change needs to be implemented within a short period of time, the speed of change must be high. A short burst of fast action can bring about the intended changes. In Figure 4.5, the speed can be seen by the slope of the arrow (in change path A, the speed between T^1 and T^2 is higher than between T^4 and T^5). On the other hand, where the change measures are less formidable and the time span for implementation is longer, the speed of change can be lower.

The variables of timing and speed of change, together with the variables of scope and amplitude of change, create a wide range of possible strategic renewal paths. Firms have many different ways of bringing about strategic change. Unavoidably, this raises the question of which route is best. Why should a firm choose one trajectory over another?

THE PARADOX OF REVOLUTION AND EVOLUTION

Nothing in progression can rest on its original plan.
We may as well think of rocking a grown man in the cradle of an infant.
Edmund Burke (1729–1797); Irish-born politician and man of letters

In selecting an approach to strategic change, most managers struggle with the question of how bold they should be. On the one hand, they usually realize that to fundamentally transform the organization a break with the past is needed. To achieve strategic renewal it is essential to turn away from the firm's heritage and to start with a clean slate. On the other hand, they also recognize the value of continuity, building on past experiences, investments and loyalties. To achieve lasting strategic renewal people in the organization will need time to learn, adapt and grow into a new organizational reality.

This distinction between disruptive change and gradual change has long been recognized in the strategic management and organizational behavior literature (e.g. Greiner, 1972; Tushman, Newman and Romanelli, 1986). Disruptive change is variably referred to as 'frame-breaking' (e.g. Baden-Fuller and Stopford, 1992; Grinyer, Mayes and McKiernan, 1987), 'radical' (e.g. Stinchcombe, 1965; Greenwood and Hinings, 1996) and 'revolutionary' (e.g. Gersick, 1991; Tushman and O'Reilly, 1996). Gradual change is variably referred to as 'incremental' (e.g. Quinn, 1980; Johnson, 1987) and 'evolutionary' (e.g. Nelson and Winter, 1982; Tushman and O'Reilly, 1996). Here the labels revolutionary and evolutionary change will be used, in keeping with the terminology used by Greiner (1972) in his classic work.

It is widely accepted among researchers that firms need to balance revolutionary and evolutionary change processes. However, most authors see this as a balancing of strategic (revolutionary) change and operational (evolutionary) change. As strategic change is far-reaching, it is often automatically equated with radical means, while gradual means are reserved for smaller-scale operational changes. Yet, in the previous section it was made clear that a radical result (a strategic change) can be pursued by both revolutionary and evolutionary means (e.g. Hayes, 1985; Krüger, 1996, Reading 4.4 in this book; Nonaka, 1988; Strebel, 1994).

While these two change processes are each other's opposites, and they seem to be at least partially contradictory, both approaches are needed within firms. In practice both change processes have valuable, but conflicting, qualities. The tension that this creates between revolution and evolution will be explored in the following sections.

The demand for revolutionary change processes

Revolution is a process whereby an abrupt and radical change takes place within a short period of time. Revolutionary change processes are those that do not build on the status quo, but overthrow it. 'Revolutionaries' revolt against the existing business system and organizational system, and attempt to push through changes that will reinvent the firm. Thus, revolution leads to a clear break with the past – a discontinuity in the firm's development path.

Such a 'big bang' approach to strategic change is generally needed when organizational rigidity is so deeply rooted that smaller pushes do not bring the firm into movement. If the firm threatens to become paralyzed by these inherited rigidities in the business system and organizational system, the only way to get moving can be to radically break with the past. Typical sources of organizational rigidity include:

- Psychological resistance to change. Many people resist change, because of the uncertainty and ambiguity that unavoidably accompanies any shift in the old way of doing business (e.g. Argyris, 1990; Pondy, Boland and Thomas, 1988). As people become accustomed to fixed organizational routines and established habits, their ability to learn and gradually adapt invariably recedes. New business methods or job descriptions are not seen as a challenging opportunity to learn, but as an unwelcome interference in the existing system. It can be necessary to break through this psychological resistance to change by imposing a new business system and/or organizational system on people (e.g. Hammer, 1990, Reading 4.1 in this book; Powell, 1991).

- Cultural resistance to change. As discussed in Chapter 2, people can easily become immune to signals that their cognitive maps are outdated, especially if they are surrounded by others with the same flawed belief system. Once an organizational culture develops that perpetuates a number of obsolete assumptions about the market or the organization, it is very difficult for organizational members to challenge and gradually reshape the organizational belief system. It can be necessary to break through this cultural resistance to change by exposing the organization to a shocking crisis or by imposing a new organizational system (e.g. Tushman, Newman and Romanelli, 1986, Reading 4.3; Senge, 1990, Reading 9.3).

- Political resistance to change. Change is hardly ever to everyone's advantage, as Machiavelli pointed out at the start of this chapter. Each organizational change leads to a different constellation of winners and losers. Generally, the potential losers reject a strategic change, although they are likely to think of some seemingly objective reasons for their opposition. Even a situation in which a person or department thinks that it might run the risk of losing power to others can be enough to block a change. Since strategic changes invariably have a significant impact on all people within an organization, there will always be a number of open, and hidden, opponents. It can be necessary to break through this political resistance by imposing a new business system and reshuffling management positions (e.g. Allison, 1969, Reading 3.3; Krüger, 1996, Reading 4.4).

- Investment lock-in. Once a firm has committed a large amount of money and time to a certain product portfolio, activity system or technology, it will find that this fixed investment locks the organization in. Any gradual movement away from the past investment will increase the risk of not earning back the sunk cost. Therefore, it can be necessary to break through the lock-in by radically restructuring or disposing of the investment (e.g. Ghemawat, 1991; Bower and Christensen, 1995).

- Competence lock-in. The better a firm becomes at something, the more a firm becomes focused on becoming even better still – which is also known as the virtuous circle of competence-building. Once a competitive advantage has been built on a particular type of competence, the natural tendency of firms is to favor external opportunities based on these competences. New people are hired that fit with the corporate competence profile and R&D spending further hones the firm's skill. But if the firm's competence base threatens to become outdated due to market or technological changes, its former advantage could become its downfall – the firm could become caught in a vicious 'competence trap', unable to gradually shift the organization to an alternative set of competences, because the entire business system and organizational system have been aligned to the old set (e.g. Leonard-Barton, 1995; Teece, Pisano and Shuen, 1997). Changing the core competence of the corporation in a comprehensive and radical manner can be the only way to 'migrate' from one competence profile to another.

- System lock-in. Firms can also become locked into an open standard (e.g. sizes in inches, GAAP accounting rules) or a proprietary system (e.g. Windows operating system, SAP enterprise resource planning software). Once the firm has implemented a standard or system, switching to another platform cannot be done gradually or at low cost. Therefore, the lock-in can usually only be overcome by a big bang transition to another platform (e.g. Arthur, 1996; Shapiro and Varian, 1998).

- Stakeholder lock-in. Highly restrictive commitments can also be made towards the firm's stakeholders. Long-term contracts with buyers and suppliers, warranties, commitments to governments and local communities and promises to shareholders can all lock firms into a certain strategic direction. To break through the stakeholders' resistance to change it can be necessary to court a crisis and aim for a radical restructuring of the firm's external relationships (e.g. Freeman, 1984; Oliver, 1991).

Besides the use of revolutionary change to overcome organizational rigidity, such a radical approach to strategic renewal is often also necessary given the short time span available for a large change. The 'window of opportunity' for achieving a strategic change can be small for a number of reasons. Some of the most common triggers for revolutionary strategic change are:

- Competitive pressure. When a firm is under intense competitive pressure and its market position starts to erode quickly, a rapid and dramatic response might be the only approach possible. Especially when the organization threatens to slip into a downward spiral towards insolvency, a bold turnaround can be the only option left to the firm.

- Regulatory pressure. Firms can also be put under pressure by the government or regulatory agencies to push through major changes within a short period of time. Such externally imposed revolutions can be witnessed among public sector organizations (e.g. hospitals and schools) and highly regulated industries (e.g. utilities and telecommunications), but in other sectors of the economy as well (e.g. antitrust break-ups, public health regulations).

- First mover advantage. A more proactive reason for instigating revolutionary change, is to be the first firm to introduce a new product, service or technology and to build up barriers to entry for late movers. Especially for know-how that is dissipation-sensitive, or for which the patent period is limited, it can be important to cash in quickly before others arrive on the market (e.g. Kessler and Chakrabarthi, 1996; Lieberman and Montgomery, 1988, 1998).

To some extent all managers recognize that their organizations are prone to inertia, and most will acknowledge that it is often vital to move quickly, either in response to external pressures or to cash in on a potential first mover advantage. It should therefore come as no surprise that most managers would like their organizations to have the ability to successfully pull off revolutionary strategic changes.

The demand for evolutionary change processes

Evolution is a process whereby a constant stream of moderate changes gradually accumulates over a longer period of time. Each change is in itself small, but the cumulative result can be large. Evolutionary change processes take the current firm as a starting point, constantly modifying aspects through extension and adaptation. Some 'mutations' to the firm prove valuable and are retained, while other changes are discarded as dysfunctional. Thus, a new business system and/or organizational system can steadily evolve out of the old, as if the organization were shedding its old skin to grow a new one (e.g. Aldrich, 1999; Kagono et al., 1985).

This 'metamorphosis' approach to strategic change is particularly important where the strategic renewal hinges on widespread organizational learning. Learning is not a process that is easily compressed into a few short bursts of activity (as anyone who has studied knows). Learning is a relatively slow process, whereby know-how is accumulated over an extended period of time. It can take years to learn things, especially if the necessary knowledge is not readily available, but must be acquired 'on the job' (e.g. Agryris, 1990; Senge, 1990, Reading 9.3 in this book). This is true for both individuals and firms. When groups of people in a firm need to develop new routines, new competences, new processes, as well as new ways of understanding the world, time is needed to experiment, reflect, discuss, test and internalize. Even in the circumstances where individuals or departments are merely asked to adjust their behaviors to new norms, the learning process is often protracted and difficult (e.g. Nelson and Winter, 1982; Pfeffer and Sutton, 1999, Reading 9.4).

While the evolutionary nature of learning is a positive factor stimulating gradual change, the organizational reality is often also that power is too dispersed for revolutionary changes to be imposed upon the firm. Where no one has enough sway in the organization to push through radical changes, a more evolutionary approach can be the only viable route forward.

To some extent all managers recognize that their firms need to continuously learn and adapt, while most will acknowledge that they do not have the absolute power to impose revolutionary changes at will. For these reasons managers generally would like their organizations to have the ability to pursue evolutionary changes.

Yet, engaging in evolutionary change is the opposite of revolutionary change. On the one hand, being opposites might make revolution and evolution complementary. Some authors suggest that organizations should be 'ambidextrous', using both revolution and evolution, contingent upon internal and external conditions (e.g. Duncan, 1976; Krüger, 1996, Reading 4.4; Tushman and O'Reilly, 1996). On the other hand, the above discussion makes clear that the two are, to a certain extent, mutually incompatible. Once the one form of change has been chosen, this will seriously limit the ability of the strategist to simultaneously, or even subsequently, use the other. Hence, managers are once again faced with a paradox, between revolution and evolution.

EXHIBIT 4.1 SHORT CASE

ALLIANZ AND DRESDNER BANK: TAKING A RISK ON ALLFINANZ?

In April 2003 Michael Diekmann took over as the new CEO of Allianz, Europe's largest insurance company and Germany's most influential corporation. Although his predecessor's resignation had come as a surprise, the troubling situation leading up to his departure was widely known. Most visibly, the company's share price had tumbled from above €400 in January 2001 to a mere €52 in March 2003, while its credit rating had deteriorated to an A−. There were several external reasons that could be blamed for this dismal performance: the economic fallout from 9/11 and the Iraq war; expensive floods in Eastern Europe; asbestos claims in North America; and the 60% fall in value of the German stock market, reducing the value of the equity portfolio of Allianz. But a significant self-inflicted wound was also apparent: the continuing huge losses incurred by Allianz from its newly acquired subsidiary, Dresdner Bank, Germany's second largest private bank by assets.

The strategy behind buying Dresdner Bank was to turn Allianz into a full range financial services company, where both retail and corporate customers could do their 'one stop shopping' for banking and insurance products. In this Allfinanz concept, a broad spectrum of products, ranging from savings and loans to investment services and insurance, would be distributed through the direct sales channel of Allianz, as well as through the extensive branch network of Dresdner. If this strategy could be made to work, sales per customer could be raised tremendously, significant cost savings could be attained, and unique financial products combining banking and insurance know-how could be introduced.

Until this Allfinanz vision was fully realized, however, Dresdner was a heavily loss-making bank, draining resources on a scale that was worrying even for a 'deep pocketed' company like Allianz: Dresdner lost €1.4 billion and consolidated Allianz lost €1.2 billion in 2002. In its corporate banking activities, Dresdner was suffering from the harsh economic climate in Germany, which was producing record numbers of bankruptcies, including headline-grabbing corporate failures, such as the collapse of the Kirch Group, Europe's formerly leading media empire. On the investment banking side, Dresdner had been clobbered by the downturn in the equity markets, and they were at any rate probably below critical size for international success. Finally, in the retail banking activities, the company was hurting from the chronic overcapacity in the German market.

Not that other German banks were doing any better. The 'big four' – Deutsche Bank, Commerzbank, HypoVereinsbank and Dresdner Bank – were all in sorry shape. Deutsche Bank, Germany's leading bank, was heavily hit by the downturn of the capital markets while aiming to turn itself into a global investment banking player, and was unable to keep its German retail and corporate banking activities profitable. In a bold strategic move, it had tried to rebrand its retail banking activities as Deutsche 24, shifting all its customers to this new outfit, but had lost a substantial amount of business in the process. Meanwhile, Commerzbank and HypoVereinsbank were both stuck in a positioning as universal bank, with no specific market focus or distinct competence profile. HypoVereinsbank had tried to fashion itself as the real estate specialist, only to run up huge losses in its portfolio. Virtually all attempts by all banks to launch tele-banking, online-banking or discount banking also proved to be costly failures. To minimize losses, the big four shed 40 000 employees between 2001 and 2003, more than a fifth of their combined workforce, and sold assets left and right to strengthen their balance sheets. However, industry experts expected that more would be necessary, predicting that ultimately every third employee would have to leave the industry, and that every second bank branch would have to be closed.

The main reason for the extreme overcapacity in the German banking market was that the country was blessed with no less than four parallel banking systems. At the end of 1999 Germany had 62 000 banking branches (more than twice as many as bakeries, and almost four times the number of gas stations) resulting in the highest branch density in the world. Next to the regular private banking sector, there were (a) the mutual banks (the *Genossenschaftssektor*), formerly farmer-based and free from shareholder pressure, (b) the savings banks (the *Sparkassensektor*), owned by the *Länder* (states), cities and communities, and (c) the government-owned postal banking system. The savings banks had supervisory boards stuffed with local politicians, and operated under de facto state guarantees. The non-private alternative banking sectors could offer credits and services to consumers and small businesses at price levels unmatchable by the private banks, which needed to meet commercial return on capital targets. The result was that the big four had only a 14.4% share of the market, and total return on equity of the German banking system during the late 1990's boom years was still only a mere 6.6%. However, in 2000 the European Commission ordered the savings banks to discard their de facto state guarantees, forcing them to become profit-oriented and triggering a restructuring of the sector. Taking this cue, the mutual banks also rapidly started consolidating and professionalizing their operations. The postal system was privatized as well, along with its banking network.

On the corporate banking side the major problem was the web of shareholdings between the big financial institutions on the one hand and the largest German industrial groups on the other. In this system, collectively known as 'Deutschland AG' (Germany Inc.), the big four banks and the two large insurers, Allianz and Munich Re, had taken large stakes in many of the major German corporations in the post-war years, to finance the rebuilding of the economy. These long-term stakes in the engines of the German economic recovery served both sides well, far into the 1980s, and gave companies such as Allianz an enormous influence in the corporate world, although this power was always wielded ever so discretely. But with the onset of more sophisticated, global capital markets, German companies began to look abroad for advanced services, while the financial players became painfully aware that their returns were far below international standards. Both sides felt locked into an outdated system. So, in 2000 the law was changed to make it possible to sell corporate shareholdings without having to pay taxes on the hidden capital gains profits, thereby opening the way to unraveling the system.

Clearly, the German banking industry was finally changing shape, and it seemed that the time to move was now. A first attempt at restructuring was undertaken by Deutsche Bank, which tried to merge with Dresdner Bank in 2000. Integration teams had almost completed the job when the merger was called off because the investment banking units could not reach an agreement over leadership. Then in 2001, Allianz pounced on Dresdner, paying €18

billion, with the intention of bringing the Allfinanz concept to the German market.

For Michael Diekmann, who had previously headed the insurance operations of Allianz in the Americas, the new position as CEO came with a number of very pressing strategic questions. First, he had to ask himself whether he shared the same Allfinanz vision as his predecessor. If not, it seemed foolhardy to keep a bleeder like Dresdner in a business it did not fully understand. He could always choose to put Dresdner up for sale again, passing it on to someone better suited to adding value to its banking business and capable of pushing through the changes necessary to stem the losses. Actually, despite the awful results in 2002, the Allianz balance sheet was strong enough to do other deals if he thought they might be beneficial. Yet, if he did want to stick to the Allfinanz idea, the main issue was how he could bring about the strategic change necessary to make it work. Transforming the organization would then be the main challenge for the years to come.

Many advisors were urging Diekmann to move swiftly and decisively to implement the Allfinanz vision. In their view the crisis was actually an opportunity to break through the lingering resistance in both, rather conservative, organizations and roll out the new policy in full force. Being a new man was an advantage, for this would give him a honeymoon period with the employees and strong unions, allowing him to take firm actions and break down barriers between the two companies. He would have to determine to what extent the two would need to be integrated, but it might be better to really shake things up, to get bankers and insurers into common units, instead of keeping them on both sides of a divide. Especially when it came to the backbone of a modern financial service company, its IT system, it seemed he would have to go all out in integrating them, if banking and insurance products would need to be offered at the same time through the same channels. But other elements might also require integration, such as the sales forces, marketing and product development. Maybe even the brands would need to be merged. And these were points for which momentum was available now, not to mention that the hypercritical stock market was watching for tangible results, after the dismal results in 2002.

Yet, others pressed Diekmann to be measured and patient. Moving too rapidly might alienate employees and antagonize the unions, leaving the company inward-looking for years to come. Moreover, it was not inconceivable that major implementation bottlenecks might disrupt operations and that customers might be left bewildered by the sudden changes. Worse yet, it might turn out that Allfinanz did not work as intended and that things would need to be changed midstream. In the end, Allianz still had a rock-solid reputation to lose. Trust, solidity and reliability were long-term core assets in the market, far more important than short-term successes and ovations from the stock market.

Almost across the street from Allianz head office in Munich was the headquarters of Munich Re, the largest reinsurance company in the world. Munich Re had over the past years quietly, and without much fanfare, moved into other financial businesses. It had now become the second largest primary insurer in Germany after Allianz, and it owned two small minority holdings in Commerzbank and HypoVereinsbank, although through clever tactics these were actually controlling stakes. While Allianz was a German household name with a brand recognition close to a 100%, only a small well-informed circle of business people even knew of Munich Re's existence. Clearly, there were several paths to becoming an Allfinanz company and Michael Diekmann wondered whether Allianz had taken the right one.

Sources: *Financial Times*, November 5 2001, June 12 2002, November 22 2002; *The Economist*, August 17 and December 21 2002; company reports.

PERSPECTIVES ON STRATEGIC CHANGE

No great thing is created suddenly, any more than a bunch of grapes or a fig. If you tell me that you desire a fig, I answer that there must be time. Let it first blossom, then bear fruit, then ripen.
Epictetus (c. 60–120); Roman philosopher

Although the demand for both revolutionary and evolutionary change is clear, this does place managers in the difficult position of having to determine how these two must be combined and balanced in a process of ongoing strategic renewal. Revolutionary change is necessary to create *discontinuity* in the renewal process – radical and swift breaks with the past. Evolutionary change is necessary to ensure *continuity* in the renewal process – moderate and gradual metamorphosis from one state into another. In finding a balance between these two demands, the question is which of the two must play a leading role and what type of change path this leads to. Does successful strategic renewal hinge on a few infrequent big bangs, with some minor evolutionary changes in the intervening time span, or is successful strategic renewal essentially a gradual process of mutation and selection, where revolutionary changes are only used in case of emergency?

Yet, as in previous chapters, we see that the strategic management literature comes up with a wide variety of answers to this question. Both among business practitioners and strategy researchers, views differ sharply about the best way of dealing with the paradox of revolution and evolution. To gain insight into the major points of disagreement between people on the issue of strategic renewal, we will again outline the two diametrically opposed perspectives here.

At one end of the virtual continuum of views, are the strategists who argue that real strategic renewal can only be achieved by radical means. Revolutionary change, although difficult to achieve, is at the heart of renewal, while evolutionary changes can only figure in a supporting role. This point of view will be referred to as the 'discontinuous renewal perspective'. At the other end of the spectrum are the strategists who argue that real strategic renewal is not brought about by an 'axe', but must grow out of the existing firm, in a constant stream of small adjustments. Evolutionary change, although difficult to sustain, is at the heart of renewal, while revolutionary changes are a fall-back alternative, if all else fails. This point of view will be referred to as the 'continuous renewal perspective'.

The discontinuous renewal perspective

According to advocates of the discontinuous renewal perspective, it is a common misconception that firms develop gradually. It is often assumed that organizations move fluidly from one state to the next, encountering minimal friction. In reality, however, strategic change is arduous and encounters significant resistance. Pressure must be exerted, and tension must mount, before a major shift can be accomplished. Movement, therefore, is not steady and constant, as a current in the sea, but abrupt and dramatic, as in an earthquake, where resistance gives way and tension is released in a short shock. In general, the more significant a change is, the more intense the shock will be.

Proponents of this perspective argue that people and organizations exhibit a natural reluctance to change. Humans have a strong preference for stability. Once general policy has been determined, most firms are inclined to settle into a fixed way of working. The organizational structure will solidify, formal processes will be installed, standard operating procedures will be defined, key competence areas will be identified, a distribution of power will emerge and a corporate culture will become established. The stability of an organization will be especially high if all of these elements form a consistent and cohesive configuration (e.g. Mintzberg, 1991; Waterman, Peters and Philips, 1982). Moreover, if a firm experiences a period of success, this usually strongly reinforces the existing way of working (e.g. Markides, 1998; Miller, 1990).

It must be emphasized that stability is not inherently harmful, as it allows people to 'get to work'. A level of stability is required to function efficiently (e.g. March and Simon, 1958; Thompson, 1967). Constant upheaval would only create an organizational mess. There would be prolonged confusion about tasks and authority, poorly structured internal communication and coordination, and a lack of clear standards and routines. The instability brought on by such continuously changing processes and structures would lead to widespread insecurity, political maneuvering and inter-departmental conflicts.

Advocates of the discontinuous renewal perspective, therefore, argue that long periods of relative stability are necessary for the proper functioning of firms. However, the downside of stability is rigidity – the unwillingness and/or inability to change, even when it is urgently required. To overcome rigidity and get the firm in motion, a series of small nudges will by no means be sufficient. A big shove will be needed. For strategic changes to really happen, measures must be radical and comprehensive. A coordinated assault is usually required to decisively break through organizational defenses and 'shock therapy' is needed to fundamentally change people's cognitive maps. Solving lock-in problems generally also demands a quick, firm-wide switchover to a new system. For instance, business process reengineering must involve all aspects of the value chain at once (e.g. Hammer, 1990, Reading 4.1; Hammer and Champy, 1993). However, proponents of the discontinuous renewal perspective emphasize that the period of turmoil must not take too long. People cannot be indefinitely confronted with high levels of uncertainty and ambiguity, and a new equilibrium is vital for a new period of efficient operations.

Therefore, the long-term pattern of strategic renewal is not gradual, but episodic. Periods of relative stability are interrupted by short and dramatic periods of instability, during which revolutionary changes take place (e.g. Greiner, 1972; Tushman, Newman and Romanelli, 1986, Reading 4.3). This pattern of development has been recognized in a variety of other sciences as well (Gersick, 1991). Following the natural historians Eldredge and Gould, this discontinuous pattern of strategic renewal is often called 'punctuated equilibrium' – stability punctuated by episodes of revolutionary change.

Some proponents of this view argue that episodes of revolutionary change are generally not chosen freely, but are triggered by crises. A major environmental jolt can be the reason for a sudden crisis (e.g. Meyer, 1982; Meyer, Brooks and Goes, 1990) – for example, the introduction of a new technology, a major economic recession, new government regulations, a novel market entrant or a dramatic event in international political affairs. However, often a misalignment between the firm and its environment grows over a longer period of time, causing a mounting sense of impending crisis (e.g. Johnson, 1988; Strebel, 1992). As tension increases, people in the firm become more receptive to submitting to the painful changes that are necessary. This increased willingness to change under crisis circumstances coincides with the physical law that 'under pressure things become fluid'. As long as the pressure persists, revolutionary change is possible, but as soon as the pressure lets up the firm will resolidify in a new form, inhibiting any further major changes (e.g. Lewin, 1947; Miller and Friesen, 1984). For this reason, managers often feel impelled to heighten and prolong the sense of crisis, to keep organization members receptive to the changes being pushed through. And where a crisis is lacking, some managers will induce one, to create the sense of urgency and determination needed to get people in the change mind-set.

Other authors argue that revolutionary changes are not always reactive responses to crisis conditions. Revolutionary change can also be proactively pursued to gain a competitive advantage, or even to change the rules of the game in the industry in which the firm is competing. If a firm decides to use a breakthrough technology or a new business model to improve its competitive position vis-à-vis rivals, this does entail that it will need to execute some major changes in a short period of time. Such innovations to the business system are inherently revolutionary. Creating novel products and developing a unique business formula requires a sharp break with the past. Old ways must be discarded before new methods can be adopted. This is the essence of what Schumpeter (1950) referred to as the process of 'creative destruction', inherent in the capitalist system. This process is not orderly and protracted, but disruptive and intense. Therefore, it is argued, to be a competitive success, firms must learn to master the skill of ongoing revolutionary change (e.g. D'Aveni, 1994; Hamel, 1996). Rapid implementation of system-wide change is an essential organizational capability – the firm needs to be able to run faster than its competitors.

It can be concluded that strategic changes, whether proactive or reactive, require an abrupt break with the status quo. Change management demands strong leadership to rapidly push through stressful, discomforting and risky shifts in the business and organizational system. Battling the sources of rigidity and turning crisis into opportunity are the key qualities needed by managers implementing strategic change. Ultimately, strategizing managers should know when to change and when it is more wise to seek stability – they should know when to trigger an 'earthquake' and when to avoid one.

EXHIBIT 4.2 THE DISCONTINUOUS RENEWAL PERSPECTIVE

CENTRICA: STEPPING ON THE GAS

In February 1997 British Gas was split into two companies – one for trading and retailing gas in the United Kingdom called Centrica, and one for producing and transporting gas (plus the international operations) called the BG Group. This radical move was a response to the pending liberalization of the residential market that the British government had planned for May 1998. British Gas had already been privatized in 1986 and had lost its monopoly for industrial and business customers in 1992, yet open competition in the household market for gas posed the biggest challenge the company had ever faced, requiring a separate company with an unequivocal focus on residential consumers.

At the moment of the split, Centrica inherited two main assets. It was given all the gas connections to British households and the brand name British Gas. However, the management of Centrica realized that both assets would rapidly decline in value within 24 months – they would have to give third parties access to their gas connections and new competitors were likely to introduce less staid brands and lower prices. Centrica's managers also recognized that along with these less than thrilling assets, the company had inherited the lumbering business practices of a giant former state-owned monopolist.

Centrica's reaction to this challenge was to radically redefine its business from simple gas provision to 'essential household services', and to rapidly transform the entire organization towards a client-centered service provider. The new 'essential household services' concept was based on the assumption that customers would value having a broad range of household services bundled into one package and paid for with one monthly bill. Within three years, Centrica expanded its product offering to include

electricity, telecommunication services (mobile, fixed and internet), credit cards, consumer credit services (through its Goldfish brand), car repair services (through the AA, Automobile Association, which Centrica bought), insurance policies, home services (plumbing repair, home security services, kitchen appliance servicing) and various other services, such as Golf England and the delivery of fine wines.

By 2001, Centrica served 67% of the gas retail market (after having dropped to little over 50% shortly after liberalization) and had become the largest residential electricity supplier. More than 55% of its sales were in non-gas services, and it had a customer relationship with 90% of all British households. It had integrated customer relationship management across all its various businesses and worked on aggressively cross-selling its services. Centrica's slogan, 'taking care of the essentials', has also been true for the financial results, allowing the company to outperform the British FTSE stock index by about 200% between the demerger in 1997 and 2002.

Sources: Company reports; Hoovers Online; *European Utilities Sector Review*, Credit Suisse Equity Research, January 2002.

The continuous renewal perspective

According to proponents of the continuous renewal perspective, if firms shift by 'earthquake' it is usually their own 'fault'. The problem with revolution is that it commonly leads to the need for further revolution at a later time – discontinuous change creates its own boom-and-bust cycle. Revolutionary change is generally followed by a strong organizational yearning for stability. The massive, firm-wide efforts to implement agonizing changes can often only be sustained for a short period of time, after which change momentum collapses. Any positive inclination towards change among employees will have totally disappeared by the time the reorganizations are over. Consequently, the firm lapses back into a stable state in which only minor changes occur. This stable situation is maintained until the next round of shock therapy becomes necessary, to jolt the organization out of its ossified state.

To supporters of the continuous renewal perspective, the boom-and-bust approach to strategic change is like running a marathon by sprinting and then standing still to catch one's breath. Yet, marathons are not won by good sprinters, but by runners with endurance and persistence, who can keep a steady pace – runners who are more inspired by the tortoise than by the hare. The same is true for companies in the marathon of competition. Some companies behave like the hare in Aesop's fable, showing off their ability to take great leaps, but burdened by a short span of attention. Other companies behave more like the tortoise, moving gradually and undramatically, but unrelentingly and without interruption, focusing on the long-term goal. In the short run, the hares might dash ahead, suggesting that making big leaps forward is the best way to compete. But in the long run, the most formidable contenders will be the diligent tortoises, whose ability to maintain a constant speed will help them to win the race.

Therefore, the 'big ideas', 'frame-breaking innovations' and 'quantum leaps' that so mesmerize proponents of the discontinuous renewal perspective are viewed with suspicion by supporters of continuous renewal. Revolution not only causes unnecessary disruption and dysfunctional crises, but also is usually the substitute of diligence. If organizations do not have the stamina to continuously improve themselves, quick fix radical change can be used as a short-term remedy. Where firms do not exhibit the drive to permanently upgrade their capabilities, revolutionary innovations can be used as the short cut to renewed competitiveness. In other words, the lure of revolutionary change is that of short-term results. By abruptly and dramatically making major changes, managers hope to rapidly book tangible progress – and instantly win recognition and promotion (Imai, 1986, Reading 4.2 in this book).

To advocates of the continuous renewal perspective, a preference for revolution usually reflects an unhealthy obsession with the short term. Continuous renewal, on the other hand, is more long term in orientation. Development is gradual, piecemeal and undramatic, but as it is constantly maintained over a longer period of time, the aggregate level of change can still be significant. Three organizational characteristics are important for keeping up a steady pace of change. First, all employees within the firm should be committed to *continuously improve*. Everyone within the firm should be driven by constructive dissatisfaction with the status quo. This attitude, that things can always be done better, reflects a rejection of stability and the acceptance of bounded instability (e.g. Beinhocker, 1999; Stacey, 1993a, Reading 9.2) – everything is open to change.

Secondly, everyone in the firm must be motivated to *continuously learn*. People within the organization must constantly update their knowledge base, which not only means acquiring new information, but challenging accepted company wisdom as well. Learning goes hand in hand with unlearning – changing the cognitive maps shared within the organization. In this respect, it is argued that an atmosphere of crisis actually inhibits continuous renewal. In a situation of crisis, it is not a matter of 'under pressure things become fluid', but 'in the cold everything freezes'. Crisis circumstances might lower people's resistance to imposed change, but it also blunts their motivation for experimenting and learning, as they brace themselves for the imminent shock. Crisis encourages people to seek security and to focus on the short term, instead of opening up and working towards long-term development (e.g. Bate, 1994; Senge, 1990, Reading 9.3).

Thirdly, everyone in the firm must be motivated to *continuously adapt*. Constant adjustment to external change and fluid internal realignment should be pursued. To this end, the organization must actively avoid inertia, by combating the forces of ossification. Managers should strive to create flexible structures and processes (e.g. Bartlett and Ghoshal, 1995; Eisenhardt and Brown, 1997), to encourage an open and tolerant corporate culture, and to provide sufficient job and career security for employees to accept other forms of ambiguity and uncertainty (e.g. Kagono et al., 1985; Nonaka, 1988).

These three characteristics of an evolutionary firm – continuous improvement, learning and adaptation – have in common that basically everyone in the organization is involved. Revolutionary change can be initiated by top management, possibly assisted and urged on by a few external consultants, and carried by a handful of change agents or champions (e.g. Maidique, 1980; Day, 1994). Evolutionary change, on the other hand, requires a firm-wide effort. Leaders cannot learn on behalf of their organizations, nor can they orchestrate all of the small improvements and adaptations needed for continuous renewal. Managers must realize that evolution can be led from the top, but not imposed from the top. For strategizing managers to realize change, hands-on guidance of organizational developments is more important than commanding organizational actions.

EXHIBIT 4.3 THE CONTINUOUS RENEWAL PERSPECTIVE

McKINSEY: 'THE FIRM' REMAINS FIRM

Ise Jingu is Japan's most sacred Shinto shrine and in the eyes of many also its most aesthetically pure and serene one. The shrine compound consists of more than 200 buildings that are constructed using 14 000 Japanese cedar wood logs, special Kaya straw and not a single nail. Every 20 years, Ise Jingu is completely razed to the ground and the priests move to an exact replica that has been built in the meantime on a parallel site. Here they will stay for the next 20 years, until it is time to move back again. In 1993, the shrine was moved for the 61st time since the year 690, a ceremony that has been maintained with only one exception, in Japan's war-torn 16th century.

Why tear down such elaborate structures only to rebuild exact replicas? The high priests of Shinto realized at the time, that the only way to maintain the know-how for constructing the shrine was to rebuild it once every 20 years, thus handing down the skills from one generation to the next. By being continuously rebuilt, Ise Jingu remains eternally young – visitors enter brand new buildings that are 1300 years old. The symbolic importance of this ritual reaches very deep. As with the construction know-how of the shrine, insight into the Shinto belief system must also be passed on to the young. By making each new generation 'rebuild' it, the Shinto belief system evolves successfully with the challenges and opportunities of the present day, without changing what is at its core.

A similar approach to change can be observed at McKinsey & Co., the international management consulting company that has such a solid position in corporate markets that it is often simply referred to as 'the Firm'. McKinsey was founded in the 1930s by Marvin Bower, who remained active in the company until his death in January 2003. From the outset, Bower imprinted a set of principles and values to guide the functioning of McKinsey and these have remained virtually unchanged over the years. He also devised a business model that is basically the same today as it was 50 years ago. And this situation is not likely to change with the election in March 2003 of a new worldwide managing partner: Ian Davis, the head of the London office, who was voted into the top job, is seen as a stern follower of 'Bowerite' values and principles.

McKinsey's profile has remained fundamentally consistent, as the firm has grabbed a position of leadership across all continents, and all industries. A McKinsey consultant in Bombay today would easily recognize the Düsseldorf operations of the 1980s or New York of the 1970s. Similarly, the profile and image of McKinsey consultants has stayed remarkably stable, independent of time and place. But how can a company that does not seem to change continuously achieve the highest recognition across such a wide range of countries, industries and times? Doesn't the fast changing world require the firm to constantly reinvent itself? In reality, McKinsey does change, only fluidly, in a continuous stream of small steps.

One of its most notorious management practices bringing about that continuous renewal is McKinsey's 'up or out policy', or more politely its 'grow or go' system. This policy forces every consultant in the firm to constantly rise through the ranks, or else to leave. Even the speed at which each career step should be taken is fixed at about a year and a half, give or take a few months. The effect of this policy is that nobody in the company can ever build a nesting place. Even senior directors must move on, leaving an open space for a rising newcomer to occupy and to learn the necessary skills for this level anew. The effect is also that as an open space is reoccupied, it is reshaped to take account of the then somewhat different external business environment, different business cycle, and change in industry or shift in regional focus. Newcomers may be in the same slot as their predecessors, and they will adhere to the same McKinsey values of 'Client First, Firm Second, everything else Third', but their job will be a changed one. Since the long-term reliance on a fixed skill base is made impossible through the 'grow or go' system, the McKinsey consultants, and with them the entire company, evolve seamlessly over time and across borders, even while remaining the same at their core. Hence, while McKinsey often advises its clients to radically restructure, for itself the firm prefers a process of continual adjustment.

Sources: *The Economist*, March 1 2003; company documents; Ise-Jingu web site.

INTRODUCTION TO THE DEBATE AND READINGS

Every act of creation is first of all an act of destruction.

Pablo Picasso (1881–1973); Spanish artist

Slow and steady wins the race.

The Hare and the Tortoise, Aesop (c. 620–560 BC); Greek writer

So, how should managers go about renewing their organizations? Should managers strive to bring about renewal abruptly, by emphasizing radical, comprehensive and dramatic changes? Or should they try to make renewal a more continuous process, accentuating ongoing improvement, learning and adaptation? As no consensus has yet developed within the field of strategic management on how to balance revolution and evolution, it is once again up to each individual to assess the arguments put forward in the debate and to form their own opinion.

As an input to the process of assessing the variety of perspectives on this issue, four readings have been selected that each can help readers to make up their own minds. Again, the first two readings will be representative of the two poles in this debate (see Table 4.1), while the second set of two readings will highlight additional arguments that are of relevance to finding a balance between the opposing demands.

As the opening reading, Michael Hammer's 'Reengineering Work: Don't Automate, Obliterate' has been selected to represent the discontinuous renewal perspective. This paper was published in *Harvard Business Review* in 1990 and was followed in 1993 by the highly influential book *Reengineering the Corporation: A Manifesto for Business Revolution*, that Hammer co-authored with James Champy. In this article, Hammer explains the concept of reengineering in much the same way as in the best-selling book. 'At the heart of reengineering,' he writes, 'is the notion of discontinuous thinking – of recognizing and breaking away from the outdated rules and fundamental assumptions that underlie operations.' In his view, radically redesigning business processes 'cannot be planned meticulously and accomplished in small and cautious steps. It's an all-or-nothing proposition with an uncertain result.' He exhorts managers to 'think big', by setting high goals, taking bold steps and daring to accept a high risk. In short, he preaches business revolution, and the tone of his article is truly that of a manifesto – impassioned, fervent, with here and there 'a touch of fanaticism'.

TABLE 4.1 Discontinuous renewal versus continuous renewal perspective

	Discontinuous renewal perspective	*Continuous renewal perspective*
Emphasis on	Revolution over evolution	Evolution over revolution
Strategic renewal as	Disruptive innovation/turnaround	Uninterrupted improvement
Strategic renewal process	Creative destruction	Organic adaptation
Magnitude of change	Radical, comprehensive and dramatic	Moderate, piecemeal and undramatic
Pace of change	Abrupt, unsteady and intermittent	Gradual, steady and constant
Lasting renewal requires	Sudden break with status quo	Permanent learning and flexibility
Reaction to external jolts	Shock therapy	Continuous adjustment
View of organizational crises	Under pressure things becomes fluid	In the cold everything freezes
Long-term renewal dynamics	Stable and unstable states alternate	Persistent transient state
Long-term renewal pattern	Punctuated equilibrium	Gradual development

Equally impassioned is the argumentation in the second reading, 'Kaizen', by Masaaki Imai, which has been selected to represent the continuous renewal perspective. This article has been taken from Imai's famous book *Kaizen: The Key to Japan's Competitive Success*. Kaizen (pronounced Ky'zen) is a Japanese term that is best translated as continuous improvement. Imai argues that it is this continuous improvement philosophy that best explains the competitive strength of so many Japanese companies. In his view, Western companies have an unhealthy obsession with one-shot innovations and revolutionary change. They are fixated on the great leap forward, while disregarding the power of accumulated small changes. Imai believes that innovations are also important for competitive success, but that they should be embedded in an organization that is driven to continuously improve.

While the articles by Hammer and Imai clearly illustrate the fundamentals of revolution and evolution, both are strongly focused on operational instead of strategic changes. To rectify this imbalance, two readings have been included that emphasize the strategic level. Reading 4.3 is 'Convergence and Upheaval: Managing the Unsteady Pace of Organizational Evolution', by Michael Tushman, William Newman and Elaine Romanelli. This often-cited 1986 article, like Hammer, takes a discontinuous renewal perspective, but develops a more sophisticated argumentation. While Hammer presents revolution as the radical measure needed to break the shackles of antiquated business systems, it is unclear what the corporation must do after it is reengineered. Tushman, Newman and Romanelli look beyond a single episode of revolution, to the longer-term pattern of development. In their view, short periods of revolutionary upheaval are usually followed by longer periods of equilibrium during which only small adaptations are made. After several years of relative stability, which they call convergence, the next wave of frame-breaking change sweeps through the organization. This leads to a cyclical pattern of convergence and sharp upheavals, referred to as punctuated equilibrium. According to Tushman, Newman and Romanelli, this pattern of strategic renewal is commonplace in practice and understandably so. They argue that piecemeal approaches to major change tend to get bogged down in politics, individual resistance to change and organizational inertia. Therefore, an abrupt, all-at-once approach to change is needed. The big challenge to top management, they believe, is to initiate upheavals proactively, instead of having to respond in the face of an unfolding crisis.

Reading 4.4 is by one of the leading German theorists on strategic change, Wilfried Krüger, whose work is unfortunately not particularly well known outside of his native country. In this article, entitled 'Implementation: The Core Task of Change Management', Krüger provides a thorough review of the challenges and approaches to strategy implementation and change, presenting many useful analytical tools and practical solutions along the way. Although he explicitly recognizes the value of both revolution and evolution (acknowledging the contributions of Hammer and Imai), his main point is that they should be explicitly combined to ensure ongoing implementation – renewal might not be entirely *continuous* (uninterrupted), but it should be *continual* (ongoing). In his words, 'change is a permanent task and challenge for general management and implementation is an integral element thereof'. Although this does not place Krüger fully in the continuous renewal 'camp', its does echo the thrust of their argumentation that managers should be constantly working towards renewal, instead of letting it erupt periodically. Krüger's emphasis on the importance of political and cultural acceptance to achieve successful strategic change and his belief that 'the overcoming of acceptance barriers must be designed as an individual and organizational learning process', fits very closely with the basic premises of the continuous renewal perspective.

Discontinuous or continuous renewal? It is now up to readers to decide whether they sympathize more with the tortoise or the hare.

Reengineering work: Don't automate, obliterate

By Michael Hammer[1]

Despite a decade or more of restructuring and downsizing, many US companies are still unprepared to operate in the 1990s. In a time of rapidly changing technologies and ever-shorter product life cycles, product development often proceeds at a glacial pace. In an age of the customer, order fulfillment has high error rates and customer inquiries go unanswered for weeks. In a period when asset utilization is critical, inventory levels exceed many months of demand.

The usual methods for boosting performance – process rationalization and automation – haven't yielded the dramatic improvements companies need. In particular, heavy investments in information technology have delivered disappointing results – largely because companies tend to use technology to mechanize old ways of doing business. They leave the existing processes intact and use computers simply to speed them up.

But speeding up those processes cannot address their fundamental performance deficiencies. Many of our job designs, work flows, control mechanisms, and organizational structures came of age in a different competitive environment and before the advent of the computer. They are geared toward efficiency and control. Yet the watchwords of the new decade are innovation and speed, service and quality.

It is time to stop paving the cow paths. Instead of embedding outdated processes in silicon and software, we should obliterate them and start over. We should 'reengineer' our businesses: use the power of modern information technology to radically redesign our business processes in order to achieve dramatic improvements in their performance.

Every company operates according to a great many unarticulated rules. 'Credit decisions are made by the credit department.' 'Local inventory is needed for good customer service.' 'Forms must be filled in completely and in order.' Reengineering strives to break away from the old rules about how we organize and conduct business. It involves recognizing and rejecting some of them and then finding imaginative new ways to accomplish work. From our redesigned processes, new rules will emerge that fit the times. Only then can we hope to achieve quantum leaps in performance.

Reengineering cannot be planned meticulously and accomplished in small and cautious steps. It's an all-or-nothing proposition with an uncertain result. Still, most companies have no choice but to muster the courage to do it. For many, reengineering is the only hope for breaking away from the antiquated processes that threaten to drag them down. Fortunately, managers are not without help. Enough businesses have successfully reengineered their processes to provide some rules of thumb for others.

What Ford and MBL did

Japanese competitors and young entrepreneurial ventures prove every day that drastically better levels of process performance are possible. They develop products twice as fast, utilize assets eight times more productively, respond to customers ten times faster. Some large, established companies also show what can be done. Businesses like Ford Motor Company and Mutual Benefit Life Insurance have reengineered their processes and achieved competitive leadership as a result. Ford has reengineered its accounts payable processes, and Mutual Benefit Life its processing of applications for insurance.

In the early 1980s, when the American automotive industry was in a depression, Ford's top management put accounts payable – along with many other departments – under the microscope in search of ways to cut costs. Accounts payable in North America alone employed more than 500 people. Management thought that by rationalizing processes and installing new computer systems, it could reduce the head count by some 20 percent.

Ford was enthusiastic about its plan to tighten accounts payable – until it looked at Mazda. While Ford was aspiring to a 400-person department,

Mazda's accounts payable organization consisted of a total of five people. The difference in absolute numbers was astounding, and even after adjusting for Mazda's smaller size, Ford figured that its accounts payable organization was five times the size it should be. The Ford team knew better than to attribute the discrepancy to callisthenics, company songs, or low interest rates.

Ford managers ratcheted up their goal: accounts payable would perform with not just a hundred but many hundreds fewer clerks. It then set out to achieve it. First, managers analyzed the existing system. When Ford's purchasing department wrote a purchase order, it sent a copy to accounts payable. Later, when material control received the goods, it sent a copy of the receiving document to accounts payable. Meanwhile, the vendor sent an invoice to accounts payable. It was up to accounts payable, then, to match the purchase order against the receiving document and the invoice. If they matched, the department issued payment.

The department spent most of its time on mismatches, instances where the purchase order, receiving document, and invoice disagreed. In these cases, an accounts payable clerk would investigate the discrepancy, hold up payment, generate documents, and all-in-all gum up the works.

One way to improve things might have been to help the accounts payable clerk investigate more efficiently, but a better choice was to prevent the mismatches in the first place. To this end, Ford instituted 'invoiceless processing.' Now when the purchasing department initiates an order, it enters the information into an on-line database. It doesn't send a copy of the purchase order to anyone. When the goods arrive at the receiving dock, the receiving clerk checks the database to see if they correspond to an outstanding purchase order. If so, he or she accepts them and enters the transaction into the computer system. (If receiving can't find a database entry for the received goods, it simply returns the order.)

Under the old procedures, the accounting department had to match 14 data items between the receipt record, the purchase order, and the invoice before it could issue payment to the vendor. The new approach requires matching only three items – part number, unit of measure, and supplier code – between the purchase order and the receipt record. The matching is done automatically, and the computer prepares the check, which accounts payable sends to the vendor. There are no invoices to worry about since Ford has asked its vendors not to send them.

Ford didn't settle for the modest increases it first envisioned. It opted for radical change – and achieved dramatic improvement. Where it has instituted this new process, Ford has achieved a 75 percent reduction in head count, not the 20 percent it would have gotten with a conventional program. And since there are no discrepancies between the financial record and the physical record, material control is simpler and financial information is more accurate.

Mutual Benefit Life, the country's eighteenth largest life carrier, has reengineered its processing of insurance applications. Prior to this, MBL handled customers' applications much as its competitors did. The long, multistep process involved credit checking, quoting, rating, underwriting, and so on. An application would have to go through as many as 30 discrete steps, spanning five departments and involving 19 people. At the very best, MBL could process an application in 24 hours, but more typical turnarounds ranged from five to 25 days – most of the time spent passing information from one department to the next. (Another insurer estimated that while an application spent 22 days in process, it was actually worked on for just 17 minutes.)

MBL's rigid, sequential process led to many complications. For instance, when a customer wanted to cash in an existing policy and purchase a new one, the old business department first had to authorize the treasury department to issue a check made payable to MBL. The check would then accompany the paperwork to the new business department.

The president of MBL, intent on improving customer service, decided that this nonsense had to stop and demanded a 60 percent improvement in productivity. It was clear that such an ambitious goal would require more than tinkering with the existing process. Strong measures were in order, and the management team assigned to the task looked to technology as a means of achieving them. The team realized that shared databases and computer networks could make many different kinds of information available to a single person, while expert systems could help people with limited experience make sound decisions. Applying these insights led to a new approach to the application-handling process, one with wide organizational implications and little resemblance to the old way of doing business.

MBL swept away existing job definitions and departmental boundaries and created a new position called a case manager. Case managers have total responsibility for an application from the time it is received to the time a policy is issued. Unlike clerks, who performed a fixed task repeatedly under the watchful gaze of a supervisor, case managers work autonomously. No more handoffs of files and responsibility, no more shuffling of customer inquiries.

Case managers are able to perform all the tasks associated with an insurance application because they are supported by powerful PC-based workstations that run an expert system and connect to a range of automated systems on a mainframe. In particularly tough cases, the case manager calls for assistance from a senior underwriter or physician, but these specialists work only as consultants and advisers to the case manager, who never relinquishes control.

Empowering individuals to process entire applications has had a tremendous impact on operations. MBL can now complete an application in as little as four hours, and average turnaround takes only two to five days. The company has eliminated 100 field office positions, and case managers can handle more than twice the volume of new applications the company previously could process.

The essence of reengineering

At the heart of reengineering is the notion of discontinuous thinking – of recognizing and breaking away from the outdated rules and fundamental assumptions that underlie operations. Unless we change these rules, we are merely rearranging the deckchairs on the Titanic. We cannot achieve breakthroughs in performance by cutting fat or automating existing processes. Rather, we must challenge old assumptions and shed the old rules that made the business underperform in the first place.

Every business is replete with implicit rules left over from earlier decades. 'Customers don't repair their own equipment.' 'Local warehouses are necessary for good service.' 'Merchandising decisions are made at headquarters.' These rules of work design are based on assumptions about technology, people, and organizational goals that no longer hold. The contemporary repertoire of available information technologies is vast and quickly expanding. Quality, innovation, and service are now more important than cost, growth, and control. A large portion of the population is educated and capable of assuming responsibility, and workers cherish their autonomy and expect to have a say in how the business is run.

It should come as no surprise that our business processes and structures are outmoded and obsolete: our work structures and processes have not kept pace with the changes in technology, demographics, and business objectives. For the most part, we have organized work as a sequence of separate tasks and employed complex mechanisms to track its progress.

This arrangement can be traced to the Industrial Revolution, when specialization of labor and economies of scale promised to overcome the inefficiencies of cottage industries. Businesses disaggregated work into narrowly defined tasks, reaggregated the people performing those tasks into departments, and installed managers to administer them.

Our elaborate systems for imposing control and discipline on those who actually do the work stem from the postwar period. In that halcyon period of expansion, the main concern was growing fast without going broke, so businesses focused on cost, growth, and control. And since literate, entry-level people were abundant but well-educated professionals hard to come by, the control systems funneled information up the hierarchy to the few who presumably knew what to do with it.

These patterns of organizing work have become so ingrained that, despite their serious drawbacks, it's hard to conceive of work being accomplished any other way. Conventional process structures are fragmented and piecemeal, and they lack the integration necessary to maintain quality and service. They are breeding grounds for tunnel vision, as people tend to substitute the narrow goals of their particular department for the larger goals of the process as a whole. When work is handed off from person to person and unit to unit, delays and errors are inevitable. Accountability blurs, and critical issues fall between the cracks. Moreover, no one sees enough of the big picture to be able to respond quickly to new situations. Managers desperately try, like all the king's horses and all the king's men, to piece together the fragmented pieces of business processes.

Managers have tried to adapt their processes to new circumstances, but usually in ways that just create more problems. If, say, customer service is poor, they create a mechanism to deliver service but overlay it on the existing organization. Bureaucracy thickens, costs rise, and enterprising competitors gain market share.

In reengineering, managers break loose from outmoded business processes and the design principles underlying them and create new ones. Ford had operated under the old rule that 'We pay when we receive the invoice.' While no one had ever articulated or recorded it, that rule determined how the accounts payable process was organized. Ford's reengineering effort challenged and ultimately replaced the rule with a new one: 'We pay when we receive the goods.'

Reengineering requires looking at the fundamental processes of the business from a cross-functional perspective. Ford discovered that reengineering only the accounts payable department was futile. The appropriate focus of the effort was what might be called the goods acquisition process, which included purchasing and receiving as well as accounts payable.

One way to ensure that reengineering has a cross-functional perspective is to assemble a team that represents the functional units involved in the process being reengineered and all the units that depend on it. The team must analyze and scrutinize the existing process until it really understands what the process is trying to accomplish. The point is not to learn what happens to form 73B in its peregrinations through the company but to understand the purpose of having form 73B in the first place. Rather than looking for opportunities to improve the current process, the team should determine which of its steps really add value and search for new ways to achieve the result.

The reengineering team must keep asking Why? and What if? Why do we need to get a manager's signature on a requisition? Is it a control mechanism or a decision point? What if the manager reviews only requisitions above $500? What if he or she doesn't see them at all? Raising and resolving heretical questions can separate what is fundamental to the process from what is superficial. The regional offices of an East Coast insurance company had long produced a series of reports that they regularly sent to the home office. No one in the field realized that these reports were simply filed and never used. The process outlasted the circumstances that had created the need for it. The reengineering study team should push to discover situations like this.

In short, a reengineering effort strives for dramatic levels of improvement. It must break away from conventional wisdom and the constraints of organizational boundaries and should be broad and cross-functional in scope. It should use information technology not to automate an existing process but to enable a new one.

Principles of reengineering

Creating new rules tailored to the modern environment ultimately requires a new conceptualization of the business process – which comes down to someone having a great idea. But reengineering need not be haphazard. In fact, some of the principles that companies have already discovered while reengineering their business processes can help jump start the effort for others.

Organize around outcomes, not tasks

This principle says to have one person perform all the steps in a process. Design that person's job around an objective or outcome instead of a single task. The redesign at Mutual Benefit Life, where individual case managers perform the entire application approval process, is the quintessential example of this.

The redesign of an electronics company is another example. It had separate organizations performing each of the five steps between selling and installing the equipment. One group determined customer requirements, another translated those requirements into internal product codes, a third conveyed that information to various plants and warehouses, a fourth received and assembled the components, and a fifth delivered and installed the equipment. The process was based on the centuries-old notion of specialized labor and on the limitations inherent in paper files. The departments each possessed a specific set of skills, and only one department at a time could do its work.

The customer order moved systematically from step to step. But this sequential processing caused problems. The people getting the information from the customer in step one had to get all the data anyone would need throughout the process, even if it wasn't needed until step five. In addition, the many handoffs were responsible for numerous errors and misunderstandings. Finally, any questions about customer requirements that arose late in the process had to be referred back to the people doing step one, resulting in delay and rework.

When the company reengineered, it eliminated the assembly-line approach. It compressed responsibility for the various steps and assigned it to one person, the 'customer service representative.' That person now oversees the whole process – taking the order, translating it into product codes, getting the components assembled, and seeing the product delivered and installed. The customer service rep expedites and coordinates the process, much like a general contractor. And the customer has just one contact, who always knows the status of the order.

Have those who use the output of the process perform the process

In an effort to capitalize on the benefits of specialization and scale, many organizations established specialized departments to handle specialized processes. Each department does only one type of work and is a 'customer' of other groups' processes. Accounting does only accounting. If it needs new pencils, it goes to the purchasing department, the group specially equipped with the information and expertise to perform that role. Purchasing finds vendors, negotiates price, places the order, inspects the goods, and pays the invoice – and eventually the accountants get their pencils. The process works (after a fashion), but it's slow and bureaucratic.

Now that computer-based data and expertise are more readily available, departments, units, and individuals can do more for themselves. Opportunities exist to reengineer processes so that the individuals who need the result of a process can do it themselves. For example, by using expert systems and databases, departments can make their own purchases without sacrificing the benefits of specialized purchasers. One manufacturer has reengineered its purchasing process along just these lines. The company's old system, whereby the operating departments submitted requisitions and let purchasing do the rest, worked well for controlling expensive and important items like raw materials and capital equipment. But for inexpensive and nonstrategic purchases, which constituted some 35 percent of total orders, the system was slow and cumbersome; it was not uncommon for the cost of the purchasing process to exceed the cost of the goods being purchased.

The new process compresses the purchase of sundry items and pushes it on to the customers of the process. Using a database of approved vendors, an operating unit can directly place an order with a vendor and charge it on a bank credit card. At the end of the month, the bank gives the manufacturer a tape of all credit card transactions, which the company runs against its internal accounting system.

When an electronics equipment manufacturer reengineered its field service process, it pushed some of the steps of the process on to its customers. The manufacturer's field service had been plagued by the usual problems: technicians were often unable to do a particular repair because the right part wasn't on the van, response to customer calls was slow, and spare-parts inventory was excessive.

Now customers make simple repairs themselves. Spare parts are stored at each customer's site and managed through a computerized inventory-management system. When a problem arises, the customer calls the manufacturer's field-service hot line and describes the symptoms to a diagnostician, who accesses a diagnosis support system. If the problem appears to be something the customer can fix, the diagnostician tells the customer what part to replace and how to install it. The old

part is picked up and a new part left in its place at a later time. Only for complex problems is a service technician dispatched to the site, this time without having to make a stop at the warehouse to pick up parts.

When the people closest to the process perform it, there is little need for the overhead associated with managing it. Interfaces and liaisons can be eliminated, as can the mechanisms used to coordinate those who perform the process with those who use it. Moreover, the problem of capacity planning for the process performers is greatly reduced.

Subsume information-processing work into the real work that produces the information

The previous two principles compress linear processes. This principle suggests moving work from one person or department to another. Why doesn't an organization that produces information also process it? In the past, people didn't have the time or weren't trusted to do both. Most companies established units to do nothing but collect and process information that other departments created. This arrangement reflects the old rule about specialized labor and the belief that people at lower organizational levels are incapable of acting on information they generate. An accounts payable department collects information from purchasing and receiving and reconciles it with data that the vendor provides. Quality assurance gathers and analyzes information it gets from production.

Ford's redesigned accounts payable process embodies the new rule. With the new system, receiving, which produces the information about the goods received, processes this information instead of sending it to accounts payable. The new computer system can easily compare the delivery with the order and trigger the appropriate action.

Treat geographically dispersed resources as though they were centralized

The conflict between centralization and decentralization is a classic one. Decentralizing a resource (whether people, equipment, or inventory) gives better service to those who use it, but at the cost of redundancy, bureaucracy, and missed economies of scale. Companies no longer have to make such trade-offs. They can use databases, telecommunications networks, and standardized processing systems to get the benefits of scale and coordination while maintaining the benefits of flexibility and service.

At Hewlett-Packard, for instance, each of the more than 50 manufacturing units had its own separate purchasing department. While this arrangement provided excellent responsiveness and service to the plants, it prevented H-P from realizing the benefits of its scale, particularly with regard to quantity discounts. H-P's solution is to maintain the divisional purchasing organizations and to introduce a corporate unit to coordinate them. Each purchasing unit has access to a shared database on vendors and their performance and issues its own purchase orders. Corporate purchasing maintains this database and uses it to negotiate contracts for the corporation and to monitor the units. The payoffs have come in a 150 percent improvement in on-time deliveries, 50 percent reduction in lead times, 75 percent reduction in failure rates, and a significantly lower cost of goods purchased.

Link parallel activities instead of integrating their results

H-P's decentralized purchasing operations represent one kind of parallel processing in which separate units perform the same function. Another common kind of parallel processing is when separate units perform different activities that must eventually come together. Product development typically operates this way. In the development of a photocopier, for example, independent units develop the various subsystems of the copier. One group works on the optics, another on the mechanical paperhandling device, another on the power supply, and so on. Having people do development work simultaneously saves time, but at the dreaded integration and testing phase, the pieces often fail to work together. Then the costly redesign begins.

Or consider a bank that sells different kinds of credit – loans, letters of credit, asset-based financing – through separate units. These groups may have no way of knowing whether another group has already extended credit to a particular customer. Each unit could extend the full $10 million credit limit.

The new principle says to forge links between parallel functions and to coordinate them while their activities are in process rather than after they are completed. Communications networks, shared databases, and teleconferencing can bring the independent groups together so that coordination is ongoing. One large electronics company has cut its product development cycle by more than 50 percent by implementing this principle.

Put the decision point where the work is performed, and build control into the process

In most organizations, those who do the work are distinguished from those who monitor the work and make decisions about it. The tacit assumption is that the people actually doing the work have neither the time nor the inclination to monitor and control it and that they lack the knowledge and scope to make decisions about it. The entire hierarchical management structure is built on this assumption. Accountants, auditors, and supervisors check, record, and monitor work. Managers handle any exceptions.

The new principle suggests that the people who do the work should make the decisions and that the process itself can have built-in controls. Pyramidal management layers can therefore be compressed and the organization flattened.

Information technology can capture and process data, and expert systems can to some extent supply knowledge, enabling people to make their own decisions. As the doers become self-managing and self-controlling, hierarchy – and the slowness and bureaucracy associated with it – disappears.

When Mutual Benefit Life reengineered the insurance application process, it not only compressed the linear sequence but also eliminated the need for layers of managers. These two kinds of compression – vertical and horizontal – often go together; the very fact that a worker sees only one piece of the process calls for a manager with a broader vision. The case managers at MBL provide end-to-end management of the process, reducing the need for traditional managers. The managerial role is changing from one of controller and supervisor to one of supporter and facilitator.

Capture information once and at the source

This last rule is simple. When information was difficult to transmit, it made sense to collect information repeatedly. Each person, department, or unit had its own requirements and forms. Companies simply had to live with the associated delays, entry errors, and costly overhead. But why do we have to live with those problems now? Today when we collect a piece of information, we can store it in an on-line database for all who need it. Bar coding, relational databases, and electronic data interchange (EDI) make it easy to collect, store, and transmit information. One insurance company found that its application review process required that certain items be entered into 'stovepipe' computer systems supporting different functions as many as five times. By integrating and connecting these systems, the company was able to eliminate this redundant data entry along with the attendant checking functions and inevitable errors.

Think big

Reengineering triggers changes of many kinds, not just of the business process itself. Job designs, organizational structures, management systems – anything associated with the process must be refashioned in an integrated way. In other words, reengineering is a tremendous effort that mandates change in many areas of the organization.

When Ford reengineered its payables, receiving clerks on the dock had to learn to use computer terminals to check shipments, and they had to make decisions about whether to accept the goods. Purchasing agents also had to assume new responsibilities – like making sure the purchase orders they entered into the database had the correct information about where to send the check. Attitudes toward vendors also had to change: vendors could no longer be seen as adversaries; they had to become partners in a shared business process. Vendors too had to adjust. In many cases, invoices formed the basis of their accounting systems. At least one Ford supplier adapted by continuing to print invoices, but instead of sending them to Ford threw them away, reconciling cash received against invoices never sent.

The changes at Mutual Benefit Life were also widespread. The company's job-rating scheme could not accommodate the case manager position, which had a lot of responsibility but no direct reports. MBL had to devise new job-rating schemes and compensation policies. It also had to develop a culture in which people doing work are perceived as more important than those supervising work. Career paths, recruitment and training programs, promotion policies – these and many other management systems are being revised to support the new process design.

The extent of these changes suggests one factor that is necessary for reengineering to succeed: executive leadership with real vision. No one in an organization wants reengineering. It is confusing and disruptive and affects everything people have grown accustomed to. Only if top-level managers back the effort and outlast the company cynics will people take reengineering seriously. As one wag at an electronics equipment manufacturer has commented, 'Every few months, our senior managers find a new religion. One time it was quality, another it was customer service, another it was flattening the organization. We just hold our breath until they get over it and things get back to normal.' Commitment, consistency – maybe even a touch of fanaticism – are needed to enlist those who would prefer the status quo.

Considering the inertia of old processes and structures, the strain of implementing a reengineering plan can hardly be overestimated. But by the same token, it is hard to overestimate the opportunities, especially for established companies. Big, traditional organizations aren't necessarily dinosaurs doomed to extinction, but they are burdened with layers of unproductive overhead and armies of unproductive workers. Shedding them a layer at a time will not be good enough to stand up against sleek startups or streamlined Japanese companies. US companies need fast change and dramatic improvements.

We have the tools to do what we need to do. Information technology offers many options for reorganizing work. But our imaginations must guide our decisions about technology – not the other way around. We must have the boldness to imagine taking 78 days out of an 80-day turnaround time, cutting 75 percent of overhead, and eliminating 80 percent of errors. These are not unrealistic goals. If managers have the vision, reengineering will provide a way.

READING 4.2 Kaizen

By Masaaki Imai[1]

Back in the 1950s, I was working with the Japan Productivity Center in Washington, D.C. My job mainly consisted of escorting groups of Japanese businessmen who were visiting American companies to study 'the secret of American industrial productivity.' Toshiro Yamada, now Professor Emeritus of the Faculty of Engineering at Kyoto University, was a member of one such study team visiting the United States to study the industrial-vehicle industry. Recently, the members of his team gathered to celebrate the silver anniversary of their trip.

At the banquet table, Yamada said he had recently been back to the United States in a 'sentimental journey' to some of the plants he had visited, among them the River Rouge steelworks in Dearborn, Michigan. Shaking his head in disbelief, he said, 'You know, the plant was exactly the same as it had been 25 years ago.'

These conversations set me to thinking about the great differences in the ways Japanese and Western managers approach their work. It is inconceivable that a Japanese plant would remain virtually unchanged for over a quarter of a century.

I had long been looking for a key concept to explain these two very different management approaches, one that might also help explain why many Japanese companies have come to gain their increasingly conspicuous competitive edge. For instance, how do we explain the fact that while most new ideas come from the West and some of the most advanced plants, institutions, and technologies are found there, there are also many plants there that have changed little since the 1950s?

Change is something which everybody takes for granted. Recently, an American executive at a large multinational firm told me his company chairman had said at the start of an executive committee meeting: 'Gentlemen, our job is to manage change. If we fail, we must change management.' The executive smiled and said, 'We all got the message!'

In Japan, change is a way of life, too. But are we talking about the same change when we talk about managing change or else changing management? It dawned on me that there might be different kinds of change: gradual and abrupt. While we can easily observe both gradual and abrupt changes in Japan, gradual change is not so obvious a part of the Western way of life. How are we to explain this difference?

This question led me to consider the question of values. Could it be that differences between the value systems in Japan and the West account for their different attitudes toward gradual change and abrupt change? Abrupt changes are easily grasped by everyone concerned, and people are usually elated to see them. This is generally true in both Japan and the West. Yet what about the gradual changes? My earlier statement that it is inconceivable that a Japanese plant would remain unchanged for years refers to gradual change as well as abrupt change.

Thinking all this over, I came to the conclusion that the key difference between how change is understood in Japan and how it is viewed in the West lies in the Kaizen concept – a concept that is so natural and obvious to many Japanese managers that they often do not even realize that they possess it! The Kaizen concept explains why companies cannot remain the same for long in Japan. Moreover, after many years of studying Western business practices, I have reached the conclusion that this Kaizen concept is non-existent, or at least very weak, in most Western companies today. Worse yet, they reject it without knowing what it really entails. It's the old 'not invented here' syndrome. And this lack of Kaizen helps explain why an American or European factory can remain exactly the same for a quarter of a century.

The essence of Kaizen is simple and straightforward: Kaizen means improvement. Moreover, Kaizen means ongoing improvement involving everyone, including both managers and workers. The Kaizen philosophy assumes that our way of life – be it our working life, our social life, or our home life – deserves to be constantly improved.

In trying to understand Japan's postwar 'economic miracle,' scholars, journalists, and businesspeople alike have dutifully studied such factors as the productivity movement, total quality control (TQC), small-group

---

[1]Source: This article was adapted with permission from Chapters 1 and 2 of *Kaizen: The Key to Japan's Competitive Success*, McGraw-Hill, New York, 1986.

activities, the suggestion system, automation, industrial robots, and labor relations. They have given much attention to some of Japan's unique management practices, among them the lifetime employment system, seniority-based wages, and enterprise unions. Yet I feel they have failed to grasp the very simple truth that lies behind the many myths concerning Japanese management.

The essence of most 'uniquely Japanese' management practices – be they productivity improvement, TQC (Total Quality Control) activities, QC (Quality Control) circles, or labor relations – can be reduced to one word: Kaizen. Using the term Kaizen in place of such words as productivity, TQC, ZD (Zero Defects), *kamban*, and the suggestion system paints a far clearer picture of what has been going on in Japanese industry. Kaizen is an umbrella concept covering most of those 'uniquely Japanese' practices that have recently achieved such world-wide fame.

The implications of TQC or CWQC (Company-Wide Quality Control) in Japan have been that these concepts have helped Japanese companies generate a process-oriented way of thinking and develop strategies that assure continuous improvement involving people at all levels of the organizational hierarchy. The message of the Kaizen strategy is that not a day should go by without some kind of improvement being made somewhere in the company.

The belief that there should be unending improvement is deeply ingrained in the Japanese mentality. As the old Japanese saying goes, 'If a man has not been seen for three days, his friends should take a good look at him to see what changes have befallen him.' The implication is that he must have changed in three days, so his friends should be attentive enough to notice the changes.

After World War II, most Japanese companies had to start literally from the ground up. Every day brought new challenges to managers and workers alike, and every day meant progress. Simply staying in business required unending progress, and Kaizen has become a way of life. It was also fortunate that the various tools that helped elevate this Kaizen concept to new heights were introduced to Japan in the late 1950s and early 1960s by such experts as W.E. Deming and J.M. Juran. However, most new concepts, systems, and tools that are widely used in Japan today have subsequently been developed in Japan and represent qualitative improvements upon the statistical quality control and total quality control of the 1960s.

Kaizen and management

Figure 4.2.1 shows how job functions are perceived in Japan. As indicated, management has two major components: maintenance and improvement. Maintenance refers to activities directed toward maintaining current technological, managerial, and operating standards; improvement refers to those directed toward improving current standards.

Under its maintenance functions, management performs its assigned tasks so that everybody in the company can follow the established SOP (Standard Operating Procedure). This means that management must first establish policies, rules, directives, and procedures for all major operations and then see to it that everybody follows SOP. If people are able to follow the standard but do not, management must introduce discipline. If people are unable to follow the standard, management must either provide training or review and revise the standard so that people can follow it.

In any business, an employee's work is based on existing standards, either explicit or implicit, imposed by management. Maintenance refers to maintaining such standards through training and discipline. By contrast, improvement refers to improving the standards. The Japanese perception of management boils down to one precept: maintain and improve standards.

The higher up the manager is, the more he is concerned with improvement. At the bottom level, an unskilled worker working at a machine may spend all his time following instructions. However, as he becomes more proficient at his work, he begins to think about improvement. He begins to contribute to

FIGURE 4.2.1 Japanese perceptions of job functions

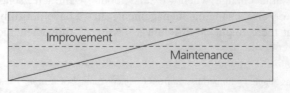

improvements in the way his work is done, either through individual suggestions or through group suggestions.

Ask any manager at a successful Japanese company what top management is pressing for, and the answer will be, 'Kaizen' (improvement). Improving standards means establishing higher standards. Once this is done, it becomes management's maintenance job to see that the new standards are observed. Lasting improvement is achieved only when people work to higher standards. Maintenance and improvement have thus become inseparable for most Japanese managers.

What is improvement? Improvement can be broken down between Kaizen and innovation. Kaizen signifies small improvements made in the status quo as a result of ongoing efforts. Innovation involves a drastic improvement in the status quo as a result of a large investment in new technology and/or equipment. Figure 4.2.2 shows the breakdown among maintenance, Kaizen, and innovation as perceived by Japanese management.

On the other hand, most Western managers' perceptions of job functions are as shown in Figure 4.2.2. There is little room in Western management for the Kaizen concept.

Sometimes, another type of management is found in the high-technology industries. These are the companies that are born running, grow rapidly, and then disappear just as rapidly when their initial success wanes or markets change.

The worst companies are those which do nothing but maintenance, meaning there is no internal drive for Kaizen or innovation, change is forced on management by market conditions and competition and management does not know where it wants to go.

Implications of QC for Kaizen

While management is usually concerned with such issues as productivity and quality, the thrust of this article is to look at the other side of the picture – at Kaizen.

The starting point for improvement is to recognize the need. This comes from recognition of a problem. If no problem is recognized, there is no recognition of the need for improvement. Complacency is the archenemy of Kaizen. Therefore, Kaizen emphasizes problem-awareness and provides clues for identifying problems.

Once identified, problems must be solved. Thus Kaizen is also a problem-solving process. In fact, Kaizen requires the use of various problem-solving tools. Improvement reaches new heights with every problem that is solved. In order to consolidate the new level, however, the improvement must be standardized. Thus Kaizen also requires standardization.

Such terms as QC (Quality Control), SQC (Statistical Quality Control), QC circles, and TQC (or CWQC) often appear in connection with Kaizen. To avoid unnecessary confusion, it may be helpful to clarify these terms here. The word *quality* has been interpreted in many different ways, and there is no agreement on what actually constitutes quality. In its broadest sense, quality is anything that can be improved. In this context, quality is associated not only with products and services but also with the way people work, the way machines are operated, and the way systems and procedures are dealt with. It includes all aspects of human behavior. This is why it is more useful to talk about Kaizen than about quality or productivity.

The English term *improvement* as used in the Western context more often than not means improvement in equipment, thus excluding the human

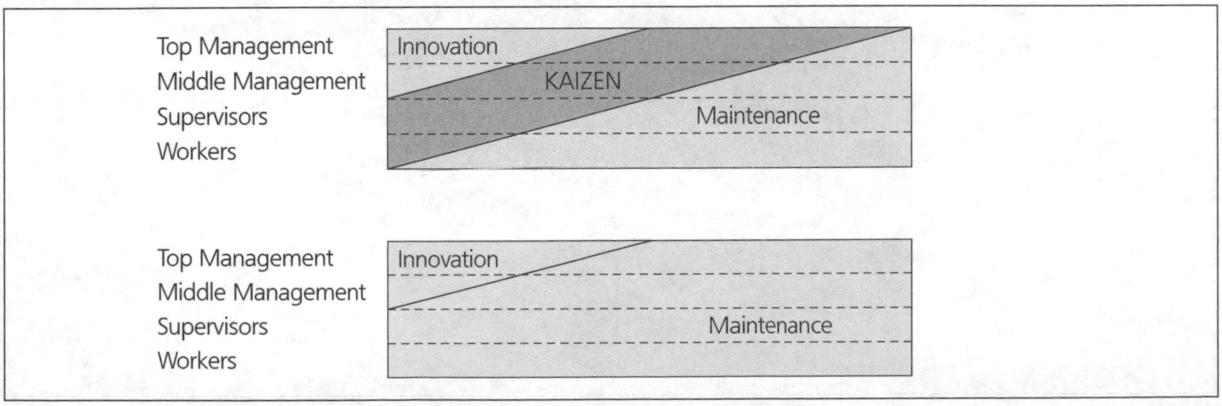

FIGURE 4.2.2 Japanese vs. Western perceptions of job functions

elements. By contrast, Kaizen is generic and can be applied to every aspect of everybody's activities. This said, however, it must be admitted that such terms as quality and quality control have played a vital role in the development of Kaizen in Japan.

In March 1950, the Union of Japanese Scientists and Engineers (JUSE) started publishing its magazine *Statistical Quality Control*. In July of the same year, W.E. Deming was invited to Japan to teach statistical quality control at an eight-day seminar organized by JUSE. Deming visited Japan several times in the 1950s, and it was during one of those visits that he made his famous prediction that Japan would soon be flooding the world market with quality products.

Deming also introduced the 'Deming cycle,' one of the crucial QC tools for assuring continuous improvement, to Japan. The Deming cycle is also called the Deming wheel or the PDCA (Plan-Do-Check-Action) cycle. (See Figure 4.2.3.) Deming stressed the importance of constant interaction among research, design, production, and sales in order for a company to arrive at better quality that satisfies customers. He taught that this wheel should be rotated on the ground of quality-first perceptions and quality-first responsibility. With this process, he argued, the company could win consumer confidence and acceptance and prosper.

In July 1954, J.M. Juran was invited to Japan to conduct a JUSE seminar on quality-control management. This was the first time QC was dealt with from the overall management perspective.

In 1956, Japan Shortwave Radio included a course on quality control as part of its educational programming. In November 1960, the first national quality month was inaugurated. It was also in 1960 that Q-marks and Q-flags were formally adopted. Then in April 1962 the magazine *Quality Control for the Foreman* was launched by JUSE, and the first QC circle was started that same year.

A QC circle is defined as a small group that *voluntarily* performs quality-control activities within the shop. The small group carries out its work continuously as part of a company-wide program of quality control, self-development, mutual education, and flow-control and improvement within the workshop. The QC circle is only *part* of a company-wide program; it is never the whole of TQC or CWQC.

Those who have followed QC circles in Japan know that they often focus on such areas as cost, safety, and productivity, and that their activities sometimes relate only indirectly to product-quality improvement. For the most part, these activities are aimed at making improvements in the workshop.

There is no doubt that QC circles have played an important part in improving product quality and productivity in Japan. However, their role has often been blown out of proportion by overseas observers who believe that QC circles are the mainstay of TQC activities in Japan. Nothing could be further from the truth, especially when it comes to Japanese management. Efforts related to QC circles generally account for only

FIGURE 4.2.3   Deming wheel

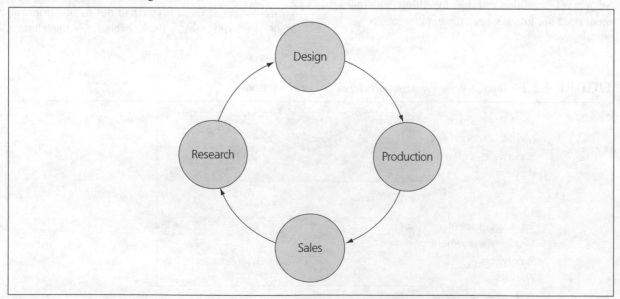

10 percent to 30 percent of the overall TQC effort in Japanese companies.

What is less visible behind these developments is the transformation of the term quality control, or QC, in Japan. As is the case in many Western companies, quality control initially meant quality control applied to the manufacturing process, particularly the inspections for rejecting defective incoming material or defective outgoing products at the end of the production line. But very soon the realization set in that inspection alone does nothing to improve the quality of the product, and that product quality should be built at the production stage. 'Build quality into the process' was (and still is) a popular phrase in Japanese quality control. It is at this stage that control charts and the other tools for statistical quality control were introduced after Deming's lectures.

Juran's lectures in 1954 opened up another aspect of quality control: the managerial approach to quality control. This was the first time the term QC was positioned as a vital management tool in Japan. From then on, the term QC has been used to mean both quality control and the tools for overall improvement in managerial performance.

At a later stage, other industries started to introduce QC for such products as consumer durables and home appliances. In these industries, the interest was in building quality in at the design stage to meet changing and increasingly stringent customer requirements. Today, management has gone beyond the design stage and has begun to stress the importance of quality product development, which means taking customer-related information and market research into account from the very start.

All this while, QC has grown into a full-fledged management tool for Kaizen involving everyone in the company. Such company-wide activities are often referred to as TQC (total quality control) or CWQC (company-wide quality control). No matter which name is used, TQC and CWQC mean company-wide Kaizen activities involving everyone in the company, managers and workers alike. Over the years, QC has been elevated to SQC and then to TQC or CWQC, improving managerial performance at every level. Thus it is that such words as QC and TQC have come to be almost synonymous with Kaizen. This is also why I constantly refer to QC, TQC, and CWQC in explaining Kaizen.

On the other hand, the function of quality control in its original sense remains valid. Quality assurance remains a vital part of management, and most companies have a QA (quality assurance) department for this.

To confuse matters, TQC or CWQC activities are sometimes administered by the QA department and sometimes by a separate TQC office. Thus it is important that these QC-related words be understood in the context in which they appear.

Kaizen and TQC

Considering the TQC movement in Japan as part of the Kaizen movement gives us a clearer perspective on the Japanese approach. First of all, it should be pointed out that TQC activities in Japan are not concerned solely with quality control. People have been fooled by the term 'quality control' and have often construed it within the narrow discipline of product-quality control. In the West, the term QC is mostly associated with inspection of finished products, and when QC is brought up in discussion, top managers, who generally assume they have very little to do with quality control, lose interest immediately.

It is unfortunate that in the West TQC has been dealt with mainly in technical journals when it is more properly the focus of management journals. Japan has developed an elaborate system of Kaizen strategies as management tools within the TQC movement. These rank among this century's most outstanding management achievements. Yet because of the limited way in which QC is understood in the West, most Western students of Japanese QC activities have failed to grasp their real significance and challenge. At the same time, new TQC methods and tools are constantly being studied and tested.

TQC in Japan is a movement centered on the improvement of managerial performance at all levels. As such, it has typically dealt with:

1 quality assurance;
2 cost reduction;
3 meeting production quotas;
4 meeting delivery schedules;
5 safety;
6 new-product development;
7 productivity improvement;
8 supplier management.

More recently, TQC has come to include marketing, sales, and service as well. Furthermore, TQC has dealt with such crucial management concerns as organizational development, cross-functional management, policy deployment, and quality deployment. In other words, management has been using TQC as a tool for improving overall performance.

Those who have closely followed QC circles in Japan know that their activities are often focused on such areas as cost, safety and productivity, and that their activities may only indirectly relate to product-quality improvement. For the most part, these activities are aimed at making improvements in the workplace.

Management efforts for TQC have been directed mostly at such areas as education, systems development, policy deployment, cross-functional management and, more recently, quality deployment.

Kaizen and the suggestion system

Japanese management makes a concerted effort to involve employees in Kaizen through suggestions. Thus, the suggestion system is an integral part of the established management system, and the number of workers' suggestions is regarded as an important criterion in reviewing the performance of these workers' supervisor. The manager of the supervisors is in turn expected to assist them so that they can help workers generate more suggestions.

Most Japanese companies active in Kaizen programs have a quality-control system and a suggestion system working in concert. The role of QC circles may be better understood if we regard them collectively as a group-oriented suggestion system for making improvements.

One of the outstanding features of Japanese management is that it generates a great number of suggestions from workers and that management works hard to consider these suggestions, often incorporating them into the overall Kaizen strategy. It is not uncommon for top management of a leading Japanese company to spend a whole day listening to presentations of activities by QC circles, and giving awards based on predetermined criteria. Management is willing to give recognition to employees' efforts for improvements and makes its concern visible wherever possible. Often, the number of suggestions is posted individually on the wall of the work-place in order to encourage competition among workers and among groups.

Another important aspect of the suggestion system is that each suggestion, once implemented, leads to a revised standard. For instance, when a special fool-proof device has been installed on a machine at a worker's suggestion, this may require the worker to work differently and, at times, more attentively.

However, inasmuch as the new standard has been set up by the worker's own volition, he takes pride in the new standard and is willing to follow it. If, on the contrary, he is told to follow a standard imposed by management, he may not be as willing to follow it.

Thus, through suggestions, employees can participate in Kaizen in the workplace and play a vital role in upgrading standards. In a recent interview, Toyota Motor chairman Eiji Toyoda said, 'One of the features of the Japanese workers is that they use their brains as well as their hands. Our workers provide 1.5 million suggestions a year, and 95 percent of them are put to practical use. There is an almost tangible concern for improvement in the air at Toyota.'

Kaizen vs. innovation

There are two contrasting approaches to progress: the gradualist approach and the great-leap-forward approach. Japanese companies generally favor the gradualist approach and Western companies the great-leap approach – an approach epitomized by the term 'innovation'.

Western management worships at the altar of innovation. This innovation is seen as major changes in the wake of technological breakthroughs, or the introduction of the latest management concepts or production techniques. Innovation is dramatic, a real attention-getter. Kaizen, on the other hand, is often undramatic and subtle, and its results are seldom immediately visible. While Kaizen is a continuous process, innovation is generally a one-shot phenomenon.

In the West, for example, a middle manager can usually obtain top management support for such projects as CAD (computer-aided design), CAM (computer-aided manufacture), and MRP (materials requirements planning), since these are innovative projects that have a way of revolutionizing existing systems. As such, they offer ROI (return on investment) benefits that managers can hardly resist.

However, when a factory manager wishes, for example, to make small changes in the way his workers use the machinery, such as working out multiple job assignments or realigning production processes (both of which may require lengthy discussions with the union as well as reeducation and retraining of workers), obtaining management support can be difficult indeed.

Table 4.2.1 compares the main features of Kaizen and of innovation. One of the beautiful things about Kaizen is that it does not necessarily require sophisti-

TABLE 4.2.1 Features of Kaizen and innovation

	Kaizen	*Innovation*
1. Effect	Long-term and long-lasting but undramatic	Short-term but dramatic
2. Pace	Small steps	Big steps
3. Timeframe	Continuous and incremental	Intermittent and non-incremental
4. Change	Gradual and constant	Abrupt and volatile
5. Involvement	Everybody	Select few 'champions'
6. Approach	Collectivism, group efforts, systems approach	Rugged individualism, individual ideas and efforts
7. Mode	Maintenance and improvement	Scrap and rebuild
8. Spark	Conventional know-how and state of the art	Technological break-throughs, new inventions, new theories
9. Practical requirements	Requires little investment but great effort to maintain it	Requires large investment but little effort to maintain it
10. Effort orientation	People	Technology
11. Evaluation criteria	Process and efforts for better results	Results and profits
12. Advantage	Works well in slow-growth economy	Better suited to fast-growth economy

cated technique or state-of-the-art technology. To implement Kaizen, you need only simple, conventional techniques. Often, common sense is all that is needed. On the other hand, innovation usually requires highly sophisticated technology, as well as a huge investment.

Kaizen is like a hotbed that nurtures small and ongoing changes, while innovation is like magma that appears in abrupt eruptions from time to time. One big difference between Kaizen and innovation is that while Kaizen does not necessarily call for a large investment to implement it, it does call for a great deal of continuous effort and commitment. The difference between the two opposing concepts may thus be likened to that of a staircase and a slope. The innovation strategy is supposed to bring about progress in a staircase progression. On the other hand, the Kaizen strategy brings about gradual progress. I say the innovation strategy 'is supposed to' bring about progress in a staircase progression, because it usually does not. Instead of following the staircase pattern, the actual progress achieved through innovation will generally follow the pattern shown in Figure 4.2.4, if it lacks the Kaizen strategy to go along with it. This happens because a system, once it has been installed as a result of new innovation, is subject to steady deterioration unless continuing efforts are made first to maintain it and then to improve on it.

In reality, there can be no such thing as a static constant. All systems are destined to deteriorate once they have been established. One of the famous Parkinson's Laws is that an organization, once it has built its edifice, begins its decline. In other words, there must be a continuing effort for improvement to even maintain the status quo.

When such effort is lacking, decline is inevitable (see Figure 4.2.4). Therefore, even when an innovation makes a revolutionary standard of performance attainable, the new performance level will decline unless the standard is constantly challenged and upgraded. Thus, whenever an innovation is achieved, it must be followed by a series of Kaizen efforts to maintain and improve it (see Figure 4.2.5).

Whereas innovation is a one-shot deal whose effects are gradually eroded by intense competition and deteriorating standards, Kaizen is an ongoing effort with cumulative effects marking a steady rise as the years go by. If standards exist only in order to maintain the status quo, they will not be challenged so long as the level of performance is acceptable. Kaizen, on the other hand, means a constant effort not only to maintain but also to upgrade standards. Kaizen strategists believe that standards are by nature tentative, akin to stepping stones, with one standard leading to another as continuing improvement efforts are made. This is the reason why

FIGURE 4.2.4   Innovation alone

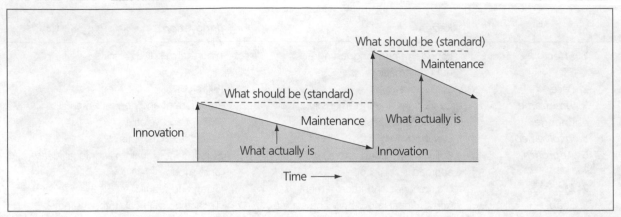

FIGURE 4.2.5   Innovation plus Kaizen

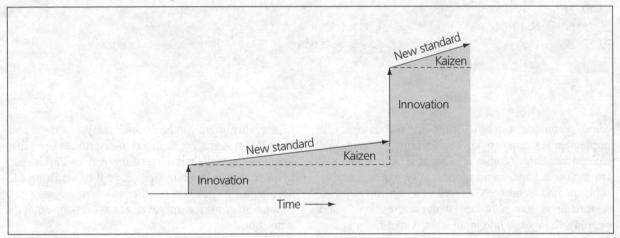

QC circles no sooner solve one problem than they move on to tackle a new problem. This is also the reason why the so-called PDCA (plan-do-check-action) cycle receives so much emphasis in Japan's TQC movement.

Another feature of Kaizen is that it requires virtually everyone's personal efforts. In order for the Kaizen spirit to survive, management must make a conscious and continuous effort to support it. Such support is quite different from the fanfare recognition that management accords to people who have achieved a striking success or breakthrough. Kaizen is concerned more with the process than with the result. The strength of Japanese management lies in its successful development and implementation of a system that acknowledges the ends while emphasizing the means.

Thus Kaizen calls for a substantial management commitment of time and effort. Infusions of capital are no substitute for this investment in time and effort.

Investing in Kaizen means investing in people. In short, Kaizen is people-oriented, whereas innovation is technology- and money-oriented.

Finally, the Kaizen philosophy is better suited to a slow-growth economy, while innovation is better suited to a fast-growth economy. While Kaizen advances inch-by-inch on the strength of many small efforts, innovation leaps upward in hopes of landing at a much higher plateau in spite of gravitational inertia and the weight of investment costs. In a slow-growth economy characterized by high costs of energy and materials, overcapacity, and stagnant markets, Kaizen often has a better payoff than innovation does. As one Japanese executive recently remarked, 'It is extremely difficult to increase sales by 10 percent. But it is not so difficult to cut manufacturing costs by 10 percent to even better effect.'

I argued that the concept of Kaizen is nonexistent or at best weak in most Western companies today.

However, there was a time, not so long ago, when Western management also placed a high priority on Kaizen-like improvement-consciousness. Older executives may recall that before the phenomenal economic growth of the late 1950s and early 1960s, management attended assiduously to improving all aspects of the business, particularly the factory. In those days, every small improvement was counted and was seen as effective in terms of building success.

People who worked with small, privately owned companies may recall with a touch of nostalgia that there was a genuine concern for improvement 'in the air' before the company was bought out or went public. As soon as that happened, the quarterly P/L (profit/loss) figures suddenly became the most important criterion, and management became obsessed with the bottom line, often at the expense of pressing for constant and unspectacular improvements.

For many other companies, the greatly increased market opportunities and technological innovations that appeared during the first two decades after World War II meant that developing new products based on the new technology was much more attractive or 'sexier' than slow, patient efforts for improvement. In trying to catch up with the ever-increasing market demand, managers boldly introduced one innovation after another, and they were content to ignore the seemingly minor benefits of improvement.

Most Western managers who joined the ranks during or after those heady days do not have the slightest concern for improvement. Instead, they take an offensive posture, armed with professional expertise geared toward making big changes in the name of innovation, bringing about immediate gains, and winning instant recognition and promotion. Before they knew it, Western managers had lost sight of improvement and put all their eggs in the innovation basket.

Another factor that has abetted the innovation approach has been the increasing emphasis on financial controls and accounting. By now, the more sophisticated companies have succeeded in establishing elaborate accounting and reporting systems that force managers to account for every action they take and to spell out the precise payout or ROI of every managerial decision. Such a system does not lend itself to building a favorable climate for improvement.

Improvement is by definition slow, gradual, and often invisible, with effects that are felt over the long run. In my opinion, the most glaring and significant shortcoming of Western management today is the lack of improvement philosophy. There is no internal system in Western management to reward efforts for improvement; instead, everyone's job performance is reviewed strictly on the basis of results. Thus it is not uncommon for Western managers to chide people with, 'I don't care what you do or how you do it. I want the results – and now!' This emphasis on results has led to the innovation-dominated approach of the West. This is not to say that Japanese management does not care about innovation. But Japanese managers have enthusiastically pursued Kaizen even when they were involved in innovation.

READING 4.3

Convergence and upheaval: Managing the unsteady pace of organizational evolution

By Michael Tushman, William Newman, and Elaine Romanelli[1]

A snug fit of external opportunity, company strategy, and internal structure is a hallmark of successful companies. The real test of executive leadership, however, is in maintaining this alignment in the face of changing competitive conditions. Consider the Polaroid or Caterpillar corporations. Both firms virtually dominated their respective industries for decades, only to be caught off guard by major environmental changes. The same strategic and organizational factors that were so effective for decades became the seeds of complacency and organization decline.

[1]Source: This article © 1986, by the Regents of the University of California. Adapted from the *California Management Review*, Vol. 29, No. 1. By permission of the Regents. All rights reserved.

Recent studies of companies over long periods show that the most successful firms maintain a workable equilibrium for several years (or decades), but are also able to initiate and carry out sharp, widespread changes (referred to here as reorientations) when their environments shift. Such upheaval may bring renewed vigor to the enterprise. Less successful firms, on the other hand, get stuck in a particular pattern. The leaders of these firms either do not see the need for reorientation or they are unable to carry through the necessary framebreaking changes. While not all reorientations succeed, those organizations which do not initiate reorientations as environments shift underperform.

This article focuses on reasons why for long periods most companies make only incremental changes, and why they then need to make painful, discontinuous, system-wide shifts. We are particularly concerned with the role of executive leadership in managing this pattern of convergence punctuated by upheaval. Here are four examples of the convergence/upheaval pattern:

■ Founded in 1915 by a set of engineers from MIT, the General Radio Company was established to produce highly innovative and high-quality (but expensive) electronic test equipment. Over the years, General Radio developed a consistent organization to accomplish its mission. It hired only the brightest young engineers, built a loose functional organization dominated by the engineering department, and developed a 'General Radio culture' (for example, no conflict, management by consensus, slow growth). General Radio's strategy and associated structures, systems, and people were very successful. By World War II, General Radio was the largest test equipment firm in the United States. After World War II, however, increasing technology and cost-based competition began to erode General Radio's market share. While management made numerous incremental changes, General Radio remained fundamentally the same organization. In the late 1960s, when CEO Don Sinclair initiated strategic changes, he left the firm's structure and systems intact. This effort at doing new things with established systems and procedures was less than successful. By 1972, the firm incurred its first loss. In the face of this sustained performance decline, Bill Thurston (a long-time General Radio executive) was made President. Thurston initiated system-wide changes. General Radio adopted a more marketing-oriented strategy. Its product line was cut from 20 different lines to three; much more emphasis was given to product-line management, sales, and marketing. Resources were diverted from engineering

to revitalize sales, marketing, and production. During 1973, the firm moved to a matrix structure, increased its emphasis on controls and systems, and went outside for a set of executives to help Thurston run this revised General Radio. To perhaps more formally symbolize these changes and the sharp move away from the 'old' General Radio, the firm's name was changed to GenRad. By 1984, GenRad's sales exploded to over $200 million (vs. $44 million in 1972). After 60 years of convergent change around a constant strategy, Thurston and his colleagues (many new to the firm) made discontinuous system-wide changes in strategy, structure, people, and processes. While traumatic, these changes were implemented over a two-year period and led to a dramatic turnaround in GenRad's performance.

■ Prime Computer was founded in 1971 by a group of individuals who left Honeywell. Prime's initial strategy was to produce a high-quality/high-price minicomputer based on semiconductor memory. These founders built an engineering-dominated, loosely structured firm which sold to OEMs and through distributors. This configuration of strategy, structure, people, and processes was very successful. By 1974, Prime turned its first profit; by 1975, its sales were more than $11 million. In the midst of this success, Prime's board of directors brought in Ken Fisher to reorient the organization. Fisher and a whole new group of executives hired from Honeywell initiated a set of discontinuous changes throughout Prime during 1975–1976. Prime now sold a full range of minicomputers and computer systems to OEMs and end-users. To accomplish this shift in strategy, Prime adopted a more complex functional structure, with a marked increase in resources to sales and marketing. The shift in resources away from engineering was so great that Bill Poduska, Prime's head of engineering, left to form Apollo Computer. Between 1975 and 1981, Fisher and his colleagues consolidated and incrementally adapted structure, systems, and processes to better accomplish the new strategy. During this convergent period, Prime grew dramatically to over $260 million by 1981. In 1981, again in the midst of this continuing sequence of increased volume and profits, Prime's board again initiated an upheaval. Fisher and his direct reports left Prime (some of whom founded Encore Computer), while Joe Henson and a set of executives from IBM initiated wholesale changes throughout the organization. The firm diversified into robotics, CAD/CAM, and office systems; adopted a divisional structure;

developed a more market-driven orientation; and increased controls and systems. It remains to be seen how this 'new' Prime will fare. Prime must be seen, then, not as a 14-year-old firm, but as three very different organizations, each of which was managed by a different set of executives. Unlike General Radio, Prime initiated these discontinuities during periods of great success.

- The Operating Group at Citibank prior to 1970 had been a service-oriented function for the end-user areas of the bank. The Operating Group hired high school graduates who remained in the 'back-office' for their entire careers. Structure, controls, and systems were loose, while the informal organization valued service, responsiveness to client needs, and slow, steady work habits. While these patterns were successful enough, increased demand and heightened customer expectations led to ever decreasing performance during the late 1960s. In the face of severe performance decline, John Reed was promoted to head the Operating Group. Reed recruited several executives with production backgrounds, and with this new top team he initiated system-wide changes. Reed's vision was to transform the Operating Group from a service-oriented back office to a factory producing high-quality products. Consistent with this new mission, Reed and his colleagues initiated sweeping changes in strategy, structure, work flows, controls, and culture. These changes were initiated concurrently throughout the back office, with very little participation, over the course of a few months. While all the empirical performance measures improved substantially, these changes also generated substantial stress and anxiety within Reed's group.

- For 20 years, Alpha Corporation was among the leaders in the industrial fastener industry. Its reliability, low cost, and good technical service were important strengths. However, as Alpha's segment of the industry matured, its profits declined. Belt-tightening helped but was not enough. Finally, a new CEO presided over a sweeping restructuring: cutting the product line, closing a plant, trimming overhead; then focusing on computer parts which call for very close tolerances, CAD/CAM tooling, and cooperation with customers on design efforts. After four rough years, Alpha appears to have found a new niche where convergence will again be warranted.

These four short examples illustrate periods of incremental change, or convergence, punctuated by discontinuous changes throughout the organization.

Discontinuous or 'frame-breaking' change involves simultaneous and sharp shifts in strategy, power, structure, and controls. Each example illustrates the role of executive leadership in initiating and implementing discontinuous change. Where General Radio, Citibank's Operating Group, and Alpha initiated system-wide changes only after sustained performance decline, Prime proactively initiated system-wide changes to take advantage of competitive/technological conditions. These patterns in organization evolution are not unique. Upheaval, sooner or later, follows convergence if a company is to survive; only a farsighted minority of firms initiate upheaval prior to incurring performance declines.

The task of managing incremental change, or convergence, differs sharply from managing frame-breaking change. Incremental change is compatible with the existing structure of a company and is reinforced over a period of years. In contrast, frame-breaking change is abrupt, painful to participants, and often resisted by the old guard. Forging these new strategy–structure–people–process consistencies and laying the basis for the next period of incremental change calls for distinctive skills.

Because the future health, and even survival, of a company or business unit is at stake, we need to take a closer look at the nature and consequences of convergent change and of differences imposed by frame-breaking change. We need to explore when and why these painful and risky revolutions interrupt previously successful patterns, and whether these discontinuities can be avoided and/or initiated prior to crisis. Finally, we need to examine what managers can and should do to guide their organizations through periods of convergence and upheaval over time.

Patterns in organizational evolution: Convergence and upheaval

Successful companies wisely stick to what works well. At General Radio between 1915 and 1950, the loose functional structure, committee management system, internal promotion practices, control with engineering, and the high-quality, premium-price, engineering mentality all worked together to provide a highly congruent system. These internally consistent patterns in strategy, structure, people, and processes served General Radio for over 35 years.

Similarly, the Alpha Corporation's customer driven, low-cost strategy was accomplished by strength in engineering and production and ever more detailed structures and systems which evaluated cost, quality, and new product development. These strengths were epitomized in Alpha's chief engineer and president. The chief engineer had a remarkable talent for helping customers find new uses for industrial fasteners. He relished solving such problems, while at the same time designing fasteners that could be easily manufactured. The president excelled at production – producing dependable, low-cost fasteners. The pair were role models who set a pattern which served Alpha well for 15 years.

As the company grew, the chief engineer hired kindred customer-oriented application engineers. With the help of innovative users, they developed new products, leaving more routine problem-solving and incremental change to the sales and production departments. The president relied on a hands-on manufacturing manager and delegated financial matters to a competent treasurer-controller. Note how well the organization reinforced Alpha's strategy and how the key people fit the organization. There was an excellent fit between strategy and structure. The informal structure also fitted well – communications were open, the simple mission of the company was widely endorsed, and routines were well understood.

As the General Radio and Alpha examples suggest, convergence starts out with an effective dovetailing of strategy, structure, people, and processes. For other strategies or in other industries, the particular formal and informal systems might be very different, but still a winning combination. The formal system includes decisions about grouping and linking resources as well as planning and control systems, rewards and evaluation procedures, and human resource management systems. The informal system includes core values, beliefs, norms, communication patterns, and actual decision-making and conflict resolution patterns. It is the whole fabric of structure, systems, people, and processes which must be suited to company strategy.

As the fit between strategy, structure, people, and processes is never perfect, convergence is an ongoing process characterized by incremental change. Over time, in all companies studied, two types of converging changes were common: fine-tuning and incremental adaptations.

Converging change: Fine-tuning

Even with good strategy–structure–process fits, well-run companies seek even better ways of exploiting (and defending) their missions. Such effort typically deals with one or more of the following:

- Refining policies, methods, and procedures.
- Creating specialized units and linking mechanisms to permit increased volume and increased attention to unit quality and cost.
- Developing personnel especially suited to the present strategy – through improved selection and training, and tailoring reward systems to match strategic thrusts.
- Fostering individual and group commitments to the company mission and to the excellence of one's own department.
- Promoting confidence in the accepted norms, beliefs, and myths.
- Clarifying established roles, power, status, dependencies, and allocation mechanisms.

The fine-tuning fills out and elaborates the consistencies between strategy, structure, people, and processes. These incremental changes lead to an ever more interconnected (and therefore more stable) social system.

Converging change: Incremental adjustments to environmental shifts

In addition to fine-tuning changes, minor shifts in the environment will call for some organizational response. Even the most conservative of organizations expect, even welcome, small changes which do not make too many waves. A popular expression is that almost any organization can tolerate a 'ten-percent change.' At any one time, only a few changes are being made; but these changes are still compatible with the prevailing structures, systems, and processes. Examples of such adjustments are an expansion in sales territory, a shift in emphasis among products in the product line, or improved processing technology in production.

The usual process of making changes of this sort is well known: wide acceptance of the need for change, openness to possible alternatives, objective examination of the pros and cons of each plausible alternative, participation of those directly affected in the preceding analysis, a market test or pilot operation where feasible, time to learn the new activities, established role models, known rewards for positive success, evaluation, and refinement.

The role of executive leadership during convergent periods is to reemphasize mission and core values and to delegate incremental decisions to middle-level managers. Note that the uncertainty created for people affected by such changes is well within tolerable limits. Opportunity is provided to anticipate and learn what is new, while most features of the structure remain unchanged. The overall system adapts, but it is not transformed.

Converging change: Some consequences

For those companies whose strategies fit environmental conditions, convergence brings about better and better effectiveness. Incremental change is relatively easy to implement and ever more optimizes the consistencies between strategy, structure, people, and processes. At AT&T, for example, the period between 1913 and 1980 was one of ever more incremental change to further bolster the 'Ma Bell' culture, systems, and structure, all in service of developing the telephone network.

Convergent periods are, however, a double-edged sword. As organizations grow and become more successful, they develop internal forces for stability. Organization structures and systems become so interlinked that they only allow compatible changes. Further, over time, employees develop habits, patterned behaviors begin to take on values (e.g. 'service is good'), and employees develop a sense of competence in knowing how to get work done within the system. These self-reinforcing patterns of behavior, norms, and values contribute to increased organizational momentum and complacency and, over time, to a sense of organizational history. This organizational history – epitomized by common stories, heroes, and standards – specifies 'how we work here' and 'what we hold important here.'

This organizational momentum is profoundly functional as long as the organization's strategy is appropriate. The Ma Bell and General Radio culture, structure, and systems – and associated internal momentum – were critical to each organization's success. However, if (and when) strategy must change, this momentum cuts the other way. Organizational history is a source of tradition, precedent, and pride which are, in turn, anchors to the past. A proud history often restricts vigilant problem solving and may be a source of resistance to change. When faced with environmental threat, organizations with strong momentum:

- may not register the threat due to organization complacency and/or stunted external vigilance (e.g., the automobile or steel industries); or
- if the threat is recognized, the response is frequently heightened conformity to the status quo

and/or increased commitment to 'what we do best.'

For example, the response of dominant firms to technological threat is frequently increased commitment to the obsolete technology (e.g. telegraph/telephone; vacuum tube/transistor; core/semiconductor memory). A paradoxical result of long periods of success may be heightened organizational complacency, decreased organizational flexibility, and a stunted ability to learn.

Converging change is a double-edged sword. Those very social and technical consistencies which are key sources of success may also be the seeds of failure if environments change. The longer the convergent period, the greater these internal forces for stability. This momentum seems to be particularly accentuated in those most successful firms in a product class (for example, Polaroid, Caterpillar, or US Steel), in historically regulated organizations (for example, AT&T, GTE, or financial service firms), or in organizations that have been traditionally shielded from competition (for example, universities, not-for-profit organizations, government agencies and/or services).

On frame-breaking change

What, then, leads to frame-breaking change? Why defy tradition? Simply stated, frame-breaking change occurs in response to or, better yet, in anticipation of major environmental changes – changes which require more than incremental adjustments. The need for discontinuous change springs from one or a combination of the following:

- Industry discontinuities. Sharp changes in legal, political, or technological conditions shift the basis of competition within industries. Deregulation has dramatically transformed the financial services and airlines industries. Substitute product technologies (such as jet engines, electronic typing, microprocessors) or substitute process technologies (such as the planar process in semiconductors or float-glass in glass manufacture) may transform the bases of competition within industries. Similarly, the emergence of industry standards, or dominant designs (such as the DC-3, IBM 360, or PDP-8) signal a shift in competition away from product innovation and towards increased process innovation. Finally, major economic changes (e.g. oil crises) and legal shifts (e.g. patent protection in biotechnology or trade/regulator barriers in pharmaceuticals or cigarettes) also directly affect bases of competition.

- Product life-cycle shifts. Over the course of a product class life-cycle, different strategies are appropriate. In the emergence phase of a product class, competition is based on product innovation and performance, where in the maturity stage, competition centers on cost, volume, and efficiency. Shifts in patterns of demand alter key factors for success. For example, the demand and nature of competition for minicomputers, cellular telephones, wide-body aircraft, and bowling alley equipment was transformed as these products gained acceptance and their product classes evolved. Powerful international competition may compound these forces.

- Internal company dynamics. Entwined with these external forces are breaking points within the firm. Sheer size may require a basically new management design. For example, few inventor-entrepreneurs can tolerate the formality that is linked with large volume; even Digital Equipment Company apparently has outgrown the informality so cherished by Kenneth Olsen. Key people die. Family investors may become more concerned with their inheritance taxes than with company development. Revised corporate portfolio strategy may sharply alter the role and resources assigned to business units or functional areas. Such pressures especially when coupled with external changes, may trigger frame-breaking change.

Scope of frame-breaking change

Frame-breaking change is driven by shifts in business strategy. As strategy shifts so too must structure, people, and organizational processes. Quite unlike convergent change, frame-breaking reforms involve discontinuous changes throughout the organization. These bursts of change do not reinforce the existing system and are implemented rapidly. For example, the system-wide changes at Prime and General Radio were implemented over 18–24-month periods, whereas changes in Citibank's Operating Group were implemented in less than five months. Frame-breaking changes are revolutionary changes of the system as opposed to incremental changes in the system. The following features are usually involved in frame-breaking change:

- Reformed mission and core values. A strategy shift involves a new definition of company mission. Entering or withdrawing from an industry may be involved; at least the way the company expects to be outstanding is altered. The revamped AT&T is a conspicuous example. Success on its new course calls for a strategy based on competition, aggressiveness, and responsiveness, as well as a revised set of core values about how the firm competes and what it holds as important. Similarly, the initial shift at Prime reflected a strategic shift away from technology and towards sales and marketing. Core values also were aggressively reshaped by Ken Fisher to complement Prime's new strategy.

- Altered power and status. Frame-breaking change always alters the distribution of power. Some groups lose in the shift while others gain. For example, at Prime and General Radio, the engineering functions lost power, resources, and prestige as the marketing and sales functions gained. These dramatically altered power distributions reflect shifts in bases of competition and resource allocation. A new strategy must be backed up with a shift in the balance of power and status.

- Reorganization. A new strategy requires a modification in structure, systems, and procedures. As strategic requirements shift, so too must the choice of organization form. A new direction calls for added activity in some areas and less in others. Changes in structure and systems are means to ensure that this reallocation of effort takes place. New structures and revised roles deliberately break business-as-usual behavior.

- Revised interaction patterns. The way people in the organization work together has to adapt during frame-breaking change. As strategy is different, new procedures, work flows, communication networks, and decision-making patterns must be established. With these changes in work flows and procedures must also come revised norms, informal decision-making/conflict-resolution procedures, and informal roles.

- New executives. Frame-breaking change also involves new executives, usually brought in from outside the organization (or business unit) and placed in key managerial positions. Commitment to the new mission, energy to overcome prevailing inertia, and freedom from prior obligations are all needed to refocus the organization. A few exceptional members of the old guard may attempt to make this shift, but habits and expectations of their associations are difficult to break. New executives are most likely to provide both the necessary drive and an enhanced set of skills more appropriate for the new strategy. While the overall number of executive changes is usually relatively small, these new executives have substantial symbolic and substantive effects on the organization. For example, frame-breaking changes at Prime, General Radio, Citibank, and Alpha Corporation were all spearheaded by a relatively small set of new executives from outside the company or group.

Why all at once?

Frame-breaking change is revolutionary in that the shifts reshape the entire nature of the organization. Those more effective examples of frame-breaking change were implemented rapidly (e.g. Citibank, Prime, Alpha). It appears that a piecemeal approach to frame-breaking changes gets bogged down in politics, individual resistance to change, and organizational inertia (e.g. Sinclair's attempts to reshape General Radio). Frame-breaking change requires discontinuous shifts in strategy, structure, people, and processes concurrently – or at least in a short period of time. Reasons for rapid, simultaneous implementation include:

- *Synergy* within the new structure can be a powerful aid. New executives with a fresh mission, working in a redesigned organization with revised norms and values, backed up with power and status, provide strong reinforcement. The pieces of the revitalized organization pull together, as opposed to piecemeal change where one part of the new organization is out of synch with the old organization.

- *Pockets of resistance* have a chance to grow and develop when frame-breaking change is implemented slowly. The new mission, shifts in organization, and other frame-breaking changes upset the comfortable routines and precedent. Resistance to such fundamental change is natural. If frame-breaking change is implemented slowly, then individuals have a greater opportunity to undermine the changes and organizational inertia works to further stifle fundamental change.

- Typically, there is a *pent-up need for change*. During convergent periods, basic adjustments are postponed. Boat-rocking is discouraged. Once constraints are relaxed, a variety of desirable improvements press for attention. The exhilaration and momentum of a fresh effort (and new team) make difficult moves more acceptable. Change is in fashion.

- Frame-breaking change is an inherently *risky and uncertain venture*. The longer the implementation period, the greater the period of uncertainty and instability. The most effective frame-breaking changes initiate the new strategy, structure, processes, and systems rapidly and begin the next period of stability and convergent change. The sooner fundamental uncertainty is removed, the better the chances of organizational survival and growth. While the pacing of change is important, the overall time to implement frame-breaking change will be contingent on the size and age of the organization.

Patterns in organization evolution

This historical approach to organization evolution focuses on convergent periods punctuated by reorientation – discontinuous, organization-wide upheavals. The most effective firms take advantage of relatively long convergent periods. These periods of incremental change build on and take advantage of organization inertia. Frame-breaking change is quite dysfunctional if the organization is successful and the environment is stable. If, however, the organization is performing poorly and/or if the environment changes substantially, frame-breaking change is the only way to realign the organization with its competitive environment. Not all reorientations will be successful (e.g. People Express' expansion and up-scale moves in 1985–86). However, inaction in the face of performance crisis and/or environmental shifts is a certain recipe for failure.

Because reorientations are so disruptive and fraught with uncertainty, the more rapidly they are implemented, the more quickly the organization can reap the benefits of the following convergent period. High-performing firms initiate reorientations when environmental conditions shift and implement these reorientations rapidly (e.g. Prime and Citibank). Low-performing organizations either do not reorient or reorient all the time as they root around to find an effective alignment with environmental conditions.

This metamorphic approach to organization evolution underscores the role of history and precedent as future convergent periods are all constrained and shaped by prior convergent periods. Further, this approach to organization evolution highlights the role of executive leadership in managing convergent periods and in initiating and implementing frame-breaking change.

Conclusion

Our analysis of the way companies evolve over long periods of time indicates that the most effective firms have relatively long periods of convergence giving support to a basic strategy, but such periods are punctuated by upheavals – concurrent and discontinuous changes which reshape the entire organization. Managers should anticipate that when environments change sharply:

- Frame-breaking change cannot be avoided. These discontinuous organizational changes will either be made proactively or initiated under crisis/turnaround condition.
- Discontinuous changes need to be made in strategy, structure, people, and processes concurrently. Tentative change runs the risk of being smothered by individual, group, and organizational inertia.
- Frame-breaking change requires direct executive involvement in all aspects of the change, usually bolstered with new executives from outside the organization.

There are no patterns in the sequence of frame-breaking changes, and not all strategies will be effective. Strategy and, in turn, structure, systems, and processes must meet industry-specific competitive issues.

Effectiveness over changing competitive conditions requires that executives manage fundamentally different kinds of organizations and different kinds of change. An executive team's ability to proactively initiate and implement frame-breaking change and to manage convergent change seem to be important factors which discriminate between organizational renewal and greatness versus complacency and eventual decline.

READING
4.4

Implementation: The core task of change management

By Wilfried Krüger[1]

Change processes do not achieve objectives or even fail. This is caused by a widespread and systematic underestimation of implementation problems. Managers tend to regard implementation as a separate stage of a standardised project procedure which comes last in the project life cycle. The corresponding activities are called 'introduction', 'realisation' or 'application'. In the worst case, implementation is reduced to a single management directive with which the people concerned just have to comply, whether they like it or not. In most cases implementation also comprises information and training activities.

This project-management type of implementation is endangered by various change barriers which have their origin in individual uncertainty and fear of disadvantages. Such problems do not just arise when people are told to follow an application directive. They also appear in early stages of change projects such as project definition and design. They are often caused by issues which are not directly related to the change program or are hidden by day-to-day business. Therefore,

a phase-oriented concept of implementation reaches its limits at lest in comprehensive and fundamental change processes. In these cases implementation has to begin at or even before the project definition, where needs and intentions are identified and then goals are established. People concerned have to be taken into account when identifying the project team, and everybody should be convinced of the need for change before the project start.

At present change management mainly concentrates on the goals of the strategic triangle 'cost, time, and quality (customer benefit)'. Conventional project solutions usually only cover a part of this triangle due to the typical conflict inherent to these three goals.

Business reengineering as a new concept tries to overcome this goal-conflict by forcing the development of innovative solutions. For example the dramatic shortening of a procedure reduces processing-time and costs and at the same time yields lower failure rates (i.e. higher quality) due to a smaller number of interfaces.

---

[1]Source: W. Krüger, 'Implementation: the Core Task of Change Management', *CEMS Business Review*, Vol. 1, 1996, Kluwer Academic/Plenum Publishers. Reproduced by permission.

However, according to Michael Hammer (the inventor and leading protagonist of business reengineering), more than 70% of all business reengineering projects fail. We suggest this happens because of the negligence of change acceptance. Conceptually 'good' solutions fail during application because they are not accepted by the people concerned. 'Giants' of conceptualisation and design are 'dwarfs' when it comes to application. Therefore, we introduce acceptance as a fourth, separate goal of change. Only if 'sufficient' acceptance is aimed for will change management realise the difficulties to be expected in time and only then can problems be solved by active implementation management. Unfortunately the acceptance goal requires activities which counteract the other goals and the strategic triangle thus assumes the form of a 'vicious square'.

Management of change

Which type of conflict and barriers arise and consequently, which kind of implementation management is appropriate depends on the kind of change and the applied change strategy. Therefore, we first introduce dimensions of change before considering tasks and tools of implementation management. The content of implementation activities depends first of all on the depth of change. It can be said that a change of 'hard facts' like strategy or information systems as well as the adjustment of structures and processes just scratches the surface of a company, whereas a change of 'soft facts' like shared values, mindsets and capabilities is comparatively profound.

Strategies for change

The implementation strategy cannot be chosen separately from the strategy for change. In the literature on the subject two main approaches to the problem are discussed: corporate transformation either as revolutionary, quantum, dramatic change ('quantum leaps') or as evolutionary, piecemeal, incremental change ('small steps'). The evolutionary model emphasises the possibility of a learning organisation and its capability to create something new step by step. Any change brings confusion and resistance, and therefore 'all but incremental change is resisted' (Pettigrew, 1985). Miller and Friesen (1984) describe a revolutionary model with a concerted quantum change in situations of crisis. A concerted quantum change is necessary because of the various interdependencies between a company's elements of structure. Here change should be rare, but then quick and dramatic.

From an analytic standpoint there are arguments in favour of and against both conceptual models of change.

The approach of *continuous improvement processes* ('Kaizen'; Imai, 1993) seems to correspond to the *evolutionary model*. Here the employees' experience and ideas are used and the starting point is the 'operating company base'. In contrast, attempts at fundamental process optimisation ('business reengineering', Hammer and Champy, 1994) demand a radical turning away from the status quo and strict directives by corporate management. This approach follows the revolutionary change model. At present both forms can be observed in German companies.

We will now turn to strategies for implementation. In practice many attempts at change are planned and prepared under the 'top secret' label and carried out with strict 'top-down' directives. Kirsch, Esser and Gabele (1979) refer to this implementation strategy as 'bombing' or as 'air raid'. Bombing implies fundamental change and corresponds to the revolutionary change model. This does not necessarily mean that revolutionary change always has to be implemented by bombing. Nevertheless, even fundamental change can be an open and participative process. For successful bombing the effect of surprise and the mastering of subsequent resistance are crucial. The apparent advantage of a quick introduction is accompanied by the disadvantage of a high acceptance risk.

The possibility of a hidden change also exists for co-operative change processes initiated by the operating company base. This concept, less often considered in the literature, can be characterised as 'guerrilla tactics'. It can only be applied up to the limits of the autonomous powers of decision enjoyed by subunits. This occurrence of informal networks which prepare for change and transform their plans into action when the time has come is also known as 'bootlegging'. Guerrilla tactics may be an evasive answer to bombing or an attempt to dilute its consequences. In this case the 'revolution ex machina' (bombing) triggers off a 'counterrevolution of the operating base' (guerrilla tactics). On the other hand the guerrilla tactics of lower and middle management could also be a sign of need for change which has been ignored by corporate management.

The special difficulty and challenge of change management is to choose the right time for action. Anticyclical change demands particular strategic courage. The public in Germany was baffled and could not understand when BMW made 3000 employees redundant in the middle of a car production boom (1991/92). Later, in the 1993 recession, its 'lean' staff helped BMW to achieve by far the best results of the German car-industry. In particular cases it may be advantageous to combine evolution and revolution in a countercurrent process (Figure 4.4.1, Krüger, 1994a). With regard to process optimisation, which at present is the focus of change management, 'kaizen' and 'business reengineering' could be combined. The framework of conditions and the direction of change are determined 'top-down' by corporate management, whereas the contents of change are rooted 'bottom-up' on impacts from the operating base. This approach can be regarded as *'controlled evolution'* (Marr, 1987; Kirsch, 1992).

Personnel barriers as the core problem of change

The core problem of change is the existence of various factual and personnel change barriers which have to be identified and handled by implementation. Implementation management is *barrier management* and comprises all three dimensions of change management we have considered. Subsequently we will discuss the regularly underestimated and neglected *personnel barriers*. With regard to the people concerned, these barriers can be roughly classified into *company-wide barriers*, *management barriers* and *employee barriers* (Krüger, 1994a).

Company-wide barriers.   The imaginary sum of values shared by all company members, their mind-sets and behavioural patterns form the central elements of corporate culture. The stronger the corporate culture, the more effective it is, but also the more difficult to change. Values and beliefs can solidify to form the 'genetic code' of a company. This code may even comprise beliefs about the structure of the industry, the basis of competitive advantage, promising strategies and the best organisational structure. If environment demands change, a strong code can militate against or even prevent change. Corporate culture assumes the characteristics of a 'flat tyre' or even 'fossilisation' (Figure 4.4.2). This may be the reason why previously successful companies often go into decline and why many change processes are so dramatic. Considerable external pressure (e.g. exerted by stakeholders) leading to a real crisis or even the intervention of external constitutional bodies (e.g. the supervisory board) is needed to trigger off change processes. An additional barrier lies in the fact that positions in the external constitutional bodies are typically held by people who share the values of corporate management (e.g. in Germany former chief executives 'retire' into the supervisory board).

Management barriers.   Specific management barriers lie in the field of *problem awareness* and *problem solution*. Problem awareness is often impeded by day-to-day business. Urgent issues are dealt with instead of the important ones. Here an effect referred to as the *'expert-doer syndrome'* (Krüger and Ebeling, 1991) can be observed. The need for rethinking is not seen. When new problems occur the 'expert' tries to apply previously successful solutions without realising that the situation has changed. When success fails to

FIGURE 4.4.1   Corporate transformation as a countercurrent process

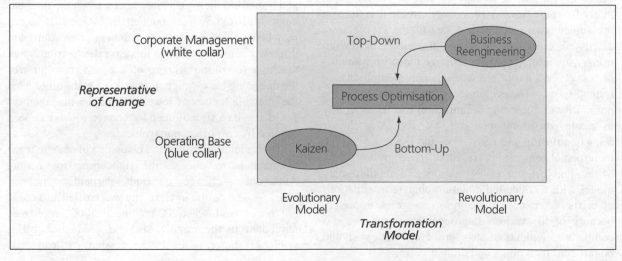

FIGURE 4.42 Possible effects of individual corporate cultures

Corporate culture is:	Up to date	Not up to date
Strong	'Accelerator'	'Fossilisation'
Weak	'Mild Breeze'	'Flat Tyre'

materialise, the expert puts even more effort into his 'reliable' solution, which cannot lead to success since it is a solution to the wrong problem. A vicious circle of effort, failure and intensification of efforts arises. In this situation neglecting the need for rethinking constitutes an *attitude barrier* to change. Often the people responsible for a solution to a problem fear loss of position and personal standing. Insecurity and a fear to assume responsibility also have to be taken into account. An '*authority fear syndrome*' can be diagnosed which yields cautious, reactive rather than proactive behaviour. These motivational barriers are *behavioural barriers* to change. In companies where lower and middle management have extensive powers of decision, management barriers have a special significance. Initiatives and impacts 'from below' must be amplified, and change within ones' own area of com-

petence must be set in motion. At times even guerrilla tactics may be appropriate if needed for the survival of the company. This means that lower and middle management walk a thin line between obedience and the refusal to carry out commands.

Employee barriers. Even when top management has opted for change, this decision still has to be executed, and the employees concerned, often including lower and middle management, must be convinced of the need for change. Various additional barriers have their root here. Psychologically these barriers, like management barriers, can be explained by individual insecurity and fear of negative consequences. These interests are articulated, represented and negotiated either by direct organisational participation or on the basis of legal rights of participation, for example by

FIGURE 4.4.3 Actors of change and their attitudes

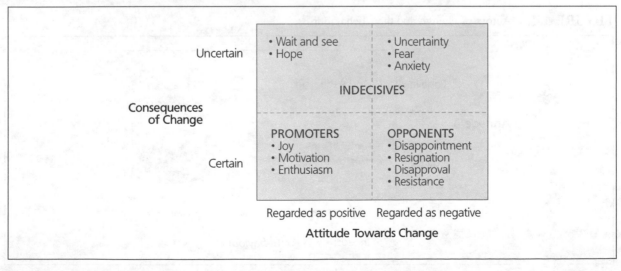

co-determination executed through workers' councils or through the workers' representatives in the supervisory board.

Change processes as fields of force

Considering the personnel barriers described above, the change process can be seen as a field of forces on which the various change participants interact (Figure 4.4.3). The promoters, clearly in favour of change, represent the proactive forces. They face a group of opponents with an aversion to change representing the opposing reactive forces, and an 'indecisive' group, that has not yet decided on its final attitude towards change. Change management has to detect the causes for the development of change barriers and, with it, the opposition or indecisiveness; then appropriate activities for implementation, namely the overcoming of barriers, can be organised.

In general, the individual employee will judge the forthcoming change according to the consequences for his own job and whether the results are obvious or uncertain. The following items will be taken into consideration:

- job security;
- working place, working time, income;
- tasks, authority, responsibility;
- requirements (qualification, motivation, behaviour);
- symbols of position and status;
- organisational environment of the position;
- peer groups;
- private relations.

On the basis of the expected advantages and disadvantages of change and the certainty or uncertainty of their occurrence, a cost-benefit analysis is performed. If the consequences can be foreseen clearly, those who expect to benefit are likely to act as promoters of change, whereas those expecting to suffer disadvantages become opponents (Figure 4.4.3). If the consequences are uncertain, it does not really matter whether they are regarded as positive or negative. Due to anxiety, fear or possibly hope, employees will remain indecisive.

The net consequence is the result of processing the available information. This cognitive process only leads to a positive or negative (internal) *attitude* towards change. In order to acquire an insight into the (external) *behaviour* of the actors of change we use two different models: the *attitude-behaviour hypothesis*, which has proved to be a helpful tool in marketing science (Kroeber-Riel, 1992), and the consideration of *attitude* and *behaviour acceptance*.

First the *attitude-behaviour hypothesis* is discussed, splitting the attitude into an 'attitude towards change in general' and an 'attitude towards personal change'. If the two attitudes match, a clear position is taken, either as promoter (positive attitudes) or as opponent (negative attitudes). Diverging attitudes result in indecisiveness, which now can be examined in more detail. Individual behaviour can be derived from the attitude towards personal change, since we expect it to be dominant. This may be different in cultures where employees may value the benefit of their social system (e.g. the company 'family') higher than individual consequences. Somebody will behave as a *potential promoter* (Figure 4.4.4) if his attitude towards change in general is posi-

FIGURE 4.4.4 Actors of change and their behaviour

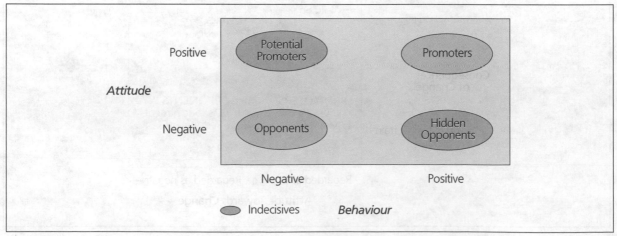

tive, but due to expected disadvantages his attitude towards personal change is negative. Often a negative attitude towards personal change can be explained by *motivational barriers* and *capability barriers*. Likewise, *hidden opponents* can be explained by a negative attitude towards change in general, but a positive attitude towards personal change due to expected advantages ('opportunists').

As research on technology acceptance has shown, there are often gaps between (internal) attitude and (external) behaviour (Wiendieck, 1992). Hence, the behaviour of potential promoters and hidden opponents can be explained by distinguishing between *attitude acceptance* and *behaviour acceptance* towards change. Opponents have negative attitude acceptance and behaviour acceptance, whereas in the case of promoters, both forms of acceptance are positive. When the two categories of acceptance diverge, the situation is less obvious. An actor whose behaviour is positive (positive behaviour acceptance) does not necessarily have a positive attitude as well. Either he helps to carry the change process more or less voluntarily or apathetically ('opportunist', 'fellow traveller'), ready to change his behaviour when necessary, or for tactical reasons he acts positively without really being convinced ('hidden opponent', Figure 4.4.4).

The counterpart is the 'potential promoter', somebody who is generally in favour of change but lacks the final conviction to act in support of change. Insufficient behaviour acceptance can be explained by lack of motivation (*motivational barriers*) and/or by insufficient know-how and skills (*capability barriers*).

Implementation management

Figure 4.4.5 shows the underlying framework for implementation management. The starting point for the internal or external actor who wants to influence and direct the 'implementation force field' is an assessment of attitude and behaviour acceptance and, with it, the classification of the four groups, promoters, potential promoters, opponents and hidden opponents. Usually the numbers of clearly identifiable promoters will be fairly small, whereas the indecisive and opposed groups will be comparatively large. Though the search for the respective groups can be quite tedious, this offers new possibilities for 'impacting' and controlling the change process.

First the three dimensions of change and implementation management (the management of perceptions and beliefs, power and politics management, and issue management) are roughly assigned to the four target groups. Here the task focus of each activity dimension can already be seen. In the first step *opponents* have to be controlled via the management of perceptions and beliefs in order to change their attitudes as far as possible in the direction of change acceptance. This 'mind forming' is supported by activities such as inducements, incentives and countertrading as well as negative sanctions. If there is no chance of overcoming the negative attitudes of opponents, it might even be necessary to consider their dismissal. For implementation management tasks involving *promoters* constitute the counterfocus. Promoters do not need to be convinced and little persuasion is needed, since they take advantage of change and, therefore, support it.

Hidden opponents are characterised by negative attitudes and positive behaviour. Here management of perceptions and beliefs supported by information (issue management) is needed to change their attitude. *Potential promoters* show the reverse attitude constellation. They behave in negative or passive ways although their attitude is positive. Power and politics management seems to be appropriate in this case, especially for creating stimuli. Depending on the situation, information and training activities may also help to change behaviour.

The common basis of all the implementation activities proposed here is a comprehensive concept of *integration* (Krüger, 1994a). The individual should become integrated in the change process in different ways in order to ensure efficiency and the effectiveness of change. Losses due to friction and stalemates have to be avoided. The general forms of integration can be used for implementation management, for example, integration by shared values (*value-based integration*), which often yields real commitment. In the same way more conventional forms usually associated with integration, such as the participation of the people affected in project teams, groups or steering-committees (*structural integration*), may be applied.

In the lower part of Figure 4.4.5 the tasks of implementation management are assigned to the six forms of integration. From left to right the diagram shows the sequence of change according to Kurt Lewin: *unfreezing*, *moving*, and *refreezing* (1947). It can be clearly seen that the beginning of the process is dominated by management of perceptions and beliefs, represented by, for example, the formulation of new visions and mission statements. This helps to defreeze patterns of thinking and behaviour. In the middle of the process, organisational units and individuals are set in motion (moving) by power and politics management,

FIGURE 4.4.5 Framework for implementation management

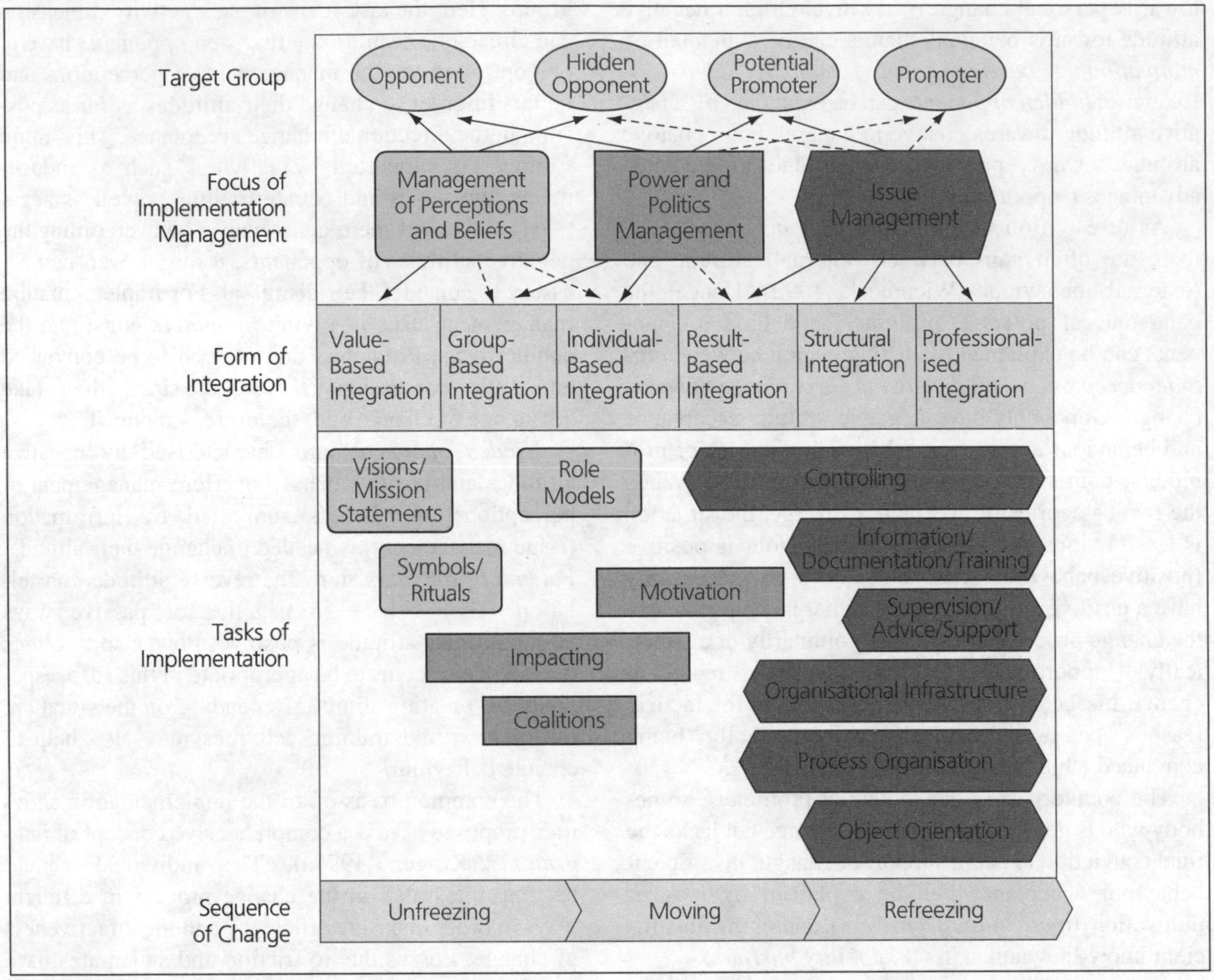

represented by motivation and impacting activities. Finally, issue management with activities such as information and training, but also supervision and control takes over. New solutions have to be learned and practised until they are rooted deeply enough for the final application (refreezing).

Management of perceptions and beliefs

Management of perceptions and beliefs aims primarily at *attitude acceptance* – target groups are identified and hidden opponents. It aims at changing existing and creating new values and beliefs. The need for change and the way in which change is to occur must be communicated. The more profound, long-lasting and important the change process is and the more development originates in the organisational units involved, the more pervasive will be the change in awareness.

A change of attitudes constitutes the *beginning* of the change process. It precedes the various activities in the area of power and politics and the discussion of single issues. The process-triggering change of attitudes can be compared with 'defreezing' or 'defrosting'. The formulation of 'inspiring' and 'thought-provoking' visions and mission statements often constitutes the first step. A good example is provided by BMW, where the board of directors proclaimed the motto 'enterprise mobility'. From the external standpoint this does not focus attention on the product 'cars', but on mobility as a specific customer need. From the internal standpoint, 'enterprise mobility' challenges every single employee and organisational unit in their behaviour. This visionary 'battle cry' is supported by a number of *action maxims* which form the mission statement. Here values, norms and behavioural patterns are anchored, as well as the employees' ability both to formulate and accept positive criticism.

But visions and mission statements in themselves are not enough. They must be lived as well. In this context *symbols* and *rituals* are of more importance than written directives. Deeply rooted and widely accepted values and norms and each employee's permanent personal commitment to these values should be the objective. This can be illustrated by an example taken from total quality management. In order to achieve fundamental quality improvements Hewlett Packard organised a steamboat trip for all employees of the units concerned. A huge rock, in which all quality faults had been engraved symbolised the 'obstacle' which had to be removed. In the middle of the lake the boat stopped and with a joint effort the rock was pushed overboard. Certainly this was an unforgettable and unequivocal ritual symbolising commitment to quality.

In practice, role models have proved to be of great importance. Individuals, teams or groups can serve as models. Sceptics can be convinced and opponents be won over by working together and sharing experiences with exemplary colleagues. A good example of this practice is Porche's employment of Japanese experts in its production line. On the other hand, top management must not only announce, but also live the values they are striving for. Real models prove the feasibility of the desired change and constitute a bridge between an ambitious concept and its application in practice. This analysis demonstrates that the management of perceptions and beliefs primarily uses *value-based integration*. The individual is offered many opportunities to identify with values. When role models are used, value-based integration is supported by *group-based* and *individual-based* integration.

Power and politics management

Power and politics management aims at *behaviour acceptance* and tries to have an impact on open opponents and potential promoters, both of which are groups with behaviour barriers. Power and politics can be exerted by individuals as well as by groups. Therefore, power and politics management primarily works with group-based and individual-based integration. *Vertical* integration is carried out by higher ranks including direct superiors as well as heads of central units and project managers. *Horizontally*, power and politics are managed by single colleagues or groups of colleagues who act as peers or peer groups. In this situation promoters who have already been identified can be used as tools to achieve multiplication effects.

Key variables and at the same time tools for integration are specific forms of power (influence) and

authority (Krüger, 1994a). First, the power to *reward* and *coerce* are explained. The power to reward (e.g. appreciation, praise, bonuses, compensations) helps to diminish possible disadvantages. In this case the effects of power are *compensatory*. Coercive power (e.g. withdrawal of support, financial disadvantages, transfers, dismissals and strike) mainly works through threats and the repression of doubt and resistance. Here the effects of power can be regarded as *repressive*. The use of coercive power is restricted by strict legal limits.

From the standpoint of motivation-theory rewards and coercion mean the granting or withdrawing of stimuli and therefore are linked to satisfaction and performance. Motivation and impacting by power and politics go hand in hand. Even the isolated change of an incentive system may be enough to trigger behavioural change. Better effects will be achieved if the activities of power and politics management and those of management of perceptions and beliefs are harmonised in an *implementation mix*, similar to marketing mix.

Witte (1973) identified a tandem structure of *promoters by power* and *promoters by know-how* as the most efficient. The *power* to *reward* and *coerce* constitute the basis for *promoters by power*. This kind of promoter mainly acts at the beginning and at the end of a change process. *Promoters by know-how* base their power mainly on *information*, i.e. knowledge and capabilities relevant for change. They usually act in the middle part of the process (moving). This expert power above all helps to emphasise the need for change and to legitimise it. From this point of view it has a *conditioning* impact, similar to the results of value-based integration. At the same time promoters by know-how and information power play an important role in issue management. The tandem structure may be supported by a process-promoter, who typically uses various forms of impacting during the whole change process (Hauschildt, 1993). Apart from reward, coercive and expert power, the process promoters relies on the power rooted in his personality which can be described as *personality power*.

Power and politics management not only means influencing single employees but managing whole systems of influence within a company (Mintzberg, 1983; Krüger, 1994a). Therefore, from the standpoint of coalition theory, implementation can be regarded as building up a *change supporting coalition*. Depending on how far-reaching the change process is, not only internal but also external coalition partners have to be considered and integrated. Quite often, a stable *bureaucratic system of influence* based on formal authority impedes change. The counterpart could be formed by a *personalised system of influence* based on the personality power of the peers and/or a *professionalised influence* based on expert power. The categories of promoters and opponents can be identified in the respective systems of influence. Active and reactive forces develop. The specific constellation of forces determines the course and the results of implementation. There is either a positive response to pressures for change or they are ignored.

Issue management

The management of issues, which is usually considered first in the discussion of change, is intentionally the last point to be examined here. The various tasks and tools are familiar from project management. In larger companies many different documents and handbooks exist in which issue management is discussed in detail. Obviously the failure of change projects and processes is not a matter of inadequate issue management, but a consequence of underestimating power and politics management and the management of perception and beliefs.

Issue management focuses on *factual barriers* to change, and the strategic triangle 'cost, time, and quality' enjoys first priority. We shall now show that there are many interrelations with personnel change barriers and the acceptance problem. Issue management and the conventional understanding of implementation typically concentrate on activities like *informing*, *training*, *documenting*, *supervising* and *consulting* the people concerned. These activities are designed to adapt employees to the new requirements of their jobs resulting from changed tasks, structures and procedures. The desired result can be described as *professionalised integration*. The individual employee is given the opportunity to meet new work requirements and to develop his professional skills by means of information and training activities. Hence, issue management is closely interrelated to the problem of *personnel change barriers*. Possible worries and fears about 'being left behind' can be eased by information, training and supervision. This also has a positive impact on attitudes and behaviour acceptance. First *capability barriers*, which are directly rooted in a lack of knowledge and skills, can be reduced and overcome. However, anybody's potential to develop is limited. This has been made clear by attempts to introduce lean management and modern manufacturing organisation. As job requirements partly exceeded the workers' capacity, the failure rate increased considerably after the introduction of work centres in the Rüsselsheim Opel

factory. Now production is reverted to the conventional-process-flow, based on the division of labour.

Information, training, supervision and other professionalised integration activities are initiated either partly or entirely *after* the decision has been taken to adopt a certain change concept. More fundamental forms of integration actively involve those concerned in the change process. Partial self-control replaces uniform top-down control. The various forms of *participation* ranging from, for example, consultation and participation in decision-making, to quality circles, project team or even self-controlled work centres must be institutionalised. The most advanced forms of self-control correspond to the idea of a *learning organisation*. Corporate management must break the ground and prepare a foundation for the concept. Then a process of continuous learning must be set in motion and maintained. 'Implementation' can no longer be a separate task or stage. Once an awareness of change has been created it has to be maintained. Implementation integrates those involved by means of organisational rules. Such approaches are forms of *structural integration*. Implementation management has to establish structures and procedures which form the *organisational implementation infra-structure*.

Process organisation is another organisational task of implementation. It is not only relevant for implementation but moulds the change process as a whole. More complex processes cannot be mastered simply by a more detailed planning which takes longer. The integration and overlapping of 'stages' associated with 'simultaneous engineering' must replace the conventional sequential project life cycle approach. Then forms of 'realisation', such as prototypes or pilot projects, can begin within the 'planning and design' stage. With shorter planning intervals and faster realisation, change and its consequences can be foreseen earlier. For those concerned the period of uncertainty is reduced while rapid improvement provides both a taste of success and learning experience. This results in higher motivation and better quality. Small first steps bringing success significantly raises the acceptance for second steps. Therefore, solutions on the level of rational decision-making like pilot projects or partial results should be used to reduce acceptance problems.

What must be done when optimising business processes is also necessary for the organisation of change processes: the dominance of functional specialisation – represented by the stages of 'feasibility', 'planning and design', 'realisation' and 'implementation' in the project life cycle – must be replaced or supplemented by an *object orientation*. In business, process-organisation-objects are modules or parts of a product, e.g. BMW, where all experts needed for the design of the body or the engine are brought together in 'modulc-teams'. For change processes in the surface layer (issue management) the objects are the corresponding subjects of change. A change team could be responsible for a new information system or technological equipment, for example. More radical change demands power and politics management and the management of perceptions and beliefs as well.

Implementation processes also need *control* and *supervision*. Deadlines, costs and the desired quantitative and qualitative results of change must be determined. Performance has to be controlled and checked. This is necessary to check results and to assess and gratify those responsible. Managing by results is very important, especially where wide powers of decision and self-control have been granted to operating units. Full commitment can only be expected if those concerned benefit personally from success. In this way the reduction of other forms of integration inherent to self-control can be compensated by *result-based integration*.

Tools for implementation

A number of tools can be used to inspire readiness for change and to achieve change acceptance (Krüger, 1994b). Their application can be seen in an analogy to marketing science. Those affected by change can be regarded as internal customers and change management as customer-oriented. From this point of view, implementation has to be regarded as project-marketing with marketing-mix instruments as tools (Reiss, 1993). A customer-oriented implementation-mix replaces an 'introduction-directive'. Figure 4.4.6 shows a selection of tools which have proved to be efficient in practice. We have deliberately refrained from a separate systematisation of these very different approaches. Instead, the diagram shows the areas of implementation management on which the tools focus, which enables us to compile an implementation-tool-box. Most of the tools have a clearly identifiable position in this implementation portfolio although the position may vary depending on the specific form of the instrument. However, for each project or process the tools chosen have to be combined in an appropriate implementation-mix.

Some instruments can be used for the conceptualisation of change as well as for its application and these are of special interest. For example *workshops* can detect the need for change and at the same time help to classify and structure the identified problem. In the

next step *project teams* may consider the question in more detail. They can take into account the best practices already in existence (*benchmarking*), the feasibility of which improves change acceptance. Meetings with *conference* character (e.g. kick-off meetings and information markets) can be used to present the authorised results and to communicate further details. *Pilot projects* and *prototypes* accelerate the change process and reduce the risk of failure. All these instruments not only have evident advantages but also improve change acceptance.

Conclusions

Figure 4.4.7 illustrates the main results of this study. Change is a permanent task and challenge for general management and implementation is an integral element thereof. It can be conceived as an iceberg with a small part above the surface of the water and the main part below the surface. The visible tip represents the rational and factual dimension of change management. Issue management concentrates on the goals of the strategic triangle 'cost, time and quality' but can only achieve results, i.e. 'float', at a level consistent with the buoyancy provided by acceptance.

The supporting base is rooted in both the interpersonal and behavioural dimension and the normative and cultural dimension, and is subject to power and politics management and to the management of perceptions and beliefs. Without this support, the rational and factual tip would sink and thereby render cost, time and quality goals unachievable. To conclude, we have derived seven propositions concerning implementation management.

(1) Implementation as an integrative element of change processes

Implementation is more than a segregated stage between 'planning' and 'realisation' in a project life-cycle. The 'introduction of a ready made solution' often merely results in the rejection of the transplant instead of the change integrated in and accepted by its environment. Implementation activities must encompass the entire change process. The raising of change awareness and the strengthening of existing forces for change are just as much part of implementation as the building up of acceptance towards results already achieved.

FIGURE 4.4.6 Implementation toolbox

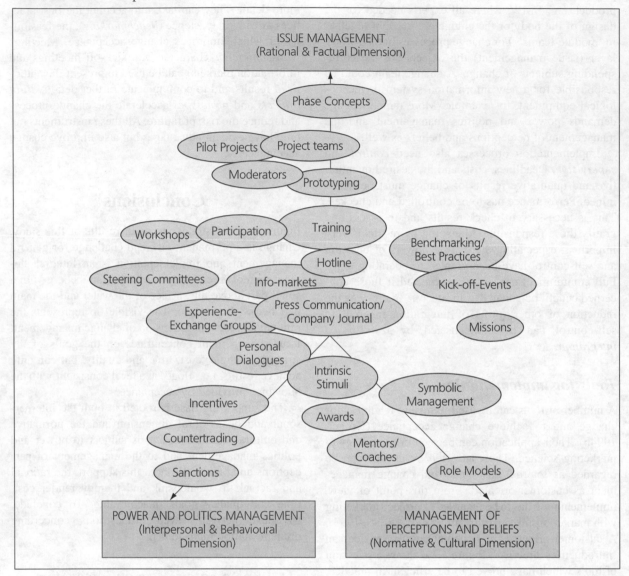

(2) Developing a contingency implementation concept

There is no 'master plan' for implementation. Instead, an implementation concept must be designed which is contingent upon the current situation. In addition to the rational and factual dimension (issue management), the interpersonal and behavioural dimension (power and politics management), as well as the normative and cultural dimension (management of perceptions and beliefs) become more and more important with increasing depth and breadth of change. Strategies must be determined for change and implementation – quantum revolution vs. evolution in steps, bombing or guerrilla

tactics. Finally, the attitude and behaviour of those concerned, the interaction between promoters, opponents and indecisive groups as well as the structure and relevance of the corresponding influence systems must be taken into account when designing and combining tasks and tools for implementation management.

(3) Acceptance as a separate implementation goal

Behavioural attitude to change can be positive or negative. It is the task of implementation management to induce or support positive and diminish negative atti-

FIGURE 4.4.7 The iceberg of change management

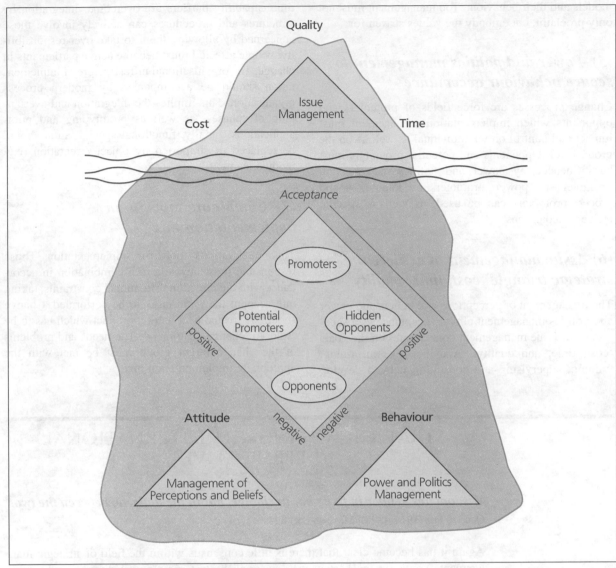

tudes and behavioural patterns among those concerned. The key problem is to identify and overcome acceptance barriers. Neither a quick and cheap nor a technically perfect solution without considering acceptance is a guarantee for success. Results can only be seen after application and maintenance or rejection and delay. Hence, a highly accepted 'imperfect patch' is better than a completely rejected 'perfect solution'. There is truth in the maxim that we should 'meet people where they are'. We understand implementation as an integrative element in change processes and, therefore, the overcoming of acceptance barriers must be designed as an individual and organisational learning process. In the best of cases the company as a whole

acquires the ability to learn – a necessary condition for building up core competencies in the competition for the future!

(4) Management of perceptions and beliefs to secure attitude acceptance

The change of attitudes – necessary above all for open and hidden opponents – occurs in the normative and cultural dimension of change. It is a task for the management of perceptions and beliefs to provide a frame of reference in the form of striking visions and clear mission statements. Symbols and rituals have also proved helpful. Finally, the feasibility of desired objectives can be demonstrated by appropriate role models and their behaviour. Top management must not only proclaim, but embody the values striven for.

(5) Power and politics management to secure behaviour acceptance

Change processes are force fields of promoters and opponents which implementation management must impact and control on the individual as well as on the group level. Opponents and potential promoters must be influenced by power and politics management. Promoters by power, promoters by know-how and process-promoters can be used, as well as specific influence coalitions.

(6) Issue management to achieve the strategic triangle 'cost, time, quality'

The management of perceptions and beliefs and power and politics management aim at acceptance as a separate goal. Issue management concentrates on the goals 'cost, time, and quality'. Activities like informing, training, supervising and consulting help to develop the required knowledge and skills, while at the same time capability barriers are overcome. Integration by structures and procedures can actively involve those concerned by allowing them to take over responsibility: people affected must become active participants in change. The organisational infrastructure of implementation should be accompanied by modern process organisation. This implies the integration and overlapping of 'phases' as well as prototyping and pilot-applications. Finally, functional specialisation should be replaced or supported by object orientation (e.g. module teams).

(7) Combining tools in an implementation mix

There are various tools for implementation. Those responsible must devise a tool combination in accordance with the prevailing situational constraints, taking into account the main tasks to be performed. Change should be treated as a market product which has to be 'sold' to 'change customers'. The needs and problems of the change target group must be met with the appropriate implementation mix.

STRATEGIC CHANGE IN INTERNATIONAL PERSPECTIVE

Wisdom lies neither in fixity nor in change, but in the dialectic between the two.
Octavio Paz (1914–1998); Mexican poet and essayist

Again it has become clear that there is little consensus within the field of strategic management. Views on the best way to accomplish strategic renewal differ sharply. Even authors from one and the same country exhibit strikingly divergent perspectives on how to deal with the paradox of revolution and evolution.

Provocatively, Reading 4.2 by Imai explicitly introduced the international dimension, suggesting that there are specific national preferences in approach to strategic change. He argues that 'Japanese companies generally favor the gradualist approach and Western companies the great-leap approach – an approach epitomized by the term innovation. Western management worships at the altar of innovation.' This general, yet fundamental, distinction is supported by other researchers such as Ouchi (1981), Pascale and Athos (1981) and Kagono et al. (1985), although all of these international comparative studies concentrate only on US–Japanese differences and are relatively old. The extensive study by Kagono and his colleagues among the top 1000 American and Japanese companies concludes that there are clearly different national change styles: 'The US-style elite-guided, logical, deductive approach achieves major innovation in strategies geared to surpass other companies. In contrast, the Japanese inductive, step-wise gradual adjustment approach seeks to steadily build upon the existing strengths to *evolve* strategy' (Kagono et al., 1985:

89–90). Other authors suggest that the United States and Japan seem to represent the two extremes, while most other industrialized countries seem to be somewhere in between (e.g. Calori and De Woot, 1994; Krüger, 1996, Reading 4.4 in this book).

Such pronounced international variance raises the question of cause. Why do firms in different countries prefer such significantly different approaches to strategic change? Which factors determine the existence of national strategic change styles? Answers to these questions might assist in defining the most appropriate context for revolutionary change, as opposed to circumstances in which evolutionary change would be more fitting. Understanding international dissimilarities and their roots should help to clarify whether firms in different countries can borrow practices from one another or are limited by their national context.

As a stimulus to the international dimension of this debate, a short overview will be given of the country characteristics mentioned in the literature as the major influences on how the paradox of revolution and evolution is dealt with in different national settings. It should be noted, however, that cross-cultural research on this topic has not been extensive. Therefore, the propositions brought forward here should be viewed as tentative explanations, intended to encourage further discussion and research.

Prevalence of mechanistic organizations

At the end of Chapter 3, the international differences in organizing work were briefly discussed. It was argued that in some countries the machine bureaucracy is a particularly dominant form of organization, while in other countries organizations are more organic. The machine bureaucracy, that is more predominant in English-speaking countries and France, is characterized by clear hierarchical authority relationships, strict differentiation of tasks, and highly formalized communication, reporting, budgeting, planning and decision-making processes. In such organizations, there is a relatively clear line separating the officers (management) from the troops, and internal relationships are depersonalized and calculative. In more organic forms of organization, management and production activities are not strictly separated, leading to less emphasis on top-down decision-making, and more on bottom-up initiatives. Job descriptions are less strictly defined and control systems are less sophisticated. Integration within the organization is not achieved by these formal systems, but by extensive informal communication and consultation, both horizontally and vertically, and by a strong common set of beliefs and a shared corporate vision. Internal relationships are based on trust, cooperation and a sense of community, leading Ouchi (1981) to call such organizations 'clans'. This type of organization is more prevalent in Japan, and to a lesser extent in, for example, Germany, the Netherlands and the Nordic countries.

Various researchers have suggested that machine bureaucracies exhibit a high level of inertia (e.g. Kanter, 1989; Mintzberg, 1994). Once formal systems have been created, they become difficult to change. As soon as particular tasks are specified and assigned to a person or group, it becomes their turf, while all else is 'not their business'. Once created, hierarchical positions, giving status and power, are not easily abolished. The consequence, it is argued, is that machine bureaucracies are inherently more resistant to change than clan-like organizations (Kagono et al., 1985). Therefore, revolution is usually the potent mode of change needed to make any significant alterations. It can be expected that in countries where organizations are more strongly mechanistic, the preference for the discontinuous renewal perspective will be more pronounced.

Clan-like organizations, on the other hand, are characterized by a strong capacity for self-organization – the ability to exhibit organized behavior without a boss being in control (Nonaka, 1988; Stacey, 1993a, Reading 9.2). They are better at fluidly, and spontaneously, reorganizing around new issues because of a lack of rigid structure, the close links between management and production tasks, the high level of group-oriented information-sharing and consensual decision-making, and the strong commitment of individuals to the organization, and vice versa. In countries where organizations are more organic in this way, a stronger preference for the continuous renewal perspective can be expected. This issue will be discussed at greater length in Chapter 9.

Position of employees

This second factor is linked to the first. A mechanistic organization, it could be said, is a system, into which groups of people have been brought, while an organic organization is a group of people, into which some system has been brought. In a machine bureaucracy, people are human resources *for* the organization, while in a clan, people *are* the organization. These two conceptions of organization represent radically different views on the position and roles of employees within organizations.

In mechanistic organizations, employees are seen as valuable, yet expendable, resources utilized by the organization. Salaries are determined by prices on the labor market and the value added by the individual employee. In the contractual relationship between employer and employee, it is a shrewd bargaining tactic for employers to minimize their dependence on employees. Organizational learning should, therefore, be captured in formalized systems and procedures, to avoid the irreplaceability of their people. Employees, on the other hand, will strive to make themselves indispensable for the organization, for instance by not sharing their learning. Furthermore, calculating employees will not tie themselves too strongly to the organization, but will keep their options open to job-hop to a better-paying employer. None of these factors contribute to the long-term commitment and receptiveness for ambiguity and uncertainty needed for continuous renewal.

In clan-like organizations the tolerance for ambiguity and uncertainty is higher, because employees' position within the organization is more secure. Information is more readily shared, as it does not need to be used as a bargaining chip and acceptance within the group demands being a team player. Employers can invest in people instead of systems, since employees are committed and loyal to the organization. These better-trained people can consequently be given more decision-making power and more responsibility to organize their own work to fit with changing circumstances. Therefore, clan-like organizations, with their emphasis on employees as permanent co-producers, instead of temporary contractors, are more conducive to evolutionary change. It is in this context that Imai concludes that 'investing in Kaizen means investing in people . . . Kaizen is people-oriented, whereas innovation is technology- and money-oriented.'

A number of factors have been brought forward to explain these international differences in the structuring of work and the position of employees. Some authors emphasize cultural aspects, particularly the level of individualism. It is argued that the mechanistic-organic distinction largely coincides with the individualism-collectivism division (e.g. Ouchi, 1981; Pascale and Athos, 1981). In this view, machine bureaucracies are the logical response to calculative individuals, while clans are more predominant in group-oriented cultures. Other authors point to international differences in labor markets (e.g. Kagono et al., 1985; Calori, Valla and De Woot, 1994). High mobility of personnel would coincide with the existence of mechanistic organizations, while low mobility (e.g. life time employment) fits with organic forms. Yet others suggest that the abundance of skilled workers is important. Machine bureaucracies are suited to dealing with narrowly trained individuals requiring extensive supervision. Clan-like organizations, however, need skilled, self-managing workers, who can handle a wide variety of tasks with relative autonomy. Kogut (1993: 11) reports that the level of workers within a country with these qualifications 'has been found to rest significantly upon the quality of education, the existence of programs of apprenticeship and worker qualifications, and the elimination of occupational distinctions.'

Based on these arguments it can be proposed that the discontinuous renewal perspective will be more prevalent in countries with a more individualistic culture, high labor mobility and less skilled workers. Conversely, the continuous renewal perspective will be more strongly rooted in countries with a group-oriented culture, low labor mobility and skilled, self-managing workers.

Role of top management

The third factor is also related to the previous points. Various researchers have observed important international differences in leadership styles and the role of top management. In some countries, top management is looked on as the 'central processing unit' of the company, making the key decisions and commanding the behavior of the rest of the organizational machine. Visible top-down leadership is the norm, and therefore, strategic innovation and change are viewed as top management responsibilities (e.g. Hambrick and Mason, 1984; Hitt et al., 1997). Strategic changes are formulated by top managers and then implemented by lower levels. Top managers are given significant power and discretion to develop bold new initiatives and to overcome organizational resistance to change. If organizational advances are judged to be insufficient or if an organization ends up in a crisis situation, a change of top management is often viewed as a necessary measure to transform or turn around the company (e.g. Boeker, 1992; Fredrickson, Hambrick and Baumrin, 1988). In nations where people exhibit a strong preference for this commander type of leadership, an inclination towards the discontinuous renewal perspective can be expected.

In other countries, top managers are viewed as the captains of the team and leadership is less direct and less visible (e.g. Kagono et al., 1985; Hofstede, 1993, Reading 1.4). The role of top managers is to facilitate change and innovation among the members of the group. It is not necessarily the intention that top managers initiate entrepreneurial activities themselves. Change comes from within the body of the organization, instead of being imposed upon it by top management. Therefore, change under this type of leadership will usually be more evolutionary than revolutionary. In nations where people exhibit a strong preference for this servant type of leadership, an inclination towards the continuous renewal perspective is more likely.

Time orientation

At the end of Chapter 3 a distinction was made between cultures that are more oriented towards the past, the present and the future. Obviously, it can be expected that cultures with a past or present orientation will be much less inclined towards change than future-oriented cultures. Among these future-minded cultures, a further division was made between those with a long-term and a short-term orientation.

Various researchers have argued that short-term oriented cultures exhibit a much stronger preference for fast, radical change than cultures with a longer time horizon. In short-term oriented cultures, such as the English-speaking countries, there are significant pressures for rapid results, which predisposes managers towards revolutionary change. Especially the sensitivity to stock prices is often cited as a major factor encouraging firms to focus on short spurts of massive change and pay much less attention to efforts and investments with undramatic long-term benefits. Other contributing factors mentioned include short-term oriented bonus systems, stock option plans and frequent job-hopping (e.g. Calori, Valla and De Woot, 1994; Kagono et al., 1985).

In long-term oriented cultures, such as Japan, China and South Korea, there is much less pressure to achieve short-term results. There is broad awareness that firms are running a competitive marathon and that a high, but steady, pace of motion is needed. Generally, more emphasis is placed on facilitating long-term change processes, instead of

Intermittently moving from short-term change to short-term change. Frequently mentioned factors contributing to this long-term orientation include long-term employment relationships, the lack of short-term bonus systems, and most importantly, the accent on growth, as opposed to profit, as firms' prime objective (e.g. Abegglen and Stalk, 1985; Hitt et al., 1997). This topic will be discussed at more length in Chapter 11.

FURTHER READING

Many excellent writings on the topic of strategic change are available, although most carry other labels, such as innovation, entrepreneurship, reengineering, revitalization, rejuvenation and learning. For a good overview of the literature, readers can consult 'Environmental Jolts and Industry Revolutions: Organizational Responses to Discontinuous Change', by Alan Meyer, Geoffry Brooks and James Goes. Paul Strebel's book *Breakpoints: How Managers Exploit Radical Business Change* also provides broad introduction to much of the work on change.

In the discontinuous renewal literature, Larry Greiner's article 'Evolution and Revolution as Organizations Grow' is a classic well worth reading. Danny Miller and Peter Friesen's landmark book *Organizations: A Quantum View* is also stimulating, although not easily accessible. More readable books on radical change are *Rejuvenating the Mature Business* by Charles Baden-Fuller and John Stopford, *Sharpbenders: The Secrets of Unleashing Corporate Potential*, by Peter Grinyer, David Mayes and Peter McKiernan, and *Crisis and Renewal*, by David Hurst. More 'hands-on' is Rosabeth Moss Kanter's *When Giants Learn to Dance*, and of course *Reengineering the Corporation: A Manifesto for Business Revolution*, by Michael Hammer and James Champy, which expands on the ideas discussed in Hammer's article in this chapter (Reading 4.1).

On the topic of innovation, Jim Utterback's book *Mastering the Dynamics of Innovation* provides a good overview, as does *Managing Innovation: Integrating Technological, Market and Organizational Change*, by Joe Tidd, John Bessant and Keith Pavitt. An excellent collection of cases is provided by Charles Baden-Fuller and Martin Pitt in their book *Strategic Innovation*.

Literature taking a continuous renewal perspective is less abundant, but no less interesting. Masaaki Imai's article in this chapter (Reading 4.2) has been reprinted from his book *Kaizen: The Key to Japan's Competitive Success*, which is highly recommended. A more academic work that explains the continuous renewal view in detail is 'The Art of Continuous Change: Linking Complexity Theory and Time-Paced Evolution in Relentlessly Shifting Organizations', by Kathleen Eisenhardt and Shona Brown. Their excellent book *Competing on the Edge: Strategy as Structured Chaos* (Brown and Eisenhardt, 1998) is also a good source. Another good academic work is *Strategic vs. Evolutionary Management: A US-Japan Comparison of Strategy and Organization*, by Tadao Kagono, Ikujiro Nonaka, Kiyonori Sakakibara and Akihiro Okumura. Ikujiro Nonaka's article 'Creating Organizational Order Out of Chaos: Self-Renewal in Japanese Firms' gives a good summary of this way of thinking.

Finally, the award-winning article 'Ambidextrous Organizations: Managing Evolutionary and Revolutionary Change', by Michael Tushman and Charles O'Reilly must be mentioned as a delightful article, in particular with regard to the way in which the authors explicitly wrestle with the paradox of revolution and evolution. Their book *Winning Through Innovation: A Practical Guide to Leading Organizational Change and Renewal* is equally stimulating.

REFERENCES

Abeggglen, J.C., and Stalk, G. (1985) *Kaisha, The Japanese Corporation*, Basic Books, New York.

Aldrich, H. (1999) *Organizations Evolving*, Sage, London.

Allaire, Y., and Firsirotu, M. (1985) 'How to Implement Radical Strategies in Large Organizations', *Sloan Management Review*, Vol. 26, No. 3, Spring, pp. 19–34.

Allison, G.T. (1969) 'Conceptual Models and The Cuban Missile Crisis', *The American Political Science Review*, No. 3, September, pp. 689–718.

Argyris, C. (1990) *Overcoming Organizational Defenses: Facilitating Organizational Learning*, Prentice Hall, Boston.

Arthur, W.B. (1996) 'Increasing Returns and the New World of Business', *Harvard Business Review*, Vol. 74, No. 4, July–August, pp. 100–109.

Baden-Fuller, C., and Pitt, M. (1996) *Strategic Innovation*, Routledge, London.

Baden-Fuller, C., and Stopford, J.M. (1992) *Rejuvenating the Mature Business*, Routledge, London.

Bartlett, C.A., and Ghoshal, S. (1995) *Transnational Management: Text, Cases, and Readings in Cross-Border Management*, Second Edition, R.D. Irwin Inc., Homewood, IL.

Bate, P. (1994) *Strategies for Cultural Change*, Butterworth-Heinemann, Oxford.

Beinhocker, E.D. (1999) 'Robust Adaptive Strategies', *Sloan Management Review*, Vol. 40, No. 3, Spring, pp. 95–106.

Boeker, W. (1992) 'Power and Managerial Dismissal: Scapegoating at the Top', *Administrative Science Quarterly*, Vol. 37, No. 4, pp. 538–547.

Bower, J.L., and Christensen, C.M. (1995) 'Disruptive Technologies: Cathing the Wave', *Harvard Business Review*, Vol. 73, No. 1, January–February, pp. 43–53.

Brown, S.L., and Eisenhardt, K.M. (1998) *Competing on the Edge: Strategy as Structured Chaos*, Harvard Business School Press, Boston, MA.

Calori, R., and de Woot, P. (eds.) (1994) *A European Management Model: Beyond Diversity*, Prentice Hall, Hemel Hempstead.

Calori, R., Valla, J.-P., and de Woot, P. (1994) 'Common Characteristics: The Ingredients of European Management', in: R. Calori, and P. de Woot (eds.), *A European Management Model: Beyond Diversity*, Prentice Hall, Hemel Hempstead.

Christensen, C.M. (1997) *The Innovator's Dilemma*, HarperBusiness, New York.

Christensen, C.M., and Overdorf, M. (2000) 'Meeting the Challenge of Disruptive Change', *Harvard Business Review*, Vol. 78, No. 2, March–April, pp. 66–76.

D'Aveni, R. (1994) *Hypercompetition: Managing the Dynamics of Strategic Maneuvering*, Free Press, New York.

Day, D.L. (1994) 'Raising Radicals: Different Processes for Championing Innovative Corporate Ventures', *Organization Science*, Vol. 5, No. 2, May, pp. 148–172.

Duncan, R.B. (1976) 'The Ambidextrous Organization: Designing Dual Structures for Innovation', in: R.H. Kilmann, L.R. Pondy, and D.P. Slevin (eds.), *The Management of Organizational Design*, Elsevier North Holland, New York, pp. 167–188.

Eisenhardt, K.M., and Brown, S.L. (1997) 'The Art of Continuous Change: Linking Complexity Theory and Time-Paced Evolution in Relentlessly Shifting Organizations', *Administrative Science Quarterly*, Vol. 42, No. 1, March, pp. 1–34.

Eisenhardt, K.M., and Brown, S.L. (1998) 'Time Pacing: Competing in Markets That Won't Stand Still', *Harvard Business Review*, March–April, Vol. 77, No. 2, pp. 8–18.

Fredrickson, J.W., Hambrick, D.C., and Baumrin, S. (1988) 'A Model of CEO Dismissal', *Academy of Management Review*, Vol. 13, No. 2, April, pp. 255–270.

Freeman, R.E. (1984) *Strategic Management: A Stakeholder Approach*, Pitman/Ballinger, Boston.

Gersick, C.J.G. (1991) 'Revolutionary Change Theories: A Multilevel Exploration of the Punctuated Equilibrium Paradigm', *Academy of Management Review*, Vol. 17, No. 1, January, pp. 10–36.

Ghemawat, P. (1991) *Commitment: The Dynamic of Strategy*, Free Press, New York.

Greenwood, R., and Hinings, C.R. (1996) 'Understanding Radical Organizational Change: Bringing Together the Old and the New Institutionalism', *Academy of Management Review*, Vol. 21, No. 4, October, pp. 1022–1054.

Greiner, L.E. (1972) 'Evolution and Revolution as Organizations Grow', *Harvard Business Review*, Vol. 50, No. 4, July–August, pp. 37–46.

Greiner, L.E., and Bhambri, A. (1989) 'New CEO Intervention and Dynamics of Deliberate Strategic Change', *Strategic Management Journal*, Vol. 10, Special issue, Summer, pp. 67–86.

Grinyer, P.H., Mayes, D., and McKiernan, P. (1987) *Sharpbenders: The Secrets of Unleashing Corporate Potential*, Blackwell, Oxford.

Hambrick, D.C., and Mason, P. (1984) 'Upper Echelons: The Organization as a Reflection of Its Top Managers', *Academy of Management Review*, Vol. 9, No. 2, April, pp. 193–206.

Hamel, G. (1996) 'Strategy as Revolution', *Harvard Business Review*, Vol. 74, No. 4, July–August, pp. 69–82.

Hammer, M. (1990) 'Reengineering Work: Don't Automate, Obliterate', *Harvard Business Review*, Vol. 68, No. 4, July–August, pp. 104–111.

Hammer, M., and Champy, J. (1993) *Reengineering the Corporation: A Manifesto for Business Revolution*, HarperCollins, New York.

Hammer, M., and Champy, J. (1994) *Business Reengineering: Die Radikalkur für das Unternehmen*, Nicholas Brealey Publishing, Frankfurt am Main-New York.

Hannan, M.T., and Freeman, J. (1984) 'Structural Inertia and Organizational Change', *American Sociological Review*, Vol. 49, No. 2, April, pp. 149–164.

Hauschildt, J. (1993) Innovationsmanagement, Vahlen, München.

Hayes, R.H. (1985) 'Strategic Planning: Forward in Reverse?', *Harvard Business Review*, Vol. 63, No. 6, November–December, pp. 111–119.

Hitt, M.A., Dacin, M.T., Tyler, B.B, and Park, D. (1997) 'Understanding the Differences in Korean and U.S. Executives' Strategic Orientations', *Strategic Management Journal*, Vol. 18, pp. 159–167.

Hofstede, G. (1993) 'Cultural Constraints in Management Theories', *Academy of Management Executive*, Vol. 7, No. 1, pp. 8–21.

Hurst, D. (1995) *Crisis and Renewal*, Harvard Business School Press, Boston.

Imai, M. (1986) *Kaizen: The Key to Japan's Competitive Success*, McGraw-Hill, New York.

Imai, M. (1993) *Kaizen: Der Schlüssel zum Erfolg der Japaner im Wettbewerb*, Third Edition, Wirtschaftsverlag, Berlin.

Ireland, R.D., and Hitt, M.A. (1999) 'Achieving and Maintaining Strategic Competitiveness in the 21st Century: The Role of Strategic Leadership', *Academy of Management Executive*, Vol. 13, No. 1, February, pp. 43–57.

Johnson, G. (1987) *Strategic Change and the Management Process*, Basil Blackwell, Oxford.

Johnson, G. (1988) 'Rethinking Incrementalism', *Strategic Management Journal*, Vol. 9, No. 1, January–February, pp. 75–91.

Kagono, T., Nonaka, I., Sakakibara, K., and Okumura, A. (1985) *Strategic vs. Evolutionary Management: A US-Japan Comparison of Strategy and Organization*, North Holland, Amsterdam.

Kanter, R.M. (1983) *The Change Masters: Innovation for Productivity in the American Corporation*, Basic Books, New York.

Kanter, R.M. (1989) *When Giants Learn to Dance*, Simon & Schuster, New York.

Kanter, R.M. (1991) 'Championing Change: An Interview With Bell Atlantic's CEO Raymond Smith', *Harvard Business Review*, Vol. 69, No. 1, January–February, pp. 119–130.

Kessler, E.H. and Chakrabarthi, A.K. (1996) 'Innovation Speed: A Conceptual Model of Context, Antecedents, and Outcomes', *Academy of Management Review*, Vol. 21, No. 4, October, pp. 1143–1191.

Kirsch, W. (1992) *Kommunikatives Handeln, Autopoesie, Rationalität. Sondierungen zu einer evolutionären Führungslehre*, München.

Kirsch, W., Esser, W.N., and Gabele, E. (1979) *Das Management des geplanten Wandels von Organisationen*, Stuttgart.

Kogut, B. (ed.) (1993) *Country Competitiveness: Technology and the Organizing of Work*, Oxford University Press, Oxford.

Kroeber-Riel, W. (1992) *Konsumentenverhalten*, Fifth Edition, Vahlen, München.

Krüger, W. (1994a) *Organisation der Unternehmung*, Third Edition, Stuttgart.

Krüger, W. (1994b) 'Umsetzung neuer Organisationsstrategien: Das Implementierungsproblem', *zfbf*, Vol. 33, pp. 197–221.

Krüger, W. (1996) 'Implementation: The Core Task of Change Management', *CEMS Business Review*, Vol. 1, pp. 77–96.

Krüger, W., and Ebeling, F. (1991) 'Psychologik: Topmanager müssen lernen, politisch zu handeln', *HARVARDmanager*, Vol. 2, pp. 47–56.

Lawrence, P.R., and Lorsch, J.W. (1967) *Organization and the Environment*, Harvard Business School, Boston, MA.

Leonard-Barton, D. (1992) 'Core Capabilities and Core Rigidities: A Paradox in Managing New Product Development', *Strategic Management Journal*, Vol. 13, Special Issue, Summer, pp. 111–125.

Leonard-Barton, D. (1995) *Wellsprings of Knowledge*, Harvard Business School Press, Boston, MA.

Lewin, K. (1947) 'Frontiers in Group Dynamics: Social Equilbria and Social Change', *Human Relations*, Vol. 1, pp. 5–41.

Lieberman, M.B., and Montgomery, D.B. (1988) 'First Mover Adavantages', *Strategic Management Journal*, Vol. 9, No. 1, January–February, pp. 41–58.

Lieberman, M.B., and Montgomery, D.B. (1998) 'First-Mover (Dis)Advantages: Retrospective and Link with the Resource-Based View', *Strategic Management Journal*, Vol. 19, No. 12, December, pp. 1111–1126.

Maidique, M.A. (1980) 'Entrepreneurs, Champions, and Technological Innovation', *Sloan Management Review*, Vol. 21, pp. 18–31.

March, J.G., and Simon, H.A. (1958) *Organizations*, Wiley, New York.

Markides, C. (1998) 'Strategic Innovation in Established Companies', *Sloan Management Review*, Vol. 39, No. 3, pp. 31–42.

Marr, R. (1987) 'Die Implementierung eines flexiblen Arbeitszeitsystems als Prozess organisatorischer Entwicklung', in: R. Marr (ed.), *Arbeitszeitmanagement*, Berlin, pp. 339–355.

McCaskey, M.B. (1982) *The Executive Challenge: Managing Change and Ambiguity*, Pitman, Boston.

Meyer, A.D. (1982) 'Adapting to Environmental Jolts', *Administrative Science Quarterly*, Vol. 27, No. 4, December, pp. 515–537.

Meyer, A., Brooks, G., and Goes, J. (1990) 'Environmental Jolts and Industry Revolutions: Organizational Responses to Discontinuous Change', *Strategic Management Journal*, Vol. 11, No. 2, February, pp. 93–110.

Miller, D. (1990) *The Icarus Paradox: How Excellent Companies Bring About Their Own Downfall*, Harper Business, New York.

Miller, D., and Friesen, P. (1984) *Organizations: A Quantum View*, Prentice Hall, Englewood Cliffs, NJ.

Mintzberg, H. (1983) *Power In and Around Organizations*, Prentice Hall, Englewood Cliffs, NJ.

Mintzberg, H (1991) 'The Effective Organization: Forces and Forms', *Sloan Management Review*, Vol. 32, No. 2, Winter, pp. 54–67.

Mintzberg, H. (1994) *The Rise and Fall of Strategic Planning*, Prentice Hall, Englewood Cliffs, NJ.

Mintzberg, H., and Westley, F. (1992) 'Cycles of Organizational Change', *Strategic Management Journal*, Vol. 13, pp. 39–59.

Morgan, G. (1986) *Images of Organization*, Sage, London.

Nelson, R.R., and Winter, S.G. (1982) *An Evolutionary Theory of Economic Change*, Harvard University Press, Cambridge, MA.

Nonaka, I. (1988) 'Creating Organizational Order Out of Chaos: Self-Renewal in Japanese Firms', *California Management Review*, Vol. 30, No. 3, Spring, pp. 9–18.

Oliver, C. (1991) 'Strategic Responses to Institutional Processes', *Academy of Management Review*, Vol. 16, No. 1, January, pp. 145–179.

Ouchi, W. (1981) *Theory Z: How American Business Can Meet the Japanese Challenge*, Addison-Wesley, Reading, MA.

Pascale, R.T., and Athos, A.G. (1981) *The Art of Japanese Management*, Simon & Schuster, New York.

Pettigrew, A.M. (1985) *The Awakening Giant: Continuity and Change in Imperial Chemical Industries*, Blackwell, Oxford.

Pettigrew, A.M. (1988) *The Management of Strategic Change*, Basil Blackwell, Oxford.

Pfeffer, J., and Sutton, R.I. (1999) 'Knowing "What" to Do is Not Enough: Turning Knowledge Into Action', *California Management Review*, Vol. 42, No. 1, Fall, pp. 83–108.

Pondy, L.R., Boland, J.R., and Thomas, H. (eds.) (1988) *Managing Ambiguity and Change*, Wiley, New York.

Powell, W.W. (1991) 'Expanding the scope of Institutional Analysis', in: W.W. Powell and P.J. DiMaggio (eds.), *The New Institutionalism in Organizational Analysis*, University of Chicago Press, Chicago, pp. 183–203.

Quinn, J.B. (1980) *Strategies for Change*, Irwin, Homewood, IL.

Reiss, M. (1993) 'Führungsaufgabe Implementierung', *Personal*, Vol. 12, pp. 551–555.

Schein, E.H. (1985) *Organizational Culture and Leadership*, Jossey-Bass, San Francisco.

Schumpeter, J.A (1950) *Capitalism, Socialism and Democracy*, Third Edition, Harper and Brothers, New York.

Senge, P.M. (1990) 'The Leader's New Work: Building Learning Organizations', *Sloan Management Review*, Vol. 32, No. 1, Fall, pp. 7–23.

Shapiro, C., and Varian, H. (1998) *Information Rules: A Strategic Guide to the Network Economy*, Harvard Business School Press, Cambridge, MA.

Stacey, R.D. (1993a) 'Strategy as Order Emerging from Chaos', *Long Range Planning*, Vol. 26, No. 1, pp. 10–17.

Stacey, R.D. (1993b) *Strategic Management and Organisational Dynamics*, Pitman Publishing, London.

Stinchcombe, A.L. (1965) 'Social Structure and Organizations', in: J.G. March (ed.), *Handbook of Organizations*, Rand McNally, Chicago, pp. 142–193.

Stopford, J.M., and Baden-Fuller, C.W.F. (1994) 'Creating Corporate Entrepreneurship', *Strategic Management Journal*, Vol. 15, No. 7, September, pp. 521–536.

Strebel, P. (1992) *Breakpoints: How Managers Exploit Radical Business Change*, Harvard Business School Press, Boston.

Strebel, P. (1994) 'Choosing the Right Change Path', *California Management Review*, Vol. 36, No. 2, Winter, pp. 29–51.

Teece, D.J., Pisano, G., and Shuen, A. (1997) 'Dynamic Capabilities and Strategic Management', *Strategic Management Journal*, Vol. 18, No. 7, August, pp. 509–533.

Thompson, J.D. (1967) *Organizations in Action*, McGraw-Hill, New York.

Tidd, J., Bessant, J., and Pavitt, K. (1997) *Managing Innovation: Integrating Technological, Market and Organizational Change*, Wiley, Chichester.

Trice, H.M., and Beyer, J.M. (1993) *The Cultures of Work Organizations*, Prentice Hall, Englewood Cliffs, NJ.

Tushman, M.L., Newman, W.H., and Romanelli, E. (1986) 'Convergence and Upheaval: Managing the Unsteady Pace of Organizational Evolution', *California Management Review*, Vol. 29, No. 1, Fall, pp. 29–44.

Tushman, M.L., and O'Reilly III, C.A. (1996) 'Ambidextrous Organizations: Managing Evolutionary and Revolutionary Change', *California Management Review*, Vol. 38, No. 4, Summer, pp. 8–30.

Tushman, M.L., and O'Reilly III, C.A. (1997) *Winning Through Innovation: A Practical Guide to Leading Organizational Change and Renewal*, Harvard Business School Press, Boston, MA.

Tushman, M., and Romanelli, E. (1985) 'Organizational Evolution: A Metamorphosis Model of Convergence and Reorientation', in: L.L. Cummings and B.M. Staw (eds.), *Research in Organizational Behavior*, JAI Press, Greenwich, CT, Vol. 7, pp. 171–222.

Utterback, J. (1994) *Mastering the Dynamics of Innovation*, Harvard Business School Press, Boston, MA.

Waterman, R.H., Peters, T.J., and Phillips, J.R. (1980) 'Structure is Not Organization', *Business Horizons*, Vol. 23, June, pp. 14–26.

Wiendieck, G. (1992) 'Akzeptanz', in: E. Frese (ed.), *Handwörter-buch der Organisation*, Third Edition, Stuttgart, pp. 89–98.

Witte, E. (1973) *Organisation für Innovationsentscheidungen: Das Promotorenmodell*, Schartz & Co., Göttingen.

STRATEGY CONTENT

Every generation laughs at the old fashions but religiously follows the new.
Henry David Thoreau (1817–1862); American philosopher

The output of the strategy process is a particular strategy that an organization follows – this is called the strategy content. 'Strategy content' is another way of saying 'the strategy itself, with all its specific characteristics'. While the strategy process section dealt with the questions of *how* strategy should be formed, *who* should be involved and *when* it should be made, the strategy content section deals with the question of *what* the strategy should be – what should be the course of action the firm should follow to achieve its purpose?

In determining what the strategy should be, two types of 'fit' are of central concern to managers. First, as discussed in Chapter 4, there needs to be a fit between the firm and its environment. If the two become misaligned, the firm will be unable to meet the demands of the environment and will start to underperform, which can eventually lead to bankruptcy or takeover. This type of fit is also referred to as 'external consonance'. At the same time, managers are also concerned with achieving an internal fit between the various parts of the firm. If various units become misaligned, the organization will suffer from inefficiency, conflict and poor external performance, which can eventually lead to its demise as well. This type of fit is also referred to as 'internal consistency'.

As external consonance and internal consistency are prerequisites for a successful strategy, they need to be achieved for each organizational unit. Most organizations have various levels, making it necessary to ensure internal and external fit at each level of aggregation within the firm. In Figure III.1 all these possible levels within a corporation have been reduced to just three general categories, and a fourth, supra-organizational level has been added. At each level the strategy followed should meet the requirements of external consonance and internal consistency:

- Functional level strategy. For each functional area, such as marketing, operations, finance, logistics, human resources, procurement and R&D, a strategy needs to be developed. At this level, internal consistency means having an overarching functional strategy that integrates various functional sub-strategies (e.g. a marketing strategy that aligns branding, distribution, pricing, product and communication strategies). External consonance means that the strategy must be aligned with the demands in the relevant external arena (e.g. the logistics or procurement environment).

- Business level strategy. At the business level, an organization can only be effective if it can integrate functional level strategies into an internally consistent whole. To achieve external consonance the business unit must be aligned with the specific demands in the relevant business area.

- Corporate level strategy. Where a company operates in two or more business areas, the business level strategies need to be aligned to form an internally consistent corporate level strategy. Between business and corporate levels there can also be divisions, but for most strategy purposes they can be approached as mini-corporations (both divisional and corporate level strategy are technically speaking 'multi-business level').

Achieving external consonance at this level of aggregation means that a corporation must be able to act as one tightly integrated unit or as many autonomous, differentiated units, depending on the demands of the relevant environment.

■ **Network level strategy.** Where various firms work together to create economic value, it sometimes is deemed necessary to align business and/or corporate level strategies to shape an internally consistent network level strategy. Such a network, or multi-company, level strategy can involve anywhere between two and thousands of companies. Here, too, the group must develop a strategy that fits with the demands in the relevant environment.

As the strategy content issues differ greatly depending on the level of aggregation under discussion, this section has been divided along the following lines. Chapter 5 will focus on business level strategy, Chapter 6 on corporate level strategy and Chapter 7 on network level strategy. Only the functional level strategies will be given no extensive coverage, as they are usually explored in great detail in functionally oriented books. It must be noted, however, that the aggregation levels used here are an analytical distinction and not an empirical reality that can always be found in practice – where one level stops and the other starts is more a matter of definition than of thick demarcation lines. Hence, when discussing strategy issues at any level, it is important to understand how they fit with higher and lower level strategy questions.

FIGURE III.1   The levels of strategy

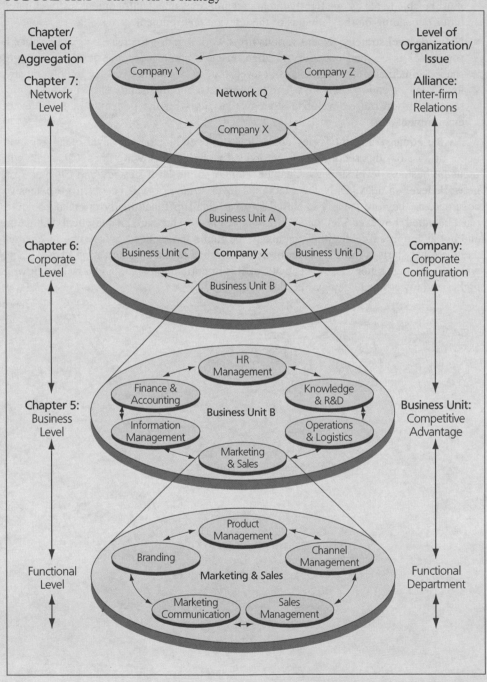

BUSINESS LEVEL STRATEGY

Advantage is a better soldier than rashness.

William Shakespeare (1564–1616); English dramatist and poet

INTRODUCTION

Strategic management is concerned with relating a firm to its environment in order to successfully meet long-term objectives. As both the business environment and individual firms are dynamic systems, constantly in flux, achieving a fit between the two is an ongoing challenge. Managers are continuously looking for new ways to align the current, and potential, strengths and weaknesses of the organization with the current, and potential, opportunities and threats in the environment.

Part of the difficulty lies in the competitive nature of the environment. To be successful, firms need to gain a competitive advantage over rival organizations operating in the same business area. Within the competitive arena chosen by a firm, it needs to accrue enough power to counterbalance the demands of buyers and suppliers, to outperform rival producers, to discourage new firms from entering the business and to fend off the threat of substitute products or services. Preferably this competitive advantage over other players in the business should be sustainable over a prolonged period of time. How firms should go about creating a (sustainable) competitive advantage in each business in which they operate is the central issue concerning managers engaged in business level strategy.

THE ISSUE OF COMPETITIVE ADVANTAGE

Whether a firm has a competitive advantage depends on the business system that it has developed to relate itself to its business environment. A business system is the configuration of resources (inputs), activities (throughput) and product/service offerings (output) intended to create value for customers – it is the way a firm conducts its business. In Figure 5.1 an overview is given of the components of a business system.

Competitive advantage can only be achieved if a business system creates superior value for buyers. Therefore, the first element in a successful business system is a superior 'value proposition'. A firm must be able to supply a product or service more closely fitted to client needs than rival firms. To be attractive, each element of a firm's 'product offering' needs to be targeted at a particular segment of the market and have a superior mix of attributes (e.g. price, availability, reliability, technical specifications, image, color, taste, ease of use, etc.). Secondly, a successful company must also have the ability to actually develop and supply the superior product offering. It needs to have the capability to perform the necessary value-adding activities in an effective and efficient manner. These value-adding activities, such as R&D, production, logistics, marketing and sales, are jointly referred to as a firm's activity system (or value chain). The third component of a business system consists of the resource base required to perform the value-adding activities. Resources such as know-how, patents, facilities, money, brands and relationships make up the stock of assets that can be employed to create the product offering. If these firm-specific assets are distinctive and useful, they can form the basis of a superior value proposition. To create a competitive advantage, alignment must be achieved between all three elements of a business system. In the following pages all three elements will be discussed in more detail.

Product offering

At the intersection between a firm and its environment, transactions take place whereby the firm supplies goods or performs services for clients in the market-place. It is here that the alignment of the firm and its environment is put to the test. If the products and services offered by the firm are more highly valued by customers than alternatives, a profitable transaction could take place. In other words, for sales to be achieved a firm must have a competitive value proposition – a cluster of physical goods, services and/or additional attributes with a superior fit to customer needs.

For the strategizing manager the key question is which products should be developed and which markets should be served. In many cases the temptation is to be everything to everybody – making a wide range of products and serving as many clients as possible. However, a number of practical constraints inhibit companies from taking such an unfocused approach to the market. Companies that do not focus on a limited set of product–market combinations run the risk of encountering a number of major problems:

■ Low economies of scale. Being unfocused is expensive, because of the low economies of scale that can be achieved. In general, the less specialized the company, the lower the opportunities to organize the activity system efficiently and leverage the resource base.

FIGURE 5.1 Components of a business system

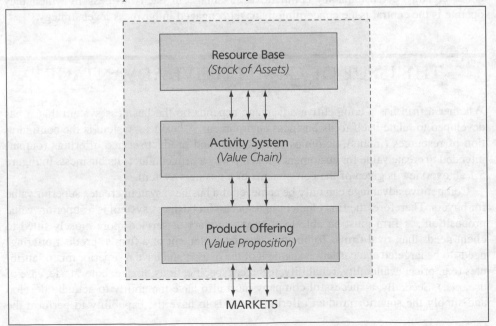

- Slow organizational learning. Being involved in a multitude of products and markets generally slows the organization's ability to build up specific knowledge and capabilities. In general, the less specialized the company, the lower the opportunity to develop a distinctive activity system and resource base.

- Unclear brand image. Unfocused companies have the added disadvantage of having a fuzzy image in the market. In general, companies that stand for everything tend to stand out in nothing.

- Unclear corporate identity. The lack of clear external image is usually compounded by a lack of internal identity within unfocused organizations. In general, a company with highly diversified activities will have difficulty explaining why its people are together in the same company.

- High organizational complexity. Highly diverse products and customers also create an exponential increase in organizational complexity. In general, the less specialized the company, the lower the opportunity to keep the organization simple and manageable.

- Limits to flexibility. Being all things to all people is often physically impossible due to the need to specify procedures, routines, systems and tools. In general, less specialized firms are often forced into certain choices due to operational necessity.

For these reasons, companies need to focus on a limited number of businesses and within each business on a limited group of customers and a limited set of products. This focus should not be arbitrary – the challenge for strategizing managers is to understand which businesses are (or can be made to be) structurally attractive and how their firm can gain a competitive advantage within each business, by offering specific value propositions to selected customer segments.

Determining a focus starts by looking for the 'boundaries' of a business – how can managers draw meaningful delineation lines in the environment, distinguishing one arena of competition from another, so that they can select some and ignore others? Ideally, the environment would be made up of neatly compartmentalized businesses, with clear borders separating them. In reality, however, the picture is much more messy. While there are usually certain clusters of buyers and suppliers interacting more intensely with one another, suggesting that they are operating in the same business, there are often numerous exceptions to any neat classification scheme. To explore how a business can be defined, it is first necessary to specify how a business differs from an 'industry' and a 'market'.

Delineating industries.   An industry is defined as a group of firms making a similar type of product or employing a similar set of value-adding processes or resources. In other words, an industry consists of producers that are much alike – there is *supply side similarity* (Kay, 1993). The simplest way to draw an industry boundary is to use product similarity as the delineation criterion. For instance, British Airways can be said to be in the airline industry, along with many other providers of the same product, such as Singapore Airlines and Ryanair. However, an industry can also be defined on the basis of activity system similarity (e.g. consulting industry and mining industry) or resource similarity (e.g. information technology industry and oil industry).

Economic statisticians tend to favor fixed industry categories based on product similarity and therefore most figures available about industries are product-category based, often making use of Standard Industrial Classification (SIC) codes. Strategists, on the contrary, like to challenge existing definitions of an industry, for instance by regrouping them on the basis of underlying value-adding activities or resources. Take the example of Swatch – how did it conceptualize which industry it was in? If they had focused on the physical product and the production process, then they would have been inclined to situate Swatch in the watch industry. However, Swatch also viewed its products as fashion accessories, placing emphasis on the key value-adding activities of fashion design and marketing. On this basis, Swatch could just as well be categorized as a member of the fashion industry (Porac, Thomas and Baden-Fuller, 1989). For the strategizing manager, the realization that Swatch can be viewed in both ways is an important insight. As creating a competitive advantage often comes from doing things differently, rethinking the definition of an industry can be a powerful way to develop a unique product offering.

Figure 5.2 gives four examples of traditionally defined 'industry columns', which Porter (1980, Reading 5.1 in this book) draws not top-down, but left-right, using the term 'value system'. These columns start with upstream industries, which are involved in the extraction/growing of raw materials and their conversion into inputs for the manufacturing sector. Downstream industries take the output of manufacturing companies and bring them to clients, often adding a variety of services into the product mix. In practice, industry columns are not as simple as depicted in Figure 5.2, as each industry has many different industries as suppliers and usually many different industries as buyers.

A second limitation of the industry columns shown in Figure 5.2 is that they are materials-flow oriented – industry boundaries are drawn on the basis of product similarity, while strategists might want to take a different angle on defining the industry. The brown blocks are some examples of alternative industry definitions, but one can imagine many

FIGURE 5.2   Alternative industry categorizations

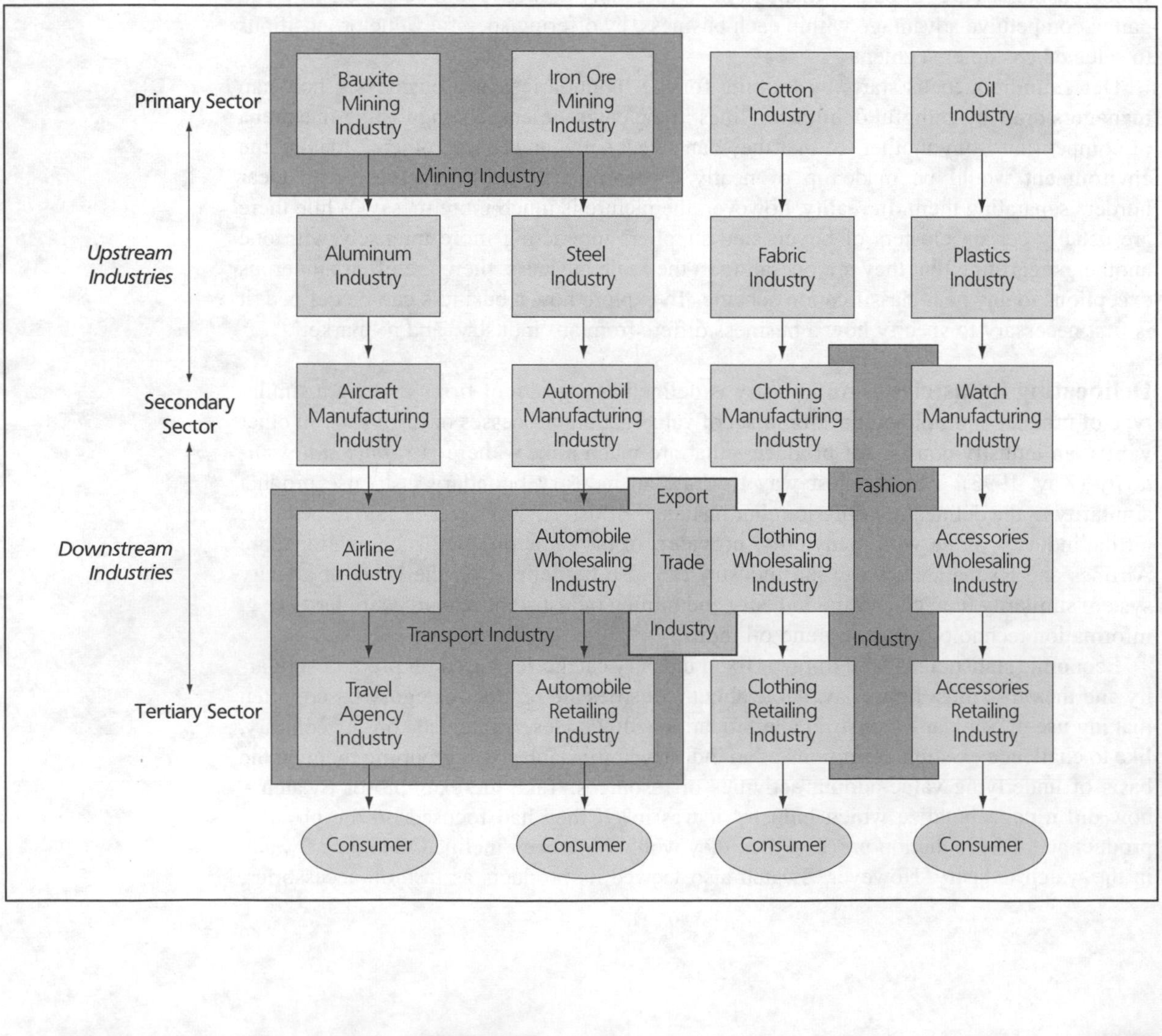

more; not only broader definitions, but also more narrow ones. For instance, it could be argued that clothing retailers with physical stores are in a distinct industry as opposed to internet/mail-order retailers.

A further downside of the industry column figure is that the 'materials-flow' angle does not really suit the two-thirds of the economy that is involved in services. Understanding who are the buyers and the suppliers of insurance, education, consultancy, advertising and healthcare requires a different way of conceiving the industry column than looking at the flow of goods. Generally, for each different type of service a different value system will exist, with a distinct web of suppliers and buyers.

Segmenting markets.   While economists see the market as a place where supply and demand meet, in the business world a market is usually defined as a group of customers with similar needs. In other words, a market consists of buyers whose demands are much alike – *demand side similarity*. For instance, there is a market for air transportation between London and Jamaica, which is a different market than for air transportation between London and Paris – the customer needs are different and therefore these products cannot be substituted for one another. But customers can substitute a British Airways London–Paris flight for one by Air France, indicating that both companies are serving the same market. Yet, this market definition (London–Paris air transport) might not be the most appropriate, if in reality many customers are willing to substitute air travel by rail travel, taking Le Shuttle through the channel tunnel, or by ferry. In this case, there is a broader London–Paris transportation market, and air transportation is a specific *market segment*. If many customers are willing to substitute physical travel by tele-conferencing or other telecommunications methods, the market might need to be defined as the 'London–Paris meeting market'.

FIGURE 5.3   Alternative market categorizations

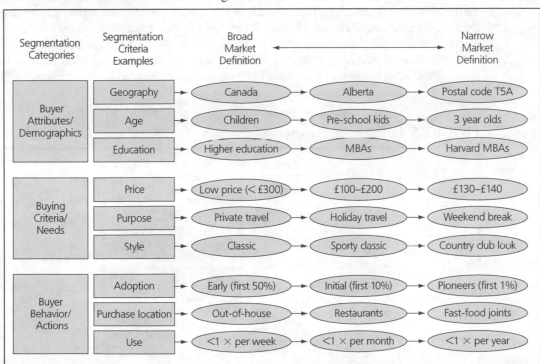

As with industries, there are many ways of defining markets, depending on which buyer characteristics are used to make a clustering. In Figure 5.3, a number of examples are given of segmentation criteria. The first group of segmentation criteria is based on buyer attributes that are frequently thought to be important predictors of actual buying criteria and buyer behavior. Such customer characteristics are commonly used to group potential clients because this information is objective and easily available. However, the pitfall of segmenting on the basis of buyer attributes is that the causal link between characteristics and actual needs and behaviors is often rather tenuous – not all Canadians need hockey sticks and not all three-year-olds nag their parents while shopping. In other words, the market can be segmented on the basis of any demographic characteristic (e.g. income, family composition, employment), but this might not lead to meaningful groups of customers with similar needs and buying behavior.

Therefore, instead of using buyer attributes as *indirect* – predictive – measures of what clients probably want, segments can also be *directly* defined on the basis of buying criteria employed and/or buyer behaviors exhibited. The advantage is that segments can then be identified with clearly similar wishes and/or behaviors. The disadvantage is that it is very difficult to gather and interpret information on what specific people want and how they really act.

For strategists, one of the key challenges is to look at existing categorizations of buyers and to wonder whether a different segmentation would offer new insights and new opportunities for developing a product offering specifically tailored to their needs. As with the redefining of industry boundaries, it is often in the reconceptualization of market segments that a unique approach to the market can be found.

Defining and selecting businesses. A business is as a set of related product–market combinations. The term 'business' refers neither to a set of producers nor a group of customers, but to the domain where the two meet. In other words, a business is a competitive arena where companies offering similar products serving similar needs rival against one another for the favor of the buyers. Hence, a business is delineated in both industry and market terms (see Figure 5.4). Typically, a business is narrower than the entire industry and the set of markets served is also limited. For instance, within the airline industry the charter business is usually recognized as rather distinct. In the charter business, a sub-set of the airline services is offered to a number of tourist markets. Cheap flights from London to Jamaica and from London to Barcelona fall within this business, while service levels will

FIGURE 5.4 Industries, markets and businesses

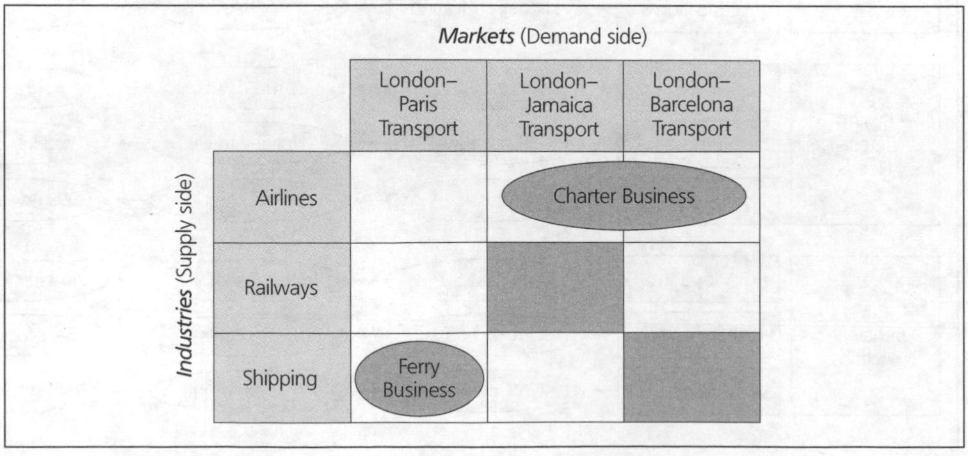

be different than in other parts of the airline industry. It should be noted, though, that just as with industries and markets, there is no best way to define the boundaries of a business (Abell, 1980).

As stated earlier, companies cannot afford to be unfocused, operating superficially in a whole range of businesses. They must direct their efforts by focusing in two ways:

1 Selecting a limited number of businesses. The first constraint that companies need to impose on themselves is to choose a limited array of businesses within which they wish to be successful. This essential strategic challenge is referred to as the issue of corporate configuration and will be examined in more detail in Chapter 6 (multi-business level strategy). Here it suffices to say that firms need to analyze the structural characteristics of interesting businesses to be able to judge whether they are attractive enough for the firm, or can be made to be attractive. In Reading 5.1 Porter presents the 'five forces analysis' as a framework for mapping the structure of industries and businesses.

2 Focusing within each selected business. Even within the limited set of businesses selected, firms need to determine what they want to be and what they want to leave aside. To be competitive, it is necessary to choose a number of distinct market segments and to target a few special product offerings to meet these customers' needs. As illustrated in Figure 5.1, these specific product offerings in turn need to be aligned with a focused activity system and resource base.

This act of focusing the overall business system to serve the particular needs of a targeted group of buyers, in a way that distinguishes the firm vis-à-vis rivals, is called positioning. This positioning of the firm in the business requires a clearly tailored product offering (product positioning), but also an activity system and resource base that closely fit with the demands of the specific group of customers and competitors being targeted.

Positioning within a business. Positioning is concerned with both the questions of 'where to compete' and 'how to compete' (Porter, 1980, Reading 5.1). Determining in which product–market combinations within a business a firm wants to be involved is referred to as the issue of competitive scope. Finding a way to beat rivals and win over customers for a product offering is the issue of competitive advantage. The two questions are tightly linked, because firms need to develop a specific advantage to be competitive within a specific product–market domain. If they try to use the same competitive advantage for too many dissimilar products and customers, they run the risk of becoming unfocused.

In selecting a competitive scope, firms can vary anywhere between being widely oriented and very tightly focused. Firms with a broad scope compete in a large number of segments within a business, with varied product offerings. Firms with a narrow scope target only one, or just a few, customer segments and have a more limited product line (see Figure 5.5). If there is a small part of the business with very specific demands, requiring a distinct approach, firms can narrowly focus on this niche as their competitive scope. In between these two extremes are firms with a segment focus and firms with a product focus, but in practice many other profiles are also possible.

In developing a competitive advantage, firms have many dimensions along which they can attempt to outdo their rivals. Some of the most important bases of competitive advantage are the following:

- Price. The most straightforward advantage a firm can have in a competitive situation is the ability to charge a lower price. All things being equal, buyers generally prefer to pay the lowest amount necessary. Hence, when purchasing a commodity product or service, most customers will be partial to the lowest priced supplier. And even when selecting among differentiated products, many customers will be inclined to buy the cheapest or at least the cheapest within a sub-group of more comparable products. For a firm

FIGURE 5.5   Determining competitive scope

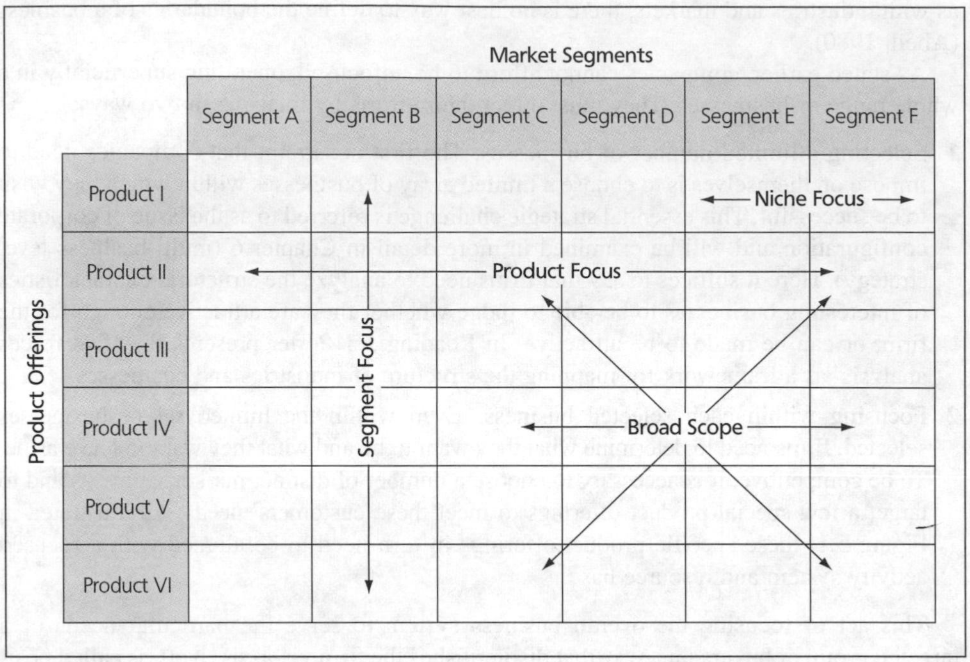

wanting to compete on price, the essential point is that it should have a *low cost* product offering, activity system and resource base to match the price positioning. After all, in the long run a firm can only survive at a lower price level if it has developed a business system that can sustainably operate at a lower cost level.

- Features. Firms can also distinguish their product offerings by having different intrinsic functional characteristics than competing offerings. There are many ways to make a product or service different, for instance by changing its size, smell, taste, color, functionality, compatibility, content, design or style. An ice cream manufacturer can introduce a new flavor and more chunky texture, a motorcycle producer can design a special 'low rider' model for women, a pay TV company can develop special channels for dog owners and science fiction addicts, and a utility company can offer environmentally friendly electricity. To be able to compete on each of these product features, firms need to command different specialized resources and activity systems. In some cases, they require significant technological knowledge and a technically sophisticated activity system, while in other cases design capabilities, marketing prowess or a satellite infrastructure are essential to the functioning of the business system.

- Bundling. Another way to offer a uniquely different value proposition is to sell a package of products and/or services 'wrapped together'. By bundling a number of separate elements into a package, the customer can have the convenience of 'one stop shopping', while also having a family of related products and/or services that fit together well. So, for instance, many customers prefer to purchase their software from one supplier because this raises the chance of compatibility. In the chocolate industry, the leading manufacturer of chocolate making machines, Rademakers, was able to gain a competitive advantage by bundling its machines with various services, such as installation, repair, spare parts and financing.

- Quality. When competing with others, a firm's product offering doesn't necessarily have to be fundamentally different, it can just be better. Customers generally appreciate products and services that exhibit superior performance in terms of usability, reliability and durability, and are often willing to pay a premium price for such quality. Excellent quality can be secured on many fronts, for instance through the materials used, the people involved, the manufacturing process employed, the quality assurance procedures followed or the distribution system used.

- Availability. The method of distribution can in itself be the main competitive edge on which a firm bases its positioning. Having a product available at the right place, at the right moment and in the right way, can be much more important to customers than features and quality. Just ask successful ice cream manufacturers – most of their revenues are from out-of-doors impulse sales, so they need to have their products available in individually wrapped portions at all locations where people have the urge to indulge. In the same way, Avon's cosmetics are not primarily sold because of their uniqueness or low price, but because of the strength of their three million sales force, who can be at the right place at the right time.

- Image. In the competition for customers' preference, firms can also gain an advantage by having a more appealing image than their rivals. In business-to-consumer markets this is particularly clear when looking at the impact of brands. Consumers often feel attracted to brands that project a certain image of the company or the products it sells. Brands can communicate specific values that consumers want to be associated with (Nike's 'just do it'), or can help to build trust among consumers who have too little information on which to base their product choices (GE's 'we bring good things to life'). But even in business-to-business markets buyers often suffer from a shortage of information about the available product offerings or lack the time to research all possible suppliers. Therefore, the image of suppliers, mostly in terms of their standing ('a leading global player') and reputation ('high quality service') can be essential to be considered at all (to be 'shortlisted') and to be trusted as business partner.

- Relations. Good branding can give customers the impression that they know the supplier, without actually being in direct contact. Yet, having a direct relation with customers can in itself be a potent source of competitive advantage. In general, customers prefer to know their suppliers well, as this gives them a more intimate knowledge of the product offering being provided. Having a relationship with a supplier can also give the customer more influence on what is offered. But besides these rational points, customers often value the personal contact, the trust and the convenience of having a long-standing relationship as well. For suppliers this means that they might acquire a competitive edge by managing their customer relationships well. To do so, however, does imply that the activity system and resource base are fit to fulfill this task.

The type of competitive advantage that a firm chooses to pursue will be influenced by what the targeted group of buyers find important. These factors of importance to potential clients are referred to as 'value drivers' – they are the elements responsible for creating value in the eyes of the customer. Which value drivers a firm will want to base its value proposition on is a matter of positioning.

According to Porter (1980, Reading 5.1 in this book) all the specific forms of competitive advantage listed above can be reduced to two broad categories, namely lower cost and differentiation. On the one hand, firms can organize their business systems in such a manner that, while their products or services are largely the same as other manufacturers, their overall cost structure is lower, allowing them to compete on price. On the other hand, firms can organize their business systems to supply a product or service that has distinctive qualities compared to rival offerings. According to Porter, these two forms of competitive advantage demand fundamentally different types of business systems and therefore are next to impossible to combine. Firms that do try to realize both at the same time run the risk of getting 'stuck in the middle' – not being able to do either properly.

Treacy and Wiersema (1995) argue that there are actually three generic competitive advantages, each requiring a fundamentally different type of business system (they speak of three distinctive 'value disciplines'). They, too, warn firms to develop an internally consistent business system focused on one of these types of competitive advantage, avoiding a 'mix-and-match' approach to business strategy:

- Operational excellence. Firms striving for operational excellence meet the buyers' need for a reliable, low cost product offering. The activity system required to provide such no-frills, standardized, staple products emphasizes a 'lean and mean' approach to production and distribution, with simple service.

- Product leadership. Firms taking the route of product leadership meet the buyers' need for special features and advanced product performance. The activity system required to provide such differentiated, state-of-the-art products emphasizes innovation and the creative collaboration between marketing and R&D.

- Customer intimacy. Firms deciding to focus on customer intimacy meet the buyers' need for a tailored solution to their particular problem. The activity system required to provide such a client-specific, made-to-measure offering emphasizes flexibility and empowerment of the employees close to the customer.

Other strategy researchers, however, argue that there is no such thing as generic competitive strategies that follow from two or three broad categories of competitive advantage (e.g. Baden-Fuller and Stopford, 1992). In their view, there is an endless variety of ways in which companies can develop a competitive advantage, many of which do not fit into the categories outlined by Porter or Treacy and Wiersema – in fact, finding a new type of competitive advantage might be the best way of obtaining a unique position in a business.

Activity system

To be able to actually make what it wants to sell, a firm needs to have an activity system in place. An activity system is an integrated set of value creation processes leading to the supply of product and/or service offerings. Whether goods are being manufactured or services are being provided, each firm needs to perform a number of activities to successfully fill the customer's wants. As these value-adding activities need to be coordinated and linked together, this part of the business system is also frequently referred to as the 'value chain' (Porter, 1985).

Activity systems can vary widely from industry to industry. The activity system of a car manufacturer is quite distinct from that of an advertising agency. Yet even within an industry there can be significant differences. Most 'bricks and mortar' bookstores have organized their value chain differently than on-line book retailers like Amazon.com. The activity systems of most 'hub-and-spoke' airline companies hardly resemble that of 'no-frills' carriers such as Southwest in the United States and easyJet in Europe.

While these examples point to radically different activity systems, even firms that subscribe to the same basic model can apply it in their own particular way. Fast-food restaurants such as McDonald's and Burger King may employ the same basic model, but their actual activity systems differ in quite a few ways. The same goes for the PC manufacturers HP and IBM, which share a similar type of activity system, but which still differ on many fronts. 'On-line mass-customization' PC manufacturer Dell, on the other hand, has a different model and consequently a more strongly differing activity system than HP and IBM.

Having such a distinct activity system often provides the basis for a competitive advantage. A unique value chain allows a firm to offer customers a unique value proposition, by doing things better, faster, cheaper, nicer or more tailored than competing firms. Developing the firm's activity system is therefore just as strategically important as developing new products and services.

Although activity systems can differ quite significantly, some attempts have been made to develop a general taxonomy of value-adding activities that could be used as an analytical framework (e.g. Day, 1990; Norman and Ramirez, 1993). By far the most influential framework is Porter's value chain, which distinguishes primary activities and support activities (see Figure 5.6). Primary activities 'are the activities involved in the physical creation of the product and its sale and transfer to the buyer, as well as after-sale assistance' (Porter, 1985: 16). Support activities facilitate the primary process, by providing purchased inputs, technology, human resources and various firm-wide functions. The generic categories of primary activities identified by Porter are:

- Inbound logistics. Activities associated with receiving, storing, and disseminating inputs, including material handling, warehousing, inventory control, vehicle scheduling and returns to suppliers.

- Operations. Activities associated with transforming inputs into final products, including machining, packaging, assembly, equipment maintenance, testing, printing and facility operations.

- Outbound logistics. Activities associated with collecting, storing and physically distributing products to buyers, including warehousing, material handling, delivery, order processing and scheduling.

- Marketing and sales. Activities associated with providing a means by which buyers can purchase the product and inducing them to do so, including advertising, promotion, sales force, quoting, channel selection, channel relations and pricing.

- Service. Activities associated with providing service to enhance or maintain the value of products, including installation, repair, training, parts supply and product adjustment.

For service industries Porter argues that the specific activities will be different, and might be performed in a different order, but can still be subdivided into these five generic categories. To ensure that the primary activities can be carried out, each firm also needs to organize four types of support activities:

- Procurement. Activities associated with the purchasing of inputs to facilitate all other activities, including vendor selection, negotiations, contracting and invoice administration.

FIGURE 5.6   The generic value chain (Porter, 1985)

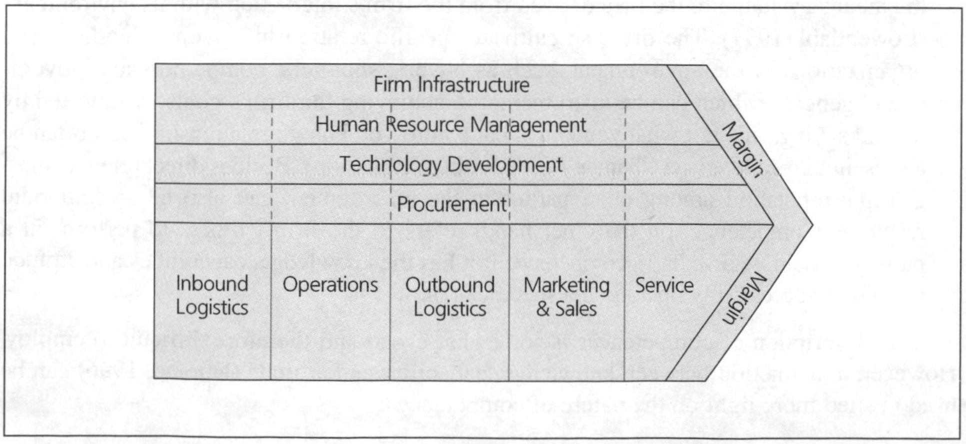

- Technology development. Activities associated with the improvement of technologies throughout the firm, including basic research, product and process design, and procedure development.

- Human resource management. Activities associated with the management of personnel throughout the organization, including recruiting, hiring, training, development and compensation.

- Firm infrastructure. Firm infrastructure consists of all general activities that support the entire value chain, including general management, planning, finance, accounting, legal, government affairs and quality management.

The uniqueness of the activity system, and its strength as the source of competitive advantage, will usually not depend on only a few specialized activities, but on the extraordinary configuration of the entire activity system. An extraordinary configuration multiplies the distinctness of a particular activity system, while often raising the barrier to imitation (Porter, 1996; Amit and Zott, 2001).

Resource base

To carry out activities and to produce goods and services, firms need resources. A firm's resource base includes all means at the disposal of the organization for the performance of value-adding activities. Other authors prefer the term 'assets', to emphasize that the resources belong to the firm (e.g. Dierickx and Cool, 1989; Itami, 1987).

Under the broad umbrella of resource-based view of the firm, there has been much research into the importance of resources for the success and even existence of firms (e.g. Penrose, 1959; Wernerfelt, 1984; Barney, 1991, Reading 5.4). No generally accepted classification of firm resources has yet emerged in the field of strategic management, however the following major distinctions (see Figure 5.7) are commonly made:

- Tangible vs. intangible resources. Tangible resources are all means available to the firm that can physically be observed (touched), such as buildings, machines, materials, land and money. Tangibles can be referred to as the 'hardware' of the organization. Intangibles, on the other hand, are the 'software' of the organization. Intangible resources cannot be touched, but are largely carried within the people in the organization. In general, tangible resources need to be purchased, while intangibles need to be developed. Therefore, tangible resources are often more readily transferable, easier to price and usually are placed on the balance sheet.

- Relational resources vs. competences. Within the category of intangible resources, relational resources and competences can be distinguished. Relational resources are all of the means available to the firm derived from the firm's interaction with its environment (Lowendahl, 1997). The firm can cultivate specific relationships with individuals and organizations in the environment, such as buyers, suppliers, competitors and government agencies, which can be instrumental in achieving the firm's goals. As attested by the old saying, 'it's not what you know, but whom you know', relationships can often be an essential resource (see Chapter 7 for a further discussion). Besides direct relationships, a firm's reputation among other parties in the environment can also be an important resource. Competence, on the other hand, refers to the firm's fitness to perform in a particular field. A firm has a competence if it has the knowledge, capabilities and attitude needed to successfully operate in a specific area.

This description of competences is somewhat broad and therefore difficult to employ. However, a distinction between knowledge, capability and attitude (Durand, 1996) can be used to shed more light on the nature of competences:

FIGURE 5.7 Types of firm resources

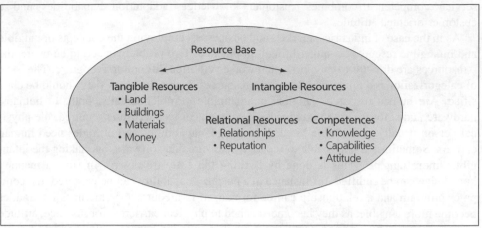

(handwritten marginal note: explain what these resources are.)

- **Knowledge.** Knowledge can be defined as the whole of rules (know-how, know-what, know-where and know-when) and insights (know-why) that can be extracted from, and help make sense of, information. In other words, knowledge flows from, and influences, the interpretation of information (Dretske, 1981). Examples of knowledge that a firm can possess are market insight, competitive intelligence, technological expertise, and understanding of political and economic developments.

- **Capability.** Capability refers to the organization's potential for carrying out a specific activity or set of activities. Sometimes the term 'skill' is used to refer to the ability to carry out a narrow (functional) task or activity, while the term 'capability' is reserved for the quality of combining a number of skills. For instance, a firm's capability base can include narrower abilities such as market research, advertising and production skills, that if coordinated could result in a capability for new product development (Stalk, Evans and Shulman, 1992).

- **Attitude.** Attitude refers to the mind-set prevalent within an organization. Sometimes the terms 'disposition' and 'will' are used in the same sense, to indicate how an organization views and relates to the world. Although ignored by some writers, every sports coach will acknowledge the importance of attitude as a resource. A healthy body (tangible resource), insight into the game (knowledge), speed and dexterity (capabilities) – all are important, but without the winning mentality a team will not get to the top. Some attitudes may change rapidly within firms, yet others may be entrenched within the cultural fabric of the organization – these in particular can be important resources for the firm. A company's attitude can, for instance, be characterized as quality-driven, internationally oriented, innovation-minded and/or competitively aggressive.

It must be noted that the term 'competences' is used in many different ways, partially due to the ambiguous definition given by its early proponents (Prahalad and Hamel, 1990, Reading 6.2 in this book). It is often used as a synonym for capabilities, while Prahalad and Hamel seem to focus more on technologically oriented capabilities ('how to coordinate diverse production skills and integrate multiple streams of technologies'). Others (e.g. Durand, 1996) have suggested that a firm has a competence in a certain area, when the firm's underlying knowledge base, capabilities and attitude are all aligned. So, Honda's engine competence is built on specific knowledge, development capabilities and the right predisposition. Wal-Mart's inventory control competence depends on specific information technology knowledge, coordination capabilities and a conducive state of mind. Virgin's service competence combines customer knowledge, adaptation capabilities and a customer-oriented attitude.

As in the case of industries, markets and businesses, employing the concepts of tangible and intangible resources is quite difficult in practice. Two problems need to be overcome – resources are difficult to categorize, but worse yet, often difficult to recognize. The issue of categorization is a minor one. For some resources it is unclear how they should be classified. Are human resources tangible or intangible? Problematically, both. In humans, hardware and software are intertwined – if an engineer's expertise is required, the physical person usually needs to be hired. Knowledge, capabilities and attitudes need human carriers. Sometimes it is possible to separate hardware and software, by making the intangibles more tangible. This is done by 'writing the software down'. In such a manner, knowledge can be codified, for instance in a patent, a capability can be captured in a computer program and a relationship can be formalized in a contract. Sometimes intangibles become more tangible, as they become attached to physical carriers – for instance, attitude can be embodied by a person or a symbol, while reputation becomes attached to a brand.

More important is the problem of resource identification. Tangible resources, by their very nature, are relatively easy to observe. Accountants keep track of the financial resources, production managers usually know the quality of their machinery and stock levels, while the personnel department will have an overview of all people on the payroll. Intangible resources, on the other hand, are far more difficult to identify (e.g. Grant, 1991; Itami, 1987). With whom does the firm have a relationship and what is the state of this relationship? What is the firm's reputation? These relational resources are hard to pin down. Competences are probably even more difficult to determine. How do you know what you know? Even for an individual it is a formidable task to outline areas of expertise, let alone for a more complex organization. Especially the *tacit* (non-articulated) nature of much organizational knowledge makes it difficult to identify the firm's knowledge base (Polanyi, 1958; Nonaka and Konno, 1998). The same is true for a firm's capabilities, which have developed in the form of organizational routines (Nelson and Winter, 1982). Likewise, the firm's attitudes are difficult to discern, because all people sharing the same disposition will tend to consider themselves normal and will tend to believe that their outlook is 'a matter of common sense' (see Chapter 2). Hence, firms intent on identifying their competences find that this is not an easy task.

While an overview of the firm's resource base is important in itself, a strategizing manager will want to compare the firm's resources to other companies to determine their relative strength. In other words, are the firm's resources unique, superior to or inferior to the resources of (potential) competitors? This type of analysis is particularly difficult, as comparison requires insight into other firms' resource bases. Especially the identification of other firms' intangible resources can be quite arduous.

Sustaining competitive advantage

A firm has a competitive advantage when it has the means to edge out rivals when vying for the favor of customers. In the previous sub-sections it was argued that competitive advantage is rooted in a unique business system, whereby the resource base, activity system and product–market position are all aligned to provide goods and/or services with a superior fit to customer needs.

A competitive advantage is said to be sustainable if it cannot be copied, substituted or eroded by the actions of rivals, and is not made redundant by developments in the environment (Porter, 1980). In other words, sustainability depends on two main factors, competitive defendability and environmental consonance:

■ Competitive defendability. Some competitive advantages are intrinsically easier to defend than others, either because they are difficult for rivals to imitate, or because rivals find it next to impossible to find an alternative route of attack. In general, a firm's competitive advantage is more vulnerable when it is based on only a limited number of distinct elements (e.g. a different packaging technology, a different delivery system or different product colors). For rivals, imitating or substituting a few elements is comparatively easy. If, however, a firm's business system has an entirely different configuration altogether, the barriers to imitation and substitution are much higher. In such a case, it is said that a firm has a distinct 'business model'. So, for instance, in the airline industry the traditional firms have tried to imitate some parts of the low cost service of Southwest in the United States, and Ryanair and easyJet in Europe, but have been largely unsuccessful because their business model as a whole is based on a different logic. Yet, many strategists note that the best defense is not to build walls around a competitive position to 'keep the barbarians out', but to have the ability to run faster than rivals – to be able to upgrade one's resources, activity system and product offering more rapidly than competitors. In this view, a competitive advantage is sustainable due to a company's capacity to stay one step ahead of rivals, *outpacing* them in a race to stay ahead (e.g. Gilbert and Strebel, 1989; Stalk, Evans and Shulman, 1992).

■ Environmental consonance. The sustainability of a firm's competitive advantage is also threatened by developments in the market. Customer needs and wants are in constant flux, distribution channels can change, government regulations can be altered, innovative technologies can be introduced and new entrants can come into the competitive arena. All of these developments can undermine the fit between the firm's competitive advantage and the environment, weakening the firm's position (Rumelt, 1980).

Yet, these two factors for sustaining competitive advantage seem to pose opposite demands on the organization. Building a distinctive business system to fend off competition would suggest that a firm should remain true to its fundamental *strengths*, especially when it comes to unique resources and activities that it has built up over a prolonged period of time. On the other hand, environmental consonance requires a firm to continually adapt its business system to the demands and new *opportunities* in the market place. The tension created by these opposite pressures will be discussed in the following section.

THE PARADOX OF MARKETS AND RESOURCES

Sell where you can, you are not for all markets.

As You Like It, William Shakespeare (1564–1616); English dramatist and poet

There must be a fit between an organization and its environment. This point is often expressed in terms of the classic SWOT analysis tool, which suggests that a sound strategy should match a firm's strengths (S) and weaknesses (W) to the opportunities (O) and threats (T) encountered in the firm's environment. The key to success is *alignment* of the two sides. Yet, fitting internal strengths and weaknesses to external opportunities and threats is often frustrated by the fact that the two sides pull in opposite directions – the distinctive resource base and activity system of a firm can point in a totally different direction compared with the developments in their current markets. Take the example of Bally, in the 1990s the worldwide market leader in pinball machines. Their strength in the manufacturing of electromechanical games was no longer aligned with developments in the market, where young people were turning to video games produced by companies such as Nintendo, Sega and Sony. As sales of pinball machines were quickly deteriorating, it was clear that Bally had to find a new fit with the market to survive. On the one hand, this meant that there was a strong pressure on Bally to adapt to market developments, for instance by upgrading its technology to also produce video games. On the other hand, Bally felt a strong pressure to exploit its current strength in electromechanical manufacturing, instead of building a new competence base from scratch. It was not self-evident for Bally how the demands for market adaptation and resource leveraging could be met simultaneously, as they seemed to be tugging the firm in diametrically opposite directions.

This tension arising from the partially conflicting demands of market adaptation and resource leveraging is referred to as the paradox of markets and resources. In the following sub-sections both sides of the paradox will be examined in more detail.

The demand for market adaptation

While adaptation to the environment is a vital requirement for the success of any organization, Bally had been very slow in responding to external developments ever since the introduction of Pac-Man. Bally had not exhibited the ability to shift its product offering to follow changing customer preferences and to respond to new entrants in the gaming market. It had lost its leading position because it no longer fully understood 'the rules of the game' in its own market. As Bally drifted further and further away from developments in the market, the misalignment was threatening the survival of its business. 'Game over' was impending.

To counter this downward trend, Bally needed to identify an attractive market opportunity that it could exploit. Not a short-term sales opportunity, but a market position that could be defended against rival firms and potential new entrants over a longer period. Ideally, this market position would serve buyers willing and able to pay a premium price, and whose loyalty could be won, despite the efforts of the competition. This market position would also need to be largely immune to substitute products and should not make the firm overly dependent on strong suppliers. Once such an opportunity had been identified, it would be essential for Bally to reorganize itself to fully meet the demands of this new positioning.

Adapting to a new market position and subsequently following the many shifts in such factors as customer preferences, competitor moves, government regulations and distribution structures, can have a significant impact on a firm. It requires significant agility in changing the product offering, activity system and resource base to remain in constant alignment with the fluctuating external circumstances. For Bally, adapting to the digital technology and software environment of the current gaming industry would have had far-reaching consequences for its entire business system. Even if Bally decided to stick to electromechanical pinball machines and to target the home market of aging pinball wizards, the company would need to make significant alterations to its business system, getting to know new distribution channels and developing new marketing competences.

The demand for resource leveraging

Yet, for Bally it was essential to build on the resource base and activity system that it had already developed. It did not want to write off the investments it had made in building up a distinctive profile – it had taken years of acquiring and nurturing resources and fine-tuning the activity system to reach its level of expertise. Its strength in electromechanical manufacturing and the development of large 'moving parts' games was much too valuable to casually throw away just because video games were currently in fashion.

However, building a new area of competence, it was understood, should not be considered lightly. It would take a considerable amount of time, effort and money to shift the resource base and reconfigure the activity system, while there would be many risks associated with this transformation process as well. On the other hand, the danger of attempting to exploit the firm's current resources would be to excel at something of increasing irrelevance. The pinball machine might be joining the buggy whip and the vacuum tube as a museum exhibit, with a real threat that Bally too could become history.

Eventually, the solution found by Bally was to give up on pinball machines altogether and to redirect its existing resources towards a much more attractive market opportunity – slot machines. This move allowed Bally to exploit its electromechanical manufacturing capability and game-making expertise, while building a strong market position in a fast growing market. But while Bally was able to find a synthesis, reconciling the two conflicting demands, not all companies are as successful. Nor do all managers agree on how the paradox of markets and resources can best be tackled.

EXHIBIT 5.1 SHORT CASE

AVON: KEEP THOSE DOORBELLS RINGING?

Few powers in the world can field an army of three million, with the ability to reach each corner of the globe. Yet, one organization has such a legion, spread across 143 countries, equipped to engage in close-range encounters, toting little more than some cosmetics samples and a few brochures. This superpower is Avon, the world's largest direct seller of beauty-related products. With 2002 annual sales exceeding US$6 billion, of which more than 60% was outside of North America, Avon is a huge player in the global market for cosmetics, fragrances and toiletries. The New York-based company has a large presence in Europe (about US$2 billion sales) and Latin America (more than US$1 billion sales), with major growth coming from emerging markets such as China. While Avon is generally known for its beauty products, more than 20% of its sales come from fashion jewelry, accessories and apparel, with another 15% realized in the areas of gifts, decorative items and home entertainment.

From its start in 1886 as the California Perfume Company, the firm has been based on the concept of independent sales representatives selling directly to women. These sales reps are independent intermediaries, who buy from Avon at a discount and then resell to their clients at list price. While men are not excluded as sales people, only a small fraction of the 'Avon Ladies' are not female. In the early years most of the sales were done 'door-to-door', making the 1950s slogan 'Ding Dong, Avon Calling' quite appropriate. Since then, large numbers of women have shifted to paid employment in most of Avon's

major markets and the company has followed them, making about a third of all sales at work. Yet, Avon's positioning has remained basically the same as at the outset – quality beauty products are provided to women of average and below average income at competitive prices, while offering personal attention and advice.

In 1999 Andrea Jung became Avon's CEO – the first female in the company's history to occupy the top job, but reflective of a management pyramid composed of more than 50% women. With years of experience in the company, Jung was acutely aware that Avon was facing a difficult battle on many fronts, particularly in its mature North American and Western European markets. On the competitive front, a number of early movers in the e-business domain, like Eve.com, ibeauty.com and women.com, had caught Avon off guard, by building up a strong direct sales channel over the Internet, while Avon had hardly taken any initiatives in this direction. At the same time, new cosmetics retailers were developing, such as the Sephora superstores in the United States, and in many countries the fragmented retailing sector was being consolidated and further professionalized. On the consumer front, Avon's brand was perceived as stale and down market, particularly by fashion-conscious younger women. Despite years of efforts to revitalize the brand, for many women Avon retained the connotation of the 1950s housewife. As Jung's predecessor, James Preston, confessed: 'I am well aware that there are many women who would not want to open their purses and pull out Avon lipstick.' To compound the image problem, Avon was finding it increasingly difficult to find new, younger recruits as Avon Ladies. For years the sales force in the mature markets had been shrinking, as younger women no longer had plenty of spare time to sell beauty products, or had better-paying alternatives open to them.

To counter these strategic weaknesses, Jung set out to bring about a 'thoughtful transformation' of Avon. Her first priority was to rejuvenate the Avon brand, and a new advertising campaign was launched around the slogan 'Let's Talk', a new tag line was added to the Avon logo ('The Company for Women'), packaging was upgraded, to create a Lancôme or Estee Lauder type luxury feel to the products and brochures were restyled to fit the new image. Jung also carried through some drastic business process redesign activities, streamlining production and logistics, indicating that she wanted to cut 8% of the workforce (3800 positions) by 2004.

Another important move Jung set out to implement was to strengthen the sales force, both in numbers and in quality. To improve the quality, Jung initiated the Beauty Advisor program, aimed at training tens of thousands of salespeople each year in the areas of beauty product knowledge and consultative selling skills. To increase the number of sales women was much more difficult since Avon, like most direct sales companies, experienced a nearly 100% turnover of its sales force each year. A core group of sales representatives – the President's Club – form the backbone of the system, generally selling full-time for many years, while the other 80% are part-timers that on average stay less than one year. To recruit more than two million salespeople each year is quite an effort, especially since Avon is not a 'network marketing' organization in which each sales representative can recruit their own resellers (multi-level sales structure). As Avon has a single level sales organization, more management time must be spent finding and training new recruits. To get the existing salespeople to assist with this task, Jung introduced a 'Sales Leadership' program, offering significant bonuses for contributing to the expansion of the sales force.

But with pressure to grow and to improve profitability, more was needed than these realignment measures. Jung was convinced that organic growth through the direct sales channels would be too limited in scale and would not catapult Avon into the top league. Therefore, Jung introduced the slogan, 'The brand is bigger than the channel', and started to look for ways to become a multi-channel company. An early experiment was the initiative to start free-standing beauty kiosks in more than 50 shopping malls around the United States, to bring shoppers into contact with Avon products. In 2000, a hugely updated Avon.com was relaunched, which allowed each sales rep to run their personalized web site, making use of the Avon platform. Much more surprisingly, Avon announced that it would be moving into retail channels, launching an entirely new, upmarket product line called beComing in 125 Sears Roebuck stores in the United States in 2001. When Sears withdrew from this agreement because of a shift in strategy, Jung signed a deal with retailer J.C. Penney to have an Avon 'store-within-a-store' at 92 locations across the United States, all focusing on the beComing line of beauty products and fashion accessories. Jung emphasized that by developing a separate, premium product line, Avon would be able to access a group of consumers not yet served by the company, without conflicting with the interests of the direct sales channel.

Next to the new beComing product line, 2001 also saw the introduction of Avon Wellness, a line of health and wellness products, including vitamins, nutritional supplements, exercise and fitness items, and self-care and stress relief items. These products were placed in a separate brochure, but were intended to be sold through the existing direct sales channel, as well as in the retail outlets.

In 2002, Avon announced that it intended to target yet another difficult, but tantalizingly lucrative, market – teenage girls and young women. Noting that females between 16 and 24 in its top 20 markets spend US$200 billion on consumer goods annually, Avon outlined a plan to develop a line of several hundred different cosmetics and related products, under the new brand name 'mark', to be launched in the United States in 2003 and globally in 2004. An integral part of this plan was to recruit teenage girls and young women into the Avon sales force to be able to sell to the target group, as well as setting up a separate system of 'mark' salespeople, to visit colleges, high schools, shopping malls and other youth-oriented spots. To run this entire operation a new unit, Avon Future, was established.

By the beginning of 2003, things seemed to be going well for Avon. The economic downturn in many of its key markets in 2002 had actually largely worked in its favor, as many women turned to its lower priced products, while others looked for part-time employment as sales representative to prop up their sagging income. Then, fairly suddenly, Avon and J.C. Penney announced that they were ending their retail alliance, and Avon indicated that it would be selling its beComing product line exclusively through its certified Avon Beauty Advisors. According to Jung 'research confirms that consumer reaction to this prestige brand has been very positive. By offering beComing through our core business, we expect to accelerate sales of the brand, advance earnings of our Beauty Advisors, and attract new customers.' However, she denied that this meant the end of Avon's retail adventure: 'Avon remains committed to a multi-brand, multi-channel strategy and we will continue to pursue opportunities to reach new customer segments that prefer a retail shopping experience,' adding that Avon's retail president, Steve Bock, was not out of a job.

Yet, the company seemed at a crossroads. Some critical observers wondered out loud whether Avon had not overstretched itself, pursuing too many divergent growth directions at the same time. At the very least it seemed that Jung would have to set clear priorities for the coming period. On the one hand, Avon could focus on the challenge of expanding and upgrading its direct sales organization to carry two new brands (beComing and mark), reaching new market segments (more affluent women and younger women) and carrying new products (for instance Avon Wellness products). This would mean that in its core, Avon would remain a direct sales organization, building on this traditional strength. On the other hand, Avon could stay on the earlier track of becoming a multi-brand, multi-channel beauty company, to make optimal use of the market opportunities identified, but then the company would need to do some serious work to achieve this objective. Whichever focus was pursued, the challenges for the coming years seemed large, calling for some clear strategic choices, not merely a cosmetic touch up.

Sources: Avon annual reports 1997–2001; Avon.com; *Fortune*, October 15 2001; *Business Week*, August 20 2002 and January 13 2003.

PERSPECTIVES ON BUSINESS LEVEL STRATEGY

Always to be best, and to be distinguished above the rest.

The Iliad, Homer (8th century BC); Greek poet

Firms need to adapt themselves to market developments and they need to build on the strengths of their resource bases and activity systems. The main question dividing managers is 'who should be fitted to whom' – should an organization adapt itself to its environment or should it attempt to adapt the environment to itself? What should be the dominant factor driving a firm, its strengths or the opportunities? Should managers take the environment as the starting point, choose an advantageous market position and then build the resource base and activity system necessary to implement this choice? Or should managers take the organization's resource base (and possibly also its activity system) as the starting point, selecting and/or adapting an environment to fit with these strengths?

As before, the strategic management literature comes with strongly different views on how managers should proceed. The variety of opinions among strategy theorists is dauntingly large, with many incompatible prescriptions being given. Here the two diametrically opposed positions will be identified and discussed in order to show the richness of differing opinions. On the one side of the spectrum, there are those managers who argue that the market opportunities should be leading, while implying that the organization should adapt itself to the market position envisioned. This point of view is called the 'outside-in perspective'. At the other end of the spectrum, many managers believe that competition eventually revolves around rival resource bases and that firms must focus their strategies on the development of unique resources and activity systems. They argue that product–market positioning is a tactical decision that can be taken later. This view is referred to as the 'inside-out perspective'.

The outside-in perspective

Managers with an outside-in perspective believe that firms should not be self-centered, but should continuously take their environment as the starting point when determining their strategy. Successful companies, it is argued, are externally oriented and market-driven (e.g. Day, 1990; Webster, 1994). They have their sights clearly set on developments in the market-place and are determined to adapt to the unfolding opportunities and threats encountered. They take their cues from customers and competitors, and use these signals to determine their own game plan (Jaworski and Kohli, 1993). For these successful companies, markets are leading, resources are following.

Therefore, for the outside-in directed manager, developing strategy begins with an analysis of the environment to identify attractive market opportunities. Potential customers must be sought, whose needs can be satisfied more adequately than currently done by other firms. Once these customers have been won over and a market position has been established, the firm must consistently defend or build on this position by adapting itself to changes in the environment. Shifts in customers' demands must be met, challenges from rival firms must be countered, impending market entries by outside firms must be rebuffed and excessive pricing by suppliers must be resisted. In short, to the outside-in manager the game of strategy is about market positioning and understanding and responding to external developments. For this reason, the outside-in perspective is sometimes also referred to as the 'positioning approach' (Mintzberg, Ahlstrand and Lampel, 1998).

Positioning is not short-term, opportunistic behavior, but requires a strategic perspective, because superior market positions are difficult to attain, but once conquered can be the source of sustained profitability. Some proponents of the outside-in perspective argue that in each market a number of different positions can yield sustained profitability. For instance, Porter suggests that companies that focus on a particular niche, and companies that strongly differentiate their product offering, can achieve strong and profitable market positions, even if another company has the lowest cost position (Porter, 1980, 1985; Reading 5.1). Other authors emphasize that the position of being market leader is particularly important (e.g. Buzzell and Gale, 1987). Companies with a high market share profit more from economies of scale, benefit from risk aversion among customers, have more bargaining power towards buyers and suppliers, and can more easily flex their muscles to prevent new entrants and block competitive attacks.

Unsurprisingly, proponents of the outside-in perspective argue that insight into markets and industries is essential. Not only the general structure of markets and industries needs to be analyzed, but also the specific demands, strengths, positions and intentions of all major forces need to be determined. For instance, buyers must be understood with regard to their needs, wants, perceptions, decision-making processes and bargaining chips. The same holds true for suppliers, competitors, potential market and/or industry entrants and providers of substitute products (Porter, 1980, 1985; Reading 5.1). Once a manager knows 'what makes the market tick' – sometimes referred to as the 'rules of the game' – a position can be identified within the market that could give the firm bargaining power vis-à-vis suppliers and buyers, while keeping competitors at bay. Of course, the wise manager will not only emphasize winning under the current rules with the current players, but will attempt to anticipate market and industry developments, and position the firm to benefit from these. Many outside-in advocates even advise firms to initiate market and industry changes, so that they can be the first to benefit from the altered rules of the game (this issue will be discussed further in Chapter 8).

Proponents of the outside-in perspective readily acknowledge the importance of firm resources and activities for cashing in on market opportunities the firm has identified. If the firm does not have, or is not able to develop or obtain, the necessary resources to implement a particular strategy, then specific opportunities will be unrealizable. Therefore, managers should always keep the firm's strengths and weaknesses in mind when choosing an external position, to ensure that it remains feasible. Yet, to the outside-in strategist, the firm's current resource base should not be the starting point when determining strategy, but should merely be acknowledged as a potentially limiting condition on the firm's ability to implement the best business strategy.

Actually, firms that are market-driven are often the first ones to realize that new resources and/or activities need to be developed and, therefore, are better positioned to build up a 'first mover advantage' (Lieberman and Montgomery, 1988, 1998). Where the firm does not have the ability to catch up with other firms' superior resources, it can always enter into an alliance with a leading organization, offering its partner a crack at a new market opportunity.

KODAK: REFOCUSING ON DIGITAL IMAGING

In 1888, inventor and entrepreneur George Eastman launched a new type of photographic camera that was pre-loaded with a roll of the light-sensitive film he had recently invented. This 'Kodak' camera marked the start of snapshot photography and ever since then the Kodak company has been inspired by Eastman's sales slogan, 'You push the button – we do the rest'. Kodak has been at the forefront of technological developments in photography, introducing color film, pocketsize cameras and photo-developing machines. Along the way, the company diversified into the related chemicals business, and from there into pharmaceuticals. By the beginning of the 1990s, Kodak was an unwieldy giant, with more than 100 000 employees, where innovation and market adaptation were slow, and growth and profitability were under pressure.

Then came the impending digital revolution. Kodak's picture-making technology was chemical-based, while the upcoming technology was IT-based, requiring different cameras and different 'information carriers'. The new digital imaging technologies promised to shake up the value system in the industry, as there would be no more need for film developers. For Kodak the initial question was how deeply its markets might be penetrated by the rival technology. Would digital imaging be largely confined to the high-end 'studio' market for professional photographers, or would it be equally successful among the midrange segment of photo-journalists and serious hobbyists? Or might it even invade the 'Point 'n Shoot' part of the market, where Kodak's 35mm film has a dominant position? Furthermore, Kodak needed to assess whether it could develop digital imaging capabilities of its own, strong enough to compete with such battle-hardened, digital savvy companies as Canon, Apple, Sony and Hewlett Packard. Not only would Kodak need to catch up technologically, but they would also need to adapt to their competitors' grueling pace of competence-building and new product development.

Alternatively, Kodak could ignore these new market developments and not step into the digital imaging 'free fighting' arena. Despite potential inroads that digital imaging might make, worldwide film sales were still predicted to grow slightly until 2000. Rather, it could look for ways to build on the chemical and printing competences it already possessed.

But this was not Kodak's perspective – they wanted to remain the world's leading imaging company, whatever competences and activity system that would require. So, ex-Motorola CEO, George Fischer was hired in 1993 and he set out to transform Kodak into a digital company. He divested Kodak's chemical and pharmaceutical businesses and poured most of the R&D budget into digital imaging technologies. Where key competences were lacking, alliances were established, for instance with Adobe (software), Hewlett Packard (inkjet printing), IBM (optical storage) and Wang (document architecture). The first digital camera for consumers was introduced in 1995, followed by a flood of new digital products and services since then. When in 2000 a successor to Fischer was sought, long-time Kodak insider Daniel Carp was selected, particularly because of his market-driven mentality.

According to Carp, 'the digital world opened up a treasure chest of possibilities . . . our strong business in traditional photography will allow us to fund our digital strategy for the long term'. In 2003 the company invested two-thirds of its US$900 million

R&D budget in digital technology, stating that within the next decade about half of Kodak's revenues should come from the digital market. According to Carp: 'We are developing new tools and new software across all digital areas. These tools will give our customers what we call the "Digital Wow Factor".'

Sources: www.kodak.com; Kodak annual reports 2000–2002; *Photo Industry Reporter*, various issues 2002–2003; *Business Week*, August 2 1999 and January 8 2003.

The inside-out perspective

Managers adopting an inside-out perspective believe that strategies should not be built around external opportunities, but around a company's strengths. Successful companies, it is argued, build up a strong resource base over an extended period of time, which offers them access to unfolding market opportunities in the medium and short term. For such companies, the starting point of the strategy formation process is the question of which resource base it wants to have. The fundamental strategic issue is which difficult-to-imitate competences and exclusive assets should be acquired and/or further refined. Creating such a resource platform requires major investments and a long breath, and to a large extent will determine the culture and identity of the organization. Hence, it is of the utmost importance and should be the central tenet of a firm's strategy. Once the long-term direction for the building of the resource infrastructure has been set, attention can be turned to identifying market opportunities where these specific strengths can be exploited. To the inside-out oriented manager the issue of market positioning is essential, as only a strong competitive position in the market will result in above-average profitability. However, market positioning must take place within the context of the broader resource-based strategy and not contradict the main thrust of the firm – selected market positions must leverage the existing resource base, not ignore it. In other words, market positioning is vital, but tactical, taking place within the boundaries set by the resource-driven strategy. For success, resources should be leading, and markets following.

Many managers taking an inside-out perspective tend to emphasize the importance of a firm's competences over its tangible resources (physical assets). Their way of looking at strategy is referred to as the competence-based view (e.g. Prahalad and Hamel, 1990, Reading 6.2; Sanchez, Heene and Thomas, 1996) or capabilities-based view (e.g. Stalk, Evans and Shulman, 1992; Teece, Pisano and Shuen, 1997). These managers point out that it is especially the development of unique abilities that is such a strenuous and lengthy process, more so than the acquisition of physical resources, such as production facilities and computer systems. Some companies might be able to achieve a competitive advantage based on physical assets, but usually such tangible infrastructure is easily copied or purchased. However, competences are not readily for sale on the open market as 'plug-and-play' components, but need to be painstakingly built up by an organization through hard work and experience. Even where a company takes a short cut by buying another organization or engaging in an alliance, it takes significant time and effort to internalize the competences in such a way that they can be put to productive use. Hence, having distinctive competences can be a very attractive basis for competitive advantage, as rival firms generally require a long time to catch up (e.g. Collis and Montgomery, 1995; Barney, 1991, Reading 5.4). And even if competitors are successful at identifying embedded competences and imitating them, the company with an initial lead can work at upgrading its competences in a race to stay ahead – this is often referred to as the dynamic capabilities view (Teece, Pisano and Shuen, 1997).

To proponents of the inside-out perspective the 'dynamic capabilities' argument accentuates the importance of committing the organization to the long-term development of a limited set of competences in which it can stay ahead of rivals. The 'nightmare scenario' for inside-out oriented strategists is where the firm flexibly shifts from one market demand to the next, building up an eclectic collection of unrelated competences, none of which are distinctive compared to competence-focused companies. In this scenario, a firm is fabulously market-driven, adaptively responding to shifts in the environment, but incapable of concentrating itself on forming the distinctive competence base needed for a robust competitive advantage over the longer term.

Most inside-out oriented managers also recognize the 'shadow side' of competences – they are not only difficult to learn, but difficult to unlearn as well. The laborious task of building up competences makes it hard to switch to new competences, even if that is what the market demands (e.g. Christensen, 1997; Rumelt, 1996). Companies far down the route of competence specialization, find themselves locked in by the choices made in the past. In the same way as few concert pianists are able (and willing) to switch to playing saxophone when they are out of a job, few companies are able and willing to scrap their competence base, just because the market is taking a turn for the worse. Becoming a concert pianist not only costs years of practice but is a way of life, with a specific way of working, network and career path, making it very unattractive to make a mid-career shift towards a more marketable trade. Likewise, companies experience that their core competences can simultaneously be their core rigidities, locking them out of new opportunities (Leonard-Barton, 1995). From an inside-out perspective, both companies and concert pianists should therefore first try to build on their unique competences and attempt to find or create a more suitable market, instead of reactively adapting to the unpredictable whims of the current environment (see Figure 5.8).

FIGURE 5.8 Two perspectives on shaping the business system

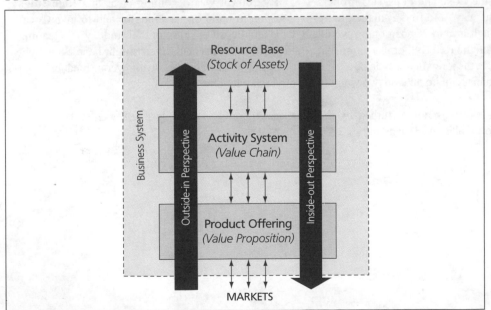

EXHIBIT 5.3 THE INSIDE-OUT PERSPECTIVE

RED BULL: BULLISH ABOUT ITS OWN WINGS

In the early 1980s, Dietrich Mateschitz, an Austrian traveling through South-East Asia, came across a local 'energy drink', containing ingredients such as taurine, caffeine and vitamins, and his entrepreneurial interest was directly spurred. Based on this example, he launched his own silver-canned energy drink, 'Red Bull', in 1987, starting an entirely new global beverage category. Soon, his little company seemed fueled by its own energy drink, and got wings. The company internationalized and experienced exponential growth throughout the 1990s. By 2001 Red Bull operated in more than 80 countries, including Japan, the United States, and most European countries, and had an estimated global market share of 70–90% in the quickly expanding energy drink category. Red Bull employed more than 1500 people, while selling 1.6 billion cans a year and realizing a turnover of €400 million.

The success of Red Bull did not go unnoticed. By the mid-1990s the first competitors entered the market with cheaper copycat products. More threatening was that the sleeping giants, Coca-Cola and PepsiCo, also awakened and moved into the branded energy drink business. Their frontal attack on Red Bull's market leadership pressured Mateschitz to explore ways to retain Red Bull's competitive advantage against the Goliaths. However, for many observers it seemed clear that Red Bull's only real option for not getting run over by the Coke and Pepsi steamrollers was to 'get out of the way' – to find a smaller, more defensible niche. Such a market positioning would have a large impact on the Red Bull organization, but it was suggested that in the long run it would be a more viable proposition than trying to take on two weighty sumo wrestlers.

However, Mateschitz was not perturbed by the prospect of taking on Coke and Pepsi, and in 2002 announced a two-pronged counter-attack. First, Mateschitz indicated that he would build further on Red Bull's existing distinctive competence, to create a slightly zany brand image and to market the experience instead of the product. To remain ahead of its lumbering competitors, Red Bull would be more agile and creative at boosting the brand. Mateschitz himself would be putting two days per week into 'generating wacky ideas' to promote Red Bull, particularly on the US home turf of Coke and Pepsi.

The second part of Red Bull's counter-attack would be to gain critical size, by introducing an entirely new drink to the market, called LunAqua. This drink, a natural spring water bottled during full moon, would be launched using the most important parts of Red Bull's resource base and activity system as its key ingredients. Crucially, Red Bull's international team of young and slightly contrarian brand-builders would cultivate an experience around LunAqua, including promotional stunts around 'full moon parties' and all types of sponsored events. Red Bull's carefully nurtured close relations with athletes and Red Bull fans would be leveraged to quickly bring LunAqua into the limelight. The Red Bull logo would also be put on the small bottle, to leverage brand awareness. Furthermore, the company would take advantage of its worldwide distribution network in retail, (sports)bars and nightclubs to get LunAqua flowing to potential customers.

By 2003 it was becoming clear that Red Bull's decision to build on its strengths and to give Coca-Cola and PepsiCo a run for their money was leading to positive results. Observers might have been right that Mateschitz and his team were 'lunatics', but obviously lunatics with wings.

Sources: *The Economist*, May 11 2002; www.red-bull.com; company reports.

INTRODUCTION TO THE DEBATE AND READINGS

One does not gain much by mere cleverness.

Marquis de Vauvenargues (1715–1747);
French soldier and moralist

Drive thy business; let it not drive thee.

Benjamin Franklin (1706–1790);
American writer and statesman

So, how can a sustainable competitive advantage be created? Should generals create a sustainable competitive advantage by first selecting a superior position in the environment (e.g. a mountain pass) and then adapt their military resources to this position, or should generals develop armies with unique resources and then try to let the battle take place where these resources can best be employed? Should football coaches first determine how they want the game to be played on the field and then attract and train players to fit with this style, or should coaches develop uniquely talented players and then adapt the team's playing style to make the best use of these resources? Whether a military, sports or business strategist, an approach to creating competitive advantage must be chosen.

As no consensus has yet developed within the field of strategic management on how to balance markets and resources, it is once again up to each individual to assess the arguments put forward in the debate and to form their own opinion. To help strategists to come to grips with the variety of perspectives on this issue, four readings have been selected that each shed their own light on the debate. As in previous chapters, the first two readings will be representative of the two poles in this debate (see Table 5.1), while the second set of two readings will bring in extra arguments to add further flavor to the discussion.

Reading 5.1, 'Competitive Strategy', has been taken from Michael Porter's 1985 book *Competitive Advantage*, but its central concepts were originally introduced in his 1980 book, *Competitive Strategy*. Since Porter is considered by all to be the most important theorist in the positioning tradition, it is only logical to start with him as representative of the outside-in perspective. In his contribution Porter argues that 'two central questions underlie the choice of competitive strategy'. First, managers must select a competitive domain with attractive characteristics and then they must position the firm vis-à-vis the five competitive forces encountered. These five forces impinging on the firm's profit potential are 'the entry of new competitors, the threat of substitutes, the bargaining power of buyers, the bargaining power of suppliers, and the rivalry among the existing competitors'. Long run above-average performance results from selecting one of the three

TABLE 5.1 Outside-in versus inside-out perspective

	Outside-in perspective	Inside-out perspective
Emphasis on	Markets over resources	Resources over markets
Orientation	Opportunity-driven (external potential)	Strength-driven (internal potential)
Starting point	Market demand and industry structure	Resource base and activity system
Fit through	Adaptation to environment	Adaptation of environment
Strategic focus	Attaining advantageous position	Attaining distinctive resources
Strategic moves	External positioning	Building resource base
Tactical moves	Acquiring necessary resources	External positioning
Competitive weapons	Bargaining power and mobility barriers	Superior resources and imitation barriers

defensible positions available to the strategist: cost leadership, differentiation or focus. According to Porter, these three options, or 'generic strategies', are the only feasible ways of achieving a sustainable competitive advantage. A firm that does not make a clear choice between one of the three generic strategies, is 'stuck in the middle' and will suffer below-average performance. For the debate in this chapter it is important to note that Porter does not explicitly advocate an exclusively outside-in approach. However, he strongly empha-sizes competitive positioning as a leading strategy principle and treats the development of firm resources as a derivative activity. Indirectly, therefore, his message to managers is that in the game of strategy it is essential to be focused on the external dynamics.

As representative of the inside-out perspective, a recent article (Reading 5.2) by Danny Miller, Russell Eisenstat and Nathaniel Foote has been selected, with the telling title 'Strategy From the Inside Out: Building Capability-Creating Organizations'. In this read-ing the authors start by emphasizing the value of 'skills, knowledge, processes, relation-ships, or outputs an organization possesses or produces' that are unique and difficult for competitors to copy or acquire – which in this book are called 'resources', but Miller, Eisenstat and Foote prefer to call 'asymmetries', to accentuate that they encompass all dif-ferences, even those that have not yet been turned to economic use. The thrust of the authors' argumentation is that 'by continually identifying and building on asymmetries, by nurturing and exploiting these within a complementary organizational design, and by leveraging them via an appropriate market focus, companies may be able to aspire realis-tically to attain sustainable competitive advantage'. To make this inside-out approach work they believe that companies must do three things well. First, they must be able to discover asymmetries and to recognize their potential. Secondly, these asymmetries must be devel-oped into a cohesive set of capabilities. Thirdly, market opportunities must be pursued that build on and leverage these capabilities. On this last point Miller, Eisenstat and Foote recognize that in the tension between markets and resources one cannot fully dominate over the other: 'Managers need to find opportunities tailored to their capabilities. Opportunities also must ultimately shape capabilities.' Yet, while they underline the value of mutual adjustment between markets and resources, they do reiterate that asymmetries and capabilities should be the drivers of this processes, not created somewhere along the line on the basis of a perceived opportunity. An important additional point brought up by the authors is that capabilities can be leveraged across two or more business units. This makes capability-based approaches to strategy equally relevant to corporate level strategy as to business level strategy (in Chapter 6, Prahalad and Hamel will pick up on this issue in Reading 6.2).

Since the early 1990s, the resource-based view of the firm has increasingly come to dominate the field of strategic management. Consequently, implicit support of the inside-out perspective on business strategy has also grown strongly. Interestingly, on the other side of the fence, in the field of marketing, the outside-in perspective is still widely expounded. Almost simultaneously with the strategy field's emphasis on resource-driven strategies, the marketing field has huddled around the concept of market-driven strategy (e.g. Jaworski and Kohli, 1993; Slater and Narver, 1998; Webster, 1994). In an effort to avoid disciplinary myopia and to keep the debate on the paradox of markets and resources open to all challenging points of view, one of the best contributions from the field of marketing has been incorporated into the chapter as Reading 5.3. In this paper, 'The Capabilities of Market-Driven Organizations', George Day argues that not all capabilities are inside-out in orientation. Capabilities in the areas of manufacturing, logistics, technol-ogy development, finances and human resource management are deployed from the inside-out, but likewise there are outside-in capabilities, such as market sensing, customer linking, channel bonding and technology monitoring. He also distinguishes spanning capa-bilities, such as purchasing, new product development and strategy development, that link inside-out and outside-in capabilities. According to Day, in a market-driven organization outside-in capabilities should 'inform and guide both spanning and inside-out capabilities'. Although he just stops short of advocating a dominant role for outside-in capabilities, it is clear that he believes that in a market-driven organization all activities become more externally oriented. In the context of the discussion in this chapter, Day's article makes more tangible what an outside-in oriented company is like, and indirectly what the profile is of an inside-out oriented company.

While much of the theoretical underpinning of the inside-out perspective comes from a stream of literature known under the umbrella term 'resource-based view of the firm', little attention has so far been paid to its fundamentals. Miller, Eisenstat and Foote also use some of the key ideas of this body of literature to build up their argument, but do not really explain the essence of this school of thought. Therefore, to add further depth to the discussion, an often-cited article by Jay Barney has been selected as a more thorough introduction to the resource-based view. In Reading 5.4, 'Firm Resources and Sustained Competitive Advantage', Barney differentiates resource-based models of competitive advantage from the Porter-like environmental models. He does not dismiss externally oriented explanations of profitability, but wishes to explore the internally oriented explanation that idiosyncratic firm resources are at the base of superior performance. He sets out on this task by pinpointing the two fundamental assumptions on which the resource-based view rests – that firms have different resources (*resource heterogeneity*) and that these resources cannot be easily transferred to, or copied by, other firms (*resource immobility*). He goes on to argue that these resources can be the basis of competitive advantage if they meet four criteria: they must be valuable and rare, while being difficult to imitate and substitute.

For readers the challenge now is to turn the arguments 'inside-out' and 'outside-in', and to determine themselves how to approach the topic of business level strategy.

READING

5.1

Competitive strategy

By Michael Porter[1]

Competition is at the core of the success or failure of firms. Competition determines the appropriateness of a firm's activities that can contribute to its performance, such as innovations, a cohesive culture, or good implementation. Competitive strategy is the search for a favorable competitive position in an industry, the fundamental arena in which competition occurs. Competitive strategy aims to establish a profitable and sustainable position against the forces that determine industry competition.

Two central questions underlie the choice of competitive strategy. The first is the attractiveness of industries for long-term profitability and the factors that determine it. Not all industries offer equal opportunities for sustained profitability, and the inherent profitability of its industry is one essential ingredient in determining the profitability of a firm. The second central question in competitive strategy is the determinants of relative competitive position within an industry. In most industries, some firms are much more profitable than others, regardless of what the average profitability of the industry may be.

Neither question is sufficient by itself to guide the choice of competitive strategy. A firm in a very attractive industry may still not earn attractive profits if it has chosen a poor competitive position. Conversely, a firm in an excellent competitive position may be in such a poor industry that it is not very profitable, and further efforts to enhance its position will be of little benefit. Both questions are dynamic; industry attractiveness and competitive position change. Industries become more or less attractive over time, and competitive position reflects an unending battle among competitors. Even long periods of stability can be abruptly ended by competitive moves.

Both industry attractiveness and competitive position can be shaped by a firm, and this is what makes the choice of competitive strategy both challenging and exciting. While industry attractiveness is partly a reflection of factors over which a firm has little influence, competitive strategy has considerable power to make an industry more or less attractive. At the same time, a firm can clearly improve or erode its position within an industry through its choice of strategy. Competitive strategy, then, not only responds to the environment but also attempts to shape that environment in a firm's favor.

The structural analysis of industries

The first fundamental determinant of a firm's profitability is industry attractiveness. Competitive strategy must grow out of a sophisticated understanding of the rules of competition that determine an industry's attractiveness. The ultimate aim of competitive strategy is to cope with and, ideally, to change those rules in the firm's favor. In any industry, whether it is domestic or international or produces a product or a service, the rules of competition are embodied in five competitive forces: the entry of new competitors, the threat of substitutes, the bargaining power of buyers, the bargaining power of suppliers, and the rivalry among the existing competitors.

The collective strength of these five competitive forces determines the ability of firms in an industry to earn, on average, rates of return on investment in excess of the cost of capital. The strength of the five forces varies from industry to industry, and can change as an industry evolves. The result is that all industries are not alike from the standpoint of inherent profitability. In industries where the five forces are favorable, such as pharmaceuticals, soft drinks, and database publishing, many competitors earn attractive returns. But in industries where pressure from one or more of the forces is intense, such as rubber, steel, and video games, few firms command attractive returns despite the best efforts of management. Industry profitability is not a function of what the product looks like or whether it embodies high or low technology, but of industry structure. Some very mundane industries such as postage meters and grain trading are extremely profitable, while some more glamorous, high-technology

---

[1] Source: This article was adapted with the permission of the Free Press, a Division of Simon and Schuster Adult Publishing Group, from *Competitive Advantage: Creating and Sustaining Superior Performance* by Michael E. Porter. © 1985, 1998 by Michael E. Porter.

industries such as personal computers and cable television are not profitable for many participants.

The five forces determine industry profitability because they influence the prices, costs, and required investment of firms in an industry – the elements of return on investment. Buyer power influences the prices that firms can charge, for example, as does the threat of substitution. The power of buyers can also influence cost and investment, because powerful buyers demand costly service. The bargaining power of suppliers determines the costs of raw materials and other inputs. The intensity of rivalry influences prices as well as the costs of competing in areas such as plant, product development, advertising, and sales force. The threat of entry places a limit on prices, and shapes the investment required to deter entrants.

The strength of each of the five competitive forces is a function of *industry structure*, or the underlying economic and technical characteristics of an industry. Its important elements are shown in Figure 5.1.1. Industry structure is relatively stable, but can change over time as an industry evolves. Structural change shifts the overall and relative strength of the competitive forces, and can thus positively or negatively influence industry profitability. The industry trends that are the most important for strategy are those that affect industry structure.

If the five competitive forces and their structural determinants were solely a function of intrinsic industry characteristics, then competitive strategy would rest heavily on picking the right industry and understanding the five forces better than competitors. But while these are surely important tasks for any firm, and are the essence of competitive strategy in some industries, a firm is usually not a prisoner of its industry's structure. Firms, through their strategies, can influence the five forces. If a firm can shape structure, it can fundamentally change an industry's attractiveness for better or for worse. Many successful strategies have shifted the rules of competition in this way.

Figure 5.1.1 highlights all the elements of industry structure that may drive competition in an industry. In any particular industry, not all of the five forces will be equally important and the particular structural factors that are important will differ. Every industry is unique and has its own unique structure. The five-forces framework allows a firm to see through the complexity and pinpoint those factors that are critical to competition in its industry, as well as to identify those strategic innovations that would most improve the industry's – and its own – profitability. The five-forces framework does not eliminate the need for creativity in finding new ways of competing in an industry. Instead, it directs managers' creative energies toward those aspects of industry structure that are most important to long-run profitability. The framework aims, in the process, to raise the odds of discovering a desirable strategic innovation.

Strategies that change industry structure can be a double-edged sword, because a firm can destroy industry structure and profitability as readily as it can improve it. A new product design that undercuts entry barriers or increases the volatility of rivalry, for example, may undermine the long-run profitability of an industry, though the initiator may enjoy higher profits temporarily. Or a sustained period of price cutting can undermine differentiation. In the tobacco industry, for example, generic cigarettes are a potentially serious threat to industry structure. Generics may enhance the price sensitivity of buyers, trigger price competition, and erode the high advertising barriers that have kept out new entrants. Joint ventures entered into by major aluminum producers to spread risk and lower capital cost may have similarly undermined industry structure. The majors invited a number of potentially dangerous new competitors into the industry and helped them overcome the significant entry barriers to doing so. Joint ventures also can raise exit barriers because all the participants in a plant must agree before it can be closed down.

Often firms make strategic choices without considering the long-term consequences for industry structure. They see a gain in the competitive position if a move is successful, but they fail to anticipate the consequences of competitive reaction. If imitation of a move by major competitors has the effect of wrecking industry structure, then everyone is worse off. Such industry 'destroyers' are usually second-tier firms that are searching for ways to overcome major competitive disadvantages, firms that have encountered serious problems and are desperately seeking solutions, or 'dumb' competitors that do not know their costs or have unrealistic assumptions about the future. In the tobacco industry, for example, the Liggett Group (a distant follower) has encouraged the trend toward generics.

The ability of firms to shape industry structure places a particular burden on industry leaders. Leaders' actions can have a disproportionate impact on structure, because of their size and influence over buyers, suppliers, and other competitors. At the same time, leaders' large market shares guarantee that anything that changes overall industry structure will affect them as well. A leader, then, must constantly balance its own competitive position against the health of the industry

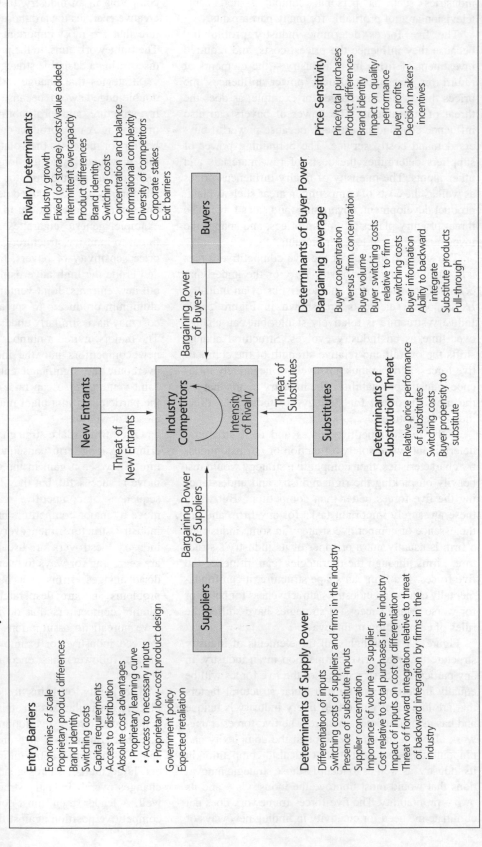

FIGURE 5.1.1 Elements of industry structure

Entry Barriers

Economies of scale
Proprietary product differences
Brand identity
Switching costs
Capital requirements
Access to distribution
Absolute cost advantages
• Proprietary learning curve
• Access to necessary inputs
• Proprietary low-cost product design
Government policy
Expected retaliation

Rivalry Determinants

Industry growth
Fixed (or storage) costs/value added
Intermittent overcapacity
Product differences
Brand identity
Switching costs
Concentration and balance
Informational complexity
Diversity of competitors
Corporate stakes
Exit barriers

Determinants of Supply Power

Differentiation of inputs
Switching costs of suppliers and firms in the industry
Presence of substitute inputs
Supplier concentration
Importance of volume to supplier
Cost relative to total purchases in the industry
Impact of inputs on cost or differentiation
Threat of forward integration relative to threat of backward integration by firms in the industry

Determinants of Buyer Power

Bargaining Leverage

Buyer concentration versus firm concentration
Buyer volume
Buyer switching costs relative to firm switching costs
Buyer information
Ability to backward integrate
Substitute products
Pull-through

Price Sensitivity

Price/total purchases
Product differences
Brand identity
Impact on quality/ performance
Buyer profits
Decision makers' incentives

Determinants of Substitution Threat

Relative price performance of substitutes
Switching costs
Buyer propensity to substitute

New Entrants
Threat of New Entrants

Industry Competitors
Intensity of Rivalry

Suppliers
Bargaining Power of Suppliers

Buyers
Bargaining Power of Buyers

Substitutes
Threat of Substitutes

as a whole. Often leaders are better off taking actions to improve or protect industry structure rather than seeking greater competitive advantage for themselves. Such industry leaders as Coca-Cola and Campbell's Soup appear to have followed this principle.

Industry structure and buyer needs

It has often been said that satisfying buyer needs is at the core of success in business endeavor. How does this relate to the concept of industry structural analysis? Satisfying buyer needs is indeed a prerequisite to the viability of an industry and the firms within it. Buyers must be willing to pay a price for a product that exceeds its cost of production, or an industry will not survive in the long run.

Satisfying buyer needs may be a prerequisite for industry profitability, but in itself is not sufficient. The crucial question in determining profitability is whether firms can capture the value they create for buyers, or whether this value is competed away to others. Industry structure determines who captures the value. The threat of entry determines the likelihood that new firms will enter an industry and compete away the value, either passing it on to buyers in the form of lower prices or dissipating it by raising the costs of competing. The power of buyers determines the extent to which they retain most of the value created for themselves, leaving firms in an industry only modest returns. The threat of substitutes determines the extent to which some other product can meet the same buyer needs, and thus places a ceiling on the amount a buyer is willing to pay for an industry's product. The power of suppliers determines the extent to which value created for buyers will be appropriated by suppliers rather than by firms in an industry. Finally, the intensity of rivalry acts similarly to the threat of entry. It determines the extent to which firms already in an industry will compete away the value they create for buyers among themselves, passing it on to buyers in lower prices or dissipating it in higher costs of competing.

Industry structure, then, determines who keeps what proportion of the value a product creates for buyers. If an industry's product does not create much value for its buyers, there is little value to be captured by firms regardless of the other elements of structure. If the product creates a lot of value, structure becomes crucial. In some industries such as automobiles and heavy trucks, firms create enormous value for their buyers but, on average, capture very little of it for themselves through profits. In other industries such as bond rating services, medical equipment, and oil field services and

equipment, firms also create high value for their buyers but have historically captured a good proportion of it. In oil field services and equipment, for example, many products can significantly reduce the cost of drilling. Because industry structure has been favorable, many firms in the oil field service and equipment sector have been able to retain a share of these savings in the form of high returns. Recently, however, the structural attractiveness of many industries in the oil field services and equipment sector has eroded as a result of falling demand, new entrants, eroding product differentiation, and greater buyer price sensitivity. Despite the fact that products offered still create enormous value for the buyer, both firm and industry profits have fallen significantly.

Industry structure and the supply/demand balance

Another commonly held view about industry profitability is that profits are a function of the balance between supply and demand. If demand is greater than supply, this leads to high profitability. Yet, the long-term supply/demand balance is strongly influenced by industry structure, as are the consequences of a supply/demand imbalance for profitability. Hence, even though short-term fluctuations in supply and demand can affect short-term profitability, industry structure underlies long-term profitability.

Supply and demand change constantly, adjusting to each other. Industry structure determines how rapidly competitors add new supply. The height of entry barriers underpins the likelihood that new entrants will enter an industry and bid down prices. The intensity of rivalry plays a major role in determining whether existing firms will expand capacity aggressively or choose to maintain profitability. Industry structure also determines how rapidly competitors will retire excess supply. Exit barriers keep firms from leaving an industry when there is too much capacity, and prolong periods of excess capacity. In oil tanker shipping, for example, the exit barriers are very high because of the specialization of assets. This has translated into short peaks and long troughs of prices. Thus industry structure shapes the supply/demand balance and the duration of imbalances.

The consequences of an imbalance between supply and demand for industry profitability also differs widely depending on industry structure. In some industries, a small amount of excess capacity triggers price wars and low profitability. These are industries where there are structural pressures for intense rivalry or powerful buyers. In other industries, periods of excess capacity have relatively little impact on profitability because of favorable structure. In oil tools, ball valves, and many other oil field equipment products, for example, there has been intense price cutting during the recent sharp downturn. In drill bits, however, there has been relatively little discounting. Hughes Tool, Smith International, and Baker International are good competitors operating in a favorable industry structure. Industry structure also determines the profitability of excess demand. In a boom, for example, favorable structure allows firms to reap extraordinary profits, while a poor structure restricts the ability to capitalize on it. The presence of powerful suppliers or the presence of substitutes, for example, can mean that the fruits of a boom pass to others. Thus industry structure is fundamental to both the speed of adjustment of supply to demand and the relationship between capacity utilization and profitability.

Generic competitive strategies

The second central question in competitive strategy is a firm's relative position within its industry. Positioning determines whether a firm's profitability is above or below the industry average. A firm that can position itself well may earn high rates of return even though industry structure is unfavorable and the average profitability of the industry is therefore modest.

The fundamental basis of above-average performance in the long run is *sustainable competitive advantage*. Though a firm can have a myriad strengths and weaknesses *vis-à-vis* its competitors, there are two basic types of competitive advantage a firm can possess: low cost or differentiation. The significance of any strength or weakness a firm possesses is ultimately a function of its impact on relative cost or differentiation. Cost advantage and differentiation in turn stem from industry structure. They result from a firm's ability to cope with the five forces better than its rivals.

The two basic types of competitive advantage combined with the scope of activities for which a firm seeks to achieve them lead to three *generic strategies* for achieving above-average performance in an industry: cost leadership, differentiation, and focus. The focus strategy has two variants, cost focus and differentiation focus. The generic strategies are shown in Figure 5.1.2.

Each of the generic strategies involves a fundamentally different route to competitive advantage, combining a choice about the type of competitive advantage sought with the scope of the strategic target in which competitive advantage is to be achieved. The cost leadership and differentiation strategies seek competitive advantage in a broad range of industry segments, while focus strategies aim at cost advantage (cost focus) or differentiation (differentiation focus) in a narrow segment. The specific actions required to implement each generic strategy vary widely from industry to industry, as do the feasible generic strategies in a particular industry. While selecting and implementing a generic strategy is far from simple, they are the logical routes to competitive advantage that must be probed in any industry.

The notion underlying the concept of generic strategies is that competitive advantage is at the heart of any

FIGURE 5.1.2 Three generic strategies

		Competitive Advantage	
		Lower Cost	Differentiation
Competitive Scope	Broad Target	1. Cost Leadership	2. Differentiation
	Narrow Target	3A. Cost Focus	3B. Differentiation Focus

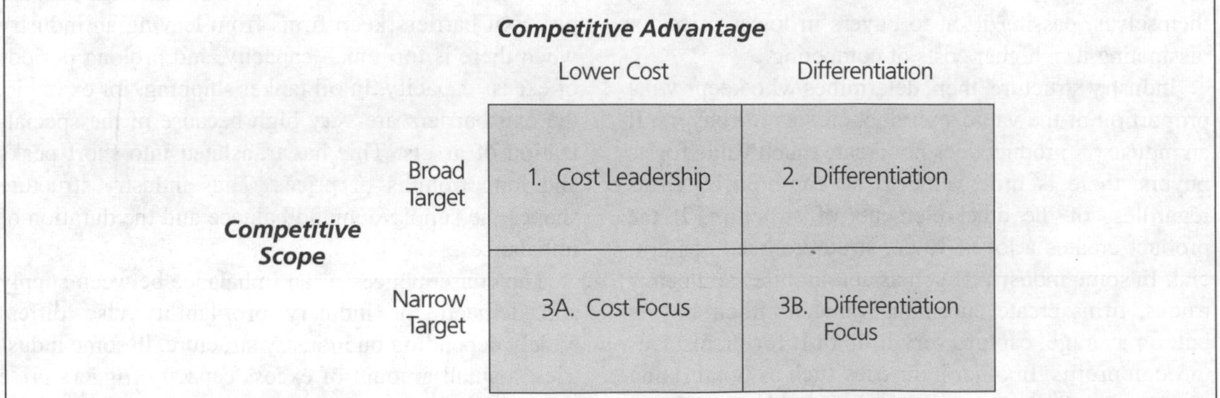

strategy, and achieving competitive advantage requires a firm to make a choice – if a firm is to attain a competitive advantage, it must make a choice about the type of competitive advantage it seeks to attain and the scope within which it will attain it. Being all things to all people is a recipe for strategic mediocrity and below-average performance, because it often means that a firm has no competitive advantage at all.

Cost leadership

Cost leadership is perhaps the clearest of the three generic strategies. In it, a firm sets out to become *the* low-cost producer in its industry. The firm has a broad scope and serves many industry segments, and may even operate in related industries – the firm's breadth is often important to its cost advantage. The sources of cost advantage are varied and depend on the structure of the industry. They may include the pursuit of economies of scale, proprietary technology, preferential access to raw materials, and other factors. In TV sets, for example, cost leadership requires efficient-size picture tube facilities, a low-cost design, automated assembly, and global scale over which to amortize research and development (R&D). In security guard services, cost advantage requires extremely low overhead, a plentiful source of low-cost labor, and efficient training procedures because of high turnover. Low-cost producer status involves more than just going down the learning curve. A low-cost producer must find and exploit all sources of cost advantage. Low-cost producers typically sell a standard, or no-frills, product and place considerable emphasis on reaping scale or absolute cost advantages from all sources.

If a firm can achieve and sustain overall cost leadership, then it will be an above-average performer in its industry provided it can command prices at or near the industry average. At equivalent or lower prices than its rivals, a cost leader's low-cost position translates into higher returns. A cost leader, however, cannot ignore the bases of differentiation. If its product is not perceived as comparable or acceptable by buyers, a cost leader will be forced to discount prices well below competitors' to gain sales. This may nullify the benefits of its favorable cost position. Texas Instruments (in watches) and Northwest Airlines (in air transportation) are two low-cost firms that fell into this trap. Texas Instruments could not overcome its disadvantage in differentiation and exited the watch industry. Northwest Airlines recognized its problem in time, and has instituted efforts to improve marketing, pas-

senger service, and service to travel agents to make its product more comparable to those of its competitors.

A cost leader must achieve *parity or proximity* in the bases of differentiation relative to its competitiors to be an above-average performer, even though it relies on cost leadership for its competitive advantage. Parity in the bases of differentiation allows a cost leader to translate its cost advantage directly into higher profits than competitors'. Proximity in differentiation means that the price discount necessary to achieve an acceptable market share does not offset a cost leader's cost advantage and hence the cost leader earns above-average returns.

The strategic logic of cost leadership usually requires that a firm be *the* cost leader, not one of several firms vying for this position. Many firms have made serious strategic errors by failing to recognize this. When there is more than one aspiring cost leader, rivalry among them is usually fierce because every point of market share is viewed as crucial. Unless one firm can gain a cost lead and 'persuade' others to abandon their strategies, the consequences for profitability (and long-run industry structure) can be disastrous, as has been the case in a number of petrochemical industries. Thus cost leadership is a strategy particularly dependent on pre-emption, unless major technological change allows a firm to radically change its cost position.

Differentiation

The second generic strategy is differentiation. In a differentiation strategy, a firm seeks to be unique in its industry along some dimensions that are widely valued by buyers. It selects one or more attributes that many buyers in an industry perceive as important, and uniquely positions itself to meet those needs. It is rewarded for its uniqueness with a premium price.

The means for differentiation are peculiar to each industry. Differentiation can be based on the product itself, the delivery system by which it is sold, the marketing approach, and a broad range of other factors. In construction equipment, for example, Caterpillar Tractor's differentiation is based on product durability, service, spare parts availability, and an excellent dealer network. In cosmetics, differentiation tends to be based more on product image and the positioning of counters in the stores.

A firm that can achieve and sustain differentiation will be an above-average performer in its industry if its price premium exceeds the extra costs incurred in being unique. A differentiator, therefore, must always seek ways of differentiating that lead to a price premium greater than the cost of differentiating. A differentiator cannot ignore its cost position, because its premium prices will be nullified by a markedly inferior cost position. A differentiator thus aims at cost parity or proximity relative to its competitors by reducing cost in all areas that do not affect differentiation.

The logic of the differentiation strategy requires that a firm choose attributes in which to differentiate itself that are *different* from its rivals'. A firm must truly be unique at something or be perceived as unique if it is to expect a premium price. In contrast to cost leadership, however, there can be more than one successful differentiation strategy in an industry if there are a number of attributes that are widely valued by buyers.

Focus

The third generic strategy is focus. This strategy is quite different from the others because it rests on the choice of a narrow competitive scope within an industry. The focuser selects a segment or group of segments in the industry and tailors its strategy to serving them to the exclusion of others. By optimizing its strategy for the target segments, the focuser seeks to achieve a competitive advantage in its target segments even though it does not possess a competitive advantage overall.

The focus strategy has two variants. In *cost focus* a firm seeks a cost advantage in its target segment, while in *differentiation focus* a firm seeks differentiation in its target segment. Both variants of the focus strategy rest on *differences* between a focuser's target segments and other segments in the industry. The target segments must either have buyers with unusual needs or else the production and delivery system that best serves the target segment must differ from that of other industry segments. Cost focus exploits differences in cost behavior in some segments, while differentiation focus exploits the special needs of buyers in certain segments. Such differences imply that the segments are poorly served by broadly targeted competitors who serve them at the same time as they serve others. The focuser can thus achieve competitive advantage by dedicating itself to the segments exclusively. Breadth of target is clearly a matter of degree, but the essence of focus is the exploitation of a narrow target's differences from the balance of the industry. Narrow focus in and of itself is not sufficient for above-average performance.

A good example of a focuser who has exploited differences in the production process that best serves different segments is Hammermill Paper. Hammermill has increasingly been moving toward relatively low-volume, high-quality speciality papers, where the larger paper companies with higher volume machines face a stiff cost penalty for short production runs. Hammermill's equipment is more suited to shorter runs with frequent setups.

A focuser takes advantage of suboptimization in either direction by broadly targeted competitors. Competitors may be *underperforming* in meeting the needs of a particular segment, which opens the possibility for differentiation focus. Broadly targeted competitors may also be *overperforming* in meeting the needs of a segment, which means that they are bearing higher than necessary cost in serving it. An opportunity for cost focus may be present in just meeting the needs of such a segment and no more.

If a focuser's target segment is not different from other segments, then the focus strategy will not succeed. In soft drinks, for example, Royal Crown has focused on cola drinks, while Coca-Cola and Pepsi have broad product lines with many flavored drinks. Royal Crown's segment, however, can be well served by Coke and Pepsi at the same time they are serving other segments. Hence Coke and Pepsi enjoy competitive advantages over Royal Crown in the cola segment due to the economies of having a broader line.

If a firm can achieve sustainable cost leadership (cost focus) or differentiation (differentiation focus) in its segment and the segment is structurally attractive, then the focuser will be an above-average performer in its industry. Segment structural attractiveness is a necessary condition because some segments in an industry are much less profitable than others. There is often room for several sustainable focus strategies in an industry, provided that focusers choose different target segments. Most industries have a variety of segments, and each one that involves a different buyer need or a different optimal production or delivery system is a candidate for a focus strategy.

Stuck in the middle

A firm that engages in each generic strategy but fails to achieve any of them is 'stuck in the middle.' It possesses no competitive advantage. This strategic position is usually a recipe for below-average performance. A firm that is stuck in the middle will compete at a disadvantage because the cost leader, differentiators, or focusers will be better positioned to compete in any segment. If a firm that is stuck in the middle is lucky enough to discover a profitable product or buyer, competitors with a sustainable competitive advantage will quickly eliminate the spoils. In most industries, quite a few competitors are stuck in the middle.

A firm that is stuck in the middle will earn attractive profits only if the structure of its industry is highly favorable, or if the firm is fortunate enough to have competitors that are also stuck in the middle. Usually, however, such a firm will be much less profitable than rivals achieving one of the generic strategies. Industry maturity tends to widen the performance differences between firms with a generic strategy and those that are stuck in the middle, because it exposes ill-conceived strategies that have been carried along by rapid growth.

Becoming stuck in the middle is often a manifestation of a firm's unwillingness to make *choices* about how to compete. It tries for competitive advantage through every means and achieves none, because achieving different types of competitive advantage usually requires inconsistent actions. Becoming stuck in the middle also afflicts successful firms, who compromise their generic strategy for the sake of growth or prestige. A classic example is Laker Airways, which began with a clear cost-focus strategy based on no-frills operation in the North Atlantic market, aimed at a particular segment of the traveling public that was extremely price sensitive. Over time, however, Laker began adding frills, new services, and new routes. It blurred its image, and suboptimized its service and delivery system. The consequences were disastrous, and Laker eventually went bankrupt.

The temptation to blur a generic strategy, and therefore become stuck in the middle, is particularly great for a focuser once it has dominated its target segments. Focus involves deliberately limiting potential sales volume. Success can lead a focuser to lose sight of the reasons for its success and compromise its focus strategy for growth's sake. Rather than compromise its generic strategy, a firm is usually better off finding new industries in which to grow where it can use its generic strategy again or exploit interrelationships.

Pursuit of more than one generic strategy

Each generic strategy is a fundamentally different approach to creating and sustaining a competitive advantage, combining the type of competitive advantage a firm seeks and the scope of its strategic target. Usually a firm must make a choice among them, or it will become stuck in the middle. The benefits of optimizing the firm's strategy for a particular target segment (focus) cannot be gained if a firm is simultaneously serving a broad range of segments (cost leadership or differentiation). Sometimes a firm may be able to create two largely separate business units within the same corporate entity, each with a different generic strategy. A good example is the British hotel firm Trusthouse Forte, which operates five separate hotel chains each targeted at a different segment. However, unless a firm strictly separates the units pursuing different generic strategies, it may compromise the ability of any of them to achieve its competitive advantage. A suboptimized approach to competing, made likely by the spillover among units of corporate policies and culture, will lead to becoming stuck in the middle.

Achieving cost leadership and differentiation is also usually inconsistent, because differentiation is usually costly. To be unique and command a price premium, a differentiator deliberately elevates costs, as Caterpillar has done in construction equipment. Conversely, cost leadership often requires a firm to forego some differentiation by standardizing its product, reducing marketing overhead, and the like.

Reducing cost does not always involve a sacrifice in differentiation. Many firms have discovered ways to reduce cost not only without hurting their differentiation but while actually raising it, by using practices that are both more efficient and effective or employing a different technology. Sometimes dramatic cost savings can be achieved with no impact on differentiation at all if a firm has not concentrated on cost reduction previously. However, cost reduction is not the same as achieving a cost advantage. When faced with capable competitors also striving for cost leadership, a firm will ultimately reach the point where further cost reduction requires a sacrifice in differentiation. It is at this point that the generic strategies become inconsistent and a firm must make a choice.

If a firm can achieve cost leadership and differentiation simultaneously, the rewards are great because the benefits are additive – differentiation leads to premium prices at the same time that cost leadership implies lower costs. An example of a firm that has achieved both a cost advantage and differentiation in its segments is Crown Cork and Seal in the metal container industry. Crown has targeted the so-called hard-to-hold uses of cans in the beer, soft drink, and aerosol industries. It manufactures only steel cans rather than both steel and aluminum. In its target segments, Crown has differentiated itself based on service, technological assistance, and offering a full line of steel cans, crowns, and canning machinery. Differentiation of this type would be much more difficult to achieve in other industry segments that have different needs. At the same time, Crown has dedicated its facilities to producing only the types of cans demanded by buyers in its chosen segments and has aggressively invested in modern two-piece steel-canning technology. As a result, Crown has probably also achieved low-cost producer status in its segments.

Sustainability

A generic strategy does not lead to above-average performance unless it is sustainable vis-à-vis competitors, though actions that improve industry structure may improve industrywide profitability even if they are imitated. The sustainability of the three generic strategies demands that a firm's competitive advantage resist erosion by competitor behavior or industry evolution. Each generic strategy involves different risks, which are shown in Table 5.1.1.

The sustainability of a generic strategy requires that a firm possess some barriers that make imitation of the strategy difficult. Since barriers to imitation are never insurmountable, however, it is usually necessary for a firm to offer a moving target to its competitors by investing in order to continually improve its position. Each generic strategy is also a potential threat to the others – as Table 5.1.1 shows, for example, focusers must worry about broadly targeted competitors and vice versa.

Table 5.1.1 can be used to analyze how to attack a competitor that employs any of the generic strategies. A firm pursuing overall differentiation, for example, can be attacked by firms that open up a large cost gap, narrow the extent of differentiation, shift the differentiation desired by buyers to other dimensions, or focus. Each generic strategy is vulnerable to different types of attacks.

In some industries, industry structure or the strategies of competitors eliminate the possibility of achieving one or more of the generic strategies. Occasionally no feasible way for one firm to gain a significant cost advantage exists, for example, because several firms

TABLE 5.1.1   Risks of the generic strategies

Risks of cost leadership	Risks of differentiation	Risks of focus
Cost leadership is not sustained ▪ competitors imitate ▪ technology changes ▪ other bases for cost leadership erode	Differentiation is not sustained ▪ competitors imitate ▪ bases for differentiation become less important to buyers	The focus strategy is imitated The target segment becomes structually unattractive ▪ structure erodes ▪ demand disappears
Proximity in differentiation is lost	Cost proximity is lost	Broadly targeted competitors overwhelm the segment ▪ the segment's differences from other segments narrow ▪ the advantages of a broad line increase
Cost focusers achieve even lower cost in segments	Differentiation focusers achieve even greater differentiation in segments	New focusers subsegment the industry

are equally placed with respect to scale economies, access to raw materials, or other cost drivers. Similarly, an industry with few segments or only minor differences among segments, such as low-density polyethylene, may offer few opportunities for focus. Thus the mix of generic strategies will vary from industry to industry.

In many industries, however, the three generic strategies can profitably coexist as long as firms pursue different ones or select different bases for differentiation or focus. Industries in which several strong firms are pursuing differentiation strategies based on different sources of buyer value are often particularly profitable. This tends to improve industry structure and lead to stable industry competition. If two or more firms choose to pursue the same generic strategy on the same basis, however, the result can be a protracted and unprofitable battle. The worst situation is where several firms are vying for overall cost leadership. The past and present choice of generic strategies by competitors, then, has an impact on the choices available to a firm and the cost of changing its position.

The concept of generic strategies is based on the premise that there are a number of ways in which competitive advantage can be achieved, depending on industry structure. If all firms in an industry followed the principles of competitive strategy, each would pick different bases for competitive advantage. While not all would succeed, the generic strategies provide alternate routes to superior performance. Some strategic planning concepts have been narrowly based on only one route to competitive advantage, most notably cost. Such concepts not only fail to explain the success of many firms, but they can also lead all firms in an industry to pursue the same type of competitive advantage in the same way – with predictably disastrous results.

READING
5.2

Strategy from the inside out: building capability-creating organizations

By Danny Miller, Russell Eisenstat and Nathaniel Foote[1]

For Citibank CEO John Reed, 1991 was a very tough year. Citi's stock had plummeted, in no small part because of its trouble-ridden global coporate bank. Some problems, such as non-performing Latin American loans, were shared by competitors. However, Citi was especially hobbled. Paradoxically, although it had banks in over 100 countries, many of these were weak. Local rivals with better ties to customers and government were strangling Citi's revenues and eroding its margins.

The choices confronting Reed seemed bleak. On the one hand, he could try to strengthen Citi's presence in lucrative markets such as Germany or Japan by copying regional rivals like Deutsche Bank. He might, for example, try to build deeper relationships with local businesses. However, Citi would always be at a disadvantage vis-à-vis local rivals, who had better government and industry contacts – relationships that for historical and political reasons Citi was unlikely to

duplicate. A more feasible strategy would be to offer new services and try to become more efficient. However, there was nothing to stop competitors from following suit and neutralizing Citi's efforts. Reed, like so many of today's CEOs, was facing a quandary.

Citibank (now Citigroup) and some two dozen other firms we studied have managed, quite craftily, to escape this predicament of how to grow sustainable capabilities. They began not be emulating best practices, but by delving constantly within themselves to discover and build on their unique, hard-to-copy assets, knowledge, relationships, and experiences. We call these emergent, potential, or hidden resources 'asymmetries'. Over time, the firms we studied evolved a set of explicit organizational processes and designs to find these asymmetries, turn them into capabilities, and leverage them across the appropriate market opportunities.

At Citi, John Reed realized that his extensive network of international banks could be of immense

---

service to large multinationals (MNCs). This was no commonplace observation as the scattered network was at the time a liability in serving MNCs. Citi's local banks gave service priority to local clients, offered products unsuitable to MNCs, and did not cooperate to facilitate cross-border business. Nor were MNCs the most profitable customers. However, Reed had a three-pronged epiphany. He realized first that no rival had Citi's global reach or could attain it easily. He also saw that by redesigning his organization, processes, and performance management systems he could make the network more responsive to MNCs. Finally, he envisioned how the international bank network could be redeployed to great advantage to serve not local firms but large clients doing extensive – and lucrative – cross-border business. In short, Reed saw how his bank was different, figured out how to make that difference an asset, and found a market that would most value that asset.

It is vital to point out that it is not only large firms such as Citi that may have potentially valuable asym-metries. The example of Shana Corp. (Exhibit 5.2.1) shows a very similar path of asymmetry identification and capability development unfolding even within a small and new firm with nowhere near the assets or relationships of a Citigroup.

The lessons from Citi and Shana are much the same: competitive advantage comes not from imitation but from using organizational processes and designs to identify emerging asymmetries and build them into capabilities. Again, asymmetries are hard-to-copy ways in which a firm differs from its rivals – ways that may ultimately bring advantage (see Exhibit 5.2.2 for the definitions of our key terms). They may consist of outputs (such as products or solutions), relationships and alliances, systems (such as Citi's global network or contacts), processes and routines, and nascent skills and knowledge (such as Shana's) – all provided that rivals cannot imitate these within practical time and cost constraints. In fact, asymmetries, because of their subtlety or uniqueness, confer a head start and discourage imitation – and that sustains their edge.

EXHIBIT 5.2.1

MOLEHILLS INTO MOUNTAINS: THE CASE OF SHANA CORP.

Shana Corp is a private Canadian software company. Some of Shana's product development efforts, combined with a few technologically related contracts, had allowed the company, over several years, to develop special expertise. It acquired the capability to create sophisticated forms completion software that was compatible between two popular operating systems. This occurred, quite fortuitously, because of the kinds of jobs Shana had worked on. However, the top managers of Shana soon became quite conscious of this emerging capability. Their firm, they realized, had learned to artfully and economically do some valuable kinds of work that its competitors simply could not do as well or as fast. Also, some natural affinities began to occur among the software developers as each began to realize more fully one another's strengths and weaknesses, and each began to specialize on certain subroutines. What had been a work group became a real team, with all of the synergies and efficiencies that entails. Soon Shana's managers began to develop training routines, work procedures, and compensa-tion and incentive policies to further improve team performance. Shana also began to use its growing body of specialized knowledge and its effective development teams to concentrate on particular clients that required its special abilities. These were clients that used the two popular operating systems but wanted the same forms software for both. The new market focus and additional product development and marketing experience it brought sharpened Shana's expertise still further, widening the skill gap between it and its rivals. This gradual convergence of the company around its capabilities and target market helped to focus new selection and training programs, project management protocols, and marketing campaigns. These allowed Shana to exploit and extend its competitive advantage.

Note that Shana did not set out to master a special capability. Nor did it perform a competitive analysis to look for promising niches. Rather, Shana's managers noticed retrospectively what their firm was unusually good at, reflected on and developed it, and pursued those clients that would most benefit from Shana's emerging talents. The firm, moreover, did not set out to emulate the competitive advantages and competencies of its most successful rivals. First, it did not have the financial or technological wherewithal to accomplish this, nor could it reasonably expect to develop it. Second, even if Shana were able to develop those competencies, by the time it did its competitors most likely would have moved ahead. Shana's managers realized that

emulation would cede to rivals product and market leadership – no competitor was a sitting target. Finally, had it attempted to do what its rivals do well, Shana would have had to share a market with a host of other imitators.

Another advantage is their accessibility. Due to accidents of history and normal variations in the skills and experiences of organizations, many companies will find that they possess asymmetries. While the capabilities or best practices of other enterprises may be almost impossible to duplicate, managers begin the hunt for asymmetries in their own back yard.

Unfortunately, *asymmetries are not resources or core competencies*. Like personal characteristics such as shyness or aggressiveness, they can serve as advantages or disadvantages. As with Citi's network they tend to be under-explored, under-funded, and unconnected to a firm's engine of value creation. However, where carefully fostered and directed, asymmetries may come to underlie the most important capabilities in a firm's competitive arsenal. By continually identifying and building on asymmetries, by nurturing and exploiting these within a complementary organizational design, and by leveraging them via an appropriate market focus, companies may be able to aspire realistically to attain sustainable advantage.

Paradoxically, a continual and intimate connection with the market environment is vital to this 'inside-out approach'. First, firms have to understand their rivals in order to know how they themselves are unique. More importantly, they need to track market reactions to discover which asymmetries are relevant. It is this ongoing ability to find the intersection between a firm's emerging asymmetries and the opportunities in the environment that is the fundamental strength of the organizations we describe here.

The three imperatives of inside-out strategy

Three imperatives are especially central to our approach. Although our presentation is necessarily linear, the process of developing inside-out strategy is emergent – full of trial and error, iteration between imperatives, and exploitation of chance.

Imperative 1: Discover asymmetries and their potential

To do well, firms need to develop important capabilities or resources that their rivals cannot. As indicated, however, it is hard for them to develop these resources unless they already have some realized or potential edge. The first step is *discovering* the asymmetries that underlie that edge, as unrecognized resources or capabilities are of little advantage.

Asymmetries can arise in a number of ways. Some, such as Citi's banking network, develop as a result of the vagaries of corporate history. Others, such as long-term contracts and distinctive patents, are consciously created. In all cases, asymmetries serve as useful starting points for creating advantage precisely because they cannot be easily copied. The search for asymmetries is the search for these inimitable differences.

The inimitability of an asymmetry may be due to legal barriers, as in the case of patents. More often, however, it is because asymmetries represent subtle and interrelated attributes and skills that have co-evolved over a significant interval – as in the case of Shana. The subtle and tacit nature of these attributes, and in some cases their lack of connection to success, keeps these asymmetries beneath the radar screens of rivals (and sometimes those of the firm itself).

Because of this subtlety, the search for asymmetries cannot be a casual process. It demands thorough and persistent inquiry across the breadth of an organization. The search must lead to an understanding of how a firm differs from its competitors in the assets it possesses, the execution processes it uses, and the combinations of these things. It should also provide insights into how these asymmetries are currently generating or may potentially generate the resources or capabilities that produce advantage. Having discovered these resources, they must be evaluated for their potential contributions to performance.

Outside search.   A good place to begin the search for internal asymmetries is to find the more obvious *external* ones – the kinds of clients and business that gravitate to a firm rather than its competitors. Managers might look for the kinds of opportunities they can capture that their competitors cannot. The types of customers and the peculiarities of their product and service demands are key clues. Asymmetries can also be spotted by asking why a company beats its rivals in capturing a particular client or market. Answers may be found in the breadth of offerings or geographic reach, reputation with a client, or intimate market knowledge.

Learning demands action as well as reflection. In fact, one of the surest ways of revealing valuable asymmetries is to launch a set of entrepreneurial initiatives, determine which ones show promise, and then try to discover why. These can be viewed as experiments and may include broaching new kinds of customers or market segments, combining existing products with services, and altering the mix of products. Such experiments bring out new fans of the firm and make clearer *emerging* asymmetries. Shana's particular talents became clearer to its managers both as it pursued different clients and new software projects. In fact, in highly emergent contexts – in e-commerce, for example, or a newly deregulated industry – required capabilities are highly ambiguous and first mover advantages are central to ultimate success. Here firms are better off moving quickly to seize opportunities. Only after carrying out their market experiments can they determine where their advantages lie.

Inside search.   Search also must take place inside a company. In many cases, the most useful asymmetries are buried deep within a firm and have to be traced back from surface abilities. Willamette Inc. is a successful medium-sized paper manufacturer. One of Willamette's apparent strengths was its ability to track the paper market by making the right grade of paper at the right time. However, the knowledge of what to make is widely available – many competitors have it. The most basic capability is an ability to convert production processes quickly and cheaply enough to take advantage of industry price changes. The reason Willamette could do this was because of its flexible equipment. The reason it had such equipment when its competitors did not was because of the experience Willamette's engineers had built up over the years converting the dilapidated plants of rivals into some of the most flexible and efficient factories in the industry. Willamette's fundamental asymmetry and its primary source of advantage was its state-of-the-art plant conversion and operating capabilities – capabilities, it turned out, that usually could not even be duplicated by the nation's top engineering consultants. It was this profound recognition of its capabilities that then allowed Willamette to allocate the human and financial resources and gear its hiring, training, promotion, and compensation approaches to support them.

Discovering asymmetries that represent *latent* resources or capabilities is particularly challenging. The case of Citigroup's global relationship banking unit was instructive because its crucial asymmetry – unrivaled geographic presence – for many years represented as much a liability as an asset. By 1980, Citi had developed a system of banks in 100 countries. Its nearest rival, Hong Kong Shanghai Bank Corp., had offices in 40 countries. However, many of Citi's banks were weak, and margins were being squeezed in developed countries by competing local banks with better ties to customers and government. Meanwhile in developing countries, market volatility and political instability were real and costly hazards. Despite these problems, then-CEO John Reed realized that the international network could *potentially* put it in a unique position to do business with far-flung multinationals that desired further globalization. Also, it was unlikely that rivals could easily imitate this resource.

Thus, asymmetry identification can take at least two forms. The first is a re-framing insight, spotting pre-existing but unexploited assets – as at Citi. The second is evolutionary and requires managers to recognize an emerging edge, frequently in intangible assets such as knowledge, relationships, and reputation. This was the case at Shana and Willamette.

Table 5.2.1 provides suggestions on how a firm can identify its own key asymmetries and capabilities. An Assessment Audit is available from the authors to guide this process.

Imperative 2: Create capability configurations – by design

Asymmetries evolve into sustainable core capabilities largely through organization design – which builds and supports capabilities by embedding them in a cohesive configuration. Design also energizes these configurations by setting up 'virtuous circles' of capability enhancement.

There are two aspects to capability configurations. First, they are made up of a *cohesive combination of resources and capabilities* that is hard to imitate. Simple resources such as patents or proprietary processes can be contrasted with more complex bundles of elements such as a distribution system. Citi's bank network, for example, encompassed a set of mutually reinforcing elements that made it easier to serve multinational clients – many banks in many countries, business and political contacts connected to and shared among the banks, and a set of common product and service standards across banks. Such resource or capability configurations tend to be far more powerful, distinctive, and tough to copy than single capabilities. Advantages of capability configurations include:

1 Configurations develop powerful complementarities around core capabilities and among resources, often by using an array of design levers.

2 Configurations embed and empower resources within a design, thereby more firmly capturing those resources, and making them more valuable to an organization than to its rivals (a condition economists call asset specificity).

3 Configurations organize capabilities into socially complex systems that are difficult for rivals to imitate.

4 Configurations embody virtuous cycles that enhance capabilities.

5 Points 2 to 4 all help to turn capabilities into sustainable competitive advantages.

However, capability configurations have an even more valuable property – they are *embedded within a*

design infrastructure that leverages, sustains, and develops them. At Citicorp, the international bank network at first was just a *potentially* valuable resource, not an actual one. The network only became a sustainable capability within the context of a supportive organizational design. As long as Citi was organized as a set of geographically based profit centers, local managers refused to give good service to multinationals that demanded bargain interest rates and service fees. John Reed was only able to unlock the value of the international network for multinationals through a new organization design. The design incorporated a group of very powerful key account managers and the multi-functional, multi-product teams needed to serve them. A flexible resource allocation system was set up to provide human, product, and knowledge resources to each multinational client – to serve that client in a globally coordinated and integrated way anywhere in the world, for a vast array of products and on demand. Reed reinforced the configuration with information systems that give all key account team members access to all client information and with a dynamic planning process that makes team members commit to specific objectives for each customer. He extracted support from local managers by having them assessed and rewarded against their ability to serve the multinationals. At Citi, then, the design of the organization was a core enabler and key component of the capability configuration (Table 5.2.2), one that dramatically enhanced its business with multinationals.

The Citi case is a good example of a firm that identified a key asymmetry (the international bank system and web of connections), realized that it could be an important resource, and developed that resource into a capability configuration by embedding it in an effective organization design. Without the configuration, the bank system resource could not be exploited or leveraged. In fact, the reason so many potentially valuable resources go undetected is because they only take on value when deployed within a complementary design configuration.

Building molehills into mountains: Virtuous cycles that enhance capabilities. One of the most advantageous aspects of design configurations is that they create 'virtuous cycles' of capability enhancement – cycles that turn the potential of an asymmetry into a real and growing capability. Virtuous cycles are simply chains of influence in which one good outcome promotes another. Companies, for example, may possess a capability that attracts talented

TABLE 5.2.1   Discovering asymmetries and capabilities

Questions	Information sought	Possible data sources
What are the differences in observable outputs between a firm and its rivals: where is the firm superior? Hints from: ■ What kinds of customers are more apt to choose this firm than its rivals and why? ■ What do they ask from the firm – and value most from its offerings?	Comparison of outputs along dimensions such as design attractiveness or functionality, service, price, solutions tailoring, reputation, guarantees, and quality. Also relevant may be the scale, scope, and reach of the firm and its EDI and logistical connections to clients.	Market facing units or key account managers; customer reactions; and data on kinds of clients drawn to firm and their reactions to firm. Indexes of performance and quality by product, geography, and plant.
Which resources and capabilities appear to underlie the above sources of superiority – and where in the firm do they reside? Which asymmetries between a firm and its rivals ultimately can be *built* into sources of superiority?	**Resources** may include those that are *property-based*: patents, control over unique supplies or channels, talent under long-term contract; *knowledge-based*: unique information about customers, segments, and tecnologies; and *relationship-based*: partnerships, alliances, reputation, and customer ties. **Capabilities** include process and product design, product development, operations, value chain integration, all aspects of marketing and customer service, and organization design.	Managers in product and process development units, market and client-facing units, and geographic units.
Which resources and capabilities would be hardest for rivals to nullify?	Target for analysis especially those resources and competencies identified above.	Market-facing managers and customers, studies of rivals' products, communications, and what is written about them.
Which capabilities and resources are most central now and for the future to a firm's competitive advantage?	Consider the degree to which each of the resources and capabilities are sustainable, drive growth and profitability, underlie other capabilities, complement other capabilities, can be enhanced and developed, and can be leveraged across a wide range of market opportunities.	Managers from different functions and SBUs.

new employees and partners whose enlistment then augments that capability. Well-managed capabilities also raise performance, which in turn fuels them with additional resources and attention.

The emergence of Denmark's International Service System (ISS), illustrates the powerful role of virtuous circles in building what is now one of the largest service firms in the world. Early in its history, ISS began to

TABLE 5.2.2 How designs build and exploit capability

Design enablers	Leadership/ governance	Values and culture	Structural mechanisms	Systems and policies
Embedding capabilities within the organization	Leaders create context to prioritize, fund, and build strategy around capabilities. TMT ensures synergy among resources and capabilities. TMT establishes policies to bring front and back units together to develop and adapt capabilities.	Corporate culture celebrates capabilities and accords prestige to units and people most central in creating those capabilities. Collaborative culture to bring together front and back units. Emphasis is on knowledge building and knowledge sharing among units.	Capability-based units such as task forces and cross-SBU teams are established to create and share knowledge. Multi-SBU, multi-function coordinating committees build and adapt capabilities. High-level management committees oversee long-term development of a specific capability.	Information and planning systems target and track capabilities by unit versus competitors. HR systems select, reward, and promote based on capabilities. Knowledge systems codify proprietary information on technologies, customers, and so on.
Enhancing capabilities	Governance bodies describe a trajectory for core capability extension and leveraging.	Informal networks bring front and back units and people together to develop capabilities.	Multi-unit teams and strategic alliances build knowledge. Communities of practice grow capabilities.	Information systems feed learning efforts: e.g., report results according to segments and customers. Training programs.
Shaping capabilities to market opportunities	Leaders link capabilities to target markets and define policy parameters for identification and sequencing of opportunities.	Entrepreneurial culture encourages managers to identify opportunities that exploit capabilities.	Opportunity-based units help shape capabilities to market segments.	HR, planning, and incentive systems create resources that can be easily leveraged across opportunities. Rewards based on firm-wide objectives to get front and back to collaborate.

accept contracts for cleaning slaughterhouses. This was a demanding task as equipment had to be disassembled for cleaning, and it was necessary to use special detergents and pressurized cleaning techniques to eradicate harmful bacteria. Also needed was expertise in testing for sterility. The experience gained with various types of clients allowed ISS to develp highly effective and efficient routines for doing the work, as well as enough financial expertise to be able to cost and price cleaning services by the machine, square meter, type of food, and so on. The proprietary technical knowledge gained in food hygiene enabled ISS to form partnerships with customers to jointly develop techniques for new products and evolving types of bacteria. This enhanced ISS's skills still further, giving them an even greater competitive advantage and an expanding client base. Eventually, ISS's expertise grew to encompass related hygiene-food businesses, including poultry and fish.

Such virtuous cycles do not happen by themselves. Design and leaders play a key role. At ISS, both executive action and the levers of design convert experience gained in a capability into policy priorities and market targets, codified knowledge, and efficient routines – which in turn extend those capabilities. For example, ISS's leadership strives to acquire 'customer density' in various segments. Scale in a segment leads not only to buying power but greater specialization, with resulting learning and customer intimacy advantages. Leaders also prioritize new opportunities that are becoming realizable because of growing skills or reputation. Information systems then build databases on costs and customers that facilitate better pricing, costing, and scheduling: this improves the capture rate of the most prized kinds of customers. Also, human resource systems codify criteria for selection and training, thereby sharpening the most important capabilities. Finally, structural mechanisms bring managers together to share knowledge across clients so that additional services can be sold to existing clients and ideas are shared around picking up additional business. Each of these design levers shapes the virtuous cycle as they help accumulate 'stocks of assets' such as reputation, technical, managerial and customer knowledge, cohesive teams and team skills, and distinctive systems and infrastructures.

Virtuous cycles have a number of things in common. They engender good performance and thus create resources to plow back into capability development. They enhance reputation, which brings opportunities. They elicit positive feedback from the market that reinforces the right kinds of people, skills, and products. Design serves as a powerful governor and amplifier of these cycles in identifying and prioritizing a capability; in assembling and coordinating the resources, people, systems, and mechanisms to develop it; in disseminating the capability within the organization; and in leveraging the capability across the right market opportunities.

Imperative 3: Pursue market opportunities that build on and leverage capabilities

The deepest capabilities and most integrated configurations are of no value unless they extract superior returns. So they have to satisfy the needs of a large enough audience who will pay amply to have that done. At the same time, emerging capabilities must be constantly unearthed and evaluated so they can be leveraged across a wider audience and set of opportunities.

A market can be looked at as a set of niches and opportunities that a firm must choose from to best leverage its capabilities. Managers must ask not only where are the opportunities, but also why should their firm be able to capture and exploit them better than potential competitors. The attractiveness of a niche must be evaluated in the context of a firm's uniqueness and the capabilities it can attain more readily than its rivals.

It is also vital that *market niches and opportunities be related or complementary in that they benefit from the same kinds of capabilities*. This consideration guided some of our most successful firms. Citi's global corporate clients, for example, are similar in that they are large, do plenty of cross-border business, and benefit from Citi's global presence and international banking services. In fact, Citi changed its pricing strategy to attract *only* those types of clients. Without this relatedness, Citi's capabilities would be underutilized or underdeveloped. Note that it is not similarity of outputs or industry boundaries that define complementarity: Citi's global clients were in many different industries and locations, and Citi sold lots of different products. Rather, complementarity is defined in terms of the ability of different opportunities to benefit from the same asymmetries and capabilities.

Citi also pursued complementarity among opportunities in developing multi-product international banking solutions tailored to specific industries. It created product packages or 'industry templates' that would appeal to *many* clients within an industry – and thus give Citi economies of product development and market knowledge. Citi's product packages built not only on the similar needs of global clients in the same industry, but also on its banking contacts and expertise in foreign exchange, global cash management, and investment banking.

Inevitably, managers will have to shape capabilities according to such related opportunities. Recall that Citi made many changes to render its international bank network valuable to global clients – for example, abolishing regional profit centers to get local managers to serve multinationals. Citi also organized its global bank into industry groups to develop its tailored product solutions and increase market penetration. Because market focus was so clear, the bank could afford to develop industry- and client-based planning and information systems. These incorporated detailed information on *each* targeted client's potential banking business, which enabled representatives to home in on the best business opportunities and develop tailored approaches to capture that business. As the examples show, when adapting asymmetries and capabilities to market opportunities, the design configuration again plays a central role.

Leveraging capabilities across new opportunities. Capabilities are especially valuable when they can be leveraged across a broadening set of market opportunities. Such leveraging must become a never-ending process. Here again virtuous cycles are useful. They strengthen current capabilities, but they also push asymmetries and capabilities into new areas. As learning occurs, a firm is able to employ capabilities or resources garnered in one situation to serve a different one. This can happen in several ways.

- The same capabilities can be applied across different products and industries. ISS leveraged its special capabilities in cleaning and sterilizing slaughterhouses to enter the hospital services field. A deep knowledge of bacteria, chemicals, sterilization, cleaning, and testing techniques allowed ISS to enter a completely different industry, with similar capability requirements.
- Customer-related expertise and reputation developed around one output can be used to sell others to the same customer. ISS-Mediclean used the reputation and customer-specific knowledge it garnered in cleaning a given hospital to get other types of service contracts with that same institution. 'Knowledge of a specific customer and a broader range of services gains Mediclean access to the customer's senior management. . . . It is this access that leads to the deepening and expanding of the relationship.'
- Segment-related expertise developed with one customer can be used with others in the same segment. ISS leveraged its knowledge across different health care institutions based on its extensive segment-specific knowledge. The company is successful in part because it thoroughly understands the needs of the British hospital customer, and because its capa-

bilities span a comprehensive array of hospital cleaning and facilitates management services.

ISS excels at all three kinds of leverage, in part because of an organization design that encompasses entrepreneurial, opportunity-seeking leadership as well as systems that gather and disseminate information on both capabilities and market opportunities. ISS's culture ensures that knowledge is easily shared across organizational boundaries, and its flexible administrative structure can manage capabilities and exploit new opportunities.

Ultimately, most capabilities become obsolete. Major sources of obsolescence include rival imitators eroding value, product lines reaching maturity, and major transformations in industry technology. The threat of imitation can often be countered by our virtuous cycles that build on capabilities fast enough to stay ahead of competitors. The threat of product obsolescence can be reduced by leveraging capabilities across new or related product areas. However, the only way to deal with technological or knowledge obsolescence is to continually look for *new* asymmetries that can be developed into capabilities that can be connected with a new set of opportunities (Christensen, 1997). This involves all three of our imperatives.

Implications for managers

In pursuing strategy from the inside out managers must learn both to pursue and trade off seeming opposites. Specifically, in discovering, building and leveraging capability they must balance reflection and action, selection and variation, resources and opportunities. Moreover, to make these tradeoffs in a quick and superior way, firms must make organizational design their source of competitive advantage. They must significantly empower their units to discover and develop the right capabilities and leverage them across the right opportunities; and they must create strong leadership and infrastructure at the center to get those units to collaborate to do this rapidly and effectively.

Three tradeoffs

Balance reflection and action: Discovering asymmetries and capabilities. Knowledge about capabilities comes in part from reflection. Managers must critically evaluate their resources and talents in looking for hidden gems – trying to determine which are the best employees, which people and units work together best, which technologies show promise, what types of projects and products succeed, and what sorts of customers are attracted to the firm. The best outcomes of reflection are imaginative 're-framings' of the value of different resources, experiences, and relationships. At Shana, for example, they led managers to see that the really valuable capabilities were not in building forms software but in bridging operating systems.

Reflection, however, is not enough. True self-knowledge demands action and experimentation. Asymmetries and capabilities are always changing and the best way to keep track is by trying things and assessing the results. At ISS experiments might include working with different types of customers, trying a new process, or changing offerings for a new market segment. These experiments provide good information on what works – cues that then can be used to shape more focused experiments that converge on capabilities and launch virtuous circles.

Given the job pressures, managers must put time aside to reflect on capabilities and initiate experiments. They might launch quarterly sessions with top management, venture teams, or 'capability teams' to explore emerging competencies and the opportunities they bring. These discussions may work especially well when members of different business or technical units or functions get together. 'Outsider' units often see creative uses for resources their counterparts deem commonplace. Gathering to address a specific market challenge or opportunity may bring some urgency to the task of surfacing capabilities.

Balance variation and selection: Developing and embedding capabilities. Leaders must determine *which* emerging capabilities are most promising and then 'select' or embed them as priorities for development. If the targeted set of capabilities is overly large or varied, resources will be too thinly spread to achieve critical mass and competitive superiority. Core or fundamental capabilities must take the lion's share of funds, talent, and visibility – even where this hurts other activities. However, to commandeer resources from 'secondary' activities, priorities must be reflected in accountabilities, performance criteria, rewards and promotions, and also in dedicated units and teams and in planning and information systems. ISS and Willamette use their planning and resource-allocation processes to drive resources towards the most promising asymmetries and capabilities. They also designate top priority capabilities and constitute teams that are appraised and rewarded according to capability development.

Variation in capabilities must also be restricted over time. Core capabilities have the highest yields when developed cumulatively over the long run and varied 'around the edges'. This requires top-level, long-term resource planning, coupled with regular follow-ups to determine how to elaborate, adapt, and fund a capability. In many of our firms, multi-functional, multi-SBU units and top-management committees assured continuity in developing longstanding capabilities. At the same time, firms searched for and experimented with capability variations – emerging but related relationships, client knowledge, expertise, and technologies. Without this exploration and 'playfulness' at the edges, a capability set narrows and loses relevance.

Balance capabilities and opportunities: Leveraging capabilities in the market. Managers need to find opportunities tailored to their capabilities. Opportunities also must ultimately shape capabilities. The faster these mutual adjustments occur, the more likely the virtuous circles, and the longer a firm is able to sustain competitive advantage. Of course, such speed is only possible when organizational designs and processes foster an ongoing, enriching dialogue between capability managers and opportunity managers.

Advantage by design

Different parts of the firm bring to bear different perspectives in building capabilities and making these tradeoffs. Units dealing with customers and markets ('front-end' units) look to leverage asymmetries in customer relationships, perhaps by broadening the product set. Units charged with engineering, R&D, and operations ('back-end' units) seek to leverage functional capabilities or products across different market opportunities. Both these pursuits are essential. Unfortunately, some product variations will unduly stretch capabilities, and some capabilities will not find a market. It is only by getting the front and back of an organization to work together that complementarity can be quickly realized between capabilities and market opportunities. This calls for organizational designs that not only empower front- and back-end units to develop opportunities and capabilities, but also create a strong center and infrastructure to get these units to collaborate.

Strong front, strong back. Back-end units must have fungible resources: flexible resources they can use to discover and develop capabilities, and ones that are free from the day-to-day pull of operations. They also require the clout to call upon resources from the front to discover the needs of customers and the strengths of the competition. Typically, this requires that some front-end resources be accountable for capability development. Front-end units also need fungible resources to identify and pursue opportunities. Moreover, they need access to resources from the back to help them adapt capabilities to the new opportunities. Back-end resources, therefore, may have to be made accountable for realizing front-end opportunities. At Citi, for example, back-end functional and product specialists were appraised according to their service to large clients.

Strong-center: Leadership and collaborative infrastructure. A strong center is needed to make front and back collaborate. This involves myriad organizational levers and processes (see Table 5.2.2), with strong leadership being primary. Leaders must establish objectives, policies, and even transfer prices for determining how front and back can work together. They need to prioritize capabilities and opportunities, or at least delineate their scope. Leaders also may act as final arbiters in disputes between front and back, the way John Reed was called to do at Citi.

However, firms do even better where front and back can work together without a leader's intervention. This is more apt to happen where corporate cultures encourage collaboration, as at Willamette, or where extensive informal networks exist, as at Citi and ISS. Such cultures are fostered by strong and clear corporate values

and by grapevines that widely disseminate reputational information so that managers can assemble effective teams. Other useful integrators are clear conflict resolution protocols, job rotation and training programs that reduce parochialism, and even virtual communities on the Internet.

Structural mechanisms such as multi-functional, multi-SBU task forces, standing committees, and integrative positions and roles can also bring together front and back. Finally, in all of the firms we studied, important roles were played by a variety of organizational systems and processes. Information and resource allocation systems, for example, identified the best human resources to serve capabilities and opportunities. Incentive systems rewarded organization-wide goals rather than departmental goals, and ensured that collaboration around capabilities and opportunities would be in the long-run interests of the firm.

Final words

Well-conceived organization processes and designs can help managers constantly identify asymmetries and potential capabilities, embed these in a configuration that grows and exploits them, and leverage those capabilities across complementary sets of market opportunities. Indeed, effective design provides the vehicle for bringing together developing resources and emerging opportunities in an ongoing process that sustains advantage.

READING 5.3 The capabilities of market-driven organizations

By George Day[1]

The marketing concept has been a paradox in the field of management. For over 40 years managers have been exhorted to 'stay close to the customer,' 'put the customer at the top of the organizational chart,' and define the purpose of a business as the creation and retention of satisfied customers. Companies that are

better equipped to respond to market requirements and anticipate changing conditions are expected to enjoy long-run competitive advantage and superior profitability.

Throughout much of its history, however, the marketing concept has been more an article of faith than a

---

[1] Source: This article was adapted from G.S. Day, 'The Capabilities of Market-Driven Organizations', *Journal of Marketing*, October, 1994, Vol. 58, No. 4, pp. 37–52. Reprinted with permission from the *Journal of Marketing*, published by the American Marketing Association.

practical basis for managing a business. Little was known about the defining features or attributes of this organizational orientation, and evidence as to the antecedents and performance consequences was mainly anecdotal. Consequently, managers had little guidance on how to improve or redirect their organizations' external orientation toward their markets.

Fortunately, this situation is changing following a 'rediscovery' in the late 1980s (Dickson 1992; Webster 1992). In the last five years, a number of conceptual and empirical studies have appeared that more clearly describe what a market orientation is and what it consists of. According to this emerging literature market orientation represents superior skills in understanding and satisfying customers (Day 1990). Its principal features are the following:

- a set of beliefs that puts the customer's interest first;
- the ability of the organization to generate, disseminate, and use superior information about customers and competitors;
- the coordinated application of interfunctional resources to the creation of superior customer value.

In addition, a modest but growing body of empirical evidence supports the proposition that a market orientation is positively associated with superior performance. Despite the recent progress in understanding what a market-driven organization does and identifying who they are, troubling gaps and shortcomings remain. Little is known, for example, about the characteristics of successful programs for building market orientation. How should these programs be designed? Should management emphasize fundamental culture change, revised work processes, organizational restructuring, new systems, redirected incentives, or some other set of plausible initiatives?

I address these issues by examining the role of capabilities in creating a market-oriented organization. Capabilities are complex bundles of skills and collective learning, exercised through organizational processes, that ensure superior coordination of functional activities. I propose that organizations can become more market oriented by identifying and building the special capabilities that set market-driven organizations apart.

Classifying capabilities

It is not possible to enumerate all possible capabilities, because every business develops its own configuration of capabilities that is rooted in the realities of its competitive market, past commitments, and anticipated requirements. None the less, certain types of capabilities can be recognized in all businesses, corresponding to the core processes for creating economic value.

Some capabilities are easier to identify than others, usually because their activities are contained within the organization. Thus, Pitney-Bowes's ability to solve customers' mail-handling problems and McDonald's Corporation's achievement of unparalleled consistency of service delivery in dispersed outlets are pointed to as distinctive capabilities that explain their durable advantages. The visibility and prevalence of these examples of capabilities that have been successfully deployed from the inside out have led some observers to argue that firms should be defined by what they are capable of doing, rather than by the needs they seek to satisfy. This perspective is unbalanced, because it is the ability of the business to use these inside-out capabilities to exploit external possibilities that matters. Thus, there has to be a matching 'outside-in' capability to sense these possibilities and decide how best to serve them.

Consider the Corning, Inc. division that manufactures fiber optic products. Its challenge was to balance demands for increased product customization and faster delivery while reducing costs to stay ahead of aggressive competition. Originally, its objective was to be the most efficient mass producer of standard fiber optics. As the fiber optic market evolved and customers began to demand more specialized products, it was necessary to convert the manufacturing capabilities from a rigid, standard-production system to a flexible manufacturing platform capable of building customized fiber products to order. This transition required both an inside-out capability to produce the low-cost, custom products on a timely basis and an outside-in capability for understanding the evolving requirements of customers and energizing the organization to respond to them.

Capabilities can be usefully sorted into three categories, depending on the orientation and focus of the defining processes (see Figure 5.3.1). At one end of the spectrum are those that are deployed from the *inside-out* and activated by market requirements, competitive challenges, and external opportunities. Examples are manufacturing and other transformation activities, logistics, and human resource management, including recruiting, training, and motivating employees. At the other end of the spectrum are those capabilities whose focal point is almost exclusively outside the organization. The purpose of these *outside-in* capabilities is to connect the processes that define the other organizational capabilities to the external environment and enable the business to compete by anticipating market requirements ahead of competitors and creating durable relationships with customers, channel members, and suppliers. Finally, spanning capabilities are needed to integrate the inside-out and outside-in capabilities. Strategy development, new product/service development, price setting, purchasing, and customer order fulfillment are critical activities that must be informed by both external (outside-in) and internal (inside-out) analyses.

Market-driven organizations have superior market sensing, customer linking, and channel bonding capabilities. The processes underlying their superior capabilities are well understood and effectively managed and deliver superior insights that inform and guide both spanning and inside-out capabilities. The effect is to shift the span of all processes further toward the external end of the orientation dimension. Consider what happens when human resources are managed by the belief that customer satisfaction is both a cause and a consequence of employee satisfaction. Key policies become market oriented: rewards are based on measurable improvements in customer satisfaction and retention, employees are empowered to resolve customer problems without approvals, recruiting is

based on customer problem-solving skills, and so forth. By contrast, the spanning and inside-out capabilities of internally oriented firms will be poorly guided by market considerations, which confines them to a narrow band toward the internal end of the orientation dimension. One reason is that the necessary outside-in processes that comprise the market sensing, customer linking, and channel bonding capabilities are likely to be poorly understood, badly managed, or deficient.

The role of spanning capabilities

Spanning capabilities are exercised through the sequences of activities that comprise the processes used to satisfy the anticipated needs of customers identified by the outside-in capabilities and meet the commitments that have been made to enhance relationships. Order fulfillment, new product development, and service delivery processes all play this role. Managing these horizontal processes so they become distinctive capabilities that competitors cannot readily match is very different from managing a vertical function in a traditional hierarchical organization.

First, process management emphasizes external objectives. These objectives may involve customers'

FIGURE 5.3.1 Classifying capabilities

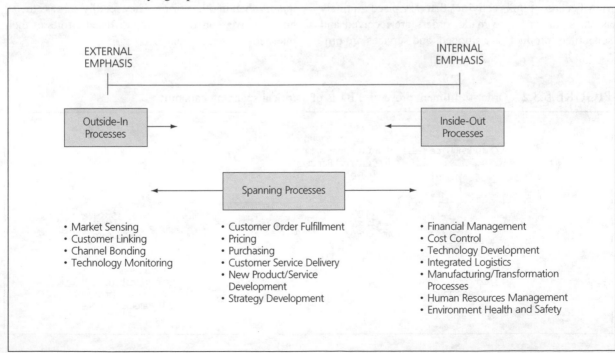

satisfaction with the outcome of the process, whether quality, delivery time, or installation assistance, or may be based on competitive performance benchmarks (e.g. cycle time, order processing time). This helps ensure that all those involved with the process are focused on providing superior value to external or internal customers. These objectives become the basis for a measurement and control system that monitors progress toward the objective.

Second, in coordinating the activities of a complex process, several jurisdictional boundaries must be crossed and horizontal connections made. These interactions require an identifiable owner of the process who can isolate sources of delay and take action to eliminate them. When no one understands the total flow of activities in an order-entry process, for example, critical time-consuming steps such as credit checks may be undertaken separately in sequence when they could have been done in parallel to save time.

Third, information is readily available to all team members, unfiltered by a hierarchy. If a question arises concerning order requirements, delivery status, or parts availability, everyone who is affected by the answer can get the information directly without having to go through an intermediary.

The order fulfillment process in Figure 5.3.2 illustrates both the problems and benefits of managing a process so it becomes a distinctive capability rather than simply a sequential series of necessary activities. Often this process is obscured from top management view because it links activities that take place routinely as sales forecasts are made, orders are received and scheduled, products are shipped, and services are pro-

vided. Things can go awry if unrealistic promises are made to customers, these promises are not kept, blame is passed around, and inventories expand as each function seeks to protect itself from the shortcomings of another (in part because no one incurs a cost for holding excess inventories).

Furthermore, the order fulfillment process has a wealth of connections to other processes. It brings together information from the outside-in processes and depends on their ability to forecast and generate a flow of orders. It depends even more on the inside-out manufacturing and logistics processes to fulfill the scheduled orders or have capacity in place to service requests and transactions. Finally, there is the allied process of cost estimation and pricing of orders. The management of this activity will significantly improve profitability, if the customer value of each order is clearly recognized and the costs of filling each order are known.

Market sensing as a distinctive capability

Every discussion of market orientation emphasizes the ability of the firm to learn about customers, competitors, and channel members in order to continuously sense and act on events and trends in present and prospective markets. In market-driven firms the processes for gathering, interpreting, and using market information are more systematic, thoughtful, and anticipatory than in other firms. They readily surpass the ad hoc, reactive, constrained, and diffused efforts of their internally focused rivals.

FIGURE 5.3.2   Order fulfillment processes: Basis of a critical spanning capability

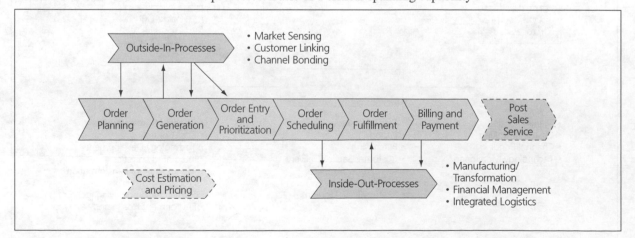

A behavioral definition of a market orientation as 'the organization-wide generation of market intelligence, dissemination of its intelligence across departments, and organization-wide responsiveness to it' (Kohli and Jaworski, 1990), captures the essence of a market sensing capability. Each element of this definition describes a distinct activity having to do with collecting and acting on information about customer needs and the influence of technology, competition, and other environmental forces. Narver and Slater (1990) offer another definition in the same spirit. They distinguish three behavioral components: customer orientation – the firm's understanding of the target market; competitor orientation – the firm's understanding of the longrun capabilities of present and prospective competitors; and interfunctional coordination – the coordinated utilization of company resources to create superior customer value.

An alternative to this behavioral perspective holds that a market orientation is part of a more deeply rooted and pervasive culture. For this purpose, Deshpandé and Webster (1989) define culture as 'the pattern of shared values and beliefs that gives the members of an organization meaning, and provides them with the rules for behavior.' A market-driven culture supports the value of thorough market intelligence and the necessity of functionally coordinated actions directed at gaining a competitive advantage. An absence of these shared beliefs and values would surely compromise the activity patterns advocated by the behavioral perspective.

The process of market sensing follows the usual sequence of information processing activities that organizations use to learn. The stylized sequence in Figure 5.3.3 can be initiated by a forthcoming decision or an emerging problem, such as explaining why performance is declining. In addition, established procedures for collecting secondary information may prompt further market-sensing activity. This step leads to the active acquisition and distribution of information about the needs and responses of the market, how it is segmented, how relationships are sustained, the intentions and capabilities of competitors, and the evolving role of channel partners. Before this information can be acted on, it has to be interpreted through a process of sorting, classification, and simplification to reveal coherent patterns. This interpretation is facilitated by the mental models of managers, which contain decision rules for filtering information and useful heuristics for deciding how to act on the information in light of anticipated outcomes. Further learning comes from observing and evaluating the results of the decisions taken on the basis of the prior information. Did the market respond as expected, and if not, why not? Organizational memory plays several roles in this process: it serves as a repository for collective insights contained within policies, procedures, routines, and rules that can be retrieved when needed; a source of answers to ongoing inquiries; and a major determinant of the ability to ask appropriate questions.

Market-driven firms are distinguished by an ability to sense events and trends in their markets ahead of their competitors. They can anticipate more accurately the responses to actions designed to retain or attract customers, improve channel relations, or thwart competitors. They can act on information in a timely, coherent manner because the assumptions about the market are broadly shared. This anticipatory capability is based on superiority in each step of the process. It is achieved through opened-minded inquiry, synergistic information distribution, mutually informed interpretations, and accessible memories.

FIGURE 5.3.3 Market sensing: Processes for learning about markets

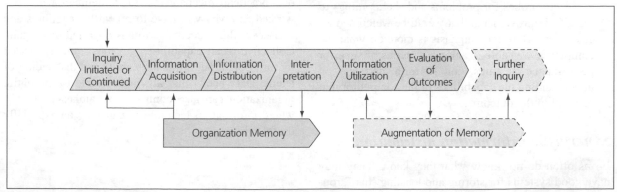

Open-minded inquiry

All organizations acquire information about trends, events, opportunities, and threats in their market environment through scanning, direct experience, imitation, or problem-solving inquiries. Market-driven organizations approach these activities in a more thoughtful and systematic fashion, in the belief that all decisions start with the market. The most distinctive features of their approach to inquiry are the following:

■ Active scanning. All organizations track key market conditions and activities and try to learn from the departures from what is normal and expected. However, this learning is usually a top-down effort because information from the front-line employees is blocked. In market-driven organizations, these front-line contacts, who hear complaints or requests for new services and see the consequences of competitive activity, are motivated to inform management systematically.

■ Self-critical benchmarking. Most firms do regular tear-down analyses of competitors' products and occasionally study firms for insights into how to perform discrete functions and activities better. Market-driven firms study attitudes, values, and management processes of nonpareils.

■ Continuous experimentation and improvement. All organizations tinker with their procedures and practices and take actions aimed at improving productivity and customer satisfaction. However, most are not very serious about systematically planning and observing the outcomes of these ongoing changes, so those that improve performance are adopted and others are dropped.

■ Informed imitation. Market-driven firms study their direct competitors so they can emulate successful moves before the competition gets too far ahead. This investigation requires thoughtful efforts to understand why the competitor succeeded, as well as further probes for problems and shortcomings to identify improvements that would be welcomed by customers. Here the emphasis is more on what the competitor was able to achieve in terms of superior performance, features, and so forth, and less on understanding the capabilities of the competitor that resulted in the outcome.

Synergistic information distribution

Firms often do not know what they know. They may have good systems for storing and locating 'hard' routine accounting and sales data, but otherwise managers have problems figuring out where in the organization a certain piece of information is known or assembling all the needed pieces in one place. This is especially true of competitor information, in which, for example, manufacturing may be aware of certain activities through common equipment suppliers, sales may hear about initiatives from distributors and collect rumors from customers, and the engineering department may have hired recently from a competitor.

Market-driven firms do not suffer unduly from organizational chimneys, silos, or smokestacks, which restrict information flows to vertical movements within functions. Instead, information is widely distributed, its value is mutually appreciated, and those functions with potentially synergistic information know where else it could be used beneficially.

Mutually informed interpretations

The simplifications inherent in the mental models used by managers facilitate learning when they are based on undistorted information about important relationships and are widely shared throughout the organization. These mental models can impede learning when they are incomplete, unfounded, or seriously distorted by functioning below the level of awareness, they are never examined. A market-driven organization avoids these pitfalls by using scenarios and other devices to force managers to articulate, examine, and eventually modify their mental models of how their markets work, how competitors and suppliers will react, and the parameters of the response coefficients in their marketing programs.

Accessible memory

Market-driven inquiry, distribution, and interpretation will not have a lasting effect unless what is learned is lodged in the collective memory. Organizations without practical mechanisms to remember what has worked and why will have to repeat their failures and rediscover their success formulas over and over again. Collective recall capabilities are most quickly eroded by turnover through transfers and rapid disbanding of teams. Data banks that are inaccessible to the entire organization can also contribute to amnesia. Here is where information technology can play an especially useful role.

Customer linking as a distinctive capability

As buyer-seller relationships continue their transformation, a customer-linking capability – creating and managing close customer relationships – is becoming increasingly important. At one time, standard purchasing practice emphasized arm's length adversarial bargaining with suppliers, aimed at achieving the lowest price for each transaction or contract. Not surprisingly, suppliers focused on individual transactions and gave little attention to the quality of the interface with the customer. They had little incentive to be open with buyers or develop superior or dedicated capabilities because they could easily lose the business to a competitor. The buyer, in turn, was unlikely to be aware of a supplier's costs and capabilities.

Now customers, as well as major channel members such as Ikea and Wal-Mart, are seeking closer, more collaborative relationships with suppliers based on a high level of coordination, participation in joint programs, and close communication links. They want to replace the adversarial model, which assumes that advantages are gained through cutting input costs, with a cooperative model that seeks advantage through total quality improvement and reduced time to market. This way of doing business suits their better suppliers, who confront intense competition that quickly nullifies their product advantages and powerful channels that control access to the market.

Despite recent emphasis on the establishment, maintenance, and enhancement of collaborative relationships, few firms have mastered this capability and made it a competitive advantage. Successful collaboration requires a high level of purposeful cooperation aimed at maintaining a trading relationship over time. The activities to be managed start with the coordination of inside-out and spanning capabilities, although these are not the means by which the relationship is managed. Instead, new skills, abilities, and processes must be mastered to achieve mutually satisfactory collaboration. These include the close communication and joint problem solving, and coordinating activities.

Close communication and joint problem solving

Suppliers must be prepared to develop team-based mechanisms for continuously exchanging information about needs, problems, and emerging requirements and then taking action. In a successful collaborative relationship, joint problem solving displaces negotiations. Suppliers must also be prepared to participate in the customer's development processes, even before the product specifications are established.

Communications occur at many levels and across many functions of the customer and supplier organizations, requiring a high level of internal coordination and a new role for the sales function. When the focus is on transactions, the salesperson is pivotal and the emphasis is on persuading the customer through features, price, terms, and the maintenance of a presence. The sales function adopts a very different – and possibly subordinate – role in a collaborative relationship. It is responsible for coordinating other functions, anticipating needs, demonstrating responsiveness, and building credibility and trust.

Coordinating activities

In addition to the scheduling of deliveries, new management processes are needed for (1) joint production planning and scheduling; (2) management of information system links so each knows the other's requirements and status and orders can be communicated electronically; and (3) mutual commitments to the improvement of quality and reliability.

Manufacturer-reseller relations has become a fertile area for the development of collaborative management capabilities, with the major grocery product firms taking the lead. The objective of each party used to be to transfer as much of their cost to the other as possible. This approach leads to dysfunctional practices such as forward buying to take advantage of manufacturer's promotional offers, resulting in excessive warehousing expenses and costly spikes in production levels. Traditionally, contacts between parties were limited to lower-level sales representatives calling on buyers who emphasized prices, quantities, and deals. Increasingly, manufacturers like Procter & Gamble and retailers like KMart are assigning multifunctional teams to deal with each other at many levels, including harmonizing systems, sharing logistics and product movement information, and jointly planning for promotional activity and product changes. The objectives of this collaborative activity are to cut total system costs while helping retailers improve sales.

Firms that have developed a distinctive capability for managing collaborative relationships find they have more integrated strategies. The integration begins with a broad-based agreement on which customers serve collaboratively. No longer is this choice left to the sales function, without regard to the impact on the manufacturing and service functions. The cross-functional coordination and information sharing required to work collaboratively with customers enhances shared understanding of the strategy and role of the different functions.

Although collaborative relationships are becoming increasingly important, they are not appropriate for every market or customer. Some customers want nothing more than the timely exchange of the product or service with minimum hassle and a competitive price. And because of the effort and resources required to support a tightly linked relationship, it may not be possible to do this with more than a few critical customers. Yet even when most relationships are purely transactional, there are still possibilities for gaining advantages by nurturing some elements of a linking capability within the organization. This process begins by analyzing which customers are more loyal or easier to retain and proceeds by seeking ways to maintain continuity with these customers through customized services or incentives.

Developing the capabilities of market-driven organizations

Initiatives to enhance market sensing and customer linking capabilities are integral to broader efforts to build a market-driven organization. The overall objective is to demonstrate a pervasive commitment to a set of processes, beliefs, and values, reflecting the philosophy that all decisions start with the customer and are guided by a deep and shared understanding of the customer's needs and behavior and competitors' capabilities and intentions, for the purpose of realizing superior performance by satisfying customers better than competitors.

Many firms have aspired to become market driven but have failed to instill and sustain this orientation. Often these aspirants underestimate how difficult a task it is to shift an organization's focus from internal to external concerns. They apparently assume that marginal changes, a few management workshops, and proclamations of intent will do the job, when in fact a wide-ranging cultural shift is necessary. To have any chance for success, change programs will have to match the magnitude of the cultural shift.

Preliminary insights into how to design change programs come from empirical research on why some organizations are more market oriented than others. For example, Jaworski and Kohli (1993) confirm the long-standing belief that top management commitment

is essential. Strong affirmation of the notion that market-driven organizations have superior capabilities comes from three of their findings. First, they found that formal and informal connectedness of functions facilitates the exchange of information whereas inter-departmental conflicts inhibit the communications that are necessary to effective market sensing. This confirms the desirability of managing this capability as a set of organization-spanning activities. Second, there was solid evidence that centralization was antithetical to market orientation. This mind-set appears to flourish when there is delegation of decision making authority and extensive participation in decision making. Finally, the use of market-based factors such as customer satisfaction for evaluating and rewarding managers was the single most influential determinant of market orientation.

Summary and conclusions

It is almost an article of faith within marketing that superior business performance is the result of superior skills in understanding and satisfying customers. This proposition has been partially validated by a growing body of research on the impact of a market orientation on business performance. This work has helped give a fuller picture of the attributes of market-driven organizations, highlighting the roles of culture, information utilization, and interfunctional coordination. These insights are not sufficient for managers, because they do not reveal how the superior skills were developed. All we see is the results of the organizational transformation. Now managers seek guidance on how to enhance the market orientation of their organization.

The emerging capabilities approach to strategy offers a valuable new perspective on how to achieve and sustain a market orientation. This approach seeks the sources of defensible competitive positions in the distinctive, difficult-to-imitate capabilities the organization has developed. The shift in emphasis to capabilities does not mean that strategic positioning is any less important. On the contrary, the choice of which capabilities to nurture and which investment commitments to make must be guided by a shared understanding of the industry structure, the needs of the target customer segments, the positional advantages being sought, and the trends in the environment.

Two capabilities are especially important in bringing these external realities to the attention of the organization. One is the market sensing capability, which determines how well the organization is equipped to continuously sense changes in its market and to anticipate the responses to marketing actions. The second is a customer-linking capability, which comprises the skills, abilities, and processes needed to achieve collaborative customer relationships so individual customer needs are quickly apparent to all functions and well-defined procedures are in place for responding to them.

READING

5.4

Firm resources and sustained competitive advantage

By Jay Barney[1]

Understanding sources of sustained competitive advantage for firms has become a major area of research in the field of strategic management. Since the 1960s, a single organizing framework has been used to structure much of this research. This framework, summarized in Figure 5.4.1, suggests that firms obtain sustained competitive advantages by implementing strategies that exploit their internal strengths, through responding to environmental opportunities, while neutralizing external threats and avoiding internal weaknesses. Most research on sources of sustained competitive advantage has focused either on isolating a firm's opportunities and threats (Porter, 1980, 1985), describing its strengths and weaknesses (Hofer and Schendel, 1978; Penrose, 1958), or analyzing how these are matched to choose strategies.

Research by Porter and his colleagues (Caves and Porter, 1977; Porter, 1980, 1985) has attempted to describe the environmental conditions that favor high levels of firm performance. Porter's 'five forces model,' for example, describes the attributes of an attractive industry and thus suggests that opportunities will be greater, and threats less, in these kinds of industries.

To help focus the analysis of the impact of a firm's environment on its competitive position, much of this type of strategic research has placed little emphasis on the impact of idiosyncratic firm attributes on a firm's competitive position. Implicitly, this work has adopted two simplifying assumptions. First, these environmental models of competitive advantage have assumed that firms within an industry (or firms within a strategic

FIGURE 5.4.1 The relationship between traditional 'strengths-weaknesses-opportunities-threats' analysis, the resource-based model, and models of industry attractiveness

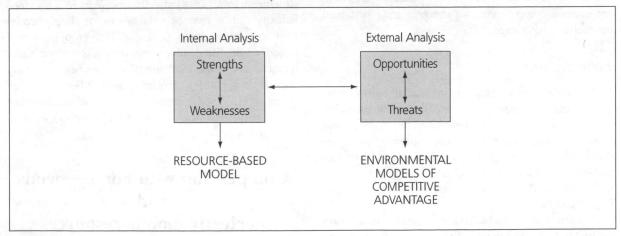

[1] Source: This article was adapted with permission from J.B. Barney, 'Firm Resources and Sustained Competitive Advantage', *Journal of Management*, Vol. 17, No. 1, 1991, pp. 99–120, © 1991 Oklahoma State University.

group) are identical in terms of the strategically relevant resources they control and the strategies they pursue. Second, these models assume that should resource heterogeneity develop in an industry or group (perhaps through new entry) that this heterogeneity will be very short lived because the resources that firms use to implement their strategies are highly mobile (i.e. they can be bought and sold in factor markets).

There is little doubt that these two assumptions have been very fruitful in clarifying our understanding of the impact of a firm's environment on performance. However, the resource-based view of competitive advantage, because it examines the link between a firm's internal characteristics and performance, obviously cannot build on these same assumptions. These assumptions effectively eliminate firm resource heterogeneity and immobility as possible sources of competitive advantage. The resource-based view of the firm substitutes two alternate assumptions in analyzing sources of competitive advantage. First, this model assumes that firms within an industry (or group) may be heterogeneous with respect to the strategic resources they control. Second, this model assumes that these resources may not be perfectly mobile across firms, and thus heterogeneity can be long lasting. The resource-based model of the firm examines the implications of these two assumptions for the analysis of sources of sustained competitive advantage.

Defining key concepts

To avoid possible confusion, three concepts that are central to the perspective developed in this reading are defined in this section. These concepts are firm resources, competitive advantage, and sustained competitive advantage.

Firm resources

In this reading, firm resources include all assets, capabilities, organizational processes, firm attributes, information, knowledge, etc. controlled by a firm that enable the firm to conceive of and implement strategies that improve its efficiency and effectiveness. In the language of traditional strategic analysis, firm resources are strengths that firms can use to conceive of and implement their strategies.

A variety of authors have generated lists of firm attributes that may enable firms to conceive of and implement value-creating strategies. For purposes of this discussion, these numerous possible firm resources can be conveniently classified into three categories: physical capital resources, human capital resources, and organizational capital resources. Those attributes of a firm's physical, human, and organizational capital that do enable a firm to conceive of and implement strategies that improve its efficiency and effectiveness are, for purposes of this discussion, firm resources. The purpose of this reading is to specify the conditions under which such firm resources can be a source of sustained competitive advantage for a firm.

Competitive advantage and sustained competitive advantage

A firm is said to have a competitive advantage when it is implementing a value creating strategy not simultaneously being implemented by any current or potential competitors. It is said to have a sustained competitive advantage when it is implementing a value creating strategy not simultaneously being implemented by any current or potential competitors and when these other firms are unable to duplicate the benefits of this strategy.

That a competitive advantage is sustained does not imply that it will 'last forever.' It only suggests that it will not be competed away through the duplication efforts of other firms. Unanticipated changes in the economic structure of an industry may make what was, at one time, a source of sustained competitive advantage, no longer valuable for a firm, and thus not a source of any competitive advantage. These structural revolutions in an industry redefine which of a firm's attributes are resources and which are not. Some of these resources, in turn, may be sources of sustained competitive advantage in the newly defined industry structure. However, what were resources in a previous industry setting may be weaknesses, or simply irrelevant, in a new industry setting. A firm enjoying a sustained competitive advantage may experience these major shifts in the structure of competition, and may see its competitive advantages nullified by such changes. However, a sustained competitive advantage is not nullified through competing firms duplicating the benefits of that competitive advantage.

Competition with homogeneous and perfectly mobile resources

Armed with these definitions, it is now possible to explore the impact of resource heterogeneity and immobility on sustained competitive advantage. This is done by examining the nature of competition when firm resources are perfectly homogeneous and mobile.

Resource homogeneity and mobility and sustained competitive advantage

Imagine an industry where firms possess exactly the same resources. This condition suggests that firms all have the same amount and kinds of strategically relevant physical, human, and organizational capital. Is there a strategy that could be conceived of and implemented by any one of these firms that could not also be conceived of and implemented by all other firms in this industry? The answer to this question must be no. The conception and implementation of strategies employs various firm resources. That one firm in an industry populated by identical firms has the resources to conceive of and implement a strategy means that these other firms, because they possess the same resources, can also conceive of and implement this strategy. Because these firms all implement the same strategies, they all will improve their efficiency and effectiveness in the same way, and to the same extent. Thus, in this kind of industry, it is not possible for firms to enjoy a sustained competitive advantage.

Resource homogeneity and mobility and first-mover advantages

One objection to this conclusion concerns so-called 'first-mover advantages' (Lieberman and Montgomery, 1988). In some circumstances, the first firm in an industry to implement a strategy can obtain a sustained competitive advantage over other firms. These firms may gain access to distribution channels, develop goodwill with customers, or develop a positive reputation, all before firms that implement their strategies later. Thus, first-moving firms may obtain a sustained competitive advantage.

However, upon reflection, it seems clear that if competing firms are identical in the resources they control, it is not possible for any one firm to obtain a competitive advantage from first moving. To be a first mover by implementing a strategy before any competing firms, a particular firm must have insights about the opportunities associated with implementing a strategy that are not possessed by other firms in the industry, or by potentially entering firms (Lieberman and Montgomery, 1988). This unique firm resource (information about an opportunity) makes it possible for the

better informed firm to implement its strategy before others. However, by definition, there are no unique firm resources in this kind of industry. If one firm in this type of industry is able to conceive of and implement a strategy, then all other firms will also be able to conceive of and implement that strategy, and these strategies will be conceived of and implemented in parallel, as identical firms become aware of the same opportunities and exploit that opportunity in the same way.

It is not being suggested that there can never be first-mover advantages in industries. It is being suggested that in order for there to be a first-mover advantage, firms in an industry must be heterogeneous in terms of the resources they control.

Resource homogeneity and mobility and entry/mobility barriers

A second objection to the conclusion that sustained competitive advantages cannot exist when firm resources in an industry are perfectly homogeneous and mobile concerns the existence of 'barriers to entry' (Bain, 1956), or more generally, 'mobility barriers' (Caves and Porter, 1977). The argument here is that even if firms within an industry (group) are perfectly homogeneous, if there are strong entry or mobility barriers, these firms may be able to obtain a sustained competitive advantage *vis-à-vis* firms that are not in their industry (group). This sustained competitive advantage will be reflected in above normal economic performance for those firms protected by the entry or mobility barrier (Porter, 1980).

However, from another point of view, barriers to entry or mobility are only possible if current and potentially competing firms are heterogeneous in terms of the resources they control and if these resources are not perfectly mobile. The heterogeneity requirement is self-evident. For a barrier to entry or mobility to exist, firms protected by these barriers must be implementing different strategies than firms seeking to enter these protected areas of competition. Firms restricted from entry are unable to implement the same strategies as firms within the industry or group. Because the implementation of strategy requires the application of firm resources, the inability of firms seeking to enter an industry or group to implement the same strategies as firms within that industry or group suggests that firms seeking to enter must not have the same strategically relevant resources as firms within the industry or group. Thus, barriers to entry and mobility only exist when competing firms are heterogeneous in terms of the strategically relevant resources they control.

The requirement that firm resources be immobile in order for barriers to entry or mobility to exist is also clear. If firm resources are perfectly mobile, then any resource that allows some firms to implement a strategy protected by entry or mobility barriers can easily be acquired by firms seeking to enter into this industry or group. Once these resources are acquired, the strategy in question can be conceived of and implemented in the same way that other firms have conceived of and implemented their strategies. These strategies are thus not a source of sustained competitive advantage.

Again, it is not being suggested that entry or mobility barriers do not exist. However, it is being suggested that these barriers only become sources of sustained competitive advantage when firm resources are not homogeneously distributed across competing firms and when these resources are not perfectly mobile.

Firm resources and sustained competitive advantage

Thus far, it has been suggested that in order to understand sources of sustained competitive advantage, it is necessary to build a theoretical model that begins with the assumption that firm resources may be heterogeneous and immobile. Of course, not all firm resources hold the potential of sustained competitive advantages. To have this potential, a firm resource must have four attributes:

- it must be valuable, in the sense that it exploits opportunities and/or neutralizes threats in a firm's environment;
- it must be rare among a firm's current and potential competition;
- it must be imperfectly imitable;
- there cannot be strategically equivalent substitutes for this resource that are valuable but neither rare or imperfectly imitable.

These attributes of firm resources can be thought of as empirical indicators of how heterogeneous and immobile a firm's resources are and thus how useful these resources are for generating sustained competitive advantages. Each of these attributes of a firm's resources are discussed in more detail below.

Valuable resources

Firm resources can only be a source of competitive advantage or sustained competitive advantage when they are valuable. As suggested earlier, resources are valuable when they enable a firm to conceive of or implement strategies that improve its efficiency and effectiveness. The traditional 'strengths–weaknesses–opportunities–threats' model of firm performance suggests that firms are able to improve their performance only when their strategies exploit opportunities or neutralize threats. Firm attributes may have the other characteristics that could qualify them as sources of competitive advantage (e.g. rareness, inimitability, non-substitutability), but these attributes only become resources when they exploit opportunities or neutralize threats in a firm's environment.

That firm attributes must be valuable in order to be considered resources (and thus as possible sources of sustained competitive advantage) points to an important complementarity between environmental models of competitive advantage and the resource-based model. These environmental models help isolate those firm attributes that exploit opportunities and/or neutralize threats, and thus specify which firm attributes can be considered as resources. The resource-based model then suggests what additional characteristics that these resources must possess if they are to generate sustained competitive advantage.

Rare resources

By definition, valuable firm resources possessed by large numbers of competing or potentially competing firms cannot be sources of either a competitive advantage or a sustained competitive advantage. A firm enjoys a competitive advantage when it is implementing a value-creating strategy not simultaneously implemented by large numbers of other firms. If a particular valuable firm resource is possessed by large numbers of firms, then each of these firms have the capability of exploiting that resource in the same way, thereby implementing a common strategy that gives no one firm a competitive advantage.

The same analysis applies to bundles of valuable firm resources used to conceive of and implement strategies. Some strategies require a particular mix of physical capital, human capital, and organizational capital resources to implement. One firm resource required in the implementation of almost all strategies is managerial talent (Hambrick, 1987). If this particular bundle of firm resources is not rare, then large numbers of firms will be able to conceive of and implement the strategies in question, and these strategies will not be a source of competitive advantage, even though the resources in question may be valuable.

To observe that competitive advantages (sustained or otherwise) only accrue to firms that have valuable and rare resources is not to dismiss common (i.e. not rare) firm resources as unimportant. Instead, these valuable but common firm resources can help ensure a firm's survival when they are exploited to create competitive parity in an industry. Under conditions of competitive parity, though no one firm obtains a competitive advantage, firms do increase their probability of economic survival.

How rare a valuable firm resource must be in order to have the potential for generating a competitive advantage is a difficult question. It is not difficult to see that if a firm's valuable resources are absolutely unique among a set of competing and potentially competing firms, those resources will generate at least a competitive advantage and may have the potential of generating a sustained competitive advantage. However, it may be possible for a small number of firms in an industry to possess a particular valuable resource and still generate a competitive advantage. In general, as long as the number of firms that possess a particular valuable resource (or a bundle of valuable resources) is less than the number of firms needed to generate perfect competition dynamics in an industry, that resource has the potential of generating a competitive advantage.

Imperfectly imitable resources

It is not difficult to see that valuable and rare organizational resources may be a source of competitive advantage. Indeed, firms with such resources will often be strategic innovators, for they will be able to conceive of and engage in strategies that other firms could either not conceive of, or not implement, or both, because these other firms lacked the relevant firm resources. The observation that valuable and rare organizational resources can be a source of competitive advantage is another way of describing first-mover advantages accruing to firms with resource advantages.

However, valuable and rare organizational resources can only be sources of sustained competitive advantage if firms that do not possess these resources cannot obtain them. These firm resources are imperfectly imitable. Firm resources can be imperfectly imitable for one or a combination of three reasons: (a) the ability of a firm to obtain a resource is dependent upon

unique historical conditions, (b) the link between the resources possessed by a firm and a firm's sustained competitive advantage is *causally ambiguous*, or (c) the resource generating a firm's advantage is *socially complex*. Each of these sources of the imperfect imitability of firm resources are examined below.

Unique historical conditions and imperfectly imitable resources. Another assumption of most environmental models of firm competitive advantage, besides resource homogeneity and mobility, is that the performance of firms can be understood independent of the particular history and other idiosyncratic attributes of firms. These researchers seldom argue that firms do not vary in terms of their unique histories, but rather that these unique histories are not relevant to understanding a firm's performance (Porter, 1980).

The resource-based view of competitive advantage developed here relaxes this assumption. Indeed, this approach asserts that not only are firms intrinsically historical and social entities, but that their ability to acquire and exploit some resources depends upon their place in time and space. Once this particular unique time in history passes, firms that do not have space- and time-dependent resources cannot obtain them, and thus these resources are imperfectly imitable.

Resource-based theorists are not alone in recognizing the importance of history as a determinant of firm performance and competitive advantage. Traditional strategy researchers often cited the unique historical circumstances of a firm's founding, or the unique circumstances under which a new management team takes over a firm, as important determinants of a firm's long-term performance. More recently, several economists (e.g. Arthur, Ermoliev and Kaniovsky, 1987; David, 1985) have developed models of firm performance that rely heavily on unique historical events as determinants of subsequent actions. Employing path-dependent models of economic performance these authors suggest that the performance of a firm does not depend simply on the industry structure within which a firm finds itself at a particular point in time, but also on the path a firm followed through history to arrive where it is. If a firm obtains valuable and rare resources because of its unique path through history, it will be able to exploit those resources in implementing value-creating strategies that cannot be duplicated by other firms, for firms without that particular path through history cannot obtain the resources necessary to implement the strategy.

The acquisition of all the types of firm resources examined in this article can depend upon the unique historical position of a firm. A firm that locates it facilities on what turns out to be a much more valuable location than was anticipated when the location was chosen possesses an imperfectly imitable physical capital resource. A firm with scientists who are uniquely positioned to create or exploit a significant scientific breakthrough may obtain an imperfectly imitable resource from the history-dependent nature of these scientist's individual human capital. Finally, a firm with a unique and valuable organizational culture that emerged in the early stages of a firm's history may have an imperfectly imitable advantage over firms founded in another historical period, where different (and perhaps less valuable) organizational values and beliefs come to dominate.

Causal ambiguity and imperfectly imitable resources.   Unlike the relationship between a firm's unique history and the imitability of its resources, the relationship between the causal ambiguity of a firm's resources and imperfect imitability has received systematic attention in the literature. In this context, causal ambiguity exists when the link between the resources controlled by a firm and a firm's sustained competitive advantage is not understood or understood only very imperfectly.

When the link between a firm's resources and its sustained competitive advantage is poorly understood, it is difficult for firms that are attempting to duplicate a successful firm's strategies through imitation of its resources to know which resources it should imitate. Imitating firms may be able to describe some of the resources controlled by a successful firm. However, under conditions of causal ambiguity, it is not clear that the resources that can be described are the same resources that generate a sustained competitive advantage, or whether that advantage reflects some other non-described firm resource. Sometimes it is difficult to understand why one firm consistently outperforms other firms. Causal ambiguity is at the heart of this difficulty. In the face of such causal ambiguity, imitating firms cannot know the actions they should take in order to duplicate the strategies of firms with a sustained competitive advantage.

To be a source of sustained competitive advantage, both the firms that possess resources that generate a competitive advantage and the firms that do not possess these resources but seek to imitate them must be faced with the same level of causal ambiguity (Lippman and Rumelt, 1982). If firms that control these resources have a better understanding of their impact on competitive advantage than firms without

these resources, then firms without these resources can engage in activities to reduce their knowledge disadvantage. They can do this, for example, by hiring away well placed knowledgeable managers in a firm with a competitive advantage or by engaging in a careful systematic study of the other firm's success. Although acquiring this knowledge may take some time and effort once knowledge of the link between a firm's resources and its ability to implement certain strategies is diffused throughout competing firms, causal ambiguity no longer exists, and thus cannot be a source of imperfect imitability. In other words, if a firm with a competitive advantage understands the link between the resources it controls and its advantages, then other firms can also learn about that link, acquire the necessary resources (assuming they are not imperfectly imitable for other reasons), and implement the relevant strategies. In such a setting, a firm's competitive advantages are not sustained because they can be duplicated.

At first, it may seem unlikely that a firm with a sustained competitive advantage will not fully understand the source of that advantage. However, given the very complex relationship between firm resources and competitive advantage, such an incomplete understanding is not implausible. The resources controlled by a firm are very complex and interdependent. Often, they are implicit, taken for granted by managers, rather than being subject to explicit analysis. Numerous resources, taken by themselves or in combination with other resources, may yield sustained competitive advantage. Although managers may have numerous hypotheses about which resources generate their firm's advantages, it is rarely possible to rigorously test these hypotheses. As long as numerous plausible explanations of the sources of sustained competitive advantage exist within a firm, the link between the resources controlled by a firm and sustained competitive advantage remains somewhat ambiguous, and thus which of a firm's resources to imitate remains uncertain.

Social complexity.   A final reason that a firm's resources may be imperfectly imitable is that they may be very complex social phenomena, beyond the ability of firms to systematically manage and influence. When competitive advantages are based in such complex social phenomena, the ability of other firms to imitate these resources is significantly constrained.

A wide variety of firm resources may be socially complex. Examples include the interpersonal relations among managers in a firm, a firm's culture (Barney, 1986), a firm's reputation among suppliers and customers. Notice that in most of these cases it is possible to specify how these socially complex resources add value to a firm. Thus, there is little or no causal ambiguity surrounding the link between these firm resources and competitive advantage. However, understanding that, say, an organizational culture with certain attributes or quality relations among managers can improve a firm's efficiency and effectiveness does not necessarily imply that firms without these attributes can engage in systematic efforts to create them. Such social engineering may be, for the time being at least, beyond the capabilities of most firms. To the extent that socially complex firm resources are not subject to such direct management, these resources are imperfectly imitable.

Notice that complex physical technology is not included in this category of sources of imperfectly imitable. In general, physical technology, whether it takes the form of machine tools or robots in factories or complex information management system, is by itself typically imitable. If one firm can purchase these physical tools of production and thereby implement some strategies, then other firms should also be able to purchase these physical tools, and thus such tools should not be a source of sustained competitive advantage.

On the other hand, the exploitation of physical technology in a firm often involves the use of socially complex firm resources. Several firms may all possess the same physical technology, but only one of these firms may possess the social relations, culture, traditions, etc. to fully exploit this technology in implementing strategies. If these complex social resources are not subject to imitation (and assuming they are valuable and rare and no substitutes exist), these firms may obtain a sustained competitive advantage from exploiting their physical technology more completely than other firms, even though competing firms do not vary in terms of the physical technology they possess.

Substitutability

The last requirement for a firm resource to be a source of sustained competitive advantage is that there must be no strategically equivalent valuable resources that are themselves either not rare or imitable. Two valuable firm resources (or two bundles of firm resources) are strategically equivalent when they each can be exploited separately to implement the same strategies. Suppose that one of these valuable firm resources is rare and imperfectly imitable, but the other is not. Firms with this first resource will be able to conceive

of and implement certain strategies. If there were no strategically equivalent firm resources, these strategies would generate a sustained competitive advantage (because the resources used to conceive and implement them are valuable, rare, and imperfectly imitable). However, that there are strategically equivalent resources suggests that other current or potentially competing firms can implement the same strategies, but in a different way, using different resources. If these alternative resources are either not rare or imitable, then numerous firms will be able to conceive of and implement the strategies in question, and those strategies will not generate a sustained competitive advantage. This will be the case even though one approach to implementing these strategies exploits valuable, rare, and imperfectly imitable firm resources.

Substitutability can take at least two forms. First, though it may not be possible for a firm to imitate another firm's resources exactly, it may be able to substitute a similar resource that enables it to conceive of and implement the same strategies. For example, a firm seeking to duplicate the competitive advantages of another firm by imitating that other firm's high quality top management team will often be unable to copy that team exactly. However, it may be possible for this firm to develop its own unique top management team. Though these two teams will be different (different people, different operating practices, a different history, etc.), they may likely be strategically equivalent and thus be substitutes for one another. If different top management teams are strategically equivalent (and if these substitute teams are common or highly imitable), then a high quality top management team is not a source of sustained competitive advantage, even though a particular management team of a particular firm is valuable, rare and imperfectly imitable.

Second, very different firm resources can also be strategic substitutes. For example, managers in one firm may have a very clear vision of the future of their company because of a charismatic leader in their firm. Managers in competing firms may also have a very clear vision of the future of their companies, but this common vision may reflect these firms' systematic, company-wide strategic planning process. From the point of view of managers having a clear vision of the future of their company, the firm resource of a charismatic leader and the firm resource of a formal planning system may be strategically equivalent, and thus substitutes for one another. If large numbers of competing firms have a formal planning system that generates this common vision (or if such a formal planning is highly imitable), then firms with such a vision derived from a charismatic leader will not have a sustained competitive advantage, even though the firm resource of a charismatic leader is probably rare and imperfectly imitable.

Of course, the strategic substitutability of firm resources is always a matter of degree. It is the case, however, that substitute firm resources need not have exactly the same implications for an organization in order for those resources to be equivalent from the point of view of the strategies that firms can conceive of and implement. If enough firms have these valuable substitute resources (i.e. they are not rare), or if enough firms can acquire them (i.e. they are imitable), then none of these firms (including firms whose resources are being substituted for) can expect to obtain a sustained competitive advantage.

The framework

The relationship between resource heterogeneity and immobility; value, rareness, imitability, and substitutability; and sustained competitive advantage is summarized in Figure 5.4.2. This framework can be applied in analyzing the potential of a broad range of firm resources to be sources of sustained competitive advantage. These analyses not only specify the theoretical conditions under which sustained competitive advantage might exist, they also suggest specific

empirical questions that need to be addressed before the relationship between a particular firm resource and sustained competitive advantage can be understood.

That the study of sources of sustained competitive advantage focuses on valuable, rare, imperfectly imitable, and non-substitutable resource endowments does not suggest – as some population ecologists would have it (e.g., Hannan and Freeman, 1977) – that managers are irrelevant in the study of such advantages. In fact, managers are important in this model, for it is managers that are able to understand and describe the economic performance potential of a firm's endowments. Without such managerial analyses, sustained competitive advantage is not likely. This is the case even though the skills needed to describe the rare, imperfectly imitable, and non-substitutable resources of a firm may themselves not be rare, imperfectly imitable, or non-substitutable.

Indeed, it may be the case that a manager or a managerial team is a firm resource that has the potential for generating sustained competitive advantages. The conditions under which this will be the case can be outlined using the framework presented in Figure 5.4.2. However, in the end, what becomes clear is that firms cannot expect to 'purchase' sustained competitive advantages on open markets. Rather, such advantages must be found in the rare, imperfectly imitable, and non-substitutable resources already controlled by a firm.

FIGURE 5.4.2   Firm resources and sustained competitive advantage

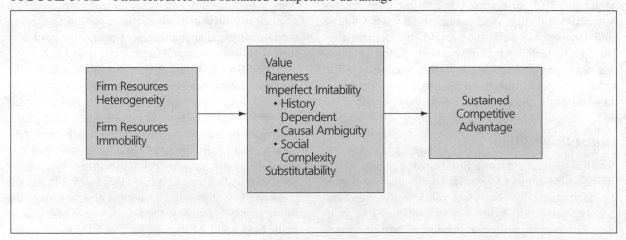

BUSINESS LEVEL STRATEGY IN INTERNATIONAL PERSPECTIVE

Whoever is winning at the moment will always seem to be invincible.

George Orwell (1903–1950); English novelist

Just as in the previous debates, it has become clear that there are various ways of dealing with the paradox of markets and resources. Each of the authors has argued a particular point of view, and it is the reader's task to judge which approach will yield the highest strategic dividends, under which set of circumstances. And as before, the chapter is concluded by explicitly looking at the issue from an international angle.

The difference between this and other chapters is that comparative management researchers have not reported specific national preferences for an inside-out or an outside-in perspective. This may be due to the fact that there actually are no distinct national inclinations when dealing with this paradox. However, it might also be the case that the late emergence of resource-based theories (starting in the early 1990s) has not yet allowed for cross-national comparisons.

As a stimulus to the debate on whether there are national differences in the approach to business level strategies, we would like to bring forward a number of factors that might be of influence on how the paradox of markets and resources is tackled in different countries. It goes almost without saying that more international research is needed to give this issue a firmer footing.

Mobility barriers

In general, industry and market positions will be of more value if there are high mobility barriers within the environment (Porter, 1980). Some of these mobility barriers can be specifically national in origin. Government regulation, in particular, can be an important source of mobility barriers. For instance, import quotas and duties, restrictive licensing systems, and fiscal regulations and subsidies, can all – knowingly or unknowingly – result in protection of incumbent firms. Such government intervention enhances the importance of obtained positions.

Other national sources of mobility barriers can be unions' resistance to change and high customer loyalty. In some economies high mobility barriers might also be imposed by powerful groups or families.

In such economies, which are more rigid due to high mobility barriers, strategists might have a strong preference to think in terms of market positions first, because these are more difficult to obtain than the necessary resources. The opposite would be true in more dynamic economies, where market positions might easily be challenged by competitors, unless they are based on distinctive and difficult to imitate resources.

Resource mobility

A second international difference might be found in the types of resources employed across countries. In nations where the dominant industries are populated by firms using relatively simple and abundant resources, market positions are far more important, since acquisition of the necessary resources is hardly a worry. However, if a national economy is composed of industries using complex bundles of resources, requiring many years of painstaking development, there might be a tendency to emphasize the importance of resources over market positions.

FURTHER READING

Although many textbooks give an overview of the variety of approaches to the topic of business level strategy, none of these introductions are as crisp as John Kay's book, *Foundations of Corporate Success: How Business Strategies Add Value*, which can be highly recommended as further reading. For a clear summary of the competing perspectives on business level strategy, see Robert Hoskisson's article 'Theory and Research in Strategic Management: Swings of a Pendulum'.

Most of what has been published on the topic of business level strategy has implicitly or explicitly made reference to the work of Michael Porter. Therefore, any follow-up readings should include his benchmark works *Competitive Strategy* and *Competitive Advantage*. It is also interesting to see how his thinking has developed and has embraced some of the resource-based concepts. In particular his articles 'Towards a Dynamic Theory of Strategy', and 'What is Strategy?' are stimulating works. Also highly recommended is the book by Robert Buzzell and Bradley Gale, *The PIMS Principles: Linking Strategy to Performance*, which has had a big impact by clarifying how market share and profitability are closely linked.

For a better insight into the resource-based approach, readers might want to go back to Edith Penrose's classic book *The Theory of the Growth of the Firm*. For a more recent introduction, the follow-up to Jay Barney's original article (Reading 5.4) is recommended. This article, written together with Mike Wright and David Ketchen, is titled 'The Resource-Based View of the Firm: Ten Years After 1991' and was part of an insightful special issue of the *Journal of Management*. David Collis and Cynthia Montgomery have also written an accessible article explaining the resource-based view, entitled 'Competing on Resources: Strategy in the 1990s'. Other important works that are more academically oriented are 'Dynamic Capabilities and Strategic Management' by David Teece, Garry Pisano and Amy Shuen, and 'The Cornerstones of Competitive Advantage: A Resource-Based View' by Margaret Peteraf. A very stimulating article bringing together outside-in and inside-out arguments is 'Strategic Integration: Competing in the Age of Capabilities', by Peter Fuchs, Kenneth Mifflin, Danny Miller and John Whitney.

Last, but not least, the works of Garry Hamel and C.K. Prahalad should be mentioned. Many of their articles in *Harvard Business Review*, such as 'Strategic Intent,' 'Strategy as Stretch and Leverage' and 'The Core Competence of the Corporation' (Reading 6.2 in this book) have had a major impact, both on practitioners and academics, and are well worth reading. Many of the ideas expressed in these articles have been brought together in their book *Competing for the Future*, which is therefore highly recommended.

REFERENCES

Abell, D. (1980) *Defining the Business: The Starting Point of Strategic Planning*, Prentice Hall, Englewood Cliffs, NJ.

Amit, R., and Zott, C. (2001) 'Value Creation in E-business', *Strategic Management Journal*, Vol. 22, pp. 493–520.

Arthur, W.B., Ermoliev, Y.M., and Kaniovsky, Y.M. (1987) 'Path Dependent Processes and the Emergence of Macro Structure', *European Journal of Operations Research*, Vol. 30, pp. 294–303.

Ashkenas, R. (1995) *The Boundaryless Organization*, Jossey-Bass, San Francisco, CA.

Baden-Fuller, C., and Stopford, J.M. (1992) *Rejuvenating the Mature Business*, Routledge, London.

Bain, J. (1956) *Barriers to New Competition*, Harvard University Press, Cambridge, MA.

Barney, J.B. (1986) 'Organizational Culture: Can It Be a Source of Sustained Competitive Advantage?', *Academy of Management Review*, Vol. 11, pp. 656–665.

Barney, J.B. (1991) 'Firm Resources and Sustained Competitive Advantage', *Journal of Management*, Vol. 17, No. 1, pp. 99–120.

Barney, J.B., Wright, M., and Ketchen, D.J. (2001) 'The Resource-Based View of the Firm: Ten Years After 1991', *Journal of Management*, Vol.27, Issue 6, pp. 625–641.

Buzzell, R.D., and Gale, B.T. (1987) *The PIMS Principles: Linking Strategy to Performance*, Free Press, New York.

Caves, R.E., and Porter, M.E. (1977) 'From Entry Barriers to Mobility Barriers: Conjectural Decisions and Contrived Deterrence to New Competition', *Quarterly Journal of Economics*, Vol. 91, pp. 241–262.

Christensen, C. (1997) *The Innovator's Dilemma*, HarperBusiness, New York.

Collis, D.J., and Montgomery, C.A. (1995) 'Competing on Resources: Strategy in the 1990s', *Harvard Business Review*, Vol. 73, No. 4, July-August, pp. 118–128.

David, P.A. (1985) 'Clio and the Economics of QWERTY', *American Economic Review Proceedings*, Vol. 75, pp. 332–337.

Day, G.S. (1990) *Market Driven Strategy, Processes for Creating Value*, The Free Press, New York.

Day, G.S. (1994) 'The Capabilities of Market-Driven Organizations', *Journal of Marketing*, Vol. 58, No. 4, October, pp. 37–52.

Deshpandé, R., and Webster Jr., F.E. (1989) 'Organizational Culture and Marketing: Defining the Research Agenda', *Journal of Marketing*, Vol. 53, pp. 3–15.

Dickson, P.R. (1992) 'Toward A General Theory of Competitive Rationality', *Journal of Marketing*, Vol. 56, pp. 69–83.

Dierickx, I., and K. Cool (1989) 'Asset Stock Accumulation and Sustainability of Competitive Advantage', *Management Science*, Vol. 35, No. 12, December, pp. 1504–1511.

Dretske, F. (1981) *Knowledge and the Flow of Information*, MIT Press, Cambridge, MA.

Durand, T. (1996) *Revisiting Key Dimensions of Competence*. Paper presented to the SMS Conference, Phoenix.

Eisenstat, R., Foote, N., Galbraith, J., and Miller, D. (2001) 'Beyond the Business Unit', *McKinsey Quarterly*, No. 1, January, pp. 54–63.

Fuchs, P.H., Mifflin, K.E., Miller, D., and Whitney, J.O. (2000), 'Strategic Integration: Competing in the Age of Capabilities', *California Management Review*, Vol. 42, No. 3, Spring, pp. 118–147.

Gilbert, X., and Strebel, P. (1989) 'From Innovation to Outpacing', *Business Quarterly*, Summer, pp. 19–22.

Grant, R.M. (2002) *Contemporary Strategy Analysis: Concepts, Techniques, Applications*, Fourth Edition, Blackwell Publishers, Oxford.

Hambrick, D. (1987) 'Top Management Teams: Key to Strategic Success', *California Management Review*, Vol. 30, pp. 88–108.

Hamel, G., and Prahalad, C.K. (1989) 'Strategic Intent', *Harvard Business Review*, May–June, pp. 63–77.

Hamel, G., and Prahalad, C.K. (1993) 'Strategy as Stretch and Leverage', *Harvard Business Review*, Vol. 71, No. 2, March–April, pp. 75–84.

Hamel, G., and Prahalad, C.K. (1994) *Competing for the Future*, Harvard Business School Press, Boston, MA.

Hannan, M.T., and Freeman, J. (1977) 'The Population Ecology of Organizations', *American Journal of Sociology*, Vol. 82, No. 5, March, pp. 929–964.

Hofer, C., and Schendel, D. (1978) *Strategy Formulation: Analytical Concepts*, West, St. Paul, MN.

Hoskisson, R.E. (1999) 'Theory and Research in Strategic Management: Swings of a Pendulum', *Journal of Management*, May–June, pp. 1–50.

Itami, H. (1987) *Mobilizing Invisible Assets*, Harvard University Press, Cambridge, MA.

Jaworski, B., and Kohli, A.K. (1993) 'Market Orientation: Antecedents and Consequences', *Journal of Marketing*, Vol. 57, No. 3, July, pp. 53–70.

Kay, J. (1993) *Foundations of Corporate Success: How Business Strategies Add Value*, Oxford University Press, Oxford.

Kohli, A.K., and Jaworski, B. (1990) 'Market Orientation: The Construct, Research Propositions, and Managerial Implications', *Journal of Marketing*, Vol. 54, pp. 1–18.

Leonard-Barton, D. (1995) *Wellsprings of Knowledge*, Harvard Business School Press, Boston, MA.

Lieberman, M.B., and Montgomery, D.B. (1988) 'First Mover Adavantages', *Strategic Management Journal*, Vol. 9, No. 1, January–February, pp. 41–58.

Lieberman, M.B., and Montgomery, D.B. (1998) 'First-Mover (Dis)Advantages: Retrospective and Link with the Resource-Based View', *Strategic Management Journal*, Vol. 19, No. 12, December, pp. 1111–1126.

Lippman, S., and Rumelt, R. (1982) 'Uncertain Imitability: An Analysis of Interfirm Differences in Efficiency under Competition', *Bell Journal of Economics*, Vol. 13, pp. 418–438.

Lowendahl, B.R. (1997) *Strategic Management of Professional Business Service Firms*, Copenhagen Business School Press, Copenhagen.

Miller, D. (1990) *The Icarus Paradox*, Harper Business, New York.

Miller, D., Eisenstat, R., and Foote, N. (2002) 'Strategy from the Inside-Out: Building Capability-Creating Organizations', *California Management Review*, Vol. 44, No. 3, Spring, pp. 37–54.

Mintzberg, H., Ahlstrand, B., and Lampel, J. (1998) *Strategy Safari: A Guided Tour Through the Wilds of Strategic Management*, The Free Press, New York.

Narver, J.C., and Slater, S.F. (1990) 'The Effect of a Marketing Orientation on Business Profitability', *Journal of Marketing*, Vol. 54, October, pp. 20–35.

Nelson, R., and Winter, S. (1982) *An Evolutionary Theory of Economic Change*, Harvard University Press, Cambridge, MA.

Nonaka, I. (1991) 'The Knowledge-Creating Company', *Harvard Business Review*, Vol. 69, No. 6, November–December, pp. 96–104.

Nonaka, I., and Konno, N. (1998) 'The Concept of Ba: Building a Foundation for Knowledge Creation', *California Management Review*, Vol. 40, No. 3, Spring, pp. 40–54.

Norman, R., and Ramirez, R. (1993) 'From Value Chain to Value Constellation: Designing Interactive Strategy', *Harvard Business Review*, July–August, pp. 65–77.

Penrose, E.T. (1958) *The Theory of the Growth of the Firm*, Wiley, New York.

Peteraf, M.A. (1993) 'The Cornerstones of Competitive Advantage: A Resource-Based View', *Strategic Management Journal*, Vol. 14, pp. 179–191.

Polanyi, M. (1958) *Personal Knowledge*, University of Chicago Press, Chicago.

Porac, J.F., Thomas, H., and Baden-Fuller, C. (1989) 'Competitive Groups as Cognitive Communities: The Case of Scottish Knitwear Manufacturers', *Journal of Management Studies*, Vol. 26, pp. 397–416.

Porter, M.E. (1980) *Competitive Strategy: Techniques for Analyzing Industries and Competitors*, Free Press, New York.

Porter, M.E. (1985) *Competitive Advantage: Creating and Sustaining Superior Performance*, Free Press, New York.

Porter, M.E. (1991) 'Towards a Dynamic Theory of Strategy', *Strategic Management Journal*, Vol. 12, pp. 95–117.

Porter, M.E. (1996) 'What is Strategy?', *Harvard Business Review*, Vol. 74, No. 6, November–December, pp. 61–78.

Prahalad, C.K., and Hamel, G. (1990) 'The Core Competence of the Corporation', *Harvard Business Review*, Vol. 68, No. 3, May–June, pp. 79–91.

Rumelt, R.P. (1980) 'The Evaluation of Business Strategy', in: W.F. Glueck (ed.), *Business Policy and Strategic Management*, Third Edition, McGraw-Hill, New York.

Rumelt, R.P. (1996) 'Inertia and Transformation', in: C.A. Montgomery (ed.), *Resource-based and Evolutionary Theories of the Firm: Towards a Synthesis*, Kluwer Academic Publishers, Boston, pp. 101–132.

Sanchez, R., Heene, A., and Thomas, H. (eds.) (1996) *Dynamics of Competence-Based Competition*, Elsevier, London.

Shay, J.P., and Rothaermel, R.T. (1999) 'Dynamic Competitive Strategy: Towards a Multi-perspective Conceptual Framework', *Long Range Planning*, Vol. 32, No. 6, pp. 559–572.

Slater S.F., and Narver, J.C. (1998) 'Customer-led and Market-oriented: Let's Not Confuse the Two', *Strategic Management Journal*, Vol. 19, No. 10, pp. 1001–1006.

Stalk, G., Evans, P., and Schulman, L.E. (1992) 'Competing on Capabilities: The New Rules of Corporate Strategy', *Harvard Business Review*, Vol. 70, No. 2, March–April, pp. 57–69.

Teece, D.J., Pisano, G., and Shuen, A. (1997) 'Dynamic Capabilities and Strategic Management', *Strategic Management Journal*, Vol. 18, No. 7, August, pp. 509–533.

Treacy, M., and Wiersema, F. (1995) *The Discipline of Market Leaders*, Addison-Wesley, Reading, MA.

Webster, F.E., Jr. (1992) 'The Changing Role of Marketing in the Corporation', *Journal of Marketing*, Vol. 56, October, pp. 1–17.

Webster, F. (1994) *Market Driven Management: Using the New Marketing Concept to Create a Customer-oriented Company*, Wiley, New York.

Wernerfelt, B. (1984) 'A Resource-Based View of the Firm', *Strategic Management Journal*, Vol. 5, No. 2, April–June, pp. 171–180.

CORPORATE LEVEL STRATEGY

We are not all capable of everything.

Virgil (70–19 BC); Roman philosopher

INTRODUCTION

As firms seek growth, they have a number of directions in which they can expand. The most direct source of increased revenue is to enlarge their market share, selling more of their current product offerings in their current market segments. Besides this growth through focused market penetration, firms can also broaden their scope by extending their product range (product development) and/or move into neighboring market segments and geographic areas (market development). All of these growth options can be pursued while staying within the 'boundaries' of a single business (see Figure 6.1). However, firms can broaden their scope even further, venturing into other lines of business, thus becoming multi-business corporations. Some multi-business firms are involved in only two or three businesses, but there are numerous corporations spanning 20, 30, or more, business areas.

This chapter deals with the specific strategic questions facing firms as they work on determining their multi-business scope. At this level, strategists must not only consider how to gain a competitive advantage in each line of business the firm has entered, but also which businesses they should be in at all. Corporate level strategy is about selecting an optimal set of businesses and determining how they should be integrated into the corporate whole. This issue of deciding on the best array of businesses and relating them to one another is referred to as the issue of 'corporate configuration'.

THE ISSUE OF CORPORATE CONFIGURATION

All multi-business firms have a particular configuration, either intentionally designed or as the result of emergent formation. Determining the configuration of a corporation can be disentangled into two main questions: (a) What businesses should the corporation be active in? and (b) How should this group of businesses be managed? This first question of deciding on the business areas that will be covered by the company is called the topic of 'corporate composition'. The second question, of deciding on the organizational system necessary to run the cluster of businesses, is labeled as the issue of 'corporate management'. In the following pages both questions will be explored in more detail.

Corporate composition

A multi-business firm is composed of two or more businesses. When a corporation enters yet another line of business, either by starting up new activities (internal growth) or by buying another firm (acquisition), this is called diversification. There are two general categories of diversification moves, vertical and horizontal. Vertical diversification, usually called vertical integration, is when a firm enters other businesses upstream or downstream within its own industry column (see Chapter 5) – it can strive for backward integration by getting involved in supplier businesses or it can initiate forward integration by entering the businesses of its buyers. The firm can also integrate related businesses at the same tier in the industry column – an example of such horizontal integration is when a newspaper and magazine publisher moves into educational publishing, as Thomson did. If a firm expands outside of its current industry, the term 'integration' is no longer employed, and the step is referred to as straightforward (horizontal) diversification (see Figure 6.1).

The issue of corporate composition deals with the question of where the firm wants to have which level of involvement. Corporate level strategists must decide where to allocate resources, build up activities and try to achieve market sales. The issue of corporate composition can be further subdivided into two parts:

- Corporate scope. First, the composition of the corporation depends on the business areas selected. The more 'business components' chosen, the broader the scope of the corporation. Deciding on the corporate scope is not only a matter of choosing out of the

FIGURE 6.1   Corporate growth directions

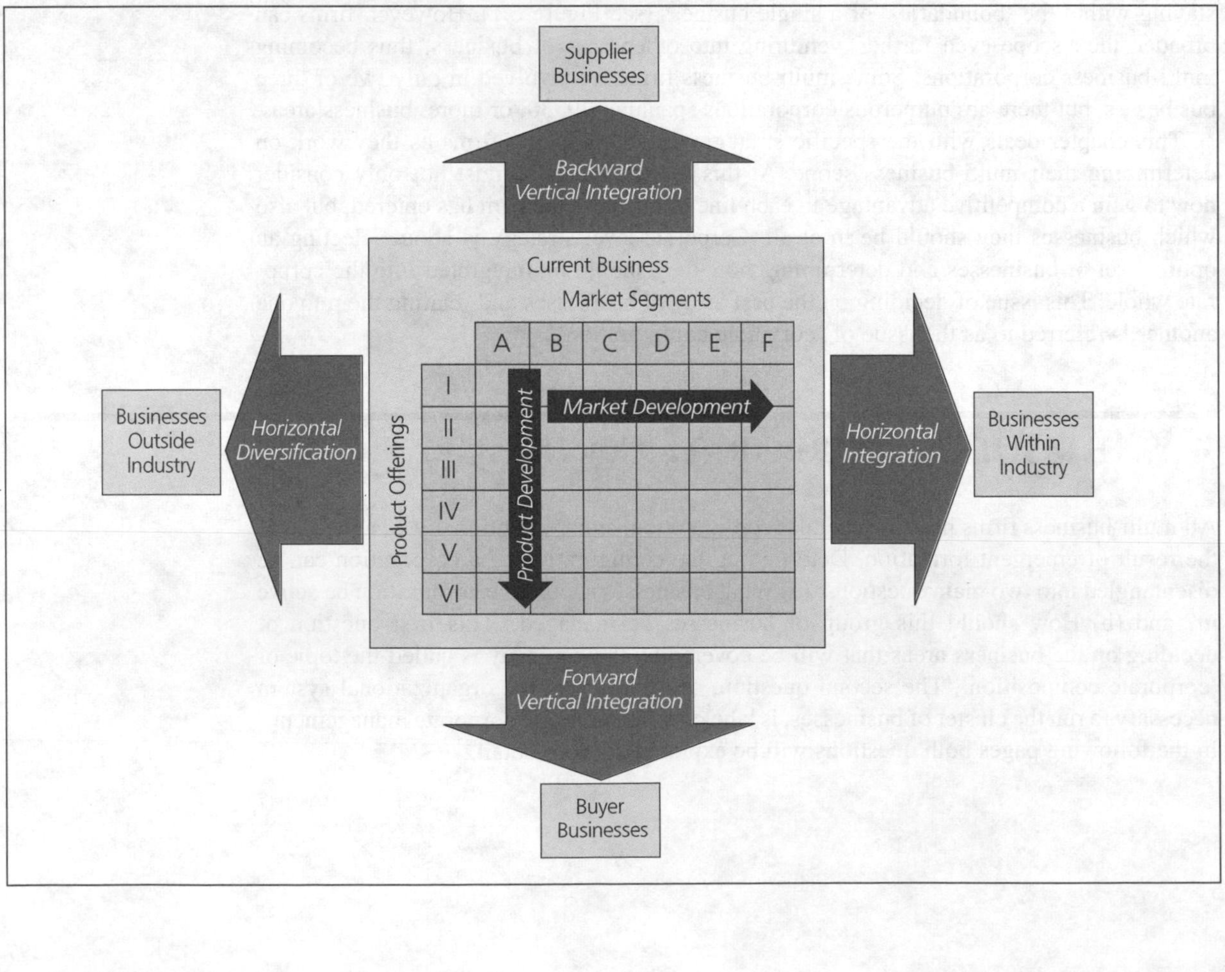

diversification options depicted in Figure 6.1, but can also work in the opposite direction, as a firm can withdraw from a certain line of business, either by divesting, or closing down, its activities.

■ Corporate distribution. The composition of the corporation also depends on the relative size of the activities in each business area covered. The distribution within the corporation is determined by the relative weight of each business component. Some corporations are equally active in all of their selected businesses, while other firms are more asymmetrical, placing more emphasis on just a few of their business activities. Deciding on the corporate distribution is a matter of determining which lines of business will receive more attention than others. Corporate level strategists need to decide which activities will be the focus of further growth and increased weight within the firm, allocating resources accordingly. However, they must also keep in mind that a certain balance within the corporation might be beneficial.

A common way of depicting the corporate composition is to plot all of the businesses in a 'portfolio matrix'. The term 'portfolio' refers to the set of business activities carried out by the corporation. In a portfolio matrix each business activity is represented as a 'bubble' in a two-dimensional grid, with the size of the bubble reflecting the revenue generated with that activity. The number of bubbles indicates the corporate scope, while the corporate distribution can be seen in the relative size of the bubbles. The intention of a portfolio matrix is not merely to give an overview of the corporate scope and distribution, but also to provide insight into the growth and profitability potential of each of the corporation's business activities and to judge the balance between the various business activities.

There are different types of portfolio matrices in use, the most well known of which (see Figure 6.2) are the Boston Consulting Group matrix (Hedley, 1977, Reading 6.1 in this book) and the General Electric business screen (Hofer and Schendel, 1978). All of these portfolio matrices are based on the same analytical format. Each business activity is mapped along two dimensions – one measuring the attractiveness of the business itself, the other measuring the strength of the corporation to compete in the business. In other words,

FIGURE 6.2   The BCG matrix and GE business screen

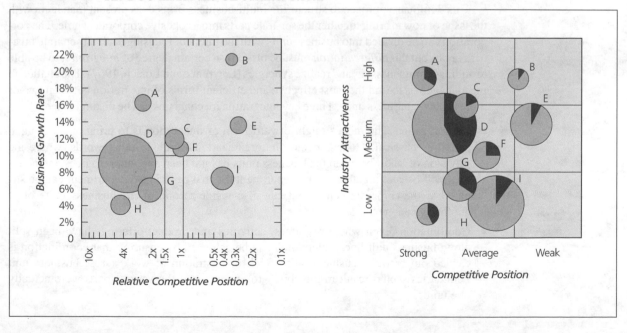

one axis is a measure of external *opportunity*, while the other axis is a measure of internal *strength* in comparison to rival firms. The major difference between the portfolio matrices is which measures are used along the axes. The BCG matrix employs two simple variables: business growth to determine attractiveness and relative market share to reflect competitive strength. The GE business screen, on the other hand, uses composite measures: both industry attractiveness and competitive position are determined by analyzing and weighing a number of different factors. Industry attractiveness will be impacted by such variables as sales growth, demand cyclicality, buyer power, supplier power, the threat of new entrants, the threat of substitutes and competitive intensity. Competitive position often reflects such factors as market share, technological know-how, brand image, customer loyalty, cost structure and distinctive competences. Another difference between the two matrices is that in the BCG portfolio grid the bubbles represent the company's sales in a line of business, while in the GE business screen the bubbles reflect the total business size, with the pie slices indicating the firm's share of the business.

Deciding which portfolio of businesses to pursue, both in terms of corporate scope and corporate distribution, will depend on how the corporate strategist intends to create value – or as Porter (1987) puts it, how the corporate strategist wants to make 'the corporate whole add up to more than the sum of its business unit parts.' After all, there must be some benefit to having the various business activities together in one corporation, otherwise each business activity could just as easily (and with less overhead) be carried out by autonomous firms. This added value of having two or more business activities under one corporate umbrella is called 'multi-business synergy' and it strongly determines the corporate composition the strategist will prefer. But before turning to the topic of synergy, the counterpart of corporate composition, namely corporate management, needs to be reviewed first.

Corporate management

It has become a widespread policy to organize multi-business firms into strategic business units (SBUs). Each strategic business unit is given the responsibility to serve the particular demands of one business area. The business units are labeled 'strategic', because each is driven by its own business level strategy.

This dominant approach to structuring multi-business firms does present managers with the issue of how to bring together the separate parts into a cohesive corporate whole. The corporation can be divided into business units with the intent of focusing each on separate business areas, but this *differentiation* must be offset by a certain degree of *integration* to be able to address common issues and realize synergies (Lawrence and Lorsch, 1967). The challenge for managers is to find the most effective and efficient forms of integration between two or more separate business units. Three key integration mechanisms can be distinguished:

- Centralization. The most straightforward form of integration is to bring resources and activities physically together into one organizational unit. In other words, where the 'division of labor' between the business units has not been applied, resources and activities will be kept together in one department. Such a centralized department can be situated at the corporate center, but can also reside at one of the business units or at another location.

- Coordination. Even where resources, activities and product offerings have been split along business unit lines, integration can be achieved by ensuring that coordination is carried out between business units. Such orchestration of work across business unit boundaries should result in the ability to operate as if the various parts were actually one unit.

- Standardization. Integration can also be realized by standardizing resources, activities and/or product offering characteristics across business unit boundaries. By having similar resources (e.g. technologies, people), standardized activities (e.g. R&D, human resource management) and common product features (e.g. operating system, high-tech positioning) such advantages as economies of scale and rapid competence development can be achieved without the need to physically centralize or continuously coordinate.

These three integration mechanisms are the tools available to managers to achieve a certain level of harmonization between the various parts of the corporate whole. Yet it is often the question who should take the initiative to realize integration – where in the management system is the responsibility vested to ensure that centralization, coordination and standardization are considered and carried out? If all business unit managers are looking after their own backyard, who is taking care of the joint issues and cross-business synergies? Basically there are two organizational means available to secure the effective deployment of the integration mechanisms (see Figure 6.3):

- Control. A straightforward way to manage activities that cross the boundaries of an individual business unit is to give someone the formal power to enforce centralization, coordination and standardization. Such a division level or corporate level manager can exert control in many ways. It can be by direct supervision (telling business units what to do), but often it is indirect, by giving business units objectives that must be met and discussing initiatives. The formal authority to secure integration does not always have to be given to a manager at the corporate center, but can be assigned to a manager within one of the business units as well. There are also various levels of authority that can be defined, ranging from full final decision-making power to 'coordinator' or 'liaison officer', who have only limited formal means at their disposal.

- Cooperation. Centralization, coordination and standardization between business units can also be achieved without the use of hierarchical authority. Business units might be willing to cooperate because it is in their interest to do so, or because they recognize the overall corporate interests. If business units believe in the importance of certain joint activities, this can be a powerful impetus to collaborate. Corporate strategists interested in such integration by mutual adjustment will focus on creating the organizational circumstances under which such self-organization can take place (See Chapter 9 for a further discussion). For instance, they might strengthen formal and informal ties between the business units in order to enhance mutual understanding and encourage the exchange of ideas and joint initiatives. They may also support cross-business career paths and try to instill a corporation-wide culture, to facilitate the communication between business units (Eisenhardt and Galunic, 2000).

It is the task of the corporate level strategist to determine the mix of control and cooperation needed to manage the corporation. In their seminal research, Goold and Campbell (1987) distinguish three general corporate control styles, each emphasizing different levels of centralization, coordination and standardization:

- Financial control style. In the financial control style the strategic business units are highly autonomous from the corporate center. Few activities are centralized or standardized (except for the financial reporting system) and the corporate center does not explicitly attempt to coordinate activities across business unit boundaries. Control is exerted by negotiating, setting and monitoring financial objectives.

- Strategic control style. In the strategic control style the strategic business units have a closer relationship with the corporate center. A number of central services exist, some systems and activities are standardized and the corporate center explicitly tries to coordinate activities that reach beyond the boundaries of only one business unit. Control is exerted by negotiating, setting and monitoring strategic objectives.

FIGURE 6.3   Corporate integration through control and cooperation

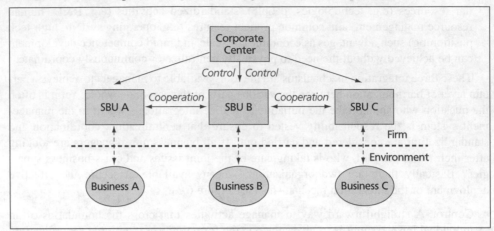

- Strategic planning style. In the strategic planning style the strategic business units have relatively little autonomy from the corporate center. Many key activities are centralized or standardized, and the corporate center is also heavily involved in securing cross-business coordination. Control is exerted by means of direct supervision.

Which corporate management style is adopted depends strongly on what the corporate strategist wishes to achieve. The preferred corporate management style will be determined by the type of multi-business synergies that the corporate strategist envisages, but also on the level of autonomy that the business units require. On the one hand, strategists will want to encourage integration to reap the benefits of having various business units together under one corporate roof and will therefore have a strong motivation to exert strong corporate center control and stimulate inter-business cooperation. On the other hand, strategists will be wary of heavy-handed head office intervention, blunt centralization, rigid standardization, paralyzing coordination meetings and excessive overhead. Recognizing that the business units need to be highly responsive to the specific demands of their own business area, corporate strategists will also be inclined to give business units the freedom to maneuver and to emphasize their own entrepreneurship. Yet, these two demands on the corporate level strategy – *multi-business synergy* and *business responsiveness* – are to a certain extent at odds with one another. How corporate strategists deal with the tension created by these conflicting demands will be examined more closely in the following section.

THE PARADOX OF RESPONSIVENESS AND SYNERGY

Nihil est ab omni parte beatum (nothing is an unmixed blessing).
Horace (65–8 BC); Roman poet

When Cor Boonstra took over as CEO of Philips Electronics in 1996, after a long career at the fast-moving consumer goods company Sara Lee, one of his first remarks to the business press was that Philips reminded him of 'a plate of spaghetti' – the company's more than 60 business units were intertwined in many different ways, sharing technologies, facilities, sales forces and customers, leading to excessive complexity, abundant bureau-

cracy, turf wars and a lack of accountability. To Boonstra the pursuit of multi-business synergy had spiraled into an overkill of centralization, coordination and standardization,
requiring direct rectification. Thus Boonstra set out to restructure Philips into, in his own
words, 'a plate of asparagus', with business units neatly lined up, one next to the other.
Over a period of five years he disposed of numerous business units and made sure that the
others were independent enough 'to hold up their own pants'. The result was a loss of some
valuable synergies, but a significant increase in the business units' responsiveness to the
demands in their own business. Then, in 2001, Boonstra handed over the reigns to a Philips
insider, Gerard Kleisterlee, who during one of his first media encounters as new CEO
stated that the business units within Philips had become too insular and narrowly focused,
thereby missing opportunities to capture important synergies. Therefore, he indicated that
it would be his priority to get Philips to work more like a team.

What this example of Philips illustrates is that corporate level strategists constantly
struggle with the balance between realizing synergies and defending business unit responsiveness. To achieve synergies, a firm must to some extent integrate the activities carried
out in its various business units. The autonomy of the business units must be partially limited, in the interest of concerted action. However, integration comes with a price tag. An
extra level of management is often required, more meetings, extra complexity, potential
conflicts of interest, additional bureaucracy – harmonization of operations costs money
and diminishes a business unit's ability to precisely tailor its strategy to its specific business environment. Hence, for the corporate strategist the challenge is to realize more *value
creation* through multi-business synergies than *value destruction* through the loss of business responsiveness (e.g. Campbell, Goold and Alexander, 1995; Prahalad and Doz, 1987).

This tension arising from the partially conflicting demands of business responsiveness
and multi-business synergy is called the paradox of responsiveness and synergy. In the
following sub-sections both sides of the paradox will be examined in more detail.

The demand for multi-business synergy

Diversification into new business areas can only be economically justified if it leads to
value creation. According to Porter (1987) entering into another business (by acquisition
or internal growth) can only result in increased shareholder value if three essential tests are
passed:

- The attractiveness test. The business 'must be structurally attractive, or capable of being
  made attractive'. In other words, firms should only enter businesses where there is a
  possibility to build up a profitable competitive position (see Chapter 5). Each new business area must be judged in terms of its competitive forces and the opportunities
  available to the firm to sustain a competitive business model.

- The cost-of-entry test. 'The cost of entry must not capitalize all the future profits.' In
  other words, firms should only enter new businesses if it is possible to recoup the investments made. This is important for internally generated new business ventures, but even
  more so for external acquisitions. Many researchers argue that, on average, firms significantly overpay for acquisitions, making it next to impossible to compensate for the
  value given away during the purchase (e.g. Sirower, 1997).

- The better-off test. 'Either the new unit must gain competitive advantage from its link
  with the corporation or vice versa.' In other words, firms should only enter new businesses if it is possible to create significant synergies. If not, then the new unit would be
  better off as an independent firm or with a different parent company, and should be cut
  loose from the corporation.

It is this last test that reveals one of the key demands of corporate level strategy. Multi-
business level firms need to be more than the sum of their parts. They need to create more

added value than the extra costs of managing a more complex organization. They need to identify opportunities for synergy between business areas and manage the organization in such a way that the synergies can be realized.

But what are the sources of synergy? For quite some time, strategists have known that potential for synergy has something to do with 'relatedness' (Rumelt, 1974). Diversification moves that were unrelated (or 'conglomerate'), for example a food company's entrance into the bicycle rental business, were deemed to be less profitable, in general, than moves that were related (or 'concentric'), such as a car-maker's diversification into the car rental business (e.g. Chatterjee, 1986; Rumelt, 1982). However, the problem has been to determine the nature of 'relatedness'. Superficial signs of relatedness do not indicate that there is potential for synergy. Drilling for oil and mining might seem highly related (both are 'extraction businesses'), but Shell found out the hard way that they were not related, selling the acquired mining company Billiton to Gencor after they were unable to create synergy (see the Shell case in Section vi). Chemicals and pharmaceuticals seem like similar businesses (especially if pharmaceuticals are labeled 'specialty chemicals'), but ICI decided to split itself in two (into ICI and Zeneca), because it could not achieve sufficient synergy between these two business areas.

Strategy researchers have therefore attempted to pin down the exact nature of relatedness (e.g. Prahalad and Bettis, 1986; Ramanujam and Varadarajan, 1989). Following the business model framework outlined in Chapter 5, the areas of relatedness that have the potential for creating synergy can be organized into three categories (see Figure 6.4): resource relatedness, product offering relatedness and activity relatedness.

FIGURE 6.4   Forms of multi-business synergy

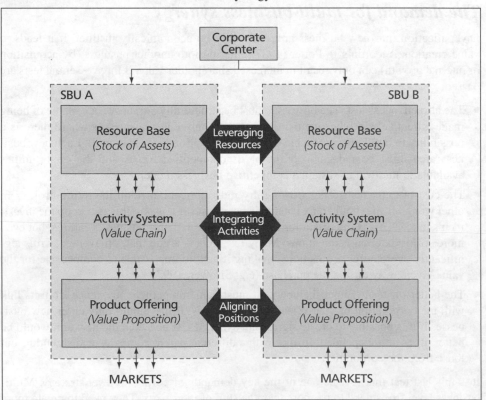

Synergy by leveraging resources.   The first area of relatedness is at the level of the businesses' resource bases. Two or more businesses are related if their resources can be productively shared between them. In principle, all types of resources can be shared, both the tangible and the intangible, although in practice some resources are easier to share than others – for example, it is easier to transfer money than knowledge. Such 'resource leveraging' (Hamel and Prahalad, 1993) can be achieved by physically reallocating resources from one business area to another, or by replicating them so they can be used in a variety of businesses simultaneously:

■ Achieving resource reallocation. Instead of leaving firm resources in the business unit where they happen to be located, a corporation can create synergy by transferring resources to other business units, where better use can be made of them. For instance, money and personnel are often shifted between business units, depending on where they are needed and the potential return is highest.

■ Achieving resource replication. While physical resources can only be used in one place at a time, intangible resources can often be copied from one business unit to another, so that the same resource can be used many times over. This happens, for example, when knowledge and capabilities are copied and reused in other business units.

Synergy by aligning positions.   A second area of relatedness is at the level of product offerings. Two or more businesses are related if they can help each other by aligning their positioning in the market. Such coordination between product–market combinations can both improve the businesses' bargaining position vis-à-vis buyers, as well as improve the businesses' competitive position vis-à-vis rival firms:

■ Improving bargaining position. Business units can improve their bargaining power vis-à-vis buyers by offering a broad package of related products and/or services to specific customer groups. Especially when the products being offered are complementary, share a common brand and have a comparable reputation, will they support each other in the market.

■ Improving competitive position. Coordination of product offerings within one firm can also prevent a number of business units from fighting fiercely amongst one another, which might have happened if all units were independent companies. Moreover, it is even possible for multiple business units to support each other in attacking a third party, for example by setting a common standard or aggressively pricing selected products. Business units can team up to create barriers to entry into the industry/market as well.

Synergy by integrating activities.   The third area of relatedness is at the level of activity systems. Two or more businesses are related if an integration of their value chains is more efficient and/or more effective than if they were totally separated. Such integration of value-creation activities can focus on the sharing of similar activities or the linking up of sequential activities:

■ Sharing value-adding activities. Business units often combine some of their value-adding activities, such as logistics, production or marketing, if this leads to significant scale advantages or quality improvements. It is also common to see that the corporate center organizes certain support activities centrally. These 'shared services' often include functions such as human resource management, procurement, quality control, legal affairs, research and development, finance and corporate communication.

■ Linking value-adding activities. Business units that are not horizontally but vertically related (see Figure 6.1) can have an internal customer–supplier relationship. Such vertical integration of sequential value-adding activities in one firm can be more efficient than operating independently where supplies need to be highly tailored to a specific type of customer demand.

Much attention in the literature has been paid to this issue of vertical integration of activities. It is also referred to as 'internalization' because firms decide to perform activities inside the firm, instead of dealing with outside suppliers and buyers. In general, companies will strive to integrate upstream or downstream activities where one or more of the following conditions are deemed important (e.g. Harrigan 1985; Mahoney, 1992):

- Operational coordination. It can be necessary for various parts of the value system to be tightly coordinated or even physically integrated, to ensure that the right components, meeting the right specifications, are available in the right quantities, at the right moment, so that high quality, low cost and/or timely delivery can be achieved. To realize this level of coordination it can be necessary to gain control over a number of key activities in the value system, instead of trying to get suppliers and buyers to cooperate.

- Avoidance of transaction costs. Reaching a deal with a supplier or buyer and transferring the goods or services to the required location may be accompanied by significant direct costs. These contracting costs can include the expenses of negotiations, drawing up a contract, financial transfers, packaging, distribution and insurance. Add to these the search costs, required to locate and analyze potential new suppliers or buyers, as well as the policing costs, which are incurred to check whether the contract is being met according to expectations and to take actions against those parties not living up to their contractual responsibilities. If a firm vertically integrates, many of these costs can be avoided, leading to potential savings (Williamson, 1975).

- Increased bargaining power. If a firm is facing a supplier or buyer with a disproportionately high level of bargaining power (for instance, a monopolist), vertical integration can be used to weaken or neutralize such a party. By fully or partially performing the activities in-house, the firm can lessen its dependence on a strong buyer or supplier. The firm can also strive to acquire the other party, to avoid the bargaining situation altogether.

- Learning curve advantages. Where vertically linked business units work closely together, exchanging knowledge and personnel, they might also learn more quickly and more efficiently than if the business units were independent. Especially where they initiate joint R&D projects and collaborate on business process improvement efforts then significant learning curve advantages can be realized.

- Implementing system-wide changes. Besides continual operational coordination and ongoing learning, there may be a need to coordinate strategic changes throughout the value system. Switching over to new technologies, new production methods and new standards can sometimes only be implemented if there is commitment and a concerted effort in various parts of the value system. Sometimes even neighboring value systems need to be involved in the changes. Vertical integration and horizontal diversification can give a firm the formal control needed to push through such changes.

Corporate level strategy is about determining the corporate configuration that offers the best opportunities for synergy, and implementing a corporate management system capable of realizing the intended synergies. However, what types of synergies can realistically be achieved, without paying a heavier penalty in terms of integration costs? Recognizing the possible benefits of bringing together various businesses under one corporate umbrella is one thing, but developing a corporate management system that does not cost more than it yields is another. Therefore, corporate strategists need to carefully consider the potential downside of resource leveraging, activity integration and position alignment – the loss of business responsiveness.

The demand for business responsiveness

Responsiveness is defined as the ability to respond to the competitive demands of a specific business area in a timely and adequate manner. A business unit is responsive if it has the capability to tightly match its strategic behavior to the competitive dynamics in its business. If a business unit does not focus its strategy on the conditions in its direct environment and does not organize its value-adding activities and management systems to fit with the business characteristics, it will soon be at a competitive disadvantage compared to more responsive rivals. Business responsiveness is therefore a key demand for successful corporate level strategy.

Yet, in multi-business firms the responsiveness of the business units is constantly under pressure. Various scope disadvantages limit the ability of the corporation to ensure business responsiveness. The major problems encountered by multi-business firms are the following:

- High governance costs. Coordinating activities within a firm requires managers. Layers of management, and the bureaucratic processes that might entail, can lead to escalating costs.

- Slower decision-making. Business units must usually deal with more layers of management, more meetings for coordination purposes, more participants in meetings, more conflicts of interest and more political infighting. This not only increases governance costs, but also slows down decision-making and action.

- Strategy incongruence. The resource leveraging, activity integration and position alignment envisioned in the corporate strategy can be more suited to the conditions in some businesses than to others. Consequently, some business units might need to compromise, adapting their business strategy to fit with the corporate strategy. However, such internal adaptation might lead to a misfit with the business demands.

- Dysfunctional control. The corporate center might not have the specific business know-how needed to judge business unit strategies, activities and results. However, the corporate center might feel the need to exert some control over business units, potentially steering them in an inappropriate direction.

- Dulled incentives. Limited autonomy combined with the aforementioned problems can have a significant negative impact on the motivation to perform optimally. This dulled incentive to be entrepreneurial and to excel can be compounded by poorly delineated responsibilities, a lack of clear accountability and the existence of 'captive' internal customers. Together these factors limit the business units' drive to be responsive.

These threats make clear that multi-business firms must determine their composition and management systems in a way that enables business units to be responsive. Yet, simultaneously, corporate strategists need to strive towards the identification and realization of synergies. The question is how these two conflicting demands can be reconciled – how can corporate level strategists deal with the paradox of responsiveness and synergy?

EXHIBIT 6.1 SHORT CASE

GUCCI: AN AFFORDABLE LUXURY?

Most people do not associate the name Ford with luxury goods – but they should. Tom Ford is the widely admired creative director of Gucci, the Italian luxury goods group that designs, produces and distributes a broad array of leather goods, shoes, watches, jewelry, fragrances, cosmetics and high-end ready-to-wear apparel. He is a celebrity with rock-star status, providing the Gucci Group with a strong external profile, while he has

▶

simultaneously been able to create a clear identity for the brands in the company's portfolio. In Gucci he has been the driving force, together with CEO Domenico De Sole, ever since both men took charge of the floundering company in 1994. The Gucci Group spans a number of famous luxury brands, besides the core Gucci name, including Yves Saint Laurent (fragrances, cosmetics and apparel), Sergio Rossi and Bottega Veneta (footwear), Boucheron (jewelry and fragrances), Balenciaga (apparel) and Bédat (watches). In 2002 global sales totaled US$2.5 billion.

Gucci's origins are much more humble than its flashy image would suggest. In 1923 Guccio Gucci opened a small shop in Florence to sell leather goods. Not satisfied with the wares offered to him, he soon opened a workshop to manufacture his own bag and shoe designs. After World War II, Gucci rapidly developed into a prime international luxury brand, opening its first foreign shop in New York in 1953. Several stores followed in other US cities and later in Europe, plus, in the early 1970s, in Japan and Hong Kong. By that time, the red-and-green striped webbing and GG-logo had become part of the domain of celebrities such as Grace Kelly and Jacqueline Onasis.

Problems within the company began after the retirement of Guccio in the 1970s and lasted throughout the 1980s. Conflicts between Guccio's two sons, Aldo and Rodolfo, and later between Rodolfo's son Maurizio and other family members were often fought out in court. To make things worse, Aldo and Maurizio were convicted of tax evasion and fraud, leading to a spell in jail. These family matters were a strong distraction, leaving the company to grow without a clear sense of direction. Production became more scattered, the distribution network became a maze and the product portfolio became highly diversified. By the late 1980s, some 22 000 products, including tennis shoes, playing cards and cigarette holders, bore the Gucci name.

In the United States, De Sole, who was then managing director of Gucci America, and one of the first professional managers in the family business, started rationalizing the operations and product portfolio. He expanded Gucci's control over distribution, by moving wholesale distribution in-house and by acquiring local franchises. Released from jail in 1989, Maurizio Gucci regained his post as chairman of Gucci and launched an ambitious restructuring program that proved to be too drastic –

losses mounted and cash flow dried up. The image of the brand was also close to 'junk status'. 'No truly discerning luxury goods client would shop at Gucci at that time', says a Gucci manager. It was only when the Bahrain-based investment company Investcorp, which had acquired 50% of the Gucci shares in 1989, eventually replaced Maurizio in 1993 that the company's fortunes improved.

It was during this period that De Sole and Ford were given the reins, with the assignment to save the company. De Sole used his experience in the US market to revamp the Gucci business in other countries. As one Gucci manager explains: 'The company was never run as a united company, as one global brand. Each company was operating on its own . . . and no information was shared.' De Sole expanded the number of directly owned and operated stores from 65 in 1995 to 126 in 1998, to get a better grip on how the brand was presented to the outside world. He also sharply reduced distribution through duty-free shops and department stores. By 1999, two-thirds of Gucci's sales came from its own stores, with the intention of increasing this share even further. In order to regain control over product quality, De Sole selected an inner circle of 25 partner-suppliers, working exclusively for Gucci, to produce 70% of the total leather goods. The other 30% was provided by a group of about 60 non-exclusive suppliers, working on yearly production agreements. A program was installed for quality control and to provide financial support and training for all suppliers. For other products similar programs and rationalizations took place, resulting in a well-managed supplier base that was entirely Italian. Only the watches were sourced from Switzerland.

Ford had been lured away from the French fashion house Yves Saint Laurent with the promise of a free hand at restyling everything in the company – products, store interiors and advertising. He successfully rejuvenated the brand for a fashionable, modern, urban consumer with an aggressively glamorous edge. Advertising budgets were increased from 3% of sales in 1993 to 13% by 2000. Ford's goal was to 'create an arresting image of a world you wanted to be part of'. Gucci made it possible for a wider range of people to enter its world by offering accessory articles. Between 1994 and 1999, Gucci's sales increased by a staggering 35% annually, without any acquisitions, with 40% of the sales coming from Asia, 30% from the United States and 30% from Europe.

This formidable growth put Gucci back on the map in the US$60 billion luxury goods industry – but the industry was also rapidly transforming. Next to the traditional segment of 'high net worth individuals' (i.e. with investible assets of over US$1 million), the industry was increasingly catering to a new segment of 'wannabees', with less money, but a ferocious appetite for luxury goods. Serving this brand-sensitive, but not brand-loyal, segment required high advertising costs and a constant flow of new designs. As a consequence, deep pockets and professional management were becoming more and more important – something most of the traditional medium-sized family-owned companies, like Bulgari, Hermès, Prada and Chanel, had in short supply. To raise cash, many medium-sized players floated their stocks during the mid-1990s, as did Gucci in 1995. Yet this opened the door to being acquired by large, professionally run, multi-brand luxury conglomerates. Of these, the French LVMH, with brands like Louis Vuitton, Moët et Chandon, TAG Heuer and Christian Dior, and the Switzerland-based Richemont, with brands like Cartier, Dunhill and Piaget, were the most prominent examples. In 1999 LVMH attempted to take over Gucci, but as Gucci management did not relish the prospect of losing control to LVMH's domineering boss Bernard Arnault, they found a white knight willing to take over Gucci, yet leave them considerable strategic freedom. The white knight was the French retailing giant Pinault-Printemps-Redoute's (PPR), run by one of the richest people in France, François Pinault, who fought a long and bitter battle with Arnault, leading to an extremely high takeover price.

Seeing the developments in the industry, De Sole also believed that increased size and professionalism were vital. Yet, in his view the growth of the Gucci brand was reaching its limits: 'a luxury brand cannot be extended infinitely – if it becomes too common, it is devalued'. Therefore, he decided to follow the lead of LVMH and Richemont, to become a multi-brand corporation. As a first step, he acquired the French company Yves Saint Laurent (YSL) in 1999, which he split into YSL Couture for ready-to-wear clothing and accessories and YSL Beauté for fragrances and cosmetics. YSL catered for the more intelligent, chic and stylish segment, compared to the more sexy and flashy Gucci segment. After this, he added a number of other brands to the portfolio – Italian footwear designers Sergio Rossi and Bottega Veneta, French jewelry and fragrance company Boucheron, French ready-to-wear clothing house Balenciaga and the young Swiss watch house Bédat. With some of the acquisitions came a number of third party licenses as well, for fragrance and cosmetics brands like Van Cleef & Arpels and Oscar de la Renta. Furthermore he raided hip UK designers Alexander McQueen and Stella McCartney from competitors to develop their own brands within the Gucci group.

With the classic brands, like YSL, Boucheron and Balenciaga, De Sole hoped to rejuvenate them in the same way as he had done with Gucci. With the new brands, like Alexander McQueen, Stella McCartney and Bédat, De Sole aimed to stake out new segments, not properly served yet. However, there were also a few challenges, not least of which was that each brand needed a lot of investment and management attention to make it a success. Furthermore, the complexity of the company had multiplied, with each brand run from a different head office, scattered across Italy and France. Each brand also had a different distribution structure – some like YSL, Sergio Rossi and Boucheron, with their own stores, while others did not.

To balance responsiveness and synergy, De Sole developed a two-pronged approach to integrating the new acquisitions. On the one side, each brand was given a dedicated management team to run the 'front end' part of the business, including the brand image, product design, the store concept, sales and marketing, communications and PR, and licensing. On the other side, the 'group management' was given responsibility for the 'back end' part of the business, where synergies would need to be realized. This includes manufacturing, technical expertise for product development in accessories, ready-to-wear and shoes, warehousing and logistics, purchasing of media, packaging and fabrics, real estate, finance and back-office activities. From Florence, where the main company headquarters are situated, the group management would direct the integration of the back end business and Ford would oversee the creative development of the front end business. De Sole wanted all managers to focus on 'group success', while he also made explicit that he expected the brand management teams to be 'entrepreneurial – managers should run their business like they own it'.

By 2002, Gucci had expanded its sales to US$2.5 billion, up from US$1.2 billion in 1999. The Gucci brand represented 60% of group sales and YSL 27%. Accessories were 31% of the business, ready-to-wear 13%, shoes 12%, fragrances and cosmetics 22%, watches 9% and jewelry 5%. Yet, business was not going well and Gucci was forced to issue two profit warnings during the year. Clearly, the economic recession was hitting all luxury goods makers very hard, but Gucci was doing even worse. Except for YSL Beauté, none of the new brands were profitable and the situation for 2003 was not expected to improve.

De Sole faced the question, whether he had not overstretched the company by simultaneously adding a large number of new brands and new businesses. Had he overestimated the ability of the Gucci team to turn lingering brands into champions? Perhaps the synergy potential between the different brands had not yet been realized sufficiently. Could it also be that he had overestimated the synergy benefits of having multiple brands and businesses in one portfolio? Was there a bottom-line compelling logic, other than the growth imperative and the emergent industry behavior, for a multi-luxury brand corporation? De Sole had to make up his mind, whether and how to pursue a multi-brand strategy – and answer the question whether Gucci could afford the luxury of keeping all of its brands, or would need to sell off some of the family jewels.

Sources: *The Economist*, January 14 1999, January 10 2002 and February 8 2003; *Harvard Business School*, Case 9-701-037; *University College Dublin*, Note 301-025-5; www.guccigroup.com.

PERSPECTIVES ON CORPORATE LEVEL STRATEGY

We must indeed all hang together, or, most assuredly, we shall all hang separately.
Benjamin Franklin (1706–1790); American politician, inventor and scientist

Corporations need to capture multi-business synergies and they need to ensure each business unit's responsiveness to its competitive environment. In other words, corporations need to be integrated and differentiated at the same time – emphasizing the *whole* and respecting the *part*. Striving towards synergy is a centripetal force, pulling the firm together into an integrated whole, while being responsive to business demands is a centrifugal force, pulling the firm apart into autonomous market-focused units (Ghoshal and Mintzberg, 1994). The main question dividing strategists is whether a corporation should primarily be a collection of parts or an integrated whole. Should corporations be loose federations of business units or tightly knit teams? Should corporations be business groups made up of distinctive parts, where only modest synergies can be realized and business units should be accorded a large measure of leeway to be responsive to their specific market conditions? Or should corporations actually be unitary organizations, with the parts serving the whole, allowing for significant synergies to be achieved, with the challenge of being responsive enough to varied business demands.

As before, the strategic management literature comes with strongly different views on how strategists should proceed. Here the two diametrically opposed positions will be identified and discussed to show the richness of differing opinions. On the one side of the spectrum, there are those strategists who believe that multi-business firms should be viewed as portfolios of autonomous business units in which the corporation has a financial stake. They argue that business responsiveness is crucial and that only a limited set of financial synergies should be pursued. This point of view is referred to as the 'portfolio organization perspective'. At the other end of the spectrum, there are strategists who believe that corporations should be tightly integrated, with a strong central core of shared resources, activities and/or product offerings keeping the firm together. They argue that corporations built up around these strong synergy opportunities can create significantly more value than is lost through limitations to responsiveness. This point of view is referred to as the 'integrated organization perspective'.

The portfolio organization perspective

In the portfolio organization perspective, responsiveness is strongly emphasized over synergy. Managers taking this perspective usually argue that each business has its own unique characteristics and demands. Firms operating in different businesses must therefore develop a specific strategy for each business and assign the responsibility for each business strategy to a separate strategic business unit. In this manner, the (strategic) business units can be highly responsive to the competitive dynamics in the business, while being a clear unit of accountability towards the corporate center. High responsiveness, however, requires freedom from corporate center interference and freedom from cross-business coordination. Hence, a high level of business unit autonomy is required, with the corporate center's influence limited to arm's length financial control.

In the portfolio organization perspective, the main reason for a number of highly autonomous business units to be in one firm is to leverage financial resources. The only synergies emphasized are financial synergies (e.g. Lubatkin and Chatterjee, 1994; Trautwein, 1990). Actually, the term 'portfolio' entered the business vocabulary via the financial sector, where it refers to an investor's collection of shareholdings in different companies, purchased to spread investment risks. Transferred to corporate strategy, the portfolio organization perspective views the corporate center as an active investor with financial stakes in a number of stand-alone business units. The role of the center is one of selecting a promising portfolio of businesses, keeping tight financial control, and allocating available capital – redirecting flows of cash from business units where prospects are dim ('cash cows' or 'dogs'), to other business units where higher returns can be expected ('stars' or 'question marks'). The strategic objective of each business unit is, therefore, also financial in orientation – grow, hold, milk or divest, depending on the business unit's position on the portfolio grid (e.g. Henderson, 1979; Hedley, 1977). A good corporate strategy strives for a balanced portfolio of mature cash producers and high potential ROI cash users, at an acceptable level of overall risk.

The financial synergies can be gained in a number of different ways (e.g. Chatterjee, 1986; Weston, Chung and Hoag, 1990). First, by having various businesses within one firm, the corporate center can economize on external financing. By internally shifting funds from one business unit to another the corporation can avoid the transaction costs and taxation associated with external capital markets. Secondly, the corporation can limit dependence on the whims of external capital providers, who might be less inclined to finance some ventures (e.g. new businesses or high risk turnarounds) at acceptable levels of capital cost. Thirdly, where the corporation does want to secure external financing, the firm's larger size, debt capacity and creditworthiness can improve its bargaining position in the financial markets. Finally, by having revenue and earning streams from two or more different businesses, the corporation can reduce its exposure to the risk of a single business. This risk balancing, or co-insurance, effect is largest where the portfolio is made up of counter-cyclical businesses. In turn, the stability and predictability of revenue and earning flows enable the corporation to plan and function more effectively and efficiently (e.g. Amit and Livnat, 1988; Seth, 1990).

The business units do not necessarily need to be 'related' in any other way than financial. In practice, the business units can be related, that is, there can be resource leveraging, activity integration and position alignment opportunities that are seized. The portfolio organization perspective does not reject the pursuit of other forms of synergy, but neither does it accommodate such efforts (Haspeslagh, 1982). Responsiveness is not compromised to achieve these synergy opportunities.

New businesses can be entered by means of internal growth, but the portfolio approach to corporate strategy is particularly well suited to diversification through acquisition. In a multi-business firm run on portfolio principles, acquired companies are simple to integrate into the corporation, because they can be largely left as stand-alone units and only need to be linked to corporate financial reporting and control systems. Proponents of the portfolio organization perspective argue that such 'non-synergistic' acquisitions can be highly profitable (Kaplan, 1989; Long and Ravenscraft, 1993). Excess cash can be routed to more attractive investment opportunities than the corporation has internally. Moreover, the acquiring corporation can shake up the management of the acquired company and can function as a strategic sounding board for the new people. In this way, the acquirer can release the untapped value potential of underperforming stand-alone businesses (Anslinger and Copeland, 1996).

The portfolio organization perspective is particularly well known for the analytical techniques that have been developed to support it. As was mentioned before, a large number of portfolio grids are in widespread use as graphical tools for visualizing corporate composition and for determining the position of each of the business units. These portfolio analysis tools have proven to be popular and much used (Goold and Lansdell, 1997), even among strategists who are not proponents of the portfolio organization perspective.

In conclusion, the basic assumption of the portfolio organization perspective is that business units must be responsible for their own competitive strategy. Business units are the main locus of strategic attention and the corporate center should understand their limited ability to get involved and stimulate synergy. Corporate centers should be modest in ambition and size, taking heed of the words of the famous 'business philosopher' Groucho Marx that 'the most difficult thing about business is minding your own'.

EXHIBIT 6.2 THE PORTFOLIO ORGANIZATION PERSPECTIVE

DEGUSSA: SPECIALTY CHEMICALS STORED SEPARATELY

Degussa is the world's largest producer of specialty chemicals, with global sales of €11.8 billion in 2002 and 48 000 employees. The company, which has its corporate headquarters in Düsseldorf, has a long industrial history in Germany, tracing its origin back to the year 1843 in Frankfurt am Main. Especially during the last ten years, Degussa has undergone an extensive series of mergers and consolidations, which have put the company at the forefront of its industry, both in terms of size and profitability (EBITDA in 2002 of 15.3%).

Degussa focuses almost exclusively on specialty chemicals because of the higher margins, lower cyclicality, higher growth rates, better differentiation, and greater value added for customers, when compared to bulk chemical suppliers. Every business of Degussa is expected to develop to be among the top three in its market. Degussa has aggressively divested every business unit that does not fit this preferred profile, amounting to more than €6 billion of divested sales between 2000 and 2002.

The key ingredient to success in the specialty chemicals market, according to Degussa, is the ability to solve problems for specific customers with specific needs. The company emphasizes as a key strategic goal to go one step further and to anticipate customer demands before customers are themselves aware of them. Responsiveness to customer demands is therefore the dominant paradigm throughout the company. In the words of the CEO, Prof. Dr. Utz-Hellmuth Felcht: 'Products, applications and processes must be developed very fast and in close cooperation with the customer. As a specialty chemicals company, there is therefore no alternative to a decentralized structure.'

Degussa has divided itself into 23 business units, with less than 150 staff members at corporate headquarters. Each business unit has global responsibility for operating results, with full control over all operating functions: sales and marketing, production, procurement, R&D and HRM. The business units (each consisting of one or more lines of business) are grouped into six divisions, which guide strategic development and are the first reporting level. There are also six global and ten site service centers providing some support activities such as IT. However, the business units are free to purchase these services from outside as well. The Figure shows their portfolio grid by line of business.

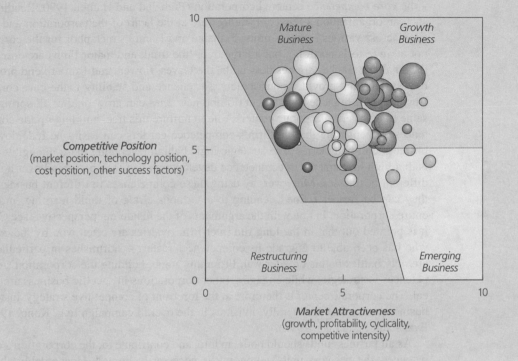

Sources: Company reports and interview with Dr. C. Grambow, Senior Vice President Corporate Development at Degussa.

The integrated organization perspective

The integrated organization perspective is fundamentally at odds with the portfolio organization perspective's minimalist interpretation of corporate level strategy. To proponents of the integrated organization perspective, a multi-business firm should be more than a loose federation of businesses held together by a common investor. Actually, a corporation should be quite the opposite – a tightly knit team of business units grouped around a common core. Having various businesses together in one corporation, it is argued, can only be justified if the corporate center has a clear conception of how strategically relevant multi-business synergies can be realized. It is not enough to capture a few operational synergies here and there – a compelling logic must lie at the heart of the corporation, creating a significant competitive advantage over rivals who operate on a business-by-business basis. The multi-business synergies generated at the core of the organization should enable the corporation to beat its competitors in a variety of business areas.

As corporate level strategists 'lead from the center' (Raynor and Bower, 2001) and develop a joint competitive strategy together with business level strategists, they must make very clear which multi-business synergies they intend to foster as the nucleus of the corporation. It is their task to determine what the core of the organization should be and to take the lead in building it. To be successful, it is necessary for them to work closely together with business level managers, whose main task it is to apply the core strengths of the corporation to their specific business area. The consequence of this joint strategy development and synergy realization is that all business units are highly interdependent, requiring continual coordination.

Many different multi-business synergies can form the core of the corporation. In the strategic management literature one specific form has received a large amount of attention – the *core competence* centered corporation (Prahalad and Hamel, 1990, Reading 6.2). In such an organization a few competences are at the heart of the corporation and are leveraged across various business units. Prahalad and Hamel's metaphor for the corporation is not an investor's portfolio, but a large tree: 'the trunk and major limbs are core products, the smaller branches are business units, the leaves, flowers and fruit are end products; the root system that provides nourishment, sustenance and stability is the core competence.' Business unit branches can be cut off and new ones can grow on, but all spring from the same tree. It is the corporate center's role to nurture this tree, building up the core competences and ensuring that the firm's competence carriers can easily be redeployed across business unit boundaries. The strategic logic behind leveraging these intangible resources is that high investments in competence development can then be spread over a number of different businesses. Moreover, by using these competences in different business settings they can be further refined, leading to a virtuous circle of rapid learning, profiting the entire corporation. In line with the arguments of the inside-out perspective (see Chapter 5), it is pointed out that in the long run inter-firm rivalries are often won by the corporation who has been able to upgrade its competences fastest – skirmishes in particular markets are only battles in this broader war. From this angle, building the corporation's core competences is strategic, while engaging other corporations in specific business areas is tactical. The corporate center is therefore at the forefront of competitive strategy, instead of the business units, that are literally divisions in the overall campaign (e.g. Kono, 1999; Stalk, Evans and Schulman, 1992).

As all business units should both tap into, and contribute to, the corporation's core competences, the business units' autonomy is necessarily limited. Unavoidably, the responsiveness to the specific characteristics of each business does suffer from this emphasis on coordination. Yet, to advocates of the core competence model, the loss of business responsiveness is more than compensated for by the strategic benefits gained.

Besides competences as the core of the corporation, other synergies can also be at the heart of a multi-business firm. For instance, corporations can focus on aligning a variety of product offerings for a group of 'core customers'. Many professional service firms, such as PricewaterhouseCoopers and Cap Gemini Ernst & Young, are involved in a broad range of businesses, with the intention of offering an integrated package of services to their selected market segments. Another type of core is where a multi-business firm is built around shared activities. Many of the large airlines, for example, have one 'core process', flying planes, but operate in the very different businesses of passenger travel and cargo transport. Yet another central synergy can be the leveraging of the firm's 'software'. For instance, Disney is such a 'core content' corporation, letting Cinderella work hard selling Disney videos, luring families to Disney theme parks, getting kids to buy Disney merchandise and enticing people to watch the Disney channel. Whichever synergy is placed center stage, to the proponents of the integrated organization perspective it should not be trivial, as such minor value-creation efforts do not provide the driving motivation to keep a corporation together. The 'glue' of the corporation must be strong enough to convince all involved that they are much better off as part of the whole than on their own.

The flip side of having a tightly knit group of businesses arranged around a common core is that growth through acquisition is generally much more difficult than in the 'plug and play' set-up of a portfolio organization. To make an acquisition fit into the corporate family and to establish all of the necessary links to let the new recruits profit from, and contribute to, the core synergies, can be very challenging. Taking the previous metaphor a step further, the corporate center will find it quite difficult to graft oak roots and elm branches on to an existing olive tree. Consequently, acquisitions will be infrequent, as the firm will prefer internal growth.

EXHIBIT 6.3 THE INTEGRATED ORGANIZATION PERSPECTIVE

SONY: INTEGRATED HOME ENTERTAINMENT

In the late 1940s a small group of engineers came together on the third floor of a Tokyo department store and started a company that would become one of the world's most admired firms – Sony. In its first three decades, Sony grew into a worldwide leader in the consumer electronics industry, introducing such innovative products as the world's first transistor radio and the Walkman. It was Sony's disappointing introduction of the Betamax video cassette recorder that convinced CEO Akio Morita, that the successful launch of new consumer hardware products was strongly dependent on having accompanying software available: Betamax had lost out to Matsushita's VHS system because Sony was unable to convince the big studios to bring out enough movies in the Betamax format. As a consequence, Morita diversified into music and films, buying the US-based CBS records in 1988 and Columbia Pictures in 1989. According to Morita, 'with the development of software, new hardware products come to life. I hope Sony will develop its software business into a large-scale operation as well, including both sound and images.'

And so it did, but not without incurring heavy losses during the first years, as it tried to learn how to manage 'creative companies' in the United States within a more technology-oriented Japanese corporation. It also remained rather sketchy how the worlds of hardware and software would be brought together to create the anticipated synergy. So, when a successor to Morita was sought in 1995, more than a dozen senior managers were bypassed to make the outspoken Nobuyuki Idei the new CEO. Idei had a clear vision that Sony needed to evolve into an integrated home entertainment company, making use of the imminent emergence of broadband networks. Instead of seeing software ('content') as a supporting ingredient for selling more stand-alone gadgets, Idei's vision was that people's enjoyment of the software content should be central and that different

types of devices for accessing this content should be networked into an integrated system. Through broadband networks, content such as music, films and games could be shared between various terminals, such as personal computers, televisions, game consoles, personal digital assistants, cellphones or any other imaginable device.

To make this happen, Idei stressed that 'collaboration between our technology and content businesses are most crucial . . . Sony as a group must work together as a single entity to create an appealing broadband environment.' To facilitate the process of transforming Sony into what had become labeled as the 'Personal Broadband Network Solutions Company', Idei reorganized Sony in 2001 into five pillars; electronics, entertainment, games, internet/communication services and financial services. While each of these pillars remained 'in charge of devising their own strategy to accomplish their mission', a strong global hub was also established, with the responsibility for 'strategically unifying the group's resources and activities for the five key business pillars'. In Idei's words, what he wanted to achieve was 'integrated, decentralized management' – only corporate strategy and some critical support services, such as accounting, finance, human resources, legal affairs, intellectual copyright, public relations, external affairs and design were centralized, but many other, decentralized, activities were closely coordinated.

Since then, Sony has made considerable steps towards providing an integrated package for the broadband networking era. Most of its new hardware products are network based, such as the Airboard, a wireless panel that can be used to watch television, send e-mail or surf the internet. To its Vaio computers it has added a RoomLink device, which can send photos, videos or music wirelessly to other devices around the house. When it comes to products and services linking hardware and software, the first steps have also been taken. For instance, through Sony's Clié personal digital assistant, people can log on to the Clié Plaza web site, to listen to music or watch a movie video. They can also play EverQuest, an on-line PlayStation2-based computer game, played by over 360 000 subscribers worldwide. Another electronics unit developed the supporting Memory Stick, which can be used to store digital data by virtually any Sony device.

As Sony's COO Kunitake Ando reiterated: 'For many years, Sony has sought to derive synergies from its manufacturing and entertainment businesses. Now, in an era when networks allow an increase in these synergies between hardware and entertainment content, more than ever our assets are uniquely suited to create new value.'

Sources: *Time Online* (www.time.com); *The Economist*, March 1 2003; www.sony.com.

INTRODUCTION TO THE DEBATE AND READINGS

Consider the little mouse, how sagacious an animal it is which never entrusts its life to one hole only.

Plautus (254–184 BC); Roman playwright

None ever got ahead of me except the man of one task.

Azariah Rossi (1513–1578); Italian physician

So, how should the corporate configuration be determined? Should corporate strategists limit themselves to achieving financial synergies, leaving SBU managers to 'mind their own business'? Or should corporate strategists strive to build a multi-business firm around a common core, intricately weaving all business units into a highly integrated whole? As before, the strategic management literature does not offer a clear-cut answer to the question of which corporate level strategies are the most successful. Many points of views have been put forward on how to reconcile the opposing demands of responsiveness and synergy, but no common perspective has yet emerged. Therefore, it is up to individual strategists to form their own opinion once again.

To help strategists to come to grips with the variety of perspectives on this issue, four readings have been selected that each shed their own light on the debate. As in previous chapters, the first two readings will be representative of the two poles in this debate (see Table 6.1), while the second set of two readings will bring extra arguments into the discussion.

TABLE 6.1 Portfolio organization versus integrated organization perspective

	Portfolio organization perspective	*Integrated organization perspective*
Emphasis on	Responsiveness over synergy	Synergy over responsiveness
Conception of corporation	Collection of business shareholdings	Common core with business applications
Corporate composition	Potentially unrelated (diverse)	Tightly related (focused)
Key success factor	Business unit responsiveness	Multi-business synergy
Focal type of synergy	Cash flow optimization and risk balance	Integrating resources, activities and positions
Corporate management style	Exerting financial control	Joint strategy development
Primary task corporate center	Capital allocation and performance control	Setting direction and managing synergies
Position of business units	Highly autonomous (independent)	Highly integrated (interdependent)
Coordination between BUs	Low, incidental	High, structural
Growth through acquisitions	Simple to accommodate	Difficult to integrate

To open the debate on behalf of the portfolio organization perspective, Barry Hedley's article 'Strategy and the Business Portfolio' has been selected as Reading 6.1. Hedley was an early proponent of the portfolio perspective, together with other consultants from the Boston Consulting Group (BCG), such as Bruce Henderson (1979). In this article, he explains the strategic principles underlying the famed growth-share grid that is commonly known as the BCG matrix. His argument is based on the premise that a complex corporation can be viewed as a portfolio of businesses, which each have their own competitive arena to which they must be responsive. By disaggregating a corporation into its business unit components, separate strategies can be devised for each. The overarching role of the corporate level can then be defined as that of portfolio manager. The major task of the corporate headquarters is to manage the allocation of scarce financial resources over the business units, to achieve the highest returns at an acceptable level of risk. Each business unit can be given a strategic mission to grow, hold or milk, depending on their prospects compared to the businesses in the corporate portfolio. This is where portfolio analysis comes in. Hedley argues that the profit and growth potential of each business unit depends on two key variables: the growth rate of the total business and the relative market share of the business unit within its business. When these two variables are put together in a grid, this forms the BCG matrix. For the discussion in this chapter, the precise details of the BCG portfolio technique are less relevant than the basic corporate strategy perspective that Hedley advocates – running the multi-business firm as a hands-on investor.

Selecting a representative for the integrated organization perspective for Reading 6.2 was a simple choice. In 1990, C.K. Prahalad and Gary Hamel published an article in *Harvard Business Review* with the title 'The Core Competence of the Corporation'. This article has had a profound impact on the debate surrounding the topic of corporate level strategy, and has inspired a considerable amount of research and writing investigating resource-based synergies. In this article, and in their subsequent book, *Competing for the Future*, Prahalad and Hamel explicitly dismiss the portfolio organization perspective as a viable approach to corporate strategy. Prahalad and Hamel acknowledge that diversified corporations have a portfolio of businesses, but they do not believe that this implies the need for a portfolio organization approach, in which the business units are highly autonomous. In their view, 'the primacy of the SBU – an organizational dogma for a generation – is now clearly an anachronism'. Drawing mainly on Japanese examples, they carry on to argue that corporations should be built around a core of shared competences. Business units should use and help to further develop these core competences. The consequence is that the role of corporate level management is much more far-reaching than in the portfolio organization perspective. The corporate center must 'establish objectives for competence building' and must ensure that this 'strategic architecture' is carried through.

The third reading has been selected to highlight a very important subject in the debate, which has only been touched on indirectly so far in this chapter – the role of acquisitions in corporate level strategy. In discussing the issue of corporate configuration, it is almost impossible not to take a view on the possibilities and impossibilities of growing the corporation by means of acquisition. Therefore, Reading 6.3, 'Understanding Acquisition Integration Approaches', by Philippe Haspeslagh and David Jemison, has been added to this chapter. This reading is a key chapter from their well-known book *Managing Acquisitions: Creating Value Through Corporate Renewal*, in which they outline three generic approaches to the integration of acquired companies. Haspeslagh and Jemison's main argument is that the integration of acquisitions depends on the levels of responsiveness and synergy that are necessary – in the terminology of Haspeslagh and Jemison these opposing forces are called the 'need for organizational autonomy' and the 'need for strategic interdependence'. This gives three different types of acquisition integration approach. Where an acquired company requires high responsiveness/autonomy and low synergy/interdependence, Haspeslagh and Jemison advise a 'preservation acquisition', in which the acquiree can retain much separate identity and freedom. In the opposite case of a high need for synergy and low responsiveness, an 'absorption acquisition' is preferred. The most difficult situation, according to the authors, is where the needs for responsiveness and synergy are both high. In such a situation they suggest a 'symbiotic acquisition', in which 'the two organizations first coexist and then gradually become increasingly interdependent'. However, they acknowledge that this approach is fraught with difficulties and it can be debated what the chances of success are likely to be.

Reading 6.4 is 'Seeking Synergies' by Andrew Campbell and Michael Goold. These researchers from the Ashridge Strategic Management Centre have been responsible for a constant stream of insightful work on corporate level strategy. One of their most recent publications has been the book *Synergy: Why Links Between Business Units Often Fail and How to Make Them Work*, from which this is the summary chapter. This reading has been selected for this chapter in order to pay more attention to the issue of realizing synergies. As a large part of the debate revolves around different views on whether synergies can actually be captured or not, it is valuable to get some more input on approaches to synergy creation and a better insight into 'synergy killers'. Campbell and Goold give a structured and practical framework for analyzing a corporation's synergy opportunities and synergy approach, followed by an analysis of the most important policies and characteristics that systematically inhibit attempts at reaping synergy advantages. In the context of this debate, it is important to note that Campbell and Goold do not necessarily side with either of the two perspectives. In their view, there are different styles of corporate strategy and different levels of synergy that can be achieved, as long as the 'parent company' develops the matching parenting capabilities and synergy parenting approach.

Strategy and the business portfolio

READING

6.1

By Barry Hedley[1]

All except the smallest and simplest companies comprise more than one business. Even when a company operates within a single broad business area, analysis normally reveals that it is, in practice, involved in a number of product-market segments which are distinct economically. These must be considered separately for purposes of strategy development.

The fundamental determinant of strategy success for each individual business segment is relative competitive position. As a result of the experience curve effect the competitor with high market share in the segment relative to competition should be able to develop the lowest cost position and hence the highest and most stable profits. This will be true regardless of changes in the economic environment. Hence relative competitive position in the appropriately defined business segment forms a simple but sound strategic goal. Almost invariably, any company which reviews its various businesses carefully in this light will discover that they occupy widely differing relative competitive positions. Some businesses will be competitively strong already, and may appear to present no strategic problem; others will be weak, and the company must face the question of whether it would be worthwhile to attempt to improve their position, making whatever investments might be required to achieve this; if this is not done, the company can only expect poor performance from the business and the best option economically will be divestment.

Even in quite small companies, the total number of possible combinations of individual business strategies can be extremely large. The difficulty of making a firm final choice on strategy for each business is normally compounded by the fact that most companies must operate within constraints established by limited resources, particularly cash resources.

The business portfolio concept

At its most basic, the importance of growth in shaping strategy choice is twofold. First, the growth of a business is a major factor influencing the likely ease – and hence cost – of gaining market share. In low-growth businesses, any market share gained will tend to require an actual volume reduction in competitors' sales. This will be very obvious to the competitors and they are likely to fight to prevent the throughput in their plants dropping. In high-growth businesses, on the other hand, market share can be gained steadily merely by securing the largest share of the growth in the business: expanding capacity earlier than the competitors, ensuring product availability and effective selling support despite the strains imposed by the *growth*, and so forth. Meanwhile competitors may even be unaware of their share loss because their actual volume of throughput has been well maintained. Even if aware of their loss of share, the competitors may be unconcerned by it given that their plants are still well loaded. This is particularly true of competitors who do not understand the strategic importance of market share for long term profitability resulting from the experience curve effect.

An unfortunate example of this is given by the history of the British motorcycle industry. British market share was allowed to erode in motorcycles world-wide for more than a decade, throughout which the British factories were still fairly full: British motorcycle production volumes held up at around 80,000 units per year throughout the sixties; in sharp contrast, Japanese export volumes leapt from only about 60,000 in 1960 to 2.5 million in 1973; their total production volumes roughly tripled in the same period. The long term effect was that while Japanese real costs were falling rapidly British costs were not: somewhat oversimplified, this is why the British motorcycle industry faced bankruptcy in the early seventies.

The second important factor concerning growth is the opportunity it provides for investment. Growth

[1]Source: This article was adapted from B. Hedley, 'Strategy and the Business Portfolio', *Long Range Planning*, February 1977, Vol. 10, No. 1, pp. 9–15, (c) 1977. With permission from Elsevier.

businesses provide the ideal vehicles for investment, for ploughing cash into a business in order to see it compound and return even larger amounts of cash at a later point in time. Of course this opportunity is also a need: the faster a business grows, the more investment it will require just to maintain market share. Yet the experience curve effect means that this is essential if its profitability is not to decline over time.

Whilst these growth considerations affect the rate at which a business will use cash, the relative competitive position of the business will determine the rate at which the business will generate cash: the stronger the company's position relative to its competitors the higher its margins should be, as a result of the experience curve effect. The simplest measure of relative competitive position is, of course, relative market share. A company's relative market share in a business can be defined as its market share in the business divided by that of the largest other competitor. Thus only the biggest competitor has a relative market share greater than one. All the other competitors should enjoy lower profitability and cash generation than the leader.

The growth–share matrix

Individual businesses can have very different financial characteristics and face different strategic options depending on how they are placed in terms of growth and relative competitive position. Businesses can basi-

cally fall into any one of four broad strategic categories, as depicted schematically in the growth–share matrix in Figure 6.1.1.

■ Stars. High growth, high share – are in the upper left quadrant. Growing rapidly, they use large amounts of cash to maintain position. They are also leaders in the business, however, and should generate large amounts of cash. As a result, star businesses are frequently roughly in balance on net cash flow, and can be self-sustaining in growth terms. They represent probably the best profit growth and investment opportunities available to the company, and every effort should therefore be made to maintain and consolidate their competitive position. This will sometimes require heavy investment beyond their own generation capabilities and low margins may be essential at times to deter competition, but this is almost invariably worthwhile for the longer term: when the growth slows, as it ultimately does in all businesses, very large cash returns will be obtained if share has been maintained so that the business drops into the lower left quadrant of the matrix, becoming a cash cow. If star businesses fail to hold share, which frequently happens if the attempt is made to net large amounts of cash from them in the short and medium term (e.g. by cutting back on investment and raising prices, creating an 'umbrella' for competitors), they will ultimately become dogs (lower right quadrant). These are certain losers.

FIGURE 6.1.1   The business portfolio or growth-share matrix

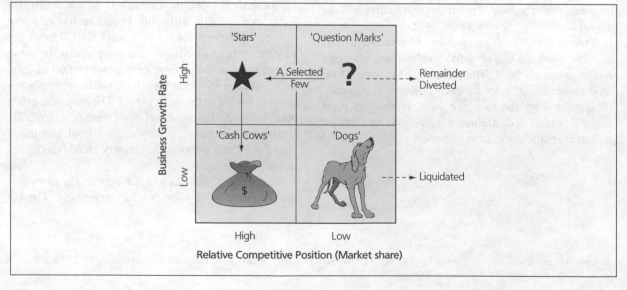

- Cash cows. Low growth, high share – should have an entrenched superior market position and low costs. Hence profits and cash generation should be high, and because of the low growth reinvestment needs should be light. Thus large cash surpluses should be generated by these businesses. Cash cows pay the dividends and interest, provide the debt capacity, pay for the company overhead and provide the cash for investment elsewhere in the company's portfolio of businesses. They are the foundation on which the company rests.

- Dogs. Low growth, low share – represent a tremendous contrast. Their poor competitive position condemns them to poor profits. Because the growth is low, there is little potential for gaining sufficient share to achieve a viable cost position at anything approaching a reasonable cost. Unfortunately, the cash required for investment in the business just to maintain competitive position, though low, frequently exceeds that generated, especially under conditions of high inflation. The business therefore becomes a 'cash trap' likely to absorb cash perpetually unless further investment in the business is rigorously avoided. The colloquial term dog describing these businesses, though undoubtedly pejorative, is thus rather apt. A company should take every precaution to minimize the proportion of its assets that remain in this category.

- Question marks. High growth, low share – have the worst cash characteristics of all. In the upper right quadrant, their cash needs are high because of their growth, but their cash generation is small because of their low share. If nothing is done to change its market share, the question mark will simply absorb large amounts of cash in the short term and later, as the growth slows, become a dog. Following this sort of strategy, the question mark is a cash loser throughout its existence. Managed this way, a question mark becomes the ultimate cash trap.

In fact there is a clear choice between only two strategy alternatives for a question mark, hence the name. Because growth is high, it should be easier and less costly to gain share here than it would be in a lower growth business. One strategy is therefore to make whatever investments are necessary to gain share, to try to fund the business to dominance so that it can become a star and, ultimately a cash cow when the business matures. This strategy will be very costly in the short term – growth rates will be even higher than if share were merely being maintained, and additional marketing and other investments will be required

to make the share actually change hands – but it offers the only way of developing a sound business from the question mark over the long term. The only logical alternative is divestment. Outright sale is preferable; but if this is not possible, then a firm decision must be taken not to invest further in the business and it must be allowed simply to generate whatever cash it can while none is reinvested. The business will then decline, possibly quite rapidly if market growth is high, and will have to be shut down at some point. But it will produce cash in the short term and this is greatly preferable to the error of sinking cash into it perpetually without improving its competitive position.

These then, are the four basic categories to which businesses can belong. Some companies tend to fit almost entirely into a single quadrant. General Motors and English China Clays are examples of predominantly cash cow companies. Chrysler, by comparison, is a dog which compounded its fundamental problem of low share in its domestic US market by acquiring further mature low share competitors in other countries (e.g. Rootes which became Chrysler UK). IBM in computers, Xerox in photocopiers, BSR in low cost record autochangers, are all examples of predominantly star businesses. Xerox's computer operation, XDS, was clearly a question mark, however, and it is not surprising that Xerox recently effectively gave it away free to Honeywell, and considered itself lucky to escape at that price! When RCA closed down its computer operation, it had to sustain a write-off of about $490m. Question marks are costly.

Portfolio strategy

Most companies have their portfolio of businesses scattered through all four quadrants of the matrix. It is possible to outline quite briefly and simply what the appropriate overall portfolio strategy for such a company should be. The first goal should be to maintain position in the cash cows, but to guard against the frequent temptation to reinvest in them excessively. The cash generated by the cash cows should be used as a first priority to maintain or consolidate position in those stars which are not self-sustaining. Any surplus remaining can be used to fund a selected number of question marks to dominance. Most companies will find they have inadequate cash generation to finance market share-gaining strategies in all their question marks. Those which are not funded should be divested either by sale or liquidation over time.

Finally, virtually all companies have at least some dog businesses. There is nothing reprehensible about this, indeed on the contrary, an absence of dogs probably indicates that the company has not been sufficiently adventurous in the past. It is essential, however, that the fundamentally weak strategic position of the dog be recognized for what it is. Occasionally it is possible to restore a dog to viability by a creative business segmentation strategy, rationalizing and specializing the business into a small niche which it can dominate. If this is impossible, however, the only thing which could rescue the dog would be an increase in share taking it to a position comparable to the leading competitors in the segment. This is likely to be unreasonably costly in a mature business, and therefore the only prospect for obtaining a return from a dog is to manage it for cash, cutting off all investment in the business. Management should be particularly wary of expensive 'turn around' plans developed for a dog if these do not involve a significant change in fundamental competitive position. Without this, the dog is a sure loser. An indictment of many corporate managements is not the fact that their companies have dogs in the portfolio, but rather that these dogs are not managed according to logical strategies. The decision to liquidate a business is usually even harder to take than that of entering a new business. It is essential, however, for the long-term vitality and performance of the company overall that it be prepared to do both as the need arises.

Thus the appropriate strategy for a multibusiness company involves striking a balance in the portfolio such that the cash generated by the cash cows, and by those question marks and dogs which are being liquidated, is sufficient to support the company's stars and to fund the selected question marks through to dominance. This pattern of strategies is indicated by the arrows in Figure 6.1.1. Understanding this pattern conceptually is, however, a far cry from being able to implement it in practice. What any company should do with its own specific businesses is of course a function of the precise shape of the company's portfolio, and the particular opportunities and problems it presents. But how can a clear picture of the company's portfolio be developed?

The matrix quantified

Based on careful analysis and research it is normally possible to divide a company into its various business segments appropriately defined for purposes of strategy development. Following this critical first step, it is usually relatively straightforward to determine the overall growth rate of each individual business (i.e. the growth of the market, not the growth of the company

within the market), and the company's size (in terms of turnover or assets) and relative competitive position (market share) within the business.

Armed with these data it is possible to develop a precise overall picture of the company's portfolio of businesses graphically. This can greatly facilitate the identification and resolution of the key strategic issues facing the company. It is a particularly useful approach where companies are large, comprising many separate businesses. Such complex portfolios often defy description in more conventional ways.

The nature of the graphical portfolio display is illustrated by the example in Figure 6.1.2. In this chart, growth rate and relative competitive position are plotted on continuous scales. Each circle in the display represents a single business or business segment, appropriately defined. To convey an impression of the relative significance of each business, size is indicated by the area of the circle, which can be made proportional to either turnover or assets employed. Relative competitive position is plotted on a logarithmic scale, in order to be consistent with the experience curve effect, which implies that profit margin or rate of cash generation differences between competitors will tend to be related to the ratio of their relative competitive positions (market shares). A linear axis is used for growth, for which the most generally useful measure is volume growth of the business concerned, as, in general, rates of cash use should be directly proportional to growth.

The lines dividing the portfolio into four quadrants are inevitably somewhat arbitrary. 'High growth', for example, is taken to include all businesses growing in excess of 10 percent per annum in volume terms. Certainly, above this growth rate market share tends to become fairly fluid and can be made to change hands quite readily. In addition many companies have traditionally employed a figure of 10 percent for their discount rate in times of low inflation, and so this also tends to be the growth rate above which investment in market share becomes particularly attractive financially.

The line separating areas of high and low relative competitive position is set at 1.5 times. Experience in using this display has been that in high-growth businesses relative strengths of this magnitude or greater are necessary in order to ensure a sufficiently dominant position that the business will have the characteristic of a star in practice. On the other hand, in low-growth businesses acceptable cash generation characteristics are occasionally, but not always, observed at relative strengths as low as 1 times; hence the addition of a

FIGURE 6.1.2 Growth rate and relative competitive position

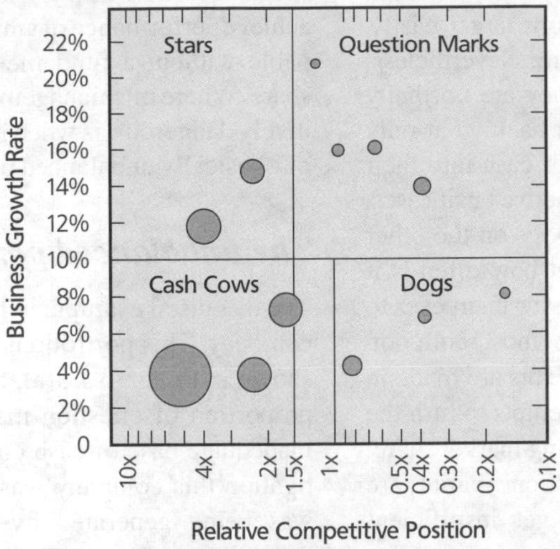

second separating line at 1 times in the low growth area, to reflect this. These lines should, of course, be taken only as approximate guides in characterizing businesses in the portfolio as dogs and question marks, cash cows and stars. In actuality, businesses cover a smooth spectrum across both axes of the matrix. There is obviously no 'magic' which transforms a star into a cash cow as its growth declines from 10.5 to 9.5 percent. It is undeniably useful, however, to have some device for broadly indicating where the transition points occur within the matrix, and the lines suggested here have worked well in practical applications of the matrix in a large number of companies.

Portfolio approaches in practice

The company shown in Figure 6.1.2 would be a good example of a potentially well-balanced portfolio. With a firm foundation in the form of two or three substantial cash cows, this company has some well-placed stars to provide growth and to yield high cash returns in the future when they mature. The company also has some question marks, at least two of which are probably sufficiently well placed that they offer a good chance of being funded into star positions at a reasonable cost, not out of proportion to the company's resources. The company is not without dogs, but properly managed there is no reason why these should be a drain on cash.

The sound portfolio, unsoundly managed

Companies with an attractive portfolio of this kind are not rare in practice. In fact Figure 6.1.2 is a disguised version of a representation of an actual UK company analyzed in the course of a Boston Consulting Group assignment. What is much rarer, however, is to find that the company has made a clear assessment of the matrix positioning and appropriate strategy for each business in the portfolio.

Ideally, one would hope that the company in Figure 6.1.2 would develop strategy along the following lines. For the stars, the key objectives should be the maintenance of market share; current profitability should be accorded a lower priority. For the cash cows, however, current profitability may well be the primary goal. Dogs would not be expected to be as profitable as the cash cows, but would be expected to yield cash. Some question marks would be set objectives in terms of increased market share; others, where gaining dominance appeared too costly, would be managed instead for cash.

The essence of the portfolio approach is therefore that strategy objectives must vary between businesses. The strategy developed for each business must fit its own matrix position and the needs and capabilities of the company's overall portfolio of businesses. In practice, however, it is much more common to find all businesses within a company being operated with a common overall goal in mind. 'Our target in this company is to grow at 10 percent per annum and achieve a return of 10 percent on capital.' This type of overall target is then taken to apply to every business in the company. Cash cows beat the profit target easily, though they frequently miss on growth. Nevertheless, their managements are praised and they are normally rewarded by being allowed to plough back what only too frequently amounts to an excess of cash into their 'obviously attractive' businesses. Attractive businesses, yes: but not for growth investment. Dogs on the other hand rarely meet the profit target. But how often is it accepted that it is in fact unreasonable for them ever to hit the target? On the contrary, the most common strategic mistake is that major investments are made in dogs from time to time in hopeless attempts to turn the business around without actually shifting market share. Unfortunately, only too often question marks are regarded very much as dogs, and get insufficient investment funds ever to bring them to dominance. The question marks usually do receive some investment, however, possibly even enough to maintain share. This is throwing money away into a cash trap. These businesses should either receive enough support to enable them to achieve segment dominance, or none at all.

These are some of the strategic errors which are regularly committed even by companies which have basically sound portfolios. The result is a serious sub-optimization of potential performance in which some businesses (e.g. cash cows) are not being called on to produce the full results of which they are actually capable, and resources are being mistakenly squandered on other businesses (dogs, question marks) in an attempt to make them achieve performance of which they are intrinsically incapable without a fundamental improvement in market share. Where mismanagement of this kind becomes positively dangerous, is when it is applied within the context of a basically unbalanced portfolio.

The unbalanced portfolio

The disguised example in Figure 6.1.3 is another actual company. This portfolio is seriously out of balance. As shown in Figure 6.1.3(a), the company has a very high proportion of question marks in its portfolio, and an inadequate base of cash cows. Yet at the time of investigation this company was in fact taking such cash as was being generated by its mature businesses and spreading it out amongst all the high-growth businesses, only one of which was actually receiving sufficient investment to enable it even to maintain share! Thus the overall relative competitive position of the portfolio was on average declining. At the same time, the balance in the portfolio was shifting: as shown in the projected portfolio in Figure 6.1.3(b), because of the higher relative growth of the question marks their overall weight in the portfolio was increasing, making them even harder to fund from the limited resources of the mature businesses.

FIGURE 6.1.3   An unbalanced portfolio

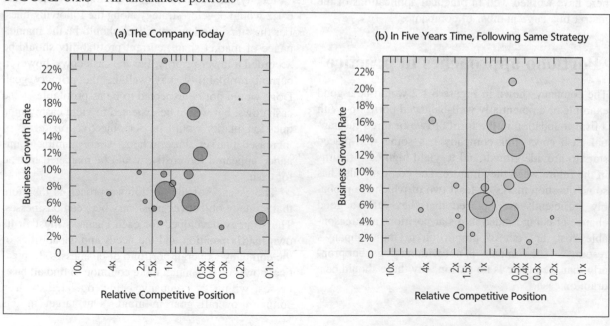

If the company continued to follow the same strategy of spreading available funds between all the businesses, then the rate of decline could only increase over time leading ultimately to disaster.

This company was caught in a vicious circle of decline. To break out of the circle would require firm discipline and the strength of will to select only one or two of the question marks and finance those, whilst cutting off investment in the remainder. Obviously the choice of which should receive investment involves rather more than selection at random from the portfolio chart. It requires careful analysis of the actual nature of the businesses concerned and particularly the characteristics and behavior of the competitors faced in those businesses. However, the nature of the strategic choice facing the company is quite clear, when viewed in portfolio terms. Without the clarity of view provided by the matrix display, which focuses on the real fundamentals of the businesses and their relationships to each other within the portfolio, it is impossible to develop strategy effectively in any multibusiness company.

<table>
<tr><td>READING
6.2</td><td># The core competence of the corporation
By C.K. Prahalad and Gary Hamel[1]</td></tr>
</table>

The most powerful way to prevail in global competition is still invisible to many companies. During the 1980s, top executives were judged on their ability to restructure, declutter, and delayer their corporations. In the 1990s, they'll be judged on their ability to identify, cultivate, and exploit the core competencies that make growth possible – indeed, they'll have to rethink the concept of the corporation itself.

Rethinking the corporation

Once, the diversified corporation could simply point its business units at particular end-product markets and admonish them to become world leaders. But with market boundaries changing ever more quickly, targets are elusive and capture is at best temporary. A few companies have proven themselves adept at inventing new markets, quickly entering emerging markets, and dramatically shifting patterns of customer choice in established markets. These are the ones to emulate. The critical task for management is to create an organization capable of infusing products with irresistible functionality or, better yet, creating products that customers need but have not yet even imagined.

This is a deceptively difficult task. Ultimately, it requires radical change in the management of major companies. It means, first of all, that top managements of western companies must assume responsibility for competitive decline. Everyone knows about high interest rates, Japanese protectionism, outdated antitrust laws, obstreperous unions, and impatient investors. What is harder to see, or harder to acknowledge, is how little added momentum companies actually get from political or macroeconomic 'relief.' Both the theory and practice of western management have created a drag on our forward motion. It is the principles of management that are in need of reform.

The roots of competitive advantage

In the short run, a company's competitiveness derives from the price/performance attributes of current products. But the survivors of the first wave of global competition, western and Japanese alike, are all converging on similar and formidable standards for product cost and quality – minimum hurdles for continued competition, but less and less important as sources of differential advantage. In the long run, competitiveness derives from an ability to build, at lower cost and more speedily than competitors, the core competencies that spawn unanticipated products. The real sources of advantage are to be found in management's ability to consolidate corporate-wide technologies and production skills into competencies that empower individual businesses to adapt quickly to changing opportunities.

Senior executives who claim that they cannot build core competencies either because they feel the autonomy of business units is sacrosanct or because their feet are held to the quarterly budget fire should think again. The problem in many western companies is not that their senior executives are any less capable than those in Japan or that Japanese companies possess greater technical capabilities. Instead, it is their adherence to a concept of the corporation that unnecessarily limits the ability of individual businesses to fully exploit the deep reservoir of technological capability that many American and European companies possess.

The diversified corporation is a large tree. The trunk and major limbs are core products, the smaller branches are business units; the leaves, flowers, and fruit are end products. The root system that provides nourishment, sustenance, and stability is the core competence. You can miss the strength of competitors by looking only at their end products, in the same way you miss the strength of a tree if you look only at its leaves (see Figure 6.2.1).

Core competencies are the collective learning in the organization, especially how to coordinate diverse production skills and integrate multiple streams of technologies. Consider Sony's capacity to miniaturize or Philips's optical-media expertise. The theoretical knowledge to put a radio on a chip does not in itself assure a company the skill to produce a miniature radio no bigger than a business card. To bring off this feat, Casio must harmonize know-how in miniaturization, microprocessor design, materials science, and ultrathin precision casing – the same skills it applies in its miniature card calculators, pocket TVs, and digital watches.

If core competence is about harmonizing streams of technology, it is also about the organization of work and the delivery of value. Among Sony's competencies is miniaturization. To bring miniaturization to its products, Sony must ensure that technologists, engineers, and marketers have a shared understanding of customer needs and of technological possibilities. The force of core competence is felt as decisively in services as in manufacturing. Citicorp was ahead of others investing in an operating system that allowed it to participate in world markets 24 hours a day. Its competence in systems has provided the company with the means to differentiate itself from many financial service institutions.

Core competence is communication, involvement, and a deep commitment to working across organizational boundaries. It involves many levels of people and all functions. World-class research in, for example, lasers or ceramics can take place in corporate laboratories without having an impact on any of the businesses

FIGURE 6.2.1   Competencies as the roots of competitiveness

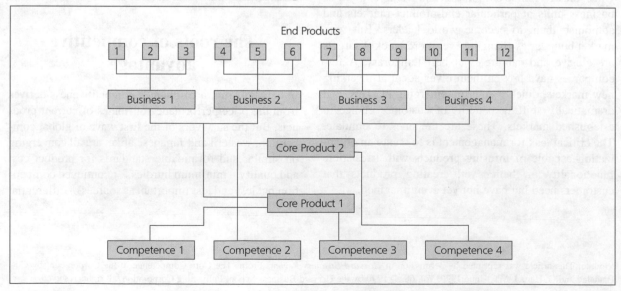

of the company. The skills that together constitute core competence must coalesce around individuals whose efforts are not so narrowly focused that they cannot recognize the opportunities for blending their functional expertise with those of others in new and interesting ways.

Core competence does not diminish with use. Unlike physical assets, which do deteriorate over time, competencies are enhanced as they are applied and shared. But competencies still need to be nurtured and protected; knowledge fades if it is not used. Competencies are the glue that binds existing businesses. They are also the engine for new business development. Patterns of diversification and market entry may be guided by them, not just by the attractiveness of markets.

Consider 3M's competence with sticky tape. In dreaming up businesses as diverse as 'Post-it' note pads, magnetic tape, photographic film, pressure-sensitive tapes, and coated abrasives, the company has brought to bear widely shared competencies in substrates, coatings, and adhesives and devised various ways to combine them. Indeed, 3M has invested consistently in them. What seems to be an extremely diversified portfolio of businesses belies a few shared core competencies.

In contrast, there are major companies that have had the potential to build core competencies but failed to do so because top management was unable to conceive of the company as anything other than a collection of discrete businesses. General Electric sold much of its consumer electronics business to Thomson of France, arguing that it was becoming increasingly difficult to maintain its competitiveness in this sector. That was undoubtedly so, but it is ironic that it sold several key businesses to competitors who were already competence leaders – Black & Decker in small electrical motors, and Thomson, which was eager to build its competence in microelectronics and had learned from the Japanese that a position in consumer electronics was vital to this challenge.

Management trapped in the strategic business unit (SBU) mind-set almost inevitably finds its individual businesses dependent on external sources for critical components, such as motors or compressors. But these are not just components. They are core products that contribute to the competitiveness of a wide range of end products. They are the physical embodiments of core competencies.

How not to think of competence

Since companies are in a race to build the competencies that determine global leadership, successful companies have stopped imagining themselves as bundles of businesses making products. Canon, Honda, Casio, or NEC may seem to preside over portfolios of businesses unrelated in terms of customers, distribution channels, and merchandising strategy. Indeed, they have portfolios that may seem idiosyncratic at times: NEC is the only global company to be among leaders in computing, telecommunications, and semiconductors *and* to have a thriving consumer electronics business.

But looks are deceiving. In NEC, digital technology, especially VLSI and systems integration skills, is fundamental. In the core competencies underlying them, disparate businesses become coherent. It is Honda's core competence in engines and power trains that gives it a distinctive advantage in car, motorcycle, lawn mower, and generator businesses. Canon's core competencies in optics, imaging, and microprocessor controls have enabled it to enter, even dominate, markets as seemingly diverse as copiers, laser printers, cameras, and image scanners. Philips worked for more than 15 years to perfect its optical-media (laser disc) competence, as did JVC in building a leading position in video recording. Other examples of core competencies might include mechantronics (the ability to marry mechanical and electronic engineering), video displays, bioengineering, and microelectronics. In the early stages of its competence building, Philips could not have imagined all the products that would be spawned by its optical-media competence, nor could JVC have anticipated miniature camcorders when it first began exploring videotape technologies.

Unlike the battle for global brand dominance, which is visible in the world's broadcast and print media and is aimed at building global 'share of mind,' the battle to build world-class competencies is invisible to people who aren't deliberately looking for it. Top management often tracks the cost and quality of competitors' products, yet how many managers untangle the web of alliances their Japanese competitors have constructed to acquire competencies at low cost? In how many western boardrooms is there an explicit, shared understanding of the competencies the company must build for world leadership? Indeed, how many senior executives discuss the crucial distinction between competitive strategy at the level of a business and competitive strategy at the level of an entire company?

Let us be clear. Cultivating core competence does not mean outspending rivals on research and development. In 1983, when Canon surpassed Xerox in world-wide unit market share in the copier business, its R&D budget in reprographics was but a small fraction of Xerox's. Over the past 20 years, NEC has spent less on R&D as a percentage of sales than almost all of its American and European competitors.

Nor does core competence mean shared costs, as when two or more SBUs use a common facility – a plant, service facility, or sales force – or share a common component. The gains of sharing may be substantial, but the search for shared costs is typically a post hoc effort to rationalize production across existing businesses, not a premeditated effort to build the competencies out of which the businesses themselves grow.

Building core competencies is more ambitious and different than integrating vertically, moreover. Managers deciding whether to make or buy will start with end products and look upstream to the efficiencies of the supply chain and downstream toward distribution and customers. They do not take inventory of skills and look forward to applying them in nontraditional ways. (Of course, decisions about competencies *do* provide a logic for vertical integration. Canon is not particularly integrated in its copier business, except in those aspects of the vertical chain that support the competencies it regards as critical.)

Identifying core competencies – and losing them

At least three tests can be applied to identify core competencies in a company. First, a core competence provides potential access to a wide variety of markets. Competence in display systems, for example, enables a company to participate in such diverse businesses as calculators, miniature TV sets, monitors for laptop computers, and automotive dashboards – which is why Casio's entry into the handheld TV market was predictable. Second, a core competence should make a significant contribution to the perceived customer benefits of the end product. Clearly, Honda's engine expertise fills this bill.

Finally, a core competence should be difficult for competitors to imitate. And it will be difficult if it is a complex harmonization of individual technologies and production skills. A rival might acquire some of the technologies that comprise the core competence, but it will find it more difficult to duplicate the more-or-less comprehensive pattern of internal coordination and learning. JVC's decision in the early 1960s to pursue the development of a videotape competence passed the three tests outlined here. RCA's decision in the late 1970s to develop a stylus-based video turntable system did not.

Few companies are likely to build world leadership in more than five or six fundamental competencies. A company that compiles a list of 20 to 30 capabilities has probably not produced a list of core competencies. Still, it is probably a good discipline to generate a list of this sort and to see aggregate capabilities as building blocks. This tends to prompt the search for licensing deals and alliances through which the company may acquire, at low cost, the missing pieces.

Most western companies hardly think about competitiveness in these terms at all. It is time to take a tough-minded look at the risks they are running. Companies that judge competitiveness, their own and their competitors', primarily in terms of the price/performance of end products are courting the erosion of core competencies – or making too little effort to enhance them. The embedded skills that give rise to the next generation of competitive products cannot be 'rented in' by outsourcing and original equipment manufacturer (OEM) supply relationships. In our view, too many companies have unwittingly surrendered core competencies when they cut internal investment in what they mistakenly thought were just 'cost centers' in favor of outside suppliers.

Of course, it is perfectly possible for a company to have a competitive product line up but be a laggard in developing core competencies – at least for a while. If a company wanted to enter the copier business today, it would find a dozen Japanese companies more than willing to supply copiers on the basis of an OEM private label. But when fundamental technologies changed or if its supplier decided to enter the market directly and become a competitor, that company's product line, along with all of its investments in marketing and distribution, could be vulnerable. Outsourcing can provide a shortcut to a more competitive product, but it typically contributes little to building the people-embodied skills that are needed to sustain product leadership.

Nor is it possible for a company to have an intelligent alliance or sourcing strategy if it has not made a choice about where it will build competence leadership. Clearly, Japanese companies have benefited from alliances. They've used them to learn from western partners who were not fully committed to preserving core competencies of their own. Learning within an alliance takes a positive commitment of resources – travel, a pool of dedicated people, test-bed facilities, time to internalize and test what has been learned. A company may not make this effort if it doesn't have clear goals for competence building.

Another way of losing is forgoing opportunities to establish competencies that are evolving in existing businesses. In the 1970s and 1980s, many American and European companies – like General Electric, Motorola, GTE, Thorn, and General Electric Company (GEC) – chose to exit the color television business, which they regard as mature. If by 'mature' they meant that they had run out of new product ideas at precisely the moment global rivals had targeted the TV business for entry, then yes, the industry was mature. But it certainly wasn't mature in the sense that all opportunities to enhance and apply video-based competencies had been exhausted.

In ridding themselves of their television businesses, these companies failed to distinguish between divesting the business and destroying their video media-based competencies. They not only got out of the TV business but they also closed the door on a whole stream of future opportunities reliant on video-based competencies.

There are two clear lessons here. First, the costs of losing a core competence can be only partly calculated in advance. The baby may be thrown out with the bath water in divestment decisions. Second, since core competencies are built through a process of continuous improvement and enhancement that may span a decade or longer, a company that has failed to invest in core competence building will find it very difficult to enter an emerging market, unless, of course, it will be content simply to serve as a distribution channel.

American semiconductor companies like Motorola learned this painful lesson when they elected to forgo direct participation in the 256k generation of DRAM chips. Having skipped this round, Motorola, like most of its American competitors, needed a large infusion of technical help from Japanese partners to rejoin the battle in the 1-megabyte generation. When it comes to core competencies, it is difficult to get off the train, walk to the next station, and then reboard.

From core competencies to core products

The tangible link between identified core competencies and end products is what we call the core products – the physical embodiments of one or more core competencies. Honda's engines, for example, are core products, linchpins between design and development skills that ultimately lead to a proliferation of end products. Core products are the components or sub-assemblies that actually contribute to the value of the end products. Thinking in terms of core products forces a company to distinguish between the brand share it achieves in end product markets (for example, 40 percent of the US refrigerator market) and the manufacturing share it achieves in any particular core product (for example, five percent of the world share of compressor output).

It is essential to make this distinction between core competencies, core products, and end products because global competition is played out by different rules and for different stakes at each level. To build or defend leadership over the long term, a corporation will probably be a winner at each level. At the level of core competence, the goal is to build world leadership in the design and development of a particular class of product functionality – be it compact data storage and retrieval, as with Philips's optical-media competence, or compactness and ease of use, as with Sony's micromotors and microprocessor controls.

To sustain leadership in their chosen core competence areas, these companies *seek to maximize their world manufacturing share in core products*. The manufacture of core products for a wide variety of external (and internal) customers yields the revenue and market feedback that, at least partly, determines the pace at which core competencies can be enhanced and extended. This thinking was behind JVC's decision in the mid-1970s to establish VCR supply relationships with leading national consumer electronics companies in Europe and the United States. In supplying Thomson, Thorn, and Telefunken (all independent companies at that time) as well as US partners, JVC was able to gain the cash and the diversity of market experience that ultimately enabled it to outpace Philips and Sony. (Philips developed videotape competencies in parallel with JVC, but it failed to build a world-wide network of OEM relationships that would have allowed it to accelerate the refinement of its videotape competence through the sale of core products.)

JVC's success has not been lost on Korean companies like Goldstar, Samsung, Kia, and Daewoo, who are building core product leadership in areas as diverse as displays, semiconductors, and automotive engines through their OEM-supply contracts with western companies. Their avowed goal is to capture investment initiative away from potential competitors, often US companies. In doing so, they accelerate their competence-building efforts while 'hollowing out' their competitors. By focusing on competence and embedding it in core products, Asian competitors have built up advantages in component markets first and have then leveraged off their superior products to move downstream to build brand share. And they are not likely to remain the low-cost suppliers forever. As their reputation for brand leadership is consolidated, they may well gain price leadership. Honda has proven this with its Acura line, and other Japanese carmakers are following suit.

Control over core products is critical for other reasons. A dominant position in core products allows a company to shape the evolution of applications and end markets. Such compact audio disc-related core products as data drives and lasers have enabled Sony and Philips to influence the evolution of the computer-peripheral business in optical-media storage. As a company multiplies the number of application arenas for its core products, it can consistently reduce the cost, time, and risk in new product development. In short, well-targeted core products can lead to economies of scale and scope.

The tyranny of the SBU

The new terms of competitive engagement cannot be understood using analytical tools devised to manage the diversified corporation of 20 years ago, when competition was primarily domestic (GE versus Westinghouse, General Motors versus Ford) and all the key players were speaking the language of the same business schools and consultancies. Old prescriptions have potentially toxic side effects. The need for new

principles is most obvious in companies organized exclusively according to the logic of SBUs. The implications of the two alternate concepts of the corporation are summarized in Table 6.2.1.

Obviously, diversified corporations have a portfolio of products and a portfolio of businesses. But we believe in a view of the company as a portfolio of competencies as well. United States companies do not lack the technical resources to build competencies, but their top management often lacks the vision to build them and the administrative means for assembling resources spread across multiple businesses. A shift in commitment will inevitably influence patterns of diversification, skill deployment, resource allocation priorities, and approaches to alliances and outsourcing.

We have described the three different planes on which battles for global leadership are waged: core competence, core products, and end products. A corporation has to know whether it is winning or losing on each plane. By sheer weight of investment, a company might be able to beat its rivals to blue-sky technologies yet still lose the race to build core competence leadership. If a company is winning the race to build core competencies (as opposed to building leadership in a few technologies), it will almost certainly outpace rivals in new business development. If a company is winning the race to capture world manufacturing share in core products, it will probably outpace rivals in improving product features and the price/performance ratio.

Determining whether one is winning or losing end-product battles is more difficult because measures of

TABLE 6.2.1 Two concepts of the corporation

	SBU	Core competence
Basis for competition	Competiveness of today's products	Interfirm competition to build competencies
Corporate structure	Portfolio of businesses related in product-market terms	Portfolio of competencies, core products, and businesses
Status of the business unit	Autonomy is sacrosanct; the SBU 'owns' all resources other than cash	SBU is a potential reservoir of core competencies
Resource allocation	Discrete businesses are the unit of analysis; capital is allocated business by business	Businesses and competencies are the unit of analysis: top management allocates capital and talent
Value added of top management	Optimizing corporate returns through capital allocation trade-offs among businesses	Enunciating strategic architecture and building competencies to secure the future

product market share do not necessarily reflect various companies' underlying competitiveness. Indeed, companies that attempt to build market share by relying on the competitiveness of others, rather than investing in core competencies and world core-product leadership, may be treading on quicksand. In the race for global brand dominance, companies like 3M, Black & Decker, Canon, Honda, NEC, and Citicorp have built global brand umbrellas by proliferating products out of their core competencies. This has allowed their individual businesses to build image, customer loyalty, and access to distribution channels.

When you think about this reconceptualization of the corporation, the primacy of the SBU – an organizational dogma for a generation – is now clearly an anachronism. Where the SBU is an article of faith, resistance to the seductions of decentralization can seem heretical. In many companies, the SBU prism means that only one plane of the global competitive battle, the battle to put competitive products on the shelf *today*, is visible to top management. What are the costs of this distortion?

Underinvestment in developing core competencies and core products

When the organization is conceived of as a multiplicity of SBUs, no single business may feel responsible for maintaining a viable position in core products or be able to justify the investment required to build world leadership in some core competence. In the absence of a more comprehensive view imposed by corporate management, SBU managers will tend to underinvest. Recently, companies such as Kodak and Philips have recognized this as a potential problem and have begun searching for new organizational forms that will allow them to develop and manufacture core products for both internal and external customers.

SBU managers have traditionally conceived of competitors in the same way they've seen themselves. On the whole, they've failed to note the emphasis Asian competitors were placing on building leadership in core products or to understand the critical linkage between world manufacturing leadership and the ability to sustain development pace in core competence. They've failed to pursue OEM-supply opportunities or to look across their various product divisions in an attempt to identify opportunities for coordinated initiatives.

Imprisoned resources

As an SBU evolves, it often develops unique competencies. Typically, the people who embody this competence are seen as the sole property of the business in which they grew up. The manager of another SBU who asks to borrow talented people is likely to get a cold rebuff. SBU managers are not only unwilling to lend their competence carriers but they may actually hide talent to prevent its redeployment in the pursuit of new opportunities. This may be compared to residents of an underdeveloped country hiding most of their cash under their mattresses. The benefits of competencies, like the benefits of the money supply, depend on the velocity of their circulation as well as on the size of the stock the company holds.

Western companies have traditionally had an advantage in the stock of skills they possess. But have they been able to reconfigure them quickly to respond to new opportunities? Canon, NEC, and Honda have had a lesser stock of the people and technologies that compose core competencies but could move them much quicker from one business unit to another. Corporate R&D spending at Canon is not fully indicative of the size of Canon's core competence stock and tells the casual observer nothing about the velocity with which Canon is able to move core competencies to exploit opportunities.

When competencies become imprisoned, the people who carry the competencies do not get assigned to the most exciting opportunities, and their skills begin to atrophy. Only by fully leveraging core competencies can small companies like Canon afford to compete with industry giants like Xerox. How strange that SBU managers, who are perfectly willing to compete for cash in the capital budgeting process, are unwilling to compete for people – the company's most precious asset. We find it ironic that top management devotes so much attention to the capital budgeting process yet typically has no comparable mechanism for allocating the human skills that embody core competencies. Top managers are seldom able to look four or five levels down into the organization, identify the people who embody critical competencies, and move them across organizational boundaries.

Bounded innovation

If core competencies are not recognized, individual SBUs will pursue only those innovation opportunities that are close at hand – marginal product-line extensions or geographic expansions. Hybrid opportunities like fax machines, laptop computers, handheld televisions, or portable music keyboards will emerge only when managers take off their SBU blinkers. Remember, Canon appeared to be in the camera business at the time it was preparing to become a world leader in copiers. Conceiving of the corporation in terms of core competencies widens the domain of innovation.

Developing strategic architecture

The fragmentation of core competencies becomes inevitable when a diversified company's information systems, patterns of communication, career paths, managerial rewards, and processes of strategy development do not transcend SBU lines. We believe that senior management should spend a significant amount of its time developing a corporate-wide strategic architecture that establishes objectives for competence-building. A strategic architecture is a road map of the future that identifies which core competencies to build and their constituent technologies.

By providing an impetus for learning from alliances and a focus for internal development efforts, a strategic architecture like NEC's C&C (computers and communication) can dramatically reduce the investment needed to secure future market leadership. How can a company make partnerships intelligently without a clear understanding of the core competencies it is trying to build and those it is attempting to prevent from being unintentionally transferred?

Of course, all of this begs the question of what a strategic architecture should look like. The answer will be different for every company. But it is helpful to think again of that tree, of the corporation organized around core products and, ultimately, core competencies. To sink sufficiently strong roots, a company must answer some fundamental questions: How long could we preserve our competitiveness in this business if we did not control this particular core competence? How central is this core competence to perceived customer benefits? What future opportunities would be foreclosed if we were to lose this particular competence?

The architecture provides a logic for product and market diversification, moreover. An SBU manager would be asked: Does the new market opportunity add to the overall goal of becoming the best player in the world? Does it exploit or add to the core competence? At Vickers, for example, diversification options have been judged in the context of becoming the best power and motion control company in the world.

The strategic architecture should make resource allocation priorities transparent to the entire organization. It provides a template for allocation decisions by top management. It helps lower-level managers understand the logic of allocation priorities and disciplines senior management to maintain consistency. In short, it yields a definition of the company and the markets it serves. 3M, Vickers, NEC, Canon, and Honda all qualify on this score. Honda knew it was exploiting what it had learned from motorcycles – how to make high-revving, smooth-running, lightweight engines – when it entered the car business. The task of creating a strategic architecture forces the organization to identify and commit to the technical and production linkages across SBUs that will provide a distinct competitive advantage.

It is consistency of resource allocation and the development of an administrative infrastructure appropriate to it that breathes life into a strategic architecture and creates a managerial culture, teamwork, a capacity to change, and a willingness to share resources, to protect proprietary skills, and to think long term. That is also the reason the specific architecture cannot be copied easily or overnight by competitors. Strategic architecture is a tool for communicating with customers and other external constituents. It reveals the broad direction without giving away every step.

Redeploying to exploit competencies

If the company's core competencies are its critical resource and if top management must ensure that competence carriers are not held hostage by some particular business, then it follows that SBUs should bid for core competencies in the same way they bid for capital. We've made this point glancingly. It is important enough to consider more deeply.

Once top management (with the help of divisional and SBU managers) has identified overarching competencies, it must ask businesses to identify the projects and people closely connected with them. Corporate officers should direct an audit of the location, number, and quality of the people who embody competence.

This sends an important signal to middle managers: core competencies are corporate resources and may be reallocated by *corporate* management. An individual business doesn't own anybody. SBUs are entitled to the services of individual employees so long as SBU management can demonstrate that the opportunity it is pursuing yields the highest possible payoff on the investment in their skills. This message is further underlined if each year in the strategic planning or budgeting process, unit managers must justify their hold on the people who carry the company's core competencies.

Also, reward systems that focus only on product-line results and career paths that seldom cross SBU boundaries engender patterns of behavior among unit managers that are destructively competitive. At NEC, divisional managers come together to identify next-generation competencies. Together they decide how much investment needs to be made to build up each future competence and the contribution in capital and staff support that each division will need to make. There is also a sense of equitable exchange. One division may make a disproportionate contribution or may benefit less from the progress made, but such short-term inequalities will balance out over the long term.

Incidentally, the positive contribution of the SBU manager should be made visible across the company. An SBU manager is unlikely to surrender key people if only the other business (or the general manager of that business who may be a competitor for promotion) is going to benefit from the redeployment. Cooperative SBU managers should be celebrated as team players. Where priorities are clear, transfers are less likely to be seen as idiosyncratic and politically motivated.

Transfers for the sake of building core competence must be recorded and appreciated in the corporate memory. It is reasonable to expect a business that has surrendered core skills on behalf of corporate opportunities in other areas to lose, for a time, some of its competitiveness. If these losses in performance bring immediate censure, SBUs will be unlikely to assent to skills transfers next time.

Finally, there are ways to wean key employees off the idea that they belong in perpetuity to any particular business. Early in their careers, people may be exposed to a variety of businesses through a carefully planned rotation program.

Competence carriers should be regularly brought together from across the corporation to trade notes and ideas. The goal is to build a strong feeling of community among these people. To a great extent, their loyalty should be to the integrity of the core competence area they represent and not just to particular businesses. In traveling regularly, talking frequently to customers, and meeting with peers, competence carriers may be encouraged to discover new market opportunities.

Core competencies are the wellspring of new business development. They should constitute the focus for strategy at the corporate level. Managers have to win manufacturing leadership in core products and capture global share through brand-building programs aimed at exploiting economies of scope. Only if the company is conceived of as a hierarchy of core competencies, core products, and market-focused business units will it be fit to fight.

Nor can top management be just another layer of accounting consolidation, which it often is in a regime of radical decentralization. Top management must add value by enunciating the strategic architecture that guides the competence acquisition process. We believe an obsession with competence building will characterize the global winners of the 1990s. With the decade underway, the time for rethinking the concept of the corporation is already overdue.

Understanding acquisition integration approaches

By Philippe Haspeslagh and David Jemison[1]

The senior members of a management team of an historically successful firm were discussing their experiences in integrating acquisitions outside their base business. When the chairman asked the management team what integration meant, the consensus answer was, 'Integrating an acquisition means making them like us.' Although that approach may be appropriate in a few instances, the chairman's reaction reflected the frustration felt by many senior executives involved in diversification activities: 'How can we do anything different with an attitude like this?'

Integration clearly means different things to different people. Most importantly, it means different things in different situations. While there are common ingredients in the process, each acquisition presents managers with a different situation and forces a choice of integration approach. Earlier writers on acquisitions have suggested several distinctions that affect the type of integration approach. For example, it has been argued that differences in the integration task are based on the relative size of the acquired firm, the acquired firm's profitability, whether the synergies are in marketing or manufacturing, and whether the cultures are similar or not. But when we compared the detailed observations from our research with such distinctions, none by itself provided a sufficient explanation of the range of integration phenomena we observed.

Our research identified two key dimensions that led to a broad logic for choosing an integration approach. This reading examines those dimensions and presents the three integration approaches that correspond to these contexts. We do not suggest that there is one best way to integrate each acquisition. Good performance is also affected by consistency and discipline in execution of what is ultimately a managerial choice. But we do advocate carefully choosing an integration approach based on the analysis of a number of key factors and then remaining flexible to adapt the approach as events unfold. In this reading we will emphasize a logic to guide integration choices and the analysis on which it can be based.

Key dimensions in acquisition integration

A firm's approach to integration can be understood by considering two central dimensions of the acquisition – its relationship to the acquiring firm and the way in which value is expected to be created. The first dimension relates to the nature of the interdependence that needs to be established between the firms to make possible the type of strategic capability transfer that is expected. The other dimension is associated with the need to preserve intact the acquired strategic capabilities after the acquisition.

Strategic interdependence need

The essential task in any acquisition is to create the value that becomes possible when the two organizations are combined, value that would not exist if the firms operated separately. The analysis, negotiation, and internal selling of an acquisition candidate and ultimately the premium offered are all predicated on this central idea. Yet managers often shy away from the integration task because of uncertainties about the fundamentals of the acquired business, because of organizational or cultural differences, or because of a fear that they will be resisted.

Capability transfer requires creating and managing interdependencies between both organizations. These interdependencies disturb the 'boundary' of the acquired company, that invisible line that distinguishes them from the acquirer. This disturbance is likely to be resented, if not resisted, by managers in the acquired firm, who want to keep their identity and their way of doing things. To transfer capabilities between firms and

[1]Source: This article was adapted with the permission of The Free Press, a Division of Simon and Schuster Adult Publishing Group, from *Managing Acquisitions: Creating Value Through Corporate Renewal* by Philippe C. Haspeslagh and David B. Jemison. © 1990 by The Free Press.

overcome possible resistance requires that the interdependence between the two firms be carefully managed. Thus, a key determinant of the integration task is the nature of the interdependence between the two firms and how that interdependence is to be managed.

The nature of the interdependence in an acquisition depends on how value will be created. We discuss three types of capability transfer (resource sharing, functional skill transfer, and general management capability transfer), as well as a number of combination benefits. Each of these four benefits implies different requirements for interdependence and, thus, for the degree to which the boundary of the acquired organization will have to be disturbed and eliminated, and, conversely, the degree to which the organizational identity of the original company should be maintained.

Some acquisitions are based primarily on *resource sharing*, which involves the combination and rationalization of operating assets. Resource sharing implies an integration process that completely dissolves the boundaries between the two subparts of the organizations that are to be rationalized. In resource sharing, value is created by combining the entities at the operating level, so that functional overlaps and duplication are eliminated. The greater efficiency of the streamlined operations is supposed to outweigh any costs associated with the rationalization. Such costs include not only those of a one-time rationalization of the firms, but also the harder-to-measure ongoing consequences of a loss of specialized focus and commitment that might derive from combining both operations.

The integration process is inherently different if the strategic capability transfer involves the *transfer of functional skills*. Skills reside in individuals, groups of people, and their procedures and practices, not in assets. They can be transferred only as people are moved across organizational boundaries or when information, knowledge, and know-how are shared. For example, the R&D capability of a chemical firm can be transferred to an acquired firm through a variety of mechanisms, including coordinated management of the R&D functions, transfer of R&D scientists in both directions, or transfer of the products or processes that are the outcome of such R&D. Although each organization retains a distinct presence in the function in question, continuing interference and involvement (or potential interference) from the acquiring company's corresponding functional managers impinge on the acquired company managers' autonomy. Because that boundary disruption comes about through essentially horizontal rather than hierarchical interactions, it is often regarded as illegitimate by the acquired managers, who want to preserve the integrity of what they still see as their firm. The transfer of *general management capability* can create value through improved strategic or operational insight, coordination, or control. These improvements can be achieved partly through direct, substantive involvement in general management decisions, or on a more permanent basis through the installation and use of systems, controls, budgets, and plans that improve both the strategic decision making and the operational efficiency of acquired management.

General management capability transfer was seen as somewhat less disruptive than the other types of strategic capability transfer. Direct involvement by hierarchical superiors was considered more legitimate than the involvement of functional counterparts from the acquirer, and after the one-time disruption of changes in systems, life inside the acquired unit could go on without further boundary disruption. Nevertheless, disruption did occur. For example, managers in the acquired firms typically regarded being subjected to the discipline of formal investment approval as a loss of freedom, even when no projects had been turned down or, to the contrary, accelerated investment had been encouraged.

Finally, any acquisition brings with it a number of *combination benefits* that are available automatically as a result of the combination and are not related to capability transfer. Some acquisitions may yield excess cash resources or borrowing capacity between the firms. In others, benefits may come from greater size, whether through the added purchasing power it provides, or through the greater market power that size brings. The merger between Metal Box of the U.K. and Carnaud of France, for example, to create CMB, one of the larger packaging firms in the world, had a clear impact on the bargaining position of Metal Box vis-à-vis British Steel, its main source of tin-plated steel. Not only did the combined firm become the largest European customer for a product that had long been cartelized by suppliers, but it also gave Metal Box access to Carnaud's integrated capacity. Given Metal Box's prior size, the immediate cost savings on its existing volume were not dramatic, but it was able to channel its new bargaining power into obtaining much more important quality and on-time delivery benefits. At the same time CMB is continuing to make acquisitions of smaller firms, and with them opportunities for a significant raw materials cost saving.

Any individual acquisition may involve benefits from several of these sources. Yet our research suggests that in most cases, independent of the varie...

number of possible synergies, it is possible, and advisable, to recognize one type of capability transfer as the *dominant* source of initial value creation.

Formally assessing the strategic interdependence needs of an acquisition has several important benefits. It helps managers develop a more unbiased, objective view of the strategic task involved in creating value with the acquisition irrespective of the ease or difficulty of implemention. At the same time, by categorizing these strategic tasks in a way that reflect the required extent of interdependence, managers can go beyond identifying potential areas of synergy and examine the organizational tasks that will be needed to bring out the expected benefits. Finally, by considering only those interdependencies regarded as critical for achieving the benefits upon which the acquisition was originally justified, managers can begin to develop a clearer sense of the strategic and organizational trade-offs involved. Before making these trade-offs, however, the organizational factors that are central to the integration process must be addressed.

Organizational autonomy need

Because we regard strategic capability transfer as the precursor to value creation, it is clearly vital to preserve the strategic capability that is to be transferred. Yet one of the paradoxes in acquisitions is that the pursuit of capability transfer itself may lead to the destruction of the capability being transferred. Whereas capability transfer requires different degrees of boundary disruption or dissolution, the preservation of capabilities requires boundary protection and, hence, organizational autonomy.

This paradox is especially evident in acquisitions where the acquired capabilities reside in people or groups of people. The disintegration of many of the financial firms that were acquired in London during the build-up to 'Big Bang' in 1986 is an example of this problem. Key people may decide to leave simply because, as we discussed earlier, they feel that value has been destroyed for them. At the heart of this problem is the issue of boundary management. Demands for organizational autonomy and 'no change' are present in every acquisition. They come from the deep-seated identification of managers, employees, and other organizational stakeholders with their original organization.

All too often, acquiring managers respond to these demands for autonomy by promising whatever it takes to make acquired managers 'accept' the takeover. They then often shroud their promises in the illusion that all expected benefits of an acquisition will be realized

without any disruptive changes. For example, a dispute over the integration of Blue Arrow, the British temporary services company, with its American acquisition of Manpower, Inc. in the United States led to the resignation of Manpower's CEO. The chairman of Blue Arrow said that it was time to look for 'back office synergies and cost savings.' At the same time, he hastily added that he would not change Manpower's culture or the way its services were marketed (*New York Times*, December 6 1998, p. 23). Statements such as this are often made for public consumption or to soothe the apprehensions of acquired managers and employees. But, as experienced acquirers well know, this sort of schizophrenic attitude often paves the way for the reverse: organizational upheaval with synergies left unrealized.

We indicated earlier that most of the organizational behavior and corporate culture research on acquisitions has focused on the issue of the impact on people and their acceptance of the acquisition. The assumption often seems to be that in an acquisition no one should be disturbed or have 'bad' things happen to them. We, too, believe that people are important in an acquisition and we believe they should be treated fairly and with dignity. But if managers lose sight of the fact that the strategic task of an acquisition is to create value, they may either grant autonomy too quickly or fall into the perilous 'no change-all synergies expected' syndrome described above. Managers and employees in acquired firms are too smart to be fooled by this syndrome.

Dealing with the perceived need for autonomy after an acquisition is one of the most important challenges a manager will face. The manager should not deviate from the strategic task – transferring capabilities to create value – unless the argument for autonomy corresponds to a real need for boundary protection. Such a real need exists when the strategic capabilities whose transfer is key to the acquisition are embedded in a distinct organization and culture and that distinction is central to the preservation of those capabilities. That is, the other firm may have been acquired precisely because it is different.

Managers in acquiring firms can consider the need for organizational autonomy in more practical terms by examining three questions: Is autonomy essential to preserve the strategic capability we bought? If so, how much autonomy should be allowed? In which areas specifically is autonomy important?

Regarding the first question, our research suggests that autonomy should be provided the acquired unit if the survival of the strategic capabilities on which the acquisition is based depends on preservation of the organizational culture from which they came. The important question, thus, is *not* how different the two cultures are, but whether *maintaining that difference* in the long term will serve a useful purpose. For example, when BASF, the German chemical giant, bought American Enka's petrochemical operations from Akzo in 1985, its main purpose was to improve the raw materials supply position of its fiber business through acquisition of the Enka plant. The economics of that facility depended very little on the organizational culture of American Akzo.

On the other hand, when BASF bought the Celanese advanced composites materials businesses in that same year, the situation was very different. The very success of that acquisition depended on BASF's ability to keep intact both the entrepreneurial culture of the former Celanese organization and its links with important aerospace and defense clients – substantial challenges for a large foreign acquirer. In such cases, allowing sufficient autonomy to preserve the acquired capabilities constitutes more than a tactic to gain acceptance and placate employees. It is vital to the success of the acquisition.

If there is a genuine need to maintain autonomy, managers must next consider whether the capabilities are widely spread or fairly isolated in the acquired organization. At one end of the spectrum the strategic capability may be embedded in a particular subunit of the organization. For example, a particular firm's value for the acquirer may derive from a specific R&D capability that, although highly dependent on a subculture within the R&D department, is fairly unrelated to the rest of the organization, from which it can be 'extracted'. In contrast, an acquired firm's value may depend on more generalized capabilities that extend well beyond a particular department to involve the entire organization. In the acquisition of the Beatrice companies by ICI, for example, the value of companies like LNP and Fiberite was based on the fact that they were close to the (leading edge) U.S. market, solution oriented, and entrepreneurial, properties that were spread throughout the organization. Another illustration is seen in the comment of the managing director of BP Nutrition, who, in the purchase of Hendrix, a Dutch animal feed company, realized that Hendrix had a very different dynamic and was most concerned about 'keeping their flywheel going', because BP would not be able to start it again.

These considerations allowed us to distinguish among the acquisitions we studied in terms of their need for autonomy. In some situations, company-wide autonomy was needed because the acquirer had virtually no experience in the business and the particular skills sought were inseparable from the culture in which they were rooted. In others, the protection of important, functionally embedded capabilities was needed, whereas other parts of the organization were less sensitive to change. Finally, in some situations the organizational differences were not at the root of the targeted benefits and hence change would not prejudice the realization of the benefits.

Managers may not always have the information to judge how different the cultures and subcultures of both organizations are before they experience those differences. Yet, we suggest, an early focus on which strategic capabilities need to be preserved, to what extent they depend on maintaining a cultural difference, and to what extent they can be contained in a subpart of the organization focus will be of critical importance in choosing an integration approach. This focus can help managers distinguish between the strategic needs of the situation and the desire of the acquired firm's management to retain its independence. It can also help to clarify the trade-offs at stake in granting or refusing autonomy to an acquired firm and help managers define decision rules for action in each setting.

Types of integration approaches

While understanding the distinctive needs for strategic interdependence and organizational autonomy can offer insights, considering them in a combined fashion helps suggest specific approaches to integration. Figure 6.3.1 positions integration approaches in light of the relationships between these two key factors. Some acquisitions have a high need for strategic interdependence, and a low need for organizational autonomy. These acquisitions call for what we label an *absorption* approach to integration. Other acquisitions, to the contrary, present a low need for strategic interdependence but a high need for organizational autonomy. We will call the integration approach associated with these acquisitions *preservation*. Other acquisitions are characterized by high needs for interdependence and high needs for organizational autonomy. We will use the term *symbiosis* to describe the integration approach called for in such acquisitions.

These three acquisition integration approaches represent, in our experience, useful metaphors to guide the integration task. In practice, of course, the degree of

FIGURE 6.3.1   Types of acquisition integration approaches

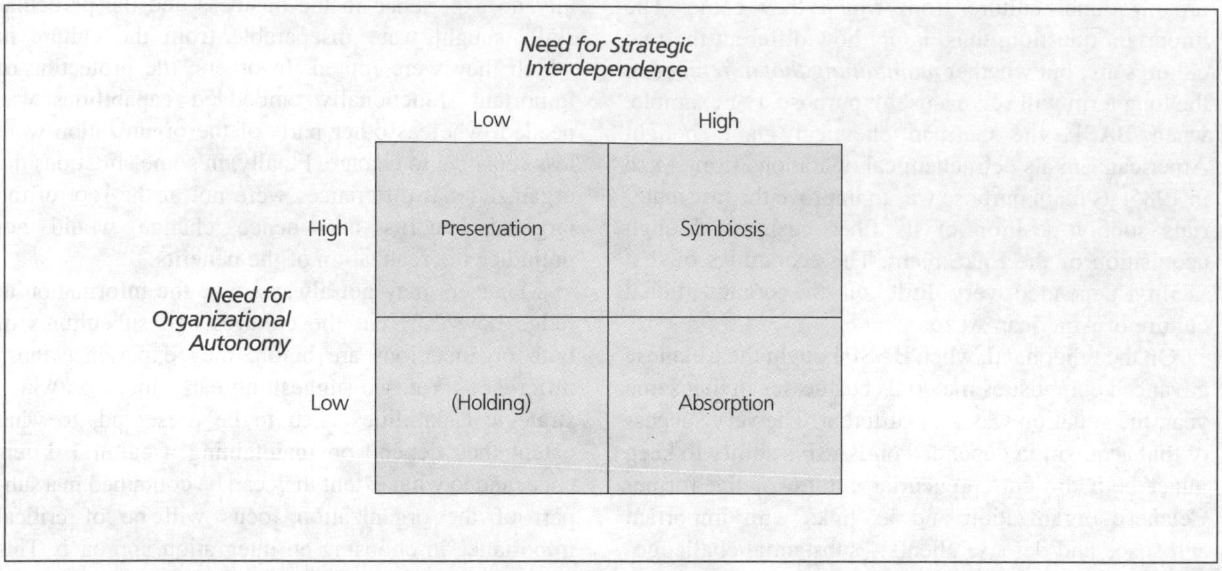

strategic interdependence and of organizational autonomy present in an acquisition integration depends on the choices managers make about how they perceive those respective needs.

The usefulness of choosing an overall metaphor for an acquisition integration does not change the fact that acquisitions bring with them many positions and capabilities, the integration of which, seen in more detailed perspective, might be best served by a different approach. A detailed analysis of the autonomy needs and interdependence needs of the main components of the acquisition helps a company determine how, within the dominant metaphor, they can try to differentiate the approach to each capability. The choice between the compromise of a fairly blanket approach and a tailor-made differentiation depends on the capability of the organization to implement the integration approach it chooses. We will describe each of these approaches more fully.

None of the acquisitions in our sample fell into the fourth quadrant in Figure 6.3.1, which could be labeled as 'holding' acquisitions: These would be acquisitions where the firm has no intention of integrating and creating value through anything except financial transfers, risk-sharing, or general management capability, even though the two firms are presumably in such similar businesses that there is no need for organizational autonomy. The only integration in such acquisitions would, in a sense, be a mere holding activity. Given our research focus on strategic

acquirers, it is not surprising that we did not encounter such acquisitions. Nevertheless, it is conceivable that such acquisitions exist. The situation of Triangle Industries, which had acquired both National Can and American Can before selling them off to the French company, Pechiney, is an example. Another is the acquisition and simultaneous holding by the financial firm McAndrews and Forbes of Revlon, Max Factor, and Barnes-Hinds, three firms in similar businesses, which were kept completely at arm's-length from each other. Such acquisitions would be made in a value-capturing perspective, as in the example of Triangle, or value creation would be based solely on the introduction of better general management.

Understanding these differences is a precondition to managing them successfully.

Absorption acquisitions

Absorption acquisitions are those in which the strategic task requires a high degree of interdependence to create the value expected but has a low need for organizational autonomy to achieve that interdependence. Integration in this case implies a full consolidation, over time, of the operations, organization, and culture of both organizations.

To eliminate all differences between both original companies may take a very long time indeed, especially if one is not just folding a small unit into a large one, but combining two sizable companies in the same businesses. The distinction that matters is one of intent at the outset: in absorption acquisitions the objective is ultimately to dissolve the boundary between both units. In this light, the key integration issue becomes a question of timing rather than how much integration should take place. In absorption acquisitions the acquiring company needs the courage of its convictions to ensure that its vision for the acquisition is carried out. Wavering because of extreme sensitivity to cultural issues is likely to limit the firm's ability to get the value expected, because the management task is to bring about the interdependence of the firms.

A recognition that the decisions can be tough but necessary is illustrated by the challenge facing ICI's Agrochemicals division after the acquisition of Stauffer. The two companies had a large degree of overlap in their sales territory in the United States. Each was set up to sell and market different products to essentially the same farmers. One company had a very direct sales approach, using its own sales force, whereas the other used independent wholesalers to provide sales and service to farmers. Whether and how to integrate the sales function and according to which model were clearly crucial and complex questions, worthy of detailed analysis. Yet a decision about whether to integrate or not had to be made very quickly. In this seasonal business, product turmoil during the crucial ordering period could mean the loss of an entire year.

Preservation acquisitions

In the preservation acquisitions there is a high need for autonomy and a low need for interdependence among the combining firms. In such situations the primary task of management is to keep the source of the acquired benefits intact, because deterioration in the acquired (and sometimes acquiring) company's ways of managing, practices, or even motivation would endanger success. Even though needs for interdependence are low in preservation acquisitions, this sort of autonomy and the protection it implies are often difficult to provide. In these situations the acquired operations are managed at arm's-length beyond those specific areas in which interdependence is to be pursued. The latter typically consist of financial/risk sharing and general management capability transfer to the extent that such capability is not industry-dependent.

In preservation acquisitions it is important to understand how sufficient value can be created to off-

set the acquisition premiums paid. The typical conception is that the main benefit is to be derived from the ability to bring funding to the acquired company. However, in the successful preservation cases we studied, money was not the main factor. In fact, all were successful enough to finance their own development completely. In these cases, value was created through a series of interactions that brought about positive changes in the ambition, risk-taking, and professionalism of the acquired company's management group. The metaphor that best captures the way value is created in preservation acquisitions is that of *nurturing*.

Nurturing the acquired firm represents only part of the value-creation potential that may be realized through a preservation approach. Another important source of value creation, which we will discuss later, is the *learning* that for the acquiring company might derive, both in terms of making further acquisitions in the newly explored area and in terms of learning for its base businesses. This learning is typically central to the purpose in the case of platform acquisitions. Exxon's ill-fated acquisitions in electronics companies; BP's entry into the nutrition business; the acquisition of Burndy, the American connector manufacturer, by Framatome, the French nuclear company; and the acquisitive development of Lafarge-Coppée New Materials' division into decorative paints are all examples of situations requiring preservation.

Symbiotic acquisitions

The third type of acquisition integration approach presents the most complex managerial challenges. Symbiotic acquisitions involve high needs for both strategic interdependence (because substantial capability transfer must take place) and organizational autonomy (because the acquired capabilities need to be preserved in an organizational context that is different from the acquirer's).

In symbiotic acquisitions the two organizations first coexist and then gradually become increasingly interdependent. This coexistence and mutual dependency are slowly achieved despite the tension arising from the conflicting needs for strategic capability transfer and the maintenance of each organization's autonomy and culture. Symbiotic acquisitions need simultaneous boundary preservation and boundary permeability. These needs can be kept in balance by protecting the boundary between both firms that shields the broad identity and character of the acquired firm at the same time that it is becoming increasingly permeable to a

ties of interactions aimed at functional as well as general management skill transfer.

The needs to preserve autonomy in symbiotic acquisitions can be gradually lifted only to the extent that the acquired company itself changes its own organizational practices to adapt to the new situation. To succeed in truly amalgamating the organizations symbiotically, each firm must take on the original qualities of the other.

Impact of other differences

The dual needs for strategic interdependence and organizational autonomy captured were by far the most important factors that we observed determining the integration approach. Two other factors, the quality and size of the acquired firm, were also found important. But, we suggest, the role these factors play in shaping the nature of the integration process is not as great as the pressures that arise from the need for strategic interdependence and the need for organizational autonomy.

| READING 6.4 | Seeking synergies |

By Andrew Campbell and Michael Goold[1]

A review of synergy management can be triggered in a number of ways. A parent manager may suspect that co-ordination opportunities are being missed, but may not be sure what is being missed, how important it is, or what to do about it. A new chief executive may sense that his predecessor's emphasis on decentralisation has led unit managers to overlook sharing opportunities. A visit to other companies that sing the praises of co-ordination may raise concerns about what is being missed. Critical press comments about the company's failure to achieve synergies across its portfolio may prompt questions about what more could be achieved. Given our concern about 'synergy bias', we counsel caution in following up vague disquiets. But an audit of how well synergy management is working can be a useful step in allaying fears or pinpointing areas that need to be addressed.

A review can also be triggered by grumbles at lower levels in the company that current co-ordination efforts are pointless or damaging or contradictory. Business managers may complain that short-term budget targets prevent them from exploring potentially valuable synergy opportunities or about the pointlessness of corporate-wide conferences at expensive resorts to promote 'family feeling'. Corridor gossip about the nega-

tive influence of the parent may percolate up to the chief executive. More direct complaints may be received from frustrated business managers. Bottom-up pressures to think again about a company's approach to synergies should be taken seriously, and, if there are widespread or deep-seated concerns, a systematic and objective stock-taking may be in order.

Some companies build a periodic review of their cross-company initiatives into their regular planning processes. We are less enthusiastic about this practice, since it can easily lead either to superficial, year-by-year reiteration of what everyone already knows about the areas of overlap between businesses or to vain attempts to come up with new ideas. Unless there is a particular reason to review linkage management, it will probably cause more frustration than enlightenment. On the whole, therefore, we believe that a review should only be undertaken when there are identifiable reasons for doing so.

Good reasons to take stock of the current approach include:

- a belief that a major category of synergies such as international rationalisation, sharing technical know-how or joint development of new business opportunities, is being systematically missed;

[1]Source: This article was adapted with permission from Chapter 7 of *Synergy: Why Links Between Business Units Often Fail and How to Make Them Work*, Capstone Publishing Ltd, Oxford, 1998.

- visible and costly failures of several recent synergy initiatives;
- evidence that business units are favouring links with third parties in preference to internal links.

While it would be useful to have a way of objectively deciding when a stock take is necessary, our experience suggests that it is best judged subjectively by thinking about how well the current organisation is working.

The purpose of a review should be to decide whether changes are needed in the overall corporate approach to synergies; to identify any specific opportunities that merit closer investigations; and to propose possible new linkage mechanisms or interventions.

A framework for a review

Our review framework is shown in Figure 6.4.1. It involves taking stock of both synergy opportunities available and the current corporate approach to cross-company linkages. The effectiveness of the approach can be assessed by testing how well it fits with the opportunities. The assessment can then be used to pin-point new initiatives that may be worth considering. The framework will bring out aspects of the overall approach that are working well or badly, and lead to proposals for changes.

The value of the framework is that it obliges companies to address some fundamental questions:

- What is our current attitude to co-ordination between our business units, and how do we go about managing it?
- What do we believe are the main synergy opportunities in our portfolio, and how fully are we grasping them?
- How well suited is our current approach, including structures, processes and staff support, to the opportunities we believe are on offer?
- What current synergy initiatives should we drop, what new opportunities should we go for, and what changes in processes and mechanisms should we consider?

FIGURE 6.4.1 Reviewing synergy parenting

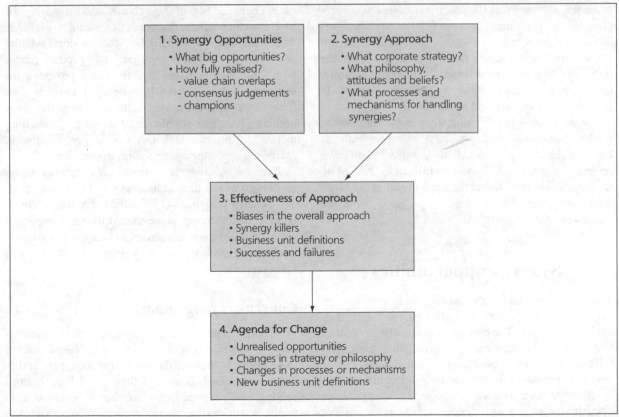

These questions can be asked of the whole company or of a multi-business division within a larger company. The framework is equally applicable when applied to any level above that of the individual business unit. However, when working at a division level, it is valuable to understand some of the broader corporate context in which the division is operating.

Although the framework provides a systematic means of tackling these questions, it should not be treated either as a straitjacket or a panacea. The emphasis of a review should depend on the concerns that prompted it. Is it primarily a matter of fine-tuning the current mechanisms and processes to work more smoothly, or are we more concerned with the underlying philosophy or structure of the company? Did we get into the review to beat the bushes to create a wide agenda of all possible new opportunities, or was it really a means of legitimising a fresh look at one or two specific issues? With different motivations for the review, the weight given to different areas of analysis will vary, the order in which activities take place will be different, and the level of effort and speed of the review will change.

We also recognise that the structured framework we suggest may not appeal to all companies. Some may have a culture that stresses a more intuitive assessment of issues, and may find the analytical approach we propose too constraining. Others may have their own preferred analyses that we have not included in our framework. We recognise that our approach is not the only way to undertake a review of linkage parenting, and we advise each company to tailor its approach to its own needs, culture and preferences.

As we discuss the different steps in the framework, readers should accordingly view our proposals as building blocks from which to construct their own review process, rather than as an inflexible 'how to do it' manual. We have found the steps useful in our work with companies, but we are not dogmatic about the framework we put forward.

Synergy opportunities

The first step in the review involves developing a list of major synergy opportunities and judging how fully they are being realised. The purpose is to unearth any important opportunities that are not currently being successfully grasped. This may prompt ideas for changes in the overall approach or for specific new interventions.

To undertake detailed analysis for every linkage opportunity as part of a general review is clearly not feasible. It would take too long and cost too much. The challenge is to find efficient ways of homing in quickly on possible areas of high unexploited potential.

In our research, we have identified three useful prompts that can help to reveal neglected potential: rough modelling of value chain overlaps; interviews, focus groups or questionnaires designed to draw out consensus from business unit and parent managers; and identification of pet projects or initiatives that are being strongly championed by individual managers.

Value chain overlaps

Businesses with value chains that overlap, or could overlap, are obvious candidates for linkage opportunities. If two businesses purchase similar components, what benefits might be available by co-ordinating their purchases? If two businesses have overseas offices in the same country, what could be saved by sharing premises, salesforces, or management? We have found that rough modelling of the extent of overlaps and of the economies of scale or utilisation available from sharing can rapidly yield a broad sizing of the benefits available in different areas. For example, a retail group was able to prioritise opportunities for joint purchasing by assessing the extent of overlaps in different product ranges between two of their chains, and estimating the level of extra purchase discounts that would be available from combined buying. Back-of-the-envelope calculations showed that there were only two product ranges with significant overlaps and, thus, real prospects for achieving better terms. More detailed analysis then focussed on these prime candidates. Although there was nothing precise or sophisticated about the modelling that led to this conclusion, it was highly effective in narrowing down the opportunities to consider.

Even rough value chain modelling can, however, be hard to do or too time consuming at the review stage. The benefits may not yet be sufficiently well-defined, or may be made up of several different component parts, or may be too numerous to analyse. An alternative is to rely on consensus judgements of informed managers.

Consensus judgement

When experienced managers agree that there is probably a worthwhile benefit to go for, their views deserve to be heard. If most of the marketing managers in different countries believe that they could benefit from sharing best practice in advertising, it is almost certainly worth trying to understand more about the opportunity. If, on the other hand, the corporate marketing director has suggested more sharing but the national marketing managers are lukewarm, it should probably be put on the backburner – at least unless the corporate director can argue convincingly that the national managers may be misjudging the opportunity. In the difficult field of synergies, the gut-feel and intuitive judgement of experienced managers should carry considerable weight.

In companies where information flows freely and managers are encouraged to express their views, it is comparatively easy for parent managers to discern an emerging consensus. In other companies, it can be much more difficult. Managers from different units may not meet together often enough to share views, or may not feel empowered to express their views to each other. They may also be constrained to follow prevailing corporate policies rather than challenge them. Whatever the reason, a structured approach to eliciting the consensus is frequently needed.

There are a variety of ways to draw out consensus judgements, ranging from questionnaires, through focus groups, to some form of systematic interviewing process. The method chosen needs to be tailored to the circumstances of the company – and we have adopted somewhat different methods in each of the companies we have worked with. In all cases, however, the objective is to discover whether informed managers generally feel that there are important unexplored opportunities going begging, and, if so, what priorities they should receive.

Championing

A third valuable prompt comes from championing. Strong and enthusiastic champions are important for the effective implementation of new interventions. We believe that they can also provide a short cut to identifying priority opportunity areas. If a manager feels so powerfully that an opportunity is worthwhile that he is willing to lobby for it, devote personal sweat equity to it, and risk the displeasure of his colleagues and bosses by repeatedly advocating it, it is usually worth taking notice.

There is little danger that strong champions will not be heard by the corporate parent. The danger is more that they will be too readily discounted. Persistent champions, particularly if their ideas challenge vested interests, can face strong opposition. Their views may be dismissed as unrealistic or irrelevant, or they may be labelled eccentrics or troublemakers. Prudent managers then pipe down, and learn to live with their frustrations. However, frustrated champions welcome any chance to promote their pet projects. A review of linkage parenting is a good opportunity to give them an objective hearing. Our advice is to listen carefully to what they have to say – even if the rest of the organisation has long ago decided not to.

Creativity and realism

In drawing up the short-list of opportunities that merit detailed consideration, we need to balance creativity and open-mindedness with realism. We want managers with new ideas to come forward, we want to encourage brainstorming that will generate fresh thinking, we want to give a hearing to highly motivated champions. Especially if the purpose of the review is to make sure we're not missing something, we should be positive about new suggestions and supportive of 'thinking the unthinkable'.

We should also be willing to accept that some promising ideas may be clouded by considerable uncertainty. In Consco, for example, there was widespread support for more sharing of best practice in training and management development. But the benefits available were somewhat nebulous. Some managers had fairly specific ideas about how course designs or materials could be shared better. Others were simply reflecting a sense that this was an increasingly important area, in which they did not feel that their units were doing a very good job. Some had anecdotes or examples to support their views. But there was considerable uncertainty about where the real opportunities lay and how they should be pursued. And, in some situations, there is intrinsic uncertainty about the nature of the benefits. In businesses in the middle of rapid technological change, such as media and communications, the benefits of collaborating to develop new businesses to some extent depend on market and technology developments that are simply not predictable. The review should encourage managers to put forward speculative or uncertain opportunities: on closer examination they may turn out to contain real nuggets of gold. But any interventions to pursue them will probably have to be exploratory, designed to find out whether there are solid benefits to be obtained or not.

In creating a short-list of ideas to examine more closely, we should, however, guard against pursuing mirages, and question whether there really are likely to be parenting opportunities to address. When we assess the short-listed ideas, we shall need to be rigorous in applying the mental disciplines to them. In drawing up the short-list, we should therefore reject ideas if there is insufficient logic or evidence to support them. For example, if the champion of a shared salesforce appears to have given little serious consideration to important details, such as salesmen's calling patterns or the purchase criteria of customers, his proposal should receive less weight. Or if, on reflection, no-one can see any possible parenting opportunities associated with the targeted benefit, we should avoid wasting time with further investigation of it. We need to blend support for fresh thinking with the reality checks and tough-mindedness that the mental disciplines provide. It is the ideas that will stand up under closer analysis that we are interested in.

Synergy approach

The next step in the review is to lay out the main features of the company's approach to synergy management. It should cover the role that synergies play within the corporate strategy. It should bring out the company's underlying philosophy, attitudes and beliefs concerning the units' relationships to each other and to the centre. And it should make explicit the mechanisms and processes that the company typically uses to deal with these issues.

Corporate strategy

In our research on corporate strategy, we have found that different companies place very different emphases on the horizontal and vertical linkages that they foster. Some companies, such as Hanson (before the breakup), Emerson, RTZ and BTR (prior to 1995), place much more weight on the value that they add through stand-alone parenting than through linkage parenting. Others, such as Banc One, Unilever, 3M, ABB and Canon, have always seen the management of synergies as a key part of their corporate strategies. Business managers in organisations such as Hanson know that the main focus of the parent's attention will be on opportunities to improve the performance of each business as a stand-alone entity, and that they will receive few brownie points for collaborative efforts with other units. By contrast, business managers in Canon or Unilever know that their bosses expect and require them to seek out and participate in opportunities for working together with other units. Furthermore, they know what sorts of synergies the parent typically promotes most energetically. In Canon, for example, the strongest drive is for new product developments that require co-operation across business unit boundaries, while in Unilever the transfer of product and market information across geographic boundaries is critical.

Exhibit 6.4.1 summarises the main sources of value creation identified in one international manufacturing and marketing company. This way of summarising the corporate strategy into a list of parenting tasks helps position the importance of synergy initiatives versus other forms of parenting.

EXHIBIT 6.4.1 SOURCES OF PARENTING VALUE CREATION

- Transferring know-how about products, markets, marketing, manufacturing and other functions from/to business units around the world.
- Helping businesses (mainly in developed economies) avoid the pitfall of under investment in new product development and consumer understanding.
- Creating a value-based performance culture that has low tolerance of unnecessary costs or weak performance, yet is capable of investing where necessary.
- Orchestrating pools of mobile management talent so that businesses can draw on them in times of need.
- Developing and appointing outstanding managers to lead each business, with skills appropriate to the particular challenges of that business.
- Helping businesses (mainly in emerging markets) to avoid common pitfalls, such as insufficient investment in local management or poor timing of major commitments.
- Developing valuable relationships with potential partners and influential governments, and building the company brand into one of the world's leading corporate brands.
- Providing cost effective central services and corporate governance activities.

In summary, the review should document the priority given to linkage issues versus other forms of parenting and record the types of linkages that feature most prominently as key sources of added value. The review should also record the direction of movement in the corporate strategy. Is the company looking to build more synergies in the future or unwind some of the links and co-ordinated activities that currently exist? The current corporate strategy and the perceived direction of movement influences the sort of synergies that managers are likely to pursue and the priority they give them.

Philosophy, attitudes and beliefs

Companies also have different underlying attitudes and beliefs about how best to handle linkages. Often these differences concern the advantages of centralisation or decentralisation. To achieve benefits from pooled purchasing power, for example, a parent with a belief in the efficacy of central initiatives may set up a central purchasing department and insist that all purchases of certain items are handled by this department. Conversely, a parent that favours decentralised networking may simply circulate data on the purchasing terms and conditions being achieved by each unit, maintaining strong pressure on the businesses to reduce their individual unit costs. Such an intervention leaves the businesses much freer to determine whether and how they wish to work with other businesses to improve their purchasing power, but gives them no direct help or guidance about what to do. Between these extremes, there are a variety of other possibilities, such as establishing joint purchasing teams with members from different businesses, nominating selected businesses to act as lead units in purchasing for different items, centralising certain aspects of negotiations on terms and conditions but allowing each business to make its own buying decisions, and hiring a central purchasing expert who is available to the businesses, but need only be used by them if they choose.

For any synergy benefit, a range of possible intervention options can be arrayed along a spectrum of more versus less centralist interventions (see Table 6.4.1). Some companies, such as Mars and Unilever, are philosophically committed to the decentralised, networking end of the spectrum. They believe that it is vital to preserve business-unit autonomy and leave decisions to business-unit managements. Wary of central interference, they prefer to rely on the 'enlightened self-interest' of unit managers to guide linkages. Other companies, such as Canon or Rentokil, are more comfortable mandating policies or decisions from the centre on a range of issues. Although they accept the importance of unit motivation and initiative, they believe that there are many important benefits that will not be realised unless the parent makes the decisions.

Differences in attitudes concerning the appropriate degree of centralisation affect the range of intervention options that a parent is likely to perceive. Those who favour decentralised solutions will tend to give little or no consideration to more mandatory central interventions. Those who typically mandate central policies and decisions will be less sensitive to how much can be accomplished through a variety of measures that encourage networking. Corporate linkage philosophies represent blinkers that constrain the options that receive attention.

Another important factor is the corporate parent's attitude to central staff resources. Should large, heavyweight staff groups be set up or not? Should the businesses be forced to work with the corporate staffs, or should their use by the businesses be voluntary? As with centralisation/decentralisation choices, companies tend to have a dominant philosophy which governs the role of staff in managing linkages. Companies such as ABB are strenuously opposed to the use of corporate staffs, wherever possible relying on decisions and resources in the business units. They fear that, lacking direct profit responsibility, staffs can easily lose touch with the needs of the businesses and take on a life of their own, in which power and empire-building take precedence over the benefits delivered to the corporation. Other companies, 3M or Cooper for instance, believe that corporate staffs, at least in selected areas, are the best way to ensure that specialist expertise is developed and shared among units. They are therefore a source of valuable linkages. These beliefs will be reflected in the synergy interventions that the parent makes.

Different philosophies therefore influence the sorts of synergies that will be pursued and the means which will be used to pursue them. Take, for example, a new product-development initiative involving joint work between two or more business units. At one extreme, a 'Hanson' approach, suspicious of shared responsibilities of this sort, would likely press for the initiative to be pursued within one of the businesses or else dropped. By contrast, a 'Unilever' approach would be to provide encouragement and, if necessary, expert assistance, while allowing the businesses to pursue the matter in their own way, within a framework of strong corporate cultural norms to guide decision-making. A 'Canon' approach would be different again, entailing willingness to give high corporate priority to the project, including assignment of numbers of both corporate

TABLE 6.4.1 Differences in linkage philosophy

	Belief in decentralisation	Mixed	Belief in central direction
Know-how sharing	■ Network facilitation	■ Some central policies ■ Centres of excellence ■ Lead units ■ Franchise	■ Mandatory central policies/directives
Tangible resources sharing	■ Internal JVs/contracts ■ Voluntary use of shared resource units set up as profit centres	■ Limited central functions and resources ■ Service level agreements	■ Mandatory central functions and resources ■ Incomplete SBUs
Pooled negotiating power	■ Information sharing ■ Joint SBU teams and initiatives	■ Lead units	■ Central functions experts
Vertical integration	■ Third party trading relationships, but first refusal in-house	■ Negotiated transfer prices ■ In-house preference ■ Centre influences relationship	■ Centre sets transfer prices and manages relationships for corporate benefit
Co-ordinated strategies	■ Centre arbitrates ■ Minimal constraints on scope/strategy	■ Restrained central role ■ Matrix structure ■ Task forces ■ Franchise	■ Centre directs ■ Low SBU autonomy
New business creation	■ SBU driven	■ Task forces drawn from centre and SBUs	■ Centrally driven

and business staff to work full-time on the project to see it through to commercialisation. Some assessment of the underlying corporate attitudes and beliefs about linkages should therefore form part of the review.

Mechanisms and processes

Companies also differ in the nature of the specific mechanisms and processes that they typically use to manage co-ordination. The review should identify the mechanisms and processes that are most frequently used, and should articulate the impact that they have on synergy management. What is the nature and importance of the budget and planning processes and how, if at all, do they affect cross-company initiatives? What sort of cross-business committees are in place and how do they work? What staff groups exist and what role do they play in linkages?

We argue that 'well-grooved' mechanisms are an important factor in gauging the ease with which a company's synergy intervention will be implemented.

Equally, ineffective or ill-suited mechanisms and processes can account for failure to realise some opportunities.

'Five lenses analysis'

As a means of describing and analysing the parent's approach to synergy issues, we have found that a display that views the characteristics of the parent through five inter-linked lenses is useful (see Goold, Campbell and Alexander, 1994 and Figure 6.4.2). The five lenses are:

■ The beliefs, knowledge or mental maps that guide the behaviour and decisions of senior managers in the parent organisation. These mental maps determine the corporate linkage strategy and philosophy, and guide the parent's thinking about the selection and implementation of linkage mechanisms and interventions.

■ The structure of the company, including the way in which the business units are defined and the nature of parenting structures to which they report, and the systems and processes through which parent managers mainly exercise influence, pressure and control. The business-unit definitions determine what links between units need to be managed; the nature of the parenting structure, for example whether there are product divisions, geographical divisions, or a matrix structure, influences the parenting opportunities that will be pursued; and the systems and processes that are in place determine how they are most likely to be handled.

- The functional staffs, central service groups, and corporate resources that are important in synergy management. The size, composition and strengths of the corporate staff and the way in which they operate are key components of the overall approach to cross-company working.

- The people in the parent organisation. The experience, skills and biases of key individuals in the parent have a major impact on synergy management.

- The extent to which authority is delegated to business managers, together with the criteria by which their performance is judged and the rewards or sanctions for good or poor performance; we refer to this as the 'decentralisation contract' for each business. The manner in which decentralisation contracts are defined influences the sorts of linkage

intervention that the parent is likely to make and that the businesses are likely to accept.

We have found that these five lenses provide a useful checklist for itemising those features of the corporate parent's approach to the management of synergies that matter most. By running through each of these headings and taking stock of the key features under each, a picture of the overall approach can be built up and made explicit. The five lenses can also be used to bring out ways in which the approach is changing, giving a direction of movement as well as a static picture.

Effectiveness of approach

The third step is to assess the effectiveness of the current synergy approach. How well does the approach match up with the opportunities? Is it working reasonably well, apart from a few specific problems? Are there any fundamental shortcomings that need to be tackled? Once the approach and the opportunities have been laid out in the first two steps of the review, the answers to these questions may be readily apparent. There are, however, some more structured questions that it may be useful to ask. These include:

- Are there biases in the overall approach that condition which opportunities will be realised?

FIGURE 6.4.2 Parenting characteristics

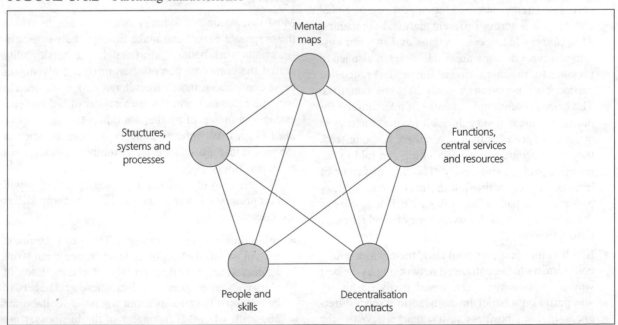

- Are there any aspects of the approach which are impeding linkages; are there any 'synergy killers'?
- Do any business unit definitions need to be changed?
- What have been the successes and failures of the approach, and what problems need addressing?

Biases in the overall approach

Earlier in this reading, we contrasted the corporate strategies and philosophies of different companies, including Hanson, Unilever, ABB and Canon. The differences in these companies' approaches to synergies mean that they will each steer away from certain sorts of interventions and towards others: their approaches bias both the types of linkages they are likely to emphasise and the means by which they will be pursued.

Nearly all companies have biases in their linkage parenting, and a value of the review is to lay out what they are. What does the corporate strategy emphasise? What are the dominant mental maps that are driving the linkage interventions that the parent chooses to make? What are the well-grooved processes that are usually chosen as the preferred way to intervene? If we can make these biases explicit, we may be able to see why certain synergy opportunities are grasped, while others are systematically overlooked; why some initiatives run smoothly, while others are always contentious and difficult.

- In one manufacturer of automotive components, the corporate strategy stressed the importance of global co-ordination across different national companies. This strategy led to cost savings and superior customer service in many areas. However, it also led to pressure for rationalisation of the product range that carried high opportunity costs in some countries. The basic presumption in favour of international co-ordination made it very difficult for the countries in question to get a fair hearing on these costs. Instead, they were accused of NIH thinking and told to fall into line with global policy. The bias in favour of international co-ordination in the corporate strategy prevented the parent from taking a balanced view of the advantages and disadvantages of product-range rationalisation.
- In a building products company, there was a strong commitment to decentralised networking as the best way to capture synergies, based partly on history and partly on a belief in the need to respect differences in each business unit's markets. When the corporate parent wanted to encourage all the businesses to adopt a common MIS system, the networking bias resulted in an endless sequence of project-team meetings, in which it was impossible to reach agreement on a new standard system for all the businesses. It was only after literally years of delay that the parent insisted on a choice being made and pushed it through. The bias in favour of networking prevented a stronger corporate lead from being taken earlier.

The biases in a company's overall approach will make it specially effective at handling certain sorts of linkages, but ineffective at others. For example, there are some parenting opportunities that require mandated central decisions and are unlikely to be grasped through interventions that simply aim to promote networking between the businesses. Hence, a parent with a bias in favour of decentralised networking is unlikely to be successful at realising these sorts of parenting opportunities. Similarly, a staff-averse company that always tends to use cross-business project teams to handle linkages will find it difficult to push through parenting opportunities for which central staffs are needed. By making explicit any biases in the approach, we may be able to understand better why some opportunities are being successfully realised while others are proving problematic. We can then decide whether to maintain the approach and endorse its biases or to consider making changes.

Synergy killers

Most discussions of synergy concern ways in which the corporate parent can make linkages between business units work better. Unfortunately, the harsh reality is that the corporate parent often inadvertently makes these connections more difficult, not easier. We need to recognise this fact, and can use a review of linkage parenting as a means of rooting out things that are impeding linkages. We refer to policies or characteristics of the parent that are systematically inhibiting linkages as 'synergy killers'.

The effectiveness of the approach to linkages will be compromised if any of the following synergy killers are present:

- Inhibiting corporate strategy. The most common way in which the corporate-level strategy can work against synergy is through lack of clarity. Lack of clarity about corporate priorities leads managers to be excessively cautious about when they collaborate and with whom. If managers in the businesses are unsure whether the corporate parent expects them to be co-ordinating their technical efforts or looking for cost savings in marketing, the uncertainty can leave them paralysed. A more obvious, if rarer, problem stems from corporate strategies that actively discourage linkages of any sort. In a notorious memorandum written after GEC's acquisition of English Electric, Lord Weinstock informed the managers of the English Electric businesses that all cross-unit committees and projects were to be disbanded forthwith. In future, they would have only one responsibility: the performance of their own units. Though few companies today take such a radical stance against synergies between businesses, some corporate-level strategies still discourage co-operation. 'In my view', stated one chief executive, 'synergy is always an illusion. What is more, it fatally damages accountability'. Not surprisingly, this attitude had a dampening effect on unit managers' attempts to work together.

- Infighting between the barons. In some companies, there are battles raging between senior managers. The battles may be about differences in corporate strategy or management philosophy. They may be about competition between managers for the top job. They may be due to personality clashes. They may be due to previous collaborations where one party felt let down. Whatever the reason, these battles have a huge negative impact on co-operation. Managers lower down are often aware of lost opportunities, but the climate of hostility between their bosses means that co-operation to pursue them is stifled. It is simply not acceptable to be seen to be 'working with the enemy'.

- Culture of secrecy. In secretive companies, people play their cards close to their chests. Information about business unit performance, new product plans, operating issues, and organisation structures is given out reluctantly. In these circumstances, co-operation is hard, not only because it is difficult to find out what is going on in other units, but also because the free flow of information and communication that is needed to oil the wheels of synergies is inhibited. Why do these cultures occur? Sometimes it is fear of competitor espionage. Sometimes it is a result of resisting corporate information requests and interference. Sometimes it is associated with baronial infighting. Whatever the cause, a culture of secrecy reduces synergy.

- Misaligned incentives. In many companies, bonus systems and promotion criteria depend largely or

exclusively on the results managers achieve in their own businesses, and give no credit for contributions to other businesses or the corporate whole. The personal incentive system then makes it more difficult for business managers to co-operate, unless they can structure a deal that rewards all the units involved. Where the synergy involves a sacrifice by one unit to help others, and there is no ready process by which to compensate the loser, the incentive system will block progress. Again and again, we encountered situations in which this prevented managers from helping colleagues in other businesses, even though there was a clear net benefit. Where win/lose trade-offs exist, reward systems should aim to make it easier for business managers to co-operate; all too often, they have precisely the reverse effect.

- Excessive performance pressure. When managers are hounded by close-to-impossible targets, they are apt to become defensive and inward-looking. In companies where business unit performance is paramount and where targets are set too high, managers often concentrate exclusively on things within their own immediate control and cease to be comfortable with situations where they must rely on their colleagues' co-operation. Oppressive targets damp down the spirit of mutuality and collaboration from which synergies flow.

- Insulation from performance pressure. At the opposite end of the spectrum from excessive performance pressure is insulation from performance pressure. If business units are insulated from performance pressures, the basic drive of enlightened self-interest, on which so many beneficial sharing initiatives depend, will be weakened. In companies where synergies thrive, such as Mars or Canon, senior managers keep up the pressure for constant improvement, knowing that this leads to more energy from working together. In companies where the parent insulates the businesses from such pressures, the businesses are less likely to seek out mutually rewarding synergies.

- Domineering corporate staff. If corporate staff groups have domineering or insensitive attitudes, business managers will automatically reject their ideas for improving linkages, however sound they may be. In a major chemical company with old-established functional baronies, the heads of the corporate staff departments were inclined to issue policies and guidelines to the businesses with little consultation or recognition of inter-company differences. Over time, the business heads became adept at passive resistance and non-cooperation, spending much more time on the tactics of opposition than on assessing whether the proposed policies were, in fact, beneficial. As a result, genuine synergy opportunities were resisted as strenuously as misguided attempts at standardisation.

- Mistrust. An atmosphere of mistrust undermines co-operation. If the businesses believe that their sister units are out to take advantage of them, or are always unwilling to put themselves out to help, relations are quickly soured to the point where even well-intentioned initiatives are blocked. Equally, if a climate of opinion has grown up where business managers believe that corporate management or staff are incompetent or untrustworthy, synergy interventions are likely to be resisted in principle. Expensive, high profile failures seriously undermine the credibility and prospects of any future proposal. Particular problems arise when the parent is suspected of having a hidden agenda, since all initiatives will be scrutinized for ulterior motives, and interpreted in the worst possible light.

All companies have some synergy killers. Our concern should be with pathological characteristics that may be causing widespread damage, not with minor irritants. Is there a strong sense that some of the parent's characteristics are really preventing collaboration? Can we see evidence from the unrealised opportunities that indicates that these synergy killers are having a real impact? How can the parent adjust the corporate context to make linkages work better?

While synergy killers inhibit linkages, their opposites create the sort of fertile ground in which co-operation flourishes. Clear corporate strategies that support high priority synergies; good personal relationships between senior managers in the businesses; an open culture that promotes sharing; incentive systems that reward attempts to create synergies; corporate pressure to raise performance through sharing best practices; competent staff units that are sensitive in their relationships with the businesses; and an atmosphere of mutual trust and support are all conducive to perceiving synergy opportunities and implementing them successfully. The parent should aim to nurture synergies through creating these fertile ground conditions. Hence, even if no real synergy killers exist, the review may still pinpoint ways in which the corporate context could be made more fertile for synergies.

Business unit definitions

The boundaries established around a group's business units are fundamental for the approach to synergies. By changing the definition of the business units, the parent automatically changes the nature of the potential links between business units. If a new European unit is set up out of previously separate national units, issues of manufacturing co-ordination that used to be handled as linkages between separate units are now managed within a single larger entity. 'Internalising' the linkages in this way makes a big difference, because there is now a single general manager for the combined business who is in a position to decide on trade-offs between the sub-units and who will be held responsible for the results of the integrated entity. This makes certain interventions much easier to push through, although it may involve some reduction in focus on the product-market niches within the larger entity.

The trade-offs between breadth and focus in business-unit definition are complex. There are, however, some business-unit definition issues that should be addressed in a review of synergy management. In particular, it is important to raise the following questions:

- Are there some important synergies that are never likely to be realised with the current business unit definitions? If so, are there alternative definitions that should be considered?
- Are certain synergies harder to achieve because of the manner in which the boundaries around the business units are set up and managed?

There are some circumstances in which co-ordination between separate businesses is never likely to be achieved, however beneficial it may be for the group. If, for example, the collective net benefits involve costs to one or more units that are hard or impossible to compensate for, the initiative is likely to be blocked. Thus, it may be almost impossible to bring about co-ordinated production planning between separate units if it involves one or more units shutting their factories and transferring production to another. To avoid the consequent reduction in power and status, the general managers of the units in question will be likely to go to any lengths to block or undermine the initiative. Conclusion: the best way to achieve this synergy benefit will probably be to redefine the business to encompass all the previously separate units, giving responsibility for optimising performance to a single management team.

Other situations in which managers should consider a redefinition of the businesses to achieve desirable synergies include the following:

■ Deeply embedded hostility and mistrust between senior managers in the different units. If the rivalry between the general managers of the units is intense, they may simply be unwilling to work together, whatever the benefits. The solution may be to redefine the business units and give responsibility for both of them to one or other of the managers.

■ Hard-to-allocate costs and revenues. If shared production facilities or the lack of an open third-party market for products traded between the units make it difficult to agree a split of costs and revenues, any form of co-operation is likely to suffer, since underlying disputes about transfer prices and allocated costs will dominate everything else. In such circumstances, it is often better to expand the business definition to include both units, with a single bottom line. Co-ordination issues then become a means to maximise aggregate profitability rather than the pretext for haggling over how to divide up the results.

■ Need for speedy and continuous resolution of trade-off judgements. Concerns about contamination and lack of focus have led many companies to create more and more separate profit centres, each with its own management and strategy. This drive for business focus creates major difficulties if the separate businesses need to be in constant touch with each other and have to resolve a series of difficult day-to-day trade-offs. For example, if two petrochemical businesses share a process plant and continuous decisions about output mix are needed to achieve the optimum overall profitability, taking account of the shifting relative prices of different inputs and of different end products, the two businesses will be locked in constant complex negotiations about how to run the plant. A structure in which a single management team is responsible for optimising both businesses is likely to work more smoothly.

The underlying issue is whether, for whatever reason, co-ordination between the separate businesses' management teams will always be much less effective than co-ordination under a single management team. Managers should therefore examine the current business-unit boundaries to see if they are preventing any important synergies from taking place. If they are, consider altering the boundaries.

Judgements about whether a redefinition of the businesses is necessary should also reflect the nature of the boundaries. If decentralisation contracts emphasise the autonomy of the business heads and provide few incentives or opportunities for them to work together, potential problems resulting from separate business definitions will be magnified. If, however, business heads do not expect to have full control over all the functions and resources they need in their businesses, and work in a context that encourages and requires frequent liaison with colleagues from other businesses and from central functions, the boundaries around the separate businesses will be more naturally permeable. In Canon, for example, business managers are very ready to work on cross-business project teams, to draw on corporate staff support, and to co-ordinate with other businesses: the corporate approach to co-ordination stresses the connections between the businesses, not the boundaries that separate them. With more permeable boundaries around the businesses, there is more flexibility to make different business definitions work well. With more separation between businesses, there is a greater premium on drawing the boundaries in ways that will internalise linkages that would otherwise become problematic.

Successes and failures

Last, but not least, the effectiveness of the overall approach can be tested in terms of evident successes and failures: well and poorly rated mechanisms and processes, fully and less fully realised synergy opportunities, patterns of success and failure that cast light on organisational strengths and weaknesses.

As part of the audit of the current approach, it is essential to canvas opinion about the effectiveness of the main systems and processes for managing synergies, and of the key staff groups that promote them. Surveys, in-depth discussions or focus groups can bring well-grooved and successful mechanisms into relief and pinpoint areas of friction or dissatisfaction. Poorly rated mechanisms should then be examined more carefully. What are the causes of dissatisfaction? Is it a mechanism for chasing mirages? Are the parenting opportunities on which it is targeted clear, or is it being driven by parenting bias? Is it wasting the time of managers at the centre or in the businesses? Should be consider other ways of intervening to realise the target benefits, or should we simply discontinue our efforts if they are not working?

Another way into the successes and failures analysis is via the synergy opportunities review. Do the unrealised opportunities indicate some underlying gap or shortcoming in our approach? Is there some mismatch between the processes or interventions we use for getting at the opportunities and the nature of the opportunities? If, for example, we are consistently failing to achieve the benefits of better capacity utilisation that vertical integration should provide, is this because there is something wrong with our transfer-pricing processes or with our approach to combined investment planning? Or are our business-specific performance measures to blame? Our quest should be to unearth new or different mechanisms for intervening that are better suited for the parenting opportunities open to us, in order to reduce the number of important unrealised opportunities.

We have also found that a retrospective analysis of patterns of success and failure with previous synergy interventions can be useful. Which synergies have we managed well – and probably taken for granted? What notorious initiatives have caused the most trouble and yielded the least benefit? What can we learn from these successes and failures?

By examining the successes, we will be able to see more clearly what mechanisms work best for us. What opportunities have we derived most benefit from? By what means did we realise these opportunities? Answers to these questions will reveal what the organisation's well-grooved mechanisms and processes are, and will help to shape thinking about how to tackle new opportunities. By examining the failures, we may discover underlying weaknesses in our skills or processes, or organisational blockages and synergy killers that lie behind our inability to implement certain types of synergies successfully. A sense of these underlying patterns is useful in assessing the effectiveness of the approach.

Agenda for change

The output from the review should be a short-list of possible new initiatives for more detailed consideration. Since the review is a broadly based stock take, the purpose is to create an agenda of possible changes, not to arrive at firm conclusions about how to move forward. Each of the possible initiatives that emerge from the review will then need to be subjected to detailed scrutiny.

The short-list should embrace:

- high priority unrealised synergy opportunities, including ways to address them;
- changes in underlying strategy or philosophy that may increase the effectiveness of the overall approach;

- changes in specific co-ordination processes or mechanisms, including elements that should be discontinued because they may be having a damaging effect, as well as new initiatives that should be considered;
- possible changes in business unit definitions.

Prioritisation of the ideas that emerge from the review is essential. The front-runners normally select themselves, either because of the size of the potential benefits (or disbenefits) or the strength of feeling among managers. But the cut-off on what to take forward is more a matter for judgement. We have four pieces of advice in forming the judgement.

First, be selective. A focused follow-through on three or four key initiatives is much more likely to yield tangible benefits than a long-drawn-out survey of a couple of dozen possibly attractive options. And if the review is not seen to lead on fairly quickly to action, its creditability will suffer and managers will lose enthusiasm.

Second, look forward, not back. Give preference to ideas that anticipate breaking trends and build links that will become increasingly valuable in the future. Avoid focusing on initiatives that deal with yesterday's problems or with issues that are likely to become less significant. Concentrate, for example, on putting in place pricing co-ordination mechanisms to avoid arbitrage in what will become an increasingly integrated European marketplace. Don't struggle to promote common design and manufacturing of components that more and more of the business units are already tending to outsource.

Third, use your rivals and competitors to guide your sense of priorities. If your main competitors are deriving much more benefit from sharing know-how than you are, move it up your priority list, unless there are good reasons why it is always likely to be less important to you than to them. If others have tried and failed with a shared-purchasing initiative, be cautious about pushing ahead with it. The concern should be with the specific achievements of known competitors, not with current general management fads and fashions. Of course, this presumes a certain level of competitive intelligence, which is not always present. However, we believe that efforts to find out about competitors' initiatives can play a valuable role in establishing a final short-list.

Fourth, recognise system effects. The five-lenses analysis brings out the connections between different aspects of the synergy approach. Successes and failures often stem from deeply rooted attitudes that underlie the use of certain mechanisms rather than others. Proposals to make changes in a given process or to address a specific opportunity may therefore entail consequential changes in other areas. Consider whether specific initiatives will work in the whole context in which they will be taken; assess the possibility that a systematic change programme to shift the overall culture may be required as a precondition for success in specific areas.

CORPORATE LEVEL STRATEGY IN INTERNATIONAL PERSPECTIVE

Growth for the sake of growth is the ideology of the cancer cell.

Edward Abbey (1927–1989); American author

As with the topic in the previous chapter, scarce attention has been paid to international differences in multi-business level strategies. Despite the high media profile of major corporations from different countries and despite researchers' fascination with large companies, little comparative research has been done. Yet, it seems not unlikely that corporate strategy practices and preferences vary across national boundaries, although these differences are not blatant. Casual observation of the major corporations around the globe quickly makes clear that one cannot easily divide the world into portfolio-oriented and integration-oriented countries. However, Goold, Campbell and Alexander do observe that in their research they have found 'there are relatively few companies in the United Kingdom, the United States, and other Western countries that pursue a full-fledged Strategic Planning style', while it is 'the most popular style among leading Japanese companies' (1994: 413). This observation has also been made by Kono (1999).

As an input to the debate whether there are international differences in corporate strategy perspectives, we would like to put forward a number of factors that might be of influence on how the paradox of responsiveness and synergy is managed in different countries. It should be noted, however, that these propositions must be viewed as tentative explanations, intended to encourage further discussion and research.

Functioning of capital and labor markets

One of the arguments leveled against the portfolio organization perspective is that there is no need for corporations that merely act as investors. With efficiently operating capital markets, investing should be left to 'real' investors. Stock markets are an excellent place for investors to spread their risks and for growing firms to raise capital. Start-up companies with viable plans can easily find venture capitalists to assist them. And all these capital providers can perform the task of financial control – portfolio-oriented corporations have nothing else to add but overhead costs. Add to this the argument that large corporations no longer have an advantage in terms of professional management skills. While in the past large firms could add value to smaller units by injecting more sophisticated managers, flexible labor markets now allow small firms to attract the same talent themselves.

Even if this general line of argumentation is true, the extent to which capital and labor markets are 'efficient' varies widely across countries. Porter (1987), an outspoken detractor of the portfolio organization perspective, acknowledges that 'in developing countries, where large companies are few, capital markets are undeveloped, and professional management is scarce, portfolio management still works'. However, he quickly adds that portfolio thinking 'is no longer a valid model for corporate strategy in advanced economies'. But are capital and labor markets equally efficient across all so-called advanced economies? Few observers would argue that venture capital markets in Asia and Europe work as well as in the United States, and the terms under which large corporations can raise capital on these continents are usually far better than for smaller companies. Neither does holding shares of a company through the stock markets of Asia and Europe give investors as much influence over the company as in the United States. In short, even in the group of developed economies, various gradations of capital market efficiency seem to exist, suggesting varying degrees to which corporations can create value by adopting the role of investors.

The same argument can be put forward for the efficiency of 'managerial labor' markets. Even if Porter is right when stating that smaller companies can attract excellent professional managers through flexible labor markets, this conclusion is not equally true across advanced economies. Lifetime employment might be a declining phenomenon in most of these countries, but not to the same extent. Job-hopping between larger and smaller companies is far more common in the United States, than in many European and Asian countries (e.g. Calori and de Woot, 1994). In many advanced economies large corporations still command a more sophisticated core of professional managers, through superior recruiting and training practices, higher compensation and status, and greater perceived career opportunities and job security. Hence, even within this group of countries, different degrees of labor market flexibility exist, suggesting that corporations in some countries might be able to create more value as developers and allocators of management talent than in other countries.

Leveraging of relational resources

With the portfolio organization perspective favoring the leveraging of financial resources and the integrated organization perspective often focusing on the leveraging of competence, the leveraging of relational resources is a topic receiving far less attention within the field of strategic management. It is widely acknowledged that 'umbrella' brands can often be stretched to include more product categories and that the corporation's reputation can commonly be employed to the business units' benefit. However, in the areas of political science and industrial organization much more attention is paid to the corporation as leverager of contacts and power. In many circumstances knowing the right people, being able to bring parties together, being able to force compliance and having the power to influence government regulations, are essential aspects of doing business. Often, corporations, either by their sheer size, or by their involvement in many businesses, will have more clout and essential contacts than can be mustered by individual businesses.

Here the international differences come in. As put forward at the end of Chapter 5, in some countries relational resources are more important than in others. Influence over government policy-making, contacts with the bureaucrats applying the rules, power over local authorities and institutions, connections with the ruling elite, access to informal networks of companies – the importance of these factors can differ from country to country. Therefore, it stands to reason that the clustering of businesses around key external relationships and power bases will vary strongly across nations. In some countries 'core contacts' centered corporations are more likely to be encountered than in others.

Costs of coordination

Coordination comes at a cost, it is argued. Individual business units usually have to participate in all types of corporate systems, file reports, ask permission, attend meetings and adapt their strategy to fit with the corporate profile. This can result in time delays, lack of fit with the market, less entrepreneurial action, a lack of accountability and a low morale. On top of this, business units have to pay a part of corporate overhead as well. The benefits of coordination should be higher than these costs.

This argument might be suffering from a cultural bias, as it assumes that individuals and businesses are not naturally inclined to coordinate. However, control by the corporate center and cooperation with other business units is not universally viewed as a negative curtailment of individual autonomy. In many countries coordination is not an unfortunate fact of life, but a natural state of affairs. Coordination within the corporate whole is often welcomed as motivating, not demotivating, especially in cultures that are more group-oriented (Hofstede, 1993, Reading 1.4 in this book). As observed in Chapter 4, if the common form of organization in a country resembles a clan, coordination might not be as difficult and costly as in other nations. Therefore, on the basis of this argument, it is reasonable to expect a stronger preference for the portfolio perspective in countries that favor mechanistic organizations.

Preference for control

The last point of international difference ties into the discussion in the next chapter. If the essence of corporate strategy is about realizing synergies between businesses, is it not possible for these businesses to coordinate with one another and achieve synergies without being a part of the same corporation? In other words, is it necessary to be owned and controlled by the same parent in order to leverage resources, integrate activities and align product offerings? Or could individual businesses band together and work as if they were one company – acting as a 'virtual corporation'?

In Chapter 7 it will be argued that there are significant international differences on this account. In some countries there is a strong preference to have hierarchical control over two businesses that need to be coordinated. In other countries there is a preference for businesses to use various forms of cooperation to achieve synergies with other businesses, while retaining the flexibility of independent ownership. Preference for control, it will be argued, depends on how managers deal with the paradox of competition and cooperation.

FURTHER READING

Readers who would like to gain a better overview of the literature on the topic of corporate level strategy have a number of good sources from which to choose. Two scholarly reviews are 'Strategy and Structure in the Multiproduct Firm' by Charles Hill and Robert Hoskisson, and 'Research on Corporate Diversification: A Synthesis', by Vasudevan Ramanujam and P. Varadarajan, although both have become somewhat dated. A more recent review is 'Why Diversify? Four Decades of Management Thinking', by Michael Goold and Kathleen Luchs. Mark Sirower's book *The Synergy Trap: How Companies Lose the Acqusition Game* also has an excellent overview of the literature as an appendix.

Much of the strategy literature taking a portfolio organization perspective is from the end of the 1970s and the beginning of the 1980s. Bruce Henderson's popular book, *On Corporate Strategy*, which explains the basic principles of the portfolio organization perspective, is from this period. However, a better review of the portfolio approach, and especially portfolio techniques, is given by Charles Hofer and Dan Schendel in *Strategy Formulation: Analytical Concepts*. Recently, there has been renewed interest in viewing the corporation as investor and restructurer. In this crop, the article 'Growth Through Acquisitions: A Fresh Look', by Patricial Anslinger and Thomas Copeland is particularly provocative.

For further reading on the integrated organization perspective, Gary Hamel and C.K. Prahalad's book *Competing for the Future* is an obvious choice. The literature on the resource-based view of the firm mentioned in the 'Further reading' section at the end of Chapter 5 is also interesting in the context of this chapter. Highly stimulating is Hiroyuki

Itami's book *Mobilizing Invisible Assets*, in which he also argues for sharing intangible resources throughout a multi-business firm.

On the topic of acquisitions, a good overview of the arguments and quantitative research is provided by Anju Seth, in his article 'Value Creation in Acquisitions: A Re-Examination of Performance Issues'. Mark Sirower's earlier mentioned book is also an excellent choice. When it comes to issues in the area of post-acquisition integration, Philippe Haspeslagh and David Jemison's book *Managing Acquisitions: Creating Value Through Corporate Renewal* from which Reading 6.3 was reprinted is a good start. The more recent book by Michael Hitt, J. Harrison, and R. Ireland, *Mergers and Acquisitions: A Guide to Creating Value for Shareholders*, is also well worth reading.

On the role of the corporate center, *Corporate-Level Strategy: Creating Value in the Multibusiness Company*, by Michael Goold, Andrew Campbell and Marcus Alexander, is highly recommended. Also stimulating is Charles Hill's article 'The Functions of the Headquarters Unit in Multibusiness Firms'. For a more academic analysis, readers are advised to turn to Vijay Govindarajan's article 'A Contingency Approach to Strategy Implementation at the Business-Unit Level: Integrating Administrative Mechanisms with Strategy'. And last but not least, for those who enjoyed Reading 6.4 by Andrew Campbell and Michael Goold, the book from which it was taken, *Synergy: Why Links Between Business Units Often Fail and How to Make Them Work*, offers more interesting insights.

REFERENCES

Amit, R., and Livnat, J. (1988) 'Diversification and the Risk-Return Trade-off', *Academy of Management Journal*, Vol. 31, No. 1, March, pp. 154–165.

Anslinger, P.L., and Copeland, T.E. (1996) 'Growth Through Acquisitions: A Fresh Look', *Harvard Business Review*, Vol. 74, No. 1, January–February, pp. 126–135.

Calori, R., and CESMA (1988) 'How Successful Companies Manage Diverse Businesses', *Long Range Planning*, Vol. 21, No. 3, pp. 80–89.

Calori, R., and de Woot, P. (eds.) (1994) *A European Management Model: Beyond Diversity*, Prentice Hall, Hemel Hempstead.

Campbell, A., and Goold, M. (1998) *Synergy: Why Links Between Business Units Often Fail and How to Make Them Work*, Capstone Publishing, Oxford.

Campbell, A., Goold, M., and Alexander, M. (1995) 'The Value of the Parent Company', *California Management Review*, Vol. 38, No. 1, Fall, pp. 79–97.

Campbell, A., and Luchs, K. (1992) *Strategic Synergy*, Butterworth Heinemann, London.

Chatterjee, S. (1986) 'Types of Synergy and Economic Value: The Impact of Acquisitions on Merging and Rival Firms', *Strategic Management Journal*, Vol. 7, No. 2, March–April, pp. 119–139.

Dundas, K.N.M., and Richardson, P.R. (1980) 'Corporate Strategy and the Concept of Market Failure', *Strategic Management Journal*, Vol. 1, pp. 177–188.

Eisenhardt, K.M., and Galunic, D.C. (2000) 'Coevolving: At Last, a Way to Make Synergies Work', *Harvard Business Review*, Vol. 78, No. 1, January–February, pp. 91–101.

Ghoshal, S., and Mintzberg, H. (1994) 'Diversification and Diversifact', *California Management Review*, Vol. 37, No. 1, Fall, pp. 8–27.

Goold, M., and Campbell, A. (1987) *Strategies and Styles: The Role of the Centre in Managing Diverse Corporations*, Basil Blackwell, Oxford.

Goold, M., Campbell, A., and Alexander M. (1994) *Corporate-Level Strategy: Creating Value in the Multibusiness Company*, Wiley, New York.

Goold, M., and Lansdell, S. (1997) *Survey of Corporate Strategy Objectives, Concepts and Tools*, Ashridge Strategic Management Centre.

Goold, M., and Luchs, K. (1993) 'Why Diversify? Four Decades of Management Thinking', *Academy of Management Executive*, Vol. 7, No. 3, August, pp. 7–25.

Govindarajan, V. (1988) 'A Contingency Approach to Strategy Implementation at the Business-Unit Level: Integrating Administrative Mechanisms with Strategy', *Academy of Management Journal*, Vol. 31, No. 4, December, pp. 828–853.

Hamel, G., and C.K. Prahalad (1993) 'Strategy as Stretch and Leverage', *Harvard Business Review*, Vo. 71, No. 2, March–April, pp. 75–84.

Hamel, G., and Prahalad, C.K. (1994) *Competing for the Future*, Harvard Business School Press, Boston, MA.

Harrigan, K.R. (1985) 'Vertical Integration and Corporate Strategy', *Academy of Management Journal*, Vol. 28, No. 2, June, pp. 397–425.

Haspeslagh, P. (1982) 'Portfolio Planning: Uses and Limits', *Harvard Business Review*, Vol. 60, No. 1, January–February, pp. 58–73.

Haspeslagh, P., and Jemison, D. (1991) *Managing Acquisitions: Creating Value Through Corporate Renewal*, Free Press, New York.

Hedley, B. (1977) 'Strategy and the "Business Portfolio"', *Long Range Planning*, Vol. 10, No. 1, February, pp. 9–15.

Henderson, B.D. (1979) *On Corporate Strategy*, Abt Books, Cambridge, MA.

Hill, C.W.L. (1994) 'The Functions of the Headquarters Unit in Multibusiness Firms', in: R. Rumelt, D. Teece, and D. Schendel (eds.), *Fundamental Issues in Strategy Research*, Harvard University Press, Cambridge, MA.

Hill, C.W.L., and Hoskisson, R.E. (1987) 'Strategy and Structure in the Multiproduct Firm', *Academy of Management Review*, Vol. 12, No. 2, April, pp. 331–341.

Hitt, M., Harrison, J., and Ireland, R. (2001) *Mergers and Acquisitions: A Guide to Creating Value for Shareholders*, Oxford Press, New York.

Hofer, C., and Schendel, D. (1978) *Strategy Formulation: Analytical Concepts*, West, St. Paul.

Hofstede, G. (1993) 'Cultural Constraints in Management Theories', *Academy of Management Executive*, Vol. 7, No. 1, pp. 8–21.

Itami, H. (1987) *Mobilizing Invisible Assets*, Harvard University Press, Cambridge, MA.

Kaplan, S. (1989) 'The Effects of Management Buyouts on Operating Performance and Value', *Journal of Financial Economics*, Vol. 24, No. 2, October, pp. 217–254.

Kogut, B., and Zander, U. (1993) 'Knowledge of the Firm and the Evolutionary Theory of the Multinational Corporation', *Journal of International Business Studies*, Vol. 24, No. 4, pp. 625–646.

Kono, T. (1999) 'A Strong Head Office Makes a Strong Company', *Long Range Planning*, Vol. 32, No. 2, pp. 225–236.

Lawrence, P.R., and Lorsch, J.W. (1967) *Organization and Environment*, Harvard University Press, Cambridge, MA.

Long, W.F., and Ravenscraft, D.J. (1993) 'Decade of Debt: Lessons from LBOs in the 1980s', in: M.M. Blair (ed.), *The Deal Decade: What Takeovers and Leveraged Buyouts Mean for Corporate Governance*, Brookings Institution, Washington.

Lubatkin, M., and Chatterjee, S. (1994) 'Extending Modern Portfolio Theory into the Domain of Corporate Diversification: Does It Apply?', *Academy of Management Journal*, Vol. 37, No. 1, pp. 109–136.

Mahoney, J.T. (1992) 'The Choice of Organizational Form: Vertical Financial Ownership versus Other Methods of Vertical Integration', *Strategic Management Journal*, Vol. 13, No. 8, pp. 559–584.

Porter, M.E. (1987) 'From Competitive Advantage to Corporate Strategy', *Harvard Business Review*, Vol. 65, No. 3, May–June, pp. 43–59.

Prahalad, C.K., and Bettis, R.A. (1986) 'The Dominant Logic: A New Linkage Between Diversity and Performance', *Strategic Management Journal*, Vol. 7, No. 6, November–December, pp. 485–601.

Prahalad, C.K., and Doz, Y. (1987) *The Multinational Mission: Balancing Local Demands and Global Vision*, Free Press, New York.

Prahalad, C.K., and Hamel, G. (1990) 'The Core Competence of the Corporation', *Harvard Business Review*, Vol. 68, No. 3, May–June, pp. 79–91.

Ramanujam, V., and Varadarajan, P. (1989) 'Research on Corporate Diversification: A Synthesis', *Strategic Management Journal*, Vol. 10, No. 6, November–December, pp. 523–551.

Raynor, M.E., and Bower, J.L. (2001) 'Lead from the Center: How to Manager Diverse Businesses', *Harvard Business Review*, Vol. 80, No. 5, May, pp. 93–100.

Rumelt, R.P. (1974) *Strategy, Structure, and Economic Performance*, Harvard University Press, Cambridge, MA.

Rumelt, R.P. (1982) 'Diversification Strategy and Profitability', *Strategic Management Journal*, Vol. 3, No. 4, October–December, pp. 359–369.

Seth, A. (1990) 'Value Creation in Acquisitions: A Re-Examination of Performance Issues', *Strategic Management Journal*, Vol. 11, No. 2, February, pp. 99–115.

Sirower, M.L. (1997) *The Synergy Trap: How Companies Lose the Acquisition Game*, Free Press, New York.

Stalk, G., Evans, P., and Schulman, L.E. (1992) 'Competing on Capabilities: The New Rules of Corporate Strategy', *Harvard Business Review*, Vol. 70, No. 2, March–April, pp. 57–69.

Trautwein, F. (1990) 'Merger Motives and Merger Prescriptions', *Strategic Management Journal*, Vol. 11, No. 4, May–June, pp. 283–295.

Weston, J.F., Chung, K.S., and Hoag, S.E. (1990) *Mergers, Restructuring, and Corporate Control*, Prentice Hall, Englewood Cliffs, NJ.

Williamson, O.E. (1975) *Markets and Hierarchies: Analysis and Antitrust Implications*, Free Press, New York.

NETWORK LEVEL STRATEGY

Alliance, n. In international politics, the union of two thieves who have their hands so deeply inserted in each other's pocket that they cannot separately plunder a third.

The Devil's Dictionary, Ambrose Bierce (1842–1914); American columnist

INTRODUCTION

A business unit can have a strategy, while a group of business units can also have a strategy together – this joint course of action at the divisional or corporate level was discussed in the previous chapter. What has not been examined yet is whether a group of companies can also have a strategy together. Is it possible that companies do not develop their strategies in 'splendid isolation', but rather coordinate their strategies to operate as a team? And is it a good idea for firms to link up with others for a prolonged period of time to try to achieve shared objectives together?

Where two or more firms move beyond a mere transactional relationship and work jointly towards a common goal, they form an alliance, partnership or network. Their shared strategy is referred to as a network level strategy. In such a case, strategy is not only 'concerned with relating a firm to its environment', as was stated in Chapter 5, but also with relating a network to its broader environment.

The existence of networks does raise a range of questions, not the least of which is whether they make strategic sense or not. Is it beneficial to engage in long-term collaborative relationships with other firms or is it more advantageous for firms to 'keep their distance' and to interact with one another in a more market-like, transactional way? Is it viable to manage a web of partnership relations or is it preferable to keep it simple, by having the firm operate more or less independently? To address these questions is to raise the issue of inter-organizational relationships – what should be the nature of the relationship between a firm and other organizations in its surroundings? This issue will be the focus of the further discussion in this chapter.

THE ISSUE OF INTER-ORGANIZATIONAL RELATIONSHIPS

No firm exists that is autarchic. All firms must necessarily interact with other organizations (and individuals) in their environment and therefore they have inter-organizational (or inter-firm) relationships. These relationships can evolve without any clear strategic intent or tactical calculation, but most managers agree that actively determining the nature of their external relations is a significant part of what strategizing is about. Even avoiding relations with some external parties can be an important strategic choice.

To gain a better understanding of the interaction between firms, four aspects are of particular importance and will be reviewed here – the who, why, what and how of inter-organizational relationships (see Figure 7.1). The first aspect is the question of who – who are the potential counterparts with whom a firm can actually have a relationship? This is referred to as the topic of 'relational actors'. The second aspect is the question of why – why do the parties want to enter into a relationship with one another? This is referred to as the topic of 'relational objectives'. The third aspect is the question of what – what type of influences determine the nature of the relationship? This is referred to as the topic of 'relational factors'. The fourth aspect is the question of how – how can relationships be structured into a particular organizational form to let them function in the manner intended? This is referred to as the topic of 'relational arrangements'.

Relational actors

In Figure 7.2 an overview is given of the eight major groups of external parties with whom the firm can, or must, interact. A distinction has been made between industry and contextual actors. The industry actors are those individuals and organizations that perform value-adding activities and/or consume the outputs of these activities. The contextual actors are those parties whose behavior, intentionally or unintentionally, sets the conditions under which the industry actors must operate. The four main categories of relationships between the firm and other industry parties are the following (e.g. Porter, 1980; Reve, 1990):

- Upstream vertical (supplier) relations. Every company has suppliers of some sort. In a narrow definition these include the providers of raw materials, parts, machinery and business services. In a broader definition the providers of all production factors (land, capital, labor, technology, information and entrepreneurship) can be seen as suppliers, if they are not part of the firm itself. All these suppliers can either be the actual producers of the input, or an intermediary (distributor or agent) trading in the product or service. Beside the suppliers with which the firm transacts directly (first-tier suppliers), the firm may also have relationships with suppliers further upstream in the industry. All these relationships are traditionally referred to as upstream vertical relations, because economists commonly draw the industry system as a column.

- Downstream vertical (buyer) relations. On the output side, the firm has relationships with its customers. These clients can either be the actual users of the product or service, or intermediaries trading the output. Besides the buyers with which the firm transacts directly, it may also have relationships with parties further downstream in the industry column.

- Direct horizontal (industry insider) relations. This category includes the relations between the firm and other industry incumbents. Because these competitors produce similar goods or services, they are said to be at the same horizontal level in the industry column.

FIGURE 7.1 Aspects of inter-organizational relations

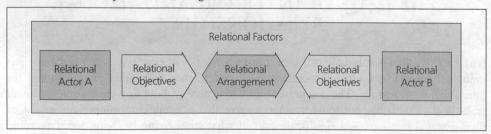

- Indirect horizontal (industry outsider) relations. Where a firm has a relationship with a company outside its industry, this is referred to as an indirect horizontal relation. Commonly, companies will have relationships with the producers of complementary goods and services (e.g. hardware manufacturers with software developers). Such a relationship can develop with the producer of a substitute good or service, either as an adversary or as an ally. A relation can also exist between a firm and a potential industry entrant, whereby the incumbent firm can assist or attempt to block the entry of the industry outsider. Furthermore, a firm can establish a relationship with a firm in another industry, with the intention of diversifying into that, or a third, industry. In reality, where industry boundaries are not clear, the distinction between direct and indirect horizontal relations is equally blurry.

Besides relationships with these industry actors, there can be many contacts with condition-setting parties in the broader environment. Employing the classic SEPTember distinction, the following rough categories of contextual actors can be identified:

- Socio-cultural actors. Individuals or organizations that have a significant impact on societal values, norms, beliefs and behaviors may interact with the firm. These could include the media, community groups, charities, religious organizations and opinion leaders.

- Economic actors. There can also be organizations influencing the general economic state of affairs, with which the firm interacts. Among others, tax authorities, central banks, employers' federations, stock exchanges and unions may be of importance.

- Political/legal actors. The firm may also interact with organizations setting or influencing the regulations under which companies must operate. These could include governments, political parties, special interest groups, regulatory bodies and international institutions.

FIGURE 7.2   The firm and its web of relational actors

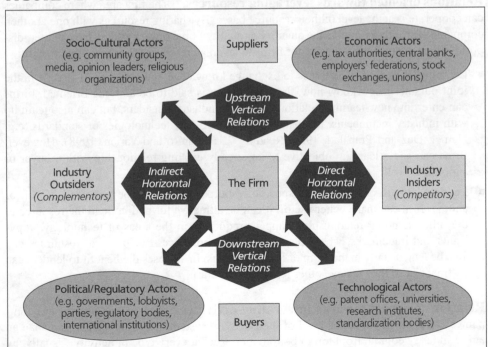

- Technological actors. There are also many organizations that influence the pace and direction of technological development and the creation of new knowledge. Among others, universities, research institutes, patent offices, government agencies and standardization bodies may be important to deal with.

As Figure 7.2 visualizes, companies can choose, but are often also forced, to interact with a large number of organizations and individuals in the environment. This configuration of external actors with which the organization interacts is referred to as the company's group of 'external stakeholders'.

Relational objectives

How organizations deal with one another is strongly influenced by what they hope to achieve (e.g. Dyer and Singh, 1998; Preece, 1995). Both parties may have clear, open and mutually beneficial objectives, but it is also possible that one or both actors have poorly defined intentions, hidden agendas and/or mutually exclusive goals. Moreover, it is not uncommon that various people within an organization have different, even conflicting, objectives and expectations with regard to an external relationship (e.g. Allison, 1969, Reading 3.3 in this book; Doz and Hamel, 1998).

Where two or more firms seek to work together with one another, they generally do so because they expect some value added – they assume more benefit from the interaction than if they had proceeded on their own. This expectation of value creation as a driver for cooperation was also discussed in Chapter 6, where two or more business units worked together to reap synergies. In fact, the same logic is at play between business units and between companies. In both cases, managers are oriented towards finding sources of added value in a potential relationship with another – either across business unit boundaries or across company boundaries. Hence, the same sources of synergy identified in the discussion on corporate level strategy are just as relevant when examining the objectives for inter-organizational cooperation (see Figure 7.3).

Relations oriented towards leveraging resources. The first area where companies can cooperate is at the level of their resource bases. By sharing resources with one another, companies can either improve the quantity or quality of the resources they have at their disposal. There are two general ways for firms to leverage resources to reap mutual benefit:

- Learning. When the objective is to exchange knowledge and skills, or to engage in the joint pursuit of new know-how, the relationship is said to be learning-oriented. Firms can enter into new learning relationships with industry outsiders, but can also team up with industry incumbents, for instance to develop new technologies or standards (e.g. Hamel, Doz and Prahalad, 1989, Reading 7.1; Shapiro and Varian, 1998). However, firms can add a learning objective to an already existing relationship with a buyer or supplier as well.

- Lending. Where one firm owns specific resources that it cannot make full use of, or another firm can make better use of, it can be attractive for both to lend the resource to the other. Lending relationships happen frequently in the areas of technology, copyrights and trademarks, where licensing is commonplace. But physical resources can also be lent, usually in the form of lease contracts. In all cases the benefit to lenders can be financial or they receive other resources in return.

Relations oriented towards integrating activities. The second area where companies can cooperate is at the level of their activity systems. Few companies can span an entire industry column from top to bottom and excel at every type of activity. Usually, by

FIGURE 7.3   Inter-organizational cooperation objectives

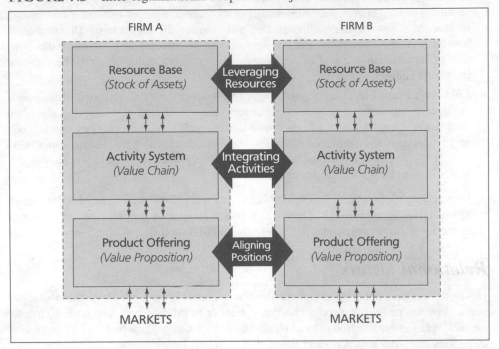

integrating their value chains with other organizations, firms can be much more efficient and effective than if they were totally separated. There are two general ways for firms to integrate their activities with others:

- Linking. The most common type of relationship in business is the vertical link between a buyer and a seller. All relationships in which products or services are exchanged fall into this category. Most firms have many linking relationships, both upstream and downstream, because they want to focus on only a limited number of value-adding activities, but need a variety of inputs, as well as clients to purchase their finished goods.

- Lumping. Where firms bring together their similar activities to gain economies of scale, the relationship is said to be oriented towards lumping. Sharing operations (e.g. airline alliances), sales infrastructure (e.g. software cross-selling deals), logistics systems (e.g. postal partnerships) or payment facilities (e.g. inter-bank settlement agreements) are examples of where firms can lump their activities together. Because the activities need to be more or less the same to be able to reap scale economies, lumping relationships are usually found between two or more industry insiders.

Relations oriented towards aligning positions.   The third area where companies can cooperate is at the level of their market positions. Even where companies want to keep their value-adding activities separate, they can coordinate their moves in the environment with the intention of strengthening each other's position. Usually, this type of coalition-building is directed at improving the joint bargaining power of the cooperating parties. These position-enhancing relationships can be further subdivided into two categories:

- Leaning. Where two or more firms get together to improve their bargaining position vis-à-vis other industry actors, it is said that they lean on each other to stand stronger. Leaning can be directed at building up a more powerful negotiation position towards suppliers, or to offer a more attractive package of products and services towards buyers. Getting together with other companies to form a consortium to launch a new industry standard can also bolster the position of all companies involved. At the same time, the cooperation can be directed at weakening the position of an alternative group of companies or even heightening the entry barriers for interested industry outsiders.

- Lobbying. Firms can also cooperate with one another with the objective of gaining a stronger position vis-à-vis contextual actors. Such lobbying relationships are often directed at strengthening the firms' voice towards political and regulatory actors, such as governments and regulatory agencies. However, firms can get together to put pressure on various other contextual actors, such as standard setting bodies, universities, tax authorities and stock exchanges as well.

In practice, cooperative relationships between organizations can involve a number of these objectives simultaneously. Moreover, it is not uncommon for objectives to shift over time and for various participants in the relationship to have different objectives.

Relational factors

How inter-organizational relationships develop is strongly influenced by the objectives pursued by the parties involved. However, a number of other factors also have an impact on how relationships unfold. These relational factors can be grouped into four general categories (e.g. Mitchell, Agle and Wood, 1997; Gulati, 1998):

- Legitimacy. Relationships are highly impacted by what is deemed to be legitimate. Written and unwritten codes of conduct give direction to what is viewed as acceptable behavior. Which topics are allowed on the agenda, who has a valid claim, how interaction should take place and how conflicts should be resolved, are often decided by what both parties accept as 'the rules of engagement'. There is said to be 'trust', where it is expected that the other organization or individual will adhere to these rules. However, organizations do not always agree on 'appropriate behavior', while what is viewed as legitimate can shift over time as well. It can also be (seen as) advantageous to act opportunistically by not behaving according to the unwritten rules (e.g. Gambetta, 1988; Williamson, 1991).

- Urgency. Inter-organizational relations are also shaped by the factor 'timing'. Relationships develop differently when one or both parties are under time pressure to achieve results, as opposed to a situation where both organizations can interact without experiencing a sense of urgency (e.g. Pfeffer and Salancik, 1978; James, 1985).

- Frequency. Inter-organizational relations also depend on the frequency of interaction and the expectation of future interactions. Where parties expect to engage in a one-off transaction they usually behave differently than when they anticipate a more structural relationship extending over multiple interactions. Moreover, a relationship with a low rate of interaction tends to develop differently than one with a high regularity of interaction (e.g. Axelrod, 1984; Dixit and Nalebuff, 1991).

- Power. Last but not least, relations between organizations are strongly shaped by the power held by both parties. Power is the ability to influence others' behavior and organizations can have many sources of power. Most importantly for inter-organizational relationships, a firm can derive power from having resources that the other organization requires. In relationships with a very high level of resource dependence, firms tend to behave differently towards each other than when they are interdependent or relatively independent of one another (e.g. Pfeffer and Salancik, 1978; Porter, 1980).

Especially the impact of power differences on inter-organizational relationships is given extensive attention in the strategic management literature. Many authors (e.g. Chandler, 1990; Kay, 1993; Pfeffer and Salancik, 1978; Porter, 1980; Schelling, 1960) stress that for understanding the interaction between firms it is of the utmost importance to gain insight into their relative power positions. One way of measuring relative power in a relationship is portrayed in Figure 7.4, where a distinction is made between the closeness of the relationship (loose vs. tight) and the distribution of power between the two parties involved (balanced vs. unbalanced). This leads to a categorization of four specific types of inter-firm relationships from the perspective of relative power position. These four categories (adapted from Ruigrok and van Tulder, 1995) are:

A Mutual independence. Organizations are independent in a relationship if they have full freedom to act according to their own objectives. Independence in an inter-organizational relationship means that organizations will only interact on their own terms and that they have the ability to break off the relationship without any penalty. In a situation of mutual independence, neither organization has significant influence over the other.

B Unbalanced independence. When two organizations work together in a loose relationship, one side (Firm A) can have more power than the other (Firm B). In such a case, it is said that Firm A is more independent than Firm B – Firm A's power gives it more freedom to act, while Firm B can be influenced by the powerful Firm A. This situation is called unbalanced independence, as both sides are independent, but one more so than the other.

C Mutual dependence. Two organizations can have a tight relationship, in which they are mutually dependent, while having an equal amount of sway over their counterpart. This type of situation, where there is a substantial, yet balanced, relationship between two or more parties, is also called interdependence.

D Unbalanced dependence. Where a tight relationship is characterized by asymmetrical dependence, one party will be able to dominate the other. In this situation of unbalanced dependence, the organization with the lower level of dependence will have more freedom to maneuver and impose its conditions than its counterpart.

FIGURE 7.4   Relative power positions in inter-organizational relationships

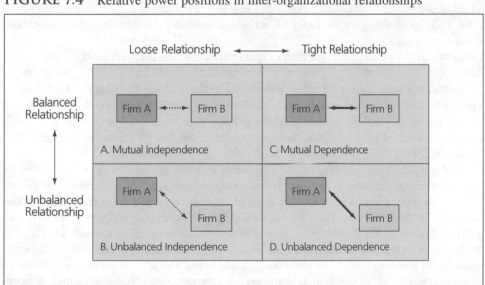

The first category, mutual independence, is what is typically expected of a normal *market* relationship, although it is not strange to also witness market relationships that fit more in the second category, unbalanced independence. At the other extreme, unbalanced dependence is very close to the situation that would occur if the dominant firm acquired its counterpart. Whether acquired or fully dependent, the dominant firm controls its behavior. For this reason it is said that in cases of unbalanced dependence the inter-organizational relationship comes close to resembling the *hierarchy*-type relationship found within a firm. Interdependence seems to be somewhere between market and hierarchy-type relationships. What this means for the structuring of these relationships will be examined below.

Relational arrangements

In the classic dichotomy, the firm and its environment are presented as rather distinct entities. Within a firm coordination is achieved by means of direct control, leading transaction cost economists to refer to this organizational form as a 'hierarchy' (Williamson, 1975, 1985). In a hierarchy a central authority governs internal relationships and has the formal power to coordinate strategy and solve inter-departmental disputes. In the environment, relationships between firms are non-hierarchical, as they interact with one another without any explicit coordination or dispute settlement mechanism. This organizational form is referred to as a 'market'.

In Chapter 6 it was argued that there are all types of activities that companies should not want to internalize and run themselves, but should leave up to the market-place. In many situations, it is much more efficient to buy inputs in the market than to make them yourself – where activities are performed by autonomous parties and outputs are sold in the market-place, costs will often be lowest. As summarized by Ouchi (1980, p. 130), 'in a market relationship, the transaction takes place between the two parties and is mediated by a price mechanism in which the existence of a competitive market reassures both parties that the terms of exchange are equitable'.

Integration of activities into the firm is only necessary where 'markets do not function properly' – where doing it yourself is cheaper or better. The firm must internalize activities, despite the disadvantages of hierarchy, where the 'invisible hand' of the market cannot be trusted to be equitable and effective. Control over activities by means of formal authority – the 'visible hand' – is needed under these conditions. This is particularly true of all of the synergy advantages mentioned in Chapter 6, that the corporation would not be able to reap if the various business activities were not brought together under one 'corporate roof'.

In reality, however, there are many organizational forms between markets and hierarchies (e.g. Håkansson and Johanson, 1993; Powell, 1990; Thorelli, 1986). These are the networks, partnerships, or alliances introduced at the start of this chapter. In networks, strategies are coordinated and disputes resolved, not through formal top-down power, but by mutual adaptation. To extend the above metaphor, networks rely neither on the visible nor invisible hand to guide relationships, but rather employ the 'continuous handshake' (Gerlach, 1992).

The organizations involved in networks can employ different sorts of collaborative arrangements to structure their ties with one another. In Figure 7.5, an overview of a number of common types of collaborative arrangements is presented. Two major distinctions are made in this overview. First, between bilateral arrangements, which only involve two parties, and multilateral arrangements, which involve three or more. Commonly, only the multilateral arrangements are referred to as networks, although here the term is employed to cover all groupings of two or more cooperating firms. The second distinction is between non-contractual, contractual and equity-based arrangements. Non-contractual arrangements are cooperative agreements that are not binding by law, while contractual arrangements do have a clear legal enforceability. Both, however, do not involve taking a financial stake in each other or in a new joint venture, while the equity-based arrangements do.

The intent of these collaborative arrangements is to profit from some of the advantages of vertical and horizontal integration, without incurring their costs. Networks are actually hybrid organizational forms that attempt to combine the benefits of hierarchy with the benefits of the market. The main benefits of hierarchy are those associated with the structural coordination of activities. In non-market relational arrangements, all parties collaborate on a more long-term basis with the intent of realizing a common goal. They will organize procedures, routines and control systems to ensure effective and efficient functioning of their joint activities and a smooth transition at their organizational interfaces. The benefits of the market that these collaborative arrangements retain are flexibility and motivation. By not being entirely locked into a fixed hierarchy, individual firms can flexibly have multiple relationships, of varying length and intensity, and can change these relationships more easily where circumstances require adaptation. The market also provides the motivation to be efficient and to optimize the pursuit of the organization's self-interest. This entrepreneurial incentive can be a strong spur for risk-taking, innovation and change.

A significant advantage of collaborative arrangements is that such relationships facilitate the process of 'co-specialization'. Much of humanity's economic progress is based on the principle of specialization by means of a division of labor. As people and firms focus more closely on performing a limited set of value-adding activities, they become more effective and efficient in their work. This division of labor assumes, however, that the value-adding activities that are outsourced by one become the specialization of another, hence co-specialization. Yet, many activities cannot be outsourced to outsiders on the basis of normal market relations, either due to the risk of dependence or because of the need for the structural coordination of activities. Under these conditions, collaborative arrangements can act as a synthesis of hierarchy and market relations, thus catalyzing the process of specialization (e.g. Best, 1990; Axelsson and Easton, 1992).

FIGURE 7.5   Examples of collaborative arrangements

	Non-Contractual Arrangements	Contractual Arrangements	Equity-based Arrangements
Multilateral Arrangements	• Lobbying coalition (e.g. European Roundtable of Industrialists) • Joint standard setting (e.g. Linux coalition) • Learning communities (e.g. Strategic Management Society)	• Research consortium (e.g. Symbian in PDAs) • International marketing alliance (e.g. Star Alliance in airlines) • Export partnership (e.g. Netherlands Export Combination)	• Shared payment system (e.g. Visa) • Construction consortium (e.g. Eurotunnel) • Joint reservation system (e.g. Galileo)
Bilateral Arrangements	• Cross-selling deal (e.g. between pharmaceutical firms) • R&D staff exchange (e.g. between IT firms) • Market information sharing agreement (e.g. between hardware and software makers)	• Licensing agreement (e.g. Disney and Coca-Cola) • Co-development contract (e.g. Disney and Pixar in movies) • Co-branding alliance (e.g. Coca-Cola and McDonald's)	• New product joint venture (e.g. Sony and Ericsson in cellphones) • Cross-border joint venture (e.g. Daimler Chrysler and Beijing Automotive) • Local joint venture (e.g. CNN Turk in Turkey)

Such co-specialization can progress to such an extent that clusters of firms work together in more of less permanent networks. Such symbiotic groups of collaborating firms can actually function as 'virtual corporations' (e.g. Chesbrough and Teece, 1996; Quinn, 1992). In such networks, the relationships between the participating firms are often very tight and durable, based on a high level of trust and perceived mutual interest. While each organization retains its individual identity, the boundaries between them become fuzzy, blurring the clear distinction between 'the organization' and 'its environment'. When a high level of trust and reciprocity has been achieved, relations can move far beyond simple contractual obligations. The collaborative relations can become more open-ended, with objectives, responsibilities, authority and results not fully determined in advance in a written contract, but evolving over time, given all parties' sincere willingness to 'work on their relationship' (e.g. Jarillo, 1988; Kanter, 1994).

While the intention of collaborative arrangements may be to blend the advantages of hierarchy with the qualities of the market, it is also possible that the weaknesses of both are actually combined. The main weakness of hierarchy is bureaucracy – creating red tape, unnecessary coordination activities and dulling the incentive to perform. In reality, collaborative arrangements might be mechanisms for structuring static relationships and dampening entrepreneurial behavior. A further danger is that the mutual dependence might become skewed, shifting the balance of power to one of the partners. Under such conditions, one or more organizations can become dependent on a dominant party, without much influence (voice) or the possibility to break off the relationship (exit). Such unbalanced dependency relationships (see Figure 7.4) might be a great benefit for the stronger party, but can easily lead to the predominance of its interests over the interests of the weaker partners (e.g. Oliver and Wilkinson, 1988; Ruigrok and van Tulder, 1995).

Simultaneously such partnerships are vulnerable to the main disadvantage of the market, namely opportunism. Companies run the risk of opportunism, that is (according to Williamson, 1985: 47):

> *self-interest seeking with guile. This includes but is scarcely limited to more blatant forms, such as lying, stealing and cheating . . . More generally, opportunism refers to the incomplete or distorted disclosure of information, especially to calculated efforts to mislead, distort, disguise, obfuscate, or otherwise confuse.*

Such behavior can be limited by clearly defining objectives, responsibilities, authority and expected results ahead of time, preferably in an explicit contract. Even then collaborative arrangements expose companies to the risk of deception, the abuse of trust and the exploitation of dependence, making their use by no means undisputed.

THE PARADOX OF COMPETITION AND COOPERATION

We have no eternal allies and we have no perpetual enemies. Our interests are eternal and perpetual, and those interests it is our duty to follow.
Lord Palmerston (Henry John Temple) (1784–1865); British prime minister

When former CEO of KLM Royal Dutch Airlines, Pieter Bouw, teamed up with Northwest Airlines in 1989, he was thrilled to have the first major transatlantic strategic alliance in the industry, involving joint flights, marketing and sales activities, catering, ground handling, maintenance and purchasing. Northwest was the fourth largest American carrier at that time, but was in 'Chapter 11', balancing on the verge of bankruptcy, and in dire need of cash. To help their new ally out, KLM gave a US$400 million capital injection, in return for 20% of the shares and the option to increase this to a majority stake within a few years. KLM and Northwest were on their way to becoming a virtual transatlantic company – a marriage 'made in the heavens'.

Commercially the deal was a success, but relationally the alliance was a Shakespearean drama. KLM gave up its hopes of an alliance with Swissair, SAS and Delta, to remain loyal to Northwest, but as soon as Northwest emerged from Chapter 11, it blocked KLM's efforts to increase its shareholding. In the resulting two-year legal shooting match between 1995 and 1997, relations deteriorated sharply and the goose laying the golden eggs threatened to be killed in the cross fire. Disappointed and dismayed, Bouw decided to give in, selling Northwest back its shares, in return for a prolongation of the alliance, after which he immediately resigned. His successor, and current CEO, Leo van Wijk, has managed the alliance since then and it is still 'up in the air', in both senses of the expression. His most important conclusion has been that a collaborative alliance is not only about working together towards a common interest, but equally about being assertive with regard to one's own interests. Alliances are not only *cooperative*, but also have *competitive* aspects.

What this example of KLM and Northwest illustrates is that firms constantly struggle with the tension created by the need to work together with others, while simultaneously needing to pursue their own interests. Firms cannot isolate themselves from their environments, but must actively engage in relationships with suppliers and buyers, while selectively teaming up with other firms inside and outside their industry to attain mutual benefit. But while they are collaborating to create joint value, firms are also each other's rivals when it comes to dividing the benefits. These opposite demands placed on organizations are widely referred to as the pressures for competition and cooperation (e.g. Brandenburger and Nalebuff, 1996; Lado, Boyd and Hanlon, 1997). In the following sections both pressures will be examined in more detail.

The demand for inter-organizational competition

Competition can be defined as the act of working against others, where two or more organizations' goals are mutually exclusive. In other words, competition is the rivalry behavior exhibited by organizations or individuals where one's win is the other's loss.

Organizations need to be competitive in their relationships with others. As the interests and/or objectives of different organizations are often mutually exclusive, each organization needs to be determined and assertive in pursuing its own agenda. Each organization needs to be willing to confront others to secure its own interests. Without the will to engage in competitive interaction, the organization will be at the mercy of more aggressive counterparts – e.g. suppliers will charge excessively for products, buyers will express stiff demands for low prices, governments will require special efforts without compensation, and rival firms will poach among existing customers. Taking a competitive posture towards these external parties means that the organization is determined to assert its own interests and fight where necessary.

The resulting competitive relations can vary between open antagonism and conflict on the one hand, and more subtle forms of friction, tension and strain on the other. Blatant competitive behavior is often exhibited towards organizations whose objectives are fully in conflict – most clearly other producers of the same goods, attempting to serve the same markets (aptly referred to as 'the competition'). Highly competitive behavior can also be witnessed where a supplier and a buyer confront each other for dominance in the industry value chain (e.g. Porter, 1980; Van Tulder and Junne, 1988). A more restrained competitive stance can be observed where organizations' objectives are less at odds, but assertiveness is still important to protect the organization's interests. Negotiation and bargaining will commonly be employed under these circumstances.

To be competitive an organization must have the power to overcome its rivals and it must have the ability and will to use its power. Many factors shape the power of an organization, but its relative level of resource dependence is one of the most important determining elements. The more independent the organization, and the more others are dependent on it, the more power the organization will wield. In competitive relationships maneuvering the other party into a relatively dependent position is a common approach. In general, calculation, bargaining, maneuvering, building coalitions and outright conflict are all characteristic for the competitive interaction between organizations.

The demand for inter-organizational cooperation

Cooperation can be defined as the act of working together with others, where two or more organizations' goals are mutually beneficial. In other words, cooperation is the collaborative behavior exhibited by organizations or individuals where both sides need each other to succeed.

Organizations need to be cooperative in their relationships with others. The interests and/or objectives of different organizations are often complementary and working together can be mutually beneficial. Therefore, organizations must be willing to behave as partners, striving towards their common good. Without the will to engage in cooperative interaction, the organization will miss the opportunity to reap the advantages of joint efforts – e.g. developing new products together with suppliers, creating a better service offering together with buyers, improving the knowledge infrastructure together with government and setting new technical standards together with other firms in the industry. Taking a cooperative posture towards these external parties means that the organization is determined to leverage its abilities through teamwork.

The resulting cooperative relations can vary between occasional alliances on the one hand, to tight-knit, virtual integration on the other. Strongly cooperative behavior can be witnessed where the long-term interests of all parties are highly intertwined. This type of symbiotic relationship can be found between the producers of complementary goods and services, where success by one organization will positively impact its partners – aptly referred to as the 'network effect' (Arthur, 1994; Shapiro and Varian, 1998). Highly cooperative behavior can also be observed where suppliers and buyers face a joint challenge (such as government regulation, an innovative technology or a new market entrant) that can only be tackled by significant mutual commitment to a shared objective.

More restrained cooperative behavior is common where there is potential for a 'positive sum game', but some parties seek to optimize their own returns to the detriment of others. Under such circumstances, exhibiting cooperative behavior does not mean being naive or weak, but creating conditions under which the long-term shared interests prevail over the short-term temptation by some to cheat their partners. An important ingredient for overcoming the lure of opportunism is to build long-term commitment to one another, not only in words and mentality, but also practically, through a high level of interdependence. Where organizations are tightly linked to one another, the pay-off for cooperative behavior is usually much more enticing than the possibility to profit from the dependence of one's partner. But to be willing to commit to such a high level of interdependence, people on both sides of a relationship need to trust each other's intentions and actions, while there must be coordination and conflict-resolution mechanisms in place to solve evolving issues (e.g. Dyer, Kale and Singh, 2001, Reading 7.4 in this book; Simonin, 1997).

EXHIBIT 7.1 SHORT CASE

MERCK: A MEDICINE AGAINST ANOREXIA?

Name an industry in which the average product takes 10 years to develop, at a cost of US$500 million a shot. Aerospace? Robotics? Logical choices, but the right answer is pharmaceuticals. Developing new drugs does not come easily or cheaply. The R&D budgets of the large pharmaceutical companies are approximately 18% of sales, placing some of them among the biggest R&D spenders in the world. With such high investments and long lead times, the pharmaceutical industry is a competitive arena that should be avoided by the short-winded and faint-hearted. Ray Gilmartin, however, does not need to reach for Prilosec, a heartburn drug – he only needs to sell the product and is doing so quite well. Since 1994, Gilmartin has been CEO of Merck & Co., the fourth largest pharmaceutical company in the world, after Pfizer, GlaxoSmithKline, and Johnson & Johnson, with sales in 2002 of US$21.4 billion and a net profit of US$6.8 billion. Merck employs more than 60 000 people around the world, many of them working in the 11 research facilities the company has in seven different countries.

Merck has competed in this high-stakes industry for more than 100 years, initially as the US subsidiary of the German company Merck. During World War I the Merck subsidiary became separated from its parent company in Darmstadt, and to this day both companies use the Merck name (the German E. Merck has sales of approximately €8 billion, half of which in pharmaceuticals). For decades, the pharmaceutical industry has enjoyed double-digit revenue growth and recession-proof high profitability, making it a stock market favorite despite the risk involved in the drug development process. But since the end of the 1990s, the industry conditions have taken a turn for the worse. After years of unchallenged price hikes, governments have started to look at the drug firms as partially responsible for the soaring cost of healthcare, threatening the industry with price regulations. In the United States, the rise of 'managed care' organizations that can buy in bulk has further enhanced the bargaining power of buyers, placing more pressure on prices. In many other countries, the healthcare insurance companies have been major players in searching for ways to clamp down on spiraling pharmaceutical expenditures.

At the same time, the highly profitable 'monopoly' period after the launch of a new drug is becoming ever shorter – successful products are soon joined by competitors' me-too products, which skillfully circumvent patent protection. And as soon as the patents actually expire, aggressive generic drug manufacturers quickly enter the market with products at cut-rate prices, often largely wiping out the sales of the patent holder. To extend their monopoly period, the research-based pharmaceutical companies have tried to devise all types of ways of getting new patents for modifications to existing drugs – only 15% of newly approved major drugs are based on 'new chemical entities' or treat illnesses in novel ways. However, some generic drug companies have responded by making court battles a 'standard operating procedure', sometimes fighting up to 100 cases a year. Most research-based drug companies realize that their best defense is to forge ahead and develop new blockbuster products. The result has been a significant growth in R&D investments, yet the stream of new products has slowed, dropping by 35% between 1997 and 2002, reaching the lowest level in 20 years. And for many companies, the product development pipeline does not seem to offer enough potential to compensate for the older products due to lose patent protection.

The US$500 million price tag and 8–15 year time span for getting the scientists' chemical compounds out of the test tube and on to the pharmacists' shelves is only partially attributable to the process of actually discovering a potential new drug. In general it takes about one to three years for a new preparation to be synthesized and tested. But once a preparation is in the pipeline, many further steps need to be taken before it becomes a sellable product. First, the preparation enters the pre-clinical development phase, which might involve animal testing. If, after a few years of tests, the results are promising, permission can be gained to proceed with clinical trials on human volunteers. At first, these are conducted on small groups, but if successful, they are enlarged to full-scale tests. The clinical trials can take five to ten years before a drug is approved for broader use and sales can begin. On average, of the 20 preparations entering pre-clinical development, only one comes out of the pipeline as a marketable drug. Obviously, pharmaceutical companies would like to increase this yield and shorten the process, but this is not proving to be easy.

▶

Merck has followed the industry trend by investing more heavily in R&D, raising its budget for 2002 to more than US$2.7 billion; double what it was just eight years before. The company seems to be spending this money well, as its scientists hold the lead in obtaining patents – between 1996 and 2002, Merck patented no less than 1933 new compounds, 400 more than second-place Pharmacia and also at the lowest cost, of 'just' US$6 million per patent. As a result, Merck claims its pipeline of upcoming new drugs is among the strongest ever. This has allowed Merck to go against another industry trend, which is to seek more intensive cooperation with others, either through alliances or mergers. Many of Merck's competitors have merged in the past few years, such as Pfizer with Pharmacia (together now number one), and Glaxo Wellcome with SmithKline Beecham (together now number two), with the intention of obtaining economies of scale in marketing and R&D. Gilmartin has been quite adamant that he prefers organic growth, seeing no value in such mega-mergers, as they only bring bureaucracy and infighting, not the innovative new products that are needed for above-average performance.

Merck has also been reluctant to join the strong movement towards all sorts of alliances, both with major pharmaceutical competitors and with small start-ups. Merck has a few joint ventures and licensing arrangements, but all on a relatively small scale. Only in 2002 did Merck's vice president and CFO, Judy Lewent, announce that the company would consider more alliances with small biotech companies, both in R&D and marketing. But the company's approach is hesitant and its philosophy towards new product development has remained largely 'do-it-yourself'. Not more than 5% of Merck's total research spending ends up outside of its own laboratories. This emphasis on doing most R&D in-house contrasts sharply with the direction being taken by the rest of the industry. All of Merck's rivals reserve between 10% and 20% of their R&D budgets for external work. In some cases only the laborious task of conducting clinical trials is outsourced, but increasingly the pharmaceutical giants are contracting out the development of new drugs to specialist firms, or licensing in the new products created by small biotech start-ups. Some analysts are predicting that the proportion of R&D performed outside of the big companies could reach 80%. Sir Richard Sykes, head of GlaxoSmithKline, has even suggested that the major drug firms will increasingly become 'virtual companies, as they concentrate on the marketing of drugs developed by the legions of small independent biotech firms.

The enthusiasm of Merck's competitors for alliances with the creative independents has been based on the view 'if you can't beat them, join them'. Despite going through a funding crisis after the bursting of the internet bubble, the number of small biotech firms has grown rapidly – in the United States alone there are more than 1800 firms active, with approximately the same number scattered around the rest of the world. All of these firms are so specialized, that at any one moment at least one of them will be ahead of any given big firm in any given technology. Most pharmaceutical giants believe that it is wise to tap into this source of new products, especially if this speeds up the process of getting newly developed drugs into their pipeline. Moreover, licensing in new drugs from the small biotech firms can usually be achieved at a fraction of the cost of doing it in-house. Most biotech firms do not have the financial stamina to shepherd their products through the years of development and trials, nor do they have the marketing and distribution infrastructure needed to reap the benefits of their labors. This gives the big firms the negotiating position to snap up promising products for considerably less than they are worth. During the past few years, hundreds of deals have been struck between small biotech firms and big pharmaceutical companies, and the number of alliances and joint ventures is still rising.

Merck, however, is strongly opposed to this policy of hollowing out. It thinks that the type of 'R&D anorexia' that its rivals are suffering from might end up being fatal. Without first class in-house scientific talent a drug firm will have problems to rapidly identify the best biotech ideas worth buying. In Merck's view, competitors are taking the easy route of shopping for new products simply because they are not clever enough to come up with their own. The president of Merck Research Laboratories, Peter Kim, has indicated that if Merck does lack certain key knowledge, he would prefer to selectively acquire smaller companies and integrate them into his research community. For example, in 2001 Merck purchased Rosetta Inpharmatics, a leading informational genomics company, to fill in a gap in its portfolio of technologies.

Of course, the question is whether Gilmartin and his team are right, while the rest of the industry is wrong. Is it necessary to keep all key activities in-house and to remain largely self-contained and independent from the outside world? Or are Merck's competitors right when they argue that the pharmaceutical industry will come to resemble Hollywood, where the big studios are focusing more on marketing and distribution, while the films are increasingly being made by small production companies? Time will tell who is right, but maybe Gilmartin should keep a bottle of Prilosec handy, just in case.

Sources: www.merck.com; *The Economist*, October 24 2002, February 13 2003; www.ims-global.com.

PERSPECTIVES ON NETWORK LEVEL STRATEGY

Concordia discors (discordant harmony).
Horace (65–8 BC); Roman poet

Firms need to be able to engage in competition and cooperation simultaneously, even though these demands are each other's opposites. Firms need to exhibit a strongly cooperative posture to reap the benefits of collaboration, and they need to take a strongly competitive stance to ensure that others do not block their interests. Some theorists conclude that what is required is 'co-opetition' (Brandenburger and Nalebuff, 1996). But while a catchy word, managers are still left with the difficult question of how to deal with these conflicting demands. To meet the pressure for cooperation, firms must actually become part of a broader 'team', spinning a web of close collaborative relationships. But to meet the pressure for competition, firms must not become too entangled in restrictive relationships, but rather remain free to maneuver, bargain and attack, with the intention of securing their own interests. In other words, firms must be *embedded* and *independent* at the same time – embedded in a network of cooperative interactions, while independent enough to wield their power to their own advantage.

The question dividing strategizing managers is whether firms should be more embedded or more independent. Should firms immerse themselves in broader networks to create strong groups, or should they stand on their own? Should firms willingly engage in long-term interdependence relationships or should they strive to remain as independent as possible? Should firms develop network level strategies at all, or should the whole concept of multi-firm strategy-making be directed to the garbage heap?

While strategy writers generally agree about the need to manage the paradox of competition and cooperation, they come to widely differing prescriptions on how to do so. Views within the field of strategic management are strongly at odds with regard to the best approach to inter-organizational relations. As before, here the two diametrically opposed positions will be identified and discussed, to show the scope of differing ideas. On the one side of the spectrum, there are strategists who believe that it is best for companies to be primarily competitive in their relationships to all outside forces. They argue that firms should remain independent and interact with other companies under market conditions as much as possible. As these strategists emphasize the discrete boundaries separating the firm from its 'competitive environment', this point of view is called the 'discrete organization perspective'. At the other end of the spectrum, there are strategists who believe that companies should strive to build up more long-term cooperative relationships with key organizations in their environment. They argue that firms can reap significant benefits by surrendering a part of their independence and developing close collaborative arrangements with a group of other organizations. This point of view will be referred to as the 'embedded organization perspective'.

The discrete organization perspective

Managers taking the discrete organization perspective view companies as independent entities competing with other organizations in a hostile market environment. In line with neoclassical economics, this perspective commonly emphasizes that individuals, and the organizations they form, are fundamentally motivated by aggressive self-interest and therefore that competition is the natural state of affairs. Suppliers will try to enhance their bargaining power vis-à-vis buyers with the aim of getting a better price, while conversely buyers will attempt to improve their negotiation position to attain better quality at lower cost. Competing firms will endeavor to gain the upper hand against their rivals if the opportunity arises, while new market entrants and manufacturers of substitute products will consistently strive to displace incumbent firms (e.g. Porter, 1980, 1985, Reading 5.1).

In such a hostile environment it is a strategic necessity for companies to strengthen their competitive position in relation to the external forces. The best strategy for each organization is to obtain the market power required to get good price/quality deals, ward off competitive threats, limit government demands and even determine the development of the industry. Effective power requires independence and therefore heavy reliance on specific suppliers, buyers, financiers or public organizations should be avoided.

The label 'discrete organization' given to this perspective refers to the fact that each organization is seen as being detached from its environment, with sharp boundaries demarcating where the outside world begins. The competitive situation is believed to be *atomistic*, that is, each self-interested firm strives to satisfy its own objectives, leading to rivalry and conflict with other organizations. Vertical interactions between firms in the industry column tend to be transactional, with an emphasis on getting the best possible deal. It is generally assumed that under such market conditions the interaction will be of a zero-sum nature, that is, a fight for who gets how much of the pie. The firm with the strongest bargaining power will usually be able to appropriate a larger portion of the 'economic rent' than will the less potent party. Therefore, advocates of the discrete organization perspective emphasize that the key to competitive success is the ability to build a powerful position and to wield this power in a calculated and efficient manner. This might sound Machiavellian to the faint-hearted, but it is the reality of the market-place that is denied at one's own peril.

Essential for organizational power is the avoidance of resource dependence. Where a firm is forced to lean on a handful of suppliers or buyers, this can place the organization in a precariously exposed position. To managers taking a discrete organization perspective, such dependence on a few external parties is extremely risky, as the other firm will be tempted to exploit their position of relative power to their own advantage. Wise firms will therefore not let themselves become overly dependent on any external organization, certainly not for any essential resources. This includes keeping the option open to exit from the relationship at will – with low barriers to exit the negotiating position of the firm is significantly stronger. Therefore the firm must never become so entangled with outsiders that it cannot rid themselves of them at the drop of a hat. The firm must be careful that in a web of relationships it is the spider, not the fly (e.g. Pfeffer & Salancik, 1978; Ruigrok and van Tulder, 1995).

Keeping other organizations at arm's-length also facilitates clear and business-like interactions. Where goods and services are bought or sold, distinct organizational boundaries help to distinguish tasks, responsibilities, authority and accountability. But as other firms will always seek to do as little as possible for the highest possible price, having clear contracts and a believable threat to enforce them, will serve as a method to ensure discipline. Arm's-length relations are equally useful in avoiding the danger of vital information leaking to the party with whom the firm must (re)negotiate.

In their relationships with other firms in the industry it is even clearer that companies' interests are mutually exclusive. More market share for one company must necessarily come at the expense of another. Coalitions are occasionally formed to create power blocks, if individual companies are not strong enough to compete on their own. Such tactical alliances bring together weaker firms, not capable of doing things independently. But 'competitive collaboration' is usually short lived – either the alliance is unsuccessful and collapses, or it is successful against the common enemy, after which the alliance partners become each other's most important rivals.

Proponents of the discrete organization perspective argue that collaborative arrangements are always second best to doing things independently. Under certain conditions, weakness might force a firm to choose an alliance, but it is always a tactical necessity, never a strategic preference. Collaborative arrangements are inherently risky, fraught with the hazard of opportunism. Due to the ultimately competitive nature of relationships, allies will be tempted to serve their own interests to the detriment of the others, by maneuvering, manipulating or cheating. The collaboration might even be a useful ploy, to cloak the company's aggressive intentions and moves. Collaboration, it is therefore concluded, is merely 'competition in a different form' (Hamel, Doz and Prahalad, 1989, Reading 7.1). Hence, where collaboration between firms really offers long-term advantages, a merger or acquisition is preferable to the uncertainty of an alliance.

Where collaboration is not the tool of the weak, it is often a conspiracy of the strong to inhibit competition. If two or more formidable companies collaborate, chances are that the alliance is actually ganging up on a third party – for instance on buyers. In such cases the term 'collaboration' is just a euphemism for collusion and not in the interest of the economy at large.

Worse yet, collaboration is usually also bad for a company's long-term health. A highly competitive environment is beneficial for a firm, because it provides the necessary stimulus for companies to continually improve and innovate. Strong adversaries push companies towards competitive fitness. A more benevolent environment, cushioned by competition-inhibiting collaboration, might actually make a firm more content and less eager to implement tough changes. In the long run this will make firms vulnerable to more aggressive companies, battle-hardened by years of rivalry in more competitive environments.

In conclusion, the basic assumption of the discrete organization perspective is that companies should not develop network level strategies, but should strive for 'strategic self-sufficiency'. Collaborative arrangements are a tactical tool, to be selectively employed. The sentiment of this perspective has been clearly summarized by Porter (1990; 224): 'alliances are rarely a solution . . . no firm can depend on another independent firm for skills and assets that are central to its competitive advantage . . . Alliances tend to ensure mediocrity, not create world leadership.'

EXHIBIT 7.2 THE DISCRETE ORGANIZAION PERSPECTIVE

McCAIN: NO SMALL FRY

Which *Belgian* invention was spread around the world by *American* fast-food restaurants and is dominated by a *Canadian* multinational? Well, a product English-speakers accidentally call *French* fries. The Canadian firm leading the international market for this golden crispy delicacy is McCain, headquartered in the small town of Florenceville in the province of New Brunswick. With worldwide sales of more than US$6 billion in 2002 and 18 000 employees scattered around the globe, McCain is no 'small fry'. The company is both in the B2C and B2B markets, selling chilled and frozen fries through supermarkets and to restaurants.

Producing French fries is a low margin, high volume business with demanding customers, particularly in the B2B market. Achieving a stable supply of potatoes at a uniform quality level is key to keeping customers happy and margins up – which is easier said than done, as potatoes are highly susceptible to the influences of the weather and natural pests. The first step in getting a good supply of quality potatoes is in breeding 'seed potatoes' that are free of diseases and suited to local growing conditions. The second step is the actual growing and harvesting of the edible potatoes. Then come the industrialized processing steps of grading, skinning, slicing and packaging. Most companies in the industry column are specialized in either breeding, growing or processing, as each step requires significantly different competences. Breeding is highly R&D intensive, oriented towards developing new, patented varieties that taste different, or have lower growing or processing costs. Potato growing has also become increasingly high-tech, but can still be carried out efficiently by relatively small-sized farms. Potato processing is an industrialized process, with high economies of scale.

In striking contrast with its specialized competitors, McCain's strategy has long been to control the entire value chain. Or as one key manager recently put it, McCain's perspective is that 'competitive strength comes from having control over every aspect of the business'. While its competitors are dependent on others in the value chain for their success, McCain has gained a high level of independence by building a substantial power base in all stages of the industry column. At the breeding stage, McCain develops its own varieties, which ensures its independence from external breeders. The company also seeks to buy patents of promising varieties before others get access to them. At the growing stage, McCain maintains a limited in-house farming capacity, yet 'outsources' most production to low cost suppliers, because potato growing has low economies of scale and a high level of risk, due to unpredictable harvests. This outsourcing is done via 'pre-harvest' contracts, on conditions very favorable to McCain – most potato growers are relatively small-scale farmers, giving McCain a powerful bargaining position. To secure uniform, high quality supplies for its factories, tightly specified contracts are used that set standards and strict delivery times. Furthermore, the firm has an 'agronomy' team that closely monitors and supports contract farmers on a day-to-day basis. Besides these contract suppliers, McCain also purchases additional supplies on the post-harvest spot market, in which large price fluctuations can occur. For this reason (but also to keep in touch with the art of potato production), McCain grows a relatively small part of its own potato supply – just enough to counter speculative 'trade strikes' by growers and traders. Well-timed 'trade strikes', whereby suppliers refuse to sell their produce, can drive up the spot market potato price, just when processors need new supplies to keep their French fry factories running.

The discrete organization perspective, which drives McCain's vertical relationships (within the value chain) is also at the basis of their horizontal relationships (with competitors and trade associations). McCain prefers to stand alone – avoiding any dependence on the trade associations that populate the potato industry. These associations, jointly paid and run by the competing firms, are mainly aimed to promote common interests vis-à-vis national and supranational (e.g. European Union) regulatory agencies and pressure groups. Apart from the occasional short-term coalition, McCain has sought to pursue its interests on its own.

Sources: *Rademakers*, 1999; www.mccain.com.

ing, Handspring outsourced manufacturing to Flextronics in Malaysia and Solectron in Mexico. Having two manufacturing partners added complexity to the system, but as Dubinsky noted, 'doing business with both helped keep each of them on their toes'. But while comparing prices and best practices, Handspring's policy was also to ensure that both partners shared in the benefits of any cost savings.

In the same way, Dubinsky went back to suppliers she knew from her days at Palm, to strike some good deals, but with a strong emphasis on fostering a win-win situation. As Colligan puts it: 'We have regular partner meetings where execs come in from various suppliers and tell us what we're doing wrong, what we're doing right and what we can do better . . . We're aggressive about making sure they feel included.' The same cooperative approach is taken to relationships with the developers of the Springboard plug-in modules. From the outset, Handspring made it highly attractive for independent developers to create modules, by making all code and specifications available free-of-charge on the Handspring web site, and providing engineering support. Customer support was also outsourced, as was order fulfillment, although Handspring was forced to switch the latter partner in 2000, due to performance shortfalls.

Reflecting on their approach to partnerships, Dubinsky says:

We've always been a little cynical and skeptical about 'Strategic Partnerships' in capital letters.

We see a lot of this in our industry: big announcements about big partnerships. We've seen a lot of them through the years be very ill defined and unsuccessful and very difficult to implement . . . At Handspring, we try to distinguish between what are real delivering partnerships and real day-to-day working partnerships, as opposed to . . . 'Barney partnerships' – a lot of 'I love you and you love me' and nothing ever happens.

At the same time, the Handspring team also wanted to avoid their Palm experience with Casio and Sharp. According to Colligan:

We were totally dependent on them – shipping, selling, marketing, doing everything. And they didn't execute, and they didn't care. It was a tiny little piece of their business. When they didn't do it, we were left holding the bag. Those were really bad partnerships.

As for the success factors of an embedded company, Dubinsky concludes: 'In structuring a relationship, know what the other party gets out of it, and understand how to structure that relationship for success for both parties, as opposed to just worrying about what it means to you.' But she also notes: 'We may get people to partner with us to execute pieces of our vision, but we're going to make it very clear that it's our vision and our direction.'

Sources: *The Economist*, September 16 1999, March 8 2001; www.handspring.com; Feldstein, Flanagan and Holloway, 2001.

INTRODUCTION TO THE DEBATE AND READINGS

The strong one is most powerful alone.

Friedrich von Schiller (1759–1805); German writer

All for one, one for all.

The Three Musketeers, Alexandre Dumas Jr. (1824–1895); French novelist

So, should managers form network level strategies or not? Should firms consciously embed themselves in a web of durable collaborative relationships, emphasizing the value of cooperative inter-organizational interactions for realizing their long-term aims? Or should firms try to remain as independent as possible, emphasizing the value of competitive power in achieving their strategic objectives? Is it 'all for one, one for all' or must the strong truly stand alone?

The debate on this issue within the field of strategy is far from being concluded. Many perspectives exist on how to reconcile the conflicting demands of competition and cooperation, and many 'best practices' have been put forward, but no consensus has thus far emerged. Therefore, individual strategists are once again in the position of needing to determine their own point of view.

To help strategists to gain more insight into the variety of perspectives on this issue, four readings have been selected that each takes a different angle on the debate. As in previous chapters, the first two readings will be representative of the two poles in this debate (see Table 7.1), while the second set of two readings will bring in additional factors to add further depth to the discussion.

To open on behalf of the discrete organization perspective, Michael Porter's reading in Chapter 5 could easily have been selected. In Reading 5.1, Porter states that 'the essence of strategy formulation is coping with competition', and that there are five sources of competitive pressure, all impinging on a firm's profit potential. These competitive forces are the threat of new entrants, powerful buyers and suppliers, rivalry among existing competitors and the threat of substitute products. Porter asserts that a company's profitability depends on how well it is able to defend itself against these 'opponents'. It is this view of the firm, as a lone organization surrounded by hostile forces, which places this reading clearly within the discrete organization perspective. While Porter does not denounce or warn against cooperative arrangements in this reading (as he does in Reading 10.3), neither does he recognize cooperation as a possibility. His message is that of *realpolitik* – in inter-organizational relationships, conflict and power are the name of the game.

Because Porter's reading is already included in Chapter 5, another classic, 'Collaborate with Your Competitors – and Win', has been selected as Reading 7.1 for this chapter to represent the discrete organization perspective. In this piece, the authors, Gary Hamel, Yves Doz and C.K. Prahalad, basically take the same stance as Porter, in assuming that inter-firm relations are largely competitive and governed by power and calculation. However, while Porter makes little mention of, or is apprehensive about, collaboration with other organizations, Hamel, Doz and Prahalad see collaboration as a useful tool for improving the firm's competitive profile. They argue that alliances with competitors 'can strengthen both companies against outsiders even if it weakens one partner vis-à-vis the other', and therefore that the net result can be positive. Yet they emphasize that companies should not be naive about the real nature of alliances – 'collaboration is competition in a different form'. An alliance is 'a constantly evolving bargain', in which each firm will be fending

TABLE 7.1   Discrete organization versus embedded organization perspective

	Discrete organization perspective	Embedded organization perspective
Emphasis on	Competition over cooperation	Cooperation over competition
Preferred position	Independence	Interdependence
Environment structure	Discrete organizations (atomistic)	Embedded organizations (networked)
Firm boundaries	Distinct and defended	Fuzzy and open
Inter-organizational relations	Arm's-length and transactional	Close and structural
Interaction outcomes	Mainly zero-sum (win/lose)	Mainly positive-sum (win/win)
Interaction based on	Bargaining power and calculation	Trust and reciprocity
Network level strategy	No	Yes
Use of collaboration	Temporary coalitions (tactical alliance)	Durable partnerships (strategic alliance)
Collaborative arrangements	Limited, well-defined, contract-based	Broad, open, relationship-based

for itself, trying to learn as much as possible from the other, while attempting to limit the partner's access to its knowledge and skills. The authors advise firms to precede cautiously with alliances, only when they have clear objectives of what they wish to learn from their allies, a well-developed capacity to learn, and defenses against their allies' probing of their skills and technologies. While Hamel, Doz and Prahalad only focus on horizontal relationships in this reading, their message is similar to that of Porter – competition in the environment is paramount and cooperation is merely an opportunistic move in the overall competitive game.

As representative of the embedded organization perspective, an article by Gianni Lorenzoni and Charles Baden-Fuller has been selected for Reading 7.2, entitled 'Creating a Strategic Center to Manage a Web of Partners'. Lorenzoni and Baden-Fuller are particularly interested in how companies structure their vertical relationships, balancing pressures for competition and cooperation. In their view, where a group of firms works together closely, they can form a 'virtual company'. This type of network can benefit from most of the advantages of being a large vertically integrated company, while avoiding most of the pitfalls of integration. But Lorenzoni and Baden-Fuller articulate that it is necessary for a network of firms to have a strategic center that can act as builder and coordinator. As builder, the strategic center can deliberately design and assemble the network components, and as coordinator it can regulate activities and resolve disputes. The authors carry on to specify the conditions under which a network of firms can be an advantageous organizational form and what is required to make them work. Overall, their main message is that durable partnerships between multiple firms are not easy, but if this interdependence can be managed well, it can give the group a strong competitive edge against others.

Reading 7.3, 'Coevolution in Business Ecosystems', by James Moore, is intended to further detail a key aspect of the debate, which both perspectives make important assumptions about – the nature of the business environment. This reading is from Moore's bestselling book *The Death of Competition*, in which he places the paradox of competition and cooperation in the broader context of 'business ecosystems'. He defines a business ecosystem as a part of the business environment where a variety of firms co-exist with one another and co-evolve on the basis of their ongoing interaction. He explains the functioning of a business ecosystem by drawing a parallel with biological ecosystems – plants and animals cannot be understood in isolation, as they co-evolve with one another in an endless cycle of change and selection. So too, the success or failure of companies cannot be understood without understanding how they have been able to nestle into the business ecosystem and how well the entire system is doing. Great companies, like great animal species, will still face extinction if their ecosystem goes into decline. Similarly, companies that want to create a new market must recognize that they actually need to create a new business ecosystem, with a lush variety of suppliers, distributors, service-providers and customers. If a firm only 'plants' its new product without engendering a broader ecosystem, it will be just as successful as a new species of tropical tree in the desert. Moore's point is that you should try to 'understand the economic systems evolving around you and find ways to contribute'. He concludes that 'competitive advantage stems principally from . . . cooperative, co-evolving relationships with a network of other contributors to the overall economic scene'. In other words, cooperation and systems level thinking are essential to the strategist – however, not to substitute competitive behavior, but rather to complement it.

Reading 7.4, 'How to Make Strategic Alliances Work', by Jeffrey Dyer, Prashant Kale and Harbir Singh, does exactly what its title suggests – it gives a thorough run down of the necessary management systems and activities needed to make strategic alliances work. This reading has been added to serve as starting point for a discussion on how to manage cooperative relationships in practice. The main argument put forward by Dyer, Kale and Singh is that managing alliances is an essential expertise, but difficult to master, and therefore that firms should build a dedicated strategic alliance function – 'a vice president or director of strategic alliance with his or her own staff and resources'. Not only can such a department help to build up the necessary know-how, but it can also provide internal coordination, assist in setting strategic priorities, draw on resources across the company and ensure clear accountability. Furthermore, having a dedicated alliance function offers internal legitimacy to alliances and signals commitment to external partners and interested parties. Dyer, Kale and Singh enthusiastically conclude that the company that 'builds a successful dedicated strategic alliance function will reap substantial rewards'. Yet, the question open for discussion is whether managing strategic alliances requires a new staff department, or whether alternative organizational forms would be better – for instance, having alliance responsibility dispersed among the line managers who need to make the relationships function 'on the work floor'.

READING
7.1

Collaborate with your competitors – and win

By Gary Hamel, Yves Doz and C.K. Prahalad[1]

Collaboration between competitors is in fashion. General Motors and Toyota assemble automobiles, Siemens and Philips develop semiconductors, Canon supplies photocopiers to Kodak, France's Thomson and Japan's JVC manufacture videocassette recorders. But the spread of what we call 'competitive collaboration' – joint ventures, outsourcing agreements, product licensings, cooperative research – has triggered unease about the long-term consequences. A strategic alliance can strengthen both companies against outsiders even as it weakens one partner *vis-à-vis* the other. In particular, alliances between Asian companies and western rivals seem to work against the western partner. Cooperation becomes a low-cost route for new competitors to gain technology and market access.

Yet the case for collaboration is stronger than ever. It takes so much money to develop new products and to penetrate new markets that few companies can go it alone in every situation. ICL, the British computer company, could not have developed its current generation of mainframes without Fujitsu. Motorola needs Toshiba's distribution capacity to break into the Japanese semiconductor market. Time is another critical factor. Alliances can provide shortcuts for western companies racing to improve their production efficiency and quality control.

We have spent more than five years studying the inner workings of 15 strategic alliances and monitoring scores of others. Our research involves cooperative ventures between competitors from the United States and Japan, Europe and Japan, and the United States and Europe. We did not judge the success or failure of each partnership by its longevity – a common mistake when evaluating strategic alliances – but by the shifts in competitive strength on each side. We focused on how companies use competitive collaboration to enhance their internal skills and technologies while they guard against transferring competitive advantages to ambitious partners.

There is no immutable law that strategic alliances *must* be a windfall for Japanese or Korean partners. Many western companies do give away more than they gain – but that's because they enter partnerships without knowing what it takes to win. Companies that benefit most from competitive collaboration adhere to a set of simple but powerful principles.

- Collaboration is competition in a different form. Successful companies never forget that their new partners may be out to disarm them. They enter alliances with clear strategic objectives, and they also understand how their partners' objectives will affect their success.

- Harmony is not the most important measure of success. Indeed, occasional conflict may be the best evidence of mutually beneficial collaboration. Few alliances remain win-win undertakings forever. A partner may be content even as it unknowingly surrenders core skills.

- Cooperation has limits. Companies must defend against competitive compromise. A strategic alliance is a constantly evolving bargain whose real terms go beyond the legal agreement or the aims of top management. What information gets traded is determined day to day, often by engineers and operating managers. Successful companies inform employees at all levels about what skills and technologies are off-limits to the partner and monitor what the partner requests and receives.

- Learning from partners is paramount. Successful companies view each alliance as a window on their partners' broad capabilities. They use the alliance to build skills in areas outside the formal agreement and systematically diffuse new knowledge throughout their organizations.

[1]Source: Reprinted by permission of *Harvard Business Review*. From 'Collaborate with your Competitors – and Win' by G. Hamel, Y.L. Doz and C.K. Prahalad, January–February 1989, Vol. 67. © 1989 by the Harvard Business School Publishing Corporation, all rights reserved.

Why collaborate?

Using an alliance with a competitor to acquire new technologies or skills is not devious. It reflects the commitment and capacity of each partner to absorb the skills of the other. We found that in every case in which a Japanese company emerged from an alliance stronger than its western partner, the Japanese company had made a greater effort to learn.

Strategic intent is an essential ingredient in the commitment to learning. The willingness of Asian companies to enter alliances represents a change in competitive tactics, not competitive goals. NEC, for example, has used a series of collaborative ventures to enhance its technology and product competences. NEC is the only company in the world with a leading position in telecommunications, computers, and semiconductors – despite its investing less in research and development (R&D) (as a percentage of revenues) than competitors like Texas Instruments, Northern Telecom, and L.M. Ericsson. Its string of partnerships, most notably with Honeywell, allowed NEC to leverage its in-house R&D over the last two decades.

Western companies, on the other hand, often enter alliances to avoid investments. They are more interested in reducing the costs and risks of entering new businesses or markets than in acquiring new skills. A senior US manager offered this analysis of his company's venture with a Japanese rival: 'We complement each other well – our distribution capability and their manufacturing skill. I see no reason to invest upstream if we can find a secure source of product. This is a comfortable relationship for us.'

An executive from this company's Japanese partner offered a different perspective: 'When it is necessary to collaborate, I go to my employees and say, "This is bad, I wish we had these skills ourselves. Collaboration is second best. But I will feel worse if after four years we do not know how to do what our partner knows how to do." We must digest their skills.'

The problem here is not that the US company wants to share investment risk (its Japanese partner does too) but that the US company has no ambition beyond avoidance. When the commitment to learning is so one-sided, collaboration invariably leads to competitive compromise.

Many so-called alliances between western companies and their Asian rivals are little more than sophisticated outsourcing arrangements. General Motors buys cars and components from Korea's Daewoo. Siemens buys computers from Fujitsu. Apple buys laser printer engines from Canon. The traffic is almost entirely one

way. These original equipment manufacturer (OEM) deals offer Asian partners a way to capture investment initiative from western competitors and displace customer-competitors from value-creating activities. In many cases this goal meshes with that of the western partner: to regain competitiveness quickly and with minimum effort.

Consider the joint venture between Rover, the British automaker, and Honda. Some 25 years ago, Rover's forerunners were world leaders in small car design. Honda had not even entered the automobile business. But in the mid-1970s, after failing to penetrate foreign markets, Rover turned to Honda for technology and product development support. Rover has used the alliance to avoid investments to design and build new cars. Honda has cultivated skills in European styling and marketing as well as multinational manufacturing. There is little doubt which company will emerge stronger over the long term.

Troubled laggards like Rover often strike alliances with surging latecomers like Honda. Having fallen behind in a key skills area (in this case, manufacturing small cars), the laggard attempts to compensate for past failures. The latecomer uses the alliance to close a specific skills gap (in this case, learning to build cars for a regional market). But a laggard that forges a partnership for short-term gain may find itself in a dependency spiral: as it contributes fewer and fewer distinctive skills, it must reveal more and more of its internal operations to keep the partner interested. For the weaker company, the issue shifts from, 'Should we collaborate?' to 'With whom should we collaborate?' to 'How do we keep our partner interested as we lose the advantages that made us attractive to them in the first place?'

There's a certain paradox here. When both partners are equally intent on internalizing the other's skills, distrust and conflict may spoil the alliance and threaten its very survival. That's one reason joint ventures between Korean and Japanese companies have been few and tempestuous. Neither side wants to 'open the kimono.' Alliances seem to run most smoothly when one partner is intent on learning and the other is intent on avoidance – in essence, when one partner is willing to grow dependent on the other. But running smoothly is not the point; the point is for a company to emerge from an alliance more competitive than when it entered it.

One partner does not always have to give up more than it gains to ensure the survival of an alliance. There are certain conditions under which mutual gain is possible, at least for a time:

- The partners' strategic goals converge while their competitive goals diverge. That is, each partner allows for the other's continued prosperity in the shared business. Philips and Du Pont collaborate to develop and manufacture compact discs, but neither side invades the other's market. There is a clear upstream/downstream division of effort.

- The size and market power of both partners is modest compared with industry leaders. This forces each side to accept that mutual dependence may have to continue for many years. Long-term collaboration may be so critical to both partners that neither will risk antagonizing the other by an overtly competitive bid to appropriate skills or competences. Fujitsu's 1 to 5 size disadvantage with IBM means it will be a long time, if ever, before Fujitsu can break away from its foreign partners and go it alone.

- Each partner believes it can learn from the other and at the same time limit access to proprietary skills. JVC and Thomson, both of whom make VCRs, know that they are trading skills. But the two companies are looking for very different things. Thomson needs product technology and manufacturing prowess; JVC needs to learn how to succeed in the fragmented European market. Both sides believe there is an equitable chance for gain.

How to build secure defenses

For collaboration to succeed, each partner must contribute something distinctive: basic research, product development skills, manufacturing capacity, access to distribution. The challenge is to share enough skills to create advantage *vis-à-vis* companies outside the alliance while preventing a wholesale transfer of core skills to the partner. This is a very thin line to walk. Companies must carefully select what skills and technologies they pass to their partners. They must develop safeguards against unintended, informal transfers of information. The goal is to limit the transparency of their operations.

The type of skill a company contributes is an important factor in how easily its partner can internalize the skills. The potential for transfer is greatest when a partner's contribution is easily transported (in engineering drawings, on computer tapes, or in the heads of a few technical experts); easily interpreted (it can be reduced to commonly understood equations or symbols); and easily absorbed (the skill or competence is independent of any particular cultural context).

Western companies face an inherent disadvantage because their skills are generally more vulnerable to transfer. The magnet that attracts so many companies to alliances with Asian competitors is their manufacturing excellence – a competence that is less transferable than most. Just-in-time inventory systems and quality circles can be imitated, but this is like pulling a few threads out of an oriental carpet. Manufacturing excellence is a complex web of employee training, integration with suppliers, statistical process controls, employee involvement, value engineering, and design for manufacture. It is difficult to extract such a subtle competence in any way but a piecemeal fashion.

So companies must take steps to limit transparency. One approach is to limit the scope of the formal agreement. It might cover a single technology rather than an entire range of technologies; part of a product line rather than the entire line; distribution in a limited number of markets or for a limited period of time. The objective is to circumscribe a partner's opportunities to learn.

Moreover, agreements should establish specific performance requirements. Motorola, for example, takes an incremental, incentive-based approach to technology transfer in its venture with Toshiba. The agreement calls for Motorola to release its microprocessor technology incrementally as Toshiba delivers on its promise to increase Motorola's penetration in the Japanese semiconductor market. The greater Motorola's market share, the greater Toshiba's access to Motorola's technology.

Many of the skills that migrate between companies are not covered in the formal terms of collaboration. Top management puts together strategic alliances and sets the legal parameters for exchange. But what actually gets traded is determined by day-to-day interactions of engineers, marketers, and product developers: who says what to whom, who gets access to what facilities, who sits on what joint committees. The most important deals ('I'll share this with you if you share that with me') may be struck four or five organizational levels below where the deal was signed. Here lurks the greatest risk of unintended transfers of important skills.

Consider one technology-sharing alliance between European and Japanese competitors. The European company valued the partnership as a way to acquire a specific technology. The Japanese company considered it a window on its partner's entire range of competences and interacted with a broad spectrum of its partner's marketing and product development staff. The company mined each contact for as much information as possible.

For example, every time the European company requested a new feature on a product being sourced from its partner, the Japanese company asked for detailed customer and competitor analyses to justify the request. Over time, it developed a sophisticated picture of the European market that would assist its own entry strategy. The technology acquired by the European partner through the formal agreement had a useful life of three to five years. The competitive insights acquired informally by the Japanese company will probably endure longer.

Limiting unintended transfers at the operating level requires careful attention to the role of gatekeepers, the people who control what information flows to a partner. A gatekeeper can be effective only if there are a limited number of gateways through which a partner can access people and facilities. Fujitsu's many partners all go through a single office, the 'collaboration section,' to request information and assistance from different divisions. This way the company can monitor and control access to critical skills and technologies.

We studied one partnership between European and US competitors that involved several divisions of each company. While the US company could only access its partner through a single gateway, its partner had unfettered access to all participating divisions. The European company took advantage of its free rein. If one division refused to provide certain information, the European partner made the same request of another division. No single manager in the US company could tell how much information had been transferred or was in a position to piece together patterns in the requests.

Collegiality is a prerequisite for collaborative success. But *too much* collegiality should set off warning bells to senior managers. CEOs or division presidents should expect occasional complaints from their counterparts about the reluctance of lower level employees to share information. That's a sign that the gatekeepers are doing their jobs. And senior management should regularly debrief operating personnel to find out what information the partner is requesting and what requests are being granted.

Limiting unintended transfers ultimately depends on employee loyalty and self-discipline. This was a real issue for many of the western companies we studied. In their excitement and pride over technical achievements, engineering staffs sometimes shared information that top management considered sensitive. Japanese engineers were less likely to share proprietary information.

There are a host of cultural and professional reasons for the relative openness of western technicians.

Japanese engineers and scientists are more loyal to their company than to their profession. They are less steeped in the open give-and-take of university research since they receive much of their training from employers. They consider themselves team members more than individual scientific contributors. As one Japanese manager noted, 'We don't feel any need to reveal what we know. It is not an issue of pride for us. We're glad to sit and listen. If we're patient we usually learn what we want to know.'

Controlling unintended transfers may require restricting access to facilities as well as to people. Companies should declare sensitive laboratories and factories off-limits to their partners. Better yet, they might house the collaborative venture in an entirely new facility. IBM is building a special site in Japan where Fujitsu can review its forthcoming mainframe software before deciding whether to license it. IBM will be able to control exactly what Fujitsu sees and what information leaves the facility.

Finally, which country serves as 'home' to the alliance affects transparency. If the collaborative team is located near one partner's major facilities, the other partner will have more opportunities to learn – but less control over what information gets traded. When the partner houses, feeds, and looks after engineers and operating managers, there is a danger they will 'go native.' Expatriate personnel need frequent visits from headquarters as well as regular furloughs home.

Enhance the capacity to learn

Whether collaboration leads to competitive surrender or revitalization depends foremost on what employees believe the purpose of the alliance to be. It is self-evident: to learn, one must want to learn. Western companies won't realize the full benefits of competitive collaboration until they overcome an arrogance borne of decades of leadership. In short, western companies must be more receptive.

We asked a senior executive in a Japanese electronics company about the perception that Japanese companies learn more from their foreign partners than vice versa. 'Our western partners approach us with the attitude of teachers,' he told us. 'We are quite happy with this, because we have the attitude of students.'

Learning begins at the top. Senior management must be committed to enhancing their companies' skills as well as to avoiding financial risk. But most learning takes place at the lower levels of an alliance. Operating employees not only represent the front lines in an effective defense but also play a vital role in acquiring knowledge. They must be well briefed on the partner's strengths and weaknesses and understand how acquiring particular skills will bolster their company's competitive position.

This is already standard practice among Asian companies. We accompanied a Japanese development engineer on a tour through a partner's factory. This engineer dutifully took notes on plant layout, the number of production stages, the rate at which the line was running, and the number of employees. He recorded all this despite the fact that he had no manufacturing responsibility in his own company, and that the alliance didn't encompass joint manufacturing. Such dedication greatly enhances learning.

Collaboration doesn't always provide an opportunity to fully internalize a partner's skills. Yet just acquiring new and more precise benchmarks of a partner's performance can be of great value. A new benchmark can provoke a thorough review of internal performance levels and may spur a round of competitive innovation. Asking questions like, 'Why do their semiconductor logic designs have fewer errors than ours?' and 'Why are they investing in this technology and we're not?' may provide the incentive for a vigorous catch-up program.

Competitive benchmarking is a tradition in most of the Japanese companies we studied. It requires many of the same skills associated with competitor analysis: systematically calibrating performance against external targets; learning to use rough estimates to determine where a competitor (or partner) is better, faster, or cheaper; translating those estimates into new internal targets; and recalibrating to establish the rate of improvement in a competitor's performance. The great advantage of competitive collaboration is that proximity makes benchmarking easier.

Indeed, some analysts argue that one of Toyota's motivations in collaborating with GM in the much-publicized NUMMI venture is to gauge the quality of GM's manufacturing technology. GM's top manufacturing people get a close look at Toyota, but the reverse is true as well. Toyota may be learning whether its giant US competitor is capable of closing the productivity gap with Japan.

Competitive collaboration also provides a way of getting close enough to rivals to predict how they will behave when the alliance unravels or runs its course. How does the partner respond to price changes? How does it measure and reward executives? How does it prepare to launch a new product? By revealing a competitor's management orthodoxies, collaboration can increase the chances of success in future head-to-head battles.

Knowledge acquired from a competitor-partner is only valuable after it is diffused through the organization. Several companies we studied had established internal clearinghouses to collect and disseminate information. The collaborations manager at one Japanese company regularly made the rounds of all employees involved in alliances. He identified what information had been collected by whom and then passed it on to appropriate departments. Another company held regular meetings where employees shared new knowledge and determined who was best positioned to acquire additional information.

Proceed with care – but proceed

After World War II, Japanese and Korean companies entered alliances with western rivals from weak positions. But they worked steadfastly toward independence. In the early 1960s, NEC's computer business was one-quarter the size of Honeywell's, its primary foreign partner. It took only two decades for NEC to grow larger than Honeywell, which eventually sold its computer operations to an alliance between NEC and Group Bull of France. The NEC experience demonstrates that dependence on a foreign partner doesn't automatically condemn a company to also-ran status. Collaboration may sometimes be unavoidable; surrender is not.

Managers are too often obsessed with the ownership structure of an alliance. Whether a company controls 51 percent or 49 percent of a joint venture may be much less important than the rate at which each partner learns from the other. Companies that are confident of their ability to learn may even prefer some ambiguity in the alliance's legal structure. Ambiguity creates more potential to acquire skills and technologies. The challenge for western companies is not to write tighter legal agreements but to become better learners.

Running away from collaboration is no answer. Even the largest western companies can no longer outspend their global rivals. With leadership in many industries shifting toward the East, companies in the United States and Europe must become good borrowers – much like Asian companies did in the 1960s and 1970s. Competitive renewal depends on building new process capabilities and winning new product and technology battles. Collaboration can be a low-cost strategy for doing both.

Creating a strategic center to manage a web of partners

READING
7.2

By Gianni Lorenzoni and Charles Baden-Fuller[1]

Strategic alliances and inter-firm networks have been gaining popularity with many firms for their lower overhead costs, increased responsiveness and flexibility, and greater efficiency of operations. Networks that are *strategically guided* are often fast-growing and on the leading edge. In 10 years, Sun Microsystems (founded in 1982) grew to $3.2 billion in sales and $284 million in profits. This remarkable growth has been achieved by Sun's strategic direction of a web of alliances.

Few would expect such rapid growth and technological success in an older and mature industry such as textiles. Yet Benetton, the famous global textile empire, is in many ways like Sun. Founded in 1964, it had by 1991 achieved more than $2 billion in sales and $235 million in profits. Benetton is widely admired in Europe and the Far East for its rapid growth and ability to change the industry's rules of the game through its strategy of 'mass fashion to young people.'

What creates and guides the successful, innovative, leading-edge interfirm network? Most research into inter-firm networks has emphasized how they can reconcile the flexibility of market relationships with the long-term commitment of hierarchically centralized management. Although all networks reflect the conscious decisions of some managers, it is becoming increasingly apparent that those networks that are not guided strategically by a 'center' are unable to meet the demanding challenges of today's markets. In this reading, we are concerned with those strategic centers that have had a very significant impact on their sectors, especially as regards innovation. They are not confined to just a few isolated sectors, but have been observed in a wide variety of circumstances, some of which are listed in Table 7.2.1.

In this reading, we examine three dimensions of the strategic center:

- as a creator of value for its partners;
- as leader, rule setter, and capability builder;
- as simultaneously structuring and strategizing.

The role of the strategic center

The strategic center (or central firm) plays a critical role as a creator of value. The main features of this role are:

- Strategic outsourcing. Outsource and share with more partners than the normal broker and traditional firm. Require partners to be more than doers, expect them to be problemsolvers and initiators.

- Capability. Develop the core skills and competencies of partners to make them more effective and competitive. Force members of the network to share their expertise with others in the network, and with the central firm.

- Technology. Borrow ideas from others which are developed and exploited as a means of creating and mastering new technologies.

- Competition. Explain to partners that the principle dimension of competition is between value chains and networks. The network is only as strong as its weakest link. Encourage rivalry between firms inside the network, in a positive manner.

From subcontracting to strategic outsourcing

All firms that act as brokers or operate networks play only a limited role in undertaking the production and delivery of the good or service to the markets in which the system is involved. What distinguishes central firms is both the extent to which they subcontract, and the way that they collect together partners who contribute to the whole system and whose roles are clearly defined in a positive and creative way.

Many organizations see their sub-contractors and partners as passive doers or actors in their quest for competitive advantage. They typically specify exactly what they want the partners to do, and leave little to the creative skills of others. They reserve a special creative role for only a few 'critical' partners. In strategic net-

[1]Source: This article © 1995, by the Regents of the University of California. Adapted from the *California Management Review*, Vol. 37, No. 3. By permission of the Regents. All rights reserved.

TABLE 7.2.1   Some central firms and their activities

Name of company and its industry	Activities of strategic center	Activities of the network
Apple (computers)	■ Hardware design ■ Software design ■ Distribution	■ Principal subcontractors manufacture ■ 3,000 software developers
Benetton (apparel)	■ Designing collections ■ Selected production ■ Developing new technology systems	■ 6,000 shops ■ 400 subcontractors in production ■ Principal joint ventures in Japan, Egypt, India, and others
Corning (glass, medical products and optical fibers)	■ Technology innovation ■ Production	■ More than 30 joint ventures world-wide
Genentech (biotechnology/DNA)	■ Technology innovation	■ J.V.s with drug companies for production and distribution, licensing in from universities
McDonald's (fast food)	■ Marketing ■ Prototyping technology and systems	■ 9,000 outlets, joint ventures in many foreign countries
McKesson (drug distribution)	■ Systems ■ Marketing ■ Logistics ■ Consulting advice	■ Thousands of retail drug outlets, and ties with drug companies, and government institutions
Nike (shoes and sportswear)	■ Design ■ Marketing	■ Principal subcontractors world-wide
Nintendo (video games)	■ Design ■ Prototyping ■ Marketing	■ 30 principal hardware subcontractors ■ 150 software developers
Sun (computers and computer systems)	■ Innovation of technology ■ Software ■ Assembly	■ Licensor/licensees for software and hardware
Toyota (automobiles)	■ Design ■ Assembly ■ Marketing	■ Principal subcontractors for complex components ■ Second tier for other components ■ Network of agents for distribution

works, it is the norm rather than an exception for partners to be innovators.

Typically each of these partnerships extends beyond a simple subcontracting relationship. Strategic centers expect their partners to do more than follow the rules, they expect them to be creative. For example, Apple worked with Canon and Adobe to design and create a laser jet printer which then gave Apple an important position in its industry. In all the cases we studied, the strategic center looked to the partners to be creative in solving problems and being proactive in the relationships. They demanded more – and obtained more –

from their partners than did their less effective counterparts that used traditional subcontracting.

Developing the competencies of the partners

How should the central firm see its own competencies *vis-à-vis* its partners? Most writers ague that current competencies should guide future decisions. Many have warned of the dangers in allowing the other partners in a joint venture or alliance to exploit the skills of the host organization. For example, Reich and Mankin (1986) noted that joint ventures between Japanese and US firms often result in one side (typically the Japanese) gaining at the expense of the other. Bleeke and Ernst (1991) found similar disappointment in that in only 51 percent of the cases they studied did both firms gain from alliances. In a study of cross border alliances, Hamel (1991) found that the unwary partner typically found that its competencies were 'hollowed out' and that its collaborator became a more powerful competitor. Badaracco (1991) examined the experiences of GM and IBM, who have signed multiple agreements, and explored the difficulties they face.

Traditional brokers and large integrated firms do not 'hand out' core skills, but the central firms we studied have ignored this advice and won. While keeping a very few skills and assets to themselves, the central firms were remarkable in their desire to transfer skill and knowledge adding value to their partners. Typically, they set out to build up the partners' ability and competencies. At Benetton, site selection and sample selection were skills which Benetton would offer to the new retail partners, either directly or through the agents. Skill transfers were also evident in the machinery networks and at Apple.

Nike brings its partners to its research site at Beaverton to show them the latest developments in materials, product designs, technologies, and markets. Sometimes the partners share some of the costs, but the prime benefit is to shorten cycle times and create a more vibrant system. Toyota's subcontractors may receive training from Toyota and are helped in their development of expertise in solving problems pertaining to their particular component. Not only does this encourage them to deliver better quality parts to the Toyota factories, but it also allows the Toyota system to generate an advantage over other car manufacturers.

In contrast to these companies, the less successful organizations we studied did not have groups of specialists to transfer knowledge to partners – nor, it seems, did they appreciate its importance. They did not enlist all their suppliers and customers to fight a common enemy. Moreover, their experiences did not encourage exploration of this approach. They spoke of past difficulties in alliances. Skill transfers between parties did not always result in mutual benefit. One defense contractor explained that their experience of skill transfers nearly always meant that the partner was strengthened and became a stronger rival.

Borrowing–developing–lending new ideas

While all firms bring in new ideas from outside, the central firms we studied have adopted an unusual and aggressive perspective in this sphere. They scan their horizons for all sorts of opportunities and utilize a formula we call *borrow–develop–lend*. 'Borrow' means that the strategic center deliberately buys or licenses some existing technological ideas from a third party; 'develop' means that it takes these outside ideas and adds value by developing them further in its own organization. This commercialization can then be exploited or 'lent' with great rapidity through its stellar system, creating new adjuncts to leverage to the greatest advantage. Borrowing ideas, which are subsequently developed and exploited, stretches the organization and forces it to grow its capabilities and competencies. It demands a new way of thinking.

In the Italian packaging machinery sector, lead producers follow this strategy. They borrow designs of a new machine from specialist designers or customers. These designs are then prototyped. From these prototypes, small and medium-sized partners or specialists often improve the design in a unique way, such as improving the flows and linkages. The focal firm then re-purchases and exploits the modified design, licensing to producers for the final development and marketing phase. Thus we see a 'to-and-fro' pattern of development between the central firm and its many partners.

Sun also used the borrow–develop–lend approach in their project to build a new workstation delivering 'more power with less cost.' They borrowed existing technology from other parties, recombined and developed them further inside Sun, and then licensed them to third parties for development and sale under the Sun brand.

The borrow–develop–lend principle helps the central firm reduce the cost of development, make progress more quickly, and, most importantly, undertake projects which would normally lie outside its scope. This approach contrasts with the procedures used by other large firms. Although these firms may buy ideas from other sources, large firms usually have a slower pace of development and rarely match the speed of exploitation achieved through networking and re-lending the idea to third parties. The strategic center seems to avoid the *not-invented-here* syndrome, where innovations and ideas are rejected because they are not internally created and developed.

From the view of independent inventors, the strategic center is an attractive organization with which to do business. The central firms have a track record of rapid commercialization (usually offering large incentives to those with ideas). They emphasize moving quickly from ideas to market by a simultaneous learning process with partners, thereby offering a competitive advantage over other developers. Finally, the willingness to involve others means rapid diffusion with fast payback, thus lessening the risks.

Perceptions of the competitive process

Firms in the same industry experience varying degrees of competitive rivalry. The joint venture, formal agreements, or the use of cross shareholdings are mechanisms used to create common ties, encourage a common view, and unite firms against others in the industry. Strategic centers also create this sense of cooperation across competing enterprises.

Competitive success requires the integration of multiple capabilities (e.g. innovation, productivity, quality, responsiveness to customers) across internal and external organizational boundaries. Such integration is a big challenge to most organizations. Strategic centers rise to this challenge and create a sense of common purpose across multiple levels in the value chain and across different sectors. They achieve a combination of

specialized capability and large-scale integration at the same time, despite the often destructive rivalry between buyers and customers. Strategic purchasing partnerships are commonly used to moderate this rivalry, but few firms are able to combine both horizontal and vertical linkages.

In building up their partner's capabilities and competencies, strategic centers convey an unusual perspective to their partners on the nature of the competitive process. This perspective permits the partners to take a holistic view of the network, seeing the collective as a unit that can achieve competitive advantage. In this respect, the whole network acts like a complex integrated firm spanning many markets.

Table 7.2.2 illustrates how the actions of the strategic center differ from other organizations. Chain stores are a good example of organizations that coordinate activities across many actors, yet at a single stage of the value chain. In contrast, the narrowly defined, vertically integrated firm coordinates across many stages but not across many markets or actors. Only the strategic center and the large multi-market, vertically integrated organization are able to coordinate across many markets and many stages of the value chain.

Beyond the hollow organization

Although the strategic center outsources more activities than most organizations, it is not hollow. Unlike the traditional broker that is merely a glorified arranger, the central firms we studied understand that they have to develop some critical core competencies. These competencies are, in general, quite different from those stressed by most managers in

TABLE 7.2.2   Different kinds of competition across sectors and stages of the value chain

	Single units within the sector	Multiple units within the sector or across related sectors
Multiple stages of the value chain	■ Vertical integration; or ■ Value-added partnerships	■ Strategic centers and their webs of partners; or ■ Large integrated multi-market organizations
Single stages of the value chain	■ Traditional adversarial firm	■ Chain stores; or ■ Simple networks

traditional firms. The agenda for the central firm consists of:

- The idea. Creating a vision in which partners play a critical role.
- The investment. A strong brand image and effective systems and support.
- The climate. Creating an atmosphere of trust and reciprocity.
- The partners. Developing mechanisms for attracting and selecting partners.

Sharing a business idea

Most of the central firms we studied are small, lean, and focused operations. They employ comparatively few people and are very selective in what they do. Yet, they have an unusual ability to conceptualize a business idea that can be shared not only internally, but with other partners. In the case of Benetton, this idea has a few key elements such as: mass fashion for young people, and the notion of a strategic network to orchestrate and fulfill this vision. In food-machinery, the key idea of the central firms is to solve the client's problems, rather than selling existing competencies, while new partners are developed in response to customer needs – a novel notion in this sector. These simple ideas are not easy to create or sustain.

These ideas have been able to capture the imagination of the employees and their partners. They also encapsulate strategy and so contain, in the language of Prahalad and Hamel (1990, Reading 6.2 in this book), the features of a clear strategic intent. Common to all the business ideas we studied, there is a notion of partnership which includes the creation of a learning culture and the promotion of systems experiments so as to outpace rival competing organizations. The strategic centers view their role as one of leading and orchestrating their systems. Their distinctive characteristics lie in their ability to perceive the full business idea and understand the role of all the different parties in many different locations across the whole value chain. The managers in the strategic center have a dream and they orchestrate others to fulfill that dream.

This vision of the organization is not just an idea in the minds of a few managers, it is a feature that is shared throughout the organization. Many of the strategic centers we studied admit that their visions have emerged over time, they are not the work of a moment. Their vision is dynamic, for as their network grows and as the environment changes, the organizational vision also changes. This is not the case in the less successful alliances. They showed the typical characteristics of most organizations, multifaceted views of the world and a less-than-clear expression of their vision.

Clearly, vision is reinforced by success. The ability of central firms to deliver profits and growth for the partners helps cement a vision in their minds and makes their claims credible. It creates a cycle where success breeds clarity, which in turn helps breed more success.

Brand power and other support

To maintain the balance of power in the network, all central firms retain certain activities. The control of the brand names and the development of the systems that integrate the network are two activities that give the organization a pivotal role and allow it to exercise power over the system.

Some of the firms we observed were involved in consumer markets where branding is important. The brand name, owned by the central firm, was promoted by the activities of the partners, who saw the brand as a shared resource. They were encouraged to ensure its success, and quite often these efforts helped the brand become famous in a short period of time. While the brand and marketing are not so vital in producer goods markets, they are still important – and the strategic center neglects these at its peril. Its importance is highlighted by the experiences of one of the less successful organizations we studied. This aerospace firm had problems as a result of the inability of its members to relinquish many of the aspects of marketing to a single central firm.

To retain its power, the central firm must ensure that the information between partners flows freely and is not filtered. Communication is a costly activity, and developing effective communication systems is always the responsibility of the strategic center. These systems are not only electronically based, but include all other methods of communication. Often there is a style for meeting among the partners, which is set and monitored by the central firm. The quality of information is a key requirement if the central firm is to mandate effectively the stream of activities scattered among different firms.

Trust and reciprocity

Leveraging the skills of partners is easy to conceive but hard to implement. The difficulties occur because it takes many partners operating effectively to make the system work, but the negative behavior of only a few can bring the whole system to a halt. The strategic vision requires all its members to contribute all the time without fail. This is a considerable demand. The typical organizational response to such a need is to circumscribe the contracts with outsiders in a tight legalistic manner. But this is not always wise; contract making and policing can be difficult and expensive. Formal contracts are relatively inflexible and are suitable only where the behavior is easy to describe and is relatively inflexible. But the relationships are creative and flexible and so very difficult to capture and enforce contractually.

The approach of the central firms we studied is to develop a sense of trust and reciprocity in the system. This trust and reciprocity is a dynamic concept and it can be very tight. The tightness is apparent in each party agreeing to perform its known obligations. This aspect has similarities to contracts in the sense that obligations are precisely understood. But Anglo-Saxon contracts are typically limited in the sense that partners are not expected to go beyond the contract. In contrast, in a network perspective, the behavior is prescribed for the unknown, each promising to work in a particular manner to resolve future challenges and difficulties as they arise. This means that each partner will promise to deliver what is expected, and that future challenges will also be addressed positively. If there are uncertainties and difficulties in the relationships, these will be resolved after the work is done. If one party goes beyond (in the positive sense) the traditional contract, others will remember and reciprocate at a later date.

Trust and reciprocity are complements, not substitutes, to other obligations. If partners do not subscribe to the trust system, they can hold the whole system hostage whenever they are asked to do something out of the ordinary, or even in the normal course of events. Such behavior will cause damage to all, and the system will break up. Only with trust can the system work in unison.

The Benetton franchising system is perhaps an extreme version of this trust system. In the continent of Europe, Benetton does not use legal contracts, rather it relies on the unwritten agreement. This, it claims, focuses everyone's attention on making the expectations clear. It also saves a great deal of time and expense. Many other strategic centers also rely on trust, but utilize contracts and formal controls as a complement. Central firms develop rules for settling disputes (for there will be disputes even in a trust system). The central firm also ensures that rewards are distributed in a manner which encourages partners to

reinforce the positive circle. Benetton has encountered limits to its approach in the US, where the cultural emphasis on law and contracts has come into conflict with Benetton's strategy.

In sharp contrast are the other less successful systems we studied. There, trust was used on a very limited scale, since most organizations had difficulty in getting partners to deliver even that which was promised. Broken promises and failed expectations were common in the defense systems. Very low anticipated expectations of partner reciprocity were a common feature of the Scottish network and appliance sectors. Most organizations believed that anything crucial had to be undertaken in-house.

Trust is delicate, and it needs fostering and underpinning. One of the ways in which positive behavior is encouraged is to ensure that the profit-sharing relationships give substantial rewards to the partners. None of the central firms we studied seeks to be the most profitable firm in the system; they are happy for others to take the bulk of the profit. In Benetton, a retailer may find his or her capital investment paid back in three years. In Corning, some partners have seen exceptional returns. This seemingly altruistic behavior, however, does not mean that the rewards to the central firm are small.

Partner selection

The central firms we studied recognize that creating success and a long-term perspective must begin with the partner selection process. In building a network, partners must be selected with great care. Initially, the central firms followed a pattern of trial and error, but following successful identification of the key points in the selection process, they became more deliberate. The many new styles of operation and new ways of doing things are not easy to grasp, and they are quite difficult to codify – especially at the early stages of the selection process. As time passes, a partner profile emerges together with a selection procedure aimed at creating the correct conditions for the relationships. These relationships require coordination among all the partners, a common long-term perspective, an acceptance of mutual adaptation, and incremental innovation.

When we looked at the details of the selection procedure, there was a difference between those central firms that had a few large partners and those that had many small-scale partners. In the case of the network composed of a few, large firm alliances, the selection criterion is typically based on careful strategic considerations. There is the question of matching capabilities and resources, as well as considerations of competition. However, most important are the organizational features based on a compatibility of management systems, decision processes, and perspectives – in short, a cultural fit.

The selection process must also be tempered by availability. Typically, there are few potential partners to fit the ideal picture. Perhaps it is for this reason that some Japanese and European firms start the process early on by deliberately spinning off some of their internal units to create potential partners. Typically these units will contain some of their best talents. However, these units will have a cultural affinity and a mutual understanding, which makes the partnership easier.

In the case of the large network composed of many small partners, the center acts as a developer of the community. Its managers must assume a different role. Apple called some of its managers 'evangelists' because they managed the relationships with 3,000 third-party developers. So that they could keep constant contact with them, they used images of the 'Figurehead' and the 'Guiding Light.'

Simultaneous structuring and strategizing

Of all the battles firms face, the most difficult is not the battle for position, nor is it even the battle between strong firms and weak firms following the same strategic approaches. Rather, it is the battle between firms adopting different strategies and different approaches to the market. In these battles, the winners are usually those who use fewer and different resources in novel combinations. The central firms we studied fit this category, for they have typically dominated their sectors by stretching and leveraging modest resources to great effect. In trying to understand these battles of stretch and leverage, others have stressed the technical achievements of central firms such as lean production, technical innovation, or flexible manufacturing and service delivery. To be sure, these advances are important and provide partial explanations for the success of Sun, Nintendo, Benetton, Apple, and others. Equally important, if not more important, are new ideas on the nature of strategizing and structuring. Strategizing is a shared process between the strategic center and its partners; structuring of the relationships between the partners goes hand in hand and is seen as a key part of the strategy.

Strategy conception and implementation of ideas is shared between central firms and their webs of partners. Here they differ from most conventional organizations, which neither share their conceptions of strategy with other organizations nor insist that their partners share their ideas with them in a constructive dialogue. While all firms form partnerships with some of their suppliers and customers, these linkages rarely involve sharing ideas systematically. Subcontracting relationships are usually deeper and more complex, and many firms share their notions of strategy with their subcontractors, but the sharing is nearly always limited. Alliances demand even greater levels of commitment and interchange, and it is common for firms involved in alliances to exchange ideas about strategy and to look for strategic fit and even reshaping of strategic directions. Networks can be thought of as a higher stage of alliances, for in the strategic center there is a conscious desire to influence and shape the strategies of the partners, and to obtain from partners ideas and influences in return.

This conscious desire to share strategy is reflected in the way in which central firms conceive of the boundaries of their operations. Most organizations view their joint ventures and subcontractors as beyond the boundaries of their firm, and even those involved in alliances do not think of partners as an integral part of the organization. Even firms that are part of a franchise system (and thus have a more holistic perspective) do not view their relationships as a pattern of multilateral contracts. Going beyond the franchise view, central firms and their participants communicate multilaterally across the whole of the value chain. In the words of Johanson and Mattsson (1992), they have a 'network theory,' a perception of governing a whole system.

Strategizing and structuring in the central firms we studied reverses Chandler's famous dictum about structure following strategy. When partner's competencies are so crucial to the developments of the business idea of the strategic center, the winners are building strategy and structure simultaneously whereas the losers are signing agreements without changing their organizational forms to match them. When each partner's resources and competencies are so essential to the success of the enterprise, new forms must be designed. To achieve this, structuring must come earlier, alongside strategizing, and both require an interaction among partners to create a platform of flexibility and capability. This behavior challenges much of what is received managerial practice and avoids some of the traps that webs of alliances face.

Like the large integrated cohesive organization, networked firms are able to believe as a single competitive entity which can draw on considerable resources.

However, the network form avoids many of the problems of large integrated firms, who typically find themselves paralyzed in the struggle between freedom and control. By focusing attention on the matters where commonality is important (e.g. product design) and by allowing each unit to have freedom elsewhere, cooperation is fostered, time and energy spent in monitoring is reduced, and resources are optimized. In this way, the networked organization succeeds in bridging the gap between centralization and decentralization. But cooperation can dull the edge of progress, and the organizations in our study have avoided this trap by fostering a highly competitive spirit.

Marketing and information sharing

The way in which information is collected and shared in the system reveals how structure and strategy go hand in hand. The gathering of information is a central activity in any organization. A strategic feature of a network of alliances is that the firms in the system are closely linked for the sharing of information. Members of the network exchange not only hard data about best practice, but also ideas, feelings, and thoughts about customers, other suppliers, and general market trends.

The central firm structures the information system so that knowledge is funneled to the areas that need it the most. Members specializing in a particular function have access to others in the system performing similar tasks, and share their knowledge. This creates a level playing field within the network system. It also provides the opportunity for the members to focus and encourage the development of competitive advantage over rivals.

One of the basic premises in our network view is that new information leading to new ways of doing things emerges in a process of interaction with people and real-life situations. It follows that the 'information ability' of the firm depends critically on a scheme of interactions. The difficulty is that the generation of new information cannot be planned, but has to emerge. Thus, the task of the manager is one of designing a structure which provides an environment favorable for interactions to form, and for new information to be generated. Such a structure is a network.

Our study found, as have others, that the availability of large amounts of high quality information on many aspects of the business facilitated more rapid responses to market opportunities. Information condensed through the network is 'thicker' than that condensed through the brokerage market, but is 'freer' than in the hierarchy.

The need for a sophisticated system was clear when we contrasted the central firms we studied with other firms. In these other firms, we often found that critical information was guarded, not shared. As is so common among organizations, individual players are either afraid of being exploited or they have a desire to exploit the power they have through knowledge. Even in traditional franchise systems, information is typically passed to the center for filtering before being shared. In the large integrated firm, centralization also causes unnecessary filtering. With centralization, the process of collecting and distributing information can be cumbersome and slow. Moreover, power to manipulate the information can be accidentally or intentionally misused by a small central group.

Some of the 'control group' of firms we studied did share their information, with adverse consequences. For example, defense contractors, unable to create an effective strategic network, found the partners sometimes used the shared information to their own advantage, and then did not reciprocate. The knowledge was exploited by partners to create superior bargaining positions. Opportunities to foster collective interest were missed, and in extreme cases, partners used the information to bolster a rival alliance to the detriment of the original information provider.

Learning races

Whereas identifying opportunities for growth is facilitated by information sharing, responding to the opportunity is more difficult. Here we see some of the clearest evidence that structure and strategy go hand in hand. First and foremost, the central firms we studied reject the idea of doing everything themselves. Instead, they seek help from others to respond to the opportunities they face. When the knowledge and capabilities exist within the network, the role of the center is to orchestrate the response so that the whole system capitalizes on the opportunity.

It frequently happens that opportunities require an innovative response, and it is common for strategic centers to set up 'learning races.' Here, partners are given a common goal (say a new product or process development) with a prize for the first to achieve the target. The prize may be monetary, but more commonly it is the opportunity to lead off the exploitation of the new development. There is a catch, the development must be shared with others in the network. Learning races create a sense of competition and rivalry, but within an overall common purpose.

Nintendo uses carefully nurtured learning races with its partners to create high quality rapid innovation. Partners are typically restricted in the number of contributions they can make. In the case of software design, the limit may be three ideas a year. These restrictions force a striving for excellence, and the consequence is a formidable pace of progress.

Learning races can be destructive rather than constructive if the partners do not have the skills and resources. The strategic centers we studied get around these difficulties by sharing knowledge and in effect allowing the whole network to 'borrow' skills and competencies from each other.

It is important to understand the role of new members in the process of creating innovations. Many central firms follow the twin strategies of internal and external development. Internal development involves offering existing partners a possibility of sharing in the growth markets. External development involves the finding of new partners to fill the gaps and accelerate the possibilities. New partners typically fit the pattern set by existing partners. These newly found 'look alike' firms allow the strategic center to truncate development of the necessary capabilities, leveraging off earlier experiences developed by the existing partners. By making growth a race between old and new partners, speed is assured and scale effects exploited. Our strategic centers fostered positive rivalry rather than hostility by ensuring that both old and new partners share in the final gains. When pursuing rapid growth, the twin tracks of internal and external development can lessen tensions. Because they are independent, existing members can respond to the new demands as they wish. But, if they do not respond positively, the central firm can sign up new partners to fill the gaps. The stresses and strains of growth can thus be reduced for each of the members of the network.

Conclusions

The strategically minded central firms in our study view the boundaries of the organization differently because their conception and implementation of strategy are shared with a web of partners. This attitude contrasts sharply with most organizations, which view their joint ventures and subcontractors as existing beyond the boundaries of their firm. Even those involved in alliances typically do not think of partners as an integral part of their organization; they rarely share their conceptions of strategy and even fewer insist that their partners share their strategy with them in a constructive dialogue. In contrast, strategic centers communicate strategic ideas and intent multilaterally across the whole of the value chain. They have a network view of governing a whole system.

Strategic centers reach out to resolve classic organizational paradoxes. Many subcontracting and alliance relationships seemed to be mired in the inability to reconcile the advantages of the market with those of the hierarchy. Strategic centers are able to create a system that has the flexibility and freedom of the market coupled with long-term holistic relationships, ensuring the requisite strategic capabilities across the whole system. Another paradox exists between creativity and discipline. Most organizations oscillate between having ample creativity and little discipline, or too much discipline and not enough creativity. Through their unusual attitude to structuring and strategizing, strategic centers attain leading-edge technological and market developments while retaining rapid decision-making processes.

All organizations have much to learn from studying strategic centers and their unusual conception of the managerial task. Strategic centers have taken modest resources and won leadership positions in a wide variety of sectors. They have brought a new way of thinking about business and organizing. Much of what they do is at the cutting edge, and they are shining examples of how firms can change the rules of the game by creative and imaginative thinking.

Coevolution in business ecosystems

By James F. Moore[1]

During the past decade, a great deal of insight has been gleaned about complex biological communities – illuminated by biologists poking around in Central American jungles, collecting insects in Asia, and observing birds in the Arctic. Much of this work has focused on the intricate and far-reaching relationships among species: predator and prey, pollinator and plant, protector and herd. What has become clear is that some ecosystems, notably those besieged by wave after wave of potential settlers, develop a special resiliency, flexibility, and resistance to catastrophes. In contrast, those that develop in isolation like Hawaii can become highly vulnerable to ecological disasters, and may even face mass extinctions.

Recent work in community ecology has dwelled on topics like 'keystone' species, the most critical of the species in an ecosystem. When they disappear from an ecosystem, life within the system itself changes radically. One example is the sea otter. Sea otters on the California coast prey on sea urchins. The urchins feast on kelp beds and other seaweeds along the ocean floor. When the otters were hunted almost to extinction during the nineteenth century, urchin populations grew exponentially and consumed much of the kelp beds, diminishing the biodiversity of the ecosystem. The ocean floor became almost barren. Through aggressive efforts, conservationists reintroduced the sea otter to the area. The urchins have now been harvested and the rich complexity along the coast restored.

Biologists have also concentrated on highly aggressive 'exotic' species that can have a particularly disruptive effect when injected into an ecosystem. The hydrilla plant, for instance, was introduced into Florida from Asia in the 1950s. Today hydrilla infests over 40 percent of the waterways in the state – choking lakes and rivers, killing native fish and other wildlife. The hydrilla is almost impossible to control and seems destined to have a permanently damaging effect on biological diversity and robustness in the region.

Unfortunately, the study of business communities lags well behind the biological. Yet close examination of the history of business innovation and the creation of wealth shows that there are important parallels between these two seemingly dissimilar worlds.

While biological analogies are often applied to the study of business, they are frequently applied much too narrowly. Almost invariably, the recurring focus is on the evolution of species. For example, some argue that in a market economy a Darwinian selection occurs in which the fittest products and companies survive. More recently, as businesses have been dissected into processes through the quality and reengineering movements, some now maintain that the fittest processes and systems of processes drive out the weak. In either instance, the 'species' are seen to be subject to genetic mutation and selection that gradually transforms them.

I have become convinced that the world is more complicated than that, and that we must think in grander terms. Species-level improvement of business processes is unquestionably crucial for keeping companies successful, and creates unmistakable value for society. But there are complementary forms of evolution that play vital but grossly underrated roles in both biology and business. They encompass the ecological and evolutionary interactions that occur across an entire ecosystem, comprising all the organisms of a particular habitat as well as the physical environment itself. Leaders who learn to understand these dimensions of ecology and evolution will find themselves equipped with a new model for devising strategy, and critical new options for shaping the future of their companies.

In biological ecosystems, changes take place over different time scales: many ecological changes occur within the lifetime of the individual organism, whereas evolutionary changes transpire over numerous generations. In business ecosystems, these two time scales collapse into one, because, unlike biological species, a business can guide its own evolution and effect dramatic evolutionary changes during its lifetime. A leader in a business ecosystem has an important edge over the species in a biological ecosystem: the ability

[1]Source: This article © 1996 by James F. Moore. Adapted from Chapter One of James F. Moore, *The Death of Competition: Leadership and Strategy in the Age of Business Ecosystems,* by permission of HarperCollins Publishers Inc.

to see the big picture and understand the dynamics of the ecosystem as a whole. This enables a business to alter its traits to better fit its ecosystem. What is more, a business can anticipate future changes in its ecosystem and evolve now so that it is well prepared to face future challenges.

Coevolution: Working together to create the future

The late anthropologist Gregory Bateson, who had a lifelong obsession with the workings of complex systems, greatly influenced my thinking. His thought-provoking theories of coevolution, culture, and addiction as they applied to natural and social systems are very intriguing, and I was struck by how he often studied systems in biological terms and then tried to understand how consciousness played its part in those systems.

In his thinking, Bateson focused on patterns. One of his observations was that behaviors within systems – companies, societies, species, families – coevolve. What does 'coevolve' mean in this context? In his book *Mind and Nature*, Bateson (1979) describes coevolution as a process in which interdependent species evolve in an endless reciprocal cycle – 'changes in species A set the stage for the natural selection of changes in species B,' and vice versa. Take the caribou and the wolf. The wolf culls the weaker caribou, which strengthens the herd. But with a stronger herd, it is imperative for wolves to evolve and become stronger themselves to succeed. And so the pattern is not simply competition or cooperation, but coevolution. Over time, as coevolution proceeds, the whole system becomes more hardy.

From Bateson's standpoint, coevolution is more important a concept than simply competition or cooperation. The same holds true in business. Too many executives focus their time primarily on day-to-day product and service-level struggles with direct competitors. Over the past few years, more managers have also emphasized cooperation: strengthening key customer and supplier relationships, and in some cases working with direct competitors on initiatives like technical standards and shared research to improve conditions for everyone.

A small number of the most effective firms in the world develop new business advantages by learning to lead economic coevolution. These companies – such as Intel, Hewlett-Packard, Shell, Wal-Mart, Creative Artists Agency, and others – recognize that they live in a rich and dynamic environment of opportunities. The job of their top management is to seek out potential centers of innovation where, by orchestrating the contributions of a network of players, they can bring powerful benefits to bear for customers and producers alike. Their executives must not only lead their current competitors and industries – whether by competition or cooperation – but hasten the coming together of disparate business elements into new economic wholes from which new businesses, new rules of competition and cooperation, and new industries can emerge.

Obliterating industry boundaries

There are certain spots on the earth – Amazon rain forests, for instance – where biological evolution proceeds at madcap speed. In these hyperdomains, nature brazenly experiments with new evolutionary loops and wrinkles, as well as new strategies for genetic invention. As a consequence, new organisms are spawned that, in due course, crawl out and populate the rest of the world.

Similar and unprecedented upheaval is astir in the world of business. There are certain identifiable hot spots of rapidly accelerating evolutionary activity in the global economy, places where the speed of business is exceedingly fast and loose. New technologies, deregulation, and changes in customer behavior are the metaphorical equivalent of floods and fires, opening up new competitive landscapes. On such newly cleared and fertile grounds, embryonic or transformed businesses are sprouting.

These new renditions are businesses with an edge. In a sense, they are renegades. In their marauding ways, they do not respect traditional industry paradigms and partitions. Indeed, what they share is a tendency to upend business and industry models and to redraw increasingly porous boundaries.

What we are seeing, in fact, is the end of industry. That's not to say that we now need to mourn the dissolution of the airline industry or the cement industry. Rather, it means the end of industry as a useful concept in contemplating business. The notion of 'industry' is really an artifact of the slowly paced business evolution during the middle of this century. The presumption that there are distinct, immutable businesses within which players scramble for supremacy is a tired idea whose time is past. It has little to do with what is shaping the world. The designation itself is simplistic, describing certain players better than others. But, in truth, the label is not much more than a crude grid used to compare and contrast businesses, a fiction conjured up by policymakers and regulators, investment analysts, and even academic students of business strategy.

There has been a profound change in management thinking of senior executives over recent years. Earlier, many senior managers could rightfully be accused of living in denial about the structural transformations of the world economy and its impact on their businesses. Today, nearly no senior management team can really be charged with living in such a state. There is no need to argue that the economic times have shifted – there is widespread agreement that this is true. The traditional industry boundaries that we've all taken for granted throughout our careers are blurring – and in may cases crumbling.

Enter a new logic to guide action

The important question for management today is not whether such changes are upon us but how to make strategy in this new world. Few management teams have been able to put together systematic approaches for dealing with the new business reality. Most find themselves struggling with varying degrees of effectiveness, but with no clear way to think about and communicate, let alone confront, the new strategic issues.

What is most needed is a new language, a logic for strategy, and new methods for implementation. Many of the old ideas simply don't work anymore. For instance, diversification strategies that emphasize finding 'attractive' industries often assume the fixedness of industry structure, yet our experience tells us that industry structures evolve very rapidly. Our traditional notions of vertical and horizontal integration fail us in the new world of cooperating communities. Competitive advantage no longer accrues necessarily from economies of scale and scope. Many firms can attain the volume of production to be efficient. Flexible systems are widely available that enable firms to customize their offers, proliferate variety, and do so at little additional cost. In the new world, scale and scope matter, but only as they contribute to a continuing innovation trajectory so that a company continually lowers its costs while increasing its performance.

Companies agitating to be leaders in the volatile new world order must transform themselves profoundly and perpetually so as to defy categorization. Is Wal-Mart a retailer, a wholesaler, or an information services and logistics company? Is Intel governed by the economic realities of the semiconductor industry, or does it lead one of several coevolving, competing personal computer-centered ecosystems? Are its competitors Texas Instruments and NEC or Microsoft and Compaq?

In place of 'industry,' I suggest an alternative, more appropriate term: *business ecosystem*. The term circumscribes the microeconomies of intense coevolution coalescing around innovative ideas. Business ecosystems span a variety of industries. The companies within them coevolve capabilities around the innovation and work cooperatively and competitively to support new products, satisfy customer needs, and incorporate the next round of innovation. Microsoft, for example, anchors an ecosystem that traverses at least four major industries: personal computers, consumer electronics, information, and communications. Centered on innovation in microprocessing, the Microsoft ecosystem encompasses an extended web of suppliers including Intel and Hewlett-Packard and myriad customers across market segments.

A second new term is 'opportunity environment,' a space of business possibility characterized by unmet customer needs, unharnessed technologies, potential regulatory openings, prominent investors, and many other untapped resources. Just as biological ecosystems thrive within a larger environment, so do business ecosystems. As traditional industry boundaries erode around us, companies often unexpectedly find themselves in fierce competition with the most unlikely of rivals. At the same time, the most creative and aggressive companies exploit these wider territories, transforming the landscape with new ecosystems. Thus, shaping cohesive strategy in the new order starts by defining an opportunity environment. Within such an environment, strategy-making revolves around devising novel ways to seize opportunities and create viable networks with other business ecosystems.

Unfortunately, most prevailing ideas on strategy today begin with the wrongheaded assumption that competition is bounded by clearly defined industries. As a result, these ideas are nearly useless in the current business climate and are sure to be even less valid in the future. Can one understand the economic events of tomorrow relying on these ideas? I very much doubt it. It is more important to see a company within its food web than in competition with superficially similar firms bundled together in an industry.

We compete in a bifurcated world. Executives today really must view strategy from two perspectives: They must pay attention to the wider opportunity environment and strive to lead in establishing the business ecosystems that will best utilize it. The dominant new ecosystems will likely consist of networks of organizations stretching across several different industries, and they will joust with similar networks, spread across still other industries.

At the same time, executives must continue to see their companies in the traditional sense, as members of homogenous industries clawing away at rivals for market share and growth. In terms of strategy, it no longer matters if the industries are old and venerable like banking and automobiles, or frisky new ones like cable television and personal computers. So understanding one's industry will be only the first step to pursuing customers, innovation, and the creation of wealth.

Learn from companies investing in the new approach

I believe that this change in conceptualizing is vitally important for three reasons. First, the conditions and challenges prevalent in the fastest-moving sectors of the global economy are spreading inexorably to all the others. The dynamics of these centers, and the challenges confronting their feistiest companies and leaders, are now relevant to us all.

Second, some of the hottest centers of economic competition – computers, communications, media, retailing, health care – are now devising fresh approaches to strategy and leadership. These approaches are not very well understood, even by many of their creators, and they surely are not appreciated by the wider public. Nevertheless, the scope of the strategic ambitions are truly breathtaking. If their creators succeed in their endeavors, their initiatives will have profound implications in our daily lives. What it already means is the end of competition as we know it.

Third, these ideas are already propagating across the general business landscape and thus are guaranteed to have a dramatic and irreversible impact on how we do business from now on. Because of these reasons, business people, no matter what business they conduct, must comprehend at least the broad outlines of what is afoot.

The special task of business leadership: Creating communities of shared imagination

In one significant respect, a strictly biological metaphor does not apply to business. Unlike biological communities of coevolving organisms, business communities are social systems. And social systems are composed of real people who make decisions. A powerful shared imagination, focused on envisioning the future, evolves in a business ecosystem that is unlike anything in biology. Conscious choice does play an important role in ecology. Animals often choose their habitats, their mates, and their behavior. In the economic world, however, strategists and policymakers and investors spend a great deal of time trying to understand the overall game and find fruitful ways to play it or change it. This consciousness is central to economic relationships.

Even more, shared imagination is what holds together economies, societies and companies. Therefore, a great deal of leadership and business strategy relies on creating shared meaning, which in turn shapes the future. For example, during 1995 millions of people from diverse backgrounds became convinced that the Internet would become a major locus for commerce, entertainment, and personal communication. They rushed to become involved and, in the act of so doing, established a foundation for the very reality they believed was coming about. While many other factors encouraged the exponential growth of interest in the Internet, Sun Microsystems played a powerful role by introducing a software language called Java. Java made it possible to create appealing animated experiences across the Internet.

Sun makes a wide range of computers. Java was the result of a small research project, outside the company mainstream. Nonetheless, Sun executives saw Java's potential to enliven the community. Sun executives chose not to treat Java as just another product. Instead, they essentially gave away Java to the rest of the world in order to feed the Internet frenzy and reinforce Sun's image as a leader of the movement. What mattered was Java the campaign – not Java the product. A widespread perception formed that Sun was prescient and well positioned for the future. Sun's sales rose, its stock appreciated, and it became more able to get other stakeholders to follow its lead.

It is the mind that imparts the harmony and the sense and the syncopation to the business ecosystem. The larger patterns of business coevolution are maintained by a complex network of choices, which depend, at least in part, on what participants are aware of. As Gregory Bateson stressed, if you change the ideas in a social system, you change the system itself. We are seeing the birth of ideas. The very fact that new ideas are coming into existence is changing the conditions. If you don't follow these new ideas, you will be totally lost.

As companies get more sophisticated in creating new ecosystems, become more like the guiding hand of a forester or gardener in an ecological environment, the more this new level of consciousness will become the dominant reality of business strategy. The game of leadership will evolve to new levels. There is a wonderful book of business history by Alfred Chandler (1977) called *The Visible Hand*. It chronicles the rise of the multidivisional organization between 1900 and 1930 and the consciousness of people like Alfred Sloane who made the development of this then new organization possible. We are witnessing the next revolution beyond multidivisional organizations and beyond the visible hand. It is the ability in an environment of immense resources, immense plasticity, and powerful information systems to make and break microeconomic relationships with enormous subtlety and velocity. We are entering an age of imagination.

In an age of imagination, the ultimate struggle among companies is for the souls of customers and the hearts of vast communities of suppliers and other associated companies. Strange things can happen in the new world of virtual organizations. In the new world, strategy based on conventional competition and cooperation gives way to strategy based on coevolution – which in turn defines a new level of competition. At this higher level, competition defines attractive futures and galvanizes concerted action. We can vividly see the tremendous power of a company like Microsoft, which leads and shapes the collective behavior of thousands of associated suppliers, even though during most of the years of its most powerful influence, Microsoft never had more than $6 billion in sales.

But heightened consciousness of the benefits of ecosystem power and influence can also make prospective partners wary of committing to a leader. Competition to lead coevolution can bring its own peculiar paranoia – and fragment a community of companies. We already see this sort of effect within the PC business, where the heightened consciousness of Microsoft's role in overturning IBM's dominion has put all participants in the computer, communications, and even the entertainment business on notice.

Now prospective allies and partners of Microsoft appreciate the costs as well as the benefits of allegiance to the company from Redmond. Many of them have become reluctant coadventurers. Worries over Microsoft's motives and leadership outweighed the genuine benefits that appeared to be achieved by working together. Such worries also helped Sun Microsystems and Java. Java appealed to some stakeholders in part because it did not originate from Microsoft. The success of Sun and Java was welcomed as a limiter of Microsoft's influence on the future.

The new ecology of business

The heart of strategy is understanding these evolutionary patterns. What is consistent from business to business is the process of coevolution, the complex interplay between competitive and cooperative business strategies.

The immense changes that have taken place in business are minor compared to what is yet to come. When an ecological approach to management becomes more common, and when an increasing number of executives become conscious of coevolution, the pace of business change will accelerate at an exponential rate. Executives whose horizons are bounded by traditional industry perspectives will miss the real challenges and opportunities facing their companies. Shareholders and directors, who perceive the new reality, will eventually oust them. For companies caught up in dynamic business ecosystems, the stakes are considerable, but the rewards are commensurate and the challenges exhilarating as never before.

How to make strategic alliances work

By Jeffrey H. Dyer, Prashant Kale and Harbir Singh[1]

Strategic alliances – a fast and flexible way to access complementary resources and skills that reside in other companies – have become an important tool for achieving sustainable competitive advantage. Indeed, the past decade has witnessed an extraordinary increase in alliances (Anand and Khanna, 2000). Currently, the top 500 global businesses have an average of 60 major strategic alliances each.

Yet alliances are fraught with risks, and almost half fail. Hence the ability to form and manage them more effectively than competitors can become an important source of competitive advantage. We conducted an in-depth study of 200 corporations and their 1,572 alliances. We found that a company's stock price jumped roughly 1% with each announcement of a new alliance, which translated into an increase in market value of $54 million per alliance (Kale, Dyer and Singh, 2000). And although all companies seemed to create some value through alliances, certain companies

– for example, Hewlett-Packard, Oracle, Eli Lilly & Co. and Parke-Davis (a division of Pfizer Inc.) – showed themselves capable of systematically generating more alliance value than others. (See Figure 7.4.1.)

How do they do it? By building a dedicated strategic-alliance function. The companies and others like them appoint a vice president or director of strategic alliances with his or her own staff and resources. The dedicated function coordinates all alliance-related activity within the organization and is charged with institutionalizing processes and systems to teach, share and leverage prior alliance-management experience and know-how throughout the company. And it is effective. Enterprises with a dedicated function achieved a 25% higher long-term success rate with their alliances than those without such a function – and generated almost four times the market wealth whenever they announced the formation of a new alliance. (See Exhibit 7.4.1.)

EXHIBIT 7.4.1

RESEARCH DESIGN AND METHODOLOGY

We conducted two types of research. From 1996 to 2000, we interviewed at companies such as Hewlett-Packard, Warner-Lambert (now part of Pfizer), Oracle, Corning, Lilly, GlaxoSmithKline and others that were reputed to have effective alliance capabilities. We also interviewed executives at companies that did not have a dedicated strategic-alliance function, many of which have had relatively poor success with alliances. We conducted a survey-based study of 203 companies (from a variety of industries) with average revenues of $3.05 billion in 1998. The analysis of alliance success and stock-market gain from alliance announcements is based

on data from 1,572 alliances formed by the companies between 1993 and 1997.

To assess the long-term success of the alliances, we collected survey data on the primary reasons that each of the alliances was formed. We then asked managers to evaluate each alliance on the following dimensions:

- the extent to which the alliance met its stated objectives;

- the extent to which the alliance enhanced the competitive position of the parent company;

- the extent to which the alliance enabled each parent company to learn some critical skills from the alliance partner; and

- the level of harmony the partners involved in the alliance exhibited.

[1]Source: This article was adapted from J.H. Dyer, P. Kale and H. Singh, 'How to Make Strategic Alliances Work' in *Sloan Management Review*, 1978, Vol. 23, No. 4, pp. 37–43. Reproduced by permission.

Managers used a standard 1–7 (1 = low and 7 = high) survey scale. Alliances that received an above-average score on the four dimensions were rated 'successes,' and those that received scores below average were rated 'failures.' Assessments of the alliance success and failure then were used to calculate an overall alliance success rate for each company. The alliance success rate is essentially a ratio of each company's 'successful' alliances to all its alliances during the study period.

In recent years, academics have begun using a market-based measure of alliance value creation and success based on abnormal stock-market gains. To estimate incremental value creation for each company, we built a model to predict stock price based on daily firm stock prices for 180 days before an alliance announcement. The model also includes daily market returns on the value-weighted S&P 500. Abnormal stock-market gains reflect the daily unanticipated movements in the stock price for each firm after an alliance announcement.

How a dedicated alliance function creates value

An effective dedicated strategic-alliance function performs four key roles: It improves knowledge-management efforts, increases external visibility, provides internal coordination, and eliminates both accountability problems and intervention problems. (See Figure 7.4.2.)

Improving knowledge management

A dedicated function acts as a focal point for learning and for leveraging lessons and feedback from prior and ongoing alliances. It systematically establishes a series of routine processes to articulate, document, codify and share alliance know-how about the key phases of the alliance life cycle. There are five key phrases, and companies that have been successful with alliances have tools and templates to manage each. (See Figure 7.4.3.)

FIGURE 7.4.1 A dedicated function improves the success of strategic alliances, 1993–1997

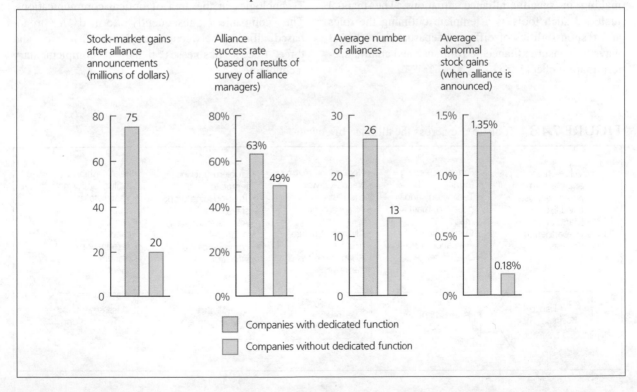

FIGURE 7.4.2   The role of the alliance function and how it creates value

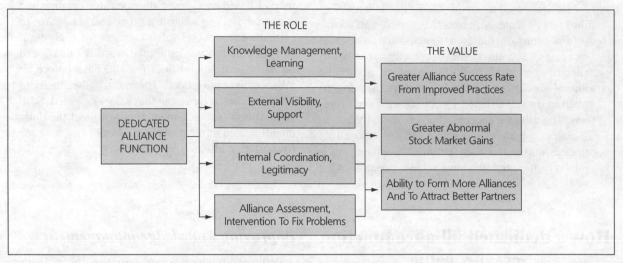

Many companies with dedicated alliance functions have codified explicit alliance-management knowledge by creating guidelines and manuals to help them manage specific aspects of the alliance life cycle, such as partner selection and alliance negotiation and contracting. For example, Lotus Corp. created what it calls its '35 rules of thumb' to manage each phase of an alliance, from formation to termination. Hewlett-Packard developed 60 different tools and templates, included in a 300-page manual for guiding decision making in specific alliance situations. The manual included such tools as a template outlining the roles and responsibilities of different departments, a list of ways to measure alliance performance and an alliance-termination checklist.

Other companies, too, have found that creating tools, templates and processes is valuable. For example, using the Spatial Paradigm for Information Retrieval and Exploration, or SPIRE, database. Dow Chemical developed a process for identifying potential alliance partners. The company was able to create a topographical map pinpointing the overlap between its patent domains and the patent domains of possible alliance partners. With this tool, the company discovered the potential for an alliance with Lucent Technologies in the area of optical communications. The companies subsequently formed a broad-based alliance between three Dow businesses and three Lucent businesses that had complementary technologies.

FIGURE 7.4.3   Tools to use across the alliance life cycle

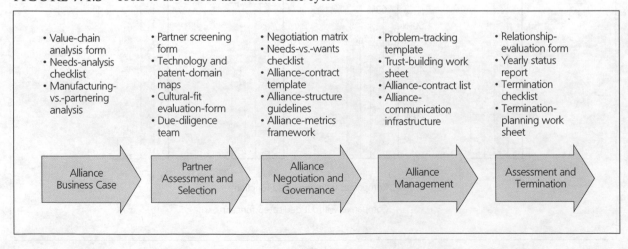

After identifying potential partners, companies need to assess whether or not they will be able to work together effectively. Lilly developed a process of sending a due-diligence team to the potential alliance partner to evaluate the partner's resources and capabilities and to assess its culture. The team looks at such things as the partner's financial condition, information technology, research capabilities, and health and safety record. Of particular importance is the evaluation of the partner's culture. In Lilly's experience, culture clashes are one of the main reasons alliances fail. During the cultural assessment, the team examines the potential partner's corporate values and expectations, organizational structure, reward systems and incentives, leadership styles, decision-making processes, patterns of human interaction, work practices, history of partnerships, and human-resources practices. Nelson M. Sims, Lilly's executive director of alliance management, states that the evaluation is used both as a screening mechanism and as a tool to assist Lilly in organizing, staffing and governing the alliance.

Dedicated alliance functions also facilitate the sharing of tacit knowledge through training programs and internal networks of alliance managers. For example, HP developed a two-day course on alliance management that it offered three times a year. The company also provided short three-hour courses on alliance management and made its alliance materials available on the internal HP alliance web site. HP also created opportunities for internal networking among managers through internal training programs, companywide alliance summits and 'virtual meetings' with executives involved in managing alliances. And the company regularly sent its alliance managers to alliance-management programs at business schools to help its managers develop external networks of contacts.

Formal training programs are one route; informal programs are another. Many companies with alliance functions have created roundtables with opportunities for alliance managers to get together and informally share their alliance experience. To that end, Nortel initiated a three-day workshop and networking initiative for alliance managers. BellSouth and Motorola have conducted similar two-day workshops for people to meet and learn from one another.

Increasing external visibility

A dedicated alliance function can play an important role in keeping the market apprised of both new alliances and successful events in ongoing alliances. Such external visibility can enhance the reputation of

the company in the marketplace and support the perception that alliances are adding value. The creation of a dedicated alliance function sends a signal to the marketplace and to potential partners that the company is committed both to its alliances and to managing them effectively. And when a potential partner wants to contact a company about establishing an alliance, a dedicated function offers an easy, highly visible point of contact. In essence, it provides a place to screen potential partners and bring in the appropriate internal parties if a partnership looks attractive.

For instance, Oracle put the partnering process on the web with Alliance Online (now Oracle Partners Program) and offered terms and conditions of different 'tiers' of partnership. Potential partners could choose the level that fit them best. At the tier I level (mostly resellers, integrators and application developers), companies could sign up for a specific type of agreement online and not have to talk with someone in Oracle's strategic-alliance function. Oracle also used its web site to gather information on its partners' products and services, thereby developing detailed partner profiles. Accessing those profiles, customers easily matched the products and services they desired with those provided by Oracle partners. The web site allowed the company to enhance its external visibility, and it emerged as the primary means of recruiting and developing partnerships with more than 7,000 tier I partners. It also allowed Oracle's strategic-alliance function to focus the majority of its human resources on its higher-profile, more strategically important partners.

Providing internal coordination

One reason that alliances fail is the inability of one partner or another to mobilize internal resources to support the initiative. Visionary alliance leaders may lack the organizational authority to access key resources necessary to ensure alliance success. An alliance executive at a company without such a function observed: 'We have a difficult time supporting our alliance initiatives, because many times the various resources and skills needed to support a particular alliance are located in different functions around the company. Unless it is a very high-profile alliance, no one person has the power to make sure the company's full resources are utilized to help the alliance succeed. You have to go begging to each unit and hope that they will support you. But that's time-consuming, and we don't always get the support we should.'

A dedicated alliance function helps solve that problem in two ways. First, it has the organizational legitimacy to reach across divisions and functions and request the resources necessary to support the company's alliance initiatives. When particular functions are not responsive, it can quickly elevate the issue through the organization's hierarchy and ask the appropriate executives to make a decision on whether a particular function or division should support an alliance initiative. Second, over time, individuals within the alliance function develop networks of contacts throughout the organization. They come to know where to find useful resources within the organization. Such networks also help develop trust between alliance managers and employees throughout the organization – and thereby lead to reciprocal exchanges.

A dedicated alliance function also can provide internal coordination for the organization's strategic priorities. Some studies suggest that one of the main reasons alliances fail is that the partnership's objectives no longer match one or both partners' strategic priorities (Bleeke and Ernst, 1993, 1998). As one alliance executive complained:

We will sometimes get far along in an alliance, only to find that another company initiative is in conflict with the alliance. For example, in one case, an internal group started to develop a similar technology that our partner already had developed. Should they have developed it? I don't know. But we needed some process for communicating internally the strategic priorities of our alliances and how they fit with our overall strategy.

Companies need to have a mechanism for communicating which alliance initiatives are most important to achieving the overall strategy – as well as which alliance partners are the most important. The alliance function ensures that such issues are constantly addressed in the company's strategy-making sessions and then are communicated throughout the organization.

Facilitating intervention and accountability

A 1999 survey by Anderson Consulting (now Accenture) found that only 51% of companies that form alliances had any kind of formal metrics in place to assess performance. Of those, only about 20% believed that the metrics they had in place were really the appropriate ones to use. In our research, we found that 76% of companies with dedicated alliance function had implemented formal alliance metrics. In con-

trast, only 30% of the companies without a dedicated function had done so.

Many executives we interviewed indicated that an important benefit of creating an alliance function was that it compelled the company to develop alliance metrics and to evaluate the performance of its alliances systematically. Moreover, doing so compelled senior managers to intervene when an alliance was struggling. Lilly established a yearly 'health check' process for each of its key alliances, using surveys of both Lilly employees and the partner's alliance managers. After the survey, an alliance manager from the dedicated function could sit down with the leader of a particular alliance to discuss the results and offer recommendations. In some cases, Lilly's dedicated strategic-alliance group found that it needed to replace the leader of a particular Lilly alliance.

When serious conflicts arise, the alliance function can help resolve them. One executive commented, 'Sometimes an alliance has lived beyond its useful life. You need someone to step in and either pull the plug or push it in new directions.' Alliance failure is the culmination of a chain of events. Not surprisingly, signs of distress are often visible early on, and with monitoring, the alliance function can step in and intervene appropriately.

How to organize an effective strategic-alliance function

One of the major challenges of creating an alliance function is knowing how to organize it. It is possible to organize the function around key partners, industries, business units, geographic areas or a combination of all four. How an alliance function is organized influences its strategy and effectiveness. For instance, if the alliance function is organized by business unit, then the function will reflect the idiosyncrasies of each business unit and the industry in which it operates. If the alliance function is organized geographically, then knowledge about partners and coordination mechanisms, for example, will be accumulated primarily with a geographic focus.

Identify key strategic parameters and organize around them

Organizing around key strategic parameters enhances the probability of alliance success. For example, a company with a large number of alliances and a few central players may identify partner-specific knowledge and partner-specific strategic priorities as critical. As a result, it may decide to organize the dedicated alliance function around central alliance partners.

Hewlett-Packard is a good example of a company that created processes to share knowledge on how to work with a specific alliance partner. (See Figure 7.4.4.) It identified a few key strategic partners with which it had numerous alliances, such as Microsoft, Cisco, Oracle and America Online and Netscape (now part of AOL Time Warner) among others. HP created a partner-level alliance-manager position to oversee all its alliances with each partner. The strategic-partner-level alliance managers had the responsibility of working with the managers and teams of the individual alliances to ensure that each of the partner's alliances would be as successful as possible. Because HP had numerous marketing and technical alliances with partners such as Microsoft, it also assigned some marketing and technical program managers to the alliance function. The managers supported the individual alliance managers and teams on specific marketing and technical issues relevant to their respective alliances. Thus HP became good at sharing partner-specific experiences and developing partner-specific priorities.

Citicorp developed a different approach. Rather than organize around key partners, the company organized its alliance function around business units and geographic areas. In some divisions, the company also used an alliance board – similar to a board of directors – to oversee many alliances. The corporate alliance function was assigned a research-and-development and coordinating role for the alliance functions that resided in each division. For instance, the e-business-solutions division engaged in alliances that were typically different from those of the retail-banking division; therefore, the alliance function needed to create alliance-management knowledge relevant to that specific division. Furthermore, to respond to differences among geographic regions, each of Citicorp's divisions created an alliance function within each region. For example, the e-business-solutions alliance group in Latin America would oversee all Citicorp's Latin American alliances in the e-business sector. The e-business division's Latin American alliance board would review potential Latin American alliances – and approve or reject them.

Organize to facilitate the exchange of knowledge on specific topics

The strategic-alliance function should be organized to make it easy for individuals throughout the organization to locate codified or tacit knowledge on a particular issue, type of alliance or phase of the alliance life cycle. In other words, in addition to developing partner-specific, business-specific or geography-specific knowledge, companies should charge certain individuals with responsibility for developing *topic-specific* knowledge.

For example, when people within the organization want to know the best way to negotiate a strategic-alliance agreement, what contractual provisions and governance arrangements are most appropriate, which metrics should be used, or the most effective way to resolve disagreements with partners, they should be able to access that information easily through the strategic-alliance function. In most cases, someone within the alliance function acts as the internal expert and is assigned the responsibility of developing and acquiring knowledge on a particular element of the alliance life cycle. For some companies, it may be important to develop expertise on specific types of alliances – for example, those tied to research and development, marketing and cobranding, manufacturing, standard setting, consolidation joint ventures or new joint ventures. The issues involved in setting up such alliances can be very different. For example, whenever the success of an alliance depends on the exchange of knowledge – as is the case in R&D alliances – equity-sharing governance arrangements are preferable because they give both parties the incentives necessary for them to bring all relevant knowledge to the table. But when each party brings to the alliance an 'easy to value' resource – as with most marketing and cobranding alliances – contractual governance arrangements tend to be more suitable.

Locate the function at an appropriate level of the organization

When done properly, dedicated alliance functions offer internal legitimacy to alliances, assist in setting strategic priorities and draw on resources across the company. That is why the function cannot be buried within a particular division or be relegated to low-level support within business development. It is critical that the director or vice president of the strategic-alliance function report to the COO or president of the company. Because alliances play an increasingly important role in overall corporate strategy, the person in charge of alliances should participate in the strategy-making processes at the highest level of the company. Moreover, if the alliance function's director reports to the company president or COO, the function will have the visibility and reach to cut across boundaries and

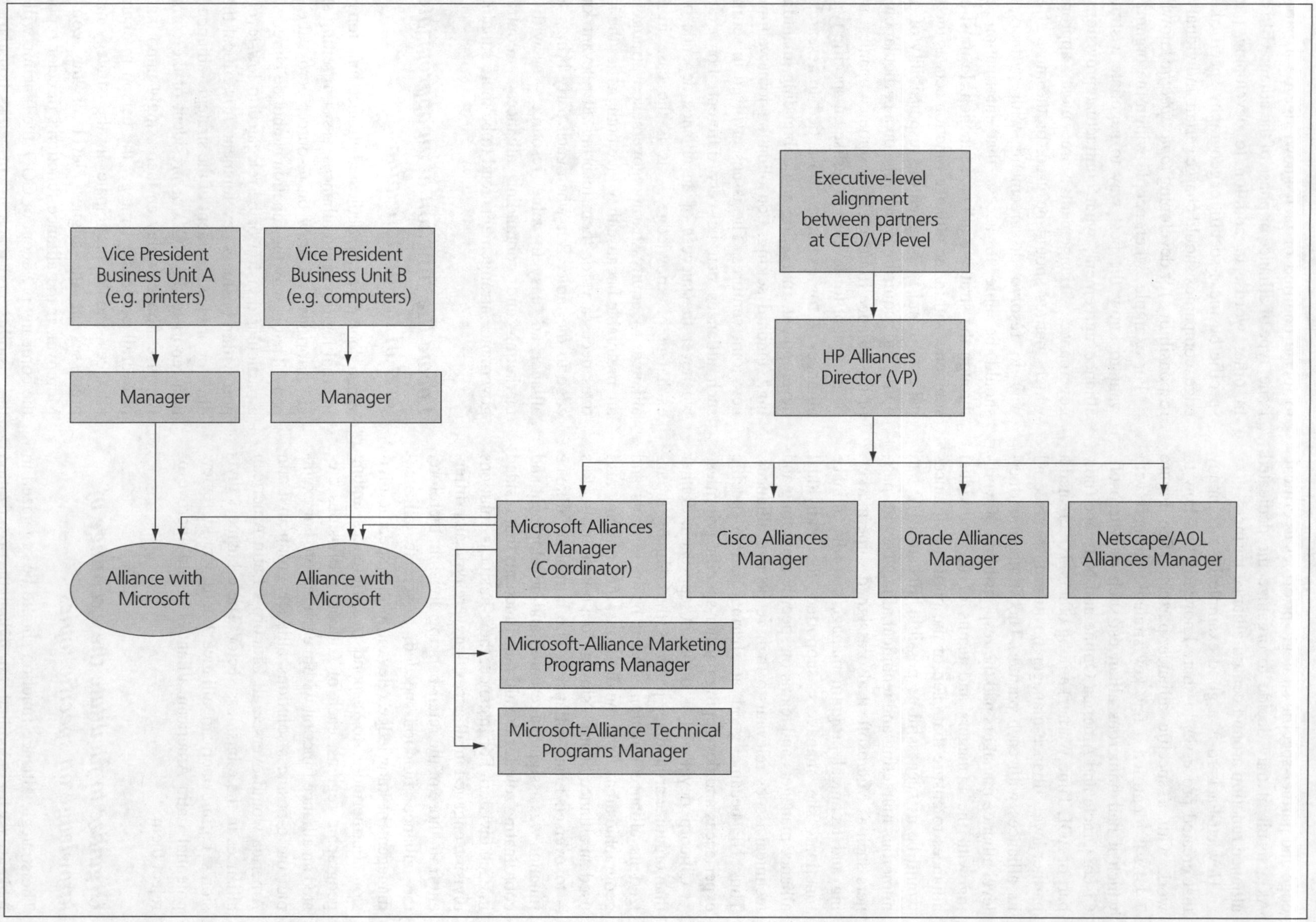

FIGURE 7.4.4 Hewlett-Packard alliance structure for key alliance partners

draw on the company's resources in support of its alliance initiatives.

A critical competence

Companies with a dedicated alliance function have been more successful than their counterparts at finding ways to solve problems regarding knowledge management, external visibility, internal coordination, and accountability – the underpinnings of an alliance-management capability.

But although a dedicated alliance function can create value, success does not come without challenges. First, setting up such a function requires a serious investment of the company's resources and its people's time. Businesses must be large enough or enter into enough alliances to cover that investment. Second, deciding where to locate the function in the organization – and how to get line managers to appreciate the role of such a function and recognize its value – can be difficult. Finally, establishing codified and consistent procedures may mean inappropriately emphasizing process over speed in decision making.

Such challenges exist. But the company that surmounts them and builds a successful dedicated strategic alliance function will reap substantial rewards. Companies with a well-developed alliance function generate greater stock-market wealth through their alliances and better long-term strategic-alliance success rates. Over time, investment in an alliance-management capability enhances the reputation of a company as a preferred partner. Hence an alliance-management capability can be thought of as a competence in itself, one that can reap rich rewards for the organization that knows its worth.

NETWORK LEVEL STRATEGY IN INTERNATIONAL PERSPECTIVE

Do as adversaries in law, strive mightily, but eat and drink as friends.
William Shakespeare (1564–1616); English dramatist and poet

Of all the debates in the field of strategic management, this one has received the most attention from comparative management researchers. Almost all of these researchers have concluded that firms from different countries display widely divergent propensities to compete and cooperate. Many authors suggest that there are recognizable national inclinations, even national styles, when it comes to establishing inter-firm relationships. For instance, Kanter (1994) notes that:

> North American companies, more than others in the world, take a narrow, opportunistic view of relationships, evaluating them strictly in financial terms or seeing them as barely tolerable alternatives to outright acquisition. Preoccupied with the economics of the deal, North American companies frequently neglect the political, cultural, organizational, and human aspects of the partnership. Asian companies are the most comfortable with relationships, and therefore they are the most adept at using and exploiting them. European companies fall somewhere in the middle.

Although Kanter's 'classification' is somewhat rough, most strategic management researchers who have done international comparative studies agree with the broad lines of her remark (e.g. Contractor and Lorange, 1988; Kagono et al., 1985).

While it is difficult to generalize at the national level, since there can be quite a bit of variance within a country, it is challenging to debate these observed international dissimilarities. Are there really national inter-organizational relationship styles and what factors might influence their existence? As a stimulus to the international dimension of this debate, a number of country characteristics are put forward as possible influences on how the paradox of competition and cooperation is dealt with in different national settings. As noted before, it is the intention of these propositions to encourage further discussion and cross-cultural research on the topic of inter-organizational relationships.

Level of individualism

At the most fundamental level, cultural values can place more emphasis on competition or cooperation. Some researchers (e.g. Hofstede, 1993, Reading 1.4; Hampden Turner and Trompenaars, 1993) point out that this has much to do with a culture's orientation toward individuals or groups. More individualist cultures accentuate the position of each single person as a distinct entity, while more collectivist cultures stress people's group affiliations. In Hofstede's research, the United States surfaced as highest scoring nation in the world on the individualism scale, closely followed by the other English-speaking countries, Australia, Great Britain, Canada and New Zealand respectively. Hofstede argues that 'in the US individualist conception, the relationship between the individual and the organization is essentially calculative, being based on enlightened self-interest', while in more collectivist cultures the relationship 'is not calculative, but moral: It is based not on self interest, but on the individual's loyalty toward the clan, organization, or society – which is supposedly the best guarantee of that individual's ultimate interest'. The willingness of individuals to forgo self-interested behavior for the good of the group is believed to be the same cultural value spurring individual firms to cooperate for the good of an entire network (e.g. Gerlach, 1992). Pascale and Athos (1981) agree that in the highly group-oriented culture of Japan, interdependence is valued, while the 'self' is regarded as an obstacle to joint development. Group members feel indebted and obligated toward one another, and trust results from a shared understanding and acceptance of interdependence.

The strong orientation of the English-speaking ('Anglo-Saxon') cultures toward individualism and the Japanese cultural emphasis on group affiliation, is also recognized by Lessem and Neubauer (1994), who place these two cultures at the extreme ends of a continuum. In the socially atomistic Anglo-Saxon nations, individuals are seen as the building blocks of society and each person is inclined to optimize her/his own interests. In the socially symbiotic Japanese culture, the whole is more important than the individual parts, so that individuals are more likely to strive towards a group's common good. Interestingly, Lessem and Neubauer (following Albert, 1991) argue that, on this point, the German and Japanese cultures are strikingly similar. Both cultures exhibit a 'wholist' worldview, in which 'management and banker, employer and employee, government and industry combine forces rather than engage in adversarial relations', to the benefit of the entire system. This collectivist bent can be observed at the multi-company level (industrial networks/ *keiretsu*), but also at the industry and national levels of aggregation, leading many analysts to speak of Japan Incorporated and Deutschland AG.

Other cultures fall somewhere between these two extremes. Italy, for instance, is often cited for its high number of networked companies (Piore and Sabel, 1984). Besides the well-known example of Benetton, there are many networks in the textile industry of Prato, the ceramics industry of Sassuolo, the farm machine industry of Reggio Emilia and the motorcycle industry of Bologna. Similar to the Germans and Japanese, Italian culture is also characterized by a strong group orientation, but the affiliations valued by Italians tend to be mostly family-like, based on blood-ties, friendships or ideological bonds between individuals. There is often a strong loyalty and trust within these family-like communities, but distrust toward the outside world. Therefore, cooperation tends to be high within these communities, but competition prevails beyond.

In France the situation is again different. In French culture, according to Lessem and Neubauer (1994), there is 'an ingrained mistrust of the natural play of forces of a free economy'. People have a strong sense that cooperation in economic affairs is important, similar to the Japanese, Germans and Italians. However, the French are unwilling to depend on the evolution of cooperation between (semi-) independent firms. Generally, there is a preference to impose cooperation top-down, by integrating companies into efficiently working bureaucracies. Such structuring of the economy usually takes place under influence, or by direct intervention, of the French government. Such *dirigisme* is based on the opposite assumption to Williamson's work (1975, 1985): hierarchical coordination is usually preferable to market transactions. Former prime minister, Edouard Balladur, summarized this assumption far more graciously, when he remarked: 'What is the market? It is the law of the jungle, the law of nature. And what is civilization? It is the struggle against nature' (*The Economist*, March 15 1997). Based on this view, even relationships with firms not absorbed into the hierarchy are of a bureaucratic nature – that is, formal, rational and depersonalized.

Type of institutional environment

Of course, the cultural values described above are intertwined with the institutional structures that have developed in each country. Some comparative management researchers focus on these institutional forces, such as governments, banks, universities and unions, to explain the divergent national views on competition and cooperation. It is generally argued that most countries have developed an idiosyncratic economic system – that is, their own distinct brand of capitalism – with a different emphasis on competition and cooperation.

One prominent analysis is that of business historian Chandler (1986, 1990), who has described the historical development of 'personal capitalism' in the United Kingdom, 'managerial capitalism' in the United States, 'cooperative capitalism' in Germany and 'group capitalism' in Japan from 1850 to 1950. The legacy of these separately evolving forms of capitalism is that, to this day, there are significantly different institutional philosophies, roles and behaviors in each of these countries. In the English-speaking nations, governments have generally limited their role to the establishment and maintenance of competitive markets (Hampden-Turner and Trompenaars, 1993). A shared belief in the basic tenets of classical economies has led these governments to be suspicious of competition-undermining collusion masquerading under the term 'cooperation'. For instance, in the United States the Sherman Antitrust Act was passed in 1890 and has been applied with vigor since then to guard the functioning of the market. Many companies that would like to cooperate have been discouraged from doing so (e.g. Teece, 1992; Dyer and Ouchi, 1993).

In the German 'cooperative capitalism' system, the situation has been quite different. The government has major shareholdings in hundreds of companies outside the public services. According to Lessem and Neubauer (1994) 'the attitude to government participation in industry is based not on ideology but on a sense of partnership with the business community. It extends to the local level where local authorities, schools, banks and businesses combine to establish policies of mutual benefit.' Especially the large German banks have played an important role in guiding industrial development, promoting cooperation and defusing potentially damaging conflicts between companies. They have had an intimate knowledge of the business and have had a long-term stake in each relationship, often expressed by a minority shareholding of the bank in the client company and/or a seat on its supervisory board. The offices of the largest bank, Deutsche Bank, hold hundreds of seats on other companies' supervisory boards, although this system has been unraveling since the late 1990s. The trade associations and unions, it should be noted, also employ a long-term, cooperative perspective.

The Japanese 'group capitalism' system is somewhat akin to the German model. In Japan, too, business and social institutions have formed a partnership to promote mutually beneficial developments. However, in Japan, the government has played a more prominent role than in Germany, through its national industrial strategies (Best, 1990). As Thurow

(1991) points out, the Japanese government has been actively involved in the indirect protection of some domestic industries, the selection of other sectors as development priorities and the funding of related research and development. Furthermore, the *keiretsu* industry groups, such as Mitsui, Mitsubishi, Sanwa, Hitachi and Sumitomo, have also formed long-term networks of cooperating companies. While some consortia have been formed to deal with a particular task at hand, firms within a *keiretsu* are familiar with one another through long historical association and have had durable, open-ended relationships, partially cemented by multilateral minority shareholdings.

In France, the dirigiste state planners play an even more prominent role than in Japan. The French model, which could be dubbed 'bureaucratic capitalism', focuses sharply on the state as industrial strategist, coordinating many major developments in the economy. It is the planners' job 'to maintain a constant pressure on industry – as part industrial consultant, part banker, part plain bully – to keep it moving in some desired direction' (Lessem and Neubauer, 1994). The unions, on the other hand, tend to be more antagonistic, particularly in their relationship to the government. On the work floor, however, a more cooperative attitude prevails.

In the 'familial capitalism' system of Italy, on the contrary, the central government plays a very small role. Instead, local networks of economic, political and social actors cooperate to create a mutually beneficial environment. Trade associations, purchasing cooperatives, educational institutions and cooperative marketing are often created to support a large number of small, specialized firms working together as a loose federation. Trust within the network is often extensive, but institutions outside of these closed communities are mistrusted, especially the central government, tax authorities, bankers and the trade unions.

Market for corporate control

Linked to the general institutional environment, is how the issue of mergers, acquisitions and takeovers is viewed in each nation. In countries such as the United States and Britain, companies whose shares are traded on the stock exchange are exposed to the threat of a takeover. This relatively open market for corporate control facilitates vertical and horizontal integration. Companies can contemplate acquiring another firm, if they believe that internal coordination is preferable to a market-based relationship. In other countries, however, the market for corporate control is less open, if not entirely absent. Where horizontal or vertical integration is difficult to achieve, but working together is still beneficial, potential acquirers often only have collaborative arrangements as an alternative.

Type of career paths

Finally, a more down to earth reason why competition or cooperation might be more prevalent in a particular country may be found at the level of personnel policy. In general, the longer people know each other and the more they interact, the more trust and cooperation that evolves (e.g. Axelrod, 1984; Teece, 1992). In countries such as Japan and Germany, where stable, long-term employment is still common, individuals are in a better position to build up durable personal relationships with people in other firms. In nations where employees frequently shift between positions and companies, establishing personal ties and gradually building mutual trust is more difficult to achieve.

Another relationship-building mechanism can be the exchange of personnel, on a temporary or permanent basis. In Japan, for instance, it is not unusual to send an employee 'on assignment' to a partner firm for a long period of time, often simultaneously accepting 'external' employees in return. In some countries, the transfer of employees between partner organizations is more permanent. France and Japan are known for their public servants' mid-career shifts to the private sector (*pantouflage* and *amakudari*, respectively), which makes building public–private partnerships much easier.

FURTHER READING

No one who wishes to delve more deeply into the topic of organizational boundaries and inter-organizational relationships can avoid running into references to the classic in this area. Oliver Williamson's *Markets and Hierarchies: Analysis and Antitrust Implications*. Williamson's writings have inspired many researchers, especially economists. Others have remarked that Williamson's transaction cost economics largely ignores the political, social and psychological aspects of business relationships. As an antidote to Williamson's strongly rationalist view of the world, another classic can be recommended. Jeffrey Pfeffer and Gerald Salancik's *The External Control of Organizations: A Resource Dependency Perspective* is an excellent book that emphasizes the political aspects of inter-organizational relationships. However, both books are quite academic and not for the faint-hearted.

A more accessible overview of the topic of inter-organizational cooperation is provided by Yves Doz and Gary Hamel in their book *The Alliance Advantage: The Art of Creating Value Through Partnering*. A very good hands-on, practitioner-oriented book is *Smart Alliances: A Practical Guide to Repeatable Success*, by John Harbison and Peter Pekar. For further reading on the subject of vertical relationships, Michael Best's *The New Competition*, and Carlos Jarillo's 'On Strategic Networks', are both excellent choices. For horizontal relationships a good starting point would be *Strategic Alliances: Formation, Implementation and Evolution*, by Peter Lorange and Johan Roos, or *The Knowledge Link: How Firms Compete Through Strategic Alliances*, by J. Badaracco. If the reader is interested in a broader view of the business ecosystem and liked James Moore's reading, then his book, *The Death of Competition: Leadership and Strategy in the Age of Business Ecosystems*, can also be recommended.

All of the above works are positively inclined towards collaboration, largely adopting the embedded organization perspective. For a more critical appraisal of networks, alliances and close relationships, by authors taking the discrete organization perspective, readers are advised to start with the article 'Outsourcing and Industrial Decline', by Richard Bettis, Stephen Bradley and Gary Hamel. Other critical accounts are John Hendry's article 'Culture, Community and Networks: The Hidden Cost of Outsourcing', and S. MacDonald's 'Too Close for Comfort?: The Strategic Implications of Getting Close to the Customer'.

For a more thorough understanding of networks within the Japanese context, Michael Gerlach's *Alliance Capitalism: The Social Organization of Japanese Business* is a good book to begin with. T. Nishiguchi's book *Strategic Industrial Sourcing: The Japanese Advantage* is particularly interesting on the topic of Japanese supplier relationships. For the Chinese view on networks, Murray Weidenbaum and Samuel Hughes book *The Bamboo Network: How Expatriate Chinese Entrepreneurs Are Creating a New Economic Superpower in Asia* is recommended, as is S. Redding's *The Spirit of Chinese Capitalism*. For an overview of European views, Ronnie Lessem and Fred Neubauer's *European Management Systems* is an excellent book, but also Roland Calori and Philippe de Woot's collection *A European Management Model: Beyond Diversity* provides challenging insights.

REFERENCES

Albert, M. (1991) *Capitalisme contre Capitalisme*, Seuil, Paris.

Allison, G.T. (1969) 'Conceptual Models and The Cuban Missile Crisis', *The American Political Science Review*, No. 3, September, pp. 689–718.

Anand, B., and Khanna, T. (2000) 'Do Companies Learn to Create Value?', *Strategic Management Journal*, Vol. 21, No. 3, March, pp. 295–316.

Anderson Consulting (1999) 'Dispelling the Myths of Alliances', *Outlook*, pp. 28.

Aoki, M., Gustafsson, B., and Williamson, O.E. (1990) *The Firm as a Nexus of Treaties*, Sage, London.

Arthur, W.B. (1994) *Increasing Returns and Path Dependence in the Economy*, University of Michigan Press, Ann Arbor, MI.

Axelrod, R. (1984) *The Evolution of Cooperation*, Basic Books, New York.

Axelsson, B., and Easton, G. (1992) *Industrial Networks: A New View of Reality*, Wiley, New York.

Badaracco, J.L. (1991) *The Knowledge Link: How Firms Compete Through Strategic Alliances*, Harvard Business School Press, Boston, MA.

Bateson, G. (1979) *Mind and Nature: A Necessary Unity*, Dutton, New York.

Best, M.H. (1990) *The New Competition: Institutions of Industrial Restructuring*, Polity, Cambridge.

Bettis, R.A., Bradley, S.P., and Hamel, G. (1992) 'Outsourcing and Industrial Decline', *Academy of Management Executive*, Vol. 6, No. 1, pp. 7–22.

Bleeke, J., and Ernst, D. (1991) 'The Way to Win in Cross Border Alliances', *Harvard Business Review*, Vol. 69, No. 6, November–December, pp. 127–135.

Bleeke, J., and Ernst, D. (1993) 'Collaborating To Compete', Wiley, New York.

Bleeke, J., and Ernst, D. (1998) 'The Way To Win in Cross-Border Alliances', *The Alliance Analyst*, March, pp. 1–4.

Brandenburger, A.M., and Nalebuff, B.J. (1996) *Co-opetition*, Currency Doubleday, New York.

Calori, R., and de Woot, P. (eds.) (1994) *A European Management Model: Beyond Diversity*, Prentice Hall, Hemel Hempstead.

Chandler, A.D. Jr. (1977) *The Visible Hand: The Managerial Revolution in American Business*, Harvard University Press, Cambridge, MA.

Chandler, A.D. (1986) 'The Evolution of Modern Global Competition', in: M.E. Porter (ed.), *Competition in Global Industries*, Harvard Business School Press, Boston, pp. 405–448.

Chandler, A.D. (1990) *Scale and Scope*, Belknop, Cambridge, MA.

Chesbrough, H.W., and Teece, D.J. (1996) 'Organizing for Innovation: When is Virtual Virtuous?', *Harvard Business Review*, Vol. 74, No. 1, January–February, pp. 65–73.

Child, J., and Faulkner, D. (1998) *Strategies for Cooperation: Managing Alliances, Networks, and Joint Ventures*, Oxford University Press, Oxford.

Contractor, F.J., and Lorange, P. (1988) *Cooperative Strategies in International Business*, Lexington Books, Lexington, MA.

Dixit, A.K., and Nalebuff, B.J. (1991) *Thinking Strategically: The Competitive Edge in Business, Politics, and Everyday Life*, W.W. Norton, New York.

Doz, Y., and Hamel, G. (1998) *The Alliance Advantage: The Art of Creating Value Through Partnering*, Harvard Business School Press, Boston, MA.

Dyer, J.H. (1996) 'Specialized Supplier Networks as a Source of Competitive Advantage: Evidence from the Auto Industry', *Strategic Management Journal*, Vol. 17, No. 4, pp. 271–291.

Dyer, J.H., Kale, P., and Singh, H. (2001) 'How to Make Strategic Alliances Work', *Sloan Management Review*, Vol. 42, No. 4, Summer, pp. 37–43.

Dyer, J.H., and Ouchi, W.G. (1993) 'Japanese-Style Partnerships: Giving Companies a Competitive Edge', *Sloan Management Review*, Fall, pp. 51–63.

Dyer, J.H., and Singh, H. (1998) 'The Relational View: Cooperative Strategy and Sources of Interorganizational Competitive Advantage', *Academy of Management Review*, Vol. 23, No. 4, pp. 660–679.

Feldstein, J., Flanagan, C.S., and Holloway, C.A. (2001) *Handspring – Partnerships*, Case #SM-79, Stanford Graduate School of Business.

Gambetta, D. (ed.) (1988) *Trust: Making and Breaking Cooperative Relations*, Blackwell, New York.

Gerlach, M. (1992) *Alliance Capitalism: The Social Organization of Japanese Business*, University of California Press, Berkeley, CA.

Gnyawali, D.R., and Madhavan, R. (2001) 'Cooperative Networks and Competitive Dynamics: A Structural Embeddedness Perspective', *Academy of Management Review*, Vol. 26, No. 3, pp. 431–445.

Gomes-Casseres, B. (1994) 'Group versus Group: How Alliance Networks Compete', *Harvard Business Review*, Vol. 72, No. 4, July–August, pp. 62–74.

Grabher, G. (ed.) (1993) *The Embedded Firm: On the Socioeconomics of Industrial Networks*, Routledge, London.

Granovetter, M.S. (1985) 'Economic Action and Social Structure: The Problem of Embeddedness', *American Journal of Sociology*, Vol. 91, pp. 481–501.

Greenhalgh, L. (2001) *Managing Strategic Relationships*, The Free Press, New York.

Gulati, R. (1998) 'Alliances and Networks', *Strategic Management Journal*, Vol. 19, No. 4, pp. 293–317.

Håkansson, H., and Johanson, J. (1993) 'The Network as a Governance Structure: Interfirm Cooperation beyond Markets and Hierarchies', in: G. Grabner (ed.), *The Embedded Firm: On the Socioeconomics of Industrial Networks*, Routledge, London, pp. 35–51.

Hamel, G. (1991) 'Competition for Competence and Inter-Partner Learning Within International Strategic Alliances', *Strategic Management Journal*, Vol. 12, Special Issue, Summer, pp. 83–103.

Hamel, G., Doz, Y.L., and Prahalad, C.K. (1989) 'Collaborate with Your Competitors – and Win', *Harvard Business Review*, Vol. 67, No. 1, January–February, pp. 133–139.

Hamilton, G.G., and Woolsey Biggart, N. (1988) 'Market, Culture and Authority: A Comparative Analysis of Management and Organization in the Far East', *American Journal of Sociology*, Vol. 94, pp. 52.

Hampden-Turner, C., and Trompenaars, A. (1993) *The Seven Cultures of Capitalism: Value Systems for Creating Wealth in the United States, Japan, Germany, France, Britain, Sweden and the Netherlands*, Doubleday, New York.

Handy, C. (1989) *The Age of Unreason*, Business Books, London.

Harbison, J., and Pekar, P. (2000) *Smart Alliances: A Practical Guide to Repeatable Success*, Josscy-Bass, San Francisco.

Harrigan, K.R. (1985) *Strategies for Joint Ventures*, D.C. Heath, Lexington, MA.

Hendry, J. (1995) 'Culture, Community and Networks: The Hidden Cost of Outsourcing', *European Management Journal*, Vol. 13, No. 2, pp. 193–200.

Hill, C.W.L. (1990) 'Cooperation Opportunism, and the Invisible Hand: Implications for Transaction Cost Theory', *Academy of Management Review*, Vol. 15, No. 3, pp. 500–513.

Hofstede, G. (1993) 'Cultural Constraints in Management Theories', *Academy of Management Executive*, Vol. 7, No. 1, pp. 8–21.

James, B.G. (1985) *Business Wargames*, Penguin, Harmondsworth.

Jarillo, J.C. (1988) 'On Strategic Networks', *Strategic Management Journal*, Vol. 9, No. 1, January–February, pp. 31–41.

Johanson, J., and Mattson, L.G. (1987) 'Interorganisational Relations in Industrial Systems: A Network Approach Compared with the Transaction Cost Approach', *International Studies in Management and Organisation*, Vol. 17, No. 1, pp. 34–48.

Johanson, J., and Mattson, L.G. (1992) 'Network Position and Strategic Action: An Analytical Framework', in: B. Axelsson and G. Easton (eds.), *Industrial Networks: A New View of Reality*, Routledge, London.

Kagono, T., Nonaka, I., Sakakibara, K., and Okumara, A. (1985) *Strategic vs. Evolutionary Management*, Amsterdam, North-Holland.

Kale, P., Dyer, J., and Singh, H. (2000) 'Alliance Capability, Stock Market Response and Long-Term Alliance Success', *Academy of Management Proceedings*, August.

Kanter, R.M. (1994) 'Collaborative Advantage: The Art of Alliances', *Harvard Business Review*, Vol. 72, No. 4, July–August, pp. 96–108.

Kay, J.A. (1993) *Foundations of Corporate Success*, Oxford University Press, Oxford.

Kim, W.C. and Mauborgne, R. (1999) 'Strategy, Value Innovation, and the Knowledge Economy', *Sloan Management Review*, Vol. 40, No. 3, Spring, pp. 41–54.

Kogut, B. (1988) 'Joint Ventures: Theoretical and Empirical Perspectives', *Strategic Management Journal*, Vol. 9, pp. 319–332.

Lado, A.A., Boyd, N.G., and Hanlon, S.C. (1997) 'Competition, Cooperation and the Search for Economic Rents: A Syncretic Model', *Academy of Management Review*, Vol. 22, No. 1, January, pp. 110–141.

Lessem, R., and Neubauer, F.F. (1994) *European Management Systems*, McGraw-Hill, London.

Lorange, P., and Roos, J. (1992) *Strategic Alliances: Formation, Implementation and Evolution*, Blackwell, Cambridge, MA.

Lorenzoni, G., and Baden-Fuller, C. (1995) 'Creating a Strategic Center to Manage a Web of Partners', *California Management Review*, Vol. 37, No. 3, Spring, pp. 146–163.

MacDonald, S. (1995) 'Too Close for Comfort?: The Strategic Implications of Getting Close to the Customer', *California Management Review*, Vol. 37, Summer, pp. 8–27.

Mahoney, J.T. (1992) 'The Choice of Organizational Form: Vertical Financial Ownership versus Other Methods of Vertical Integration', *Strategic Management Journal*, Vol. 13, No. 8, pp. 559–584.

Miles, R.E., and Snow, C.C. (1986) 'Network Organizations: New Concepts for New Forms', *California Management Review*, Vol. 28, Spring, pp. 62–73.

Mitchell, R.K., Agle, B.R., and Wood, D.J. (1997) 'Toward a Theory of Stakeholder Identification and Salience: Defining the Principle of Who and What Really Counts', *Academy of Management Review*, Vol. 22, No. 4, October, pp. 853–886.

Moore, J.F. (1993) 'Predators and Prey: A New Ecology of Competition', *Harvard Business Review*, Vol. 71, No. 3, pp. 75–86.

Moore, J.F. (1996) *The Death of Competition: Leadership and Strategy in the Age of Business Ecosystems*, HarperBusiness, New York.

Nalebuff, B.J., and Brandenburger, A.M. (1997) 'Co-opetition: Competitive and Cooperative Business Strategies for the Digital Economy', *Strategy and Leadership*, Vol. 25, No. 6, November–December, pp. 28–35.

Nishiguchi, T. (1994) *Strategic Industrial Sourcing: The Japanese Advantage*, Oxford University Press, New York.

Oliver, N., and Wilkinson, B. (1988) *The Japanization of British Industry*, Basil Blackwell, London.

Ouchi, W.G. (1980) 'Markets, Bureaucracies, and Clans', *Administrative Science Quarterly*, Vol. 25, No. 1, pp. 129–142.

Parolini, C. (1999) *The Value Net*, Wiley, Chichester.

Pascale, R.T., and Athos, A.G. (1981) *The Art of Japanese Management*, Simon & Schuster, New York.

Pfeffer, J., and Salancik, G.R. (1978) *The External Control of Organizations: A Resource Dependency Perspective*, Harper & Row, New York.

Piore, M., and Sabel, C.F. (1984) *The Second Industrial Divide*, Basic Books, New York.

Porter, M.E. (1979) 'How Competitive Forces Shape Strategy', *Harvard Business Review*, March–May, pp. 137–145.

Porter, M.E. (1980) *Competitive Strategy: Techniques for Analyzing Industries and Competitors*, Free Press, New York.

Porter, M.E. (1985) *Competitive Advantage*, Free Press, New York.

Porter, M.E. (1990) *The Competitive Advantage of Nations*, Macmillan, London.

Powell, W. (1990) Neither Market nor Hierarchy: Network Forms of Organization, *Research in Organizational Behavior*, Vol. 12, pp. 295–336.

Prahalad, C.K., and Hamel, G. (1990) 'The Core Competence of the Corporation', *Harvard Business Review*, Vol. 68, No. 3, May–June, pp. 79–91.

Preece, S.B. (1995) 'Incorporating International Strategic Alliances into Overall Firm Strategy: A Typology of Six Managerial Objectives', *The International Executive*, Vol. 37, No. 3, May–June, pp. 261–277.

Quinn, J.B. (1992) *The Intelligent Enterprise: A Knowledge and Service Based Paradigm for Industry*, Free Press, New York.

Rademakers, M.F.L. (1999) *Managing Inter-Firm Cooperation in Different Institutional Environments: A Comparison of the Dutch and UK Potato Industries*, PhD Series in General Management, Rotterdam School of Management, Rotterdam.

Redding, S.G. (1990) *The Spirit of Chinese Capitalism*, Walter de Gruyter, Berlin.

Reich, R., and Mankin, E. (1986) 'Joint Ventures with Japan Give Away Our Future', *Harvard Business Review*, Vol. 64, No. 2, March–April, pp. 78–86.

Reve, T. (1990) 'The Firm as a Nexus of Internal and External Contracts', in: M. Aoki, B. Gustafsson and O.E. Williamson (eds.), *The Firm as a Nexus of Treaties*, Sage, London.

Richardson, G. (1972) 'The Organization of Industry', *Economic Journal*, Vol. 82, pp. 833–896.

Ruigrok, W., and van Tulder, R. (1995) *The Logic of International Restructuring*, Routledge, London.

Schelling, T. (1960) *The Strategy of Conflict*, Harvard University Press, Cambridge, MA.

Shapiro, C., and Varian, H. (1998) *Information Rules: A Strategic Guide to the Network Economy*, Harvard Business School Press, Cambridge, MA.

Simonin, B. (1997) 'The Importance of Collaborative Know-How', *Academy of Management Journal*, Vol. 40, No. 5, pp. 1150–1174.

Teece, D.J. (1992) 'Competition, Cooperation, and Innovation: Organizational Arrangements for Regimes of Rapid Technological Progress', *Journal of Economic Behavior and Organization*, Vol. 18, pp. 1–25.

Thorelli, H.B. (1986) 'Networks: Between Markets and Hierarchies', *Strategic Management Journal*, Vol. 7, No. 1, January–February, pp. 37–51.

Thurow, L. (1991) *Head to Head*, MIT Press, Cambridge, MA.

Van Tulder, R., and Junne, G. (1988) *European Multinationals and Core Technologies*, Wiley, London.

Weidenbaum, M., and Hughes, S. (1996) *The Bamboo Network: How Expatriate Chinese Entrepreneurs Are Creating a New Economic Superpower in Asia*, Free Press, New York.

Williamson, O.E. (1975) *Markets and Hierarchies: Analysis and Antitrust Implications*, Free Press, New York.

Williamson, O.E. (1979) 'Transaction Cost Economics: The Governance of Contractual Relations', *Journal of Law and Economics*, Vol. 22, pp. 223–261.

Williamson, O.E. (1985) *The Economic Institutions of Capitalism*, Free Press, New York.

Williamson, O.E. (1991) 'Strategizing, Economizing, and Economic Organization', *Strategic Management Journal*, Vol. 12, Special Issue, Winter, pp. 75–94.

STRATEGY CONTEXT

Circumstances? I make circumstances!

Napoleon Bonaparte (1769–1821); French emperor

The strategy context is the set of circumstances surrounding strategy-making – the conditions under which both the strategy process and the strategy content are formed. It could be said that strategy context is concerned with the *where* of strategy – where (i.e. in which firm and which environment) the strategy process and strategy content are embedded.

Most strategizing managers have an ambivalent relationship with their strategy context. On the one hand, strategizing is about creating something new, and for this a healthy level of disregard, or even disrespect, for the present circumstances is required. Much like Napoleon, managers do not want to hear about current conditions limiting their capability to shape the future – they want to create their own circumstances. On the other hand, managers recognize that many contextual limitations are real and that wise strategists must take these circumstances into account. In this section, this fundamental tension between *shaping* the context and *adapting* to it will be at the center of attention.

As visualized in Figure IV.1, the strategy context can be dissected along two different dimensions: industry versus organization, and national versus international. This gives the three key contexts that will be explored in Chapters 8, 9 and 10:

- The industry context. The key issue here is how industry development takes place. Can the individual firm influence its industry and to what extent does the industry context dictate particular types of firm behavior?

- The organizational context. The key issue here is how organizational development takes place. Can strategizing managers influence their own organizational conditions and to what extent does the organizational context determine particular types of firm behavior?

- The international context. The key issue here is how the international context is developing. Must firms adapt to ongoing global convergence or will international diversity remain a characteristic with which firms will need to cope?

FIGURE IV.1   Parts of the strategy context

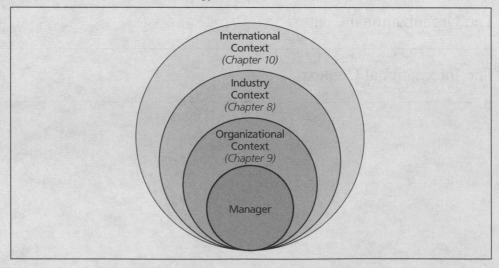

THE INDUSTRY CONTEXT

Know the other and know yourself: Triumph without peril.
Know nature and know the situation: Triumph completely.

Sun Tzu (5th century BC); Chinese military strategist

INTRODUCTION

If strategic management is concerned with relating a firm to its environment, then it is essential to know this environment well. In the previous chapters the factors and actors that shape the external context of the firm have been thoroughly reviewed. While the entire outside world was taken into consideration, emphasis was placed on the direct environment in which a firm needs to compete – its industry context. It was concluded that an understanding of competitors, buyers, suppliers, substitutes and potential new entrants, as well as the structural factors that influence their behavior, is invaluable for determining a successful strategy.

A constant theme in the strategy process and strategy content sections was industry change. Knowing the current industry context, it became clear, is not enough to secure an ongoing alignment between a firm and its environment. Strategizing managers need to recognize in which direction the industry is developing to be able to maintain a healthy fit. However, what was not addressed in these discussions is how industry development actually takes place. Important questions such as 'what are the drivers propelling industry development?' and 'what patterns of development do industries exhibit?' have not yet been examined. Nor has it been established whether industries develop in the same way and at the same speed, and whether change is always accompanied by the same opportunities and threats. In this chapter, these questions surrounding the issue of industry development will be at the center of attention.

For strategizing managers, however, the most important question linked to the issue of industry development is how a firm can move beyond *adapting* to *shaping*. How can a firm, or a group of collaborating firms, modify the structure and competitive dynamics in their industry to gain an advantageous position? How can the industry's evolutionary path be proactively diverted into a particular direction? If a firm would be capable of shaping its industry environment instead of following it, this would give them the potential for creating a strong competitive advantage – they could 'set the rules of the competitive game' instead of having to 'play by the rules' set by others. This topic of industry leadership – shaping events as opposed to following them – will be the key focus throughout this chapter.

THE ISSUE OF INDUSTRY DEVELOPMENT

When strategists look at an industry, they are interested in understanding 'the rules of the game' (e.g. Prahalad and Doz, 1987; Hamel, 1996). The industry rules are the demands dictated to the firm by the industry context, which limit the scope of potential strategic behaviors. In other words, industry rules stipulate what must be done to survive and thrive in the chosen line of business – they determine under what conditions the competitive game will be played. For example, an industry rule could be 'must have significant scale economies', 'must have certain technology' or 'must have strong brand'. Failure to adhere to the rules leads to being selected out.

The industry rules arise from the structure of the industry (e.g. Porter, 1980; Tirole, 1988). All of Porter's five forces can impose constraints on a firm's freedom of action. Where the rules are strict, the degrees of freedom available to the strategist are limited. Strict rules imply that only very specific behavior is allowed – firms must closely follow the rules of the game or face severe consequences. Where the rules are looser, firms have more room to maneuver and exhibit distinctive behavior – the level of managerial discretion is higher (e.g. Hambrick and Abrahamson, 1995; Carpenter and Golden, 1997).

As industries develop, the rules of competition change – vertical integration becomes necessary, certain competences become vital or having a global presence becomes a basic requirement. To be able to play the competitive game well, strategizing managers need to identify which characteristics in the industry structure and which aspects of competitive interaction are changing. This is the topic of 'dimensions of industry development', which will be reviewed in more detail below. To determine their response, it is also essential to understand the nature of the change. Are the industry rules gradually shifting or is there a major break with the past? Is the industry development more evolutionary or more revolutionary? A process of slow and moderate industry change will demand a different strategic reaction than a process of sudden and dramatic disruption of the industry rules. This topic of 'paths of industry development' will also be examined more closely.

As strategists generally like to have the option to shape instead of always being shaped, they need to recognize the determinants of industry development as well. What are the factors that cause the industry rules to change? This subject can be divided into two parts. First, the question of what the drivers of industry development are, pushing the industry in a certain direction. Secondly, the question of what the inhibitors of industry development are, placing a brake on changes. Together, these forces of change and forces for stability will determine the actual path of development that the industry will follow. How these four topics are interrelated is outlined in Figure 8.1.

Dimensions of industry development

Industry development means that the structure of the industry changes. In Chapter 5, the key aspects of the industry structure have already been discussed. Following Porter (1980), five important groups of industry actors were identified (i.e. competitors, buyers, suppliers, new entrants and substitutes) and the underlying factors determining their behavior were reviewed. Industry development (which Porter calls 'industry evolution', see Reading 8.1) is the result of a change in one or more of these underlying factors.

As Porter already indicates, the industry structure can be decomposed into dozens of elements, each of which can change, causing a shift in industry rules. Here it is not the intention to go through all of these elements, but to pick out a number of important structural characteristics that require special attention. Each one of these structural characteristics represents a dimension along which significant industry developments can take place:

FIGURE 8.1   The issue of industry development

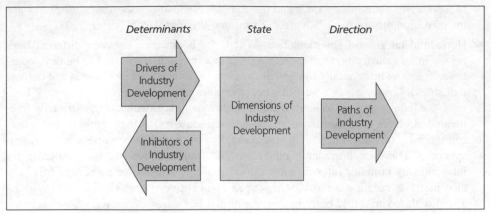

- Convergence–divergence. Where the business models that firms employ increasingly start to resemble each other, the industry is said to be moving towards convergence (e.g. insurance and airline industries). In contrast, where many firms introduce new business models, the industry is said to be developing towards more diversity (e.g. car retailing and restaurant industries). Higher diversity can be due to the 'mutation' of existing firms, as they strive to compete on a different basis, or the result of new entrants with their own distinct business model. Convergence is the consequence of adaptation by less successful firms to a 'dominant design' in the industry and the selecting out of unfit firms incapable of adequate and timely adaptation (e.g. Hannan and Freeman, 1977; Porter, 1980). Generally, patterns of divergence and convergence can be witnessed in all industries, although the amount of mutation and the pressure for convergence can greatly differ, as can the overall cycle time of an 'evolutionary phase' of mutation and selection (e.g. Aldrich, 1999; Baum and Singh, 1994).

- Concentration–fragmentation. Where an increasing share of the market is in the hands of only a few companies, the industry is said to be developing towards a more concentrated structure (e.g. aircraft and food retailing industries). Conversely, where the average market share of the largest companies starts to decrease, the industry is said to be moving towards a more fragmented structure (e.g. airline and telecom services industries). Concentration can be due to mergers and acquisitions, or the result of companies exiting the business. Fragmentation can happen when new companies are formed and grab a part of the market, or through the entry of existing companies into the industry. In a concentrated industry it is much more likely that only one or two firms will be dominant than in a fragmented industry, but it is also possible that the industry structure is more balanced.

- Vertical integration–fragmentation. Where firms in the industry are becoming involved in more value-adding activities in the industry column, the industry is said to be developing towards a more vertically integrated structure (e.g. media and IT service providers). Conversely, where firms in the industry are withdrawing from various value-adding activities and 'going back to the core', the industry is said to be moving towards a more, disintegrated, layered or vertically fragmented structure (e.g. telecom and automotive industries). It is even possible that the entire vertical structure changes if a new business model has major consequences upstream and/or downstream. In recent years, technological changes surrounding IT and the internet have triggered a number of such instances of industry reconfiguration (e.g. travel and encyclopedia industries). However, even though we are now equipped with more fashionable terms (e.g.

'deconstruction'), such industry-wide transformations of the value-creation process are in themselves not new (e.g. PCs and the computer industry in the 1980s; airplanes and the travel industry in the 1950s) (e.g. Evans and Wurster, 1997; Porter, 2001).

- Horizontal integration–fragmentation. Where the boundaries between different businesses in an industry become increasingly fuzzy, the industry is said to be developing towards a more horizontally integrated structure (e.g. consumer electronics and defense industries). Conversely, where firms become more strictly confined to their own business, the industry is said to be moving towards a more segmented or horizontally fragmented structure (e.g. construction and airline industries). Links between businesses can intensify or wane, depending on the mobility barriers and potential cross-business synergies. However, horizontal integration and fragmentation are not limited to the intra-industry domain. Inter-industry integration between two or more industries can also increase, creating a more or less open competitive space (Hamel and Prahalad, 1994) with few mobility barriers (e.g. the digital industries). Inter-industry integration can also occur where the producers of different products and services are complementary and/or converge on a common standard or platform (e.g. Palm OS and Linux), making them 'complementors' (e.g. Cusumano and Gawer, 2002; Moore, 1996, Reading 7.3). Yet, the opposite trend is possible as well, whereby an industry becomes more isolated from neighboring sectors (e.g. accountancy).

- International integration–fragmentation. Where the international boundaries separating various geographic segments of an industry become increasingly less important, the industry is said to be developing towards a more internationally integrated structure (e.g. food retailing and business education industries). Conversely, where the competitive interactions in an industry are increasingly confined to a region (e.g. Europe) or country, the industry is said to be moving towards a more internationally fragmented structure (e.g. satellite television and internet retailing). These developments will be more thoroughly examined in Chapter 10, which deals with the international context.

- Expansion–contraction. Industries can also differ with regard to the structural nature of the demand for their products and/or services. Where an industry is experiencing an ongoing increase in demand, the industry is said to be in growth or expansion. Where demand is constantly receding, the industry is said to be in decline or contraction. If periods of expansion are followed by periods of contraction, and vice versa, the industry is said to be cyclical. A prolonged period of expansion is usually linked to the growth phase of the industry life cycle (e.g. Moore, 2000; Porter, 1980, Reading 8.1), while contraction is linked to the decline phase, but often it is rather difficult to apply the 'life cycle' concept to an entire industry (as opposed to a product or technology). As industry growth (expansion) can easily follow a period of industry decline (contraction), the life cycle model has little descriptive value – what does it mean to be mature? – and even less predictive value.

Paths of industry development

The development of an industry can be mapped along any one of the dimensions listed above. The most popular is to track the pattern of expansion and contraction, to gain some indication of the life cycle phase in which the industry might have arrived. Another frequently analyzed characteristic is the level of concentration, commonly using a concentration index to measure the market share of the four or eight largest companies. But it is equally viable to trace the trajectory of vertical, horizontal or international integration. In Figure 8.2 examples of these paths of industry development are given.

In Figure 8.3 one particular element of the convergence–divergence dimension has been selected for further magnification. As discussed above, in the development of an industry

FIGURE 8.2 Examples of industry development paths

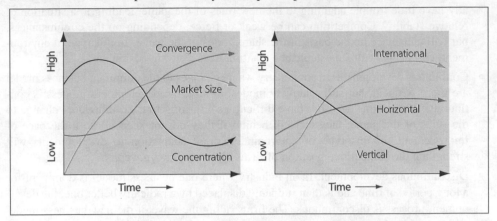

a particular business model can become the dominant design around which the rest of the industry converges. A strategically relevant development occurs when the dominant business model is replaced by a new business model that offers customers higher value. In Figure 8.3, four generic patterns of industry development are outlined, each describing a different type of transition from the old dominant model to the new (Burgelman and Grove, 1996; D'Aveni, 1999):

- Gradual development. In an industry where one business model is dominant for a long period of time and is slowly replaced by an alternative that is a slight improvement, the

FIGURE 8.3 Patterns of dominant business model development

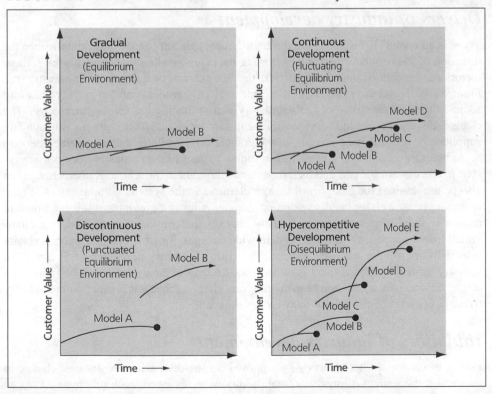

development process is gradual. The firms adhering to the dominant design will generally have little trouble adapting to the new rules of the game, leading to a situation of relative stability. Competition can be weak or fierce, depending on the circumstances, but will take place on the basis of the shared rules of the game. In this type of environment, companies with an established position have a strong advantage.

- Continuous development. In an industry where changes to the dominant business model are more frequent, but still relatively modest in size, the development process is continuous. While firms need not have difficulties adjusting to each individual change to the rules of the game, they can fall behind if they do not keep up with the pace of improvement. In this type of environment, rapid adaptation to developments will strengthen the competitive position of firms vis-à-vis slow movers.

- Discontinuous development. In an industry where one business model is dominant for a long period of time and is then suddenly displaced by a radically better one, the development process is discontinuous. The firms riding the wave of the new business model will generally have a large advantage over the companies that need to adjust to an entirely different set of industry rules. Where industry incumbents are themselves the 'rule breakers' (Hamel, 1996), they can strongly improve their position vis-à-vis the 'rule takers' in the industry. But the business model innovator can also be an industry outsider, who gains entrance by avoiding competition with established players on their terms (e.g. Bower and Christensen, 1995; Slywotsky, 1996).

- Hypercompetitive development. In an industry where business models are frequently pushed aside by radically better ones, the development process is hypercompetitive (D'Aveni, 1994). The rules of the game are constantly changing, making it impossible for firms to build up a sustainably dominant position. The only defense in this type of environment is offense – being able to outrun existing competitors, being innovative first and being able to outperform new rule breakers at their own game.

Drivers of industry development

There is an endless list of factors in the environment that can change and can influence the direction of industry development. Following the categorization made in Chapter 7, these factors can be divided into change drivers that are external or internal to the industry (see Figure 8.4). The change drivers in the contextual environment can be roughly split into socio-cultural, economic, political/regulatory and technological forces for change. The change drivers in the industry environment can be divided into groups surrounding suppliers, buyers, incumbent rivals, new entrants, and substitutes and complementors.

As the arrows indicate, change in a complex system like an industry does not always start in one discernible part and then reverberate throughout the whole. Rather, change can also be the result of the interplay of various elements in the system, without any clear start or ending point. Yet, for the discussion on shaping industry development it is important to recognize the distinction between industry changes that are largely triggered by an individual firm, as opposed to broader, system-wide changes, for which no one actor can claim responsibility. Where one firm is the major driver of industry development, it can claim industry leadership. But if there is no industry leader and the evolution of the industry is due to the complex interaction of many different change drivers, it is said that the industry dynamics determine the path of industry development.

Inhibitors of industry development

Forces of change do not always go unopposed. In the discussion on strategic change in Chapter 4, the sources of organizational rigidity were reviewed, each of which acts as an

FIGURE 8.4 Drivers of industry development

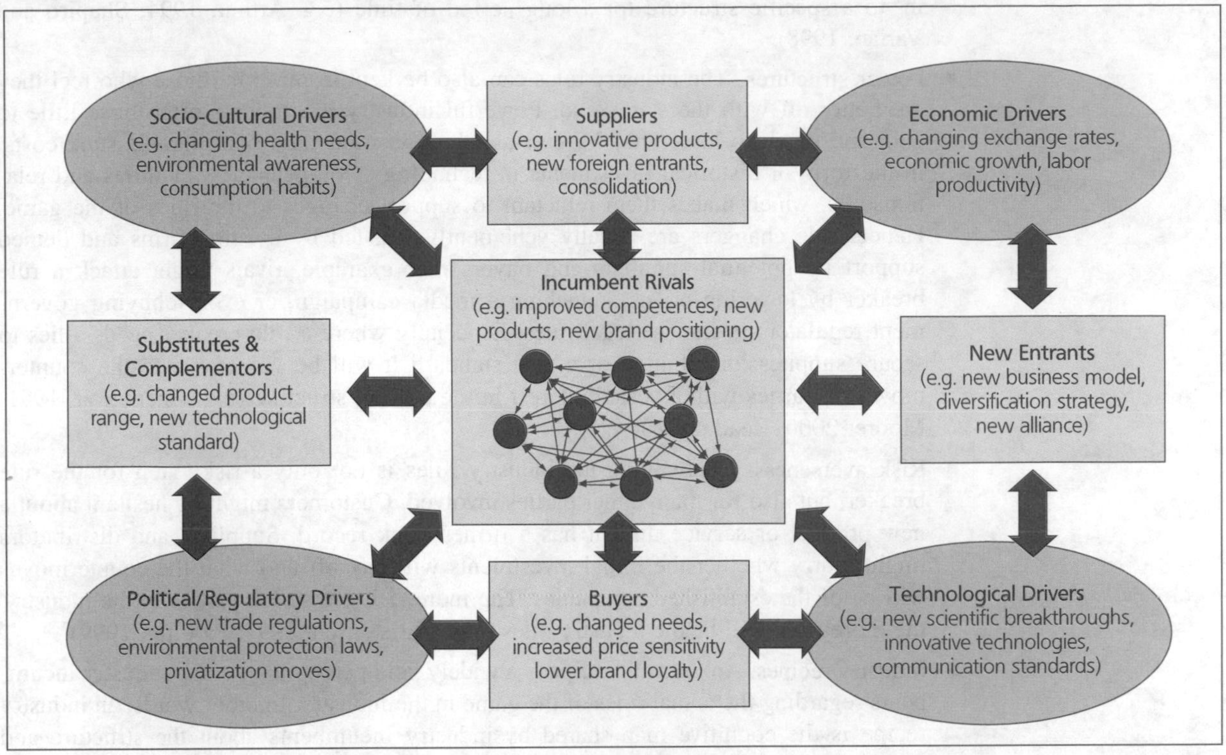

inhibitor to organizational change. In the same way, there are many sources of industry rigidity, making the industry rules much more difficult to bend or break. Industry rigidity can be defined as the lack of susceptibility to change. If an industry is rigid, the rules of the game cannot be altered and competitive positions are relatively fixed. The opposite term is industry plasticity – an industry's susceptibility to change.

A large number of factors can contribute to rigidity, thereby inhibiting industry development. Some of the most important ones are the following:

- Underlying conditions. Basically, some rules might be immutable because the underlying industry conditions cannot be changed. In some industries economies of scale are essential (e.g. airplane manufacturing, merchant shipping), where in others economies of scale are not of importance (e.g. wedding services, dentistry services). In some industries buyers are fragmented (e.g. newspapers, moving services), while in others they are highly concentrated (e.g. defense systems, harbor construction). In some industries buyers value product differentiation (e.g. clothing, restaurants), while in others bulk producers must compete on price (e.g. chemicals, general construction). Many of these structural factors are inherent to the industry and defy any attempts to change them (e.g. Bain, 1959; Porter, 1980).

- Industry integration. Besides the limited plasticity of individual aspects of the industry context, it is also important to recognize that some industries are particularly rigid because of the complex linkages between various aspects of the industry. For example, to be a rule breaking music company not only requires developing new delivery methods via the internet, but also getting electronics manufacturers to adopt the new standards, finding ways to safeguard copyrights, working together with governments to find new policing methods, and not least to change the buying behavior of consumers. Such interrelations between various elements of the industry can make it particularly difficult to actually influence the direction of events over time. The industry can become 'locked in' to a specific structure for a long period of time (e.g. Arthur, 1994; Shapiro and Varian, 1998).

- Power structures. The industry rules can also be kept in place by those who feel they are better off with the status quo. Powerful industry incumbents often have little to gain and much to lose. They have established positions and considerable sunk costs, in the form of historical investments in technology, competencies, facilities and relationships, which makes them reluctant to support changes to the rules of the game. Hence, rule changers are usually vehemently resisted by existing firms and denied support by potential suppliers and buyers. For example, rivals might attack a rule breaker by lowering prices, launching a media campaign, or even lobbying government regulators to impose legal rules. Especially where a rule breaker needs allies to secure supplies, distribution or a new standard it will be vulnerable to the countermoves of parties with a vested interest in the current structure (e.g. Ghemawat, 1991; Moore, 2000, Reading 8.3).

- Risk averseness. Challenging the industry rules is not only a risky step for the rule breaker, but also for many other parties involved. Customers might be hesitant about a new product or service until it has a firmer track record. Suppliers and distributors might worry whether the initial investments will pay off and what the countermoves will be of the established companies. The more risk averse the parties in the industry, the more rigid will be the industry rules (e.g. Christensen, 1997; Parolini, 1999).

- Industry recipes. An industry recipe is a widely held perception among industry incumbents regarding the actual rules of the game in the industry. In other words, an industry recipe is the cognitive map shared by industry incumbents about the structure and demands of an industry. Such a common understanding of the rules of the game can develop over time through shared experiences and interaction – the longer people are in the industry and converse with each other, the greater the chance that a consensus will grow about 'what makes the industry tick'. Thus, the industry recipe can limit people's openness to rule changers who challenge the industry orthodoxy (e.g. Baden-Fuller and Stopford, 1992, Reading 8.2; Spender, 1989).

- Institutional pressures. While the industry recipe is a shared understanding of how the industry actually functions, industry incumbents usually also share norms of what constitutes socially acceptable economic behavior. Companies experience strong pressures from government, professional associations, customers, consultants, trade unions, pressure groups and other industry incumbents prescribing permissible strategies and actions, and generally internalize these behavioral standards. Such conformity to institutional pressures gives companies legitimacy, but makes them less willing to question industry conventions, let alone work together with a maverick rule breaker (e.g. Aldrich and Fiol, 1994; Oliver, 1997).

Taken together, these historically determined factors inhibit developments in the industry. It is said that industry evolution is path dependent – the path that the industry has traveled in the past will strongly limit how and in which direction it can develop in the future. In other words, 'history matters', setting bounds on the freedom to shape the future.

THE PARADOX OF COMPLIANCE AND CHOICE

When people are free to do as they please, they usually imitate each other.
Eric Hoffer (1902–1983); American philosopher

Yet, the question is whether firms should attempt to shape their industries at all, given the required effort and apparent risk of failure. There might be attractive rewards if a firm can lead industry developments, but trying to break industry rules that turn out to be immutable can be a quick way to achieve bankruptcy. Being an industry leader might sound very proactive, and even heroic, but it is potentially suicidal if the industry context defies being shaped.

This duality of wanting to change the industry rules that are malleable, while needing to adapt to the industry rules that are fixed, is the tension central to dealing with the industry context. On the one hand, managers must be willing to irreverently transgress widely acknowledged industry rules, going against what they see as the industry recipe. On the other hand, managers must respectfully accept many characteristics of the industry structure and play according to existing rules of the competitive game. Yet, these conflicting demands of being irreverent and respectful towards the industry rules are difficult for strategists to meet at the same time.

Where firms cannot influence the structure of their industry, *compliance* to the rules of the game is the strategic imperative. Under these circumstances, the strategic demand is for managers to adapt the firm to the industry context. Where firms do have the ability to manipulate the industry structure, they should exercise their freedom of *choice* to break the industry rules. In such a case, the strategic demand is for managers to try to change the terms of competition in their own favor.

This tension between compliance and choice has been widely acknowledged in the strategic management literature (e.g. Porter, 1980, Reading 8.1; Hrebiniak and Joyce, 1985). The pressure for compliance has usually been presented as a form of environmental determinism, as the industry developments force firms to adapt or be selected out (e.g. Astley and Van der Ven, 1983; Wilson, 1992). The freedom of choice has often been labeled as organizational voluntarism, to convey the notion that industry developments can be the result of the willful actions of individual organizations (e.g. Bettis and Donaldson, 1990; Child, 1972). In the following sections both compliance and choice will be further examined.

The demand for firm compliance

It goes almost without saying that organizations must, to a large extent, adapt themselves to their environments. No organization has the ability to shape the entire world to fit its needs. Therefore, to be successful, all organizations need to understand the context in which they operate and need to play by most of the rules of the game.

After all, the alternative of ignoring the rules is fraught with danger. Probably the most common cause of 'corporate death' is misalignment between the organization and its environment. And misalignment can happen very quickly, as most industries are constantly in flux. Companies can misinterpret the direction of the changes, can fail to take appropriate corrective action, or can be plainly self-centered, paying insufficient attention to external developments. Most companies have enough difficulty just staying attuned to the current rules of the competitive game, let alone anticipating how the industry context will change in the future.

To achieve compliance with the industry rules, firms must develop structures, processes and a culture in which listening and adapting to the environment becomes engrained.

Firms must learn to become customer and market-oriented, reacting to the 'pull' of the market, instead of 'pushing' their standard approach and pet projects at an unwilling audience. Firm compliance means avoiding the pitfall of organizational arrogance – knowing better than the market and imposing an approach that no one is waiting for (e.g. Miller, 1990; Whitley, 1999).

The demand for strategic choice

While compliance to the industry rules can be very beneficial, contradicting them can also be strategically valuable. If firms only play by the current rules, it is generally very difficult for them to gain a significant competitive advantage over their rivals. After all, adapting to the current industry structure means doing business in more or less the same way as competitors, with few possibilities to distinguish the organization. In other words, 'compliance' might be another way of saying 'follow a me-too strategy'.

To be unique and develop a competitive advantage, firms need to do something different, something that does not fit within the current rules of the game. The more innovative the rule breaker, the larger will be the competitive advantage over rivals stuck with outdated business models. The more radical the departure from the old industry recipe, the more difficult it will be for competitors to imitate and catch up. Where companies are capable of constantly leading industry developments, they will have the benefit of capturing attractive industry positions before less proactive competitors eventually follow. In other words, there is a strong pressure for firms to attempt to shape the industry rules.

To achieve organizational choice, firms must find ways of escaping the pitfall of organizational conformity – the strict adherence to current industry rules. Firms must develop structures, processes and a culture in which the current industry recipe is constantly questioned, challenged and changed. Managers must come to see that in the long run the easy path of following the industry rules will be less productive than the rocky road of innovation and change (e.g. Hamel and Prahalad, 1994; Kim and Mauborgne, 1999, Reading 8.4).

EXHIBIT 8.1 SHORT CASE

PALM: WAVING PALMS OR SWEATY PALMS?

The name 'Palm' engenders different connotations depending to whom you speak. Some people will picture white sand, turquoise water and waving palm trees, while others will picture white foam, brown ale and waving customers, trying to order another round of Belgium's famous Palm beer. Yet others will think of PDAs – personal digital assistants – small handheld computers for minor administrative tasks, such as jotting down notes, making a 'to do' list, performing calculations, updating a calendar, keeping track of expenses and filing telephone numbers and addresses. Palm was not the first company to introduce a PDA to the market, but it was the first company to do so successfully, launching the PalmPilot in 1996. Within four years, Palm's annual revenues soared to US$564 million,

with a 70% share of the 10 million PDAs sold around the world, making the company just as well known as the trees and more profitable than the beer.

The company was established in 1992 by Jeff Hawkins, a software designer, and he was soon joined by ex-Apple director, Donna Dubinsky. They entered an industry that was already littered with the broken dreams of many high-tech firms. Since the late 1980s, various companies from the computer and consumer electronics industries, including Apple, Microsoft, Sony, IBM, Motorola, Psion and Sharp, had tried to introduce PDAs to the presumed technology-hungry masses. Yet, all attempts had failed, some silently, others with a big bang. And in each case the flop could be attributed to more or less the same problem – companies were selling a brick. The PDAs were too large and heavy, or too expensive, or both. Moreover, none had found a convenient data entry method, instead using impossibly small keyboards or primitive handwriting recognition software. At the basis of these failures was an implicit belief that the device should be a small-sized substitute for the notebook computer. This belief was rooted in an evolutionary logic – first there was the mainframe, then the personal computer, then came the notebook computer and next would obviously be the handheld computer. However, neither the technology, nor the customer, seemed ready for the industry envisioned.

Initially, Palm followed this industry recipe as well. In 1993, its first device, the Zoomer, zoomed to an early death soon after its market launch. Unlike its companions in misfortune, however, Palm was triggered by the debacle to fundamentally rethink its assumptions about the industry during a full year of investigations. The result was a new insight that was simple, but revolutionary. Instead of striving to produce a substitute for a notebook computer, Palm devised a substitute for paper and pencil, which could be used as a complement to any PC. This insight led to the development of the PalmPilot: a small, fast and affordable PDA, with a simple operating system and a stylus as data entry tool.

To quickly build on its early success and establish a dominant position in the PDA industry, Palm set a high pace of new product introductions, grabbing the limelight as innovation leader. Sales were aggressive, distributing products via all possible channels – through distributors to large retailers, directly to retailers, directly via an online store to consumers and via a direct sales force to business customers. The success of the PalmPilot hardware also paved the way for Palm's Operating System (OS) software to become the industry standard, with a market share of more than 80% in 2001.

But the juicy PDA market, which was forecast to grow to 30 million units per year by 2004, was much too attractive to remain Palm's private domain for long. Many competitors saw PDAs as the future mobile access points to the internet and at the very least as a device for controlling many networked machines around the house and in the office. One formidable contender lured in by this promising future was Microsoft. In 1998, Microsoft stepped up its attempts to extend Windows to the PDA environment, launching Windows CE 2.0. At the same time, Microsoft introduced the Palm PC, and later the Pocket PC, which looked very similar to Palm's

PDAs and had about the same price as well. The result was that Palm started to lose market share to Microsoft, made worse by a slow down in Palm's new model releases after founders Hawkins and Dubinsky left to start Handspring.

Compounding the looming problems, another competitor, Psion, released the EPOC operating system, which combined PDA and wireless communications technology. Via a coalition called Symbian, EPOC was successfully promoted among the world's largest cellular telephone manufacturers, including Nokia, Ericsson and Motorola. These giants wanted to enhance their cell phones by adding PDA functions, thus creating 'smartphones', and ultimately making conventional PDAs obsolete.

The introduction of the Windows CE and EPOC operating systems caused quite a few sweaty palms at the headquarters of Palm in Santa Clara, California. Palm's strategy was to keep its operating system to itself, as the main competitive advantage of its PDAs. But with such powerful rivals as Microsoft, Nokia and Motorola, many were worried that Palm might suffer the same fate as Apple – being the owner of a proprietary operating system with insufficient critical mass to attract application software developers and a large community of interconnected users. To be able to stay at the forefront of the PDA industry, Palm would have to convince software developers that its large and growing group of users would make it profitable to keep on creating new applications based on Palm OS. Simultaneously, Palm would need to convince consumers that its PDAs would remain the industry standard, ensuring a steady stream of compatible new applications and facilitating the future exchange of data between Palm PDAs and other devices. Therefore, Palm decided to defend its 'network effect' advantage by licensing its operating system to other hardware manufacturers, including IBM, Sony, Handspring, Dell and Sun Microsystems. Palm also made a deal with Qualcomm and Samsung to incorporate Palm OS into their cellular phones, while Symbol Technologies started using it for process control devices. As a consequence, in 2000 more than 50 000 developers had signed up with Palm.

By 2003 it had become clear that Palm's licensing strategy was working – Palm OS had retained its leading position, being incorporated into three-quarters of all PDAs being sold. The downside, however, was that Palm's hardware had taken a

▶

beating, dropping to less than 40% market share and slipping fast. Yet, Palm's handhelds were still responsible for 95% of the company's revenues, while licensing only brought in a meager 5%. This did not bode well for Palm's long-term viability vis-à-vis larger manufacturers of computers and consumer electronics, with their scale economies and huge R&D budgets. Especially the fact that new PDAs were being introduced that actually did resemble genuine handheld PCs was rather worrying, as this conflicted with Palm's focus on simplicity, speed, reliability and style as distinguishing factors. It also seemed to suggest that the domains of PCs and PDAs were finally starting to converge, tilting the field in favor of Microsoft's Windows CE that from the start was intended to bridge these two worlds. Other industry watchers were even more pessimistic, predicting the end of the PDA device in its current form altogether. They pointed to emerging customer preferences to combine many of the functions of cell phones, PDAs, PCs and game consoles into one 'smartphone' gadget. If this trend continued to gather momentum, the members of the Symbian alliance (Psion and the cellular phone manufacturers) would be best positioned to profit.

Palm's response to these threats was three-fold. First, Palm decided to spin off its operating system activities to raise cash. The new company, Palm Source, would continue to focus on building powerful, but simple and fault-free, operating systems to prolong its leading position in the industry. Secondly, to fight back in the segment for business people and the techno savvy, Palm decided to follow the trend towards highly advanced PDAs with PC-like applications and the latest features including wireless communication. Thirdly, the company decided to broaden Palm's appeal beyond current segments, branching out to serve non-conventional customers. By tapping into new markets that were less technology-oriented, such as 'busy suburban moms', Palm would be able to play its old game of offering a simple, small and affordable PDA. Contrary to its competitors, these PDAs would not be sold through electronics shops, but via department stores, supermarkets and gasoline stations.

Not everyone was confident that Palm's new strategy would work. Some analysts feared that Palm's response was 'too little, too late' – much too compliant with the current rules of the game to really gain a significant competitive advantage vis-à-vis the circling scavengers. Palm would have to come up with a path breaking innovation to regain control over its own destiny. Others observed that, as the PDA industry had become mature, no such new breakthroughs could be expected, and that Palm would be wise to find ways to remain competitive without hoping for a miracle. Palm should adjust to the well-known rules of a maturing hardware industry and get ready to survive, and perhaps take advantage of, the coming shakeout. Clearly, Palm still had some tough choices to make – no time for waving palms, only for sweaty palms, at the moment.

Sources: *The Economist*, June 2 2001; *Financial Times*, August 9 2002; *FEM Business*, April 5 2003; www.palm.com; Yoffie and Kwak (2001).

PERSPECTIVES ON THE INDUSTRY CONTEXT

A wise man will make more opportunity than he finds.
Francis Bacon (1561–1624); Lord Chancellor of England

Once again the strategizing manager seems 'stuck between a rock and a hard place'. The pressures for both compliance and choice are clear, but as opposites they are at least partially incompatible. Developing an organizational culture, structure and processes attuned to compliance will to some extent be at odds with the culture, structure and processes needed to shape an industry. An organization well rehearsed in the art of adaptation and skillful imitation is usually quite different than one geared towards business innovation and contrarian behavior. How should managers actually deal with the issue of industry development – should they lead or follow?

In the strategic management literature many answers to this question are given – unfortunately, many contradictory ones. The views among management theorists differ sharply, as they emphasize a different balance between the need to comply and the need to choose. To gain a better overview of the range of conflicting opinions, here the two diametrically opposed positions will be identified and discussed. On the one hand, there are strategists who argue that industry development is an autonomous process, which individual firms can hardly hope to shape. They believe that compliance to shifting industry characteristics is mandatory – adjust or risk being selected out. This point of view will be referred to as the 'industry dynamics perspective'. On the other hand, many strategists believe that the industry context can be shaped in an infinite variety of ways by innovative firms. Therefore, industry development can be driven by firms willing and able to take a leading role. This point of view will be referred to as the 'industry leadership perspective'.

The industry dynamics perspective

To those taking an industry dynamics perspective, the popular notion that individual firms have the power to shape their industry is an understandable, but quite misplaced, belief. Of course, the illusion of control is tempting – most people, especially managers, would like to control their own destiny. Most individuals assume they have a free will and can decide their own future. Many governments suppose that they can shape society and many cultures assume that they control nature. In the same way, it is seductive to believe that the individual firm can matter, by influencing the development of its industry.

Unfortunately, this belief is largely a fallacy, brought on by a poor understanding of the underlying industry dynamics. In reality, according to advocates of the industry dynamics perspective, industries are complex systems, with a large number of forces interacting simultaneously, none of which can significantly direct the long-term development of the whole. Firms are relatively small players in a very large game – their behaviors may have some impact on industry development, but none can fundamentally shape the direction of changes. On the contrary, as industries evolve, all firms that do not meet the changing demands of the environment are weeded out. Firms not suited to the new circumstances die, while firms complying with the changing rules prosper. Hence, through selection the industry context determines the group of industry survivors and through the pressures for adaptation the behavior of the remaining firms is determined. In short, the industry shapes the firm, not the other way around.

The industry dynamics perspective is often also referred to as the industry evolution perspective, due to the strong parallel with biological evolution. Both evolutionary processes, it is argued, share a number of basic characteristics. In nature, as in business, the survival and growth of entities depends on their fit with the environment. Within each environment variations to a successful theme might come about. These new individuals will thrive, as long as they suit the existing circumstances, but as the environment changes, only those that meet the new demands will not be selected out. Hence, Darwin's well-known principle of 'survival of the fittest' is based on a cycle of variation and environmental selection. Many proponents of the industry dynamics perspective think that this biological view of evolution is a good model for what happens in industries – new organizations arise as mutations and only the fittest mutations survive. However, it is usually pointed out that in a business environment, organizations do not vary 'at random', but purposefully, and they possess the ability to adapt to selection pressures during the evolution process (e.g. Nelson and Winter, 1982; Baum and Singh, 1994). Therefore, organizations have much more flexibility to evolve along with the unfolding industry dynamics than life forms generally do. This process of mutual adaptation and development between entities in the system is called 'co-evolution' (e.g. Aldrich, 1999; Moore, 1996, Reading 7.3). To proponents of the industry dynamics perspective, the objective of a firm should be to co-evolve with its environment, instead of trying to conquer it.

Supporters of the industry dynamics perspective do not deny that every once in a while a rule breaker comes along, turning an industry upside down and spawning dozens of case studies by admiring business professors and hours of television interviews. But these successes must be put into perspective, just as a lottery winner should not encourage everyone to invest their life savings into buying lottery tickets. Yes, some business innovators are successful, but we have no idea of how many challengers were weeded out along the way – only the most spectacular failures make it into the media, but most go unreported. This is called the 'survivor's bias', and the emphasis on case-based reasoning in the field of strategy makes theorists and practitioners equally susceptible to fall into this trap. But even where a firm has been able to pull off a major industry change once, this does not make them the industry leader going into the future. They might have been the right company in the right place at the right time, able to push the industry in a certain direction once, but to assume that they will win the lottery twice is not particularly realistic.

The conclusion drawn by advocates of the industry dynamics perspective is that 'winning big' by changing the rules of the game sounds easy, fast and spectacular – but isn't. If one thing has been learnt from the internet bubble, it is that changing the rules of the game is extremely difficult, slow and hazardous, and should be left up to those 'high rollers' willing to play for 'high stakes' with only a low chance of success (i.e. venture capitalists and entrepreneurs). For regular companies, such an approach cannot be the mainstay of their strategy. Their basic approach must be to stick close to the shifting currents in their industry, which is challenging enough in most cases. Competitive advantage can be sought, but through hard work within the rules of the game.

The bad news is that this leaves limited freedom to maneuver and that the general level of profitability that a firm can achieve is largely predetermined. Once in a poor industry, a firm's growth and profit potential are significantly limited (Porter, 1980). The good news is that this still leaves plenty of room for a firm to score above the industry average, by positioning better than competitors, but also by adapting better to the ongoing industry changes, or even anticipating changes more skillfully and reacting appropriately.

EXHIBIT 8.2 THE INDUSTRY DYNAMICS PERSPECTIVE

WESTJET: GO WITH THE FLOW

Everyone visiting the world's largest rodeo, the Calgary Stampede, knows that it doesn't matter who gets out of the gate first – the winner is who stays on the wild horse's back longest. This lesson has not been lost on the entrepreneurs David Neeleman and Clive Beddoe, who started their airline, WestJet, in Calgary in 1996. WestJet was by no means the first Southwest Airlines clone in Canada, offering low-fare, no-frills, point-to-point air travel. But while they were not first movers, and did not attempt to rewrite the rules of the game in the airline industry, they are still on the bronco's back, while many of their competitors have been sent flying to the ground. Within only a few years, WestJet has become

Canada's second largest, and most profitable, airline, not by being more innovative than its rivals, but by steadfastly rolling out its business model in accordance with the emerging industry rules.

WestJet did not take off immediately. In the first few years, WestJet was a small pioneering outfit, with three Boeing 737–200s, struggling to overcome initial barriers, such as strict safety-related licensing regulations and a lack of capital. It also needed time to build up a good reputation and a route structure. But WestJet's growth was disciplined, and after 1999 expansion started to accelerate, to 35 aircraft in 2002, and plans to operate 94 modern Boeing 737–700s by 2008.

In 2002, one of WestJet's main competitors, Canada 3000, went bankrupt. It propelled WestJet into the position of Canada's second largest airline. Air Canada, the country's largest airline, used the collapse of Canada 3000 to quickly capture 80% of the domestic market. Industry stakeholders, disliking Air Canada's dominance, started to court WestJet. Medium-sized cities came begging for WestJet's service to break Air Canada's stranglehold, foreign airlines looked for alternatives to Air Canada's steep rates for connecting flights and the international airline alliance Oneworld started to court WestJet, hoping to get a Canadian partner to complement their international network. However, WestJet was cautious about overextending itself under these favorable market circumstances. The company decided that it was not ready to internationalize yet, and turned down Oneworld and its foreign carrier suitors. WestJet did, however, join the global distribution system Sabre in 2002. CEO Beddoe explained: 'We did not want to do that, but gradually we found that we had to give it a try.' Sabre rapidly represented a significant portion of WestJet's bookings.

Looking back over the past few years, it can be seen that WestJet's business model has evolved along with the developments in the industry. Starting as a straightforward Southwest Airlines clone, WestJet has gradually moved away from point-to-point services, towards the hub-and-spoke model typical of the industry incumbents. Its home base, Calgary, already was a mini-hub and nearby Edmonton was soon given the same function. Another change, whereby WestJet has moved along with shifting external circumstances, has been to refocus on more long-haul routes. Initially WestJet had targeted car travelers, luring them to switch to air travel for shorter distances. But with a new security charge of C$24 on each round-trip imposed by the Canadian government, short hops have become less competitive compared to driving. At the same time, WestJet's new Boeing 737s have opened up new longer-haul opportunities.

The skies looked bright for WestJet. Clearly, the rules of the game in the domestic airline industry had tilted in favor of low-costs no-frills carriers. Even the industry leader, Air Canada, had shifted capacity to its in-house no-frills brand Tango and was about to launch Zip, another low-cost carrier. Referring to Air Canada's latest move, Beddoe stated: 'Imitation is the greatest form of flattery.' He should know, as WestJet was no stranger to the practice of flattering the right examples.

Sources: *Financial Times*, August 2 and 26 2002, October 21 2002; *Airline Business*, October 1 2002.

The industry leadership perspective

Strategists taking an industry leadership perspective fundamentally disagree with the determinism inherent in the industry dynamics perspective. Even in biology, breeders and genetic engineers consistently attempt to shape the natural world. Of course, in industries, as in biology, some rules are immutable. Certain economic, technological, social and political factors have to be accepted as hardly changeable. But the remaining environmental factors that can be manipulated leave strategists with an enormous scope for molding the industry of the future. This belief is reflected in the remark by the Dutch poet Jules Deelder that 'even within the limits of the possible, the possibilities are limitless'. It is up to the strategist to identify which rules of the game must be respected and which can be ignored in the search for new strategic options. The strategist must recognize both the limits on the possible and the limitless possibilities.

Advocates of the industry leadership perspective do not deny that in many industries the developments are largely an evolutionary result of industry dynamics. For an understanding of the development paths of these 'leaderless' industries, the industry dynamics perspective offers a powerful explanatory 'lens' – many industries do evolve without a clear industry leader. However, these industries only followed this path because no firm was creative and powerful enough to actively shape the direction of change. A lack of leadership is not the 'natural state of affairs', but simply weakness on behalf of the industry incumbents. Industry developments can be shaped, but it does require innovative companies willing to take on the leadership role (e.g. Baden-Fuller and Stopford, 1992, Reading 8.2; Hamel and Prahalad, 1994).

A leadership role, supporters of this perspective argue, starts with envisioning what the industry of tomorrow might look like. The firm's strategists must be capable of challenging the existing industry recipe and building a new conception of how the industry could function in the future. They must test their own assumptions about which industry rules can be changed and must, in fact, think of ways of 'destroying their current business'. Hamel and Prahalad (1994) refer to this as intellectual leadership, noting that smart strategists also develop 'industry foresight', anticipating which trends are likely to emerge, so that they can be used to the firm's advantage.

Not only must a firm have the intellectual ability to envision the industry's future, but it must also be able to communicate this vision in a manner that other firms and individuals will be willing to buy in. If a vision of the industry of tomorrow is compelling enough, people inside and outside the company will start to anticipate, and will become committed to, that future, making it a self-fulfilling prophecy. This 'inevitableness' of an industry vision can be important in overcoming risk averseness and resistance from industry incumbents (e.g. Levenhagen, Porac and Thomas, 1993; Moore, 2000, Reading 8.3).

To actually change the rules of the competitive game in an industry, a firm must move beyond a compelling vision, and work out a new competitive business model. If this new business model is put into operation and seems to offer a competitive advantage, this can attract sufficient customers and support to gain 'critical mass' and break through as a viable alternative to the older business models. To shape the industry, the firm will also need to develop the new competences and standards required to make the new business model function properly. The better the firm is at building new competences and setting new standards, alone or in cooperation with others, the more power it will have to determine the direction of industry development (e.g. D'Aveni, 1999; Hamel, 1996).

All of the above points together add up to quite a considerable task. But then, industry leadership is not easy and changing the industry rules rarely happens overnight. Rather, it can take years, figuring out which rules can be broken and which cannot. It can be a marathon, trying to get the business model right, while building competences and support. Therefore, organizations require perseverance and commitment if they are to be successful as industry shapers (Hamel and Prahalad, 1994).

EXHIBIT 8.3 THE INDUSTRY LEADERSHIP PERSPECTIVE

AUTONATION: DRIVEN TO RULE

Wayne Huizenga has a reputation for being a serial rule breaker. When as a young man he first got involved in the waste disposal business in the United States, he was struck by the conservatism and lack of entrepreneurship in the industry. Companies were satisfied to remain relatively small and keep on working as they had done for years, which to Huizenga seemed like the ideal type of competitors to have. Garbage smelt like a great opportunity and Huizenga went on to make his fortune building up a more innovative, large-scale company, Waste Management. But instead of retiring early and taking

up golf, Huizenga started to look for other industries populated by small, unimaginative companies, stuck in an old business model. This eventually brought him to the video rental business, with its many 'Mom and Pop' stores. Here too, Huizenga swept through the industry, creating a large-scale professional organization, Blockbuster Video. Yet, even after this adventure, the golf course did not beckon. Huizenga once again went hunting for a fragmented industry wedded to outdated business recipes, and he found car retailing.

When Huizenga spotted the US car retailing industry in the mid-1990s, total revenues in the sector exceeded US$1 trillion per year. But while the sales were enormous, individual car retailers were comparatively small. Most car dealers were local or regional, and carried only one or two brands. This industry structure had suited the car manufacturers well, as they had more or less dedicated sales channels, which had limited bargaining power to extract a high margin from the car producers. This is where Huizenga saw an opportunity to change the rules of the game. By establishing a large-scale professional retailing organization, Huizenga believed that he could gain significant purchasing power vis-à-vis the car manufacturers, while creating a more appealing service offering towards consumers. So, in 1996 he started AutoNation and within only four years became the largest car retailer in the United States.

The business model of AutoNation is based on a branded value proposition of high service at a relatively low price. Key to the high service perception is the 'one-price, no-hassle' car selling process, removing many buyers' frustration of having to deal with high-pressure salespeople. AutoNation also offers multiple brands at each location, saving consumers the trouble of needing to drive around town to many dealerships. In addition, AutoNation's car service departments offer longer hours, completion of work within the agreed budget, and free service if work is not finished on time. AutoNation also does more than other car retailers to develop its own brand into a trusted household name.

Keeping prices low means keeping costs low, which in turn requires economies of scale. AutoNation's approach has been to strive for at least a 15% share of each local market, allowing them to run large retailing outlets, attract more expensive professional management and have a larger marketing budget than rivals, while still having a competitive cost structure. To gain such a large market share quickly, AutoNation market entry has been through the acquisition of the top two or three car dealerships, predominantly in the most lucrative market areas in the United States. Generally, these dealerships already had the best management teams, good reputations, excellent market knowledge, reasonable retail capabilities, and clean operations, making it easier for AutoNation to quickly accelerate. Additional benefits of this acquisition policy have been that no extra capacity has been added to the market spoiling prices and that potential copycats will have to settle for buying the third or fourth best dealerships if they want to take on AutoNation.

'We feel we have found the approach that will change the automobile retailing industry,' says Huizenga, and the results seem to back up this assertion. By 2003 AutoNation owned and operated more than 400 outlets, employing about 30 000 people. The firm's sales of new vehicles (60% of total), used cars (20% of total), and service, financing and insurance (20% of total) were approximately US$20 billion, with the highest profitability in the industry. The question on everyone's mind now is whether Huizenga will finally head for the golf course, or whether other industries are on his list to be re-created.

Sources: Sexton (2001); http://corp.AutoNation.com.

INTRODUCTION TO THE DEBATE AND READINGS

The pilot cannot mitigate the billows or calm the winds.

Plutarch (c. 46–c. 120);
Greek biographer and philosopher

The reasonable man adapts himself to the world; the unreasonable one persists in trying to adapt the world to himself. Therefore, all progress depends on the unreasonable man.

George Bernard Shaw (1856–1950);
Irish playwright and critic

So, how should managers deal with the industry context? Should they concentrate on adapting to the dynamics in the industry, honing their ability to respond to changing demands and to adjust their business model to meet new requirements? Or should they take a more proactive role in shaping the future of the industry, changing the rules of the competitive game to suit their own needs? As the views within the field of strategic management are so far apart and no consensus seems to be emerging, managers must once again determine their own view on the topic, finding some way of balancing compliance and choice.

As an input to the process of assessing the variety of perspectives on this issue, four readings have been selected that each shed their own light on the debate. As in previous chapters, the first two readings will be representative of the two poles in this debate (see Table 8.1), while the second pair has been chosen to bring additional arguments into the discussion.

Actually, Reading 8.1 is not entirely representative of the industry dynamics perspective. In selecting a reading, we were faced by the problem that almost all contributions to the strategic management literature by researchers taking an industry dynamics perspective have been written in academic journals and do not make for easy reading. There are many excellent works, but none that are accessible enough to act as the opening article in this debate. Few strategists like to hear that they have little influence over their industry and that they should play by the rules – this message is hardly inspiring, if not outright frustrating, and it definitely does not sell books, which might partially explain why few proponents of the industry dynamics perspective have written for an audience of practicing managers.

As a compromise, therefore, the debate in this chapter will be started off by an author who is strongly affiliated with the industry dynamics perspective, but who is not fully in their camp. This author is Michael Porter, and the article selected is appropriately titled 'Industry Evolution'. In this reading, taken from his classic book *Competitive Strategy*, Porter expands on his basic premises, which were discussed in Chapter 5. In his view, a company's profitability is heavily influenced by the structure of the industry in which it competes. Some industries have a poor structure, making it difficult for even the best firms to make a profit. Other industries, however, have a more advantageous structure, making it much easier to show a good performance. In Porter's opinion, how the game of competition is played in each industry is largely determined by the underlying economics. The industry structure presents the strict rules with which companies must comply. As an industry's structure evolves, Porter sees two processes at work that determine which companies will survive and profit over the longer term. On the one hand, Porter recognizes 'natural selection' processes, whereby only the fittest survive and firms that are not suited to the new environment become extinct. For instance, Porter argues that the selection of fit companies is particularly strong as industries move into a mature phase of development: 'when growth levels off in an industry . . . there is a period of turmoil as intensified rivalry

TABLE 8.1   Industry dynamics versus industry leadership perspective

	Industry dynamics perspective	Industry leadership perspective
Emphasis on	Compliance over choice	Choice over compliance
Industry development	Uncontrollable evolutionary process	Controllable creation process
Change dynamics	Environment selects fit firms	Firm creates fitting environment
Firm success due to	Fitness to industry demands	Manipulation of industry demands
Ability to shape industry	Low, slow	High, fast
Normative implication	Play by the rules (adapt)	Change the rules (innovate)
Development path	Convergence towards dominant design	Divergence, create new design
Firm profitability	Largely industry-dependent	Largely firm-dependent

weeds out the weaker firms'. On the other hand, Porter also believes that companies can adapt themselves to changes in the industry's structure, although he emphasizes that they first must understand the drivers of change. So far, Porter's arguments fully coincide with the industry dynamics perspective. However, besides compliance with the industry context, Porter mentions the possibility of 'co-makership' as well. Or, in his own terms, he believes that firms can have some influence on the evolution of the industry's structure. Thus, each company does have a certain degree of strategic freedom to determine its own fate, but ultimately the autonomous development of the industry structure is crucially important to the survival and profitability of the company.

To open the debate on behalf of the industry leadership perspective, Reading 8.2 by Charles Baden-Fuller and John Stopford has been selected, with the telling title 'The Firm Matters, Not the Industry'. In a direct reference to Porter, they state that their view 'contrasts sharply with the popular, but misguided, school of thought that believes that the fortune of a business is closely tied to its industry'. They point out that only a fraction of the differences in profitability between companies can be attributed to industry characteristics, while more than half of the profit variations are due to the choice of strategy. Their conclusion is that the given industry circumstances are largely unimportant – it's how a firm plays the game that matters. In their opinion, high profitability is not the consequence of complying with some preset rules, but the result of acting creatively and imaginatively. For instance, they challenge the widely held belief that high market share is important for profitability. Nor do they agree that the competitive game dictates generic strategies, as Porter suggested in Chapter 5. They do not even believe that there is such a thing as a mature industry. In their view, the industry context does not present any fixed rules that cannot be avoided or changed by innovative companies. Their advice, therefore, is to remain imaginative and to adopt approaches that counter traditional solutions.

The second set of two readings starts with a recent work by Geoffrey Moore entitled 'Living on the Fault Line', which has been taken from the book of the same name (note that there are more Moores; Geoffrey's namesake in the previous chapter was James Moore). This reading has been added to bring in an issue of vital importance to industry development – the introduction of new technology. Of all the drivers of industry development, the adoption of disruptive technologies is probably the most prominent. Disruptive technologies are those that do not complement established technologies, but displace them. As such, Moore points out, disruptive technologies can cause dramatic shifts in an industry as 'competitive advantage positions that once seemed secure are abruptly overthrown and management teams . . . must scramble to recover'. Moore's central thesis is that for the innovators, championing a new technology, creating a mainstream market requires going through a number of phases, each with its own inherent strategic logic. He describes these phases of market development, making use of the widely known technology adoption life cycle. The first phase, or 'early market', is where technology enthusiasts and visionaries adopt the innovation. This phase is generally followed by a 'chasm', which is a period of no adoption, which needs to be bridged to get to the second phase, called the 'bowling alley', where early pragmatists 'knock' others into also adopting the new technology. Once adoption starts picking up speed, the third phase is entered, the 'tornado', where high growth is experienced. Finally, the technology achieves the fourth phase of broad acceptance, called 'Main Street'. Key to success in each phase, Moore concludes, is realizing that the strategy of the previous phase is no longer appropriate and that a new strategy must be developed. In his argumentation Moore focuses his attention on customer acceptance, paying less attention to the reactions of competitors and other industry actors. As such, his contribution is more to understanding market development and less to highlighting overall industry development. However, this reading still provides invaluable insight into the difficult process of changing the rules of the game based on technological innovation.

The last article (Reading 8.4) is 'Strategy, Value Innovation, and the Knowledge Economy', by W. Chan Kim and Renée Mauborgne. This reading has been selected as a counterweight to Moore's emphasis on technology-enabled innovation and the role of disruptive technologies in industry development. Kim and Mauborgne are equally interested in innovation, but particularly in fundamentally new and superior ways of creating value for buyers, which often has nothing to do with new technology, and which they call 'value innovation'. To engage in value innovation a company does not need to be a technology leader, but needs to redefine customers' problems, find hidden demand or create totally new demand, and then needs to develop an offering that provides superior value in the eyes of the customer. In such an approach to strategizing, Kim and Mauborgne argue, the competition is largely irrelevant. They find that companies that focus on competitors usually are imitative, reactive and unknowledgeable about customer demands, while companies that focus on customers are usually more innovative, proactive and value-oriented. Their conclusion is that strategy theories that accentuate 'competitive strategy' and 'competitive advantage' might have placed an unhealthy emphasis on fighting a zero-sum game, instead of finding new ways to create value for customers. In the context of this chapter, their message is that industry development is not only driven by the factor technology, but that the new products and business models fueling industry development can also be the product of customer-oriented value innovations.

With so many competing opinions on the nature of the industry context, readers may now want to 'select the fittest one'. Or maybe readers will have to conclude that one view has rewritten the rules of competition in the strategy industry. Whichever way, it is up to each individual reader to form their own judgment on how to deal with the paradox of compliance and choice.

READING

8.1

Industry evolution

By Michael Porter[1]

Structural analysis gives us a framework for understanding the competitive forces operating in an industry that are crucial to developing competitive strategy. It is clear, however, that industries' structures change, often in fundamental ways. Entry barriers and concentration have gone up significantly in the US brewing industry, for example, and the threat of substitutes has risen to put a severe squeeze on acetylene producers.

Industry evolution takes on critical importance for formulation of strategy. It can increase or decrease the basic attractiveness of an industry as an investment opportunity, and it often requires the firm to make strategic adjustments. Understanding the process of industry evolution and being able to predict change are important because the cost of reacting strategically usually increases as the need for change becomes more obvious and the benefit from the best strategy is the highest for the first firm to select it. For example, in the early post-war farm equipment business, structural change elevated the importance of a strong exclusive dealer network backed by company support and credit. The firms that recognized this change first had their pick of dealers to choose from.

This article will present analytical tools for predicting the evolutionary process in an industry and understanding its significance for the formulation of competitive strategy.

Basic concepts in industry evolution

The starting point for analyzing industry evolution is the framework of structural analysis (see Chapter 5). Industry changes will carry strategic significance if they promise to affect the underlying sources of the five competitive forces; otherwise changes are important only in a tactical sense. The simplest approach to analyzing evolution is to ask the following question: Are there any changes occurring in the industry that will affect each element of structure? For example, do

any of the industry trends imply an increase or decrease in mobility barriers? An increase or decrease in the relative power of buyers or suppliers? If this question is asked in a disciplined way for each competitive force and the economic causes underlying it, a profile of the significant issues in the evolution of an industry will result.

Although this industry-specific approach is the place to start, it may not be sufficient, because it is not always clear what industry changes are occurring currently, much less which changes might occur in the future. Given the importance of being able to predict evolution, it is desirable to have some analytical techniques that will aid in anticipating the pattern of industry changes we might expect to occur.

The product life cycle

The grandfather of concepts for predicting the probable course of industry evolution is the familiar product life cycle. The hypothesis is that an industry passes through a number of phases or stages – introduction, growth, maturity, and decline – illustrated in Figure 8.1.1. These stages are defined by inflection points in the rate of growth of industry sales. Industry growth follows an S-shaped curve because of the process of innovation and diffusion of a new product. The flat introductory phase of industry growth reflects the difficulty of overcoming buyer inertia and stimulating trials of the new product. Rapid growth occurs as many buyers rush into the market once the product has proven itself successful. Penetration of the product's potential buyers is eventually reached, causing the rapid growth to stop and to level off to the underlying rate of growth of the relevant buyer group. Finally, growth will eventually taper off as new substitute products appear.

As the industry goes through its life cycle, the nature of competition will shift. I have summarized in Table 8.1.1 the most common predictions about how an

[1]Source: Reprinted with the permission of the Free Press, a Division of Simon and Schuster Adult Publishing Group, from *Competitive Strategy: Techniques for Analyzing Industries and Competitors* by Michael E. Porter. © 1980, 1988 by The Free Press.

FIGURE 8.1.1   Stages of the life cycle

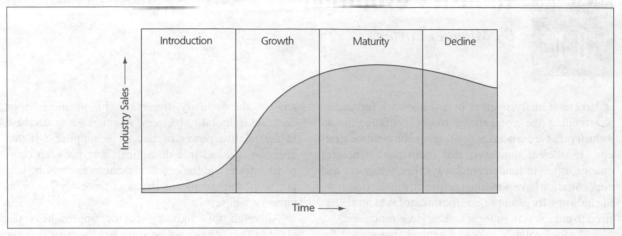

industry will change over the life cycle and how this should affect strategy.

The product life cycle has attracted some legitimate criticism:

- The duration of the stages varies widely from industry to industry, and it is often not clear what stage of the life cycle an industry is in. This problem diminishes the usefulness of the concept as a planning tool.

- Industry growth does not always go through the S-shaped pattern at all. Sometimes industries skip maturity, passing straight from growth to decline. Sometimes industry growth revitalizes after a period of decline, as has occurred in the motorcycle and bicycle industries and recently in the radio broadcasting industry. Some industries seem to skip the slow takeoff of the introductory phase altogether.

- Companies can *affect* the shape of the growth curve through product innovation and repositioning, extending it in a variety of ways. If a company takes the life cycle as given, it becomes an undesirable self-fulfilling prophesy.

- The nature of competition associated with each stage of the life cycle is *different* for different industries. For example, some industries start out highly concentrated and stay that way. Others, like bank cash dispensers, are concentrated for a significant period and then become less so. Still others begin highly fragmented; of these some consolidate (automobiles) and some do not (electronic component distribution). The same divergent patterns apply to advertising, research and development (R&D)

expenditures, degree of price competition, and most other industry characteristics. Divergent patterns such as these call into serious question the strategic implications ascribed to the life cycle.

The real problem with the product life cycle as a predictor of industry evolution is that it attempts to describe *one* pattern of evolution that will invariably occur. And except for the industry growth rate, there is little or no underlying rationale for why the competitive changes associated with the life cycle will happen. Since actual industry evolution takes so many different paths, the life cycle pattern does not always hold, even if it is a common or even the most common pattern of evolution. Nothing in the concept allows us to predict when it will hold and when it will not.

A framework for forecasting evolution

Instead of attempting to describe industry evolution, it will prove more fruitful to look underneath the process to see what really drives it. Like any evolution, industries evolve because some forces are in motion that create incentives or pressures for change. These can be called *evolutionary processes*.

Every industry begins with an *initial structure* – the entry barriers, buyer and supplier power, and so on that exist when the industry comes into existence. This structure is usually (though not always) a far cry from the configuration the industry will take later in its development. The initial structure results from a combination of underlying economic and technical

TABLE 8.1.1 Predictions of product life cycle theories about strategy, competition, and performance

	Introduction	Growth	Maturity	Decline
Buyers and buyer behavior	■ High-income purchaser ■ Buyer inertia ■ Buyers must be convinced to try the product	■ Widening buyer group ■ Consumer will accept uneven quality	■ Mass market ■ Saturation ■ Repeat buying ■ Choosing among brands is the rule	■ Customers are sophisticated buyers of the product
Products and product change	■ Poor quality ■ Product design and development key ■ Many different product variations; no standards ■ Frequent design changes ■ Basic product designs	■ Products have technical and performance differentiation ■ Reliability key for complex products ■ Competitive product improvements ■ Good quality	■ Superior quality ■ Less product differentiation ■ Standardization ■ Less rapid product changes – more minor annual model changes ■ Trade-ins become significant	■ Little product differentiation ■ Spotty product quality
Marketing	■ Very high advertising/sales ■ Creaming price strategy ■ High marketing costs	■ High advertising, but lower percent of sales than introductory ■ Most promotion of ethical drugs ■ Advertising and distribution key for nontechnical products	■ Market segmentation ■ Efforts to extend life cycle ■ Broaden line ■ Service and deals more prevalent ■ Packaging important ■ Advertising competition ■ Lower advertising/sales	■ Low advertising/ sales and other marketing
Manufacturing and distribution	■ Overcapacity ■ Short production runs ■ High skilled-labor content ■ High production costs ■ Specialized channels	■ Undercapacity ■ Shift toward mass production ■ Scramble for distribution ■ Mass channels	■ Some overcapacity ■ Optimum capacity ■ Increasing stability of manufacturing process ■ Lower labor skills ■ Long production runs with stable techniques ■ Distribution channels pare down their lines to improve their margins ■ High physical distribution costs due to broad lines ■ Mass channels	■ Substantial overcapacity ■ Mass production ■ Specialty channels
R&D	■ Changing production techniques			
Foreign trade	■ Some exports	■ Significant exports ■ Few imports	■ Falling exports ■ Significant imports	■ No exports ■ Significant imports
Overall strategy	■ Best period to increase market share ■ R&D, engineering are key functions	■ Practical to change price or quality image ■ Marketing the key function	■ Bad time to increase market share, particularly if low-share company ■ Having competitive costs becomes key ■ Bad time to change price image or quality image ■ 'Marketing effectiveness' key	■ Cost control key

TABLE 8.1.1 *continued*

	Introduction	Growth	Maturity	Decline
Competition	■ Few companies	■ Entry ■ Many competitors ■ Lots of mergers and casualties	■ Price competition ■ Shakeout ■ Increase in private brands	■ Exits ■ Fewer competitors
Risk	■ High risk	■ Risks can be taken here because growth covers them up	■ Cyclicality sets in	
Margins and profits	■ High prices and margins ■ Low profits ■ Price elasticity to individual seller not as great as in maturity	■ High profits ■ Highest profits ■ Fairly high prices ■ Lower prices than introductory phase ■ Recession resistant ■ High P/Es ■ Good acquisition climate	■ Falling prices ■ Lower profits ■ Lower margins ■ Lower dealer margins ■ Increased stability of market shares and price structure ■ Poor acquisition climate – tough to sell companies ■ Lowest prices and margins	■ Low prices and margins ■ Falling prices ■ Prices might rise in late decline

characteristics of the industry, the initial constraints of small industry size, and the skills and resources of the companies that are early entrants. For example, even an industry like automobiles with enormous possibilities for economies of scale started out with labor-intensive, job-shop production operations because of the small volumes of cars produced during the early years.

The evolutionary processes work to push the industry toward its *potential structure*, which is rarely known completely as an industry evolves. Embedded in the underlying technology, product characteristics, and nature of present and potential buyers, however, there is a range of structures the industry might possibly achieve, depending on the direction and success of research and development, marketing innovations, and the like.

It is important to realize that instrumental in much industry evolution are the investment decisions by both existing firms in the industry and new entrants. In response to pressures or incentives created by the evolutionary process, firms invest to take advantage of possibilities for new marketing approaches, new manufacturing facilities, and the like, which shift entry barriers, alter relative power against suppliers and buyers, and so on. The luck, skills, resources, and orientation of firms in the industry can shape the evolutionary path the industry will actually take. Despite potential for structural change, an industry may not actually change because no firm happens to discover a feasible new marketing approach; or potential scale economies may go unrealized because no firm possesses the financial

resources to construct a fully integrated facility or simply because no firm is inclined to think about costs. Because innovation, technological developments, and the identities (and resources) of the particular firms either in the industry or considering entry into it are so important to evolution, industry evolution will not only be hard to forecast with certainty but also an industry can potentially evolve in a variety of ways at a variety of different speeds, depending on the luck of the draw.

Evolutionary processes

Although initial structure, structural potential, and particular firms' investment decisions will be industry-specific, we can generalize about what the important evolutionary processes are. There are some predictable (and interacting) dynamic processes that occur in every industry in one form or another, though their speed and direction will differ from industry to industry:

- long-run changes in growth;
- changes in buyer segments served;
- buyer's learning;
- reduction of uncertainty;
- diffusion of proprietary knowledge;
- accumulation of experience;
- expansion (or contraction) in scale;
- changes in input and currency costs;
- product innovation;

- marketing innovation;
- process innovation;
- structural change in adjacent industries;
- government policy change;
- entries and exits.

Key relationships in industry evolution

In the context of this analysis, *how* do industries change? They do not change in a piecemeal fashion, because an industry is an *interrelated system*. Change in one element of an industry's structure tends to trigger changes in other areas. For example, an innovation in marketing might develop a new buyer segment, but serving this new segment may trigger changes in manufacturing methods, thereby increasing economies of scale. The firm reaping these economies first will also be in a position to start backward integration, which will affect power with suppliers – and so on. One industry change, therefore, often sets off a chain reaction leading to many other changes.

It should be clear from the discussion here that whereas industry evolution is always occurring in nearly every business and requires a strategic response, there is no one way in which industries evolve. Any single model for evolution such as the product life cycle should therefore be rejected. However, there are some particularly important relationships in the evolutionary process that I will examine here.

Will the industry consolidate?

It seems to be an accepted fact that industries tend to consolidate over time, but as a general statement, it simply is not true. In a broad sample of 151 four-digit US manufacturing industries in the 1963–72 time period, for example, 69 increased in four-firm concentration more than two percentage points, whereas 52 decreased more than two percentage points in the same period. The question of whether consolidation will occur in an industry exposes perhaps the most important interrelationships among elements of industry structure – those involving competitive rivalry, mobility barriers, and exit barriers.

Industry concentration and mobility barriers move together

If mobility barriers are high or especially if they increase, concentration almost always increases. For

example, concentration has increased in the US wine industry. In the standard-quality segment of the market, which represents much of the volume, the strategic changes (high advertising, national distribution, rapid brand innovation, and so on) have greatly increased barriers to mobility. As a result, the larger firms have gotten further ahead of smaller ones, and few new firms have entered to challenge them.

No concentration takes place if mobility barriers are low or falling

Where barriers are low, unsuccessful firms that exit will be replaced by new firms. If a wave of exit has occurred because of an economic downturn or some other general adversity, there may be a temporary increase in industry concentration. But at the first signs that profits and sales in the industry are picking up, new entrants will appear. Thus a shakeout when an industry reaches maturity does not necessarily imply long-run consolidation.

Exit barriers deter consolidation

Exit barriers keep companies operating in an industry even though they are earning subnormal returns on investment. Even in an industry with relatively high mobility barriers, the leading firms cannot count on reaping the benefits of consolidation if high exit barriers hold unsuccessful firms in the market.

Long-run profit potential depends on future structure

In the period of very rapid growth early in the life of an industry (especially after initial product acceptance has been achieved), profit levels are usually high. For example, growth in sales of skiing equipment was in excess of 20 percent per year in the late 1960s, and nearly all firms in the industry enjoyed strong financial results. When growth levels off in an industry, however, there is a period of turmoil as intensified rivalry weeds out the weaker firms. All firms in the industry may suffer financially during this adjustment period. Whether or not the remaining firms will enjoy above-average profitability will depend on the level of mobility barriers, as well as the other structural features of the industry. If mobility barriers are high or have increased as the industry has matured, the remaining firms in the industry may enjoy healthy financial results even in the new era of slower growth. If mobility barriers are low, however, slower growth probably means the end of above-average profits for the industry. Thus mature industries may or may not be as profitable as they were in their developmental period.

Changes in industry boundaries

Structural change in an industry is often accompanied by changes in industry boundaries. Industry evolution has a strong tendency to shift these boundaries. Innovations in the industry or those involving substitutes may effectively enlarge the industry by placing more firms into direct competition. Reduction in transportation cost relative to timber cost, for example, has made timber supply a world market rather than one restricted to continents. Innovations increasing the reliability and lowering the cost of electronic surveillance devices have put them into effective competition with security guard services. Structural changes making it easier for suppliers to integrate forward into the industry may well mean that suppliers effectively become competitors. Or buyers purchasing private label goods in large quantities and dictating product design criteria may become effective competitors in the manufacturing industry. Part of the analysis of the strategic significance of industry evolution is clearly an analysis of how industry boundaries may be affected.

Firms can influence industry structure

Industry structural change can be influenced by firms' strategic behavior. If it understands the significance of structural change for its position, the firm can seek to influence industry change in ways favorable to it, either through the way it reacts to strategic changes of competitors or in the strategic changes it initiates.

Another way a company can influence structural change is to be very sensitive to external forces that can cause the industry to evolve. With a head start, it is often possible to direct such forces in ways appropriate to the firm's position. For example, the specific form of regulatory changes can be influenced; the diffusion of innovations coming from outside the industry can be altered by the form that licensing or other agreements with innovating firms take; positive action can be initiated to improve the cost or supply of complementary products through providing direct assistance and help in forming trade associations or in stating their case to the government; and so on for the other important forces causing structural change. Industry evolution should not be greeted as a fait accompli to be reacted to, but as an opportunity.

READING

8.2

The firm matters, not the industry

By Charles Baden-Fuller and John Stopford[1]

Introduction

It is the firm that matters, not the industry. Successful businesses ride the waves of industry misfortunes; less successful businesses are sunk by them. This view contrasts sharply with the popular, but misguided, school of thought that believes that the fortune of a business is closely tied to its industry. Those who adhere to this view believe that some industries are intrinsically more attractive for investment than others. They (wrongly) believe that if a business is in a profi-

table industry, then its profits will be greater than if the business is in an unprofitable industry.

The role of the industry in determining profitability

Old views can be summarized as follows:

- Some industries are intrinsically more profitable than others.

- In mature environments it is difficult to sustain high profits.

---

[1]Source: This article has been adapted from Chapter 2 of *Rejuvinating the Mature Business*, Routledge, pp. 13–14. Used with permission.

- It is environmental factors that determine whether an industry is successful, not the firms in the industry.

New views can be summarized as follows:

- There is little difference in the profitability of one industry versus another.

- There is no such thing as a mature industry, only mature firms; industries inhabited by mature firms often present great opportunities for the innovative.

- Profitable industries are those populated by imaginative and profitable firms; unprofitable industries have unusually large numbers of uncreative firms.

This notion that there are 'good' and 'bad' industries is a theme that has permeated many strategy books. As one famous strategy writer (Porter, 1980) put it:

> *The state of competition in an industry depends on five basic competitive forces. . . . The collective strength of these forces determines the ultimate profit potential in the industry, where profit potential is measured in terms of long-run return on invested capital. . . . The forces range from intense in industries like tires, paper and steel – where no firm earns spectacular returns – to relatively mild like oil-field equipment and services, cosmetics and toiletries – where high returns are quite common.*

Unfortunately, the writer overstates his case, for the evidence does not easily support his claim. Choosing good industries may be a foolish strategy; choosing good firms is far more sensible. As noted in Table 8.2.1, recent statistical evidence does not support the view that the choice of industry is important. At best only 10 per cent of the differences in profitability

between one business unit and another can be related to their choice of industry. By implication, nearly 90 per cent of profitability variations are not explained by the choice of industry, and *at least half appear to be attributable to the choice of strategy*. Put simply, the correct choice of strategy appears to be at least five times more important than the correct choice of industry.

Mature industries offer good prospects for success

It is often stated that market opportunities are created rather than found. Thus market research would never have predicted the large potential of xerography, laptop computers, or the pocket cassette recorder. Leaps of faith may be required. By analogy, low-growth mature markets or troubled industries are arguably ones that may offer greater chances of rewards than ones that appear to be glamorous and profitable. Our reasoning is simple. In general, profitable industries are more profitable because they are populated by more imaginative and more creative businesses. These businesses create an environment that attracts customers, grows the industry revenues, and makes the industry attractive. But creative and innovative businesses are also more fiercely competitive. To win in such environments may be difficult, as the pace of change may be rapid and the minimum standards high. In contrast, many less profitable industries are populated by sleepy, uncreative businesses that fail to innovate. In such environments, the potential for success by a creative newcomer is greater. The demands of competition may be less exacting and the potential for attracting customers is better.

We do not wish to overstate our case, but rather to force the reader to focus attention away from the

TABLE 8.2.1   The role of industry factors determining firm performance

Percentage of business units' profitability explained by	
Choice of industry	8.3 percent
Choice of strategy	46.4 percent
Parent company	0.8 percent
Not explained – random	44.5 percent

Adapted from Rumelt (1991).

mentality of labeling and prejudging opportunities based only on industry profitability. For example, outsiders often point to low-growth industries and suggest that the opportunities are less than those in high-growth industries. Yet the difference in growth rates may be dependent on the ability of businesses in these industries to be creative and innovative. Until Honda came, the motorcycle market was in steady decline. By their innovations – of new bicycles with attractive features sold at reasonable prices – the market was once again revived. Thus we suggest that the growth rate of the industry is a reflection of the kinds of businesses in the industry, not the intrinsic nature of the environment.

Large market share is the reward, not the cause of success

We believe that many managers are mistaken in the value they ascribe to market share. A large share of the market is often the symptom of success, but it is not always its cause. Banc One and Cook achieved significant positions in their industries because they were successful. For these organizations the sequence of events was success followed by growth, which was then cemented into greater success. Banc One has been doing things differently from many of its competitors for many years. It emphasized operational efficiency and it quickly captured a significant position as a low cost, high quality data processor for other banks and financial service companies. It also emphasized service, in particular service to retail and commercial customers, which contrasted with the approach of many other banks that sought to compete solely on price or failed to appreciate what the customer really wanted.

Mergers and growth have been an important part of Banc One's strategy, but in every case, the merged organizations have been changed to fit the philosophy of Banc One.

Market share and profitability

Old views can be summarized as follows:

- Large market share brings lower costs and higher prices and so yields greater profits.
- Small-share firms cannot challenge leaders.

New views can be summarized as follows:

- Large market share is the reward for efficiency and effectiveness.
- If they do things better, small-share firms can challenge the leaders.

For creative organizations we see an upward spiral (Figure 8.2.1), and for organizations that are not creative, we see the cycles shown in Figure 8.2.2.

Our assertions run counter to much of what has been written in conventional books on strategy, and what is believed in many corporate boardrooms (see Exhibit 8.1.1). There is a common but incorrect belief among managers that being number one or number two in an industry gives the business unique advantages and that these are greatest in industries characterized by slow growth. With a large market share, it is often argued, the business can achieve lower costs and charge higher prices than its rivals. In slow-growth markets, it is argued, this may prove to be a decisive factor. This thinking ignores the importance of innovation, and believes that it is the size of the business that confers the advantage, not the new ways of doing things.

FIGURE 8.2.1 Upward spiral of creative business

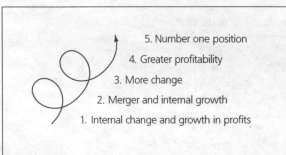

5. Number one position

4. Greater profitability

3. More change

2. Merger and internal growth

1. Internal change and growth in profits

FIGURE 8.2.2 Downward spiral of unchanging business

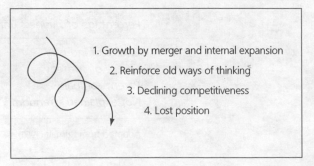

1. Growth by merger and internal expansion

2. Reinforce old ways of thinking

3. Declining competitiveness

4. Lost position

EXHIBIT 8.1.1 MARKET SHARE AND PROFITABILITY

There is a lively debate on the importance of market share in *explaining* business unit profitability. By *explaining* we do not mean *causing*. High market share could be the consequence of profitability, or the cause of both.

Those who advocate that large market share *leads* to greater profits point to the importance of several causal factors. First, large market share gives rise to the need to deliver large volumes of the service or good. These increased volumes in turn give rise to opportunities for costs savings by exploiting scale economies in production, service delivery, logistics, and marketing. Second, large market share permits the firm to benefit from experience or learning effects that also lower costs. Third, larger market share may allow the firm to charge higher prices. A product or service with a large share may seem intrinsically less risky to consumers. Finally, with a large market share, new entrants may be discouraged because they perceive the incumbent to have a substantial commitment to the industry through perceived or actual sunk costs.

In contrast, there are several who argue that these supposed benefits of large share are overrated. It is innovation that matters, innovators that realize new ways of competing can achieve their advantages by new approaches that do not necessarily need large market shares. However, those with new approaches may win market share, in which case large share is a reward for success. This Darwinian view of the market suggests that the competitive process is one where success goes to the firm that successfully innovates.

The strongest proponents of the importance of market share as a cause of success are Buzzell and Gale. Using the PIMS database drawn from a very large sample of business units across a range of industries, they asserted the existence of a strong relationship between relative market share and profitability. The figures below (Buzzell and Gale, 1987) suggest that a firm that has first rank in an industry will be more than twice as profitable as one of fourth rank.

Industry rank (by market share)	1	2	3	4	≤5
Pretax profits/sales (per cent)	12.7	9.1	7.1	5.5	4.5

However, these figures are misleading, for in a very large proportion of the industries studied, the firm with largest rank was *not* the most profitable. Often the picture is quite different; indeed according to the statistics published in Buzzell and Gale (1987) only 4 percent of the differences in profitability of one business unit versus another could be explained by differences in market share. Schmalensee (1985), in his extensive study of more than 400 firms in US manufacturing, found that less than 2 percent of the variations in profitability between one business and another could be explained by differences in market share. Market share effects appear to be relatively unimportant across a wide sample of industries. Of course, market share may be important in specific instances, but this only goes to reinforce our basic point that the critical success is dependent on getting the right strategy.

These false beliefs are widespread. They appear in many guises. At one extreme there are chief executives who say, 'We are only interested in industries where we hold a number one or number two position.' Such statements, if unaccompanied by an emphasis on innovation, will give out the wrong signal that high share will lead to success. At a more mundane level, managers are encouraged to write in their plans, 'We should dominate the industry and seek success by capturing a number one position.' Again, such statements are dangerous where the writer and reader believe that share by itself will bring success.

Growing market share is not the panacea for an organization's ills, not even in mature slow-growing markets. The belief that gaining market share will lead to greater profitability comes from confusing cause and effect. Many successful businesses do have a large market share, but the causality is usually from success to share, not the other way. Successful businesses often (but not always) grow because they have discovered an overwhelming source of competitive advantage, such as quality at low cost. Such advantages can be used to displace the market share of even the most entrenched incumbents.

It has been fashionable to suggest that there are a few *stable generic strategies* that offer fundamental choices to the organization. Typically these are described as a choice between a *low cost strategy* or a *differentiated strategy*. The low cost strategy involves the sacrifice of something – speed, variety, fashion, or even quality – in order to keep costs low, the lowest in the industry. In contrast, the high cost, differentiated strategy involves the focus on the very factors ignored by the others. The advocates of generic strategy make an (implicit or explicit) assertion: that the opposites cannot be reconciled. According to the generic strategists, it is not possible to be both low cost and high quality, or low cost and fashionable, or low cost and speedy. Trying to reconcile the opposites means being *stuck in the middle*. This, it is suggested, is the worst of both worlds.

Generic strategies are a fallacy. The best firms are striving all the time to reconcile the opposites. Cook did find a way to be both high quality and low cost, so, too, many of the other creative firms we studied. At any point in time, there are some combinations that have not yet been resolved, but firms strive to resolve them. Until McDonald's, the idea of consistency and low price for fast food had not been achieved on a large scale. McDonald's solved that problem. Benetton was but one of many firms that resolved the dilemma of fashion at low cost. Given the enormous rewards that accrue to those who can resolve the dilemmas of the opposites, it is not surprising that there are no *lasting or enduring generic strategies*.

Competing recipes

The crucial battles amongst firms in an industry are often centered around differing approaches to the market. Even in the so-called mature industries, where incumbent strategies have evolved and been honed over long time periods, it is new ideas that displace the existing leaders. Traditional wisdom has overstated the power of the generic approach (see Exhibit 8.2.2) and underplayed the role of innovation. Banc One established its premier position by rejecting conventional orthodoxy and emphasizing aspects hitherto neglected by industry leaders. Cook won in the steel castings industry by emphasizing quality and service to the customer. Hotpoint emphasized variety and quality in its approach to both the retailers and the final consumers. No single approach works well in all industries, but rather a multiple set of approaches. Here we emphasize the more fundamental point: the real competitive battles are fought out between firms with a diversity of approaches to the market.

The dynamics of competition in traditional industries

The old view is:

- Competition is based on firms following well-defined traditional (or generic) approaches to the market.

The new view is:

- The real battles are fought among firms taking different approaches, especially those that counter yesterday's ideas.

Conclusions

Organizations that have become mature and suffer from poor performance typically view themselves as prisoners of their environment. Often their managers blame everyone but themselves for their poor performance. Labelling their environment as mature or hostile, they identify excess capacity, unfair competition, adverse exchange rates, absence of demand, and a host of other factors to explain why they are doing badly. Alas, too often these external factors are not really the causes of their demise but rather the symptoms of their failure. This conclusion is not so new; others have made the point before, yet their words appear to have been forgotten. Hall (1980) in an article in the *Harvard Business Review* noted:

Even a cursory analysis of the leading companies in the eight basic industries leads to an important observation: survival and prosperity are possible even when the business environment turns hostile and industry trends change from favourable to unfavourable. In this regard, the casual advice frequently offered to competitors in basic industries – that is diversify, dissolve or be prepared for below average returns – seems oversimplified and even erroneous.

Of course all industries experience the roller coaster of economic upswings and downswings, but there are organizations that appear to ride the waves and others that appear to be submerged by them.

Those who are submerged all too often clutch at the wrong things in trying to escape their drowning. Seeking simple solutions such as industry recipes, the value of market share, or the need to amass large resources, they fail to appreciate the extent to which the rules of the game in an industry are always changing.

READING 8.3

Living on the fault line

By Geoffrey Moore[1]

The technology adoption life cycle models the response of any given population to the offer of a discontinuous innovation, one that forces the abandonment of traditional infrastructure and systems for the promise of a heretofore unavailable set of benefits. It represents this response as a bell curve, separating out five sub-populations, as illustrated in Figure 8.3.1.

The bell curve represents the total population of people exposed to a new technology offer. The various segments of the curve represent the percentage of peo-

ple predicted to adopt one or another of the five different strategies for determining when and why to switch allegiance from the old to the new. The five strategies unfold sequentially as follows:

1 The *technology enthusiast strategy* is to adopt the new technology upon its first appearance, in large part just to explore its properties to determine if it is 'cool'. The actual benefits provided may not even be of interest to this constituency, but the

FIGURE 8.3.1   The technology adoption life cycle

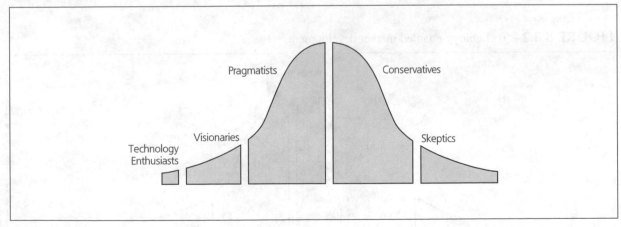

[1]Source: © 2000 Geoffrey Moore

mechanism by which they are provided is of great interest. If they are entertained by the mechanism, they often adopt the product just to be able to show it off.

2 The *visionary strategy* is to adopt the new technology as a means for capturing a dramatic advantage over competitors who do not adopt it. The goal here is to be first to deploy an advantaged system and use that head start to leapfrog over the competition, establishing a position so far out in front that the sector realigns around its new leader. Visionaries are mavericks who want to break away from the herd and differentiate themselves dramatically.

3 The *pragmatist strategy* is directly opposed to the visionary. It wants to stay with the herd, adopting the new technology if and only if everyone else does as well. The goal here is to use the wisdom of the marketplace to sort out what's valuable and then to be a fast follower once the new direction has clearly emerged. Pragmatists consult each other frequently about who's adopting what in an effort to stay current but do not commit to any major change without seeing successful implementations elsewhere first.

4 The *conservative strategy* is to stick with the old technology for as long as possible (a) because it works (b) because it is familiar, and (c) because it is paid for. By putting off the transition to the new platform, conservatives conserve cash and avoid hitting the learning curve, making themselves more productive in the short run. Long term, when they do switch, the system is more completely debugged, and that works to their advantage as well. The

downside of the strategy is that they grow increasingly out of touch for the period they don't adopt and can, if they wait too long, get isolated in old technology that simply will not map to the new world.

5 Finally, the *skeptic strategy* is to debunk the entire technology as a false start and refuse to adopt it at all. This is a winning tactic for those technologies that never do gain mainstream market acceptance. For those that do, however, it creates extreme versions of the isolation problems conservatives face.

Each of these strategies has validity in its own right, and a single individual is perfectly capable of choosing different strategies for different offers. But for any given technology, the market will develop in a characteristic pattern due to the aggregate effects of a population distributing its choices in the proportions outlined by the bell curve. The resulting market development model is shown in Figure 8.3.2.

The model segments the evolution of a technology-based market as follows:

- The first phase, or *early market*, is a time when early adopters (technology enthusiasts and visionaries) take up the innovation while the pragmatic majority holds back. The market development goal at this stage is to gain a few prestigious flagship customers who help publicize the technology and celebrate its potential benefits.

- The early market is followed by a *chasm*, a period of no adoption, when the early adopters have already made their choices, but the pragmatist

FIGURE 8.3.2 Technology-enabled market development

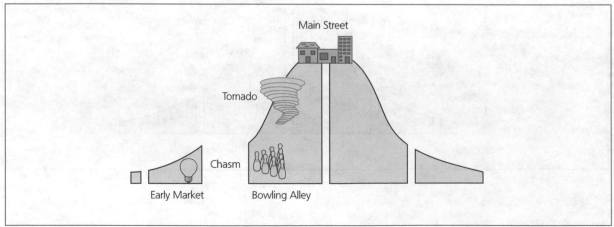

majority is still holding back. The barrier to further progress is that pragmatists are looking to other pragmatists to be references, but no one wants to go first. The market development goal at this stage is to target an initial beachhead segment of pragmatists who can lead the second wave of adoption.

- In the development of most technology-enabled markets, specific niches of pragmatic customers adopt the new technology before the general pragmatist population. We call this period the *bowling alley* because the market development goal is to use the first group of adopters as references to help win over the next group, and the next, and so on. Typically the 'head bowling pin' is a niche of pragmatists who have a major business problem that cannot be solved with current technology but that does respond to a solution built around the new innovation. These are the *department managers in charge of a broken, mission-critical process*. Once this first group starts to move it takes much less of a motive to overcome the inertia of the next group.

- As pragmatist adoption builds in niches, one of two futures emerges. In one, adoption continues to remain localized to niche markets, creating a pattern we call 'bowling alley forever'. In this pattern, each niche's solution is relatively complex and differentiated from every other niche's. As a result, no mass market emerges, and the market development goal is simply to expand existing niches and create new ones as the opportunity arises. In the other pattern, a 'killer app' emerges – a single application of the innovative technology that provides a compelling benefit that can be standardized across multiple niches. The killer app transforms niche adoption into mass adoption, creating an enormous uptick in demand for the new technology across a wide range of sectors. We call this period the *tornado* because the onrush of mass demand is so swift it creates a vortex that sucks the supply out of the market and puts the category into hypergrowth for a number of years. The market development goal here is to win as much market share as possible during a period when the entire market is choosing its supplier for the new class of technology-enabled offering.

- Once the supply side of the market finally catches up with the backlog of demand, the tornado phase subsides, and the market reaches a state we call *Main Street*. The new technology has been broadly deployed and, with the support of conservatives, now settles down to a (hopefully) long engagement as the incumbent technology. The market development goal here is to continuously improve the value of the offering, decreasing its base costs, and recouping margins by increasing the number of value-adding extensions that can supplement it. The ultimate extension in many cases is to convert the offering from a product sale to a services subscription, allowing the customer to gain the benefit of the product without having to take on the responsibility for maintaining it.

It is important to note that the end of the technology adoption life cycle does not represent the end of technology's productive market life. The category of offering can be sustained indefinitely on Main Street, coming to an end only when the next discontinuous innovation renders the prior technology obsolete. Indeed, despite all the emphasis on shortening life cycles, Main Street markets normally last for decades after complete absorption of the enabling technology – witness the car, the telephone, the television, the personal computer, and the cell phone. Importantly, however, the marketplace pecking order set by market share that emerges during the bowling alley and tornado phases tends to persist for the life of Main Street. That is, while Main Street represents the final and lasting distribution of competitive advantage, its boundaries get set prior to arrival. Thus success in every prior stage in the life cycle is key to building sustainable Main Street market success.

Stage-one adoption: The early market

Value-chain strategy

The early market begins with the ambitions of two constituencies who live at opposite ends of the value chain (see Figure 8.3.3). On the left is the *technology provider*, the supplier of the discontinuous innovation, with ambitions of constructing an entirely new marketplace based on a new platform. On the right are one or more visionary executives, in the role of *economic buyer*, who also have ambitions of their own. They want to rearchitect the marketplaces they participate in to install their company as the new market leader – and they want to do it fast. They see in the new technology an opportunity to disrupt the established order and insert themselves into the lead.

Between these two poles, however, there is at present no existing value chain that can link their ambitions. Indeed, the existing value chain is appalled by

FIGURE 8.3.3   Early-market value chain

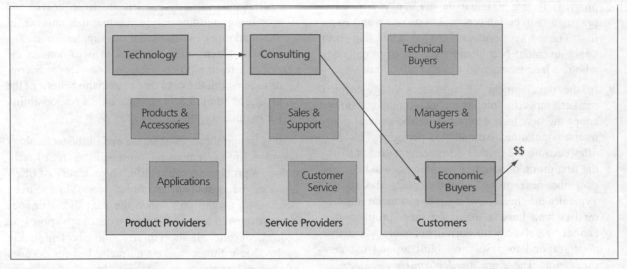

them. There is, however, one institution in the market that can bridge the gulf between the two, can transform the technology provider's magic into the economic buyer's dream, and that is the *consulting firm*. Rather than try to incubate a value chain in the marketplace, this consultancy will instead create a temporary value chain to serve a single project's specific needs. That is, they will pull together the products, the applications, the sales and support, the customer service, and in extreme cases even substitute their own people for the customer's technical buyer (and even for the customer's end users), all to make the value chain work *in a single instance for a single customer*.

Needless to say, this is an expensive proposition. But if it pays off, if the sponsoring company really does leapfrog over its competition in a new market order, then the visionary becomes a hero, and whatever money was spent was pocket change by comparison to the appreciation in the customer company's stock price.

Competitive advantage in the early market

The primary competitive-advantage strategy for the early market consists of being first to catch the new technology wave. This is often called *first-mover advantage*. Amazon.com, by catching the Web retail wave first, has created a powerful brand that its competitors cannot hope to replicate, regardless of how much they spend. By being first to introduce auctions onto the Web, eBay gained first-mover advantage also, so that even when assaulted by an alliance of extremely

powerful companies – Microsoft, Dell, Lycos, Excite – it has been able to sustain market share. Four years into Web advertising, the top ten sites, with Yahoo! leading the list, garner as much as 85 percent of the total spending – largely because of first-mover advantage. The Sabre system for airline and other travel-related reservations has had a similar track record, even as Apollo and Galileo and others have entered the market. Same with United Airlines' and American Airlines' frequent-flyer systems.

In every case, first-mover advantage equates to getting the market started around your unique approach and making the others play catch-up. It is a great strategy – when it works. The risk, of course, is that the market never goes forward to adopt the paradigm. At the time when the visionaries make their moves, this is a high probability. Visionaries are always bucking the odds in that most markets, like most mutations, die out before they can reproduce themselves sufficiently to gain persistence. Indeed, market creation is very much like the origin of species in nature, with the early market equating to the emergence of at least a few vital representatives of the new order.

The key metric of competitive advantage at this stage is simply the existence of proof of having one or more such representatives. For the technology provider, the test is one or more major corporate commitments from prestigious customers who champion the new paradigm as a platform for change in their industries. For the customer, the test is whether on top of this new platform an industry-changing offer can be promulgated. Neither measure is financial. Neither measure uses market share. The goal in both cases is just to validate the category. That puts the new wave on the map, enters it in the race.

The benefit to the company sponsoring this new initiative is that it gets a lot of attention. This attracts prospective customers to it at no additional cost of marketing. It also positions it as something of a thought leader in its industry. At the same time, however, it starts a timer ticking, with the expectation that within some definable period dramatic results will appear. If they do not, then the customers lose face, and the technology providers lose their company.

Value disciplines for the early market

In order to execute on a winning agenda, management teams must understand that the early market rewards discontinuous innovation and product leadership and penalizes customer intimacy and operational excellence. Thus optimal results are gained by elevating the former and suppressing the latter, as follows:

- Elevate discontinuous innovation and product leadership. The early market is driven by the demands of visionaries for offerings that create dramatic competitive advantages of the sort that would allow them to leapfrog over the other players in their industry. Only discontinuous innovation offers such advantage. In order to field that innovation, however, it must be transformed into a product offering that can be put to work in the real world. Hence the need for product leadership.
- Suppress customer intimacy and operational excellence. When technologies are this new, there are no target markets as yet and thus customer intimacy is not practical. Moreover, discontinuous innovations demand enormous customer tolerance and sacrifice as they get debugged, again not a time for celebrating putting the customer first. At the same time, because everything is so new and so much is yet to be discovered, it is equally impractical to target operational excellence. There is just too much new product, process, and procedure to invent and then shake out before pursuing this value discipline would be reasonable. Instead, one has to make peace with the strategy 'Go ugly early.'

Looking at the above, it is not surprising that engineering-led organizations, who resonate with the value disciplines in favor, are much more successful at early-market initiatives than marketing-led or operations-led organizations, who lean toward the value disciplines that should be suppressed. Going forward, as we look

at each subsequent phase of the life cycle, we will see that the rewarded and penalized disciplines change and so will the types of organizations that can be most successful.

Stage-two adoption: Crossing the chasm into the bowling alley

For technologies to gain persistent marketplace acceptance, they must cross the chasm and take up a position on the other side. Now we are in the realm of the pragmatists. To get pragmatists to move at all, companies must rethink their marketing objective from the early market. There the goal was to win a customer, and then another, and another. To cross the chasm, however, you have to *win a herd*. Here's why:

- Pragmatists only feel comfortable moving in herds. That's why they ask for references and use word of mouth as their primary source of advice on technology purchase decisions. Selling individual pragmatists on acting ahead of the herd is possible but very painful, and the cost of sales more than eats up the margin in the sale itself.
- Pragmatists evaluate the entire value chain, not just the specific product offer, when buying into a new technology. Value chains form around herds, not individual customers. There has to be enough repeatable business in the pipeline to reward an investment in specializing in the new technology. Sporadic deals, regardless of how big they are, do not create persistent value chains.

The visible metric for crossing the chasm, therefore, is to *make a market* and *create a value chain* where there were no market and no value chain before. This is a difficult undertaking. To increase its chances for success, and to decrease the time it takes to achieve, it is best to focus the effort on creating a niche market first before trying to create a mass market. It is simply prudent to minimize the number of variables at risk.

Think of a niche market as a self-contained system of commerce with its own local set of specialized needs and wants. Isolated from the mainstream market, which does not serve these special needs, it offers a *value-chain incubator* for emerging technology-enabled markets. That is, its isolation protects the fragile new chain from direct competitive attacks from the incumbent value chain. The customer community, in effect, nurtures the fledgling enterprise because it hopes to gain great benefit from it.

Value-chain strategy

To visualize the changes in moving from the early market to the bowling alley, let us return to our value-chain diagram, this time focusing on a new set of market makers (see Figure 8.3.4).

At the right-hand end of the chain, the *managers* in the customer domain represent the preassembled herd, an aggregation of relatively homogeneous demand. These are the department managers in charge of a broken, mission-critical process, all huddled in a mass. At the other end, the *application provider* in the product domain offers a relatively homogeneous solution to this herd's problem. It will bring its solution to market through a sales and support organization where it is the *support function* that really counts. That is because at the outset of a market the remaining value-chain partners are just getting recruited and cannot be relied upon to assemble the whole product correctly on their own. Later on these same partners will compete to take over the support function – and the enlightened application provider will let them, as it will greatly expand its market and its reach – but for now it is all just too new. So the application provider's support team must take the lead in working through all the glitches until a working whole product is in place, even when the problem is with someone else's part of the offering and not their own.

Note that the money-recycling arrow has now been restored to the diagram. This is the whole point of the niche-market strategy. We are now creating for the first time a self-funding persistent market where the economic gains of the customer lead to increasing and ongoing investment in the products and services that bring them about. Even if no other market ever adopts this technology, it will still be economically viable to maintain this niche. To be sure, the returns will not be all that the investors hoped for, but it will not be a total bust either. That is because niche markets have persistent competitive advantages that allow them to sustain themselves even when the marketplace in general is unsupportive of their efforts. Moreover, if the value chain extends its reach into additional niches, then it can add market growth to its already attractive price margins to produce highly attractive returns indeed.

The major beneficiary of this strategy are the application providers. It is they who harness the new wave of technology to the specific needs of the target segment, and they who rally the rest of the value chain to support this effort. Because the application provider is the company that really does 'make the market', it gains a dominant market-specific competitive advantage during this market formation period. This advantage will persist indefinitely, even after the technology adoption life cycle goes forward, since once any market falls into a particular pecking order, it is loath to change.

Everyone else in the value chain – the core technology providers, the hardware and software product companies, the business consultants and the systems integrators, the customer service staff, and even the client's own technical staff – all happily take a backseat. That's because they will all be operating primarily as cost-effective generalists, making relatively minor

FIGURE 8.3.4 Bowling alley value chain

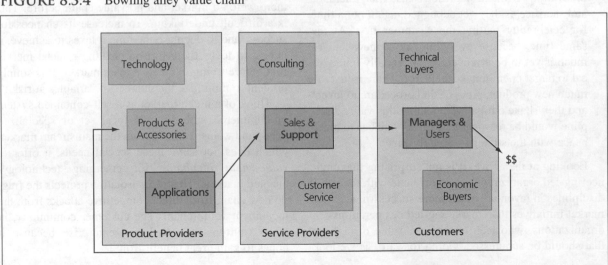

modifications to their way of doing business, whereas the application vendor, interacting intimately with the problem-owning department managers, must operate as a value-creating specialist and invest significantly to be able to do so effectively.

Competitive advantage in the bowling alley

The ability to harness the technology wave to solve the critical problem of one or more specific niche markets is what creates power at this stage, and that power goes primarily to the application provider. As more and more of the pragmatist department managers in the niches see their colleagues getting out of the soup, they, too, will come forward and insist on buying this vendor's application. Thus every other company in the value chain becomes dependent on that one vendor's good graces to get into the good deals. In effect, this creates a form of value-chain domination, but it is restricted solely to the niches served, and so it has very different properties – and a very different valuation – from the kind of broad horizontal-market domination we will see develop inside the tornado.

Because they reap the bulk of the rewards, it is relatively easy for application providers to understand and adopt niche marketing, especially if the alternative is to spend another year in the chasm. It is much more problematic, however, for a platform product or a transaction services company to embrace it. Their business plans are normally predicated on either broad horizontal adoption across a multitude of business segments or a broad cross-section of consumers. They are not well positioned to go after niche markets. Vertical industry domain expertise holds little value for them, and voluntarily subordinating themselves to an application vendor just to gain entry into one little niche seems like a huge price to pay. Moreover, even if the tactic proves successful, the resulting order stream will be relatively modest, and worse, may inappropriately cause the rest of the market to misperceive the company as a niche player. For all these very good reasons, platform-products and transaction-services vendors tend to shy away from taking the niche approach to crossing the chasm. And yet it is still a mistake. Here's why.

As we shall see shortly, platform products are optimised for tornado markets, and transaction-services offers are optimised for Main Street markets. Those are the phases of the life cycle in which they will shine. So their strategy should be to accelerate technology adoption to get to 'their' phase as quickly as possible. Time

spent in the chasm for either strategy represents a huge opportunity cost, giving their competitors a chance to catch up to first-mover advantage while making no progress for themselves at all. This makes exiting the chasm as quickly as possible their top strategic imperative – hence their need to perform the admittedly unnatural act of niche marketing. To be sure, it is a little bit like asking a caterpillar who has a stated goal to be a butterfly to first spin itself into a cocoon and melt – the intermediate step is so disconnected from the end result that it is hard to warrant taking it. But there is now sufficient history to show that not taking the step is fatal – as demonstrated by the market development failures of ISDN networking, object-oriented databases, IBM's OS/2 operating system, pen-based PCs, infrared connectivity protocols, and artificial intelligence.

To be sure, once an initial niche market is established, the winning strategy for platform products and transaction services does indeed split off from the application providers. For the latter, the most powerful path forward is to stay in the bowling alley – this is their sweet spot – expanding niche to niche, following a bowling pin strategy. In this manner, such companies can chew their way through multiple markets with a very high probability of securing dominant positions in the majority of their niches. It is a 'bowling alley forever' strategy focused on *preserving complexity* in order to create a source of profit margins for themselves and their service partners. It ends up trading off massive scale in favor of locally dominant roles and eventually makes the transition to Main Street as a leader in a set of mature vertical markets.

By contrast, for platform-product and transaction-services companies, the goal should be to get beyond niches altogether as soon as possible. Their quest instead should be for a single, general-purpose 'killer app' – a word-processing program, a spreadsheet, e-mail, voice-mail, a Web site, an e-commerce server – something that can be adopted by whole sectors of the economy all at once, thereby leveraging their horizontal business models' strength in being able to scale rapidly. But students of the life cycle should note that in the era prior to pervasive word processing, there were segment-specific solutions for lawyers, doctors, consultants, and governmental functions. These were a critical stepping stone toward getting to a mass market.

Value disciplines for the bowling alley

To execute on a niche strategy in an emerging technology-enabled market, companies must realign their value discipline orientation to meet a new set of market priorities, as follows:

- Elevate product leadership and customer intimacy. The bowling alley is driven by the demands of pragmatists for a whole product that will fix a broken mission-critical business process. The fact that the process will not respond to conventional treatment calls out the need for product leadership. The fact that the required whole product will have to integrate elements specific to a particular vertical segment calls out the need for customer intimacy.
- Suppress discontinuous innovation and operational excellence. Pragmatist department managers under pressure to fix a broken process have neither the time nor the resources to support debugging a discontinuous innovation. At the same time, their need for special attention is incompatible with the kind of standardization needed for operational excellence.

Marketing-led organizations are best at crossing the chasm, specifically those that combine strong domain expertise in the targeted market segment with a solutions orientation. Operations-led organizations struggle with the amount of customization required that cannot be amortized across other segments, all of which offends their sense of efficiency. Engineering-led organizations struggle with the lack of product symmetry resulting from heavily privileging one niche's set of issues over a whole raft of other needed enhancements.

To win with this strategy, the critical success factor is focus – specifically, focus on doing whatever it takes to get that first herd of pragmatist customers to adopt en masse the new technology. Hedging one's bet by sponsoring forays targeted at additional herds at the same time is bad strategy. Both engineering- and operations-oriented organizations, however, are drawn to this approach because they fear that the company is putting all its eggs into one basket. Of course, that is precisely what it *is* doing. The reason it is good strategy to do so is that only by creating critical mass can one move a market and bring into existence a new value chain. Unless they can leverage tornado winds blowing in other markets, alternative initiatives subtract from the needed mass and, ironically, increase rather than decrease market risk.

Stage-three adoption: inside the tornado

A tornado occurs whenever pragmatists across a variety of market sectors all decide simultaneously that it is time to adopt a new paradigm – in other words, when the pragmatist herd stampedes. This creates a dramatic spike in demand, vastly exceeding the currently available supply, calling entire categories of vendors to reconfigure their offerings to meet the needs of a new value chain.

Value-chain strategy

The overriding market force that is shaping the tornado value chain is the desire for everyone in the market, beginning with the customer but quickly passing through to all vendors, to drive the transition to a new paradigm as quickly as possible. That calls to the fore the three constituencies highlighted in Figure 8.3.5.

Each of these constituencies is well positioned to benefit from standardization for rapid deployment.

- In the product sphere, it is *products*, not technology and not applications, that get the privileged position. The problem with technology is that it is too malleable to be mass-produced and thus does not lend itself to rapid proliferation of common, standard infrastructure. The problem with applications is that they must be customized to sector-specific processes, and so again they do not deploy as rapidly as desired. By contrast, products, and specifically those that serve as platforms for a broad range of applications, are the ideal engine for paradigm proliferation.

  Now, to be sure, there must be at least one application that warrants the purchase of the platform in the first place, but in a tornado that application must be essentially the same for every sector. Such an application is called 'the killer app', and it becomes the focus for horizontal expansion across multiple sectors of the economy. *Accounting* was the killer app for mainframes, *manufacturing automation* for minicomputers, *word processing* for PCs, *computer-aided design* for workstations, and *electronic mail* for local area networks. But in every case, it was the platform product providers, not the killer app vendors, who were ultimately the big tornado winners because as other applications came on-line, they created still more demand for their platforms.

- In the services sphere, it is the sales and support function, with the emphasis on *sales*, that carries the

FIGURE 8.3.5 Tornado value chains

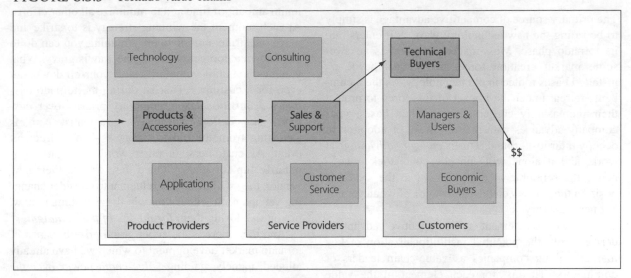

day. The drawback with consulting is that its projects are too complex, take too long, and require resources that are too scarce to ever permit a tornado to go forward. The drawback with customer service is that it is too focused on serving existing customers at a time when the overwhelming emphasis has to be on acquiring new customers.

Generating sales in the tornado is not a problem of winning over the customer so much as it is of beating the competition. It is critical, therefore, to field the most competitive sales force you can at this time. Because so much wealth is changing hands, and because the long-term consequences of market share are so great, tornado sales tactics are brutal, and sales aggressiveness is the core discipline. This is the time when nice guys do finish last.

On the support side, the key issue is to get new customers up and running on a minimal system as quickly as possible and then move on to the next new customer. The more cookie-cutter the process, the faster it replicates, and the more new customers you can absorb. The push is for operational excellence, not customer intimacy. This is not a normal support profile, so once again focusing the team on the right value discipline is a critical executive responsibility.

■ On the customer side of the value chain, it is the *technical buyer*, not the end-user departments and not the economic buyer, who becomes the key focus. The problem with end users is that they inevitably seek customization to meet their department-specific needs. Not only is such complexity

contrary to the vendor's wishes, it also works against the host institution's imperative to roll out the new infrastructure to everyone in the company as quickly as possible. Such rapid deployment requires a one-size-fits-all approach for the initial roll-out, something that the technical buyer understands far better than the end user. It is also not the time to court senior executives in their role as economic buyers. Once the tornado is under way, they sense the need to get over to the new infrastructure and delegate the task, including the selection process, to their technical staff.

When technical buyers become the target customer, their compelling reason to buy drives sales outcomes. High on their list is conformance to common standards, followed by market leadership status, which initially is signalled by partnerships with other market leaders, and later on confirmed by market share. The technical buyers' biggest challenge is systems integration, and this is where the support function can contribute to faster roll-outs by building standard interfaces to the most prevalent legacy systems.

The tornado, in essence, is one big land grab – a fierce struggle to capture as many new customers as possible during the pragmatist stampede to the new paradigm. Increasing shareholder value revolves entirely around maximizing market share, and to that end there are three sources of competitive-advantage leverage to exploit.

Competitive advantage in the tornado

The primary source of competitive advantage is simply to be riding the new technology wave as it enters into its tornado phase. Mass-market adoption is an awesome market creation force that wreaks havoc on installed bases rooted in old technology. As the incumbents retreat under the impact of this force to protect their increasingly conservative installed bases, your company advances with the new wave of adoption to occupy their lost ground. This is *category advantage* at work, and it alone will enhance your stock price – hence the scramble of every vendor in the sector to position themselves on the bandwagon of whatever this hot new category is.

The second element of competitive advantage derives from the potential institutionalization of key market-making companies as value-chain leaders or dominators. That is, for each element in the value chain, tornado markets seek out a single market-leading provider to set the de facto standards for that component. That role normally goes to the company that garners the most new customers early in the race. In addition, when a single company can gain power over the rest of the value chain, typically by leveraging the power to withhold its proprietary technology and thereby stymie the entire offer, the market accords even more privilege to it.

The power of market-share leadership is rooted in the pragmatist preference to make the safe buy by going with the market leader. That is, rather than rely on their own judgment, pragmatist prefer to rely on the group's. Once that judgment has been made clear, once one vendor has emerged as the favorite, then pragmatists naturally gravitate to that choice, which of course further increases that company's market share, intensifying its gravitational attraction.

This cycle of positive feedback not only spontaneously generates market leaders, but once they are generated, works to keep them in place. That is, the value-chain advantage a market leader gains over its direct competitors is that it has become the default choice for any other company in the chain to round out its offers. Thus the company gains sales that it never initiated and gets invited into deals its competitors never see. Such sales not only add to revenues but to margins, since the absence of competition removes much of the pressure to discount price. In short, winning the market-share prize is a very sweet deal, which, if it is not working for you, is working against you. Hence the need to focus all guns on market share.

Thus the essence of tornado strategy is simply to capture the maximum number of customers in the minimum amount of time and to minimize all other efforts. At each moment the winning strategy is to strike and move on, strike and move on. Anything you can do to slow down a competitor along the way is gravy. What you must not do is voluntarily slow yourself down, not even for a customer. That is, during the tornado *customer acquisition* takes temporary priority over *customer satisfaction*. The entire pragmatist herd is switching from the old to the new – not a frequent event. As customers, in other words, they are temporarily 'up for grabs'. Once they choose their new vendor, they will be highly reluctant to consider changing yet again. So either you win these customers now, or you risk losing them *for the life of the paradigm*.

And then there is the super grand prize bonanza of tornado market development to which we have already alluded, namely, gaining *value-chain power over the other vendors in the value chain*. As noted, this occurs when a single vendor has monopoly control of a crucial element in the value chain, the way Microsoft and Intel each do for the personal computer, the way Cisco does for the Internet, the way Qualcomm appears to do for the future of wireless telephony. In such cases, as the market tornado unfolds, the standard whole product that forms around the killer app incorporates a piece of your proprietary technology. Going forward, for the value-chain offering as a whole to evolve, it must take your technology along with it – and there is no substitute for it. This makes everyone in the chain dependent upon you, which in turn allows you to orchestrate the behavior of the rest of the chain. This can include pressuring value-chain partners to adopt or support some of your less successful products so that you gain power across a much broader portion of your product line than its actual features and benefits would normally merit.

Value disciplines for the tornado

Whatever position one achieves during the tornado market depends largely on your company's ability to execute a market-share land-grab strategy. To this end, the market rewards a third alignment of value disciplines, as follows:

- Elevate product leadership and operational excellence. The tornado is driven by the demands of infrastructure buyers for standard, reliable offerings suitable for rapid mass deployment. Here product leadership gets translated into shipping the next release with the new set of features ahead of the competition and thereby grabbing additional market share from them. Operational excellence is critical to this effort because if there is any hiccup in the process, the market can still shift to an alternative vendor, with major market-share consequences that will last for the duration of the paradigm.

■ Suppress discontinuous innovation and customer intimacy. Any form of discontinuous innovation during a tornado creates opportunity for error, putting rapid mass deployment at risk, and is thus anathema. Customer intimacy is also suppressed for the duration of the roll-out for the same reason, sacrificed to the end of achieving reliable, consistent deployment. Once the infrastructure is set in place, then there will be time to come back and meet customer-specific requests.

Operations-led organizations tend to have the edge in a tornado, where meeting deadlines, shipping in quantity, and minimizing returns all take priority over innovation and customer delight. Marketing-led organizations, by contrast, typically flounder because they cannot bear to relinquish their commitment to customer intimacy and customer satisfaction. They need to realize that, in a tornado, just getting the new systems installed and working properly is grounds for customer satisfaction.

Stage-four adoption: On Main Street

Main Street begins as the market-share frenzy that drives tornado winds subsides. The overwhelming bulk of the pragmatists in the market have chosen their vendor, made their initial purchases, and rolled out the first phase of a multiphase deployment. Only a fraction of the total forecastable sales in the segment have actually been made at this point, but from here on out the market-share boundaries are relatively fixed. This has significant implications for the value chain.

Value-chain strategy

Here is the fourth and final mutation in the value chain. This one will endure for the life of the paradigm. In effect, it is the value chain we have been setting up all along (see Figure 8.3.6).

There is a key change underlying this entire value chain, which is that the technology adoption life cycle as a whole has evolved from the pragmatist to the conservative agenda, and every constituency in the value chain is affected by this change. Let's start with the customer.

When companies adopt new paradigms, conservative customers at first hang back, preferring to eke out some last bit of value from the old system. But once it is clear that the new system must supplant the old one, then they seek to put their stamp on the new vendor relationship. They remind all these new arrivals that most of the promises that were made on behalf of their

FIGURE 8.3.6 Main Street value chain

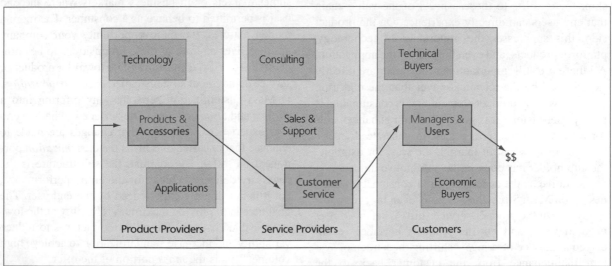

products and services are as yet far from true, and they work to keep everyone focused on making incremental improvements going forward. In effect, they transform what heretofore was a discontinuous innovation into what will from now on be a system of continuous innovation.

In mature – or maturing – markets, both the economic buyer and the technical buyer recede in importance. The economic buyer is no longer looking for competitive advantage or to support a manager in fixing a broken business process; now the issue is simply staying within budget, and that can be delegated. And the technical buyer is no longer concerned about how to either manage or postpone the introduction of a disruptive technology; now the concern is simply to stay compliant with established standards, and that, too, can be delegated. Even within the user community, the managers are now taking the new systems for granted, assuming that it must be doing pretty much what it was bought to do (a naive, but all too frequent point of view). Thus it is only *end users*, the people who actually interact with the system on a frequent basis, that (a) know anything about how it really works, and (b) have a stake in sponsoring improvements to it.

If these end users do not voice their desires, then the offering becomes a complete commodity, with the purchasing department driving a *supplier relationship* going forward. If they do voice their desires, however, and gain their managers' approval, then end users can drive a *vendor relationship*, a condition that allows a company to earn margins above commodity levels. We are long past the time for customers to embrace you in a *strategic partner relationship*, something that is confined to earlier phases in the life cycle.

To earn preferred margins from end-user sponsorship, focus shifts to those aspects of the value chain that end users can directly experience. On the product side, this suppresses the importance of technology, platform products, and even the core of the application. All these are still important, but they are more directly experienced by the technical buyer than the end user. By contrast, any product element that is consumable, is highly user visible. It is here that minor enhancements for a modest increase in price can generate dramatic changes in gross profit margin, the way, for example, the cup holder has done in the automotive industry.

Lucrative as the accessories and consumables business is on Main Street, however, an even bigger opportunity lies in the product-service shift. What customers used to value and buy as products becomes reconceived as service offerings – shifting the burden of system maintenance from the customer back to the vendor. Thus the move from answering machine to voice-mail, from videotapes to pay-per-view, from bar bells to health clubs.

The primary organization tasked with masterminding this shift is *customer service*. Historically this has been a challenge because that organization was not constructed nor were its personnel recruited with the thought that it would eventually become a lead contributor to the P&L and market valuation of the company. In the age of the Internet, however, investors are now actively pursuing companies that have been founded from day one with just such an agenda in mind.

Competitive advantage on Main Street

The technology wave has crested and broken and no longer provides market development leverage. The value chain is already formed, and whatever place you have in it is not going to change without massive and usually unwarranted investment. There is always the possibility of you finding an underserved market segment here or there, but the speed of market penetration now will be much slower, the impact on any local value chain much less, and thus the rewards more modest than they would have been during the bowling alley phase. And so it is that we get to the domain of company execution, to which we shall turn in a moment, and differentiated offerings.

There are classically two types of differentiation strategies that succeed on Main Street. The first is being the low-cost provider, a strategy that works best in commodity markets where it is not the end user but the purchasing manager acting as economic buyer who is the real decision maker. The other type is a customer-delight strategy, which works best in consumer markets or in business markets where the end user is permitted to behave as a consumer. The more a market matures, the more opportunity your company has to deliver on both of these propositions to be competitive. To do so it must gravitate toward a product or service deployment strategy called *mass customization*.

Mass customization separates any offering into a *surface* and a *substructure*. The surface is what the end user experiences. It is here that changes are made to enhance that experience. This is the *customization* portion of the offer. By contrast, the substructure is the necessary delivery vehicle for the entire performance, but it is not directly experienced by the end user. The goal here is to provide maximum reliability at the lowest possible cost, and the preferred tactic is to reduce variability and increase standardization to achieve high volume. This is the *mass* portion of the offer.

To combine the two without sacrificing the benefits of either, the customizing portion must often be done downstream in the value chain in a separate step from the mass portion. This typically leads to a need to redesign the value chain, creating new opportunities for service providers to create customization value at the point of customer contact. Think of how cell phones are provided, and you get the idea. Everything upstream from the retail outlet is totally standardized; everything downstream is customizable – the phone itself, its accessories, service options, program pricing, and the like. Prior to retail, everything is sold as a commodity; after retail, it is a value-added offering.

The implications of this restructuring of the market are far-reaching, and not just for service providers. Consumables have the same potential to deliver customized value. Consider, for example, the razor-to-razor-blade transition in Gillette's history, or Kodak's move from cameras to film, or HP's transition from inkjet printers to inkjet cartridges. In every case once Main Street is reached, it is the consumable at the surface, and not the underlying engine at the core, that becomes the basis of differentiation and the locus of high profit margins.

Alternatively, service transactions can also replace the serviced commodity as the locus of value creation. This has been the case in the automobile industry, where the bulk of the profits are made not from selling new cars but from financing the purchase, insuring the vehicle, supplying the consumables, and providing the maintenance services. In every case margins are affected by the end user's experience during these transactions. That is why companies like Lexus have been so successful with their customer-care offers. It is also why traditional car dealerships are failing with their customer-unfriendly approach to purchase and financing, driving their customers to brokers and to the Web instead.

In large part the promise of the Internet is based on it being a universal platform for value-adding customization in Main Street value chains. The systems are not yet completely in place to fulfill this proposition today, but forward-thinking executives and enlightened investors can see how with incremental improvements they will be able to generate scaleable, low-cost, high-touch offerings of the sort that create attractive profit margins on Main Street.

Value disciplines

To execute on this strategy of mass customization, companies as elsewhere in the life cycle must learn to elevate one pair of value disciplines and suppress the other:

- Elevate operational excellence and customer intimacy. Main Street markets are supported by conservative customers seeking incremental gains in value. These can be achieved either through decreasing the costs of the current set of offers – the domain of operational excellence – or by introducing a new set of offers improved through readily absorbed continuous innovations – the domain of customer intimacy.

- Suppress discontinuous innovation and product leadership. Discontinuous innovation runs directly contrary to the interests of Main Street customers and is simply not welcome. Even offers based on product leadership are problematic. If they require retooling the existing infrastructure, they usually just aren't worth it. What development teams must realize is that now product improvements should be focused either on keeping the core product viable, with operational excellence as a guide, or on making cosmetic changes at the surface, with customer intimacy providing the direction.

Of all the pairings, this particular set should be the most familiar to established companies in mature markets. They should see themselves as the champions of the first pair, and those wretched dotcoms assaulting their marketplace as the purveyors of the second. Note that in this pairing the established company's existing customers are very much on its side, not on the dotcoms'. That's because they, like the company itself, are ruled by conservative interests. It is instead the flock of new customers who are entering the tornado for the next big thing that are undermining this company's stock price going forward.

Implications of living on the fault line

The four market states are set out in a side-by-side comparison in Table 8.3.1.

The table maps the working out of the competitive-advantage hierarchy over the course of a technology-enabled market's development. The columns lay out the life-cycle phases these markets evolve through. The rows lay out the changes in focus that organizations must make to adapt to this evolution. The first row sets forth the layer in the competitive-advantage hierarchy that has the most impact during each phase. The next three rows highlight the value-chain elements that

TABLE 8.3.1 Comparison of market states

	Early market	Bowling alley	Tornado	Main Street
Primary competitive advantage	Catching technology wave	Market-segment domination	Market-share leadership	Differentiated offerings
Product focus	Technology	Applications	Platform products	Consumables
Service focus	Consulting	Support	Sales	Customer service
Customer focus	Economic buyer	Department manager	Technical buyer	End user

create the most impact during the phase because they are best suited to leveraging the type of competitive advantage available.

Even a cursory glance, shows that the changes companies have to make in order to adapt to these forces are dramatic indeed. Moreover, the time allotted to make them is painfully short. As a result, it should surprise no one that few real-world organizations are very good at actually making them. Indeed, the larger and more successful a company becomes, the less likely it is to attempt making them at all.

Strategy, value innovation, and the knowledge economy

W. Chan Kim and Renée Mauborgne[1]

For the past twenty years, competition has occupied the center of strategic thinking. Indeed, one hardly speaks of strategy without drawing on the vocabulary of competition – competitive strategy, competitive benchmarking, competitive advantages, outperforming the competition. In fact, most strategic prescriptions merely redefine the ways companies build advantages over the competition. This has been the strategic objective of many firms, and, in itself, nothing is wrong with this objective. After all, a company needs some advantages over the competition to sustain itself in the marketplace. When asked to build competitive advantage, however, managers typically assess what competitors do and strive to do it better. Their strategic thinking thus regresses toward the competition. After expending tremendous effort, companies often achieve no more than incremental improvement – imitation, not innovation.

Consider what happened in the microwave oven and VCR industries. As a result of competitive benchmarking, product offerings were nearly mirror images of each other and, from the customer's perspective, they were overdesigned and overpriced. Most buyers had no use for most of the features and found them confusing and irritating. These companies may have outdone one another, but they missed an opportunity to capture the mass market by offering microwaves and VCRs that were easy to use at accessible prices.

Another classic example is the battle of IBM versus Compaq in the PC market. In 1983, when Compaq launched its IBM-compatible machines with technologically superb quality at a 15 percent lower price than IBM's, it rapidly won the mass of PC buyers. Once roused by Compaq's success, IBM started a race to beat Compaq; Compaq likewise focused on beating

[1]Source: This article was adapted from W.C. Kim and R. Mauborgne, 'Strategy, Value Innovation, and the Knowledge Economy' in *Sloan Management Review*, 1999, Vol. 40, No. 3, pp. 41–54. Reproduced by permission.

IBM. Trying to outperform one another in sophisticated feature enhancements, neither company foresaw the emergence of the low-end PC market in which user-friendliness and low price – not the latest technology – were keys to success. Both companies created a line of overly designed and overpriced PCs, and both companies missed the emerging low-end market. When IBM walked off the cliff in the late 1980s, Compaq was following closely.

These cases illustrate that strategy driven by the competition usually has three latent, unintended effects:

- Imitative, not innovative, approaches to the market. Companies often accept what competitors are doing and simply strive to do it better.
- Companies act reactively. Time and talent are unconsciously absorbed in responding to daily competitive moves, rather than creating growth opportunities.
- A company's understanding of emerging mass markets and changing customer demands becomes hazy.

Over the past decade, we have studied companies of sustained high growth and profits vis-à-vis their less successful competitors. Regardless of size, years of operation, industry conditions, and country of origin, the strategy these companies pursue is what we call *value innovation*. Value innovation is quite different from building layers of competitive advantages and is not about striving to outperform the competition. Nor is value innovation about segmenting the market and accommodating customers' individual needs and differences. Value innovation makes the competition irrelevant by offering fundamentally new and superior buyer value in existing markets and by enabling a quantum leap in buyer value to create new markets.

Take, for example, Callaway Golf, the U.S. golf club manufacturer, which in 1991 launched its 'Big Bertha' golf clubs. The product rapidly rose to dominate the market, wresting market share from its rivals and expanding the total golf club market. Despite intense competition, Callaway did not focus on its competitors. Rival golf clubs looked alike and featured sophisticated enhancements, a result of attentive benchmarking of the competitors' products. In the meantime, Callaway pondered the 'country club' markets of golf and tennis. Many people play tennis because they find the task of hitting a little golf ball with a little golf club head too daunting. Recognizing a business opportunity, Callaway made a golf club with a larger head that made playing golf less difficult and more fun. The result: not only were new players drawn into the market, but Callaway captured an overwhelming share of existing players as well.

Similar examples of value innovation arise in diverse industries. Consider CNN in news broadcasting, Wal-Mart in discount retailing, Compaq in computers (after its turnaround), Kinepolis in cinema, IKEA in home products retail, Charles Schwab & Co. in investment and brokerage account management, Home Depot in home improvement retail, SAP in business application software, Barnes & Noble in book retailing, Southwest Airlines in short-haul air travel, and others. Their steady growth and high profits are not a consequence of daring young organizational members, of being a small entrepreneurial start-up, of being in attractive industries, or of making big commitments in the latest technology. Instead, the superperforming companies that we studied are united in their pursuit of innovation outside a conventional context. That is, they do not pursue innovation as technology, but as value. The companies cited above created quantum leaps in some aspect of value; many have nothing to do with new technology. This is why we call these companies value innovators.

Many high achievers excel despite bad industry conditions. Instead of falling victim to industry conditions, these value innovators focus on creating opportunities in their fields. They ask, 'How can we offer buyers greater value that will result in soaring profitable growth irrespective of industry or competitive conditions?' Because they question everything about a particular industry and their competitors, they explore a far wider range of strategic options than other companies. This broadens their creative scope, allowing them to find opportunities where other companies can see only constraints imposed by external conditions.

To achieve sustained profitable growth, companies must break out of the competitive and imitative trap. Rather than striving to match or outperform the competition, companies must cultivate value innovation. Emphasis on value places the buyer, not the competition, at the center of strategic thinking; emphasis on innovation pushes managers to go beyond incremental improvements to totally new ways of doing things.

Consider our recent study of the profitable growth consequences of more than a hundred new business launches. We found that while 86 percent of these business launches were 'me too' businesses or businesses with value improvements over the competition, they generated only 62 percent of total revenues and 39 percent of total profits. In contrast, the remaining 14 percent of the business launches – those that were value innovators – generated 38 percent of total revenues and a whopping 61 percent of total profits. The performance of value innovators far exceeds that of companies focusing on matching or beating their competitors. Companies pursuing value innovation are on the rise. Value innovation fuels small companies to grow profitably and regenerates the fortunes of big companies.

Shifting the basis of strategy

Why has competition been the key building block of strategy in theory and practice? Think of the competitive penetration of Japanese companies into U.S. industries that awakened U.S. companies to the reality of global competition. After a period of denial, U.S. companies vigorously responded, making competition the centerpiece of their strategic thinking. In neoclassical economics, firms and innovations are treated as 'black boxes'. What firms do is determined by market conditions because market conditions are assumed to be beyond the influence of individual companies. In such a setting, innovations are random events exogenous to firms. If market conditions and innovations are treated as given sets of the external environment, a firm strategically chooses a distinctive cost or differentiation position that best fits with its internal systems and capabilities to counter the competition in that particular environment. In such a situation, innovation is not endogenous to its system, so cost and product performance are seen as trade-offs.

Competition-based strategy, however, has waning power in today's economy in which, in many industries, supply exceeds demand. Competing for a share of contracting markets is a marginal and 'second best' strategy. Such a zero-sum strategy is cutthroat and does not create new wealth. A 'first best' strategy in today's economy stimulates the demand side of the economy. It expands existing markets and creates new markets. Such a non-zero-sum strategy generates new wealth and has high payoffs. In regard to profitable growth, creating shareholder value, and generating new jobs and wealth for society, companies pursuing the first-best strategy through value innovation far outperform companies following the second-best strategy. In our studies, we see this happening in the business world today.

During the past two decades, for example, we have seen a rapid change in the *Fortune* 500 list – both in rankings and those who qualify for the list; some 60 percent have disappeared from the list. Value innovators are now among the most rapidly growing companies. In less than forty years, a value innovator like Wal-Mart, for example, has become the world's eighth largest company in revenues and the world's second largest employer (825,000 people).

Shareholder value and wealth created by value innovators are equally compelling. The market value of SAP, for example, exceeds that of 150-year-old Siemens; Microsoft's market value towers over the combined values of General Motors and Ford. In 1995, with $6 billion in revenues and $7 billion in assets, the market value of Microsoft was 1.5 times that of GM with $168 billion in revenues and $217 billion in assets.

Why do value innovators such as SAP have such high market valuations despite their much smaller physical and fiscal assets? What do investors value in these companies that is not reflected on their balance sheets? As far as the market is concerned, their high stock of *knowledge* portends tremendous wealth-creating potential despite their much smaller sizes. In creating wealth, knowledge is increasingly taking a front seat to the traditional factors of production, that is, physical and fiscal assets. The gap between a company's market value and its tangible asset value is widening; the key variable explaining this gap is a firm's stock of knowledge. Unlike land, labor, and capital – the economist's traditional, finite factors of production – knowledge and ideas are infinite economic goods that can generate increasing returns through their systematic use, as SAP and Nintendo prove.

In a world in which industry conditions no longer dictate corporate well-being because companies can transcend these conditions through the systematic pursuit of innovation, a firm need not compete for a share of given demand – it can create new demand. Moreover, low cost and differentiation do not have to be an either-or choice because innovation can be a sustainable strategy (Hill, 1988). In fact, to innovate in this knowledge economy, companies employing the first best strategy often pursue low cost and differentiation simultaneously. Rising companies, small or large, that have achieved sustained high growth and profits are those that have pursued value innovation. Their strategic focus was not on outcompeting within given industry conditions, but on creating fundamentally new and superior value, making their competitors irrelevant. They went beyond competing in existing markets to expand the demand side of the economy.

Value and innovation

Value innovation places equal emphasis on *value* and *innovation*. Value without innovation tends to focus on improving the buyer's net benefit or value creation on an incremental scale. Innovation without value can be too strategic or wild (by betting on a company's long-term industry foresight) or too technology-driven or futuristic (shooting far beyond what buyers are ready to accept). Value innovation anchors innovation with buyer value. Hence, value innovation is not the same as *value creation*. Value creation as a concept of strategy is too broad because no boundary condition specifies the direction a company should follow to bring about successful strategic actions. Value creation on an incremental scale, for example, still creates some value but is not sufficient for high performance.

Value innovation also differs from *technology innovation*. As previously mentioned, technology innovation is not a requisite for value innovation; value innovation can occur with or without new technology. Moreover, technology innovation does not necessarily produce value innovation. For example, although Ampex innovated video recording technology in the 1950s, the company failed to convert this new technology into a value innovation cheap enough for mass buyers. As a result, later value innovators, such as Sony and JVC, profited greatly by unlocking the mass market at almost 1 percent of Ampex's initial price. Value innovators are not necessarily first entrants to their markets in technological terms. In this sense, they are not necessarily technology pioneers, but they are value pioneers.

Value innovation links innovation to what the mass of buyers value. To value innovate, companies must ask two questions: (1) Are we offering customers radically superior value? (2) Is our price level accessible to the mass of buyers in our target market? High-growth companies understand that offering a new and superior product or service at a price that most buyers cannot afford is like laying an egg that other companies will hatch. (See Figure 8.4.1 for the relationships among value creation, value innovation, and technology innovation.)

While technology innovators such as Ampex failed to capture profits for themselves, their technological discoveries often benefited the overall economy because later value innovators eventually use these technological discoveries successfully. In light of this, the distinction between technology innovation and value innovation may not be relevant to economists whose main concern is a theory of growth at the macro level. Such a distinction, however, is important to those whose interest is in building a theory of firm growth. Who will capture the profit is a pertinent and critical issue to individual firms.

Many innovation and creativity studies have focused on improving or redefining solutions to problems with technology as a central component of the discussions. Researchers attempted to explain how an organization develops technological solutions to customers' problems. Because technologies are seen as solutions to problems, most innovation studies have been solution driven. Unlike technology innovation, value innovation focuses on redefining the problems themselves. This is how value innovation makes the competition irrelevant. By redefining the problem an industry focuses on, a value innovator shifts the performance criteria that mater to customers. This creates new market space. To redefine customers' problems, market insights are needed to discover existing but 'hidden' demand or to create totally new demand. Value innovation is a consequence of such market insights gained from creative strategic thinking.

Callaway Golf, for example, created its Big Bertha golf club after redefining the consumer's need, that is, a desire to hit the ball more easily. Rivals focused on offering better solutions to hitting the ball farther –

FIGURE 8.4.1   Relationships among value creation, value innovation, and technology innovation

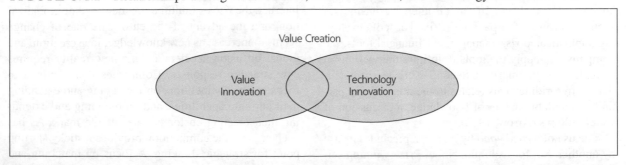

some were cost leaders and some were differentiators in solving this particular problem. By addressing a redefined problem, Big Bertha expanded the total market by attracting new customers who had not previously played golf. The company gained this market insight by thinking in terms of alternative industries – golf versus tennis – as opposed to thinking in terms of its industry competitors. Its main strategic question was why people choose tennis over golf in the country club market. Callaway Golf did not concentrate on how to outperform other golf club manufacturers by offering a *better* solution to the conventional goal of hitting the fall farther.

The concept of value innovation is consistent with the Schumpeterian notion (1934) of 'creative destruction' in the sense that it is about creating fundamentally new and superior value, hence making existing things and ways of doing things irrelevant. But whereas the entrepreneur is the major input in creating Schumpeterian innovation, knowledge and ideas are the major inputs for value innovation. Whether an executive or a factory worker, anyone can have a good idea; value innovation can occur in any organization and at any time in a sustainable manner with the proper process. In contrast, the realization of Schumpeterian innovation is subject to the availability of entrepreneurs who are in short supply. Hence, while an understanding of entrepreneurship and the entrepreneur as an economic hero are critical to Schumpeterian innovation, it is not with value innovation.

Market dynamics of value innovation

The transition from a production to a knowledge economy has two new consequences. First, it creates the potential for increasing returns (Arthur, 1996). This is easy to understand in the software industry in which, for example, producing the first copy of the Windows 95 operating system cost Microsoft millions, whereas subsequent copies involved no more than the near trivial cost of a diskette. In capital-intensive businesses such as Enron's, after paying the fixed cost of developing sophisticated risk management financial tools, the company can apply the tools to infinite transactions at insignificant marginal cost. Second, it creates the potential for free-riding. This relates to the nonrival and partially excludable nature of knowledge, a discussion of which follows (Arrow, 1962).

The use of a *rival good* by one firm precludes its use by another. So, for example, Nobel Prize-winning scientists employed by IBM cannot simultaneously be employed by another company. Nor can scrap steel consumed by Nucor be simultaneously consumed for production by other minimill steel makers. In contrast, the use of a *nonrival good* by one firm does not limit its use by another. Ideas fall into this category. So, for example, when Virgin Atlantic Airways launched its 'Upper Class' value innovation – a new concept in business class travel that essentially combined the huge seats and leg room of traditional first class with the price of business class tickets – other airlines could apply this idea to their own business class service without limiting Virgin's ability to use it. This makes competitive imitation not only possible but less costly, as the cost and risk of developing the innovative idea is borne by the value innovator, not the follower.

Of course, were it possible to get a patent and formal legal protection for innovative ideas, the risk of free-riding would be considerably lower. Pharmaceutical companies, for example, have long enjoyed the benefit of formal patent protection to prevent the free-riding of other drug companies on their scientific discoveries for a specified time. But, how do you patent a radically superior concept for a coffee store such as Starbuck's, which has tremendous value but in itself consists of no new technological discoveries? It is the arrangement of the items that adds fundamentally new value, that is, the way they are combined, not the items themselves. While collectively this represents a new, creative, and explosive concept, little about the Starbuck's concept is scientifically new and, hence, patentable and excludable. Starbuck's, like The Body Shop, Home Depot, Schwab, Virgin Atlantic Airways, Amazon.com, Borders, and Barnes & Noble, is not about patentable technology innovation, but value innovation.

Shifting strategy focus

The underlying foundation of business is shifting in unprecedented ways. Consider the emergence of the Internet, the rise of multimedia, the speed of globalization, and the advent of the euro. The rate of change seems to increase as new knowledge, idea creation, and global diffusion accelerate. This new reality requires new strategic responses. Companies that continue to focus on the competition, on leveraging and extending their current capabilities, and on retaining and extending their existing customers are off the mark. As has been argued, the competition provides a sticky starting point for strategic thinking. A focus on matching and beating the competition leads to reactive, incremental, and often imitative strategic moves – not what is needed in a knowledge economy. The irony of competition is this: intense competition makes innovation indispensable, but an obsessive focus on the competition makes innovation difficult to attain.

At the same time, thinking beyond a company's boundaries is necessary. Since the field of strategy emerged, its focus has been on building and leveraging a company's strengths. The basic argument here is that firms possess unique resources, reputation, and skills – capabilities that should be nurtured and leveraged to guide their strategic decisions. Extended and refined over time, this basic argument persists in theory and practice. An inwardly driven focus on capabilities within a company, however, significantly limits a company's opportunity horizon and introduces resistance to change if the market is evolving away from a company's forte. As we enter an era of the modular society in which networks become more prevalent, companies can increasingly pursue strategic relations with other firms to capture emerging opportunities on the basis of their respective strengths.

The central quest of a value innovator's strategic mind-set is to create radically new and superior value. The conventional focus on retaining and better satisfying existing customers tends to promote hesitancy to challenge the status quo for fear of losing or dissatisfying existing customers. However, companies must focus on capturing the mass of buyers, even if that means losing some existing customers. Value innovators monitor existing customers but, more importantly, follow noncustomers closely because they provide deep insights into trends and changes.

After radically superior value is discovered, value innovators deploy capabilities that exist both inside and outside their companies to actualize an opportunity. Value innovators often have a network of partners that provide complementary assets, capabilities, products, and services.

SMH's innovative Swatch idea did not originate with the competition. The company did not have a core competency in mass-market watches, in plastic molding, or in contemporary design. At the time of the Swatch introduction, the young mass-market customers were not SMH customers. What did SMH have in its favor? Hayek had a relentless desire to offer buyers radically superior value, an idea (to create a watch exuding *joie de vivre*), and the insight to create, buy, or borrow the expertise needed to produce the watches. Likewise, SAP possessed no core competencies or distinctive resources. At the time of its founding more

than twenty-five years ago, SAP did not own computers to use in writing its software. Yet, SAP not only created its first value innovation, R/2 business application software for the mainframe environment, but repeatedly launched value innovations, including R/3, client-server business application software. As Hasso Plattner, SAP cofounder, put it: 'The only resource we had was our brains and the idea of how to build powerful software.' Later SAP leveraged the resources and capabilities of others, including Andersen Consulting, which served as SAP's marketing and implementation arm; Oracle, which supplied the necessary sophisticated database; and IBM, which supplied hardware. SAP has continuously renewed its customer base by moving aggressively from mainframe users, to client-server users, and to midsized and small companies to capitalize on emerging market opportunities. 'Noncustomers often offer the greatest insights into where the market is moving and what we should be doing fundamentally differently,' remarked Plattner. 'We never look at what the competition is doing.' As a result, SAP is the global leader in business application software.

Making value innovation happen

To make value innovation happen, top management must clearly communicate the company's commitment to value innovation as the key strategy component by articulating its underlying logic. The aim is to drive out of the organization conventional competition-based thinking that usually leads to only incremental market improvements. The CEO and his or her top management team play a critical role in initiating this change (Kanter, 1996). Through strategic retreats, corporate communications, and by continuously challenging proposed strategic plans on the basis of value innovation, staff members will gradually orient themselves toward the principles of value innovation. Five key questions, which contrast conventional competition-based logic with that of value innovation, can serve as a guide to reframing strategic thinking toward the new mind-set.

What type of organization best unlocks the ideas and creativity of its employees to achieve this end? In our studies, two structural characteristics are common to value innovation companies.

■ Small autonomous units or teams focusing on a common business or product goal rather than organization on the basis of function, region, or channel type. Although top managers must clearly specify that the strategic goal is to value innovate (as opposed to benchmarking the competition), teams must freely explore how to achieve these objectives. Some degree of freedom heightens a sense of ownership among team members, promotes creativity, and ensures that individual expertise is fully exploited.

- Team members of diverse backgrounds and perspectives. This seems most conducive to higher levels of creativity.

When putting value innovation strategies into action, structural conditions create only the *potential* for individuals to share their best ideas and knowledge. To *actualize* this potential, a company must cultivate a corporate culture conducive to willing collaboration.

How to promote voluntary cooperation among organizational members is critical to value innovation efforts. An organization must supply and create knowledge and ideas effectively, because these are the primary inputs for value innovation. Unlike traditional production factors, such as land, labor, and capital, knowledge and ideas are intangible assets locked in the human mind. Even in ideal organizational conditions, creating and sharing knowledge – intangible activities – cannot be supervised or forced; they happen only when individuals cooperate voluntarily.

The distinction between compulsory and voluntary cooperation is worth noting. Compulsory cooperation is in accordance with organizational rules, regulations, and acceptable standards, whereas voluntary cooperation goes beyond the call of duty: individuals exert effort, energy, and initiative to the best of their abilities on behalf of the organization. Companies can mandate compulsory cooperation by using organizational force; voluntary cooperation is not achievable without trust and commitment that can only be cultivated purposefully. Compulsory cooperation alone cannot effectively supply and generate the knowledge required to formulate value innovation plans.

Voluntary cooperation is also essential because effectively executing planned value innovation usually involves major changes in how a company functions. This often requires behavioral changes. The collaborative initiative and spontaneity that is characteristic of voluntary cooperation are key to adapting to change.

As we studied successes and failures in this area, one central theme repeatedly emerged whether we were working with senior executives or shop floor employees: individuals are most likely to share ideas and cooperate voluntarily when the company acknowledges their intellectual and emotional worth. Individuals are gratified when the company solicits and

thoughtfully considers their ideas and shares opinions with them. Recognizing individuals as human beings worthy of respect regardless of hierarchical level rather than 'labor', 'personnel', or 'human resources' engenders loyalty and willingness to collaborate for the welfare of the company.

Value innovation as strategy

In the coming decade, what is the key strategic agenda for corporate giants like Microsoft, Intel, Compaq, Enron, SAP, Proctor & Gamble, Johnson & Johnson, Motorola, Chrysler, SMH, 3M, Sony, Toyota, and Samsung? For example, Proctor & Gamble's strategic goal for the next decade is to double its $35 billion business through assertive efforts to achieve business breakthroughs. As we participated in, heard, and read about their management training, strategic planning discussions, and executive retreats, we unfailingly noted that all these companies aspire to attain breakthroughs in their markets.

We believe that value innovation is the essence of strategy in the knowledge economy. It must be supported by the proper tactics to prolong and maximize an innovation's profit-making potential, distancing it from emulators. After a value innovation is created, business line extensions and continuous improvements can maximize profits before another value innovation is launched. However, these business and operational improvements are not strategies; they are tactics (Porter, 1996). Value innovation as strategy creates a pattern of punctuated equilibrium, in which bursts of value innovation that reshape the industrial landscape are interspersed with periods of improvements, geographic and product line extensions, and consolidation.

In some industrial and regional sectors of the economy, however, many companies will still be successful on the basis of competition-driven strategy without spurts of value innovation. We predict that these dormant sectors of the economy will increasingly dwindle as value innovation and its globalization penetrates farther into the economy. Nevertheless, other successful strategies exist. Along with value innovators, cost leaders and differentiators can achieve profitable growth. In markets where value innovation occurs, however, the space for success of cost leaders and differentiators narrows as value innovators occupy the core of markets by attracting the mass of buyers. For example, since Wal-Mart has grown to dominate the discount retail market by capturing its core, successful cost leaders and differentiators in this market are those pursuing a rock-bottom pricing strategy (Dollar General, Family Dollar, Dollar Tree) or targeting high-end segments (specialty stores). As value innovation further penetrates into markets, strategies of cost leadership and differentiation are likely to succeed best at the low end (cost leaders) and the high end (differentiators). As happened in discount retailing, cost leaders and differentiators may become peripheral players relative to value innovators that emerge to capture the core of expanded markets. It is important to note here that value innovators do capture the core of the market not at the direct expense of other market players since they expand the market by creating new demand.

THE INDUSTRY CONTEXT IN INTERNATIONAL PERSPECTIVE

How many things are looked upon as quite impossible until they have been actually effected.
Pliny the Elder (23–79); Roman writer

In the field of strategy, views differ sharply on whether the industry context can be shaped or not, although these differences of opinion usually remain implicit – few practicing managers or strategy theorists make a point of expounding their assumptions about the nature of the environment. For this reason, it is difficult to identify whether there are national preferences when it comes to industry context perspective. Yet, it seems not unlikely that strategists in different countries have different inclinations on this issue. Although it is always difficult to generalize, it seems that strategists in some nations gravitate more towards an industry leadership perspective than in other nations.

As an input to the debate whether there are international differences in industry context perspective, we would like to put forward a number of factors that might be of influence on how the paradox of compliance and choice is viewed in different countries. It should be noted, however, that these propositions are intended to encourage discussion and constitute only tentative explanations for cross-cultural differences in perspective. More specific international research is needed to give this debate a firmer basis.

Locus of control

Culture researchers have long recognized international differences in how people perceive the power of individuals to shape their environment. In some cultures the view that an individual is at the mercy of external events is more predominant, while in other cultures there is a stronger belief in the freedom of individuals to act independent of the environment and even to create their own circumstances. Psychologists refer to this as the perceived 'locus of control' (e.g. Miller, Kets de Vries and Toulouse, 1982). People with an internal locus of control believe that they largely control their own fate. Their efforts will shape their circumstances – success is earned and failure is one's own fault. People with an external locus of control, on the other hand, believe that their fate is largely the result of circumstances beyond their control. Any effort to improve one's position, if at all possible, should be directed toward complying with external demands – fortune favors those who go with the flow. In the most extreme case, however, people with an external locus of control are fatalistic, that is, they assume no efforts will change that which is inevitable.

Obviously, in countries where the culture is more inclined towards an internal locus of control, it is reasonable to expect that the industry leadership perspective will be more widespread. It is in such nations that one might expect remarks, such as that by the 19th century English essayist Sydney Smith: 'When I hear any man talk of an unalterable law, the only effect it produces on me is to convince me that he is an unalterable fool.' In cultures with a strong emphasis on external locus of control, the industry dynamics perspective is likely to be more predominant.

Time orientation

As was identified in Chapter 4, cultures can also differ with respect to their time orientation. Some cultures are directed towards the past, while others are more focused on the present or on the future. In countries with a future-orientation, the belief is widespread that change is progress. People generally welcome change as an opportunity for advancement. Therefore, in future-oriented cultures, people are even willing to initiate painful change processes, in the expectation that this will lead to future benefits. In these countries a stronger inclination towards the industry leadership perspective is most likely.

In past-oriented cultures, the belief is widespread that change is decay. People generally actively resist change and protect the status quo. In these cultures, external changes will only be adapted to if strictly necessary. In present-oriented cultures, the belief is widespread that change is relatively unimportant. People live for the day and adapt to changes as they come. In both types of culture, the industry dynamics perspective is more likely to be more predominant.

Role of government

Internationally, opinions also differ on the role that governments can play in encouraging the shaping of industries. In some countries the predominant view is that governments should facilitate industry change by creating good business circumstances and then staying out of the way of company initiatives. Governments are needed to set basic rules of business conduct, but firms should not be impeded by other governmental intervention in the functioning of industries and markets. Individual companies are seen as the primary drivers of industry development and if companies are given enough leeway, excellent ones can significantly shape their industry context. Such economic liberalism is particularly strong in the English-speaking nations, and it is here that governments attempt to actually facilitate firms' industry shaping efforts. Unsurprisingly, the industry leadership perspective is rather pronounced in these countries.

In other nations the predominant view is that Adam Smith's free market ideal often proves to be dysfunctional. A fully liberal market, it is believed, can lead to short-termism, negative social consequences, mutually destructive competition, and an inability to implement industry-wide changes. Governments must therefore assume a more proactive role. They must protect weaker parties, such as workers and the environment, against the negative side effects of the market system, and actively create a shared infrastructure for all companies. Furthermore, the government can develop an industrial policy to encourage the development of new industries, force companies to work together where this is more effective, and push through industry-wide changes, if otherwise a stalemate would occur. Such a 'managed competition' view has been prevalent in Japan and France, and to a lesser extent in Germany (e.g. Hampden-Turner and Trompenaars, 1993; Lessem and Neubauer, 1994). In these countries the industry leadership perspective is not as strongly held as in the English-speaking nations – industries can be shaped, but few companies have the power to do so without a good industrial policy and government backing.

Network of relationships

This factor is linked to the discussion in the previous chapter. In countries where the discrete organization perspective is predominant, companies often strive to retain their independence and power position vis-à-vis other companies. As these firms are not embedded in complex networks, but operate free from these constraining relationships, they are more at liberty to challenge the existing rules of the game. In other words, where firms are not entangled in a web of long-term relationships, they are better positioned for rule breaking behavior – every firm can make a difference. In these countries an industry leadership perspective is more prevalent.

However, in nations where firms are more inclined to operate in networks, each individual firm surrenders a part of its freedom in exchange for long-term relationships. The ability of the individual firm to shape its industry thus declines, as all changes must be discussed and negotiated with its partners. Hence, in these countries, the industry leadership perspective is generally less strongly held than in the countries favoring discrete organizations. It should be noted that a group of firms, once in agreement, is often more powerful than each individual firm and therefore more capable of shaping the industry. However, it is acknowledged that getting the network partners to agree is a formidable task and a significant limit on the firm's ability to shape its environment.

FURTHER READING

For a good academic overview of the debate on 'who shapes whom' readers are advised to consult the special edition of *Academy of Management Review* (July 1990) that focused on this issue. In particular, the article 'Market Discipline and the Discipline of Management' by Richard Bettis and Lex Donaldson is very insightful. For a broader discussion on the issue of determinism and voluntarism, good readings are 'Central Perspective and Debates in Organization Theory', by W. Graham Astley and Andrew van der Ven, and 'Organizational Adaptation: Strategic Choice and Environmental Determinism', by Lawrence Hrebiniak and William Joyce. Also useful is the recent work on managerial discretion, which attempts to measure how much leeway top managers have in shaping the future of their firm in different industries. Of these, the article 'Managerial Discretion: A Bridge Between Polar Views of Organizational Outcomes', by Donald Hambrick and Sydney Finkelstein, is interesting for its theoretical base, while 'Assessing the Amount of Managerial Discretion in Different Industries: A Multi-Method Approach', by Donald Hambrick and Eric Abrahamson is interesting for its analysis of various industry environments. All of these studies, it should be mentioned, do not have an audience of practitioners in mind.

The same is true for all further literature taking an industry dynamics perspective. A good book outlining the population ecology view of industry and firm development is the classic *Organizational Ecology* by Michael Hannan and John Freeman. For an excellent overview of the work in the area of industry and organizational evolution see Howard Aldrich's recent book, *Organizations Evolving*. Other constraints on the freedom of firms to shape their own fate are brought forward by institutional theory and resource dependence theory, both of which have not been represented in this debate. Christine Oliver gives a good overview of these two approaches in her article 'Strategic Responses to Institutional Processes'. The classic in the field of institutional theory is Paul DiMaggio and Walter Powell's article 'The Iron Cage Revisited: Institutional Isomorphism and Collective Rationality in Organizational Fields', while Scott's book *Institutions and Organizations* is a good, more recent work. The classic in the field of resource dependence is Jeffrey Pfeffer and Gerald Salancik's book *The External Control of Organizations*.

Readers interested in the industry leadership perspective might want to start by looking at J.-C. Spender's book *Industry Recipe: An Enquiry into the Nature and Sources of Managerial Judgement*. The book from which Charles Baden-Fuller and John Stopford's article was taken, *Rejuvenating the Mature Business*, is also excellent follow-up reading. The same is true of Gary Hamel and C.K. Prahalad's book *Competing for the Future*. In this context, Richard D'Aveni's book *Hypercompetition* is also worth reviewing. For a more complete view of Geoffrey Moore's line of argumentation, his book *Living on the Fault Line* is an interesting and entertaining read.

For those who want to understand what happened during the internet bubble and whether there was anything to the New Economy, we advise starting with Michael Porter's article 'Strategy and the Internet'. Also valuable is Michael Cusumano and Annabelle Gawer's article 'The Elements of Platform Leadership' which describes the functioning of industry standards, as does Carl Shapiro and Hal Varian's excellent book, *Information Rules*.

REFERENCES

Aldrich, H.E. (1979) *Organizations and Environments*, Prentice Hall, Englewood Cliffs, NJ.

Aldrich, H.E. (1999) *Organizations Evolving*, Sage, London.

Aldrich, H.E., and Fiol, C.M. (1994) 'Fools Rush In? The Institutional Context of Industry Creation', *Academy of Management Review*, Vol. 19, No. 4, pp. 645–670.

Arrow, K.J. (1962) 'Economic Welfare and the Allocation of Resources for Inventions', in: R.R. Nelson (ed.), *The Rate and Direction of Inventive Activity*, Princeton University Press, Princeton, NJ.

Arthur, W.B. (1994) *Increasing Returns and Path Dependence in the Economy*, University of Michigan Press, Ann Arbor, MI.

Arthur, W.B. (1996) 'Increasing Returns and the New World of Business', *Harvard Business Review*, Vol. 74, No. 4, July–August, pp. 100–109.

Astley, W.G., and van der Ven, A.H. (1983) 'Central Perspectives and Debates in Organization Theory', *Administrative Science Quarterly*, Vol. 28, No. 2, June, pp. 245–273.

Baden-Fuller, C.W.F., and Stopford, J.M. (1992) *Rejuvenating the Mature Business*, Routledge, London.

Bain, J.S. (1959) *Industrial Organizations*, Wiley, New York.

Baum, A.C., and Singh, J.V. (eds.) (1994) *Evolutionary Dynamics of Organizations*, Oxford University Press, New York.

Beinhocker, E.D. (1997) 'Strategy at the Edge of Chaos', *The McKinsey Quarterly*, No. 1, pp. 24–39.

Bettis, R.A., and Donaldson, L. (1990) 'Market Discipline and the Discipline of Management', *Academy of Management Review*, Vol. 15, No. 3, July, pp. 367–368.

Bower, J.L., and Christensen, C.M. (1995) 'Disruptive Technologies: Cathing the Wave', *Harvard Business Review*, Vol. 73, No. 1, January–February, pp. 43–53.

Burgelman, R.A., and Grove, A.S. (1996) 'Strategic Dissonance', *California Management Review*, Vol. 38, No. 2, pp. 106–131.

Buzzell, R.D., and Gale, B.T. (1987) *The PIMS Principles: Linking Strategy to Performance*, Free Press, New York.

Carpenter, M.A., and Golden, B.R. (1997) 'Perceived Managerial Discretion: A Study of Cause and Effect', *Strategic Management Journal*, Vol. 18, No. 3, March, pp. 187–206.

Child, J. (1972) 'Organizational Structure, Environment, and Performance: The Role of Strategic Choice', *Sociology*, January, pp. 2–22.

Christensen, C.M. (1997) *The Innovator's Dilemma*, HarperBusiness, New York.

Cusumano, M.A., and Gawer, A. (2002) 'The Elements of Platform Leadership', *Sloan Management Review*, Vol. 43, No. 3, Spring, pp. 51–58.

D'Aveni, R.A. (1994) *Hypercompetition*: *Managing the Dynamics of Strategic Maneuvering*, Free Press, New York.

D'Aveni, R.A. (1999) 'Strategic Supremacy through Disruption and Dominance', *Sloan Management Review*, Vol. 40, No. 3, pp. 127–135.

DiMaggio, P.J., and Powell, W.W. (1983) 'The Iron Cage Revisited: Institutional Isomorphism and Collective Rationality in Organizational Fields', *American Sociological Review*, Vol. 48, No. 2, April, pp. 147–160.

Evans, P.B., and Wurster, T.S. (1997) 'Strategy and the New Economics of Information', *Harvard Business Review*, Vol. 76, No. 5, September–October, pp. 71–82.

Finkelstein, S., and Hambrick, D.C. (1996) *Strategic Leadership: Top Executives and Their Effects on Organizations*, West, St. Paul.

Freeman, J., and Boeker, W. (1984) 'The Ecological Analysis of Business Strategy', *California Management Review*, Spring, pp. 73–86.

Ghemawat, P. (1991) *Commitment: The Dynamic of Strategy*, Free Press, New York.

Gilbert, X., and Strebel, P. (1989) 'Taking Advantage of Industry Shifts', *European Management Journal*, December, pp. 398–402.

Hall, W.K. (1980) 'Survival Strategies in a Hostile Environment', *Harvard Business Review*, Vol. 58, No. 5, September–October, pp. 75–85.

Hambrick, D.C., and Abrahamson, E. (1995) 'Assessing the Amount of Managerial Discretion in Different Industries: A Multi-Method Approach', *Academy of Management Journal*, Vol. 38, No. 5, October, pp. 1427–1441.

Hambrick, D.C., and Finkelstein, S. (1987) 'Managerial Discretion: A Bridge Between Polar Views of Organizational Outcomes', in: B.M. Staw and L.L. Cummings (eds.), *Research in Organizational Behavior*, Vol. 9, JAI, Greenwich, CT, pp. 369–406.

Hamel, G. (1996) 'Strategy as Revolution', *Harvard Business Review*, Vol. 74, No. 4, July–August, pp. 69–82.

Hamel, G., and Prahalad, C.K. (1994) *Competing for the Future*, Harvard Business School Press, Boston.

Hampden-Turner, C., and Trompenaars, A. (1993) *The Seven Cultures of Capitalism: Value Systems for Creating Wealth in the United States, Japan, Germany, France, Britain, Sweden and the Netherlands*, Doubleday, New York.

Hannan, M.T., and Freeman, J. (1977) 'The Population Ecology of Organizations', *American Journal of Sociology*, Vol. 82, No. 5, March, pp. 929–964.

Hannan, M.T., and Freeman, J. (1989) *Organizational Ecology*, Harvard University Press, Cambridge, MA.

Hill, C.W.L. (1988) 'Differentiation Versus Low Cost or Differentiation and Low Cost', *Academy of Management Review*, Vol. 13, July, pp. 401–412.

Hrebiniak, L.G., and Joyce, W.F. (1985) 'Organizational Adaptation: Strategic Choice and Environmental Determinism', *Administrative Science Quarterly*, Vol. 30, No. 3, September, pp. 336–349.

Kanter, R.M. (1996) 'When a Thousand Flowers Bloom: Structural, Collective, and Social Conditions, for Innovation in Organizations', in: P.S. Myers (ed.), *Knowledge Management and Organization Design*, Butterworth-Heinemann, Boston, pp. 169–211.

Kim, W.C. and Mauborgne, R. (1999) 'Strategy, Value Innovation, and the Knowledge Economy', *Sloan Management Review*, Vol. 40, No. 3, Spring, pp. 41–54.

Lawrence, P.R., and Lorsch, J.W. (1967) *Organization and Environment*, Harvard University Press, Cambridge, MA.

Lessem, R., and Neubauer, F.F. (1994) *European Management Systems*, McGraw-Hill, London.

Levenhagen, M., Porac, J.F., and Thomas, H. (1993) 'Emergent Industry Leadership and the Selling of Technological Visions: A Social Constructionist View', in: J. Hendry, G. Johnson, and J. Newton (eds.), *Strategic Thinking: Leadership and the Management of Change*, Wiley, Chichester.

Markides, C. (1997) 'Strategic Innovation', *Sloan Management Review*, Vol. 38, No. 3, Spring, pp. 9–23.

Markides, C. (1998) 'Strategic Innovation in Established Companies', *Sloan Management Review*, Vol. 39, No. 3, Spring, pp. 31–42.

Miles, R.E., and Snow, C.C. (1978) *Organizational Strategy: Structure and Process*, McGraw-Hill, New York.

Miller, D. (1990) *The Icarus Paradox: How Excellent Companies Bring About Their Own Downfall*, Harper Business, New York.

Miller, D., Kets de Vries, M., and Toulouse, J.M. (1982) 'Top Executive Locus of Control and its Relationship to Strategy-making, Structure and Environment', *Academy of Management Journal*, Vol. 25, pp. 237–253.

Moore, G.A. (2000) *Living on the Fault Line: Managing for Shareholder Value in the Age of the Internet*, HarperBusiness, New York.

Moore, J.F. (1993) 'Predators and Prey: A New Ecology of Competition', *Harvard Business Review*, May–June, pp. 75–86.

Moore, J.F. (1996) *The Death of Competition: Leadership & Strategy in the Age of Business Ecosystems*, HarperBusiness, New York.

Nelson, R.R., and Winter, S.G. (1982) *An Evolutionary Theory of Economic Change*, Harvard University Press, Reading, MA.

Oliver, C. (1991) 'Strategic Responses to Institutional Processes', *Academy of Management Review*, Vol. 16, No. 1, January, pp. 145–179.

Oliver, C. (1997) 'Sustainable Competitive Advantage: Combining Institutional and Resource-based Views', *Strategic Management Journal*, Vol. 18, No. 9, October, pp. 697–713.

Parolini, C. (1999) *The Value Net*, Wiley, Chichester.

Pfeffer, J., and Salancik, G. (1978) *The External Control of Organizations: A Resource Dependency Perspective*, Harper & Row, New York.

Porter, M.E. (1980) *Competitive Strategy: Techniques for Analyzing Industries and Competitors*, Free Press, New York.

Porter, M.E. (1985) *Competitive Advantage: Creating and Sustaining Superior Performance*, Free Press, New York.

Porter, M.E. (1996) 'What is Strategy?', *Harvard Business Review*, Vol. 74, No. 6, November–December, pp. 61–78.

Porter, M.E. (2001) 'Strategy and the Internet', *Harvard Business Review*, Vol. 80, No. 3, March, pp. 62–78.

Prahalad, C.K., and Doz, Y.L. (1987) *The Multinational Mission: Balancing Local Demands and Global Vision*, Free Press, New York.

Rumelt, R. (1991) 'How Much Does Industry Matter?', *Strategic Management Journal*, Vol. 12, No. 3, March, pp. 167–186.

Schmalensee, R. (1985) 'Do Markets Differ Much?', *American Economic Review*, June, pp. 341–351.

Schumpeter, J.A. (1934) *The Theory of Economic Development*, Harvard University Press, Cambridge, MA.

Scott, W.R. (1995) *Institutions and Organizations*, Sage, Thousand Oaks, CA.

Sexton, D.L. (2001) 'Wayne Huizenga: Entrepreneur and Wealth Creator', *Academy of Management Executive*, Vol. 15, No. 1, pp. 40–48.

Shapiro, C.E., and Varian, H.R. (1998) *Information Rules*, HBS Press, Boston, MA.

Shapiro, C.E., and Varian, H.R. (1999) 'The Art of Standard Wars', *California Management Review*, Vol. 41, No. 2, Winter, pp. 8–32.

Slywotsky, A.J. (1996) *Value Migration*, Harvard Business School Press, Boston.

Spender, J.C. (1989) *Industry Recipe: An Enquiry into the Nature and Sources of Managerial Judgement*, Basil Blackwell, New York.

Tirole, J. (1988) *The Theory of Industrial Organization*, MIT Press, Cambridge, MA.

Whitley, R.D. (1999) *Divergent Capitalisms: The Social Structuring and Change of Business Systems*, Oxford University Press, Oxford.

Wilson, D.C. (1992) *A Strategy of Change*, London, Routledge.

Yoffie, D.B., and Kwak, M. (2001) 'Mastering Strategic Movement at Palm', *Sloan Management Review*, Vol. 43, Iss. 1, pp. 55–63.

THE ORGANIZATIONAL CONTEXT

We shape our environments, then our environments shape us.

Winston Churchill (1874–1965); British statesman and writer

INTRODUCTION

In organizations, just as in families, each new generation does not start from scratch but inherits properties belonging to their predecessors. In families, a part of this inheritance is in the form of genetic properties, but other attributes are also passed down such as family traditions, myths, habits, connections, feuds, titles and possessions. People might think of themselves as unique individuals, but to some degree they are an extension of the family line, and their behavior is influenced by this inheritance. In firms the same phenomenon is observable. New top managers may arrive on the scene, but they inherit a great deal from the previous generation. They inherit traditions and myths in the form of an organizational culture. Habits are passed along in the form of established organizational processes, while internal and external relationships and rivalries shape the political constellation in which new managers must function. They are also handed the family jewels – brands, competences and other key resources.

In Chapter 4 it was pointed out that such inheritance is often the source of organizational rigidity and inertia (e.g. Hannan and Freeman, 1977; Rumelt, 1995). Inheritance limits 'organizational plasticity' – the capacity of the organization to change shape. As such, organizational inheritance can partially predetermine a firm's future path of development – which is referred to as path dependency, or sometimes simply summed up as 'history matters' (e.g. Aldrich, 1999; Nelson and Winter, 1982). Therefore, it was concluded that for strategic renewal to take place, some inherited characteristics could be preserved, but others needed to be changed, by either evolutionary or revolutionary means.

What was not discussed in Chapter 4 was *who* should trigger the required strategic changes. Who should initiate adaptations to the firm's business system and who should take steps to reshape the organizational system? Typically, managers will have some role to play in all developments in the organizational context, but the question is what role. It is unlikely that any manager will have complete influence over all organizational developments, or would even want to exert absolute control. Inheritance and other organizational factors limit 'organizational malleability' – the capacity of the organization to be shaped by someone. As such, managers need to determine what power they do have and where this power should be applied to achieve the best results. At the same time, managers will generally also look for opportunities to tap into the capabilities of other people in the firm to contribute to ongoing organizational adaptation.

So, the question can be summarized as 'what is the role of managers in achieving a new alignment with the environment and what input can be garnered from other organizational members?'. This question is also referred to as the issue of organizational development and will be the central topic of further discussion in this chapter.

THE ISSUE OF ORGANIZATIONAL DEVELOPMENT

When it comes to realizing organizational development, managers generally acknowledge that they have some type of leadership role to play. Leadership refers to the act of influencing the views and behaviors of organizational members with the intention of accomplishing a particular organizational aim (e.g. Selznick, 1957; Bass, 1990). Stated differently, leadership is the act of getting organizational members to follow. From this definition it can be concluded that not all managers are necessarily leaders, and not all leaders are necessarily managers. Managers are individuals with a formal position in the organizational hierarchy, with associated authority and responsibilities. Leaders are individuals who have the ability to sway other people in the organization to get something done.

To be able to lead organizational developments, managers need power. Power is the capability to influence. They also need to know how to get power, and how and where to exert it. In the following sections, these three topics will be examined in more detail. First, the sources of leadership influence will be described, followed by the levers of leadership influence. Finally, the arenas of leadership influence will be explored.

Sources of leadership influence

To lead means to use power to influence others. Leaders can derive their potential influence from two general sources – their position and their person (Etzioni, 1961). 'Position power' comes from a leader's formal function in the organization. 'Personal power' is rooted in the specific character, knowledge, skills and relationships of the leader. Managers always have some level of position power, but they do not necessarily have the personal power needed to get organizational members to follow them. These two main types of power can be further subdivided into the following categories (French and Raven, 1959):

- Legitimate power. Legitimate power exists when a person has the formal authority to determine certain organizational behaviors and other employees agree to comply with this situation. Examples of legitimate power are the authority to assign work, spend money and demand information.

- Coercive power. People have coercive power when they have the capability to punish or withhold rewards to achieve compliance. Examples of coercive power include giving a poor performance review, withholding a bonus and dismissing employees.

- Reward power. Reward power is derived from the ability to offer something of value to a person in return for compliance. Examples of reward power include giving praise, awarding wage raises and promoting employees.

- Expert power. Expert power exists when organizational members are willing to comply because of a person's superior knowledge or skills in an important area. Such expert power can be based on specific knowledge of functional areas (e.g. marketing, finance), technologies (e.g. pharmaceuticals, information technology), geographic areas (e.g. South-East Asia, Florida) and/or businesses (e.g. mining, automotive).

- Referent power. When organizational members let themselves be influenced by a person's charismatic appeal, this is called referent power. This personal attraction can be based on many attributes, such as likeableness, forcefulness, persuasiveness, visionary qualities and image of success.

The first three types of power are largely determined by the organizational position of leaders and their willingness to exert them – coercive and reward capabilities without the credibility of use are not a viable source of power. The last two sources of power, expert and referent power, are largely personal in nature, and also more subjective. Whether someone is seen as an expert and therefore accorded a certain level of respect and influence depends strongly on the perceptions of the people being lead. Expert power can be made more tangible by wearing a white lab coat, putting three pens in your breast pocket or writing a book, but still perceived expertise will be in the eyes of the beholder. The same is true for referent power, as people do not find the same characteristics equally charismatic. What is forceful to one follower might seem pushy to someone else; what is visionary to one person might sound like the murmurings of a madman to others (e.g. Klein and House, 1998; Waldman and Yammarino, 1999).

In practice, leaders will employ a mix of all five types of power to achieve the influence they desire. However, leadership styles can differ greatly depending on the relative weight placed on the various sources of power within the mix.

Levers of leadership influence

The sources of power available to the leader need to be used to have influence. There are three generic ways for leaders to seek influence, each focused on a different point in the activities of the people being influenced. These levers of leadership influence are:

- Throughput control. Leaders can focus their attention directly at the actions being taken by others in the organization. Throughput control implies getting involved hands-on in the activities of others, either by suggesting ways of working, engaging in a discussion on how things should be done, leading by example or simply by telling others what to do. This form of direct influence does require sufficiently detailed knowledge about the activities of others to be able to point out what should be done.

- Output control. Instead of directly supervising how things should be done, leaders can set objectives that should be met. Output control implies reaching agreement on certain performance targets and then monitoring how well they are being lived up to. The targets can be quantitative or qualitative, financial or strategic, simple or complex, realistic or stretch-oriented. And they can be arrived at by mutual consent or imposed by the leader. The very act of setting objectives can have an important influence on people in the organization, but the ability to check ongoing performance and to link results with punishment and rewards can further improve a person's impact.

- Input control. Leaders can also choose to influence the general conditions under which activities are carried out. Input control implies shaping the circumstances preceding and surrounding the actual work. Before activities start a leader can influence who is assigned to a task, which teams are formed, who is hired, where they will work and in what type of environment. During the execution of activities the leader can supply physical and financial resources, mobilize relationships and provide support. Not unimportantly, the leader can also be a source of enthusiasm, inspiration, ambition, vision and mission.

Of these three, throughput control is the most direct in its impact and input control the least. However, throughput control offers the lowest leverage and input control the highest, allowing a leader to influence many people over a longer period of time, while leaving more room for organizational members to take on their own responsibilities as well. In practice, leaders can combine elements of all three of the above, although leadership styles differ greatly with regard to the specific mix.

Arenas of leadership influence

As leaders attempt to guide organizational development, there are three main organizational arenas where they need to direct their influence to achieve strategic changes. These three overlapping arenas are the parts in the organization most resistant to change – they are the sub-systems of the firm where organizational inheritance creates its own momentum, resisting a shift into another direction (e.g. Miller and Friesen, 1980; Tushman, Newman and Romanelli, 1986):

- The political arena. While most top managers have considerable position power with which they can try to influence the strategic decision-making process within their organization, very few top managers can impose their strategic agenda on the organization without building widespread political support. Even the most autocratic CEO will need to gain the commitment and compliance of key figures within the organization to be able to successfully push through significant changes. In practice, however, there are not many organizations where the 'officers and the troops' unquestioningly follow the general into battle. Usually, power is more dispersed throughout organizations, with different people and units having different ideas and interests, as well as the assertiveness to pursue their own agenda. Ironically, the more leaders that are developed throughout the organization, the more complex it becomes for any one leader to get the entire organization to follow – broad leadership can easily become fragmented leadership, with a host of strong people all pointing in different directions. For top management to gain control of the organization they must therefore build coalitions of supporters, not only to get favorable strategic decisions made, but also to ensure acceptance and compliance during the period of implementation. Otherwise strategic plans will be half-heartedly executed, opposed or silently sabotaged. However, gaining the necessary political support in the organization can be very difficult if the strategic views and interests of powerful individuals and departments differ significantly. Cultural and personality clashes can add to the complexity. Yet, top managers cannot recoil from the political arena, for it is here that new strategic directions are set (e.g. Allison, 1969, Reading 3.3 in this book; Pfeffer, 1992).

- The cultural arena. Intertwined with the process of gaining political influence in the organization, there is the process of gaining cultural influence. After all, to be able to change the organization, a leader must be able to change people's beliefs and associated behavioral patterns. Yet, affecting cultural change is far from simple. A leader must be capable of questioning the shared values, ideas and habits prevalent in the organization, even though the leader has usually been immersed in the very same culture for years. Leaders must also offer an alternative worldview and set of behaviors to supercede the old. All of this requires exceptional skills as visionary – to develop a new image of a desired future state for the firm – and as missionary – to develop a new set of beliefs and values to guide the firm. Furthermore, the leader needs to be an excellent teacher to engage the organizational members in a learning process to adapt their beliefs, values and norms to the new circumstances. In practice, this means that leaders often have to 'sell' their view of the new culture, using a mix of rational persuasion, inspirational appeal, symbolic actions, motivational incentives and subtle pressure (e.g. Senge, 1990b, Reading 9.3; Ireland and Hitt, 1999).

- The psychological arena. While leaders need to influence the political process and the cultural identity of the organization, attention also needs to be paid to the psychological needs of individuals. To affect organizational change, leaders must win both the hearts and minds of the members of the organization. People must be willing to, literally, 'follow the leader' – preferably not passively, but actively, with commitment, courage and even passion (e.g. Bennis and Nanus, 1985; Kelley, 1988). To achieve such 'followership', leaders must gain the respect and trust of their colleagues. Another important factor in winning people over is the ability to meet their emotional need for certainty, clarity and continuity, to offset the uncertainties, ambiguities and discontinuities surrounding them (e.g. Argyris, 1990; Pfeffer and Sutton, 1999b, Reading 9.4).

Even where political, cultural and psychological processes make the organization difficult to lead, managers might still be able to gain a certain level of control over their organizations. Yet, there will always remain aspects of the organizational system that managers cannot control, and should not even want to control, and this will be discussed in the following section.

THE PARADOX OF CONTROL AND CHAOS

Of all men's miseries the bitterest is this, to know so much and to have control over nothing.
Herodotus (5th century BC); Greek historian

In general, managers like to be in control. Managers like to be able to shape their own future, and by extension, to shape the future of their firm. Managers do not shy away from power – they build their power base to be able to influence events and steer the development of their organization. In short, to be a manager is to have the desire to be in charge.

Yet, at the same time, most managers understand that their firms do not resemble machines, where one person can sit at the control panel and steer the entire system. Organizations are complex social systems, populated by numerous self-thinking human beings, each with their own feelings, ideas and interests. These people need to decide and act for themselves on a daily basis, without the direct intervention of the manager. They must be empowered to weigh situations, take initiatives, solve problems and grab opportunities. They must be given a certain measure of autonomy to experiment, do things differently and even constructively disagree with the manager. In other words, managers must also be willing to 'let go' of some control for the organization to function at its best.

Moreover, managers must accept that in a complex system, like an organization, trying to control everything would be a futile endeavor. With so many people and so many interactions going on in a firm, any attempt to run the entire system top-down would be an impossible task. Therefore, letting go of some control is a pure necessity for normal organizational functioning.

This duality of wanting to control the development of the organization, while understanding that letting go of control is often beneficial, is the key strategic tension when dealing with the organizational context. On the one hand, managers must be willing to act as benevolent 'philosopher kings', autocratically imposing on the company what they see as best. On the other hand, managers must be willing to act as constitutional monarchs, democratically empowering organizational citizens to take their own responsibilities and behave more as entrepreneurs. The strategic paradox arises from the fact that the need for top-down *imposition* and bottom-up *initiative* are conflicting demands that are difficult for managers to meet at the same time.

On one side of this strategy paradox is 'control', which can be defined as the power to direct and impose order. On the other side of the paradox is the need for 'chaos', which can be defined as disorder or the lack of fixed organization. The paradox of control and chaos is a recurrent theme in the literature on strategy, organization, leadership and governance. In most writings the need for control is presented as a pressure for a directive leadership style and/or an autocratic governance system (e.g. Tannenbaum and Schmidt, 1958; Vroom and Jago, 1988). The need for chaos is presented as a pressure for a participative leadership style and/or a democratic governance system (e.g. Ackoff, 1980; Stacey, 1992). In the following sub-sections both control and chaos will be further examined.

The demand for top management control

As Herodotus remarked, it would be bitter indeed to have control over nothing. Not only would it be a misery for the frustrated managers, who would be little more than mere administrators or caretakers. It would also be a misery for their organizations, which would need to constantly adjust course without a helmsman to guide the ship. Managers cannot afford to let their organizations drift on the existing momentum. It is a manager's task and responsibility to ensure that the organization changes in accordance to the environment, so that the organizational purpose can still be achieved.

Top management cannot realize this objective without some level of control. They need to be able to direct developments in the organization. They need to have the power to make the necessary changes in the organizational structure, processes and culture, to realign the organization with the demands of the environment. This power, whether positional or personal, needs to be applied towards gaining sufficient support in the political arena, challenging existing beliefs and behaviors in the cultural arena, and winning the hearts and minds of the organizational members in the psychological arena.

The control that top management needs is different from the day-to-day control built in to the organizational structure and processes – they need *strategic control* as opposed to *operational control*. While operational control gives managers influence over activities within the current organizational system, strategic control gives managers influence over changes to the organizational system itself (e.g. Goold and Quinn, 1990; Simons, 1994). It is this power that managers require to be able to steer the development of their organization.

The demand for organizational chaos

To managers the term 'chaos' sounds quite menacing – it carries connotations of rampant anarchy, total pandemonium and a hopeless mess. Yet, chaos only means disorder, coming from the Greek term for the unformed original state of the universe. In the organizational context chaos refers to situations of disorder, where phenomena have not yet been organized, or where parts of an organizational system have become 'unfreezed'. In other words, something is chaotic if it is unformed or has become 'disorganized'.

While this still does not sound particularly appealing to most managers, it should, because a period of disorganization is often a prerequisite for strategic renewal. Unfreezing existing structures, processes, routines and beliefs, and opening people up to different possibilities might be inefficient in the short run, as well as making people feel uncomfortable, but it is usually necessary to provoke creativity and to invent new ways of seeing and doing things. By allowing experimentation, skunk works, pilot projects and out-of-the-ordinary initiatives, managers accept a certain amount of disorder in the organization, which they hope will pay off in terms of organizational innovations.

But the most appealing effect of chaos is that it encourages 'self-organization'. To illustrate this phenomenon, one should first think back to the old Soviet 'command economy', which was based on the principle of control. It was believed that a rational, centrally planned economic system, with strong top-down leadership, would be the most efficient and effective way to organize industrial development. In the West, on the other hand, the 'market economy' was chaotic – no one was in control and could impose order. Everyone could go ahead and start a company. They could set their own production levels and even set their own prices! As entrepreneurs made use of the freedom offered to them, the economy 'self-organized' bottom-up. Instead of the 'visible hand' of the central planner controlling and regulating the economy, it was the 'invisible hand' of the market that created relative order out of chaos.

As the market economy example illustrates, chaos does not necessarily lead to pandemonium, but can result in a self-regulating interplay of forces. A lack of top-down control frees the way for a rich diversity of bottom-up ventures. Managers who also want to release the energy, creativity and entrepreneurial potential pent up in their organizations must therefore be willing to let go and allow some chaos to exist. In this context, the role of top management is comparable to that of governments in market economies – creating suitable conditions, encouraging activities and enforcing basic rules.

EXHIBIT 9.1 SHORT CASE

LE MÉRIDIEN: CHARGE OF THE FIVE STAR GENERAL?

On September 8 2001 a press release was sent to the international media: 'The independent luxury hotel group Le Méridien, announces a widespread £850 million (US$1204 million) global investment program designed to dramatically upgrade its facilities and catapult the brand to the top of the hotel industry rankings in three years.' Le Méridien, with such hotels as The Ritz in Madrid and Barcelona, The Eden in Rome and Le Parker Méridien in New York, ambitiously, yet confidently, declared that they would push through major changes to become the leader in the five star segment of the hotel business. Just three days later came 9/11. For hotels around the world the shock was enormous. Occupancy rates dropped, followed by profitability.

Yet Jürgen Bartels, CEO of Le Méridien, was not pessimistic. He believed that gains could be made in any market: 'My bottom line is that there are winners and losers in all conditions . . . it is not that everyone loses equally in a holding pattern.' Jürgen Bartels was known as JB to the industry, and his voice counted. A veteran of the hospitality business, with more than 40 years of experience, JB was known to be as eccentric as he was successful. He founded Renaissance Hotels, was CEO of Carlson Hospitality, and moved on to become CEO and chairman of the Westin Hotels and Resorts. Under his leadership, the group staged its impressive growth in the 1990s and merged with Starwood Hotels and ITT Sheraton Hotels and Resorts.

Eventually JB was lured away by Guy Hands of the Principal Finance Group (PFG), a subsidiary of the Japanese bank Nomura, to help with the acquisition of Le Méridien. After a bidding war with the Marriott Hotel Group, Le Méridien was purchased by PFG in July 2001 for £1.9 billion, which was quite expensive for a company with annual sales of just over £1 billion. Yet JB was bullish, even putting in £10 million of his own money. His goal was not merely to shake up Le Méridien, but to establish a new benchmark for modern luxury hotels. The global investment program he had planned would be the 'largest R&D effort . . . ever undertaken in the industry'.

The challenge facing JB was quite formidable, even without the events of 9/11. With 140 Le Méridien hotels in 55 countries, JB had gained formal control over a very diverse family of hotels, often with long histories and idiosyncratic practices. In each hotel different conditions, customer demands and business habits had grown into differing local market approaches. In Japan, for example, the wedding market is a major income earner for a hotel, and therefore an in-house chapel and wedding package are essential. In Barcelona, on the other hand, weekend travelers are an important market segment, while in Dubai more emphasis is needed for the stopover traveler. Yet, the differences between the hotels ran much deeper than distinctive client profiles, seasonal cycles of supply and demand, local labor force issues, government regulations, municipal sanitary conditions and local food supplies – many hotels had unique personalities, strongly rooted in their local environment.

The diversity of Le Méridien's hotels was matched by its diversity of ownership. The company had changed hands four times in only seven years, from Air France to the British Forte Group, then to the Granada Group, then to the catering giant Compass Group, and then to PFG. Every owner had left its own imprint on the company. Furthermore, Le Méridien held many hotel properties under an operating license only, with the actual hotel owner being a real estate or other type of investor. These license agreements came in many different shapes and forms, giving the owners varying degrees of influence on management practice and strategic direction.

In response to the variety of local conditions, the managing directors of the individual hotels had generally been granted far-reaching autonomy. Both the

▶

pricing in the local market, the management of the local work force, and the need to respond immediately to customers' requests required the entrepreneurial talents of local bosses. But even they had only one pair of eyes and hands, and needed to sleep at night, relying on their organizations to create the luxury experience, 365 days and nights around the clock. Unlike in a manufacturing environment, in hotels product reworking is not possible – lousy service to guests cannot be undone. Managers have to rely on the organizational systems in the hotel, and the improvisation skills of their staff, to get things right the first time, every time.

Yet, despite the autonomy given to local managing directors, the financial performance of Le Méridien was below par, even before the economic downturn. While industry leader Four Seasons managed a 36% earnings margin on sales in 2000, Le Méridien achieved only 15%. The brand also lacked the pulling power required in the five star segment of the market, which the Ritz Carltons or the Mandarin Orientals for instance had. Therefore, it was JB's task as new CEO to reinvigorate the company and to make the whole worth more than the sum of its individual locations. As a private equity investor, PFG had set the financial targets high for JB, in effect requiring Le Méridien to outperform the industry within three years. In order to achieve these ambitious goals, JB developed a two-pronged strategy: one was called 'Art & Tech', and the other was called 'treasure hunting'.

Art & Tech was based on JB's vision to combine the power of a worldwide brand with the avant-garde appeal of local boutique hotels. Approximately 5000 of the 40 000 hotel rooms at Le Méridien would be converted to this concept, and the others would contain several elements of it. The 'Tech' part of the concept consisted of such features as a 42 inch plasma TV screen, high speed dataport/internet access in the room, showering and bathing facilities with thick water jets, specially engineered beds 'providing the ultimate sleep experience in crisp white cotton duvets' and 'advanced lighting technologies electronically controlled to create a series of different moods'. The 'Art' component included various artistic elements throughout the room, creating a 'space that will not only provide luxury accommodation but an environment that will engage, surprise and intrigue Le Méridien's guests'. Each hotel would have specially commissioned photographs and art themes inspired from the local-

ity of the hotel, nearby museums or their collections. In all, 'the Art & Tech room is designed to offer today's increasingly sophisticated traveler the ultimate in innovative luxury'.

The second prong of JB's strategy was the treasure hunt. The moneymaking parts of a hotel are its rooms and its conference facilities. But inside a typical hotel, a lot of space is used as staff rooms, management offices and apartments, which do not directly contribute to hotel revenue. In JB's view, these could be converted into rooms, and cheaper space could be rented outside of the main building for the administrative and supply functions. Likewise, low-income space usages such as swimming pools, fitness areas, shopping malls and restaurants could be reduced to the minimum, using the surplus space as conference facilities. In this way, JB believed that he could significantly increase the revenue potential for a given piece of real estate, adding a total of 1600 bedrooms and more than 2000 square meters of conferencing rooms throughout the group at comparatively minor cost.

Once JB arrived in July 2001, he lost no time starting to implement his strategy. Top management was almost completely replaced by hand-picked recruits, who were often industry outsiders. For instance, his new marketing chief came from American Express, which JB hoped would bring fresh ideas into the company. Even the designer responsible for fashioning the Art & Tech look was an unconventional outside choice, with a background in museum design.

However, by early 2003, half way into JB's three-year plan, not much could yet be seen of Le Méridien climbing to the top. Given the overall economic climate, this was hardly surprising. Times were such that mere survival was reason to celebrate. The business travel market that Le Méridien was targeting was the hardest hit of all. Of the £850 million investment program that had been announced in September of 2001, little had actually been spent – most of the money had been pledged by the hotel property owners to convert hotels to the Art & Tech concept and few were inclined to proceed with this plan after 9/11.

While putting on a brave face, this situation was a severe blow to JB's ambitions. With only a year and a half left to achieve the above-average profitability needed to pay off its high debts, JB could not afford to sit back and wait for the world economy to rebound. To many people around him it was now the moment of truth – to see whether JB had the leadership abilities to take decisive action and to pilot the organization into a safe haven. In particular, Le Méridien's owner, PFG, was very anxious to see whether JB, with all his industry experience and wealth of contacts, could push through the measures necessary to improve the company's long-term, and short-term prospects.

Other observers, however, were doubtful whether JB's strategy would have worked, even without 9/11. In their view, JB's top-down approach to rejuvenating the company was bound to run into the sand anyway, due to the complexity and diversity of the organization. Local managing directors were unlikely to be very thrilled with wild ideas coming from headquarters that paid scant attention to local conditions and the uniqueness of each hotel. Even where they broadly agreed with JB, it would not have been easy to get local owners, staff and management to accept all the required changes and implement them in such a short period of time.

For JB, with a career and £10 million at stake, the pressing question was what he could still do to revitalize Le Méridien. Should he charge forward, leading the 40 000 troops, or were there more effective ways to keep himself, and the hotels, occupied?

Sources: *Financial Times*, March 25, April 3, May 24 and September 27 2002; Company reports; 'Four Seasons goes to Paris', *Academy of Management Executive*, 2002, Vol. 16 No. 4.

PERSPECTIVES ON THE ORGANIZATIONAL CONTEXT

I claim not to have controlled events, but confess plainly that events have controlled me.

Abraham Lincoln (1809–1865); American president

While the pressures for both control and chaos are clear, this does leave managers with the challenging question of how they must reconcile two opposite, and at least partially incompatible, demands. Gaining a considerable level of top management control over the development of the organization will to some extent be at odds with a policy of accepting, or even encouraging, organizational chaos. To control or not to control, that is the question.

And yet again managers should not hope to find widespread consensus in the strategic management literature on what the optimal answer is for dealing with these two conflicting pressures. For among strategy academics and business practitioners alike, opinions differ strongly with regard to the best balance between control and chaos. Although many writers do indicate that there may be different styles in dealing with the paradox and that these different styles might be more effective under different circumstances (e.g. Strebel, 1994; Vroom and Jago, 1988), most authors still exhibit a strong preference for a particular approach – which is duly called the 'modern' or 'new' style, or better yet, '21st century practices' (Ireland and Hitt, 1999).

Following the dialectical inquiry method used in previous chapters, here the two diametrically opposed positions will be identified and discussed. On the one hand, there are those who argue that top managers should lead from the front. Top managers should dare to take on the responsibility of imposing a new strategic agenda on the organization and should be at the forefront in breaking away from organizational inheritance where necessary. This point of view, with its strong emphasis on control and leading top-down, will be referred to as the 'organizational leadership perspective'. This view is also known as the strategic leadership perspective (e.g. Cannella and Monroe, 1997; Rowe, 2001), but to avoid confusion with the industry leadership perspective discussed in Chapter 8, here the prefix 'organizational' is preferred. On the other hand, there are people who believe that managers rarely have the ability to shape their organizations at will, but rather that organizations develop according to their own dynamics. These strategists argue that in most organizations no one is really in control and that managers should not focus their energy on attempting to impose developments top-down, but rather focus on facilitating processes of self-organization. This point of view, with its strong emphasis on chaos and facilitating bottom-up processes, will be referred to as the 'organizational dynamics perspective'.

The organizational leadership perspective

To proponents of the organizational leadership perspective, top management can – and should – take charge of the organization. In their view, organizational inertia and a growing misfit between the organization and its environment are not an inevitable state of affairs, but result from a failure of leadership. Bureaucracy, organizational fiefdoms, hostile relationships, inflexible corporate cultures, rigid competences and resistance to change – all of these organizational diseases exist, but they are not unavoidable facts of organizational life. 'Healthy' organizations guard against falling prey to such degenerative illnesses, and when symptoms do arise it is a task of the leader to address them. If organizations do go 'out of control', it is because weak leadership has failed to deal with a creeping ailment. The fact that there are many sick, poorly controllable companies does not mean that sickness should be accepted as the natural condition.

At the basis of the organizational leadership perspective lies the belief that if people in organizations are left to 'sort things out' by themselves, this will inevitably degenerate into a situation of strategic drift (see Chapter 4). Without somebody to quell political infighting, set a clear strategic direction, force through tough decisions, and supervise disciplined implementation, the organization will get bogged down in protracted internal bickering. Without somebody to champion a new vision, rally the troops and lead from the front, the organization will never get its heavy mass in motion. Without somebody who radiates confidence and cajoles people into action, the organization will not be able to overcome its risk averseness and conservatism. In short, leaders are needed to counteract the inherent inertia characteristic of human organization.

As organizational order and direction do not happen spontaneously, the 'visible hand' of management is indispensable for the proper functioning of the organization (e.g. Child, 1972; Cyert, 1990, Reading 9.1). And this hand must be firm. Managers cannot afford to take a *laissez-faire* attitude towards their task as leader – to lead means to get the organizational members to follow, and this is usually plain hard work (e.g. Bennis and Nanus, 1985; Kelley, 1988). To convince people in the organization to let themselves be led, managers cannot simply fall back on their position power. To be able to steer organizational developments managers need considerable personal power. To be successful, managers must be trusted, admired and respected. The forcefulness of their personality and the persuasiveness of their vision must be capable of capturing people's attention and commitment. And as leaders, managers must also be politically agile, able to build coalitions where necessary to get their way.

Of course, not all managers have the qualities needed to be effective leaders – either by nature or nurture. Some theorists emphasize the importance of 'nature', arguing that managers require specific personality traits to be successful leaders (e.g. House and Aditya, 1997; Tucker, 1968). Yet, other theorists place more emphasis on 'nurture', arguing that most effective leadership behavior can be learned if enough effort is exerted (e.g. Kotter, 1990; Nanus, 1992). Either way, the importance of having good leadership makes finding and developing new leaders one of the highest priorities of the existing top management team.

To proponents of the organizational leadership perspective, being a leader does not mean engaging in simple top-down, command-and-control management. There are circumstances where the CEO or the top management team design strategies in isolation and then impose them on the rest of the organization. This type of direct control is sometimes necessary to push through reorganizations or to make major acquisitions. In other circumstances, however, the top managers can control organizational behavior more indirectly. Proposals can be allowed to emerge bottom-up, as long as top management retains its power to approve or terminate projects as soon as they become serious plans (e.g. Bourgeois and Brodwin, 1983; Quinn, 1980, Reading 3.2). Some authors suggest that top management might even delegate some decision-making powers to lower level managers, but still control outcomes by setting clear goals, developing a conducive incentive system and fostering a particular culture (e.g. Senge, 1990b, Reading 9.3; Tichy and Cohen, 1997).

What leaders should not do, however, is to relinquish control over the direction of the organization. The strategies do not have to be their own ideas, nor do they have to carry out everything themselves. But they should take upon themselves the responsibility for leading the organization in a certain direction and achieving results. If leaders let go of the helm, organizations will be set adrift, and will be carried by the prevailing winds and currents in directions unknown. Someone has to be in control of the organization, otherwise its behavior will be erratic. Leadership is needed to ensure that the best strategy is followed.

In conclusion, the organizational leadership perspective holds that the upper echelons of management can, and should, control the strategy process and by extension the strategy content. The CEO, or the top management team (e.g. Finkelstein and Hambrick, 1996; Hambrick and Mason, 1984), should have a grip on the organization's process of strategy formation and should be able to impose their will on the organization. Leaders should strive to overcome organizational inertia and adapt the organization to the strategic direction they intend. This type of controlled strategic behavior is what Chandler (1962) had in mind when he coined the aphorism 'structure follows strategy' – the organizational structure should be adapted to the strategy intended by the decision-maker. In the organizational leadership perspective it would be more fitting to expand Chandler's maxim to 'organization follows strategy' – all aspects of the company should be matched to the strategist's intentions.

EXHIBIT 9.2 THE ORGANIZATIONAL LEADERSHIP PERSPECTIVE

NISSAN: NEW DRIVER AT THE WHEEL

In 1998 car-maker Nissan was heading for a brick wall at high speed. Its market share in Japan had been sliding for 26 years straight, and while its key domestic rivals Honda and Toyota were reporting record profits, Nissan had not been able to make a profit for seven of the eight previous years. Daimler Chrysler had declined to buy Nissan, even for the symbolic amount of one dollar, while Ford, too, had lost interest. Eventually it was French car-maker Renault who took the opportunity to gain a controlling stake in March 1999. Just three years later,

Nissan was one of the most profitable automobile manufacturers in the world, even surpassing Toyota, and was set to recapture the number two market share position in Japan. Seldom has a turnaround been so dramatic, so complete and so attributable to one person – Carlos Ghosn.

Between 1992 and 1998, three different presidents had been behind the wheel at Nissan, but none were able to get the skidding company under control. No fewer than four restructuring plans were announced, but nothing seemed capable of avoiding the imminent crash. So when Renault eventually stepped in and sent the 45-year-old, non-Japanese speaking, Brazil-born French/Lebanese Carlos

Ghosn to take control of Nissan in summer 1999, his task was widely hailed as 'Mission Impossible'. Later in that year, this assessment was toned down to 'Mission Improbable', and in 2002 *Fortune* named Carlos Ghosn 'Asia's Businessman of the Year'. What did he do that predecessors were incapable of doing?

According to one senior executive at Nissan, 'Ghosn stresses action, speed and results. He follows up closely. If there are any deviations he goes after them immediately. He is relentless in following up.' In his own words at the time:

I have one goal, that Nissan will be profitable in 2001. . . This is not like buying a Persian rug: the guy says he wants 100, but if he gets 50 he will be happy. We want 100, and we are going to get 100. If we do not get it in 2001, that's it, we will resign . . . From now on, financial objectives will entail accountability.

Accountability is Ghosn's credo. He sees no value in business relationships that are not characterized by clear and controllable targets. Starting at the top, the number of directors on the board was reduced from 43 to nine. The traditional lifetime employment and seniority-based reward system was completely revamped. Several hundred key managers received stock options instead. Promotion and rewards were linked to performance against an annual set of objectives. Ghosn created six program directors with worldwide profit responsibility for a range of cars under their management. Externally, by the end of 2002, Nissan's 67 equity investments in Keiretsu (group) companies were reduced to 25, while all 1400 cross-shareholdings with other Japanese companies were undone. The 300 global banking relationships were centralized into a single treasury function. The number of suppliers was reduced by half to 600, with each remaining supplier committing to at least a 20% cost reduction over three years.

The pressure was equally fierce inside the company. Headcount was reduced by almost 20%, dropping from 148 000 to 127 000 employees, and five manufacturing plants were closed. Yet, at the same time Ghosn planned to introduce 28 new car models within three years. In order to achieve all that, one of Ghosn's first actions in office was to install nine cross-functional teams with up to ten middle managers and hundreds of sub-team members, to work out the entire 'Nissan Revival Plan' within only two months. Team members were not responsible for implementation, but their recommendations had to be aggressive, specific, backed up by numbers and not respectful towards current practices. Any team that did not live up to these targets was sent straight back to work.

In May 2002, having achieved the turnaround one year ahead of schedule, Ghosn unveiled the new Nissan 180 plan – by 2005, Nissan would increase car sales almost 40%, from 2.6 to 3.6 million vehicles, reach 8% operating profit on sales (top of the industry), and have reduced net automotive debt to zero. To industry insiders, this sounded like 'Mission Impossible' all over again, but if anyone could pull off this assignment, it would be Carlos Ghosn.

Sources: *Business Week,* January 18 2000, June 21 2001, January 13 2003; Interview with Carlos Ghosn in *Harvard Business Review,* January–February 2002; Yoshino, 2002.

The organizational dynamics perspective

To proponents of the organizational dynamics perspective, such an heroic depiction of leadership is understandable, but usually more myth than reality. There might be a few great, wise, charismatic managers that rise to the apex of organizations, but unfortunately, all other organizations have to settle for regular mortals. Strong leaders are an exception, not the norm, and even their ability to mold the organization at will is highly exaggerated – good stories for best-selling (auto)biographies, but legend nevertheless (e.g. Chen and Meindl, 1991; Kets de Vries, 1994). Yet, the belief in the power of leadership is quite popular, among managers and the managed alike (e.g. Meindl, Ehrlich and Dukerich, 1985; Pfeffer, 1977). Managers like the idea that as leaders of an organization or organizational unit, they can make a difference. To most, 'being in control' is what management is all about. They have a penchant for attributing organizational results to their own efforts (e.g. Calder, 1977; Sims and Lorenzi, 1992). As for 'the managed', they too often ascribe organizational success or failure to the figurehead leader, whatever that person's real influence has been – after all, they too like the idea that somebody is in control. In fact, both parties are subscribing to a seductively simple 'great person model' of how organizations work. The implicit assumption is that an individual leader, by the strength of personality, can steer large groups of people, like a present-day Alexander the Great.

However seductive, this view of organizational functioning is rarely a satisfactory model. A top manager does not resemble a commander leading the troops into battle, but rather a diplomat trying to negotiate a peace. The top manager is not like a jockey riding a thoroughbred horse, but more like a cowboy herding mules. Organizations are complex social systems, made up of many 'stubborn individuals' with their own ideas, interests and agendas (e.g. Greenwood and Hinings, 1996; Stacey, 1993a). Strategy formation is therefore an inherently political process, that leaders can only influence depending on their power base. The more dispersed the political power, the more difficult it is for a leader to control the organization's behavior. Even if leaders are granted, or acquire, significant political power to push through their favored measures, there may still be considerable resistance and guerilla activities. Political processes within organizations do not signify the derailment of strategic decision-making – politics is the normal state of affairs and few leaders have real control over these political dynamics.

Besides such political limitations, a top manager's ability to control the direction of a company is also severely constrained by the organization's culture. Social norms will have evolved, relationships will have been formed, aspirations will have taken root and cognitive maps will have been shaped. A leader cannot ignore the cultural legacy of the organization's history, as this will be deeply etched into the minds of the organization's members. Any top manager attempting to radically alter the direction of a company will find out that changing the underlying values, perceptions, beliefs and expectations is extremely difficult, if not next to impossible. As Weick (1979) puts it, an organization does not have a culture, it is a culture – shared values and norms are what make an organization. And just as it is difficult to change someone's identity, it is difficult to change an organization's culture (e.g. Schein, 1993; Smircich and Stubbart, 1985). Moreover, as most top managers rise through the ranks to the upper echelons, they themselves are a product of the existing organizational culture. Changing your own culture is like pulling yourself up by your own bootstraps – a great trick, too bad that nobody can do it.

In Chapters 5 and 6, a related argument was put forward, as part of the resource-based view of the firm. One of the basic assumptions of the resource-based view is that building up competences is an arduous task, requiring a relatively long period of time. Learning is a slow process under the best of circumstances, but even more difficult if learning one thing means unlearning something else. The stronger the existing cognitive maps (knowledge), routines (capabilities) and disposition (attitude), the more challenging it is to 'teach an old dog new tricks'. The leader's power to direct and speed up such processes, it was argued, is quite limited (e.g. Barney, 1991, Reading 5.4; Leonard-Barton, 1995).

Taken together, the political, cultural and learning dynamics leave top managers with relatively little direct power over the system they want to steer. Generally, they can react to this limited ability to control in one of two basic ways – they can squeeze tighter or let go. Many managers follow the first route, desperately trying to acquire more power, to gain a tighter grip on the organization, in the vain attempt to become the heroic leader of popular legend. Such a move to accumulate more power commonly results in actions to assert control, including stricter reporting structures, more disciplined accountability, harsher punishment for non-conformists and a shakeout among managers. In this manner, control comes to mean restriction, subordination or even subjugation. Yet, such a step towards authoritarian management will still not bring managers very much further towards having a lasting impact on organizational development.

The alternative route is for managers to accept that they cannot, but also should not try to, tightly control the organization. As they cannot really control organizational dynamics, all heavy-handed control approaches will have little more result than making the organization an unpleasant and oppressive place to work. If managers emphasize control, all they will do is run the risk of killing the organization's ability to innovate and learn. Innovation and learning are very difficult to control, especially the business innovation and learning happening outside of R&D labs. Much of this innovation and learning is sparked by organizational members, out in the markets or on the work floor, questioning the status quo. New ideas often start 'in the margins' of the organization and grow due to the room granted to offbeat opinions. Fragile new initiatives often need to be championed by their owners lower down in the hierarchy and only survive if there is a tolerance for unintended 'misfits' in the organization's portfolio of activities. Only if employees have a certain measure of freedom and are willing to act as intrapreneurs, will learning and innovation be an integral part of the organization's functioning (e.g. Amabile, 1998; Quinn, 1985).

In other words, if managers move beyond their instinctive desire for control and recognize the creative and entrepreneurial potential of self-organization, they will not bemoan their lack of control. They will see that a certain level of organizational chaos can create the conditions for development (e.g. Levy, 1994; Stacey, 1993a, Reading 9.2). According to the organizational dynamics perspective, the task for managers is to use their limited powers to facilitate self-organization (e.g. Beinhocker, 1999; Wheatley and Kellner-Rogers, 1996). Managers can encourage empowerment, stimulate learning and innovation, bring people together, take away bureaucratic hurdles – all very much like the approach by most governments in market economies, who try to establish conditions conducive to entrepreneurial behavior instead of trying to control economic activity. Managers' most important task is to ensure that the 'invisible hand of self-organization' functions properly, and does not lead to 'out-of-hand disorganization'.

So, does the manager matter? Yes, but in a different sense than is usually assumed. The manager cannot shape the organization – it shapes itself. Organizational developments are the result of complex internal dynamics, which can be summarized as strategy follows organization, instead of the other way around. Managers can facilitate processes of self-organization and thus indirectly influence the direction of development, but at the same time managers are also shaped by the organization they are in.

EXHIBIT 9.3 THE ORGANIZATIONAL DYNAMICS PERSPECTIVE

SEMCO: PUMPING SUCCESS

When Ricardo Semler took over his father's pump-making business in 1980, Semco was a US$4 million company, focused on the domestic Brazilian market, and heading for bankruptcy in a severe recession that was to last for most of the decade. By 2003, Semco had expanded beyond pumps to dishwashers, digital scanners, cooling units and mixers for anything from bubble gum to rocket fuel, operating as a federation of ten businesses, with revenues totaling US$160 million and about 3000 employees. While a fascinating business success,

Semco's turnaround is all the more interesting because it was achieved without the leadership of a charismatic CEO – actually, it was achieved without having a CEO at all.

Semco has no traditional organizational hierarchy for decision-making and control. Major decisions affecting the entire organization, such as the purchase of a new plant site or an acquisition, are put to a democratic vote, while other decisions are taken consensually by all employees involved. There are no internal audit groups, no controls on travel expenses, and inventory and storage rooms remain unlocked – but all information is made available to everyone, encouraging self-control. According to Semler: 'Freedom is no easy thing. It does not make life carefree – because it introduces difficult choices.' To stimulate information exchange, the offices have no walls and all memos must be kept to one page, without exception. Furthermore, everyone is trained to read financial statements, and everybody knows the profit and loss statements of the company and their business unit.

The alternative organizational configuration of Semco is made up of four concentric circles. The innermost circle consists of six Counselors, who serve as the executive team and take turns as chairperson every six months. Despite being the 90% owner of the company, Semler is only one of these six. Around the Counselors is a circle of Partners, who act as business unit managers. Around them is a circle of Coordinators, who function as first-line supervisors. Everybody else is in the fourth circle, and is called Associate. Additionally there are 'Nucleuses of Technology Innovation', which are 'no-boss' temporary project teams who are freed from their day-to-day work in order to focus on some kind of business improvement project, a new product, a cost reduction program, a new business plan or the like.

The members of Semco decide among themselves what their pay will be. The amount is made transparent to all others by regular participation in salary surveys, thus everybody knows what the pay is of everyone else. Furthermore, every member is part of the company-wide profit sharing program that pays out 23% of a business unit's profits per quarter to the employees. In fact, the payout ratio of 23% was also decided by the employees. Members of a Nucleus of Technology Innovation receive royalties on the achievements of their projects.

At any given moment, who belongs to the Semco company and who doesn't, can be rather fuzzy. Semler explains:

When we walk through our plants, we rarely even know who works for us. Some of the people in the factory are full-time employees; some work for us part-time; some work for themselves and supply Semco with components or services; some work for themselves under contract to outside companies (even competitors); and some of them work for each other. We could decide to find out which is which and who is who, but . . . we think it is all useless information.

As for strategy, Semco has no grand design. Semler readily admits that he has no idea what the company will be making in ten years time: 'I think that strategic planning and vision are often barriers to success.' Semco's approach is largely to let strategy emerge on the basis of opportunities identified by employees close to the market. Where new initiatives can muster enough support among colleagues, they are awarded more time and money to bring them to fruition. In this way, Semco can make the best possible use of the engagement and entrepreneurship of its employees.

Summing up the Semco philosophy, Semler told the *Financial Times*:

At Semco, the basic question we work on is: how do you get people to come to work on a gray Monday morning? This is the only parameter we care about, which is a 100% motivation issue. Everything else – quality, profits, growth – will fall into place, if enough people are interested in coming to work on Monday morning.

Sources: Semler (1994); *Financial Times*, May 15 1997; *Guardian Unlimited*, April 17 2003; Semler (1995, 2003).

INTRODUCTION TO THE DEBATE AND READINGS

An institution is the lengthened shadow of one man.

Ralph Waldo Emerson (1803–1882);
American essayist and poet

Chaos often breeds life, when order breeds habit.

Henry Brooks Adams (1838–1919);
American writer and historian

So, how should organizational development be encouraged? Can the top management of a firm shape the organization to fit with their intended strategy or does the organizational context determine the strategy that is actually followed? And should top management strive to have a tight grip on the organization, or should they leave plenty of room for self-organization?

As before, views differ strongly, both in business practice and in academia; not only in the field of strategy, but also in neighboring fields such as organizational behavior, human resource management and innovation management. And not only in the management sciences, but more broadly in the humanities, including sociology, economics, political science and psychology as well. The economic sociologist Duesenberry once remarked that 'economics is all about how people make choices; sociology is all about how they don't have any choices to make'. Although half in jest, his comment does ring true. Much of the literature within the field of economics assumes that people in organizations can freely make choices and have the power to shape their strategy, while possible restraints on their freedom usually come from the environment. Sociological literature, but also psychological and political science work, often features the limitations on individual's freedom. These different disciplinary inclinations are not absolute, but can be clearly recognized in the debate.

With so many conflicting views and incompatible prescriptions on the issue of organizational development, it is again up to each individual strategist to form their own opinion on how best to deal with the paradox of control and chaos. But to help strategists to come to grips with the variety of perspectives on this issue, four readings have been selected that each shed their own light on the topic. As in previous chapters, the first two readings will be representative of the two poles in this debate (see Table 9.1), while the second set of two readings will bring in extra angles to add further depth to the discussion.

To open the debate on behalf of the organizational leadership perspective, Reading 9.1 has been selected entitled 'Defining Leadership and Explicating the Process', which is by one of the 'godfathers' of organizational theory, Richard Cyert. In this article, Cyert starts by summarizing the functions of a leader: determining the organizational structure, selecting managers, setting strategic objectives, controlling internal and external information flows, maintaining morale and making important decisions. But while some authors who take an organizational leadership perspective tend to conjure up an image of the leader as an octopus, with many long arms performing all of these tasks at the same time, Cyert has a more human, two-armed individual in mind. His view of the leader is not the control freak who wants to run the organization single-handedly, but a person who can 'heavily influence the process of determining the goals of the organization', and then can 'have the participants in the organization behave in the ways that the leader believes are desirable'. This definition of leadership has two important ingredients. First, Cyert argues that leaders need to take the initiative in determining a vision and organizational goals, although they do this in interaction with other organizational members. Secondly, Cyert argues that leaders need to focus on modifying the people's behaviors. To get people to move in the desired direction, he states that it is not so important what a leader decides or tells people to do. Rather, an effective leader 'controls the allocation of the attention focus of the participants in the organization . . . so that their attention is allocated to the areas that the leader considers important'. In this way, Cyert believes, organizational members will voluntarily align their behaviors with where the leader wants to go. He admits that 'this conception of leadership might strike some as making the leader a manipulative person', but feels that if leaders have a genuine belief in what they are doing and have an honest dedication to the people in the organization, exerting this type of leadership is justified. Although Cyert is well aware that organizations are complex systems of interacting human beings, his unquestioned supposition throughout the reading is that leadership is *possible* and *necessary*. As many writers taking an organizational leadership perspective, the demand for top management control is an implicit assumption – the main issue discussed is how to get power and how to exert control. Cyert's preference is for more indirect control, implicitly leaving some room for bottom-up self-organization.

As the opening reading to represent the organizational dynamics perspective (Reading 9.2), an article by Ralph Stacey has been selected, entitled 'Strategy as Order Emerging from Chaos'. Stacey argues that top managers cannot, and should not even try, to control the organization and its strategy. In his view, the organizational dynamics involved in strategy formation, learning and change are too complex to simply be controlled by managers. He states that 'sometimes the best thing a manager can do is to let go and allow things to happen'. The resulting chaos, he argues, does not mean that the organization will be a mess – a lack of control, he assures, does not mean that the organization will be adrift. His reasoning is that non-linear feedback systems, such as organizations, have a self-organizing ability, which 'can produce controlled behavior, even though no one is in control'. In his view, real strategic change requires the chaos of contention and conflict to destroy old recipes and to encourage the quest for new solutions. The 'self-organizing processes of political interaction and complex learning' ensure that chaos does not result in disintegration. Hence, in Stacey's opinion, it is management's task to help create a situation of bounded instability in which strategy can emerge. Managers do have a role in organizations, but it can hardly be called leadership – 'leaders' must direct their efforts at influencing the organizational context in such a way that the right conditions prevail for self-organization to take place. 'Leaders' are largely facilitators, making it possible for new and unexpected strategies to develop spontaneously.

To complement the two 'opening statements' in the debate, two additional readings have been selected for this chapter that shed more light on aspects of the organizational

TABLE 9.1 Organizational leadership versus organizational dynamics perspective

	Organizational leadership perspective	Organizational dynamics perspective
Emphasis on	Control over chaos	Chaos over control
Organizational development	Controllable creation process	Uncontrollable evolutionary process
Development metaphor	The visible hand	The invisible hand
Development direction	Top-down, imposed organization	Bottom-up, self-organization
Decision-making	Authoritarian (rule of the few)	Democratic (rule of the many)
Change process	Leader shapes new behavior	New behavior emerges from interactions
Change determinants	Leader's vision and skill	Political, cultural and learning dynamics
Organizational malleability	High, fast	Low, slow
Development driver	Organization follows strategy	Strategy follows organization
Normative implication	Strategize, then organize	Strategizing and organizing intertwined

context that have not yet been sufficiently accentuated. Reading 9.3 is 'Building Learning Organizations' by Peter Senge. This reading summarizes many of the major points of Senge's (1990a) acclaimed book *The Fifth Discipline: The Art and Practice of the Learning Organization*. This reading has been selected to delve more deeply into the role of learning in the organizational development process. Both the organizational leadership perspective and the organizational dynamics perspective acknowledge that learning is an important part of ongoing organizational adaptation, but the two sides emphasize different aspects of the learning process. Proponents of the organizational leadership perspective, like Cyert, highlight the role of leaders in guiding organizational learning and stress how learning needs to be channeled in the most appropriate direction to be valuable. However, advocates of the organizational dynamics perspective, like Stacey, point to the need for organizational members to think for themselves and to strike out in bold new directions, unlimited by rigid organizational paradigms or corporate 'thought police'. In his contribution Senge takes arguments from both sides in an attempt to find a way to 'build a learning organization'. Senge agrees with Stacey that leaders cannot learn on behalf of their organizations and then push through the strategic changes they believe should be made. In his view, leaders must facilitate organizational learning – leaders 'are responsible for building organizations where people are continually expanding their capabilities to shape their future'. Creating organizations that want to adapt, learn and evolve means avoiding the traditional sources of inertia. Senge believes that one of the keys to continuous learning is motivation. He suggests that the drive to learn can best be stimulated by establishing a creative tension between the current reality and a compelling vision of the future. But, Senge points out, creating a shared vision and designing the organization in a way that enables learning, instead of impeding it, are clearly leadership tasks. This is where he swings more to Cyert's point of view. In his opinion, leaders are needed to perform these important formative tasks, as well as to act as organizational teachers. A teacher is not someone with all the right answers, but a leader who can ask challenging questions and can shake up existing cognitive maps. Together, these 'new tasks' of leaders give them plenty of scope to influence the future direction of the firm, while at the same time leaving enough room for organizational members to also contribute to the organization's development.

The final reading is 'The Knowing-Doing Gap', by Jeffrey Pfeffer and Robert Sutton, an article based on their (1999b) book *The Knowing-Doing Gap: How Smart Companies Turn Knowledge Into Action*. This reading has been selected to review many of the sources of inertia that frustrate organizational development and to highlight the role of knowledge management, both as a driver and a major inhibitor of organizational development. The main thesis of Pfeffer and Sutton is that most organizations actually know what they should do, but somehow don't do it – most organizations don't suffer from *ignorance*, but only from a lack of *implementation*. And where there is a gap between 'ignorance and knowing', this is easier to bridge than the gap between 'knowing and doing'. This observation does not fit well with the conception of strong top management control put forward by the organizational leadership perspective, because implementation should in theory be something that is easily controllable, using either throughput or output controls. Yet, Pfeffer and Sutton argue that various organizational processes are at work, which interfere with the translation of organizational knowledge into concrete organizational action. In their view, managers can play an important role in solving the knowing-doing problem, but not by engaging in traditional control-oriented behavior, imposing programs on docile employees. Their practical advice for managers is to create conditions for *knowing through doing* – emphasizing action and getting organizational members to learn along the way. In this approach, managers have influence on what is going on in the organization, by outlining a vision, teaching others hands-on, rewarding action, encouraging cooperation and measuring progress, but the engagement of all organizational members is required to shape the firm together. Pfeffer and Sutton do not use the word self-organization, but their advocacy of active participation of all people in the firm in realizing organizational development shows that they clearly appreciate the importance of organizational chaos as well.

READING 9.1

Defining leadership and explicating the process

Richard M. Cyert[1]

It is true that organizations, whether for-profit or not-for-profit, are in need of leadership. Most people in leadership positions in organizations tend to be managers rather than leaders. They administer, allocate resources, resolve conflicts, and go home at night convinced that they have done a good day's work. They may have, but they have not provided the organization with the critical ingredient that every organization needs – leadership (Zalesnik, 1977; Bavelas, 1964).

It is possible to generalize three broad functions that a leader performs. I specify these functions as organizational, interpersonal, and decisional. The organizational function involves the development of the organizational structure and the selection of people to manage the various segments of an organization. It involves the determination of the goal structure and the control of the internal and external information flows. This function requires the leader to make certain that the participants in the organization and the relevant groups external to the organization are knowledgeable about the organization.

The interpersonal function involves the maintenance of morale in the organization. It reflects the degree of concern about the humanness of the organization. It requires the leader to pay attention to individual concerns.

The decision function involves the making of decisions that must be made in order for the organization to progress toward the achievement of its goals. This is the function that has traditionally been associated with leadership.

Nature of leadership

Although there is little agreement on the definition of leadership, most students of leadership would agree that the three functions just described are clearly a part of the definition. In a broad sense, the leader is attempting to have the participants in the organization behave in the ways that the leader believes are desirable. A major step in performing the organizational function is to define desirable behavior.

Desirability is determined by the goals of the organization. The leader should heavily influence the process of determining the goals of the organization. The determination of a goal structure for an organization is the result of a series of interactions among the participants and between the participants and the leader. The goal structure represents the vision of the leader and of the organization's other members. Projecting a vision for the organization is another characteristic that is commonly associated with leadership.

The vision embedded in the goal structure is essentially a map that is used as a guide for the direction of the organization. Clearly, the map is more detailed as one's view shifts to sub-units within the organization. At the top leadership position, a number of broad principles are specified to guide the overall construction of the vision.

These principles relate to the process by which the organization's vision can be constantly modified and reshaped. The specification of strategic principles and of the process by which the vision is modified is another characteristic of leadership. The leader is the helmsman, and the goal structure, together with the strategic principle, is the means by which the leader steers the organization. But, an organization is an interactive system of human beings, and its performance depends on the behavior of individuals. Regardless of the policies that are promulgated, the participants in the organization will determine the destiny of the organization by their productivity.

The goal structure is important in the leading of an organization. However, organizations can have conflicting goals (Cyert and March, 1963), primarily because they tend to goals sequentially. Also, each unit in an organization can focus on different goals. These goals may conflict, but they can all be embraced by the organization (Birnbaum, 1988).

[1]Source: This article was adapted from 'Defining Leadership and Explicating the Process', R.M. Cyert: © 1990 Jossey-Bass Inc. Publishers. This material is used by permission of John Wiley & Sons, Ltd.

A definition of leadership

The concept of attention focus is one of the most important variables in organization theory (March and Simon, 1958; Cyert and March, 1963). Participants in an organization allocate their attention to a variety of matters. The amount of attention allocated to each matter has been a subject of study. It can affect the organization in crucial ways. For example, if attention is not given to problems concerned with the future, the organization may flounder from myopia – too much attention to immediate problems. Clearly, the problems, concerns, ideas, concepts, and so on to which the participants pay attention will determine the long-run viability of the organization. The control of this allocation of attention is vital to the organization.

In discussing the formation of the organizational coalition, Cyert and March (1963, p. 39) argue that one of the five basic mechanisms for a theory of coalition formation is 'an attention-focus mechanism'; however, 'we know rather little about the actual mechanisms that control this attention factor.' In this paper, I argue that the leadership function is one of the mechanisms that controls the attention factor.

In fact, my definition of leadership is that the leader controls the allocation of the attention focus of the participants in the organization. The leader of any organization, no matter how small or large it is, affects the allocation of attention by participants. In a decentralized, structured organization, standard operating procedures determine the allocation of attention if the leader does not intervene. In general, in any organization where managers dominate, structured rules tend to influence the allocation of attention, but the leader will try to capture the attention focus of the participants so that their attention is allocated to the areas that the leader considers important.

The issues or problems on which the leader attempts to focus attention reflect, at least in part, the vision of the organization that exists in the leader's mind. This vision will generally have been developed from discussions with relevant participants, from the leader's experience and knowledge, and from his or her assessment of the organization's future in the light of existing information. This vision will change over time as the leader gets feedback from the organization's performance. As the vision changes, so does the priority of individual issues and problems to which the leader wishes to allocate the attention of participants. Organizations are dynamic, and attention allocation is an ongoing and always necessary process. Leadership, in the sense in which I have defined it here, must also be continuous.

Leadership, as I define it here, must also have substance. A leader cannot succeed in allocating attention without a strong intellectual position for a particular attention focus. This position can only come from a knowledge of the organization and of the area in which it functions. This need for specific knowledge is one of the reasons why it is difficult for executives to move from an organization in one industry to an organization in a different industry. The executive may be able to function as a manager, but he or she will have more difficulty functioning as a leader.

A second definition of leadership

Subgroups develop in every organization. Participants involved in the same department or in similar endeavors form a natural alliance (March and Simon, 1958). Important individuals in an organization can constitute subgroups in and of themselves. The point is that subgroups can develop a goal structure of their own, and this goal structure may conflict with that of the central organization.

The leader must bring about conformity between subgroup goals and the goals of the central organization. In other words, the leader must convince the members of the subgroup to give up or modify their goals and adopt the central organization's goals. In some cases, of course, the leader may decide that the central goals should be changed in the direction of the subgroup's goals. The point is that the leader cannot tolerate conflicting goals in the organization (Vroom and Jago, 1988). There must be a single goal structure, and everyone in the organization must accept it if the organization's goals are to be achieved. The concept of teamwork – of everyone working together – is a necessity for any organization.

Definitions of leadership and the three leadership functions

Having defined leadership, it is now logical for us to discuss the methods that one uses in the act of leadership. However, before we move to that topic, it will be useful to relate our two definitions of leadership – which really are essentially one – to the three functions of leadership discussed earlier.

In order to understand the leader's role, we need to go back to the distinction between managers and leaders. Every leader must perform some managerial functions, even though every manager cannot take a leadership role.

For example, in an effort to change organizational performance, many managers attempt to change the structure of their organizations. Currently, in an effort to reduce costs, many managers are attempting to reduce the number of hierarchical levels. Sometimes, the structure is changed by modifying the reporting relationship among units. The level at which decisions are made can also be changed. The organization can become more centralized or more decentralized with respect to decision making. Yet, changes in organizational structure alone are not likely to have any lasting impact on the organization's performance unless the structure affects the basic desire of participants to improve their performance.

The leader recognizes that it is necessary to focus the attention of participants on factors that will change performance. Thus, the leader makes changes in structure for their effect on attention focus, not because he or she believes that organizational structure alone can change the performance of participants. If the leader wishes to focus attention on costs, he or she looks at changes in the organization's structure that will encourage participants to allocate their attention to costs. Increased decentralization will often accomplish such a shift. The point is that leaders look at organizational tasks with a view to the impact that their actions will have on the attention focus of participants. Attention focus is central to the performance of the organizational function of leadership.

A similar statement can be made about the interpersonal function. The leader's role is to relate to the participants in ways that will affect their attention focus. The interpersonal function of leadership is sometimes viewed as one that holds the leader responsible for making everyone in the organization feel good. Friendliness and openness can be good for an organization if they help participants to focus their attention on the elements that the leader deems to be important. The interpersonal function is extremely important, but the leader must relate his or her actions in this area to the desired impact on attention focus. There is ample evidence that there is a low correlation between high morale and high productivity (Misumi, 1985).

The relation between the decisional function and attention focus is perhaps the most interesting of the three. Bavelas (1964, p. 206) defined leadership in terms of decision-making: 'leadership consists of the continuous choice-making process that permits the organization as a whole to proceed toward its objectives despite all sorts of internal and external perturbations.' More explicitly, he regards leadership as consisting of the reduction of uncertainty; this reduction is achieved by making choices.

This definition, which is close to the commonly accepted view of leadership, is quite different from those propounded here. My definitions focus on the leader's responsibility for modifying the behavior of participants in the organization. They assume that behavior is affected by the items to which individuals allocate their attention. The leader is able to capture the attention focus of participants. The leader gets participants to allocate attention to the items that he or she deems to be important. There is no question that the decisions that a leader makes are ways of making the priorities for attention clear. That is the aspect of decision making that in my view is part of leadership, not the fact that decision making reduces uncertainty. Nevertheless, it could be argued that influencing the allocation of attention tends to reduce uncertainty.

Studies of decision-making tend to show that decisions are rarely made by a single individual without regard to the views of the members of the organization. Leadership in an organization has to be less individualistic than it is in a combat situation where the leader may single-handedly eliminate a machine gun nest. Decision making in an organization must take into account the fact that members of the organization are interested in the direction that the organization takes. If the leader has captured the attention focus of the members, then it is possible to demonstrate 'the highest expressions of personal leadership' (Bavelas, 1964) and carry the organization along with those expressions.

Methods of leadership

If leadership is adequately encompassed by my definitions, we may ask how leadership is actually implemented in an organization. How does a person act in an organization when he or she plays a leadership role and wants to exert leadership?

There are at least three general approaches that are taken. They can be classified as communication, role modeling, and reward systems. I will discuss each of these approaches.

Communication

The first action that influences attention focus is oral interaction. These talks are ways of capturing the attention focus of participants. The ultimate aim is to change the behavior of people in the organization by influencing their focus. The underlying theory is that individuals' behavior is controlled by their attention focus. Put another way, the leader brings about the behavior that he or she desires by convincing participants to focus their attention on the ideas and actions that the leader considers important.

The interesting and difficult problem is that the methods of communication in organizations, are not well defined (March and Simon, 1958). In general, it is best to use a variety of communication channels. These channels can vary from one-on-one discussions to departmental meetings and meetings of the whole faculty and staff.

The leader also uses written communication. Again, different approaches must be found. Written communications can vary from personal letters to letters to the whole organization and formal reports. Even articles written for newspapers or other publications can be used to explicate the leader's desired priorities for the allocation of attention among participants.

Communication is perhaps the most important mechanism of leadership. The leader must have a clear understanding of the message that he or she is communicating, and he or she must be aware that the goal of communication is to influence the allocation of attention of the organization's members.

Role model

As a way of continuing to communicate with members of the organization, the leader must take into account the impact of his or her behavior on the attention focus of participants. The actions of the leader clearly represent the ideas that he or she considers to be important. If a university president is trying to emphasize research as an activity of importance, he or she should engage in research activity as well as emphasize research in the direct communications that he or she makes. Role modeling is a case in which actions speak as loudly as words.

The leader's activities are widely known among the members of any organization. Thus, the leader has ample opportunity to affect the attention focus of participants by demonstrating the factors that are important in his or her own behavior. In other words, role modelling is a form of communication. The leader's behavior exerts leadership whether the leader intends it or not.

Reward system

The reward system that the leader establishes is another way of reinforcing the attention focus of members. The relationship between particular rewards and performance is not well established. An organization cannot offer a specific monetary award and achieve a particular performance. However, a leader can use rewards to reinforce the priority system for attention allocation that he or she has established. The reward system can lead to both honor and money for recipients. The reward system is also a means of communicating the leader's priorities to participants. Obviously, a reward system cannot guarantee that performance in teaching will improve, but it can supplement the leader's effort to capture the attention focus of participants and allocate attention to areas that the leader considers important.

Conclusion

The theory of leadership just outlined is essentially a simple one. It assumes that participants in an organization behave in accordance with their focus attention. Behavior follows from the items on which they focus. From this perspective, leadership is the effort to capture the attention focus of the members of an organization. Three mechanisms help to perform the leadership function: communication between leader and participants, role modeling, and reward systems. The three mechanisms are alike in that all are ways of communicating the matters on which the leader wants members to focus their attention. There are other, related mechanisms. My list is not exhaustive. In all cases, the effort is to capture the attention focus of participants.

This conception of leadership might strike some as making the leader a manipulative person (Glassman, 1986). The key is that the leader must believe in what he or she is expressing. Mintzberg (1989) has put it exactly right: 'To my mind, key to the development of an organization idcology, in a new or existing organization, is a leadership with a genuine belief in mission and an honest dedication to the people who must carry it out.'

It is obvious, although I have not emphasized it, that a leader must have the ability and the knowledge needed to select the right items for the attention focus of participants (Mintzberg, 1982). That is, the items singled out for attention must enable the organization to attain its goals. The process of capturing the attention focus is also a dynamic one. The items on which the leader wishes participants to focus will change, and the leader must be perceptive enough to select the new items properly.

Although I have simplified the nature of leadership and the methods by which leadership can be exerted, I do not mean to imply that leadership is anything but complex. In any organization of significant size, the leader uses a system composed of many variables. To attend to the appropriate constituencies and focus their attention on the appropriate items requires thought, planning, energy, conviction, and an ability to persuade.

Strategy as order emerging from chaos

READING 9.2

By Ralph Stacey[1]

There are four important points to make on the recent discoveries about the complex behaviour of dynamic systems, all of which have direct application to human organizations.

Chaos is a form of instability where the specific long-term future is unknowable

Chaos in its scientific sense is an irregular pattern of behavior generated by well-defined nonlinear feedback rules commonly found in nature and human society. When systems driven by such rules operate away from equilibrium, they are highly sensitive to selected tiny changes in their environments, amplifying them into self-reinforcing virtuous and vicious circles that completely alter the behavior of the system. In other words, the system's future unfolds in a manner dependent upon the precise detail of what it does, what the systems constituting its environments do, and upon chance. As a result of this fundamental property of the system itself, specific links between cause and effect are lost in the history of its development, and the specific path of its long-term future development is completely unpredictable. Over the short term, however, it is possible to predict behavior because it takes time for the consequences of small changes to build up.

Is there evidence of chaos in business systems? We would conclude that there was if we could point to small changes escalating into large consequences; if we could point to self-reinforcing vicious and virtuous circles; if we could point to feedback that alternates between the amplifying and the damping. It is not difficult to find such evidence.

Creative managers seize on small differences in customer requirements and perceptions to build significant differentiators for their products. Customers may respond to this by switching from other product offerings, leading to a virtuous circle; or they may switch away, causing the kind of vicious circle that Coca-Cola found itself caught up in when it made that famous soft drink slightly sweeter.

Managers create, or at the very least shape, the requirements of their customers through the product offerings they make. Sony created a requirement for personal hi-fi systems through its Walkman offering, and manufacturers and operators have created requirements for portable telephones. Sony and Matsushita created the requirement for video recorders, and when companies supply information systems to their clients, they rarely do so according to a complete specification – instead, the supplier shapes the requirement. When managers intentionally shape customer demands through the offerings they make, this feeds back into customer responses, and managers may increase the impact by intentionally using the copying and spreading effects through which responses to product offerings feed back into other customers' responses. When managers do this, they are deliberately using positive feedback – along with negative feedback controls to meet cost and quality targets, for example – to create business success.

A successful business is also affected by many amplifying feedback processes that are outside the control of its managers and produce effects that they did not intend. Successful businesses are quite clearly characterized by feedback processes that flip between the negative and the positive, the damping and the amplifying; that is, they are characterized by feedback patterns that produce chaos. The long-term future of a creative organization is absolutely unknowable, and no one can intend its future direction over the long term or be in control of it. In such a system long-term plans and visions of future states can be only illusions.

But in chaos there are boundaries around the instability

While chaos means disorder and randomness in the behavior of a system at the specific level, it also means that there is a qualitative pattern at a general, overall level. The future unfolds unpredictably, but it always does so according to recognizable family-like resemblances. This is what we mean when we say that his-

[1]Source: This article was reprinted from *Long Range Planning*, Vol. 26, No. 1, R. Stacey, 'Strategy as Order Emerging from Chaos', pp. 23–29, © 1993. With permission from Elsevier.

tory repeats itself, but never in the same way. We see this combination of unpredictable specific behavior within an overall pattern in snowflakes. As two nearby snowflakes fall to the earth, they experience tiny differences in temperature and air impurities. Each snowflake amplifies those differences as they form, and by the time they reach the earth they have different shapes – but they are still clearly snowflakes. We cannot predict the shape of each snowflake, but we can predict that they will be snowflakes. In business, we recognize patterns of boom and recession, but each time they are different in specific terms, defying all attempts to predict them.

Chaos is unpredictable variety within recognizable categories defined by irregular features, that is, an inseparable intertwining of order and disorder. It is this property of being bounded by recognizable qualitative patterns that makes it possible for humans to cope with chaos. Numerous tests have shown that our memories do not normally store information in units representing the precise characteristics of the individual shapes or events we perceive. Instead, we store information about the strength of connection between individual units perceived. We combine information together into categories or concepts using family resemblance-type features. Memory emphasizes general structure, irregular category features, rather than specific content. We remember the irregular patterns rather than the specific features and we design our next actions on the basis of these memorized patterns. And since we design our actions in this manner, chaotic behavior presents us with no real problem. Furthermore, we are adept at using analogical reasoning and intuition to reflect upon experience and adapt it to new situations, all of which is ideally suited to handling chaos.

Unpredictable new order can emerge from chaos through a process of spontaneous self-organization

When nonlinear feedback systems in nature are pushed far from equilibrium into chaos, they are capable of creating a complex new order. For example, at some low temperature the atoms of a particular gas are arranged in a particular pattern and the gas emits no light. Then, as heat is applied, it agitates the atoms causing them to move, and as this movement is amplified through the gas it emits a dull glow. Small changes in heat are thus amplified, causing instability, or chaos,

that breaks the symmetry of the atoms' original behavior. Then at a critical point, the atoms in the gas suddenly all point in the same direction to produce a laser beam. Thus, the system uses chaos to shatter old patterns of behavior, creating the opportunity for the new. And as the system proceeds through chaos, it is confronted with critical points where it, so to speak, makes a choice between different options for further development. Some options represent yet further chaos and others lead to more complex forms of orderly behavior, but which will occur is inherently unpredictable. The choice itself is made by spontaneous self-organization amongst the components of the system in which they, in effect, communicate with each other, reach a consensus, and commit to a new form of behavior. If a more complex form of orderly behavior is reached, it has what scientists call a dissipative structure, because continual attention and energy must be applied if it is to be sustained – for example, heat has to be continually pumped into the gas if the laser beam is to continue. If the system is to develop further, then the dissipative structure must be short-lived; to reach an even more complex state, the system will have to pass through chaos once more.

It is striking how similar the process of dealing with strategic issues in an organization is to the self-organizing phenomenon just outlined. The key to the effectiveness with which organizations change and develop new strategic directions lies in the manner in which managers handle what might be called their strategic issue agenda. That agenda is a dynamic, unwritten list of issues, aspirations, and challenges that key groups of managers are attending to. Consider the steps managers can be observed to follow as they handle their strategic issue agenda:

- Detecting and selecting small disturbances. In open-ended strategic situations, change is typically the result of many small events and actions that are unclear, ambiguous, and confusing, with consequences that are unknowable. The key difficulty is to identify what the real issues, problems, or opportunities are, and the challenge is to find an appropriate and creative aspiration or objective. In these circumstances the organization has no alternative but to rely on the initiative of individuals to notice and pursue some issue, aspiration, or challenge. In order to do this, those individuals have to rely on their experience-based intuition and ability to detect analogies between one set of ambiguous circumstances and another.

- Amplifying the issues and building political support. Once some individual detects some potential issue, that individual begins to push for organizational attention to it. A complex political process of building special interest groups to support an issue is required before it gains organizational attention and can thus be said to be on the strategic issue agenda.

- Breaking symmetries. As they build and progress strategic issue agendas, managers are in effect altering old mental models, existing company and industry recipes, to come up with new ways of doing things. They are destroying existing perceptions and structures.

- Critical points and unpredictable outcomes. Some issues on the agenda may be dealt with quickly, while others may attract attention, continuous or periodic, for a very long time. How quickly an issue is dealt with depends upon the time required to reach enough consensus and commitment to proceed to action. At some critical point, an external or internal pressure in effect forces a choice. The outcome on whether and how to proceed to action over the issue is unpredictable because it depends upon the context of power, personality, and group dynamic within which it is being handled. The result may or may not be action, and action will usually be experimental at first.

- Changing the frame of reference. Managers in a business come to share memories of what worked and what did not work in the past – the organizational memory. In this way they build up a business philosophy, or culture, establishing a company recipe and in common with their rivals an industry recipe too. These recipes have a powerful effect on what issues will subsequently be detected and attended to; that is, they constitute a frame of reference within which managers interpret what to do next. The frame of reference has to be continually challenged and changed because it can easily become inappropriate to new circumstances. The dissipative structure of consensus and commitment is therefore necessarily short-lived if an organization is to be innovative.

These phases constitute a political and learning process through which managers deal with strategic issues, and the key point about these processes is that they are spontaneous and self-organizing: no central authority can direct anyone to detect and select an open-ended issue for attention, simply because no one knows what it is until someone has detected it; no one can centrally organize the factions that form around specific issues; nor can anyone intend the destruction of old recipes and the substitution of new ones since it is impossible to know what the appropriate new ones are until they are discovered. The development of new strategic direction requires the chaos of contention and conflict, and the self-organizing processes of political interaction and complex learning.

Chaos is a fundamental property of nonlinear feedback systems, a category that includes human organizations

Feedback simply means that one action or event feeds into another; that is, one action or event determines the next according to some relationship. For example, one firm repackages its product and its rival responds in some way, leading to a further action on the part of the first, provoking in turn yet another response from the second, and so on. The feedback relationship may be linear, or proportional, and when this is the case, the first firm will repackage its product and the second will respond by doing much the same. The feedback relationship could be nonlinear, or nonproportional, however, so that when the first firm repackages its product, the second introduces a new product at a lower price; this could lead the first to cut prices even further, so touching off a price war. In other words, nonlinear systems are those that use amplifying (positive) feedback in some way. To see the significance of positive feedback, compare it with negative feedback.

All effective businesses use negative or damping feedback systems to control and regulate their day-to-day activities. Managers fix short-term targets for profits and then prepare annual plans or budgets, setting out the time path to reach the target. As the business moves through time, outcomes are measured and compared with annual plan projections to yield variances. Frequent monitoring of those variances prompts corrective action to bring performance indicators back onto their planned paths; that is, variances feed back into corrective action and the feedback takes a negative form, so that when profit is below target, for example, offsetting action is taken to restore it. Scheduling, budgetary, and planning systems utilize negative feedback to keep an organization close to a predictable, stable equilibrium path in which it is adapted to its environment. While negative feedback controls a system according to prior intention, positive feedback produces explosively unstable equilibrium where changes are amplified, eventually putting intolerable pressure on the system until it runs out of control.

The key discovery about the operation of nonlinear feedback systems, however, is that there is a third choice. When a nonlinear feedback system is driven away from stable equilibrium toward explosive unstable equilibrium, it passes through a phase of bounded instability – there is a border between stability and instability where feedback flips autonomously between the amplifying and the damping to produce chaotic behavior; a paradoxical state that combines both stability and instability.

All human interactions take the form of feedback loops simply because the consequences of one action always feed back to affect a subsequent one. Furthermore, all human interactions constitute nonlinear feedback loops because people under- and over-react. Since organizations are simply a vast web of feedback loops between people, they must be capable of chaotic, as well as stable and explosively unstable, behavior. The key question is which of these kinds of behaviors leads an organization to success. We can see the answer to this question if we reflect upon the fundamental forces operating on an organization.

All organizations are powerfully pulled in two fundamentally different directions:

- Disintegration. Organizations can become more efficient and effective if they divide tasks, segment markets, appeal to individual motivators, empower people, promote informal communication, and separate production processes in geographic and other terms. These steps lead to fragmenting cultures and dispersed power that pull an organization toward disintegration, a phenomenon that can be seen in practice as companies split into more and more business units and find it harder and harder to maintain control.

- Ossification. To avoid this pull to disintegration, and to reap the advantages of synergy and coordination, all organizations are also pulled to a state in which tasks are integrated, overlaps in market segments and production processes managed, group goals stressed above individual ones, power concentrated, communication and procedures formalized, and strongly shared cultures established. As an organization moves in this direction it develops more and more rigid structures, rules, procedures, and systems until it eventually ossifies, consequences that are easy to observe as organizations centralize.

Thus, one powerful set of forces pulls every organization toward a stable equilibrium (ossification) and another powerful set of forces pulls it toward an explosively unstable equilibrium (disintegration). Success lies at the border between these states, where managers continually alter systems and structures to avoid attraction either to disintegration or to ossification. For example, organizations typically swing to centralization in one period, to decentralization in another, and back again later on. Success clearly lies in a nonequilibrium state between stable and unstable equilibria; and for a nonlinear feedback system, that is chaos.

Eight steps to create order out of chaos

When managers believe that they must pull together harmoniously in pursuit of a shared organizational intention established before they act, they are inevitably confined to the predictable – existing strategic directions will simply be continued or innovations made by others will simply be imitated. When, instead of this, managers create the chaos that flows from challenging existing perceptions and promote the conditions in which spontaneous self-organization can occur, they make it possible for innovation and new strategic direction to emerge. Managers create such conditions when they undertake actions of the following kind.

Develop new perspectives on the meaning of control

The activity of learning in a group is a form of control that managers do not normally recognize as such. It is a self-organizing, self-policing form of control in which the group itself discovers intention and exercises control. Furthermore, we are all perfectly accustomed to the idea that the strategic direction of local communities, nation-states, and international communities is developed and controlled through the operation of political sytems, but we rarely apply this notion to organizations. When we do, we see that a sequence of choices and actions will continue in a particular direction only while those espousing that direction continue to enjoy sufficient support. This constitutes a form of control that is as applicable to an organization when it faces the conflicts around open-ended change, as it is to a nation. The lesson is that self-organizing processes can produce controlled behavior even though no one is in control – sometimes the best thing a manager can do is to let go and allow things to happen.

Design the use of power

The distribution of power and the way in which it is used provide very important boundaries around the group learning process from which new strategic directions emerge. The application of power in particular forms has fairly predictable consequences for group dynamics. Where power is applied as force and consented to out of fear, the group dynamic will be one of submission, or where such power is not consented to, the group dynamic will be one of rebellion, either covert or overt. Power may be applied as authority, and the predictable group dynamic here is one in which members of the group suspend their critical faculties and accept instructions from those above them. Groups in states of submission, rebellion, or conformity are incapable of complex learning, that is, the development of new perspectives and new mental models.

The kind of group dynamics that are conducive to complex learning occur when highly competitive win/lose polarization is removed, and open questioning and public testing of assertions encouraged. When this happens, people use argument and conflict to move toward periodic consensus and commitment to a particular issue. That consensus and commitment cannot, however, be the norm when people are searching for new perspectives – rather, they must alternate between conflict and consensus, between confusion and clarity. This kind of dynamic is likely to occur when they most powerfully alternate the form in which they use their power: sometimes withdrawing and allowing conflict; sometimes intervening with suggestions; sometimes exerting authority.

Encourage self-organizing groups

A group will be self-organizing only if it discovers its own challenges, goals, and objectives. Mostly, such groups need to form spontaneously – the role of top managers is simply to create the atmosphere in which this can happen. When top managers do set up a group to deal with strategic issues, however, they must avoid the temptation to write terms of reference, set objectives, or prod the group to reach some predetermined view. Instead top managers must present ambiguous challenges and take the chance that the group may produce proposals they do not approve of. For a group of managers to be self-organizing, it has to be free to operate as its members jointly choose, within the

boundaries provided by their work together. This means that when they work together in this way, the normal hierarchy must be suspended for most of the time. Members are there because of the contributions they are able to make and the influence they can exert through those contributions and their own personalities. This suspension of the normal hierarchy can take place only if those on higher levels behave in a manner that indicates that they attach little importance to their position for the duration of the work of the group.

Provoke multiple cultures

One way of developing the conflicting countercultures required to provoke new perspectives is to rotate people between functions and business units. The motive here is to create cultural diversity as opposed to the current practice of using rotation to build a cadre of managers with the same management philosophy. Another effective way of promoting countercultures is that practiced by Canon and Honda, where significant numbers of managers are hired at the same time, midway through their careers in other organizations, to create sizeable pockets of different cultures that conflict with the predominant one.

Present ambiguous challenges instead of clear long-term objectives or visions

Agendas of strategic issues evolve out of the clash between different cultures in self-organizing groups. Top managers can provoke this activity by setting ambiguous challenges and presenting half-formed issues for others to develop, instead of trying to set clear long-term objectives. Problems without objectives should be intentionally posed to provoke the emotion and conflict that lead to active search for new ways of doing things. This activity of presenting challenges should also be a two-way one, where top executives hold themselves open to challenge from subordinates.

Expose the business to challenging situations

Managers who avoid taking chances face the certainty of stagnation and therefore the high probability of collapse in the long term, simply because innovation depends significantly on chance. Running for cover because the future is unknowable is in the long run the riskiest response of all. Instead, managers must intentionally expose themselves to the most challenging of situations. In his study of international companies, Michael Porter concludes that those who position themselves to serve the world's most sophisticated and demanding customers, who seek the challenge of competing with the most imaginative and competent competitors, are the ones who build sustainable competitive advantage on a global scale.

Devote explicit attention to improving group learning skills

New strategic directions emerge when groups of managers learn together in the sense of questioning deeply held beliefs and altering existing mental models rather than simply absorbing existing bodies of knowledge and sets of techniques. Such a learning process may well be personally threatening and so arouse anxiety that leads to bizarre group dynamics – this is perhaps the major obstacle to effective organizational learning. To overcome it, managers must spend time explicitly exploring how they interact and learn together – the route to superior learning is self-reflection in groups.

Create resource slack

New strategic directions emerge when the attitudes and behavior of managers create an atmosphere favourable to individual initiative and intuition, to political inter-

action, and to learning in groups. Learning and political interaction are hard work, and they cannot occur without investment in spare management resources. A vital precondition for emergent strategy is thus investment in management resources to allow it to happen.

Conclusion

Practicing managers and academics have been debating the merits of organizational learning as opposed to the planning conceptualization of strategic management. That debate has not, however, focused clearly on the critical unquestioned assumptions upon which the planning approach is based, namely, the nature of causality. Recent discoveries about the nature of dynamic feedback systems make it clear that cause and effect links disappear in innovative human organizations, making it impossible to envision or plan their long-term futures. Because of this lack of causal connection between specific actions and specific outcomes, new strategic directions can only emerge through a spontaneous, self-organizing political and learning process. The planning approach can be seen as a specific approach applicable to the short-term management of an organization's existing activities, a task as vital as the development of a new strategic direction.

READING **9.3**

Building learning organizations
By Peter Senge[1]

Human beings are designed for learning. No one has to teach an infant to walk, or talk, or master the spatial relationships needed to stack eight building blocks that don't topple. Children come fully equipped with an insatiable drive to explore and experiment. Unfortunately, the primary institutions of our society are oriented predominantly toward controlling rather than learning, rewarding individuals for performing for others rather than for cultivating their natural curiosity

and impulse to learn. The young child entering school discovers quickly that the name of the game is getting the right answer and avoiding mistakes – a mandate no less compelling to the aspiring manager.

'Our prevailing system of management has destroyed our people,' writes W. Edwards Deming, leader in the quality movement. 'People are born with intrinsic motivation, self-esteem, dignity, curiosity to learn, joy in learning. The forces of destruction begin

[1]Source: This article was reprinted from 'The Leader's New Work: Building Learning Organizations', *Sloan Management Review*, Fall, 1990. Reproduced by permission.

with toddlers – a prize for the best Halloween costume, grades in school, gold stars, and on up through university. On the job, people, teams, divisions are ranked – reward for the one at the top, punishment at the bottom. Management by Objectives (MBO), quotas, incentive pay, business plans, put together separately, division by division, cause further loss, unknown and unknowable.'

Ironically, by focusing on performing for someone else's approval, corporations create the very conditions that predestine them to mediocre performance. Over the long run, superior performance depends on superior learning.

If anything, the need for understanding how organizations learn and accelerating that learning is greater today than ever before. The old days when a Henry Ford, Alfred Sloan, or Tom Watson learned for the organization are gone. In an increasingly dynamic, interdependent, and unpredictable world, it is simply no longer possible for anyone to 'figure it all out at the top.' The old model, 'the top thinks and the local acts,' must now give way to integrating thinking and acting at all levels. While the challenge is great, so is the potential payoff.

Adaptive learning and generative learning

The prevailing view of learning organizations emphasizes increased adaptability. Given the accelerating pace of change, or so the standard view goes, 'the most successful corporation of the 1990s,' according to *Fortune* magazine, 'will be something called a learning organization, a consummately adaptive enterprise.'

But increasing adaptiveness is only the first stage in moving toward learning organizations. The impulse to learn in children goes deeper than desires to respond and adapt more effectively to environmental change. The impulse to learn, at its heart, is an impulse to be generative, to expand our capability. This is why leading corporations are focusing on *generative* learning, which is about creating, as well as *adaptive* learning, which is about coping.

The total quality movement in Japan illustrates the evolution from adaptive to generative learning. With its emphasis on continuous experimentation and feedback, the total quality movement has been the first wave in building learning organizations. But Japanese firms' view of serving the customer has evolved. In the early years of total quality, the focus was on 'fitness to standard,' making a product reliably so that it would do what its designers intended it to do and

what the firm told its customers it would do. Then came a focus on 'fitness to need,' understanding better what the customer wanted and then providing products that reliably met those needs. Today, leading-edge firms seek to understand and meet the 'latent need' of the customer – what customers might truly value but have never experienced or would never think to ask for.

Generative learning, unlike adaptive learning, requires new ways of looking at the world, whether in understanding customers or in understanding how to better manage a business. For years, US manufacturers sought competitive advantage in aggressive controls on inventories, incentives against overproduction, and rigid adherence to production forecasts. Despite these incentives, their performance was eventually eclipsed by Japanese firms who saw the challenges of manufacturing differently. They realized that eliminating delays in the production process was the key to reducing instability and improving cost, productivity, and service. They worked to build networks of relationships with trusted suppliers and to redesign physical production processes to reduce delays in materials procurement, production setup, and in-process inventory – a much higher-leverage approach to improving both cost and customer loyalty.

As Boston Consulting Group's George Stalk has observed (Stalk, Evans and Shulman, 1992), the Japanese saw the significance of delays because they saw the process of order entry, production scheduling, materials procurement, production, and distribution as an integrated system. 'What distorts the system so badly is time,' observes Stalk – the multiple delays between events and responses. 'These distortions reverberate throughout the system, producing disruptions, waste, and inefficiency.' Generative learning requires seeing the systems that control events. When we fail to grasp the systemic source of problems, we are left to 'push on' symptoms rather than eliminate underlying causes. The best we can ever do is adaptive learning.

The leader's new work

Our traditional view of leaders – as special people who set the direction, make the key decisions, and energize the troops – is deeply rooted in an individualistic and nonsystemic worldview. Especially in the West, leaders are heroes – great men (and occasionally women) who rise to the fore in times of crisis. So long as such myths prevail, they reinforce a focus on short-term events and charismatic heroes rather than on systemic forces and collective learning.

Leadership in learning organizations centers on subtler and ultimately more important work. In a learning organization, leaders' roles differ dramatically from that of the charismatic decision maker. Leaders are designers, teachers, and stewards. These roles require new skills: the ability to build shared vision, to bring to the surface and challenge prevailing mental models, and to foster more systemic patterns of thinking. In short, leaders in learning organizations are responsible for building organizations where people are continually expanding their capabilities to shape their future – that is, leaders are responsible for learning.

Creative tension: The integrating principle

Leadership in a learning organization starts with the principle of creative tension. Creative tension comes from seeing clearly where we want to be, our 'vision,' and telling the truth about where we are, our 'current reality.' The gap between the two generates a natural tension.

Creative tension can be resolved in two basic ways: by raising current reality toward the vision, or by lowering the vision toward current reality. Individuals, groups, and organizations who learn how to work with creative tension learn how to use the energy it generates to move reality more reliably toward their visions.

Without vision there is no creative tension. Creative tension cannot be generated from current reality alone. All the analysis in the world will never generate a vision. Many who are otherwise qualified to lead fail to do so because they try to substitute analysis for vision. They believe that, if only people understood current reality, they would surely feel the motivation to change. They are then disappointed to discover that people resist the personal and organizational changes that must be made to alter reality. What they never grasp is that the natural energy for changing reality comes from holding a picture of what might be that is more important to people than what is.

But creative tension cannot be generated from vision alone; it demands an accurate picture of current reality as well. Vision without an understanding of current reality will more likely foster cynicism than creativity. The principle of creative tension teaches that *an accurate picture of current reality is just as important as a compelling picture of a desired future*.

Leading through creative tension is different from solving problems. In problem solving, the energy for change comes from attempting to get away from an aspect of current reality that is undesirable. With creative tension, the energy for change comes from the vision, from what we want to create, juxtaposed with current reality. While the distinction may seem small, the consequences are not. Many people and organizations find themselves motivated to change only when their problems are bad enough to cause them to change. This works for a while, but the change process runs out of steam as soon as the problems driving the change become less pressing. With problem solving, the motivation for change is extrinsic. With creative tension, the motivation is intrinsic. The distinction mirrors the distinction between adaptive and generative learning.

New roles

The traditional authoritarian image of the leader as 'the boss calling the shots' has been recognized as oversimplified and inadequate for some time. According to Edgar Schein (1985), 'Leadership is intertwined with culture formation.' Building an organization's culture and shaping its evolution is the 'unique and essential function' of leadership. In a learning organization, the critical roles of leadership – designer, teacher, and steward – have antecedents in the ways leaders have contributed to building organizations in the past. But each role takes on new meaning in the learning organization and, as will be seen in the following sections, demands new skills and tools.

Leader as designer

The functions of design, or what some have called social architecture, are rarely visible; they take place behind the scenes. The consequences that appear today are the result of work done long in the past, and work today will show its benefits far in the future. Those who aspire to lead out of a desire to control, or gain fame, or simply to be at the center of the action will find little to attract them to the quiet design work of leadership.

But what, specifically, is involved in organizational design? 'Organization design is widely misconstrued as moving around boxes and lines,' says Hanover's O'Brien. 'The first task of organization design concerns designing the governing ideas of purpose, vision, and core values by which people will live.' Few acts of leadership have a more enduring impact on an organization than building a foundation of purpose and core values.

If governing ideas constitute the first design task of leadership, the second design task involves the policies, strategies, and structures that translate guiding ideas into business decisions. Leadership theorist Philip Selznick calls policy and structure the 'institutional embodiment of purpose.' 'Policy making (the rules that guide decisions) ought to be separated from decision making,' says Jay Forrester. 'Otherwise, short-term pressures will usurp time from policy creation.'

Traditionally, writers like Selznick and Forrester have tended to see policy making and implementation as the work of a small number of senior managers. But that view is changing. Both the dynamic business environment and the mandate of the learning organization to engage people at all levels now make it clear that this second design task is more subtle. Henry Mintzberg has argued that strategy is less a rational plan arrived at in the abstract and implemented throughout the organization than an 'emergent phenomenon.' Successful organizations 'craft strategy' according to Mintzberg, as they continually learn about shifting business conditions and balance what is desired and what is possible. The key is not getting the right strategy but fostering strategic thinking.

Behind appropriate policies, strategies, and structures are effective learning processes; their creation is the third key design responsibility in learning organizations. This does not absolve senior managers of their strategic responsibilities. Actually, it deepens and extends those responsibilities. Now they are not only responsible for ensuring that an organization has well-developed strategies and policies but also for ensuring that processes exist whereby these are continually improved.

In the early 1970s, Shell was the weakest of the big seven oil companies. Today, Shell and Exxon are arguably the strongest, both in size and financial health. Shell's ascendance began with frustration. Around 1971 members of Shell's Group Planning in London began to foresee dramatic change and unpredictability in world oil markets. However, it proved impossible to persuade managers that the stable world of steady growth in oil demand and supply they had known for 20 years was about to change. Despite brilliant analysis and artful presentation, Shell's planners realized, in the words of Pierre Wack (1985), that they 'had failed to change behavior in much of the Shell organization.' Progress would probably have ended there, had the frustration not given way to a radically new view of corporate planning.

As they pondered this failure, the planners' view of their basic task shifted: 'We no longer saw our task as producing a documented view of the future business environment five or ten years ahead. Our real target was the microcosm (the 'mental model') of our decision makers.' Only when the planners reconceptualized their basic task as fostering learning rather than devising plans did their insights begin to have an impact. The initial tool used was 'scenario analysis,' through which planners encouraged operating managers to think through how they would manage in the future under different possible scenarios. It mattered not that the managers believed the planners' scenarios absolutely, only that they became engaged in ferreting out the implications. In this way, Shell's planners conditioned managers to be mentally prepared for a shift from low prices to high prices and from stability to instability. The results were significant. When the Organisation of Petroleum Exporting Countries (OPEC) became a reality, Shell quickly responded by increasing local operating company control (to enhance maneuverability in the new political environment), building buffer stocks, and accelerating development of non-OPEC sources – actions that its competitors took much more slowly or not at all.

Somewhat inadvertently, Shell planners had discovered the leverage of designing institutional learning processes whereby, in the words of former planning director De Geus, 'Management teams change their shared mental models of their company, their markets, and their competitors.' Since then, 'planning as learning' has become a byword at Shell, and Group Planning has continually sought out new learning tools that can be integrated into the planning process. Some of these are described below.

Leader as teacher

Leader as teacher does *not* mean leader as authoritarian expert whose job it is to teach people the 'correct' view of reality. Rather, it is about helping everyone in the organization, oneself included, to gain more insightful views of current reality. This is in line with a popular emerging view of leaders as coaches, guides, or facilitators. In learning organizations, this teaching role is developed further by virtue of explicit attention to people's mental models and by the influence of the systems perspective.

The role of leader as teacher starts with bringing to the surface people's mental models of important issues. No one carries an organization, a market, or a state of technology in his or her head. What we carry in our heads are assumptions. These mental pictures of how the world works have a significant influence on how we perceive problems and opportunities, identify courses of action, and make choices.

One reason that mental models are so deeply entrenched is that they are largely tacit. Ian Mitroff, in his study of General Motors, argues that an assumption that prevailed for years was that, in the United States, 'Cars are status symbols. Styling is therefore more important than quality.' The Detroit automakers didn't say, 'We have a *mental model* that all people care about is styling.' Few actual managers would even say publicly that all people care about is styling. So long as the view remained unexpressed, there was little possibility of challenging its validity or forming more accurate assumptions.

But working with mental models goes beyond revealing hidden assumptions. Reality, as perceived by most people in most organizations, means pressures that must be borne, crises that must be reacted to, and limitations that must be accepted. Leaders as teachers help people *restructure their views of reality* to see beyond the superficial conditions and events into the underlying causes of problems and therefore to see new possibilities for shaping the future.

Specifically, leaders can influence people to view reality at three distinct levels: events, patterns of behavior, and systemic structure.

Systemic Structure (Generative)
↓
Patterns of Behavior (Responsive)
↓
Events (Reactive)

The key question becomes 'Where do leaders predominantly focus their own and their organization's attention?'

Contemporary society focuses predominantly on events. The media reinforces this perspective, with almost exclusive attention to short-term, dramatic events. This focus leads naturally to explaining what happens in terms of those events: 'The Dow Jones average went up 16 points because high fourth-quarter profits were announced yesterday.'

Pattern-of-behavior explanations are rarer in contemporary culture than event explanations, but they do occur. Trend analysis is an example of seeing patterns of behavior. A good editorial that interprets a set of current events in the context of long-term historical changes is another example. Systemic, structural explanations go even further by addressing the question 'What causes the patterns of behavior?'

In some sense, all three levels of explanation are equally true. But their usefulness is quite different.

Event explanations – who did what to whom – doom their holders to a reactive stance toward change. Pattern-of-behavior explanations focus on identifying long-term trends and assessing their implications. They at least suggest how, over time, we can respond to shifting conditions. Structural explanations are the most powerful. Only they address the underlying causes of behavior at a level such that patterns of behavior can be changed.

By and large, leaders of our current institutions focus their attention on events and patterns of behavior, and under their influence, their organizations do likewise. That is why contemporary organizations are predominantly reactive, or at best responsive – rarely generative. On the other hand, leaders in learning organizations pay attention to all three levels, but focus especially on systemic structure; largely by example, they teach people throughout the organization to do likewise.

Leader as steward

This is the subtlest role of leadership. Unlike the roles of designer and teacher, it is almost solely a matter of attitude. It is an attitude critical to learning organizations.

While stewardship has long been recognized as an aspect of leadership, its source is still not widely understood. I believe Robert Greenleaf (1977) came closest to explaining real stewardship, in his seminal book *Servant Leadership*. There, Greenleaf argues that 'the servant leader *is* servant first. . . . It begins with the natural feeling that one wants to seve, to serve *first*. This conscious choice brings one to aspire to lead. That person is sharply different from one who is leader first, perhaps because of the need to assuage an unusual power drive or to acquire material possessions.'

Leaders' sense of stewardship operates on two levels: stewardship for the people they lead and stewardship for the larger purpose or mission that underlies the enterprise. The first type arises from a keen appreciation of the impact one's leadership can have on others. People can suffer economically, emotionally, and spiritually under inept leadership. If anything, people in a learning organization are more vulnerable because of their commitment and sense of shared ownership. Appreciating this naturally instills a sense of responsibility in leaders. The second type of stewardship arises from a leader's sense of personal purpose and commitment to the organization's larger mission. People's natural impulse to learn is unleashed when they are engaged in an endeavor they consider worthy of their fullest commitment. Or, as Lawrence Miller puts it, 'Achieving return on equity does not, as a goal, mobilize the most noble forces of our soul.'

New skills

New leadership roles require new leadership skills. These skills can only be developed, in my judgment, through a lifelong commitment. It is not enough for one or two individuals to develop these skills. They must be distributed widely throughout the organization. This is one reason that understanding the disciplines of a learning organization is so important. These disciplines embody the principles and practices that can widely foster leadership development.

Three critical areas of skills (disciplines) are building shared vision, surfacing and challenging mental models, and engaging in systems thinking.

Building shared vision

The skills involved in building shared vision include the following:

- Encouraging personal vision. Shared visions emerge from personal visions. It is not that people only care about their own self-interest – in fact, people's values usually include dimensions that concern family, organization, community, and even the world. Rather, it is that people's capacity for caring is personal.

- Communicating and asking for support. Leaders must be willing to continually share their own vision, rather than being the official representative of the corporate vision. They also must be prepared to ask, 'Is this vision worthy of your commitment?' This can be difficult for a person used to setting goals and presuming compliance.

- Visioning as an ongoing process. Building shared vision is a never-ending process. At any one point there will be a particular image of the future that is predominant, but that image will evolve. Today, too many managers want to dispense with the 'vision business' by going off and writing the Official Vision Statement. Such statements almost always lack the vitality, freshness, and excitement of a genuine vision that comes from people asking, 'What do we really want to achieve?'

- Blending extrinsic and intrinsic visions. Many energizing visions are extrinsic – that is, they focus on achieving something relative to an outsider, such as a competitor. But a goal that is limited to defeating an opponent can, once the vision is achieved, easily become a defensive posture. In contrast, intrinsic goals like creating a new type of product, taking an established product to a new level, or setting a new standard for customer satisfaction can call forth a new level of creativity and innovation. Intrinsic and extrinsic visions need to coexist; a vision solely predicated on defeating an adversary will eventually weaken an organization.

- Distinguishing positive from negative visions. Many organizations only truly pull together when their survival is threatened. Similarly, most social movements aim at eliminating what people don't want: for example, antidrug, antismoking, or antinuclear arms movements. Negative visions carry a subtle message of powerlessness: people will only pull together when there is sufficient threat. Negative visions also tend to be short term. Two fundamental sources of energy can motivate organizations: fear and aspiration. Fear, the energy source behind negative visions, can produce extraordinary changes in short periods, but aspiration endures as a continuing source of learning and growth.

Surfacing and testing mental models

Many of the best ideas in organizations never get put into practice. One reason is that new insights and initiatives often conflict with established mental models. The leadership task of challenging assumptions without invoking defensiveness requires reflection and inquiry skills possessed by few leaders in traditional controlling organizations.

- Seeing leaps of abstraction. Our minds literally move at lightning speed. Ironically, this often slows our learning, because we leap to generalizations so quickly that we never think to test them. We then confuse our generalizations with the observable data upon which they are based, treating the generalizations as if they were data.

- Balancing inquiry and advocacy. Most managers are skilled at articulating their views and presenting them persuasively. While important, advocacy skills can become counterproductive as managers rise in responsibility and confront increasingly complex issues that require collaborative learning among different, equally knowledgeable people. Leaders in learning organizations need to have both inquiry and advocacy skills.

- Distinguishing espoused theory from theory in use. We all like to think that we hold certain views, but often our actions reveal deeper views. For example, I may proclaim that people are trustworthy, but never lend friends money and jealously guard my possessions. Obviously, my deeper mental model (my theory in use), differs from my espoused theory. Recognizing gaps between espoused views and theories in use (which often requires the help of others) can be pivotal to deeper learning.

- Recognizing and defusing defensive routines. As one CEO (chief executive officer) in our research program puts it, 'Nobody ever talks about an issue at the eight o'clock business meeting exactly the same way they talk about it at home that evening or over drinks at the end of the day.' The reason is what Chris Argyris calls defensive routines, entrenched habits used to protect ourselves from the embarrassment and threat that come with exposing our thinking. For most of us, such defenses began to build early in life in response to pressures to have the right answers in school or at home. Organizations add new levels of performance anxiety and thereby amplify and exacerbate this defensiveness. Ironically, this makes it even more difficult to expose hidden mental models, and thereby lessens learning. The first challenge is to recognize defensive routines, then to inquire into their operation. Those who are best at revealing and defusing defensive routines operate with a high degree of self-disclosure regarding their own defensiveness.

Systems thinking

We all know that leaders should help people see the big picture. But the actual skills whereby leaders are supposed to achieve this are not well understood. In my experience, successful leaders often are 'systems thinkers' to a considerable extent. They focus less on day-to-day events and more on underlying trends and forces of change. But they do this almost completely intuitively. The consequence is that they are often unable to explain their intuitions to others and feel frustrated that others cannot see the world the way they do.

One of the most significant developments in management science today is the gradual coalescence of managerial systems thinking as a field of study and practice. This field suggests some key skills for future leaders:

- Seeing interrelationships, not things, and processes, not snapshots. Most of us have been conditioned throughout our lives to focus on things and to see the world in static images. This leads us to linear explanations of systemic phenomenon.

- Moving beyond blame. We tend to blame each other or outside circumstances for our problems. But it is poorly designed systems, not incompetent or unmotivated individuals, that cause most organizational problems. Systems thinking shows us that there is no outside – that you and the cause of your problems are part of a single system.

- Distinguishing detail complexity from dynamic complexity. Some types of complexity are more important strategically than others. Detail complexity arises when there are many variables. Dynamic complexity arises when cause and effect are distant in time and space, and when the consequences over time of interventions are subtle and not obvious to many participants in the system. The leverage in most management situations lies in understanding dynamic complexity, not detail complexity.

- Focusing on areas of high leverage. Some have called systems thinking the 'new dismal science' because it teaches that most obvious solutions don't work – at best, they improve matters in the short run, only to make things worse in the long run. But there is another side to the story. Systems thinking also shows that small, well-focused actions can produce significant, enduring improvements, if they are in the right place. Systems thinkers refer to this idea as the principle of leverage. Tackling a difficult problem is often a matter of seeing where the high leverage lies, where a change – with a minimum of effort – would lead to lasting, significant improvement.

- Avoiding symptomatic solutions. The pressures to intervene in management systems that are going awry can be overwhelming. Unfortunately, given the linear thinking that predominates in most organizations, interventions usually focus on symptomatic fixes, not underlying causes. This results in only temporary relief, and it tends to create still more pressures later on for further, low-leverage intervention. If leaders acquiesce to these pressures, they can be sucked into an endless spiral of increasing intervention. Sometimes the most difficult leadership acts are to refrain from intervening through popular quick fixes and to keep the pressure on everyone to identify more enduring solutions.

The consequences of leaders who lack systems-thinking skills can be devastating. Many charismatic leaders manage almost exclusively at the level of events. They deal in visions and in crises, and little in-between. Under their leadership, an organization hurtles from crisis to crisis. Eventually, the worldview of people in the organization becomes dominated by events and reactiveness. Many, especially those who are deeply committed, become burned out. Eventually, cynicism comes to pervade the organization. People have no control over their time, let alone their destiny.

Similar problems arise with the 'visionary strategist,' the leader with vision who sees both patterns of change and events. This leader is better prepared to manage change. He or she can explain strategies in terms of emerging trends, and thereby foster a climate that is less reactive. But such leaders still impart a responsive orientation rather than a generative one.

Many talented leaders have rich, highly systemic intuitions but cannot explain those intuitions to others. Ironically, they often end up being authoritarian leaders, even if they don't want to, because only they see the decisions that need to be made. They are unable to conceptualize their strategic insights so that these can become public knowledge, open to challenge and further improvement.

Developing leaders and learning organizations

In a recently published retrospective on organization development in the 1980s, Marshall Sashkin and N. Warner Burke observe the return of an emphasis on developing leaders who can develop organizations. They also note Schein's critique that most top executives are not qualified for the task of developing culture. Learning organizations represent a potentially significant evolution of organizational culture. So it should come as no surprise that such organizations will remain a distant vision until the leadership capabilities they demand are developed. 'The 1990s may be the period,' suggest Sashkin and Burke, 'during which organization development and (a new sort of) management development are reconnected.'

I believe that this new sort of management development will focus on the roles, skills, and tools for leadership in learning organizations. Undoubtedly, the ideas offered above are only a rough approximation of this new territory. The sooner we begin seriously exploring the territory, the sooner the initial map can be improved – and the sooner we will realize an age-old vision of leadership:

The wicked leader is he who the people despise.
The good leader is he who the people revere.
The great leader is he who the people say, 'We did it ourselves.'
(Lao Tsu)

READING 9.4 The knowing-doing gap

By Jeffrey Pfeffer and Robert I. Sutton[1]

Why do so much education and training, management consulting, and business research and so many books and articles produce so little change in what managers and organizations actually do? In 1996, more than 1,700 business books were published in the United States, and more are published each year. Many of these books are filled with the same analyses and prescriptions, albeit using different language and graphics, as could be found in similar books published the year before. In fact, many of the ideas proclaimed as new each year can be found in similar books printed decades earlier. Yet these books find a ready market because the ideas, although often widely known and proven to be useful and valid, remain unimplemented. So, authors try, in part through repackaging and updating, to somehow get managers to not only *know* but to *do* something with what they know. And managers continue to buy the books filled with ideas they already know because they intuitively understand that knowing isn't enough. They hope that by somehow buying and reading one more book they will finally be able to translate this performance knowledge into organizational action.

Each year, more than $60 billion is spent on training in and by organizations, particularly management training. Much of this training, on subjects such as Total Quality Management (TQM), customer service and building customer loyalty, leadership, and organizational change is based on knowledge and principles that are fundamentally timeless – unchanged and unchanging. Nevertheless, the training often is repeated. Regardless of the quality of the content, the delivery, or the frequency of repetition, management education is often ineffective in changing organizational practices.

Professor Mark Zbaracki (1998) studied Total Quality Management training in five organizations in which senior executives believed that TQM methods could enhance the quality of their products and services and that the training had changed how people performed their jobs. Zbaracki found, however, that the quantitative TQM methods were not used *at all* in four of the organizations and only on a limited basis in the fifth. This result is not unique to TQM – we observed it repeatedly during our research.

Each year, billions of dollars are spent on management consultants by organizations seeking advice – one estimate for 1996 was $43 billion. But that advice is seldom implemented. One consultant, making a presentation to obtain work from a large U.S. bank, showed an overhead slide that had the recommendations from four previous consulting studies conducted in just the prior six years for that bank. All four studies had come to the same conclusions, which is not surprising given that smart people from four different firms looked at essentially the same data. The presenter, selling implementation and change rather than analytical services, asked the assembled executives, 'Why do you want to pay for the same answer a fifth time?' He and his firm got the job. As another example of knowing but not doing in the world of management consulting, two consultants from one of the leading firms worked on a project for a large electrical utility in Latin America that was facing deregulation. They were chagrined to discover that management already

had a four-year-old, 500-page document with extensive plans and recommendations produced by a different consulting firm in a previous engagement. They reported:

> *The old document was very good. It had benchmarking cost studies from best-practice utilities all around the world, summaries of the most successful training systems in other industrial companies, and pretty detailed implementation calendars. . . . As our analysis was based on the same . . . information that was given to the last consultants four years before . . . our recommendations were basically the same. The problem was not analysis. It was implementation. Although we could identify some new areas for improvement, the core was almost a copy of the old document. . . . The client already had the basic information we were giving them.*

Each year the hundreds of business schools in the United States graduate more than 80,000 MBAs and conduct numerous research studies on business topics. Business education and research are growing in scope and prominence in countries around the world. Yet the translation of this research and management education into practice proceeds slowly and fitfully. There is little evidence that being staffed with people who have an advanced education in business is consistently related to outstanding organizational performance. Many top-performing firms – Southwest Airlines, Wal-Mart, The Men's Wearhouse, Service-Master, PSS/World Medical, SAS Institute, AES, Whole Foods Market, and Starbucks – don't recruit at the leading business schools and don't emphasize business degree credentials in their staffing practices. Numerous researchers have found that 'little of what is taught in college or even business schools really prepares would-be managers for the realities of managing.' One study reported that 73 percent of the surveyed MBA program graduates said 'that their MBA skills were used "only marginally or not at all" in their first managerial assignments.'

Did you ever wonder why so much education and training, management consultation, organizational research, and so many books and articles produce so few changes in actual management practice? Did you ever wonder why the little change that does occur often happens with such great difficulty? Why is it that, at the end of so many books and seminars, leaders report being enlightened and wiser, but not much happens in their organizations?

Implementation or ignorance: Does a knowing doing gap really exist?

How do we know that knowledge isn't always implemented and that this is a problem affecting organizational performance? And perhaps even more important, how can organizations discover to what degree they are not actually doing what they think they should? These are important, but relatively straightforward, issues.

Evidence of knowing-doing gaps

There are a number of studies within single industries demonstrating that there are superior ways of managing people and organizing their work. Yet although these superior management practices are reasonably well known, diffusion proceeds slowly and fitfully, and backsliding is common. A study of apparel manufacturing demonstrated that modular production, with an emphasis on team-based production, produced far superior economic performance along a number of dimensions compared with the traditional bundle system of manufacturing using individual piece work and limited training. Trade publications, industry associations, and the relevant unions have favored modular production since the early 1980s. Nonetheless, in 1992 about 80 percent of all garments were still sewn using the bundle method, and some plants that had adopted modular production abandoned it and returned to the bundle system.

Similarly, evidence for the advantages of flexible or lean production in automobile assembly is compelling. This knowledge is widely diffused within the industry and has been for some time. Nevertheless, a five-year follow-up study of the diffusion of flexible manufacturing systems found that there was only modest implementation of flexible arrangements and that 'some plants undertook only minor changes in their use of high-involvement work practices . . . and still others showed modest decreases.' And a large-scale study of semi-conductor fabrication revealed substantial differences in performance, as measured by cycle time, line yield, and defect density, based on the management practices used. Yet the study found substantial variation in these practices, even in an industry that was characterized by geographic concentration, particularly of corporate headquarters, and substantial movement of personnel between firms. In these and other studies the evidence seems compelling that, although there are better ways of managing and organizing, these superior practices are not necessarily quickly or readily adopted.

Some other examples illustrate the frequently large gap between knowing that something is important and actually doing it. For instance, the Association of Executive Search Consultants conducted a survey in which 'three-quarters of the responding CEOs said companies should have "fast track" programs, [but] fewer than half have one at their own companies.' As noted in a *Fortune* article commenting on this study, 'Maybe chief executives don't say what they mean, and maybe they have trouble implementing what they say.' Our research indicates that it is the latter problem – implementing what leaders say and know – that is more pervasive.

Evidence from various industry studies, and from studies of firms in multiple industries, shows that knowledge of how to enhance performance is not readily or easily transferred *across* firms. Moreover, there is evidence that knowledge of how to enhance performance doesn't transfer readily even *within* firms. There are persistent and substantial differences in performance within facilities in the same company. One study of 42 food plants in a single company doing essentially the same manufacturing tasks with similar technologies found differences in performance of 300 percent between the best- and worst-performing plants. The best plant earned 80 percent more than the mean, and the worst plant earned 40 percent less than the mean for all the plants. A study of oil refineries reported little consistency in performance in multirefinery organizations. There was no evidence of a 'company effect' on performance, indicating that there was not much consistency in management practices or philosophy across different facilities within the same company.

An intensive study of an effort to make a Hewlett-Packard (HP) manufacturing unit more effective reported: 'By interviewing thirteen such stakeholders from other departments, including procurement, process generation, engineering, and finance, design team members discovered that communication between departments was poor, thus limiting the degree to which they learned from each other. . . . Opportunities to share innovative process technologies or other sources of competitive advantage were being overlooked.' The problems associated with transferring knowledge within HP have led Lew Platt, the CEO, to lament, 'I wish we knew what we know at HP.' Another study of the transfer of best practices, or knowledge, within firms, noted:

You would think that . . . better practices would spread like wildfire in the entire organization. They don't. As William Buehler, senior vice president at Xerox, said, 'You can see a high-performance factor or office, but it just doesn't spread.'. . . One Baldrige winner [said], 'We can have two plants right across the street from one another, and it's the damnedest thing to get them to transfer best practices.'

Does the knowing-doing gap matter?

The answer to the question of whether the knowing-doing gap actually matters for organizational performance is not as obvious as it might at first seem. It is possible that differences in organizational performance come from differences in what firms *know* – the quality and depth of their insights about business strategy, technologies, products, customers, and operations – rather than from their ability to translate that knowledge into action. There are, however, numerous reasons to doubt this is the case. We do not deny that there are important differences in knowledge across firms, such as differences in the sophistication of their understanding of management and operations. But we argue that such differences are only part of the reason for differences in firm performance, and that a much larger source of variation in performance stems from the ability to turn knowledge into action.

Why do we argue that the gap between knowing and doing is more important than the gap between ignorance and knowing? First, because there are too many activities and organizations involved in acquiring and disseminating knowledge to plausibly maintain that there are many important performance 'secrets.' Consider the plethora of books, articles, consultants, and training programs we have already described. All of these have as one of their objectives the transmission of information. There are organizations that specialize in collecting knowledge about management practices, storing it, and then transferring the information to those who need such information about enhancing performance. These organizations, sometimes called *knowledge brokers*, make a business of transferring performance knowledge. Major consulting firms have units that specialize in transferring knowledge about best practices learned from work with past clients to current clients who did not know, or at least did not use, such information (Hargadon, 1998).

Although the market for information about 'best practices' may not be as efficient as financial or capital markets are reputed to be, it is nonetheless implausible to presume that better ways of doing things can remain secret for long. There are few managers who can resist the temptation to tell their counterparts at other firms or the business press about what they are doing to achieve organizational success. Managers of successful firms are also frequently interviewed and hired by competing firms in the same industry and by firms in other industries that hope to learn and implement the practices of these firms.

Southwest Airlines is a firm that uses fairly simple business practices that are widely known, but it continues to have the best financial performance in the airline industry. Numerous books, case studies, and television shows have described Southwest's management approach, but the firm's competitors have either not tried to imitate what it does or, when they have, like the United Shuttle did, they have not been nearly as successful as Southwest.

Second, research demonstrates that the success of most interventions designed to improve organizational performance depends largely on implementing what is already known, rather than from adopting new or previously unknown ways of doing things. Consider one representative study. A field experiment was conducted with an electrical wholesale company with headquarters in Melbourne, Australia. The experiment compared sales changes in branches that used benchmarking with branches that set high performance goals. In the more-effective benchmarking treatment, 'at the beginning of each month . . . each branch was sent a "League Ladder" showing the percentage improvement [in sales] and ranking of all the branches in that group for the past month. In addition, they were sent a list of "Best Practices" hints compiled . . . from information provided by managers of the best-performing branches' (Mann, Samson & Dow, 1998). Over a three-month period, these branches improved their sales performance by almost 6 percent.

The 'Best Practice' hints were actually:

well-known practices, with the extra dimension that they were reinforced and carried out reliably in the better performing branches. . . . Most managers agreed with the hints, but claimed they were already aware of and employing most of them. . . . Given the nature of the 'Best Practice' hints, we can rule out discovery and communication of highly original and effective practices as the reason for improvement in the benchmarking group.

Using regular schedules to plan weekly activities, conducting meetings of branch staff to review and discuss branch staff performance, training sales representatives in understanding and interpreting sales trend reports, and using practices that ensure fast and reliable customer service are far from rocket science. They are, in fact, common sense. It is interesting how uncommon common sense is in its implementation.

Or consider Honda's efforts to enhance the performance of its suppliers, which resulted in productivity increases averaging 50 percent at the 53 suppliers participating in Honda's BP (Best Practice, Best Process, Best Performance) program. A study of Honda's process noted that 'the underlying scientific knowledge for the reengineering of production lines was primarily concrete and simple rather than abstract and complex' (MacDuffie and Helper, 1997). The changes were consistent with the idea of *kaizan*, or continuous improvement, most of them being small, simple, and in many cases, quite commonsensical given the particular manufacturing process. The genius of the Honda system was in its implementation, not in particularly novel or complicated technical ideas for enhancing productivity.

If there is widespread diffusion of information on 'best' (or at least 'better') practices, and if the evidence suggests that many successful interventions rely more on implementation of simple knowledge than on creating new insights or discovering obscure or secret practices used by other firms, then our position that the gap between knowing and doing is important for firm performance follows logically. This conclusion means that although knowledge creation, benchmarking, and knowledge management may be important, transforming knowledge into organizational action is at least as important to organizational success.

How knowledge management contributes to the knowing-doing problem

One might think that with the current interest in 'knowledge management' and intellectual capital, there wouldn't be a knowing-doing problem. After all, there is general acceptance that 'knowledge has become increasingly important as a contributor to a country's and individual firm's success in industrial competition.' Tomas Stewart's conclusion (1998) is typical: 'The new economy is about the growing value

of knowledge as an input and output, making it the most important ingredient of what people buy and sell.' But the view of knowledge taken by many consultants, organizations, and management writers is of something to be acquired, measured, and distributed – something reasonably tangible, such as patents. There are two problems with this conception of knowledge or knowhow. First, the conception of knowledge as something explicit and quantifiable draws a problematic distinction between knowledge as a tangible good and the use of that good in ongoing practice. The emphasis that has resulted has been to build the stock of knowledge, acquiring or developing intellectual property (note the use of the term *property*) under the presumption that knowledge, once possessed, will be used appropriately and efficiently. As we have seen, this presumption is often not valid.

There is some attention in both the management literature and in management practice to knowledge in use, but this perspective is comparatively rare. Commenting on the papers at a conference on knowledge management, Don Cohen (1998) noted, 'In the U.S., most knowledge practice focuses on collecting, distributing, re-using, and measuring existing codified knowledge and information. Practitioners often look to information technology to capture and distribute this explicit knowledge; firms measure success by near-term economic returns on knowledge investment.' An Ernst & Young survey of 431 firms conducted in 1997 is quite revealing about why most firms' efforts in knowledge management are not likely to do much good and may even be counterproductive regarding turning knowledge into organizational action. According to data from that survey (see Figure 9.4.1), most firms' efforts consist of investing in knowledge repositories such as intranets and data warehouses, building networks so that people can find each other, and implementing technologies to facilitate collaboration. These are all activities that treat knowledge pretty much like steel or any other resource, to be gathered, shared, and distributed. What firms haven't done very much is build knowledge into products and services, or develop new products and services based on knowledge. Furthermore, there is no item on this list of knowledge management projects that reflects implementing knowledge on an ongoing basis.

One of the main reasons that knowledge management efforts are often divorced from day-to-day activities is that the managers, consulting firms, and information technologists who design and build the systems for collecting, storing, and retrieving knowl-

FIGURE 9.4.1 Project priorities

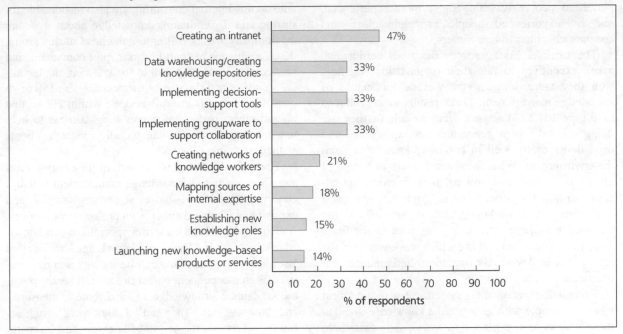

Source: Data from Ruggles (1998).

edge have limited, often inaccurate, views of how people actually use knowledge in their jobs. Sociologists call this 'working knowledge' (Harper, 1987). Knowledge management systems rarely reflect the fact that essential knowledge, including technical knowledge, is often transferred between people by stories, gossip, and by watching one another work. This is a process in which social interaction is often crucial. A recent study of 1,000 employees in business, government, and nonprofit organizations reported that 'most workplace learning goes on unbudgeted, unplanned, and uncaptured by the organization. . . . Up to 70 percent of workplace learning is informal.' This study by the Center for Workforce Development found that informal learning occurs in dozens of daily activities, including participating in meetings, interacting with customers, supervising or being supervised, mentoring others, communicating informally with peers, and training others on the job.

Yet, most knowledge management efforts emphasize technology and the storage and transfer of codified information such as facts, statistics, canned presentations, and written reports. A June 1997 Conference Board conference on creating and leveraging intellectual capital reported: 'Most corporate initiatives to manage intellectual capital are focused on specific projects, the most common of which deploy technol-

ogy to share and leverage knowledge and best practices.' There is an unfortunate emphasis on technology, particularly information technology, in these efforts. For instance, one recent article on making knowledge management a reality asserted that 'it's clear that an intranet is one of the most powerful tools for achieving results within this [knowledge management] arena.' Another article asserted that 'knowledge management starts with technology.' We believe that this is precisely wrong. As the Conference Board report noted, 'Dumping technology on a problem is rarely an effective solution.' When knowledge is transferred by stories and gossip instead of solely through formal data systems, it comes along with information about the process that was used to develop that knowledge. When just reading reports or seeing presentations, people don't learn about the subtle nuances of work methods – the failures, the tasks that were fun, the tasks that were boring, the people who were helpful, and the people who undermined the work.

Formal systems can't store knowledge that isn't easily described or codified but is nonetheless essential for doing the work, called *tacit knowledge*. So, while firms keep investing millions of dollars to set up knowledge management groups, most of the knowledge that is actually used and useful is transferred by the stories people tell to each other, by the trials and errors that occur as people develop knowledge and skill, by inexperienced people watching those more experienced, and by experienced people providing close and constant coaching to newcomers.

The Ernst & Young survey described earlier also asked executives to rate their organizations on how well they were doing in the various dimensions of knowledge management. These results are reproduced in Figure 9.4.2. Managers seem to believe they are doing a good job in generating new knowledge and even doing pretty well in obtaining knowledge from the environment. What they aren't doing very well at all, by their own assessments, is transferring knowledge *within* the organization. And perhaps most important, Ernst & Young didn't even ask if the knowledge in these firms was being used by the firms – not just in decision making which was covered in the survey, but in day-to-day operations and management practices.

Knowledge management systems seem to work best when the people who generate the knowledge are also those who store it, explain it to others, and coach them as they try to implement the knowledge. For example, Hewlett-Packard's Strategic Planning, Analysis, and Modeling group has had success transferring knowledge about supply chain management that has been implemented in many HP divisions. One of the reasons

the group has been successful is that the same people who do this internal consulting are also responsible for storing and disseminating knowledge about it within the company. Corey Billington, the head of this group, describes his job as 'part librarian, part consultant, and part coach.' He is responsible for knowing the technical solutions and the stories surrounding the 150 or so consulting jobs his group has done within HP so that he and others in his group can suggest ideas to help new internal clients and can actually coach the clients as they implement the ideas.

The second problem with much of the existing literature and practice in knowledge management is that it conceptualizes knowledge as something tangible and explicit that is quite distinct from philosophy or values. As Don Cohen (1998), a writer specializing on knowledge issues, put it, 'The noun "knowledge" implies that knowledge is a thing that can be located and manipulated as an independent object or stock. It seems possible to "capture" knowledge, to "distribute," "measure," and "manage" it. The gerund "knowing" suggests instead a process, the action of knowers and inseparable from them.' A leading Japanese scholar in the area of knowledge in organizations made a simple but important point (Nonaka and Konno, 1998): 'Knowledge is embedded in . . . these shared spaces, where it is then acquired through one's own experience

FIGURE 9.4.2   Good or excellent performance

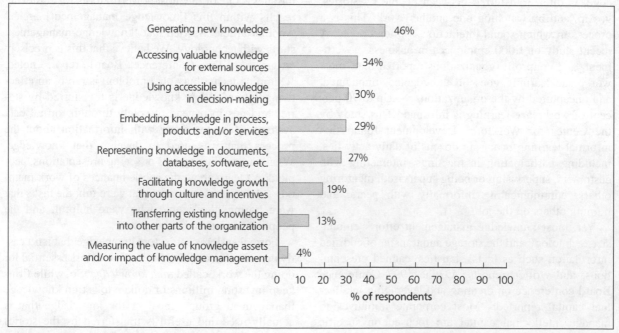

Source: Data from Ruggles (1998).

or reflections on the experiences of others. . . . Knowledge is intangible.'

The fact that knowledge is acquired through experience and is often intangible and tacit produces a third problem in turning knowledge into action. One important reason we uncovered for the knowing-doing gap is that companies overestimate the importance of the tangible, specific, programmatic aspects of what competitors, for instance, do, and underestimate the importance of the underlying philosophy that guides what they do and why they do it. Although specific practices are obviously important, such practices evolve and make sense only as part of some system that is often organized according to some philosophy or metatheory of performance. As such, there is a knowing-doing gap in part because firms have misconstrued what they should be knowing or seeking to know in the first place.

Why has it been so difficult for other automobile manufacturers to copy the Toyota Production System (TPS), even though the details have been described in books and Toyota actually gives tours of its manufacturing facilities? Because 'the TPS techniques that visitors see on their tours – the *kanban* cards, *andon* cords, and quality circles – represent the surface of TPS but not its soul' (Taylor, 1997). The Toyota Production System is about philosophy and perspective, about such things as people, processes, quality, and continuous improvement. It is not just a set of techniques or practices:

> On the surface, TPS appears simple. . . . Mike DaPrile, who runs Toyota's assembly facilities in Kentucky, describes it as having three levels: techniques, systems, and philosophy. Says he: Many plants have put in an andon cord that you pull to stop the assembly line if there is a problem.

> A 5-year-old can pull the cord. But it takes a lot of effort to drive the right philosophies down to the plant floor.

A similar perspective is evident in the study examining how Honda creates lean suppliers. Honda chooses its supplier-partners in large part based on the attitudes of the companies' management. In the words of Rick Mayo, the Honda engineer directing these activities, 'We are a philosophy-driven company . . . Honda felt it was easier to teach the technical knowledge associated with a different product or process technology than to find a technically-capable supplier possessing the combination of risk-taking attitude, motivation to improve, responsiveness to future needs, and overall competence that is valued so highly' (MacDuffie and Helper, 1997).

Nor is this emphasis on philosophy just the view of some Japanese automobile companies. The importance of values and philosophy is a theme that was repeated by Howard Behar, president of Starbucks International, the coffee company; David Russo, vice president of human resources for SAS Institute, a software firm recently ranked by *Fortune* as the third-best company to work for in the United States; and George Zimmer, founder and chairman of The Men's Wearhouse, a rapidly growing, extremely profitable off-price retailer of tailored and casual men's clothing. All three of these organizations have been financially successful, and all are renowned for their people management practices. In all three instances, the message was the same: What is important is not so much what we do – the specific people management techniques and practices – but *why* we do it – the underlying philosophy and view of people and the business that provides a foundation for the practices. Attempting to copy just *what* is done – the explicit practices and

EXHIBIT 9.4.1 WHY TYPICAL KNOWLEDGE MANAGEMENT PRACTICES MAKE KNOWING-DOING GAPS WORSE

- Knowledge management efforts mostly emphasize technology and the transfer of codified information.

- Knowledge management tends to treat knowledge as a tangible thing, as a stock or quantity, and therefore separates knowledge as some thing from the use of that thing.

- Formal systems can't easily store or transfer tacit knowledge.

- The people responsible for transferring and implementing knowledge management frequently don't understand the actual work being documented.

- Knowledge management tends to focus on specific practices and ignores the importance of philosophy.

policies – without holding the underlying philosophy is at once a more difficult task and an approach that is less likely to be successful. Because of the importance of values and philosophy in the management processes of many successful companies, the emphasis on the tangible, explicit aspects of knowledge that characterizes most knowledge management projects is unlikely to provide much value and may be, at worst, a diversion from where and how companies should be focusing their attention.

Turning knowledge into action

Knowledge and information are obviously crucial to performance. But we now live in a world where knowledge transfer and information exchange are tremendously efficient, and where there are numerous organizations in the business of collecting and transferring best practices. So, there are fewer and smaller differences in *what firms know* than in their *ability to act* on that knowledge. It is widely recognized that many firms have gaps between what they know and what they do, but the causes have not been fully understood. Harlow Cohen (1998) has called this gap between knowing and doing the performance paradox: 'Managers know what to do to improve performance, but actually ignore or act in contradiction to either their strongest instincts or to the data available to them.'

There are no simple analyses or easy answers for the knowing-doing problem. The problem is not just costs, or leadership, or some single organizational practice that can be changed to remedy the problem. The knowing-doing gap arises from a constellation of factors and it is essential that organizational leaders understand them all and how they interrelate. Nonetheless, there are some recurring themes that help us understand the source of the problem and, by extension, some ways of addressing it.

1. Why before how: Philosophy is important.

Why has General Motors in the past had so much difficulty learning from Saturn or NUMMI? Why have executives from so many firms toured Toyota's facilities but failed to comprehend the essence of the Toyota Production System? Why have so few firms copied The Men's Wearhouse, SAS Institute, Whole Foods Market, AES, PSS/World Medical, Kingston Technology, or the many other successful firms that people read about, visit, but then fail to learn from? One reason is that too many managers want to learn 'how' in terms of detailed practices and behaviors and techniques, rather than 'why' in terms of philosophy and general guidance for action.

Saturn, Toyota, Honda, IDEO Product Development, AES, the SAS Institute, The Men's Wearhouse, and many of the other organizations we have discussed begin not with specific techniques or practices but rather with some basic principles – a philosophy or set of guidelines about how they will operate. AES has a set of four core values – fun, fairness, integrity, and social responsibility – that guide its behavior. It also has a set of core assumptions about people that it tries to implement in its management approach: that people (1) are creative, thinking individuals, capable of learning; (2) are responsible and can be held accountable; (3) are fallible; (4) desire to make positive contributions to society and like a challenge; and (5) are unique individuals, deserving of respect, not numbers or machines (Pfeffer, 1997a). SAS Institute has a philosophy of treating everyone fairly, equally, and with trust and respect – treating people in accordance with the firm's stated belief in their importance to the organization. The Men's Wearhouse philosophy comes from founder George Zimmer's background: 'He'd grown up in the mid-sixties to early seventies . . . and was definitely interested in alternative forms of social organization (Pfeffer, 1997b). Zimmer believes very strongly that there is tremendous untapped human potential and that it is his company's job to help people realize that potential. 'What creates longevity in a company is whether you look at the assets of your company as the untapped human potential that is dormant within thousands of employees, or is it the plant and equipment? . . . If you ask me how I measure the results of my training program, I can't. I have to do it on . . . trust in the value of human potential.' That is why Zimmer has stated that the company is in the people business, not the suit business.

These firms learn and change and do things consistent with implementing their general principles to enhance organizational performance. Operating on the basis of a general business model or theory of organizational performance, a set of core values, and an underlying philosophy permits these organizations to avoid the problem of becoming stuck in the past or mired in ineffective ways of doing things just because they have done it that way before. They don't let precedent or memory substitute for thinking. No particular practice, in and of itself, is sacred. What is constant and fundamental are some basic business and operating principles. Consequently, these firms are able to learn and adapt, to communicate with newcomers and across large geographic distances, and to do so in ways consistent with their basic understanding of what creates success and high performance in their particular business.

2. Knowing comes from doing and teaching others how.

In a world of conceptual frameworks, fancy graphics presentations, and, in general, lots of *words*, there is much too little appreciation for the power, and indeed the necessity of not just talking and thinking but of *doing* – and this includes explaining and teaching – as a way of knowing. Rajat Gupta, managing director of McKinsey since 1994, had this to say about the importance of apprenticeship and experience in developing leadership within the firm: 'The notion of apprenticeship and mentoring is that you learn by observation, learn from doing together with someone who's done it before. . . . You [also] learn a lot when you're thrown into a situation and you don't have a lot of help.'

Teaching is a way of knowing, and so is doing the work, trying different things, experimenting. As David Sun of Kingston Technology said, 'If you do it, then you will know.' Honda's emphasis on putting people where they could see the actual part and the actual situation reflects the idea that seeing and touching, being closely involved in the actual process, is imperative for real understanding and learning.

The notion that learning is best done by trying a lot of things, learning from what works and what does not, thinking about what was learned, and trying again is practiced with religious zeal at IDEO Product Development, the largest and most successful product design consulting firm in the world. CEO David Kelley likes to say that 'enlightened trial and error outperforms the planning of flawless intellects.' As in the other action-oriented firms we studied, Kelley doesn't just talk about the virtues of learning through trial and error. They live it at IDEO. As engineer Peter Skillman puts it, 'Rapid prototyping is our religion. When we get an idea, we make it right away so we can see it, try it, and learn from it.' Kelley, Skillman, and many others at IDEO also regularly teach classes to managers, engineers, and artists in which they explain their philosophy and have students enact it by designing, building, demonstrating, and pitching their inventions to others.

What an out-of-fashion idea – being in proximity to what you are learning, using experience as a teacher, learning by doing and teaching! We live in an era of distance learning. We have companies that sell CD-Roms so that people can learn things alone by interacting with their computers. We have a plethora of seminars in which people sit and listen to ideas and concepts. We human beings can learn some things

those ways – mostly specific cognitive content. But many things, about organizations, operations, and people, can only be learned by firsthand experience. The tangible, physical, material aspects of knowledge acquisition and knowledge transfer, learning by doing, learning by coaching and teaching, are critical.

Knowing by doing is, unfortunately, a less cost-efficient way of transmitting knowledge. There is less ability to leverage the Internet or to put lots of people in a large room with one instructor, which are, unfortunately, the modes of instruction at most business schools today. But both the evidence and the logic seem clear: Knowing by doing develops a deeper and more profound level of knowledge and virtually by definition eliminates the knowing-doing gap.

3. Action counts more than elegant plans and concepts.

A number of years ago, Tom Peters and Robert Waterman (1982) talked about the virtues of a 'ready, fire, aim' approach to running organizations. We have seen that this principle of acting even if you haven't had the time to fully plan the action has two advantages. First, it creates opportunities for learning by doing. Without taking some action, without being in the actual setting and confronting the actual 'part,' learning is more difficult and less efficient because it is not grounded in real experience. Second, the idea of 'firing' and then 'aiming' – or doing and then planning – helps to establish a cultural tone that action is valued and that talk and analysis without action are unacceptable.

Greg Brenneman, the COO of Continental Airlines and one of the architects of its successful turnaround, attributed the turnaround to an action orientation: 'If you sit around devising elegant and complex strategies and then try to execute them through a series of flawless decisions, you're doomed. We saved Continental because we acted and we never looked back.' In a world where sounding smart has too often come to substitute for doing something smart, there is a tendency to let planning, decision making, meetings, and talk come to substitute for implementation. People achieve status through their words, not their deeds. Managers come to believe that just because a decision has been made and there was discussion and analysis, something will happen. As we have seen, that is often not the case.

A while ago we worked with the World Bank as it was trying to transform its culture. One of the problems that the bank faced was a set of human resource policies and practices that clashed with the culture the bank thought it wanted and that it needed to implement to fulfill its evolving role in the world economy. So the bank embarked on an effort to change those practices. But what this particular change effort largely entailed, and this was true in many other instances of change in the bank, was preparing a white paper laying out options, providing rationales, talking about implementation plans, and providing supporting data. The white paper on human resource practices was then critiqued by senior officials and revised on the basis of those critiques. And the process continued – analysis, writing, critique, and revision. There was great concern to produce an outstanding paper about human resource policies and practices, but much less concern with actually making any changes. This sort of process came naturally in an environment of people with advanced degrees who had learned to write journal articles in precisely this way – write, get comments, revise, and produce yet another draft. But behavior that may be useful for writing articles in scientific journals can be quite unproductive for organizations trying to change. In the time it took the people at the bank to analyze, document, propose, and revise descriptions of possible changes to management practices, they could have implemented many actual changes, learned what worked and what did not and why, and could have made revisions based on that experience numerous times.

4. There is no doing without mistakes. What is the company's response?

In building a culture of action, one of the most critical elements is what happens when things go wrong. Actions, even those that are well planned, inevitably entail the risk of being wrong. What is the company's response? Does it provide, as PSS/World Medical does, 'soft landings'? Or does it treat failure and error so harshly that people are encouraged to engage in perpetual analysis, discussion, and meetings but not to do anything because they are afraid of failure?

Warren Bennis and Burt Nanus (1997) defined learning as an extension of the word trying and asserted that 'all learning involves some "failure," something from which one can continue to learn.' They proposed a general rule for all organizations: 'Reasonable failure should never be received with anger,' which they illustrated with the following story about Thomas Watson Sr., IBM's founder and CEO for many decades:

A promising junior executive of IBM was involved in a risky venture for the company and managed to lose over $10 million in the gamble. It was a

disaster. When Watson called the nervous executive into his office, the young man blurted out, 'I guess you want my resignation?' Watson said, 'You can't be serious. We just spent $10 million dollars educating you!'

5. Fear fosters knowing-doing gaps, so drive out fear.

Fear in organizations causes all kinds of problems. Greg Brenneman, COO of Continental Airlines, noted: 'Pressure and fear often make managers do erratic, inconsistent, even irrational things.' No one is going to try something new if the reward is likely to be a career disaster. The idea of rapid prototyping – trying things out to see if they work and then modifying them on the basis of that experience – requires a culture in which failure is not punished because failure provides an opportunity for learning. Clayton Christensen, a professor at Harvard Business School, has said, 'What companies need is a forgiveness framework and not a failure framework, to encourage risk taking and empower employees to be thinking leaders rather than passive executives.' Fear produces sentiments like the following, which we often hear when we teach executives about high-performance work cultures and ask why their firms don't implement these ideas: 'We may not be doing very well, but at least our performance is predictable. And, no one has gotten fired for doing what we're doing. So why should we try something new that has risk involved?'

That is why firms that are better able to turn knowledge into action drive out fear. They don't go on missions to find who has erred, but rather attempt to build cultures in which even the concept of failure is not particularly relevant. Livio DeSimone, Minnesota Mining and Manufacturing's CEO, commented: 'We don't find it useful to look at things in terms of success or failure. Even if an idea isn't successful initially, we can learn from it.' Such firms put people first and act as if they really care about their people. If they have too many people – as the New Zealand Post did or as Continental Airlines did when it began paring back its routes – those who are redundant are treated humanely, with dignity and respect. At Continental, many managers had come in under Frank Lorenzo, CEO and hostile takeover king. Many of these managers were replaced because they drove fear in rather than out of the organization, clashing with the new culture. As routes were restructured, other people had to leave. But, 'cleaning house needn't be a brutal or humiliating experience. . . . If you fire people inhumanely, you'll be left with a bunch of employees who don't trust the company or their coworkers.'

Putting people first and driving out fear are not just ideas to be implemented when times are good. You can downsize, you can even close a facility; but do it in a way that maintains employee dignity and well-being and, as a consequence, productivity and performance. The people at the Newcastle Steelworks of the Australian firm BHP learned in April 1997 that the works would have to be closed. There was overcapacity in steel making within BHP and this particular plant required excessive capital for modernization. Extensive evidence suggests that 'at least half of the plants facing closure experience between limited to extreme productivity losses.' A case study of the Newcastle plant, however, revealed that in the time after the closing announcement, the plant enjoyed *higher* productivity, better quality, and better safety. Why did this occur? The plant management did a number of things right, many of the same things that Levi Strauss did when it implemented plant closings. One of the most important was to make and keep a commitment to look after the employees. The company implemented a program called Pathways, 'a structured set of initiatives aimed at assessing employees both to decide their future direction (path) after leaving ... and to receive intensive support to achieve it.' That program, coupled with open communication and lots of employee and union involvement, created an atmosphere of trust and mutual respect. If this success in both performance and maintaining employee morale and spirit can be achieved under the difficult and demanding experience of a plant closure, think what can be achieved under more favorable circumstances by organizations committed to building a workplace in which people aren't afraid of the future.

Fear starts, or stops, at the top. It is unfortunate, but true, that a formal hierarchy gives people at the top the power to fire or harm the careers of people at lower levels. Fear of job loss reflects not only the reality of whether or not one can readily find another job, but also the personal embarrassment that any form of rebuke causes. Organizations that are successful in turning knowledge into action are frequently characterized by leaders who inspire respect, affection, or admiration, but not fear.

Hierarchy and power differences are real. But firms can do things to make power differences less visible and, as a consequence, less fear-inducing. This is possibly one of the reasons why removing status markers and other symbols that reinforce the hierarchy can be so useful and important. Those symbols of hierarchy serve as reminders that those farther down have their jobs, their salaries, and their futures within the firm mostly at the sufferance of those in superior positions. Although to some extent this is always true, removing visible signs of hierarchy – things such as reserved parking spaces, private dining rooms, elaborate, separate offices, differences in dress – removes physical reminders of a difference in hierarchical power that can easily inspire fear among those not in the highest-level positions.

6. Beware of false analogies: Fight the competition, not each other.   Cooperation has somehow developed a bad reputation in many organizations. Collaborative, cooperative organizations, where people worry about the welfare of each other and the whole instead of just themselves, seem to remind some people of socialism. Yet, cooperation means that 'the result is the product of common effort, the goal is shared, and each member's success is linked with every other's. ... Ideas and materials, too, will be shared, labor will sometimes be divided, and everyone in the group will be rewarded for successful completion of the task' (Kohn, 1992). There is a mistaken idea that because competition has apparently triumphed as an economic system, competition *within* organizations is a similarly superior way of managing. This is not just a sloppy use of analogies, but has real consequences that hurt real people and real organizations. Following this suspect logic, firms establish all sorts of practices that intensify internal rivalry: forced-curve performance rankings, prizes and recognition for relatively few employees, raises given out in a zero-sum fashion, and individual rewards and measurements that set people against each other.

We have shown that these ideas and the practices they produce almost certainly undermine organizational performance as well as employee well being. British Petroleum enjoyed a turnaround in the 1990s because it encouraged business units to learn from each other and had senior leaders that worked to build a culture of cooperation that made doing so possible. The Men's Wearhouse has succeeded in selling clothes by emphasizing team selling and the fact that employees succeed only as their colleagues succeed. 'The customer doesn't care about who gets the commission. All he remembers is the store's atmosphere. That's why we use "team selling." One wardrobe consultant can offer the customer a cup of coffee; another can offer to press his clothing while he's in our dressing rooms; and another can take his kids to watch the videos we keep in some of our stores.' One of the reasons that SAS Institute's turnover is so low is that people actually prefer working in a place where they don't have to always look over their shoulder to see who is doing them in. In contrast, learning within Fresh Choice, particularly following the Zoopa acquisition, was inhibited by the competition for internal status and related feelings of insecurity and fearfulness. Learning with General Motors was similarly hampered by unproductive internal competition that left people reluctant to learn from each other or to share their knowledge with internal competitors.

There is also much evidence that people prefer collaborative and cooperative work arrangements. For instance, a study of 180 people from five organizations found that 'employees with compatible goals had high expectations, exchanged resources, and managed conflicts. Cooperative interactions improved the work relationship, employee morale, and task completion' (Tjosvold, 1986).

Turning knowledge into action is easier in organizations that have driven fear and internal competition out of the culture. The idea that the stress of internal competition is necessary for high levels of performance confuses *motivation* with *competition*. It is a perspective that mistakes internal competition and conflict, accompanied by a focus on 'winning' internal contests, for an interest in enhancing *organizational* performance and winning the battle in the marketplace.

7. Measure what matters and what can help turn knowledge into action.

'The foundation of any successfully run business is a strategy everyone understands coupled with a few key measures that are routinely tracked.' But this simple notion is frequently ignored in practice. Organizations proliferate measures. 'Mark Graham Brown (1998) reports working with a telecommunications company that expected its managers to review 100 to 200 pages of data a week.' The readily available computer hardware and software that make data capture and analysis easy also make it hard to resist the temptation to confuse data with information and to measure more and more things.

The dictum that what is measured is what gets done has led to the apparent belief that if a company measures more things, more will get done. But that is not at all the case. Southwest Airlines focuses on the critical measures of lost bags, customer complaints, and on-time performance – keys to customer satisfaction and therefore to success in the airline industry. AES focuses on plant utilization (uptime), new business development, and environmental and safety compliance, the factors that are critical to success in the electric power generation business. SAS Institute measures employee retention, important in an intellectual capital

business. A few measures that are directly related to the basic business model are better than a plethora of measures that produce a lack of focus and confusion about what is important and what is not.

Organizations tend to measure the past. Typical information systems can tell you what has happened – how much has been sold, what costs have been, how much has been invested in capital equipment – but the systems seldom provide information that is helpful in determining *why* results have been as they have or what is going to happen in the near future. We sit in too many meetings in which too much time is spent discussing what has occurred but too little time is spent on discussing why or, more important, what is going to be done to create a different and better future.

Organizations tend to measure outcomes instead of processes. We know what the quality of our output is, but we don't know why it is so good or so bad. One of the important lessons of the quality movement is the importance of measuring processes so that process improvement is possible. As we saw, when General Motors became more serious about implementing lean or flexible manufacturing, attention switched to enhancing measures of intermediate outcomes and in-process indicators.

Even fewer organizations measure knowledge implementation. Typical knowledge management systems and processes focus instead on the stock of knowledge, the number of patents, the compilation of skills inventories, and knowledge captured on overheads or reports and made available over some form of groupware. Holding aside whether these systems even capture the tacit, experiential knowledge that is probably more important than what can be easily written down, such systems certainly don't capture whether or not this knowledge is actually being used. Organizations that are serious about turning knowledge into action should measure the knowing-doing gap itself and do something about it.

8. What leaders do, how they spend their time and how they allocate resources, matters.

The difference between Barclays Global Investors, IDEO, or British Petroleum in the late 1990s and the many organizations that have greater difficulty in turning knowledge into action is not that one set of firms is populated by smarter, better, or nicer people than the other. The difference is in the systems and the day-to-day management practices that create and embody a culture that values the building and transfer of knowledge and, most important, acting on that knowledge. Leaders of companies that experience smaller gaps between what they know and what they do understand that their most important task is not necessarily to make strategic decisions or, for that matter, many decisions at all. Their task is to help build systems of practice that produce a more reliable transformation of knowledge into action. When Dennis Bakke of AES says that in 1997 he only made one decision, he is not being cute or facetious. He understands that his job is not to know everything and decide everything, but rather to create an environment in which there are *lots* of people who both know and do. Leaders create environments, reinforce norms, and help set expectations through what they do, through their actions and not just their words.

When Dave House left Intel to become CEO of Bay Networks, a company that was experiencing extremely poor performance, he knew he had to change the existing culture and do so quickly. The company suffered from its creation through a merger of two competitors, Synoptics and Wellfleet Communications, two firms of about equal size, one headquartered on the East Coast and one on the West. Following the merger, the company had tried to take on the best products and ideas of both companies, but what had resulted was product proliferation and slow decision making in a rapidly moving market. 'Bay engineers were working on twice as many new products as the company had the resources to ship.' What House did was create a set of courses to teach business practices he believed could help the company, and House taught many of the sessions himself. By actually delivering the material, House showed he was serious about the ideas and about making change happen. Larry Crook, Bay's director of global logistics, described the impact of House's training sessions: 'They blew my mind. . . . He showed us that he was serious about how we conducted ourselves – and that if we wanted to be successful, we had to get down to basics.'

Skip LeFauve told us that the CEO of General Motors teaches in GM University, reinforcing the importance of the knowledge building and sharing activity. David Kearns, when he was CEO at Xerox, applied quality principles to the top management team as he encouraged their implementation throughout the company. For instance, he and his colleagues thought about who their customers were and realized that these were managers one and two levels below who looked to them for advice and for strategic direction. So Kearns instituted practices to gather information on how well the senior leadership was actually helping executives below them to do their jobs.

The remarkable success of the product development firm IDEO is not simply because the firm has somehow been able to attract 'better' designers. Its success is dependent in large measure on a set of management practices that come from a philosophy that values an 'attitude of action' and the importance of learning by trying new things. For instance, David Kelley believes that, even when a designer knows a lot about a product, there are advantages in trying to feel and act 'stupid.' By pretending to be naïve and asking 'dumb' questions, and even trying to design solutions that are known to be wrong, product designers can overcome the hazards of being too knowledgeable. The ability of product designers at IDEO to think and act in this fashion comes from the fact that this is how Kelley himself behaves, and from his efforts to create consistent norms for management behavior throughout the company.

Knowing about the knowing-doing gap is not enough

We now have a better understanding of some of the organizational processes and factors that hinder efforts to turn knowledge into action. But even if we do understand something more about why organizations fail to turn knowledge into action, these insights are insufficient to solve the problem. *Knowing* about the knowing-doing gap is different from *doing* something about it. Understanding causes is helpful because such understanding can guide action. But by itself, this knowing is insufficient – action must occur.

THE ORGANIZATIONAL CONTEXT IN INTERNATIONAL PERSPECTIVE

So long as men worship the Caesars and Napoleons, Caesars and Napoleons will duly arise and make them miserable.
Aldous Huxley (1894–1963); English novelist

Again it has become clear that there is little consensus in the field of strategy. Views on the nature of the organizational context vary sharply. Even authors from one and the same country have contrasting opinions on the paradox of control and chaos. However, looking back on the readings in the sections on strategy process and strategy content, it is striking how few of the authors make a point of expounding their outlook on organizational development. The assumptions on which their theories are built are largely left implicit.

For this reason, it is difficult to identify whether there are national preferences when it comes to organizational context perspective. Yet, it seems not unlikely that strategists in different countries have different inclinations on this issue. In large-scale field work carried out by researchers at Cranfield Business School in the United Kingdom (Kakabadse et al., 1995), significantly different 'leadership styles' were recognized among European executives. The predominant approach in Sweden and Finland was typified as the 'consensus' style (low power distance, low masculinity), while executives in Germany and Austria had a style that was labeled 'working towards a common goal' (specialists working together within a rule-bound structure). In France, the most popular style was 'managing from a distance' (focus on planning, high power distance), while executives from the United Kingdom, Ireland, and Spain preferred 'leading from the front'. This last leadership style, according to the researchers, relies 'on the belief that the charisma and skills of some particular individuals will lead to either the success or the failure of their organizations'. This finding suggests that the organizational leadership perspective will be more popular in these three countries (as well as in other 'Anglo-Saxon' and 'Latin' cultures), than in the rest of Europe. Other cross-cultural theorists also support this supposition (e.g. Hampden-Turner and Trompenaars, 1993; Lessem and Neubauer, 1994).

As an input to the debate whether there are international differences in perspective, we would like to put forward a number of factors that might be of influence on how the paradox of control and chaos is viewed in different countries. It should be noted, however, that these propositions are intended to encourage discussion and constitute only tentative explanations for cross-cultural differences in perspective. More specific international research is needed to give this debate a firm footing.

Locus of control

This point can be kept short, as it was also raised in Chapter 8. People with an internal locus of control believe that they can shape events and have an impact on their environment. People with an external locus of control believe that they are caught up in events that they can hardly influence. Cross-cultural researchers have argued that cultures can differ significantly with regard to the perceived locus of control that is predominant among the population.

Obviously, in countries where the culture is more inclined towards an internal locus of control, it is reasonable to expect that the organizational leadership perspective will be more widespread. Managers in such 'just do it' cultures will be more strongly predisposed to believe that they can shape organizational circumstances. In cultures that are characterized by a predominantly external locus of control, more support for the organizational dynamics perspective can be expected.

Level of uncertainty avoidance

A cultural characteristic related to the previous point, is the preference for order and structure that prevails in some countries. Hofstede (1993, Reading 1.4) refers to this issue as uncertainty avoidance. In some cultures, there is a low tolerance for unstructured situations, poorly defined tasks and responsibilities, ambiguous relationships and unclear rules. People in these nations exhibit a distinct preference for order, predictability and security – they need to feel that things are 'in control'. In other cultures, however, people are less nervous about uncertain settings. The tolerance for situations that are 'unorganized' or 'self-organizing', is much higher – even in relatively chaotic circumstances, the call for 'law and order' will not be particularly strong. It can be expected that there will be a more pronounced preference for the organizational leadership perspective in countries that score high on uncertainty avoidance, than in nations with a low score.

Prevalence of mechanistic organizations

In Chapters 3 and 4, different international views on the nature of organizations were discussed. A simple distinction was made between mechanistic and organic conceptions of organizations. In the mechanistic view, organizations exist as systems that are staffed with people, while in the organic view organizations exist as groups of people into which some system has been brought.

When it comes to organizational development, people taking a mechanistic view will see leaders as mechanics – the organizational system can be redesigned, reengineered and restructured to pursue another course of action where necessary. Success will depend on leaders' design, engineering and structuring skills, and their ability to overcome resistance to change by the system's inhabitants. If a leader does not function well, a new one can be installed, and if employees are too resistant, then they can be replaced. In countries where the mechanistic view of organizations is more predominant, a leaning towards the organizational leadership perspective can be expected.

People taking an organic view will see a leader as the head of the clan, bound by tradition and loyalty, but able to count on the emotional commitment of the members. Success in reshaping the organization will depend on reshaping the people – changing beliefs, ideas, visions, skills and interests. Important in reorienting and rejuvenating the organization is the leader's ability to challenge orthodox ideas, motivate people and manage the political processes. In countries where the organic view of organizations is more predominant, a leaning towards the organizational dynamics perspective can be expected.

FURTHER READING

Readers interested in pursuing the topics of leadership and organizational dynamics have a rich body of literature from which to choose. An excellent overview of the subject is provided by Sydney Finkelstein and Donald Hambrick, in their book *Strategic Leadership: Top Executives and Their Effects on Organizations*. Also recommended as overview of the leadership literature is Yukl's *Leadership in Organizations*. In the category of more academically oriented works, the special issue of *Organization Studies* entitled 'Interpreting Organizational Leadership', and edited by Susan Schneider gives a rich spectrum of ideas.

The same is true for the special edition of the *Strategic Management Journal* entitled 'Strategic Leadership', and edited by Donald Hambrick.

For more specific readings taking an organizational leadership perspective, the classics with which to start are John Kotter's *The General Managers* and Gordon Donaldson and Jay Lorsch's *Decision Making at the Top: The Shaping of Strategic Direction*. Good follow-up readings are the book by Warren Bennis, *On Becoming a Leader*, and the book by Burt Nanus, *Visionary Leadership: Creating a Compelling Sense of Direction for Your Organization*. For leadership literature further away from the 'control pole', readers are advised to turn to Peter Senge's book *The Fifth Discipline: The Art and Practice of the Learning Organization* and Edward Schein's *Organizational Culture and Leadership*. The book by Henry Sims and Peter Lorenzi, *The New Leadership Paradigm: Social Learning and Cognition in Organizations*, is also a challenging book, but not easy to read.

For a critical reaction to the leadership literature, Manfred Kets de Vries has many excellent contributions. His article 'The Leadership Mystique' is very good, as are his books with Danny Miller, entitled *The Neurotic Organization* and *Unstable at the Top*. Miller also has many thought-provoking works to his name, of which *The Icarus Paradox: How Excellent Companies Can Bring About Their Own Downfall* is highly recommended. In the more academic literature, stimulating commentaries are given in the articles 'The Romance of Leadership' by James Meindl, S. Ehrlich and J. Dukerich, and in 'The Ambiguity of Leadership', by Jeffrey Pfeffer. The reading by Pfeffer and Robert Sutton in this chapter is based on their book, *The Knowing-Doing Gap*, which is quite accessible and very interesting.

For a good reading highlighting the importance of organizational dynamics for both strategy process and strategy content, Ralph Stacey's book *Strategic Management and Organizational Dynamics* is a good place to start. Gerry Johnson's *Strategic Change and the Management Process* also provides provocative ideas about the relationship between strategy and the organizational context. Richard Pascale's *Managing on the Edge: How Successful Companies Use Conflict to Stay Ahead* is also stimulating reading. Finally, for the academically more adventurous, Joel Baum and Jitendra Singh's volume, *Evolutionary Dynamics of Organizations*, gives plenty of food for thought, as does Howard Aldrich's recent *Organizations Evolving*.

REFERENCES

Ackoff, R.L. (1980) *Creating the Corporate Future*, Wiley, Chichester.

Aldrich, H. (1999) *Organizations Evolving*, Sage, London.

Allison, G. (1969) 'Conceptual Models and The Cuban Missile Crisis', *The American Political Science Review*, Vol. 63, No. 3, September, pp. 689–718.

Amabile, T.M. (1998) 'How to Kill Creativity', *Harvard Business Review*, Vol. 76, No. 5, September–October, pp. 76–87.

Argyris, C. (1990) *Overcoming Organizational Defenses: Facilitating Organizational Learning*, Allyn & Bacon, Needham, MA.

Arrow, K.J. (1963) *Social Choice and Individual Values*, Yale University Press, New Haven, CT.

Barney, J.B. (1991) 'Firm Resources and Sustained Competitive Advantage', *Journal of Management*, Vol. 17, No. 1, pp. 99–120.

Bass, B.M. (1990) *Bass and Stogdill's Handbook of Leadership*, Third Edition, The Free Press, New York.

Baum, J.A.C., and Singh, J.V. (eds.) (1994) *Evolutionary Dynamics of Organizations*, Oxford University Press, Oxford.

Bavelas, A. (1964) 'Leadership: Man and Function', in: H.H. Leavitt and L.R. Pondy (eds.), *Readings in Managerial Psychology*, University of Chicago Press, Chicago.

Beinhocker, E.D. (1999) 'Strategy at the Edge of Chaos', *The McKinsey Quarterly*, No. 1, pp. 24–39.

Bennis, W. (1989) *On Becoming a Leader*, Addison-Wesley, Reading, MA.

Bennis, W., and Nanus, B. (1985) *Leaders: The Strategies for Taking Charge*, Harper & Row, New York.

Bennis, W., and Nanus, B. (1997) *Leaders: Strategies for Taking Charge*, HarperBusiness, New York, p. 60.

Birnbaum, R. (1988) *How Colleges Work: The Cybernetics of Academic Organization and Leadership*, Jossey-Bass, San Francisco.

Bourgeois, L.J., and Brodwin, D.R. (1983) 'Putting Your Strategy into Action', *Strategic Management Planning*, March–May.

Bower, J.L. (ed.) (1991) *The Craft of General Management*, Harvard Business School Publications, Boston.

Brown, M.G. (1998) 'Using Measurement to Boost Your Unit's Performance, *Harvard Management Update*, Vol. 3, p. 1.

Calder, B. (1977) 'An Attribution Theory of Leadership', in: B. Staw and B. Salancik (eds.), *New Directions in Organizational Behavior*, St. Clair, Chicago.

Cannella, A.A., and M.J. Monroe (1997) 'Contrasting Perspectives on Strategic Leaders: Toward a More Realistic View of Top Managers', *Journal of Management*, Vol. 23, No. 3, pp. 213–237.

Chandler, A.D. (1962) *Strategy and Structure: Chapters in the History of the American Industrial Enterprise*, MIT Press, Cambridge, MA.

Chandler, A.D. (1977) *The Visible Hand*, Harvard University Press, Cambridge, MA.

Chen, C.C., and Meindl, J.R. (1991) 'The Construction of Leadership Images in the Popular Press: The Case of Donald Burr and People Express', *Administrative Science Quarterly*, Vol. 36, No. 4, December, pp. 521–551.

Child, J. (1972) 'Organizational Structure, Environment, and Performance: The Role of Strategic Choice', *Sociology*, January, pp. 2–22.

Cohen, D. (1998) 'Toward a Knowledge Context: Report on the First Annual U.C. Berkeley Forum on Knowledge and the Firm', *California Management Review*, Vol. 40, No. 3, Spring, p. 23.

Cohen, H. (1998) 'The Performance Paradox', *Academy of Management Executive*, Vol. 12, p. 30.

Conger J.A. (1999) 'Charismatic and Transformational Leadership in Organizations', *The Leadership Quarterly*, Vol. 10, No. 2, Summer, pp. 145–179.

Cyert, R.M. (1990) 'Defining Leadership and Explicating the Process', *Non-Profit Management and Leadership*, Vol. 1, No. 1, Fall, pp. 29–38.

Cyert, R.M., and March, J.G. (1963) *A Behavioral Theory of the Firm*, Prentice Hall, Englewood Cliffs.

De Geus, A. (1988) 'Planning as Learning', *Harvard Business Review*, March–April, pp. 70–74.

Donaldson, G., and Lorsch, J.W. (1983) *Decision Making at the Top: The Shaping of Strategic Direction*, Basic Books, New York.

Drucker, P. (1973) *Management: Tasks, Responsibilities, Practices*, Harper & Row, New York.

Etzioni, A. (1961) *A Comparative Analysis of Complex Organizations*, Free Press, New York.

Finkelstein, S. (1992) 'Power in Top Management Teams: Dimensions, Measurement, and Validation', *Academy of Management Journal*, Vol. 35, No. 3, August, pp. 505–538.

Finkelstein, S., and Hambrick, D.C. (1996) *Strategic Leadership: Top Executives and Their Effects on Organizations*, West, St. Paul.

French, J., and Raven, B.H. (1959) 'The Bases of Social Power', in: D. Cartwright (ed.), *Studies of Social Power*, Institute for Social Research, Ann Arbor.

Glassman, R.M. (1986) 'Manufactured Charisma and Legitimacy', in: R.M. Glassman and W.H. Swatos, Jr. (eds.), *Charisma, History, and Social Structure*, Glenwood Press, New York.

Goold, M., and Quinn, J.J. (1990) *Strategic Control: Milestones for Long-Term Performance*, Hutchinson, London.

Greenleaf, R.K. (1977) *Servant Leadership: A Journey into the Nature of Legitimate Power and Greatness*, Paulist Press, New York.

Greenwood, R., and Hinings, C.R. (1996) 'Understanding Radical Organizational Change: Bringing Together the Old and the New Institutionalism', *Academy of Management Review*, Vol. 21, No. 4, October, pp. 1022–1054.

Greiner, L.E. (1972) 'Evolution and Revolution as Organizations Grow', *Harvard Business Review*, July–August, pp. 37–46.

Hambrick, D.C. (1987) 'The Top Management Team: Key to Strategic Success', *California Management Review*, Vol. 30, No. 1, Fall, pp. 88–108.

Hambrick, D.C. (ed.) (1989) 'Guest Editor's Introduction: Putting Top Managers Back in the Strategy Picture', *Strategic Management Journal*, Vol. 10, Special Issue, Summer, pp. 5–15.

Hambrick, D.C., and Finkelstein, S. (1987) 'Managerial Discretion: A Bridge between Polar Views of Organizational Outcomes', in: B.M. Staw and L.L. Cummings (eds.), *Research in Organizational Behavior* (Vol. 9), JAI, Greenwich, CT, pp. 369–406.

Hambrick, D.C., and Mason, P.A. (1984) 'Upper Echelons: The Organization as a Reflection of Its Top Managers', *Academy of Management Review*, Vol. 9, No. 2, April, pp. 193–206.

Hampden-Turner, C., and Trompenaars, A. (1993) *The Seven Cultures of Capitalism: Value Systems for Creating Wealth in the United States, Japan, Germany, France, Britain, Sweden, and the Netherlands*, Doubleday, New York.

Hannan, M.T., and Freeman, J. (1977) 'The Population Ecology of Organizations', *American Journal of Sociology*, Vol. 82, No. 5, March, pp. 929–964.

Hargadon, A. (1998) 'Firms as Knowledge Brokers', *California Management Review*, Vol. 40, No. 3, Spring, pp. 209–227.

Harper, D. (1987) *Working Knowledge: Skill and Community in a Small Shop*, University of Chicago Press, Chicago.

Hedberg, B.L.T., Bystrom, P.C., and Starbuck, W.H. (1976) 'Camping on Seesaws: Prescriptions for a Self-Designing Organization', *Administrative Science Quarterly*, Vol. 21, No. 1, March, pp. 41–65.

Hofstede, G. (1993) 'Cultural Constraints in Management Theories', *Academy of Management Executive*, Vol. 7, No. 1, pp. 8–21.

House, R.J. (1971) 'A Path-Goal Theory of Leadership Effectiveness', *Administrative Science Quarterly*, Vol. 16, No. 3, September, pp. 321–339.

House, R.J., and Aditya, R.N. (1997) 'The Social Science Study of Leadership: Quo Vadis?', *Journal of Management*, Vol. 23, No. 3, May–June, pp. 409–474.

Ireland, R.D., and Hitt, M.A. (1999) 'Achieving and Maintaining Strategic Competitiveness in the 21st Century: The Role of Strategic Leadership', *Academy of Management Executive*, Vol. 13, No. 1, February, pp. 43–57.

Jensen, M.C., and Meckling, W.H. (1994) 'The Nature of Man', *Journal of Applied Corporate Finance*, Vol. 7, No. 2, Summer, pp. 4–19.

Johnson, G. (1987) *Strategic Change and the Management Process*, Blackwell, Oxford.

Johnson, G. (1988) 'Rethinking Incrementalism', *Strategic Management Journal*, Vol. 9, No. 1, January–February, pp. 75–91.

Kakabadse, A., Myers, A., McMahon, T., and Spony, G. (1995) 'Top Management Styles in Europe: Implications for Business and Cross-National Teams', *European Business Journal*, Vol. 7, No. 1, pp. 17–27.

Kelley, R.E. (1988) 'In Praise of Followers', *Harvard Business Review*, Vol. 66, No. 6, November–December, p. 142.

Kets de Vries, M.F.R. (1994) 'The Leadership Mystique', *Academy of Management Executive*, Vol. 8, No. 3, August, pp. 73–92.

Kets de Vries, M.F.R., and Miller, D. (1984) *The Neurotic Organization*, Jossey-Bass, San Francisco.

Kets de Vries, M.F.R., and Miller, D. (1988) *Unstable at the Top: Inside the Troubled Organization*, New American Library, New York.

Khandwalla, P.N. (1977) *The Design of Organizations*, Harcourt, Brace, Jovanovich, New York.

Klein, K.J., and House, R.J. (1998) 'Further Thoughts on Fire: Charismatic Leadership and Levels of Analysis', in: F. Dansereauand and F.J. Yammarino (eds.), *Leadership: The Multi-Level Approaches*, JAI Press, Stamford, CT, Vol. 2, pp. 45–52.

Kohn, A. (1992) *No Contest: The Case Against Competition*, Houghton Mifflin, Boston, MA.

Kotter, J.P. (1982) *The General Managers*, Free Press, New York.

Kotter, J.P. (1990) 'What Leaders Really Do', *Harvard Business Review*, Vol. 68, No. 3, May–June, p. 103.

Lawrence, P.R., and Lorsch, J.W. (1967) 'Differentiation and Integration in Complex Organizations', *Administrative Science Quarterly*, March, pp. 1–47.

Leavy, B., and Wilson, D. (1994) *Strategy and Leadership*, Routledge, London.

Leonard-Barton, D. (1995) *Well-Springs of Knowledge: Building and Sustaining the Sources of Innovation*, Harvard Business School Press, Boston.

Lessem, R., and Neubauer, F.F. (1994) *European Management Systems*, McGraw-Hill, London.

Levy, D. (1994) 'Chaos Theory and Strategy: Theory, Application, and Managerial Implications', *Strategic Management Journal*, Vol. 15, pp. 167–178.

Lorange, P. (1974) 'A Framework for Management Control Systems', *Sloan Management Review*, Vol. 16, No. 1, Fall, pp. 41–56.

Lorange, P., Scott, M.F., and S. Ghoshal (1986) *Strategic Control*, West, St. Paul.

MacDuffie, J.P., and Helper, S. (1997) 'Creating Lean Suppliers: Diffusing Lean Production Through the Supply Chain', *California Management Review*, Vol. 39, No. 4, Summer, pp. 118–150.

Mann, L., Samson, D., and Dow, D. (1998) 'A Field Experiment on the Effects of Benchmarking and Goal Setting on Company Sales Performance', *Journal of Management*, Vol. 24, p. 82.

March, J.G., and Simon, H.A. (1958) *Organizations*, Wiley, New York.

Meindl, J.R., Ehrlich, S.B., and Dukerich, J.M. (1985) 'The Romance of Leadership', *Administrative Science Quarterly*, Vol. 30, No. 1, March, pp. 78–102.

Meyer, J.W., and Zucker, L.G. (1989) *Permanently Failing Organizations*, Sage Publications, Newbury Park.

Miles, R.E., and Snow, C.C. (1978) *Organizational Strategy: Structure and Process*, McGraw-Hill, New York.

Miller, D. (1990) *The Icarus Paradox: How Excellent Companies Can Bring About Their Own Downfall*, Harper Business, New York.

Miller, D., and Friesen, P.H. (1980) 'Momentum and Revolution in Organizational Adaptation', *Academy of Management Journal*, Vol. 23, No. 4, December, pp. 591–614.

Miller, D., and Kets de Vries, M. (1987) *Unstable at the Top*, New American Library, New York.

Mintzberg, H. (1979) *The Structure of Organizations*, Prentice Hall, Englewood Cliffs, NJ.

Mintzberg, H. (1982) 'If You're Not Serving Bill and Barbara, Then You're Not Serving Leadership', in: J.G. Hunt, U. Sekaran, and C.A. Schreisheim (eds.), *Leadership: Beyond Establishment Views*, Southern Illinois University, Carbondale.

Mintzberg, H. (1989) *Mintzberg on Management*, Free Press, New York.

Mintzberg, H. (1991) 'The Effective Organization: Forces and Forms', *Sloan Management Review*, Vol. 32, No. 2, Winter, pp. 54–67.

Misumi, J. (1985) *The Behavioral Science of Leadership*, University of Michigan Press, Ann Arbor.

Morgan, G. (1986) *Images of Organization*, Sage, London.

Nadler, D.A., and Tushman, M.L. (1990) 'Beyond the Charismatic Leader: Leadership and Organizational Change', *California Management Review*, Vol. 32, No. 2, Winter, pp. 77–97.

Nanus, B. (1992) *Visionary Leadership: Creating a Compelling Sense of Direction for Your Organization*, Jossey-Bass, San Francisco.

Nelson, R.R., and Winter, S.G. (1982) *An Evolutionary Theory of Economic Change*, Harvard University Press, Reading, MA.

Nonaka, I. (1988) 'Creating Organizational Order Out of Chaos: Self-Renewal in Japanese Firms', *California Management Review*, Vol. 30, No. 3, Spring, pp. 57–73.

Nonaka, I., and Konno, N. (1998) 'The Concept of "Ba": Building a Foundation for Knowledge Creation', *California Management Review*, Vol. 40, No. 3, Summer, pp. 40–41.

Pascale, R.T. (1990) *Managing on the Edge: How Successful Companies Use Conflict to Stay Ahead*, Viking Penguin, London.

Peters, T.J., and Waterman, R.H. (1982) *In Search of Excellence*, Harper & Row, New York.

Pettigrew, A. (1985) *The Awakening Giant*, Blackwell, Oxford.

Pfeffer, J. (1977) 'The Ambiguity of Leadership', *Academy of Management Review*, Vol. 2, No. 1, January, pp. 104–112.

Pfeffer, J. (1982) *Organizations and Organization Theory*, Pitman, Boston.

Pfeffer, J. (1992) *Managing With Power: Politics and Influence in Organizations*, Harvard Business School Press, Boston, MA.

Pfeffer, J. (1997a) *Human Resources at the AES Corporation: The Case of the Missing Department, Case SHR-3*, Graduate School of Business, Stanford University, Stanford, CA.

Pfeffer, J. (1997b) *The Men's Wearhouse: Success in a Declining Industry, Case HR-5*, Graduate School of Business, Stanford University, Stanford, CA.

Pfeffer, J., and Salancik, G. (1978) *The External Control of Organizations: A Resource Dependency Perspective*, Harper & Row, New York.

Pfeffer, J., and Sutton, R.I. (1999a) 'Knowing "What" to Do is Not Enough: Turning Knowledge Into Action', *California Management Review*, Vol. 42, No. 1, Fall, pp. 83–108.

Pfeffer, J., and Sutton, R.I. (1999b) *The Knowing-Doing Gap: How Smart Companies Turn Knowledge Into Action*, Harvard Business School Press, Boston, MA.

Pondy, L.R., Boland, J.R., and Thomas, H. (eds.) (1988) *Managing Ambiguity and Change*, Wiley, New York.

Porter, M.E. (1990) *The Competitive Advantage of Nations*, Macmillan, London.

Quinn, J.B. (1980) 'Managing Strategic Change', *Sloan Management Review*, Summer, pp. 3–20.

Quinn, J.B. (1985) 'Managing Innovation: Controlled Chaos', *Harvard Business Review*, Vol. 63, No. 3, May–June, pp. 73–84.

Rowe, W.G. (2001) 'Creating Wealth in Organizations: The Role of Strategic Leadership', *Academy of Management Executive*, Vol. 15, No. 1, February, pp. 81–94.

Ruggles, R. (1998) 'The State of the Notion: Knowledge Management in Practice', *California Management Review*, Vol. 40, No. 3, p. 83.

Rumelt, R.P. (1995) 'Inertia and Transformation', in: C.A. Montgomery (ed.), *Resource-based and Evolutionary Theories of the Firm: Towards a Synthesis*, Kluwer Academic Publishers, Boston, pp. 101–132.

Schein, E.H. (1985) *Organizational Culture and Leadership*, Jossey-Bass, San Francisco.

Schein, E.H. (1993) 'On Dialogue, Culture, and Organizational Learning', *Organizational Dynamics*, Vol. 22, No. 2, pp. 40–51.

Schneider, S.S. (ed.) (1991) 'Interpreting Organizational Leadership', *Organization Studies*, Special Issue, Vol. 12.

Selznick, P. (1957) *Leadership in Administration: A Sociological Interpretation*, Harper & Row, New York.

Semler, R. (1994) 'Why My Employees Still Work for Me', *Harvard Business Review*, January–February, p. 64.

Semler, R. (1995) *Maverick*, Arrow Business, London.

Semler, R. (2003) *The Seven-day Weekend*, Century.

Senge, P. (1990a) *The Fifth Discipline: The Art and Practice of the Learning Organization*, Doubleday, New York.

Senge, P.M. (1990b) 'The Leader's New Work: Building Learning Organizations', *Sloan Management Review*, Vol. 32, No. 1, Fall, pp. 7–23.

Simons, R. (1991) 'Strategic Orientation and Top Management Attention to Control Systems', *Strategic Management Journal*, Vol. 12, No. 1, pp. 49–62.

Simons, R. (1994) 'How New Top Managers Use Control Systems as Levers of Strategic Renewal', *Strategic Management Journal*, Vol. 15, No. 3, March, pp. 169–189.

Simons, R. (1995) *Levers of Control: How Managers Use Innovative Control Systems to Drive Strategic Renewal*, HBS Press, Boston, MA.

Sims, H.P., and Lorenzi, P. (1992) *The New Leadership Paradigm: Social Learning and Cognition in Organizations*, Sage, London.

Smircich, L., and Stubbart, C. (1985) 'Strategic Management in an Enacted World', *Academy of Management Review*, Vol. 10, No. 4, pp. 724–736.

Stacey, R.D. (1992) *Managing Chaos: Dynamic Business Strategies in an Unpredictable World*, Kogan Page, London.

Stacey, R.D. (1993a) 'Strategy as Order Emerging from Chaos', *Long Range Planning*, Vol. 26, No. 1, pp. 10–17.

Stacey, R.D. (1993b) *Strategic Management and Organizational Dynamics*, Pitman, London.

Stalk, G., Evans, P., and Shulman, L.E. (1992) 'Competing on Capabilities: The New Rules of Corporate Strategy', *Harvard Business Review*, Vol. 70, No. 2, March–April, pp. 57–69.

Stewart, T.A. (1998) 'Knowledge, the Appreciating Commodity', *Fortune*, October 12, pp. 199.

Stopford, J.M., and Baden-Fuller, C. (1990) 'Corporate Rejuvenation', *Journal of Management Studies*, July, pp. 399–415.

Strebel, P. (1994) 'Choosing the Right Change Path', *California Management Review*, Vol. 36, No. 2, Winter, pp. 29–51.

Tannenbaum, R., and Schmidt, W.H. (1958) 'How to Choose a Leadership Pattern', *Harvard Business Review*, Vol. 36, No. 2, March–April, pp. 95–101.

Taylor, A. III (1997) 'How Toyota Defies Gravity', *Fortune*, December, p. 8.

The Conference Board (1997) *HR Executive Review*, Vol. 5, No. 3, p. 3.

Tichy, N., and Cohen, E. (1997) *The Leadership Engine: How Winning Companies Build Leaders at Every Level*, HaperCollins, New York.

Tichy, N., and Devanna, M. (1987) *The Transformational Leader*, Wiley, New York.

Tichy, N.M., and Ulrich, D.O. (1984) 'SMR Forum: The Leadership Challenge – A Call for the Transformational Leader', *Sloan Management Review*, Vol. 26, No. 1, Fall, pp. 59–68.

Tjosvold, D. (1986) *Working Together to Get Things Done*, D.C. Heath, Lexington, MA.

Trice, H.M., and Beyer, J.M. (1993) *The Cultures of Work Organizations*, Prentice Hall, Englewood Cliffs, NJ.

Tucker, R.C. (1968) 'The Theory of Charismatic Leadership', *Daedalus*, Vol. 97, No. 3, pp. 731–756.

Tushman, M.L., Newman, W.H. and Romanelli, E. (1986) 'Convergence and Upheaval: Managing the Unsteady Pace of Organizational Evolution', *California Management Review*, Vol. 29, No. 1, Fall, pp. 29–44.

Vroom, V.H., and Jago, A.G. (1988) *The New Leadership: Managing Participation in Organizations*, Prentice Hall, Englewood Cliffs, NJ.

Wack, P. (1985) 'Scenarios: Uncharted Waters Ahead', *Harvard Business Review*, Vol. 64, No. 5, September–October, pp. 73–89.

Waldman, D.A., and Yammarino, F.H. (1999) 'CEO Charismatic Leadership: Levels-of-Management and Levels-of-Analysis Effects', *Academy of Management Review*, Vol. 24, No. 2, pp. 266–285.

Weick, K.E. (1979) *The Social Psychology of Organizing*, Random House, New York.

Wheatly, M.J., and Kellner-Rogers, M. (1996) 'Self-Organization: The Irresistible Future of Organizing', *Strategy, and Leadership*, Vol. 24, No. 4, pp. 18–25.

Yoshino, M. (2002) *Nissan Motor Co. 2002*, Harvard Business School Press, Boston, MA.

Yukl, G. (1994) *Leadership in Organizations*, Third Edition, Prentice Hall, Englewood Cliffs, NJ.

Zalesnik, A. (1977) 'Managers and Leaders: Are They Different?', *Harvard Business Review*, Vol. 55, No. 3, May–June, pp. 67–78.

Zalesnik, A. (1989) *The Managerial Mystique: Restoring Leadership in Business*, Harper & Row, New York.

Zbaracki, M. (1998) 'The Rhetoric and Reality of Total Quality Management', *Administrative Science Quarterly*, Vol. 43, pp. 602–636.

THE INTERNATIONAL CONTEXT

There never were, since the creation of the world, two cases exactly parallel.

Philip Dormer Stanhope (1694–1773); English Secretary of State

INTRODUCTION

As firms move out of their domestic market on to the international stage, they are faced with differing business arenas. The nations they expand to can vary with regard to consumer behavior, language, legal system, technological infrastructure, business culture, educational system, labor relations, political ideology, distribution structures and fiscal regime, to name just a few. At face value, the plurality of the international context can seem daunting. Yet, the question is how important the international differences are for firms operating across borders. Do firms need to adapt to the international diversity encountered, or can they find ways of overcoming the constraints imposed by distinct national systems, structures and behaviors? This matter of understanding and dealing with international variety is one of the key topics for managers operating across borders.

A second question with regard to the international context is that of international linkages – to what extent do events in one country have an impact on what happens in other countries? When a number of nations are tightly linked to one another in a particular area, this is referred to as a case of international integration. If, on the other hand, there are very weak links between developments in one country and developments elsewhere, this is referred to as a situation of international fragmentation. The question for managers is how tightly linked nations around the world actually are. Countries might be quite different, yet developments in one nation might significantly influence developments elsewhere. For instance, if interest rates rise in the United States, central bankers in most other countries cannot ignore this. If the price of oil goes down on the spot market in Rotterdam, this will have a 'spill over effect' towards most other nations. And if a breakthrough chip technology is developed in Taiwan, this will send a shockwave through the computer industry around the world. If nations are highly integrated, the manager must view all countries as part of the same system – as squares on a chessboard, not to be judged in isolation.

When looking at the subjects of international variety and linkages, it is also important to know in which direction they have been moving, and will develop further, over time. Where a development towards lower international variety and tighter international linkages on a worldwide scale can be witnessed, a process of globalization is at play. Where a movement towards more international variety and a loosening of international linkages is apparent, a process of localization is taking place.

For managers operating in more than one nation, it is vital to understand the nature of the international context. Have their businesses been globalizing or localizing, and what can be expected in future? Answers to these questions should guide strategizing managers in choosing which countries to be active in and how to manage their activities across borders. Taken together, these international context questions constitute the issue of international configuration, and will be the focus of the further discussion in this chapter.

THE ISSUE OF INTERNATIONAL CONFIGURATION

How a firm configures its activities across borders is largely dependent on how it deals with the fundamental tension between the opposite demands of globalization and localization. To understand these forces, pulling the organization in contrary directions, it is first necessary to further define them. Globalization and localization are terms used by many, but explained by few. This lack of uniform definition often leads to an unfocused debate, as different people employ the same terms, but actually refer to different phenomena. Therefore, this discussion will start with a clarification of the concepts of globalization and localization. Subsequently, attention will turn to the two central questions facing the international manager: which countries should the firm be active in and how should this array of international activities be managed? This first question, of deciding on which geographic areas the organization should be involved in, is the issue of international composition. The second question, of deciding on the organizational structure and systems needed to run the multi-country activities, is the issue of international management.

Dimensions of globalization

Clearly, globalization refers to the process of becoming more global. But what is global? Although there is no agreement on a single definition, most writers use the term to refer to one or more of the following elements (see Figure 10.1):

- Worldwide scope. 'Global' can simply be used as a geographic term. A firm with operations around the world can be labeled a global company, to distinguish it from firms that are local (not international) or regional in scope. In such a case, the term 'global' is primarily intended to describe the *spatial* dimension – the broadest possible international scope is to be global. When this definition of global is employed, globalization is the process of international expansion on a worldwide scale (e.g. Patel and Pavitt, 1991).

- Worldwide similarity. 'Global' can also refer to homogeneity around the world. For instance, if a company decides to sell the same product in all of its international markets, it is often referred to as a global product, as opposed to a locally tailored product. In such a case, the term 'global' is primarily intended to describe the *variance* dimension – the ultimate level of worldwide similarity is to be global. When this definition of global is employed, globalization is the process of declining international variety (e.g. Levitt, 1983, Reading 10.1 in this book).

- Worldwide integration. 'Global' can also refer to the world as one tightly linked system. For instance, a global market can be said to exist if events in one country are significantly impacted by events in other geographic markets. This as opposed to local markets, where price levels, competition, demand and fashions are hardly influenced by developments in other nations. In such a case, the term 'global' is primarily intended to describe the *linkages* dimension – the ultimate level of worldwide integration is to be global. When this definition of global is employed, globalization is the process of increasing international interconnectedness (e.g. Porter, 1986).

FIGURE 10.1   Internationalization and globalization of the firm

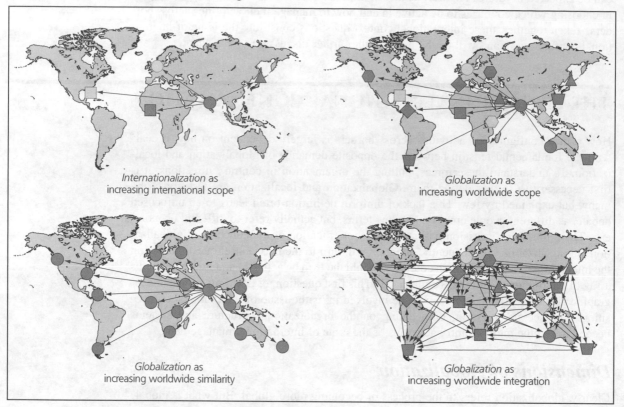

So, is for example McDonald's a global company? That depends along which of the above three dimensions the company is measured. When judging the international scope of McDonald's, it can be seen that the company is globalizing, but far from global. The company operates in approximately half the countries in the world, but in many of these only in one or a few large cities. Of McDonald's worldwide revenues, more than half is still earned in the United States. This predominance of the home country is even stronger if the composition of the company's top management is looked at (Ruigrok and Van Tulder, 1995). However, when judging McDonald's along the dimension of international similarity, it is simple to observe that the company is relatively global, as it takes a highly standardized approach to most markets around the world. Although, it should be noted that on some aspects as menu and interior design there is leeway for local adaptation. Finally, when judging McDonald's along the dimension of international integration, the company is only slightly global, as it is not very tightly linked around the world. Some activities are centralized or coordinated, but in general there is relatively little need for concerted action.

As for localization – the opposite of the process of globalization – it is characterized by decreasing international scope, similarity and integration. From the angle of international strategy the most extreme form of localness is when firms operate in one country and there is no similarity or integration between countries (e.g. the hairdressing and driving school businesses). However, this equates local with national, while firms and businesses can be even more local, all the way down to the state/province/department/district and municipal playing fields.

Levels of globalization

The second factor complicating a clear understanding of the concept of globalization is that it is applied to a variety of subjects, while the differences are often not made explicit. Some people discuss globalization as a development in the economy at large, while others debate globalization as something happening to industries, markets, products, technologies, fashions, production, competition and organizations. In general, debates on globalization tend to concentrate on one of three levels of analysis:

- Globalization of companies. Some authors focus on the micro level, debating whether individual companies are becoming more global. Issues are the extent to which firms have a global strategy, structure, culture, workforce, management team and resource base. In more detail, the globalization of specific products and value-adding activities is often discussed. Here it is of particular importance to acknowledge that the globalization of one product or activity (e.g. marketing) does not necessarily entail the globalization of all others (e.g. Prahalad and Doz, 1987; Bartlett and Ghoshal, 1987, Reading 10.4).

- Globalization of businesses. Other authors are more concerned with the *meso* level, debating whether particular businesses are becoming more global. Here it is important to distinguish those who emphasize the globalization of markets, as opposed to those accentuating the globalization of industries (see Chapter 5 for this distinction). The issue of globalizing markets has to do with the growing similarity of worldwide customer demand and the growing ease of worldwide product flows (e.g. Levitt, 1983, Reading 10.1; Douglas and Wind, 1987, Reading 10.2). For example, the crude oil and foreign currency markets are truly global – the same commodities are traded at the same rates around the world. The markets for accountancy and garbage collection services, on the other hand, are very local – demand differs significantly, there is little cross-border trade and consequently prices vary sharply. The globalization of industries is quite a different issue, as it has to do with the emergence of a set of producers that compete with one another on a worldwide scale (e.g. Prahalad and Doz, 1987; Porter, 1990a, 1990b). So, for instance, the automobile and consumer electronics industries are quite global – the major players in most countries belong to the same set of companies that compete against each other all around the world. Even the accountancy industry is relatively global, even though the markets for accountancy services are very local. On the other hand, the hairdressing and retail banking industries are very local – the competitive scene in each country is relatively uninfluenced by competitive developments elsewhere.

- Globalization of economies. Yet other authors take a macro level of analysis, arguing whether or not the world's economies in general are experiencing a convergence trend. Many authors are interested in the macroeconomic dynamics of international integration and its consequences in terms of growth, employment, inflation, productivity, trade and foreign direct investment (e.g. Kay, 1989; Krugman, 1990). Others focus more on the political realities constraining and encouraging globalization (e.g. Klein, 2000; McGrew and Lewis, 1992). Yet others are interested in the underlying dynamics of technological, institutional and organizational convergence (e.g. Dunning, 1986; Kogut, 1993).

Ultimately, the question in this chapter is not only whether economies, businesses and companies are actually globalizing, but also whether these developments are a matter of choice. In other words, is global convergence or continued international diversity an uncontrollable evolutionary development to which firms (and governments) must comply, or can managers actively influence the globalization or localization of their environment?

International composition

An international firm operates in two or more countries. When a firm starts up value-adding activities in yet another country, this process is called internationalization. In Figure 10.2 an overview is presented of the most common forms of internationalization. One of the earliest international growth moves undertaken by firms is to sell their products to foreign buyers, either directly (internet or telephone sales), through a traveling sales-person, or via a local agent or distributor. Such types of export activities are generally less taxing for the organization than the establishment of a foreign sales subsidiary (or sales unit). Serving a foreign market by means of a sales subsidiary often requires a higher level of investment in terms of marketing expenditures, sales force development and after-sales service provision. A firm can also set up a foreign production subsidiary (or 'off-shore' production unit), whose activities are focused on manufacturing goods to be exported back to the firm's other markets. Alternatively, a firm can begin an integrated foreign subsidiary that is responsible for a full range of value-adding activities, including production and sales. In practice, there are many variations to these basic forms of internationalization, depending on the specific value-adding activities carried out in different countries. For example, some subsidiaries have R&D, assembly and marketing their portfolio of activities, while others do not (Birkenshaw and Hood, 1998).

When establishing a foreign subsidiary the internationalizing firm must decide whether to purchase an existing local company (entry by acquisition) or to start from scratch (greenfield entry). In both cases the firm can work independently or by means of a joint venture with a local player or foreign partner. It is also possible to dispense with the estab-lishment of a subsidiary at all, by networking with local manufacturers, assemblers, sales agents and distributors (as discussed in Chapter 7).

The issue of international composition deals with the question of where the firm wants to have a certain level of involvement. The firm's strategists must decide where to allocate resources, build up activities and try to achieve results. The issue of international composition can be further subdivided into two parts:

FIGURE 10.2   International growth options

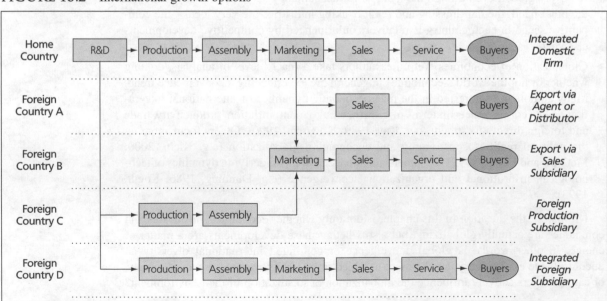

- International scope. The international composition of the firm depends first of all on the countries selected to do business in. The geographic spectrum covered by the firm is referred to as its international scope. The firm's strategists must decide how many countries they want to be active in, and which countries these should be.

- International distribution. The international composition of the firm also depends on how it has distributed its value-adding activities across the countries selected. In some firms all national subsidiaries carry out similar activities and are of comparable size. However, in many firms activities are distributed less symmetrically, with, for example, production, R&D and marketing concentrated in only a few countries (Porter, 1986). Commonly some countries will also contribute much more revenue and profits than others, but these might not be the countries where new investments can best be made. It is the task of the firm's strategists to determine how activities can best be distributed and how resources can best be allocated across the various countries.

Just as a corporation's portfolio of businesses could be visualized by means of a portfolio grid, so too can a business's portfolio of foreign sales markets be displayed using such a matrix. In Figure 10.3 a fictitious example is given of a firm's international sales portfolio using the GE business screen as analysis tool. Instead of industry attractiveness along the vertical axis, country attractiveness is used, calculating items such as market growth, competitive intensity, buyer power, customer loyalty, government regulation and operating costs. Following a similar logic, firms can also evaluate their international portfolios of, for instance, production locations and R&D facilities.

Deciding which portfolio of countries to be active in, both in terms of international scope and distribution, will largely depend on the strategic motives that have stimulated the firm to enter the international arena in the first place. After all, there must be some good reasons why a firm is willing to disregard the growth opportunities in its home market and to enter into uncertain foreign adventures. There must be some advantages to being international that offset the disadvantages of foreignness and distance. These advantages

FIGURE 10.3 Example of a foreign sales market portfolio

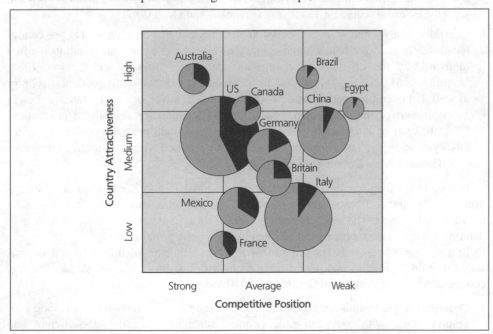

of having activities in two or more countries – cross-border synergies – will be discussed in more detail, after an account of the second international configuration question, the issue of international management.

International management

A firm operating in two or more countries needs to find some way of organizing itself to deal with its border-spanning nature. As managing across borders is difficult and costly, the simplest solution would be to organize all operations on a country-by-country basis, and to leave all country units as autonomous as possible. Yet, internationalization is only economically rational if 'the international whole is more than the sum of the country parts' (see Chapter 6). In other words, internationalization only makes sense if enough cross-border synergies can be reaped to offset the extra cost of foreignness and distance.

Therefore, the firm needs to have international integration mechanisms to facilitate the realization of cross-border synergies. The three most important integration mechanisms used in international management are:

- Standardization. An easy way to reap cross-border synergies is to do the same thing in each country, without any costly adaptation. Such standardization can be applied to all aspects of the business model (see Chapter 5) – the product offerings, value-adding activities and resources employed. Standardization is particularly important for achieving economies of scale (e.g. Hout, Porter and Rudden, 1982; Levitt, 1983), but can be equally valuable for serving border-crossing clients who want to encounter a predictable offering (e.g. Hamel and Prahalad, 1985; Yip, 1993).

- Coordination. Instead of standardizing products or activities, international firms can also align their varied activities in different countries by means of cross-border coordination. Getting the activities in the various countries aligned is often inspired by the need to serve border-crossing clients in a coordinated manner (e.g. global service level agreements), or to counter these clients' policy of playing off the firm's subsidiaries against one another (e.g. cross-border price shopping). International coordination can be valuable when responding to, or attacking, competitors as well. A coordinated assault on a few markets, financed by the profits from many markets (i.e. cross-subsidization), can sometimes lead to competitive success (Prahalad and Doz, 1987).

- Centralization. Of course, activities within the firm can also be integrated at one central location, either in the firm's home country or elsewhere. Such centralization is often motivated by the drive for economies of scale (e.g. Buckley and Casson, 1985; Dunning, 1981), but might be due to the competitive advantage of a particular country as well. For example, production costs might be much lower, or quality much higher, in a certain part of the world, making it a logical location for centralized production. Centralization of knowledge intensive activities is sometimes also needed, to guard quality or to ensure faster learning than could be attained with decentralized activities (e.g. Porter, 1990b; Dunning, 1993).

It is up to the firm's strategists to determine the most appropriate level of standardization, coordination and centralization needed to function efficiently and effectively in an international context. The level chosen for each of these three characteristics will largely determine the organizational model adopted by the international firm.

In their seminal research, Bartlett and Ghoshal (1989) distinguish four generic organizational models for international firms, each with its own mix of standardization, coordination and centralization (see Figure 10.4):

- Decentralized federation. In a decentralized federation, the firm is organized along geographic lines, with each full-scale country subsidiary largely self-sufficient and

FIGURE 10.4 Generic organizational models for international firms (adapted from Bartlett and Ghoshal, 1995)

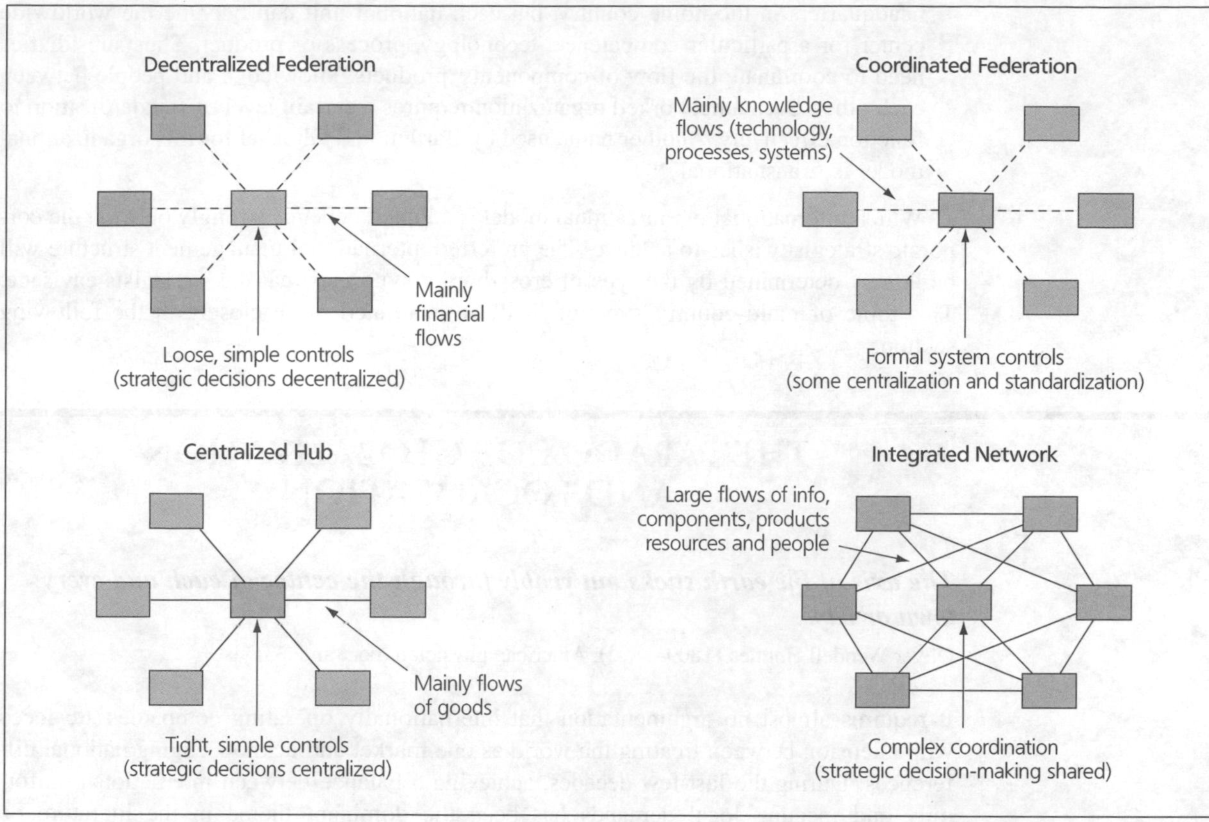

autonomous from international headquarters in the home country. Few activities are centralized and little is coordinated across borders. The level of standardization is also low, as the country unit is free to adapt itself to the specific circumstances in its national environment. Bartlett and Ghoshal refer to this organizational model as 'multinational'. Another common label is 'multi-domestic' (e.g. Prahalad and Doz, 1987; Stopford and Wells, 1972).

- Coordinated federation. In a coordinated federation, the firm is also organized along geographic lines, but the country subsidiaries have a closer relationship with the international headquarters in the home country. Most of the core competences, technologies, processes and products are developed centrally, while other activities are carried out locally. As a consequence, there is some standardization and coordination, requiring some formalized control systems (i.e. planning, budgeting, administration). Another name employed by Bartlett and Ghoshal to refer to this organizational model is 'international'.

- Centralized hub. In a centralized hub, national units are relatively unimportant, as all main activities are carried out in the home country. Generally a highly standardized approach is used towards all foreign markets. As centralization and standardization are high, foreign subsidiaries are limited to implementing headquarters' policies in the local markets. Coordination of activities across countries is made easy by the dominance of headquarters. Bartlett and Ghoshal use the term 'global' to describe this organizational model.

- Integrated network. In an integrated network, the country subsidiaries have a close relationship with international headquarters, just as in the coordinated federation, but also have a close relationship with each other. Very little is centralized at the international headquarters in the home country, but each national unit can become the worldwide center for a particular competence, technology, process or product. Thus subsidiaries need to coordinate the flow of components, products, knowledge and people between each other. Such a networked organization requires a certain level of standardization to function effectively. Another name used by Bartlett and Ghoshal for this organizational model is 'transnational'.

Which international organizational model is adopted depends strongly on what the corporate strategist wishes to achieve. The preferred international management structure will be largely determined by the type of cross-border synergies that the strategists envisage. This topic of multi-country synergies will be examined more closely in the following section.

THE PARADOX OF GLOBALIZATION AND LOCALIZATION

The axis of the earth sticks out visibly through the center of each and every town or city.

Oliver Wendell Holmes (1809–1894); American physician, poet and essayist

It requires almost no argumentation that internationally operating companies are faced with a tension between treating the world as one market and acknowledging national differences. During the last few decades, achieving a balance between international uniformity and meeting local demands has been the dominant theme in the literature on international management. All researchers have recognized the tension between international standardization and local adaptation. The key question has been whether international firms have the *liberty* to standardize or face the *pressure* to adapt.

However, since the mid-1980s, this standardization-adaptation discussion has progressed significantly as strategy researchers have moved beyond the organizational design question, seeking the underlying strategic motives for standardization and adaptation (e.g. Bartlett and Ghoshal, 1987; Porter, 1986; Prahalad and Doz, 1987). It has been acknowledged that international standardization is not a matter of organizational convenience that companies naturally revert to when the market does not demand local adaptation. Rather, international standardization is a means for achieving cross-border synergies. A firm can achieve cross-border synergies by leveraging resources, integrating activities and aligning product offerings across two or more countries. Creating additional value in this way is the very *raison d'être* of the international firm. If internationalizing companies would fully adapt to local conditions, without leveraging a homegrown quality, they would have no advantage over local firms, while they would be burdened by the extra costs of international business (e.g. overcoming distance and foreignness). Therefore, international companies need to realize at least enough cross-border synergies to compensate for the additional expenses of operating in multiple countries.

Much of the theoretical discourse has focused on the question which cross-border synergies can be achieved on the ultimate, global scale. Most researchers identify various potential opportunities for worldwide synergy, yet recognize the simultaneous demands to meet the specific conditions in each local market (e.g. Dicken, 1992; Yip, 1993). These possibilities for reaping global synergy will be examined first, followed by the countervailing pressures for local responsiveness.

The demand for global synergy

Striving for cross-border synergies on as large a scale as possible can be an opportunity for an international firm to enhance its competitive advantage. However, realizing global synergies is often less an opportunity than a competitive demand. If rival firms have already successfully implemented a global strategy, there can be a severe pressure to also reap the benefits of globalization through standardization, coordination and/or centralization.

There are many different types of cross-border synergies. In accordance with the business model framework described in Chapter 5, these synergies can be organized into three categories: aligning product offerings, integrating activities and leveraging resources (see Figure 10.5).

Synergy by aligning positions.   The first way to create cross-border synergies is to align market positions in the various countries in which the firm operates. Taking a coordinated approach to different national markets can be necessary under two circumstances – namely to provide a concerted cross-border product offering to customers and to stage a concerted cross-border attack on competitors:

- Dealing with cross-border customers. An international firm is ideally placed to offer border-crossing customers an internationally coordinated product and/or service offering. Whether it is for a tourist who wants to have the same hotel arrangements around the world, or for an advertiser who wants to stage a globally coordinated new product introduction, it can be important to have a standardized and coordinated offering across various nations. It might be equally necessary to counter the tactics of customers

FIGURE 10.5   Forms of cross-border synergies

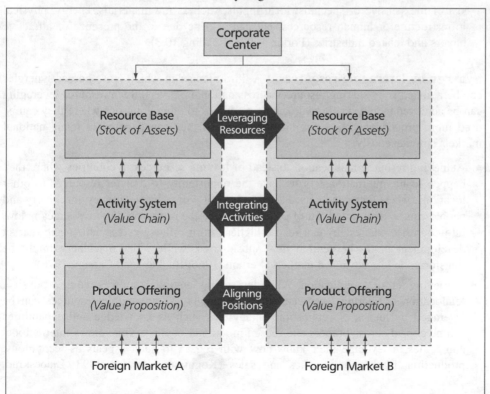

shopping around various national subsidiaries for the best deals, or to meet the customer's demand to aggregate all global buying via one central account.

- Dealing with cross-border competition. An international firm is also in an ideal position to successfully attack locally oriented rivals, if it does not spread its resources too thinly around the world, but rather focuses on only a few countries at a time. By coordinating its competitive efforts and bringing its global power to bear on a few national markets, an international firm can push back or even defeat local rivals country-by-country. Of course, an international company must also have the capability of defending itself against such a globally coordinated attack by a rival international firm.

Synergy by integrating activities.   Cross-border synergies can also be achieved by linking the activity systems of the firm in its various national markets. Integrating the value-creation processes across borders can be useful to realize economies of scale and to make use of the specific competitive advantages of each nation:

- Reaping scale advantages. Instead of organizing the international firm's activity system on a country-by-country basis, certain activities can be pooled to reap economies of scale. Commonly this means that activities must be centralized at one or a few locations, and that a certain level of product and/or process standardization must be accepted. Economies of scale can be realized for many activities, most notably production, logistics, procurement and R&D. However, scale advantages might be possible for all activities of the firm. Although scale advantages are often pursued by means of centralization, it is often possible to achieve economies by standardizing and coordinating activities across borders (e.g. joint procurement, joint marketing campaigns).

- Reaping location advantages. For some activities certain locations are much more suited than others, making it attractive to centralize these activities in the countries that possess a particular competitive advantage. A national competitive advantage can consist of inexpensive or specialist local inputs, such as raw materials, energy, physical infrastructure or human resources, but can also be due to the presence of attractive buyers and related industries (Porter, 1990a, Reading 10.3).

Synergy by leveraging resources.   A third manner in which cross-border synergies can be realized is by sharing resources across national markets. Such resource leveraging can be achieved by physically reallocating resources to other countries where they can be used more productively, or by replicating them so they can be used in many national markets simultaneously:

- Achieving resource reallocation. Instead of leaving resources in countries where they happen to be, international firms have the opportunity to transfer resources to other locations, where they can be used to more benefit. For example, money, machinery and people can be reallocated out of countries where the return on these resources is low, into countries where they can reap a higher return. Managers specializing in market development might be sent to new subsidiaries, while older machinery might be transferred to less advanced markets (Vernon, 1966; Buckley and Casson, 1976).

- Achieving resource replication. While leveraging tangible resources requires physical reallocation or sharing (see reaping scale advantages), intangible resources can be leveraged by means of replication. Intangibles such as knowledge and capabilities can be copied across borders and reused in another country. This allows international companies to leverage their know-how with regard to such aspects as technology, production, marketing, logistics and sales (Kogut and Zander, 1993; Liebeskind, 1996).

For all of these cross-border synergies it holds that the wider the geographic scope, the greater the potential benefit. Where possible, realizing these synergies on a global scale would result in the highest level of value creation.

These opportunities for global synergy represent a strong demand on all companies, both international and domestic. If a company can reap these synergies more quickly and successfully than its competitors, this could result in a strong offensive advantage. If other companies have a head start in capturing these global synergies, the firm must move quickly to catch up. Either way, there is a pressure on companies to seek out opportunities for global synergy and to turn them to their advantage.

The demand for local responsiveness

Yet the pressure to pursue global synergies is only half the equation. Simultaneously, companies must remain attuned to the specific demands of each national market and retain the ability to respond to these particular characteristics in a timely and adequate manner. In other words, firms must have the capability to be responsive to local conditions. If they lose touch with the distinct competitive dynamics in each of their national markets, they might find themselves at a competitive disadvantage compared to more responsive rivals.

While business responsiveness is always important, it becomes all the more pressing when the differences between various national markets are large. The more dissimilar the national markets, the more pressure on the international firm to be attuned to these distinct characteristics. The most important differences between countries include:

- Differences in market structure. Countries can differ significantly with regard to their competitive landscape. For example, in some national markets there are strong local competitors, requiring the international firm to respond differently than in countries where it encounters its 'regular' international rivals. Another difference is that in some countries there are only a few market parties, while in other countries the market is highly fragmented among numerous competitors. There can also be large differences from country to country in the background of competitors – in some countries conglomerates dominate the business scene, while in other countries single business competitors are more frequent.

- Differences in customer needs. Customers in each national market can have needs that are significantly different than the needs exhibited in other countries. The nature of these customer differences can vary from divergent cultural expectations and use circumstances, to incompatible technical systems and languages employed.

- Differences in buying behavior. Not only the customers' needs can differ across countries, but so can their buying behavior. For example, customers can be different with regard to the way they structure buying decisions, the types of information they consider and the relationship they wish to have with their suppliers.

- Differences in substitutes. National markets can also differ with regard to the types of indirect competition that needs to be faced. In some countries, for instance, beer brewers have to deal with wine as an important rival product, while in other markets tea or soft drinks might be the most threatening substitutes.

- Differences in distribution channels. Countries can exhibit remarkable differences in the way their distribution channels work. For example, countries can vary with regard to the kinds of distribution channels available, the number of layers in the distribution structure, their level of sophistication, their degree of concentration and the negotiating power of each player.

- Differences in media structure. National markets can have very different media channels available for marketing communication purposes. In the area of television, for instance, countries vary widely with regard to the number of stations on the air (or on the cable), the types of regulation imposed, the amount of commercial time available, and its cost and effectiveness. In the same way, all other media channels may differ.

- Differences in infrastructure. Many products and services are heavily dependent on the type of infrastructure available in a country. For example, some products rely on a digital telephone system, high-speed motorways, 24-hour convenience stores, or a national healthcare system. Some services require an efficient postal service, poor public transport, electronic banking or cable television.

- Differences in supply structure. If a company has local operations, the differences between countries with regard to their supply structures can also force the company to be more locally responsive. Not only the availability, quality and price of raw materials and components can vary widely between countries, but the same is true for other inputs such as labor, management, capital, facilities, machinery, research, information and services.

- Differences in government regulations. As most government regulations are made on a country-by-country basis, they can differ significantly. Government regulations can affect almost every aspect of a company's operations, as they range from antitrust and product liability legislation, to labor laws and taxation rules.

Responsiveness to these local differences is not only a matter of adaptation. Simple adaptation can be reactive and slow. Being responsive means that the firm has to have the ability to be proactive and fast. As each market develops in a different way and at a different pace, the international firm needs to be able to respond quickly and adequately to remain in tune.

It is clear that international managers cannot afford to neglect being responsive to local conditions. Yet, at the same time, they need to realize cross-border synergies to create additional value. Unfortunately for managers, these two key demands placed on the international firm are, at least to some extent, in conflict with one another. Striving for cross-border synergies on a global scale will interfere with being locally responsive and vice versa. Therefore, the question is how these two conflicting demands can be reconciled – how can the international manager deal with the paradox of globalization and localization?

EXHIBIT 10.1 SHORT CASE

WAL-MART: ANOTHER BRICK IN THE WALL?

Bentonville, Arkansas. Small-town America. On one side of the street is Colleen's Beauty Chalet; on the other is a three-story warehouse with a brick facade. Although rather unremarkable, this is the headquarters of the largest company in the world, Wal-Mart. By reaching revenues exceeding US$246 billion in 2002, Wal-Mart overtook General Motors and Exxon-Mobil, which had previously topped the global sales list. Drawn by rock-bottom prices and friendly service, 100 million customers push their shopping carts through the aisles of Wal-Mart's stores every week. There they can find everything, ranging from food and clothing to hardware, elec-

tronics and medicine. At the same time they can do their banking, have their weekend's pictures developed, get their eyes checked and have the oil changed in their car. The company that started as a humble discount retailer in small-town America now operates some 4400 stores in ten countries, employing 1.4 million people, also making it the largest private employer in the world.

Sam Walton and his brother James 'Bud' Walton opened up their first Discount City Store in 1962, selling a broad range of general merchandise and soon started adding new stores to this chain. While most of their American rivals in the 'low price department store' category, like K-Mart and Target, focused on urban areas, Wal-Mart stores were typically located in small and medium-sized towns, where they faced only fragmented competition and profited from lower operating costs. As the Walton brothers offered prices equal to, or lower than, prices in nearby cities, this made them very popular among local shoppers. Sam Walton, who died in 1992, was an ambitious man: whenever his wife pressed him to stop building new stores, his answer was always 'just one more, dear'. To keep on growing, Wal-Mart eventually broadened beyond its rural base, expanding into metropolitan areas. Wal-Mart also expanded into grocery retailing, by creating Wal-Mart Supercenters, which combine the inventories of a discount store with a full-line supermarket. Furthermore, Wal-Mart set up a chain of membership-based warehouse stores focused on bulk sales, called Sam's Clubs.

By the beginning of the 1990s Wal-Mart had become the largest retailer in the United States, and started to look to foreign markets to sustain the 30% annual growth rate that it had averaged throughout the 1980s. Not only capital markets had come to expect this pace of growth, but so did Wal-Mart's employees, many of whom have significant amounts of shares through the company's stock purchase plan. The first step abroad was into Mexico in 1991, where the company started a 50–50 joint venture with Mexico's largest retailer, Cifra, and then to Puerto Rico in 1992. The following moves showed that Wal-Mart wanted to have the large markets in the Americas as its initial international focus – in 1994 a 60–40 joint venture was established with Lojas Americana in Brazil, followed later in the year by the acquisition and rebranding of 122 Woolco stores in Canada, and a greenfield entry into Argentina in 1995. By 1996 Wal-Mart felt confident enough to shift its expansion focus to Asia, first entering China, and in 1998 South Korea, both by means of joint ventures with local players. To the surprise of many, Wal-Mart also signaled that it wanted to break into the more mature European markets, acquiring the 21-store Wertkauf chain in Germany in 1998, quickly followed up by the purchase of 74 German Interspar grocery stores in 1999. In the same year Wal-Mart rolled into Britain, taking over the 229-outlet ASDA supermarket group. After a short pause, Wal-Mart again surprised many by taking a minority stake in the Japanese retailer Seiyu in 2002, with the option of increasing its stake to 66.7% before 2008. By the end of 2002 Wal-Mart had more than 1200 stores outside of the United States, employing 300 000

people and generating revenues exceeding US$35 billion. It also had plans to invest about US$2 billion in 2003 to renovate existing stores abroad and to open about 130 new ones.

In this international expansion, Wal-Mart has attempted to replicate the competitive advantages it had already developed in its home market. At the heart of Wal-Mart's success has been its enormous bargaining power with multinational suppliers, which has helped it to sell branded products at 'everyday low prices', undercutting all other discount retailers. But there is much more to the Wal-Mart business model than buying and selling cheaply. On the buying side, Wal-Mart requires vendors to hook-up to its supply chain management system, to keep order entry and processing costs low, while keeping stock buffers in the supply chain to a bare minimum. Most merchandise is then shipped to Wal-Mart's advanced distribution centers, which have been tactically placed to be able to serve between 150 and 200 stores within a day's drive. These highly automated distribution centers operate 24 hours per day, using cross-docking techniques, whereby goods received at one end are quickly used to fill orders at the other. Wal-Mart's own fleet of trucks then supply the stores. This distribution and logistics infrastructure saves Wal-Mart transportation costs (only full truck loads are sent), while still ensuring that all the shelves are stocked, with a minimum of back-room inventory. At the same time, the sales and inventory data per store are analyzed to understand trends, to anticipate growing needs and to avoid being stuck with slow-moving stocks. Furthermore, Wal-Mart is known for having a dedicated and highly productive workforce that provides outstanding customer service. It achieves this loyalty and effectiveness by such policies as profit sharing, incentive bonuses, performance-based promotion from within and team-building.

Yet, from the beginning of its international expansion the question has been whether the Wal-Mart formula is exportable to all countries around the world. According to Craig Herkert, Chief of Operations of Wal-Mart International, there can be no doubt: 'Every day low prices, quality assortment and exceptional service are Wal-Mart principles that transcend borders, language and cultural differences.' Many analysts agree, pointing to Wal-Mart's many successes so far in transplanting its corporate DNA to other nations. In Canada, for instance, Wal-Mart was able to quickly turn around the acquired

▶

Woolco chain, increasing sales per square foot three-fold in only three years and increasing market share from roughly 20% to over 50%, making them the largest retailer in the country, with more than 200 stores. In Mexico, Wal-Mex operates approximately 600 stores, making them the largest retailer and private employer around. As one local put it, 'this idea that the customer comes first is a great gringo strategy'.

In entering foreign markets, Wal-Mart has been cautious not to bluntly apply its US store formats and range of merchandise. For example, in China the company experimented with a number of different store sizes (supercenters and smaller satellite stores) and added a range of local delicacies to the cooked food section. It also quickly became clear to the company that you can't sell electric stoves to Mexicans (they cook with natural gas), golf clubs to Brazilians (too few people are rich enough to play) or tenderized T-bone steaks to Argentineans (they prefer specially-cut rump steaks). Yet, the thrust of Wal-Mart's approach has been to 'standardize unless'. Mexicans have been turned in to avid bagel eaters, while donuts have been a runaway success in China. As a *Newsweek* reporter put it, 'the Wal-Mart effect is already homogenizing global consumer tastes. Sam Walton built his chain on the idea that you could sell the same stuff everywhere, and major Wal-Mart suppliers such as Proctor & Gamble and Heinz now often deliver the same sauces and soaps to Berlin, Mexico City and Houston.'

However, Wal-Mart's internationalization track record is not all fame and glory. Take its operations in Germany, where since its entry in 1997 the firm has suffered five consecutive years of negative results, losing US$100–200 million per year on sales of about US$3 billion. The first blow was that Wal-Mart encountered much stiffer competition than expected from another global retailing chain, Metro, which was on its home-turf, but equally from tough local chains such as Aldi and Lidl, who were trying to gain a larger share of a stagnant market with low prices and no-frills service. Moreover, the German managers running Wertkauf and Interspar were not amused by American 'mentors' telling them how to run their business when they didn't even speak German or know the German market. To make things worse, suppliers did not take kindly to being forced to switch to a new supply system and to send merchandise to Wal-Mart's new centralized warehouses, leaving Wal-Mart's shelves regularly empty. To start exerting pressure on suppliers, Wal-Mart would need to triple its market share to 6% and double the number of stores, but to their despair they have found that regulations protecting small neighborhood stores can add five or more years to the launching of a new hypermarket. Other rules are just as limiting, including store closing hours and labor laws. Wal-Mart also collided with fair-competition regulators, who forced them to raise prices on milk, butter and some other staples, which it was selling below cost. Top management had to concede they underestimated the challenge: 'We just walked in and said "we're going to lower prices, we're going to add people to the stores and we're going to remodel the stores, because inherently, that's correct", and it wasn't', Wal-Mart's CEO, Lee Scott, admitted.

To improve its international performance, Scott hired John Menzer as chief of Wal-Mart's International Division in 2000. Menzer hired a German as country head and delegated more authority in buying, logistics, building design and other operational decisions, not only in Germany, but across the board, cutting the international staff in Bentonville from 450 to less than 150 people. 'We could get very specific on what should be on an end cap [a store display at the end of an aisle] . . . I think we've matured', says Scott. In Germany, Wal-Mart is working with suppliers to boost centralized distribution efforts. Instead of the expensive renovations to 'Walmartize' 24 stores in 2000, the company switched to more modest facelifts and opened two new stores in 2001, instead of the intended 50. Says Menzer: 'We set ourselves back a few years, and now we're rebounding.'

Others are not convinced, wondering whether Wal-Mart's internationalization has not hit a brick wall: 'We don't see Wal-Mart as a threat anymore', says Hong Sun Sang of E-Mart, a 35-store chain in South Korea, indicating that Wal-Mart's 'headquarters knows best' mind-set is their Achilles' heel. With few top managers that aren't American and few people around that speak more than one language, critics point out that it will be difficult for Wal-Mart to ever become more than a US company with an international division. Moreover, critics argue that Wal-Mart might be able to enter less developed retailing markets like China, but are in for trouble in mature markets such as Europe and Japan. And even in China, Wal-Mart will need to become more Chinese to withstand the pressure of copycat competitors, while at the same time being up against more experienced international competitors such as Carrefour, Tesco, Ahold and Metro.

As Wal-Mart wants to keep up its pace of international expansion, a key question for Scott and Menzer is where the 'Wal-Martians' should land next – what should be the next brick in the wall? But just as important is the question of how the company should manage itself internationally, to gain a strong competitive position in each country of operation. Despite all international problems, both inside and outside the company, one thing was clear to Scott: 'The chances this company has to grow are as big as it ever had in the past.' If Sam Walton were still around, he certainly would agree.

Sources: *Business Week*, September 3 2001; *Newsweek*, May 20 2002; *Fortune*, May 13 2002; Wal-Mart Annual Report 2002; Govindarajan and Gupta, 1999; www.walmartstores.com.

PERSPECTIVES ON THE INTERNATIONAL CONTEXT

Nothing is more dangerous than an idea, when you have only one idea.
Alain (Emile-Auguste Chartier) (1868–1951); French poet and philosopher

When doing business in an international context, it is generally accepted that the challenge for firms is to strive for cross-border synergies, while simultaneously being responsive to the local conditions. It is acknowledged that international managers need to weigh the specific characteristics of their business when reconciling the paradox of globalization and localization – some businesses are currently more suited for a global approach than others. Where opinions start to diverge is on the question of which businesses will become more global, or can be made more global, in the near future. To some managers it is evident that countries are rapidly becoming increasingly similar and more closely interrelated. To them globalization is already far advanced and will continue into the future, wiping out the importance of nations as it progresses. Therefore, they argue that it is wise to anticipate, and even encourage, a 'nationless' world, by focusing on global synergies over local responsiveness. Other managers, however, are more skeptical about the speed and impact of globalization. In their view, much so-called globalization is quite superficial, while at a deeper level important international differences are not quickly changing and cross-border integration is moving very slowly. They also note that there are significant counter-currents creating more international variety, with the potential of loosening international linkages. Therefore, wise managers should remain highly responsive to the complex variety and fragmentation that characterizes our world, while only carefully seeking out selected cross-border synergy opportunities.

These differing opinions among international strategists are reflected in differing views in the strategic management literature. While there is a wide spectrum of positions on the question of how the international context will develop, here the two opposite poles in the debate will be identified and discussed. On the one side of the spectrum, there are the managers who believe that globalization is bringing Lennon's dream of the 'world living as one' closer and closer. This point of view is called the 'global convergence perspective'. At the other end of the spectrum are the managers who believe that deep-rooted local differences will continue to force firms to 'do in Rome as the Romans do'. This point of view is referred to as the 'international diversity perspective'.

The global convergence perspective

 According to proponents of the global convergence perspective, the growing similarity and integration of the world can be argued by pointing to extensive economic statistics, showing significant rises in foreign direct investment and international trade. Yet, it is simpler to observe things directly around you. For instance, are you wearing clothing unique to your country, or could you mingle in an international crowd without standing out? Is the television you watch, the vehicle you drive, the telephone you use and the timepiece you wear specific to your nation, or based on the same technology and even produced by the same companies as those in other countries? Is the music you listen to made by local bands, unknown outside your country, or is this music equally popular abroad? Is the food you eat unique to your region, or is even this served in other countries? Now compare your answers to what your parents would have answered 30 years ago – the difference is due to global convergence.

Global convergence, it is argued, is largely driven by the ease, low cost and frequency of international communication, transport and travel. This has diminished the importance of distance. In the past world of large distances, interactions between countries were few and international differences could develop in relative isolation. But the victory of technology over distance has created a 'global village', in which goods, services and ideas are easily exchanged, new developments spread quickly and the 'best practices' of one nation are rapidly copied in others. Once individuals and organizations interact with one another as if no geographic distances exist, an unstoppable process towards cultural, political, technological and economic convergence is set in motion – countries will become more closely linked to one another and local differences will be superseded by new global norms.

Of course, in the short run there will still be international differences and nations will not be fully integrated into a 'world without borders'. Managers taking a global convergence perspective acknowledge that such fundamental and wide-ranging changes take time. There are numerous sources of inertia – e.g. vested interests, commitment to existing systems, emotional attachment to current habits and fear of change. The same type of change inhibitors could be witnessed during the industrial revolution, as well. Yet, these change inhibitors can only slow the pace of global convergence, not reverse its direction – the momentum caused by the shrinking of distance can only be braked, but not stopped. Therefore, firms thinking further than the short term, should not let themselves be guided too much by current international diversity, but rather by the emerging global reality (Ohmae, 1990).

For individual firms, global convergence is changing the rules of the competitive game. While in the past most countries had their own distinct characteristics, pressuring firms to be locally responsive, now growing similarity offers enormous opportunities for leveraging resources and sharing activities across borders – e.g. production can be standardized to save costs, new product development can be carried out on an international scale to reduce the total investments required, and marketing knowledge can easily be exchanged to avoid reinventing the wheel in each country. Simultaneously, international integration has made it much easier to centralize production in large-scale facilities at the most attractive locations and to supply world markets from there, unrestrained by international borders. In the same manner, all types of activities, such as R&D, marketing, sales and procurement, can be centralized to profit from worldwide economies of scale.

An equally important aspect of international integration is that suppliers, buyers and competitors can also increasingly operate as if there are no borders. The ability of buyers to shop around internationally makes the world one global market, in which global bargaining power is very important. The ability of suppliers and competitors to reap global economies of scale and sell everywhere around the world creates global industries, in which competition takes place on a worldwide stage, instead of in each nation separately. To deal with such global industries and global markets, the firm must be able to align its market activities across nations.

These demands of standardization, centralization and coordination require a global firm, with a strong center responsible for the global strategy, instead of a federation of autonomous national subsidiaries focused on being responsive to their local circumstances. According to proponents of the global convergence perspective, such global organizations, or 'centralized hubs' (Bartlett and Ghoshal, 1995), will become increasingly predominant over time. And as more companies switch to a global strategy and a global organizational form, this will in turn speed up the general process of globalization. By operating in a global fashion, these firms will actually contribute to a further decrease of international variety and fragmentation. In other words, globalizing companies are both the consequence and a major driver of further global convergence.

EXHIBIT 10.2 THE GLOBAL CONVERGENCE PERSPECTIVE

SIX CONTINENTS: 'THE WORLD'S MOST GLOBAL HOTEL GROUP'

In the summer of 1951, Kemmons Wilson, the founder of Holiday Inn, took his family on 'the road trip that changed the world'. Unable to find lodgings for his family at an affordable price, Wilson decided to enter the hotel business himself. Now, some 50 years later, more travelers have stayed at a Holiday Inn than at any other hotel chain, making it the most recognized name in mid-range lodging around the world. Together with the luxurious InterContinental hotel chain and the business-class Crowne Plaza, Holiday Inn is now part of the Six Continents hotel group, which owns 3300 hotels in some 100 countries, selling 28 million hotel nights per year. 'Six Continents is a name which emphasizes the global spread of the company', according to Tim Clarke, chief executive of Six Continents Holding. Yet, worldwide scope is not the only thing that makes the hotel group global in character.

The distinct policy of Six Continents Hotels is that its ethos, culture and services should transcend national boundaries. With the mission of 'building the world's preferred places to meet, relax, and dream', Six Continents wants to offer its guests the same experience irrespective of the continent that they happen to be on. 'Our aim is to make our hotels the preferred choice of our guests, so that they return again and again, finding exactly the same level of service and the amenities they want, wherever they are', says Thomas Oliver, chairman and CEO of Six Continents Hotels. To achieve this level of conformity every hotel goes through the same service quality award program – 'our Quality Excellence Award sets the standard for all Six Continents hotels around the world', according to the Annual Report 2001. Guests can also make use of the global reservation system, Holidex, become members of the global loyalty program, Priority Club, and watch the same television programs around the world, provided by a global uniform broadcasting platform.

Behind the scenes, the company's global offerings are complemented by an impressive global infrastructure, managed from the company's headquarters in Atlanta and London. For instance, all Six Continents hotels make use of the same property management system, OPERA, reap the benefits of the corporation's alliances with product and service providers, and are able to make use of procurement systems that allow large-scale purchasing around the world. Marketing is often executed on a global scale as well. For instance, when the InterContinental in Hong Kong was refurbished, hotels such as the ones in Beirut, Chicago, London, New York, São Paulo and Tokyo had to join in for a fix up launch, supported by a US$25 million marketing campaign around the world. Taken together, this level of international service standardization and back-office coordination and centralization seems to justify Six Continents' claim to be the 'most global hotel group in the world'.

Sources: *Financial Times*, November 8 2002; Annual Report 2001; www.6c.com.

The international diversity perspective

To managers taking an international diversity perspective, the 'brave new world' outlined in the previous sub-section is largely science fiction. People around the world might be sporting a Swatch or a Rolex, munching Big Macs and drinking Coke, while sitting in their Toyota or Nissan, but to conclude that these are symptoms of global convergence is a leap of faith. Of course, there are some brand names and products more or less standardized around the world, and their numbers might actually be increasing. The question is whether these manufacturers are globalizing to meet increasing worldwide similarity, or whether they are actually finally utilizing the similarities between countries that have always existed. The actual level of international variety may really be quite consistent.

It is particularly important to recognize in which respects countries remain different. For instance, the world might be drinking the same soft drinks, but they are probably doing it in different places, at different times, under different circumstances and for different reasons in each country. The product might be standardized worldwide, but the cultural norms and values that influence its purchase and use remain diverse across countries. According to proponents of the international diversity perspective, it is precisely these fundamental aspects of culture that turn out to be extremely stable over time – habits change slowly, but cultural norms and values are outright rigid. Producers might be lucky to find one product that fits in with such cultural diversity, but it would be foolish to interpret this as worldwide cultural convergence.

Other national differences are equally resilient against the tides of globalization. No countries have recently given up their national language in favor of Esperanto or English. On the contrary, there has been renewed emphasis on the local language in many countries (e.g. Ireland and the Baltic countries) and regions (e.g. Catalonia and Quebec). In the same way, political systems have remained internationally diverse, with plenty of examples of localization, even within nations. For instance, in Russia and the United States the shift of power to regional governments has increased policy diversity within the country. Similar arguments can be put forward for legal systems, fiscal regimes, educational systems and technological infrastructure – each is extremely difficult to change due to the lock-in effects, vested interests, psychological commitment and complex decision-making processes.

For each example of increasing similarity, a counter-example of local initiatives and growing diversity could be given. Some proponents of the international diversity perspective argue that it is exactly this interplay of divergence and convergence forces that creates a dynamic balance preserving diversity. While technologies, organizing principles, political trends and social habits disperse across borders, resulting in global convergence, new developments and novel systems in each nation arise causing international divergence (Dosi and Kogut, 1993). Convergence trends are usually easier to spot than divergence – international dispersion can be more simply witnessed than new localized developments. To the casual observer, this might suggest that convergence trends have the upper hand, but after more thorough analysis, this conclusion must be cast aside.

Now add to this enduring international diversity the reality of international economic relations. Since World War II attempts have been made to facilitate the integration of national economies. There have been some regional successes (e.g. the North American Free Trade Association and the European Union) and some advances have been made on a worldwide scale (e.g. the World Trade Organization). However, progress has been slow and important political barriers remain.

The continued existence of international diversity and political obstacles, it is argued, will limit the extent to which nations can become fully integrated into one borderless world. International differences and barriers to trade and investment will frustrate firms' attempts to standardize and centralize, and will place a premium on firms' abilities to adapt and decentralize. Of course, there will be some activities for which global economies of scale can be achieved and for which international coordination is needed, but this will not become true for all activities. Empowering national managers to be responsive to specific local conditions will remain an important ingredient for international success. Balancing globalization and localization of the firm's activities will continue to be a requirement in the future international context.

Ideally, the internationally operating company should neither deny nor regret the existence of international diversity, but regard it as an opportunity that can be exploited. Each country's unique circumstances will pose different challenges, requiring the development of different competences. Different national 'climates' will create opportunities for different innovations. If a company can tap into each country's opportunities and leverage the acquired competences and innovations to other countries, this could offer the company an important source of competitive advantage. Naturally, these locally leveraged competences and innovations would subsequently need to be adapted to the specific circumstances in other countries. This balancing act would require an organization that combined strong local responsiveness with the ability to exchange and coordinate internationally, even on a worldwide scale. International organizations blending these two elements are called 'transnational' (Bartlett and Ghoshal, 1995), or 'heterarchical' (Hedlund, 1986). However, in some businesses the international differences will remain so large that an even more locally responsive organizational form might be necessary, operating on a federative basis.

EXHIBIT 10.3 THE INTERNATIONAL DIVERSITY PERSPECTIVE

HSBC: THE WORLD'S LOCAL BANK

When Scotsman Thomas Sutherland arrived in Hong Kong in 1865, he soon realized that the growing trade between China and Europe was creating considerable demand for local banking services, so he founded the Hongkong and Shanghai Banking Corporation (HSBC). As international trade grew and spread, so did HSBC, establishing offices around South-East Asia. By the 1950s, HSBC began to acquire subsidiaries farther afield, such as the Imperial Bank of Persia, the Cyprus Popular Bank, New York's Marine Midland Bank and CCF, one of France's largest banks. Nowadays the HSBC Group has some 7000 offices worldwide, employing 170 000 people, serving over 30 million customers in 81 countries. In 2002, HSBC ranked second in the world and first in Europe in terms of market capitalization, and received the 'Best Global Bank Award'.

HSBC is headed by Sir John Bond, a distinguished Hong Kong Anglo-Saxon, who has been with the bank since he was 19. When he became group chairman of HSBC Holding in 1998, he started a review of the firm's international strategy, questioning whether a globally standardized approach was the best route for the future. He wanted to blend the company's many acquisitions and subsidiaries into an integrated worldwide organization that could deliver high quality services around the globe, yet also strongly believed that the bank needed to embrace local cultures and conform to different regulatory regimes. To quote Bond:

Success for HSBC means operating in a globalizing world . . . but we don't want to Americanize the world; we want to enjoy the world in all its diversity. If globalization is about cultural hegemony, we disapprove. If it is about better products and services for host countries, and it benefits the citizens of a country, then we are for it.

In 2002 HSBC started a marketing campaign, positioning itself as the 'World's Local Bank'. The company's international strategy is 'to be a Chinese bank in China, a Brazilian bank in Brazil and a French bank in France', while still sharing core values around the world and creating a global back-office infrastructure. At the group's head office in London a global digital network, Hexagon, is at the core of HSBC's transaction, data and communication traffic.

All staff members around the world are also trained to use common operating platforms and conform to internal standards, based on 'a cast-iron set of universal values which we practice wherever we are in the world'. Within these boundaries, the various local subsidiaries are encouraged to develop products and services tailored to local circumstances by local staff. For instance, for countries with large Muslim populations HSBC has created an Islamic banking unit that conducts business according to the principle in the Koran, forbidding the charging of interest. Another example is that in Saudi Arabia women-only branches have been opened. Summing up HSBC's philosophy, Bond has remarked that 'we need to be constantly aware that we view the world through the distorting lens or our own culture, and that sometimes we need to change our perspective. In our business we aim to adjust to cultural requirements wherever needed.'

Sources: *Business Week*, September 20 1999; *The Banker*, September 1 2002; www.HSBC.com.

INTRODUCTION TO THE DEBATE AND READINGS

You may say I'm a dreamer,
but I'm not the only one;
I hope some day you'll join us,
and the world will live as one.

John Lennon (1940–1980);
British musician and songwriter

When I am at Milan,
I do as they do at Milan;
but when I go to Rome,
I do as Rome does.

St. Augustine (354–430);
Roman theologian and philosopher

So, is the international context moving towards increased similarity and integration, or will it remain as diverse and fragmented as at the moment? And what does this mean for the international configuration of firms? Should managers anticipate and encourage global convergence by emphasizing global standardization, centralization and coordination? They would choose to place more emphasis on realizing value creation by means of global synergies, accepting some value destruction due to a loss of local responsiveness. Or should managers acknowledge and exploit international diversity by emphasizing local adaptation, decentralization and autonomy? They would then focus on being locally responsive, accepting that this will frustrate the realization of cross-border synergies.

Again, the strategic management literature does not provide a uniform answer to the question of which international strategy firms can best pursue. On the contrary, the variety of opinions among strategy theorists is dauntingly large, with many incompatible prescriptions being given. At the core of the debate within the field of strategy is the paradox of globalization and localization. Many points of view have been expounded on how to reconcile these opposing demands, but no common perspective has yet emerged. Hence, it is up to individual managers to find their own approach in dealing with the challenge of the international context.

To help strategizing managers to come to grips with the variety of perspectives on this issue, four readings have been selected that each shed their own light on the debate. As in previous chapters, the first two readings will be representative of the two poles in this debate (see Table 10.1), while the second set of two readings will bring in extra arguments to add further flavor to the discussion.

Reading 10.1, representing the global convergence perspective, is 'The Globalization of Markets' by Theodore Levitt. This article, published in the early 1980s, has probably been the most influential at starting the debate about globalization in the business literature. Levitt's thesis is that the world is quickly moving towards a converging commonality. He

TABLE 10.1 Global convergence versus international diversity perspective

	Global convergence perspective	International diversity perspective
Emphasis on	Globalization over localization	Localization over globalization
International variety	Growing similarity	Remaining diversity
International linkages	Growing integration	Remaining fragmentation
Major drivers	Technology and communication	Cultural and institutional identity
Diversity and fragmentation	Costly, convergence can be encouraged	Reality, can be exploited
Strategic focus	Global-scale synergies	Local responsiveness
Organizational preference	Standardize/centralize unless	Adapt/decentralize unless
Innovation process	Center-for-global	Locally leveraged
Organizational structure	Global (centralized hub)	Transnational (integrated network)

believes that 'the world's needs and desires have been irrevocably homogenized'. The force driving this process is technology, which has facilitated communication, transport and travel, while allowing for the development of superior products at low prices. His conclusion is that 'the commonality of preference leads inescapably to the standardization of products, manufacturing and the institutions of trade and commerce'. The old-fashioned multinational corporation, that adapted itself to local circumstances is 'obsolete and the global corporation absolute'. While a clear proponent of the global convergence perspective, it should be noted that Levitt's bold prediction of global convergence is focused on the globalization of markets. In particular, he is intent on pointing out that converging consumer demand in international markets facilitates – even necessitates – the reaping of economies of scale through the standardization of products, marketing and production. With this emphasis on the demand side, Levitt pays far less attention to the supply side – the globalization of industries and the competition within industries – that other global convergence proponents tend to accentuate (see Reading 10.3). And although he strongly advises companies to become 'global corporations', he does not further detail what a global company should look like (see Reading 10.4). Overall, Levitt views globalization more as growing international similarity, while paying less attention than some other authors to the possibility of growing international integration.

As a direct response to 'the sweeping and somewhat polemic character' of Levitt's argumentation, Susan Douglas and Yoram Wind's article, 'The Myth of Globalization', has been selected for Reading 10.2 as representative of the international diversity perspective. Douglas and Wind believe that many of the assumptions underlying Levitt's global standardization philosophy are contradicted by the facts. They argue that the convergence of customer needs is not a one-way street; divergence trends are noticeable as well. Furthermore, they believe that Levitt is mistaken in arguing that economies of scale in production and marketing are an irreversible force driving globalization. According to Douglas and Wind, many new technologies have actually lowered the minimum efficient scale of operation, while there are also plenty of industries where economies of scale are not an important issue. The authors conclude by outlining the specific circumstances under which a strategy of global standardization might be effective. Under all other circumstances, Douglas and Wind reiterate, the international strategist will have to deal with the existence of international diversity and search for the right balance between global standardization and local adaptation.

In Reading 10.3, 'The Competitive Advantage of Nations', Michael Porter introduces a different angle to the debate on globalization. Porter agrees with proponents of the global convergence perspective that the world is becoming highly integrated, although in some industries more than others (see Porter, 1986). However, Porter does not agree that the world is in all ways becoming more similar. In fact, Porter argues the opposite – growing international integration encourages international diversity. Global integration, according to Porter, does not make geographic location and nationality unimportant, as some authors seem to suggest (e.g. Ohmae, 1989), but in some ways more important. This is due to the process of local specialization, by which clusters of interconnected buyers, suppliers, competitors, and related and supporting industries evolve, that reinforce each other in innovating and becoming more competitive. Porter argues that such local clusters of firms operating in a particular sector will develop if there is a strong national diamond, that is, a challenging competitive environment with advantageous factor and demand conditions, and a strong infrastructure of related and supporting industries. And once a strong diamond has been established, it can have a self-perpetuating momentum, by winning in global competition and by attracting excellent companies and individuals from other countries. Porter therefore concludes that companies should recognize the specific characteristics of the national diamond in their home country and try to exploit and improve its unique strengths. He also advises companies to seek out and tap into strong local clusters abroad, to supplement their home-based advantages and to compensate for any home-based disadvantages. In short, international diversity is a reality, but can be exploited by the internationally operating company.

In the final reading, 'Transnational Management', Christopher Bartlett and Sumantra Ghoshal bring the issue of organization into the debate on globalization. Bartlett and Ghoshal do not take a direct stance on the issue of global convergence and international diversity. They are more concerned with clarifying the various pressures on international organizations and outlining the different organizational forms that can be adopted. The thrust of their argument is that globalization has forced the international company to manage across borders, as opposed to the old multinational corporation that was organized on a country-by-country basis. In the old multinational, emphasis was placed on strong *geographic management* to be responsive to the local circumstances. But to deal with, and benefit from, international integration and similarities, companies have to be able to do more. *Global functional management* is needed to learn and transfer competences worldwide, while *global business management* with global product responsibilities is needed to achieve worldwide efficiency. Bartlett and Ghoshal argue that optimizing learning, efficiency and responsiveness simultaneously is the challenge facing the new transnational organization. They believe that every organization must find its own dynamic balance between these forces; there is not one best organizational response to globalization, because the extent of globalization is never the same.

READING

10.1

The globalization of markets

By Theodore Levitt[1]

A powerful force drives the world toward a converging commonality, and that force is technology. It has proletarianized communication, transport, and travel. It has made isolated places and impoverished peoples eager for modernity's allurements. Almost everyone everywhere wants all the things they have heard about, seen, or experienced via the new technologies.

The result is a new commercial reality – the emergence of global markets for standardized consumer products on a previously unimagined scale of magnitude. Corporations geared to this new reality benefit from enormous economies of scale in production, distribution, marketing, and management. By translating these benefits into reduced world prices, they can decimate competitors that still live in the disabling grip of old assumptions about how the world works.

Gone are accustomed differences in national or regional preference. Gone are the days when a company could sell last year's models – or lesser versions of advanced products – in the less developed world. And gone are the days when prices, margins, and profits abroad were generally higher than at home.

The globalization of markets is at hand. With that, the multinational commercial world nears its end, and so does the multinational corporation.

The multinational and the global corporation are not the same thing. The multinational corporation operates in a number of countries, and adjusts its products and practices in each – at high relative costs. The global corporation operates with resolute constancy – at low relative cost – as if the entire world (or major regions of it) were a single entity; it sells the same things in the same way everywhere.

Which strategy is better is not a matter of opinion but of necessity. World-wide communications carry everywhere the constant drumbeat of modern possibilities to lighten and enhance work, raise living standards, divert, and entertain. The same countries that ask the world to recognize and respect the individuality of their cultures insist on the wholesale transfer to them of modern goods, services, and technologies. Modernity is not just a wish but also a widespread practice among those who cling, with unyielding passion or religious fervor, to ancient attitudes and heritages.

Who can forget the televized scenes during the 1979 Iranian uprisings of young men in fashionable French-cut trousers and silky body shirts thirsting with raised modern weapons for blood in the name of Islamic fundamentalism?

In Brazil, thousands swarm daily from preindustrial Bahian darkness into exploding coastal cities, there quickly to install television sets in crowded corrugated huts and, next to battered Volkswagens, make sacrificial offerings of fruit and fresh-killed chickens to Macumban spirits by candlelight.

A thousand suggestive ways attest to the ubiquity of the desire for the most advanced things that the world makes and sells – goods of the best quality and reliability at the lowest price. The world's needs and desires have been irrevocably homogenized. This makes the multinational corporation obsolete and the global corporation absolute.

Living in the Republic of Technology

Daniel J. Boorstin, author of the monumental trilogy *The Americans*, characterized our age as driven by 'the Republic of Technology (whose) supreme law . . . is convergence, the tendency for everything to become more like everything else.'

In business, this trend has pushed markets toward global commonality. Corporations sell standardized products in the same way everywhere – autos, steel, chemicals, petroleum, cement, agricultural commodities and equipment, industrial and commercial construction, banking and insurance services, computers, semiconductors, transport, electronic instruments, pharmaceuticals, and telecommunications, to mention some of the obvious.

[1]Source: Reprinted by permission of *Harvard Business Review*. From 'The Globalization of Markets' by T. Levitt, May–June 1983, Vol. 61. © 1983 by Harvard Business School Publishing Corporation, all rights reserved.

Nor is the sweeping gale of globalization confined to these raw material or high-tech products, where the universal language of customers and users facilitates standardization. The transforming winds whipped up by the proletarianization of communication and travel enter every crevice of life.

Commercially, nothing confirms this as much as the success of McDonald's from the Champs Elysées to the Ginza, of Coca-Cola in Bahrain and Pepsi-Cola in Moscow, and of rock music, Greek salad, Hollywood movies, Revlon cosmetics, Sony televisions, and Levi jeans everywhere. 'High-touch' products are as ubiquitous as high-tech.

Starting from opposing sides, the high-tech and the high-touch ends of the commercial spectrum gradually consume the undistributed middle in their cosmopolitan orbit. No one is exempt and nothing can stop the process. Everywhere everything gets more and more like everything else as the world's preference structure is relentlessly homogenized.

Consider the cases of Coca-Cola and Pepsi-Cola, which are globally standardized products sold everywhere and welcomed by everyone. Both successfully cross multitudes of national, regional, and ethnic taste buds trained to a variety of deeply ingrained local preferences of taste, flavor, consistency, effervescence, and aftertaste. Everywhere both sell well. Cigarettes, too, especially American-made, make year-to-year global inroads in territories previously held in the firm grip of other, mostly local, blends.

These are not exceptional examples. (Indeed their global reach would be even greater were it not for artificial trade barriers.) They exemplify a general drift toward the homogenization of the world and how companies distribute, finance, and price products. Nothing is exempt. The products and methods of the industrialized world play a single tune for all the world, and all the world eagerly dances to it.

Ancient differences in national tastes or modes of doing business disappear. The commonality of preference leads inescapably to the standardization of products, manufacturing, and the institutions of trade and commerce. Small nation-based markets transmogrify and expand. Success in world competition turns on efficiency in production, distribution, marketing, and management, and inevitably becomes focused on price.

The most effective world competitors incorporate superior quality and reliability into their cost structures. They sell in all national markets the same kind of products sold at home or in their largest export market. They compete on the basis of appropriate value – the best combinations of price, quality, reliability, and delivery for products that are globally identical with respect to design, function, and even fashion.

That, and little else, explains the surging success of Japanese companies dealing world-wide in a vast variety of products – both tangible products like steel, cars, motorcycles, hi-fi equipment, farm machinery, robots, microprocessors, carbon fibers, and now even textiles, and intangibles like banking, shipping, general contracting, and soon computer software. Nor are high-quality and low-cost operations incompatible, as a host of consulting organizations and data engineers argue with vigorous vacuity. The reported data are incomplete, wrongly analyzed, and contradictory. The truth is that low-cost operations are the hallmark of corporate cultures that require and produce quality in all that they do. High quality and low costs are not opposing postures. They are compatible, twin identities of superior practice.

To say that Japan's companies are not global because they export cars with left-side drives to the United States and the European continent, while those in Japan have right-side drives, or because they sell office machines through distributors in the United States but directly at home, or speak Portuguese in Brazil is to mistake a difference for a distinction. The same is true of Safeway and Southland retail chains operating effectively in the Middle East, and to not only native but also imported populations from Korea, the Philippines, Pakistan, India, Thailand, Britain, and the United States. National rules of the road differ, and so do distribution channels and languages. Japan's distinction is its unrelenting push for economy and value enhancement. That translates into a drive for standardization at high quality levels.

Vindication of the Model T

If a company forces costs and prices down and pushes quality and reliability up – while maintaining reasonable concern for suitability – customers will prefer its world-standardized products. The theory holds at this stage in the evolution of globalization, no matter what conventional market research and even common sense may suggest about different national and regional tastes, preferences, needs, and institutions. The Japanese have repeatedly vindicated this theory, as did Henry Ford with the Model T. Most important, so have their imitators, including companies from South Korea (television sets and heavy construction), Malaysia (personal calculators and microcomputers), Brazil (auto parts and tools), Colombia (apparel), Singapore (optical equipment), and yes, even from the United States (office copiers, computers, bicycles, castings), Western Europe (automatic washing machines), Rumania (housewares), Hungary (apparel), Yugoslavia (furniture), and Israel (pagination equipment).

Of course, large companies operating in a single nation or even a single city don't standardize everything they make, sell, or do. They have product lines instead of a single product version, and multiple distribution channels. There are neighborhood, local, regional, ethnic, and institutional differences, even within metropolitan areas. But although companies customize products for particular market segments, they know that success in a world with homogenized demand requires a search for sales opportunities in similar segments across the globe in order to achieve the economies of scale necessary to compete.

Such a search works because a market segment in one country is seldom unique; it has close cousins everywhere precisely because technology has homogenized the globe. Even small local segments have their global equivalents everywhere and become subject to global competition, especially on price.

The global competitor will seek constantly to standardize his offering everywhere. He will digress from this standardization only after exhausting all possibilities to retain it, and he will push for reinstatement of standardization whenever digression and divergence have occurred. He will never assume that the customer is a king who knows his own wishes.

Trouble increasingly stalks companies that lack clarified global focus and remain inattentive to the economics of simplicity and standardization. The most endangered companies in the rapidly evolving world tend to be those that dominate rather small domestic markets with high value-added products for which there are smaller markets elsewhere. With transportation costs proportionately low, distant competitors will enter the now-sheltered markets of those companies with goods produced more cheaply under scale-efficient conditions. Global competition spells the end of domestic territoriality, no matter how diminutive the territory may be.

When the global producer offers his lower costs internationally, his patronage expands exponentially. He not only reaches into distant markets, but also attracts customers who previously held to local preferences and now capitulate to the attractions of lesser prices. The strategy of standardization not only responds to world-wide homogenized markets but also expands those markets with aggressive low pricing.

The new technological juggernaut taps an ancient motivation – to make one's money go as far as possible. This is universal – not simply a motivation but actually a need.

The hedgehog knows

The difference between the hedgehog and the fox, wrote Sir Isaiah Berlin in distinguishing between Dostoevski and Tolstoy, is that the fox knows a lot about a great many things, but the hedgehog knows everything about one great thing. The multinational corporation knows a lot about a great many countries and congenially adapts to supposed differences. It willingly accepts vestigial national differences, not questioning the possibility of their transformation, not recognizing how the world is ready and eager for the benefit of modernity, especially when the price is right. The multinational corporation's accommodating mode to visible national differences is medieval.

By contrast, the global corporation knows everything about one great thing. It knows about the absolute need to be competitive on a world-wide basis as well as nationally and seeks constantly to drive down prices by standardizing what it sells and how it operates. It treats the world as composed of few standardized markets rather than many customized markets. It actively seeks and vigorously works toward global convergence. Its mission is modernity and its mode, price competition, even when it sells top-of-the-line, high-end products. It knows about the one great thing all nations and people have in common: scarcity.

Nobody takes scarcity lying down; everyone wants more. This in part explains division of labor and specialization of production. They enable people and nations to optimize their conditions through trade. The median is usually money.

Experience teaches that money has three special qualities: scarcity, difficulty of acquisition, and transience. People understandably treat it with respect. Everyone in the increasingly homogenized world market wants products and features that everybody else wants. If the price is low enough, they will take highly standardized world products, even if these aren't exactly what mother said was suitable, what immemorial custom decreed was right, or what market-research fabulists asserted was preferred.

The implacable truth of all modern production – whether of tangible or intangible goods – is that large-scale production of standardized items is generally cheaper within a wide range of volume than small-scale production. Some argue that CAD/CAM (computer aided design/computer aided manufacturing) will allow companies to manufacture customized products on a small scale – but cheaply. But the argument misses the point. If a company treats the world as one or two distinctive product markets, it can serve the world more economically than if it treats it as three, four, or five product markets.

Different cultural preferences, national tastes and standards, and business institutions are vestiges of the past. Some inheritances die gradually; others prosper and expand into mainstream global preferences. So-called ethnic markets are a good example. Chinese food, pitta bread, country and western music, pizza, and jazz are everywhere. They are market segments that exist in world-wide proportions. They don't deny or contradict global homogenization but confirm it.

Many of today's differences among nations as to products and their features actually reflect the respectful accommodation of multinational corporations to what they believe are fixed local preferences. They believe preferences are fixed, not because they are but because of rigid habits of thinking about what actually is. Most executives in multinational corporations are thoughtlessly accommodating. They falsely presume that marketing means giving the customer what he says he wants rather than trying to understand exactly what he'd like. So they persist with high-cost, customized multinational products and practices instead of pressing hard and pressing properly for global standardization.

I do not advocate the systematic disregard of local or national differences. But a company's sensitivity to such differences does not require that it ignore the possibilities of doing things differently or better.

With persistence and appropriate means, barriers against superior technologies and economics have always fallen. There is no recorded exception where reasonable effort has been made to overcome them. It is very much a matter of time and effort.

A failure in global imagination

Many companies have tried to standardize world practice by exporting domestic products and processes without accommodation or change – and have failed miserably. Their deficiencies have been seized on as evidence of bovine stupidity in the face of abject impossibility. Advocates of global standardization see them as examples of failures in execution.

In fact, poor execution is often an important cause. More important, however, is failure of nerve – failure of imagination.

Consider the case for the introduction of fully automatic home laundry equipment in Western Europe at a time when few homes had even semiautomatic machines.

The growing success of small, low-powered, low-speed, low-capacity, low-priced Italian machines, even against the preferered but highly priced and highly promoted brand in West Germany, was significant. It contained a powerful message that was lost on managers confidently wedded to a distorted version of the marketing concept according to which you give the customer what he says he wants. In fact the customers said they wanted certain features, but their behavior demonstrated they'd take other features provided the price and the promotion were right.

In this case it was obvious that under prevailing conditions, people preferred a low-priced automatic over any kind of manual or semiautomatic machine and certainly over higher priced automatics, even though the low-priced automatics failed to fulfil all their expressed preferences. The supposedly meticulous and demanding German consumers violated all expectations by buying the simple, low-priced Italian machines.

This case illustrates how the perverse practice of the marketing concept and the absence of any kind of marketing imagination let multinational attitudes survive when customers actually want the benefits of global standardization. People were asked what features they wanted in a washing machine rather than what they wanted out of life. Selling a line of products individually tailored to each nation is thoughtless. Managers who took pride in practicing the marketing concept to the fullest did not, in fact, practice it at all. Data do not yield information except with the intervention of the mind. Information does not yield meaning except with the intervention of imagination.

Cracking the code of Western markets

Since the theory of the marketing concept emerged a quarter of a century ago, the more managerially advanced corporations have been eager to offer what customers clearly want rather than what is merely convenient. They have created marketing departments supported by professional market researchers of awesome and often costly proportions. And they have proliferated extraordinary numbers of operations and product lines – highly tailored products and delivery systems for many different markets, market segments, and nations.

Significantly, Japanese companies operate almost entirely without marketing departments or market research of the kind so prevalent in the West. Yet, in the colorful words of General Electric's chairman John F. Welch Jr., the Japanese, coming from a small cluster of resource-poor islands, with an entirely alien culture and an almost impenetrably complex language, have cracked the code of Western markets. They have done it not by looking with mechanistic thoroughness at the way markets are different but rather by searching for meaning with a deeper wisdom. They have discovered the one great thing all markets have in common – an overwhelming desire for dependable, world-standard modernity in all things, at aggressively low prices. In response, they deliver irresistible value everywhere, attracting people with products that market-research technocrats described with superficial certainty as being unsuitable and uncompetitive.

The wider a company's global reach, the greater the number of regional and national preferences it will encounter for certain product features, distribution systems, or promotional media. There will always need to be some accommodation to differences.

In its highly successful introduction of Contac 600 (the timed-release decongestant) into Japan, SmithKline Corporation used 35 wholesalers instead of the 1000-plus that established practice required. Daily contacts with the wholesalers and key retailers, also in violation of established practice, supplemented the plan, and it worked.

Denied access to established distribution institutions in the United States, Komatsu, the Japanese manufacturer of lightweight farm machinery, entered the market through over-the-road construction equipment dealers in rural areas of the Sunbelt, where farms are smaller, the soil sandier and easier to work. Here inexperienced distributors were able to attract customers on the basis of Komatsu's product and price appropriateness.

In cases of successful challenge to prevailing institutions and practices, a combination of product reliability and quality, strong and sustained support systems, aggressively low prices, and sales-compensation packages, as well as audacity and implacability, circumvented, shattered, and transformed very different distribution systems. Instead of resentment, there was admiration.

The differences that persist throughout the world despite its globalization affirm an ancient dictum of economics – that things are driven by what happens at the margin, not at the core. Thus, in ordinary competitive analysis, what's important is not the average price but the marginal price, what happens not in the usual case but at the interface of newly erupting conditions. What counts in commercial affairs is what happens at the cutting edge. What is most striking today is the underlying similarities of what is happening now to national preferences at the margin. These similarities at the cutting edge cumulatively form an overwhelming, predominant commonality everywhere.

To refer to the persistence of economic nationalism (protective and subsidized trade practices, special tax aids, or restrictions for home market producers) as a barrier to the globalization of markets is to make a valid point. Economic nationalism does have a powerful persistence. But, as with the present almost totally smooth internationalization of investment capital, the past alone does not shape or predict the future.

Reality is not a fixed paradigm, dominated by immemorial customs and derived attitudes, heedless of powerful and abundant new forces. The world is becoming increasingly informed about the liberating and enhancing possibilities of modernity. The persistence of the inherited varieties of national preferences rests uneasily on increasing evidence of, and restlessness regarding, their inefficiency, costliness, and confinement. The historic past, and the national differences respecting commerce and industry it spawned and fostered everywhere, is now subject to relatively easy transformation.

Cosmopolitanism is no longer the monopoly of the intellectual and leisure classes; it is becoming the established property and defining characteristic of all sectors everywhere in the world. Gradually and irresistibly it breaks down the walls of economic insularity, nationalism, and chauvinism. What we see today as escalating commercial nationalism is simply the last violent death rattle of an obsolete institution.

The successful global corporation does not abjure customization or differentiation for the requirements of markets that differ in product preferences, spending patterns, shopping preferences, and institutional or legal arrangements. But the global corporation accepts and adjusts to these differences only reluctantly, only after relentlessly testing their immutability, after trying in various ways to circumvent and reshape them.

READING

10.2

The myth of globalization

By Susan Douglas and Yoram Wind[1]

In recent years, globalization has become a key theme in every discussion of international strategy. Proponents of the philosophy of 'global' products and brands, such as Professor Theodore Levitt of Harvard, and the highly successful advertising agency, Saatchi & Saatchi, argue that in a world of growing internationalization, the key to success is the development of global products and brands, in other words, a focus on standardized products and brands world-wide. Others, however, point to the numerous barriers to standardization, and suggest that greater returns are to be obtained from adapting products and marketing strategies to the specific characteristics of individual markets.

The growing integration of international markets as well as the growth of competition on a world-wide scale implies that adoption of a global perspective has become increasingly imperative in planning strategy. However, to conclude that this mandates the adoption of a strategy of universal standardization appears naive and oversimplistic. In particular, it ignores the inherent complexity of operations in international markets, and the formulation of an effective strategy to penetrate these markets. While global products and brands may be appropriate for certain markets and in targeting certain segments, adopting such an approach as a universal strategy in relation to all markets may not be desirable, and may lead to major strategic blunders. Furthermore, it implies a product orientation, and a product-driven strategy, rather than a strategy grounded in a systematic analysis of customer behavior and response patterns and market characteristics.

The purpose of this article is thus to examine critically the notion that success in international markets necessitates adoption of a strategy of global products and brands. Given the restrictive characteristic of this philosophy, a somewhat broader perspective in developing global strategy is proposed which views standardization as merely one option in the range of possible strategies which may be effective in global markets.

The traditional perspective on international strategy

Traditionally, discussion of international business strategy has been polarized around the debate concerning the pursuit of a uniform strategy world-wide versus adaptation to specific local market conditions. On the one hand, it has been argued that adoption of a uniform strategy world-wide enables a company to take advantage of the potential synergies arising from multicountry operations, and constitutes the multinational company's key competitive advantage in international markets. Others however, have argued that adaptation of strategy to idiosyncratic national market characteristics is crucial to success in these markets.

Fayerweather, in his seminal work in international business strategy, described the central issue as one of conflict between forces toward unification and those resulting in fragmentation. He pointed out that within a multinational firm, internal forces created pressures toward the integration of strategy across national boundaries. On the other hand, differences in the sociocultural, political, and economic characteristics of countries as well as the need for effective relations with the host society, constitute fragmenting influences that favor adaptation to the local environment.

Recent discussion of global competitive strategy echoes the same theme of the dichotomy between the forces that have triggered the globalization of markets and those that constitute barriers to global competition. Factors such as economies of scale in production, purchasing, faster accumulation of learning from operating world-wide, decrease in transportation and distribution costs, reduced costs of product adaptation, and the emergence of global market segments have encouraged competition on a global scale. However, barriers such as governmental and institutional constraints, tariff barriers and duties, preferential treatment of local firms, transportation costs, differences in customer demand, and so on, call for nationalistic or 'protected niche' strategies.

[1]Source: This article was reprinted from *Columbia Journal of World Business*, Winter 1987, S. Douglas and Y. Wind, 'The Myth of Globalization', pp. 19–29, (c) 1987. With permission of Elsevier.

Compromise solutions such as 'pattern standardization' have also been proposed. In this case, a global promotional theme or positioning is developed, but execution is adapted to the local market. Similarly, it has been pointed out that even where a standardized product is marketed in a number of countries, its positioning may be adapted in each market. Conversely, the positioning may be uniform across countries, but the product itself adapted or modified.

Although this debate first emerged in the 1960s, it has recently taken on a new vigor with the widely publicized pronouncements of proponents of 'global standardization' such as Professor Levitt and Saatchi & Saatchi.

The sweeping and somewhat polemic character of their argument has sparked a number of counterarguments as well as discussion of conditions under which such a strategy may be most appropriate. It has, for example, been pointed out that the potential for standardization may be greater for certain types of products such as industrial goods or luxury personal items targeted to upscale consumers, or products with similar penetration rates. Opportunities for standardization are also likely to occur more frequently among industrialized nations, and especially the Triad countries where customer interests as well as market conditions are likely to be more similar than among developing countries.

The role of corporate philosophy and organizational structure in influencing the practicality of implementing a strategy of global standardization has also been recognized. Here, it has been noted that few companies pursue the extreme position of complete standardization with regard to all elements of the marketing mix, and business functions such as R&D, manufacturing, and procurement in all countries throughout the world. Rather, some degree of adaptation is likely to occur relative to certain aspects of the firm's operations or in certain geographic areas. In addition, the feasibility of implementing a standardized strategy will depend on the autonomy accorded to local management. If local management has been accustomed to substantial autonomy, considerable opposition may be encountered in attempting to introduce globally standardized strategies.

An examination of such counterarguments suggests that there are a number of dangers in espousing a philosophy of global standardization for all products and services, and in relation to all markets world-wide. Furthermore, there are numerous difficulties and constraints to implementing such a strategy in many markets, stemming from external market conditions (such as government and trade regulation, competition, the marketing infrastructure, and so on), as well as from the current structure and organization of the firm's operations.

The global standardization philosophy: The underlying assumptions

An examination of the arguments in favor of a strategy of global products and brands reveals three key underlying assumptions:

- Customer needs and interests are becoming increasingly homogeneous world-wide.
- People around the world are willing to sacrifice preferences in product features, functions, design, and the like for lower prices at high quality.
- Substantial economies of scale in production and marketing can be achieved through supplying global markets.

There are, however, a number of pitfalls associated with each of these assumptions. These are discussed here in more detail.

Homogenization of the world's wants

A key premise of the philosophy of global products is that customers' needs and interests are becoming increasingly homogeneous world-wide. But while global segments with similar interests and response patterns may be identified in some product markets, it is by no means clear that this is a universal trend. Furthermore, there is substantial evidence to suggest an increasing diversity of behavior within countries, and the emergence of idiosyncratic country-specific segments.

Lack of evidence of homogenization. In a number of product markets ranging from watches, perfume, and handbags to soft drinks and fast foods, companies have successfully identified global customer segments, and developed global products and brands targeted to these segments. These include such stars as Rolex, Omega and Le Baume & Mercier watches, Dior, Patou or Yves St. Laurent perfume. But while these brands are highly visible and widely publicized, they are often, with a few notable exceptions such as Classic Coke or McDonald's, targeted to a relatively restricted upscale international customer segment.

Numerous other companies, however, adapt lines to idiosyncratic country preferences, and develop local brands or product variants targeted to local market segments. The Findus frozen food division of Nestlé, for example, markets fish cakes and fish fingers in the United Kingdom, but beef bourguignon and coq au vin in France, and vitello con funghi and braviola in Italy. Similarly, Coca-Cola in Japan markets Georgia, cold coffee in a can, and Aquarius, a tonic drink, as well as Classic Coke and Hi-C.

Growth of intracountry segmentation price sensitivity.

Furthermore, there is a growing body of evidence that suggests substantial heterogeneity within countries. In the United States, for example, the VALS (Value of American Lifestyles) study has identified nine value segments, while other studies have identified major differences in behavior between regions and subcultural segments. Many other countries are also characterized by substantial regional differences as well as different lifestyle and value segments.

Similarly, in industrial markets, while some global segments, often consisting of firms with international operations, can be identified, there also is considerable diversity within and between countries. Often local businesses constitute an important market segment and, especially in developing countries, may differ significantly in technological sophistication, business philosophy and strategy, emphasis on product quality, and service and price, from large multinationals.

The evidence thus suggests that the similarities in customer behavior are restricted to a relatively limited number of target segments, or product markets, while for the most part, there are substantial differences between countries. Proponents of standardization counter that the international strategist should focus on similarities among countries rather than differences. This may, however, imply ignoring a major part of a local market, and the potential profits that may be obtained from tapping other market segments.

Universal preference for low price at acceptable quality

Another critical component of the argument for global standardization is that people around the world are willing to sacrifice preferences in product features, functions, design, and the like for lower prices, assuming equivalent quality. Aggressive low pricing for quality products that meet the common needs of customers in markets around the world is believed to further expand the global markets facing the firm.

Although an appealing argument, this has three major problems.

Lack of evidence of increased price sensitivity.

Evidence to suggest that customers are universally willing to trade off specific product features for a lower price is largely lacking. While in many product markets there is invariably a price-sensitive segment, there is no indication that this is on the increase. On the contrary, in many product and service markets, ranging from watches, personal computers, and household appliances to banking and insurance, an interest in multiple product features, product quality, and service appears to be growing.

Low price positioning is a highly vulnerable strategy.

Also, from a strategic point of view, emphasis on price positioning may be undesirable, especially in international markets, since it offers no long-term competitive advantage. A price-positioning strategy is always vulnerable to new technological developments that may lower costs, as well as to attack from competitors with lower overhead, and lower operating or labor costs. Government subsidies to local competitors may also undermine the effectiveness of a price-positioning strategy. In addition, price-sensitive customers typically are not brand or source loyal.

Standardized low price can be overpriced in some countries and underpriced in others.

Finally, a strategy based on a combination of a standardized product at a low price, when implemented in countries that vary in their competitive structure as well as the level of economic development, is likely to result in products that are overdesigned and overpriced for some markets and underdesigned and underpriced for others. Cost advantages may also be negated by transportation and distribution costs as well as tariff barriers and/or price regulation.

Economies of scale of production and marketing

The third assumption underlying the philosophy of global standardization is that a key force driving strategy is product technology, and that substantial economies of scale can be achieved by supplying global markets. This does, however, neglect three critical and interrelated points:

1 Technological developments in flexible factory automation enable economies of scale to be

achieved at lower levels of output and do not require production of a single standardized product.

2 Cost of production is only one and often not the critical component in determining the total cost of the product.

3 Strategy should not be solely product driven but should take into account the other components of a marketing strategy, such as positioning, packaging, brand name, advertising, PR, consumer and trade promotion and distribution.

Developments in flexible factory automation. Recent developments in flexible factory automation methods have lowered the minimum efficient scale of operation and have thus enabled companies to supply smaller local markets efficiently, without requiring operations on a global scale. However, diseconomies may result from such operations due to increased transportation and distribution costs, as well as higher administrative overhead, and additional communication and coordination costs.

Furthermore, decentralization of production and establishment of local manufacturing operations enables diversification of risk arising from political events, fluctuations in foreign exchange rates, or economic instability. Recent swings in foreign exchange rates, coupled with the growth of offshore sourcing have underscored the vulnerability of centralizing production in a single location. Government regulations relating to local component and/or offset requirements create additional pressures for local manufacturing. Flexible automation not only implies that decentralization of manufacturing and production may be cost efficient but also makes minor modifications in products or models in the latter stages of production feasible, so that a variety of model versions can be produced without major retooling. Adaptations to product design can thus be made to meet differences in preferences from one country to another without loss of economies of scale.

Production costs are often a minor component of total cost. In many consumer and service industries, such as cosmetics, detergents, pharmaceuticals, or financial institutions, production costs are a small fraction of total cost. The key to success in these markets is an understanding of the tastes and purchase behavior of target customers' distribution channels, and tailoring products and strategies to these rather than production efficiency. In the detergent industry, for example, mastery of mass-merchandising tech-

niques and an effective brand management system are typically considered the key elements in the success of the giants in this field, such as Procter & Gamble (P&G) or Colgate-Palmolive.

The standardization philosophy is primarily product driven. The focus on product- and brand-related aspects of strategy in discussions of global standardization is misleading since it ignores the other key strategy variables. Strategy in international markets should also take into consideration other aspects of the marketing mix, and the extent to which these are standardized across country markets rather than adapted to local idiosyncratic characteristics.

Requisite conditions for global standardization

The numerous pitfalls in the rationale underlying the global standardization philosophy suggests that such a strategy is far from universally appropriate for all products, brands, or companies. Only under certain conditions is it likely to prove a 'winning' strategy in international markets. These include:

- the existence of a global market segment;
- potential synergies from standardization;
- the availability of a communication and distribution infrastructure to deliver the firm's offering to target customers world-wide.

Existence of global market segments

As noted previously, global segments may be identified in a number of industrial and consumer markets. In consumer markets these segments are typically luxury- or premium-type products. Global segments are, however, not limited to such product markets, but also exist in other types of markets, such as motorcycle, record, stereo equipment, and computer, where a segment with similar needs and wants can be identified in many countries.

In industrial markets, companies with multinational operations are particularly likely to have similar needs and requirements world-wide. Where the operations are integrated or coordinated across national boundaries, as in the case of banks or other financial institutions, compatibility of operational systems and equipment may be essential. Consequently, they may seek vendors who can supply and service their operations world-wide, in some cases developing global contrasts for such purchases. Similarly, manufacturing companies with world-wide operations may source globally in order to ensure uniformity in quality, service and price of components, and other raw materials throughout their operations.

Marketing of global products and brands to such target segments and global customers enables development of a uniform global image throughout the world. In some markets such as perfume or fashions, association with a specific country of origin or a foreign image in general may carry a prestige connotation. In other cases, for example, Sony electronic equipment, McDonald's hamburgers, Hertz or Avis car rental, IBM computers, or Xerox office equipment, it may help to develop a world-wide reputation for quality and service. Just as multinational corporations may seek uniformity in supply world-wide, some consumers who travel extensively may be interested in finding the same brand of cigarettes and soft drinks, or hotels, in foreign countries. This may be particularly relevant in product markets used extensively by international travelers.

While the existence of a potential global segment is a key motivating factor for developing a global product and brand strategy, it is important to note that the desirability of such a strategy depends on the size and economic viability of the segment in question, the strength of the segment's preference for the global brand, as well as the ability to reach the segment effectively and profitably.

Synergies associated with global standardization

Global standardization may also have a number of synergistic effects. In addition to those associated with a global image noted above, opportunities may exist for the transfer of good ideas for products or promotional strategies from one country to another.

The standardization of strategy and operations across a number of countries may also enable the acquisition or exploitation of specific types of expertise that would not be feasible otherwise. Expertise in assessing country risk or foreign exchange risk, or in identifying and interpreting information relating to multiple country markets, for example, may be developed.

Such synergies are not, however, unique to a strategy of global standardization, but may also occur wherever operations and strategy are coordinated or integrated across country markets. In fact, only certain scale economies associated with product and advertising copy standardization, and the development of a global image as discussed earlier, are unique to global standardization.

Availability of an international communication and distribution infrastructure

The effectiveness of global standardization also depends to a large extent on the availability of an international infrastructure of communications and distribution. As many corporations have expanded overseas, service organizations have followed their customers abroad to supply their needs world-wide.

Advertising agencies such as Saatchi & Saatchi, McCann Erickson, and Young & Rubicam now have an international network of operations throughout the world, while many research agencies can also supply services in major markets world-wide. With the growing integration of financial markets, banks, investment firms, insurance and other financial institutions are also becoming increasingly international in orientation and are expanding the scope of their operations in world markets. The physical distribution network of shippers, freight forwarding, export and import agents, customs clearing, invoicing and insurance agents is also becoming increasingly integrated to meet demand for international shipment of goods and services.

Improvements in telecommunications and in logistical systems have considerably increased capacity to manage operations on a global scale and hence facilitate adoption of global standardization strategies. The spread of telex and fax systems, as well as satellite linkages and international computer linkages, all contribute to the shrinking of distances and facilitate globalization of operations. Similarly, improvements in transportation systems and physical logistics such as containerization and computerized inventory and handling systems have enabled significant cost savings as well as reducing time required to move goods across major distances.

Operational constraints to effective implementation of a standardization strategy

While adoption of a standardized strategy may be desirable under certain conditions, there are a number of constraints that severely restrict the firm's ability to develop and implement a standardized strategy.

External constraints to effective standardization

The numerous external constraints that impede global standardization are well recognized. Here, four major categories are highlighted, namely

1 government and trade restrictions;
2 differences in the marketing infrastructure, such as the availability and effectiveness of promotional media;
3 the character of resource markets, and differences in the availability and costs of resources;
4 differences in competition from one country to another.

Government and trade restrictions. Government and trade restrictions, such as tariff and other trade barriers, product, pricing or promotional regulation, frequently hamper standardization of the product line, pricing, or promotional strategy. Tariffs or quotas on the import of key materials, components, or other resources may, for example, affect production costs and thus hamper uniform pricing or alternatively result in the substitution of other components and modifications in product design. Local content requirements or compensatory export requirements, which specify that products contain a certain proportion of components manufactured locally or that a certain volume of production is exported to offset imports of components or other services, may have a similar impact.

The existence of cartels such as the European steel cartel, or the Swiss chocolate cartel, may also impede or exclude standardized strategies in countries covered by these agreements. In particular, they may affect adoption of a uniform pricing strategy as the cartel sets prices for the industry. Cartel members may also control established distribution channels, thus preventing use of a standardized distribution strategy. Extensive grey markets in countries such as India, Hong Kong, and South America may also affect administered pricing systems, and require adjustment of pricing strategies.

The nature of the marketing infrastructure. Differences in the marketing infrastructure from one country to another may hamper use of a standardized strategy. These may, for example, include differences in the availability and reach of various promotional media, in the availability of certain distribution channels or retail institutions, or in the existence and effi-

ciency of the communication and transportation network. Such factors may, therefore, require considerable adaptation of strategy of local market conditions.

Interdependencies with resource markets. Yet another constraint to the development of standardized strategies is the nature of resource markets, and their operation in different countries throughout the world as well as the interdependency of these markets with marketing decisions. Availability and cost of raw materials, as well as labor and other resources in different locations, will affect not only decisions regarding sourcing of and hence the location of manufacturing activities but also marketing strategy decisions such as product design. For example, in the paper industry, availability of cheap local materials such as jute and sugar cane may result in their substitution for wood fiber.

Cost differentials relative to raw materials, labor, management, and other inputs may also influence the trade-off relative to alternative strategies. For example, high packaging cost relative to physical distribution may result in use of cheaper packaging with a shorter shelf life and more frequent shipments. Similarly, low labor costs relative to media may encourage a shift from mass media advertising to labor-intensive promotion such as personal selling and product demonstration.

Availability of capital, technology, and manufacturing capabilities in different locations will also affect decisions about licensing, contract manufacturing, joint ventures, and other 'make-buy' types of decisions for different markets, as well as decisions about countertrade, reciprocity, and other long-term relations.

The nature of the competitive structure. Differences in the nature of the competitive situation from one country to another may also suggest the desirability of adaptation strategy. Even in markets characterized by global competition, such as agricultural equipment and motorcycles, the existence of low-cost competition in certain countries may suggest the desirability of marketing stripped-down models or lowering prices to meet such competition. Even where competitors are predominantly other multinationals, preemption of established distribution networks may encourage adoption of innovative distribution methods or direct distribution to short-circuit an entrenched position. Thus, the existence of global competition does not necessarily imply a need for global standardization.

All such aspects thus impose major constraints on the feasibility and effectiveness of a standardized strategy, and suggest the desirability or need to adapt to specific market conditions.

Internal constraints to effective standardization

In addition to such external constraints on the feasibility of a global standardization strategy, there are also a number of internal constraints that may need to be considered. These include compatibility with the existing network of operations overseas, as well as opposition or lack of enthusiasm among local management toward a standardized strategy.

Existing international operations. Proponents of global standardization typically take the position of a novice company with no operations in international markets, and hence fail to take into consideration the fit of the proposed strategy with current international activities. In practice, however, many companies have a number of existing operations in various countries. In some cases, these are joint ventures, or licensing operations or involve some collaboration in purchasing, manufacturing or distribution with other companies. Even where foreign manufacturing and distribution operations are wholly owned, the establishment of a distribution network will typically entail relationships with other organizations, for example, exclusive distributor agreements.

Such commitments may be difficult if not impossible to change in the short run, and may constitute a major impediment to adoption of a standardized strategy. If, for example, a joint venture with a local company has been established to manufacture and market a product line in a specific country or region, resistance from the local partner (or government authorities) may be encountered if the parent company wishes to shift production or import components from another location. Similarly, a licensing contract will impede a firm from supplying the products covered by the agreement from an alternative location for the duration of the contract, even if it becomes more cost efficient to do so.

Conversely, the establishment of an effective dealer or distribution network in a country or region may constitute an important resource to a company. The addition of new products to the product line currently sold or distributed by this network may therefore provide a more efficient utilization of company resources than expanding to new countries or geographic regions with the existing line, as this would require substantial investment in the establishment of a new distribution network.

In addition, overseas subsidiaries may currently be marketing not only core products and brands from the company's domestic business, but may also have added or acquired local or regional products and brands in response to local market demand. In some cases, therefore, introduction of a global product or brand may be likely to cannibalize sales of local or regional brands.

Advocates of standardization thus need to take into consideration the evolutionary character of international involvement, which may render a universal strategy of global products and brands suboptimal. Somewhat ironically, the longer the history of a multinational corporation's involvement in foreign or international markets, and the more diversified and far-flung its operations, the more likely it is that standardization will not lead to optimal results.

Local management motivation and attitudes. Another internal constraint concerns the motivation and attitudes of local management with regard to standardization. Standardized strategies tend to facilitate or result in centralization in the planning and organization of international activities. Especially if input from local management is limited, this may result in a feeling that strategy is 'imposed' by corporate headquarters, and/or not adequately adapted or appropriate in view of specific local market characteristics and conditions. Local management is likely to take the view 'it won't work here – things are different,' which will reduce their motivation to implement a standardized strategy effectively.

A framework for classifying global strategy options

The adoption of a global perspective should not be viewed as synonymous with a strategy of global products and brands. Rather, for most companies such a perspective implies consideration of a broad range of strategic options of which standardization is merely one.

In essence, a global perspective implies planning strategy relative to markets world-wide rather than on a country-by-country basis. This may result in the identification of opportunities for global products and brands and/or integrating and coordinating strategy across national boundaries to exploit potential synergies of operating on an international scale. Such opportunities should, however, be weighed against the benefits of adaptation to idiosyncratic customer characteristics.

The development of an effective global strategy thus requires a careful examination of all international options in terms of standardization versus adaptation open to the firm.

A firm's international operations are likely to be characterized by a mix of strategies, including not only global products and brands, but also some regional products and brands and some national prod-ucts and brands. Similarly, some target segments may be global, others regional, and others national. Hybrid strategies of this nature thus enable a company to take advantage of the benefits of standardization and potential synergies from operating on an international scale, while at the same time not losing those afforded by adaptation to specific country characteristics and customer preferences.

READING 10.3

The competitive advantage of nations

By Michael Porter[1]

Companies, not nations, are on the front line of international competition. Yet, the characteristics of the home nation play a central role in a firm's international success. The home base shapes a company's capacity to innovate rapidly in technology and methods and to do so in the proper directions. It is the place from which competitive advantage ultimately emanates and from which it must be sustained. A global strategy supplements and solidifies the competitive advantage created at the home base; it is the icing, not the cake. However, on the one hand, while having a home base in the right nation helps a great deal, it does not ensure success. On the other hand, having a home base in the wrong nation raises fundamental strategic concerns.

The most important sources of national advantage must be actively sought and exploited, unlike low fac-tor costs obtainable simply by operating in the nation. Internationally successful firms are not passive bystanders in the process of creating competitive advantage. Those we studied were caught up in a never-ending process of seeking out new advantages and struggling with rivals to protect them. They were positioned to benefit the most their national envi-ronment. They took steps to make their home nation (and location within the nation) an even more favorable environment for competitive advantage. Finally, they amplified their home-based advantages and offset home-based disadvantages through global strategies that tapped selectively into advantages available in other nations.

Competitive advantage ultimately results from an effective combination of national circumstances and company strategy. Conditions in a nation may create an environment in which firms can attain international competitive advantage, but it is up to a company to seize the opportunity.

The context for competitive advantage

These imperatives of competitive advantage constitute a mind-set that is not present in many companies. Indeed, the actions required to create and sustain advantage are unnatural acts. Stability is valued in most companies, not change. Protecting old ideas and techniques becomes the preoccupation, not creating new ones.

The long-term challenge for any firm is to put itself in a position where it is most likely to perceive, and best able to address, the imperatives of competitive advantage. One challenge is to expose a company to new market and technological opportunities that may be hard to perceive. Another is preparing for change by upgrading and expanding the skills of employees and improving the firm's scientific and knowledge base. Ultimately, the most important challenge is

[1]Source: Reprinted and edited with the permission of the publishers, Palgrave, and The Free Press, a Division of Simon and Schuster Adult Publishing Group, from *The Competitive Advantage of Nations* by Michael E Porter. © 1990, 1998 by Michael E. Porter.

overcoming complacency and inertia to act on the new opportunities and circumstances.

The challenge of action ultimately falls on the firm's leader. Much attention has rightly been placed on the importance of visionary leaders in achieving unusual organizational success. But where does a leader get the vision, and how is it transmitted in a way that produces organizational accomplishment? Great leaders are influenced by the environment in which they work. Innovation takes place because the home environment stimulates it. Innovation succeeds because the home environment supports and even forces it. The right environment not only shapes a leader's own perceptions and priorities but provides the catalyst that allows the leader to overcome inertia and produce organizational change.

Great leaders emerge in different industries in different nations, in part because national circumstances attract and encourage them. Visionaries in consumer electronics are concentrated in Japan, chemicals and pharmaceuticals in Germany and Switzerland, and computers in America. Leadership is important to any success story, but is not in and of itself sufficient to explain such successes. In many industries, the national environment provides one or two nations with a distinct advantage over their foreign competitors. Leadership often determines which particular firm or firms exploit this advantage.

More broadly, the ability of any firm to innovate has much to do with the environment to which it is exposed, the information sources it has available – and consults – and the types of challenges it chooses to face. Seeking safe havens and comfortable customer relationships only reinforces past behavior. Maintaining suppliers who are captive degrades a source of stimulus, assistance, and insight. Lobbying against stringent product standards sends the wrong signal to an organization about norms and aspirations.

Innovation grows out of pressure and challenge. It also comes from finding the right challenges to meet. The main role of the firm's leader is to create the environment that meets these conditions. One essential part of the task is to take advantage of the national 'diamond' (see Figure 10.3.1 and Exhibit 10.3.1) that currently describes competition in the industry.

The new rules for innovation

A company should actively seek out pressure and challenge, not try to avoid them. Part of the task is to take advantage of the home nation in order to create the impetus for innovation. Some of the ways of doing so are:

- Sell to the most sophisticated and demanding buyers and channels. Some buyers (and channels) will stimulate the fastest improvement because they are knowledgeable and expect the best performance. They will set a standard for the organization and provide the most valuable feedback. However, sophisticated and demanding buyers and channels need not be the firm's only customers. Focusing on

FIGURE 10.3.1 The diamond

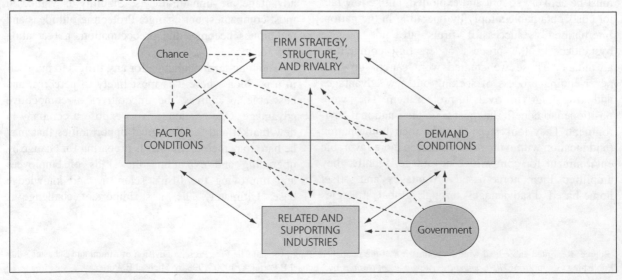

them exclusively may unnecessarily diminish long-term profitability. Nevertheless, serving a group of such buyers, chosen because their needs will challenge the firm's particular approach to competing, must be an explicit part of any strategy.

- Seek out the buyers with the most difficult needs. Buyers who face especially difficult operating requirements (such as climate, maintenance requirements, or hours of use), who confront factor cost disadvantages in their own businesses that create unusual pressures for performance, who have particularly tough competition, or who compete with strategies that place especially heavy demands on the firm's product or service, are buyers that will provide the laboratory (and the pressure) to upgrade performance and extend features and services. Such buyers should be identified and cultivated. They become part of a firm's R&D program.

- Establish norms of exceeding the toughest regulatory hurdles or product standards. Some localities (or user industries) will lead in terms of the stringency of product standards, pollution limits, noise guidelines, and the like. Tough regulating standards are not a hindrance but an opportunity to move early to upgrade products and processes. Older or simplified models can be sold elsewhere.

- Source from the most advanced and international home-based suppliers. Suppliers who themselves possess competitive advantage, as well as the insight that comes from international activities, will challenge the firm to improve and upgrade as well as provide insights and assistance in doing so.

- Treat employees as permanent. When employees are viewed as permanent instead of as workers who can be hired and fired at will, pressures are created that work to upgrade and sustain competitive advantage. New employees are hired with care, and continuous efforts are made to improve productivity instead of adding workers. Employees are trained on an ongoing basis to support more sophisticated competitive advantages.

EXHIBIT 10.3.1 ELEMENTS OF THE DIAMOND

COMPETITIVE ADVANTAGES AND DISADVANTAGES

The 'diamond' provides a framework for assessing important areas of competitive strength and weakness.

Factor conditions. International rivals will differ in the mix and cost of available factors and the rate of factor creation. Swedish automobile firms, for example, benefit from the solidarity wage system that makes the wages of Swedish auto workers closer to those of other Swedish industries, but relatively lower than the wages of auto workers in other advanced nations.

Demand conditions. Competitors from other nations will face differing segment structures of home demand, differing home buyer needs, and home buyers with various levels of sophistication. Demand conditions at their home base will help predict foreign competitors' directions of product change as well as their likely success in product development, among other things.

Related and supporting industries. Competitors based in other nations will differ in the availability of domestic suppliers, the quality of interaction with supplier industries, and the presence of related industries. Italian footwear firms and leather goods producers, for example, have early access to new tanned leather styles because of the world-leading Italian leather tanning industry.

Firm strategy, structure, and rivalry. The environment in their home nation will strongly influence the strategic choices of foreign rivals. Italian packaging equipment firms, for example, reflect their Italian context. They are mostly small and managed by strong, paternal leaders. Owners of firms have personal relationships with significant buyers. This makes them unusually responsive to market trends and provides the ability to custom-tailor machinery to buyer circumstances.

- Establish outstanding competitors as motivators. Those competitors who most closely match a company's competitive advantages, or exceed them, must become the standard of comparison. Such competitors can be a source of learning as well as a powerful focal point to overcome parochial concerns and motivate change for the entire organization.

The true costs of stability

These prescriptions may seem counterintuitive. The ideal would seem to be the stability growing out of obedient customers, captive and dependent suppliers, and sleepy competitors. Such a search for a quiet life, an understandable instinct, has led many companies to buy direct competitors or form alliances with them. In a closed, static world, monopoly would indeed be the most comfortable and profitable solution.

In reality, however, competition is dynamic. Complacent firms will lose to other firms who come from a more dynamic environment. Good managers always run a little scared. They respect and study competitors. Seeking out and meeting challenges is part of their organizational norm. By contrast, an organization that values stability and lacks self-perceived competition breeds inertia and creates vulnerabilities.

In global competition, the pressure of demanding local buyers, capable suppliers, and aggressive domestic rivalry are even more valuable and necessary for long-term profitability. These drive the firm to a faster rate of progress and upgrading than international rivals, and lead to sustained competitive advantage and superior long-term profitability. A tough domestic industry structure creates advantage in the international industry. A comfortable, easy home base, in contrast, leaves a firm vulnerable to rivals who enjoy greater dynamism at home.

Perceiving industry change

Beyond pressure to innovate, one of the most important advantages an industry can have is early insight into important needs, environmental forces, and trends that others have not noticed. Japanese firms had an early and clear warning about the importance of energy efficiency. American firms have often gotten a jump in seeing demand for new services, giving them a head start in many service industries. Better insight and early warning signals lead to competitive advantages. Firms gain competitive position before rivals perceive an opportunity (or a threat) and are able to respond.

Perceiving possibilities for new strategies more clearly or earlier comes in part from simply being in the right nation at the right time. Yet it is possible for a firm to more actively position itself to see the signals of change and act on them. It must find the right focus or location within the nation, and work to overcome the filters that distort or limit the flow of information.

- Identify and serve buyers (and channels) with the most anticipatory needs. Some buyers will confront new problems or have new needs before others because of their demographics, location, industry, or strategy.

- Discover and highlight trends in factor costs. Increases in the costs of particular factors or other inputs may signal future opportunities to leapfrog competitors by innovating to deploy inputs more effectively or to avoid the need for them altogether. A firm should know which markets or regions are likely to reflect such trends first.

- Maintain ongoing relationships with centers of research and sources of the most talented people. A firm must identify the places in the nation where the best new knowledge is being created that is now or might become relevant to its industry. Equally important is to identify the schools, institutions, and other companies where the best specialized human resources needed in the industry are being trained.

- Study all competitors, especially the new and unconventional ones. Rivals sometimes discover new ideas first. Innovators are often smaller, more focused competitors that are new to the industry. Alternatively, they may be firms led by managers with backgrounds in other industries not bound by conventional wisdom. Such 'outsiders,' with fewer blinders to cloud their perception of new opportunities and fewer perceived constraints in abandoning past practices, frequently become industry innovators.

- Bring some outsiders into the management team. The incorporation of new thinking in the management process is often speeded by the presence of one or more 'outsiders' – managers from other companies or industries or from the company's foreign subsidiaries.

Interchange within the national cluster

A firm gains important competitive advantages from the presence in its home nation of world-class buyers, suppliers, and related industries. They provide insight into future market needs and technological developments. They contribute to a climate for change and improvement, and become partners and allies in the innovation process. Having a strong cluster at home unblocks the flows of information and allows deeper and more open contact than is possible when dealing with foreign firms. Being part of a cluster localized in a small geographic area is even more valuable.

Buyers, channels, and suppliers

The first hurdle to be cleared in taking advantage of the domestic cluster is attitudinal. It means recognizing that home-based buyers and suppliers are allies in international competition and not just the other side of transactions. A firm must also pursue:

- regular senior management contact;
- formal and ongoing interchange between research organizations;
- reciprocity in serving as test sites for new products or services;
- cooperation in penetrating and serving international markets.

Working with buyers, suppliers, and channels involves helping them upgrade and extend their own competitive advantages. Their health and strength will only enhance their capacity to speed the firm's own rate of innovation. Open communications with local buyers or suppliers, and early access to new equipment, services, and ideas, are important for sustaining competitive advantage. Such communication will be freer, more timely, and more meaningful than is usually possible with foreign firms.

Encouraging and assisting domestic buyers and suppliers to compete globally is one part of the task of upgrading them. A company's local buyers and suppliers cannot ultimately sustain competitive advantage in many cases unless they compete globally. Buyers and suppliers need exposure to the pressures of world-wide competition in order to advance themselves. Trying to keep them 'captive' and prevent them from selling their products abroad is ultimately self-defeating.

An orientation toward closer vertical relationships is only just starting to take hold in many American companies, though it is quite typical in Japanese and Swedish companies. Interchange with buyers, channels, and suppliers always involves some tension, because there is inevitably the need to bargain with them over prices and service. In global industries, however, the competitive advantage to be gained from interchange more than compensates for some sacrifice in bargaining leverage. Interchange should not create dependence but interdependence. A firm should work with a group of suppliers and customers, not just one.

Related industries

Industries that are related or potentially related in terms of technology, channels, buyers, or the way buyers obtain or use products are potentially important to creating and sustaining competitive advantage. The presence in a nation of such industries deserves special attention. These industries are often essential sources of innovation. They can also become new suppliers, buyers, or even new competitors.

At a minimum, senior management should be visiting leading companies in related industries on a regular basis. The purpose is to exchange ideas about industry developments. Formal joint research projects, or other more structured ways to explore new ideas, are advisable where the related industry holds more immediate potential to affect competitive advantage.

Locating within the nation

A firm should locate activities and its headquarters at those locations in the nation where there are concentrations of sophisticated buyers, important suppliers, groups of competitors, or especially significant factor-creating mechanisms for its industry (such as universities with specialized programs or laboratories with expertise in important technologies). Geographic proximity makes the relationships within a cluster closer and more fluid. It also makes domestic rivalry more valuable for competitive advantage.

Serving home base buyers who are international and multinational

To transform domestic competitive advantage into a global strategy, a firm should identify and serve buyers at home that can also serve abroad. Such buyers are domestic companies that have international operations, individuals who travel frequently to other nations, and local subsidiaries of foreign firms. Targeting such buyers has two benefits. First, they can provide a base of demand in foreign markets to help offset the costs of entry. More important, they will often be sophisticated buyers who can provide a window into international market needs.

Improving the national competitive environment

Sustaining competitive advantage is not only a function of making the most of the national environment. Firms must work actively to improve their home base by upgrading the national diamond (see Figure 10.3.1 and Exhibit 10.3.1). A company draws on its home nation to extend and upgrade its own competitive advantages. The firm has a stake in making its home base a better platform for international success.

Playing this role demands that a company understands how each part of the 'diamond' best contributes to competitive advantage. It also requires a long-term perspective, because the investments required to improve the home base often take years or even decades to bear fruit. What is more, short-term profits are elevated by foregoing such investments, and by shifting important activities abroad instead of upgrading the ability to perform them at home. Both actions will diminish the sustainability of a firm's competitive advantages in the long run.

Firms have a tendency to see the task of ensuring high-quality human resources, infrastructure, and scientific knowledge as someone else's responsibility. Another common misconception is that, because competition is global, the home base is unimportant. Too often, US and British companies in particular leave investments in the national diamond to others or to the government. The result is that companies are well managed but lack the human resources, technology, and access to capable suppliers and customers needed to succeed against foreign rivals.

Where and how to compete

A firm's home nation shapes where and how it is likely to succeed in global competition. Germany is a superb environment for competing in printing equipment, but does not offer one conducive to international success in heavily advertised consumer packaged goods. Italy represents a remarkable setting for innovation in fashion and furnishing, but a poor environment for success in industries that sell to government agencies or infrastructure providers.

Within an industry, a nation's circumstances also favor competing in particular industry segments and with certain competitive strategies. Given local housing conditions, for example, Japan is a good home base for competing globally in compact models of appliances and in appliances that are inherently compact (such as microwave ovens) but a poor home base for competing in full-size refrigerators. Within compact appliances, the Japanese environment is particularly conducive to differentiation strategies based on rapid new model introduction and high product quality.

The national diamond becomes central to choosing the industries to compete in as well as the appropriate strategy. The home base is an important determinant of a firm's strengths and weaknesses relative to foreign rivals.

Understanding the home base of foreign competitors is essential in analyzing them. Their home nation yields them advantages and disadvantages. It also shapes their likely future strategies. The diamond serves as an important tool for competitor analysis in international industries.

Choosing industries and strategies

The likelihood that a firm can achieve breakthroughs or innovations of strategic importance in an industry is also influenced by its home nation. Innovation and entrepreneurial behavior is partly a function of chance. But it also depends to a considerable degree on the environment in which the innovator or entrepreneur works. The diamond has a strong influence on which nation (and even on which region within that nation) will be the source of an innovation.

Important innovations in Denmark, for example, have occurred in enzymes for food processing, in natural vitamins, in measuring instruments related to food processing, and in drugs isolated from animal organs (insulin and the anticoagulant heparin). These are hardly random in a nation whose exports are dominated by a large cluster of food-and-beverage-related industries. A firm or individual has the best odds of succeeding in innovation, or in creating a new business, where the national diamond provides the best environment.

The national circumstances most significant for competitive advantage depend on a firm's industry and strategy. In a resource- or basic factor-driven industry, the most important national attribute is a supply of superior or low-cost factors. In a fashion-sensitive industry, the presence of advanced and cutting-edge customers is paramount. In an industry heavily based on scientific research, the quality of factor-creating mechanisms in human resources and technology, coupled with access to sophisticated buyers and suppliers, is decisive.

Cost-oriented strategies are more sensitive to factor costs, the size of home demand, and conditions that favor large-scale plant investments. Differentiation strategies tend to depend more on specialized human resources, sophisticated local buyers, and world-class local supplier industries. Focus strategies rest on the presence of unusual demand in particular segments or on factor conditions or supplier access that benefits competing in a particular product range.

As competition globalizes, and as developments such as European trade liberalization and free trade between the United States and Canada promise to eliminate artificial distortions that have insulated domestic firms from market forces, firms must increasingly compete in industries and segments where they have real strengths. This must increasingly be guided by the national diamond.

A firm can raise the odds of success if it is competing in industries, and with strategies, where the nation provides an unusually fertile environment for competitive advantage. The questions in Figure 10.3.2 are designed to expose such areas. Of major importance is a forward-looking view in answering these questions. The focus must be on the nature of evolving competition, not the past requirements for success.

Diversification

While diversification is part of company strategy in virtually every nation, its track record has been mixed at best. Widespread diversification into unrelated industries was rare among the international leaders we studied. They tended instead to compete in one or two core industries or industry sectors, and their commitment to these industries was absolute. For every widely diversified Hitachi or Siemens, there were several Boeings, Koenig & Bauers, FANUCs, Novo Industries, and SKFs, who are global competitors but heavily focused on their core industry.

Internal diversification, not acquisition, has to a striking degree been the motivation for achieving leading international market positions. Where acquisitions were involved in international success stories, the acquisitions were often modest or focused ones that served as an initial entry point or reinforced an internal entry. The reasons for this track record in diversification are not hard to understand when viewed in light of my theory.

Internal diversification facilitates a transfer of skills and resources that is quite difficult to accomplish when acquiring an independent company with its own history and way of operating. Internal entry tends to increase the overall rate of investment in factor creation. There is also an intense commitment to succeed in diversification into closely related fields because of the benefits that accrue to the base business and the effect on the overall corporate image. Unrelated diversification, particularly through acquisition, makes no contribution to innovation. The implications of my theory for diversification strategy are as follows:

- New industries for diversification should be selected where a favorable national diamond is present or can be created. Diversification proposals should be screened for the attractiveness of the home base.

- Diversification is most likely to succeed when it follows or extends clusters in which the firm already competes.

- Internal development of new businesses, supplemented by small acquisitions, is more likely to create and sustain competitive advantage than the acquisition of large, establishment companies.

- Diversification into businesses lacking common buyers, channels, suppliers, or close technological connections is not only likely to fail but will also undermine the prospects for sustaining advantage in the core businesses.

Locating regional headquarters

The principles I have described carry implications for the choice of where to locate the regional headquarters responsible for managing a firm's activities in a group of nations. Regional headquarters are best placed not for administrative convenience but in the nation with the most favorable national diamond. Of special importance is choosing a location that will expose the firm to significant needs and pressures lacking at home. The purpose is to learn as well as raise the odds that information passes credibly back to the home base.

Selective foreign acquisitions

Foreign acquisitions can serve two purposes. One is to gain access to a foreign market or to selective skills. Here the challenge of integrating the acquisition into the global strategy is significant but raises a few unusual issues. The other reason for a foreign acquisition is to gain access to a highly favorable national

FIGURE 10.3.2   The home base diamond

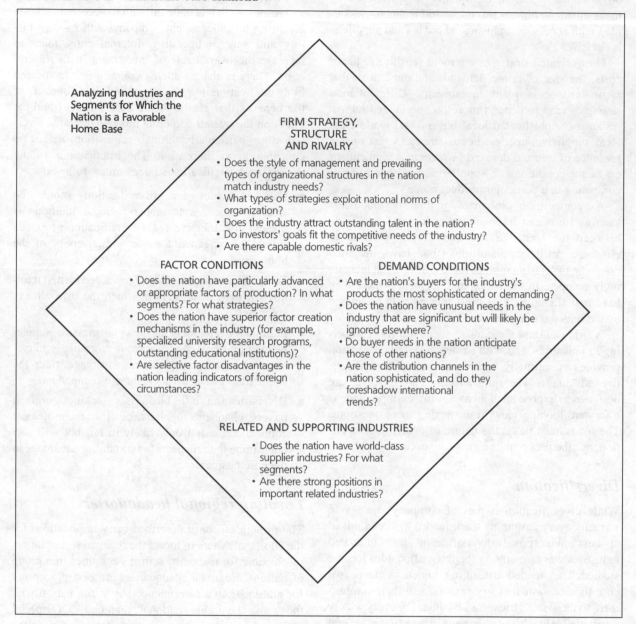

Analyzing Industries and Segments for Which the Nation is a Favorable Home Base

FIRM STRATEGY, STRUCTURE AND RIVALRY

- Does the style of management and prevailing types of organizational structures in the nation match industry needs?
- What types of strategies exploit national norms of organization?
- Does the industry attract outstanding talent in the nation?
- Do investors' goals fit the competitive needs of the industry?
- Are there capable domestic rivals?

FACTOR CONDITIONS

- Does the nation have particularly advanced or appropriate factors of production? In what segments? For what strategies?
- Does the nation have superior factor creation mechanisms in the industry (for example, specialized university research programs, outstanding educational institutions)?
- Are selective factor disadvantages in the nation leading indicators of foreign circumstances?

DEMAND CONDITIONS

- Are the nation's buyers for the industry's products the most sophisticated or demanding?
- Does the nation have unusual needs in the industry that are significant but will likely be ignored elsewhere?
- Do buyer needs in the nation anticipate those of other nations?
- Are the distribution channels in the nation sophisticated, and do they foreshadow international trends?

RELATED AND SUPPORTING INDUSTRIES

- Does the nation have world-class supplier industries? For what segments?
- Are there strong positions in important related industries?

diamond. Sometimes the only feasible way to tap into the advantages of another nation is to acquire a local firm because an outsider is hard-pressed to penetrate such broad, systemic advantages. The challenge in this latter type of acquisition is to preserve the ability of the acquired firm to benefit from its national environment at the same time as it is integrated into the company's global strategy.

The role of alliances

Alliances, or coalitions, are final mechanisms by which a firm can seek to tap national advantages in other nations. Alliances are a tempting solution to the dilemma of a firm seeking the home-base advantages of another nation without giving up its own. Unfortunately, alliances are rarely a solution. They can achieve selective benefits, but they always involve significant costs in terms of coordination, reconciling goals with an independent entity, creating a competitor, and giving up profits. These costs make many alliances temporary and destined to fail. They are often transitional devices rather than stable arrangements.

No firm can depend on another independent firm for skills and assets that are central to its competitive advantage. If it does, the firm runs a grave risk of los-ing its competitive advantage in the long run. Alliances tend to ensure mediocrity, not create world leadership. The most serious risk of alliances is that they deter the firm's own efforts at upgrading. This may occur because management is content to rely on the partner. It may also occur because the alliance has eliminated a threatening competitor.

READING 10.4

Transnational management

By Christopher Bartlett and Sumantra Ghoshal[1]

Changes in the international operating environment have forced MNCs to optimize global efficiency, national responsiveness, and world-wide learning simultaneously. For most companies, this new challenge implies not only a fundamental strategic reorientation, but also a major change in organizational capability.

Implementing such a complex three-pronged strategic objective would be difficult under any circumstances, but in a world-wide company the task is complicated even further. The very act of 'going international' multiplies a company's organizational complexity. Most companies find it difficult enough balancing product divisions that carry overall responsibility for achieving operating efficiency and strategic focus with corporate staffs whose functional expertise allows them to play an important counterbalance and control role. The thought of adding capable geographically oriented management and maintaining a three-way balance of organizational perspectives and capabilities among product, function, and area is intimidating. The difficulty is further increased because the resolution of tensions among the three different management groups must be accomplished in an organization whose operating units are often divided by distance and time and whose key members are separated by barriers of culture and language.

Beyond structural fit

Because the choice of a basic organizational structure has such a powerful influence on the management process in an MNC, much of the earlier attention of managers and researchers alike was focused on trying to find which formal structure provided the right 'fit' under various conditions. The most widely recognized study on this issue was Stopford and Wells's (1972) research on the 187 largest US-based MNCs in the late 1960s. Their work resulted in a 'stages model' of international organization structure that became the benchmark for most work that followed.

Stopford and Wells defined two variables to capture strategic and administrative complexity that faced most companies as they expanded abroad: the number of products sold internationally ('foreign product diversity,' shown on the vertical axis in Figure 10.4.1) and the importance of international sales to the company ('foreign sales as a percentage of total sales,' shown on the horizontal axis). Plotting the structural change in their sample of 187 companies, they found that world-wide corporations typically adopt different organizational structures at different stages of international expansion.

According to this model, world-wide companies typically manage their international operations through an international division at the early stage of foreign expansion, when both foreign sales and the diversity of products sold abroad are limited. Subsequently, those companies that expand their sales abroad without significantly increasing foreign product diversity typically adopt an area structure. Other companies that expand by increasing their foreign product diversity tend to adopt the world-wide product division structure. Finally, when both foreign sales and foreign product

[1]Source: Reprinted from Chapter 5 of *Transnational Management: Text, Cases, and Readings in Cross-Border Management*, second edition, R.D. Irwin Inc., 1995. Permission applied for.

FIGURE 10.4.1 Stopford and Wells's international structural stages model (adapted from Stopford and Wells, 1972)

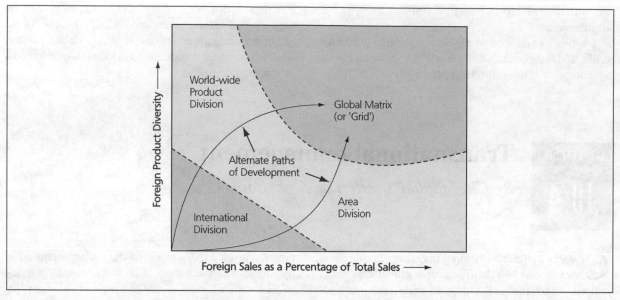

diversity are high, companies resort to the global matrix.

Although these ideas were presented as a descriptive model, consultants, academics, and managers alike soon began to apply them prescriptively. For many companies, it seemed that structure followed fashion more than strategy. And in the process, the debate was often reduced to generalized discussions of the comparative value of product versus geography-based structures and to simplistic choices between 'centralization' and 'decentralization.'

Confronted with the increasing complexity, diversity, and change in the 1980s, managers in many world-wide companies looked for ways to restructure. Conventional wisdom provided a ready solution: the global matrix. But for most companies, the result was disappointing. The promised land of the global matrix turned out to be an organizational quagmire from which they were forced to retreat.

Failure of the matrix

In theory, the solution should have worked. Having front-line managers report simultaneously to different organizational groups (such as business managers reporting to both the area and the functional groups or area managers reporting along functional and business lines) should have enabled the companies to maintain the balance among centralized efficiency, local respon-

siveness, and world-wide knowledge transfer. The multiple channels of communication and control promised the ability to nurture diverse management perspectives, and the ability to shift the balance of power within the matrix theoretically gave it great flexibility. The reality turned out to be otherwise, however, and the history of companies that built formal global matrix structures was an unhappy one.

Dow Chemical, a pioneer of global matrix organization, eventually returned to a more conventional structure with clear lines of responsibility being given to geographic managers. Citibank, once a textbook example of the global matrix, similarly discarded this mode of dual reporting relationships after a few years of highly publicized experimentation. And so too did scores of other companies that experimented with this complex and rather bureaucratic structure.

Most encountered the same problems. The matrix amplified the differences in perspectives and interests by forcing all issues through the dual chains of command so that even a minor difference could become the subject of heated disagreement and debate. While this strategy had proven useful in highly concentrated domestic operations, the very design of the global matrix prevented the resolution of differences among managers with conflicting views and overlapping responsibilities. Dual reporting led to conflict and confusion; the proliferation of channels created informational logjams; and overlapping responsibilities resulted in turf battles and a loss of accountability.

Separated by barriers of distance, time, language, and culture, managers found it virtually impossible to clarify the confusion and resolve the conflicts.

As a result, the management process was slow, acrimonious, and costly. Communications were routinely duplicated, approval processes were time-consuming, and constant travel and frequent meetings raised the company's administrative costs dramatically. In company after company, the initial appeal of the global matrix structure quickly faded into a recognition that a different solution was required.

Building organizational capability

The basic problem underlying a company's search for a structural fit was that it focused on only one organizational variable – formal structure – and this single tool proved to be unequal to the task of capturing the complexity of the strategic task facing most MNCs. First, as indicated earlier, this focus often forced managers to ignore the multidimensionality of the environmental forces as they made choices between product versus geographically-based structures and debated the relative advantages of centralization versus decentralization. Furthermore, structure defined a static set of roles, responsibilities, and relationships in a dynamic and rapidly evolving task environment. And finally, restructuring efforts often proved harmful, as organizations were bludgeoned into a major realignment of roles, responsibilities, and relationships overnight.

In an increasing number of companies, managers now recognize that formal structure is a powerful but blunt instrument of strategic change. Moreover, given the complexity and volatility of environmental demands, structural fit is becoming both less relevant and harder to achieve. Success in coping with managers' multidimensional strategic task now depends rather more on building strategic and organizational flexibility.

To develop multidimensional and flexible strategic capabilities, a company must go beyond structure and expand its fundamental organizational capabilities. The key tasks become to reorient managers' thinking and reshape the core decision-making systems. In doing so, the company's entire management process – the administrative system, communication channels, and interpersonal relationships – become the tools for managing such change.

Administrative heritage

While industry analysis can reveal a company's strategic challenges and market opportunities, its ability to fulfill that promise will be greatly influenced – and often constrained – by existing asset configurations, its historical definition of management responsibilities, and the ingrained organizational norms. A company's organization is shaped not only by current external task demands but also by past internal management biases. In particular, each company is influenced by the path by which it developed – its organizational history – and the values, norms, and practices of its management – its management culture. Collectively, these factors constitute a company's administrative heritage. It can be, at the same time, one of the company's greatest assets – the underlying source of its key competencies – and also a significant liability, since it resists change and thereby prevents realignment or broadening of strategic capabilities. As managers in many companies have learned, often at considerable cost, while strategic plans can be scrapped and redrawn overnight, there is no such thing as a zero-based organization. Companies are, to a significant extent, captives of their past, and any organizational transformation has to focus at least as much on where the company is coming from – its administrative heritage – as on where it wants to get to.

The importance of a company's administrative heritage can be illustrated by contrasting the development of a typical European MNC whose major international expansion occurred in the decades of the 1920s and 1930s, a typical American MNC that expanded abroad in the 1940s and 1950s, and a typical Japanese company that made its main overseas thrust in the 1960s and 1970s. Even if these companies were in the same industry, the combined effects of the different historical contexts in which they developed and the disparate internal cultural norms that influenced their management processes led to their adopting some very different strategic and organizational models.

Decentralized federation

Expanding abroad in a period of rising tariffs and discriminatory legislation, the typical European company found its budding export markets threatened by local competitors. To defend its various market positions, it was forced to build local production facilities. With their own plants, various national subsidiaries were able to modify products and marketing approaches to meet widely differing local market needs. The increasing independence of these fully integrated national units was reinforced by the transportation and communications barriers that existed in that era, limiting the headquarters' ability to intervene in the management of the company's spreading world-wide operations.

The emerging configuration of distributed assets and delegated responsibility fit well with the ingrained management norms and practices in many European companies. Because of the important role of owners and bankers in corporate-level decision making, European companies, particularly those from the United Kingdom, the Netherlands, and France, developed an internal culture that emphasized personal relationships rather than formal structures, and financial controls more than coordination of technical or operational detail. This management style, philosophy, and capability tended to reinforce companies' willingness to delegate more operating independence and strategic freedom to their foreign subsidiaries. Highly autonomous national companies were often managed

more as a portfolio of offshore investments rather than as a single international business.

The resulting organization and management pattern was a loose federation of independent national subsidiaries, each focused primarily on its local market. As a result, many of these companies adopted what we have described as the multinational strategy and developed a decentralized federation organization model that is represented in Figure 10.4.2.

Coordinated federation

US companies, many of which enjoyed their fastest international expansion in the 1950s and 1960s, developed under very different circumstances. Their main strength lay in the new technologies and management processes they had developed as a consequence of being located in the world's largest, richest, and most technologically advanced market. After the war, their foreign expansion focused primarily on leveraging this strength, particularly in response to demands generated by postwar reconstruction and the

FIGURE 10.4.2 Organizational configuration models

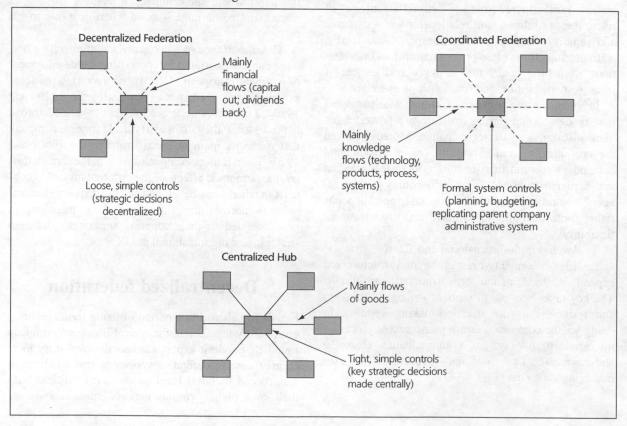

Decentralized Federation
Mainly financial flows (capital out; dividends back)
Loose, simple controls (strategic decisions decentralized)

Coordinated Federation
Mainly knowledge flows (technology, products, process, systems)
Formal system controls (planning, budgeting, replicating parent company administrative system

Centralized Hub
Mainly flows of goods
Tight, simple controls (key strategic decisions made centrally)

granting of independence to previously colonized nations.

Reinforcing this strategy was a professional managerial culture in most US-based companies that contrasted with the 'old boy network' that typified the European companies' processes. The management approach in most US-based companies was built on a willingness to delegate responsibility, while retaining overall control through sophisticated management systems and specialist corporate staffs. The systems provided channels for a regular flow of information, to be interpreted by the central staff. Holding the managerial reins, top management could control the free-running team of independent subsidiaries and guide the direction in which they were headed.

The main handicap such companies faced was that parent-company management often adopted a parochial and even superior attitude toward international operations, perhaps because of the assumption that new ideas and developments all came from the parent. Despite corporate management's increased understanding of its overseas markets, it often seemed to view foreign operations as appendages whose principal purpose was to leverage the capabilities and resources developed in the home market.

None the less, the approach was highly successful in the postwar decades, and many US-based companies adopted what we have described as the international strategy and a coordinated federation organizational model shown in Figure 10.4.2. Their foreign subsidiaries were often free to adapt products or strategies to reflect market differences, but their dependence on the parent company for new products, processes, and ideas dictated a great deal more coordination and control by headquarters than in the decentralized federation organization. This was facilitated by the existence of formal systems and controls in the headquarters-subsidiary link.

Centralized hub

In contrast, the typical Japanese company, making its main international thrust since the 1970s, faced a greatly altered external environment and operated with very different internal norms and values. With limited prior overseas exposure, it chose not to match the well-established local marketing capabilities and facilities that its European and US competitors had built up. (Indeed, well-established Japanese trading companies often provided it with an easier means of entering foreign markets.) However, it had new, efficient, scale-intensive plants, built to serve its rapidly expanding domestic market, and it was expanding into a global environment of declining trade barriers. Together, these factors gave it the incentive to develop a competitive advantage at the upstream end of the value-added chain. Its competitive strategy emphasized cost advantages and quality assurance and required tight central control of product development, procurement, and manufacturing. A centrally controlled, export-based internationalization strategy represented a perfect fit with the external environment and the company's competitive capabilities.

Such an approach also fit the cultural background and organizational values in the emerging Japanese MNC. At the foundation of the internal processes were the strong national cultural norms that emphasized group behavior and valued interpersonal harmony. These values had been enhanced by the paternalism of the zaibatsu and other enterprise groups. They were also reflected in the group-oriented management practices of *nemawashi* and *ringi* that were at the core of Japanese organizational processes. By keeping primary decision making and control at the center, the Japanese company could retain this culturally dependent management system that was so communications intensive and people dependent.

Cultural values were also reflected in one of the main motivations driving the international expansion of Japanese MNCs. As growth in their domestic market slowed and became increasingly competitive, these companies needed new sources of growth so they could continue to attract and promote employees. In a system of lifetime employment, growth was the engine that powered organizational vitality and self-renewal. It was this motivation that reinforced the bias toward an export-based strategy managed from the center rather than the decentralized foreign investment approach of the Europeans. As a result, these companies adopted what we have described as a global strategy, and developed a centralized hub organizational model, shown in Figure 10.4.2, to support this strategic orientation.

The transnational challenge

We advanced the hypothesis that many world-wide industries have been transformed in the 1980s from traditional multinational, international, and global forms toward a transnational form. Instead of demanding efficiency, responsiveness, or learning as the key capability for success. these businesses now require participating firms to achieve the three capabilities simultaneously to remain competitive.

Table 10.4.1 summarizes the key characteristics of the decentralized federation, coordinated federation, and centralized hub organizations as the supporting forms for companies pursuing the multinational, international, and global strategies. A review of these characteristics immediately reveals the problems each of the three archetypal company models might face in responding to the transnational challenge.

With its resources and capabilities consolidated at the center, the global company achieves efficiency primarily by exploiting potential scale economies in all its activities. In such an organization, however, the national subsidiaries' lack of resources and responsibilities may undermine their motivation and their ability to respond to local market needs. Similarly, while the centralization of knowledge and skills allows the global company to be highly efficient in developing and managing innovative new products and processes, the central groups often lack adequate understanding of the market needs and production realities outside their home market. Limited resources and the narrow implementation role of its overseas units prevent the company from tapping into learning opportunities outside its home environment. These are problems that a global organization cannot overcome without jeopardizing its trump card of global efficiency.

The classic multinational company suffers from other limitations. While its dispersed resources and decentralized decision making allows national subsidiaries to respond to local needs, the fragmentation of activities also leads to inefficiency. Learning also suffers, because knowledge is not consolidated and does not flow among the various parts of the company. As a result, local innovations often represent little more than the efforts of subsidiary management to protect its turf and autonomy, or reinventions of the wheel caused by blocked communication or the not-invented-here (NIH) syndrome.

In contrast, the international company is better able to leverage the knowledge and capabilities of the parent company. However, its resource configuration and operating systems make it less efficient than the global company, and less responsive than the multinational company.

The transnational organization

There are three important organizational characteristics that distinguish the transnational organization from its multinational, international, or global counterparts. It builds and legitimizes multiple diverse internal perspectives able to sense the complex environmental demands and opportunities; its physical assets and

TABLE 10.4.1 Key organizational characteristics

	Decentralized federation	Coordinated federation	Centralized hub
Strategic approach	Multinational	International	Global
Key strategic capability	National responsiveness	World-wide transfer of home country innovations	Global-scale efficiency
Configuration of assets and capabilities	Decentralized and nationally self-sufficient	Sources of core competencies centralized, others decentralized	Centralized and globally scaled
Role of overseas operations	Sensing and exploiting local opportunities	Adapting and leveraging parent-company competencies	Implementing parent-company strategies
Development and diffusion of knowledge	Knowledge developed and retained within each unit	Knowledge developed at the center and transferred to overseas units	Knowledge developed and retained at the center

management capabilities are distributed internationally but are interdependent; and it has developed a robust and flexible internal integrative process. In the following paragraphs, we will describe and illustrate each of these characteristics.

Multidimensional perspectives

Managing in an environment in which strategic forces are both diverse and changeable, the transnational company must develop the ability to sense and analyze the numerous and often conflicting opportunities, pressures, and demands it faces world-wide. Having a limited or biased management perspective through which to view developments can constrain a company's ability to understand and respond to some potential problems or opportunities.

The transnational organization must have broad sensory capabilities able to reflect the diverse environmental opportunities and demands in the internal management process. Strong national subsidiary management is needed to sense and represent the changing needs of local consumers and the increasing pressures from host governments; capable global business management is required to track the strategy of global competitors and to provide the coordination necessary to respond appropriately; and influential functional management is needed to concentrate corporate knowledge, information, and expertise, and facilitate its transfer among organizational units.

Unfortunately, however, in many companies, power is concentrated with the particular management group that has historically represented the company's most critical strategic tasks – often at the cost of allowing other groups to represent different needs. For example, in multinational companies, key decisions were usually dominated by the country management group since they made the most critical contribution to achieving national responsiveness, which lay at the center of the strategic approach of such companies. In global companies, by contrast, managers in world-wide product divisions were typically the most influential, since strong business management played the key role in the company's efforts to seek global efficiency. And in international companies, functional management groups often came to assume this position of dominance because of their roles in building, accumulating, and transferring the company's skills, knowledge, and capabilities.

In transnational companies, however, biases in the decision-making process are consciously reduced by building up the capability, credibility, and influence of the less powerful management groups while protecting the morale and capabilities of the dominant group. The objective is to build a multidimensional organization in which the influence of each of the three management groups is balanced.

Distributed, interdependent capabilities

Having sensed the diverse opportunities and demands it faces, the transnational organization must then be able to make choices among them and respond in a timely and effective manner to those that are deemed strategically important. When a company's decision-making process and organizational capabilities are concentrated at the center – as they are in the global organization's centralized hub configuration – it is often difficult to respond appropriately to diverse world-wide demands. Being distant from the front-line opportunities and threats, the central group's ability to act in an effective and timely manner is constrained by its reliance on complex and intensive international communications. Furthermore, the volume and diversity of demands made on the central group often result in central capabilities being overloaded, particularly where scarce technological or managerial resources are involved.

On the other hand, multinational organizations with their response capabilities spread throughout the decentralized federation of independent operations suffer from duplication of effort (the reinventing-the-wheel syndrome), inefficiency of operations (the 'locally self-sufficing scale' problem), and barriers to international learning (the not-invented-here syndrome).

In transnational organizations, management breaks away from the restricted view that assumes the need to centralize activities for which global scale or specialized knowledge is important. They ensure that viable national units achieve global scale by giving them the responsibility of becoming the company's world source for a given product or expertise. And they tap into important technological advances and market developments wherever they are occurring around the globe. They do this by securing the cooperation and involvement of the relevant national units in upgrading the company's technology, developing its new products, and shaping its marketing strategy.

One major consequence of the distribution of assets and responsibilities is that the interdependence of world-wide units automatically increases. Simple structural configurations like the decentralized federation, the coordinated federation, and the centralized hub are inadequate for the task facing the transnational corporation. What is needed is a structure we term the *integrated network* (see Figure 10.4.3).

In the integrated network configuration, national units are no longer viewed only as the end of a delivery pipeline for company products, or as implementors of centrally defined strategies, or even as local adapters and modifiers of corporate approaches. Rather, the assumption behind this configuration is that management should consider each of the world-wide units as a source of ideas, skills, capabilities, and knowledge that can be harnessed for the benefit of the total organization. Efficient local plants may be converted into international production centers; innovative national or regional development labs may be designated the company's 'center of excellence' for a particular product or process development; and creative subsidiary marketing groups may be given a lead role in developing world-wide marketing strategies for certain products or businesses. The company becomes a truly integrated network of distributed and interdependent resources and capabilities.

Flexible integrative process

Having established management groups representing multiple perspectives to reflect the variety of environmental demands and pressures and a configuration based on distributed and interdependent assets and organizational capabilities, the transnational organization requires a management process that can resolve the diversity of interests and perspectives and integrate the dispersed responsibilities. However, it cannot be bound by the symmetry of organizational process that follows when the task is seen in simplistic or static terms (e.g. 'Should responsibilities be centralized or decentralized?'). It is clear that the benefits to be gained from central control of world-wide research or manufacturing activities may be much more important than those related to the global coordination of the sales and service functions. We have also seen how the pattern of functional coordination varies by business and by geographic area (aircraft engine companies need central control of more decisions than multinational food packagers; operations in developing countries may need more central support than those in advanced countries). Furthermore, all coordination needs change over time due to changes in the international operating environment, the life cycles of products and technologies, or the company's stage of development.

Thus, management must be able to differentiate its operating relationships and change its decision-making roles by function, across businesses, among geographic units, and over time. The management process must be able to change from product to product, from country to country, and even from decision to decision.

This requires the development of rather sophisticated and subtle decision-making machinery based on three different but interdependent management processes. The first is a supportive but constrained escalation process that allows top management to intervene directly in the content of certain decisions – a subtle and carefully managed form of *centralization*. The second is a managed organizational process in which the key management task is to structure individual roles and supportive systems to

FIGURE 10.4.3 Integrated network model

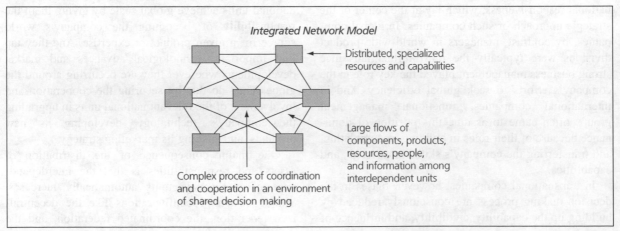

influence specific key decisions through *formalization*. The third is a self-regulatory capability in which top management's role is to establish a broad culture and set of relationships that provide an appropriate organizational context for delegated decisions – a sophisticated management process driven by *socialization*.

THE INTERNATIONAL CONTEXT IN INTERNATIONAL PERSPECTIVE

A truth on this side of the Pyrenees, a falsehood on the other.

Montaigne (1533–1592); French moralist and essayist

What a curious title, one might be inclined to think: 'The international context in international perspective'. Isn't this a case of the snake biting itself in its own tail? Of course, the answer is no. Similar to all previous chapters, an international angle can be used to view the debate between proponents of the global convergence perspective and those of the international diversity perspective. The question of interest is whether strategists in certain countries are more inclined towards a specific perspective. In other words, are there nations where the global convergence perspective is more prevalent, while in other nations the international diversity perspective is more widespread?

This is a tantalizing question, but as before, it must be concluded that little comparative research has been done on the issue. As a stimulus to the debate whether there are national differences in international context perspective, we would like to put forward a number of factors that might be of influence on how the paradox of globalization and localization is dealt with in different countries. It goes without saying that more international comparative research is required before a clear picture can be formed about the actual international differences.

Of course, if the proponents of the global convergence perspective are entirely right, the factors mentioned below will become less and less important as countries grow more similar. All of the international differences in strategic management preferences discussed in the concluding pages of each of the preceding chapters will also wither away. However, if international diversity remains a characteristic of our world, the way strategy paradoxes are dealt with differently in each country will continue to be an important issue to discuss.

Level of nationalism

The prospect of global convergence is a dream to some, but a nightmare to others. It is inspiring for those who would like to see a borderless world, in which like-minded people would see eye-to-eye. It is frightening for those who prefer to keep a diverse world, in which local autonomy and retaining of national culture are highly valued. Although global convergence enthusiasts and detractors can be found in each country, some nations seem more troubled by the prospect of further globalization than others. In some countries the belief is widespread that foreign values, norms, habits and behaviors are being imposed, that are undermining the national culture, and that the country's ability to decide its own fate is being compromised. This leads many to argue that global convergence should be, and will be, curtailed. In other countries such nationalism is far less pronounced, and the advantages of globalization are more widely accepted. In general, it can be expected that strategists from countries with a strong streak of nationalism will gravitate more toward the international diversity perspective, while strategists from less nationalist countries will be more inclined toward the global convergence perspective.

Size of country

In general, smaller countries are more exposed to the international context than larger countries. Smaller countries commonly export more of their gross domestic product than larger countries, and import more as well. Hence, their companies are more used to dealing with, and adapting to, a high number of foreign suppliers, customers and competitors. Moreover, companies from smaller countries, confronted with a limited home market, are forced to seek growth in foreign markets earlier than their counterparts in larger countries. During this early internationalization, these companies do not have the benefit of scale economies in the home market and therefore are usually more inclined to adapt themselves to the demands of foreign markets. Companies in larger markets normally grow to a significant size at home, thereby achieving certain economies of scale through national standardization, while also establishing a domestically oriented management style. When they do move abroad, as a more mature company, their international activities will tend to be modest compared to domestic operations and therefore they will be less inclined to be locally adaptive.

It stands to reason that this difference in exposure to the international context has an influence on how strategists from different countries perceive developments in the international context. Generally, strategists from smaller countries, to whom adaptation to international variety has become second nature, will favor the view that international diversity will remain. Strategists from larger countries will be more inclined to emphasize the growing similarities and to seek opportunities for international standardization.

Preference for central decision-making

This point is linked to the debate in the previous chapter, where the paradox of control and chaos was discussed. It was argued that in some countries there is a stronger emphasis on the role of top management in running the firm. In these countries there is usually a strong chain of command, with clear authority and responsibilities, and a well-developed control system. To remain manageable from the top, the organization must not become too complex to comprehend and steer. Usually this means that business units are structured along simple lines and that strategy is not too varied by product or geographic area. As soon as each product or geographic area requires its own specific strategy, the ability to run things centrally will diminish. Strategists with a strong preference for central decision-making will therefore be less inclined to acknowledge pressures for local responsiveness. Quite the opposite, they will be searching for opportunities to standardize their approach to different countries, which will allow for a more centralized decision-making structure. Strategists from countries with a tradition of more decentralized decision-making, are more likely to accept international diversity as a workable situation (e.g. Calori, Valla and De Woot, 1994; Turcq, 1994; Yoneyama, 1994).

FURTHER READING

There have been few writers as radical as Theodore Levitt, but quite a large number of stimulating works from the global convergence perspective. A good place for the interested reader to start would be Kenichi Ohmae's *The Borderless World: Power and Strategy in the Interlinked Economy* and George Yip's *Total Global Strategy*. For a stronger balancing of perspectives, the reader should turn to *The Multinational Mission*, by C.K. Prahalad and Yves Doz, and *Competition in Global Industries* by Michael Porter. For a critical review of the globalization literature, *The Logic of International Restructuring* by Winfried Ruigrok and Rob van Tulder makes for stimulating reading.

Most of this literature emphasizes strategy content issues, while largely neglecting strategy process aspects. A well-known exception is the article 'Strategic Planning for a Global Business' by Balaji Chakravarthy and Howard Perlmutter. With regard to the management of large international companies, *Managing Across Borders: The Transnational Solution*, by Christopher Bartlett and Sumantra Ghoshal, is highly recommended.

REFERENCES

Bartlett, C.A., and Ghoshal, S. (1987) 'Managing Across Borders: New Organizational Responses', *Sloan Management Review*, Vol. 29, No. 1, Fall, pp. 43–53.

Bartlett, C.A., and Ghoshal, S. (1989) *Managing Across Borders: The Transnational Solution*, Harvard Business School Press, New York.

Bartlett, C.A., and Ghoshal, S. (1995) *Transnational Management: Text, Cases, and Readings in Cross-Border Management*, Second Edition, R.D. Irwin Inc., New York.

Birkenshaw, J., and Hood, N. (1998) *Multinational Corporate Evolution and Subsidiary Development*, Macmillan, London.

Buckley, P.J., and Casson, M.C. (1976) *The Future of the Multinational Enterprise*, Macmillan, London.

Buckley, P.J., and Casson, M.C. (1985) *The Economic Theory of the Multinational Enterprise*, Macmillan, London.

Calori, R., Valla, J.-P., and de Woot, P. (1994) 'Common Characteristics: The Ingredients of European Management', in: R. Calori, and P. de Woot (eds.), *A European Management Model*, Prentice Hall, London.

Chakravarthy, B.S., and Perlmutter, H.W. (1985) 'Strategic Planning for a Global Business', *Columbia Journal of World Business*, Vol. 20, Summer, pp. 3–10.

Dicken, P. (1992) *Global Shift: The Internationalisation of Economic Activity*, Chapman, London.

Dosi, G., and Kogut, B. (1993) 'National Specificities and the Context of Change: The Co-evolution of Organization and Technology', in: B. Kogut (ed.), *Country Competitiveness: Technology and the Organizing of Work*, Oxford University Press, Oxford.

Douglas, S.P., and Wind, Y. (1987) 'The Myth of Globalization', *Columbia Journal of World Business*, Vol. 22, Winter, pp. 19–29.

Dunning, J. (1986) *Japanese Participation in British Industry: Trojan Horse or Catalyst for Growth?*, Croom Helm, Dover, NH.

Dunning, J. (1993) *The Globalization of Business*, Routledge, London.

Dunning, J.H. (1981), *International Production and the Multinational Enterprise*, Allen and Unwin, London.

Ghoshal, S., and Nohria, N. (1993) 'Horses for Courses: Organizational Forms for Multinational Companies', *Sloan Management Review*, Winter, pp. 23–35.

Govindarajan, V., and Gupta, A.K. (1999) 'Taking Wal-Mart Global: Lessons from Retailing's Giant', *Strategy and Business*, No. 4.

Gupta, A.K., and Govindarajan, V. (2000) 'Managing Global Expansion: A Conceptual Framework', *Business Horizons*, Vol. 43, No. 2, March–April, pp. 45–54.

Hamel, G., and Prahalad, C.K. (1985) 'Do You Really Have a Global Strategy?', *Harvard Business Review*, Vol. 63, No. 4, July–August, pp. 139–148.

Hedlund, G. (1986) 'The Hypermodern MNC – A Heterarchy?', *Human Resource Management*, Vol. 25, pp. 9–35.

Hout, T.M., Porter, M.E., and Rudden, E. (1982) 'How Global Companies Win Out', *Harvard Business Review*, Vol. 60, No. 5, September–October, pp. 98–108.

Kay, J. (1989) 'Myths and Realities', in: Davis, E. (ed.), *1992: Myths and Realities*, Centre for Business Strategy, London.

Klein, N. (2000) *No Logo, Taking Aim at the Brand Bullies*, Flamingo, London.

Kogut, B. (1985) 'Designing Global Strategies: Comparative and Competitive Value-Added Chains', *Sloan Management Review*, Summer, pp.15–28.

Kogut, B. (ed.) (1993) *Country Competitiveness: Technology and the Organizing of Work*, Oxford University Press, Oxford.

Kogut, B., and Zander, U. (1993) 'Knowledge Of The Firm And The Evolutionary Theory Of The Mul', *Journal of International Business Studies*, Vol. 24, No. 4; pp. 625–645.

Krugman, P.R. (1990) *Rethinking International Trade*, MIT Press, Cambridge, MA.

Levitt, T. (1983) 'The Globalization of Markets', *Harvard Business Review*, Vol. 61, No. 3, May–June, pp. 92–102.

Liebeskind, J. (1996) 'Knowledge, Strategy and the Theory of the Firm', *Strategic Management Journal*, Vol. 17, Special Issue, Winter, pp. 93–107.

McGrew, A.G. and Lewis, P.G. (eds.) (1992) *Global Politics: Globalisation and the Nation-State*, Polity Press, Cambridge.

Morrison, A.J., Ricks, D.A., and Roth, K. (1991) 'Globalization versus Regionalization: Which Way for the Multinational?', *Organizational Dynamics*, Winter, pp. 17–29.

Ohmae, K. (1989) 'Managing in a Borderless World', *Harvard Business Review*, Vol. 67, No. 3, May–June, pp. 152–161.

Ohmae, K. (1990) *The Borderless World: Power and Strategy in the Interlinked Economy*, Fontana, London.

Patel, P., and Pavitt, K. (1991) 'Large Firms in the Production of the World's Technology: An Important Case of "Non-Globalisation"', *Journal of International Business Studies*, Vol. 22, No. 1, pp. 1–21.

Pitt, M. (1996) 'IKEA of Sweden: The Global Retailer', in: C. Baden-Fuller and M. Pitt (eds.), *Strategic Innovation*, Routledge, London.

Porter, M.E. (1986) *Competition in Global Industries*, Free Press, New York.

Porter, M.E. (1990a) *The Competitive Advantage of Nations*, MacMillan, London.

Porter, M.E. (1990b) 'New Global Strategies for Competitive Advantage', *Planning Review*, Vol. 18, No. 3, May–June, pp. 4–14.

Prahalad, C.K., and Doz, Y. (1987) *The Multinational Mission: Balancing Local Demands and Global Vision*, Free Press, New York.

Reich, R. (1991) *The Work of Nations: Preparing Ourselves for 21st Century Capitalism*, Alfred Knopf, New York.

Rodrik, D. (1997) 'Has Globalization Gone Too Far', *California Management Review*, Vol. 39, No. 3, Spring, pp. 29–53.

Ruigrok, W., and van Tulder, R. (1995) *The Logic of International Restructuring*, Routledge, London.

Stopford, J.M., and Wells L.T. (1972) *Strategy and Structure of Multinational Enterprise*, Basic Books, New York.

Teece, D.J. (1981) 'The Multinational Enterprise: Market Failure and Market Power Considerations', *Sloan Management Review*, Spring, pp.4–17.

Turcq, D. (1994) 'Is There a US Company Management Style in Europe?', in: R. Calori, and P. de Woot (eds.), *A European Management Model*, Prentice Hall, London.

Vernon, R. (1966) 'International Investment and International Trade in the Product Life Cycle', *Quarterly Journal of Economics*, Vol. 80, No. 2, May, pp. 190–207.

Vernon, R., and Wells, L.T. (1986) *The Economic Environment of International Business*, Fourth Edition, Prentice Hall, Englewood Cliffs, NJ.

Wortzel, L.H. (1990) 'Global Strategies: Standardization Versus Flexibility', in: H. Vernon-Wortzel and L.H. Wortzel (eds.), *Global Strategic Management*, Wiley, New York.

Yip, G.S. (1993) *Total Global Strategy: Managing for Worldwide Competitive Advantage,* Prentice Hall, London.

Yoneyama, E. (1994) 'Japanese Subsidiaries: Strengths and Weaknesses', in: R., Calori, and P. de Woot (eds.), *A European Management Model*, Prentice Hall, London.

PURPOSE

ORGANIZATIONAL PURPOSE

Corporation, n. An ingenious device for obtaining individual profit without individual responsibility.

The Devil's Dictionary, Ambrose Bierce (1842–1914); American columnist

INTRODUCTION

At the beginning of this book, strategy was defined as a course of action for achieving an organization's purpose. Subsequently, nine chapters were spent looking at strategy from many different angles, but scant attention was paid to the organizational purposes that firms want to achieve. How to set a course for the organizational vessel through turbulent waters was discussed, but the question of why the journey was being undertaken in the first place was hardly raised – the focus was on means, not on ends. This lack of attention to the subject of organizational purpose is a notable feature of the strategic management literature. This might be due to the widespread assumption that it is obvious why business organizations exist. Some writers might avoid the topic because it is highly value-laden and somehow outside the realm of strategic management.

Yet, in practice, managers must constantly make choices and seek solutions based on an understanding of what their organization is intended to achieve. It is hardly possible for strategizing managers to avoid taking a stance on what they judge to be the purpose of their organization. They are confronted with many different claimants who believe that the firm exists to serve their interests. Demands are placed on the firm by shareholders, employees, suppliers, customers, governments and communities, forcing managers to weigh whose interests should receive priority over others. Even when explicit demands are not voiced, managers must still determine who will be the main beneficiary of the value-creation activities of the firm.

Where managers have a clear understanding of their organization's purpose, this can provide strong guidance during processes of strategic thinking, strategy formation and strategic change. The organizational purpose can function as a fundamental principle, against which strategic options can be evaluated. Yet, while of central importance, organizations can be guided by more principles than organizational purpose alone. For example, they can be strongly influenced by certain business philosophies and values. The broader set of fundamental principles giving direction to strategic decision-making, of which organizational purpose is the central element, is referred to as the 'corporate mission'.

Determining the corporate mission is a challenging task, not least because there are so many different views on how it should be done. In this chapter, the issue of corporate mission will be explored in more detail, with the intention of uncovering the conflicting perspectives on the subject of organizational purpose that lie at the heart of the divergent opinions.

THE ISSUE OF CORPORATE MISSION

Corporate mission is a rather elusive concept, often used to refer to the wooly platitudes on the first few pages of annual reports. To many people, mission statements are lists of lofty principles that have potential public relations value, but have little bearing on actual business, let alone impact on the process of strategy formation. Yet, while frequently employed in this hollow manner, a corporate mission can be very concrete and play an important role in determining strategic actions.

A good way to explain the term's meaning is to go back to its etymological roots. 'Mission' comes from the Latin word *mittere*, which means 'to send' (Cummings and Davies, 1994). A mission is some task, duty or purpose that 'sends someone on their way' – a motive or driver propelling someone in a certain direction. Hence, 'corporate mission' can be understood as the basic drivers sending the corporation along its way. The corporate mission consists of the fundamental principles that mobilize and propel the firm in a particular direction.

The corporate mission contributes to 'sending the firm in a particular direction' by influencing the firm's strategy. To understand how a mission impacts strategy, two topics require closer attention. First, it is necessary to know what types of 'fundamental principles' actually make up a corporate mission. These elements of corporate mission will be described below. Secondly, it needs to be examined what types of roles are played by a corporate mission in the strategy formation process. These functions of corporate mission will also be described (see Figure 11.1).

Besides the 'what' of corporate mission, it is equally important to explore the 'who' – who should determine a corporate mission. In the previous chapters the implicit assumption has consistently been that managers are the primary 'strategic actors' responsible for setting the direction of the firm. But in fact, their actions are formally monitored and controlled by the board of directors. In this way, the direction of the firm must be understood as a result of the interaction between management ('the executives') and the board of directors. As the name would imply, directors have an important influence on direction.

The activities of the board of directors are referred to as 'corporate governance' – directors govern the strategic choices and actions of the management of a firm. And because they have such an important role in setting the corporate mission and strategy, their input will be examined here as well. First, an overall review will be presented of the various

FIGURE 11.1   Corporate mission and corporate governance

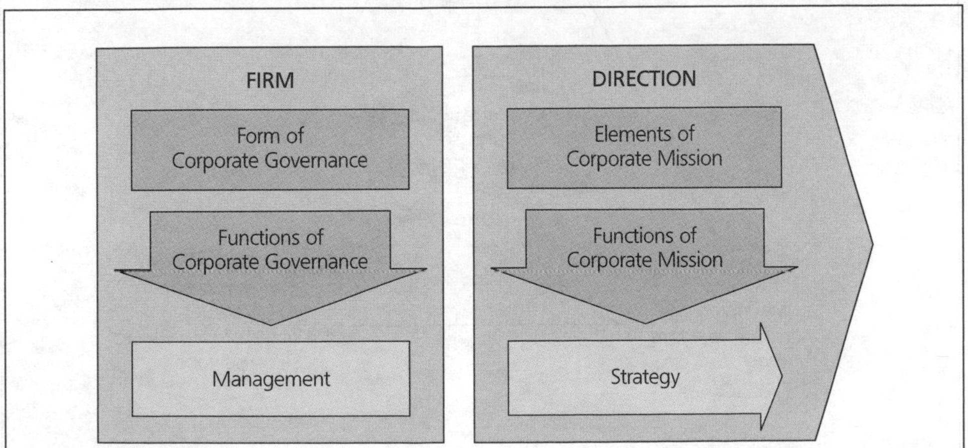

functions of corporate governance. Then it will be examined what the different forms of corporate governance are, as this can significantly influence the eventual mission and strategy that are followed (see Figure 11.1).

Elements of corporate mission

Organizational purpose can be defined as the reason for which an organization exists. It can be expected that the perception that managers have of their organization's purpose will give direction to the strategy process and influence the strategy content (e.g. Bartlett and Ghoshal, 1994; Campbell and Tawadey, 1990). Sometimes strategizing managers consciously reflect on, or question, the organizational purpose as they make strategic choices. However, more often their view of the organization's purpose will be a part of a broader set of business principles that steers their strategic thinking. This enduring set of fundamental principles, that forms the base of a firm's identity and guides its strategic decision-making, is referred to as the corporate mission.

While the purpose of an organization is at the heart of the corporate mission, three other components can also be distinguished (see Figure 11.2):

- Organizational beliefs. All strategic choices ultimately include important assumptions about the nature of the environment and what the firm needs to do to be successful in its business. If people in a firm do not share the same fundamental strategic beliefs, joint decision-making will be very protracted and conflictual – opportunities and threats will be interpreted differently and preferred solutions will be very divergent (see Chapter 2). To work swiftly and in unison, a common understanding is needed. The stronger the set of shared beliefs subscribed to by all organizational members, the easier communication and decision-making will become, and the more confident and driven the group will be. Where researchers refer to the organizational ideology ('system of ideas') as their 'collective cognitive map' (Axelrod, 1976), 'dominant logic' (Prahalad and Bettis,

FIGURE 11.2   Elements of a corporate mission

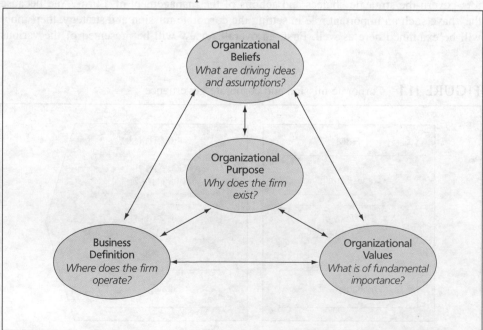

1986) or 'team mental model' (Klimoski and Mohammed, 1994), companies themselves usually simply speak of their beliefs or philosophy.

- Organizational values. Each person in an organization can have their own set of values, shaping what they believe to be good and just. Yet, when an organization's members share a common set of values, determining what they see as worthwhile activities, ethical behavior and moral responsibilities, this can have a strong impact on the strategic direction (e.g. Falsey, 1989; Hoffman, 1989). Such widely embraced organizational values also contribute to a clear sense of organizational identity, attracting some individuals, while repelling others. Although it can be useful to explicitly state the values guiding the organization, to be influential they must become embodied in the organization's culture (e.g. McCoy, 1985; Collins and Porras, 1994).

- Business definition. For some firms, any business is good business, as long as they can make a reasonable return on investment. Yet, if any business is fine, the firm will lack a sense of direction. In practice, most firms have a clearer identity, which they derive from being active in a particular line of business. For these firms, having a delimiting definition of the business they wish to be in strongly focuses the direction in which they develop. Their business definition functions as a guiding principle, helping to distinguish opportunities from diversions (e.g. Abell, 1980; Pearce, 1982). Of course, while a clear business definition can focus the organization's attention and efforts, it can lead to shortsightedness and the missing of new business developments (e.g. Ackoff, 1974; Levitt, 1960).

The strength of a corporate mission will depend on whether these four elements fit together and are mutually reinforcing (Campbell and Yeung, 1991). Where a consistent and compelling corporate mission is formed, this can infuse the organization with a sense of mission, creating an emotional bond between organizational members and energizing them to work according to the mission.

A concept that is often confused with mission is vision. Individuals or organizations have a vision if they picture a future state of affairs they wish to achieve (from the Latin *vide* – to see; Cummings and Davies, 1994). While the corporate mission outlines the fundamental principles guiding strategic choices, a strategic vision outlines the desired future at which the company hopes to arrive. In other words, vision provides a business aim, while mission provides business principles (see Figure 11.3).

FIGURE 11.3   Corporate mission and strategic vision

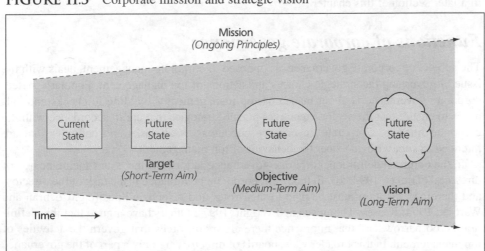

Generally, a strategic vision is a type of aim that is less specific than a short-term target or longer-term objective. Vision is usually defined as a broad conception of a desirable future state, of which the details remain to be determined (e.g. Senge, 1990; Collins and Porras, 1996). As such, strategic vision can play a similar role as corporate mission, pointing the firm in a particular direction and motivating individuals to work together towards a shared end.

Functions of corporate mission

The corporate mission can be articulated by means of a mission statement, but in practice not everything that is called a mission statement meets the above criteria (e.g. David, 1989; Piercy and Morgan, 1994). However, firms can have a mission, even if it has not been explicitly written down, although this does increase the chance of divergent interpretations within the organization.

In general, paying attention to the development of a consistent and compelling corporate mission can be valuable for three reasons. A corporate mission can provide:

- **Direction.** The corporate mission can point the organization in a certain direction, by defining the boundaries within which strategic choices and actions must take place. By specifying the fundamental principles on which strategies must be based, the corporate mission limits the scope of strategic options and sets the organization on a particular heading (e.g. Bourgeois and Brodwin, 1983; Hax, 1990).

- **Legitimization.** The corporate mission can convey to all stakeholders inside and outside the company that the organization is pursuing valuable activities in a proper way. By specifying the business philosophy that will guide the company, the chances can be increased that stakeholders will accept, support and trust the organization (e.g. Klemm, Sanderson and Luffman, 1991; Freeman and Gilbert, 1988).

- **Motivation.** The corporate mission can go a step further than legitimization, by actually inspiring individuals to work together in a particular way. By specifying the fundamental principles driving organizational actions, an *esprit de corps* can evolve, with the powerful capacity to motivate people over a prolonged period of time (e.g. Campbell and Yeung, 1991; Peters and Waterman, 1982).

Especially these last two functions of a corporate mission divide both management theorists and business practitioners. What is seen as a legitimate and motivating organizational purpose is strongly contested. What the main factors of disagreement are will be examined in a later section of this chapter.

Functions of corporate governance

The subject of corporate governance, as opposed to corporate management, deals with the issue of governing the strategic choices and actions of top management. Popularly stated, corporate governance is about managing top management – building in checks and balances to ensure that the senior executives pursue strategies that are in accordance with the corporate mission. Corporate governance encompasses all tasks and activities that are intended to supervise and steer the behavior of top management.

In the common definition, corporate governance 'addresses the issues facing boards of directors' (Tricker, 1994: xi). In this view, corporate governance is the task of the directors and therefore attention must be paid to their roles and responsibilities (e.g. Cochran and Wartick, 1994; Keasey, Thompson and Wright, 1997). Others have argued that this definition is too narrow, and that in practice there are more forces that govern the activities of top management. In this broader view, boards of directors are only a part of the governance system. For instance, regulation by local and national authorities, as well as pressure from societal groups, can function as the checks and balances limiting top management's discretion (e.g. Mintzberg, 1984; Demb and Neubauer, 1992, Reading 11.3 in this book).

Whether employing a narrow or broad definition, three important corporate governance functions can be distinguished (adapted from Tricker, 1994):

- **Forming function.** The first function of corporate governance is to influence the forming of the corporate mission. The task of corporate governance is to shape, articulate and communicate the fundamental principles that will drive the organization's activities. Determining the purpose of the organization and setting priorities among claimants are part of the forming function. The board of directors can conduct this task by, for example, questioning the basis of strategic choices, influencing the business philosophy, and explicitly weighing the advantages and disadvantages of the firm's strategies for various constituents (e.g. Freeman and Reed, 1983, Reading 11.2; Yoshimori, 1995, Reading 11.4).

- **Performance function.** The second function of corporate governance is to contribute to the strategy process with the intention of improving the future performance of the corporation. The task of corporate governance is to judge strategy initiatives brought forward by top management and/or to actively participate in strategy development. The board of directors can conduct this task by, for example, engaging in strategy discussions, acting as a sounding board for top management, and networking to secure the support of vital stakeholders (e.g. Baysinger and Hoskisson, 1990; Donaldson and Davis, 1995; Zahra and Pearce, 1989).

- **Conformance function.** The third function of corporate governance is to ensure corporate conformance to the stated mission and strategy. The task of corporate governance is to monitor whether the organization is undertaking activities as promised and whether performance is satisfactory. Where management is found lacking, it is a function of corporate governance to press for changes. The board of directors can conduct this task by, for example, auditing the activities of the corporation, questioning and supervising top management, determining remuneration and incentive packages, and even appointing new managers (e.g. Parkinson, 1993; Spencer, 1983).

These functions give the board of directors considerable influence in determining and realizing the corporate mission. As such, they have the ultimate power to decide on the organizational purpose. Therefore, it is not surprising that the question to whom these functions should be given is extremely important.

Forms of corporate governance

There is considerable disagreement on how boards of directors should be organized and run. Currently, each country has its own system of corporate governance and the international differences are large. Yet even within many countries, significant disagreements are discernible. In designing a corporate governance regime, three characteristics of boards of directors are of particular importance (adapted from Tricker, 1994):

- Board structure. Internationally, there are major differences between countries requiring a two-tier board structure (e.g. Germany, the Netherlands and Finland), countries with a one-tier board (e.g. United States, Britain and Japan), and countries in which companies are free to choose (e.g. France and Switzerland). In a two-tier system there is a formal division of power, with a management board made up of the top executives and a distinct supervisory board made up of non-executives with the task of monitoring and steering the management board. In a one-tier (or unitary) board system, executive and non-executive (outside) directors sit together on one board (see Figure 11.4).

FIGURE 11.4 Two- vs. one-tier board structure

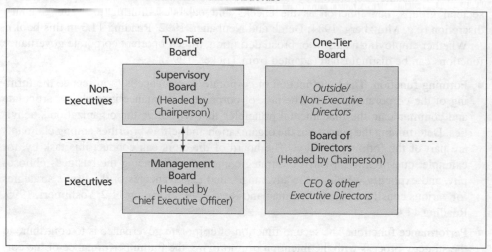

- Board membership. The composition of boards of directors can vary sharply from company to company and from country to country. Some differences are due to legal requirements that are not the same internationally. For instance, in Germany by law half of the membership of a supervisory board must represent labor, while the other half represents the shareholders. In French companies labor representatives are given observer status on the board. In other countries there are no legal imperatives, yet differences have emerged. In some cases outside (non-executive) directors from other companies are common, while in other nations fewer outsiders are involved. Even within countries, differences can be significant, especially with regard to the number, stature and independence of outside (non-executive) directors.

- Board tasks. The tasks and authority of boards of directors also differ quite significantly between companies. In some cases boards meet infrequently and are merely asked to vote on proposals put in front of them. Such boards have little formal or informal power to contradict the will of the CEO. In other companies, boards meet regularly and play a more active role in corporate governance, by formulating proposals, proactively selecting new top managers, and determining objectives and incentives. Normally, the power of outside (non-executive) directors to monitor and steer a company only partly depends on their formally defined tasks and authority. To a large degree their impact is determined by how proactive they define their own role.

The question in the context of this chapter is how a board of directors should be run to ensure that the organization's purpose is best achieved. What should be the structure, membership and tasks of the board of directors, to realize the ends for which the organization exists?

THE PARADOX OF PROFITABILITY AND RESPONSIBILITY

Property has its duties as well as its rights.
Thomas Drummond (1797–1840); English public administrator

Discussions on what firms should strive to achieve are not limited to the field of strategic management. Given the influential position of business organizations in society, the purpose they should serve is also discussed by theorists in the fields of economics, political science, sociology, ethics and philosophy. Since the industrial revolution, and the rise of the modern corporation, the role of business organizations within the 'political economic order' has been a central theme in many of the social sciences. It has been the topic that has filled libraries of books, inspired society-changing theories and stirred deep-rooted controversies.

The enormous impact of corporations on the functioning of society has also attracted political parties, labor unions, community representatives, environmentalists, the media and the general public to the debate. All take a certain position on the role that business organizations should play within society and the duties that they ought to shoulder. Here, too, the disagreements can be heated, often spilling over from the political arena and negotiating tables into the streets.

In countries with a market economy, it is generally agreed that companies should pursue strategies that ensure economic profitability, but that they have certain social responsibilities that must be fulfilled as well. But this is where the consensus ends. Opinions differ sharply with regard to the relative importance of profitability and responsibility. Some people subscribe to the view that profitability is the very purpose of economic organizations and that the only social responsibility of a firm is to pursue profitability within the boundaries of the law. However, other people argue that business corporations are not only economic entities, but also social institutions, embedded in a social environment, which brings along heavy social responsibilities. In this view, organizations are morally obliged to behave responsibly towards all parties with a stake in the activities of the firm, and profitability is only a means to fulfill this duty.

Most managers accept that both economic profitability and social responsibility are valuable goals to pursue. Yet, as organizational purpose, profitability and responsibility are at least partially contradictory. If managers strive towards profit maximization, shareholders might be enamored, but this will bring managers into conflict with the optimization of benefits for other stakeholders. In other words, to a certain extent there is a tension between the profitability and responsibility (e.g. Cannon, 1992; Demb and Neubauer, 1992, Reading 11.3; Drucker, 1984; Yoshimori, 1995, Reading 11.4).

The demand for economic profitability

It is clear that business organizations must be profitable to survive. Yet simple profitability, that is having higher income than costs, is not sufficient. To be an attractive investment, a company must earn a higher return on the shareholders' equity than could be realized if the money were deposited in the bank. Put differently, investors must have a financial incentive to run a commercial risk; otherwise they could just as well bring their money to the bank or buy low risk government bonds.

Yet, offsetting the risk carried by investors is but a small part of the larger picture. Once a corporation has established a track record of profitability, this inspires trust among financiers. Such trust makes it much easier to raise new capital, either through borrowing (at more attractive rates) or by issuing new shares. And of course, new capital can be used to further the competitive objectives of the organization. Where companies have not been particularly profitable in the past, and cannot authoritatively project an attractive level of profitability in the future, they will find it difficult or virtually impossible to find new financing. This can significantly weaken the position of the firm and undermine its long-term competitiveness.

For publicly traded corporations strong profitability is usually reflected in higher share prices, which is not only beneficial to the shareholders at that moment, but also makes it easier to acquire other firms and to pay with shares. Moreover, a high share price is the best defense against a hostile takeover and the best negotiating chip for a friendly one. In both publicly and privately held companies, retained profits can also be an important source of funds for new investments.

In short, profitability is not only a *result*, but also a *source*, of competitive power. Profitability provides a company with the financial leeway to improve its competitive position and pursue its ambitions.

The demand for social responsibility

As economic entities engaging in formalized arrangements with employees, suppliers, buyers and government agencies, corporations have the legal responsibility to abide by the stipulations outlined in their contracts. Equally, they are bound to stay within the 'letter of the law' in each jurisdiction in which they operate. However, being good corporate citizens entails more than just staying out of court.

Companies are more than just 'economic machines' regulated by legal contracts. They are also networks of people, working together towards a common goal. And as members of a social group, people within a company need to develop a sense of 'community' if they are to function properly. One of the most basic needs is to build a level of trust among people – a feeling of security that each individual's interests will be taken into account. Trust evolves where people feel certain that others will behave in a socially responsible manner, instead of letting their own self-interest prevail without limitation. Once there is enough trust between people, they can engage in productive teamwork and invest in their mutual relationships.

Hence, social responsibility – that is, acting in the interest of others, even when there is no legal imperative – lies at the basis of trust. And where there is trust, people are generally willing to commit themselves to the organization, both emotionally and practically. Emotionally, they will become involved with, and can become strongly connected to, the organization, which can lead to a sense of pride and loyalty. Practically, they will be willing to invest years acquiring firm-specific knowledge and skills, and in building a career. Such commitments make people dependent on the organization, as they will be less able and inclined to job-hop. It is therefore vital that the organization rewards such commitment by acting responsibly, even where this hurts profitability; otherwise the bond of trust can be seriously damaged.

Acting in the interest of all employees is a limited form of social responsibility. Just as it is beneficial for trust to evolve within organizations, it is important for trust to develop between the organization and its broader environment of buyers, suppliers, governments, local communities and activist groups. Therefore, it is important that these organizations also come to trust that the organization is willing to act in a socially responsible way, even when this entails sacrificing profitability.

EXHIBIT 11.1 SHORT CASE

GOLDMAN SACHS: HITTING THE JACKPOT?

Freud probably would have had a good explanation why the name Goldman Sachs exerts such a strong pull on university graduates. However, an alternative explanation is that Goldman Sachs is the world's premier investment bank and working there is the ultimate career ambition of many 'high potentials'. Despite the fact that its employees are reputed to work the hardest and the longest in the industry, the prestige of Goldman Sachs encourages many of the top people to try to get a job with the firm. By 2002, the company employed over 20 000 employees in 20 offices around the world, with the reputation of being the very best analysts, traders and associates around.

Goldman Sachs is active in the areas of investment banking, asset management and securities services, with a particular strength in initial public offerings (IPOs) and mergers and acquisitions (M&A). Since its establishment in 1869, the firm has added many of the world's blue chip companies to its client list. A typical aspect of its culture is that it combines a strongly proactive attitude towards fulfilling its clients' needs with a cautious stance towards the financial markets. A famous saying within the firm is: 'Good companies worry about their competition, great companies worry about their clients.' This way of thinking translates into high levels of client commitment and client care, with a strong emphasis on preserving relationships and reputation. To insiders it came as no surprise that Goldman Sachs' cautious stance helped it to stay away from the reckless behavior that got its competitors like Merrill Lynch, Lehman Brothers and Morgan Stanley into difficulties in the 1980s.

In hiring new employees, the firm has (quoting its web site) a specific approach:

Although our activities are measured in billions of dollars, we select our people one by one. In a service business we know that without the best people we cannot be the best firm . . . so we aggressively recruit the very best professionals. But where we differ most from some of the other Wall Street firms is in the attention we pay to retention. Goldman's standards of care of its professionals are simply the best in the industry.

Which might be true, but in practice the firm's most powerful tool for retaining professionals has always been the prospect of partnership. These top-of-class professionals have been willing to work 14–18 hour days for 10–15 years at salaries often lower than they could earn elsewhere, in the hope of hitting the jackpot – becoming a partner in the firm. This jackpot has consisted of an eight-figure compensation package and the prestige of belonging to an exclusive club. Of course, only the happy few have made it to the top of this pyramid scheme, but those who have, have shared in the yearly profits. And these profits, a newspaper once remarked, have regularly surpassed the national income of a country like Tanzania, but have only needed to be distributed among approximately 200 people. Over the course of their careers, Goldman Sachs partners have had the prospect of earning at least US$25 million.

By the 1990s, this partnership structure made Goldman Sachs the odd-man out on Wall Street, where all other investment banks had long before become public companies. But the pros and cons of the partnership model were hotly debated in the firm. On the one hand, many partners argued that 'if it ain't broke, don't fixed it'. They felt that for more than 100 years the partnership structure had ensured a high commitment of the partners to work towards maximizing the firm's value – partners could only cash in their shares after a number of years and therefore had a strong incentive to keep the value of the shares high. These partners also felt little need to share their hard-earned profits with outside shareholders. On the other hand, many partners were increasingly worried about the risks that the partners needed to bare. As they became more and more reliant on trading to boost profitability, they also became more exposed to the risk of a single trader losing millions in a day, as happened at Barings. Furthermore, the partnership was vulnerable to groups of partners leaving and taking their equity with them, as happened during the 1994 bond crash. At the same time, competitors were merging and getting bigger, often becoming a part of a large financial service conglomerate. It was believed that these dinosaurs had little extra competitive power, but would be better placed to survive the next shakeout during a prolonged bear market. This left many partners feeling small and vulnerable. Finally, it was argued that for Goldman Sachs to grow by acquisition, it would be much easier to pay in shares than in cash.

A first move by Goldman Sachs to find a solution to the downsides of the partnership structure was to switch to a limited liability partnership status. The firm also extended the period that partners had to wait before being allowed to sell their shares, to slow the cash drain, as well as limiting the number of people entitled to a share of the profits. But then disaster hit. Goldman Sachs was accused of IPO spinning – giving special IPO allocations to key clients in exchange for investment bank business. This led to an investigation into conflicts of interest by the Securities and Exchange Commission (SEC) and ended up costing the firm a significant fine and a dented reputation.

With the SEC threatening further probes, the partners started to feel ever more vulnerable. With each one of them having so much of their personal wealth tied up in the company, partners felt overexposed to the threat of one big mistake wiping out the company. So, after ample discussion, the partners decided to float a small part of their company (12.6%) on the stock market. In November 1999, the initial public offering was made, raking in US$3.6 billion and valuing the entire company at US$33 billion – a healthy four times book value. Approximately 50% of the equity capital was still owned by the 221 former partners, making them worth an average of US$75 million per person. Another 20% of the shares were owned by non-partner employees, with the remaining shares in the hands of retired partners and other long-time investors.

The fear that the partners-turned-employees would be less eager to pursue financial success now they had to share it with thousands of outside shareholders has not yet been borne out. The market circumstances have been rather difficult since 2001, leading the new top management team to fire some employees and push through pay cuts, but the financial results of Goldman Sachs have still been respectable. In 2002, revenues were down for the second year in a row (from US$16.5 to US$14 billion), as were earnings (from US$3 to US$2 billion), but the firm was doing well compared to the carnage around it. In a letter to the shareholders the board wrote 'this performance also reflected, as it has throughout the 133 years since the firm's founding, in good and bad times, the quality of the people of Goldman Sachs and their ability to develop and execute business'.

Which 'people of Goldman Sachs' the board saw as responsible for the reasonable performance became clear soon after the presentation of the 2002 annual report. In a mandatory annual statement of information to shareholders, a new compensation plan was announced for the company's 29 most senior employees, in which each was promised a bonus of up to 1% of before-tax profits, on top of their multi-million dollar base salaries. To avoid the appearance of excess, the bonuses would be limited to US$35 million per executive. The rationale for the compensation plan according to the company was 'to perpetuate the sense of partnership'. Over 2002, the CEO, Henry Paulson, had earned US$10 million, but this amount was deemed to be inadequate for the purpose of 'the perpetuation of the sense of partnership', hence the need to introduce more stimulating bonuses. In justifying Paulson's pay for 2002, the compensation committee of the board of management called him a 'strong voice for Goldman Sachs and the industry as a whole' and praised him for taking steps to restore trust in the integrity of corporate management.

The question on the minds of many shareholders and employees was whether this compensation plan was a necessary investment to ensure the future success of the company, or whether it was more the reflection of the true purpose of the firm – to make its partners/executives rich. With the old partners still in power, it seemed as if they were still running the show primarily to serve their own interests. To many it seemed that the 'sense of partnership' was another way to say 'a continued partnership, but by another means'. For many shareholders, this was not what they had expected of a publicly traded company. And for many employees, especially those sacked or whose pay had been cut, this was not the type of responsibility they had hoped would come with the demise of the partnership pyramid. But then, were their expectations justified? After all, whose company is it in the first place?

But for the Goldman Sachs top management team, these gripes sounded odd. To most insiders it was clear that Goldman Sachs would continue to be run by its partners, for its partners, with a few public shareholders allowed to climb aboard for the ride. As one manager summarized it: 'We're going to let you in. Now shut up and sit back and we'll let you know how much you made.'

Sources: *The Economist*, April 4 1999 and March 20 2003; *Business Week*, May 19 1999; Goldman Sachs web site.

PERSPECTIVES ON ORGANIZATIONAL PURPOSE

Perfection of means and confusion of goals . . . characterize our age.
Albert Einstein (1879–1955); German-American physicist

Firms require a certain measure of economic profitability if they want to compete and survive, and they need to exhibit a certain amount of social responsibility if they are to retain the trust and support of key stakeholders. In itself, this creates a tension, as the two demands can be at odds with one another. Often, socially responsible behavior costs money, which can only be partially recouped by the increased 'social dividend' it brings. But if profitability and responsibility are both seen as the ultimate purpose of business firms, then the tension is even stronger, as optimizing the one will be in conflict with maximizing the other. Emphasizing profitability means subjecting all investments to an economic rationale – socially responsible behavior should only be undertaken if the net present value of such an investment is attractive or there is no legal way of avoiding compliance. Emphasizing responsibility means subjecting all activities to a moral and/or political rationale – asking who has a legitimate and pressing claim to be included as a beneficiary of the activities being undertaken, which can severely depress profitability.

Hence, it is not surprising to find that the paradox of profitability and responsibility strongly divides people across many walks of life, not only business managers and management theorists. The main point of contention is whether firms should primarily be run for the financial benefit of the legal owners, or for the broader benefit of all parties with a significant interest in the joint endeavor. Should it be the purpose of firms to serve the interests of their shareholders or of their stakeholders? Should profitability be emphasized because economic organizations belong to the providers of risk capital, or should responsibility be emphasized because organizations are joint ventures bringing together various resource providers by means of a social contract?

While there are many points of view on the 'right' organizational purpose in the strategy literature, here the two diametrically opposed positions will be identified and discussed. At the one pole of the debate are those people who argue that corporations are established to serve the purposes of their owners. Generally, it is in the best interest of a corporation's shareholders to see the value of their stocks increase through the organization's pursuit of profitable business strategies. This point of view is commonly referred to as the 'shareholder value perspective'. At the other end of the spectrum are those people who argue that corporations should be seen as joint ventures between shareholders, employees, banks, customers, suppliers, governments and the community. All of these parties hold a stake in the organization and therefore can expect that the corporation will take as its responsibility to develop business strategies that are in accordance with their interests and values. This point of view will be referred to as the 'stakeholder values perspective'.

The shareholder value perspective

To proponents of the shareholder value perspective it is obvious that companies belong to their owners and therefore should act in accordance with the interests of the owners. Corporations are instruments whose purpose it is to create economic value on behalf of those who invest risk-taking capital in the enterprise. This clear purpose should drive companies, regardless of whether they are privately or publicly held. According to Rappaport (1986, p. xiii, Reading 11.1), 'the idea that business strategies should be judged by the economic value they create for shareholders is well accepted in the business community. After all, to suggest that companies be operated in the best interests of their owners is hardly controversial.'

There is some disagreement between advocates of this perspective with regard to the best way of advancing the interests of the shareholders, particularly in publicly held companies. Many people taking this point of view argue that the well-being of the shareholders is served if the strategy of a company leads to higher share prices and/or higher dividends (e.g. Hart, 1995; Rappaport, 1986). Others are less certain of the stock markets' ability to correctly value long-term investments, such as R&D spending and capital expenditures. In their view, stock markets are excessively concerned with the short term and therefore share prices myopically overemphasize current results and heavily discount investments for the future. To avoid being pressured into short-termism, these people advocate that strategists must keep only one eye on share prices, while the other is focused on the long-term horizon (e.g. Charkham, 1994; Sykes, 1994).

According to supporters of the shareholder value perspective, one of the major challenges in large corporations is to actually get top management to pursue the shareholders' interests. Where ownership and managerial control over a company have become separated, it is often difficult to get the managers to work on behalf of the shareholders, instead of letting managers' self-interest prevail. This is known as the principal-agent problem (e.g. Jensen and Meckling, 1976; Eisenhardt, 1989) – the managers are agents, working to further the interests of their principals, the shareholders, but are tempted to serve their own interests, even when this is to the detriment of the principals. This has led to a widespread debate in the academic and business communities, especially in Britain and the United States, about the best form of corporate governance. The most important players in corporate governance are the outside, or non-executive, members on the board of directors. It is one of the tasks of these outsiders to check whether the executives are truly running the company in a way that maximizes the shareholders' wealth. For this reason, many proponents of the shareholder value perspective call for a majority of independent-minded outside directors on the board, preferably owning significant amounts of the company's stock themselves.

The emphasis placed on profitability as the fundamental purpose of firms does not mean that supporters of the shareholder value perspective are blind to the demands placed on firms by other stakeholders. On the contrary, most exponents of this view argue that it is in the interest of the shareholders to carry out a 'stakeholder analysis' and even to actively manage stakeholder relations. Knowing the force field of stakeholders constraining the freedom of the company is important information for the strategy process. It is never advisable to ignore important external claimants such as labor unions, environmental activists, bankers, governmental agencies and community groups. Few strategists would doubt that proactive engagement is preferable to 'corporate isolationism'. However, recognizing that it is expedient to pay attention to stakeholders does not mean that it is the corporation's purpose to serve them. If parties have a strong bargaining position, a firm might be forced into all types of concessions, sacrificing profitability, but this has little to do with any moral responsibility of the firm towards these other powers. The only duty of a company is to maximize shareholder value, within the boundaries of what is legally permissible.

The important conclusion is that in this perspective it might be in the interest of shareholders to treat stakeholders well, but that there is no moral obligation to do so. For instance, it might be a good move for a troubled company not to lay off workers if the resulting loyalty and morale improve the chances of recovery and profitability later on. In this case the decision not to fire workers is based on profit-motivated calculations, not on a sense of moral responsibility towards the employees. Generally, proponents of the shareholder value perspective argue that society is best served by this type of economic rationale. By pursuing enlightened self-interest and maintaining market-based relationships between the firm and all stakeholders, societal wealth will be maximized. Responsibility for employment, local communities, the environment, consumer welfare and social developments are not an organizational matter, but issues for individuals and governments (Friedman, 1970).

GENERAL ELECTRIC: YOUR COMPANY

Few companies are as widely known and admired as General Electric. In 2002 it was elected 'The World's Most Respected Company' for the fifth consecutive year by a panel of 1000 CEOs from around the globe. This impressive achievement is all the more surprising given the fact that GE defies the conventional industry wisdom that conglomerates should have become extinct. With its US$132 billion in sales coming from such businesses as airplane engines, television broadcasting, medical equipment, household appliances, plastics, locomotives and financial services, GE is a highly diversified company, but without the 'conglomerate discount' applied to its share price. On the contrary, for years GE shares have traded at a very high price/earnings level, to the envy of many focused competitors.

Much of the popularity of GE has been due to the man who was at the helm of the company from 1981 to 2001, Jack Welch. After taking over as CEO in 1981, Welch quickly acquired his nickname, Neutron Jack, due to his hard-nosed approach to restructuring, in which he was said to have the same impact as a neutron bomb – the buildings were left standing, but all of the people were gone. During these early years of his tenure, he thoroughly shook up the company, introducing the rule that GE should exit any business in which it could not be number one or two, on the premise that only these two top spots hold the promise of superior profitability. Subsequently, he drove the company hard, with one clear focus: maximizing shareholder value. His style at the corporate center was that of a very demanding and challenging sparring partner for the business units, constantly setting high financial targets for each to achieve.

Welch's impact has been enormous. GE is characterized by a results-oriented culture, in which financial performance is the name of the game. The clear sense of purpose within the company has made a mission statement redundant – it is engrained in the firm that success means giving the shareholders 10%-plus earnings growth per year and 20%-plus return on total capital per year. Executive compensation packages are strongly tied to financial performance, to encourage them to pursue what is best for the shareholders. And to further motivate employees to serve the interests of the owners, GE has stimulated widespread share ownership within the company, which currently totals approximately 10% of the company's stock.

Welch's relentless focus on shareholder value has been very beneficial for this group. During his reign the market capitalization of GE grew 23% annually (rising 62-fold). GE was one of the few companies to consistently outperform the S&P 500, which rose on average 15% per year in the same period. Furthermore, in 2002 the company raised its annual dividend for the 27th consecutive year – an unparalleled performance. In 2003, GE was one of the nine companies left in the world holding the prized triple-A credit rating.

The focus on shareholder value has not meant that GE has disregarded its employees or other stakeholders. For instance, GE has recognized that investing in human resources is an important means for achieving the purpose of shareholder value creation. Similarly, GE has been at the forefront of the development of environment-friendly technologies, particularly in engines and turbines, but with the clear objective of making money by pleasing customers.

When in 2001 Jeffrey Immelt took on the daunting task of filling Welch's shoes, he emphasized continuity of goals and management practices. It is clear that he plans to follow the same type of shareholder value-driven strategy as Welch. Yet, things have not been easy for Immelt, with an economic downturn and a scandal surrounding the extravagant retirement perks of Welch. In 2002, GE shares underperformed the S&P 500, and analysts and shareholders have started arguing whether there is enough reason to keep the industrial and financial businesses of GE together in one company. But whatever happens next, Immelt has promised GE shareholders that 'your GE team' is committed to maximizing the value of 'your company'.

Sources: www.ge.com; *The Economist*, May 4 2002.

The stakeholder values perspective

Advocates of the stakeholder values perspective do not see why the supplier of one ingredient in an economic value-creation process has a stronger moral claim on the organization than the providers of other inputs. They challenge the assumption that individuals with an equity stake in a corporation have the right to demand that the entire organization work on their behalf. In the stakeholder values perspective, a company should not be seen as the instrument of shareholders, but as a coalition between various resource suppliers, with the intention of increasing their common wealth. An organization should be regarded as a joint venture in which the suppliers of equity, loans, labor, management, expertise, parts and service all participate to achieve economic success. As all groups hold a stake in the joint venture and are mutually dependent, it is argued that the purpose of the organization is to serve the interests of all parties involved (e.g. Berle and Means, 1932; Freeman and Reed, 1983, Reading 11.2).

According to endorsers of the stakeholder values perspective, shareholders have a legitimate interest in the firm's profitability. However, the emphasis shareholders place on stock price appreciation and dividends must be balanced against the legitimate demands of the other partners. These demands are not only financial, as in the case of the shareholders, but also qualitative, reflecting different values held by different groups (e.g. Clarke, 1998; Freeman, 1984). For instance, employees might place a high value on job security, occupational safety, holidays and working conditions, while a supplier of parts might prefer secure demand, joint innovation, shared risk-taking and prompt payment. Of course, balancing these interests is a challenging task, requiring an on-going process of negotiation and compromise. The outcome will in part depend on the bargaining power of each stakeholder – how essential is its input to the economic success of the organization? However, the extent to which a stakeholder's interests are pursued will depend on the perceived legitimacy of their claim as well. For instance, employees usually have a strong moral claim because they are heavily dependent on the organization and have a relatively low mobility, while most shareholders have a spread portfolio and can 'exit the corporation with a phone call' (Stone, 1975).

In this view of organizational purpose, managers must recognize their responsibility towards all constituents (e.g. Clarkson, 1995; Alkhafaji, 1989). Maximizing shareholder value to the detriment of the other stakeholders would be unjust. Managers in the firm have a moral obligation to consider the interests and values of all joint venture partners. Managing stakeholder demands is not merely a pragmatic means of running a profitable business – serving stakeholders is an end in itself. These two interpretations of stakeholder management are often confused. Where it is primarily viewed as an approach or technique for dealing with the essential participants in the value-adding process, stakeholder management is *instrumental*. But if it is based on the fundamental notion that the organization's purpose is to serve the stakeholders, then stakeholder management is *normative* (e.g. Buono and Nichols, 1985; Donaldson and Preston, 1995).

Most proponents of the stakeholder values perspective argue that, ultimately, pursuing the joint interests of all stakeholders it is not only more just, but also more effective for organizations (e.g. Jones, 1995; Solomon, 1992). Few stakeholders are filled with a sense of mission to go out and maximize shareholder value, especially if shareholders bear no responsibility for the other stakeholders' interests (e.g. Campbell and Yeung, 1991; Collins and Porras, 1994). It is difficult to work as a motivated team if it is the purpose of the organization to serve only one group's interests. Furthermore, without a stakeholder values perspective, there will be a deep-rooted lack of trust between all of the parties involved in the enterprise. Each stakeholder will assume that the others are motivated solely by self-interest and are tentatively cooperating in a calculative manner. All parties will perceive a constant risk that the others will use their power to gain a bigger slice of the pie, or even rid themselves of their 'partners'. The consequence is that all stakeholders will vigorously guard their own interests and will interact with one another as adversaries. To advocates of the stakeholder values perspective, this 'every person for themselves' model of organizations is clearly inferior to the partnership model in which sharing, trust and symbiosis are emphasized. Cooperation between stakeholders is much more effective than competition (note the link with the embedded organization perspective in Chapter 7).

Some exponents of the stakeholder values perspective argue that the narrow economic definition of stakeholders given above is too constrictive. In their view, the circle of stakeholders with a legitimate claim on the organization should be drawn more widely. Not only should the organization be responsible to the direct participants in the economic value-creation process (the 'primary stakeholders'), but also to all parties affected by the organization's activities. For example, an organization's behavior might have an impact on local communities, governments, the environment and society in general, and therefore these groups have a stake in what the organization does as well. Most supporters of the stakeholder values perspective acknowledge that organizations have a moral responsibility towards these 'secondary stakeholders' (e.g. Carroll, 1993; Langtry, 1994). However, opinions differ whether it should actually be a part of business organizations' purpose to serve this broader body of constituents.

The implication of this view for corporate governance is that the board of directors should be able to judge whether the interests of all stakeholders are being justly balanced. This has led some advocates of the stakeholder values perspective to call for representatives of the most important stakeholder groups to be on the board (e.g. Guthrie and Turnbull, 1994). Others argue more narrowly for a stronger influence of employees on the choices made by organizations (e.g. Bucholz, 1986; Blair, 1995). Such co-determination of the corporation's strategy by management and workers can, for instance, be encouraged by establishing work councils (a type of organizational parliament or senate), as is mandatory for larger companies in most countries of the European Union. Yet others emphasize measures to strengthen corporate social responsibility in general. To improve corporate social performance, it is argued, companies should be encouraged to adopt internal policy processes that promote ethical behavior and responsiveness to societal issues (e.g. Epstein, 1987; Wartick and Wood, 1998). Corporate responsibility should not be, to quote Ambrose Bierce's sarcastic definition, 'a detachable burden easily shifted to the shoulders of God, Fate, Fortune, Luck, or one's neighbor'.

EXHIBIT 11.3 THE STAKEHOLDER VALUES PERSPECTIVE

MEDTRONIC: FULL VALUE THROUGH FULL LIFE

When opening the annual shareholders' meeting each year, William George, chairman of Medtronic is crystal clear: 'Medtronic is not in the business of maximizing shareholder value. We are in the business of maximizing value to the patients we serve.' And nobody doubts for one moment that he means what he is saying – Medtronic lives by this principle. As the world's leading medical device company for all types of inner organs, with sales in 2001 exceeding US$5.5 billion, Medtronic is driven by its purpose of bringing medical technology to a higher level and improving the quality of life of its patients.

Illustrative is Medtronic's Mission and Medallion Ceremony, which has been conducted since the founding of the company in the early 1960s, where George meets every new employee personally to review the mission of the company and to present them with a bronze medallion. The medallion has a picture of a person rising off an operating table, with the words 'towards full life' inscribed around the perimeter. The employees are urged to put the medallion on their desk and to remind themselves that they work at Medtronic not just to make money for themselves or the company, but to restore people to fuller lives. After completing five major

▶

acquisitions in 1998/99, George personally conducted Mission and Medallion Ceremonies for more than 9000 employees around the world.

In 2001 George was named 'Executive of the Year' by the US-based Academy of Management. In his address to the Academy members he outlined his view that many corporations espouse lofty values, such as serving customers, quality, integrity, respect for employees and good citizenship, but what matters is what you actually live by. Values have to be constantly reinforced and consistently reflected in the actions of management at all levels. At Medtronic, all employees are asked each year to sign a detailed compliance statement, confirming that they have behaved in accordance with the company's values. Individuals who deviate from this statement or falsify their responses are asked to leave the company immediately.

According to George, long-term success requires companies to be driven by an inspiring purpose, to have a strong set of shared values at the core of the organization, and to have an adaptable business strategy. The real flaw in having the maximization of shareholder value as sole purpose, argues George, is the inability to motivate a large group of employees to exceptional performance. The shareholder value theme has little or no meaning, even if the employees benefit from the stock performance. Instead, employees should be inspired by a mission that motivates them to achieve superior performance in serving their customers. Innovative product ideas will be copied by competitors, but an organization of highly motivated people is extremely difficult to duplicate.

The intensive attention to stakeholders produces tangible results. *The Economist* labels Medtronic as 'the most innovative and market-savvy firm in the medical device industry and Mr. George is one of the best strategists in healthcare'. Medtronic is introducing new medical devices at breakneck speed – it wants to have 70% of its revenues coming from products launched in the previous two years. Lead times for developing medical devices are a mere 18 months.

And the shareholders? From 1986 to 2001, the company's revenues grew from US$363 million to US$5.5 billion, an 18% compound annual growth rate. Earnings per share went from US$0.04 in 1985 to US$1.05 in 2001, and shareholder value grew in that period from US$1.1 billion to US$60 billion (having peaked at US$70 billion in 2000), representing a 37% compound annual growth rate. Even in the worldwide recession year 2002, Medtronic reported an increase in earnings per share to US$1.21. Shareholders, it seems, are also enjoying a full life at Medtronic.

Sources: *Academy of Management Executive*, 2001, Vol. 15, No. 4; company reports; *The Economist*, August 31 2000.

INTRODUCTION TO THE DEBATE AND READINGS

The business of America is business.

Calvin Coolidge (1872–1933); American president

A business that makes nothing but money is a poor kind of business.

Henry Ford (1863–1947); American industrialist

So, what should be the purpose of a firm? Should managers strive to maximize shareholder value or stakeholder values? Should it be the purpose of business organizations to pursue profitability on behalf of their owners, or should firms serve the interests and promote the values of all of their stakeholders in a balanced way?

This debate has been going on for some time now, made all the more relevant by the mounting political pressure in many countries to reform their system of corporate governance. The proponents of the shareholder value perspective are lobbying for more receptiveness to the interests of the shareholders on the part of the board, to increase top management accountability and to curb perceived executive self-enrichment at the expense of shareholders. The advocates of the stakeholder values perspective are vying for a system that would bring more receptiveness to the interests of stakeholders, to ensure that firms do not become more myopically 'bottom line' oriented. While both sides do agree on one or two points (e.g. corporate governance is generally too weak), on the whole, little consensus can be found on how to deal with the paradox of profitability and responsibility. Therefore, again, managers cannot look to the strategy literature to glean the best practice and apply it to their own situation, but will need to determine their own point of view on what they believe should be the purpose of the organization.

To help managers make up their own mind, this section will present four readings. As before, the first set of two readings will represent the two poles in the debate (see Table 11.1), so that the reader can gain a sharper understanding of the breadth of opinions on this topic. The second set of two readings will add extra arguments to the debate, to further deepen the discussion. In this case, both readings will focus on the international differences in thinking about organizational purpose. In all other chapters, the international perspective was only introduced at the end of the readings section, but here the international dimension is too predominant to keep out of the debate for so long. The international differences in view, and the divergent corporate governance systems, have such a strong influence on the debate, that they warrant two readings in this chapter.

Selecting the first reading to represent the shareholder value perspective was a simple task. Alfred Rappaport's highly influential book *Creating Shareholder Value* is the classic text in the field. Although the largest part of his book details how the shareholder value approach can be applied to planning and performance evaluation processes, the first chapter is a compelling exposition of his underlying views on the purpose of a business organization. This first chapter, entitled 'Shareholder Value and Corporate Purpose', has been reprinted as Reading 11.1. Rappaport's argument is straightforward – the primary purpose of corporations should be to maximize shareholder value. Therefore, 'business strategies should be judged by the economic returns they generate for shareholders, as measured by dividends plus the increase in the company's share price'. Unlike some other proponents of the shareholder value perspective, Rappaport does not explicitly claim that shareholders have the moral right to demand the primacy of profitability. His argument is more pragmatic – failing to meet the objective of maximizing shareholder value will be punished by more expensive financing. A company's financial power is ultimately determined by the stock markets. Hence, management's ability to meet the demands of the various corporate constituencies depends on the continuing support of its shareholders. Creating shareholder value, therefore, precedes the satisfaction of all other claims on the corporation. It should be noted, however, that Rappaport's arrows are not directed at the demands of employees, customers, suppliers or debtholders, but at top management. He carefully states that senior

TABLE 11.1 Shareholder value versus stakeholder values perspective

	Shareholder value perspective	*Stakeholder values perspective*
Emphasis on	Profitability over responsibility	Responsibility over profitability
Organizations seen as	Instruments	Joint ventures
Organizational purpose	To serve owner	To serve all parties involved
Measure of success	Share price and dividends (shareholder value)	Satisfaction among stakeholders
Major difficulty	Getting agent to pursue principal's interests	Balancing interests of various stakeholders
Corporate governance through	Independent outside directors with shares	Stakeholder representation
Stakeholder management	Means	End and means
Social responsibility	Individual, not organizational matter	Both individual and organizational
Society best served by	Pursuing self-interest (economic efficiency)	Pursuing joint-interests (economic symbiosis)

executives may in some situations pursue objectives that are not to the benefit of share-holders. His preferred solution is not to change corporate governance structures, but to more tightly align the interests of both groups, for example by giving top managers a rel-atively large ownership position and by tying their compensation to shareholder return per-formance (in later writings he does favor more structural reforms; e.g. Rappaport, 1990).

The opening reading on behalf of the stakeholder values perspective (Reading 11.2) is also a classic – 'Stockholders and Stakeholders: A New Perspective on Corporate Governance', by Edward Freeman and David Reed. This article in *California Management Review* and Freeman's subsequent book *Strategic Management: A Stakeholder Approach* were instrumental in popularizing the stakeholder concept. In their article, Freeman and Reed challenge 'the view that stockholders have a privileged place in the business enter-prise'. They deplore the fact that 'it has long been gospel that corporations have obliga-tions to stockholders . . . that are sacrosanct and inviolable'. They argue that there has been a long tradition of management thinkers who believe that corporations have a broader responsibility towards stakeholders other than just the suppliers of equity financing. It is their conviction that such a definition of the corporation, as a system serving the interests of multiple stakeholders, is superior to the shareholder perspective. Their strong preference for the stakeholder concept is largely based on the pragmatic argument that, in reality, stakeholders have the power to seriously affect the continuity of the corporation. Stakeholder analysis is needed to understand the actual claims placed by constituents on the firm and to evaluate each stakeholder's power position. Stakeholder management is a practical response to the fact that corporations cannot afford to ignore or downplay the interests of the claimants. Only here and there do Freeman and Reed hint that corporations have the moral responsibility to work on behalf of all stakeholders (which Freeman does more explicitly in some of his later works, e.g. Freeman and Gilbert, 1988; Freeman and Liedtka, 1991). In their opinion, the consequence of the stakeholder concept for corporate governance is that 'there are times when stakeholders must participate in the decision-making process'. However, they believe that if boards of directors adopt a stakeholder out-look and become more responsive to the demands placed on corporations, structural reforms to give stakeholders a stronger role in corporate governance will not be necessary.

Reading 11.3 is intended to bring the international perspective directly into the debate (rather than introducing cross-cultural differences at the end of the chapter). This reading by Ada Demb and Friedrich Neubauer, entitled 'The Corporate Board: Confronting the Paradoxes', is a journal article summarizing the main points of their book of the same name. While Rappaport and Freeman and Reed argue more broadly about the purpose of the organization, Demb and Neubauer relate the topic of organizational purpose directly to corporate governance issues. They start by taking a broad view of corporate governance, as 'the process by which corporations are made responsive to the rights and wishes of stakeholders'. This definition of corporate governance not only includes the board of direc-tors as the mechanism for achieving corporate accountability, but also encompasses three other 'governance institutions': influencing through the *ownership* structure, imposing *regulations* and codes of conduct, and exerting direct *social pressure*. However, the main thrust of their argument is directed at the functioning of boards of directors, in particular to international differences therein. Very similar to our approach of identifying strategy paradoxes, Demb and Neubauer uncover three corporate governance paradoxes, pulling firms in opposite directions. Their first paradox is between the demand for board supervi-sion and the demand for management control – both the board and management need to steer the organization, but 'without diminishing the initiative and motivation of the other'. The second paradox is between the demand for critical, in-depth evaluation and the demand for independent, detached judgment – the board needs to be intimately involved enough to have a fine grasp of company issues, but distant enough to consider the issues without being politically, financially or intellectually captive. The third paradox is between the demand for a strong team and the demand for strong individuals – 'the board needs the trusting familiarity of a tight-knit group, yet members must be independent personalities who can resist "groupthink" and raise critical questions'. Demb and Neubauer argue that these three paradoxes are dealt with differently in each country, leading to a large measure of variety in the international arena. They conclude that there is no one best way to structure boards, but that the various national governance structures have a lot to learn from each other. Interestingly, they do not recognize the more fundamental paradox of profitability and responsibility as a key issue facing boards. Rather, they conclude their article by pointing to a new era where business leaders 'in order to achieve both societal and business objectives, . . . [foster] a new concept of partnership between business, governments and the public'. But how the inherent tension between business profitability and these societal responsibilities will be dealt with is not addressed.

In Reading 11.4 the paradox of profitability and responsibility is recognized, and reviewed from an international perspective. In this article, 'Whose Company Is It? The Concept of the Corporation in Japan and the West', Masaru Yoshimori compares the Japanese view of organizational purpose with European and American conceptions. He points out that the ultimate issue dividing the shareholder value and stakeholder values perspectives is their view of organization ownership. Yoshimori has looked at this issue by asking middle managers in Britain, France, Germany, the United States, and Japan the simple question 'In whose interest should the firm be managed?'. He reports that the countries studied fall into three categories. In Britain and the United States, the shareholder value perspective, which he refers to as the 'monistic' concept of the corporation, is most prevalent. In Japan, on the other hand, the stakeholder values perspective is by far the predominant outlook. In the Japanese 'pluralistic' concept of the corporation, the employees' interests take precedence, closely followed by those of the main banks, major suppliers, subcontractors, and distributors. According to Yoshimori, most managers in Germany and France exhibit a 'dualistic' concept of the corporation, in which shareholder and employee interests are both taken into consideration. Yoshimori carries on to explain the most important differences between these five countries, and he weighs the costs and benefits of each. He concludes that in all countries corporate governance is poorly developed, and that nations have a lot to learn from one another. In his opinion, international cross-fertilization will lead to a partial convergence of corporate governance systems in the various countries. However, 'the concept of the corporation is firmly rooted in the historic, economic, political and even socio-cultural traditions of the nation', and therefore it is improbable 'that any one concept should drive out another at least in the foreseeable future'.

READING

11.1

Shareholder value and corporate purpose

By Alfred Rappaport[1]

Corporate mission statements proclaiming that the primary responsibility of management is to maximize shareholders' total return via dividends and increases in the market price of the company's shares abound. While the principle that the fundamental objective of the business corporation is to increase the value of its shareholders' investment is widely accepted, there is substantially less agreement about how this is accomplished.

On the cover of its 1984 annual report Coca-Cola states that 'to increase shareholder value over time is the objective driving this enterprise.' On the very next page the company goes on to say that to accomplish its objective 'growth in annual earnings per share and increased return on equity are still the names of the game.' In contrast, Hillenbrand Industries, a producer of caskets and hospital equipment, also declares its intention to provide a superior return to its shareholders, but to accomplish that objective management is focusing not on earnings but rather on creating 'shareholder value,' which, it explains in the 1984 annual report, 'is created when a company generates free cash flow in excess of the shareholders' investment in the business.'

Both Coca-Cola and Hillenbrand Industries acknowledge their responsibility to maximize return to their respective shareholders. However, Coca-Cola emphasizes accounting indicators, earnings-per-share growth, and return on equity, while Hillenbrand Industries emphasizes the cash-flow based shareholder value approach to achieve shareholder returns. There are material differences between these two approaches to assessing a company's investment opportunities. Maximizing earnings-per-share growth or other accounting numbers may not necessarily lead to maximizing return for shareholders.

The growing interest

Numerous surveys indicate that a majority of the largest industrial companies have employed the share-

holder value approach in capital budgeting for some time. Capital budgeting applications deal with investment projects such as capacity additions rather than total investment at the business level. Thus, we sometimes see a situation where capital projects regularly exceed the minimum acceptable rate of return, while the business unit itself is a 'problem' and creates little or no value for shareholders. This situation can arise because capital expenditures typically represent only a small percentage of total company outlays. For example, capital expenditures amount to about 10 percent of total outlays at General Motors, a particularly capital intensive company.

During the past 10 years, the shareholder value approach has been frequently applied not only to internal investments such as capacity additions, but also to opportunities for external growth such as mergers and acquisitions. Recently a number of major companies such as American Hospital Supply, Combustion Engineering, Hillenbrand Industries, Libbey-Owens-Ford, Marriott, and Westinghouse have found that the shareholder value approach can be productively extended from individual projects to the entire strategic plan. A strategic business unit (SBU) is commonly defined as the smallest organizational unit for which integrated strategic planning, related to a distinct product that serves a well-defined market, is feasible. A strategy for an SBU may then be seen as a collection of product-market related investments and the company itself may be characterized as a portfolio of these investment-requiring strategies. By estimating the future cash flows associated with each strategy, a company can assess the economic value to shareholders of alternative strategies at the business unit and corporate levels.

The interest in shareholder value is gaining momentum as a result of several recent developments.

- The threat of corporate take-overs by those seeking undervalued, undermanaged assets.
- Impressive endorsements by corporate leaders who have adopted the approach.

[1]Source: This article was adapted with the permission of The Free Press, a Division of Simon & Schuster Adult Publishing Group, from *Creating Shareholder Value: The New Standard for Business Performance* by Alfred Rappaport. © 1986 by Alfred Rappaport.

- The growing recognition that traditional accounting measures such as EPS and ROI are not reliably linked to increasing the value of the company's shares.

- Reporting of returns to shareholders along with other measures of performance in the business press such as *Fortune's* annual ranking of the 500 leading industrial firms.

- A growing recognition that executives' long-term compensation needs to be more closely tied to returns to shareholders.

Endorsements of the shareholder value approach can be found in an increasing number of annual reports and other corporate publications. One of the more thoughtful statements appears in Libbey-Owens-Ford's 1983 annual report and is reproduced as Exhibit 11.1.1. Combustion Engineering's vice president for finance states that 'a primary financial objective for Combustion Engineering is to create shareholder value by earning superior returns on capital invested in the business. This serves as a clear guide for management action and is the conceptual framework on which CE's financial objectives and goals are based.'

EXHIBIT 11.1.1 LIBBEY-OWENS-FORD STATEMENT

A GREATER EMPHASIS ON SHAREHOLDER VALUE

Libbey-Owens-Ford's mission statement specifies that its primary responsibility is to its shareholders, and that the company has a continuing requirement to increase the value of our shareholders' investment in LOF. This is not just a contemporary business phrase, but the basis for a long-term company strategy. It evaluates business strategies and plans in terms of value to our shareholders, not just on the incremental income that the results will contribute to the bottom line. It requires a greater emphasis on developing strategies and plans that will increase shareholder value as measured by the market appreciation of our stock and dividends.

Traditional Accounting Measures May Not Tell the Entire Story

Traditionally, the most popular way to determine whether a company is performing well is through such accounting measurements as earnings per share (EPS) and return on investment. These measures do, of course, give an indication of a company's performance, but they can be misleading in that often they do not measure the increase or decrease in shareholder value. Sustained growth as measured by EPS does not necessarily reflect an increase in stock value.

This occurs because earnings do not reflect changes in risk and inflation, nor do they take into account the cost of added capital that may have been invested in the business to finance its growth. Yet these are critical considerations when you are striving to increase the value of the shareholders' investment.

Cash Flow Analysis is Emphasized

LOF stresses the importance of cash flow measurement and performance. Individual operating companies must analyze the cash flow effects of running their businesses. Where cash comes from and what cash is used for must be simply and clearly set forth. LOF's cash and short-term investments increased $46.3 million during 1983.

The Shareholder Value Approach

The shareholder value approach taken by LOF emphasized economic cash flow analysis in evaluating individual projects and in determining the economic value of the overall strategy of each business unit and the corporation as a whole. Management looks at the business units and the corporation and determines the minimum operating return necessary to create value. It then reviews the possible contribution of alternative strategies and evaluates the financial feasibility of the strategic plan, based on the company's cost of capital, return on assets, the cash flow stream and other important measurements.

This disciplined process allows LOF to objectively evaluate all its corporate investments, including internal projects and acquisitions, in light of our primary goal to increase shareholder value.

Source: Libbey-Owens-Ford Company 1983 Annual Report.

Whether or not executives agree with the well-publicized tactics of raiders such as Carl Icahn and T. Boone Pickens, they recognize that the raiders characterize themselves as champions of the shareholders. The raiders attack on two fronts. First, they are constantly searching for poorly managed companies, where aggressive changes in strategic directions could dramatically improve the value of the stock. Second, they identify undervalued assets that can be redeployed to boost the stock price. As a result, many executives recognize a new and compelling reason to be concerned with the performance of their company's stock.

Executives have also become increasingly aware that many accrual-based accounting measures do not provide a dependable picture of the current and future performance of an organization. Numerous companies have sustained double-digit EPS growth while providing minimal or even *negative* returns to shareholders. Hillenbrand Industries, for example, points out in its 1984 annual report (p. 4) that 'public companies that focus on achieving short-term earnings to meet external expectations sometimes jeopardize their ability to create long-term value.'

Considerable attention has focused recently on the problems associated with rewarding executives on the basis of short-term accounting-based indicators. As a reflection of the increasing scrutiny under which executive compensation has come, business publications such as *Fortune* and *Business Week* have begun to publish compensation surveys that examine the correlation between the executives' pay and how well their companies have performed based on several measures – including returns to shareholders. For example, *Business Week*'s executive compensation scoreboard now includes a 'pay-performance index' for 255 companies in 36 industries. The index shows how well the top two executives in each company were paid relative to how shareholders fared. The index is the ratio of the executive's three-year total pay as a percent of the industry average to the shareholders' total three-year return as a percent of the industry average. If an executive's pay and shareholders' return are both at the industry average, the index is 100. The lower the index, the better shareholders fared. The broad range in the pay-performance index, even within industries, has further fueled the interest in achieving shareholder value. For the 1982–1984 period, for example, *Business Week* reported a pay-performance index of 59 for Roger Smith, CEO of General Motors, and an index of 160 for Phillip Caldwell, CEO of Ford Motor.

When the shareholder value approach first gained attention toward the end of the 1970s, even the executives who found the concept an intriguing notion tended to think that the approach would be very difficult to implement. The task of educating managers seemed substantial, and they were also not eager to develop a new planning system if it might involve upheaval in the corporate information system. Recent advances in technology have put impressive analytical potential at management's disposal. Managers' decisions are now greatly facilitated by microcomputer software. New approaches thus can more readily be incorporated without displacing existing information systems.

Management versus shareholder objectives

It is important to recognize that the objectives of management may in some situations differ from those of the company's shareholders. Managers, like other people, act in their self-interest. The theory of a market economy is, after all, based on individuals promoting their self-interests via market transactions to bring about an efficient allocation of resources. In a world in which principals (e.g. stockholders) have imperfect control over their agents (e.g. managers), these agents may not always engage in transactions solely in the best interests of the principals. Agents have their own objectives and it may sometimes pay them to sacrifice the principals' interests. The problem is exacerbated in large corporations where it is difficult to identify the interests of a diverse set of stockholders ranging from institutional investors to individuals with small holdings.

Critics of large corporations often allege that corporate managers have too much power and that they act in ways to benefit themselves at the expense of shareholders and other corporate constituencies. The argument is generally developed along the following lines. Responsibility for administering companies or 'control' is vested in the hands of professional managers and thereby has been separated from 'ownership.' Since the ownership of shares in large corporations tends to be diffused, individual shareholders are said to have neither influence on nor interest in corporate governance issues such as the election of board members. Therefore, boards are largely responsive to management which, in turn, can ignore shareholders and run companies as they see fit.

The foregoing 'separation of ownership and control' argument advanced by Berle and Means in 1932 has been a persistent theme of corporate critics during the intervening years. There are, however, a number of factors that induce management to act in the best interests of shareholders. These factors derive from the fundamental premise that the greater the expected unfavorable consequences to the manager who decreases the wealth of shareholders, the less likely it is that the manager will, in fact, act against the interests of shareholders.

Consistent with the above premise, at least four major factors will induce management to adopt a shareholder orientation: (1) a relatively large ownership position, (2) compensation tied to shareholder return performance, (3) threat of take-over by another organization, and (4) competitive labor markets for corporate executives.

Economic rationality dictates that stock ownership by management motivates executives to identify more closely with the shareholders' economic interests. Indeed, we would expect that the greater the proportion of personal wealth invested in company stock or tied to stock options, the greater would be management's shareholder orientation. While the top executives in many companies often have relatively large percentages of their wealth invested in company stock, this is much less often the case for divisional and business unit managers. And it is at the divisional and business unit levels that most resource allocation decisions are made in decentralized organizations.

Even when corporate executives own shares in their company, their viewpoint on the acceptance of risk may differ from that of shareholders. It is reasonable to expect that many corporate executives have a lower tolerance for risk. If the company invests in a risky project, stockholders can always balance this risk against other risks in their presumably diversified portfolios. The manager, however, can balance a project failure only against the other activities of the division or the company. Thus, managers are hurt by the failure more than shareholders.

The second factor likely to influence management to adopt a shareholder orientation is compensation tied to shareholder return performance. The most direct means of linking top management's interests with those of shareholders is to base compensation, and particularly the incentive portion, on market returns realized by shareholders. Exclusive reliance on shareholder returns, however, has its own limitations. First, movements in a company's stock price may well be greatly influenced by factors beyond management control such as the overall state of the economy and stock market. Second, shareholder returns may be materially influenced by what management believes to be unduly

optimistic or pessimistic market expectations at the beginning or end of the performance measurement period. And third, divisional and business unit performance cannot be directly linked to stock price.

Rather than linking incentive compensation directly to the market returns earned by shareholders, most *Fortune* 500 companies tie annual bonuses and long-term performance plans to internal financial goals such as earnings or accounting return on investment. These accounting criteria can often conflict with the way corporate shares are valued by the market. If incentives were largely based on earnings, for example, management might well be motivated to pursue economically unsound strategies when viewed from the perspective of shareholders. In such a situation what is economically irrational from the shareholder viewpoint may be a perfectly rational course of action for the decision-making executives.

The third factor affecting management behavior is the threat of take-over by another company. Tender offers have become a commonly employed means of transferring corporate control. Moreover the size of the targets continues to become larger. During the 1979–1985 period, 77 acquisitions each in excess of $1 billion were completed. The threat of take-over is an essential means of constraining corporate managers who might choose to pursue personal goals at the expense of shareholders. Any significant exploitation of shareholders should be reflected in a lower stock price. This lower price, relative to what it might be with more efficient management, offers an attractive take-over opportunity for another company which in many cases will replace incumbent management. An active market for corporate control places limits on the divergence of interests between management and shareholders and thereby serves as an important counterargument to the 'separation of ownership and control' criticisms.

The fourth and final factor influencing management's shareholder orientation is the labor market for corporate executives. Managerial labor markets are an essential mechanism for motivating management to function in the best interests of shareholders. Managers compete for positions both within and outside of the firm. The increasing number of executive recruiting firms and the length of the 'Who's News' column in the *Wall Street Journal* are evidence that the managerial labor market is very active. What is less obvious is how managers are evaluated in this market. Within the firm, performance evaluation and incentive schemes are the basic mechanisms for monitoring managerial performance. As seen earlier, the question here is whether these measures are reliably linked to the market price of the company's shares.

How managers communicate their value to the labor market outside of their individual firms is less apparent. While the performance of top-level corporate officers can be gleaned from annual reports and other publicly available corporate communications, this is not generally the case for divisional managers. For corporate level executives, the question is whether performance for shareholders is the dominant criterion in assessing their value in the executive labor market. The question in the case of division managers is, first, how does the labor market monitor and gain insights about their performance and second, what is the basis for valuing their services.

'Excellence' and restructuring

Two of the most visible business phenomena of the first half of the 1980s have been the publication of Peters and Waterman's *In Search of Excellence* and the unprecedented surge in the restructuring of companies. The 'excellence phenomenon' certainly provided no obvious encouragement for management to link its decisions more closely with the objective of maximizing returns to shareholders. In contrast, the more recent restructuring movement is clearly a manifestation of top management's growing concern with its company's share price and shareholder returns.

As US corporations began the 1980s, saddled with a decade of inflation and lagging productivity, nothing could have come as better news than the idea that not all excellent companies are Japanese. It was in this climate that *In Search of Excellence*, published in 1982, became an absolute sensation. Its longevity on the top of the best-seller list along with its wide coverage in the business press provided an extraordinary platform for the authors' ideas.

The basic purpose of *In Search of Excellence* was to identify key attributes of corporate excellence that are common among successful American corporations. To choose the 'excellent' companies, Peters and Waterman began by assembling a list of 62 US companies that were considered 'successful' by business leaders, consultants, members of the business press, and business school professors. From that list they selected 36 'excellent' companies based on superior performance for such financial measures as return on total capital, return on equity, return on sales, and asset growth. Eight attributes of corporate excellence were identified – a bias for action; staying close to the customer; autonomy and entrepreneurship; productivity through people; hands-on, value-driven management; sticking to the knitting; simple organization form and lean staff; and simultaneous loose-tight properties.

Even though the 'excellent' firms exhibited superior financial (accounting) performance over the 1960–1980 period, they did not provide consistently superior returns to shareholders via dividends plus share price appreciation. The excellent companies did not perform significantly better than the market. Indeed, they did not consistently outperform their respective industry groups or closest competitors. These results once again raise questions about the use of accounting measures to gauge the economic performance of corporations. Since the eight attributes of corporate excellence are not associated with systematically superior returns to shareholders, efforts to emulate these attributes may be ill-advised.

While *In Search of Excellence* became 'must reading' in many organizations during 1982 and 1983, a certain degree of disenchantment set in during the following two years as a number of 'excellent' companies experienced strategic setbacks. Atari, Avon Products, Caterpillar Tractor, Digital Equipment, Hewlett-Packard, Levi Strauss, and Texas Instruments serve as examples.

But if emulating excellent companies has lost some of its luster, a new focal point of interest has captured the imagination of management during the past couple of years – restructuring. Hardly a day passes without some company announcing a major restructuring of its businesses or capital structure. Restructuring involves diverse activities such as divestiture of underperforming businesses or businesses that do not 'fit,' spinoffs directly to shareholders, acquisitions paid for with 'excess cash,' stock repurchases, debt swaps, and liquidation of overfunded pension funds. In many cases, these restructurings are motivated by a desire to foil a take-over bid by so-called 'raiders' who look for undermanaged companies where changes in strategic direction could dramatically increase the value of the stock, and for companies with high liquidation values relative to their current share price. There is, of course, no better means of avoiding a take-over than increasing the price of the stock. Thus, increasing share price has become the fundamental purpose of corporate restructuring.

In contrast to the earlier euphoria over emulating excellent companies, the current restructuring movement is solidly based on shareholder value creation principles. In 1985, the Standard & Poor's 500 appreciated 26 percent in price. Goldman Sachs estimates that corporate restructuring accounted for about 30 percent of that price change. However, the early stage of the restructuring movement, which I call 'Phase I restructuring,' is largely based on one-time transactions such as those listed above rather than changes in day-to-day management of the business.

The necessary agenda for the second half of the 1980s seems clear. Companies need to move from Phase I restructuring to Phase II restructuring. In Phase II, the shareholder value approach is employed not only when buying and selling businesses or changing the company's capital structure, but also in the planning and performance monitoring of all business strategies on an ongoing basis. Frequently, the most difficult issue in this area is how to go about estimating the impact of strategies on shareholder value. Fortunately, relatively straightforward approaches do exist for estimating the shareholder value created by a business strategy, and an increasing number of major companies have begun to use them.

Most companies already use the same discounted cash-flow techniques used in the shareholder value approach to assess the attractiveness of capital investment projects and to value prospective acquisition targets. This approach can be extended to estimate the value creation potential of individual business units and the strategic plan for the entire company.

In Phase II restructuring it will also become increasingly important that executive compensation be tied closely to the shareholder value driven plans so that management will be strongly motivated to make decisions consistent with creating maximum returns to shareholders. A successful implementation of Phase II restructuring not only ensures that management has met its fiduciary responsibility to develop corporate performance evaluation systems consistent with the parameters investors use to value the company, but also minimizes the Phase I concern that a take-over of an undermanaged company is imminent.

Rationale for shareholder value approach

Business strategies should be judged by the economic returns they generate for shareholders, as measured by dividends plus the increase in the company's share price. As management considers alternative strategies, those expected to develop the greatest sustainable competitive advantage will be those that will also create the greatest value for shareholders. The 'shareholder value approach' estimates the economic value of an invest-

ment (e.g. the shares of a company, strategies, mergers and acquisitions, capital expenditures) by discounting forecasted cash flows by the cost of capital. These cash flows, in turn, serve as the foundation for shareholder returns from dividends and share-price appreciation.

The case for why management should pursue this objective is comparatively straightforward. Management is often characterized as balancing the interests of various corporate constituencies such as employees, customers, suppliers, debtholders, and stockholders. As Treynor (1981) points out, the company's continued existence depends upon a financial relationship with each of these parties. Employees want competitive wages. Customers want high quality at a competitive price. Suppliers and debtholders each have financial claims that must be satisfied with cash when they fall due. Stockholders as residual claimants of the firm look for cash dividends and the prospect of future dividends which is reflected in the market price of the stock.

If the company does not satisfy the financial claims of its constituents, it will cease to be a viable organization. Employees, customers, and suppliers will simply withdraw their support. Thus, a going concern must strive to enhance its cash-generating ability. The ability of a company to distribute cash to its various constituencies depends on its ability to generate cash from operating its businesses and on its ability to obtain any additional funds needed from external sources.

Debt and equity financing are the two basic external sources. The company's ability to borrow today is based on projections of how much cash will be generated in the future. Borrowing power and the market value of the shares both depend on a company's cash-generating ability. The market value of the shares directly impacts the second source of financing, that is, equity financing. For a given level of funds required, the higher the share price, the less dilution will be borne by current shareholders. Therefore, management's financial power to deal effectively with corporate claimants also comes from increasing the value of the shares. Treynor, a former editor of the *Financial Analysts Journal*, summarizes this line of thinking best:

Those who criticize the goal of share value maximization are forgetting that stockholders are not merely the beneficiaries of the corporation's financial success, but also the referees who determine management's financial power.

Any management – no matter how powerful and independent – that flouts the financial objective of maximizing share value does so at its own peril.

Stockholders and stakeholders: A new perspective on corporate governance

By Edward Freeman and David Reed[1]

Management thought has changed dramatically in recent years. There have been, and are now underway, both conceptual and practical revolutions in the ways that management theorists and managers think about organizational life. The purpose of this article is to understand the implications of one of these shifts in world view; namely, the shift from 'stockholder' to 'stakeholder.'

The stakeholder concept

It has long been gospel that corporations have obligations to stockholders, holders of the firm's equity, that are sacrosanct and inviolable. Corporate action or inaction is to be driven by attention to the needs of its stockholders, usually thought to be measured by stock price, earnings per share, or some other financial measure. It has been argued that the proper relationship of management to its stockholders is similar to that of the fiduciary to the *cestui que trustent*, whereby the interests of the stockholders should be dutifully cared for by management. Thus, any action taken by management must ultimately be justified by whether or not it furthers the interests of the corporation and its stockholders.

There is also a long tradition of departure from the view that stockholders have a privileged place in the business enterprise. Berle and Means (1932) were worried about the 'degree of prominence entitling (the corporation) to be dealt with as a major social institution.' Chester Barnard argued that the purpose of the corporation was to serve society, and that the function of the executive was to instill this sense of moral purpose in the corporation's employees (Barnard, 1938). Public relations and corporate social action have a history too long to be catalogued here. However, a recent development calls for a more far-reaching change in the way that we look at corporate life, and that is the good currency of the idea of 'stakeholders.'

The stakeholder notion is indeed a deceptively simple one. It says that there are other groups to whom the corporation is responsible in addition to stockholders: those groups who have a stake in the actions of the corporation. The word *stakeholder*, coined in an internal memorandum at the Stanford Research Institute in 1963, refers to 'those groups without whose support the organization would cease to exist.' The list of stakeholders originally included shareowners, employees, customers, suppliers, lenders, and society. Stemming from the work of Igor Ansoff and Robert Stewart (in the planning department at Lockheed) and, later, Marion Doscher and Stewart (at SRI), stakeholder analysis served and continues to serve an important function in the SRI corporate planning process.

From the original work at SRI, the historical trail diverges in a number of directions. In his now classic *Corporate Strategy: An Analytic Approach to Business Policy for Growth and Expansion*, Igor Ansoff (1965) makes limited use of the theory:

> While as we shall see later, 'responsibilities' and 'objectives' are not synonymous, they have been made one in a 'stakeholder theory' of objectives. This theory maintains that the objectives of the firm should be derived by balancing the conflicting claims of the various 'stakeholders' in the firm: managers, workers, stockholders, suppliers, vendors.

Ansoff goes on to reject the stakeholder theory in favor of a view which separates objectives into 'economic' and 'social' with the latter being a 'secondary modifying and constraining influence' on the former.

In the mid-1970s, researchers in systems theory, led by Russell Ackoff (1974) 'rediscovered' stakeholder analysis, or at least took Ansoff's admonition more seriously. Propounding essentially an open systems view of organizations, Ackoff argues that many social problems can be solved by the redesign of fundamental institutions with the support and interaction of stakeholders in the system.

A second trail from Ansoff's original reference is the work of William Dill, who in concert with Ackoff, sought to move the stakeholder concept from the

[1]Source: © 1982, by the Regents of the University of California. Reprinted from the *California Management Review*, Vol. 25, No. 3. By permission of the Regents.

periphery of corporate planning to a central place. In 1975 Dill argued:

For a long time, we have assumed that the views and the initiative of stakeholders could be dealt with as externalities to the strategic planning and management process: as data to help management shape decisions, or as legal and social constraints to limit them. We have been reluctant, though, to admit the idea that some of these outside stakeholders might seek and earn active roles with management to make decisions. The move today is from stakeholder influence towards stakeholder participation.

Dill went on to set out a role for strategic managers as communicators with stakeholders and considered the role of adversary groups such as Nader's Raiders in the strategic process. For the most part, until Dill's paper, stakeholders had been assumed to be nonadversarial, or adversarial only in the sense of labor-management relations. By broadening the notion of stakeholder to 'people outside . . . who have ideas about what the economic and social performance of the enterprise should include,' Dill set the stage for the use of the stakeholder concept as an umbrella for strategic management.

A related development is primarily responsible for giving the stakeholder concept a boost; namely, the increase in concern with the social involvement of business. The corporate social responsibility movement is too diverse and has spawned too many ideas, concepts, and techniques to explain here. Suffice it to say that the social movements of the sixties and seventies – civil rights, the antiwar movement, consumerism, environmentalism, and women's rights – served as a catalyst for rethinking the role of the business enterprise in society. From Milton Friedman to John Kenneth Galbraith, there is a diversity of arguments. However, one aspect of the corporate social responsibility debate is particularly relevant to understanding the good currency of the stakeholder concept.

In the early 1970s the Harvard Business School undertook a project on corporate social responsibility. The output of the project was voluminous, and of particular importance was the development of a pragmatic model of social responsibility called 'the corporate social responsiveness model' (Ackerman and Bauer, 1976). It essentially addressed Dill's question with respect to social issues: 'How can the corporation respond proactively to the increased pressure for positive social change?' By concentrating on responsive-

ness instead of responsibility, the Harvard researchers were able to link the analysis of social issues with the traditional areas of strategy and organization.

By the late 1970s the need for strategic management processes to take account of nontraditional business problems in terms of government, special interest groups, trade associations, foreign competitors, dissident shareholders, and complex issues such as employee rights, equal opportunity, environmental pollution, consumer rights, tariffs, government regulation, and reindustrialization had become obvious. To begin to develop these processes, The Wharton School began, in 1977 in its Applied Research Center, a 'stakeholder project.' The objectives of the project were to put together a number of strands of thought and to develop a theory of management which enabled executives to formulate and implement corporate strategy in turbulent environments. Thus, an action research model was used whereby stakeholder theory was generated by actual cases.

To date the project has explored the implications of the stakeholder concept on three levels: as a management theory; as a process for practitioners to use in strategic management; and as an analytical framework.

At the theoretical level the implications of substituting *stakeholder* for *stockholder* needs to be explicated. The first problem at this level is the actual definition of *stakeholder*. SRI's original definition is too general and too exclusive to serve as a means of identifying those external groups who are strategically important. The concentration on generic stakeholders, such as society and customers, rather than specific social interest groups and specific customer segments produces an analysis which can only be used as a background for the planning process. Strategically useful information about the actions, objectives, and motivations of specific groups, which is needed if management is to be responsive to stakeholder concerns, requires a more specific and inclusive definition.

We propose two definitions of *stakeholder*: a wide sense, which includes groups who are friendly or hostile, and a narrow sense, which captures the essence of the SRI definition. but is more specific.

■ The wide sense of stakeholder. Any identifiable group or individual who can affect the achievement of an organization's objectives or who is affected by the achievement of an organization's objectives. (Public interest groups, protest groups, government agencies, trade associations, competitors, unions, as well as employees, customer segments, shareowners, and others are stakeholders, in this sense.)

- The narrow sense of stakeholder. Any identifiable group or individual on which the organization is dependent for its continued survival. (Employees, customer segments, certain suppliers, key government agencies, shareowners, certain financial institutions, as well as others are all stakeholders in the narrow sense of the term.)

While executives are willing to recognize that employees, suppliers, and customers have a stake in the corporation, many resist the inclusion of adversary groups. But from the standpoint of corporate strategy, *stakeholder* must be understood in the wide sense: strategies need to account for those groups who can affect the achievement of the firm's objectives. Some may feel happier with other words, such as *influencers*, *claimants*, *publics*, or *constituencies*. Semantics aside, if corporations are to formulate and implement strategies in turbulent environments, theories of strategy must have concepts, such as the wide sense of *stakeholder*, which allow the analysis of all external forces and pressures whether they are friendly or hostile. In what follows we will use *stakeholder* in the wide sense, as our primary objective is to elucidate the questions of corporate governance from the perspective of strategic management.

A second issue at the theoretical level is the generation of prescriptive propositions which explain actual cases and articulate regulative principles for future use. Thus, a *post hoc* analysis of the brewing industry and the problem of beverage container legislation, combined with a similar analysis of the regulatory environments of public utilities have led to some simple propositions which serve as a philosophical guideline for strategy formulation. For example:

- Generalize the marketing approach: understand the needs of each stakeholder, in a similar fashion to understanding customer needs, and design products, services, and programs to fulfill those needs.

- Establish negotiation processes: understand the political nature of a number of stakeholders, and the applicability of concepts and techniques of political science, such as coalition analysis, conflict management, and the use and abuse of unilateral action.

- Establish a decision philosophy that is oriented towards seizing the initiative rather than reacting to events as they occur.

- Allocate organizational resources based on the degree of importance of the environmental turbulence (the stakeholders' claims).

Other prescriptive propositions can be put forth, especially with respect to issues of corporate governance. One proposition that has been discussed is to 'involve stakeholder groups in strategic decisions,' or 'invite stakeholders to participate in governance decisions.' While propositions like this may have substantial merit, we have not examined enough cases nor marshalled enough evidence to support them in an unqualified manner. There are cases where participation is appropriate. Some public utilities have been quite successful in the use of stakeholder advisory groups in matters of rate setting. However, given the breadth of our concept of stakeholder we believe that co-optation through participation is not always the correct strategic decision.

The second level of analysis is the use of stakeholder concepts in strategy formulation processes. Two processes have been used so far: the *Stakeholder Strategy Process* and the *Stakeholder Audit Process*. The Stakeholder Strategy Process is a systematic method for analyzing the relative importance of stakeholders and their cooperative potential (how they can help the corporation achieve its objectives) and their competitive threat (how they can prevent the corporation from achieving its objectives). The process is one which relies on a behavioral analysis (both actual and potential) for input, and an explanatory model of stakeholder objectives and resultant strategic shifts for output. The Stakeholder Audit Process is a systematic method for identifying stakeholders and assessing the effectiveness of current organizational strategies. By itself, each process has a use in the strategic management of an organization. Each analyzes the stakeholder environment from the standpoint of organizational mission and objectives and seeks to formulate strategies for meeting stakeholder needs and concerns.

The use of the stakeholder concept at the analytical level means thinking in terms which are broader than current strategic and operational problems. It implies looking at public policy questions in stakeholder terms and trying to understand how the relationships between an organization and its stakeholders would change given the implementation of certain policies.

One analytical device depicts an organization's stakeholders on a two-dimensional grid map. The first dimension is one of 'interest' or 'stake' and ranges from an equity interest to an economic interest or marketplace stake to an interest or stake as a 'kibitzer' or influencer. Shareowners have an equity stake; customers and suppliers have an economic stake; and single-issue groups have an influencer stake. The second dimension of a stakeholder is its power, which ranges from the formalistic or voting power of stock-holders to the economic power of customers to the political power of special interest groups. By *economic power* we mean 'the ability to influence due to market-place decisions' and by *political power* we mean 'the ability to influence due to use of the political process.'

Figure 11.2.1 represents this stakeholder grid graphically. It is of course possible that a stakeholder has more than one kind of both stake and power, especially in light of the fact that there are stakeholders who have multiple roles. An employee may be at once shareholder, customer, employee, and even kibitzer. Figure 11.2.1 represents the prevailing world view. That is, shareholders and directors have formal or voting power; customers, suppliers, and employees have economic power; and government and special interest groups have political power. Moreover, management concepts and principles have evolved to treat this 'diagonal case.' Managers learn how to handle stock-holders and boards via their ability to vote on certain key decisions, and conflicts are resolved by the procedures and processes written into the corporate charter or by methods which involve formal legal parameters. Strategic planners, marketers, financial analysts, and operations executives base their decisions on marketplace variables, and an entire tradition of management principles is based on the economic analysis of the marketplace. Finally, public relations and public affairs managers and lobbyists learn to deal in the political arena. As long as the real world approximately fits into the diagonal, management processes may be able to deal effectively with them.

A more thoughtful examination, however, reveals that Figure 11.2.1 is either a straw man or that shifts of position have occurred. In the auto industry, for instance, one part of government has acquired economic power in terms of the imposition of import quotas or the trigger price mechanism. The Securities and Exchange Commission might be looked at as a kibitzer with formal power in terms of disclosure and accounting rules. Outside directors do not necessarily have an equity stake, especially those women, minorities, and academics who are becoming more and more normal for the boards of large corporations. Some kibitzer groups are buying stock and acquiring an equity stake, and while they also acquire formal power, their main source of power is still political. Witness the marshalling of the political process by church groups in bringing up, at annual meetings, issues such as selling infant formula in the Third World or investing in South Africa. Unions are using their political power as well as their formal clout as managers of large portions of pension funds to influence the company. Customers are being organized by consumer advocates to exercise the voice option and to politicize the marketplace. In short, the real world looks more like Figure 11.2.2. (Of course, each organization will have its own individual grid.) Thus, search for alternative applications of traditional management processes must begin, and new concepts and techniques are needed to understand the shifts that have occurred and to manage in the new environment.

There is a need to develop new and innovative management processes to deal with the current and future

FIGURE 11.2.1   Classical grid

FIGURE 11.2.2 'Real world' stakeholder grid

	Formal or Voting Power	Economic Power	Political Power
Equity Stake	• Stockbrokers • Directors • Minority interests		• Dissident stockholders
Economic Stake		• Suppliers • Debt holders • Customers • Unions	• Local governments • Foreign governments • Consumer groups • Unions
Influencers	• Government • SEC • Outside directors	• EPA/OSHA	• Nader's Raiders • Government • Trade associations

complexities of management issues. At the theoretical level, stakeholder analysis has been developed to enrich the economic approach to corporate strategy by arguing that kibitzers with political power must be included in the strategy process. At the strategic level, stakeholder analysis takes a number of groups into account and analyzes their strategic impact on the corporation.

Stakeholder analysis and corporate democracy

The debate on corporate governance and, in particular, corporate democracy has recently intensified. Proposals have been put forth to make the corporation more democratic, to encourage shareholder participation and management responsiveness to shareholder needs, and to make corporations more responsive to other stakeholder needs and, hence, to encourage the participation of stakeholders in the governance process. Reforms from cumulative voting to audit committees have been suggested.

Corporate democracy has come to have at least three meanings over the years, which prescribe that corporations should be made more democratic: by increasing the role of government, either as a watchdog or by having public officials on boards of directors; by allowing citizen or public participation in the managing of its affairs via public interest directors and the like; or by encouraging or mandating the active participation of all or many of its shareholders. The analysis of the preceding section has implications for each of these levels of democratization.

The propositions of stakeholder analysis advocate a thorough understanding of a firm's stakeholders (in the wide sense) and recognize that there are times when stakeholders must participate in the decision-making process. The strategic tools and techniques of stakeholder analysis yield a method for determining the timing and degree of such participation. At the absolute minimum this implies that boards of directors must be aware of the impact of their decisions on key stakeholder groups. As stakeholders have begun to exercise more political power and as marketplace decisions become politicized, the need for awareness to grow into responsiveness has become apparent. Thus, the analytical model can be used by boards to map carefully the power and stake of each group. While it is not the proper role of the board to be involved in the implementation of tactical programs at the operational level of the corporation, it must set the tone for how the company deals with stakeholders, both traditional marketplace ones and those who have political power. The board must decide not only whether management is managing the affairs of the corporation, but indeed, what are to count as the affairs of the corporation. This involves assessing the stake and power of each stakeholder group.

Much has been written about the failure of senior management to think strategically, competitively, and globally. Some have argued that American businesspersons are 'managing [their] way to economic decline' (Hayes and Abernathy, 1980). Executives have countered the critics with complaints about the increase in the adversarial role of government and in the number of hostile external interest groups. Yet if the criteria for success for senior executives remains fixated on economic stakeholders with economic power and on short-term performance on Wall Street, the rise of such a turbulent political environment in a free and open society should come as no surprise. If the board sees itself as responsive only to the shareholder in the short term, senior management will continue to manage towards economic decline.[2] We have argued that the problem of governing the corporation in today's world must be viewed in terms of the entire grid of stakeholders and their power base. It is only by setting the direction for positive response and negotiation at the board level that the adversarial nature of the business-government relationship can be overcome.

If this task of stakeholder management is done properly, much of the air is let out of critics who argue that the corporation must be democratized in terms of increased direct citizen participation. Issues which involve both economic and political stakes and power bases must be addressed in an integrated fashion. No longer can public affairs, public relations, and corporate philanthropy serve as adequate management tools. The sophistication of interest groups who are beginning to use formal power mechanisms, such as proxy fights, annual meetings, the corporate charter, to focus the attention of management on the affairs of the corporation has increased. Responsive boards will seize these opportunities to learn more about those stakeholders who have chosen the option of voice over the Wall Street Rule. As boards direct management to respond to these concerns, to negotiate with critics, to trade off certain policies in return for positive support, the pressure for mandated citizen participation will subside.

[2] It is arguable whether responsiveness to nonmarket stakeholders is in the long-term interest of the corporation. We believe that there is no need to appeal to utilitarian notions of greatest social good or altruism or social responsibility. Rather the corporation fulfills its obligations to shareholders in the long term only through proper stakeholder management. In short we believe that enlightened self-interest gives both reasons why (personal motivation) and reasons for (social justification) taking stakeholder concerns into account. The development of this argument is, however, beyond our present scope.

READING

11.3

The corporate board: Confronting the paradoxes

By Ada Demb and F.-Friedrich Neubauer[1]

Corporate governance is *the process by which corporations are made responsive to the rights and wishes of stakeholders*. It is the issue of corporate accountability which every country and society has had to deal with since the days of the merchant traders. Most societies use four mechanisms to achieve corporate accountability: they influence corporate behaviour through: board structures, ownership, regulations or codes, and direct social pressure.

Ownership has shifted dramatically during this century, with the most recent change coming in the role of the institutional investor. In Japan and Germany institutional investors with complex cross-holdings form a tight business community which lends stability to the industrial environment by concentrating power in the hands of a small group. In the U.K., the U.S. and the Netherlands, while institutional investors seem to be taking a more active role, the effect of their new behaviour remains a mystery. Although more active, the pension funds, for example, are tied to a competitive market which limits their independence compared with an institution like Deutsche Bank. Further, despite global capital markets, arcane cross-boundary trading procedures still

[1]Source: This article was adapted from *Long Range Planning*, Vol. 25, No. 3, A. Demb and F.F. Neubauer, 'The Corporate Board: Confonting the Paradoxes', pp. 9–20, © 1992. With permission from Elsevier.

EXHIBIT 11.3.1 THE RESEARCH APPROACH

Seventy-one directors from 11 multinational corporations agreed to participate with us in exploring the question of corporate governance and the role of boards. The companies are headquartered in Canada (1), France (1), Finland (1), Germany (1 company plus two independent directors), the Netherlands (1), Switzerland (1), the U.K. (4) and Venezuela (1). The Dutch, Finnish and German companies work with two-level boards; the others are unitary. Two companies are primarily state-owned, the rest publicity-traded. None is family-owned. Three are in the energy business, one in heavy industry, two in health care, two consumer, one utility, two manufacturing. Their annual turnover ranges from US $2.5bn to US $50bn, and they employ between 28,000 and 260,000 people.

Each company gave us access to a minimum of five directors, for confidential, in-depth interviews, lasting 2–3 hours. The minimum set included: the Chairman, the CEO, the Corporate Secretary, two Executive Directors, and two outside, Non-Executive Directors. For those companies with a two-level board structure, we interviewed members of both the Supervisory and Management boards. In some cases we interviewed as many as seven or eight directors. Two of the companies included labour representatives to the board among our interviewees. The sample included 30 executive, or inside directors, 31 outside, or non-executive directors, and 11 corporate secretaries. The average age was 58. All were university educated, with the majority holding advanced professional degrees. Among them, these directors serve on 500 boards in Europe, North and South America.

For the purposes of international comparisons, our sample consists of the directors, rather than the companies. The reason is obvious: conclusions about national differences cannot be drawn from samples of one, two or four companies. On the other hand, comparisons can be made between British and German directors, between executives and non-executives, between the chairmen of single, and two-tier companies. The companies served as the unit of analysis for understanding how decision-making, structure, role, culture and personality affected the behaviour of a single board.

FIGURE 11.3.1 Interviewees by nationality and board structure

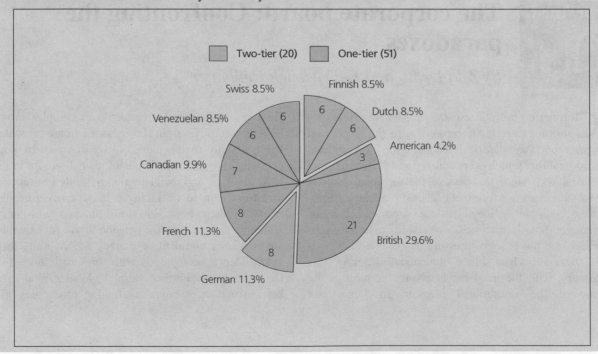

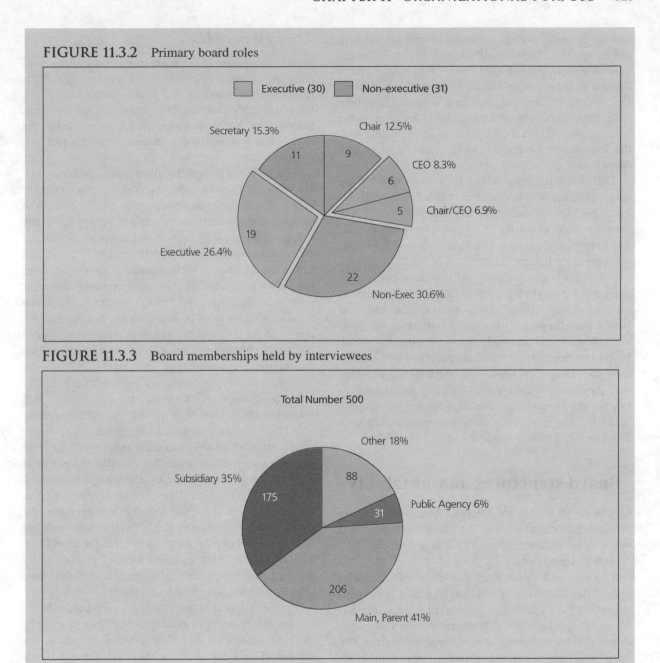

FIGURE 11.3.2 Primary board roles

Executive (30) Non-executive (31)

Secretary 15.3% | 11 | 9 | Chair 12.5%

CEO 8.3% | 6

Chair/CEO 6.9% | 5

Executive 26.4% | 19

22 | Non-Exec 30.6%

FIGURE 11.3.3 Board memberships held by interviewees

Total Number 500

Other 18% | 88

Subsidiary 35% | 175

31 | Public Agency 6%

206

Main, Parent 41%

hamper investors who wish to own the stocks of companies headquartered in 'foreign' countries.

Regulatory environments are remarkably similar among western economies. Regulations cover all aspects of corporate activity, from taxes and antitrust to employment conditions and toxic waste. Relatively speaking, they are strictly enforced. We see changes occurring in many settings, as a result of more complex definitions of accountability. Switzerland, whose banking industry has been a very private haven for the world's riches, is considering banking regulation to permit scrutiny of accounts under certain conditions in order to respond to a global community concerned about stock manipulation and the laundering of drug money. It is bizarre to find Burger King prosecuted for child labour violation in 1989 – regulations growing out of the sweatshops of the early part of the century.

However, the tough approach taken by federal prosecutors toward recent Exxon and Shell oil spills is serious for business because it reflects a fundamental change in governments' attitudes toward oil industry pollution. The Valdez spill elicited criminal charges against Exxon. A year later, Shell faced a very heavy fine for an on-shore spill in the U.K. in spring of 1990. Discussions addressing the earth's natural resource base have begun in a serious way, yet they falter because we still lack a conceptual base for dealing with the importance of the Antartic, or the tropical rain forests, as a *global commons*.

Difference in *social habits* for putting direct pressure on companies are deeply rooted in history and culture – perhaps the one aspect of governance which will vary between countries. Still, judicial systems seek solutions to many issues which are common, for example, corporate liability in the case of risk to employee health. This issue is already an important concern to companies considering participation in the redevelopment of central Europe. Local management and local labour have been working for 30–40 years with old technologies and in many cases, substances which have since been determined harmful. How will companies who decide to move into these settings ensure that they do not face a crisis similar to Bhopal, or inherit the seemingly unending chain of liability faced by American corporations in conjunction with cancer-related asbestos suits?

Board structures and instability

Of course, all boards are different. Boards must reflect the special circumstances of their company and national environment. Hence, the argument that they cannot be compared.

Our research shows first, that all boards deal with almost the same sets of tasks, and second, that board structures have evolved to respond to a basic instability resulting from three structural tensions or *paradoxes*, that are independent of national boundaries. The most straightforward illustration of the similarities comes from responses to the question: what is the mandate, or 'job' of the board?

Why are those who argue the differences so forceful? Most often it stems from a conviction that the differences between one- and two-tier boards, proportions of executive to non-executive membership, and different requirements for labour participation are too big to overcome. We take the view that these structural differences are attempts to cope with three paradoxes faced by all boards as they seek to carry out their mandates effectively.

The first paradox

Legally, the board is the highest authority in the company, the 'fountain of power', yet top management naturally tends to exercise that power. On the one hand, the board bears clear legal responsibility; on the other, management has the infrastructure, the knowledge, the time – and frequently the appetite – to shoulder this responsibility.

The paradox is how to allow *both* the board and management to retain effective control without diminishing the initiative and motivation of the other. The paradox creates tensions which are vexing for many corporations, causing friction and considerable loss of energy. Circumstances often dictate a fluid situation; at times the pendulum of influence may swing more toward the board, and at other times more toward management. Because the board carries governance responsibility, it must be in a position to influence the course of the corporation, and to exercise a reasonable degree of control. In practice, is the board in a position to exercise this control?

Responsibility, control and influence are tightly interwoven elements of power. It is popular to talk about boards as centres of power, but we believe the term has become over-used. In governance, power cumulates from an ability to exert authority of different types, at different moments. Specifically, the power of a board can be understood by assessing four factors: the personal influence of key players, participation in the selection of the CEO and top management, the board's ability to shape strategy, and the board's ability to monitor and control progress towards the objectives. The balance of responsibility, control and authority between the board and management reflects their relative positions on these four factors.

Do the different board structure predispose a board toward management or board control? Not really. For example, American, British and Dutch boards in our sample all have experience with CEOs whose personal influence, built on a track record and national standing inhibits outside directors from challenging their proposals. Similarly, there are boards in each country where certain outside directors, by virtue of their own corporate responsibilities and standing, easily provide the counter-balance to a strong management.

In those countries with two-tier boards, one explicit mandate of the Supervisory Board is the selection of the Management Board, e.g. the CEO and top managers. Thus, it would seem the structure supports more 'outside director' control. In practice, in discussing CEO and top management selection with directors, we found no difference in the CEO's influence on the choice of *successor*, for example. In fact, those one-tier boards with 'nominating committees' or 'human resource and compensation committees' consisting of outside directors often played a stronger role in the selection of the next CEO. *The key was a committee structure* which supported strong outside director integration among themselves, and shifted the centre of gravity of the selection process to the outside directors. A Supervisory Board which meets only four times a year, and which does not have such a committee is disadvantaged in this process. Among all of our boards we found the CEO was the key player on selecting *top management* for a variety of obvious reasons: in-depth knowledge of the candidates, and the prerogative of selecting his own 'team'.

The issues of participation in strategy and control depend more upon the frequency of board interaction and the nature of strategic planning processes than on board structure. Having said that, as two-tier boards tend to meet only quarterly, there is a tendency toward management dominance of strategy in those settings. Of our three two-tier boards, this was true for two of them. Formal planning processes lend themselves to more board interaction than entrepreneurial modes.

The second paradox

Board members are expected to provide critical judgement on management performance – which requires an in-depth knowledge of, and intimacy with the affairs of the corporation – and at the same time to assure that this judgement is independent – which requires detachment and distance. The central question of this paradox is: how to bring the board to the point where it can exercise judgement which is both critical and independent? *Critical* means discriminating. Exercising critical judgement means knowing the situation well enough to distinguish the important from the flashy trends from temporary aberrations. In order to be critical the board needs individuals with a fine grasp of the company – its history, strengths, weaknesses, and the industry – its competitive dynamics, technology cycles. *Independent* means judgement free from the bias of self-interest. The board must attend to broader consideration involving stakeholders' interest, public responsibilities, and trends which may affect the life of the industry itself. Board members need a certain detachment from the company itself – they must be independent of financial and other vested interests in order to comment intelligently on the performance of the company and to define the proper context. The board needs to feel that it

belongs without being captive. Evaluating the contribution of individual board members on these dimensions is a necessary first step to creating balance across the group – and a revealing exercise.

An executive defines self-interest in terms of the company or even a business and is, therefore, very involved. It is difficult for an executive director who also heads a business to gain sufficient detachment from the development needs of the business to take a corporate view, for example. While the CEO may be able to take an integrated and synthetic view of the company, the CEO's stature, reputation and personal wealth remain tied to the company and often prevent a detached view of stakeholder perspectives. How do insiders detach themselves sufficiently, for their natural involvement with the company and businesses they manage, to exercise independent judgement? While an executive director brings to the table a fine understanding of the dynamics of the company and its businesses, after a career of 20 or 25 years becoming more and more expert in the businesses, the executive succumbs to some degree of *tunnel vision*?

By contrast, most non-executives come to the board with a certain detachment from the company; they are affiliated only through their board responsibilities, which, in our group, rarely exceeded 15 per cent of their total professional activity. Exceptions were those brought in by the Chairman or CEO for personal support, some whose fees are so high that they, too, depend upon the company for stature and personal wealth, and of course, owners. Most non-executives are relatively ignorant of company details but bring with them experience in other industries and sectors, such as government or work in the community.

Basically, the pool of candidates who can serve on the board can be described as variations of insiders and outsiders who bring quite different amounts of the four key ingredients to the boardroom: a *depth* of understanding about the company and its industry, a *breadth* of perspective which brings the larger context into focus, *involvement* and commitment to the objectives of the company's businesses, and a sense of *detachment* from any encumbering affiliation. The capacity of a board depends on a combining of these ingredients like the flavours in a gourmet meal, on the quality of their participation and the relationships among the executive and non-executive directors.

The third paradox

The working style of the board must build its collective strength: the board needs the trusting familiarity of a close-knit group, yet members must be independent personalities who can resist 'groupthink' and raise critical questions of colleagues. The core of this paradox is to forge a set of relationships among a group of strong individuals that will permit information to be shared, recommendations challenged, and actions evaluated, while at the same time, avoiding the trap of becoming a group so trusting, familiar and comfortable with itself, that judgement is undermined by cosy self-satisfaction.

Boards suffer the hazards of all small groups. These include the potential for 'groupthink', for a few individuals (possibly the CEO) to dominate discussions and decision-making, and for avoiding conflict. It is the *collective* strength of the directors that gives the board its capability for judgement – the capability that translates into a distinct, additive role.

American, Canadian, Swiss and German supervisory boards – those composed primarily of outside directors – are vulnerable to the opposite effect – the 'all-star' syndrome. 'All-star' sports teams put together at the end of a season to represent a region or league, draw 'most valuable players' from member teams. The resulting 'all-star' team has the best individual talent the league can offer. As a group, however, the time available to turn the talents into the coordinated synergy of a *championship* team is severely limited. So, despite their individual abilities, all-star teams are rarely a match for even a mediocre team that has played together for an entire season. Similarly, infrequent meetings, a sparse committee structure, and, perhaps, a Chairman and CEO who prefers to retain power, reduce the ability of 'all-star' boards to build their collective strength.

At the other end of the spectrum are teams who have played together so long that they function like a well-oiled machine. A quick nod takes the place of complicated signals, sending an entire team into a pre-arranged formation. In the board setting, goals, values and styles are shared to a point where meetings become very efficient – questions can be anticipated and presentations geared to individual concerns. However, as personal relationships and trust grow, what was once a robust, challenging forum, can deteriorate into a mutual-admiration society. It is a variation on the theme, 'success is our greatest enemy'.

A newly-formed board, or a board accommodating new members finds itself with 'strangers' in the group, and therefore with a reduced ability to access its collective judgement. As the group continues to work together over a period of years, the familiarity may lead to complacency and a tendency to seek new members who 'fit' with existing members. Slowly and incrementally the board's critical ability, its ability to challenge, deteriorates. Mueller (1989) called this a 'concinnity bias', e.g. 'many boards tend to develop a clubbable, if elusive, characteristic of organizations which place internal harmony and fitness before such attributes as objectivity and independent judgement'.

Four factors contribute to the collective strength of the board: (1) *The personality and style of the Chairman and CEO*, including the combination or split in Chairman and CEO roles; (2) The *culture*, or *climate* of board meetings: how open, frank, and discursive a forum, the size of the board, how decisions are taken and the agenda is set, and relationships among directors; (3) The *people* involved: the composition of the board, and how directors come to be on the board; (4) The *degree of common purpose*, how well directors understand their roles. We find these factors no matter what is the formal structure of the board, or its legal context.

While the two-tier structures do address the split of Chairman and CEO roles, they bring a different problem pertinent to resolving this paradox: The separation of the two boards means that management can form an *insider's club* which relegates the outside directors to a secondary role. Further it reduces management's access to outside perspectives.

Few boards choose their roles. Some, however, have developed *mission statements* which outline their goals, and values, to whom and for what the board should be accountable. The mission concept is a central theme in discussions of corporate strategy. In a board, as in a company, the goal is to create 'alignment' – where board members can combine their individual purposes with commitment to a common purpose. An aligned board would be anything but a rubber-stamp organization. Aligned groups often have more open disagreement and apparent conflict than less aligned groups. 'In fact, a high degree of alignment is really a necessary condition for creative disagreement, since the quality of interpersonal relationships in a highly aligned organization allows people to argue about ideas without fearing loss of acceptance or damaged relationships' (Kiefer and Senge, 1987).

Long experience with group dynamics and team-building in organizations suggests that these shared missions at the board level, supported by working procedures, should help to focus the board judgement and attention.

Synthesizing national experience

Does the existence of paradoxes mean that trouble is brewing? The opposite seems to be true: 'Excellence in an organization seems to involve the tension of paradox' (Cameron, 1986). Finding balance for the tensions created by the paradoxes is like resolving the structural tensions in designing a bridge. The bridge must be strong, but not unwieldy. It must be stable enough to carry the load, yet flexible enough to move with wind or earthquakes. There are many different, equally effective, solutions to the problem of building a good bridge. Similarly, boards use different approaches to resolve their structural tensions. Because most board dysfunction can be traced to a distortion in one of these fundamental tensions, it is useful to summarize how the different national board structures resolve them. From them we can derive nine principles which are the base for effective board performance in these national settings.

1 A balance of executive and non-executive board members is key. The balance is important in resolving the issues of both the first and second paradoxes. British, Dutch, Finnish and German boards in our study benefited from the combination of perspectives, and balance of power. Non-executives should represent either a majority of board members or a substantial proportion, i.e. no fewer than three. However, examining paradox 2 reveals that a board needs more than the CEO as the insider. Executives as well as non-executives, should serve on the board and carry formal legal board responsibility. The two-tier structures, and the British boards demonstrate the importance legal responsibility brings: it demands of the executives a broader consideration of stakeholder perspectives. There is less possibility for scapegoating the board as well. U.S., Swiss and Canadian boards comprised of outsiders (and, perhaps the CEO) often overcome the problems of the second paradox with committees that provide opportunities for outsiders to interact with executives. This solution does not make the same demand of executives as formal, legal board membership.

2 The roles of Chairman and CEO should either be separate or, if combined, carefully balanced with processes and structures that empower the outside directors. Chairman and CEO roles are separate by law in Germany, the Netherlands and Finland; in Britain, and in Australia, there is active discussion now about a legal separation. In Canada, Britain, and Switzerland we find companies cycling through 'combination Chairman and CEO – then separation for succession – then recombination'. In effective boards, where the role is combined, the Swiss and British have strong outside director committees. The separation may be desirable; however, legislation which prescribes an organizational structure unnecessarily reduces flexibility – and does nothing to overcome the disadvantage of promoting the former CEO to Chairman made clear by a systematic analysis along the lines of the second paradox!

3 Outside directors need opportunities to interact on strategy and access to good information through formal and informal channels. One French Chairman and CEO used the telephone to keep in contact with key outside board members. Our British boards offered a combination of unedited monthly management reports, specially-prepared trend data, and annual 2- or 3-day strategy reviews.

4 Meetings should be frequent. In Britain, Finland, and for the Swiss Chairman's committee this meant meeting a minimum of 6–8 times each year, and not uncommonly 10 or 11 times. In Germany and the Netherlands where boards meet only 3–4 times each year, the balance clearly shifted to the management boards. The law simply sets a minimum number of meetings and does not prevent a company from scheduling more.

5 Committees should be established to provide both more in-depth exposure (paradox 2) and better control (paradox 1). Committee structure provide opportunities for outsiders to understand the company, its executive talent pool, businesses and industry better. Audit committees, almost the norm in the U.S., are being established in Britain and Germany. Strategy and finance or investment committees are becoming more common. Management compensation and human resource committees put executive review and CEO selection more firmly in the hands of the non-executives.

6 The establishment of a nominating committee of outside directors who represent the centre of gravity for bringing new outside directors onto the board. This helps avoid the dangers of the third paradox – deterioration into a cosy club. It also balances the power of a combined Chairman and CEO.

7 Smaller boards, of eight to ten. Smaller boards such as those in Britain, the U.S. and some Swiss, companies, create informal environments where more forceful discussions can be sustained. They are

more vulnerable to the dangers of paradox 3, and therefore, may require a majority of non-executives, who meet frequently, and who control the nomination of new outside directors.

8   Boards should use both retreats and specific discussions of board purpose and mission to create the coherence that focuses energy on key issues. Developing a clear understanding of the ways in which the board can add-value to the company and to management's role is a first step in avoiding power struggles, and creating a good working environment. The focus helps identify the characteristics desirable in outside board members, defines the mandates of key committees, and makes obvious the type of information board members require in order to contribute effectively.

9   Boards should review their performance. A small, but growing number of boards, regularly review the performance of the board and of outside directors. Term appointment and firm retirement ages for non-executives add to the board's ability to recognize contributors and non-performers. Without a performance review, the board is hard put to design the mechanisms, and processes that can enable it to balance the tensions of power, judgement and trust embodied in the paradoxes. We found boards in Britain and the U.S. who had structured criteria and review processes to assess board performance.

In devising their solutions within the limits of national legislation, individual companies have made an implicit choice between a board structure which is basically stable and reliable, by contrast with one which is highly manoeuvrable, but perhaps only under ideal conditions.

Management-dominated boards permit companies to respond quickly to changes in markets or technology. A combined Chairman and CEO can be decisive. Some situations require this manoeuvrability: start-ups, companies in high-tech industries fighting for market share, perhaps turnarounds. The Supervisory Board structure in Germany, Finland, Norway and the Netherlands basically puts a brake on a manoeuvrable management board. British, Canadian and American boards call for substantial outside director involvement for the same reason. A board has to decide what mix of manoeuvrability and stability is desirable. Is it going to be a high performance but unstable board, or reliable and stable, but perhaps, unexciting? The goal is to use committee structures, composition and agendas to create a board portfolio that meets the needs of the company within the limits of reliability. An unexciting board does not imply an unexciting company, and there is much to be said for both! Fine companies can be found in both categories.

The governance challenge

The ten largest employers in the world include Indian, Italian, German, British, American and Dutch companies and among them employ 4.3 million people. Simple multiplication by any standard family size (4 or 5) means that a population between that of New York State or the combined Scandinavian countries is dependent upon these companies for their well-being. When corporate board structures were conceived, did policymakers foresee that fewer than 200 directors would bear the responsibility for the welfare of some 17–21 million people?

How did board structures or governance frameworks change to keep pace with this explosion in size, complexity and responsibility? While annual reports are certainly a dubious source for information about the actual workings of boards, a statement by Hilmar Kopper, Chairman of Daimler-Benz, gives no indication of any substantial change in their board activity, 'In the four Supervisory Board meetings of the past year and by means of written and verbal reports, we have been informed in detail and have consulted with the Board of Management on the state of the corporation and on principal matters of corporate policy'.

These realities drive home the urgent need to redefine our standards for board performance, and to devise new approaches to corporate governance in a global context. In the 1990s and for the foreseeable future, we do not simply speak of 'substantial contributions' by corporations. We speak of corporations *leading, undertaking, and underwriting* such enormous tasks as the redevelopment of central and eastern Europe.

A first major transition occurred during the first sixty years of the twentieth century, as we watched the responsibility for corporate governance shift from the boardroom to the public domain – with the dispersion of ownership through stock markets, and public pressure to direct corporate activity through regulations. Now we are experiencing a second transition, as we come to terms with the reality of the dependence of our societies on corporate activity for the achievement not only of economic, but also social objectives. Corporations have come to play a role in our societies which is much more central, much broader and more tied to the achievement of social goals than we anticipated as late as 1960. The dependence requires a shift in the definition of corporate governance from controlling corporations, to forming a *partnership* with them.

The transitions and the issues that accompany them are common to all modern societies. Earlier, as *individual* players, the impact of individual company activity was swamped by the collective impact of 'industries', and government. That is no longer the case. No matter how different the value base for addressing corporate accountability, there is a long list of basic issues which are common to all of our countries, and a growing list for whose resolution we are inextricably interdependent. This is the new challenge of the second governance transition. The second transition will culminate in a new vision for corporate governance based on partnership and mutual responsibility. A leader member of the Australian business community, Sir Eric Neal, puts it this way:

Directors must look beyond the narrow goal of what is good for the company and the shareholders and accept that the health of the economy as a whole is of direct interest to all of us, including the shareholders we serve.

The new vision will not happen overnight. The challenge to business leaders, i.e. board members, is twofold; to continue to carry the board's key role in the governance system, while working with governments and others to define and institutionalize an approach to corporate governance that recognizes the new realities: (1) In order to achieve both societal and business objectives, we need a governance approach that fosters a new concept of *partnership* between business, governments and the public – one which takes into account a scope of business activity which transcends financial, geographic and technical boundaries. (2) Businesses have been an effective engine for societal development, and therefore the governance demands should assist business to maintain a *platform of profitability and innovation*. (3) Business and boards must approach their activities with full understanding of the *broader responsibilities* that the present scale and impact of business activity entails. Boards will remain integral to the process of corporate governance, but recognition of their inherent instability will lead to new thinking about board roles and structures. We have a common need to help boards overcome their essential instabilities in the short run, so that we can work together to devise frameworks to support corporate and social objectives for the long run.

READING 11.4

Whose company is it? The concept of the corporation in Japan and the West

By Masaru Yoshimori[1]

Available evidence seems to suggest that in terms of corporate governance countries may be divided into three groups: with monistic, dualistic and pluralistic concepts of the corporation. The monistic outlook is shareholder-oriented and looks at the firm as the private property of its owners. This concept is prevalent in the United States and the UK. The dualistic concept also puts a premium on the shareholder interest, but the interests of employees are taken into account as well. This is an adapted form of the monistic concept and is widely shared in Germany and to a lesser degree in

France. The view that the firm is a social institution where people develop themselves freely ranked first among six alternative definitions, according to Albach's survey of leading German companies in 1975, though it slipped to the third rank in 1991 (Albach, 1994).

The pluralistic approach assumes that the firm belongs to all the stakeholders, with the employees' interests taking precedence. This is the concept specific to Japan which manifests itself in the form of long-term employment for employees and long-term trading

[1]Source: This article was adapted from *Long Range Planning*, Vol. 28, No. 4, M. Yoshimori, 'Whose Company Is It? The Concept of the Corporation in Japan and the West', pp. 33–45, © 1995. With permission from Elsevier.

relations among various other stakeholders (the main bank, major suppliers, subcontractors, distributors), loosely called *Keiretsu*.

This three-part categorization is supported by the results of a mail survey undertaken by the author with managers and executives in the five countries under review (see Figure 11.4.1). The shareholder-centred Anglo-American outlook starkly contrasts with the employee-centred Japanese perspective, with Germany and France in between but significantly more oriented towards 'shareholder value' than Japan. The findings on Japan are consistent with the results of other studies. For instance, a survey carried out in 1990 by *Nippon Keizai Shimbun* on 104 employees of large corporations showed a majority of 80 percent replying that the company belongs to its employees; 70 percent believed that the company exists for the benefit of society as a whole. The concept that the firm is the property of shareholders ranked third with 67 percent.

Clearly Japan puts the interest of employees before that of shareholders. Her current unemployment rate of around three percent even in a prolonged recession is a testimony to this. Though increasingly challenged, job security is still defended as the main-

stream ideology, as two major spokesmen of the Japanese business community recently proclaimed: Fumio Sato, Chairman of Toshiba Corporation, said that to discharge employees is 'the most serious sin' a president can commit and Takeshi Moroi, Chairman of Chichibu Cement, said that job security is the 'responsibility of the corporation'.

Key implications of the different approaches

The central characteristic of the Japanese pluralistic concept is the alignment of the company's goals and interests with those of the stakeholders. This leads to a higher degree of cohesion between the firm's stakeholders, i.e. shareholders, management, employees, the main bank, major suppliers and distributors. They pull together toward a common purpose: the company's survival and prosperity. They share the implicit consensus that their respective interests are realized and promoted through their long-term commitment and cooperation with the firm. Maximization of general benefit, or the firm's

FIGURE 11.4.1   Whose company is it?

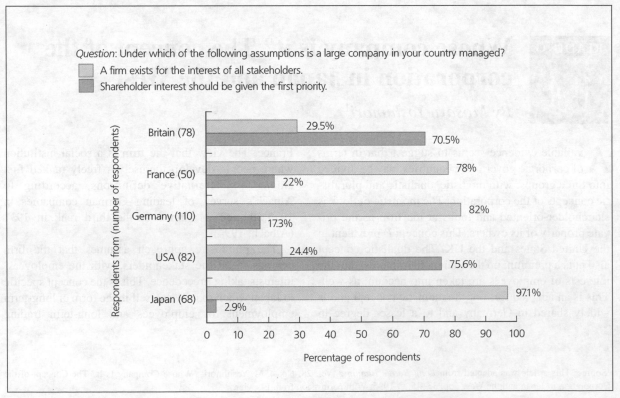

Question: Under which of the following assumptions is a large company in your country managed?
- A firm exists for the interest of all stakeholders.
- Shareholder interest should be given the first priority.

Respondents from (number of respondents):

Britain (78): 29.5% / 70.5%
France (50): 78% / 22%
Germany (110): 82% / 17.3%
USA (82): 24.4% / 75.6%
Japan (68): 97.1% / 2.9%

Percentage of respondents

'wealth maximizing capacity', as Drucker (1991) puts it, and not self-interest, is the name of the game. Michael Porter characterizes such relationship as 'a greater community of interest' and categorizes it as 'quasi integration', that is an intermediate form between long-term contracts and full ownership. According to Porter (1980), this type of interdependent relationship among the stakeholders combines some of the benefits of vertical integration without incurring the corresponding costs. Suzuki and Wright (1985) argue that a Japanese company, though legally independent, should be regarded rather as a division of a big conglomerate. This 'network structure' provides a system of collective security in time of crisis, as will be illustrated later.

Within the Japanese concept of the corporation, the company president is the representative of both the employees and the other stakeholders. The source of legitimacy of the president is derived primarily from his role as the defender of job security for the employees. This is understandable given the fact that the employees constitute the most important power base for the president, as Figure 11.4.2 indicates. His secondary role is as the arbitrator for the divergent interests of the stakeholders so that a long-term balance of interests is achieved.

In contrast, under the Anglo-American 'monistic' concept where shareholders' interests are given primacy, the CEO represents the interests of the shareholders as their 'ally', according to Abegglen and Stalk, though their respective objectives may diverge at times. Understandably other stakeholders also seek to maximize their respective interests. In this 'zero-sum game', the firm ends up as a mere vehicle by which to satisfy the self-centred needs of the different stakeholders. The company then becomes an organization 'external' to the interests of its stakeholders, as Abegglen and Stalk (1985) point out, with no one caring about the long-term destiny of the firm itself. This makes a turnaround process more difficult, once a firm is confronted with financial difficulties.

The relationship between the firm and its main bank

In the Japanese *Keiretsu* the main bank assumes a pivotal role owing to its monitoring and disciplinary

FIGURE 11.4.2   Job security or dividends?

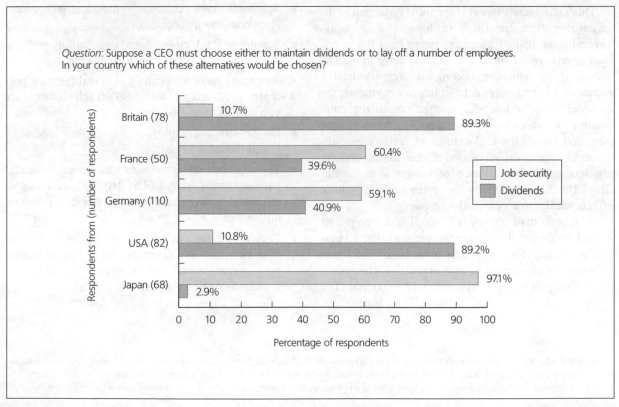

function based on its financial and equity claims. The main bank is not to be confused with the *Zaibatsu*[2] institution, as any bank, whether *Zaibatsu* or non-*Zaibatsu* in origin, can assume this role. The firm's main bank relations are characterized as follows:

- The main bank is typically the largest or one of the largest providers of loans and makes available on a preferential basis long-term and comprehensive financial services covering deposits, discounting of notes, foreign exchange transactions, advice in financial planning, agents on other loans, etc.

- Cross-shareholdings and interlocking directorships result in information sharing through official and personal contacts.

- The rescue of a client firm is attempted when it is targeted in a hostile take-over bid. Thus none of the hostile take-over attempts by a well-known raider, Minebea, were successful. An attempt to acquire Janome, a sewing machine maker, was thwarted by its main bank, Saitama Bank, another raid on Sankyo Seiki was frustrated by its main bank, Mitsubishi Bank who later arranged for an equity participation by Nippon Steel.

- Direct intervention in the turnaround process occurs in case the borrower company faces serious financial distress.

This main bank support is the most important motivation for Japanese firms to have a main bank. Typically the bailout measures range from the provision of emergency finance at an early stage in the crisis to, if the situation becomes more serious, the reduction of or exemption from interest payments, the engineering of a financial reorganization, the bank sending its own executives to supervise the reorganization, and finally the replacement of ineffectual management, the reorganization of the assets and an arrangement for an alliance or merger with another firm. The intervention by the main bank may have effects similar to an external take-over.

A recent mail survey of 305 listed companies excluding financial corporations suggests that 70 percent of them believe that their main bank would provide them with support in case of a crisis. The results of another poll of 354 corporations of Nikkeiren (The Japanese Federation of Employers' Associations) published in August 1994, indicated that 81.6 percent are in favour of maintaining the main bank system.

A Japan–US comparison of stakeholder relations

The relations among stakeholders in Japan, in particular the firm–main bank relations, may be better understood when a firm faces a crisis. The turnaround processes of Toyo Kogyo, manufacturer of Mazda passenger cars, and of Chrysler are contrasted.

Toyo Kogyo

In 1974, Toyo Kogyo was confronted with a financial crisis due to its large stockpile of unsold cars. Mazda cars powered by Wankel rotary engines were less fuel-efficient, a serious disadvantage after the first oil crisis of 1973. Sumitomo Bank, the main bank, played a vital role in the bailout operations.

- Sumitomo Bank made a public assurance to stand by the distressed company, and a commitment to carry any new loans.

- Sumitomo Bank sent a team of seven directors to control and implement the reorganization process.

- Sumitomo Bank replaced the president with a new, more competent successor.

- Sumitomo Bank co-ordinated negotiations with the other lenders to establish a financial package.

- Sumitomo group companies switched their car purchases to Mazda and bought 8000 vehicles over six years.

- No lay-off of employees but factory operators joined the sales force.

- The suppliers and subcontractors agreed to extend payment terms from 189 to 210 days, resulting in estimated savings in interest payments of several billion yen.

- They also agreed to price reductions of 14 percent over two and a half years. Joint cost reduction programmes were also implemented, with cost reductions of ¥123 billion over 4 years.

---

[2] *Zaibatsu* is a prewar conglomerate under family ownership and control. Mitsubishi, Mitsui, Sumitomo, and other *Zaibatsu* controlled a majority of Japan's large industrial, financial and service firms before World War II. They were broken up by the Occupation forces after the war. Today the firms of a former *Zaibatsu* form a loose federation based on their common tradition and business relationship.

FIGURE 11.4.3 The Japanese CEO's most important power base

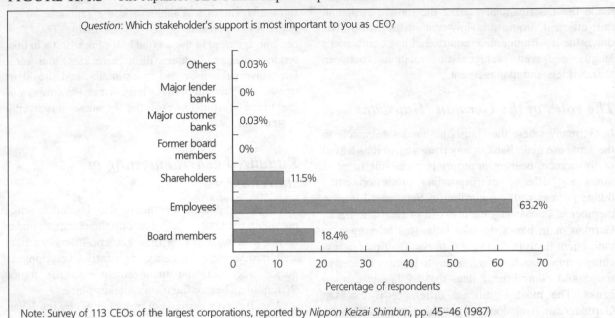

Question: Which stakeholder's support is most important to you as CEO?

Others — 0.03%
Major lender banks — 0%
Major customer banks — 0.03%
Former board members — 0%
Shareholders — 11.5%
Employees — 63.2%
Board members — 18.4%

Percentage of respondents

Note: Survey of 113 CEOs of the largest corporations, reported by *Nippon Keizai Shimbun*, pp. 45–46 (1987)

- The employees accepted rescheduling of bonus payments, contributing ¥4 billion in increased annual cash flow. They also agreed to restraints in wage and bonus increases.

Chrysler

In the turnaround process at Chrysler, the stakeholders – the banks, the union, and the dealers – distrusted each other, were afraid of being stuck with an unfair burden and shunned responsibility for saving the firm. Its lead bank, Manufacturers Hanover Trust, did not or could not make an assurance to bail Chrysler out, although the bank's chairman had been on the Chrysler board for years. The chairman declared that he would approve no more unguaranteed loans to Chrysler because of its fiduciary responsibility to its shareholders and depositors. Lack of solidarity of the lenders and other stakeholders made the turnaround process dependent on government guarantees. As Iacocca sarcastically wrote, 'it took longer to get $655 million in concessions from the four hundred lending institutions than it did to get the loan guarantees of $1.5 billion passed by the entire US Congress'. For him, 'the congressional hearings were as easy as changing a flat tire on a spring day, compared to dealing with the banks'. Such financial concerns occupied top management for most of one year.

- Manufacturers Hanover Trust arranged for an agreement on a $455 million revolving credit with 80 American banks.

- Manufacturers Hanover Trust's chairman pleaded in Congress for a Federal loan guarantee for Chrysler.

- Manufacturers Hanover Trust urged its colleagues to accept Chrysler's packages of concessions.

- The labour union agreed to a wage restraint and curtailment of paid days off.

- Suppliers agreed to price reductions.

Legal restrictions on banks in the United States

Contrary to Japan and Germany, the United States traditionally put a premium on investor protection by insisting on complete and accurate disclosure of company information, portfolio diversification and on a sharp line of demarcation between investor and manager roles. Thus the Glass-Steagall Act, the Bank Holding Company Act of 1956, the Investment Company Act of 1940, the ERISA Act of 1974 and finally the rules against insider trading all combine to prohibit or inhibit investing funds of banks and pension plans in the stock of any single corporation, and participation in the management of the portfolio and borrower companies. This legal framework coupled with banks' preference for liquidity over investment has made the US financial market the most transparent, fair, efficient, liquid and low-cost in the world. The downside is fragmented equity holding, and arm's length or even antagonistic relations between shareholders and management.

The roles of the German 'Hausbank'

In Germany where the Hausbank has a similar role to the Japanese main bank, many firms regard it as a kind of 'insurance, bearing appropriate premiums in good times and offering corresponding protection when things go less well', according to Schneider-Linné, a member of the Management Board of Deutsche Bank. German main banks do take initiatives to reorganize their client firms in financial distress. Their part in rescuing companies, however, seems to be more limited in scope and commitment than that of Japanese main banks. The most significant difference is that the German main bank does not get directly involved in the management of the distressed firm and that the rescue concept itself is usually left to management consultancy firms. The German bank usually confines itself to rescheduling interest and principal payments or reducing interest charges and debts, giving advice to management and bringing in suitable new management.

The flaws in the Japanese concept of the corporation

Needless to say, Japan's close-knit, inward-looking concept of the corporation has its downsides. The most serious one is inefficient monitoring of top management. Indeed, there has been practically no control exercised over top management except through the product market. Through cross-shareholdings, cross-directorships and long-term business relations, Japanese managers have isolated themselves from take-over threats and shareholder pressures and thus have been able to pursue expansionist strategies throughout the post-war period, particularly during the high-growth period up until the mid-1970s. Certainly their growth-oriented strategies have been beneficial to companies, as many Japanese firms rose to dominant positions in the international market. In the process managers have not generally sought to maximize their personal income as in some other countries. The remuneration level of Japanese top executives is much lower than international levels.

But the potential risk of ineffective monitoring of top management was inherent in the Japanese governance system, as it is also in Germany. This flaw became apparent in the second half of the 1980s in horrendous wastes of capital through reckless and unrelated diversifications and investments, and illegal or unethical behaviour of many large firms. We now examine major dysfunctions of the Japanese monitoring system.

Ritualized general meeting of shareholders

The Japanese general meeting of shareholders is without doubt the least effective among the countries under review as a monitor over management. It has degenerated into a mere formality, as nearly everything is decided between the management and the major shareholders before the meeting takes place.

A mail survey carried out in June 1993 by the Japan Association of Statutory Auditors on 1106 public corporations revealed that nearly 80 percent of their general meetings of shareholders ended in less than half an hour including recess time. Less than three percent last for more than an hour. At the meeting not a single question was posed by shareholders in 87 percent of the companies studied, not to speak of shareholder proposals which were not made at all in 98 percent of the companies.

Limited monitoring power of the chairman of the board

Unlike in Anglo-American and French companies, board chairmanship and presidency of Japanese corporations are seldom assumed concurrently by the same person. At first sight, therefore, the supervisory function of the chairman and the executive function of the president seem to be clearly separated. Theoretically the chairman is expected to exercise control over the president. But this is not the case, because the Japanese board chairmanship is usually an honorary, symbolic or advisory position, the last step on the ladder before retirement from the company after having been president for several years. The chairman rarely interferes with the day-to-day managerial activities of the president, though his advice may be occasionally sought on major strategic decisions or on the appointment of key managerial positions. He spends most of his time representing the firm at external functions and activities, such as meetings of trade and economic associations, government commissions etc. This 'half-retired' position of the chairman of the board is well illustrated by the fact that in 96 percent of the firms the president, not the chairman, presides over the general meeting of shareholders.

Board members are appointed by the president

The fundamental cause of the board's dysfunction is that in most large firms nearly all of the board members are appointed by the president and naturally pledge their allegiance to him. In addition there are no or very few outside directors. If any, they are typically representatives from affiliated companies such as suppliers, subcontractors, etc. with little influence on the president. There is no distinction, therefore, between directors and officers. The board members are supposed to monitor the president who is their immediate superior, with obvious adverse consequences.

Boards are too large

The average board in Japanese companies is larger than in any of the other industrialized nations examined here. Sakura Bank, second largest bank in revenue in 1993, is the champion with 62 board members. The average board size for the top three construction firms is about 52, for the top three trading companies close to 50, and for the three largest automobile and banking companies around 43.

This inflation of board sizes is due to the fact that board membership is often a reward for long and faithful service or major contributions to the company. The title of board member is useful to obtain business from major customers. In short, the Japanese board of directors has been transformed into a motivating and marketing tool. With such a large board with most directors engaged in day-to-day line activities, it is practically impossible to discuss any matter of importance in detail, let alone advise and sanction the president.

Ineffective statutory auditors

Large listed corporations are legally subject to two monitoring mechanisms: statutory auditors and independent certified public accountants. Neither is functioning properly. The primary auditing function of statutory auditors is to prevent any decisions by the directors to be taken or implemented which are judged to be in violation of laws or articles of incorporation, or otherwise detrimental to the company. Statutory audi-

tors thus perform both accounting and operating audits to protect the interests of the company and the stakeholders by forestalling any adverse decisions and actions before it is too late. On paper they are given powerful authority, including the right to suspend illegal actions by a board member. But actual use of this power is unheard of. The root cause of the lack of monitoring by the statutory auditors is that they are selected by the president whom they are supposed to monitor.

A study conducted by Kobe University reveals that 57 percent of statutory auditors are selected by the president and 33 percent by directors or the executive committee and endorsed by the president. This shows that 90 percent of the statutory auditors are indeed chosen by the president for perfunctory approval at the shareholders' meeting.

Flawed corporate governance in the West

Nor do the monitoring capabilities of Western boards function perfectly due firstly to the CEO assuming the board chairmanship (except in Germany where this is legally prohibited), secondly due to the psychological and even economic dependence of outside (non-executive) directors on the CEO/chairman, and lastly due to multiple directorships.

CEO/chairman duality – USA, UK, and France

These three countries share the same problem as expressed by the chairman of Delta Metal; 'The problem with British companies is that the chairman marks his own papers'. In the United States, 75 percent of large manufacturing companies are run by the CEO-chairman, according to a survey by Rechner and Dalton (1989). CEO duality is also prevalent in the UK where in 60 percent of large firms including financial corporations the chairman is also the CEO, according to a Korn Ferry International survey. In France firms can opt either for the conventional single board or the two-tier board system inspired by the German model. An overwhelming majority of large firms have the traditional single board where in most cases the chairman is also the CEO, as the title Président Directeur-Général indicates.

In Germany the separation between the supervisory board and the management board is legally assured as no member of the one board is allowed to be a member of the other at the same time. Theoretically, the German system precludes the power concentration on the CEO-chairman as seen in other countries, thus assuring independent monitoring by the chairman of the supervisory board over the management board. But the reality does not altogether reflect the intention of the legislation. According to an empirical study by Gerum (1991) on 62 large firms, this monitoring mechanism functions effectively only in firms whose supervisory board is dominated by one or more block-vote holders. The study shows that in a majority of 64 percent of the sample firms the management board influences the supervisory board. Only in 13 percent of firms does the supervisory board discharge its over-sight functions over the management board. In the remaining 23 percent of firms, the supervisory board is strongly involved in the decision making of the man-agement board, a power concentration similar to the Anglo-American, French and Japanese situations. The researcher concludes that this represents 'pathological traits' in the light of the objectives sought by the law (Gerum, 1991).

Lack of neutrality of outside directors – USA and Europe

In the United States the board chairman (who is often also the CEO as mentioned already) recommends can-didates for outside directors in 81 percent of the 600 firms surveyed by Korn Ferry International. In the UK 80 percent of the non-executive (outside) directors are selected from among the 'old-boy network', reducing their monitoring potential, as reported by Sir Adrian Cadbury. A similar situation is observed in France where new candidates for board membership are rec-ommended by the CEO-chairman in 93.5 percent of the firms controlled by owner-managers, and in 92 percent of firms under managerial control, according to a study by Charreaux and Pitol-Belin (1990). In Germany, no hard data are available, but the preced-ing findings of Gerum on the dominance of the man-agement board over the supervisory board lead us to infer that in a majority of large firms it is the man-agers on the management board that effectively deter-mine who will be the members of the supervisory board.

Multiple directorships – USA and Europe

This is a phenomenon that does not exist in Japan. All the Western countries reviewed here share this conven-tion. In the United States 72 percent of the CEOs of the largest 50 corporations serve on the board of other firms and 50 percent of them have more than 6 outside directorships, according to Bassiry and Denkmejian (1990). In Germany the maximum number of board memberships is set at 10 without counting director-ships in subsidiary companies. Bleicher's study of directors (1987) shows that 36 percent of his sample assume directorship in more than three corporations. Whenever there is spectacular corporate mismanage-ment, further reduction in the maximum number of directorships is urged, often to five. In the UK 58 per-cent of directors assume non-executive directorship positions in other companies and 81 percent of them hold two to four directorships (Nash, 1990). In France the legal limit is eight directorships plus five at sub-sidiary firms. Of 13,000 directors, 47 percent have one to 13 outside director positions, two percent have 14 to 50 positions, according to a survey by Bertolus and Morin (1987).

The question is to what extent they can be counted on to be an effective monitor and advisor. They surely have enough problems in managing their own com-pany. They do not have in-depth knowledge or infor-mation on the business and internal problems of the other companies where they serve as outside directors.

Which system will win out?

The inevitable and tempting question which follows from this kind of international comparison is which system has superiority, if any at all, over the other in the long run in the light of two fundamental criteria: efficiency and equity.

As for efficiency we have limited evidence but one of the first empirical studies revealing a positive corre-lation between efficiency and the pluralistic concept of the corporation was offered by Kotter and Heskett (1992). They report that firms with cultures that emphasized the importance of all the stakeholders (customers, stockholders, and employees) outper-formed by a huge margin firms that did not (see Table 11.4.1). If sufficient similar evidence is accumulated, we may conclude that the pluralistic concept does enhance a firm's efficiency.

The pluralistic concept seems to be more conducive to an equitable distribution of the firm's income, and fairer sharing of risk and power among the stakehold-ers. This will increase organizational cohesion and sur-vivability, as we have seen in the comparative case studies. Under the monistic concept of the corporation, employees tend to incur a disproportionately higher

TABLE 11.4.1 The pluralistic concept may bring better performance – a US study

11-year growth	Firms emphasizing value to customers, shareholders & employees (%)	Other firms
Revenue	682	166
Workforces	282	36
Stock prices	901	74
Income	756	1

Study carried out between August 1987 and January 1991 with 202 US firms.
Based on: John P. Kotter and James L. Heskett, *Corporate Culture and Performance*, p. 11 (1992).

risk, as their job security is jeopardized in favour of shareholder/manager interests. They are usually the first to bear the brunt of poor decision making by top management, even if they are not responsible for it. This makes it difficult to expect a high commitment from them, under normal conditions or in crisis situations.

Applicability of the pluralistic concept

The pluralistic concept of the corporation may find wider applicability in countries outside Japan and may be a more viable and universal way for the modern corporation to promote efficiency and equity. It is not an ideology unique to Japan. An almost identical concept of the corporation was put forward in 1917 in Germany by Walther Rathenau and in the United States by Adolf Berle/Gardiner Means in 1932, and by Ralph Cordiner in the 1950s.

Walther Rathenau, who was to become Foreign Minister later, succeeded his father as the CEO of the electric engineering firm AEG. In an influential article in 1917 he asserted that 'a big business is not only a product of private interests but it is, individually and collectively, a part of the national economy and of the whole community' (Rathenau, 1923). This thesis is believed to have been instrumental in the later development of the concept of 'the firm itself' (*Unternehmen an sich*), which is close to the pluralistic approach. It paved the way for a dilution of shareholder rights, the protection of management positions, the post-World War II co-determination, and the justification of 'hidden reserves' and shares with multiple votes.

Most probably influenced by Rathenau (quoted twice in their seminal work), Berle and Means (1932) conclude their book with exactly the same proposition. In the last chapter titled *'The New Concept of the Corporation'*, they suggest:

> neither the claims of ownership nor those of control can stand against the paramount interests of the community. . . . The passive property right (i.e. diffused ownership) . . . must yield before the largest interests of the society. It is conceivable indeed it seems almost essential if the corporate system is to survive that the 'control' of the great corporation should develop into a purely neutral technocracy, balancing a variety of claims by various groups in the community and assigning to each a portion of the income stream on the basis of the public policy rather than private cupidity.

A similar ideology was espoused by Ralph Cordiner, CEO of General Electric in the 1950s who advocated that top management, as a trustee, was responsible for managing the company 'in the best interest of shareholder, customers, employees, suppliers, and plant community cities'. This concept of the corporation did not last, however, primarily because of the rise of the hostile take-over in the late 1970s, according to Peter Drucker.

Emerging convergence

The concept of the corporation is firmly rooted in the historic, economic, political and even socio-cultural traditions of the nation. Each approach has its own positive and adverse sides. It would be improbable nor would it be necessary, therefore, that any one concept should drive out another at least in the foreseeable future. Through the cross-fertilization process, nations will be correcting the flaws in their systems, while retaining the core norms. In the process different concepts of the corporation may slowly converge, but certainly not totally. Some signs of such partial convergence are already discernible.

Japan

Japan and Germany are edging towards the Anglo-American model for increased openness and transparency, emphasis of shareholder interest and shorttermism. In Japan the traditional emphasis on job security is being eroded and the process seems to be irreversible in the long run for various reasons: firms' tendency to place merit before seniority, perspectives of low growth economy, the changing industrial structure, competitive pressures from the rapidly developing Asian countries, the increasingly detached attitude of young employees to their company, and so on.

Yotaro Kobayashi, Chairman of Fuji Xerox, for instance, made an almost unprecedented declaration for a Japanese executive to the effect that Japanese management giving top priority to employees was no longer tenable. Several companies recently announced their target return on equity to show their emphasis on shareholder wealth. Mitsubishi Corporation has declared that it will raise ROE from currently 0.6 percent to eight percent by the year 2000. Other listed corporations such as Marubeni, Omron, Daikin, etc. are following suit.

The amended Commercial Code came into force in October 1993, albeit under the usual (salutary) pressure from the United States. Every large company is now required to increase the minimum number of statutory auditors from two to three. The newly introduced stockholders' representative action makes it easier for shareholders to bring lawsuits against company directors as the court fee has been fixed at a flat rate of only ¥8,200 per case, regardless of the size of the claim. The number of shareholders eligible for access to confidential financial documents has been expanded to those with at least three percent ownership, down from the former 10 percent. This revision may be a small step forward but it is still progress.

USA

In the United States, conversely, the traditional restrictions on concentration of funds in a single investment and of board representation at portfolio companies are breaking down. Anti-take-over regulations have been introduced in a number of States, so that the interests of the company, i.e. all stakeholders and particularly employees, are taken into account. Employees are regarded as a major stakeholder and are involved in small group activities and share ownership. Long-term business relations are being introduced notably in the automobile industry between subcontractors and assemblers.

Germany

In Germany legislation against insider trading is finally being passed. The US style audit committee is advocated by senior executives and by scholars as one of the effective remedies to ensure the proper monitoring of the supervisory board. Shareholder activism by Anglo-American institutional shareholders as well as domestic individual shareholders is increasing. In an unprecedented move the CEO and CFO of Metallgesellschaft were simply fired for their responsibility in the alleged mismanagement of oil futures business. Increased reliance on the New York capital markets and the future location of the EU's central bank in Frankfurt am Main will certainly accelerate the Anglo–Americanization process. Disclosure by Daimler-Benz of its hidden assets to conform to the SEC regulations for listing on the New York Stock Exchange is symbolic.

Conclusion

The business organization is one of the few social institutions where the deficit of democracy is pronounced, compared with the national governance system. Lack of consensus as to whose interest the company should be promoting, and insufficient checks and balances among various corporate governance mechanisms are some of the evidence. As Prof. Rappaport (1990) of the Northwestern University stresses, corporate governance is 'the last frontier of reform' of the public corporation. This reform is a daunting challenge, but it will determine the economic fate of any industrialized nation in the next century.

FURTHER READING

Readers interested in delving deeper into the topic of organizational purpose have a richness of sources from which to choose. A good introductory work is the textbook *International Corporate Governance* by Robert Tricker, which also contains many classic readings and a large number of interesting cases. One of the excellent readings reprinted in Tricker's book is Henry Mintzberg's article 'Who Should Control the Corporation?', which provides a stimulating insight into the basic questions surrounding the topic of organizational purpose. Another good overview of the issues and literature in the area of corporate governance is presented in the book *Strategic Leadership: Top Executives and Their Effects on Organizations* by Sydney Finkelstein and Donald Hambrick.

Other worthwhile follow-up readings on the topic of corporate governance include the book by Ada Demb and Friedrich Neubauer, *The Corporate Board: Confronting the Paradoxes*, and an excellent comparison of five national governance systems given in the book *Keeping Good Company*, by Jonathan Charkham. Recent edited volumes well worth reading are *Capital Markets and Corporate Governance*, by Nicolas Dimsdale and Martha Prevezer, and *Corporate Governance: Economic, Management and Financial Issues*, by Kevin Keasey, Steve Thompson and Mike Wright.

For further reading on the topic of shareholder value, Alfred Rappaport's book *Creating Shareholder Value* is the obvious place to start. A good follow-up reading is Michael Jensen's article 'Corporate Control and the Politics of Finance'. For a very fundamental point of view, Milton Friedman's classic article 'The Social Responsibility of Business is to Increase Its Profits', is also highly recommended. For a stinging attack on the stakeholder concept, readers are directed to 'The Defects of Stakeholder Theory', by Elaine Sternberg.

For a more positive view of stakeholder theory, Edward Freeman's *Strategic Management: A Stakeholder Approach* is still the book at which to begin. Only recently has stakeholder theory really attracted significant academic attention. Excellent works in this new crop include 'Instrumental Stakeholder Theory: A Synthesis of Ethics and Economics', by Thomas Jones, and 'The Stakeholder Theory of the Corporation: Concepts, Evidence, and Implications', by Thomas Donaldson and Lee Preston.

On the topic of corporate social responsibility, there are a number of good books that can be consulted. Archie Carroll's, *Business and Society: Ethics and Stakeholder Management* can be recommended, while the book *International Business and Society*, by Steven Wartick and Donna Wood, has a stronger international perspective. Good articles include 'The Corporate Social Policy Process: Beyond Business Ethics, Corporate Social Responsibility and Corporate Social Responsiveness', by Edwin Epstein, and the more academic 'A Stakeholder Framework For Analyzing and Evaluating Corporate Social Performance', by Max Clarkson.

For an explicit link between strategy and ethics, the book *Corporate Strategy and the Search For Ethics*, by Edward Freeman and Daniel Gilbert, provides a good point of entry. The more recent article 'Strategic Planning As If Ethics Mattered', by LaRue Hosmer, is also highly recommended. Many books on the general link between ethics and business, such as Thomas Donaldson's *Ethics in International Business*, deal with major strategy issues as well.

Finally, on the topic of corporate mission a very useful overview of the literature is given in the reader *Mission and Business Philosophy*, edited by Andrew Campbell and Kiran Tawadey. Good follow-up works not in this reader are Derek Abell's classic book *Defining the Business: The Starting Point of Strategic Planning*, and the article 'Mission Analysis: An Operational Approach', by Nigel Piercy and Neil Morgan. An interesting book emphasizing the importance of vision is *Built To Last: Successful Habits of Visionary Companies*, by James Collins and Jerry Porras.

REFERENCES

Abbeglen, J., and Stalk, G. (1985) *Kaisha, the Japanese Corporation*, Basic Books, New York.

Abell, D. (1980) *Defining the Business: The Starting Point of Strategic Planning*, Prentice Hall, Englewood Cliffs, NJ.

Ackermann, R.W., and Bauer R.A. (1976) *Corporate Social Performance: The Modern Dilemma*, Reston, Reston, VA.

Ackoff, R.L. (1974) *Redesigning the Future*, Wiley, New York.

Albach, H. (1994) 'Wertewandel Deutscher Manager', in: H. Albach, (ed.), *Werte und Unternehmensziele im Wandel der Zeit*.

Alkhafaji, A.F. (1989) *A Stakeholder Approach to Corporate Governance: Managing a Dynamic Environment*, Quorum Books, Westport, CT.

Ansoff, I. (1965) *Corporate Strategy: An Analytic Approach to Business Policy for Growth and Expansion*, McGraw-Hill, New York.

Axelrod, R. (1976) *The Structure of Decision: The Cognitive Maps of Political Elites*, Princeton University Press, Princeton, NJ.

Barnard, C. (1938) *The Function of the Executive*, Harvard University Press, Cambridge, MA.

Bartlett, C.A., and Ghoshal, S. (1994) 'Changing the Role of Top Management: Beyond Strategy to Purpose', *Harvard Business Review*, November–December, pp. 79–88.

Bassiry, G.R., and Denkmejian, H. (1990) 'The American Corporate Elite: A Profile', *Business Horizons*, May–June.

Baysinger, B.D., and Hoskisson, R.E. (1990) 'The Composition of Boards of Directors and Strategic Control: Effects of Corporate Strategy', *Academy of Management Review*, Vol. 15, No. 1, January, pp. 72–81.

Berle, A.A., and Means, G.C. (1932) *The Modern Corporation and Private Property*, Transaction Publishers, Mcmillan, New York.

Bertolus, J., and Morin, F. (1987) 'Conseil d'Administration', *Science et Vie Économie*, Vol. 33, November.

Blair, M. (1995) *Ownership and Control: Rethinking Corporate Governance for the Twenty-First Century*, Brookings Institution, Washington.

Bleicher, K. (1987) *Der Aufsichtsrat im Wandel, Verlag Bertelsmann-Stiftung*, Guetersloh.

Bourgeois, L.J., and Brodwin, D.R. (1983) 'Putting Your Strategy into Action', *Strategic Management Planning*, March–May.

Bucholz, R.A. (1986) *Business Environment and Public Policy*, Prentice Hall, Englewood Cliffs, NJ.

Buono, A.F., and Nichols, L.T. (1985) *Corporate Policy, Values and Social Responsibility*, Praeger, New York.

Cameron, K.S. (1986) 'Effectiveness as a Paradox: Consensus and Conflict in Conceptions of Organizational Effectiveness', *Management Science*, 549, May.

Campbell, A., and Tawadey, K. (1990) *Mission and Business Philosophy*, Butterworth-Heinemann, Oxford.

Campbell, A., and Yeung, S. (1991) 'Creating a Sense of Mission', *Long Range Planning*, Vol. 24, No. 4, August, pp.10–20.

Cannon, T. (1992) *Corporate Responsibility*, Pitman, London.

Carroll, A.B. (1993) *Business and Society: Ethics and Stakeholder Management*, Second Edition, South-Western Publishing, Cincinnati.

Charkham, J. (1994) *Keeping Good Company: A Study of Corporate Governance in Five Countries*, Oxford University Press, Oxford.

Charreaux, G., and Pitol-Belin, J. (1990) *Le Conseil d'Administration*.

Clarke, T. (1998) 'The Stakeholder Corporation: A Business Philosophy for the Information Age', *Long Range Planning*, Vol. 31, No. 2, April, pp. 182–194.

Clarkson, M.B.E. (1995) 'A Stakeholder Framework For Analyzing and Evaluating Corporate Social Performance', *Academy of Management Review*, Vol. 20, No. 1, January, pp. 92–117.

Cochran, P.L., and Wartick, S.L. (1994) 'Corporate Governance: A Review of the Literature', in: R.I. Tricker (ed.), *International Corporate Governance: Text, Readings and Cases*, Prentice-Hall, Singapore.

Collins, J.C., and Porras, J. (1994) *Built To Last: Successful Habits of Visionary Companies*, Random House, London.

Collins, J.C., and Porras, J. (1996) 'Building Your Company's Vision', *Harvard Business Review*, Vol. 75, No. 5, September–October, pp. 65–77.

Cummings, S., and Davies, J. (1994) 'Mission, Vision, Fusion', *Long Range Planning*, Vol. 27, No. 6, December, pp. 147–150.

David, F.R. (1989) 'How Companies Define Their Mission', *Long Range Planning*, Vol. 22, No. 1, February, pp. 90–97.

Demb, A., and Neubauer, F.F. (1992) *The Corporate Board: Confronting the Paradoxes*, Oxford University Press, Oxford.

Dill, W.R. (1975) 'Public Participation in Corporate Planning: Strategic Management in a Kibitzer's World', *Long Range Planning*, pp. 57–63.

Dimsdale, N., and Prevezer, M. (eds.) (1994) *Capital Markets and Corporate Governance*, Oxford University Press, Oxford.

Donaldson, L., and Davis, J.H. (1995) 'Boards and Company Performance: Research Challenges the Conventional Wisdom', *Corporate Governance*, Vol. 2, pp. 151–160.

Donaldson, T. (1989) *Ethics in International Business,* Oxford University Press, London.

Donaldson, T., and Preston, L.E. (1995) 'The Stakeholder Theory of the Corporation: Concepts, Evidence, and Implications', *Academy of Management Review*, Vol. 20, No. 1, January, pp. 65–91.

Drucker, P.F. (1984) 'The New Meaning of Corporate Social Responsibility', *California Management Review*, Vol. 26, No. 2, Winter, pp. 53–63.

Drucker, P.F. (1991) 'Reckoning with the Pension Fund Revolution', *Harvard Business Review,* March–April.

Eisenhardt, K.M. (1989) 'Agency Theory: An Assessment and Review', *Academy of Management Review*, Vol. 14, No. 1, January, pp. 57–74.

Emshoff, J.R., and Freeman, R.E. (1981) 'Stakeholder Management: A Case Study of the U.S. Brewers Association and the Container Issue', in: R. Schultz, (ed.), *Applications of Management Science*, JAI Press, Greenwich.

Epstein, E.M. (1987) 'The Corporate Social Policy Process: Beyond Business Ethics, Corporate Social Responsibility, and Corporate Social Responsiveness', *California Management Review*, Vol. 29, No. 3, Spring, pp. 99–114.

Falsey, T.A. (1989) *Corporate Philosophies and Mission Statements*, Quorum Books, New York.

Finkelstein, S., and Hambrick D.C. (1996) *Strategic Leadership: Top Executives and Their Effects on Organizations*, West, St. Paul.

Forbes, D.P., and Milliken F.J. (1999) 'Cognition and Corporate Governance: Understanding Boards of Directors as Strategic Decision-Making Groups', *Academy of Management Review*, Vol. 24, No. 3, July, pp. 489–505.

Freeman, R.E. (1984) *Strategic Management: A Stakeholder Approach*, Pitman/Ballinger, Boston.

Freeman, R.E., and Gilbert Jr., D.R. (1988) *Corporate Strategy and the Search for Ethics*, Prentice Hall, Englewood Cliffs, NJ.

Freeman, R.E., and Liedtka, J. (1991) 'Corporate Social Responsibility: A Critical Approach', *Business Horizons*, July-August.

Freeman, R.E., and Reed, D.L. (1983) 'Stockholders and Stakeholders: A New Perspective on Corporate Governance', *California Management Review*, Vol. 25, No. 3, Spring, pp. 88–106.

Friedman, M. (1970) 'The Social Responsibility of Business is to Increase Its Profits, *The New York Times Magazine*, September 13.

Gerum, E. (1991) 'Aufsichtratstypen: Ein Beitrag zur Theorie der Organisation der Unternehmungsführung', *Die Betriebswirtschaft*, No. 6.

Goodpaster, K.E. (1991) 'Business Ethics and Stakeholder Analysis', *Business Ethics Quarterly*, January.

Guthrie, J., and Turnbull, S. (1994) 'Audit Committees: Is There a Role for Corporate Senates and/or Stakeholder Councils?', *Corporate Governance*, Vol. 3, pp. 78–89.

Harrison, J.R. (1987) 'The Strategic Use of Corporate Board Committees', *California Management Review*, Vol. 30, pp. 109–125.

Hart, O.D. (1995) *Firms, Contracts and Financial Structure*, Clarendon Press, Oxford.

Hax, A.C. (1990) 'Redefining the Concept of Strategy and the Strategy Formation Process', *Planning Review*, May–June, pp. 34–40.

Hayes, R., and Abernathy, W. (1980) 'Managing Our Way to Economic Decline', *Harvard Business Review*, Vol. 58, No. 4, pp. 66–77.

Hoffman, W.M. (1989) 'The Cost of a Corporate Conscience', *Business and Society Review*, Vol. 94, Spring, pp. 46–47.

Hosmer, L.T. (1994) 'Strategic Planning as if Ethics Mattered', *Strategic Management Journal*, Vol. 15, Summer, pp. 17–34.

Jensen, M.C. (1991) 'Corporate Control and the Politics of Finance', *Journal of Applied Corporate Finance*, Vol. 4, pp. 13–33.

Jensen, M.C., and Meckling, W.H. (1976) 'Theory of the Firm, Managerial Behavior, Agency Costs, and Ownership Structure', *Journal of Financial Economics*, Vol. 3, No. 4, October, pp. 305–360.

Jones, T.M. (1995) 'Instrumental Stakeholder Theory: A Synthesis of Ethics and Economics', *Academy of Management Review*, Vol. 20, No.2 , April, pp. 404–437.

Keasey, K., Thompson, S., and Wright, M. (eds.) (1997) *Corporate Governance: Economic, Management, and Financial Issues*, Oxford University Press, Oxford.

Kiefer, C.F., and Senge, P.M. (1987) *Metanoic Organizations: Experiments in Organizational Innovation*, Innovation Associates, Framingham, MA.

Klemm, M., Sanderson, S., and Luffman, G. (1991) 'Mission Statements', *Long Range Planning*, Vol. 24, No. 3, June, pp. 73–78.

Klimoski, R., and Mohammed, S. (1994) 'Team Mental Model: Construct or Metaphor', *Journal of Management*, Vol. 20, pp. 403–437.

Kotter, J.P., and Heskett, J.L. (1992) *Corporate Culture and Performance*, The Free Press, New York.

Langtry, B. (1994) 'Stakeholders and the Moral Responsibilities of Business', *Business Ethics Quarterly*, Vol. 4, pp. 431–443.

Levitt, T. (1960) 'Marketing Myopia', *Harvard Business Review*, Vol. 38, July–August, pp. 45–56.

McCoy, C.S. (1985) *Management of Values*, Ballinger, Cambridge, MA.

Mintzberg, H. (1984) 'Who Should Control the Corporation?', *California Management Review*, Vol. 27, No. 1, Fall, pp. 90–115.

Mitchell, R.K., Agle, B.R., and Wood, D.J. (1997) 'Toward a Theory of Stakeholder Identification and Salience: Defining the Principle of Who and What Really Counts', *Academy of Management Review*, Vol. 22, No. 4, October, pp. 853–886.

Mohn, R. (1989) *Success Through Partnership*, Bantam, London.

Mueller, R.K. (1989) *Board Compass*, Lexington Books, Lexington, MA.

Nash, T. (1990) 'Bit Parts and Board Games', *Director*, October.

Parkinson, J.E. (1993) *Corporate Power and Responsibility*, Oxford University Press, Oxford.

Pearce, J.A. (1982) 'The Company Mission as a Strategic Tool', *Sloan Management Review*, Spring, pp. 15–24.

Peters, T.J., and Waterman, R.H. (1982) *In Search of Excellence*, Harper & Row, New York.

Piercy, N.F., and Morgan, N.A. (1994) 'Mission Analysis: An Operational Approach', *Journal of General Management*, Vol. 19, No. 3, pp. 1–16.

Porter, M.E. (1980) *Competitive Strategy: Techniques for Analyzing Industries and Competitors*, Free Press, New York.

Prahalad, C.K., and Bettis, R.A. (1986) 'The Dominant Logic: A New Linkage Between Diversity and Performance', *Strategic Management Journal*, November–December, pp. 485–601.

Rappaport, A. (1986) *Creating Shareholder Value: The New Standard for Business Performance*, The Free Press, New York.

Rappaport, A. (1990) 'The Staying Power of the Public Corporation', *Harvard Business Review*, January–February, Vol. 68, No. 1, p. 96.

Rathenau, W. (1923) *Vom Aktienwesen, eine geschäftliche Betrachtung*, Fischer, Berlin.

Rechner, P.L., and Dalton, D.R. (1989) 'The Impact of CEO as Board Chairperson on Corporate Performance: Evidence vs. Rhetoric', *The Academy of Management Executive*, Vol. 3, No. 2, pp. 141–144.

Senge, P. (1990) *The Fifth Discipline: The Art and Practice of the Learning Organization*, Doubleday, New York.

Solomon, R.C. (1992) *Ethics and Excellence: Cooperation and Integrity in Business*, Oxford University Press, New York.

Spencer, A. (1983) *On the Edge of the Organization: The Role of the Outside Director*, Wiley, New York.

Sternberg, E. (1997) 'The Defects of Stakeholder Theory', *Corporate Governance: An International Review*, Vol. 5, No. 1, January, pp. 3–10.

Stone, C.D. (1975) *Where the Law Ends*, Harper & Row, New York.

Suzuki, S., and Wright, R.W. (1985) 'Financial Structure and Bankruptcy Risk in Japanese Companies', *Journal of International Business Studies*, Spring, pp. 97–110.

Sykes, A. (1994) 'Proposals for Internationally Competitive Corporate Governance in Britain and America', *Corporate Governance*, Vol. 2, No. 4, pp. 187–195.

Treynor, J.L. (1981) 'The Financial Objective in the Widely Held Corporation', *Financial Analysts Journal*, March–April, pp. 68–71.

Tricker, R.I. (ed.) (1994) *International Corporate Governance: Text, Readings and Cases*, Prentice Hall, Singapore.

Walsh, J.P., and Seward, J.K. (1990) 'On the Efficiency of Internal and External Corporate Control Mechanisms', *Academy of Management Review*, Vol. 15, pp. 421–458.

Wartick, S.L., and Wood, D.J. (1998) *International Business and Society*, Blackwell, Oxford.

Yoshimori, M. (1995) 'Whose Company Is It? The Concept of the Corporation in Japan and the West', *Long Range Planning*, Vol. 28, pp. 33–45.

Zahra, S.A., and Pearce, J.A. (1989) 'Boards of Directors and Corporate Financial Performance: A Review and Integrative Model', *Journal of Management*, Vol. 15, pp. 291–334.

CASES

CASE 1

FedEx Corporation: Structural transformation through e-business

By Ali F. Farhoomand and Pauline Ng[1]

[FedEx] has built superior physical, virtual and people networks not just to prepare for change, but to shape change on a global scale: to change the way we all connect with each other in the new Network Economy.

(1999 Annual Report)

[FedEx] is not only reorganizing its internal operations around a more flexible network computing architecture, but it's also pulling-in and in many cases locking-in customers with an unprecedented level of technological integration.

(Janah and Wilder, 1997)

Since its inception in 1973, Federal Express Corporation ('FedEx') had transformed itself from an express delivery company to a global logistics and supply-chain management company. Over the years, the Company had invested heavily in IT systems, and with the launch of the Internet in 1994, the potential for further integration of systems to provide services throughout its customers' supply-chains became enormous. With all the investment in the systems infrastructure over the years and the US$88 million acquisition of Caliber Systems, Inc., in 1998, the Company had built a powerful technical architecture that had the potential to pioneer in Internet commerce. However, despite having all the ingredients for the makings of a successful e-business, the Company's logistics and supply-chain operations were struggling to shine through the historical image of the Company as simply an express delivery business. Furthermore, competition in the transportation/express delivery industry was intense and there were reports that FedEx's transportation volume growth was slowing down, even though they were poised to take advantage of the surge in traffic that e-tailing and electronic commerce (EC) were supposed to generate. Hence, on 19 January, 2000, FedEx announced major reorganisations in the Group's operations in the hope of mak-ing it easier to do business with the entire FedEx family. The mode of operation for the five subsidiary companies was to function independently but to compete collectively. In addition to streamlining many functions, the Group announced that it would pool its sales, marketing and customer services functions, such that customers would have a single point of access to the whole Group. The reorganisation was expected to cost US$100 million over three years. Was this simply a new branding strategy or did FedEx have the right solution to leverage its cross-company synergies and its information and logistics infrastructure to create e-business solutions for its customers?

The express transportation and logistics industry

FedEx invented the air/ground express industry in 1973. Although UPS was founded in 1907 and became America's largest transportation company, it did not compete with FedEx directly in the overnight delivery market until 1982. Competition began with a focus on customer segmentation, pricing and quality of service. For most businesses, physical distribution costs often accounted for 10–30 per cent of sales or more. As competition put pressure on pricing, businesses began to look at ways to cut costs yet improve customer service. The solution was to have a well-managed logistics operation to reduce the length of the order cycle and thus generate a positive effect on cash flow.

The growth of the express transportation and logistics industry was brought about by three main trends: the globalisation of businesses, advances in information technology (IT) and the application of new technology to generate process efficiencies, and the changing market demand for more value-added services. As businesses expanded beyond national boundaries and extended their global reach to take advantage of new markets and cheaper resources, so the movement of goods created new demands for the transportation and logistics industry. With this, the competitiveness of transportation companies depended upon their global network of distribution centres and their ability to deliver to wherever their customers conducted business. Speed became of significance to achieve competitiveness, not only for the transportation companies but also for their customers. The ability to deliver goods quickly shortened the order-to-payment cycle, improved cash flow, and created customer satisfaction.

Advances in IT promoted the globalisation of commerce. The ability to share information between operations/departments within a company and between organisations to generate operation efficiencies, reduce costs and improve customer services was a major breakthrough for the express transportation industry. However, of even greater significance was the way in which new technology redefined logistics. At a time when competition within the transportation industry was tough and transportation companies were seeking to achieve competitive advantages through value-added services, many of these companies expanded into logistics management services. Up until the 1980s, logistics was merely the handling, warehousing and transportation of goods. By combining the functions of materials management and physical distribution, logistics took on a new and broader meaning. It was concerned with inbound as well as outbound material flow, within companies as well as the movement of finished goods from dock-to-dock. With this, the transportation industry responded by placing emphasis not only on the physical transportation, but also on the co-ordination and control of storage and movement of parts and finished goods. Logistics came to include value-added activities such as order processing, distribution centre operations, inventory control, purchasing, production and customer and sales services. Interconnectivity, through the Internet and Intranets and the integration of systems enabled businesses to redefine themselves and to re-engineer their selling and supply-chains. Information came to replace inventory. Just-in-time inventory management helped to reduce costs and improve efficiency. With the advent of IT, express transportation became an aggregation of two main functions: the physical delivery of parcels, and the management and utilisation of the flow of information pertaining to the physical delivery (i.e., control over the movement of goods).

FedEx Corp.

FedEx was the pioneer of the express transportation and logistics industry. Throughout the 27 years of its operation, FedEx's investment in IT had earned the Company a myriad of accolades. Since 1973 FedEx had won over 194 awards for operational excellence. Fundamental to the success of the FedEx business was the vision of its founder.

The visionary behind the business

If we're all operating in a day-to-day environment, we're thinking one to two years out. Fred's thinking five, ten, fifteen years out.
(William Conley, VP, FedEx Logistics, Managing Director Europe)

Fred Smith, Chairman, President and Chief Executive Officer of FedEx Corporation, invented the express distribution industry in March 1973. By capitalising on the needs of businesses for speed and reliability of deliveries, FedEx shortened lead-times for companies. Its next-day delivery service revolutionised the distribution industry. The success of FedEx's distribution business in those early days rested on Smith's commitment to his belief that the opportunities open to a company that could provide reliable overnight delivery of time-sensitive documents and packages were excellent. Despite losses in the first three years of operation due to high capital investments in the physical transportation infrastructure of the business, FedEx began to see profits from 1976 onwards. To compete on a global basis, the key components of the physical infrastructure had to be in place to connect the world's GDP. The underlying philosophy was that wherever business was conducted, there was going to have to be the movement of physical goods.

Under Smith's leadership, the Company had set a few records with breakthrough technology. In the 1980s, FedEx gave away more than 100,000 sets of PCs loaded with FedEx software, designed to link and log customers into FedEx's ordering and tracking systems. FedEx was also the first to issue hand-held scanners to its drivers that alerted customers of when packages were picked up or delivered. Then in 1994, FedEx became the first big transportation company to launch a Website that included tracking and tracing capabilities. Very early on, Smith could foresee that the Internet was going to change the way businesses would operate and the way people would interact. By applying IT to the business, FedEx leapfrogged the rest of the industry. Smith was the visionary who forced his company and other companies to think outside of the proverbial one. The core of FedEx's corporate strategy was to use IT to help customers take advantage of international markets. By 1998, FedEx was a US$10 billion company spending US$1 billion annually on IT developments plus millions more on capital expenditure. It had an IT workforce of 5,000 people.

Building the transportation and logistics infrastructure

In the early years of the FedEx transportation business, Smith insisted that the Company should acquire its own transportation fleet, while competitors were buying space on commercial airlines and sub-contracting their shipments to third parties. The strategy of expanding through acquiring more trucks and planes continued. By the tenth year of operation FedEx earned the accolade of being the first US company to achieve the US$1 billion revenues mark within a decade without corporate acquisitions and mergers.

FedEx was quoted as being the inventor of customer logistics management (Bruner and Bulkley, 1995). As early as 1974, FedEx started logistics operations with the Parts Bank. In those days, a few small set-ups approached FedEx with their warehousing problems and decided on the idea of overnight distribution of parts. With those propositions, FedEx built a small warehouse on the end of its sorting facilities at Memphis. This was FedEx's first attempt at multiple-client warehousing. Customers would call up and order the despatch of parts and the order would be picked up on the same day. That was also FedEx's first value-added service beyond basic transportation. From there, the logistics side of the business snowballed.

Throughout the next three decades, FedEx's transportation business growth was attributable to a number of external factors that FedEx was quick to capitalise on. These included:

- Government deregulation of the airline industry, which permitted the landing of larger freight planes, thus reducing operating costs for FedEx.
- Deregulation of the trucking industry, which allowed FedEx to establish a regional trucking system to lower costs further on short-haul trips.
- Trade deregulation in Asia Pacific, which opened new markets for FedEx. Expanding globally became a priority for FedEx.
- Technological breakthroughs and applications innovations promoted significant advances for customer ordering, package tracking and process monitoring.
- Rising inflation and global competition gave rise to greater pressures on businesses to minimise the costs of operation, including implementation of just-in-time inventory management systems, etc. This also created demands for speed and accuracy in all aspects of business.

As of January 2000, FedEx served 210 countries (making up more than 90 per cent of the world's GDP), operated 34,000 drop-off locations and managed over 10 million square feet of warehouse space worldwide. It had a fleet of 648 aircraft and more than 60,000 vehicles, with a staff of nearly 200,000. It was the world's largest overnight package carrier, with about 30 per cent market share.

Building the virtual information infrastructure

We are really becoming a technology company enabled by transportation.

(David Edmonds, VP,
Worldwide Services Group, FedEx)

Even as early as 1979, a centralised computer system – Customer, Operations, Service, Master On-line System (COSMOS) – kept track of all packages handled by the Company. This computer network relayed data on package movement, pickup, invoicing and delivery to a central database at Memphis headquarters. This was made possible by placing a bar-code on each parcel at the point of pickup and scanning the bar-code at each stage of the delivery cycle.

In 1984, FedEx started to launch a series of technological systems, the PowerShip programme, aimed at improving efficiency and control, which provided the most active customers (over 100,000) with proprietary on-line services (see Exhibit 1). In summary, these PowerShip systems provided additional services to the customer, including storing of frequently used addresses, label printing, on-line package pick-up requests, package tracking, and much more.

EXHIBIT 1　FEDEX'S RECORD OF SYSTEMS INNOVATIONS

1979　COSMOS (Customer Oriented Services and Management Operating System), a global shipment tracking network based on a centralised computer system to manage vehicles, people, packages, routes and weather scenarios on a real-time basis. COSMOS integrated two essential information systems: information about goods being shipped and information about the mode of transportation.

1980　DADS (Digitally Assisted Dispatch System) co-ordinated on-call pickups for customers. It allowed couriers to manage their time and routes through communications via a computer in their vans.

1984　FedEx introduces the first PC-based automated shipping system, later named FedEx PowerShip; a standalone DOS-based system for customers with five or more packages per day. The customer base was immediately transformed into a network that allowed customers to interact with the FedEx system and download software and shipping information.

1984　PowerShip Plus, a DOS-based shipping system integrated with customers' order-entry, inventory-control and accounting systems, for customers who ship more than 100 packages per day.

1985　FedEx was the first to introduce barcode labelling to the ground transportation industry.

1986　The SuperTracker, a hand-held barcode scanner system that captures detailed package information.

1989　FedEx launches an on-board communications system that uses satellite tracking to pinpoint vehicle location.

1991　Rite Routing demonstrates the value of a nationwide, centralised transportation management service.

1991　PowerShip PassPort, a Pentium-class PC system that combines best of PowerShip and PowerShip Plus for customers who ship more than 100 packages a day (1,500 users).

1993　MultiShip, the first carrier-supplied customer automation system to process packages shipped by other transportation providers.

1993　FedEx ExpressClear Electronic Customs Clearance System expedites regulatory clearance while cargo is en route.

1993　PowerShip 3, a client-server shipping system for customers who ship three or more packages per day.

1994　The FedEx Website debuts at www.fedex.com, the first to offer on-line package status tracking so that customers can actually conduct business via the Internet.

1994　DirectLink, a software that lets customers receive, manage and remit payments of FedEx invoices electronically.

1995　FedEx Ship, a Windows-based shipping and tracking software allows customers to process and manage shipping form their desktop (650,000 users). It extended the benefits of PowerShip to all FedEx's customers, providing software and toll-free dial-up to the FedEx network.

1995　FedEx launches the AsiaOne network, a transportation routing system.

1996　FedEx became the first company to allow customers to process shipments on the Internet with FedEx interNetShip, available through www.fedex.com (65,000 users). This allowed customers to create shipping labels, request courier pick-ups and send e-mail notifications to recipients of the shipments, all from the FedEx Website.

1996　FedEx VirtualOrder, a software that links Internet ordering with FedEx delivery and on-line tracking. It also puts customers' catalogues on their Websites for them.

1997   FedEx introduces e-Business Tools for easier connection with FedEx shipping and tracking applications.

1998   FedEx Ship for Workgroups, a Windows-based software housed on a server that lets users share information, such as address-book information, access to shipping logs and a tracking database. The server can be connected to FedEx via either modem or the Internet.

1998   PowerShip mc, a multi-carrier electronic shipping system.

1999   The FedEx Marketplace debuts at www.fedex.com, providing easy access to on-line merchants that offer fast, reliable FedEx express shipping.

1999   The EuroOne network was launched to link 16 cities to FedEx's Paris hub by air and another 21 cities by road-air. Like AsiaOne, this was a transportation routing system.

1999   FedEx MarketPlace, a convenient link to on-line shopping. Through this new portal, shoppers had one-click access to several top on-line merchants that utilised FedEx's delivery services, including Value America, L.L. Bean, and HP Shopping Village (Hewlett-Packard's consumer EC Website).

1999   FedEx made a deal with Netscape to offer a suite of delivery services at its Netcenter portal. This entailed automatically integrating Netscape with the FedEx site. Although customers of Netscape could choose not to use FedEx, the use of an alternative shipper meant that they would not benefit from the efficiencies of the integrated systems. Considering the Netscape Netcenter had more than 13 million members, the deal was a winner for FedEx.

Note: PowerShip had 850,000 on-line customers worldwide; PowerShip, PowerShip 3 and PowerShip PassPort were hardware-based products.

The emergence of electronic data interchange (EDI) and the Internet allowed companies to build one-to-one relationships with their customers. This was the perfect scenario for many manufacturers: the ability to match supply to demand without wastage. FedEx took advantage of such new technologies and started to track back along the supply-chain to the point of raw materials. As they did so, they identified points along the supply-chain where they could provide management services. Often, these services included transportation, order processing and related distribution centre operations, fulfilment, inventory control, purchasing, production and customer and sales services. The ability to interconnect and distribute information to ally the players in a supply-chain became the focus of FedEx's attention. For many of its customers, logistics was viewed as a key means for differentiating their products or services from those of their competitors (see Exhibit 2 for examples of some customer solutions). In other words, logistics became a key part of strategy formulation. As businesses were placing more emphasis on the order cycle as the basis for evaluating customer service levels, FedEx's role in providing integrated logistics systems formed the basis of many partnership arrangements. By helping them to redefine sources and procurement strategies so as to link in with other parties in the supply-chain, such as raw materials suppliers, customers were outsourcing their supply-chain management functions to FedEx, functions that were seen as peripheral to the core of their business (see Figures 1 and 2 for FedEx's coverage of the supply chain through integrated systems). By improving, tightening and synchronising the various parts to the supply-chain, customers saw the benefits of squeezing time and inventory out of the system. Tighter supply-chain management was no longer viewed as a competitive advantage but a competitive imperative.

EXHIBIT 2 CUSTOMER SOLUTIONS

Dell Computers pioneered the direct selling model in the computer industry and succeeded because it was able to keep inventory very low. FedEx provided the system to track and monitor the assembly of each PC on order. Because the assembly line could be in any one of five manufacturing locations around the world, however, FedEx described itself as the conveyor belt for that manufacturing line. FedEx was a key partner for Dell, allowing customised, built-to-order products to be delivered within days of a customer placing an order, a huge advantage in an industry whose components become obsolete at the rate of two per cent per month.

Five years ago, **National Semiconductor Corp.** decided to outsource its warehousing and distribution to FedEx. By 1999, virtually all of NatSemi's products, manufactured by six factories (three being subcontractors) were shipped directly to FedEx's distribution warehouse in Singapore. Hence, FedEx had control over the goods, the warehouse and the despatch of orders (via FedEx transportation, of course). Having complete visibility of NatSemi's order systems allowed FedEx to reduce the average customer delivery cycle from four weeks to two days, and distribution costs from 2.9 per cent of sales to 1.2 per cent. FedEx could pack and fulfil orders without NatSemi having to notify them. In effect, it became the logistics department of NatSemi. Furthermore, this arrangement enabled NatSemi to dispense with seven regional warehouses in the US, Asia and Europe. NatSemi reported savings in the region of US$8 million over the five-year period (see Figure 2).

For **Omaha Steaks**, when orders were received, they would be relayed from Omaha Steaks' IBM AS/400 to its warehouse and simultaneously to FedEx by dedicated line. FedEx would generate the tracking and shipping labels and the orders would be delivered to one of FedEx's regional hubs for onward delivery.

Cisco Systems is a Silicon Valley Internet hardware maker that transacts 80 per cent of its business over the Web. At the end of 1999, FedEx had signed an agreement with Cisco to co-ordinate all of Cisco's shipping over the next two years, and to gradually eliminate Cisco's warehousing over the following three years. How could this be possible? Cisco had factories in the US, Mexico, Scotland, Taiwan and Malaysia. The finished parts were stored in warehouses near the factories awaiting completion of the whole order before it was despatched to the customer. But Cisco did not want to build more warehouses, pay for reshipping and hold massive volumes of inventory in transit. So the solution was to merge the orders in transit. As soon as parts were manufactured, they would be shipped to customers. Once all the parts had arrived at the customer's site, assembly would take place, thus doing away with warehousing. (This was known as the 'merge-in-transit' programme offered to companies such as Micron Computers.) FedEx created a unique system for Cisco that would automatically select routes and pick the most effective and economical mode of transportation, which included carriers other than FedEx's fleet of trucks and planes. Just as critical, however, was that the real-time information status of the synchronisation operation was constantly available on the Internet.

Businesses sought ways to improve their return on investment and became interested in any business process that could be integrated and automatically triggered (e.g., proof of delivery and payment) as opposed to being separately invoked. So not only was FedEx pushing its customers for integration, but its innovative customers were also demanding greater integration. Some customers had even jumped ahead of FedEx. Cisco, for example, had developed an extranet that allowed its customers to order FedEx services without leaving the Cisco Website. By integrating its services within the supply-chain of its customers, and thus generating increases in customer loyalty and in customers' switching costs, FedEx managed to effectively raise the barriers to entry for competitors.

The Internet refined the COSMOS system. Whenever new information was entered into the system by FedEx or by customers through the Internet, all related files and databases were automatically

FIGURE 1 Fedex solutions for the entire supply-chain

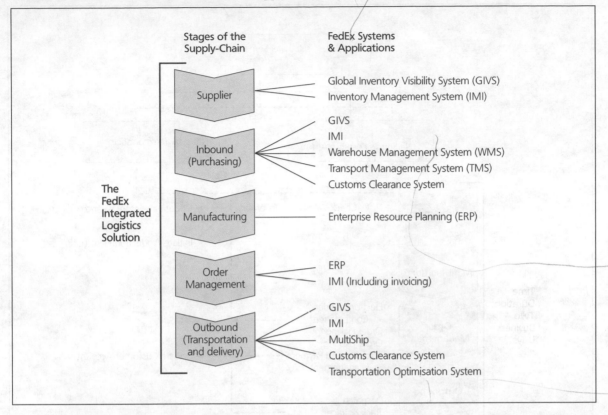

updated. For example, when a FedEx customer placed an order through fedex.com, the information would find its way to COSMOS, FedEx's global package-tracking system. The courier's Route Planner – an electronic mapping toll – would facilitate the pickup and delivery of the order from the customer. A product movement planner would schedule the order through the Company's global air and courier operations. The customer would be able to track the status of the shipment through PowerShip or FedEx Ship. The COSMOS system handled 54 million transactions per day in 1999.

In 1998, FedEx decided to overhaul its internal IT infrastructure under Project GRID (Global Resources for Information Distribution). The project involved replacing 60,000 terminals and some PCs with over 75,000 network systems. The decision to go with network computers was made to avoid the 'desktop churn' found with PCs. The network computers linked over a global Internet Protocol network aimed to enhance the quality and quantity of services FedEx could deliver to its customers. For example, FedEx employees at any location at any time could track a package through

the various steps in the FedEx chain. Other applications planned to be launched included COSMOS Squared, which allowed Non-Event Tracking, a feature that triggered alerts when scheduled events, such as the arrival of a package, did not occur. Through a 24-hour, seven-day operation called the Global Operations Command Centre, the central nervous system of FedEx's worldwide system in Memphis, FedEx was able to provide efficient gathering and dissemination of real-time data. The operation housed huge screens covering the walls that tracked world events, weather patterns and the real-time movement of FedEx trucks and aircraft. New systems were also introduced to predict with greater accuracy the amount of inbound traffic. This system allowed FedEx to prioritise the hundreds of variables involved in the successful pickup, processing and delivery of a parcel. Senior managers at FedEx believed that having current and accurate information helped them to reduce failure in the business.

As well as the data centre in Memphis, FedEx operated other centres in Colorado Springs, Orlando, Dallas-Fort Worth, Singapore, Brussels and Miami.

FIGURE 2 Example of integrated customer order process management: National Semiconductor

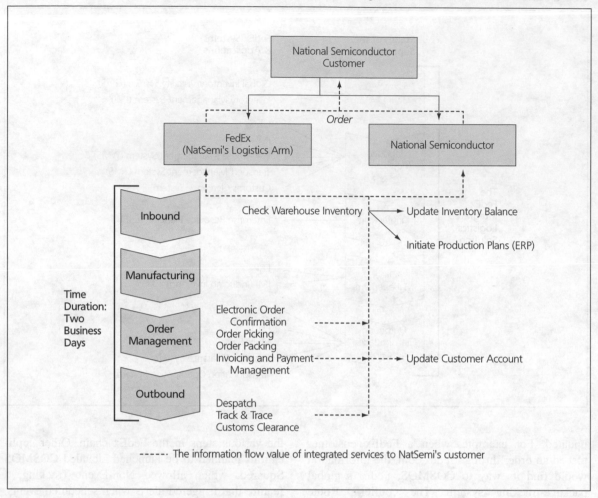

National Semiconductor Customer

Order

FedEx (NatSemi's Logistics Arm)

National Semiconductor

Inbound

Check Warehouse Inventory → Update Inventory Balance

Initiate Production Plans (ERP)

Manufacturing

Time Duration: Two Business Days

Order Management

Electronic Order Confirmation
Order Picking
Order Packing
Invoicing and Payment Management → Update Customer Account

Outbound

Despatch
Track & Trace
Customs Clearance

- - - - - The information flow value of integrated services to NatSemi's customer

Also in 1999, FedEx signed an agreement with Netscape to adopt Netscape software as the primary technology for accessing its corporate intranet sites. FedEx's intranet included more than 60 Websites, created for its end users and in some cases by its end users. Customers could build integrated Websites using FedEx Applications Programming Interfaces (API) or FedEx intraNetShip (free downloads from fedex.com) and incorporate a link that would allow them to track packages directly from their own site. Over 5000 Websites fed hundreds of thousands of tracking requests through to the fedex.com site.

Our API solutions are designed to give global visibility and access across the supply-chain, from manufacturing to customer service to invoicing. We've managed to wipe out those irritating WISMO (Where Is My Order) calls because we've seamlessly linked our customers to their customers.

(Mike Janes, former VP, Electronic Commerce & Logistics Marketing, FedEx: Gentry, 1998)

At the beginning of 1999, FedEx launched an enhancement to its package-tracking service. Customers could query and receive package status information for up to 25 shipments simultaneously, and forward this information on to up to three e-mail recipients. Furthermore, users in France, Japan, Italy, Germany, the Netherlands and Portuguese- and Spanish-speaking countries could access this information on-line in their native languages through fedex.com.

FedEx claimed to have the largest on-line client server network in the world that operated in real-time. Information became an extremely critical part of its business.

We're in the express transportation business, but we've discovered how to lock up a lot of value in the information that we have.

(Mark Dickens, VP, Electronic Commerce & Customer Services: Janah and Wilder, 1997)

... even when on the physical side of the business, we outsource, for instance, the pick-up or the delivery or the warehousing activity for a customer, we have never outsourced the information. Protecting the brand has always been very, very critical for us.

(William Conley)

The benefits of these services were not limited to FedEx's customers. For FedEx, its on-line services, which in 1999 handled 60 million transactions per day, saved FedEx the cost of 200,000 customer service employees. In turn, the Company reported spending 10 per cent of its US$17 billion annual revenue on IT in 1999. Information had allowed FedEx to lower its costs such that the cost to customers of using FedEx in 1999 was lower than it was 25 years ago.

Going beyond delivery services, FedEx aimed to fully integrate its corporate partners every step of the way along the supply-chain. Fundamental to FedEx's strategy for establishing its e-business and logistics operations was how well it could forge technology links with customers.

It's all about integration, whether it's inside FedEx, with our technology partners, or with our customer.

(Laurie Dicker, Senior VP, Logistics Electronic Commerce & Catalog: Janah and Wilder, 1997)

Integration of Internet services with our transportation offerings is not an addition to our core business; it is our core business.

(Dennis Jones, CIO: Cone and Duvall, 1999)

When it comes to managing synergies across businesses, we've found that seamless information integration is a critical component.

(1999 Annual Report)

Branding and business structure up until 19 January, 2000

In the first 21 years of business, FedEx operated under the corporate name of Federal Express Corporation. Its customers came to recognise it as 'FedEx' in short and the brand took off as the Company grew and expanded its service offerings under the purple and orange flag. Hence in 1994, it seemed natural that the Company should change its brand name to 'FedEx'.

The Parts Bank was given official recognition when it became a division of FedEx Corp. In 1988 and became known as Business Logistics Services (BLS). It operated as a separate and independent company. In line with the express transportation side of the business, BLS developed expertise in the high-value, high-tech industries. It was involved in the express inbound, outbound and redistribution of goods. However, it focused mainly on the small parcel business. FedEx based its solutions on just-in-time logistics. As the business grew, concern was raised that the logistics business was not generating revenue for the express transportation business, but rather feeding this through to other carriers. Hence in 1994, BLS was renamed FedEx Logistics, and it became mandatory for the logistics business to include FedEx transportation as part of its solution to customers. In 1996, the division changed its name yet again, to FedEx Logistics and Electronic Commerce (FLEC). The Company started to focus its resources on doing business on the Internet, and the name change was to reflect the changes in the marketplace.

Following the acquisition of Caliber Systems Inc. in 1998, five separate subsidiary companies were formed: Federal Express, RPS, Roberts Express, Viking Freight and FDX Logistics. The latter four were Caliber businesses. Each subsidiary was managed independently and was responsible for its own accounts (see Exhibit 3). However, Caliber and FedEx's logistics operations were fundamentally different in that they had completely distinct customer bases and service offerings. Caliber developed expertise in moving raw materials, plates of steel and steel bars and managing work-in-progress. It would manage the manufacturing of cars and fork-lift trucks. Caliber provided an elaborate logistics operation concentrating mainly on high-priced goods industries, and it provided a fuller supply-chain solution than

FLEC did, whereas FLEC was primarily focused on finished goods, transportation logistics and reverse logistics (i.e., handling returns). One was concentrating its business at the front-end of the supply chain (e.g., receiving, work-in progress) while the other was more involved in the back-end operations of the supply chain (i.e. warehousing, transportation). Hence the two operations continued to operate independently of each other. Logistics systems and applications were also developed independently. Caliber Logistics became a subsidiary company under FDX Logistics, while FLEC continued as a division within Federal Express, the express transportation arm.

EXHIBIT 3 SUBSIDIARY COMPANIES OF FEDEX FOLLOWING THE ACQUISITION OF CALIBER SYSTEMS INC. IN 1998

- **Federal Express** was the world leader in global express distribution, offering 24–48-hour delivery to 211 countries that comprised 90 per cent of the world's GDP. In 1998, FedEx was the undisputed leader in the overnight package delivery business. It had a fleet of 44,500 ground vehicles and 648 planes that gave support to the US$14 plus billion business. It had 34,000 drop-off locations, and 67 per cent of its US domestic shipping transactions were generated electronically. Goods shipped ranged from flowers to lobsters to computer components. This company was constantly running in crisis mode, seeking to move packages through all weather and conditions to fulfil shipments overnight. The underlying philosophy that ensured high service levels was that every package handled could make a difference to someone's life. The company handled nearly three million shipments per day in 1998.

- **RPS** was North America's second-largest provider of business-to-business ground small-package delivery. It was a low-cost, non-union, technology-savvy company acquired with the Caliber purchase. The company specialised in business-to-business shipments in one to three days, a service that FedEx could not attract because it was unable to offer prices low enough to attract enough volume. Being a 15 year-old company, RPS prized itself on having one of the lowest cost models in the transportation industry. It employed only owner-operators to deliver its packages. In terms of volume and revenue growth, RPS outperformed FedEx. For the future, plans were to grow RPS's business-to-consumer delivery service to take advantage of the growth of electronic commerce, thus carving a niche in the burgeoning residential delivery market. In 2000, the company owned 8,600 vehicles, achieved annual revenues of US$1.9 billion and employed 35,000 people, including independent contractors. It handled 1.5 million packages per day.

- **Viking Freight** was the first less-than-truckload freight carrier in the western United States. The company employed 5,000 people, managed a fleet of 7,660 vehicles and 64 service centres, and shipped 13,000 packages per day.

- **Roberts Express** was the world's leading surface-expedited carrier for non-stop, time-critical and special-handling shipments. The service offered by Roberts Express has been likened to a limousine service for freight. In 1999, the company handled more than 1,000 shipments per day. It was the smallest company within the FedEx Group. Urgent shipments could be loaded onto trucks within 90 minutes of a call and shipments would arrive within 15 minutes of the promised time 96 per cent of the time. Once loaded, shipments could be tracked by satellite every step of the way. Goods such as works of art or critical manufacturing components often required exclusive-use truck services. Exclusivity allowed customers greater control but at a price. This service was an infrequent necessity for most customers. Roberts had exclusive use of a handful of FedEx aircrafts, but the company still had to pay for use and for crew time.

- **Caliber Logistics** was a pioneer in providing customised, integrated logistics and warehousing solutions worldwide. The acquisition of

Caliber in January 1998 brought with it over-the-road transportation and warehousing capabilities. Since the acquisition, FedEx tried to move away from traditional logistics offerings to providing total supply-chain management solutions, and Caliber Logistics was renamed FDX Logistics. To the customer, this meant that FedEx could provide warehousing services, but only if this was part of a bigger deal. In September 1999, FedEx bought its first freight forwarder, Caribbean Transport Services (formerly GeoLogistics Air Services). Caribbean had a strong overseas network. FDX Logistics was the parent company of FedEx Supply-chain Services and Caribbean Transportation Services.

The acquisition served to reinforce FedEx's commitment to becoming more than just an express delivery company. Yet commentators and customers continued to associate the FedEx brand with transportation, and FedEx fought to transform the image of the Company outside of this mould. One solution was to rename the Company. With the acquisition, the Company created a holding company, 'FDX Corporation'. However, FedEx did very little to promote its new FDX corporate brand. Furthermore, its transportation subsidiary continued to operate under the Federal Express name with the purple and orange FedEx brand on its trucks and vans. The FedEx brand lived on, but with no advertising or aggressive promotion of FDX, the name did not resonate in the marketplace. While the likes of UPS had the advantage of promoting just one brand – UPS – to sell the entire company and its many service offerings, FedEx was trying to promote five different subsidiary companies with completely unrelated names and business logos under the FDX banner through distinctly separate sales and customer service teams. Furthermore, with two separate logistics businesses within the Group, separate sales forces selling services offered by different parts of the Company, separate customer services staff to deal with different queries and IT resources spread across the Group, customers were confused and resources were duplicated.

Despite the confusion, by 1999 FedEx purported to offer companies 'total one-stop shopping' for solutions at all levels of the supply-chain. Each subsidiary continued to operate independently, with separate accounting systems and customer service staff, while competing collectively. However, while maintaining the autonomy of each subsidiary company, the challenge for FedEx was how to bring the companies closer together to create those synergies. Providing customers with a single point of access to the whole Group was the ultimate goal. In practical terms, the task was to decide how each of the subsidiary companies should leverage its skills and services to a broader audience.

Events leading up to the January 2000 reorganisation

FedEx needed to address a number of factors that would affect the prospects of the Company.

FedEx's performance

In the year ending 31 May, 1999, the Company had out-performed analyst expectations, posting record earnings of 73 per cent, an increase of 28 per cent over the previous year (Gelsi, 1999). Net income had risen 30 per cent to US$221 million. However, results took a downturn in the following financial year. For the first quarter ended 31 August, 1999, FedEx announced that rising fuel prices had severely impacted upon the Company's net income, causing it to miss its first-quarter target. With no sign of improvements in fuel prices and with the US domestic market growth slowing down, FedEx warned that earnings for the second quarter and the full fiscal year may fall below analyst expectations. Bearing in mind that the express transportation business (mainly Federal Express and RPS) accounted for over 80 per cent of the Group's revenue, and that the US market accounted for approximately US$10 billion of the Group's revenue, both trends had a significant negative impact on net income.

Sure enough, FedEx reported that for the quarter ended 30 November, 1999, operating income was down by 10 per cent on the previous year and net income was down by six per cent. The Company was not achieving the level of US domestic growth as expected. Rising fuel prices continued to erode operating income. However, operations other than express transportation (i.e., Viking Freight, Roberts Express, FDX Logistics and Caribbean Transportation Services) achieved revenue and operating income increases of 27 per cent and 12 per cent respectively in the second quarter. With the adverse fuel prices alone, the Company anticipated that operating income could be down by more than US$150 million for the year ending 31 May, 2000. This called for some immediate remedial action.

Other trends within the express transportation and logistics market were also putting pressure on the Company to re-think its business strategy.

The Internet market and e-tailing

The Internet changed the basis for competition for most businesses. Its low cost and diversity of applications made it appealing and accessible. The Internet levelled the playing field such that, once a company was on-line, as long as it fulfilled its orders to the expectations of its customers, the size of the company was of no significance. The impact of the Internet on FedEx was twofold. Firstly, it opened up opportunities in logistics management for FedEx as businesses were using the Internet to re-engineer their supply-chains. So long as customers were satisfied, it really did not matter whether the goods were warehoused or not, whether the goods came directly from a factory in some distant location or whether the goods had been made to order. Integration with customer supply-chains was the key.

Secondly, the express transportation needs associated with the growth in e-tailing (expected to reach US$7 billion in 2000) and business-to-business EC (expected to reach US$327 billion by 2002) presented enormous opportunities for companies such as FedEx (Lappin, 1996; Erwin et al., 1997).

FedEx was sure that it had the right business model to take advantage of these opportunities.

> *We're right at the centre of the new economy. . . . Businesses are utilising the Internet to re-engineer the supply-chain. In the new economy, the Internet is the neural system. We're the skeleton – we make the body move.*

> (Fred Smith)

But so were its competitors.

The competition

In January 2000, CBS MarketWatch Live reported that FedEx's express delivery business was maturing

and was not growing as fast as it used to (Adamson, 2000). Furthermore, the industry was loaded with companies, local and global, that provided a myriad of transportation services to a wide range of businesses. Competition was fierce. All major transportation and delivery companies were betting big on technology. Although FedEx pioneered the Web-based package-tracking system, such systems became the industry norm rather than a competitive advantage.

The four leading companies in the international courier business were DHL, FedEx, UPS and TNT. Between them they held more than 90 per cent of the worldwide market (Murphy and Hernly, 1999).

UPS. Since 1986, UPS had spent US$9 billion on IT and had formed five alliances in 1997 to disseminate its logistics software to electronic commerce users. However, while FedEx developed all its IS software in-house, UPS made a point in stating that it was not a software developer and that companies taking that route were 'trying to go a bridge too far' (Blackmon, 1999).

In early 1998, UPS formed a strategic alliance with Open Market, Inc., a US-based provider of Internet software, to deliver a complete Internet commerce solution providing integrated logistics and fulfilment. They were also working with IBM and Lotus to standardise formats on their Website.

In 1999, UPS raised US$5.47 billion through its initial public offering, the largest in the US IPO history. The company shipped more than 55 per cent of goods ordered over the Internet and offered over the full range of logistics solutions to its customers.

DHL. In 1993, DHL announced a four-year US$1.25 billion worldwide capital spending programme aimed at investing in handling systems, automation, facilities and computer technology. The company launched its Website in 1995. It was 25 per cent owned by Deutsche Post and 25 per cent owned by Lufthansa Airlines. Plans were under way for an initial public offering in the first half of 2001. Though the company dominated the UK market, it projected an increase in worldwide turnover of 18 per cent to US$5.26 billion (Exelby, 2000).

TNT. In 1998, TNT launched a Web Collection facility on the Internet. Later the same year, TNT launched the world's first global Price Checker service on its Website that allowed customers to calculate the price of sending a consignment from one place to another anywhere in the world. Other applications were under development that would allow customers to integrate with TNT's on-line services. Then in 1999, TNT launched QuickShipper, a one-stop on-line access to TNT's entire range of distribution services, from pricing to delivery. This new service was to be integrated with existing on-line tools such as Web Collection and Price Checker.

Also in March 1999, TNT launched the express industry's first dedicated customer extranet, Customised Services environment. This offered regular customers easy access to detailed and personalised shipment information through the use of user IDs and passwords. With this came a host of service offerings.

While FedEx had pioneered many logistics solutions that had helped it to achieve economies of scale faster than its competitors, the advantages were quickly eroding as newer technologies became even more powerful and less expensive.

The January 2000 announcement

On 19 January, 2000, FedEx announced three major strategic initiatives:

1 A new branding strategy that involved changing the Company's name to 'FedEx Corporation', and extending the 'FedEx' brand to four of its five subsidiary companies. The subsidiary companies became:

   - FedEx Express (formerly Federal Express)
   - FedEx Ground (formerly RPS)
   - FedEx Custom Critical (formerly Roberts Express)
   - FedEx Logistics (formerly Caliber Logistics)
   - Viking Freight (no change).

2 Major reorganisations such that there would be one point of access to sales, customer services, billing and automation systems. With these consolidations, the Company announced intentions to form a sixth subsidiary called FedEx Corporate Services Corp. in June 2000 (see Figure 3 for new Group structure). The new subsidiary would pool together the marketing, sales, customer services, information technology and electronic commerce resources of the Group. The invoicing functions would also be combined for all the companies.

3 Introduction of a new low-cost residential delivery service, FedEx Home Delivery, to be launched in the US.

Of significance was the merging of the two logistics operations (Caliber Logistics and FLEC) into FedEx Logistics. The two companies seemed to complement each other in terms of their service offerings and customer base. Both had a few of the same customers but many different ones. Furthermore, Caliber's presence was mainly in North America and Europe, while FLEC had expanded into other continents. FedEx Logistics brought together all the splintered operations of logistics in all the subsidiary companies, streamlining costs, presenting one menu of logistics service offerings to customers, and aligning R&D of systems upon common, agreed platforms. This reorganisation also brought about another major change in operations. It was no longer mandatory for the logistics business to use FedEx transportation as part of its solutions to customers. Being 'carrier-agnostic' meant that FedEx Logistics would use FedEx transportation where it fitted, both in terms of cost and in terms of geographic coverage. The decision would also rest on customer preference and the kind of goods being transported. For example, Caliber was transporting fork-lift trucks, cars and steel plates that FedEx did not have the physical capacity to handle.

Combining the two operations brought together the IT expertise and the know-how of the logistics business. Under one CIO, standards were set for the development of systems on a worldwide basis, including vendor selection. In the past, regions developed their own solutions and operated in isolation. However, the Internet forced the Company to consolidate its systems and solutions as customers demanded global solutions. Through the IT groups located in Memphis, Leiden (Holland) and Singapore, the Company resolved to develop global systems for worldwide implementation, with functions such as multiple currencies and multiple languages. FedEx Logistics forecast a 70 per cent growth rate in the year ending 31 May, 2000. However, the business so far failed to generate any profit. The company aimed to build on its expertise in the five market segments: health care, industrial, high-tech, automotive and consumer.

The Company anticipated having to spend US$100 million on these changes over three years.

FIGURE 3 Group structure

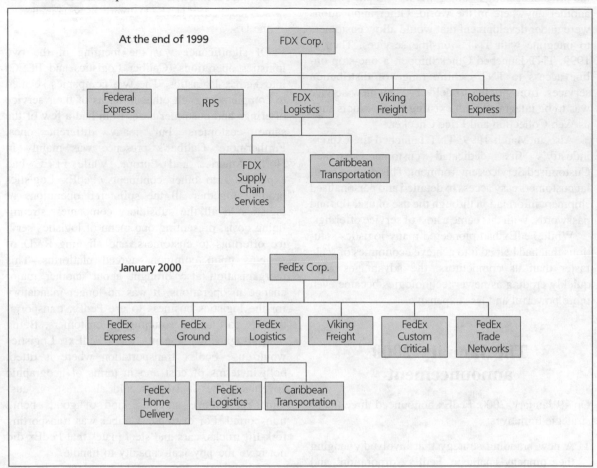

The intention was to take advantage of one of its greatest assets, the FedEx brand name; the name that customers could count on for 'absolutely, positively' reliable service and cutting-edge innovation. The value of the brand had been ignored, particularly when the Company decided to change its corporate name to FDX in 1998. Realising its mistake, the renaming of the Company as FedEx Corporation and the extension of the brand to its subsidiaries fell in line with its intention to provide customers with an integrated set of business solutions. Customers wanted to deal with one company to meet their transportation and logistics needs.

Each subsidiary company was to continue operating independently, but collectively the Group would provide a wide range of business solutions. It was this collective synergy of solutions that FedEx believed would form the competitive advantage of the Company in the future. For customers, the benefits included easier means of doing business with

FedEx. There was to be one toll-free telephone number, one Website, one invoice and account number, one sales team, one customer service team and a streamlined customer automation platform to handle electronic transactions for small and large businesses (see Table 1 for details of the changes following reorganisation). The new organisation was aimed at helping businesses of all sizes to achieve their shipping, logistics, supply-chain and e-business objectives. However, analysts questioned whether the new Group structure would work, given that there would still be different teams of delivery and pick-up staff for the different operations. Hence, one person could pick up one package sent by ground and another person could pick up another package sent by express from the same company. Companies such as UPS, on the other hand, would have one person pick up both types of packages.

In addition to these changes, FedEx anticipated growth in consumer electronic commerce and planned

TABLE 1 Before and after the reorganisation

Before	After
Multiple brands under FDX umbrella	A single branding system leveraging the power of the FedEx brand so more customers can use FedEx reliability as a strategic competitive advantage
Separate sales force with directed co-operation	A single, expanded sales force especially targeting small and medium-sized businesses, cross-selling a wide portfolio of services and pricing schemes
Multiple invoices and account numbers	A single invoice and single account number from FedEx
Multiple automation platforms offering all FDX services	Streamlined customer automation systems to handle electronic transactions and database management needs for small and large businesses
Separate customer service, claims trace functions	Single customer service, claims and trace functions by calling 1-800-Go-FedEx® (800-463-3339) or visiting its Website at www.fedex.com.

to start a new service called FedEx Home Delivery (within the FedEx Ground subsidiary company) to meet the needs of businesses specialising in business-to-consumer e-tailing. FedEx had been successful in providing services to the business-to-business electronic commerce market. Now it aimed to achieve the same leadership status in the business-to-consumer electronic commerce market. However, expanding the residential delivery business was one segment that FedEx consciously made a decision not to pursue throughout the 1990s. This gave UPS the opportunity to lead in residential delivery services.

In late 1997, Smith was quoted as saying:

We've made huge investments in our networks, and now that bow wave has passed. We think we have a good chance of harvesting a lot of that investment.

(Grant, 1997)

In the two years that followed, the results of the Company showed few signs of a harvest. Was the January restructuring going to bring in the harvest? The announcement certainly served to tell investors that they were making some major changes to address some competitive issues. However, analysts took a pragmatic view to the announcement, saying that, 'the proof of the pudding is in the eating'. Was the reorganisation going to leverage the power of the

networks and the information and logistics infrastructures that FedEx had built? Did it provide the right ingredients to achieve the objectives of creating value for FedEx customers while at the same time improving profitability for FedEx? Given the speed at which technology and the marketplace were changing, would the new organisation structure be adaptable to the changing business environment? Were there better alternative solutions that the Company could have considered?

References

Adamson, D., 'FDX Corp. Changes Name to FedEx', *CBS MarketWatch-Live*, 19 January, 2000.

Blackmon, D. A., 'Ante Up! Big Gambles in the New Economy: Overnight Everything Changed for FedEx', *The Wall Street Journal Interactive Edition*, URL: http://www.djreprints.com/jitarticles/trx0001273701443 html, 4 November, 1999.

Bruner, R. F. and Bulkley, D., 'The Battle for Value: Federal Express Corporation versus United Parcel Service of America Inc. (Abridged)', University of Virginia Darden School Foundation, 1995.

Cone, E. and Duvall, M., 'UPS Keeps Truckin'; FedEx: A Documented Success', *Inter@ctive Week*, 16 November, 1999.

Erwin, B., Modahl, M. A. and Johnson, J., 'Sizing Intercompany Commerce', *Business Trade & Technology Strategies*, 1 (1), Forrester Research, Cambridge, MA, 1997.

Exelby, J., 'Interview – DHL UK Foresees Tough Market', URL: http://biz.yahoo.com/rf/000117/mq.html, 17 January, 2000.

Gelsi, S., 'FDX Posts Stronger-than-Expected Profit', *CBS MarketWatch*, 30 June, 1999, URL:http://cbs.marketwatch. com/archive.../current/fdx.htm'?source=&dist=srch, February 2000.

Gentry, C., 'FedEx API's Create Cinderella Success Stories', October 1998, URL:http://www.fedex.com/us/about/api. html.

Grant, L., 'Why FedEx is Flying High', 10 November, 1997, URL:http://pathfinder.com/fortune/1997/971110/fed.html.

Janah, M. and Wilder, C., 'Special Delivery', *Information Week*, URL: http://www.FedExcorp.com/media/infowktop100. html, 1997.

Lappin, T., 'The Airline of the Internet', *Wired*, 4 (12), December 1996, URL: http://www.wired.com/wired/4.12/ features/ffedex.html.

Murphy, D. and Hernly, K., 'Air Couriers Soar Despite Mainland Gloom, *South China Morning Post*, 30 May, 1999.

CASE 2

Reconciling managerial dichotomies at Honda Motors

By Andrew Mair[1]

*By following a corporate policy that stresses
originality, innovation, and efficiency in every
facet of its operations – from product
development and manufacturing to marketing –
Honda has striven to attain its goal of satisfying
its customers.*

(Honda Annual Report, 1997)

Honda Motor Co., the Japan-based manufacturer of cars, motorcycles and power products like lawnmowers and small boat engines, is one of the great success stories of the post-war Japanese economy (see Exhibit 1 and Tables 1 and 2). Established in 1948, since the 1970s Honda has been widely recognized as a pioneering Japanese manufacturer and as one of the world's leading motor industry companies. Honda was the first Japanese manufacturer to make its products in Europe, when its Belgian motorcycle factory opened in 1963. Honda became the first Japanese firm to manufacture automobiles in North America when it opened its Ohio assembly plant in 1982. Honda took the risk of entering into a long and complex relationship during the 1980s with a European company universally considered to be one of the least capable automobile manufacturers in the West, British Leyland (now Rover Group).

EXHIBIT 1 SIGNIFICANT MILESTONES IN HONDA'S DEVELOPMENT

1946   Soichiro Honda sets up Honda Technical Research Institute in Hamamatsu, producing auxiliary engines for bicycles, and later, machine tools.

1948   Company renamed Honda Motor Co. Ltd. First production Honda vehicle, 90cc B-type motorcycle.

1952   Exports begin (to Philippines).

1954   Soichiro Honda visits European car manufacturers. First exports (of 200cc K-type 'Juno' scooter) to USA.

1955   Honda becomes largest Japanese motorcycle manufacturer.

1959   American Honda Motor Co. Inc. [sales subsidiary] established.

1961   European Honda GmbH (now Honda Deutschland GmbH) [sales subsidiary] established in Hamburg.

1962   NV Honda Motor SA (now Honda Belgium NV) established to assemble and sell mopeds in Europe (production begins 1963) [the first manufacturing facility opened by any Japanese company in the West].

1963   T360 lightweight truck and S360 sports car, first Honda 4-wheeled vehicles, go on sale.

1965   Honda UK Ltd. [sales subsidiary] established in London.

1968   First exports of N360 and N600 microcars. Cumulative motorcycle production passes 10 million.

1971   CVCC low emission automobile engine announced.

1972   First generation Civic automobile introduced.

1973   Soichiro Honda and Takeo Fujisawa retire to become Supreme Advisors.

1976   First generation Accord announced. Civic production reaches 1 million after 4 years.

[1]Source: This case was written by Andrew Mair, Birkbeck College, University of London. A previous version of this case study appeared as 'Honda Motors: a paradoxical approach to growth,' in C. Baden-Fuller and M. Pitt (eds), *Strategic Innovation: An International Casebook*, Routledge, London, 1996, pp. 435–61. The author acknowledges the helpful comments of Charles Baden-Fuller and Martyn Pitt. This version has been updated and revised. Copyright © 1997 by Andrew Mair.

1977 IAP Industriale SpA (now Honda Italia Industriale SpA) established in Italy [subsidiary to manufacture motorcycles].

1978 Honda of America Manufacturing, Inc. set up to make motorcycles in the USA (production begins 1979). Cumulative production of motorcycles exceeds 30 million. Cumulative car production exceeds 5 million.

1979 Company signs technical collaboration with British Leyland [now Rover Group], covering BL production of Triumph Acclaim car (production in the United Kingdom begins 1981) [first of several joint car developments between the firms lasting until late 1990s].

1982 European Head Office established in Belgium. Honda of America begins car production.

1984 Plans to double Honda of America car manufacturing capacity to 300,000 units/year. Honda Research of America (now Honda R&D North America) established.

1985 Plans announced to double car production in Canada from 40,000 to 80,000 cars/year.

1986 Honda of America begins engine manufacture.

1988 Plans announced for second US car assembly plant. VTEC variable valve timing system principle announced. Plans announced to build R&D centre in Europe.

1989 Soichiro Honda inducted into America's Automotive Hall of Fame [as first Japanese]; Honda Accord becomes overall best selling automobile model in the United States.

1990 Agreement with Rover under which Honda acquires minority shareholding in Rover. Accord Aerodeck becomes the first American built car model to be exported both to Japan and to Europe.

1992 European production of Honda Accord begins at Swindon, United Kingdom.

1994 Honda unwinds formal relationship with Rover and BMW purchases Rover from its parent company; announcement of further investments in North America to take annual production capacity from 600,000 to 800,000 by 1999, with 150,000 of these vehicles exported.

1995/6 Successful entry into growing 'light truck' market niches in Japan and North America with Odyssey minivan and CR-V sports utility vehicle.

1997 Production of new 'Asian car' (City model) starts in Thailand as overseas production approaches half of total car production at Honda.

Source: Excerpted from *Honda European Information Handbook* (1991–1992) and Honda Annual Reports.

TABLE 1   Growth of Honda's world-wide automobile production, 1960–1995

Year	Automobiles/Light trucks (000 units)
1960	0
1965	52
1970	393
1975	414
1980	957
1985	1,363
1990	1,928
1995	1,794

Source: Honda Annual Reports, Japan Automobile Manufacturers Association.

TABLE 2   Snapshot of Honda activities, 1997

Product range	Annual unit sales (000s)	Percentage of sales by value
Motorcycles	5,198	13.0
Automobiles	2,184	79.9
Power products	2,648	7.1

(engines, tillers, portable generators, outboard motors, lawnmowers, etc.)

- **Focus on internal combustion engines**

  Honda produced over 10 million internal combustion engines world-wide in 1996–7, or about 40,000 per day.

- **Regional sales breakdown by value**

Japan	34%
North America	42%
Europe	11%
Others	13%

- **Factories**

  Honda has a wide international production network, with 89 production facilities in 33 countries.

- **Employees**

  Honda directly employs 101,100 people, approximately 1/3 of them in Japan.

Source: Honda Annual Report 1996–7.

By the late 1980s, only 25 years after the firm entered the automobile industry, the 'industry of industries', Honda had become one of the world's top ten producers. Indeed, automobile production had come to dominate Honda's activities, responsible for nearly four-fifths of its turnover. By the mid 1990s Honda also stood head and shoulders above other leading automobile producers in international sales (with 77 percent of its sales by volume outside its home market region), and had become the most international of all automobile companies in production, with 46 percent of its manufacturing output by volume outside its home market region (see Table 3).

Compared to its Japanese rivals, Honda has remained a relatively small player in its domestic market, with market share consistently under 10 percent, on a par with Mazda and Mitsubishi, not far ahead of Daihatsu and Suzuki. But from a global perspective, Honda's early and rapid internationalization, first of sales during the 1970s, then of production during the 1980s, propelled the company spectacularly out of the ranks of mid-sized Japanese automobile producers to a status alongside Toyota

and Nissan as one of the global Japanese 'Big Three' automobile producers. And Honda was now significantly more international than either Toyota or Nissan in both sales and production. Continued growth of sales and production during the first half of the 1990s was hindered – as in the early 1970s – by world recession. But the geographical spread of Honda's activities meant that, unlike some of its Japanese competitors, the firm was able to sustain profitability right through the post-'bubble economy' slump in the Japanese economy during the early 1990s (see Table 4).

In the global automobile industry, Honda's achievements on the technology front are well recognized, ranging from its cutting-edge low pollution and low fuel consumption engine technologies to its achievement in powering World Champion Formula 1 (F-1) racing cars for six years in a row during the 1980s. In 1989 the company's founder, Soichiro Honda, became the first Japanese to be accepted into Detroit's symbolic Automotive Industry Hall of Fame.

It is perhaps not surprising that examples of strategic management practice at Honda became

TABLE 3 World production and sales of new passenger cars in 1994

Producers	Production 1994 (Output in 1000s)	Geographic distribution of production (in %)				Geographic distribution of sales (in %)			
		North America	Europe	Japan	Others	North America	Europe	Japan	Others
Ford	3,959	54.6	37.1		8.3	53.3	35.8	0.2	10.7
Ford (& Mazda)	4,928	46.6	29.8	16.7	7.0	49.3	32.3	5.5	12.9
General Motors	5,486	59.7	30.1		10.2	61.4	28.4	0.4	9.8
GM (& Isuzu)	5,537	59.1	29.9	0.9	10.1	60.8	28.1	0.5	10.6
Honda	1,561	38.9	3.3	54.1	3.7	53.2	10.7	23.0	13.0
Nissan	2,081	22.0	9.8	64.5	3.7	31.7	18.3	36.5	13.5
Toyota	3,836	12.7	2.2	72.2	12.9	21.4	8.2	36.9	33.5
V.A.G.	2,980	8.2	71.8		20.1	9.3	63.3	1.2	26.2
Fiat	2,137		62.7		37.3	0.1	60.2	0.2	39.6
Renault	1,613		86.5		13.5	0.0	81.0	0.1	18.9
PSA Peugot-Citroën	1,798		98.5		1.5	0.0	84.9	0.3	14.7
BMW-Rover	1,027	(*)	97.8		2.2	8.7	75.6	2.9	12.8
Mercedes	599	(*)	97.5		2.5	12.9	69.9	5.6	11.6

Source: Bélis-Bergouignan, Bordenave and Lung (1998).
(*) New plants have been opened in North America since 1994.

widely quoted in the management literature during the 1980s. An undoubtedly successful firm was attracting the attention it deserved. But was that success a result of good management or was it due to a series of fortunate coincidences? One problem with the way Honda has been analyzed in the management literature is that its management innovations have been treated as a series of isolated stories frequently described in only a few sentences, and seemingly brought forth to justify or legitimize this or that new theory (Mair, 1998).

Is there anything more fundamental, more deep-seated, that underlies Honda's recognized proclivity for innovative and pioneering management strategies?

Reconciling dichotomies: A method for innovative strategic thinking?

Underlying Honda's innovative strategic management, there appears to lie a process that might be described as 'reconciling dichotomies'. To see how it seems to work consider the dozens of dichotomous categories that pervade management thinking and permeate all aspects and functions. There are dichotomies in buyer-supplier relations (e.g. vertical integration and market relationships), work organization (e.g. efficient and humane), product development processes (e.g. sequential and simultaneous development), and business strategy (e.g. cost and differentiation), to name but a few.

Why are these dichotomies important? Strangely, although we can come up with lists of them, few Western managers consider them to be of any significance. And yet if we were to consider them as paradoxes or poles that implicitly require to be solved, we would discover a novel method for developing new ideas about traditional management problems.

In the West, the traditional, ingrained and implicit approach to the puzzles that dichotomous concepts represent has been twofold:

1 Assume a trade-off between them: hence, to take the example of the group–individual dichotomy, to gain the advantages of individualism it is necessary to sacrifice some of the benefits of the group, and vice versa.

2 Conceive of change management in terms of switching from one dichotomized – and mutually

TABLE 4 Honda's recent financial performance

Fiscal year*	Net sales (¥bn)	Net income of sales (%)	Research and development (¥bn)
1985	2,740	4.7	114
1986	3,009	4.9	135
1987	2,961	2.8	150
1988	3,229	3.1	164
1989	3,489	2.8	184
1990	3,853	2.1	186
1991	4,302	1.8	194
1992	4,391	1.4	192
1993	4,132	0.9	199
1994	3,863	0.6	189
1995	3,966	1.6	203
1996	4,252	1.7	221
1997	5,293	4.2	251

*Ends 28th February up to 1987, 31st March from 1988. Fiscal year therefore includes 9 or 10 months of previous calendar year. Figures for 1988 are author's estimate for comparative purposes, based on 12/13 of previous 13 months.

All yen conversions are at then-current exchange rates. During the above period, the value of the US dollar declined from 251 yen in February 1985 to 89 yen in March 1995 and then rose to 124 yen in March 1997. During the same period, Honda's unit automobile sales in North America remained roughly constant, proportionately, at approximately half of world-wide Honda sales.

exclusive – pole to the other. Any attempt to sit in the middle (trying to keep elements of both group- and individual-oriented organizational forms, for instance) has been thought of as 'muddling through', ending up with 'the worst of both worlds'.

If these ways of thinking seem self-evidently true to many in the West, to Honda they do not. The case study examines Honda's very different way of thinking.

An example: 'Right-first-time' or 'build in quality'

To illustrate the Honda approach, let us look at a very significant instance of the thought process that characterizes dichotomy reconciliation and observe how it works. This example is well understood in Japan (it was not invented by Honda) and has also increasingly been accepted by many Western managers in recent years.

Western management thinking has traditionally assumed trade-offs between product quality, cost and

delivery: high quality cost more and took longer; low cost meant low quality too; fast delivery cost more and risked low quality. But the Japanese-developed 'right-first-time' principle inherent in the 'just-in-time' production system has revealed that there are better ways to manage these dichotomies. By focusing on how to 'build in quality' to products rather than 'test in quality' afterwards, it is possible to reduce costs (less waste and downtime) and to rationalize production with minimal stocks, hence reducing delivery lead times too.

This example involves a strategic approach to manufacturing, and it has widespread ramifications for marketing, product positioning and competitive strategy. Yet significant as the example is, it has been taken up almost in isolation in the West. Few realize that it represents just one example of a wholly different way of strategic thinking rather than a solution to one particular management problem. There are many more dichotomies waiting to be discovered and reconciled, thereby providing innovative impetus to strategic thinking across the range of management functions.

Nobuhiko Kawamoto's reforms

Shortly after taking office as company president in 1991, Nobuhiko Kawamoto introduced significant reforms to the top management structure at Honda. Since the retirement in 1973 of the joint company founders, inventive engineer Soichiro Honda and financial mastermind Takeo Fujisawa, during their company's 25th anniversary year (see Exhibit 2), Honda had become well known in the business world for the collective decision-making process utilized by its top executives, a process in which few of them seemed to have clear individual responsibilities. The collective process was symbolized in the physical layout of the Honda headquarters 'board room', in which none of the executives had their own offices, but instead shared an open space where there were not only individual desks but also various areas for them to meet, sit and talk together.

There was no doubt that Kawamoto's new ideas were significant. He established a clear hierarchy at executive level, with two leading executives joining him to form an innermost leadership circle. He also announced that executives could have private offices if they so wished. Moreover, Honda's global management structure was reorganized with clear and direct lines of responsibility to the top management group.

Kawamoto's reforms made front page news in the Western business press. *The Wall Street Journal* ran the headline 'Just as US Firms Try Japanese Management, Honda is Centralizing: Kawamoto Finds "Teamwork" Is No Longer Enough To Boost Market Share: Coming Soon: Private Offices'

(Chandler and Ingrassia, 1991). *Fortune* followed suit, with 'A US-Style Shakeup at Honda: CEO Kawamoto has abandoned consensus management for American-looking organization charts. Result: Communications and decision-making are getting faster' (Taylor, 1991). As far as strategic decision making was concerned, the clear impression given was that Honda's penchants for groupism and horizontal communication were on the way out, with individualism and vertical structure the order of the new day. Apparently a Japanese company with a particularly Japanese management style had now decided that a Western style was superior after all.

But was this interpretation valid? Was Honda a firm whose strategic management decision making switched from a collectivist mode to an individualist mode? In fact, the true picture is rather different, and the view presented in the Western business press is, arguably, uninformed.

The joint board room had actually been set up in the mid 1960s by Takeo Fujisawa, who saw it as an adjunct structure to Soichiro Honda's highly individualistic style, a means of encouraging executives to talk about problems and solutions with each other, and to prepare younger managers for the day the founders would retire. In other words, the organizational structure to promote collective decision making existed alongside the individualist Honda (who is said once to have hit an engineer over the head with a spanner to drive home a point!).

Kawamoto's changes were only one of a series of periodic reorganizations at Honda. When Honda and Fujisawa retired in 1973, new president Kiyoshi Kawashima shifted Honda further towards a collec-

EXHIBIT 2 HONDA'S LEADERS

- Soichiro Honda, founded company 1948; retired 1973.
- Takeo Fujisawa, joined company 1949, in effect business manager, leaving Soichiro Honda free to concentrate on engineering and product strategy; retired 1973.
- Kiyoshi Kawashima, joined company 1947, before it was officially formed; ran works motor racing teams in 1960s; company president, 1973–83.
- Tadashi Kume, joined company 1953; ran works motor racing teams in 1960s; principal engineer in design and development of Life and Civic models; company president, 1983–90.
- Nobuhiko Kawamoto, joined company 1963; consecutively chief engineer, director and president of Honda R&D, 1970–91; company president and CEO, 1991–.

tive decision-making mode with the wide-ranging committee structure that he set up. When Tadashi Kume in turn succeeded Kawashima as president in 1983, he too instituted his own changes. Thus each new president has deliberately sent a shock wave of reorganization (of interrelationships as much as of people) through the firm. Indeed Kawamoto was by no means dispensing with collective decision making; what he was doing was injecting a strong dose of individual responsibility into the existing framework.

Kawamoto's changes are best interpreted less as a switch to a new type of structure, as the Western press had it, from one pole of a dichotomy to another, than as a change in emphasis. A useful way to visualize this process is to think of the organization as a sailing ship on a narrow tack against the wind, progressing in a zig-zag fashion, first towards individualism and vertical structure, then back towards collectivism and horizontal structure, then back again. All the while, the ship moves forward despite sailing against the wind, as each tack builds on the achievements of the last, despite the apparently dramatic changes of direction (see Figure 1).

Reconciling dichotomies at Honda

Honda's approach to the individual–group dichotomy in the strategic decision-making process is exemplary of Honda's approach to innovation in management. Honda appears to have implemented a systematic approach to resolving some of the great dilemmas of twentieth-century management.

Traditional dichotomous pairs of concepts are used in the West as an underlying framework to think about management. Thus in the case of Kawamoto's reforms, there is, first, the collective (or group) versus the individual, and second, vertical structure and horizontal structure. 'Reconciliation' in this context refers to an approach in which the two poles are somehow (and that is the challenge) made compatible with each other.

The way in which Kawamoto 'changed tacks' from a group-based to an individual-based trajectory (not structure) is a classic example of dichotomy reconciliation, Honda-style. Honda's strategic thinking rejects the typical Western simple trade-off and emphatically rejects the typical Western idea that failure to select clearly one or the other pole leads to indecision. Honda's solution to the group–individual dichotomy and the horizontal–vertical dichotomy is to progress flexibly with a 'tacking' motion along a well-defined and fairly narrow path. In other words, the reconciliation sought is always one which incorporates 'the best of both worlds' (see Figure 2).

The refusal to accept static trade-offs, and the rejection of any obligation to choose one pole or the other, lie behind many of Honda's strategic innovations. The process can be seen at work across a wide range of activities at Honda, and constitutes the hallmark of its strategic innovation.

FIGURE 1 The 'tacking ship' vision of progress

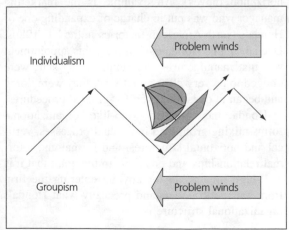

FIGURE 2 Visualizing dichotomy reconciliation

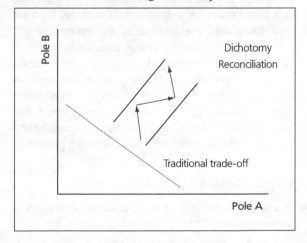

Organizational process: Competition and the individual

Let us take a closer look at how the individual–group dichotomy is played out at Honda. Honda has a remarkable penchant for praising the successes of individual employees and for encouraging a sense of competition among them. Company-wide quality circle (called NH Circles; for New, Now, Next Honda) competitions have focused on the achievements of individual people (albeit, characteristically, working in small groups). Within Honda R&D, the subsidiary company that develops Honda products, competitive and individual-based basic research activities deliberately foster individual inventiveness. The competitive nature of employee suggestion schemes at Honda's North American operations, with awards given to annual 'winners', also fosters individualism.

In similar vein, individual managers remain closely associated with the projects and products for which they have been responsible; Tadashi Kume was lauded as the principal engineer behind the Life and Civic automobiles. Kawamoto has been known as 'Mr NSX' after the aluminium-bodied supersports car Honda developed in the late 1980s, and he was also associated with Honda's successes in the 1980s on the Grand Prix racing circuit.

What is most interesting, however, is that individualism and competition are not stressed over and above loyalty and cooperation; each 'pole' within the individual–group dichotomy is a tendency that 'has its place' in a way that maximizes the contribution each can make, while minimizing any negative impacts of overemphasis on either individual or group. Hence alongside the stress on individual achievement can be observed the promotion of group processes: collective decision making, in the corporate board room for instance; team working, the tight and disciplined cooperation of the various people involved in F-1 racing being communicated as a model of behaviour for all employees; and interdepartmental cooperation in the product development process, which is organized into highly cooperative 'SED' (Sales-Engineering-Development) teams that are explicitly differentiated from the individualist and competitive character of the basic research process.

Organizational structure

A classic dichotomy in organizational structures is between vertical and horizontal structures. Recently many consultants have been advising large companies to dispense with vertical, hierarchical structures in favour of process-oriented horizontal linkages. Indeed a driving force behind reform of organizational structure at Honda has been the avoidance of 'big business disease'. In the Honda view, when a company grows bigger and adopts overly rigid vertical structures of organizational control, it can lose the small-firm vitality and the horizontal linkages and communication that are so vital to innovation and dynamism.

At Honda there are regular drives to battle 'big business disease'. But significantly, these take place within, rather than replacing, a strongly hierarchical structural framework. Thus after he became Honda President in 1983, Tadashi Kume launched a series of initiatives to prevent bureaucratic structures from hardening. These included round-table meetings between executives and front-line supervisors to cut across layers of vertical hierarchy, regular round-table meetings between executives and middle-level managers, and the encouragement of 'diagonal' linkages whereby manufacturing managers, for instance, held discussions to share viewpoints with front-line sales staff.

In similar vein, strategic thinking about the career paths of individuals has been woven into organizational thinking to keep structure flexible and innovative. Honda's 'expert' system, developed during the 1950s and 1960s, allows technical experts to be promoted in a clearly vertical fashion without having to enter the ranks of management, on the grounds that the latter would be a sure-fire route to poor lower-level management since many technical experts desire promotion but do not actually want to manage other people. Moreover, managers can follow diagonal promotion paths (simultaneous vertical and horizontal moves). An example is the marketing manager who was put in charge of expanding one of Honda's North American factories in the late 1980s. One advantage Honda gained from this appointment was that manufacturing and engineering staff were obliged to be very clear about what they were doing and began to question taken-for-granted procedures.

Honda has pursued web-like organizational forms mixing group and individual processes, vertical and horizontal structures, and formal and informal relationships and positions to the point that it is well-nigh impossible for anyone entering the firm from outside to understand precisely what Honda's organizational structure is.

Is Honda a 'Japanese' firm?

One dichotomy pervasive in the Western management literature is the grand division between Western firms and management methods, on the one hand, and Japanese firms and methods on the other hand. Many management theorists and practitioners have held to the idea that Japanese firms are fundamentally different from Western firms: whether in organizational structures, company cultures, labour relations, inter-firm relationships, manufacturing systems, work organization, or marketing strategies. Analysts created a 'Japanese model' of management diametrically opposed, in classic dualist fashion, to the Western model. Their argument was that adherence to this Japanese model explained much of Japan's economic successes during the 1970s and 1980s (see Table 5).

It may therefore seem strange even to pose the question of whether Honda can be considered a 'Japanese' firm. But remember that only one third of Honda's turnover now derives from Japan, and the company runs over eighty manufacturing facilities throughout the world, nearly all of them outside Japan. The crux of the issue, however, is whether Honda is actually managed in a 'Japanese' way. Many assume that it must be, given its roots in a country with a particularly strong and unique culture. And yet Japanese analysts agree that Honda does not easily fit the 'Japanese model'. In Japan Honda has deliberately set out to counter what it views as negative traits of 'Japanese-ness'. It deliberately stresses decentralized management structures, praises the achievements of individuals, makes merit the key to promotion, and awards responsibility

TABLE 5 The 'Japanese model' seen as diametrically opposed to the 'Western model'

'Western management model'	'Japanese management model'
Overall description	
▪ Mass	▪ Lean
▪ Standardized	▪ Flexible
▪ Fordist	▪ Post-Fordist
Work process	
▪ Taylorist	▪ Post-Taylorist
▪ Do workers	▪ Think workers
▪ Unskilled	▪ Polyvalent
Production organization and logistics	
▪ Large-lot production	▪ Small-lot production
▪ Just-in-case	▪ Just-in-time
▪ Push system	▪ Pull system
Organization	
▪ Vertical	▪ Horizontal
▪ Fragmented duties	▪ Broad duties
▪ Individual as responsible	▪ Group as responsible
Labour relations	
▪ Job control focus	▪ Employment conditions focus
▪ Cross-company unions	▪ Enterprise unions
▪ Hire and fire	▪ Job-for-life
Industry organization	
▪ Separated firms	▪ *Keiretsu* families
▪ Distant inter-firm relations	▪ Close inter-firm relations

to younger employees: all this in a Japanese society founded on centralization, collective decision making and responsibility, status and seniority, and respect for elders. The point to grasp is that Honda has struggled to overcome the innovation-deadening impacts of these cultural forces. Soichiro Honda himself has been the model, portrayed as exemplary of an individualist who cared nothing for the position of his supposed 'betters', deliberately crossed status barriers, and promoted younger individuals across seniority levels. The result is that in Japan Honda is commonly viewed as a peculiarly 'un-Japanese' firm.

Thus Honda has injected so-called Western attributes into the way it functions, which co-exist with the 'Japanese' features that employees bring with them – the results of their upbringing in Japan – as they enter the firm. Rather than pursuing a 'Japanese model' distinct from a 'Western model', the big picture reveals Honda's innovation to be its simultaneous incorporation of both models so as to work consciously and deliberately with elements of each: precisely what we saw earlier in Kawamoto's reforms.

Product strategy: Guiding the technology development process

A recognized source of competitive advantage for Honda has been its 'core competence' in the advanced internal combustion engines which power the whole range of its products. But Honda's product strength goes far deeper: a dichotomy-reconciling approach characterizes both the mental process of technology research and the philosophy behind the actual product designs. The technology and design features of Honda products are the embodiments of successful reconciliations of dichotomies which deliver direct and immediate competitive advantage.

The classic example of Honda's technology is the CVCC (compound vortex controlled combustion) engine, designed during the 1969–71 period. Indeed the CVCC engine is used within the firm to represent and communicate Honda's approach to technology. The compromise tackled and overcome by the CVCC engine was widely accepted in the world's automobile industry, namely a trade-off among the various pollutants emitted from internal combustion engines. According to the traditional view, attempts to reduce emissions of one chemical inevitably led to increases in others. The only way out of the dilemma, it was believed, was to add a process (e.g. catalytic conversion) to clean up the pollutants after combustion.

Honda engineers proceeded from the assumption that it would be more rational not to create pollutants in the first place than to have to clean them up. The CVCC engine design therefore denied the taken-for-granted compromises. The technical solution was to place two connected combustion chambers in each cylinder. A fuel-thin mixture of fuel and air was injected into a main combustion chamber. A fuel-rich mixture was injected into a smaller chamber where the spark plug was located. When the spark ignited the mixture, combustion spread from the smaller to the main chamber, with the result that the fuel and oxygen burned more completely, and with less fuel used, compared to a conventional engine. Each of these characteristics helped reduce a different pollutant, resulting in an engine in which the old trade-offs were overcome (see Exhibit 3).

The thinking embodied in the VTEC (variable valve timing and lift electronic control) family of engines that Honda first introduced in 1989 derives from a similar approach. The conventional

---

EXHIBIT 3 HOW THE CVCC ENGINE SIMULTANEOUSLY REDUCED POLLUTANTS IN A WAY PREVIOUSLY THOUGHT IMPOSSIBLE

Regular engine

- Supply of a denser mixture of air and fuel decreases NOx but increases CO and HC.

- Supply of a thinner mixture of air and fuel decreases CO and HC but increases NOx.

- As the mixture grows thinner, NOx and CO will decrease but the engine may die.

Sources of pollutants

- The higher the temperature of the gas in the cylinder, the greater the amount of NOx emitted.

- The more quickly the temperature of the gas in the cylinder falls in the process of expansion, the greater the amount of unignited fuel emitted as HC.

- The greater the amount of dense fuel supplied, the greater the amount of CO emitted due to lack of oxygen resulting from oxidation.

Merits of CVCC engine
- Decrease in NOx by lowering the maximum combustion temperature.

- Decrease in HC by prolonging the time the temperature of oxidation is maintained.
- Decrease in CO by supplying very thin mixed gas so as to make sufficient oxygen available.

Source: Mito (1990).

dichotomy and associated trade-off tackled by the VTEC engines was fuel economy versus engine power; to improve fuel economy meant losing power. However, in the VTEC engine the innovative variable valves (the mechanisms which let fuel and air in and out of the combustion chamber), in conjunction with the electronically controlled fuel injection system, control the ratio of fuel to air according to driving conditions. In normal mode, a fuel-thin mixture provides fuel economy. But at high engine speeds with the driver's foot pressed hard on the accelerator a fuel-richer mixture provides significantly more power. Figure 3 illustrates both the

performance economy trade-off of Honda's conventional engines, and the dichotomy-reconciling leap achieved by VTEC engines in Honda Accord automobiles.

While in product terms Honda is perhaps best known for its technologically innovative engines, refusal to accept taken-for-granted trade-offs characterizes all aspects of Honda's strategic approach to technological change. This is well illustrated in the revealing language used by a Honda engineer describing an apparently mundane technological advance made by Honda R&D at its North American operations (see Exhibit 4).

FIGURE 3 The VTEC engine compared to the conventional fuel consumption-acceleration trade-off

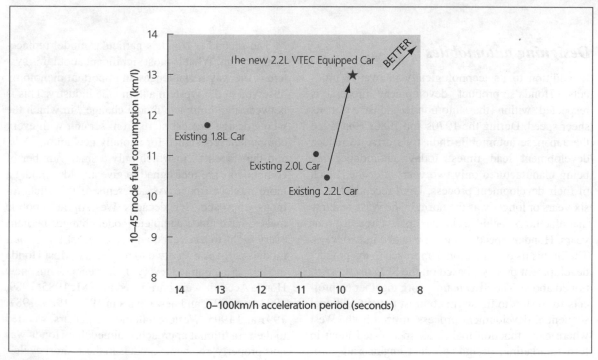

Source: Japan Autotech Report (1993).

EXHIBIT 4 WE AREN'T INTERESTED IN TRADE-OFFS

When it comes to weight reduction, the auto industry's appetite is insatiable. Honda is no exception.

As part of a corporate goal to reduce weight in its automobiles, Honda of America Manufacturing Inc. in Marysville, Ohio, is the first automaker in the United States to use a lightweight underbody coating, or sound deadener, with expanded polymeric microspheres supplied by Pierce & Stevens Corp. of Buffalo, NY.

Besides lightweight, Honda sought several other attributes from any new underbody coating, including reduced volatile organic compound emissions and an improved durability standard.

Honda also wanted improved 'line-side workability' – the ease-of-use characteristics judged by those who work with the product on the production line.

In addition, the product could not require any modifications to the existing sound-deadener delivery and application systems.

It was a tall order, but according to Trish Peters, assistant manager of the Marysville plant's auto paint department, reformulations either meet all of Honda's standards or they aren't used at all.

'We aren't interested in trade-offs', she said. 'We won't accept lesser performance in any aspect of a product to get improvement in some other aspect. Our sound-deadener suppliers – there are several – know this. They accepted our goals and came back to us with formulations that included polymeric microspheres – what we call 'plastic balloons.'

'We reduced the weight of the deadener by 30 to 40 percent', said Lee Manville of the Marysville auto paint production staff. 'We got better adhesion of the product to the body surface and were able to reduce film build (the amount applied) while improving our durability standard'.

'We're satisfied with the performance of the reformulated sound deadener – for now', said Peters. 'Honda has trained us not to make or accept assumptions about the performance of anything we use. Our department's goals – to improve existing materials and find new materials – are like our corporate goals to improve quality and drive down costs. They never end'.

Source: Fleming (1993).

Designing automobiles

In addition to its technologically innovative products, Honda's product development process is respected within the automobile industry for its sheer speed. During the 1970s and 1980s Honda led the Japanese automobile industry's drive to reduce development lead times: today automobiles are being manufactured only two years after the launch of their development process. Until recently five to six years or longer was the norm in the West, and few manufacturers achieve better than three to four years. Honda's speed has been attained in two ways. The first is its organizational approach to the product development process, based on the SED teams mentioned above. The SED teams work together on projects from start to finish, in contrast to the traditional sequential development process utilized in the West where each function makes its specialized input in turn (marketing, design, product engineering, production engineering and manufacturing).

The second is Honda's particular model replacement system. What is most significant about this system is the way it challenges an important dichotomy observed in the Western automobile industry. This is between the 'complete model change', in which the whole design process starts from scratch with every component redesigned for a totally new automobile, and the 'facelift', in which only a small number of components are redesigned to give an older model a more modern image. As adherents of this dichotomous approach, for decades Western automobile makers have made complete model changes perhaps every eight to ten years, and given facelifts to their models perhaps every two to four years. Most Honda models are changed every four years. Thus new Honda Accords were introduced in 1981, 1985, 1989, 1993 and 1997, and new Civics in 1979, 1983, 1987, 1991 and 1995. Western automobile makers, wedded to their traditional approach, claimed that Honda was not 'properly' replacing models in these short cycles, but simply giving its models a cosmetic facelift.

Yet Honda's strategic approach to model replacement means that it does not face the same dichotomous choices. The process at Honda can be described schematically as follows. Honda's model changes are neither complete changes nor mere facelifts. Instead, every four years, when a Honda model is 'officially' replaced, the components the driver can see or otherwise notice are replaced: the exterior body shape, the interior design, the lights. Then, also every four years with a two-year lag after the official model change, vital unseen components are changed, and new engines, gearboxes, braking systems, for instance, are introduced. The outcome is best described as a 'rolling' or 'iterative' model change programme with significant and regular changes to each model (and hence a regular boost to customer interest). The traditional distinction between complete change and facelift is dispensed with in favour of a smoother, more fluid and flexible approach. Manufacturing systems (for instance, sizes and shapes of machinery) and whole vehicle design configurations (for instance, sizes and shapes of components and the spaces they fit in) are pre-planned as far as possible to allow for the expected evolution of models and components.

This iterative process of model evolution is put into practice in three 'dimensions'. The first is over time, as described above. Thus the 1993 replacement for the Today model, sold in Japan, shared 40 percent of its components with its predecessor. Second, it is practiced laterally, in the development of parallel, 'sister' models for different market segments. The third dimension is geographical, in which models developed for different world markets are frequently spin-offs from existing models (neither entirely different, nor mere cosmetic changes). Hence both the Accord and Civic models that Honda was manufacturing in Europe in the mid-1990s were spin-offs, with significant engineering changes, from automobiles first manufactured for the Japanese market.

Strategies for production and logistics: The assembly line

What philosophy guides how Honda actually makes its products? Honda has sought to combine the advantages inherent in what have normally been seen in the West as dichotomous and mutually exclusive production and logistics systems.

Honda first experimented with a 'free-flow' assembly line at its Kumamoto motorcycle plant on the Japanese island of Kyushu in the late 1970s. This system was an attempt to combine productive efficiency with human dignity. Efficiency and dignity have been treated as polar opposites in the traditional Western strategy for manufacturing design which regarded the mind-numbing and alienating continuous assembly line, with its fragmentation of tasks carefully orchestrated by time-and-motion staff, as the epitome of efficiency, and viewed the efforts of the Swedish automobile manufacturers Volvo and Saab to develop more personally satisfying forms of 'group work' in the 1970s and 1980s as necessarily sacrificing efficiency.

Honda's free-flow assembly line, the first of its type in the Japanese motor industry, was based on a series of separate carriers upon which partially completed vehicles were placed (or hung). The carriers followed each other from work-station to work-station but their speed of movement was not controlled centrally as with the traditional chain-driven line. Advantages were sought in terms of efficiency and dignity. On the one hand both manual and automated assembly tasks could be undertaken more accurately since the separate carriers could stop at each work-station. Moreover, work could be completed satisfactorily before the carrier was sent on its way. On the other hand production workers could be given a sense of control over the production process since they could make the decision that the task had been executed properly and that the carrier should now move to the next work-station. The free-flow principle was later adopted for the new third automobile assembly line built at the Suzuka factory in the late 1980s, where Honda has continued to experiment with it.

Production planning

Honda has also developed an innovative strategy for the planning of production, a strategy which exhibits characteristics of both the traditional dichotomous poles. One pole is 'large-lot mass production', in which manufacturing is organized so that thousands of identical or virtually identical products are made in a row, or series. This implies the use of dedicated machinery and, indeed, in the Western automobile industry each factory frequently can make only a single automobile model, which is changed every few years. To many, the automobile industry is the epitome of large-lot mass production. In this system the goal is to reduce costs, achieved at the expense of product variety (the trade-off within the Western mass production system).

At the other extreme is the 'one-piece-flow' production system said to characterize at least some firms in the Japanese automobile industry. In this system each assembly line can handle several different models with minimal if any changeover time, and the partly finished vehicles coming down the line are sequenced in 'lots of one', i.e. each vehicle is different from that preceding and following it (colours, options, engines, numbers of doors, models). The objective of this system is to permit far greater product variety (to the point of 'customized' products individually ordered). One drawback is the very complex logistics system needed to supply components to the assembly line in the correct order. In general terms, the Toyota-developed 'just-in-time' production and logistics system can be seen as a dichotomy reconciliation permitting both product variety and productive efficiency.

Honda's own innovative strategy for production planning has been to develop a 'small batch' production system based around the key number 60 and its factors (30, 15, 12, etc.). Automobiles are sent down the assembly lines in batches in which each vehicle is exactly the same (including colour). Workers therefore execute exactly the same tasks for each batch. Components are delivered to the assembly line in batches (lot sizes, colours, optional extras) which exactly match the vehicles they will be fitted into. The objective is to combine the advantages of large-lot production (simpler logistics and quality control, less likelihood of error, easier to programme production schedules) and of small-lot production (ability to offer a wider range of products to consumers and greater worker involvement and satisfaction).

Making production planning and product marketing coherent

This small batch production system is closely linked to Honda's strategy towards marketing and sales. Honda has tended not to offer its customers the spectacular breadth of choice developed by other Japanese automobile manufacturers during the Japanese 'bubble economy' of the late 1980s. Some firms expanded product variety so far that Japanese customers could choose among several dozen different steering wheels per model, a level of consumer choice which was soon recognized to have got out of hand. Honda's strategy emphasizes the high technology built into all its products and it was quick to

offer features like advanced engines (though often available in only two sizes per model), anti-lock brakes, electric windows and sun-roofs as standard rather than optional extras, thus simplifying product variety within each model type.

In operations management, an important dichotomy distinguishes 'push'-based production planning and logistical systems from 'pull'-based systems. In the former, said to be typically Western, production schedules for particular models are set out months in advance, and alignment of output levels with customer demand tends to focus on sales strategy (e.g. discounting may be necessary). In the latter, said to be typically Japanese, automobiles are only made to customer order.

Honda's approach to production planning is to operate a combination push-pull system. When planning at the annual scale, production levels of particular models can be varied up or down as a function of demand, because flexible equipment means that production lines can be used for various models (in gross terms, a pull system). When undertaking monthly planning, an 'un-Japanese' push system fixes the total mix of products and appropriate schedules several months in advance, based on market forecasts. Simultaneously a small-scale inventory pull system is utilized for everyday production planning, where it helps deal with unforeseen difficulties: if, for instance, there is a problem with a certain colour of paint in the paint shops, components makers may be alerted in a matter of hours that the production schedule has been altered and they will need to respond accordingly. The outcome at Honda is the simultaneous operation of pull- and push-based production planning systems rather than dominance of one type over the other.

Relationships with components makers

In the analysis of inter-firm relationships, in particular buyer-supplier relations in the components supply chain, a distinction is traditionally made in the West between vertical integration and market relationships (reflected in the 'make or buy?' decision). Honda's approach to relationships with its components suppliers transcends this dichotomy and others associated with supply chain management. In Japan Honda has only a handful of components makers that might be considered to belong to its supplier 'family', and is the only firm in the Japanese automobile industry not to organize its own 'suppliers association' as a forum for suppliers to meet and solve common problems. Honda does build long-term relationships with its suppliers, but these are not buttressed by the institutional mechanisms (cross-shareholding, 'family' relationships, supplier associations) often said to govern long-term relationships in Japan.

In North America, where a substantial network of more than 80 Japanese 'transplant' component makers has developed to supply Honda with components, Honda invested its own capital in a number of the early arrivals as a means of reducing the risk for its smaller Japanese partners. Other than this, formal linkages in North America are non-existent. And yet in operational terms Honda intervenes directly in the 'internal' activities of its component makers when it believes this necessary. For a number of components Honda arranges the purchase of the raw materials, for example steel and aluminium, two or three tiers back along the supply chain, which will eventually find their way into Honda automobiles, gaining advantages in price and quality. Honda engineers also visit suppliers regularly, and may be stationed in their factories for a time if serious problems arise in components delivery and quality.

Thus relationships with component makers are based on complex combinations of close control and open, commercial relationships, creating a structure which defies the polar types in traditional views of buyer–supplier relations. The goal is clearly to reconcile the dichotomy to gain the advantages accruing from each polar type of organizing.

The same refusal to fit easily into traditional categories holds for the number of supplier firms from which Honda sources each component. The traditional dichotomous choice between 'dual/multiple' sourcing strategy versus 'single' sourcing strategy is bypassed by Honda, where sourcing strategy is based on elements of both. Thus Honda sources a certain type of seat (the basic version, say) for its Accord model from supplier A, in single-sourcing fashion, and simultaneously sources a different type of seat (perhaps a high-tech electronic version) from supplier B, also in single-sourcing fashion. The two suppliers are not in direct competition, yet Honda can subtly play them off (in dual-sourcing fashion) since each is aware of the other's existence and willingness to expand its market share when plans are made for the next Accord model change. Honda gains the advantage of both single sourcing (stable relationships with one supplier) and dual sourcing (an element of competition).

Honda's ability to find solutions even reaches into the geographical pattern of its relationships with component makers in North America. The traditional approach is to choose between purchasing from component makers located very long distances away, often to allow cheap labour sources in other regions and countries to be exploited (a feature of the 'Western model'), and the spatially concentrated production system at Toyota City in Japan, where hundreds of supplier companies and nearly all Toyota's production capacity are concentrated into a few square kilometres, which is particularly advantageous for just-in-time logistics.

In North America, where Honda has greatly influenced the general location choices made by its Japanese component makers, the geographical pattern reflects both spatial dispersal and spatial concentration. In Ohio, where Honda's main manufacturing base has been constructed, there are now more than 40 Japanese-owned firms making automobile components, nearly all of which supply Honda. Concentration within a two-hour travel-time permits just-in-time 'pull' logistics to be operated on a day-to-day basis. However, within Ohio the factories are dispersed to small town locations 10 to 20 miles apart; this way, their local labour markets are separated and the new investments and jobs they represent will not drive up local wages. Distant from Honda too, they can offer wages only half to two-thirds those paid at the automobile assembly plant. In other words, Honda's network of component makers is designed to combine the advantages of spatial concentration and spatial dispersal.

Honda's strategic challenges

How does Honda manage the key dichotomies of strategic management: planning vs. learning, market positioning vs. developing internal resources, and within the resource-based perspective, product-related core competencies vs. process-related core capabilities? The many Western observers of Honda from the academic and consultancy worlds in recent years have tended to lay the emphasis on one pole to the exclusion of the other, and have battled it out among themselves to claim that Honda is *either* a planner *or* a learner, *either* a market positioner *or* a resource builder, *either* a competency-based diversifier *or* a capabilities predator. Similarly, followers of trends in multinational enterprise organization have been quick to claim that Honda exemplifies a polar position as a 'post-national' or 'stateless' corporation operating in a 'borderless' world (Mair, 1997, 1998).

Judging by the evidence of Honda's strategic capability to reconcile dichotomies, these analysts may be missing the point. As the energies of debate have been channelled into ceaseless either/or argument, meanwhile Honda may have been focusing its strategic effort, and mobilizing its dichotomy-reconciling strategic capability, precisely on reconciling the apparently incompatible poles of strategic dichotomies in a way that consigns these debates to the irrelevant margins.

Have Honda's strategists therefore implemented detailed planned strategies with precision whilst simultaneously learning and adjusting strategy to business environment change? One clue may be found by reversing the normal assumption that the formulation and execution of detailed strategic plans is inevitably a long-term process such that learning from environmental change can only extend to marginal tweaks. What if learning were the long term and planning the short term? A strategically agile company might be able to make operational (treat as short-term variables) parameters previously considered strategic (necessarily fixed in the short term). The strategy process would then consist of a series of rapid formulation-implementation pulses over time. And indeed Honda's rapid and iterative new product development process and flexifactory manufacturing infrastructure appear to support just such an approach.

Can a market positioning and resource-based view of strategy content be reconciled in innovative ways? Here Honda appears to have faced difficult challenges at a number of points in its history, without always succeeding, particularly in reconciling the company's core competencies in engine design as well as its engineers' pursuit of technological mastery to the evolution of market demand. Significantly, notwithstanding Honda's image as a designer of sporty and technically innovative cars, fully three-quarters of the company's global sales comprise the relatively conservative and simple Civic and Accord models, which, broadly speaking, occupy the market position (once thought unattainable) which combines high quality with low cost based on core capabilities residing at the heart of Honda's product design and production process. What core-competency related product technology breakthroughs might provide the basis for novel and successful market positions in future? Not surprisingly, along with other industry companies, Honda

has recently invested huge resources into developing new low-pollution power sources for its vehicles (electric, solar power, for example), in the drive to focus its competencies on potential breakthrough market positions.

Which matters most to the consumer, Honda's core competencies in mechanical technologies, or its core capabilities in managing the whole value chain from raw materials to dealer networks via product design and production processes? This dichotomy seems plainly false, at Honda at least. The company focuses on both resources because both matter to purchasers of its products: if to varying degrees. Purchasers of the top-of-the-range super sports NSX model are presumably attracted by the car's driving and handling characteristics, features intimately related to product technology, whereas purchasers of a small engine three-door Civic model may focus more on cost, quality, and reliability (hence in some countries, notably the United Kingdom, Honda has struggled to shake off a market image as a maker of cars for the over 60s), product features associated more with core design and production process capabilities.

The grand dichotomies of business and corporate strategy are clearly more complex, multilayered concepts and practices than those associated with operations, human resources and other functional-level strategies. Yet Honda seems destined to pitch the company's collective intellect full-force into the struggle to find ways of reconciling them for competitive advantage. Each time Honda succeeds in finding new solutions, the competitive map in its chosen industries will be redrawn, just as it has been at regular intervals over the past 50 years.

References

Bélis-Bergouignan, M.-C., Bordenave, G., and Lung, Y. (1998) Global strategies in the automobile industry, *Regional Studies* (forthcoming).

Chandler, C. and Ingrassia, P. (1991) Just as US Firms Try Japanese Management, Honda is Centralizing: Kawamoto Finds 'Teamwork' Is No Longer Enough To Boost Market Share: Coming Soon: Private Offices, *The Wall Street Journal*, 4th November, pp. 1 and A10.

Fleming, A. (1993) Honda switches to lighter underbody coating, *Automotive News*, 12th April, p. 20.

Japan Autotech Report (1993) Vol. 175, p. 23.

Mair, A. (1997) Strategic localization: the myth of the post-national enterprise, in Cox, K.R. (ed.), *Spaces of Globalization: Reasserting the Power of the Local*, Guildford, New York, pp. 64–88.

Mair, A. (1998) Learning from Honda, *Journal of Management Studies*.

Mito, S. (1990) *The Honda Book of Management: A Leadership Philosophy for High Industrial Success*, Kogan Page, London.

Taylor III, A. (1991) A US-Style Shakeup at Honda: CEO Kawamoto has abandoned consensus management for American-looking organization charts. Result: Communications and decision-making are getting faster, *Fortune*, 20 December.

The house that Branson built: Virgin's entry into the new millennium

By Robert Dick, Kets de Vries and Raoul de Vitry d' Avaucourt[1]

Reflecting in 1999 on significant events in the history of the Virgin Group, Richard Branson, its chairman, remained extremely ambivalent about the most momentous decision of his business career – a decision that had been made seven years earlier. It concerned his acceptance of a £510 million cash offer from Thorn EMI, a UK conglomerate with extensive music interests, for his record label Virgin Music. A private company with tangible assets of less than £4 million, Virgin Music was, symbolically, the heart of the Virgin Group, having its roots in the late 1960s, when Branson and his first collaborators founded a record mail-order business in London. Its sale, therefore, meant a great deal more to Branson than simply another business transaction. He would part company with many people he had known since childhood and hand over a business that had been built painstakingly on cash flow using a combination of guile, flair, and luck.

In March 1992, Branson was a reluctant seller, but he was also a realist. He recognized that the cards were heavily stacked against him. The world economy – the airline industry in particular – was in the doldrums in the aftermath of the Gulf War. Virgin Atlantic, the airline he had founded in the mid '80s, had been badly affected by the turmoil in the Middle East. Moreover, it was being targeted in a competitive war by British Airways, which (it would later transpire) was using dubious tactics to gain advantage. Further complicating matters, the media were speculating on Virgin's financial health (prompted, if Branson's allegations are accurate, by misleading stories fed to journalists by British Airways); and behind the scenes, Virgin's bankers were pressing ever more strongly for a sale to reduce debt, reinforcing Branson's disdain for financial organizations that he saw as fair-weather friends.

More personally, Simon Draper, Branson's cousin and the creative force behind Virgin Music, had made it clear that he wanted to cash in his equity and do something different with his life. A vehement opponent of Virgin's move into the airline business from the outset, he envisaged his life's work collapsing with the airline, which was surviving only on the cash flow and guarantees provided by Virgin Music. And Virgin Music provided strong support indeed: only months before, the music label had signed the Rolling Stones, a sign of the position it had attained in the worldwide music business.

Branson realized that the sale of Virgin Music would transform Virgin's financial situation. After settling with the Japanese company Fujisankei, a 25 percent shareholder, and with Simon Draper and Ken Berry (a key collaborator and minority shareholder who had started at Virgin as an accounts clerk and who now runs Thorn EMI's music business), Branson would be left with over £350 million in cash – more than enough to 'fulfill [my] wildest dreams.' (Branson 1998: p. 413).

Growing a business: A strategy for fun

Richard Branson's business career started when, at the age of seventeen, he founded *Student* magazine – the 'Voice of Youth' – while still at boarding school. Based on co-operative principles, the magazine employed fellow students as workers and a nearby public pay phone as an office. *Student* was a product of the 1960s, the decade when the post-war 'baby boomers' came of age. Across Western Europe and North America, young people enjoyed educational, employment, and lifestyle opportunities unknown to their parents, all made possible by rapid economic growth. The decade became known for its promotion of a youth culture in which authority was challenged, fashions changed rapidly, and rock stars were the global gurus of a new age.

[1]Source: © 2000 INSEAD, Fontainebleau, France. All rights reserved.

The initial success of the magazine (Branson optimistically claimed a circulation of 100,000) was not sustained. Seeking new activities to boost his flagging business, he decided to try to tap the potential he saw in the sale of records, still overpriced despite the abolition of retail price maintenance, a UK government policy designed to support certain industries by allowing manufacturers and suppliers to 'recommend' prices to retailers.

Lacking the capital to start a retail outlet, Branson and his associates simply placed an advertisement in the last issue of *Student* to test the market, listing only records likely to appeal to young people. Prices discounted those offered in stores by as much as 15 percent, and orders (accompanied by cash) came flooding in. Casting around for a name for his new business, he finally accepted a suggestion made jokingly by one of his coterie, who claimed that what they needed was a name that proclaimed their commercial innocence but also had a certain shock value, in keeping with the anti-establishment mood of the times. What better, therefore, than 'Virgin'? The name appealed to Branson and was adopted despite objections from the registration authorities, who deemed it to be in poor taste.

Branson quickly realized that buying and selling records in bulk required proper controls and systems. He turned to a childhood friend, Nik Powell, to help him manage his new business, offering in return a 40 percent stake in the company. Methodical where Branson was erratic, cautious where Branson would overextend himself, Nik Powell became the ideal counterbalance in the record mail-order company.

In 1971 a national postal strike threatened to push the mail-order company into bankruptcy. Immediately Branson rented retail space, transferred his stock of records, and launched Virgin Retail. True to the emerging Virgin style, the shop's decor was a mix of the outrageous and the shabby, attracting customers more bent on enjoying an experience than spending money. Later that year, Virgin received its first overseas order. Realizing that records intended for export could be purchased by Virgin tax-free, Branson gave in to the temptation to make a quick cash profit by selling 'exported' records through his London store – until the tax authorities pounced.

Shocked and humiliated, Branson spent an uncomfortable night in prison. He was released only after a tearful appeal to his parents to put up £30,000 bail, using their home as security. Eventually, formal charges were dropped in return for an out-of-court financial settlement. Later, Branson would laughingly dismiss his night in a cell, but the pain and embarrassment he caused his parents made him resolve to 'avoid sleepless nights and pay taxes.' Even so, Branson remains an unwilling tax payer and holds his Virgin shareholding in secret off-shore family trusts, preferring 'to reinvest profits in the business.'

While these setbacks were taking place, Branson had a piece of good fortune. Simon Draper persuaded him to consider backing Mike Oldfield, a nervous, troubled, and talented young musician who arrived at Virgin clutching a handful of recording tapes. Having already been rejected by the major recording studios, the young man was looking for friends and supporters. At Virgin he found them, and his first recording, *Tubular Bells*, was to launch him and Virgin into the big time.

Tubular Bells *and the Sex Pistols*

Released in 1973, *Tubular Bells* was an immediate hit, eventually selling over five million copies worldwide. The massive inflow of funds transformed the company. For Branson, this was the ideal opportunity to launch the Virgin record label and join the ranks of the small independent record producers that were active in the UK market at that time. Within two years, however, financial pressure forced Virgin to reassess its position to avoid becoming a one-hit record label. Its original creative policy, which focused on non-mainstream artists, was not working. Branson needed something fast to re-establish the Virgin name with the record-buying public. He achieved his aim in 1977 with a notorious punk rock band: the Sex Pistols. Debauched and drug-crazed, foul-mouthed and obscene, the Sex Pistols were the subject of intense media coverage and speculation until one of its members, already facing a murder charge, died of a drug overdose and the band disintegrated. But their short existence was a considerable fillip for Virgin.

By the end of the '70s, Virgin comprised a record label, recording studios, music retail outlets, music and book publishing, night-clubs, and cinemas. Virgin had prospered in a buoyant UK market. But as the decade closed, recession and high inflation, combined with changing consumer tastes, severely affected the music business worldwide.

Sales contracted and few record companies earned profits. Virgin registered losses of £400,000 in 1980 and £900,000 in 1981. Although well-established, the record company was still a small player living hand-to-mouth in a business dominated by large multinationals.

With financial pressure mounting, Branson was forced to act. Looking to Nik Powell for solutions, he was offered belt-tightening measures that inevitably included laying off personnel, a task Branson has always found daunting and has avoided whenever possible, usually by delegation. The anxiety and ill-feeling that the various measures caused led to talk of union representation.

To some extent Branson himself had inflamed discontent in his company. His personal business philosophy was simple: Why worry about the past? It is over and done. Look to the future to solve difficulties through new opportunities, expansion, and growth. Even as the company was firing staff, closing its US office, and cutting its roster of bands, Branson used scarce financial resources to purchase two night-clubs – Heaven, London's largest venue for homosexuals, and the struggling Roof Garden. He also launched a new London entertainment guide, *Event*, founded to challenge the strike-bound market leader, *Time Out*. The launch was unsuccessful; within a year *Event* closed at a cost to Virgin of £750,000.

Branson's expansion-oriented actions created tension between him and his senior management, particularly Nik Powell. As Powell's working relationship with Branson soured, he realized that his ambitions were likely to remain unfulfilled while he was number two. Matters came to head over creative policy. Despite limited funds, Simon Draper wanted to invest in new bands and to continue financing existing artists whom he believed would eventually be profitable. Nik Powell, advocating a more cautious, corporate-type approach, pressed for the pruning of loss-making bands. Obligated to make the choice that would settle matters, Branson, with some reluctance and sadness, backed Draper's artistic judgement over the more conventional approach offered by Powell.

His instinct proved right: within a short span of time, Virgin had some of the most profitable bands of the '80s – Phil Collins, Human League, Simple Minds, and the hugely successful Culture Club, led by the transvestite Boy George. Virgin successfully maneuvered itself out of the recession, nearly doubling its turnover from £48 million in 1982 to £94

million in 1983, with profits soaring to over £11 million. But Nik Powell was not around to share the success. Dissatisfied with his position, he had left the company in 1981, selling his shareholding in return for £1 million, Virgin's cinema interests, and a video recording studio. Branson was once again the 100 percent owner of Virgin, with two trusted lieutenants: Simon Draper and Ken Berry. (Both later acquired holdings in the record company after lengthy negotiations.) Branson, depending on Draper for creative decisions and on Berry for contracts and management, kept himself out of the day-to-day administration of the company to concentrate on new ventures.

In France, Germany, and Italy, Virgin companies were established to add local artists to the company roster and to represent UK bands. In the US, the Virgin label was re-established. The huge success of Virgin artists attracted increasing numbers of established and emerging bands to the Virgin stable, creating a portfolio of talent that challenged the industry leaders. In circumstances such as these, conventional business practice would dictate that success should be consolidated and expansion restricted to complementary activities. Such, however, was not to be Branson's way. He wanted to expand his company in a completely new direction. To the astonishment of music industry observers, the horror of Simon Draper, and the ridicule of the music press, Richard Branson was off on a new path: he was going to found an airline.

'Never let the facts get in the way of a good idea'

In early 1984, Branson received a call from Randolph Fields, the 31-year-old California-born lawyer who had founded British Atlantic, a transatlantic airline not yet off the ground that hoped to target business travelers. Fields, one of an increasing number of people arriving at Branson's door with ideas that needed backing, was seeking additional financing to get his airline airborne. Branson was all too aware of the dangers in entering the airline business: his company had no experience in that arena, the business was capital intensive, and revenue was highly seasonal. Furthermore, he recalled the recent experience of a UK cut-price airline, Laker Airlines, which had been pushed into bankruptcy by high debts, currency fluctuations, and ferocious competition from established national airlines. The industry

Goliaths had slaughtered the upstart David in a battle whose echoes were still straining UK/US trade diplomacy in the mid '80s.

Yet, despite all these reservations and obstacles, Branson was persuaded by Fields's proposal. Within a week – 'We can decide something in the morning and have it running in the afternoon' is Branson's proud boast – he had formed a partnership with Fields, renaming the airline Virgin Atlantic. It was later dubbed by jokers the airline that Boy George built, a reference to the supposed source of cash injected by Branson into his new project. The launch in June 1984 saw him playing to the cameras dressed as a World War I pilot in leather jacket and goggles, the first in a long line of publicity stunts that were to become Branson's trademark.

One of a number of ex-Laker managers recruited by Branson was David Tait, now President of Virgin Atlantic North America, based in Norwalk, Connecticut. Recalling the launch of the airline he said:

> I thought that Virgin was the most stupid name ever for an airline, and I told him that his plan [for business class only] was not a good idea and explained why. But with Richard, you never let the facts get in the way of a good idea! ... Despite what people think, it was never a budget proposition either – more a mix of economy and business class, which in those days only Air Florida had tried with success. Since we went into Newark and not JFK, we could also offer lower fares with less chance of reprisal. But our real secret was to offer value-for-money. Charge the same or slightly less for a much better product: first-class travel at business-class rates.

The creation of his airline took Branson into unfamiliar territory. His business needed skills not previously required in the unregulated, open-market environment of the record industry. The airline business, by contrast, was – and remains – highly political: the awarding of jealously guarded international landing rights to (mostly) nationalized airlines involved protracted inter-governmental negotiations, requiring Branson to lobby the Thatcher government. Informally advised by Freddy Laker, Branson also had an eye to the future; he anticipated predatory pricing from the major airlines that would jeopardize his cost advantage – the Laker scenario all over again.

Randolph Fields, who had brought the airline idea to Branson, did not stay long with Virgin. His management style, Branson concluded, did not fit either the Virgin ethos or the detailed operation of an airline, although Branson recognized Fields's contribution in putting together the initial proposal. Behind the scenes, relations between the two became so acrimonious that Branson felt forced to oust Fields in 1985, buying his shareholding for £1 million. Fields later said that he had fallen in love with Branson on the day they met, but that Branson had fallen in love only with Fields's idea.

From the rock market to the stock market

In late 1986 a series of press and TV advertisements appeared in the UK under the slogan 'From the rock market to the stock market.' The advertisement invited the public to buy shares in the Virgin Group. Richard Branson, for so long a champion of private company status and the independence of entrepreneurs, had succumbed to the blandishments of City investment bankers to sell part of his company during the '80s bull market. He saw the move as an opportunity to raise capital quickly to reduce the company's dependence on short-term bank borrowing – and what Branson saw as demanding and short-sighted bankers – and to further expand without losing control of his company. (When the public company was eventually floated, Branson and his senior collaborators retained control of 63 percent of the voting stock.)

Much of the detail work of the flotation had been handled by Don Cruickshank, appointed Group Managing Director in 1984. A Scottish accountant with an MBA from Manchester Business School, Cruickshank had worked for the consulting firm McKinsey and had been in general management in the media industry. At ease in City circles, he was the kind of executive with whom bankers felt comfortable, an important factor in Branson's decision to recruit him via head-hunters.

Despite the demand for shares, the stock market flotation was not the success that Branson or the investors had expected. Although recording better-then-expected profits, Virgin's share price performed badly post-flotation and later fell precipitously when the London exchange crashed in October 1987. Moreover, relations between Virgin management and City analysts were at best uneasy. Branson was unsuited to cultivating the type of relationship that the chairman of a public company must have with institutional investors. While appreciating the discipline that being a public company had imposed on his company, he nevertheless felt that the City undervalued Virgin and failed to understand the entrepreneurial nature of his business, especially the music division. The analysts in turn were uncomfortable with the vagaries of a business where, it seemed to them, most of the assets – rock musicians and their creative output – were valued against the ephemeral nature of public taste. (More recently there has been evidence to show that established artists can create a steady revenue stream against which investment decisions can be calculated. The sale in 1997 of David Bowie's work via a securitized bond placement is a case in point.)

The analysts' doubts and concerns were reinforced by the unpredictable nature of the Chairman and the demands on his time from his publicity stunts, airline business, and charitable activities. Unwilling to tolerate the constraints placed upon him but determined to help the many small investors who had seen the value of their investment diminish, Branson finally resolved to quit the stock market. In July 1988 he announced his decision to raise privately £200 million to be used to buy out the publicly held shares at the original asking price, in effect compensating the original shareholders, both private and corporate, who at that point faced a considerable paper loss. Richard Branson thus honored a moral debt he felt he owed and was once more master of his own destiny.

Too old to rock, too young to fly

The unsuccessful flotation had forced Branson to review Virgin's activities and modus operandi. With a major debt to repay and still in need of a substantial capital injection to finance his ambitions for the company, Branson recognized that he needed external investors. However, his approach in the light of his stock market experience was to be more circumspect.

In the years following privatization, Branson, while still an opportunistic entrepreneur, nevertheless followed a path of growth through joint ventures with established companies. This approach permitted his company to expand, in terms of both product and geography. The most significant deal was the sale in 1989 of 25 percent of Virgin Records to Fujisankei, Japan's largest media company, for £115 million. That same year, another Japanese company – Seibu Saison, the hotel chain – paid £10 million for 10 percent of Virgin Travel, which had recently

acquired landing rights in Tokyo through Virgin Atlantic.

In the UK, Virgin's retail interests were consolidated around the Megastore concept in a joint venture with a major retailer. In prestige locations in major cities, Megastores began to sell home-entertainment products – music, videos, and books – on a large scale. They replaced the string of small secondary retail outlets for which Virgin had become known. The success of the Megastore concept was exported to major cities throughout the world, frequently through joint ventures.

Virgin Atlantic had also advanced dramatically from the original operation envisaged by Randolph Fields. Although still a relatively small player, it now competed with the major carriers on the same routes out of London, winning awards for innovation and service as well as plaudits from vital business travelers. Virgin Atlantic had become a serious threat to the major airlines – none more so than British Airways (BA), the UK's national carrier, led by the ebullient and forthright Lord King.

However, the airline had suffered financially as a result of the recession and the Gulf War, perhaps more than Branson was prepared to admit publicly. He was reconciled to finding a major capital investment to ensure the airline's long-term survival, an ambition close to his heart. Internally, such capital could realistically come only from the sale of the record business – the jewel in the Virgin crown and the largest remaining independent record company in the world.

After long discussions with his immediate team, and wrenching soul-searching, Branson, advised by the investment bank Goldman Sachs, entered into negotiations with Bertelsmann of Germany and Thorn EMI, calculating that the time was ripe to conclude a sale on his terms. Thorn's offer of cash or shares (Branson took the cash) to a value of £510 million won the day, allowing Branson to clear his debts and to plan the expansion of his airline in the way he sought. Commercial to the last, Branson and Berry managed to win £9 million on currency speculation by delaying payment to Fujisankei to the last contractual moment.

Virgin Music was combined with EMI records, creating a music business with 18 percent of the world market. City comments that Thorn had overpaid for Virgin were quickly discounted. A rationalization of Virgin staff and bands improved Thorn's profits by more than £80 million in 1993–94. At the time of the sale, some Virgin Music employees felt that they had been let down by Branson. They had assumed they would share in the profits from the sale of the company, although no promises had been made. Many of the long-serving staff attended an emotional farewell party where a tearful Branson and Draper assured them that Ken Berry would be staying with Virgin and that its future independence within the Thorn EMI group was guaranteed. After the sale, Branson said, 'Too many entrepreneurs have gone down because they were not prepared to cash in their chips at the right time.'

The battle between British Airways and Virgin Atlantic, personalized around its two leaders (Lord King dismissing Richard Branson as 'too old to rock and too young to fly'), became increasingly acrimonious. Matters came to a head when a television program alleged that BA had used dirty tricks against Virgin Atlantic, breaking into its computer system to target its customers, spreading misinformation about Virgin's financial state, and diverting its customers at US airports to BA flights. Branson immediately sued BA for damages, claiming £11 million. Lord King's rebuttal was libellous and Branson won substantial damages, humiliating the BA chairman and accelerating his retirement after an otherwise distinguished business career. As a gesture to the airline staff, Branson divided the damages among them.

Coming of age?

The sale of the record company in 1992 saw the departure of many long-serving staff. This, combined with the evolutionary changes in retail, the growth of the airline, and the creation of new companies, moved Virgin away from its roots and previous management structure. From 1992 to 1997, the company was overseen by a triumvirate: Richard Branson, Trevor Abbott (the Group's Finance Director, brought in by Cruickshank), and Robert Devereux (Branson's brother-in-law, who headed the media and entertainment interests). These latter are no longer with Virgin. Robert Devereux, now a wealthy man, has achieved his aim of 'semi-retiring at forty' and spends his time climbing mountains; Trevor Abbott took his own life, motivated, it is believed, by serious personal problems and his diminishing role at Virgin. Their functions are now fulfilled by Simon Burke and Steven Murphy, respectively.

Research on the Virgin brand name in the early 1990s demonstrated the impact over time of quirky advertising and publicity stunts. The brand was recognised by 96 percent of UK consumers, and Richard Branson was correctly identified by 95 percent as the company's founder. The Virgin name was associated by respondents with words such as fun, innovation, success, and trust and identified with a range of businesses, confirming what Branson and others had believed: in principle, there were no product or service boundaries limiting a brand name, provided it was associated with a quality offering.

Encouraged by the research, Virgin began entering new sectors outside of its core activities of travel and retail. Virgin businesses as diverse as radio broadcasting, book publishing, and computer games found a home in the same stable as hotels, railways, personal computers, cola drinks, cinemas, and financial services. To manage this complex empire, Virgin increasingly employed the type of structure and people more usually associated with conventional companies. Branson continued to work at the center, supported by a small business-development group, a press office, and key senior advisors in the areas of strategy and finance. Although the firm is now housed in more elegant surroundings, the early Virgin style of informality and openness remains. There is not the feel of a traditional corporate head office: neckties are rarely worn, denim jeans are common, and everybody is on first-name terms.

Building on that evolutionary process started in the mid '80s, Virgin today is more likely to employ people (particularly at the management level) with direct experience of a relevant business activity, either through a career at Virgin or through training with a competitor. The policy of promotion-from-within that Branson practiced in the early days remains in force, especially in the larger companies, but has become more organized and less driven by short-term exigencies and Branson's whims. In acknowledgement of the fact that promotion cannot always provide the best candidate, the use of headhunters is now an established practice for senior posts. Human resource tools such as assessment centers, personality profiling, and employee development are commonly used. Moreover, many managers have formal business training and qualifications, along with experience with multinationals or management consultancies, a profile that would have been unknown at Virgin in its early days. Despite this, there is still a belief, held by most of the senior management, that there are 'Virgin people' – those who, through their personality, style, or outlook on life, are better suited than others for the organization (see Exhibit 1: Virgin People).

EXHIBIT 1 VIRGIN PEOPLE

Is there a 'Virgin person'? From Richard Branson to the most humble employee, those who work for Virgin seem to believe that only a certain type of person will fit into the sprawling Virgin empire, despite its diverse range of businesses. What follows are selected extracts from interviews with Virgin staff, who talked about what it takes to work at Virgin:

Stephen Murphy, Group Financial Director based in Geneva: *We like to hire smart people who have had all the schooling and education but who are pissed off with management consultancies, investment banks, and the like. We had one woman who was thrown out of a well-known consultancy because she had a nose earring. We took her on. We don't have those kinds of prejudices.*

Dan Higgott, International Brand Development Manager, Megastores (formerly Manager of the flagship Megastore on London's Oxford Street): *After five years with Virgin, I still find it difficult to describe a Virgin person. You need common sense and need not to be overly concerned with status and formality, but these could apply to any successful business. There are no preconceptions about people at Virgin, and I'm a good example. My training was in fashion, and I fell into retail management by accident. In Virgin Retail we have quite a formal process for developing people, so I've been given opportunities to progress. At twenty-nine I was running a £35 million business. I believe those opportunities genuinely apply to any of the 230 people who worked for me at the Oxford Street store.*

Kenneth Ibbett, Chairman, Virgin Media Group: *I joined Virgin so that I could come to work on a bicycle and not wear a tie – and took a 25 percent pay cut! We don't necessarily pay the best rates, and we're quite open about that. One problem at Virgin is that senior people with creativity and flair move on when they cash in their options. We miss people like that – Robert Devereux is a good example. When recruiting, you have to be open-minded and recognize that you're not looking for clones. I've just recruited someone who has nothing in common with me, but she's just right to run our TV business. As to the attributes we look for, it's probably easier to list the negatives to avoid: complacency, fear of failure, lack of integrity, and stupidity are probably the important ones.*

Lene Byrne, Flight Supervisor, Virgin Atlantic: *I came from Denmark to college in England and had wanted to fly for a couple of years. That was nine years ago. We've grown a lot since then and are more systemized, less easygoing, but we also have more chance to be transferred or promoted. I like the way we have fun at Virgin; it's more like a family where I know everyone, and that wouldn't be the same at BA, for example. To be employed at Virgin Atlantic you have to have the Virgin Flair – that's the big one – which means thinking young, having a sense of humor, being easygoing but professional at the same time. The longer you're here, the more you get to know Richard. Personally he's a very nice man, very genuine; but when it comes to business, he doesn't do anything without a reason – he's good at it!*

Will Whitehorn, Director of Corporate Affairs, Virgin Group: *Virgin has grown a lot recently and brought in a lot of new people. [To avoid difficulties in a start-up,] a new team will be made up of Virgin people plus new people. The new telecommunications business is a good example of that. We've brought in technical expertise and linked it to our marketing skills. The kind of people we look for are those who want to be the boss sometime and can work in the culture here at Virgin that gives you the confidence to do that. We want people with a clear idea of why they want to be with us, who don't beat around the bush when it comes to expressing a vision they may have. The organization doesn't like 'yes' people or political people; we want people who are happy to enter a discourse and debate things.*

Tim McIntosh, Manager, Union Square Megastore, New York: *In New York the staff do have the feeling that they work for Richard Branson and an English company because they've seen him and talked to him when he comes by for [promotional] events. For many of them this is their first job, but they know the history because of the book [Branson's autobiography] and the Virgin record label. We look at resumes [of potential recruits] and on paper they look good but not when you meet them. We're looking for personality – someone you'll notice, friendly and upbeat, people who look like they're going to try. It takes time to find the right people. Once they're here, they have to do a pretty bad thing to* *get fired – stealing, racial slurs, drinking, fighting, and that kind of thing. At a senior level, one bad business decision won't get a hatchet thrown at you, but you don't make that decision again.*

Whatever the profile of the Virgin Person, the company should not have difficulty in persuading young people to join, at least in the UK. According to a 1999 survey, UK graduates ranked Virgin Group second only to the BBC as the best place to work, ahead of its rival British Airways (ranked sixth) and the accounting and consulting firms.

Having a center did not mean a centralized operation, a notion that Branson resisted – at least until recently. Each operating unit was expected to stand alone, having little interaction with either the head office or other units. Unit managers networked informally (usually at parties and similar events) but were not obliged to follow prescriptive corporate policies; these were 'understood' rather than codified. For example, there was no common human resource policy. Managers knew that employees must be treated 'fairly,' since 'that is what Richard would want,' and they complied in their own way, whether in the UK or overseas. Similarly, there was no group information-technology strategist or central purchasing function, because Branson believed that those roles would constitute interference and discourage managerial creativity. In the same way there was no systematic seeking out of synergy, either at the center or by unit managers. Whenever synergy emerged, it was because the unit managers saw mutual advantage, not because a corporate policy dictated it.

This strategy was Virgin's modus operandi until 1999, when a chance remark from one of his senior executives made Branson rethink his approach. The executive mentioned to Branson that the managing director of a rival organization had commented that if Virgin companies ever decided to collaborate, they would be unstoppable. To test whether this was true, Branson immediately – and for the first time – brought together all his managing directors (some thirty in all) for a retreat at his hotel in Mallorca. The agenda was open, but two themes dominated – e-commerce and a proposed unifying document, the Virgin Charter.

During the discussion at the Mallorca meeting, the participants realized that, more by happenstance than planning, Virgin had found itself in businesses 'that are ideally suited to e-commerce and in which growth is expected to occur – travel, financial services, publishing, music, entertainment.' To exploit this potential, the participants decided to use tomorrow's technology to give all Virgin customers a small mobile device from which they could purchase any Virgin product – from a rail or cinema ticket to a CD or a savings product – and streamline online services with a single Virgin web address: Virgin.com. Virgin Net, another venture, is an Internet service provider created as a joint venture between Virgin and the UK subsidiary of NTL, a US computer technology company. Virgin is responsible for creative content and marketing; NTL provides the backup systems and software. Virgin Net targets the UK consumer market and wants to compete on 'value-for-money, speed, excellent customer service, and compelling content,' according to David Clarke, Managing Director. Much of its content is sourced from specialist suppliers (for example, the *Independent* newspaper for news). This idea took off in 1999; Virgin Net became a free service, and Virgin.com continued its expansion in e-commerce with a wide range of connections from Megastores online to train booking facilities (total internet revenues 1999 – £150 million).

During the meeting in Mallorca, the group also endorsed Branson's proposed Virgin Charter. Running to some sixty pages, the charter is an agreement between Virgin Management Ltd (in effect, the holding company) and all the subsidiaries. It defines the role of the center vis-à-vis the subsidiaries. The principal benefit the Virgin Charter is expected to bring is to create clearer information and communication flows between the Virgin shareholders, Virgin Management Ltd, and the Virgin companies. It covers topics such as taxation, legal affairs, intellectual property, and real estate, but it also outlines closer links in areas previously left to individual units: IT, people, purchasing. Thus the charter sets out ways for Virgin companies to tackle common activities with a common approach (Exhibit 2 shows Richard Branson's introduction to the charter).

EXHIBIT 2 RICHARD BRANSON'S INTRODUCTION TO THE VIRGIN CHARTER

Virgin is a unique brand, and behind that brand sits an equally unique corporate structure. Over the years Virgin has evolved into something between a branded venture capital organization and a Japanese-style *keiretsu* (family of businesses).

The consequences of this evolving structure have been twofold. Firstly, each business has become focused and been able to develop in a more autonomous and entrepreneurial environment than their equivalent subsidiaries in large conglomerates. Secondly, the Virgin brand has built up a world-wide reputation out of all proportion to the actual size and market share of any individual Virgin company. Much in the way that other brands have become household names without being associated to any one product, so Virgin is becoming a household name, bound only by the attributes that people want to associate it with – namely, value for money, quality, innovation, challenge and fun.

In a hectic and dynamic business environment, however, autonomy can have its downside – and communication links are usually the first to suffer. This can lead to flaws in the decision-making process and, ultimately, to companies acting on their own and without the common good of the Virgin shareholders in mind. As more responsibility is devolved to a range of individually significant businesses in their own right, links become stretched and frustrated and information stops flowing.

We need to prevent this from happening while respecting and maintaining the spirit of Virgin. Hence the Virgin Charter.

It is intended that the Virgin Charter will evolve into a management system that will allow all Virgin companies to be the best they can possibly be, without the need for obstructive hierarchies which can so easily impede rapid decision-making by those who know their own business.

In the longer term we hope that the Virgin Charter will become a mechanism through which both the individual companies, Virgin Management Ltd and the Virgin brand can quickly take advantage of the truly exciting opportunities that lie ahead, both in our core businesses and the new frontiers of global electronic commerce. As we move into the twenty-first century there is a real opportunity to turn Virgin into one of the leading global brands, by looking at strategic opportunities for the existing businesses and by forming new ones.

Finally, please don't forget that Virgin's success, both now and in the future, rests with each of us. We are a people brand and a people business in the purest sense of the word.

My greatest hope is that the Virgin Charter will continue to create a culture of praise rather than blame, and family rather than alienation. If that alone can be achieved then all our efforts will have been worthwhile.

Branson has compared his current operation to a venture capital firm based on the Virgin brand. At the center, ideas (whether sourced internally or externally) are debated and analyzed, deals are struck, and new ventures are created. Potentially good ideas are disseminated outwards – quite often by Branson, who will 'call up [a manager] in his half-apologetic way and ask you to think about a suggestion.' When deals or joint ventures are finalized, the implementation is delegated out, usually with considerable autonomy. A small example of the process is Virgin Brides. In 1995 Ailsa Petchley joined Virgin Atlantic as a member of its cabin crew. On one of her early flights she met Branson and got talking about weddings and the poor, often disjointed service offered to prospective brides. When she mentioned that she had a business idea offering a comprehensive service, she was given a few months to put together a plan. The net result was the creation of Virgin Brides, with Ailsa in the role of marketing manager, working in collaboration with a bridal-wear specialist from the US. The company is established but has a way to go to be profitable.

Along with the development of Virgin.com, Branson's last bold move at the close of the century was his deal with Singapore Airlines. During 1999 Branson had intimated that he might float part of the airline to raise capital for expansion. As the year was closing, however, he announced a surprise deal with Singapore Airlines that, in terms of fleet and revenues, is about three times the size of Virgin Atlantic. If the deal goes through, in 2000 Singapore will acquire a 49% stake in Virgin Atlantic at a cost of £600 million. The two airlines will work in partnership to maximise cost cutting synergies (e.g. maintenance, ground facilities, code sharing) but retain their respective identities and develop their own products. Industry observers saw the logic of the deal since in many ways the two airlines are complementary – their routes do not overlap and they both enjoy excellent reputations for service and innovation. There were, however, doubts expressed

at the price that Singapore was paying, valuing Virgin Atlantic at more than £1.2 billion, a high figure in many observers' view.

The Virgin Group in 2000 comprised twenty-four individual companies or groups of companies (see Exhibits 3 and Table 1 for commentary and summary). Nearly all are private and owned entirely by the Virgin Group or by Richard Branson's family trusts; Branson sits on the board of most of the companies and usually, but by no means always, attends board meetings. He relies on others to bring serious problems to his attention: he has little time for reading long operational reports, market research, financial statements, and the like.

EXHIBIT 3 VIRGIN GROUP OF COMPANIES IN 1999: COMMENTARY ON MAJOR OPERATIONS

It is generally acknowledged, both within and outside Virgin, that **Virgin Travel**, especially Virgin Atlantic, is the company closest to Branson's heart. It is the only company in which employees have Branson's direct telephone number and are encouraged to call or write to him with ideas or feedbacks on customer satisfaction. Branson regularly travels on his planes, helping to serve meals, talking to passengers and cabin crew, and generally listening for suggestions for improvements.

With twenty-nine aircraft and routes from London to about a dozen major cities outside Europe, **Virgin Atlantic** remains a niche player in an industry dominated by global carriers and state airlines. Since its founding, the airline has relied on service, value-for-money, and innovation, dished up with panache and flair, to differentiate itself in the market. On the first flights, cabin crew in business class were dressed as butlers, serving bought in food from Maxims. Later, in-flight magicians, masseuses, and musicians were used; a limousine service to the airport for upper-class passengers was instituted; and multi-channel music and video systems that can be customized to a passenger's individual needs were installed. More recently, luxurious Virgin Atlantic clubhouses have appeared at London's two airports as well as in Hong Kong, Washington, and San Francisco. Not all of these ideas originated at Virgin, but Branson will hap-

pily copy good practice if he sees an advantage. Judging by the numerous awards and citations the airline has won, his approach seems to work.

Also included in the deal with Singapore Airlines are the other divisions of Virgin Atlantic – Virgin Holidays, Virgin Sun and Virgin Aviation Services, the group's cargo division. Managing Director Ron Simms describes **Virgin Holidays** as 'the world's largest long-haul tour operator in terms of numbers carried.' The holiday company grew on the back of the airline and has recently moved into the short-haul business. The main destination is Florida, where Virgin is the Disney hotels' biggest customer.

Virgin Entertainment owns **Virgin Cinemas**, a cinema chain formed from the purchase of MGM cinemas. Virgin sold the ninety small sites it acquired, retaining the remainder for conversion to 'Megaplexes.' After substantial refurbishment, Megaplexes offer café/bars, shops, and spacious seating; those that offer 'Premium Screen' also have personalized service – coats are taken, drinks are served at the seat, extra legroom is provided. Virgin plans to develop the chain through purpose-built Megaplexes.

Virgin Entertainment is also the Virgin partner in joint ventures that run overseas Megastores. The Megastore concept is exported and refined to adapt to the local culture, but it retains its core values: fun, good design, value-for-money, and choice.

Virgin Retail's core activity is the chain of fifty-plus Megastores in the UK, in partnership with W.H. Smith, a retail chain. It also owns Caroline International, an importer/exporter of music and video media and has an interest in Sound & Media, a specialist music supplier.

Based in Brussels, **Virgin Express Holdings Plc** is a scheduled airline company serving the main European cities, offering single-class airfares substantially below the norm. If offers its customers a no-frills, simple-to-understand service in which even ticketing has been reduced to a booking confirmation number.

Virgin Direct and **Virgin Direct Personal Finance** were founded to bring Virgin into the personal financial services market, where Branson saw an industry 'ripe for reform': poor service, high charges, disreputable practices, dissatisfied customers. In addition, the market was forecast to grow as people took more responsibility for their own financial security in old age.

Relying for competitive advantage on the Virgin brand's association with trust and value-for-money, Virgin Direct was initially a joint venture with Norwich Union Assurance, a large insurance group that supplied the technology and back-office support while Virgin supplied the marketing. Norwich Union withdrew shortly after the launch in favor of Australian Mutual Provident.

Virgin Direct differentiates itself in several ways. First, it does not use a commission-led sales force or agents, relying instead on advertising and telesales, contrary to accepted industry practice. Second, it offers simple saving products, based on tracking financial indices, that the average person can understand. Simplicity of product and lack of commission mean lower costs, which are passed on as lower administration charges. The transparency of its charges are a key selling point in its advertising. In 1999, after four years in operation, Virgin Direct has over 200,000 customers with more than £1 billion under management. Its main products are PEPS (a tax-efficient personal equity plan under a 'tax wrapper'), personal pensions, and life insurance.

Virgin Direct Personal Finance links Virgin Direct with Royal Bank of Scotland to offer the *One* account, a combined, highly flexible mortgage and bank account with a single rate for all lending purposes: car loan, house purchase, overdraft, credit card, etc.

The most recent major investments by Virgin, **Virgin Rail** consists of twenty-year franchises to operate two networks: CrossCountry, a series of routes that traverse the UK, and West Coast, the main route from London to Glasgow and intermediate stations. The franchises were awarded by competitive tendering as part of the long-term denationalisation program of the Conservative government. Virgin inherited rolling stock, ticketing offices, and staff, all previously under British Rail ownership and management. The tracks, signaling, and stations are owned and operated by Railtrack.

British Rail was not seen as a customer-friendly and efficient organization. Furthermore, years of under-investment had had an impact on the infrastructure. The result was high prices, unhappy customers, and demotivated (sometimes antagonistic) staff. Industry observers, City analysts, and media commentators all had reservations about the prospects for franchisees given the major turnaround required. In Virgin's case, they forecast considerable damage to the brand. Branson recognized that there was a risk but believed that his project to undertake major investment in modern trains and convert the staff to a customer-service culture would pay off in the long term, particularly with passenger numbers forecast to rise. In the short term, however, Virgin Rail has suffered from poor public relations, with horror stories surfacing frequently about delayed trains, poor food, and dirty trains. Virgin Rail management explains that improvements cannot come overnight.

Virgin Rail was initially a joint venture between Virgin and venture capitalists. In 1998, Branson made plans to float Virgin Rail, intending to offer part of the equity to the public to allow the initial investors to withdraw. There were doubts in the City about whether this would be a success. At the last moment, Brian Souter, chairman of Stagecoach, a private bus company operating mainly in the UK but also overseas, offered to take a 49 percent holding. A Scottish entrepreneur from a modest background, Souter is a born-again Christian with a reputation for running a tight and hard-nosed operation. His company has been accused of predatory actions against competitors, for example. His business was founded in the early '80s and prospered when the Thatcher government privatised many bus companies. With the reputation for being somewhat eccentric (i.e., in the Branson mold), Souter sees synergy between his bus networks and trains.

Obliged by contract to stay out of the music business for three years after the sale of Virgin Music, **V2 Music** is Branson's return to the industry that got him started. It was founded as a global business with a presence in many countries. Still a small, loss-making operator, V2 Music has yet to sign any major artists, but it is investing in creative personnel to seek out new talent.

Virgin Net is an Internet service provider created as a joint venture between Virgin and the UK subsidiary of NTL, a US computer technology company. Virgin is responsible for creative content and marketing; NTL provides the backup systems and software. Virgin Net targets the UK consumer market and wants to compete on 'value-for-money, speed, excellent customer service, and compelling content,' according to David Clarke, Managing Director. Much of its content is sourced from specialist suppliers (for example, the *Independent* newspaper for news).

TABLE 1 Virgin Group of companies in 1999

Virgin company	% Virgin interests	Other major shareholders	Turnover 97/98 £m*	Employees	Trading location(s)	Launch date
Virgin Travel Group	100%			4,750	Worldwide	
Virgin Atlantic Airways	100%		678			1984
Virgin Holidays	100%		177			1985
Virgin Aviation Services	90%	Held by management	15			1985
Virgin Entertainment Group	70%	Texas Pacific Group, Colony Capital				
Cinemas	100%		100	800	UK	1995
US Megastores	100%		80	400	USA	1992
Japan Megastores	50%	Marui Co	68	100	Japan	1990
European Megastores	100%		150	300	Continental Europe	1988
Virgin Retail Group	100%					
Virgin Retail (Our Price, UK Megastores)	25%	W H Smith	500	4,500	UK	1971
Caroline International	100%		20	62	UK	1972
Sound & Media	50%	Held by management	8	68	UK	1994
Virgin Trading Group	100%					
Virgin Cola, Virgin Vodka	100%		21	45	UK	1994
Virgin Limobikes	100%		0.3	5	UK	1996
V Entertainment Group	100%					
Virgin Digital Studios (525, Rushes, WITV)	100%		27	340	UK, USA	1986
Virgin Publishing	60%	Robert Devereux	10	42	Worldwide	1991
John Brown Enterprises	20%	John Brown	12	68	UK	1984
Rapido TV	50%	Rapido TV Investments	4	12	Mexico	1991
Ginger Media Group	20%	Chris Evans, Apax partners				
Virgin Radio	100%		18	64	UK	1993

TABLE 1 *cont.*

Virgin company	% Virgin interests	Other major shareholders	Turnover 97/98 £m*	Employees	Trading location(s)	Launch date
Virgin Express Holdings Plc	50.1%	Guarantee Nominees Ltd management	150	800	Continental Europe	1996
Virgin Hotels Group	100%					
Virgin Clubs, La Residencia,						
Woodhouse Securities, Cribyn	100%		21	587	UK, Spain	1988
Le Manoir Aux Quat' Saisons	50%	Held by management	7	120	UK	1994
Virgin Direct Ltd	50%	Australian Mutual Provident (AMP)				
Virgin Direct Personal Services	100%		608**	450	UK	1995
Virgin Direct Personal Finance	25%	AMP, Royal Bank of Scotland		150	UK	1998
Victory Corporation Plc	49%	Clerical Medical, Foreign & Colonial, GRE				
Virgin Vie	100%		2.5	150	UK	1997
Virgin Clothing	100%			57	UK	1998
Virgin Rail Group	51%	Stagecoach Group	423	3,450	UK	1997
West Coast Trains	100%					
CrossCountry Trains	100%					
V2 Music	66%	McCarthy Corporation	10	200	UK	1996
Virgin Net	51%	NTL	10	60	UK	1996
Vanson Developments (property)	100%		30	14	UK	1983
Virgin Bride	100%		0.9	25	UK	1996
Neckar (island resort)	100%		2.5	33	Virgin Islands	1984
Heaven	100%		3	43	London	1982
Virgin Vouchers	100%		0.1	2	UK	1996
London Broncos	50.1%	BAT Trustees (Jersey), King Investments	2	50	London	1997
Virgin Helicopters	100%		0.8	12	UK	1997
The Lightship Group	50%	Lightship America	9	215	UK, USA	1990
Virgin Airships & Balloons	75%	Nerorate	8	47	UK	1987
Storm Model Management	50%	Held by management	6	22	Worldwide	1985

* Financial year-ends not concurrent.
** Gross sales.
Plc indicates publicly quoted company.

Richard Branson: A Portrait

Richard Branson was born in July 1950, the first child and the only son of Ted Branson and his wife, Eve, née Huntley-Flint. He was later joined by two sisters, Lindi and Vanessa. The family has remained close, all enjoying what Richard was later to describe as a 'happy and secure' childhood.

Both Ted and Eve came from comfortable Establishment backgrounds. Ted was the son and grandson of eminent lawyers, a fact impressed on young Richard when he visited Tussaud's waxworks museum in London with his father and saw models of murderers sentenced to hang by Sir George Branson, his grandfather. Following family tradition, Ted left his Quaker-run school to study law at Cambridge University. After military service in World War II, he eventually qualified as a lawyer, but (perhaps because of his Quaker education or his naturally kindly disposition) his career in advocacy, where adversarial skills are vital, was slow to get started.

Eve Huntley-Flint came from a family of clerics, farmers, and stockbrokers whose womenfolk were expected to have horizons beyond the home. While still a young girl, she trained as a dancer and appeared in London theatres, both in dance reviews and as an actress, a somewhat risqué career for someone of her background. By the time she met Ted Branson, she had become an air stewardess, travelling to South America when air travel still contained a significant element of adventure and danger. Determined, self-assured and ambitious, at twenty-seven Eve was an attractive, outgoing young woman when she married Ted Branson, the reserved and fair-minded young lawyer.

Eve had decided views on child-rearing. While she was never a martinet, she pushed her children to be self-reliant and responsible, to take control of their own destinies rather than relying on others. One summer afternoon as she and four-year-old Richard were on their way home after visiting his grandparents, Eve told Richard to get out of the car and try to find his own way back. The farmhouse where they were staying was not far, but Richard got lost, ending up at the neighbour's farm to be collected by his alarmed parents. Eve Branson now admits that she may have been overly enthusiastic about encouraging Richard's independence, but she has never regretted it. Clearly, Eve admired strength of character. Furthermore, she was convinced that shyness in children was simply bad manners and a self-indulgence to be discouraged. She believed that her children's ability to overcome challenges would encourage the kind of spirit she wanted to see in them. Accordingly, she used her own considerable energy to organize activities, games, and projects for her children that were not only fun but also served a useful purpose. Holidays, weekends, and other free time were used productively. In line with that goal, the Branson household had no television, since it was 'time-wasting.' If money was short (as it was in the early days, when Ted's father cut off his allowance to protest his precipitate marriage), a solution could always be found in small money-making schemes that Eve thought up. Bemoaning one's lot was never acceptable to Eve, and she lived up to her own standards.

Ted Branson was never a strict and remote father figure. Rather, he acted as a calm and considerate backdrop to Eve's daily management of the children. Sympathetic and supportive by preference, a half-hearted disciplinarian if really necessary, Ted was less directly ambitious for his children than Eve, who expected, for example, that 'Richard [would] one day be Prime Minister.'

Richard grew up to be the archetypal naughty boy, frequently in minor scrapes, scolded for innumerable misdemeanours, and hyperactive in all he did. His parents found him both endearing and fatiguing. According to his father, Branson began his first business venture when he was eleven or twelve years old. He planted a thousand seedlings and then went back to school convinced that he would make a killing selling Christmas trees. Rabbits soon ate the trees, however. About a year later he tried another venture. This time the scheme involved budgerigars, a highly fecund type of small parrot. Another failure.

Richard's parents were particularly concerned about his progress at school, where – thanks to a strong physique and a competitive spirit – his main accomplishments were on the sports field. His schoolboy heroes were sportsmen, particularly cricketers, and adventurers such as Scott of the Antarctic, the famous British explorer and a distant relation by marriage. A serious leg injury, however, forestalled a promising career in athletics, while a period of forced intensive study finally gained his admittance to Stowe School, an exclusive English boys' private school with a liberal reputation. His indifference to schoolwork (not helped by long-undetected poor eyesight and dyslexia) continued, and he achieved only average results, ruling out a legal or other professional career. By contrast, *Student* magazine excited Branson with its possibilities and offered a timely and convenient exit from the educational treadmill. So, with his parents' reluctant blessing – his father's support was particularly influential – he quit school.

Branson left few friends behind him. While he was not unpopular, his energetic and single-minded pursuit of that which pleased him left little room for others. His indifference to the contemporary social mores and allegiances common in a school like Stowe left him somewhat isolated. His few friends were those he managed to inveigle into his varied and numerous projects. Commenting on the end of his schooldays, Branson said, 'Having left school without going to university, I decided to make money . . . . I never considered failure.' His headmaster had definite views about his future: 'Richard, you will either go to prison or become a millionaire.'

Working with family and friends

For a long time, Branson's office and home shared quarters in a canal houseboat. One bedroom served as the office of his two secretaries, while Branson operated from a dining table in the small sitting room. On occasion the bathroom served as the boardroom, with Branson conducting meetings from his bath. Eventually, when his two children 'started to answer the phones,' Branson was forced to move to a larger home, but he kept the houseboat as a private office. Nowadays, he runs his business empire from a large, elegant townhouse situated in London's diplomatic quarter. His home is in a similar building nearby.

His (second) wife, a down-to-earth Glaswegian from a working-class background, has no interest or role in his business life. She remains out of the limelight in the interests of their two children, providing an intimate family life to which Branson can retreat. Her stance is something of an anomaly at Virgin. Contrary to conventional wisdom, Branson has always been a great believer in working with family and friends, convinced that the advantages outweigh the risks. Over time, his cousins, aunts, school and childhood friends, parents, and former girlfriends have all been drawn into his various business activities. His first wife found the situation difficult to accept, but even she is now in a joint venture with Branson, developing hotels in Spain.

The charges of nepotism that such arrangements usually gender were muted at Virgin, because of Branson's promotion-from-within policy. He has given many of his staff opportunities that their gender, lack of experience, or training would have precluded in more conventional companies. Of course, Virgin has been unconventional in other ways, too. Somehow, Branson has created the impression that people work at Virgin for fun rather than simply as a means of earning a living ('More than any other element, fun is the secret of Virgin's success,' he believes: Branson, 1998, p. 431). Notoriously indifferent to material possessions and unconcerned about everyday financial matters, the young Branson saw no problem in paying modest salaries provided people enjoyed themselves and felt part of an idiosyncratic enterprise that had a heart. If people were down, a party would revive spirits and, incidentally, give Branson the chance to play a practical joke on newcomers, an embarrassing rite of passage at Virgin that is partially maintained to this day. For example, when Branson hands out 'wings' to newly appointed cabin crew, he douses them in champagne. Similarly, the traditional annual company party that Branson used to throw at the recording studios (and now holds at his country home) has grown from a small Sunday event for 200 or so in the '70s, to a marathon jamboree to which all Virgin staff and their family and friends can come.

A business philosophy

Much of Virgin's operating style was established not so much by design as by the exigencies of the time when Virgin was getting started. Nonetheless, it has proved to be a successful model that Branson believes he can replicate. His practice is to immerse himself in a new venture until he understands the ins and outs of the business, then hand it over to a good managing director and financial controller, the two of whom are usually given a stake and then expected to make the company take off. (Branson can usually be relied on to engage in a publicity stunt of some kind that will give the company some initial awareness, jumpstarting the process. In the case of Virgin Bride, for example, he shaved off his beard and was photographed in a bridal gown).

Branson knows that expansion through the creation of additional discrete legal entities not only protects the Virgin Group but also give people a sense of involvement with and loyalty to the smaller unit to which they belong, particularly if he trusts the managers of subsidiaries with full authority and offers them minority share options. He is proud of the fact that Virgin has produced a considerable number of millionaires. He has said that he does not want his best people to leave the company to start a venture outside; he prefers to make millionaires within.

His use of joint ventures, an extension of this model, has been reinforced by his dealings with the Japanese. Branson has been impressed by the Japanese approach to business, admiring their commitment to the long term and the way they take time to build through organic growth rather than acquisitions. He sees similarities between the Japanese *keiretsu* system (small companies interlocking in a collaborative network) and the structure he has created at Virgin, with numerous small companies around the world operated quasi-independently by the right people. Both systems embody the maxims 'Small is beautiful' and 'People matter.'

Branson explained these and other business maxims that he believes are necessary for success in a speech to the Institute of Directors in London in 1993. 'Staff first, then customers and shareholders' – this should be the chairman's priority if an organization wants better performance, according to Branson. Happy staff who are proud of their company make for happy customers who return. Job satisfaction is hampered when management is remote from all levels of staff, relying, for example, on trade unions for communication. Branson cites his decision to keep 200 airline staff on the payroll, rather than lay them off during a recession, as a practical manifestation of this staff-first philosophy. Businesses should be 'shaped around the people,' Branson believes, citing his experience of subdividing the record company as it grew. Each new record label was given to up-and-coming managers, creating in-house entrepreneurs who were 'far more motivated to build a business' with which they, and the staff, identified. In accordance with that maxim, Branson has never made a major acquisition (as that term is usually understood).

His rivalry with British Airways illustrates his views on competition: 'Be best not biggest: compete on quality as well as price.' And his habit, since the early days, of recording good ideas in notebooks (dozens of these books have accumulated over time) supports his notion that the innovative business must 'capture every fleeting idea.' In a restless, creative business with an emphasis on experiment and devel-opment, 'ideas are lifeblood.' 'Drive for change' is another guiding principle in the Branson business philosophy. Branson is impatient with what he sees as the risk-aversive nature of British industry and commerce, and indeed society at large. 'It is great for tourism . . . and airlines . . . but has no place in industry. . . . We [at Virgin] experiment endlessly with new methods, new companies, and new marketing, especially when we can get others to pay for it!'

Formally expounding a business philosophy, however, is not a regular Branson activity. Indeed, in his autobiography he commented, 'Academics analyze . . . we just hit the phones and get on with the business' (Branson, 1998: p. 12).

'Hero of the world'

In 1990, Richard Branson found himself in northern Japan preparing for take-off in an attempt to make the first-ever trans-Pacific crossing in a hot-air balloon, an event timed to coincide with Virgin Atlantic's inaugural flight to Tokyo. His Japanese hosts had invited a huge crowd to witness the event, and banners had been hung declaring him to be the 'Hero of the World.'

The attempt was just one in a series of exploits undertaken by Branson. They began in 1985 when he attempted to cross the Atlantic in a high-powered speedboat to win the coveted Blue Riband, the prize awarded to the vessel and crew with the fastest time. The vessel sank off Ireland, but a similar attempt the following year was successful. In 1987, he and Per Lindstrand, an experienced balloonist, attempted the fastest trans-Atlantic balloon crossing, an aim achieved – but only after both barely escaped with their lives when the balloon made a forced landing in the Irish Sea. His latest endeavour, a round-the-world balloon flight, has now been abandoned following a rival's successful attempt.

Branson is happy to admit that these exploits were started as an inexpensive way of publicizing his trans-Atlantic airline, but with time they seemed to gain a momentum of their own. Asked how the chairman of a major corporation can justify the risks and expense, he replied, 'People who have to ask the question don't understand.'

Whatever his motives, Branson has come to be seen as a modern buccaneer with an appealing, devil-may-care attitude to physical danger as well as business risks. At the same time, he supports charitable, radical, and humanitarian causes. For example, he still funds a sex counselling clinic that he helped found in his *Student* days when his girlfriend became pregnant and they had nowhere to turn for advice. He also launched a new brand of condoms, Mates, as a response to the government's *laissez-faire* attitude towards AIDS and condom use. This is the kind of project that appeals to Branson: there is a benefit for society, money is raised for charity, and he has fun doing it. More controversially, he boycotted a magazine that refused to carry advertisements supporting the legalization of marijuana, although he personally dislikes illegal drugs following an ill-fated experiment with LSD. 'Richard could not stand to be out of control,' according to his girlfriend at the time.

Branson's exploits and causes are diverse, ranging from a health-care foundation supporting AIDS research to financial support for a new political publication. He bought and published a banned video on security matters, used his aircraft to rescue people trapped by the Gulf War, and led an initiative to help unemployed teenagers (although the initiative soon wound down). He submitted a bid to run the new National Lottery in the UK on a charitable rather than profit-making basis. He lost, later claiming that the winning consortium's representative had tried to bribe him to withdraw from the bidding. The representative sued but lost in court, paying heavy damages to Branson and standing down from his position.

Branson's esteem in UK public opinion at all levels is regularly demonstrated. In the 1980s he was the darling of the former Prime Minister, Margaret Thatcher; in the late 1990s he enjoyed good relations with Tony Blair's Labour government. He has been nominated for awards for enterprise, voted the most popular businessman, and named in polls by Londoners as the preferred choice for the new post of mayor, even though he has never put his name forward. In recognition of his services to entrepreneurship, the Blair government nominated Branson for a knighthood in the new millennium honours list. The soon-to-be Sir Richard Branson expressed his delight at the award, noting that 'neither I nor Virgin have made a political donation', underlining his long-held apolitical stance.

In general, Branson is the point of reference whenever comparisons are made between the traditional business leader and emerging entrepreneurs of the '80s and '90s. He is, however, a man of contrasts. The public persona is that of a warm, friendly, idealistic family man. Yet he is also a highly competitive workaholic and an extremely tough negotiator who thrives on bargaining.

The 'real' Richard Branson

Richard Branson has become an international celebrity, the subject of numerous profiles in gossip magazines; the business press, and television programmes. Generally, this coverage has been sympathetic – especially in the UK, where he has achieved folk-hero status. Writers focus on his eccentric lifestyle, derring-do exploits, and new business ventures, comparing him favourably to more staid and conventional business leaders. Even the London tabloids, not known for their generosity to celebrities – indeed, often seeking out sensational stores about their private lives – seem willing to give Branson a relatively soft ride. They generally adopt a tone of friendly mockery about his exploits (although the failure to meet expectations in his rail company is starting to encourage negative press). He is frequently cited as a role model by young people wanting a successful business career that does not compromise personal ethics.

His detractors see Branson in different terms: a me-too operator, simply copying other people's ideas; an arch manipulator, fooling staff and consumers with warm words to mask his own grasping ambition; a fool with a death wish, driven by demons from his childhood to undertake ever-more risky exploits – whether commercial or physical – until eventually everything collapses about him.

Whichever point of view is right, in material terms Branson is undoubtedly successful. He became one of the UK's richest people before he turned forty, and recently he ranked as the eleventh-wealthiest person in the UK, with an estimated net worth of £900 million. Asked to explain the strategy that got him to this point, he talks of minimizing risks: 'Protect the downside, always be ready to walk away,' he says. 'But I have never thought of myself as a businessman. In my first venture I saw myself as an editor, only becoming a businessman to make sure my magazine survived.'

Over the years he has made strategic statements that, with hindsight, have not related closely to subsequent events. Most frequently, however, he eschews strategy in favour of fun: he says he simply wants to enjoy himself. But can a strategy for fun really explain the creation of a music company by a founder who, paradoxically, has little interest in or knowledge of music? Equally, it is difficult to explain how a shy man, ill at ease when speaking publicly or in private conversation with strangers, can become a supreme self-publicist. Or how an establishment-born figure with intrinsically conventional views can become the champion of radical and libertarian causes. Or how the man who is almost obsessive about fair play can negotiate ferociously for the last penny in a deal.

A London *Sunday Times* report on the British Airways affair quoted Lord King as saying, 'If Richard Branson had worn a pair of steel-rimmed glasses, a double-breasted suit and shaved off his beard, I would have taken him seriously. As it was I couldn't. . . . I underestimated him.' Perhaps Lord King is not alone in being misled by the hippie entrepreneur image that surrounds Branson. But if that image is not the real Richard Branson, then what is?

Virgin in the new millennium

In the year 2000, when Richard Branson celebrates his fiftieth birthday, he will have been leading Virgin for thirty-two years (see Exhibit 4 for key dates). How many more years will he be at the helm? Can a company founded on youth, fun, and anti-establishment sentiments be run by someone with retirement on the horizon? Indeed, will Richard Branson ever *want* to retire? If not, what implications would his continuation have for Virgin and its management? If he does plan to withdraw, either partly or wholly, what impact would his retirement have, given that his persona is so closely associated in the eyes of the public and investors with Virgin and its ethos? Is there anyone else who could act as the public face of Virgin, who could step into Branson's shoes? He has children, but they are still in their teens; the elder, his daughter has ambitions to become a doctor.

EXHIBIT 4 KEY DATES

1968	First issue of *Student* magazine published.
1970/71	Virgin mail order operation started; first Virgin record shop opened in Oxford Street.
1971/73	First Virgin recording studio opened at The Manor near Oxford; *Tubular Bells* released; Virgin record label launched, music publishing operation established in the UK.
1977	The Sex Pistols signed by Virgin.
1978/80	First Virgin night-club (The Venue) opened; Human League signed to Virgin; Virgin Records presence in overseas markets expanded.
1981/82	Phil Collins, Boy George, and Culture Club signed to Virgin.
1983/84	Virgin Vision formed: film and video distribution, TV, broadcasting; Virgin Games launched; Virgin Atlantic and Virgin Cargo launched; first luxury hotel launched (in Mallorca); the Music Channel, a 24-hour satellite-delivered music station, launched by Virgin Vision, which also produced the award-winning film *1984*, starring Richard Burton and John Hurt.
1985/86	Business Enterprise Award for company of the year won by Virgin; Virgin Holidays formed; £25 million raised via convertible stock; Virgin Group floated on London stock exchange.
1987	Virgin Records America launched; Japanese subsidiary established; Rushes Video, London, acquired; 525, Virgin Communications LA-based post-production facility, launched; Virgin served as founding member of British Satellite Broadcasting Plc; majority holding in Music Channel sold; UK distribution rights for Sega computer games acquired; Virgin balloon company launched; first results from Virgin Group Plc made available – turnover: £279 million; pbt: £28 million.

1988 Olympic Recording Studios opened in London; Virgin Classics established to specialize in high-quality classical music repertoire; first Virgin Megastores opened in Australia, Glasgow, and Paris; smaller UK retail outlets sold to W.H. Smith for £23 million; Virgin Broadcasting formed to further develop Virgin's interests in radio and TV; three major business-class awards won by Virgin Atlantic, designated Britain's second-most-popular long-haul carrier; management buyout announced by Branson following the 1987 October stock market crash.

1989 Doubled pre-tax profits at £10 million announced by Virgin Atlantic, which also established its own engineering operations; 10 percent of Virgin Travel sold to Seibu Saison, Japan; 25 percent of Virgin Music sold to Fujisankei, Japan; long-term European distribution for Sega Video Games signed by Virgin Mastertronics as Sega became the number-one brand for video games in Europe; Virgin Vision sold to Management Company Entertainment Group (MCEG) of Los Angeles for $83 million.

1990 Virgin Music Group launched second US record company based in New York; Megastores opened in Marseilles, Bordeaux, and Belfast; West One Television, a UK post-production company, created by Virgin Communications; joint venture signed with Marui retail group to operate Megastores in Japan.

1991 Ruling by the Civil Aviation Authority (CAA) won by Virgin Atlantic, allowing it to operate extra services to Tokyo by transfer of rights from BA; right won by Virgin Atlantic to operate services out of Heathrow (London) in addition to Gatwick (London), along with UK government approval to fly to South Africa; Virgin Mastertronic, Virgin Communications' European computer games distributor, sold to Sega of Japan for £40 million (though Virgin Communications retained the publishing division and began a rapid expansion of Virgin Games); Virgin Book Publishing formed in joint venture with W.H. Smith and Allison & Busby.

1992 Virgin Music Group sold to Thorn EMI Plc; first video-game software in Europe released by Virgin Games; Westwood Studios Inc., a Las Vegas-based developer of computer software, acquired; Virgin Games SA established in Paris; purchase of DC-3 announced to establish new US carrier Vintage Airtours, to operate a daily service of nostalgic trips from Orlando to the Florida Keys; UK's first national radio rock station launched in joint venture with TV-am Plc; post-production interests consolidated by Virgin TV, which also planned international expansion; Megastores opened in Spain, Netherlands, Australia, USA; joint venture formed by Virgin Retail with Blockbuster of Florida to expand Megastores in Europe, Australia, and North America; Euro-Magnetic, a specialist supplier of PC consumables, acquired by Virgin.

1993 Libel settlement of £610,000 against Lord King and BA won by Virgin Atlantic, which was voted Executive Travel's Airline of the Year for the third year running; Virgin Games K.K. established in Tokyo by Virgin Games, which sold minority interests to Hasbro Inc and Blockbuster; the PC market entered by Virgin Euromagnetics, which launched its first range of personal computers; first management contract obtained by Virgin Hotels; daily flight to Hong Kong and San Francisco launched by Virgin Atlantic; joint venture announced with Wheelock Pacific to form Virgin Megastores Hong Kong, aimed at Chinese-speaking Asia market; Our Price chain in UK acquired by Virgin Retail; Saehan Virgin Megastores Korea established in joint venture with Saehan Media.

1994 Virgin Games renamed Virgin Interactive Entertainment (VIE) and Blockbuster raise stake to 75 percent; creative design and brand-development consultancy formed in partnership with Rodney Fitch and Co; Virgin City Jet service launched in January between Dublin and London City Airport; joint venture formed by Virgin Hotels with Shirayama Shokusan to develop London's County Hall; management contracts for four UK hotels awarded to Virgin Hotels; 100 percent ownership of three hotels previously held in joint venture taken by Virgin Hotels, which also acquired 50 percent ownership of the luxury restaurant Le Manoir aux Quai' Saisons; Virgin Hotels Marketing launched to promote owner-managed small hotels operating in Virgin style; Virgin Television Mexico formed; Virgin Trading formed to market FMCG under the Virgin brand name, with first venture in partnership with W. Grant and Sons to market Virgin Vodka; Virgin Radio awarded FM license in London; Virgin Cola Company formed by Virgin Retail and COTT of Canada.

1995   Agreement reached by Virgin Atlantic and Malaysian Airways to operate a twice-daily flight to Kuala Lumpur; agreement between Virgin Atlantic and Delta Airways approved by the US Department of Transportation; Virgin Direct Financial Services launched in a joint venture with Norwich Union Insurance; joint venture formed to acquired MGM Cinemas; Norwich Union bought out by Australian Mutual Provincial (AMP); Virgin Atlantic voted airline of the year by Executive Travel magazine; Virgin Cola launched to compete with Coca-Cola and Pepsi; British Airways sued again by Branson, who this time claimed damages in the US.

1996   Flights started by Virgin Atlantic to Orlando and Washington DC; Euro Belgian Airlines acquired by Virgin Travel, which renamed it Virgin Express; Virgin Bride, Europe's largest bridal-wear shop, opened; Virgin Net formed to enter the Internet market; V2 Music launched, signing its first two bands; £3 billion contract to build Channel Tunnel Link and operate Eurostar services to Paris and Brussels awarded to London and Continental Railways, in which Virgin is a minority shareholder; Virgin Rail awarded franchise to operate rail passenger service covering 130 stations in England, Scotland, and Wales; Virgin Atlantic voted best business class and best transatlantic carrier by Executive Travel magazine for the sixth year running.

1997   Virgin Rail awarded InterCity West Coast franchise; three hotels in Wales acquired by Virgin Hotels; 50 percent share in London Broncos rugby team acquired by Branson; Virgin Express quoted on the Brussels and NASDAQ exchanges; Virgin Cinemas and Virgin Megastores World-wide (excluding the UK) merged to form Virgin Entertainment Group; four stores in UK opened by Virgin Vie, a joint venture in cosmetics and beauty care; first banking product – Virgin One Account – launched by Virgin Direct (Financial Services) in joint venture with Royal Bank of Scotland; Virgin Radio sold for £85 million; COTT's share of Virgin Cola bought out by Virgin Trading.

1998   Richard Branson wins G-Tech court case, involving G-Tech the lottery equipment supplier and Guy Snowden its former chairman; 'Diana', the tribute album for Diana, Princess of Wales, released by V2 Records on behalf of the record industry raises over £40m for charity; Virgin Sun, Virgin Holidays' first foray into short-haul holidays is launched; Virgin Express starts flights from Stansted to Continental Europe; Rail Regulator, John Swift, approves Virgin Trains' and Railtrack's massive upgrade of the UK's West Coast Main Line; Stagecoach buys 49% of Virgin Rail Group and Virgin increases its stake from 41% to 51%; Virgin Entertainment Group buys W.H. Smith's 75% holding in Virgin Our Price retail chain in Great Britain and Ireland.

1999   Virgin Rail Group completes the financing of new high speed tilting trains for both its franchises – West Coast and Cross Country. A total of over £4 billion of private sector investment secured with the introduction of the new trains still on track for 2001–2002. The first new 'Pendolino' destined for the West Coast Mainline rolls off the production line in December 1999; Virgin Atlantic announces further expansion plans on the back of continuing growth and increased profitability. 1999 will see the launch of new routes to Chicago, Shanghai and other destinations. Virgin Sun's first charter flights commence in May 1999. Virgin Atlantic's fleet of wide body jets grows to 28. In December, Singapore Airlines and Virgin announce that the former will buy a 49% stake in Virgin Atlantic for £600m cash. In the same month, Virgin Atlantic also announces a deal with Air India which will give the airline access to the sub-continent for the first time, with flights due to start in July 2000; Virgin Group announces its intention to enter the telecommunications business; Virgin Net goes free and Virgin continues its expansion in e-commerce with a wide range of connections from Megastores online to train booking facilities (total internet revenues 1999 – £150 million); Virgin Mobile, Virgin's first consumer telecommunications venture, announces creation of 500 jobs in Trowbridge, West Wiltshire. The company will establish a management, customer service and call centre from which to market mobile telephony products (joint venture with Deutsche Telekom's One2One unit); Virgin Megastores continue their expansion world-wide with store openings in Miami, Glasgow, Piccadilly Circus, Bluewater, Strasburg, Okayama in Japan, bringing the total of Megastores up to 381 stores world-wide. As a result of its more focused retail strategy, Virgin Entertainment Group accepts an offer of £215m from UGC of France to buy Virgin Cinemas, the deal completes in November 1999; Virgin Active launches the first of its expected chain health and lifestyle centres, in Preston, Leeds and Stockley Park; Virgin Express starts a new service from Stansted to Berlin. Virgin also confirms the intention to set up a new independent low cost airline in Australia; Virgin opens its first game park in South Africa. The company also confirms that it has sold some of its smaller UK hotels to a private investor as part of its plan to refocus on exclusive properties around the world.

2000   Virgin Spectrum Limited is formed to participate in SpectrumCo. A new company formed by a number of shareholders to bid for a 3rd Generation Mobile Telephony license in the UK in March 2000. Other partners in the bid include Tesco, EMI, Sonera, Nextel, Marconi and a number of large private equity funds; Virgin Rail Group confirms its intention to bid for the East Coast Mainline; Virgin confirms its intention to launch Virgin.com/cars, a new e-commerce business, selling a wide range of cars direct to the consumer online.

Typically, entrepreneurs do not pass on their heritage successfully. What needs to be done to ensure that Virgin endures? What potential dangers are there, and what preventative steps should be taken? Will it take a commercial or other calamity to force Branson to take a back seat, or will someone (family? friend? business associate?) be able to 'control' his instinctive tendency for expansion, growth, and risk taking, directing his energies towards an orderly transition?

Or is the only real danger the sudden loss of Branson himself? Branson argues that he is not the sole source of the company's success, that each major Virgin company could stand alone, led by an experienced management team. The Virgin brand, he says, is an independent entity that has an existence beyond its association with him. Moreover, the organization has the momentum and strength that would see it through a crisis. Is this assertion correct? If Branson goes, would the company lose the impetus for innovation and the 'can-do' culture that has for so long been its hallmark? Who would maintain the elaborate structure of financial deals, joint ventures, and interlinked companies? Would the abrupt departure of Richard Branson create a crisis of confidence so severe as to endanger the very survival of Virgin?

As time passes, questions about the future of Virgin (often brought to the fore by Branson's dangerous exploits) will increasingly be in the minds of

shareholders, bankers, senior managers, potential partners, and myriad other interested parties. Has Virgin come of age to face a robust future, or is it on the cusp, about to enter terminal decline?

References

Branson, R., *Losing My Virginity*, London, Virgin Publishing, 1998.

The Toyoko Inn Group

By Miles Dodd[1]

It was April 2001. Norimasa Nishida, president of the Toyoko Inn group, sat back in his car and relaxed as his driver adjusted the navigation system to route them home. He was an excellent golfer, and was pleased that, with his hotel business now well established and very successful, he could take time away from the office to play. It had been a good day on the golf course, and he now settled down for the long drive back to his home in central Tokyo. He had always regretted not spending more time studying the fundamentals of business, and as another way of using his time, had recently enrolled in a part-time MBA course.

One of the things bothering him was how he should organise the future of Toyoko Inn, the western style hotel chain that he had founded. From its start in Kamata in Ota-ku, south-west Tokyo, in 1986, the group had expanded rapidly to become one of the largest chains in Japan. There were now over 50 hotels in Japan, offering more than 8,000 rooms

(see Figure 1). In 2000 the occupancy rate was 81% and annual sales were over ¥10 billion (US$80 million at ¥125 = US$1). The first Toyoko Inn outside Japan would open shortly in Shenyang, Liaoning province in China.

Nishida was the sole owner of the Toyoko Inn group and had a reputation as a 'one man boss'. He was aware that his strong personality had laid the basis for his success, but wondered what the best system was for managing the company in future as he reduced his own influence and explored opportunities in other fields.

Roots

In 1945, Ota-ku was a miserable place. It was a bombed land, barren and burned, full of rubble and ruin. Yet like seeds stirring in an old field, there was promise of new life. Nishida's father had returned

FIGURE 1 Toyoko Inn growth, 1986–2002

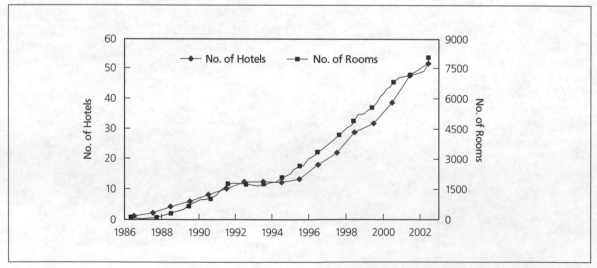

[1]Source: © 2002 Miles Dodd, Visiting Professor, Nihon University, Tokyo.

there after the war, and in 1947 had started an electrical engineering company in Kamata called Shotoku Denki Shokai. With the onset of the Korean War in the early 1950s many small entrepreneurial engineering factories in Ota-ku experienced a business boom and Shotoku Denki quickly became the largest electrical contracting company in the area.

Nishida was a spoiled child. As Shotoku Denki grew the family became quite wealthy. He was not a motivated student but when his father refused him a yacht unless he became top of the class, Norimasa won his yacht.

At Nihon University he did little work, but he was a tall and athletic youth. He had a golf handicap of 2 and played on the university golf team which was one of the best in Japan.

After university, Nishida briefly moved away to Osaka. However, he eventually returned to Kamata and was working as a manager in Shotoku Denki's general affairs department when, in 1979, his father unexpectedly died. A measure of the company's status in the community was that over 3,000 people attended the funeral. Young Nishida was 32 years old. One of his uncles had worked in the firm for some time, and everyone expected that the uncle would become president. However, after the funeral, as they were waiting to greet close friends and relatives, as is customary after a Japanese funeral, Nishida suddenly decided to ask his mother to announce that he himself, and not the uncle, would take over the company. This was a big surprise to all present, and not everyone welcomed it. He had remembered his father's often-expressed wish that his son would take over the company. Nishida got on with his uncle well enough, but did not like the idea of having to report to him. Besides, he could see no point in waiting until he was older to take charge.

After he became president, however, things went badly for Shotoku Denki. Many factories were abandoning Ota-ku, which by then had become heavily polluted, and orders had dropped off drastically because of the 'oil shock'. Also, 'I was a bit of a playboy,' Nishida admitted, and some staff left Shotoku to form a competing company. 18 months after he took over, only 15 of the 50 staff remained in Shotoku Denki, yet it remained a good steady business.

However, Nishida did not see a dynamic future for Shotoku. He saw that there was little money in construction, and that greater benefit accrued to the person who controlled the building itself. This interested him, and he soon discovered that he had a talent for identifying exactly what kind of building would be most appropriate in a given location. He started advising friends informally and with considerable success, but discovered that they were more likely to consult him if they paid for the service, so he established a property consultancy called Shotoku Biru Kikaku – the Shotoku Building Planning Company. This was successful but Nishida quickly realised that he was giving people advice from which they, not he, would reap the principal reward. He therefore decided to invest in building himself, leasing out offices to tenants. His first building was completed in 1980 in Kamata, quickly followed by another in Ebisu, a fast growing office and entertainment district in west central Tokyo.

Into the hotel business

Early in 1984, Nishida's friend Kono was facing a problem. His family owned a traditional wooden *ryokan* inn in Kamata. The fire prevention authorities were no longer prepared to license it and Kono had decided to pull it down and erect a seven storey building on the site. He had arranged to lease the three lower floors to a *yobiko* (a type of crammer school to prepare students for university entrance), the next three floors would be let out as small residential apartments, and he and his mother would live on the top floor. Unfortunately the *yobiko* went bankrupt before construction started, and Kono asked Nishida to advise how the building should be reconfigured.

Nishida told him that the only viable business was to use the lower six floors as a hotel. Kono did not like this idea. As the son of a *ryokan* owner he had too many memories of drunken guests returning from the city's bars in the early hours of the morning, loudly demanding to be let in. He was definitely not going to build a hotel! For several evenings Kono and Nishida met to discuss what could be done, but Nishida would not change his recommendation. Finally one evening after several rounds of *saké*, Kono challenged Nishida. 'OK, if you think it's such a great idea, do it yourself.' Never one to resist a challenge, Nishida thereupon agreed to enter the hotel business.

The Japanese hotel business

Most major cities in Japan had large western style hotels, some with famous western brand names.

They were modelled on the typical European or American hotel, with western style bedrooms, bathrooms, and public rooms, and with restaurants offering western food. They had also acquired a substantial social function, providing rooms for corporate and group gatherings, wedding and funeral reception facilities, and large banquet rooms. Many were originally 'railway' hotels close to stations. When the Japan City Hotel Association was established in 1918, it was authorised by the then Ministry of Railways. Typically, such hotels had many permanent managerial and service staff and were very labour intensive. Nishida considered their management structure to be bureaucratic and hierarchical and basically outdated.

Among other hotel categories in Japan were resort hotels for domestic tourists; traditional Japanese *ryokan* inns; high-quality 'limited service' hotels; and 'business' hotels, which were often of inferior design and quality and which lacked sophisticated reservation or marketing systems. In 1999, the Japanese hotel industry had 205,000 rooms, of which 6% were in the deluxe class, 22% first class, 54% economy/budget, and 18% were 'resort' hotels in holiday destinations.

In most areas of Japanese business and industry there are many *gyokai*. These are trade associations in which companies active in a certain business sector join together to represent and protect the collective interest. Many also play a role as a lobbying group and have a close relationship with local and national politicians. Nishida's plan to establish a hotel in Kamata brought him face to face with the local *ryokan gyokai*. While it would have been difficult for them to stop Nishida opening the hotel, they made a very strong effort to influence his decisions on pricing. While the *ryokan gyokai* might oppose the opening of a Toyoko Inn, the local chambers of commerce welcomed it since, while in most hotels the food and other services were included in the hotel itself, Toyoko Inn guests relied on services in the town. Nishida calculated that each guest would benefit the local community by ¥4,000.

Nishida could not entirely ignore the *gyokai* since Shotoku Denki undertook electrical work for many of their members. His original idea was to charge ¥4,500 per single room but the *gyokai* pressured him to increase it by several thousand yen. Nishida knew that the average *salariman* travelling on business had a daily allowance of around ¥8,000, out of which he would have to pay for meals. ¥6,000 thus seemed reasonable, and he fixed that rate feeling that he had compromised sufficiently towards the *gyokai*. It would provide a satisfactory return on an occupancy rate of only 55%. He was confident that would be easy to reach. In 2001 the rates for Toyoko Inn hotels ranged from ¥5,800 to ¥6,800. They had remained virtually unchanged since the company was founded in 1985. Toyoko Inn occupancy rates in 2001 were well over 80%.

Developing the Toyoko Inn concept

Nishida did not follow any accepted model but based his hotel concept on his own experience and common sense. How could he provide guests with acceptable and pleasing western-style accommodation at a moderate price that made sense for both him and the customer? He intended to concentrate on the market for businessmen, and saw no point in supplying facilities which they would not use. He minimised staff-intensive areas, such as restaurants, and concentrated on essentials delivered to a high standard. Rooms would be comfortable and practical and have all necessary facilities but no unnecessary luxuries. For example, there would be a refrigerator in each room, but it would be empty: 'Guests can go to a convenience store and pick up drinks for ¥100. If we supplied them, we would have to charge ¥120/130,' explained Nishida. There would be no room service; the reception desk would close from 10.00 a.m. to 4.00 p.m., between those times the hotel would be closed, except for guests still in residence, to allow vacated rooms to be cleaned and made ready for new guests. In order to avoid heavy staff overhead costs he hired part-time staff to clean the rooms, and to serve buffet style breakfast in the mornings.

Every Toyoko Inn room was supplied with a colour television, a refrigerator, a video machine, tea-making equipment, toiletries, a hair dryer, shaving kit, and morning and evening newspapers. In each hotel there were coin-operated machines for laundry; food and drink; fax; and copying. Room design was constantly improved, and new facilities added. Internet access had become standard throughout the group.

Hotel management model

While Nishida did not consult any hotel business 'experts' on the running of his first hotel, he did have a useful adviser. She was Mrs Kono, the mother of his friend, who lived, as had been planned, on the 7th floor of the first Toyoko Inn. Having run the family *ryokan* she knew how things should be done. She insisted that everything should be perfectly clean, and that service down to the last detail should be the main point of emphasis. For example rather than greeting guests with the standard '*irrashaimase*' (welcome) greeting, Mrs. Kono recommended that '*okaerinasai*' (welcome home) should be used, a practice that Toyoko Inn staff follow to this day.

To start with Toyoko Inn employed both male and female staff. However, as he put it 'men are careless and clumsy, and are not good at cleaning or other day-to-day tasks. The male of the human species is a hunter, he is not good at service, his place is not indoors.' He therefore adopted a policy of employing women as managers at his hotels.

The first manager was a wise and experienced woman who had managed a drinking establishment in Kamata that Nishida had regularly frequented. She felt the time had come to give up that business, and readily agreed when Nishida suggested that she become the manager of his first Toyoko Inn. As Nishida put it, she had plenty of experience dealing with people in all sorts of situations, she was familiar with the business side having run her own establishment, and had plenty of worldly wisdom. In 2001 women managed all but one of the group hotels.

There were few opportunities for mature women to take positions of real responsibility in Japan even at the start of the 21st century. However, Nishida's view was that women with broad experience were very well adapted to manage the microcosm of life which he felt his hotels represented. Many of the Toyoko Inn managers had grown-up children, and some were divorcees: as Nishida said, divorcees had a rounded view of life, and their views of men had 'moved beyond the romantic stage'.

Some might consider that the women in charge of the hotels could be placed in an unduly vulnerable position. However, experience showed that, on the contrary, men who might otherwise be rowdy or violent calm down and become less aggressive when dealing only with women. The female manager of one of the Toyoko Inn hotels with seven years experience said that such problems were not an important issue for her. Her main concern was the risk of infra-structure problems. For example the main electrical supply might fail, or a major plumbing disaster would occur.

Hotel managers were answerable for the entire operation in their respective hotels. They produced the accounts and profit and loss statements, kept bondholders informed of occupancy levels (on which the bonds' interest rates were based – see following section) and were also responsible for staff, hotel maintenance and local advertising. They therefore had a very broad responsibility.

In addition to the hotel managers, Toyoko Inn was unusual in the number of women it employed overall. 96.6% of the 300 permanent employees ('*seishain*') and 700 part-timers were women. The manager of the hotel operations division is Ms. Shinkai who reports directly to Nishida.

Toyoko Inn obtained ISO 9002 certification in 2001. The authorising body, the Japan Quality Association, would willingly have granted certification on the basis of inspecting one hotel, but Nishida felt that the process and discipline of obtaining certification had a real value in itself. He insisted that all hotels go through the process while noting that he was not in agreement with the entire ISO system, and so had changed and adapted some of the requirements.

Hotel ownership model

Kono, landlord of the original Toyoko Inn, had wanted to retain ownership of his building, so he agreed to negotiate a lease with Nishida. This worked well and in fact became a model for the future (see Figure 2). Nishida realised that many first-generation entrepreneurs wanted to retire, but did not trust their children with the legacy of their labours. He could resolve the problem for the parents by getting them to fund the construction of a hotel building in accordance with Toyoko Inn's design, and then leasing it to Toyoko Inn for a 30 year period. During that time the capital would be secure while the children obtained a regular monthly income from the lease. Rental was increased automatically by 3% every three years. This became the established pattern for Toyoko Inn's development, and it also had substantial tax advantages for the group.

Although construction cost was the responsibility of the owner, Toyoko Inn still had to provide lease guarantee money (*hoshoukin*) to the landlord, a customary practice in Japan equivalent to 20% of the

FIGURE 2 Toyoko Inn – ownership model

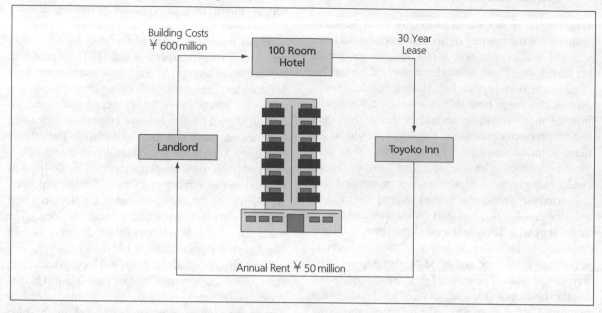

building cost. If a hotel cost ¥600 million (US$4.8 million) to build, the *hoshoukin* thus amounted to ¥120 million (US$960,000).

In order to raise funds for the *hoshoukin*, Toyoko Inn sometimes issued private bonds repayable in annual instalments over five years. The interest was determined by the occupancy rate of the hotel, with a guaranteed minimum of 2.5% per annum and a maximum of 6.5%. In 2001, this interest rate was exceptionally high for Japan – most saving methods yield interest less than 1.5%. In 2001 Toyoko Inn obtained bond ratings from both a domestic and a foreign rating-services company in order to establish its credibility and financial reputation. The bond for the Morioka Toyoko Inn for example returned 5.8% interest in 2001.

Nishida became very keen on the bond system. Bondholders were, as he put it, 'unpaid salesmen' since they urged everyone they knew to use 'their' hotel in order to push up the occupancy rate. However government regulations restricted companies to two bond issues per year, so Nishida resorted to bank borrowing for the *hoshoukin* for the third and any subsequent hotels within each financial year.

Nishida was the sole owner of Toyoko Inn. He preferred to retain control himself rather than floating the company on the stock market. He avoided shared family ownership believing it only caused quarrels and arguments: however his daughter, in her early 20s, worked in the company.

The weekend problem

Toyoko Inn occupancy rates were generally very high on weekdays but fell off steeply on Sundays. In June 2001 the Sunday rate was 54.1% while the Saturday rate was 86.1% and for all other days 89.6%, giving an overall rate of 84.3%. Nishida and his management team were considering how to improve the Sunday occupancy rate, and had introduced a number of incentive schemes. For example, guests aged 60 or over attracted special concessionary rates at weekends.

Reservation system

In 1991, a friend told Nishida that the Internet system would have a great future, so Nishida invested in a hotel reservation system that he named 'Hornet' (http://www.inn-info.co.jp). His intention was to establish a business hotel reservation system which not only handled reservations for the Toyoko Inn group but for other non-group hotels. As long as occupancy rates at group hotels were high, the system was a useful way of accommodating overflow bookings. It also helped clients looking for a place to stay in cities where there was no Toyoko Inn (for example in Hiroshima).

The Toyoko Inn name

The name 'Toyoko' combines the first kanji characters of Tokyo and Yokohama. Coincidentally 'Toyoko' is very similar to 'Tokyu' – the name of another hotel chain which has 46 hotels throughout Japan. It is also all too easy to confuse 'Toyoko' with 'Tokyu'. Initially, Toyoko Inn might have benefited from the confusion but with an established brand of its own, the similarity may have begun to work against it.

The Toyoko Inn management system

Each Toyoko Inn was treated as a separate business unit, with the manager acting as the *de facto* CEO. This delegation was an important way of keeping head office costs at a reasonable level. It also gave managers themselves a real sense of responsibility and satisfaction. As local people, they knew their territory well, and were not moved from one hotel to another as might happen in other large chains. In some cases, a separate legal company wholly owned by the group was actually created for financial reasons.

The top management team, representing every part of the organisation, held regular Friday meetings. Those attending were Shigeta, Director and Vice-President; Mineno, Finance and Accounting; Hibiya, head of Toyoko Inn Development, and Sawada, his deputy; Kubota, head of System Denken K.K.; Ms Koezuka, Reservations; Rokukawa, Standing Auditor (*kansayaku*); Koyasu, Special Adviser, and Nishida himself. According to both Shigeta and Rokukawa, there was always discussion at the meetings, and 'Nishida listens'. At the same time, there was never any doubt who was the boss and ultimate decision-maker.

Kunimori Shigeta had been working in a trading company and was approached by Hibiya, who was already with Toyoko Inn, when the need for senior managers grew as the group expanded. On joining Toyoko Inn he had been surprised to find that the company organisation was quite unlike the traditional Japanese management 'pyramid' to which he had been accustomed in the past. Despite the outward impression that Nishida, as president, ran a 'one-man' company, the Toyoko Inn organisation was quite flat. Nishida was not so much the king of the castle, but the hub of the wheel: the various activities of the Toyoko Inn organisation radiate out from him. Every month all the hotel managers gathered in Tokyo for a meeting to exchange views and discuss new developments or needs. If one hotel was having problems, a more senior hotel manager might be asked to act as advisor to help improve performance. Shigeta commented that one of this main functions is to 'act as a consultant' to the hotel managers.

Koyasu, the special adviser, managed the monthly meetings. He had been manager in the US for a major Japanese bank, and was an experienced executive. In addition to the hotel managers, the meeting included all the head office managers and managers of the subsidiary companies. Every participant was provided with detailed results and figures for the preceding month. Discussion was always active and there was a high degree of participation. Koyasu was tough but always fair in reviewing the figures. After the review, various committees would report. Committees were nearly all formed of three of four hotel managers. Nishida was always present at the meetings but commented only occasionally. His interruptions were interesting. On one occasion, a committee had been charged with redesigning the Toyoko Inn credit card. In the new design, the head office hotel telephone number had been removed from the back of the card because of shortage of space. Nishida interjected that the number must be shown, 'customers must always be able to contact us directly', he said. On another occasion, a committee had produced a short video showing how chairs could be easily refurbished. Nishida ordered the video remade, 'those are men's hands', he said, 'all our managers are women, remake the tape showing women's hands'.

While he was happy with his existing management team, and the competence with which it managed Toyoko Inn's operation and growth, Nishida was not sure how he should proceed in future. He wondered whether he should sell the Toyoko Inn group to a foreign organisation that might approach him, or perhaps suggest to the managers that they finance a management buyout. Alternatively, he could appoint one of his present directors to replace him or even bring in a new president from the outside. Maybe there was a member of his family who could join the company and eventually take over. Of course he could stay on and just take it easy, but he felt that he had done enough to lay the foundation for The Toyoko Inn group and was looking for new challenges.

Toyoko Inn bonus schemes

Three different bonus systems operated within Toyoko Inn. Most staff received 15.5 months' salary each year. This is the usual Japanese salary structure in which the bonus is not performance related, but consists of winter and summer lump sum payments made to staff automatically in accordance with an agreed formula.

For staff working on the hotel reception desks there was a 14-month basic salary. In addition each receptionist received ¥5 per person staying on nights when they were on duty plus an additional bonus of ¥2,500 for each 'full house' night. Nishida realised that the most difficult time of the month for many women was the week just before the monthly salary was received. He therefore arranged for the 'full house' bonus to be paid out on the 10th of each month. He commented that some women appreciated this almost as much as their actual salary payment!

The third bonus scheme was for Toyoko Inn Development Company staff. Their basic pay is generous, however they earn a further ¥2,000,000 for every hotel development project successfully completed.

New construction and maintenance – System Denken K.K.

The original electrical contracting business had been absorbed into the Toyoko Inn group under the name System Denken K.K. and was a vital part of group activity. By managing construction, renewal, and maintenance work in-house, costs for these essential works were about half what Nishida estimated the company would have to pay on the open market. Every five years group hotels are refurbished throughout.

System Denken also arranged the manufacturing of prefabricated module bathrooms, which were incorporated into the new hotels as they were built. Thirty workers had recently come over from China to observe and learn so that they could work on the new hotel in Shenyang, Toyoko Inn's first overseas investment.

Nishida's philosophy

Nishida called his business philosophy *sanpou ichiryou doku*, an expression dating from the Edo era in Japan. It literally means that each of three persons with an interest in a venture should earn one gold coin from it. Toyoko Inn's business partners – the building owner, the customer, and Toyoko Inn itself – should all benefit. In 2001, he decided to make a 'millennium gesture' to customers by absorbing the 5% Japanese consumer tax without raising prices, a 'gesture' worth between US$4 and US$5 million per year.

Nishida recounted how in the late 1980s he had intended to build deluxe US$800,000 condominiums in Honolulu aimed at Japanese buyers who were flocking to Hawaii at the time. However, he read an article reporting how Hawaiian residents were suffering from inflated property prices due to the Japanese boom, and immediately redesigned for the block to have units at the more affordable price of US$300,000 for Hawaiian residents. Nishida did not regret that decision. The market for expensive condominiums in Hawaii collapsed after the 'bubble' burst in Japan in 1991 and many developers went bankrupt. Nishida on the other hand, had no problem selling his more modestly priced units.

Nishida lay back in the car and closed his eyes. As the car sped along the highway towards the lights of Tokyo he felt pleased that the group he had established was now a significant player in the Japanese hotel market, and his thoughts returned to the question of succession and how he could ensure the continuing success of the group while satisfying his own interest in developing new ventures.

CASE 5

PowerGen: Strategy and corporate planning

By David Jennings[1]

Prior to the reorganisation of the electricity industry in England and Wales in 1989 and its subsequent privatisation in 1991, the Central Electricity Generating Board (CEGB) was responsible for the generation and transmission of electricity.

By the mid-1980s the number of power stations was declining, from 262 in 1958 to 79 in 1986. At the same time the technical complexity of power stations was increasing. In 1987 the CEGB reorganised to reflect these changes, adopting a structure based on functional specialisation, replacing regional management by providing resources on a national scale to address the generic problems of the power stations.

In 1990 the CEGB's generating activities were split between three companies, non-nuclear generating capacity was divided to form two organisations, National Power and PowerGen; nuclear generation formed the basis for a third company, Nuclear Electric. The CEGB's transmission function (the national grid) was placed within the joint ownership of the 12 electricity supply companies, the regional electricity companies (RECs). The RECs were to continue their function of supplying electricity to the final customer, metering and billing. Until 1998 customers with a demand below 100kW were to be exclusively supplied by the local RECs, after which time the market was to be opened to competition. Supply to customers over 100kW was progressively opened to all competitors in 1990 and 1994.

The reorganised industry was to be regulated by a director general of electricity supply, whose duties included the promotion of competition in the generation and supply of electricity.

PowerGen's functions were conferred in March 1990. In March 1991 PowerGen was privatised through the sale of 60% of its shares in a public offer (the remaining 40% in 1995). At vesting, PowerGen was allocated 21 power stations, generating approximately 30% of the electricity supplied to the transmission and distribution networks in England and Wales (National Power 48%, Nuclear Power 17%). Over 94% of PowerGen's output was generated from coal and dual-fired (coal/oil) power stations, all of which were first commissioned in the mid- to late 1960s and early 1970s.

The generators were to sell electricity into an electricity pool, from which the suppliers (RECs) would buy. The pool operated on the basis of competitive bidding by generators. The national grid determined which sets of generating plant needed to run to meet demand. The bid price of the last set required (i.e. the most expensive) became the price for that (half-hour) period.

As pool prices could vary significantly over short periods, they were often hedged by agreements between a generator and a supplier to specify a price and quantity for a particular time. The contracts resulted in payments by generator to supplier when the pool price exceeded the agreed price, or supplier to generator when the pool price was lower than the strike price.

Organisation and planning, 1989–92

In 1988 the McKinsey consulting company was employed to help develop a strategy and organisational structure for PowerGen. A structure was proposed that was based on well-defined functional responsibilities and few layers of management (Figure 1, asterisks indicate those involved in managing the planning process). Each function formed a division, within which units were termed business units.

The McKinsey review also considered the planning process, recommending a five-stage process

---

[1]Source: This case was prepared by Dr David Jennings of Nottingham Business School, Nottingham Trent University, UK. It is intended as a basis for class discussion and not as an illustration of either good or bad management practice. © D. Jennings, 1999.

FIGURE 1   Organisation structure, 1990

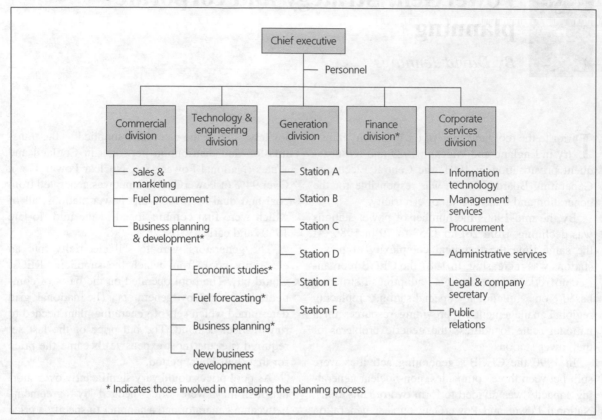

* Indicates those involved in managing the planning process

(Figure 2) that was introduced in 1990, along with the new organisation structure.

The planning process was led and managed by the commercial division, within which a large group of planners assisted the development of corporate strategy and the company's diversification through the new business development unit. The planning process retained a high degree of centralisation. Staff in the business planning and development department constructed a number of scenarios concerning market share, pool prices and competitor analysis for the core business (the generation division). The decisions that could be made by each unit (power station) were essentially those that had been available to

them within the CEGB, with planning focused on developing the resource implications of a centrally determined strategy. The plans from the business units were aggregated to provide divisional plans. Financial projections from these exercises were consolidated by the finance division.

Strategic development

The centralised approach to planning associated with the CEGB began to lose relevance with the opening of the market for electricity, the wholesale electricity pool (April 1990). The operation of the pool became

FIGURE 2   Corporate planning cycle, 1990

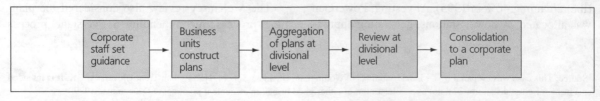

the focus of PowerGen's strategy, requiring the development of both a strong commercial orientation and increased operational flexibility.

At an early stage PowerGen's chief executive (and from 1996 also chairman), Ed Wallis stated that the company was 'first and foremost, a power generation business'. 'We concentrated our early energies on totally reshaping the core electricity business' to become 'a low-cost producer on a world class basis.' In addition, the company would 'seek the opportunity to reintegrate generation with supply', implying merger with a regional electricity company.

PowerGen began to develop its generating capacity to better fit commercial and environmental requirements, through improving the flexibility of the coal units and developing gas-fired stations. By October 1990, plans had been announced for three CCGT power stations at a cost of £500 million. By 1996 the three gas-fired stations would provide over a third of PowerGen's output. Similar investments were being made by National Power.

Gas has numerous benefits for a generator. Compared with coal-fired stations the plant has relatively low capital costs, a shorter construction time, operates at high efficiency and productivity levels and has a lower emission of pollutants than coal generation. At the same time the availability of gas-fired technology lowered the barriers facing would-be entrants to electricity generation.

In gas supply the privatised company British Gas retained effective control of the supply of North Sea gas to business and households. PowerGen formed a joint venture with Conoco, Kinetica. Plans included the supply of gas to power stations, including PowerGen's, and large businesses with factories near the route of its £200 million pipeline. The pipeline was projected to supply 20% of UK gas consumption.

The national grid forecast a growth in electricity demand of only 0.6% a year for the period 1990–97, with demand peaking at 50,000 MW, against industry capacity of 61,000 MW in 1990/91. PowerGen engaged in a series of power station closures that would adjust the company's capacity to the new operating and commercial environment; this included the closure of coal-fired plant that was up to 34 years old. By April 1993, PowerGen had shut down 3275 MW of plant since privatisation.

The company's strategy anticipated that PowerGen would suffer an inevitable reduction in market share together with pressures for price reduction. Consequently, the company recognised that growth in the medium and longer term would require the establishment of new income streams in other energy-related areas where its core competences could create value. Early attention was given to developing a portfolio of new businesses based in the UK; international developments were believed to take longer to contribute to profits.

Upstream gas activities were seen as a logical extension of PowerGen's downstream activities, and assets were acquired in the North Sea and Liverpool Bay. Downstream, there was the partnership in the gas supply and transportation company, Kinetica. Also in the UK, Combined Heat and Power (CHP) was established to design, install, own and operate plant providing combined heat and power under agreements with specific industrial companies.

Overseas, the increasing international demand for power and the opening up of electricity markets to foreign investment presented opportunities for PowerGen's diversification. In the USA, the world's biggest energy consumer, energy demand was predicted to grow by 30% over the next two decades. Within the developing countries the rate of growth in electricity consumption was considerably greater than that in the UK, China and India averaging increases of 9 and 10% respectively between 1985 and 1991. The tendency throughout the developing countries for utilities to charge too little for the power they generated would require in some cases considerably higher prices (as much as a 50% increase) to attract outside capital investment. Projected investments also faced the possible effect of depreciating exchange rates over the 20-year life of most investments and future changes in government regulation of the industry. Nevertheless, the growth prospects were sufficiently attractive to invite investment proposals from power-related businesses around the world. In addition, the privatisation of state-owned utilities presented PowerGen with potential opportunities to enter markets and apply acquired expertise in project management, the operation of plant and deregulation. By the middle of the 1990s, PowerGen had made power station and mining acquisitions in eastern Germany and Hungary, with construction projects in Portugal and Indonesia.

Reorganisation, 1992

In 1992 PowerGen introduced a number of organisational changes that were profoundly to affect the corporate planning process. The company was reorganised from a functional form to three divisions: New Ventures (containing PowerGen International, North Sea (gas) and Combined Heat and Power), UK Electricity (UK generation, including sales and marketing) and Engineering and Business Services (Figure 3). Each division was given its own managing director.

The existing large, central planning team was replaced by planning staff within the divisions. A smaller central strategic planning function was introduced, responsible for both corporate strategy and corporate planning. The separate task of financial planning was located within the finance department.

All business units became either profit or cost centres. The business units were given a wider role in decision making, with their managers provided, often for the first time, with a profit-and-loss format and support from finance staff newly located in their division.

In the New Ventures division the business units were to have considerable influence over their own revenue. North Sea Gas actively bought and sold gas, Combined Heat and Power had its own client contracts. The increased freedom also extended to UK Electricity. The power station managers were empowered to take a wide range of decisions that would reduce costs, including through questioning the purchase of a range of central services. The process of devolution and the internal market extensively reduced PowerGen's central staff and helped to empower business-level management.

Within the new structure the planning process operated at a number of levels. The central strategic planning staff developed the corporate strategy. Each unit in the organisation produced a business plan, which was consolidated by the divisional board and again at corporate level to form the corporate plan. Guidance for the planning exercise was provided by corporate-level planning staff. The guidelines included overall business and economic assumptions, scenarios and profit targets (in place of expenditure limits for various categories of spend), anticipated output required from each power station and, for a non-generating unit, the corporate challenges and targets that the business unit was expected to contribute to achieving. The challenges and targets encouraged units to explore their potential rather than meet a set target.

The scope of options available to the business units had been considerably widened and provided

FIGURE 3 Organisation structure, 1992

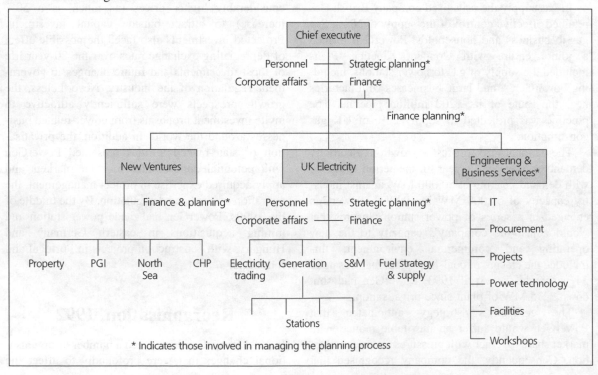

* Indicates those involved in managing the planning process

with a commercial focus. The level of detail required in business unit plans was reduced to provide a plan that could be expressed in a few sheets of paper. The time required to carry out the corporate planning process had also changed, from a year, or more, to a nine-month process.

Planning problems: 1993–94

During 1993–94 several developments occurred that would affect the future profitability of the core business, UK Electricity. These included an agreement with the industry regulator to cap wholesale prices in the electricity pool and also for the company to sell 2 GW of power plant. The effect on profit forecasts was compounded by an unexpected increase in electricity supplied by Nuclear Electric.

For any organisation, planning is inherently an iterative process, but during the 1993–94 planning cycle presentation of the corporate plan to the board was delayed by the need for substantial reworking of the plan to reflect PowerGen's financial priorities more fully. The 1993 planning cycle revealed a rift between strategic decisions and the group's financial requirements. In part the problem was seen as a result of the way in which planning responsibilities had been assigned within the company. The company's strategic planner, reporting to the chief executive, was responsible for both the development of corporate strategy and production of the corporate plan, an arrangement that limited the influence of the finance department in shaping the corporate plan early in the planning cycle. Responsibility for the plan and for managing the corporate planning process was passed to the director of finance, effectively increasing the influence of financial considerations in the planning process.

The planning difficulties also reflected a failure by the centre to communicate scenario information fully. The centre had considered that such an event as 'capping' could occur, but had not communicated that early enough for it to be a part of the context for developing the business plans. PowerGen adopted the practice that, as part of the strategic review, the core businesses should themselves develop a number of scenarios as to how the market might develop, and the plans that followed were to be robust to those possibilities.

The difficulties experienced in the 1993 planning cycle were added to by the divisional form of organisation that PowerGen had adopted in 1992. From the perspective of managing the planning process, the divisions could add a level of bureaucracy to the process and affect communication with the business units. Priorities and issues that were identified at corporate level were filtered, and often new arguments added, before being addressed by business unit planners.

Merger with an REC

At the end of 1995/96, sales to the electricity pool remained the core business of PowerGen, accounting for 70% of group turnover. PowerGen continued to face increasing pressures on market share and lower electricity prices. Although overall electricity demand in England and Wales in 1995/96 had risen by over 3% in the year, as a result of the continuing economic upturn and a cold winter, PowerGen's share of the market had fallen.

In 1995 the government's 'golden share' in the RECs expired, leading to a flurry of takeover activity with a range of UK and overseas companies, from within the generating industry and outside it, bidding to acquire RECs. Motives varied but included the belief that the five-yearly review of prices left the RECs comparatively weakly regulated: domestic electricity prices had fallen by only 4% since privatisation. PowerGen made an agreed offer of £1.9 billion for Midlands Electricity plc, a regional electricity company. Although this was the sixth bid that had occurred for an REC, and the government had recently allowed Scottish Power's £1.1 billion offer for Manweb, the industry regulator voiced concern. The merger, together with a similar proposed merger by National Power with Manweb, was referred to the Monopolies and Mergers Commission (MMC).

As an REC, Midlands had a local monopoly of supply in its geographical area for customers of less than 100 kW, customers whose annual electricity bills ranged from £12,000 (small business) to £300 (domestic customer). In total RECs had 23 million such customers, accounting for half of all electricity demand by volume and two-thirds by value. In the over 100 kW (competitive) market – large customers throughout England and Wales – MEB had a 6% share. PowerGen was the largest supplier to that market, with a share of 16%. Under its operating licence MEB was allowed to generate up to 88 MW, 15% of its requirements at vesting, and had interests in five power stations with a total capacity of 2688 MW.

Analysis presented to the MMC pointed to the conclusion that PowerGen had been able to use its generating facilities (non-baseload) to set pool prices for a large proportion of the time, about 35%, in 1995/96. The MMC considered that without the merger that figure would reduce to between 27 and 30% by 2000/01. The merger raised the prospect of acquired information and influence supporting higher prices than would otherwise occur. Other concerns addressed the industry regulator's ability to enforce prohibitions on cross-subsidy and the requirement for economic purchasing. At the same time the increased size of the merged company and its wider skill base was seen as enhancing the ability to compete in international markets, where international energy companies were emerging.

The overall conclusion arrived at by the MMC was that the adverse effects of the merger need not justify its prohibition. The government, however, decided to block the merger. However, chief executive Ed Wallis responded by restating his intention to buy an REC, although accepting that PowerGen might have to wait until after the next general election. Wallis predicted that merger activity was leading to the creation of five or six super-utilities that would emerge to dominate the privatised electricity market.

In November 1996 the company had sufficient cash, partly due to sale of its stake in MEB, to carry out its third share buy-back in two years, totalling a third of its shares since the completion of its privatisation in 1995.

Reorganisation, 1996

By the mid-1990s several of the businesses with the New Venture division had developed to a stage where they justified their own management, on a level with that of UK Electricity. In addition, within the core, the signalled liberalisation of the electricity market (1998) argued for sales and marketing to be given greater autonomy and separation from generation.

In September 1996 PowerGen underwent a reorganisation that reflected these developments, replacing the divisional form of organisation with new clusters of business units (Figure 4). Each cluster, such as UK Production, was headed by a managing director. Typically the MD was assisted by a finance manager whose role included, as part of their financial responsibilities, managing the planning process.

Similarly, it was common practice for a specific member of staff to be given the role of developing business unit strategy.

The reorganisation improved the focus of unit managers on the particular circumstances associated with their businesses; it also enabled corporate staff to develop targets that more exactly addressed the individual business.

Within the new structure a group MD had been established to act as MD responsible for all the business units. The role of the chief executive focused on the development of corporate strategy, the finance director was mainly concerned with the financial aspects of plans, and the group MD was concerned with business unit strategy. As a team they engaged in a continuing dialogue concerning the overall strategic and financial direction of PowerGen. The corporate strategist (with a team of three staff) and corporate planner (four staff) assisted this debate and the development of business strategies and plans.

Environment and scenarios

A number of developments acted to increase the environmental complexity and uncertainty facing PowerGen. These included industry and geographical diversification, increasing competition in the UK generation industry (the core business for revenue) and the actions and reactions occurring at the company/regulator/government interface. As a consequence, the company placed a great deal of effort into managing the interface with regulatory, political and environmental developments continually absorbing the external perspective and assessing its implications for strategic options.

Prior to the planning cycle, in July and August, a number of scenarios were developed. The past practice of centralised scenario development had been replaced by a devolved process based on one or more business units and the corporate strategist.

The principal scenario exercises in the planning round primarily concerned the inputs and outputs of PowerGen's businesses, the markets and prices for gas, coal and electricity. Price information was developed in the context of the larger, world pictures, with the prices based on views concerning possible futures that may for example include the composition of the industry, how those in the industry might behave, the role of wider sources of supply such as Russian gas and conditions in the UK energy markets.

FIGURE 4 Organisation structure, 1996

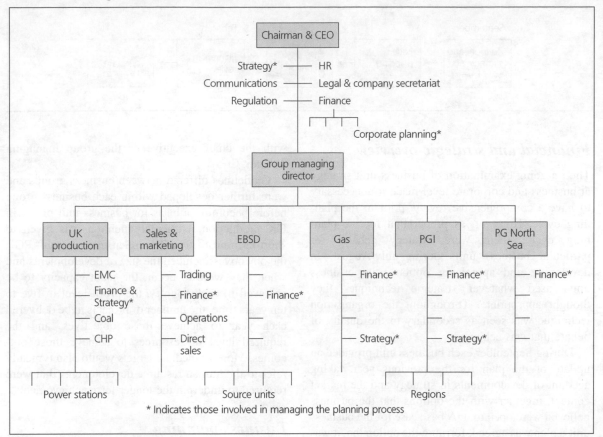

Other scenarios were also developed, for example, as part of strategy development for UK production a scenario would be developed for the evolution of the UK electricity market. Given that PowerGen was a major supplier, the company would have some influence in how that situation might develop. In such a case the scenario exercise became part of strategy development.

Scenarios came to be developed by a team drawn from a number of functions and businesses to represent the various groups with a significant interest in the output from the scenario. The team would be led by a representative of the unit that either has the most expertise or involvement in the area on which the scenario was focused. In general, outside experts were not involved as team members; however, the advice of external people was sought and they made presentations to the team. The scenarios were developed by trying to identify the key drivers for the industry. This involved the use of quantitative trends and qualitative analysis concerning industry structure, government intervention and the behaviour of

the various players in the market. Brainstorming then focused on how different futures might evolve. Information from the scenario exercises formed part of the planning guidance.

The corporate planning process, 1996–98

The planning system encouraged initiatives by the business units within a corporate context; it also addressed the need for co-ordination between a number of the business units. In the UK, PowerGen was seeking to build an integrated gas and electricity business. The businesses that made up the UK electricity and gas value chain had to have consistent strategies and objectives for achieving that end. There was also a need for co-ordination between UK generation and the developing overseas operations, a skills transfer that required integration of human resource planning. The planning cycle is detailed in Figure 5.

FIGURE 5   Corporate planning cycle, 1998

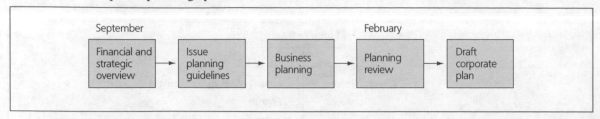

Financial and strategic overview

The on-going examination of business unit strategy at business and corporate level made it unnecessary to have a comprehensive review prior to the planning cycle. However, as preparation for the planning cycle, there were strategy debates for particular business units during July/August. In developing and appraising options, the business units used whatever strategic techniques they thought appropriate. Throughout the organisation technique was seen as secondary to the quality of debate that was achieved.

During September each business unit provided an update of the plan for the previous year, taking account of developments in strategy and the market context, together with the options that the business believed were open to it. A base case for the business unit's plan was agreed, forming the option that it was expected would be developed in the subsequent business planning. Business unit strategy was established before developing detailed planning guidance. Partly this reflected the need for co-ordination. However, there was scope for flexibility: issues affecting business unit strategies often emerged and had to be addressed within the subsequent stages of the corporate planning process, prior to board approval.

Following its consolidation this information was examined by the corporate staff for its strategic and financial fit against the overall priorities of the company. Conclusions from this comparison supported the development of guidelines, the corporate context of strategic and financial priorities and targets agreed with each business unit within which business planning was conducted.

Planning guidelines

Typically this stage in the planning process involved a great deal of discussion and lobbying between the corporate strategy and planning staff and business unit managers. The guidelines were formally agreed with the chief executive or the group managing director.

Guidelines differed between business groups and were further developed within each business group before becoming a basis for business unit plans. In UK production, particular attention was given to short-term profit. For PowerGen International (PGI) the objectives included the size of developments and when they were to occur, the plant capacity to be achieved in each country, the profit level in five to ten years time, the number of projects to be delivered each year to achieve those objectives, and the required level of resources to achieve those outcomes. More immediate targets would also typically refer to the human resource developments that were required to underpin the longer-term achievements.

Business planning

All units, including corporate staff units, produced a plan with a five-year horizon. Typically a plan was a brief document clearly stating the business unit objectives and how they expected to meet them, the key issues facing the business, how the business was going to develop and the expected financial performance.

Planning review

The planning review stage involved the corporate planning staff, business planners and business directors. Once business units had submitted their individual plans, the team examined the overall financial picture that the plans presented and whether in total they met the group requirements. This led to feedback into the business reviews, where the group MD and financial director reviewed the plans of individual business units with the unit's MD.

The final stage in the planning process involved amalgamating the business plans and drafting the corporate plan.

Performance review

Following the presentation of the plan to the board, the performance of the managing directors of the various businesses was reviewed. A bonus scheme operated with three components: individual performance, the performance of the director's business and corporate performance. While corporate performance typically involved earnings per share, business performance included the year's contribution to achieving the longer-term key achievements that the business was trying to deliver over the next five years, such as market share, developing the business's capabilities and other forms of business development. All of the financial and strategic targets were specified in the business plan for the previous year.

Industry and company developments, 1998

During 1997/98, competition from over 30 other generators contributed to a further fall in PowerGen's share of UK generation, by 2.1% to 19.5%. In the supply of electricity to industrial and commercial customers, the company retained its leading position with a market share of 16%.

In the same period the upstream gas business, PowerGen North Sea, delivered a strong performance. This was originally established to secure low-cost gas to support PowerGen's CCGT programme and to enable the group to gain expertise and knowledge of the business. Further growth would require the injection of considerable capital and the decision was taken to find a buyer for the business.

PowerGen was involved in the production, transportation, marketing and trading of gas, meeting its own long-term needs through long-term contracts with gas producers. In gas supply PowerGen had achieved agreements to supply gas for household use, as well as electricity, to two of the regional electricity companies. PowerGen already supplied 10% of the industrial and commercial gas market.

PowerGen's combined heat and power business successfully commissioned a further two new CHP plants, for Conoco and Iggesund Paperboard, bringing the total of PowerGen's CHP capacity to 180 MW of electricity on five sites.

In international activities, by 1998 PowerGen had achieved a total committed investment of £700 million in plant and projects overseas. The operations in Australia, Hungary and Germany had produced improved results, although continuing difficult market conditions in Australia (accounting for 55% of the company's operational overseas generating capacity) depressed the company's international profits. During the next two years the completion of major projects in India, Indonesia and Portugal, to a total of 5455 MW, would more than double PowerGen's international operating capacity. A further three projects in Hungary, India and Thailand, totalling 2367 MW, were due to come into operation by 2002/03. By 2001 PowerGen expected to earn £100 million a year from outside the UK.

Within the UK the increased use of gas and the consequent loss of jobs in the coal-mining industry became a politically sensitive issue for the power industry. In 1997 the newly elected Labour government announced its intention to limit further construction of gas-powered generating plant. The industry regulator observed that this would act as a barrier to industry entry, arguing, if necessary, for the break-up of National Power and PowerGen. The government announced its intention to review the operation of the electricity pool and prices in distribution. Government proposals included replacing the pool with bilateral trading arrangements between large users (big industrial consumers and supply companies) and the generators, in an attempt to lower the wholesale price of electricity.

The government continued to hold a 'golden share' in both PowerGen and National Power, protecting them from takeover. Nevertheless, a consortium of overseas financial and industrial companies had planned a hostile bid for National Power with the intention of demerging the company, whose share price was depressed by a profit warning and potential power plant disposals. It was not clear that the government would oppose an offer that promoted competition and assisted realisation of its energy policy.

By 1997 only one REC remained independent, Southern Electric, with more than half the original 12 companies held by US companies. In September 1998 PowerGen was given government permission to proceed with a second bid to acquire East Midlands Electricity from Dominion Resources, an American utility, for £1.9 billion, £300 million more than Dominion had paid 18 months earlier. A further referral to the MMC would have delayed the signing of long-term coal contracts, which the government believed would safeguard thousands of jobs in the mining industry. The government's condition for the merger was that PowerGen would carry out the disposal of two large coal-fired power stations, amounting to 4002 MW of its 13,600 MW coal- and gas-fired capacity. The disposals were expected to raise about £900 million.

The acquisition of EME provided PowerGen with its long-sought integration with the supply industry, in addition enabling the company to sell both electricity and gas to household customers. The merger also provided a wider base of expertise for PowerGen to use in bidding for overseas contracts, many of which involved running distribution networks as well as generation.

In September 1998 the liberalisation of the under 100 kW (household) market began, to be completed during 1999. Liberalisation replaced the monopoly supply of the RECs with a competitive market in which consumers were encouraged to find best value from over 15 potential suppliers, whose offers included lower prices and the dual supply of gas and electricity. At an early stage British Gas had succeeded in attracting 400,000 electricity customers. Its 150 door-to-door salespeople, together with sales through the Sainsbury supermarket chain, were intended to raise the total to 3.5 million customers.

PowerGen's vision was to build one of the world's leading integrated electricity and gas businesses, using the experience gained in the UK liberalisation process as a basis for developing opportunities in other liberalising markets. PowerGen had entered into negotiations with Houston Industries, America's ninth largest utility, to form a £10 billion group. Previous merger talks with another US company, Cinergy, had broken down in 1997, partly due to strains between the two chairmen. Houston was also to be deterred, this time by the prospect of a changing UK regulatory climate that might include the forced divestment of a substantial part of PowerGen's generating capacity. Other US companies had started to

lose interest in the UK for similar reasons, including the government's imposition in 1997 of a windfall tax on industry profits (£202 million for PowerGen) and the increasing level of competition in the domestic market.

PowerGen continued to assess opportunities to enter the US market, creating a new holding company, PowerGen 1998, to more easily meet US regulatory demands in the event of a merger and to increase the financial flexibility of the group.

Between April 1990 and March 1994 prices paid to generators were set by the pool without an upper limit. For the period April 1994 to April 1996, the DGES obtained voluntary undertakings from PowerGen and National Power to bid into the pool in such a way that average pool prices would be below a specified level, 'the cap'.

In 1996 the Monopolies Commission concluded that within the electricity pool market share by output (non-baseload sector) was a broad indicator of a generator's ability to set pool prices. CCGT (gas-powered plant) can be technically operated as 'baseload' (continuous demand) as well as 'mid-merit', which involves turning the plant on and off at least once in 24 hours. The report of the MMC concluded that market shares of around 17% for PowerGen and 21% for National Power would provide a 'broadly satisfactory competitive environment' in generation.

In 1996 PowerGen and National Power completed an undertaking to the DGES by disposing of a total of 6000 MW of plant through a leasing arrangement to Eastern Electricity. By 1998 Eastern had become a vertically integrated company (generator and REC) with a 9% share of the generation market. In that year evidence emerged that the Eastern group had been able to use its capacity to achieve higher pool prices. The development of market share over the years is given in Table 1.

TABLE 1 Market share in England and Wales

	Generator's share of total output of electricty in England and Wales (%)							
	1991	1992	1993	1994	1995	1996	1997	1998
National Power	45.5	43.5	40.9	35.0	34.0	32.6	24.1	20.9
PowerGen	28.4	28.2	27.0	26.0	26.0	24.2	21.5	19.7
Nuclear Electric	17.4	18.6	21.4	23.2	22.2	22.3	24.2	24.7
Scottish and French interconnectors	7.1	8.0	8.2	8.0	8.7	8.5	9.3	9.1
Others	1.6	1.7	2.5	7.8	9.1	12.4	20.9	25.6

The industry regulator estimated that, as a result of 'gaming', in December 1998 wholesale (pool) prices for electricity had been £90 million higher than they should have been, a figure equal to 10% of that month's pool sales. PowerGen's performance and group interests are set out in Table 2 and Exhibit 1, respectively.

TABLE 2 PowerGen performance, 1991–98

	Years ended							
	1991	1992	1993	1994	1995	1996	1997	1998
Turnover (£ million)								
Generation (pool)	2412	2667	2537	2225	2252	2184	2071	1897
Direct sales to end customer	239	430	651	707	615	674	656	622
Other energy and hydrocarbon sales	–	–	–	–	18	75	128	156
Gas trading and retail	–	–	–	–	–	–	43	257
Total turnover	2651	3097	3188	2932	2885	2933	2898	2932
Sources of profit (£ million)								
Generation	237	323	422	509	547			
Direct sales	7	(1)	28	(18)	–			
Other	(3)	3	(1)	(14)	(16)			
International operations						12	12	9
Combined heat and power						(1)	1	5
Operating profit	241	325	449	477	531	693	511	*591
Profit before tax	272	359	425	476	545	687	577	**211
Operating profit margin (%)	9.1	10.5	14.1	16.3	18.4			
Average number of employees	8840	7771	5715	4782				
Employees: UK business					4122	3558	2833	2865
International business					49	590	534	591

PowerGen does not analyse its results by business segment in its statutory accounts, figures for 1991–1995 are from the company's submission to the MMC.

* 1998, before exceptional items of £369m for plant rationalisation and restructuring costs, £339m of which follows a review of the companys UK plant portfolio in the light of increased competition and market changes.
** Pre-tax profit is before windfall tax.
Source: 1991–1995, MMC; 1996–98 PowerGen Co. Report

EXHIBIT 1 POWERGEN GROUP AND ASSOCIATED UNDERTAKINGS

By 1998 PowerGen held a 100% interest in the following group undertakings:

PowerGen CHP Ltd
Sale of energy services involving the construction of combined heat and power plant

PowerGen North Sea Ltd
Oil- and gas-related activities

Kinetica Ltd
Transportation and marketing of natural gas in the UK

Wavedriver Ltd
Development of electric-vehicle-related technology

It also held the following investments in associated undertakings (% equity owned):

Yallourn Energy (49.95%)
Australia, mining of brown coal and production and sale of electricity from coal-fired power station

Saale Energie (50%)
Germany, holding and management company for the group's interest in Schkopau power station

MIBRA GmbH (33.33%)
Germany, mining, refinement and sale of brown coal and generation and sale of electricity

Turbogas Productora Energetica (49.99%)
Portugal, construction of gas-fired power-station plant

Csepel Power Company
Generation and sale of electricity (Hungary)

PT Jawa Power (35%)
Indonesia, construction of coal-fired power-station plant

Gujarat Torrent Energy Corporation (27.8%)
India, construction of gas-fired power-station plant

Cottam Development Centre (50%)
UK, construction and operation of gas-fired power-station plant to develop, test and commercially operate the next generation of gas-powered plant technology, a joint venture with Siemens

CASE

6

KAO Corporation

By Sumantra Ghoshal and Charlotte Butler[1]

Dr Yoshio Maruta introduced himself as a Buddhist scholar first, and as President of the Kao Corporation second. The order was significant, for it revealed the philosophy behind Kao and its success in Japan. Kao was a company that not only learned, but 'learned how to learn.' It was, in Dr Maruta's word's, 'an educational institution in which everyone is a potential teacher.'

Under Dr Maruta's direction, the scholar's dedication to learning had metamorphosed into a competitive weapon which, in 1990, had led to Kao being ranked ninth by *Nikkei Business* in its list of excellent companies in Japan, and third in terms of corporate originality (see Table 1). As described by Fumio Kuroyanagi, Director of Kao's overseas planning department, the company's success was due not merely to its mastery of technologies nor its efficient marketing and information systems, but to its ability to integrate and enhance these capabilities through learning. As a result Kao had come up with a stream of new products ahead of its Japanese and foreign competitors and, by 1990, had emerged as the largest branded and packaged goods company in Japan and the country's second largest cosmetics company.

Since the mid 1960s Kao had also successfully used its formidable array of technological, manufacturing and marketing assets to expand into the neighbouring markets of SE Asia. Pitting itself against long established multinationals like Procter & Gamble and Unilever, Kao had made inroads into the detergent, soap and shampoo markets in the region. However, success in these small markets would not make Kao a global player, and since the mid-1980s, Kao had been giving its attention to the problem of how to break into the international markets beyond the region. There, Kao's innovations were being copied and sold by its competitors, not by Kao itself, a situation the company was keen to remedy. But would Kao be able to repeat its domestic success in the US and Europe? As Dr. Maruta knew, the company's ability to compete on a world-wide basis would be measured by its progress in these markets. This, then, was the new challenge to which Kao was dedicated: how to transfer its learning capability, so all-conquering in Japan, to the rest of the world.

TABLE 1 Ranking of Japanese excellent companies 1990 (*Nikkei Business*, April 9, 1990)

Company	Points*
1. Honda Motors	79.8
2. IBM-Japan	79.4
3. SONY	78.4
4. Matsushita Electrics	74.5
5. Toshiba	69.9
6. NEC	69.8
7. Nissan Motors	69.8
8. Asahi Beer	67.4
9. KAO	66.6
10. Yamato Transportation	66.4
11. Fuji-Xerox	66.3
12. Seibu Department Store	66.2
13. Suntory	65.8
14. Nomura Security	65.4
15. NTT	65.3
16. Omron	65.1
17. Ajinomoto	64.3
18. Canon	64.3
19. Toyota Motors	63.9
20. Ohtsuka Medicines	63.8

*Points are calculated on the basis of the following criteria:
1. the assessment by Nikkei Business committee members with regard to corporate originality, corporate vision, flexibility, goodness;
2. the result of research among consumers.

[1]Source: © 1992 INSEAD-EAC, Fontainebleau, France. All rights reserved

The learning organization

Kao was founded in 1890 as Kao Soap Company with the prescient motto, 'Cleanliness is the foundation of a prosperous society.' Its objective then was to produce a high-quality soap that was as good as any imported brand, but at a more affordable price for the Japanese consumer, and this principle had guided the development of all Kao's products ever since. In the 1940s Kao had launched the first Japanese laundry detergent, followed in the 1950s by the launch of dishwashing and household detergents. The 1960s had seen an expansion into industrial products to which Kao could apply its technologies in fat and oil science, surface and polymer science. The 1970s and 1980s, coinciding with the presidency of Dr Maruta, had seen the company grow more rapidly than ever in terms of size, sales and profit, with the launching of innovative products and the start of new businesses. Between 1982 and 1985 it had successfully diversified into cosmetics, hygiene and floppy disks.

A vertically integrated company, Kao owned many of its raw material sources and had, since the 1960s, built its own sales organization of wholesalers who had exclusive distribution of its products throughout Japan. The 1980s had seen a consistent rise in profits, with sales increasing at roughly 10 percent a year throughout the decade, even in its mature markets (see Table 2). In 1990, sales of Kao products had reached ¥620.4 billion ($3,926.8 million), an 8.4 percent increase on 1989. This total consisted of laundry and cleansing products (40 percent), personal care products (34 percent), hygiene products (13 percent), specialty chemicals and floppy disks (9 percent) and fatty chemicals (4 percent) (see Figure 1). Net income had increased by 1.7 percent, from ¥17.5 billion ($110 million) in 1989 to ¥17.8 billion ($112.7 million) in 1990.

Kao dominated most of its markets in Japan. It was the market leader in detergents and shampoo, and was vying for first place in disposable diapers and cosmetics. It had decisively beaten off both foreign and domestic competitors, most famously in two particular instances: the 1983 launch of its disposable diaper brand Merries which, within 12 months, had overtaken the leading brand, Procter & Gamble's Pampers and the 1987 launch of its innovative condensed laundry detergent, the aptly named Attack; as a result of which the market share of Kao's rival, Lion, had declined from 30.9 percent (1986) to 22.8 percent (1988), while in the same period Kao's share had gone from 33.4 percent to 47.5 percent.

The remarkable success of these two products had been largely responsible for Kao's reputation as a creative company. However, while the ability to introduce a continuous stream of innovative, high quality products clearly rested on Kao's repertoire of core competences, the wellspring behind these was less obvious: Kao's integrated learning capability.

TABLE 2 Kao's performance

| Years ended March 31 | Billions of yen | | | | | | Millions of US$* |
	1985	1986	1987	1988	1989	1990	1990
Net sales	398.1	433.7	464.1	514.4	572.2	620.4	3,926.8
Net sales increase (%)		8.9	7.0	10.9	11.2	8.4	
Operating income	16.5**	19.9**	31.7	36.5	41.4	43.5	275.5
Operating income increase (%)				15.2	13.5	5.1	
Net income	9.4	10.5	12.9	13.4	17.5	17.8	112.7
Net income increase (%)		12.3	22.5	4.2	30.4	1.7	
Total assets	328.3	374.4	381.0	450.4	532.3	572.8	3,625.5
Total shareholders' equity	114.4	150.9	180.2	210.7	233.8	256.6	1,624.1

*The US dollar amounts are translated, for convenience only, at the rate of ¥156 = $1, the approximate exchange rate prevailing on March 30, 1990.
**non-consolidated

FIGURE 1   Review of operations

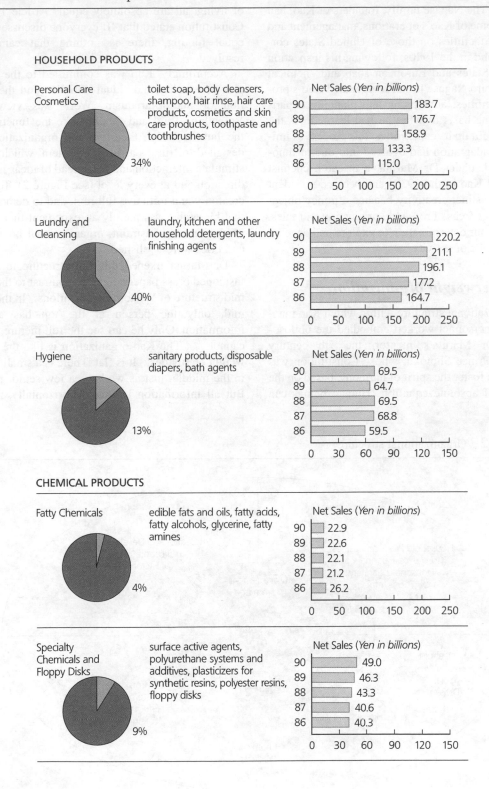

HOUSEHOLD PRODUCTS

Personal Care Cosmetics — toilet soap, body cleansers, shampoo, hair rinse, hair care products, cosmetics and skin care products, toothpaste and toothbrushes — 34%

Net Sales (*Yen in billions*)
90 — 183.7
89 — 176.7
88 — 158.9
87 — 133.3
86 — 115.0

Laundry and Cleansing — laundry, kitchen and other household detergents, laundry finishing agents — 40%

Net Sales (*Yen in billions*)
90 — 220.2
89 — 211.1
88 — 196.1
87 — 177.2
86 — 164.7

Hygiene — sanitary products, disposable diapers, bath agents — 13%

Net Sales (*Yen in billions*)
90 — 69.5
89 — 64.7
88 — 69.5
87 — 68.8
86 — 59.5

CHEMICAL PRODUCTS

Fatty Chemicals — edible fats and oils, fatty acids, fatty alcohols, glycerine, fatty amines — 4%

Net Sales (*Yen in billions*)
90 — 22.9
89 — 22.6
88 — 22.1
87 — 21.2
86 — 26.2

Specialty Chemicals and Floppy Disks — surface active agents, polyurethane systems and additives, plasticizers for synthetic resins, polyester resins, floppy disks — 9%

Net Sales (*Yen in billions*)
90 — 49.0
89 — 46.3
88 — 43.3
87 — 40.6
86 — 40.3

This learning motif had been evident from the beginning. The Nagase family, founders of Kao, had modeled some of Kao's operations, management and production facilities on those of United States corporations and in the 1940s, following his inspection of United States and European soap and chemical plants, Tomiro Nagase II had reorganized Kao's production facilities, advertising and planning departments on the basis of what he had learned. As the company built up its capabilities, this process of imitation and adaptation had evolved into one of innovation until, under Dr Maruta, a research chemist who joined Kao in the 1930s and became president in 1971, 'Distinct creativity became a policy objective in all our areas of research, production and sales, supporting our determination to explore and develop our own fields of activity.'

The paperweight organization

The organizational structure within which Kao managers and personnel worked embodied the philosophy of Dr Maruta's mentor, the 7th century statesman Prince Shotoku, whose Constitution was designed to foster the spirit of harmony, based on the principle of absolute equality; 'Human beings can live only by the Universal Truth, and in their dignity of living, all are absolutely equal.' Article 1 of his Constitution stated that 'If everyone discusses on an equal footing, there is nothing that cannot be resolved.'

Accordingly, Kao was committed to the principles of equality, individual initiative and the rejection of authoritarianism. Work was viewed as 'something fluid and flexible like the functions of the human body,' therefore the organization was designed to 'run as a flowing system' which would stimulate interaction and the spread of ideas in every direction and at every level (see Figure 2). To allow creativity and initiative full rein, and to demonstrate that hierarchy was merely an expedient that should not become a constraint, organizational boundaries and titles were abolished.

Dr Maruta likened this flat structure to an old fashioned brass paperweight, in contrast to the pyramid structure of Western organizations: 'In the pyramid, only the person at the top has all the information. Only he can see the full picture, others cannot . . . The Kao organization is like the paperweight on my desk. It is flat. There is a small handle in the middle, just as we have a few senior people. But all information is shared horizontally, not fil-

FIGURE 2   Organizational structure

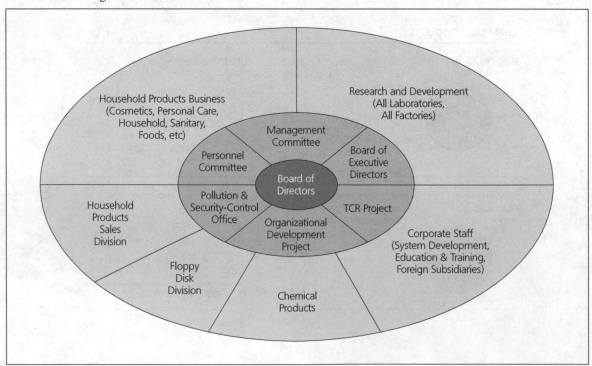

tered vertically. Only then can you have equality. And equality is the basis for trust and commitment.'

This organization practiced what Kao referred to as 'biological self control.' As the body reacted to pain by sending help from all quarters, 'If anything goes wrong in one department, the other departments should know automatically and help without having to be asked.' Small group activities were encouraged in order to link ideas or discuss issues of immediate concern. In 1987, for example, to resolve the problem of why Kao's Toyohashi factory could achieve only 50 percent of the projected production of Nivea cream, workers there voluntarily formed a small team consisting of the people in charge of production, quality, electricity, process and machinery. By the following year, production had been raised to 95 percent of the target.

In pursuit of greater efficiency and creativity, Kao's organization has continued to evolve. A 1987 programme introduced a system of working from home for sales people, while another will eventually reduce everyone's working time to 1800 hours a year from the traditional level of 2100 hours. Other programmes have aimed at either introducing information technology or revitalizing certain areas. 1971 saw the 'CCR movement,' aimed at reducing the workforce through computerization. 'Total Quality Control' came in 1974, followed in 1981 by Office Automation. The 1986 'Total Cost Reduction' programme to restructure management resources evolved into the 'Total Creative Revolution' designed to encourage a more innovative approach. For example, five people who were made redundant following the installation of new equipment, formed, on their own initiative, a special task force team, and visisted a US factory which had imported machinery from Japan. They stayed there for three months until local engineers felt confident enough to take charge. Over time, this group became a flying squad of specialists, available to help foreign production plants get over their teething troubles.

Managing information

Just as Dr Maruta's Buddha was the enlightened teacher, so Kao employees were the 'priests' who learned and practiced the truth. Learning was 'a frame of mind, a daily matter,' and truth was sought through discussions, by testing and investigating concrete business ideas until something was learned, often without the manager realizing it. This was 'the quintessence of information . . . something we actu-

ally see with our own eyes and feel with our bodies.' This internalized intuition, which coincides with the Zen Buddhist phrase *kangyo ichijo*, was the goal Dr Maruta set for all Kao managers. In reaching it, every individual was expected to be a coach; both to himself and to everyone else, whether above or below him in the organization.

Their training material was information. Information was regarded not as something lifeless to be stored, but as knowledge to be shared and exploited to the utmost. Every manager repeated Dr Maruta's fundamental assumption: 'in today's business world, information is the only source of competitive advantage. The company that develops a monopoly on information, and has the ability to learn from it continuously, is the company that will win, irrespective of its business.' Every piece of information from the environment was treated as a potential key to a new positioning, a new product. What can we learn from it? How can we use it? These were the questions all managers were expected to ask themselves at all times.

Access to information was another facet of Kao's commitment to egalitarianism: as described by Kuroyanagi, 'In Kao, the "classfied" stamp does not exist.' Through the development of computer communication technologies, the same level of information was available to all: 'In order to make it effective to discuss subjects freely, it is necessary to share all information. If someone has special and crucial information that the others don't have, that is against human equality, and will deprive us and the organization of real creativity.'

Every director and most salesmen had a fax in their homes to receive results and news, and a bi-weekly Kao newspaper kept the entire company informed about competitors' moves, new product launches, overseas development or key meetings. Terminals installed throughout the company ensured that any employee could, if they wished, retrieve data on sales records of any product for any of Kao's numerous outlets, or product development at their own or other branches. The latest findings from each of Kao's research laboratories were available for all to see, as were the details of the previous day's production and inventory at every Kao plant. 'They can even,' said Dr. Maruta, 'check up on the president's expense account.' He believed that the increase in creativity resulting from this pooling of data outweighed the risk of leaks. In any case, the prevailing environment of *omnes flux* meant that things moved so quickly 'leaked information instantly becomes obsolete.'

The task of Kao managers therefore, was to take information directly from the competitive environment, process it and, by adding value, transform it into knowledge or wisdom.

Digesting information from the market place in this way enabled the organization to maintain empathy with this fast moving environment. The emphasis was always on learning and on the future, not on following an advance plan based on previous experience. 'Past wisdom must not be a constraint, but something to be challenged,' Dr Maruta constantly urged. Kao managers were discouraged from making any historical comparisons. 'We cannot talk about history,' said Mr Takayama, Overseas Planning Director. 'If we talk about the past, they (the top management) immediately become unpleasant.' The emphasis was rather, what had they learnt today that would be useful tomorrow? 'Yesterday's success formula is often today's obsolete dogma. We must continuously challenge the past so that we can renew ourselves each day,' said Dr Maruta.

'Learning through cooperation' was the slogan of Kao's research and development (R&D); the emphasis was on information exchange, both within and outside the department, and sharing 'to motivate and activate.' Glycerine Ether, for example, an emulsifier important for the production of Sofina's screening cream, was the product of joint work among three Kao laboratories. Research results were communicated to everyone in the company through the IT system, in order to build a close networking organization. Top management and researchers met at regular R&D conferences, where presentations were made by the researchers themselves, not their section managers. 'Open Space' meetings were offered every week by the R&D division, and people from any part of the organization could participate in discussions on current research projects.

A number of formal and informal systems were created to promote communication among the research scientists working in different laboratories. For example, results from Paris were fed daily into the computer in Tokyo. The most important of these communication mechanisms, however, were the monthly R&D working conferences for junior researchers which took place at each laboratory in turn. When it was their own laboratory's turn to act as host, researchers could nominate anyone they wished to meet, from any laboratory in the company, to attend that meeting. In addition, any researcher

could nominate him or herself to attend meetings if they felt that the discussions could help their own work, or if they wanted to talk separately with someone from the host laboratory. At the meetings, which Dr Maruta often attended to argue and discuss issues in detail, researchers reported on studies in progress, and those present offered advice from commercial and academic perspectives.

The decision process

'In Kao, we try collectively to direct the accumulation of individual wisdom at serving the customer.' This was how Dr Maruta explained the company's approach to the decision process. At Kao, no one owned an idea. Ideas were to be shared in order to enhance their value and achieve enlightenment in order to make the right decision. The prevailing principle was *tataki-dai*; present your ideas to others at 80 percent completion so that they could criticize or contribute before the idea became a proposal. Takayama likened this approach to heating an iron and testing it on one's arm to see if it was hot enough. 'By inviting all the relevant actors to join in with forging the task,' he said, 'we achieve *zoawase*; a common perspective or view.' The individual was thus a strategic factor, to be linked with others in a union of individual wisdom and group strategy.

Fumio Kuroyanagi provided an illustration. Here is the process by which a problem involving a joint venture partner, in which he was the key person, was resolved:

I put up a preliminary note summarizing the key issues, but not making any proposals. I wanted to share the data and obtain other views before developing a proposal fully . . . This note was distributed to legal, international controllers to read . . . then in the meeting we talked about the facts and came up with some ideas on how to proceed. Then members of this meeting requested some top management time. All the key people attended this meeting, together with one member of the top management. No written document was circulated in advance. Instead, we described the situation, our analysis and action plans. He gave us his comments. We came to a revised plan. I then wrote up this revised plan and circulated it to all the people, and we had a second meeting at which everyone agreed with the plan. Then the two of us attended the actual meeting with the partner. After the meeting I debriefed other members, discussed and circulated a draft of the letter to the partner which, after everyone else had seen it and given their comments, was signed by my boss.

The cross fertilization of ideas to aid the decision process was encouraged by the physical lay out of the Kao building. On the 10th floor, known as the top management floor, sat the chairman, the president, four executive vice presidents and a pool of secretaries (see Figure 3). A large part of the floor was open space, with one large conference table and two smaller ones, and chairs, blackboards and overhead projectors strewn around: this was known as the Decision Space, where all discussions with and among the top management took place. Anyone passing, including the president, could sit down and join in any discussion on any topic, however briefly. This layout was duplicated on the other floors, in the

laboratories and in the workshop. Workplaces looked like large rooms; there were no partitions, but again tables and chairs for spontaneous or planned discussions at which everyone contributed as equals. Access was free to all, and any manager could thus find himself sitting round the table next to the president, who was often seen waiting in line in Kao's Tokyo cafeteria.

The management process, thus, was transparent and open, and leadership was practiced in daily behaviour rather than by memos and formal meetings. According to Takayama, top management 'emphasizes that 80 percent of its time must be spent on communication, and the remaining 20 percent on decision making.' While top mangement regularly visited other floors to join in discussions, anyone attending a meeting on the 10th floor then had to pass on what had happened to the rest of his colleagues.

FIGURE 3 Layout of Kao offices

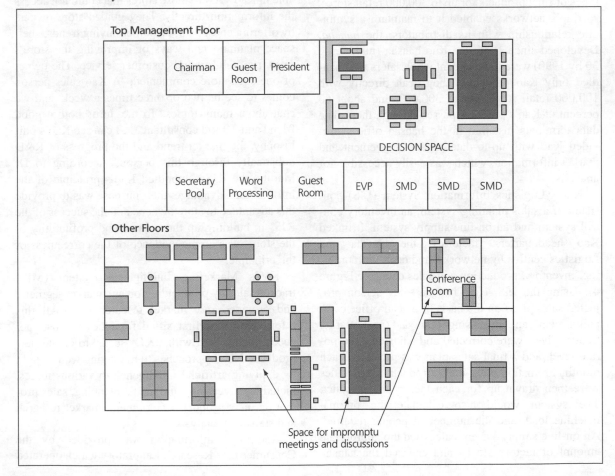

Space for impromptu meetings and discussions

Information technology

Information Technology (IT) was one of Kao's most effective competitive weapons, and an integral part of its organizational systems and management processes. In 1982, Kao made an agreement to use Japan Information Service Co's VAN (Value Added Networks) for communication between Kao's head office, its sales companies and its large wholesalers. Over time, Kao built its own VAN, through which it connected upstream and downstream via information linkages. In 1986 the company added DRESS, a new network linking Kao and the retail stores receiving its support.

The objective of this networking capability was to achieve the complete fusion and interaction of Kao's marketing, production and R&D departments. Fully integrated information systems controlled the flow of materials and products; from the production planning of raw materials to the distribution of the final products to local stores: no small task in a company dealing with over 1,500 types of raw materials from 500 different suppliers, and producing over 550 types of final products for up to 300,000 retail stores.

Kao's networks enabled it to maintain a symbiotic relationship with its distributors, the *hansha*. Developed since 1966, the Kao hansha (numbering 30 by 1990) were independent wholesalers who handled only Kao products. They dealt directly with 100,000 retail stores out of 300,000, and about 60 percent of Kao's products passed through them. The data terminals installed in the hansha offices provided Kao with up-to-date product movement and market information, which was easily accessible for analysis.

Kao's Logistics Information System (LIS) consisted of a sales planning system, an inventory control system and an on-line supply system. It linked Kao headquarters, factories, the hansha and Logistics centres by networks, and dealt with ordering, inventory, production and sales data (see Figure 4). Using the LIS, each hansha sales person projected sales plans on the basis of a head office campaign plan, an advertising plan and past market trends. These were corrected and adjusted at corporate level, and a final sales plan was produced each month. From this plan, daily production schedules were then drawn up for each factory and product. The system would also calculate the optimal machine load, and the number of people required. An on-line supply system calculated the appropriate amount of factory stocks and checked the hansha inventory. The next day's supply was then computed and automatically ordered from the factory.

A computerized ordering system enabled stores to receive and deliver products within 24 hours of placing an order. Through a POS (point of sale) terminal, installed in the retail store as a cash register and connected to the Kao VAN, information on sales and orders was transmitted to the hansha's computer. Via this, orders from local stores, adjusted according to the amount of their inventory, were transmitted to Kao's Logistics centre, which then supplied the product.

Two other major support systems, KAP and RRS, respectively helped the wholesale houses in ordering, stocking and accounting, and worked with Kao's nine distribution information service companies: the Ryutsu Joho Service Companies (RJSs). Each RJS had about 500 customers, mainly small and medium-sized supermarkets who were too small to access real-time information by themselves. The RJSs were essentially consulting outfits, whose mandate was to bring the benefits of information available in Kao VAN to those stores that could not access the information directly. They guided store owners by offering analysis of customer buying trends, shelf space planning and ways of improving the store's sales, profitability and customer service. The owner of one such store commented: 'A Kao sales person comes to see us two or three times a week, and we chat about many topics. To me, he is both a good friend and a good consultant . . . I can see Kao's philosophy, the market trend and the progress of R&D holistically through this person.' According to Dr Maruta, the RJSs embodied Kao's principle of the information advantage: their purpose was to provide this advantage to store owners, and the success of the RJSs in building up the volume and profitability of the stores was ample evidence of the correctness of the principle.

Kao's Marketing Intelligence System (MIS) tracked sales by product, region and market segment, and provided raw market research data. All this information was first sifted for clues to customer needs, then linked with R&D 'seeds' to create new products. New approaches to marketing were sought by applying artificial intelligence to various topics, including advertising and media planning, sales promotion, new product development, market research and statistical analysis.

Additional information was provided by the Consumer Life Research Laboratory which operated

FIGURE 4 Kao's information network (*Nikkei Computer*, Oct. 9, 1989)

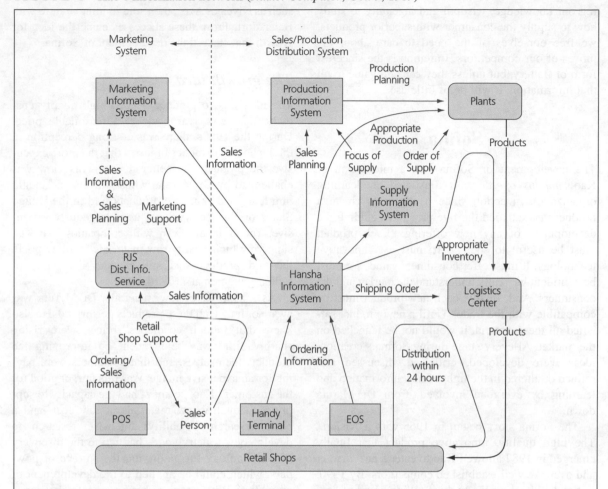

ECHO, a sophisticated system for responding to telephone queries about Kao products. In order to understand and respond immediately to a customer's question, each phone operator could instantly access a video display of each of Kao's 500 plus products. Enquiries were also coded and entered into the computer system on-line, and the resulting data base provided one of the richest sources for product development or enhancement ideas. By providing Kao with 'a direct window on the consumer's mind,' ECHO enabled the company to 'predict the performance of new products and fine tune formulations, labelling and packaging.' Kao also used a panel of monitor households to track how products fitted into consumers' lives.

In 1989, Kao separated its information systems organization and established a distinct entity called Kao Software Development. The aim was to pene-

trate the information service industry which, according to Japan Information, was projected to reach a business volume of ¥12,000 billion ($80 billion) by the year 2000. In 1989, the market was ¥3,000 billion ($20 billion). One IBM sales engineer forecast, 'by 2000, Kao will have become one of our major competitors, because they know how to develop information technology, and how to combine it with real organization systems.'

In 1989 Kao's competitors, including Lion and Procter & Gamble, united to set up Planet Logistics, a system comparable to Kao's VAN. Through it, they aimed to achieve the same information richness as Kao. But Dr Maruta was not worried by this development. Irrespective of whatever information they collected, he believed that the competitors would not be able to add the value and use it in the same way as Kao did: 'As a company we do not spend our time chasing after what our rivals do. Rather, by mustering our knowledge, wisdom and ingenuity to study how to supply the consumer with superior products, we free ourselves of the need to care about the moves of our competitors. Imitation is the sincerest form of flattery, but unless they can add value to all that information, it will be of little use.'

Sofina

The development of Sofina was a microcosm of Kao's *modus operandi*. It illustrated the learning organization in action since it sought to create a product that satisfied the five principles guiding the development of any new offering: 'Each product must be useful to society. It must use innovative technology. It must offer consumers value. We must be confident we really understand the market and the consumers. And, finally, each new product must be compatible with the trade.' Until a new product satisfied all these criteria, it would not be launched on the market. At every stage during Sofina's creation, ideas were developed, criticized, discussed and refined or altered in the light of new information and learning by everyone involved, from Dr Maruta down.

The Sofina story began in 1965 with a 'vision.' The high quality, innovative product that finally emerged in 1982 allowed Kao to enter a new market and overtake well-established competitors. By 1990, Sofina had become the highest selling brand of cosmetics in Japan for most items except lipsticks.

The vision

The vision, according to Mr Daimaru (the first director of Sofina marketing), was simple: to help customers avoid the appearance of wrinkles on their skin for as long as possible. From this vision an equally simple question arose. 'What makes wrinkles appear?' Finding the answer was the spring that set the Kao organization into motion.

Kao's competence until then had been in household and toiletry personal care products. However, Kao had long supplied raw materials for the leading cosmetics manufacturers in Japan, and had a technological competence in fats and soap that could, by cross pollination, be adapted to research on the human skin. Accordingly, the efforts of Kao's R&D laboratories were directed towards skin research, and

the results used in the company's existing businesses such as Nivea or Azea, then sold in joint venture with Beiersdorf. From these successes came the idea for growth that steered the development of Sofina.

The growth idea

The idea was to produce a new, high quality cosmetic that gave real vlaue at a reasonable price. During the 1960s, there was a strong perception in the Japanese cosmetics industry that the more expensive the product, the better it was. This view was challenged by Dr Maruta, whose travels had taught him that good skin care products sold in the United States or Europe were not as outrageously expensive. Yet in Japan, even with companies like Kao supplying high quality raw materials at a low price, the end product was still beyond the reach of ordinary women at ¥10–20,000.

As a supplier of raw materials, Dr Maruta was aware of how well these products performed. He also knew that though cosmetics' prices were rising sharply, little was being spent on improving the products themselves, and that customers were paying for an expensive image. Was this fair, or good for the customer? Kao, he knew, had the capacity to supply high quality raw materials at low cost, and a basic research capability. Intensive research to develop new toiletry goods had led to the discovery of a technology for modifying the surface of powders, which could be applied to the development of cosmetics. Why not use these assets to develop a new, high quality, reasonably priced product, in keeping with Kao's principles?

To enter the new market would mean a heavy investment in research and marketing, with no guarantee that their product would be accepted. However, it was decided to go ahead; the product would be innovative and, against the emotional appeal of the existing competition in terms of packaging and image, its positioning would embody Kao's scientific approach.

This concept guided the learning process as Sofina was developed. It was found that the integration of Kao's unique liquid crystal emulsification technology and other newly developed materials proved effective in maintaining a 'healthy and beautiful skin.' This led Kao to emphasize skin care, as opposed to the industry's previous focus on make-up only. All the research results from Kao's skin diagnosis and dermatological testing were poured into the new product and, as Dr Tsutsumi of the Tokyo Research Laboratory recalled, in pursuing problems connected with the product, new solutions emerged. For example, skin irritation caused by the new chemical was solved by developing MAP, a low irritant, and PSL, a moisturiser. By 1980, most of the basic research work had been done. Six cosmetics suitable for the six basic skin types had been developed, though all under the Sofina name.

During this stage, Kao's intelligence collectors were sent out to explore and map the new market environment. Information on products, pricing, positioning, the competition and above all, the customers, was analyzed and digested by the Sofina marketing and R&D teams, and by Kao's top management. Again and again Dr Maruta asked the same two questions: How would the new product be received? Was it what customers wanted?

The growth process

Test marketing began in September 1980, in the Shizuoka prefecture, and was scheduled to last for a year. Shizuoka was chosen because it represented three percent of the national market and an average social mix; neither too rich nor too poor, neither too rural nor too urban. Its media isolation meant that television advertisements could be targeted to the local population, and no one outside would question why the product was not available elsewhere. The local paper also gave good coverage. In keeping with Kao's rule that 'the concept of a new product is that of its advertising,' the Sofina advertisements were reasoned and scientific, selling a function rather than an image.

Sofina was distributed directly to the retail stores through the Sofina Cosmetics Company, established to distinguish Sofina from Kao's conventional detergent business and avoid image blurring. No mention was made of Kao. Sofina's managers found, however, that retailers did not accept Sofina immediately, but put it on the waiting list for display along with other new cosmetics. The result was that by October 1980, Kao had only succeeded in finding 200 points of sale, against an object of 600. Then, as the real parentage of Sofina leaked out, the attitude among retailers changed, and the Sofina stand was given the best position in the store. This evidence of Kao's credibility, together with the company's growing confidence in the quality and price of the product, led to a change of strategy. The 30-strong sales force was instructed to put the Kao name first and, by November, 600 outlets had been found.

Sofina's subsequent development was guided by feedback from the market. Direct distribution enabled Kao to retain control of the business and catch customer responses to the product at first hand. To Mr Masashi Kuga, Director of Kao's Marketing Research Department, such information 'has clear added value, and helps in critical decision making.' During the repeated test marketing of Sofina, Kao's own market research service, formed in 1973 to ensure a high quality response from the market with the least possible distortion, measured the efficacy of sampling and helped decide on the final marketing mix. This activity was usually supported by 'concept testing, focus group discussions, plus product acceptance research.' Mr Daimaru visited the test market twice or three times each month and talked to consumers directly. Dr Maruta did the same.

Every piece of information and all results were shared by the Sofina team, R&D, Kao's top management, corporate marketing and sales managers. Discussions on Sofina's progress were attended by all of these managers, everyone contributing ideas about headline copy or other issues on an equal basis. Wives and friends were given samples and their reactions were fed back to the team.

From the reactions of customers and stores, Kao learned that carrying real information in the advertisements about the quality of the product had been well received, despite differing from the normal emphasis on fancy packaging. This they could never have known from their detergent business. Another finding was the importance of giving a full explanation of the product with samples, and of a skin analysis before recommending the most suitable product rather than trying to push the brand indiscriminately. They also learned the value of listening to the opinion of the store manager's wife who, they discovered, often had the real managing power, particularly for cosmetics products.

Decisions were implemented immediately. For example, the decision to improve the design for the sample package was taken at 3.30 p.m., and by 6.30 p.m. the same day the engineer in the factory had begun re-designing the shape of the bottle.

The results of this test marketing, available to the whole company, confirmed the decision to go ahead with Sofina. Kao was satisfied that the product would be accepted nationally, though it might take some time. A national launch was planned for the next year. Even at this stage, however, Mr Maruta was still asking whether consumers and retail store owners really liked Sofina.

The learning extended

Sofina finally went on nationwide sale in October 1982. However, the flow of learning and intelligence gathering continued via the hansha and MIS. Kao, the hansha, the retailers and Sofina's customers formed a chain, along which that was a free, two-way flow of information. The learning was then extended to develop other products, resulting in production of the complete Sofina range of beauty care. In 1990, the range covered the whole market, from basic skin care to make-up cosmetics and perfumes.

In fact, the product did not achieve real success until after 1983. Dr Tsutsumi dated it from the introduction of the foundation cream which, he recalled, also faced teething problems. The test result from the panel was not good; it was too different from existing products and was sticky on application. Kao, however, knowing it was a superior product that lasted longer, preserved and used their previous experience to convert the stickiness into a strength: the product was repositioned as 'the longest lasting foundation that does not disappear with sweat.'

In the early 1980s, while market growth was only two to three percent, sales of Sofina products increased at the rate of 30 percent every year. In 1990, sales amounted to ¥55 billion, and Kao held 15.6 percent of the cosmetic market behind Shiseido and Kanebo, though taken individually, Sofina brands topped every product category except lipsticks.

Within Japan, Sofina was sold through 12,700 outlets. According to Mr Nakanishi, director of the Cosmetics Division, the marketing emphasis was by that time being redirected from heavy advertising of the product to counselling at the point of sale. Kao was building up a force of beauty counsellors to educate the public on the benefits of Sofina products. A Sofina store in Tokyo was also helping to develop hair care and cosmetics products. A Sofina newspaper had been created which salesmen received by fax, along with the preveious month's sales and inventory figures.

Knowledge gathered by the beauty advisers working in the Sofina shops was exploited for the development of the next set of products. Thus, Sofina 'ultra-violet' care, which incorporated skin lotion, uv care and foundation in one, was positioned to appeal to busy women and advertised as 'one step less.' The Sofina cosmetics beauty care consultation system offered advice by phone, at retail shops or by other means to consumers who made enquiries.

From their questions, clues were sought to guide new product development.

A staff of Field Companions visited the retail stores to get direct feedback on sales. Every outlet was visited once a month, when the monitors discussed Kao products with store staff, advised on design displays and even helped clean up. Dr Maruta himself maintained an active interest. Mr Kuroyanagi described how Dr Maruta recently 'came down to our floor' to report that while visiting a certain town, he had 'found a store selling Sofina products, and a certain shade sample was missing from the stand.' He asked that the store be checked and the missing samples supplied as soon as possible.

Despite Sofina's success, Kao was still not satisfied. 'To be really successful, developing the right image is important. We've lagged behind on this, and we must improve.'

As the Sofina example showed, in its domestic base Kao was an effective and confident company, renowned for its ability to produce high quality, technologically advanced products at relatively low cost. Not surprising then, that since the 1960s it had turned its thoughts to becoming an important player on the larger world stage. But could the learning organization operate effectively outside Japan? Could Kao transfer its learning capability into a very different environment such as the US or Europe, where it would lack the twin foundations of infrastructure and human resource? Or would internationalization demand major adjustments to its way of operating?

Kao International

When the first cake of soap was produced in 1890, the name 'Kao' was stamped in both Chinese characters and Roman letters in preparation for the international market. A century later, the company was active in 50 countries but, except for the small neighbouring markets of South East Asia, had not achieved a real breakthrough. Despite all its investments, commitment and efforts over 25 years, Kao remained only 'potentially' a significant global competitor. In 1988, only 10 percent of its total sales was derived from overseas business, and 70 percent of this international volume was earned in SE Asia. As a result, internationalization was viewed by the company as its next key strategic challenge. Dr Maruta made his ambitions clear; 'Procter and Gamble,

Unilever and L'Oréal are our competitors. We cannot avoid fighting in the 1990s.' The challenge was to make those words a reality.

The strategic infrastructure

Kao's globalization was based not on a company-wide strategy, but on the product division system. Each product division developed its own strategy for international expansion and remained responsible for its world-wide results. Consequently, the company's business portfolio and strategic infrastructure varied widely from market to market.

South East Asia. As Table 3 illustrates, Kao had been building a platform for production and marketing throughout South East Asia since 1964, when it created its first overseas subsidiary in Thailand. By 1990 this small initial base had been expanded, mainly through joint ventures, and the company had made steady progress in these markets. The joint ventures in Hong Kong and Singapore sold only Kao's consumer products, while the others both manufactured and marketed them.

One of Kao's biggest international battles was for control of the Asian detergent, soap and shampoo markets, against rivals like P&G and Unilever. In the Taiwanese detergent market, where Unilever was the long established leader with 50 percent market share, Kao's vanguard product was the biological detergent, Attack. Launched in 1988, Attack increased Kao's market share from 17 percent to 22 percent. Subsequently, Kao decided on local production, both to continue serving the local market and for export to Hong Kong and Singapore. Its domestic rival, Lion (stationary at 17 percent) shortly followed suit. In Hong Kong, Kao was the market leader with 30 percent share and in Singapore, where Colgate-Palmolive led with 30 percent, had increased its share from five percent to 10 percent. Unilever, P&G and Colgate-Palmolive had responded to Kao's moves by putting in more human resources, and consolidating their local bases.

In Indonesia, where Unilever's historic links again made it strong, Kao, Colgate-Palmolive and P&G competed for the second position. In the Philippines, Kao had started local production of shampoo and liquid soap in 1989, while in Thailand it had doubled its local facilities in order to meet increasing demand. To demonstrate its commitment to the Asian market where it was becoming a major

player, Kao had established its Asian headquarters in Singapore. In that market, Kao's disposable diaper Merry had a 20 percent share, while its Merit shampoo was the market leader.

North America

Step 1 – Joint venture: In 1976, Kao had embarked on two joint ventures with Colgate-Palmolive Company, first to market hair care products in the US, and later to develop new oral hygiene products for Japan. The potential for synergy seemed enormous; Colgate-Palmolive was to provide the marketing expertise and distribution infrastructure, Kao would contribute the technical expertise to produce a high quality product for the top end of the United States market.

In 1977 there was a considerable exchange of personnel and technology, and a new shampoo was specially developed by Kao for the United States consumer. Despite the fact that tests in three major United States cities, using Colgate-Palmolive's state-of-the-art market research methods, showed poor market share potential, the product launch went ahead. The forecasts turned out to be correct, and the product was dropped after 10 months due to Colgate-Palmolive's reluctance to continue. A Kao manager explained the failure thus:

> First, the product was not targeted to the proper consumer group. High-price, high-end products were not appropriate for a novice and as yet unsophisticated producer like us. Second, the United States side believed in the result of the market research too seriously and did not attempt a second try . . . Third, it is essentially very difficult to penetrate a market like the shampoo market. Our partner expected too much short-term success. Fourth, the way the two firms decided on strategy was totally different. We constantly adjust our strategy flexibly. They never start without a concrete and fixed strategy. We could not wait for them.

The alliance was dissolved in 1985. However, Kao had learned some valuable lessons about United States marketing methods, Western lifestyles and, most of all, about the limitations of using joint ventures as a means of breaking into the United States market.

Step 2 – Acquisition: In 1988, Kao had made three acquisitions. In May, it bought the Andrew Jergens

TABLE 3 The history of Kao's internationalization

	Company	Year	Capital %	Main products
ASIA				
Taiwan	Taiwan Kao Co. Ltd	1964	90	detergent, soap
Thailand	Kao Industrila Co. Ltd	1964	70	hair care products
Singapore	Kao Private Ltd	1965	100	sales of soap, shampoo, detergents
Hong Kong	Kao Ltd	1970	100	sales of soap, shampoo, detergents
Malaysia	Kao Ptc. Ltd	1973	45	hair care products
Philippines	Pilippinas Kao Inc.	1977	70	fats and oils
Indonesia	P.T. PoleKao	1977	74	surfactants
Philippines	Kao Inc.	1979	70	hair care products
Indonesia	P.T. Dino Indonesia Industrial Ltd	1985	50	hair care products
Malaysia	Fatty Chemical Sdn. Bdn.	1988	70	alcohol
Singapore	Kao South-East Asia Headquarters	1988		
Philippines	Kao Co. Philippines Laboratory			
NORTH AMERICA				
Mexico	Qumi-Kao S.A. de C.V.	1975	20	fatty amines
	Bitumex	1979	49	asphal
Canada	Kao-Didak Ltd	1983	89	floppy disk
USA	Kao Corporation of Americal (KCOA)	1986	100	sales of household goods
	High Point Chemical	1987	100 (KCOA)	ingredients
	Kao Infosystems Company	1988	100 (KCOA)	duplication of software
	The Andrew Jergens	1988	100 (KCOA)	hair care products
USA	KCOA Los Angeles Laboratories			
EUROPE				
W. Germany	Kao Corporation GmbH (KCG)	1986	100	sales of household goods
	Kao Perfekta GmbH	1986	80 (KCG)	toners for copier
	Guhl Ikebana GmbH	1986	50 (KCG)	hair care products
Spain	Kao Corporation S.A.	1987	100	surfactants
W. Germany	Goldwell AG	1989	100	cosmetics
France	Kao Co. S.A. Paris Laboratories			
Spain	Kao Co. S.A. Barcelona Laboratories			
W. Germany	Kao Co. GmbH Berlin Laboratories			

Company, a Cincinnati soap, body lotion and shampoo maker, for $350 million. To acquire Jergens' extensive marketing know-how and established distribution channels, Kao beat off 70 other bidders, including Beiersdorf and Colgate-Palmolive, and paid 40 percent more than the expected price. Since then, Kao has invested heavily in the company, building a new multi-million dollar research centre and doubling Jergens' research team to over 50. Cincinnati was the home town of P&G, who have since seen Jergens market Kao's bath preparations in the United States.

High Point Chemical Corporation of America, an industrial goods producer, was also acquired in 1988. As Kao's United States chemical manufacturing arm, it had since begun 'an aggressive expansion of its manufacturing facilities and increased its market position.' The third acquisition, Info Systems (Sentinel) produced application products in the field of information technology.

In Canada, Kao owned 87 percent of Kao-Didak, a floppy disk manufacturer it bought out in 1986. A new plant, built in 1987, started producing 3.5 inch and 5.25 inch diskettes, resulting in record sales of $10 million that same year. Kao viewed floppy disks as the spearhead of its thrust into the United States market. As Mr Kuroyanagi explained: 'This product penetrates the US market easily. Our superior technology makes it possible to meet strict requirements for both quantity and quality. Our experience in producing specific chemicals for the floppy disk gives us a great competitive edge.' In what represented a dramatic move for a Japanese company, Kao relocated its world-wide head office for the floppy disk business to the United States, partly because of Kao's comparatively strong position there (second behind Sony) but also because it was by far the biggest market in the world. The United States headquarters was given complete strategic freedom to develop the business globally. Under the direction of this office a plant was built in Spain.

Europe.   Within Europe, Kao had built a limited presence in Germany, Spain and France. In Germany, it had established a research laboratory, and through its 1979 joint venture with Beiersdorf to develop and market hair care products, gained a good knowledge of the German market. The strategic position of this business was strengthened in 1989 by the acquisition of a controlling interest in Goldwell AG, one of Germany's leading suppliers of hair and skin care products to beauty salons. From studying Goldwell's network of beauty salons across Europe, Kao expected to expand its knowledge in order to be able to develop and market new products in Europe.

Kao's French subsidiary, created in January 1990, marketed floppy disks, skin toner and the Sofina range of cosmetics. The research laboratory established in Paris that same year was given the leading role in developing perfumes to meet Kao's worldwide requirements.

Kao's vanguard product in Europe was Sofina, which was positioned as a high quality, medium priced product. Any Japanese connection had been removed to avoid giving the brand a cheap image. While Sofina was produced and packaged in Japan, extreme care was taken to ensure that it shared a uniform global positioning and image in all the national markets in Europe. It was only advertised in magazines like Vogue, and sales points were carefully selected; for example in France, Sofina was sold only in the prestigious Paris department store, Galeries Lafayette.

Organizational capability

Organizationally, Kao's international operations were driven primarily along the product division axis. Each subsidiary had a staff in charge of each product who reported to the product's head office, either directly or through a regional product manager. For example, the manager in charge of Sofina in Spain reported to the French office where the regional manager responsible for Sofina was located, and he in turn reported to the Director of the Divisional HQ in Japan. Each subsidiary was managed by Japanese expatriate managers, since Kao's only foreign resource was provided by its acquired companies. Thus, the German companies remained under the management of its original directors. However, some progress was made towards localization; in Kao Spain (250 employees) there were 'only six to ten Japanese, not necessarily in management.' Kao's nine overseas R&D laboratories were each strongly connected to both the product headquarters and laboratories in Japan through frequent meetings and information exchange.

Mr Takayama saw several areas that needed to be strengthened before Kao could become an effective global compeititor. Kao, he believed 'was a medium-sized company grown large.' It lacked international experience, had fewer human resource assets, especially in top management and, compared with competitors like P&G and Unilever, had far less accumulated international knowledge and experience of Western markets and consumers. 'These two companies know how to run a business in the West and have well established market research techniques, whereas the Westernization of the Japanese lifestyle has only occurred in the last 20 years,' he explained. 'There are wide differences between East and West in, for example, bathing habits, that the company has been slow to comprehend.'

Kao attempted to redress these problems through stronger involvement by headquarters' managers in supporting the company's foreign operations. Mr Kuroyanagi provided an insight into Kao's approach to managing its overseas units. He described how, after visiting a foreign subsidiary where he felt change was necessary, he asked a senior colleague in Japan to carry out a specific review. The two summarized their findings, and then met with other top management members for further consultation. As a result, his colleague was temporarily located in the foreign company to lead certain projects. A team was formed in Japan to harmonize with locals, and sent to work in the subsidiary. Similarly, when investigating the reason for the company's slow penetration of the shampoo market in Thailand, despite offering a technologically superior product, headquarters' managers found that the product positioning, pricing and packaging policies developed for the Japanese market were unsuitable for Thailand. Since the subsidiary could not adapt these policies to meet local requirements, a headquarters' marketing specialist was brought in, together with a representative from Dentsu – Kao's advertising agent in Japan – to identify the source of the problem and make the necessary changes in the marketing mix.

Part of Mr Kuroyanagi's role was to act as a 'liaison officer' between Kao and its subsidiaries. Kao appointed such managers at headquarters to liaise with all the newly acquired companies in Europe and Asia; their task was to interpret corporate strategies to other companies outside Japan and ensure that 'We never make the same mistake twice.' He described himself as 'the eyes and ears of top management, looking round overseas moves, competitors' activities and behaviours and summarizing them.' He was also there to 'help the local management abroad understand correctly Kao as a corporation, and give hints about how to overcome the cultural gap and linguistic difficulties, how to become open, aggressive and innovative.'

Kao's 1990 global strategy was to develop 'local operations sensitive to each region's characteristics and needs.' As Mr Takayama explained, these would be able 'to provide each country with goods tailored to its local climate and customs, products which perfectly meet the needs of its consumers.' To this end, the goals of the company's research centres in Los Angeles, Berlin, Paris and Santiago de Compostela in Spain, had been redefined as: 'to analyze local market needs and characteristics and integrate them into the product development process,' and a small market research unit had been created in Thailand to support local marketing of Sofina. Over time, Kao hoped, headquarters' functions would be dispersed to SE Asia, the US and Europe, leaving to the Tokyo headquarters the role of supporting regionally based, locally managed operations by giving 'strategic assistance.' There were no plans to turn Jergens or other acquired companies into duplicate Kaos; as described by Dr Maruta 'We will work alongside them rather than tell them which way to go.'

The lack of overseas experience among Kao's managers was tackled via a new ¥9 billion training facility built at Kasumigaura. The 16 hectare campus, offering golf, tennis and other entertainment opportunities was expected to enjoy a constant population of 200, with 10 days' training becoming the norm for all managers. To help Kao managers develop a broader and more international outlook, training sessions devoted considerable attention to the cultural and historical heritages of different countries. A number of younger managers were sent to Europe and the United States, spending the first year learning languages and the second either at a business school, or at Kao's local company offices.

'If you look at our recent international activity,' said Mr Kuroyanagi, 'we have prepared our stage. We have made our acquisitions . . . the basis for globalization in Europe, North America and South East Asia has been facilitated . . . We now need some play on that stage.' Kao's top management was confident that the company's R&D power, 'vitality and open, innovative and aggressive culture' would ultimately prevail. The key constraints, inevitably, were people. 'We do not have enough talented people to direct these plays on the stage.' Kao could not and did not wish to staff its overseas operations with Japanese nationals, but finding, training and keeping suitable local personnel was a major challenge.

Kao expected the industry to develop like many others until 'there were only three or four companies operating on a global scale. We would like to be one of these.' Getting there looked like taking some time, but Kao was in no rush. The perspective, Dr Maruta continually stressed, was very long term, and the company would move at its own pace:

We should not think about the quick and easy way, for that can lead to bad handling of our products. We must take the long term view . . . and spiral our activity towards the goal . . . We will not, and need not hurry our penetration of foreign markets. We need to avoid having unbalanced growth. The harmony among people, products and world-wide operations is the most important philosophy to keep in mind . . . only in 15 years will it be clear how we have succeeded.

CASE 7

Continental: Liberating entrepreneurial energy

By Heike Bruch and Bernd Vogel[1]

At the beginning of the 1990's the Germany (Hanover) based company Continental AG was first and foremost active in the rubber industry. Car as well as truck tires and other technical products with a high rubber content were its core products with total sales amounting to €4,372.1 million in 1990 (see Table 1).

In 1991 Continental's serious decline started: While the company was market leader in Germany in the core-product area, tires, it ranked no. 2 in the European tire market. But in the world market the company controlled only 7% and occupied fourth-place, with a great gap behind the 'Big Three' – Michelin (20%), Goodyear (16.4%) and Bridgestone

TABLE 1 Continental AG 11-year statistics

		1990	1991	1992	1993	1994	1995	1996	1997	1998	1999	2000
Fixed assets and investments	million €	1,458.9	1,747.0	1,817.3	1,949.8	1,843.3	1,781.9	1,797.3	1,797.7	3,999.3	4,220.6	4,381.6
Currents assets	million €	1,694.5	1,652.7	1,791.3	1,696.6	1,642.4	1,645.5	1,629.4	2,112.6	2,766.4	3,183.2	3,233.6
Balance sheet total	million €	3,153.4	3,399.7	3,608.6	3,646.4	3,485.7	3,427.4	3,426.7	3,910.3	6,765.7	7,403.8	7,615.2
Shareholders' equity	million €	842.6	725.1	765.3	780.2	756.6	764.2	816.7	1,232.3	1,329.1	1,760.6	1,844.1
Minority interests	million €	48.2	49.4	61.5	88.5	100.1	102.7	134.5	149.5	174.5	142.4	145.7
Long-term borrowed funds	million €	1,068.5	1,344.6	1,452.4	1,399.7	1,356.8	1,102.5	1,245.7	1,268.5	3,003.4	2,343.9	2,855.2
Spending on fixed assets	million €	352.5	424.0	362.7	319.1	263.2	302.3	282.0	282.6	416.3	581.5	682.8
Equity ratio	in %	26.7	21.3	21.2	21.4	21.7	22.3	23.8	31.5	19.6	23.8	24.2
Financing of fixed assets and investments & inventories with shareholders' equity and l-t borrowed funds	in %	89.6	89.0	90.0	86.3	90.1	79.4	85.1	104.6	93.1	83.4	91.5
Indebtedness	million €	790.4	1,100.8	1,235.7	1,170.6	1,089.3	1,016.8	836.9	283.4	1,919.0	1,712.8	2,017.9
Internal financing ratio	in %	68.1	52.1	133.8	86.4	113.5	122.9	132.9	173.7	117.1	135.3	112.5
Liquidity ratio	in %	77.1	74.6	76.5	68.3	76.6	61.3	68.7	107.1	82.5	69.3	79.8
Sales	million €	4,372.1	4,794.3	4,954.4	4,790.3	5,050.0	5,242.0	5,333.1	5,719.4	6,743.2	9,132.2	10,115.0
Share outside Germany	in %	61.8	62.8	63.9	65.4	67.6	66.5	66.1	67.4	66.4	68.6	68.9
Cost of sales[2]	in %	75.9	74.7	73.2	74.1	74.0	73.9	73.4	71.9	74.0	78.6	79.7
Selling expenses[2]	in %	14.7	14.8	15.0	16.7	16.3	15.6	15.8	16.0	14.4	11.6	11.1
Administrative expenses[2]	in %	5.9	6.5	6.7	6.2	6.2	5.7	5.5	5.3	4.7	3.9	3.8
EBIT	million €	152.8	171.2	239.4	151.8	154.2	198.2	268.0	320.4	380.3	511.3	432.4
Staff costs	million €	1,548.4	1,654.7	1,709.4	1,683.7	1,669.4	1,673.9	1,672.2	1,751.5	1,937.1	2,387.7	2,580.8
Depreciation[3]	million €	193.3	271.5	257.0	284.7	298.3	282.6	311.5	306.8	395.7	576.5	654.7
Cash flow	million €	260.8	269.0	358.6	296.0	320.0	378.2	416.5	490.9	567.0	849.7	866.3
Value added	million €	1,766.5	1,697.4	1,904.7	1,835.5	1,823.5	1,872.0	1,899.2	2,071.9	2,317.4	2,899.0	3,013.2
Net income for the year	million €	47.8	−65.5	68.0	33.3	36.2	79.4	98.4	164.5	138.2	234.7	204.7
Employees (average)	1.000	48.4	50.8	50.4	49.8	49.0	48.4	46.4	44.8	50.2	62.6	63.5

The consolidated financial statements as of 1998 are drawn up in accordance with US GAAP. Prior to 1998 they were drawn up to the German Commercial Code. This explains the drop in the annual profit as of 1998, which – at DM413.9 million – would not have occurred if the profit for the year had been calculated to HGB.

[1] without minority interests   [2] of sales   [3] without depreciation on financial assets

[1]Source: This case was written by Dr Heike Bruch, Assistant Professor at the University of St Gallen, Switzerland and Dipl. Ök. Bernd Vogel, Lecturer at the University of Hanover, Germany. It is intended to be used as a basis of discussion rather than to illustrate either effective or ineffective handling of a business situation. Reprinted with permission of Heike Bruch and Bernd Vogel.

(16.2%) (see Table 2). Moreover the demand for tires was flat and the innovative potential of the core product tires seemed to be nearly exhausted. Internally Continental was a monolithic, unprofitable company driven by managers that tended to administrative activities rather than taking initiatives in the areas for which they were accountable. Finally, in 1991 Continental suffered from a record loss of €65.5 million.

Ten years later, in 2000, Continental has fundamentally altered its core target market; it was a highly innovative supplier of automotive chassis aspiring to become a leading global provider of automotive systems. During the years 1991–2000, Continental had undergone some radical changes that reversed the record loss of €65.5 million in 1991 to a record profit of €204.7 million in 2000. Its development from a manufacturer of rubber products to a specialist for automotive chassis was the result of a fundamental transformation. It implied company-wide liberating of entrepreneurial energy of Continental's managers and employees. In 2001, this process was not fully completed. In fact, maintaining the entrepreneurial spirit was seen as the key challenge.

Setting the agenda for strategic change

At the beginning of the 90's the world tire industry was in the midst of a serious recession marked by considerable overcapacities and a decline in vehicle registrations. Despite this, Continental and other tire industry producers pursued growth strategies in their traditional markets to achieve economies of scale. The result was a fierce price war.

As a consequence Continental slipped into the red in just two years. Its earnings plummeted from a profit of €116.6 million in 1989 to a mere €47.8 million in 1990, followed by losses of €65.5 million in 1991. At the same time, sales grew by about €42.2 million. Acquisitions in this time period led to a ballooning of net indebtedness to €1.2 billion.

TABLE 2 Sales of major tire producers 1990–1999

		Bridgestone	Michelin	Goodyear	Continental	Sumitomo	Pirelli	Yokohama	Cooper	Toyo	Kumho
1999	Sales in millions of €	13,500.0	13,500.0	11,515.6	4,900.0	3,413.8	2,725.2	2,408.2	1,557.1	1,254.7	1,195.0
	Rank	1	2	3	4	5	6	7	8	9	10
	% of total sales	74	92	85	50	76	40	70	71	60	59
1998	Sales in millions of €	12,634.8	12,916.3	11,311.0	4,334.0	3,750.0	3,005.8	2,193.5	1,447.4	1,120.2	965.5
	Rank	2	1	3	4	5	6	7	8	9	10
	% of total sales	74	93	85	58	75	49	70	77	60	91
1997	Sales in millions of €	12,920.0	12,718.0	11,850.0	4,355.0	3,800.0	3,020.0	2,343.0	1,449.0	1,283.0	1,241.0
	Rank	1	2	3	4	5	6	7	8	9	10
	% of total sales	72	93	85	68	75	46	70	80	59	89
1996	Sales in millions of €	12,900.0	13,100.0	11,705.0	4,866.0	4,000.0	3,000.0	2,600.0	1,372.0	1,378.0	1,355.0
	Rank	2	1	3	4	5	6	7	9	8	10
	% of total sales	72	94	84	70	75	45	70	85	57	89
1995	Sales in millions of €	12,740.0	12,240.0	10,105.0	4,938.0	3,975.0	2,987.0	2,860.0	1,267.0	1,524.0	1,147.0
	Rank	1	2	3	4	5	6	7	9	8	10
	% of total sales	71	92	77	69	70	90	71	85	57	83
1994	Sales in millions of €	11,100.0	11,000.0	9,428.0	4,415.0	3,426.0	2,717.0	2,651.0	1,193.0	1,410.0	847.0
	Rank	1	2	3	4	5	6	7	9	8	10
	% of total sales	71	91	77	68	72	90	72	85	58	80
1993	Sales in millions of €	9,471.9	9,500.0	8,853.3	3,719.3	3,223.0	2,747.5	2,522.5	1,014.6	1,295.8	876.3
	Rank	2	1	76	4	5	6	7	9	8	10
	% of total sales	65	84	3	65	71	90	70	85	56	79
1992	Sales in millions of €	9,345.0	10,500.0	8,166.9	3,980.3	3,275.6	2,874.8	2,431.7	1,000.0	1,263.0	843.5
	Rank	2	1	3	4	5	6	7	9	8	10
	% of total sales	67	83	69	64	71	86	71	85	57	79
1991	Sales in millions of €	8,688.0	10,020.0	7,849.0	3,613.0	3,050.0	2,756.0	2,320.0	830.0	1,194.0	703.0
	Rank	2	1	3	4	5	6	7	9	8	10
	% of total sales	65	84	72	64	71	85	69	83	58	79

Source: European Rubber Journal

EXHIBIT 1 PIRELLI'S ATTEMPTED TAKEOVER

Alongside the challenges posed by regular business operations in these years, Continental's independence was threatened by a takeover attempt on the part of its competitor, Pirelli, at the time no. 5 on the worldwide tire market. Presentation of Pirelli's merger proposal on September 15, 1990 kicked off a protracted tug-of-war between the Executive Board, the Supervisory Board, banks, politicians and Pirelli representatives. Round-table talks were agreed to by the two companies for the purpose of investigating the situation. They led, in the end, to the departure of Executive Board chairman Horst W. Urban on May 10, 1991. The takeover endeavors were ultimately laid to rest in April 1993 with the transfer of the Pirelli-controlled block of shares to a bank consortium.

In addition to competitive influences, internal factors were particularly responsible for this development. Poor profits in a number of corporate divisions were one of the major factors. While the 'Tire Production' division did, in fact, report a profit, a segment of the division, the original equipment business with the automotive industry, reported a loss of €51 million on sales of €256 million.

Moreover, Continental was running into trouble integrating the companies acquired as part of its growth strategy. These included, among others, Uniroyal 1979, Semperit 1985, General Tire 1987. The European tire brands such as Uniroyal and Semperit were positioned similarly to the parent brand in the replacement market and ended up competing for the same target customers. Thus both market areas – the original equipment business with the automotive industry and the replacement market – were in trouble through internal difficulties.

One of the causes of this was the company's generally bureaucratic and centralistic structure and culture. With areas like 'Tire production', 'Tire marketing/sales', 'Corporate finance, controlling and logistics' and 'Technical products', the corporate structure was tuned primarily to functional responsibilities and remained largely insensitive to markets or customers (see Figure 1). This structure was correspondingly reflected in the centralized control philosophy.

We saw ourselves subjected to a high degree of centralization as far as decision-making was concerned. The units enjoyed little autonomy. We were characterized by a strong finance and controlling orientation and were, bottom line, a control company.

(Wilhelm Schäfer, 1993–1995
Board member – Car Tires)

Thus major internal reasons for Continental's crisis were: a lack of awareness of the sources of the company's losses, poor management of internal competition, suppression of decentral innovative potential and the absence of entrepreneurial initiative on the part of managers and employees.

FIGURE 1 Functional structure of Continental AG in 1991

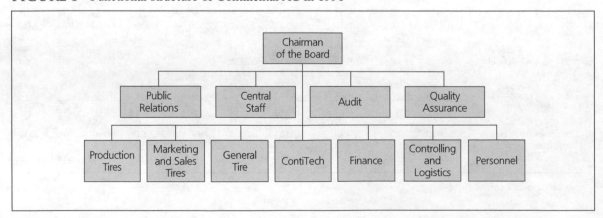

Giving priority to profit and innovation

When Dr. Hubertus von Grünberg left his post as president and CEO of the ITT Automotive Group to take over as Continental Executive Board chairman on July 20, 1991, the corporate situation was characterized by fierce predatory competition, a sharp drop in results, loss-making operations in the corporation and the threat of takeover by Pirelli (see Exhibit 1). Early on Dr. von Grünberg shifted the corporation's focus. At a press conference on August 30, 1991, he outlined the direction Continental would take in the future.

> *The main goal is that of stabilizing the corporation's profitability and of bringing about a sustained improvement. . . . There must not be any taboos in pursuit of these goals.*

To ensure the company's future survival, growth was no longer to be fueled by additional acquisitions but by successful innovations achieved by the company on its own strength and through its own entrepreneurial forces.

On December 2, 1991, Dr. von Grünberg reinforced his emphasis on profit and innovation presenting his 10-point program:

1 Growth through successful in-house developments and profitable production structures

2 Investments in sales revenues, not in size

3 Strategic alliances

4 Fewer acquisitions, with new focal points

5 Technological leadership and a wide range of systems

6 Expansion of market position in Eastern Europe

7 Pro-active environmental protection

8 Rescue operation for General Tire

9 Decentral responsibility: Fight losses and improve earnings

10 Figures well into the black in 1992

The program highlighted strategic topics and placed immediate demands on Continental's managers to intensify Continental's focus in the next years on two basic perspectives. First, the company and its managers had to follow a clear profit orientation marking a departure from its previous growth strategy, which instead had been aimed strictly as higher sales. Second, Dr. von Grünberg stressed the absolute importance of innovations for the corpora-

tion if it was to be able to claim technology leadership in the tire sector. Profitability became the corporate guideline for all direct and indirect areas. In figures this meant that after the drop in corporate profitability in 1993, he envisioned a sustained annual rate of return after taxes of 2.5% and a long-term target of 4%.

Implanting profitability: Towards a new growth strategy

Connected with this was the demand, or compulsion, to achieve widespread productivity growth in all units, especially those operating at a loss.

> *When the changes got under way, the motto was 'Cut the losses!'. The basic assumption was that it was easier, and thus quicker, to do away with operations making losses than to raise those units doing well to an even higher level of profit. In so doing, the tense earnings situation in the corporation was turned inside out.*
> (Dr. Dieter von Herz, Head of Corporate Communications until 1998)

Continental was aware that a fundamental restructuring was necessary in order to make it clearer where profits were being generated, and where losses were being made. Transparency of profits and losses was seen as a central precondition for transferring responsibility to managers.

> *We broke everything down organizationally until we arrived at units that weren't earning anything. A young employee was then sent in to straighten out the unit.*
> (Dr. Hubertus von Grünberg, Chairman of the Supervisory Board of Continental AG; Chairman of the Executive Board of Continental AG from 1991 to 1999)

Here Dr. von Grünberg could take advantage of the experience gained in the successful decentralization of ContiTech. Back on January 1, 1991, the company had already pulled apart the tightly knit structure of the non tire operations. Eight legally independent companies had been set up. Each of them had a separate range of products and its own market segments and was run by managers who had to report on revenue matters. In this way it was possible to directly read off the market success or failure of each unit.

For the tire area, restructuring the previous functional orientation took off on February 1, 1992. The board areas 'Tire Production' on the one hand and 'Marketing/Sales' on the other, each of them responsible for both car and truck tires, were dissolved and replaced by two separate product-driven Board-level divisions – 'Passenger Tires' and 'Commercial Vehicle Tires/Environment/Research' (see Figure 2). Both divisions were given responsibility for the whole production and marketing process. Market success could be measured directly and the division managers themselves took on business responsibility for the products' market results. Furthermore, the greater degree of transparency made it possible to impose more explicitly formulated profit demands on top management in the tire divisions.

In the wake of this fundamental reorientation, decentralization worked its way deeper and deeper into the hierarchy of the organization. This did not occur all at once but in a series of steps. Small units with profit responsibility were created, which, despite their size, incorporated cross-functional processes. In this way, useless runaround in the hierarchy could be avoided.

(Axel Witt, Head of Corporate Human Resources, Development & Internal Consulting)

The organizational split-up of the passenger tire division into two business units at the beginning of 1996 provides an example of how loss-making areas were pinpointed and then changed. The highly profitable replacement business was separated organizationally from the loss-making original equipment business. Therefore the results of the latter area were no longer subsumed in the results for car tires as a whole but were clear for all to see.

Dr. Kessel took over at the helm of an independent original equipment business unit furnished with the requisite resources, e.g. four production plants assigned directly to it and full responsibility for running the business and for reducing the €51 million in losses. These entrepreneurial possibilities and the adoption of a strategic policy to no longer accept the automotive industry's pricing policy did the trick. The original equipment business succeeded in getting back in the black in 1997.

Profit-orientation of service functions

The demand for profitability and direct responsibility applied to indirect functions too. They were also expected to generate earnings and to reduce cost.

The now entrepreneurial orientation led to a fundamental questioning of the service functions. Each area was required to make a visible contribution for the benefit of the corporation.

(Klaus Friedland, Board member in charge of Finance, Controlling, Human Resources and Law)

As a consequence, IT operations, for example, were largely outsourced in 1996. About 370 employees were transferred to a company operated jointly by IBM and Continental. In 1995, a management buyout transformed large parts of the previous human resources development department into an independent company, Contur GmbH.

FIGURE 2 Organizational structure of tire operations in 1992

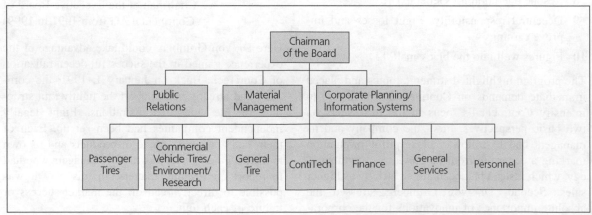

New standards regarding the contribution made to improving earnings were applied to the corporation's purchasing processes, as well. By 1996, Continental's annual purchasing volume had risen to around €2.7 billion, corresponding to 50% of corporate sales. Procurement thus represented a significant field of action for achieving competitive advantages, yet one that had hardly been noticed until the early '90s. The example of steel cord procurements provides a clear illustration of the new thinking (Exhibit 2).

The new way of thinking was also evident in the marketing organization of the car tire division. The acquisitions in the '80s had given Continental a number of brands – Continental, Uniroyal, Semperit, General Tire, Gislaved, Mabor, Sava, Viking and Barum. Each of these had a separate management accountable for the respective brand's profitability. However, the brands overlapped somewhat in terms of positioning and target groups and tended to turn down one another's market shares.

To put customers and markets at the center of attention, a switch from brand orientation to market orientation was adopted at the end of 1993. General market managers were made accountable for the results in regional business segments on a mix of all brands. The managers were thus given much more latitude in dealing with the customers in their territory. These increased opportunities arose because the brands were no longer in direct competition with one another. The multibrand strategy attempted, instead, to create a clear distinction among the brands, with each of them focusing on specific target groups. And so, for example even in

2001 'Continental' was for all practical purposes the premium brand and 'Barum' the budget brand. The target groups were defined, however, not only on the basis of quality but also on the basis of the type of application they were best suited for. Uniroyal, for example, was positioned as the rain tire and Semperit as the winter tire.

Central coordination of decentral activities

As a means of guarding against inefficient decentralization and to prevent the decentral units from drifting apart, certain functions – controlling, finance, technology or purchasing – were retained as central units.

> *Corporate headquarters started and continues to define targets that serve as a framework and pose a challenge. Rigorous adherence and pursuit of these targets is expected from those in charge of the autonomous divisions and units.*
>
> (Axel Witt, Head of Corporate Human Resources, Development & Internal Consulting)

Despite the extensive decentralization, Dr. von Grünberg continued to exert direct influence, particularly on investment activity.

> *Under certain circumstances – for example, if it did not appear plausible that the anticipated return could actually be realized – he was known to reject investment requests that had already gotten the go-ahead from those*

EXHIBIT 2 THE EXAMPLE OF STEEL CORD PROCUREMENT

In 1995 tire makers were very much at the mercy of a monopolistic structure to satisfy their requirements for steel cord – a key basic material in the tire production. Despite high prices, the previous purchasing staff shied away from switching to a different supply source and thereby running the risk of compromised quality. This being the case, a parallel project group was instituted to track down new possibilities for obtaining this material. In the face of opposition from purchasing itself and from the production plants, the

project group proposed buying steel cord from Russia. This involved, however, development of a much-expanded purchasing concept to allay the fears of those opposed to the switch and to dispel any reservations regarding quality. The future suppliers were involved in the planning activities. They worked together simultaneously with purchasers, quality staff and product developers to upgrade the products. In exchange for this preparatory work, long-term contracts were concluded with the new suppliers.

respectively in charge of line functions or central units. He always attached great importance to keeping the reasons for his rejection transparent, though, so that those in positions of responsibility could learn something from the case at hand.

(Dr. Bernadette Hausmann, Head of Corporate Purchasing and Strategic Technology)

Fostering strategic innovation

Striving for technological leadership

Already in 1991, in the first few months of his time as chairman of the Executive Board, Dr. von Grünberg set about implementing a reorientation of the corporation's business. He called on the company to strive for the leading position in technology in the sector on the basis of the innovative capability of the individual employees in all areas of the company. Notwithstanding the fact that the tire area's innovative potential seemed to have been almost exhausted, he continued to count on further product and process innovations.

> *Alone or in partnership with others, we were looking for access to fields of technology not already occupied.*
>
> (Dr. Hubertus von Grünberg)

The importance was demonstrated by substantial investments in R&D – even during the crisis. Approximately 4% of sales revenue was plowed back into the R&D. This was the absolute limit for investments that could be retrieved from the market via prices. This initial investment activity resulted for example in a new tire line, Eco-Contact, in 1992 and the development of a one-stage tire building machine in 1994.

Bundling innovative force

To make more efficient use of available resources and to increase the corporation's innovative power, Dr. von Grünberg made incursions into R&D's existing structure. After a two-year period of restructuring, a technology center was inaugurated in Hanover, in the immediate vicinity of Continental AG corporate headquarters, in April 1996. It was to supply the innovations the corporation required and underlined the significance of R&D as a sort of technological clamp around an increasingly decentral-

ized corporation. In the face of considerable resistance at the decentral research locations, the R&D resources from the former brand locations in Traiskirchen (Semperit) and Aachen (Uniroyal) were brought together in Hanover. Representing an investment of €51 million, the technology center thus created employed 1000 engineers and technicians engaged in producing market-oriented innovations for car/truck tires and automotive systems.

RDE-meetings: Innovation meets market demands

The innovation activities were subject to exactly the same profit demands as had been formulated for the other corporate processes. At so-called research-development-engineering meetings (RDE-meetings), Continental researchers and developers were dealt with as if they were entrepreneurs and directly confronted with the demands of managers from market and customer units.

> *In 1992, Dr. von Grünberg introduced these quarterly RDE-meetings as a means of conducting research and development innovations. The sessions brought together the Board member for the tire division and those in charge of the R&D areas for a presentation of new projects and a review of the progress made so far. Alongside material prospects, the marketability of the technological innovation was introduced as a key criterion in the evaluation of these innovations. The RDE-meetings thus determined in large measure Continental's specific technological orientation, which was clearly market- and customer-driven.*
>
> (Heinrich Huinink, Head of Strategic Technology)

> *The RDE-meetings offered a platform for display of new business ideas and systems solutions, e.g. by linking existing products with other technologies and with the market areas.*
>
> (Wolf-Dieter Gogoll, Head of Corporate Human Resources until 2000)

Towards a systems supplier for the automotive industry

Dr. von Grünberg held to the ambition that Continental AG was itself capable of developing and marketing cutting-edge technology. From 1992 on, he therefore pursued a competitively induced reorientation of the company's strategic activities in the direction of the systems business with the automotive industry. As part of this, the tire product range was expanded to incorporate technical chassis components to form complete systems that could be supplied as such to the automotive industry.

We believed and continue to be convinced that over the medium and long term, suppliers of complete systems will play the dominant role in the automotive industry of the future.

(Dr. Hubertus von Grünberg)

In the long run, the delivery of technically sophisticated components is intended to cushion the strategic problems inherent in the supplier/automaker relationship. The latter includes the limited technological development potential of tires as products, the secondary importance of tires for the automotive industry and uncertain growth potential because of dependence on auto industry production volumes. In view of the tendency in the auto industry to reduce the number of suppliers, it was generally assumed that Continental could no longer expect to remain a direct supplier if the corporation stuck almost exclusively to the production of tires. The company ran the risk of seeing its status downgraded to that of secondary supplier, with only minimal impact on development. To avoid this, tires were to be combined with other technical components and supplied to the auto industry as systems.

A major move towards acquiring the status of systems supplier to the automotive industry was the founding of a separate Board area 'Automotive Systems' in 1994 (see Figure 3) to be headed by Albert Beller, a former manager at ITT Industries with formative experience in the chassis business.

The division established itself initially as supplier of pre-assembled wheel/tire systems. Starting with 10,000 tires in 1994, production was increased to three million tires pre-assembled in 1996. This was accompanied by the development of a series of innovative product ideas for the chassis – TPMS, CECC, CASS, SWT, to cite just the major ones.[2] These ideas did not immediately have an impact on profit but formed the basis for the systems business as future added-value potential.

By establishing the Board area Automotive Systems, Dr. von Grünberg made clear where he wanted to position the corporation. Even if the development fields he had his sights on were very small at Continental in comparison to what the competition maintained, it significantly demonstrated the direction the corporation was heading for.

(Heinrich Huinink, Head of Strategic Technology)

FIGURE 3   Corporate structure of Continental AG in 2001

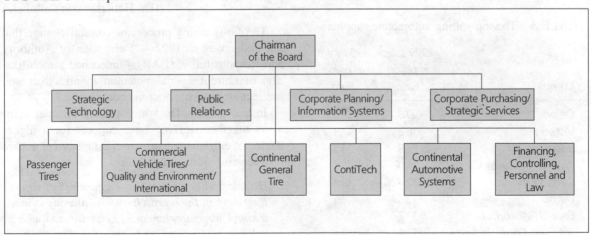

[2] TPMS (Tire Pressure Monitoring System); CECC (Continental Electronic Chassis Control, an electronically controlled brake system); CASS (Continental Air Suspension System for passenger cars); SWT (Sidewall Torsion Sensor, provides electronic information on the deformation of the tire during driving).

Acquisition of Teves

This acquisition of Teves – ITT Industries' brake and chassis operations – in 1998 marked the first time that Dr. von Grünberg went outside the corporation in pursuit of systems supplier status. Up to that point, he had worked to position the company in the systems field strictly on the basis of its own entrepreneurial strength and innovation potential. He invested a good €1.5 billion in this acquisition, which gave the corporation competence, sales and revenue in chassis technology.

Teves' major products were the antilock braking system (ABS) and the electronic stability program (ESP). The additional sales that Teves contributed to the company heaved it into the no. 9 slot among automotive suppliers (see Table 3). At the same time it gave the company as a whole a development capacity and technological innovation force of around 2500 researchers and developers.

As a result Continental was enabled to play a major role in the further development of the worldwide automotive industry. For automakers it made more sense to technically and economically optimize whole modules than to work on individual components. Thus Continental positioned itself as a global systems and technology partner in the automotive industry.

With the joint competence now available, Dr. von Grünberg's aspirations continued to evolve, however. He emphasized the goal of supplying unique products that could not be copied, therefore generating sustainable competitive advantages.

TABLE 3   The top-selling automotive suppliers

Company	1999 sales in billion Euro	1998 sales in billion Euro
Delphi	27.6	28.5
Visteon	18.3	17.8
Bosch	16.9	16.5
TRW Auto/Lucas Varity	16.0	11.5
Dana Corporation	12.4	12.8
Denso	13.8	12.6
Lear/UT Automotive	11.7	12.1
Johnson Controls Auto	11.4	9.3
Continental	9.1	6.7
Valeo/ITT Electrical Syst.	7.7	8.9
Magna International	7.0	6.6

For Continental these new possibilities opened the way to an electronically controlled chassis that considerably enhanced driving safety and riding comfort.

(Dr. Hubertus von Grünberg)

Already in 1999 this division contributed €2.6 billion in sales (see Table 4).

Unleashing managers' entrepreneurial energy

Guidelines for entrepreneurial activity

From the previous development it was evident that restructuring gave managers a great deal of latitude. Already in December 1991 Dr. von Grünberg called upon the corporation's managers to put this extra freedom to good use by adopting an entrepreneurial mindset and, above all, by acting in an entrepreneurial manner:

Everywhere in the company, it is necessary to think and act more entrepreneurially. I want to have entrepreneurs in our company who assert themselves against any and all resistance. Who have well thought-out ideas and see to it that they lead to profitable results. (. . .) I would often like to see more daring and more willingness to take risks. (. . .) The basic principle for the future is the precedence of earnings over quantity. To this end I would like to provide all senior executives with profit responsibility.

(Dr. Hubertus von Grünberg)

The far-reaching process of cultural change that got under way in 1992 – 'Delegation of Authority and Responsibility' (DAR) – unleashed a mobilization of entrepreneurial potential in all direct and indirect areas throughout the company.

In this process Dr. von Grünberg brought managers together working on a concept for a higher degree of entrepreneurship extending beyond a mere restructuring of the units.

He selected those persons – regardless of where they were in the hierarchy – who already evinced a knack for entrepreneurial behavior and who exhibited a willingness to enforce a larger quantum of entrepreneurship at Continental. No specific project with the title DAR was founded. The process was powered by drivers who were

TABLE 4 Sales and EBIT[1] shares of the various corporate divisions (in million Euro)

	Automotive Systems		Car Tires		Commercial Vehicle Tires		Continental General Tire		ContiTech	
	Sales	EBIT	Sales	EBIT	Sales	EBIT	Sales	EBIT	Sales	EBIT
1993			2,011	129	527	−25	1,150	11	1,084	48
1994			1,998	107	549	−15	1,122	21	1,266	58
1995			2,082	128	597	3	1,054	28	1,427	62
1996			2,158	171	548	−12	1,053	42	1,515	91
1997			2,223	207	669	11	1,203	64	1,580	91
1998	630	−5	2,389	241	759	48	1,230	71	1,704	78
1999	2,544	59	2,547	270	879	49	1,494	74	1,716	130
2000	3,023	216	2,639	177	976	36	1,763	12	1,787	139

[1] EBIT (earnings before interest and taxes)

already actively living out the idea and who had thus made entrepreneurship their business.

(Axel Witt, Head of Corporate Human Resources, Development & Internal Consulting)

The process led to the formulation of a concrete call for entrepreneurial, profit-oriented action on the part of Continental managers and employees:

- Cross-functional action instead of functional thinking.
- Result responsibility instead of mere plan fulfillment.
- Customer orientation instead of functional-hierarchical orientation.
- Agreement on targets instead of those on top dictating what is to be done.
- Internal service units instead of central staff functions.

Creating internal competition

Benefiting from an increasingly decentralized structure and managers increasingly sensitized for entrepreneurial thinking and acting. Dr. von Grünberg pinpointed corporate units with poor earnings or especially high costs and kept at the top managers in charge to get the situation into line financially. He focused his interest on these 'burning platforms' and kept a close eye on the development of their units.

The pattern for this 'burning platform' approach was characterized by high pressure on those in charge of certain selected units to effect change, backed up, above all, by corresponding figures and the unambiguous call to put an end to the miserable situation. Dr. von Grünberg always sketched an escape route and offered far-reaching support for the steps that had to be taken to unleash the necessary change.

(Wolf-Dieter Gogoll, Head of Corporate Human Resources until 2000)

By way of stepping up the pressure for change, he consciously put units in competition with one another.

Internal competition was an important, intensively used instrument for generating the pressure for change. In the end it helped to meet the targets set by encouraging those involved to think in terms of alternatives. Of course, this internal competition often involved painful processes for the company and caused a lot of unnecessary trouble. The tension it generated was laid to rest by the ensuing success. The success worked like a drug that welded the units in the company together.

(Dr. Bernadette Hausmann, Head of Corporate Purchasing and Strategic Technology)

Dr. von Grünberg made purposeful use of this instrument in the production area. Regularly he had productivity comparisons drawn up at the various plants. At the same time he entrusted the plants with a greater degree of authority to control performance processes. The plant in Mount Vernon, Illinois, was assigned the status of benchmark in 1993. Furthermore, in 1995 and 1996 Dr. von Grünberg announced that one of the existing plants would be closed because of the production quantities in most of the plants being uneconomically small. However, he did not explicitly name the plant. The performance and productivity ratios at the individual plants was under permanent review and served as the basis for deciding which plant was to be shut down. In this very direct way Dr. von Grünberg made abundantly clear to the plant managers and employees the absolute inevitability of change. The outcome of this process was the closure of the plant in Dublin in 1996 and the transfer of the production of 2 million tires from Traiskirchen to the plant in Otrokovice, Czech Republic.

Internal benchmarking continued to be practiced in the following years, with the prospect of a further plant shutdown. In November 1999 the production in Newbridge, Scotland, was closed. And so for years on end Dr. von Grünberg succeeded in asserting unrelenting pressure on a number of corporate units to change and increase earnings.

Creative destruction of the status quo

Dr. von Grünberg was not only unswerving in his insistence on improved profit, he also encouraged top managers to constantly and fundamentally question the status quo in their respective areas. In a major departure from the prevailing mindset at the time he joined the company, he strongly encouraged risk-taking. Risks were no longer regarded as negative but as genuinely positive. He expected his employees to exhibit a willingness and the initiative to avoid solutions that upheld the status quo and to engage instead in wide-ranging processes of change. The related risk was supported and even explicitly solicited.

> *Several times Dr. von Grünberg employed Schumpeter's mental construct of 'creative destruction'. To encourage managers to break up the status quo, he directed the attention of those involved at first on the idea of destruction. The second aspect – the creative element – was emphasized later after they had opened up.*
>
> (Wilhelm Schäfer, Executive Board member responsible for Passenger Tires from 1993 to 1995)

Underlining the permanent challenge of the status quo Dr. von Grünberg rejected, above all, the argumentation of managers that certain processes in the tire business were off limits to change by merit of their traditional status. Many in positions of responsibility at Continental tended to think along these lines and numerous processes were very firmly anchored in the corporate culture. Dr. von Grünberg strongly rejected this line of thought viewing these arguments as excuses for avoiding the strain connected with the questioning of given processes and their alteration. Therefore this procedure was internally called 'no-excuse management'.

Dr. von Grünberg, however, preferred to focus on the incentive to look for innovative solutions that would break existing principles as well as habits and themselves define new rules for the market and for internal processes.

> *Dr. von Grünberg was always open to new, radical ideas put forth by the employees.*
>
> (Dr. Bernadette Hausmann, Head of Corporate Purchasing and Strategic Technology)

Parallel to the existing structure, Dr. von Grünberg formed teams that were to overcome the status quo by working on pilot conceptional experiments. Examples of this were the MMP project and the purchasing processes. He gave the affected line positions time to understand the impact of these projects and to become actively involved in the process. After giving those concerned a certain time to accept the new procedures, consequent measures were taken against employees who persistently disregarded the new ideas and refused to get involved in the process of change. In certain cases employees even had to leave the company.

Another key building block for the success of Continental's transformation was that more emphasis was placed on actually implementing changes than on engaging in planning of these changes. Previously planning had enjoyed priority at Continental. Dr. von Grünberg attached greater importance, however, to the actual realization of new concepts and ideas. He ensured this for example by confronting developers with internal customers in the RDE-meetings. But in other areas as well, employees who had developed a new concept were given the job of implementing it. In this way, a stronger link between conception and realization was established.

EXHIBIT 3 MODULAR MANUFACTURING PROCESS (MMP): A NEW PRODUCTION CONCEPT FOR TIRES

The production of tires was traditionally geared to the type of mass production that accommodated the markets' broad demand for similar products. Despite the fact that there still was a sizable market – 10–15% of customers – demanding high product diversity in small lots, production was still organized to high volumes rather than small batches. The goal of the MMP project unveiled in 1997 was to efficiently satisfy this heterogeneous demand by means of a new process that yielded a fit of high product flexibility and low stocktaking ('built-to-order' principle).

The project provoked a great deal of internal resistance, confronting, as it did, most engineers with a fundamental challenge to the aforementioned mass production model. Dr. von Grünberg got around this by setting up a parallel project team. With MMP he succeeded in splitting the production process up into two stages to develop a kind of platform strategy. This put an end to the necessity of manufacturing tires in a continuous process in one factory. Basic tire modules were first manufactured en masse. Final production of limited-volume articles could then be carried out in small factories located in the new target markets.

The project proved successful. The first plant for 'basic modules' was started up in Romania in 2000. It was planned to have 15% of car tire production made in MMP plants by 2003, covering 60% of the product spectrum.

Dr. von Grünberg himself provided a living example of rigorous orientation to implementation of strategic decisions. Departing from the way things had traditionally been done at Continental, he pushed through unpopular decisions in the face of considerable internal opposition. Examples of this were the closure of the Dublin plant and the transfer of production capacities from Traiskirchen, Austria, to the low wage plant in Otrokovice, Czech Republic.

Appointing 'entrepreneurs' to key positions

One effect of Dr. von Grünberg's policies was that the personnel structure reflected the process of change, both by way of dismissals and in the form of enhanced career opportunities. Managers – even Board members – who did not adhere to the new entrepreneurial requirements were let go. Examples of this were the departure of Günter H. Sieber, Board member for the passenger cars/marketing and tire sales area in 1993 and Klaus-Dieter Röker's removal from the post of Board member in charge of commercial vehicle tires, research and environment in 1997. Responsibility for profit and loss thus manifested itself in negative and positive personnel consequences.

Dr. von Grünberg employed sanctioning with a persistence and to an extent previously unknown at the company. Above all the dismissal of managers who failed to deliver had a shock effect for Continental, which had been more accustomed to a consensus-oriented corporate culture. This really shook up the company.
(Dr. Bernadette Hausmann, Head of Corporate Purchasing and Strategic Technology)

At the same time, the personnel policy offered major chances for young, venturesome managers who accepted and exemplified the new entrepreneurial mindset. Dr. von Grünberg took the risk and entrusted young senior executives with tasks, authority and responsibility.

Via tailored departments, he brought young managers into 'combat-like' situations and pushed them to the utmost limits of their performance capability.
(Heinrich Huinink, Head of Strategic Technology)

To provide a living example of entrepreneurship, Dr. von Grünberg himself took over operative responsibility for the car tire division early in 1996, exercising this function alongside that of Board chairman.

Dr. von Grünberg was of the opinion that a living example of entrepreneurial action was the best way to let employees know what was expected of them. Those who adhered to this

EXHIBIT 4   DISMISSAL OF MANAGERS AS A RADICAL BREAK IN CORPORATE CULTURE

General Tire, Continental's US-American tire subsidiary, was incurring huge losses as a result of obsolete production structures and poor market positioning. To revitalize the company, General Tire was reorganized as an independent decentralized Board area and provided with a large scope of entrepreneurial freedom. In spite of this, Board member Alan Ockene still did not manage to achieve the turnaround demanded. And so the company dismissed Ockene on December 31, 1994, downgraded GT to only a division under the management of an officer with full powers to act on behalf of the corporation (general power of attorney) and bound GT closely to the systems and R&D in Europe ('transatlantic union'). Following the successful development of the division under Bernd Frangenberg, General Tire 1998 was reinstated as a separate Board area.

---

style were allowed an extremely high degree of freedom in their positions.

(Klaus Friedland, Board member in charge of Finance, Controlling, Human Resources and Law)

Proving oneself in difficult situations formed the basis for a fast promotion to important leadership positions in the corporation. In this way Dr. von Grünberg consciously bypassed the established routes for promotion and assigned concrete crisis areas to young senior executives. So, in January 1995, Dr. Bernadette Hausmann, just 34 at the time, was appointed head of Corporate Purchasing and Procurement Strategy. In April 1997 she was made manager with general power of attorney and additionally given responsibility for strategic tire technology, and thus for Continental's central technological competence. In 1995 Dr. Stephan Kessel was just 42 when he was put in charge of cutting losses and reorienting the original equipment business. In April 1997, he was appointed Board member for Commercial Tires, in which position he was charged with bringing about a turnaround in the division.

Developing entrepreneurial competencies

A key task for the human resources department was to identify those young executives who were able and willing to get involved in the progress of the corporation. To promote the entrepreneurial development of young managers it was also necessary to transfer competence for the innovative handling of processes of change.

The premise of our work was and is that change cannot be achieved by management decision or per order. We as a corporation can, however, lay the groundwork for change in the human resources department. We have to find employees with a high tolerance for ambiguity, as this quality is needed in initiating change and dealing with it. For the selection of these key people we worked out the 'Big 6' for Continental. It encompasses the requirements for managers generally and for processes of change in particular. Our criteria for competence are: Knowledge, learning, capability for change, drive, interaction and vision

(Wolf-Dieter Gogoll, Head of Corporate Human Resources until 2000)

For about ten years, management development ran a Junior Management Training Program (JMTP) intended to promote the qualities expected of managers, namely the ability to challenge the status quo, on the one hand, and the capability to get things done, on the other hand. Young executives with a very high performance and potential rating were given a business puzzle to work on, alongside their regular tasks. Over a period of seven months they were expected to develop a concept and an implementation strategy. To assure that there was a real problem pressure as well as a clear 'customer' for their solutions the topics for the business puzzles were proposed by the Executive Board and senior executives of other business units. The results were presented in front of the 85 top managers and the full Board so that an immediate project commitment could be issued, where appropriate, and implementation could get under way immediately.

EXHIBIT 5 RUBBER 'LIFTING BELTS' AS A PRODUCT OF COORDINATED CORPORATE ENTREPRENEURSHIP

An example of a successful entrepreneurial initiative and business idea worked out at one of these development programs was the proposal to operate lifts with rubber 'lifting belts' instead of steel cables. Overcoming internal resistance a group of program members followed their idea consequently and it proved possible to sell this idea to ContiTech Antriebssysteme (drive systems) in Dannenberg. After gathering initial project results, the Dannenberg plant became development partner to the US elevator manufacturer, Otis, the world's leading company in this sector, which was working on the same idea. A new generation of elevators was jointly developed through to production readiness. The new elevators have no machine room, smaller drive motors and require minimum maintenance. In the meantime the products are already in use and ContiTech has netted a supply contract for around four million meters of belting a year.

Future challenges for Continental AG in 2001

When Dr. von Grünberg took over the chairmanship of Continental's Executive Board in 1991, the company was very strained economically. After the year's profit plunged again in 1993, to just €33.3 million, the reorientation that had been initiated finally began to pay off. Entrepreneurially driven managers in key positions, the company's innovative capabilities and its new strategic position helped increase profit in the following years (see Table 1). In 1998 all divisions contributed positively to corporate earnings. In 1998 commercial vehicle operations ended the year in the black for the first time since the founding of the division in 1992. The overall profit for the year came to €138.6 million, with an annual rate of return after taxes of 3.1%.

When the Board chairmanship passed to Dr. Stephan Kessel on June 1, 1999, Continental was a healthy, highly profitable company well placed in a new market. It had accomplished an important step in its transformation to a corporation with an entrepreneurial mindset.

However, Continental was aware that the process of change was not yet completed. Continental was called upon to prove itself in generating prerequisites for sustained corporate renewal. In fact, maintaining the then liberated entrepreneurial energy was seen as a key task of the new CEO. More precisely, Dr. Kessel saw his challenge in terms of the basic new cultural maxim. It involved managers constantly questioning the status quo in an entrepreneurial manner and accepting the change process as an ongoing personal task.

Stretch in the core area of competence – chassis systems

In 2001 Continental found itself immersed in the concrete implementation of its sustainable strategic reorientation to an automotive industry systems supplier.

The company evolved from a manufacturer of outstanding products to a specialist for automotive chassis. It did this by bundling its know-how in the area of tires, tire sensors, brakes and suspension systems.

(Dr. Stephan Kessel, Chairman of the Executive Board of Continental AG)

By establishing chassis systems as core competence, it targeted the systems supply business as its prime growth market.

Electronics make up about 15 to 17 percent of the value of a standard-size vehicle. The general estimate is that in five years time this will have increased to 35 to 40 percent.

(Dr. Stephan Kessel)

To take advantage of this growth market and to expand its competitive position with a lasting effect, it was necessary to maintain employees' ongoing innovative activities and profit orientation.

Integrating tires and chassis components

A seminal point of the future strategy was the expansion of the Automotive Systems division through realization of further synergies to be derived from the collaboration of Continental Teves with the tire divisions. Hence it was necessary that managers and the workforce developed an awareness of the win-win situation available to truly realize a joint, cross-functional identity as chassis specialist. The introduction and, above all, the implementation of a new policy – the so-called BASICS – provided the sustainable framework for this (see Exhibit 7).

The primary goal of the BASICS is to create value. That is not necessarily anything new. The difference is that we want to create value that benefits all of our stakeholders. In other words, our shareholders and owners, our customers and employees and, last but not least, the general public as well. To this end we have developed the clear targets enunciated in the BASICS.

(Dr. Stephan Kessel)

Dr. Kessel initiated a company wide balanced scorecard process for the purpose of firmly establishing these guidelines within Continental. He involved a great number of managers in this strategic process of integrating the various corporate competencies. At workshops and with the support of internal multiplicators, a balanced scorecard was prepared for each business unit as well as for the indirect service areas. The scorecard was aligned to the prevailing policy – in other words, to the strategic reorientation – and was to be reviewed annually. Having each unit work through the BASICS each year the global strategic understanding and the cross-functional entrepreneurial thinking of managers and employees increased. Furthermore, the company wide use of the balanced scorecard provided a better handling of corporate divisions using fewer performance figures. This was of value as control information and allowed for fast responses.

Alongside these processes, the success of joint technology-driven projects played a crucial role, first in realizing the synergies envisioned from collaboration between the tire divisions and Automotive Systems, and second in gaining a technological edge on competition. The newly founded Strategic Technology unit played an important role in this regard.

The demand on the newly founded corporate unit Strategic Technology embodied in exemplary fashion the corporation's altered way of thinking. The collaboration between the four products and research areas – tires, chassis, brakes and technical products – is to be guaranteed by means of profit- and action-oriented networking. This is a perfect example of the company's reorientation to a systems supplier. The objective is system optimization rather than optimization of several individual components from various divisions. This unit

---

EXHIBIT 6   STRATEGIC POSITION AS SYSTEMS SUPPLIER TO THE AUTOMOTIVE INDUSTRY

As a systems supplier, Continental had to avoid ending up in the same type of position it found itself in as a tire manufacturer.

In the tire business we were no. 4 and our chances of surviving were seen as meager. With our reorientation and the acquisition of Teves, we captured the no. 9 slot worldwide among automotive industry suppliers. We had, to be sure, also achieved competence in the combination of tires, chassis and electronics that could not yet be copied

(Axel Witt, Head of Corporate Human Resources, Development & Internal Consulting)

The Teves acquisition and the reorientation brought Continental into a new market. With sales of €9 billion it lagged behind its key competitors in the supplier sector, however (see also Table 3). For this reason it was crucial for Continental to maintain price leadership by further innovative development of those products and systems that provide sales and profit. By marketing innovative products not yet offered by competitors Continental expected to escape downward price pressure. The company also moved ahead with further globalization so as to quickly realize advantages in new markets and in the immediate vicinity of automotive industry plants.

EXHIBIT 7 BASICS: THE NEW CONTINENTAL POLICY

OUR TASK: SHAPE CONTINENTAL TOGETHER

Our Vision

- **We make individual mobility safer and more comfortable**.
  Thanks to our core competence, our products and our services, we, together with our customers, improve the safety, comfort and fun of driving.

- **We will be the global technology leader in all our business areas**.
  As international manufacturer of components, modules and systems, we are a backbone of the global automotive industry, setting standards worldwide and helping vehicle manufacturers to fulfill their product promises.

Overall Focus – Value Creation

- **Value creation is a central management task**.
  In the interest of the entire corporation and our stakeholders, we will pursue every opportunity to create value.

Focus – Stakeholders

- **Our obligation to all involved** – Getting things done alone is history.

- **Customer and market orientation** – We aim to delight our customers.

- **Shareholder value** – Our goal is creating value.

- **With and for our employees** – Our employees make Continental strong.

- **Social responsibility** – We stand by our social responsibility.

- **The environment** – We are committed to environmental protection.

- **Partnerships** – We believe in partnerships.

- **Suppliers** – We appreciate the contributions of our suppliers.

Focus – Products and Services

- **Superior technology and services** – We will be the best.

- **Technology leadership and innovation** – Technology is our passion.

- **Quality without compromise** – We set market standards.

Focus – Corporate Spirit

- **A culture of high performance** – Our culture rewards excellence.

- **Striving for the best** – Only the best is good enough.

- **Cooperation and teamwork** – We cooperate with each other.

- **Responsibility and management** – Everybody must be accountable for his or her action.

- **Learning and knowledge management** – Competitive advantages is based on knowledge.

---

ensures, moreover, the leading position in terms of technological innovation and allows the corporation to be a trendsetter rather than just a fast follower. The upshot of this was not only incremental improvements but also technological shakeups that provided the impetus for product development.

(Heinrich Huinink, Head of Strategic Technology)

The specific implementation took the form of the cross-divisional '30-meter car' and 'global chassis control' projects. The '30-meter car' project stands for the goal of optimizing the interplay of tires and chassis electronics to such an extent that a car traveling at 100 km/h comes to a full stop in thirty-meters. The 'global chassis control' project takes on the overall architecture of the chassis to interlink all components synergistically and without frictions.

Maintaining entrepreneurial energy

In 2001 Continental saw itself constrained to further maintain the once achieved awareness for ongoing extraordinary change and entrepreneurial activities it had nurtured.

Up to the beginning of the '90s, Continental tended to shake off any pressure to change. The development introduced in the early '90s brought about a more global awareness of change. This awareness is now borne by the entire company.

(Klaus Friedland, Board member in
charge of Finance, Controlling,
Human Resources and Law)

The question that concerned the company was how long an organization and its members can summon up the energy needed for new processes of change and thus for extreme situations. An important source of energy was Continental's experience that the corporation was capable, for the most part, of relying on its own resources to effect change. A successful pattern took shape that was characterized by blunt exposure of the company's weaknesses, development of its strengths, and buildup of new possibilities in the light of a new product philosophy and the potential of entrepreneurial managers and employees.

A major step in the future may be that of quickly putting managers in decision-making situations with regard to their work processes. This makes it possible to arrive at positive or negative decisions early on. Significant steps can be made in this direction by continuously turning away from 'hypercaution' in the company's activities and by nurturing an even more assertive willingness to take risks in business. We need this in order to keep going.

(Dr. Stephan Kessel)

The comeback of Caterpillar, 1985–2001

By Isaac Cohen[1]

For three consecutive years, 1982, 1983, and 1984, the Caterpillar Company lost one million dollars a day. Caterpillar's major competitor was a formidable Japanese company called Komatsu. Facing a tough global challenge, the collapse of its international markets, and an overvalued dollar, Caterpillar had no choice. It had to reinvent itself, or die.

Caterpillar managed to come back as a high-tech, globally competitive, growth company. Over a period of 15 years, and throughout the tenure of two CEOs – George Schaefer (1985–1990) and Donald Fites (1990–1999) – Caterpillar had transformed itself. George Schaefer introduced cost-cutting measures and employee involvement programs, outsourced machines, parts, and components, and began modernizing Caterpillar's plants. Donald Fites diversified Caterpillar's product line and reorganized the company structurally. He also completed Caterpillar's plant modernization program, revitalized Caterpillar's dealership network, and altered radically Caterpillar's approach to labor relations.

As Donald Fites retired in February 1999, Glen Barton was elected CEO. Barton was in an enviable position. The world's largest manufacturer of construction and mining equipment, and a Fortune 100 company, Caterpillar generated 21 billion dollars in revenues in 1998, the sixth consecutive record year. Leading its industry while competing globally, Caterpillar recorded a $1.5 billion profit in 1998, the second best ever.

Notwithstanding Caterpillar's dramatic comeback, Barton could not count on the continual prosperity of the company because the US construction industry was moving into a grinding economic downturn. At the time Barton completed his first year as CEO, on February 1, 2000, the company announced its 1999 result: sales declined by 6 percent and earnings by 37 percent. In March 2000,

Caterpillar share price was trading close to its 52 week low ($36 against a high of $66) and one industry analyst declared: 'The stock for the foreseeable future is dead money.'[2]

What should Barton do? Should Barton follow the strategies implemented by Schaefer and Fites to enhance Caterpillar's competitive position relative to its principal rivals, Komatsu, John Deere, and CNH Global (CNH is the product of a 2000 merger between Case Corp. and New Holland)? Should he, instead, reverse some of the policies introduced by his predecessors? Or should he, rather, undertake whole new strategies altogether?

To assess Barton's strategic choices in improving Caterpillar's results, the case looks back at the experience of his two predecessors. How precisely did both Schaefer and Fites manage to turn Caterpillar around?

The heavy construction equipment industry

The heavy construction equipment industry supplied engineering firms, construction companies, and mine operators. The industry's typical product line included earthmovers (bulldozers, loaders, and excavators), road building machines (pavers, motor graders, and mixers), mining related equipment (off-highway trucks, mining shovels), and large cranes. Most machines were offered in a broad range of sizes, and a few were available with a choice of wheels or crawler tracks. Most were used for the construction of buildings, power plants, manufacturing plants, and infra-structure projects such as roads, airports, bridges, tunnels, dams, sewage systems, and water lines. On a global basis, earthmoving equipment accounted for about half of the industry's total sales in the 1990s (Table 1). Among earthmovers,

[1]Source: This case was presented at the October 2001 Meeting of the North American Case Research Association (NACRA) at Memphis, Tennessee. Copyright by Isaac Cohen and NACRA. Reprinted with permission. All rights reserved.
[2]Michael Arndt, 'This Cat Isn't so Nimble,' *Business Week*, February 21, 2000. Start p. 148. Online. Lexis-Nexis. Academic Universe; Mark Tatge, 'Caterpillar's Truck-Engine Sales May Hit Some Breaking', *Wall Street Journal*, March 13, 2000.

hydraulic excavators accounted for 45 percent of the sales. Excavators were more productive, more versatile, and easier to use in tight spaces than either bulldozers or loaders. Off-highway trucks that hauled minerals, rocks, and dirt, were another category of fast selling equipment.[3]

Global demand for heavy construction machinery grew at a steady rate of 4.5 percent in the 1990s. The rate of growth, however, was faster among the developing nations of Asia, Africa, and Latin America than among the developed nations. In the early 2000s, North America and Europe were each expected to account for 25 percent of the industry's sales, Japan for 20 percent, and the developing nations for the remaining 30 percent.[4]

The distinction between original equipment and replacement parts was an essential feature of the industry. Replacement parts and 'attachments' (work tools) made up together over a quarter of the total revenues of the heavy construction equipment industry (Table 1), but accounted for a substantially larger share of the industry's earnings for two reasons: first, the sale of replacement parts was more profitable than that of whole machines; and second, the market for replacement parts was less cyclical than that for original equipment.[5] As a rule of thumb, the economic life of a heavy construction machine was 10 to 12 years, but in many cases, especially in developing countries, equipment users kept their machines in service much longer, perhaps 20 to 30 years, thus creating an ongoing stream of revenues for parts, components, and related services.[6]

Another characteristic of the industry was the need to achieve economies of scale. According to industry observers, the optimal scale of operation was about 90,000 units annually. In other words, up to a production level of 90,000 units a year, average equipment unit cost declined as output increased, and therefore capturing a large market share was critical for benefiting from economies of scale.[7] The relatively low volume of global sales – 200,000 to 300,000 earthmoving equipment units per year (1996)[8] – further intensified competition over market share among the industry's leading firms.

Successful marketing also played an important role in gaining competitive advantage. A widespread distribution service network had always been essential for competing in the heavy construction equipment industry because 'downtime' resulting from the inability to operate the equipment at a construction site was very costly. Typically, manufacturers used a worldwide network of dealerships to sell machines, provide support, and offer after sales service. Dealerships were

TABLE 1 Global demand of heavy construction equipment by major categories, 1985–2005

Percentage of total demand	1985	1994	2000	2005*
Earthmoving Equipment	50	49	49	49
Off Highway Trucks	8	7	7	7
Construction Cranes	9	11	10	10
Mixers, Pavers, and Related Equipment	6	6	7	7
Parts & Attachments	27	27	27	26
Total Demand (billions of US $)	38	56	72	90

*Percentages do not add up to 100 because of rounding.
Source: Andrew Gross and David Weiss, 'Industry Corner: The Global Demand for Heavy Construction Equipment,' *Business Economics*, July 1996, p. 56.

[3]Andrew Gross and David Weiss, 'Industry Corner: The Global Demand for Heavy Construction Equipment,' *Business Economics*, 31:3 (July 1996), pp. 54–55.
[4]Gross and Weiss, 'Industry Corner,' p. 54
[5]Ibid.
[6]Donald Fites, 'Making Your Dealers Your Partners,' *Harvard Business Review*, March–April 1996, p. 85.
[7]U. Srinivasa Rangan, 'Caterpillar Tractor Co.,' in Christopher Bartlett and Sumantra Ghoshal, *Transatlantic Management: Text, Cases, and Readings in Cross Border Management* (Homewood IL: Irwin, 1992), p. 296.
[8]Fites, 'Making Your Dealers Your Partners,' p. 85.

independent, company owned, or both, and were normally organized on an exclusive territorial basis. Since heavy construction machines operated in a tough and inhospitable environment, equipment wore out and broke down frequently, parts needed to be rebuilt or replaced often, and therefore manufacturers placed dealers in close proximity to equipment users, building a global service network that spread all over the world.

Manufacturers built alliances as well. Intense competition over market share drove the industry's top firms to form three types of cooperative agreements. The first were full scale joint ventures to share production. Caterpillar's joint venture with Mitsubishi Heavy Industries was a notable case in point. The second were technology sharing agreements between equipment manufacturers and engine makers to ensure access to the latest engine technology. The joint venture between Komatsu and Cummins Engine, on the one hand, and the Case Corporation and Cummins, on the other, provided two examples. The third type of agreements were technology sharing alliances between major global firms and local manufacturers whereby the former gained access to new markets, and in return, supplied the latter with advanced technology. Caterpillar utilized such an arrangement with Shanghai Diesel in China, and Komatsu did so with the BEML company in India.[9]

History of Caterpillar

At the turn of the century, farmers in California faced a serious problem. Using steam tractors to plow the fine delta land of the San Joaquin valley, California farmers fitted their tractors with large drive wheels to provide support on the moist soil; nevertheless, despite their efforts, the steamer's huge wheels – measuring up to 9 feet high – sank deeply into the soil. In 1904, Benjamin Holt, a combine maker from Stockton California, solved the problem by spreading weight on a broader surface. Holt, in addition, replaced the heavy steam engine with a gasoline engine, thus improving the tractor's mobil-

ity further by reducing its weight (a steam tractor weighed up to 20 tons). He nicknamed the tractor 'Caterpillar', acquired the 'Caterpillar' trade mark, and applied it to several crawler-type machines that his company manufactured and sold. By 1915 Holt tractors were sold in 20 countries.[10]

Outside agriculture, crawler tractors were first used by the military. In 1915, the British military invented the armor tank, modeling it after Holt's machine, and during World War I, the United States and its allies in Europe utilized Holt's track-type tractors to haul artillery and supply wagons. In 1925, the Holt Company merged with another California firm, the Best Tractor Company, to form Caterpillar (Cat). Shortly thereafter, Caterpillar moved its corporate headquarters and manufacturing plants to Peoria, Illinois. The first company to introduce a diesel engine on a moving vehicle (1931), Caterpillar discontinued its combine manufacturing during the 1930s and focused instead on the production of road-building, construction, logging, and pipelaying equipment. During World War II, Caterpillar served as the primary supplier of bulldozers to the US Army; its sales volume more than tripled between 1941 and 1944 to include motor graders, diesel engines, and electric generators, apart from tractors and wagons.[11]

Demand for Caterpillar products exploded in the early post-war years. Cat's equipment was used to reconstruct Europe, build the US interstate highway system, erect the giant dams of the Third World, and lay out the major airports of the world. The company managed to differentiate itself from its competitors by producing reliable, durable and high quality equipment, offering quick after-sales service, and providing a speedy delivery of replacement parts. As a result, during the 1950s and 1960s, Caterpillar had emerged as the uncontested leader of the heavy construction equipment industry, far ahead of any rival. By 1965, Caterpillar had established foreign manufacturing subsidiaries – either wholly owned or joint ventures – in Britain, Canada, Australia, Brazil, France, Mexico, Belgium, India, and Japan. Caterpillar's 50/50 joint venture with Mitsubishi in Japan, established in 1963, had become one of the

[9]Gross and Weiss, 'Industry Corner,' p. 58.
[10]William L. Naumann, *The Story of Caterpillar Tractor Co.* (New York: the Newcomen Society, 1997), pp. 7–9.
[11]'Caterpillar Inc.,' *Hoover's Handbook of American Business 1999* (Austin: Hoover Business Press, 1999), p. 328; 'The Story of Caterpillar,' Online. Caterpillar.Com. Retrieved March 9, 2000.

most successful, stable, and enduring alliances among all American-Japanese joint ventures.[12]

Caterpillar's distribution and dealership network also contributed to the company's worldwide success. From the outset, the company's marketing organization rested on a dense network of independent dealers who sold and serviced Cat equipment. Strategically located throughout the world, these dealers were self sustaining entrepreneurs who invested their own capital in their business, derived close to 100 percent of their revenues from selling and supporting Cat equipment, and cultivated close relationships with Caterpillar customers. On average, a Caterpillar dealership had remained in the hands of the same family – or company – for over 50 years. Indeed, some dealerships, including several located overseas, predated the 1925 merger that gave birth to Caterpillar.[13] In 1981, on the eve of the impending crisis, the combined net worth of Cat dealers equaled that of the company itself, the total number of employees working for Cat dealers was slightly lower than the company's own workforce.[14]

The crisis of the early 1980s

Facing weak competition both at home and abroad, Caterpillar charged premium prices for its high quality products, paid its production workers, union-scale wages, offered its shareholders high rates of return on their equity, and enjoyed superior profits. Then, in 1982, following a record year of sales and profits, Caterpillar suddenly plunged into three successive years of rising losses totaling nearly 1 $billion. 'Quite frankly, our long years of success made us complacent, even arrogant,'[15] Pierre Guerindon, an executive vice president at Cat conceded.

The crisis of 1982–84 stemmed from three sources, a global recession, a costly strike, and unfavorable currency exchange rates. First, the steady growth in demand for construction machinery, dating back to 1945, came to an end in 1980, as highway construction in the US slowed down to a halt while declining oil prices depressed the world-wide market for mining, logging, and pipelaying equipment. Second, Caterpillar's efforts to freeze wages and reduce overall labor cost triggered a seven month strike (1982–83) among its US employees, led by the United Auto Workers (UAW) union, the strike accounted for a sizable portion of the company's three year loss. The third element in Caterpillar's crisis was a steep rise in the value of the dollar (relative to the Yen and other currencies) that made US exports more expensive abroad, and US imports (shipped by Caterpillar's competitors) cheaper at home. 'The strong dollar is a prime factor in Caterpillar's reduced sales and earnings . . . [and] is undermining manufacturing industries in the United States,'[16] said Cat's annual reports for 1982 and 1984.

Taking advantage of the expensive dollar, Komatsu Limited had emerged as Caterpillar's principal rival. Komatsu ('little pine tree' in Japanese) had initially produced construction machinery for the Japanese and Asian markets, then sought to challenge Caterpillar's dominance in the markets of Latin America and Europe, and eventually penetrated the United States to rival Caterpillar in its domestic market. Attacking Caterpillar head-on, Komatsu issued a battle cry, 'Maru C,' meaning 'encircle Cat.' Launching a massive drive to improve quality while reducing costs, Komatsu achieved a 50 percent labor productivity advantage over Caterpillar, and in turn, underpriced Caterpillar's products by as much as 30 percent. The outcome was a dramatic change in market share. Between 1979 and 1984 Komatsu global market share more than doubled to 25 percent while Caterpillar's fell by almost a quarter to 43 percent.[17]

[12]Michael Yoshino and U. Srinivasa Rangan, *Strategic Alliances: An Entrepreneurial Approach to Globalization* (Boston: Harvard Business School Press, 1995), p. 93; Naumann, 'Story of Caterpillar,' pp. 12–14; William Haycraft, *Yellow Power: The Story of the Earthmoving Equipment Industry* (Urbana, Illinois: University of Illinois Press, 2000), pp. 118–122, 159–167, 196–203.

[13]Fites, 'Making Your Dealers Your Partners,' p. 94.

[14]Rangan, 'Caterpillar Tractor Co.,' p. 304; James Risen, 'Caterpillar: A Test of U.S. Trade Policy,' *Los Angeles Times*, June 8, 1986, Online. Lexis-Nexis, Academic Universe.

[15]Cited in Kathleen Deveny, 'For Caterpillar, the Metamorphosis Isn't Over,' *Business Week*, August 31, 1987, p. 72.

[16]Cited in Dexter Hutchins, 'Caterpillar's Triple Whammy,' *Fortune*, October 27, 1986, p. 91. See also Robert Eckley, 'Caterpillar's Ordeal: Foreign Competition in Capital Goods,' *Business Horizons*, March–April 1989, pp. 81–83.

[17]James Abegglen and George Stalk, *Kaisha, the Japanese Corporation* (New York: Basic Books, 1985), pp. 62, 117–118; Yoshino and Rangan, *Strategic Alliances*, pp. 94–95; 'Komatsu Ltd.,' *Hoover's Handbook of World Business*, 1999, p. 320.

Turnaround: George Schaefer's Caterpillar, 1985–1990

Competition with Komatsu and the crisis of 1982–84 forced Caterpillar to reexamine its past activities. Caterpillar's new CEO (1985), George Schaefer, was a congenial manager who encouraged Cat executives to openly admit the company's past mistakes. 'We have experienced a fundamental change in our business – it will never again be what it was,' Schaefer said as he became CEO. 'We have no choice but to respond, and respond vigorously, to the new world in which we find ourselves.'[18] Under Schaefer's direction, Caterpillar devised and implemented a series of strategies that touched upon every important function of the company, including purchasing, manufacturing, marketing, personnel, and labor relations.

Global outsourcing

Traditionally, Caterpillar functioned as a vertically integrated company that relied heavily on in-house production. To ensure product quality as well as an uninterrupted supply of parts, Cat self-produced two-thirds of its parts and components, and assembled practically all of its finished machines. Under the new policy of 'shopping around the world,' Caterpillar sought to purchase parts and components from low-cost suppliers who maintained high quality standards. Working closely with its suppliers, Caterpillar moved towards the goal of outsourcing 80 percent of its parts and components.[19]

An additional goal of the policy was branding, that is, the purchase of final products for resale. Through its branding program, Caterpillar sold outsourced machines under its own brand name, taking advantage of its superior marketing organization, and keeping production costs down. Beginning in the mid 1980s, Cat contracted to buy lift trucks from a Norwegian company, hydraulic excavators from a West German manufacturer, paving machines from an Oklahoma corporation, off-highway trucks from a British firm, and logging equipment from a Canadian company, and resell them all under the Cat nameplate. Ordinarily, Caterpillar out-sourced product manufac-turing but not product design. By keeping control over the design of many of its out-sourced products, Caterpillar managed to retain in-house design capability, and ensure quality control.[20]

Broader product line

For nearly a decade, the DC10 bulldozer had served as Caterpillar's signature item. It stood 15 feet tall, weighed 73 tons, and sold for more than $500,000 (1988). It had no competitors. But as demand for highway construction projects dwindled, Caterpillar needed to reevaluate its product mix because heavy equipment was no longer selling well. Sales of light construction equipment, on the other hand, were fast increasing. Between 1984 and 1987, accordingly, Caterpillar doubled its product line from 150 to 300 models of equipment, introducing many small machines that ranged from farm tractors to backhoe loaders (multi-purpose light bulldozers), and diversified its customer base. Rather than focusing solely on large clients, i.e. multinational engineering and construction firms like the Bechtel corporation – a typical user of heavy bulldozers – Cat began marketing its light-weight machines to a new category of customers: small-scale owner operators and emerging contractors. Still, the shift in Cat's product mix had a clear impact on the company's bottom line. Unlike the heavy equipment market where profit margins were wide, intense competition in the market for light products kept margins slim and pitted Caterpillar against John Deere and the Case corporation, the light equipment market leaders.[21]

Labor relations

To compete successfully, Caterpillar also needed to repair its relationship with the union. In 1979, following the expiration of its collective bargaining agreement, Caterpillar experienced an 80 days strike, and three years later, in 1982, contract negotiations erupted in a 205 days strike, the longest company-wide work stoppage in the UAW history.[22] Named CEO in 1985, George Schaefer led the next two rounds of contract negotiations.

[18]Quoted in Yoshino and Rangan, *Strategic Alliances*, p. 96.
[19]Yoshino and Rangan, *Strategic Alliances*, p. 97; Eckley, 'Caterpillar's Ordeal,' p. 84.
[20]Eckley, 'Caterpillar's Ordeal,' p. 84; *Business Week*, August 31, 1987, p. 73; Yoshino and Rangan, *Strategic Alliances*, p. 97.
[21]Ronald Henkoff, 'This Cat is Acting like a Tiger,' *Fortune*, December 19, 1988, pp. 67, 72, 76; *Business Week*, August 31, 1987, p. 73.
[22]Eckley, 'Caterpillar's Ordeal,' pp. 81, 83.

Schaefer's leadership style was consensual. By contrast to the autocratic style of his predecessors, Schaefer advocated the free flow of ideas between officers, managers, and production workers, and promoted open communication at all levels of the company. A low-key CEO who often answered his own phone, Schaefer possessed exceptional people skills. Asked to evaluate Schaefer's performance, John Stark, editor of *Off Highway Ledger*, a trade journal, said: 'Schaefer is probably the best manager the construction machinery industry has ever had.'[23]

Schaefer's social skills led to a significant improvement in Cat's relations with the UAW. Not a single strike broke out over contract negotiations during Schaefer's tenure; on the contrary, each cycle of bargaining was settled peacefully. Under Schaefer's direction, furthermore, the union agreed to reduce the number of labor grades and job classifications, and to streamline seniority provisions, a move that enhanced management flexibility in job assignment, and facilitated the cross utilization of employees.[24] More important, improved labor relations contributed to the success of two programs that played a critical role in Caterpillar's turnaround strategy, namely, an employee involvement plan based on team work, and a reengineering effort of plant modernization and automation.

Employee involvement

An industry-wide union famous for its cooperative labor-management efforts at the Saturn corporation, the NUMMI plant (a GM-Toyota joint-venture in Fremont California), and elsewhere, the UAW lent its support to Caterpillar's employee involvement program. Called the Employee Satisfaction Process (ESP), and launched by Schaefer in 1986, the program was voluntary. ESP members were organized in work teams, met weekly with management, and offered suggestions that pertained to many critical aspects of the manufacturing process, including production management, workplace layout, and quality enhancement. Implemented in a growing number of

US plants, the program resulted (1990) in productivity gains, quality improvements, and increased employee satisfaction. At the Cat plant in Aurora Illinois, for example, the local ESP chairman recalled: the ESP program 'changed everything: the worker had some say over his job. . . . [and t]op management was very receptive. We zeroed in on quality, anything to make the customer happy.' Management credited the ESP teams at Aurora with a steep fall in the rate of absenteeism, a sharp decline in the number of union grievances filed, and cost savings totaling $10 million.[25] At another ESP plant, a Cat assembly-line worker told a *Fortune* reporter in 1988: 'Five years ago the foreman wouldn't even listen to you, never mind the general foreman or plant supervisor. . . . Now everyone will listen.' Caterpillar applied the ESP program to outside suppliers as well. Typically, ESP teams made up of Caterpillar machinists visited suppliers' plants to check and certify equipment quality. The certified vendors received preferential treatment, mostly in the form of reduced inspection, counting, and other controls. Only 0.6 percent of the parts delivered by certified suppliers were rejected by Caterpillar compared to a reject rate of 2.8 percent for non-certified suppliers.[26]

Plant with a future

Caterpillar's employee involvement plan went hand in hand with a $1.8 billion plant modernization program launched by Schaefer in 1986.[27] Dubbed 'Plant with a Future' (PWAF), the modernization program combined just-in-time inventory techniques, a factory automation scheme, a network of computerized machine tools, and a flexible manufacturing system. Several of these innovations were pioneered by Komatsu late in the 1970s. The industry's technological leader, Komatsu had been the first construction equipment manufacturer to introduce both the just-in-time inventory system, and the 'quick changeover tooling,' technique, a flexible tooling method designed to produce a large variety of equipment models in a single plant.[28]

[23]Quoted in *Fortune*, December 19, 1988, p. 76.
[24]Eckley, 'Caterpillar's Ordeal,' p. 84, *Fortune*, December 19, 1988, p. 76; Alex Kotlowitz, 'Caterpillar Faces Shutdown with UAW,' *Wall Street Journal*, March 5, 1986. Online. ABI data base.
[25]Barry Bearak, 'The Inside Strategy: Less Work and More Play at Cat,' *Los Angeles Times*, May 16, 1995. Online. Lexis-Nexis. Academic Universe.
[26]*Fortune*, December 19, 1988, p. 76.
[27]Brian Bremner, 'Can Caterpillar Inch Its Way Back to Heftier Profits?' *Business Week*, September 25, 1989, p. 75.
[28]Abegglen and Stalk, *Kaisha*, p. 118.

To challenge Komatsu, top executives at Caterpillar did not seek merely to imitate the Japanese. This was not enough. They studied, instead, the modernization efforts of several manufacturing companies, and arrived at two important conclusions: it was necessary 1) to change the layout of an entire plant, not just selected departments within a plant; and 2) to implement the program company-wide, that is, on a global basis both at home and abroad. Implementing such a comprehensive program took longer than expected, however, lasting seven years, four under Schaefer's direction, and three more under the direction of his successor, Donald Fites.[29]

The traditional manufacturing process at Caterpillar known as 'batch' production, was common among US assembly plants in a number of industries. Under batch production, subassembly lines produced components (radiators, hydraulic tanks, etc.) in small lots. Final assembly lines put together complete models, and the entire production system required large inventories of parts and components owing to the high level of 'work in progress' (models being built at any one time). Under batch production, furthermore, assembly tasks were highly specialized, work was monotonous and dull, and workers grew lax and made mistakes. Correcting assembly mistakes, it should be noted, took more time than the assembly process itself because workers needed to disassemble components in order to access problem areas. Parts delivery was also problematic. Occasionally, delays in delivery of parts to the assembly areas forced workers to leave the line in order to locate a missing part. Occasionally, the early arrival of parts before they were needed created its own inefficiencies.[30]

To solve these problems, Caterpillar reconfigured the layout of its manufacturing plants into flexible work 'cells.' Grouped in cells, workers used computerized machine tools to perform several manufacturing steps in sequence, processing components from start to finish and sending them 'just-in-time' to an assembly area, as the following example suggests.

To manufacture steel tractor-tread under the batch production layout, Cat workers were required to cut, drill, and heat-treat steel beams on three distinct assembly lines. Under cellular manufacturing, by contrast, all three operations were carried out automatically in single tractor-tread cells linked together by computers.[31]

Caterpillar, in addition, reduced material handling by means of an automated electrified monorail which delivered parts to storage and assembly areas, traveling on a long aluminum track throughout the modernized plant. When parts arrived at the delivery point, a flash light alerted the assembly line workers, semi-automatic gates (operated by infrared remote control) opened, and a lift lowered the components directly onto an assembly. Don Western, a manufacturing manager at Cat Aurora plant, observed: 'Materials now [1990] arrive at the assembly point only when required – and in the order required. At most, we hold about a 4 hour supply of large parts and components on the line.'[32]

Caterpillar, finally, improved product quality. Formerly, components moved down the assembly line continuously, not intermittently, and therefore workers were unable to respond quickly to quality problems. Managers alone controlled the speed of the line. Under the new assembly plan, on the other hand, components moved automatically between work areas and remained stationary during the actual assembly operation. More important, under the PWAF plan, managers empowered production workers to change the speed of the assembly line at will, granting them the flexibility necessary to resolve quality and safety problems.[33]

The PWAF program resulted in productivity and quality gains across the board in many of Caterpillar's plants. At the Aurora plant in Illinois, for instance, factory workers managed to reduce the assembly process time four-fold, building and shipping a customer order in four rather than 16 days, and cutting product defects by one-half in four years (1986–1990).[34] At the Cat plant in Grenoble, France, to mention another case, workers slashed the time it

[29]*Fortune*, December 19, 1988, pp. 72, 74; *Business Week*, September 25, 1989, p. 75.
[30]Karen Auguston, 'Caterpillar Slashes Lead Times from Weeks to Days,' *Modern Materials Handling*, February 1990, p. 49.
[31]Barbara Dutton, 'Cat Climbs High with FMS,' *Manufacturing Systems*, November 1989, pp. 16–22; *Business Week*, August 31, 1987, p. 73, September 25, 1989, p. 75.
[32]Quoted in Auguston, 'Caterpillar Slashes Lead Times,' p. 49.
[33]Auguston, 'Caterpillar Slashes Lead Times,' pp. 50–51.
[34]Auguston, 'Caterpillar Slashes Lead Times,' pp. 49, 51.

took to assemble machinery parts from 20 to 8 days in three years (1986–1989). Company wide changes were equally impressive: collectively, Caterpillar's 30 worldwide plants cut inventory levels by 50 percent and manufacturing space by 21 percent in three years.[35]

Looking back at Schaefer's five year-long tenure, Caterpillar had reemerged as a globally competitive company, lean, flexible, and technologically advanced. Caterpillar's world market share rebounded from 43 percent to 50 percent (1984–1990),[36] revenues increased by 66 percent (1985–1989), and the company was profitable once again. As Caterpillar prospered, Komatsu was retrenching. In 1989, Caterpillar's sales totaled over $11 billion or nearly twice the sales reported by Komatsu, Caterpillar's profit margins exceeded Komatsu's, and the gap between the two companies – in terms of both market share and income on sales – was growing (Table 2).

TABLE 2   Caterpillar versus Komatsu

	CAT		KOMATSU	
	Sales ($Bil.)	Income as % of sales	Sales ($Bil.)	Income as % of sales
1985	6.7	2.9	____*	1.8
1986	7.3	1.0	____*	2.8
1987	8.2	3.9	5.1	1.3
1988	10.4	5.9	6.2	0.4
1989	11.1	4.5	6.0	2.6

*Sales are available only in Yen (1985, 796 billion Yen; 1986, 789 billion Yen).
Source: For Caterpillar, *Hoover's Handbook of American Business*, 1995, p. 329; For Komatsu, *Hoover's Handbook of World Business*, 1995–96, p. 291.

The transformation continued: Donald Fites' Caterpillar, 1990–1999

Notwithstanding Schaefer's achievements, the transformation of Caterpillar was far from over. For one thing, the company stock lagged far behind its earnings. Cat shares underperformed the S&P 500 index by over 50 percent for five years (1987–1992).[37] For another, Caterpillar was facing an industry-wide downturn in both its domestic and international markets. Partly as a result of the cyclical nature of the construction equipment industry, and also as a result of an increase in the value of the dollar (a weak dollar in the late 1980s helped Caterpillar's foreign sales), Caterpillar revenues and profits fell. During the two years following Schaefer's retirement, the company actually lost money.

Replacing Schaefer in the winter of 1990, Donald Fites viewed Caterpillar's financial troubles as an opportunity to introduce change: 'I certainly didn't count on . . . [a] recession . . . but [the recession] made it easier to accept the fact that we needed to change.'[38] 'It's hard to change an organization when you're making record profits.'[39]

Leadership

Fites' leadership style stood in a stark contrast to Schaefer's. 'George was . . . a consensus builder' while '[Don] expects people to challenge him forcefully,'[40] one Cat executive said, and another (former Cat CEO Lee Morgan) described Fites as 'one of the most determined men I've ever met.'[41] Fites was a hard line executive, feared by his subordinates, respected by his peers, and cheered by Wall Street. An imposing man standing six feet five, Fites led by explicit command rather than persuasion, asserted the company's 'right to manage' in face of mounting union opposition, and did not hesitate to cut thousands of management and production jobs at a stroke.

---

[35]*Business Week*, September 25, 1989, p. 75.
[36]Yoshino and Rangan, *Strategic Alliances*, p. 98.
[37]Jennifer Reingold, 'CEO of the Year,' *Financial World*, March 28, 1995, p. 68.
[38]Quoted in 'An Interview with Caterpillar Inc. Chairman and CEO Donald V. Fites,' *Inter-Business Issues*, December 1992, p. 32.
[39]Quoted in Tracy Benson, 'Caterpillar Wakes Up,' *Industry Week*, May 20, 1991, p. 36.
[40]Quoted in Reingold, 'CEO of the Year,' p. 74.
[41]Quoted in Kevin Kelly, 'Caterpillar's Don Fites: Why He Didn't Blink,' *Business Week*, August 10, 1992, p. 56.

The son of a subsistence corn farmer, Fites had joined Caterpillar in 1956, rising through the ranks, and spending 16 years overseas. A career marketer, he worked for Cat in South Africa, Germany, Switzerland, Brazil, Japan, and other countries. In 1971, Fites had earned an MBA from MIT, writing a thesis entitled 'Japan Inc.: Can US Industry Compete?' and soon thereafter, he received an assignment in Japan, serving nearly five years as the marketing director of Caterpillar-Mitsubishi joint venture. Fites' Japanese experience resonated throughout the remainder of his career. He was impressed, first of all, by the ways in which the Japanese trained their managers, rotating executives through functional departments in order to educate them in all aspects of the business. Returning from Japan to Peoria in the mid 1970s, Fites revamped Cat's product development process, utilizing an integrated approach based on Japanese-style functional teams. He also admired Japanese labor relations. Historically, American unions had been organized on an industry-wide basis and therefore labor relations in the United States were often adversarial. Trade unions in Japan, by contrast, were company-based organizations, loyal, cooperative, and in Fites' words, 'deeply dedicated to the success of the [firm].'[42] Leading Caterpillar in the 1990s, Fites sought to bring Caterpillar's labor relations closer to the Japanese model.

Reorganization

A marketing manager, Fites was convinced that Caterpillar did not pay sufficient attention to customer needs because global pricing decisions were made at the company's headquarters in Peoria with little knowledge of the local market conditions around the world. In 1985, as he took charge of Cat's worldwide marketing organization, Fites delegated district offices the authority to set prices, thereby pushing responsibility down the chain of command to the lowest possible level. Promoted to President in 1989, Fites applied the same principle to Caterpillar's entire structure, developing a company-wide reorganization plan under Schaefer's direction.[43]

Caterpillar's old organizational structure was archaic. It was a functional structure suitable for a small company that operated just a few plants, all located within the United States. A centralized body with only four primary functions – engineering, manufacturing, marketing, and finance – the old structure served Caterpillar well until World War II, but as the company expanded globally in subsequent decades, the limitations of such a structure had become apparent. First, decisions were made at the top of each functional unit, and executives were reluctant to delegate authority to mid-level or low-level managers. Second, each functional unit tended to focus on its own goal rather than the enterprise's objectives (marketing was preoccupied with market share, engineering with product safety, manufacturing with assembly problems, etc.), making it difficult for top management to coordinate functional goals.[44] And third, the bureaucratization of the decision making process impaired effective communication. Under the old structure, Fites recalled, the flow of information upwards was 'so filtered with various prejudices – particularly functional prejudice[s] – that you didn't know whether you were really looking at the facts or looking at someone's opinion.'[45]

To equip Caterpillar with the flexibility, speed, and agility necessary to operate in the global economy, Fites broke the company into 17 semi-autonomous divisions or 'profit centers,' 13 responsible for products (tractors, engines, etc.), and four for services.[46] He then required each division to post a 15 percent rate of return on assets, and threatened to penalize any division that fell behind. He stood by his words. When Caterpillar's forklift division failed to improve its return on assets in 1992, Fites transferred it into an 80 percent–20 percent joint venture controlled by Mitsubishi.[47]

Caterpillar's new divisional structure facilitated downsizing. Under the new structure, Caterpillar cut 10,000 jobs in three years, 1990–1993 (Table 3). Of the 7,500 employees who lost their jobs between January 1990 and August 1992, 2,000 were salaried

---

[42]Quoted in *Business Week*, August 10, 1992, pp. 56–57.
[43]*Business Week*, August 10, 1992, p. 57.
[44]Quoted in Benson, 'Caterpillar Wakes Up,' p. 32.
[45]'An Interview with Fites,' *Inter-Business Issues*, p. 32.
[46]Benson, 'Caterpillar Wakes Up,' p. 33.
[47]*Business Week*, August 10, 1992, p. 56.

managers and 5,500 hourly workers.[48] As Caterpillar's sales grew from $10 billion to $15 billion in the first half of the 1990s, the number of managers employed by the company fell by 20 percent.[49] In addition, the move from a functional into a divisional structure, coupled with the drive for profit making, brought about a change in the methods of managerial compensation. Traditionally, Cat managers were paid in proportion to the size of the budget they controlled or the number of employees they supervised. Under the new plan, Caterpillar based all its incentive compensation schemes on return on assets.[50] Lastly, Caterpillar decentralized its research and development activities. With each division controlling its own product development programs and funding, R&D activities under the new plan were more customer driven than at any other period in the past.[51]

TABLE 3 Donald Fites' Caterpillar: employment and sales

	Number of employees	Sales ($Bil.)
1990	60,000	11.4
1991	56,000	10.2
1992	52,000	10.2
1993	50,000	11.6
1994	54,000	14.3
1995	54,000	16.1
1996	57,000	16.5
1997	60,000	18.9
1998	64,000	21.0

Source: For 1990–1997, *Hoover's Handbook of American Business*, 1999, p. 329; for 1998, *Caterpillar Inc. 1999 Annual Report*, p. 1.

Marketing and dealerships

Caterpillar's reorganization plan affected the company's distribution network as well. Under the new structure, dealers seeking assistance could contact any of the 17 product and service profit-centers directly, saving time and money; they no longer needed to call the General Office in their search for assistance within the company.[52] The new structure also facilitated a more frequent interaction between Caterpillar's managers and dealers, a development of which resulted in '[v]irtually everyone from the youngest design engineer to the CEO' having 'contact with somebody in [a] dealer organization [wrote Fites].' Ordinarily, low level managers at Caterpillar communicated daily with their counterparts at Cat dealerships; senior corporate executives, several times a week.[53]

Caterpillar's network of dealerships was extensive. In 1999, 207 independent dealers served Caterpillar, 63 of whom were stationed in the US and 144 abroad. The number of employees working for Cat dealers exceeded the company's own workforce (67,000) by nearly one third; the combined net worth of Cat dealers surpassed Caterpillar's stockholders' equity ($5.5 billion)[54] by nearly one quarter (Table 4). Many of Caterpillar's dealerships were privately owned, a few were public companies. On average, the annual sales of a Caterpillar dealership amounted to $150 million (1996); several of the large dealerships, however, generated annual revenues of up to $1 billion.

To Caterpillar, the information relationships between the company and its dealers were far more important than the formal contractual relations. Dealership agreements ran only a few pages, had no expiration date, and allowed each party to terminate the contract at will, following 90-days notice. Notwithstanding the open ended nature of the contract, turnover among Cat dealerships was extremely low. Caterpillar actively encouraged its dealers to keep the business in their families, running seminars on tax issues and succession plans for dealers, holding regular conferences in Peoria for the sons and

[48]J. P. Donlon, 'Heavy Metal,' *Chief Executive*, September 1995, p. 50.
[49]Andrew Zadoks, 'Managing Technology at Caterpillar,' *Research Technology Management*, January 1997, pp. 49–51, Online. Lexis-Nexis, Academic Universe.
[50]*Business Week*, August 10, 1992, p. 56.
[51]Donlon, 'Heavy Metal,' p. 50.
[52]Benson, 'Caterpillar Wakes Up,' p. 36.
[53]Fites, 'Make Your Dealers Your Partners,' p. 93.
[54]*Caterpillar Inc. 1999 Annual Report*, p. 34.

TABLE 4 Caterpillar dealerships, 1999

	Inside U.S.	Outside U.S.	Worldwide
Dealers	63	144	207
Branch Stores	382	1,122	1,504
Employees	34,338	54,370	88,709
Service Bays	6,638	5,529	12,167
Estimated Net Worth (billion US $)	3.22	3.54	6.77

Source: *Caterpillar Inc. 1999 Annual Report*, p. 43.

daughters of 'dealer Principals' (dealership owners), and taking concrete steps to encourage a proper succession from one generation to another.[55]

While Caterpillar had always protected its dealers against failure, under Fites' direction, Caterpillar did so more aggressively than before, assisting individual dealers who were subjected to intense price competition by rival manufacturers. To help a dealer, Caterpillar sometimes offered discounted prices, sometimes helped reduce the dealer's costs, and occasionally launched a promotion campaign in the dealer's service territory, emphasizing the lower lifetime cost of a Cat machine relative to a competitor's. Caterpillar also protected dealers during recessions. Despite the company's losses during the industry slump of 1991–92, Fites' Caterpillar helped vulnerable Cat dealers survive the downturn, stay in the business, and order equipment in advance of the 1993 upturn. Caterpillar's competitors, in contrast, saw several of their dealers go out of business during the recession.[56]

Fites' Caterpillar cooperated with dealers in other ways. During the 1990s, Caterpillar worked together with its dealers to conduct surveys among customers in order to improve customer service and parts delivery. Sending out 90,000 survey forms annually, Cat received a response rate of nearly 40 percent. Through its 'Partners in Quality' program, Caterpillar involved dealers in quality control discussions, linking personnel at Cat plants and dealerships, and sponsoring quarterly meetings. Periodically, Caterpillar invited its entire body of independent dealers to a week long conference in

Peoria to review corporate strategy, manufacturing plants, and marketing policies. A firm believer in strong personal business ties, Fites explained:

Dealers can call me or any senior corporate office at any time, and they do. Virtually any dealer in the world is free to walk in my door: I'll know how much money he made last year and his market position. And I'll know what is happening in his family. I consider the majority of dealers personal friends. Of course, one reason I know the dealers so well is that I rose through our distribution organization.[57]

Caterpillar's worldwide distribution system, according to Fites, was the company's single greatest advantage over its competitors. It was a strategic asset whose importance was expected to grow in the future: '[u]ntil about 2010,' Fites predicted, 'distribution' – that is, after-sales support, product application, and service information – 'will be what separates the winners from the losers in the global economy.'[58] Contrasting American and Japanese manufacturing firms, Fites elaborated:

Although many Japanese companies had the early advantage in manufacturing excellence, US companies may have the edge this time around. . . . [T]hey know more about distribution than anyone else. . . . Quite frankly, distribution traditionally has not been a strength of Japanese companies. Marketing people and salespeople historically have been looked down upon in Japanese society.[59]

[55]Fites, 'Make Your Dealers Your Partners,' pp. 89, 91–92, 94.
[56]Fites, 'Make Your Dealers Your Partners,' pp. 92–93.
[57]Quoted in Fites, 'Make Your Dealers Your Partners,' p. 94, but see also pp. 90, 93.
[58]Quoted in Donlon, 'Heavy Metal,' p. 50.
[59]Quoted in Fites, 'Make Your Dealers Your Partners,' p. 86.

Information technology

Fites' Caterpillar invested generously in expanding and upgrading Caterpillar's worldwide computer network – a system linking together factories, distribution centers, dealers, and large customers. By 1996, the network connected 1,000 locations in 160 countries across 23 time zones, providing Caterpillar with the most comprehensive and fastest part delivery system in the industry. Although Caterpillar had long guaranteed a 48-hours delivery of parts anywhere in the world, by 1996, Cat dealers supplied 80 percent of the parts a customer needed at once; the remaining 20 percent – not stocked by the dealers – was shipped by the company on the same day the parts were ordered. With 22 distribution centers spread all around the world, Caterpillar serviced a total of 500,000 different parts, keeping over 300,000 in stock, and manufacturing the remainder on demand.[60]

A critical element in Caterpillar's drive for technological leadership was an electronic alert information system the company was developing under Fites. The new system was designed to monitor machines remotely, identify parts which needed to be replaced, and replace them before they failed. Once fully operational in the early 2000's, the new IT system was expected first, to help dealers repair machines before they broke down, thereby reducing machine downtime, on the one hand, and saving repair costs, on the other; and second, provide Caterpillar and its dealers with the opportunity to slash their inventory costs. In 1995, the value of the combined inventories held by Caterpillar and its dealers amounted to $2 billion worth of parts.[61]

Diversification

Fites' Caterpillar expanded its sales into farm equipment, forest products, and compact construction machines, introducing new lines of products, one at a time. Between 1991 and 1999, Caterpillar entered a total of 38 mergers and joint venture agreements, many of which contributed to the company's efforts to diversify.[62]

The growth in Caterpillar's engine sales was the company's largest. Caterpillar had traditionally produced engines for internal use only, installing them on Cat machines, but beginning in the mid 1980s, as the company was recovering from its most severe crisis, Cat embarked on a strategy of producing engines for sale to other companies. In 1999, engine sales accounted for 35 percent of Cat's revenues, up from 21 percent in 1990, and Cat engines powered about one-third of the big trucks in the United States. Apart from trucking companies, Caterpillar produced engines for a variety of other customers including petroleum firms, electric utility companies, and shipbuilding concerns. Only 10 percent of the diesel engines manufactured by Caterpillar in 1999 were installed on the company's own equipment.[63]

Two important acquisitions by Caterpillar helped the company compete in the engine market. In 1996, Donald Fites purchased the MaK Company – a German maker of engines for power generation. Partly because governments of developing countries were reluctant to build large power plants, and partly because the utility industry in the United States deregulated and new electrical suppliers entered the market, worldwide demand for generators was fast increasing. The rise in demand helped Caterpillar increase its sales of power generators by 20 percent annually between 1995 and 1999.[64]

Similarly, in 1998, Fites bought Britain's Perkins Engines, a manufacturer of engines for compact construction machinery, for $1.3 billion. The new acquisition contributed to Caterpillar's efforts to increase its share in the small equipment market which was growing at a rate of 10 percent a year. Perkins' best selling engine powered the skid steer loader. A compact wheel tractor operated by one person and capable of maneuvering in tight spaces, the skid dug ditches, moved dirt, broke up asphalt, and performed a wide variety of other tasks.[65]

[60]Myron Magnet, 'The Productivity Payoff Arrives,' *Fortune*, June 27, 1994, pp. 82–83; Benson, 'Caterpillar Wakes Up,' p. 36; Fites, 'Make Your Dealers Your Partners,' pp. 88–89.
[61]Quoted in Steven Prokesch, 'Making Global Connections in Caterpillar,' *Harvard Business Review*, March–April 1996, p. 89, but see also p. 88, and Donlon, 'Heavy Metal,' p. 50.
[62]'Caterpillar's Growth Strategies,' Copyright 1999. Online. Caterpillar.Com.
[63]*Wall Street Journal*, March 13, 2000; David Barboza, 'Aiming for Greener Pastures,' *New York Times*, August 4, 1999.
[64]De'Ann Weimer, 'A New Cat on the Hot Seat,' *Business Week*, March 9, 1998, p. 61; *Wall Street Journal*, March 13, 2000.
[65]*Business Week*, March 9, 1998; *Wall Street Journal*, March 13, 2000.

Labor relations

Perhaps no other areas of management had received more attention than Caterpillar's labor relations under Fites. For nearly seven years, 1991–1998, Fites fought the UAW in what had become the longest U.S. labor dispute in the 1990s. On the one side, a union official described the UAW relationship with Fites as 'the single most contentious . . . in the history of the union;' on the other, a Wall Street analyst called Fites 'the guy who broke the union, pure and simple.'[66]

In part, Fites' opposition to the UAW was ideological: it 'is not so much a battle about economics as it is a battle about who's going to run the company.'[67] Yet economics did matter, and Fites was determined to ensure Caterpillar's global competitiveness by cutting the company's labor cost. His principal target was a UAW 'pattern' agreement, a collective bargaining contract modeled on agreements signed by the UAW and Caterpillar's domestic competitors, John Deere, the Case Corporation, and others (a pattern agreement tied separate labor contracts together so that changes in one led to similar changes in others within the same industry). Fites rejected pattern bargaining because Caterpillar was heavily dependent on the export of domestically manufactured products, selling over 50 percent of its American-made equipment in foreign markets, and thus competing head-to-head with foreign-based, global companies like Komatsu. Cat's US-based competitors, by contract, exported a far smaller proportion of their domestically made goods. Because Cat's global competitors paid lower wages overseas than the wages paid by Cat's American-based competitors at home, Fites argued, Caterpillar could not afford paying the UAW pattern of wages.[68]

The first Caterpillar strike erupted in 1991, at a time when Caterpillar's 17,000 unionized employees were working under a contract. The contract was set to expire on September 30, and Fites was prepared.

He had built up enough inventory to supply customers for six months, giving Cat dealers special incentives to buy and stock parts and equipment in case a strike shut down the company's US plants. Caterpillar's contract offer included three principal demands: no pattern on wages, flexible work schedules, and a two-tier wage system. The union rejected the offer outright and staged a strike. About 50 percent of the strikers were within six years of retirement, and as the strike prolonged, 30 percent of the strikers crossed the picket line. Five months into the strike, Fites threatened to replace the strikers permanently if they did not return to work within a week. Shortly thereafter, the union called off the strike, the strikers went back to work 'unconditionally,' and Cat's unionized employees continued working without a contract under the terms of the rejected offer.[69]

One casualty of the 1991–1992 strike was Caterpillar's Employee Satisfaction Process. The strike, effectively put an end to Cat's ESP program which George Schaefer had launched in 1986 and strove so painstakingly to persevere. As the climate of labor relations at Caterpillar deteriorated, the number of unresolved grievances increased. At the Aurora plant at Illinois, the number of grievances at the final stage before arbitration rose from less than 20 prior to the strike to over 300 in the year following the end of the strike. When Cat employees began wearing their own ESP buttons to read 'Employee Stop Participating,' Caterpillar terminated the program altogether.[70]

During 1992–1994, Caterpillar's unionized employees continued to resist Fites' hard-line stand against the UAW. They organized shopfloor disruptions ('informational picketing'), slowdowns ('Work to Rule'), wildcat strikes in selected plants, and picket lines at Cat's dealerships.[71] Fites, in the meantime, trained managers and office workers to operate factory machinery and reassigned many of them to the shopfloor of plants undergoing short-term

[66]The quotations, in order, are from Reingold, 'CEO of the Year,' p. 72; Carl Quintanilla, 'Caterpillar Chairman Fites to Retire,' *Wall Street Journal*, October 15, 1998. Online. ABI data base.
[67]Quoted in Reingold, 'CEO of the Year,' p. 72.
[68]'An Interview with Fites,' *Inter Business Issues*, pp. 34–45; 'What's Good for Caterpillar,' *Forbes*, December 7, 1992. Online. ABI data base.
[69]Michael Cimini, 'Caterpillar's Prolonged Dispute Ends,' *Compensation and Working Conditions*, Fall 1998, pp. 5–6; Kevin Kelly, 'Cat May be Trying to Bulldoze the Immovable,' *Business Week*, December 2, 1991, p. 116, 'Cat VS. Labor: Hardhats Anyone?' *Business Week*, August 26, 1991, Start p. 48. Lexis-Nexis. Academic Universe.
[70]Michael Verespej, 'Bulldozing Labor Peace at Caterpillar,' *Industry Week*, February 15, 1993, Start p. 19. Online. ABI data base.
[71]'Caterpillar: Union Bull,' *Economist*, January 9, 1993, Start p. 61. Online. Lexis-Nexis. Academic Universe; Cimini 'Caterpillar's Prolonged Dispute Ends,' pp. 7–9.

work-stoppages. Once again, he was fully prepared for a long stike.

The 1994–95 strike broke out in June 1994, lasted 17 months, was bitterly fought by the striking unionists, and came to an abrupt end when the UAW ordered its members to return to work 'immediately and unconditionally' in order to save their jobs.[72] During the strike, Caterpillar supplemented its workforce with 5,000 reassigned white collar employees, 3,700 full-time and part-time new hires, 4,000 union members who crossed the picket line, and skilled workers borrowed from its dealerships. The company, furthermore, shifted work to non-union plants in the South. Additionally, Caterpillar supplied the US market with equipment imported from its plants in Europe, Japan, and Brazil.[73]

Operating effectively all through the strike, Caterpillar avoided massive customer defection, and managed to keep up production, expand sales, increase profits, and drive up the company stock price. In 1995, the company earned record profits for the second year in a row (Table 5). During the two years following the end of the strike, the shopfloor struggle between Cat management and the union resumed. Caterpillar issued strict rules of workplace conduct, limiting employees' behavior as well as speech. Union activists, in response, launched a work-to-rule campaign in Cat's unionized plants. The UAW, in addition, filed numerous charges with the National Labor Relations Board (NLRB), alleging that the company committed unfair labor practices. Accepting many of these charges, the NLRB issued formal complaints.[74] Meanwhile, in 1997, Caterpillar racked up record profits for the fourth year in a row.

In February 1998, at long last, Caterpillar and the union reached an agreement. The terms of the 1998 agreement clearly favored Caterpillar. First and most important, the contract allowed Caterpillar to break away from the long-standing practice of pattern bargaining. Second, the contract allowed Caterpillar to introduce a two-tier wage system and pay new employees 70 percent of the starting union scale. A third clause of the contract provided for a more flex-ible work schedule, allowing management to keep employees on the job longer than eight hours a day and during weekends (without paying overtime). The contract also granted management the right to hire temporary employees at certain plants without the union's approval, and reduce the number of union jobs below a certain level. Running for six years rather than the typical three years, the contract was expected to secure Caterpillar with a relatively long period of industrial peace.[75]

Several provisions of the contract were favorable to the union. The contract's key economic provisions included an immediate wage increase of 2–4 percent and future increases of 3 percent in 1999, 2001, and 2003; cost of living allowances; and substantial gains in pension benefits (the average tenure of the 1994–95 strikers was 24 years). Another provision favorable to the UAW was a moratorium on most plant closings. But perhaps the most significant union gain was simply achieving a contract, as AFL-CIO Secretary Treasurer Rich Trumka observed: 'The message to corporate America is this: Here's one of the biggest companies, and they couldn't walk away from the union.'[76]

TABLE 5   Caterpillar's financial results during the labor disputes of the 1990s

	Sales ($Mil.)	Net Income ($Mil.)	Income as % of Sales	Stock Price Close ($)
1991	10,182	(404)	–	10.97
1992	10,194	(2,435)	–	13.41
1993	11,615	652	5.6	22.25
1994	14,328	955	6.7	27.56
1995	16,072	1,136	7.1	29.38
1996	16,522	1,361	8.2	37.63
1997	18,925	1,665	8.8	48.50

Source: *Hoover's Handbook for American Business*, 1999, p. 329.

[72]Cimini, 'Caterpillar's Prolonged Dispute Ends,' p. 9; Robert Rose, 'Caterpillar Contract with UAW May be Tough to Sell to Workers,' *Wall Street Journal*, February 17, 1998 Online. ABI data base; Reingold, 'CEO of the Year,' p. 72.
[73]Cimini, 'Caterpillars Prolonged Dispute Ends,' pp. 8–9.
[74]Ibid.
[75]Carl Quintanilla, 'Caterpillar Touts Its Gains as UAW Battle Ends,' *Wall Street Journal*, March 24, 1998; Dirk Johnson, 'Auto Union Backs Tentative Accord with Caterpillar,' *New York Times*, February 14, 1998.
[76]Quoted in Philip Dine, 'Gulf Remains Wide in Caterpillar's Home,' *St. Louis Post Despatch*, March 29, 1998. Online. Lexis-Nexis. Academic Universe. See also Cimini, 'Caterpillar's Prolonged Dispute Ends,' p. 11.

Why, then, was Fites willing to sign a contract? Why did a company which operated profitably year after year without a contract, and operated efficiently during strikes, suddenly seek to reach an agreement with the UAW?

Fites' decision was influenced by two developments. First, Caterpillar's record revenues and profits during 1993–97 came to an end in 1998–99, as the industry was sliding into a recession. Revenues and profits were declining as a result of a strong dollar coupled with a weak demand for Cat products. Caterpillar, therefore, needed a flexible wage agreement, stable employment relations, and a more cooperative workforce in order to smooth its ride during the impending downturn. Another reason why Fites sought accommodation with the union was the need to settle some 400 unfair labor practice charges filed by the NLRB against the company during the dispute. These charges were not only costly to adjudicate but could have resulted in huge penalties which the company had to pay in cases where the NLRB ruled in favor of the UAW. One of Caterpillar's principal demands in the 1998 settlement – to which the UAW agreed – was dropping these unfair labor practice charges.[77]

The future: Glen Barton's Caterpillar 1999–

As Fites retired in February 1999, Glen Barton, a 39-year Cat veteran, assumed the company's leadership. During his first year in office, Barton lost two potential allies on the Cat Board of Directors, Glen Schaefer and Donald Fites. In January 2000, Caterpillar's Board of Directors revised the company's corporate governance guidelines to prohibit retired Cat employees from sitting on the board. The move was intended to safeguard the interests of stockholders and prevent the company's inside directors from opposing swift actions proposed by the board's outside members.[78]

Barton faced other difficulties. In 1999, Caterpillar's profits fell 37 percent to $946 million, the worst results since 1993, and its North American market, which accounted for half of Cat's sales and nearly 2/3 of its profits, was in a slump.[79]

Barton believed that the downturn in the US construction market could be offset by an upturn in the international market. He thought that Caterpillar could take advantage of its global positioning to cushion the US decline by increasing sales in Asia and Latin America whose economies were rebounding. But being cautious, Barton also realized that he needed to ensure the future of Caterpillar in the long run. He therefore embarked on four growth strategies: the expansion into new markets; diversification; the development of a new distribution channel; and the build up of alliances with global competitors.

New markets

In 1999, 80 percent of the world's population lived in developing countries, and Caterpillar's sales to developing nations accounted for only 23 percent of the total company's sales. Developing countries had limited access to water, electricity, and transportation, and therefore needed to invest in building highways, bridges, dams, and waterways. Under Barton's leadership, increased sales of Caterpillar's equipment to the developing nations of Asia, Latin America, Eastern Europe, and the Commonwealth of Independent States (the former Soviet Union) was a top strategic priority.[80]

Diversification

Just as globalization protected Caterpillar from the cyclical movements of boom and bust, so did diversification. Cat's expansion into the engine business is a case in point. In 1999, Caterpillar's overall sales fell by 6 percent, yet its engine sales rose by 5 percent. Cat's engine business itself was further diversified, with truck-engine sales making up just over one-third of all Cat's engine sales in 1999 (Table 6). Such a diversification, according to Barton, ensured the company that any future decline in truck engine sales could be offset, at least in part, by an increase in sales of non-truck engines. By 2010, Caterpillar's total engine sales were expected to double to nearly $14 billion.[81]

[77]'The Caterpillar Strike: Not Over Till It's Over,' *Economist*, February 28, 1998.
[78]*Business Week*, February 21, 2000, Start p. 148.
[79]Ibid.
[80]'Growth Strategies,' Caterpillar.Com, p. 2.
[81]*Wall Street Journal*, March 13, 2000.

TABLE 6 Cat engine sales to end users

Percentage of Total Sales	1999	2000
Trucks	34	27
Electric Power Generators	26	33
Oil Drilling Equipment	20	19
Industrial Equipment	11	13
Ships and Boats	9	8

Source: Caterpillar Inc. 1999 *Annual Report*, p. 24; and 2000 *Annual Report*.

Of all Cat engine sales, the growth in sales of electric diesel generators – 20 percent a year since 1996 – had been the fastest (Table 7). Caterpillar's energy business clearly benefited from the energy crisis. Large corporations, manufacturing facilities, internet server centers, and utility companies had installed back up diesel generators for standby or emergency use; in the nine months ending May 2001, Cat sales of mobile power modules (trailer equipped with a generator) quadrupled.[82]

TABLE 7 Caterpillar's sales of power generators

	Sales ($Bil.)	As % of Total Revenues
1996	1.2	7.3
1997	1.3	6.9
1998	1.6	7.6
2000	1.8	9.1
2001	2.3	11.4

Source: David Barboza, 'Cashing In On the World's Energy Hunger,' *The New York Times*, May 22, 2001.

The world's largest manufacturer of diesel generators, Caterpillar nevertheless faced a serious challenge in its efforts to transform itself into an ET (energy technology) company: diesel generators produced far more pollution than other sources of power. To address this problem, Barton's Caterpillar accelerated its shift towards cleaner micro power. In 2001, only 10 percent of Caterpillar's generators were powered by natural gas; in 2011, the corresponding figure was expected to climb to 50 percent.[83]

To diversify the company in still another way, Barton planned to double its farm equipment sales in five years (1999–2004).[84] In the agricultural equipment market, Caterpillar needed to compete head-to-head with the John Deere Co. and the CNH Corporation (former Case Corp. and New Holland), the leading US manufacturers.

A new distribution channel

Under Barton's direction, Caterpillar expanded its rental equipment business, reaching a new category of customers both at home and abroad. Formerly, Caterpillar sold or rented equipment to rental centers, and these centers, in turn, re-rented the equipment to end-users. Rarely did Caterpillar rent directly to customers. Now Barton was making aggressive efforts to help Cat dealers diversify into rentals. Nearly half of all Cat's machines sold in North America in 2000 entered the market through the rental distribution channel, and the fastest growing segment of the business was short-term rentals. Implemented by Barton in 1999–2000, the Cat Rental Store Program was designed to assist dealers in operating a one-stop rental shop that offered a complete line of rental equipment from heavy bulldozers and tractors to light towers, work platforms, and hydraulic tools.[85]

[82]David Barboza, 'Cashing In On the World's Energy Hunger,' *New York Times*, May 22, 2001.
[83]*New York Times*, May 22, 2001; 'Energy Technology: Beyond the Bubble,' *Economist*, April 21, 2001.
[84]Heather Landy, 'Putting More Cats Down on the Farm,' *Chicago Sun Times*, March 28, 1999. Online. Lexis-Nexis. Academic Universe.
[85]Michael Roth, 'Seeing the Light,' *Rental Equipment Register*, January 2000. Online. Lexis-Nexis. Academic Universe; Nikki Tait, 'Cat Sharpens Claws to Pounce Again,' *Financial Times*, November 8, 2000; Online. Lexis-Nexis. Academic Universe.

Joint ventures

Increasingly, Caterpillar had used joint ventures to expand into new markets and diversify into new products. In November 2000, Barton's Caterpillar announced a plan to form two joint ventures with DaimlerChrysler, the world's leading manufacturer of commercial vehicles. One was for building medium-duty engines, the other was for manufacturing fuel systems. The combined share of the two companies in the medium-duty engine market was only 10 percent, yet the medium-duty engine market generated world-wide sales of $10 billion annually.

The sales of fuel systems were even more promising. Fuel systems were designed to increase the efficiency of diesel engines and thereby reduce diesel emissions. Participating in the two joint ventures were Cat and DaimlerChrysler plants in four US states (South Carolina, Georgia, Illinois, and Michigan) and at least five other countries.[86]

Future prospects

Notwithstanding their initial prospects, Barton's strategic initiatives failed to address adequately two major concerns that could have effected the company's future. One had to do with the state of labor relations, particularly Cat's employee satisfaction program which Schaefer had introduced and Fites terminated. Implemented effectively by Schaefer, the ESP program, we have seen, contributed to increased labor productivity, improved product quality, enhanced employee satisfaction, and reduced

TABLE 8   Caterpillar: Five year financial summary (Million US $. except per share data)

	2000	1999	1998	1997	1996
Sales and Revenues	20,175	19,702	20,977	18,925	16,522
Profits	1,053	946	1,513	1,665	1,361
Profits as % of Sales & Revenues	5.2	4.8	7.2	8.8	8.2
Profits per Share	3.04	2.66	4.17	4.44	3.54
Dividends per Share	1.345	1.275	1.150	0.950	0.775
Return on Equity (%)	19.0	17.9	30.9	37.9	36.3
Capital Expenditures, Net	723	790	925	824	506
R&D Expenses	854	814	838	700	570
R&D Expenses as % of Sales & Revenues	4.2	4.1	4.0	3.7	3.4
Wage, Salaries & Employee Benefits	4,029	4,044	4,146	3,773	3,437
Number of Employees	67,200	66,225	64,441	58,366	54,968
Total Assets Consolidated	28,464	26,711	25,128	20,756	18,728
Machinery & Engines	16,554	16,158	15,619	14,188	13,066
Financial Products	14,618	12,951	11,648	7,806	6,681
Long Term Debt Consolidated	11,334	9,928	9,404	6,942	5,087
Machinery & Engines	2,854	3,099	2,993	2,367	2,018
Financial Products	8,480	6,829	6,411	4,575	3,069
Total Debt Consolidated	15,067	13,802	12,452	8,568	7,469
Machinery & Engines	3,427	3,317	3,102	2,474	2,176
Financial Products	11,957	10,796	9,562	6,338	5,433

Source: *Caterpillar Inc. 2000 Annual Report*, p. 39.
For additional financial data, as reported in the company's annual reports and other financial documents, check out Caterpillar's web site at www.caterpillar.com

[86]Joseph Hallinan, 'Caterpillar, DaimlerChrysler Team Up,' *Wall Street Journal*, November 23, 2000.

employee absenteeism. Should Barton, then, reintroduce Cat's employee satisfaction program and thereby improve the climate of labor relations at the company's US plants? Would Barton be able to cooperate closely with the local union leadership to persuade shopfloor employees to join the program?

Another challenge Barton faced pertained to the impact of E-commerce. How could Caterpillar take advantage of the opportunities offered by E-commerce without undermining its distribution system? How, in other words, could Caterpillar benefit from utilizing the internet for the marketing, distributing, and service of its products without weakening its strong dealers' networks?

Barton wondered, 'What should I do next?'

CASE 9

Metro: A modern newspaper for a modern people?

By Heather A. Hazard[1]

We are committed to our aggressive international expansion, as we have demonstrated with out two most recent launches. This expansion, as well as the development of Metro in Sweden and our 15 other editions is our primary focus. Everyday has fulfilled our expectations in terms of readership growth, but advertisers remain to be convinced and we prefer to focus our efforts on the Metro free morning newspaper business, which continues to grow strongly.

With these upbeat (but cautious) words, on 15 March 2001 Pelle Törnberg, President and CEO of Metro International SA announced that his company would publicly give up the battle for the attention of the evening commuter in Stockholm. Still Metro had only begun the publication of *Everyday* the August before as a companion to its flagship product, the morning Metro. Metro was launched in 1995 but while the idea of giving away free newspapers was not a new one the idea of using an urban transit system for distribution was. And what an idea it was – to publish a free newspaper carrying only 'headline' local, regional, national, and international news in a standardized accessible format that commuters could read during a typical journey of about 20 minutes. The income was to be derived solely from advertising. What would make Metro more appealing to advertisers than a standard 'light weight' freebie? The demographic make-up of the readers (employed and therefore with high average income) and the captive nature of their attention were exactly the characteristics advertisers were looking for.

The Kinnevik group launched Metro in 1995. Kinnevik had made its first investment in the Astra satellite consortium in the mid 1980s. Each of the Kinnevik products had been launched with the intention of finding a lucrative niche in a market where

rivalry was limited. The company styled itself as 'pioneers in the Scandinavian media market'. In 1988, Kinnevik set up an arm (the Modern Times Group) to oversee its TV and media ventures. While the stated focus was on TV, MTG also sought to obtain benefits from cross-promotion, co-ordination of advertising sales, customer service, and production. Pelle Törnberg was present at the creation and became vice-president of the Kinnevik Group in 1993. In 1995 he was rewarded for his commitment by being made the President and CEO of MTG. When a decision was made to capitalize Metro in August of 2000 (by floating it on both the Swedish and NASDAQ stock exchanges) he was made the President of Metro International SA.

The strategy behind Metro was clear. They would attempt to develop each of their newspapers into the leading newspapers within their market (as they indeed had with their first launch in Stockholm) and to capitalize upon the Metro concept by replicating it in other cities including using the same name whenever possible to develop the brand. Replicating the concept was important not only because they would be utilizing a known and refined business model but because they hoped to attract advertisers who would buy space in all of their publications in addition to the standard local customers. Each local paper would be run with only a lean local editorial team who would create a local adaptation (language, 'feel', etc.) only to the most limited extent they could. As the editor of the Philadelphia edition, Mary Ellen Bornak, put it: 'We don't drill down, but we have most of the news that the other papers have just in a brief format. And that is all that most people think they need to know.' Printing and distribution would be outsourced to keep operating costs at a low level and news and photos would be purchased from third parties. The strategy also called for the specific pre-emption of competitors by entering only markets where rivals did not pre-exist. By doing this, Metro

[1]Source: © 2002 SIMI, Scandinavian International Management Institute. Reprinted with permission of SIMI and Heather Hazard.

executives hoped to be a successful player in two markets at once. The would 'buy' the attention of readers with advertising and editorial content and then turn around and resell this attention to advertisers in exchange for revenues. But while they were playing the traditional broker role they were doing so in a new way by forgoing the subscription and per copy revenues from readers that most newspapers depended on (see Figure 1).

The fact that Metro chose free distribution gave it a hidden advantage in its earliest launches – the existing newspapers didn't take it seriously. As a result they didn't react and Metro was able to pursue its strategic objective of increasing the number of ad pages (and revenues) relatively unimpeded. While executives had planned for profitability by year three they were able to achieve that performance target in the very first year. Media analyst Alan Wilson felt that Metro single handedly changed the reading patterns of Swedes and that it is all that the young people (coveted by advertisers for their disposable income) read. Thomas Axen, president of *Dagens Nyheter*, admitted 'We didn't look on it as a real newspaper. We didn't think that it was a real threat because we didn't believe anybody would read it.' *Dagens Nyheter* was looking down from a position of tremendous strength as the city's largest newspaper, over 350,000 subscriptions and almost no single copy sales. Five years later Axen regretted their lack of response that had allowed Metro to grow into the city's second largest newspaper with over 250,000 distributed copies and an estimated readership of twice that. Moreover, Axen admitted both that 'people view it as a newspaper of high quality' and that 'Metro sells lots of ads and makes tons of money'.

By the time they launched their afternoon edition in Stockholm however, the Swedish Press Subsidy Board was not so complacent, however, Karl Erik Gustafsson of the Board felt that the launch would provoke 'a tougher competition . . . and the profit margin will very likely shrink' for other newspapers in Stockholm. The successful launch in Stockholm was followed first by companion national launches in Gothenburg and Malmo and later by international launches in Hungary and the Netherlands.

By this time, however, competitors were learning from *Dagens Nyheter*'s mistaken impassivity and taking the threat seriously. The Norwegian publisher Schibsted was quick to recognize the unpleasant consequences an entry Metro would have on its sales and ad revenues both from its broad sheet *Aftenposten* and its upscale tabloid, *Verdens Gang*.

Schibsted made preemptive claims that it would launch a free transit newspaper in Oslo. Metro backed off – the market would now fail its no direct competitor criteria. Schibsted was never forced to fulfill its threat and only launched a free home-delivered newspaper, *Newspaper 1*. Delivered only twice a week and only to customers who didn't already subscribe to *Aftenposten*, Schibsted was able to keep Metro at bay and limit cannibalisation of its other products and revenues. Moreover, they used the launch and communication strategy to realize synergistic effects with *Aftenposten*.

The unhampered launches of the early years were only a pleasant memory by the time MTG decided to role out a London edition. Associated Newspapers was already well established within the market as the publisher of the *Mail* titles and of the *Evening Standard*. When they picked up rumors of MTG's intentions they quickly entered talks with the London Underground. In order to create the management capacity, Associated undertook a major reshuffle and created a new products division. While the division was new though the leadership was well seasoned as Associated put Kevin Beatty in charge as its executive director and expected him to bring in all the experience he had gained as the managing director of the *Mail on Sunday*. The London Underground also understood the potential and entered into 'commercially sensitive' discussions with several publishers simultaneously. Associated also moved quickly to strike at the core of MTG's strategy by licensing the Metro name for its own use. MTG attempted to fight this maneuver legally but lost and gave up the venture. Pelle Törnberg tried to put a cheerful face on the loss when he told the *World* reporter that he really didn't mind the loss as it gave him more cash to put into his venture in Philadelphia and the latitude to seriously consider entry into San Francisco. Others, including Constantine Kamaris of the World Association of Newspapers, thought that Associated had won big, however. He told the *Editor and Publisher Market Guide* that 'the project has quickly transformed itself into an aggressive, product-development venture which taps into a very important market – young, non-newspaper readers. Other newspapers should recognize this is a new paradigm and take advantage of it.'

Associated also learned from the Schibsted model. While they did make good their threat to produce a free transit newspaper they negotiated an agreement with the London Underground in their

FIGURE 1 Traditional and emerging revenue models in publishing

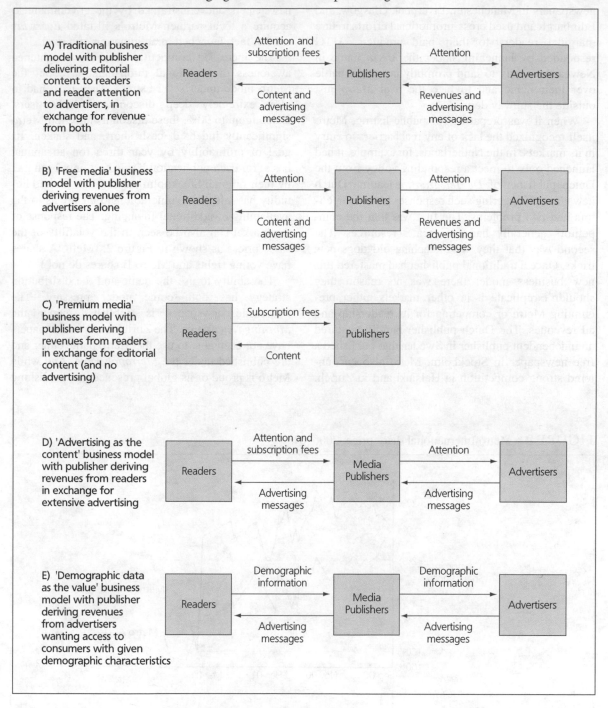

A) Traditional business model with publisher delivering editorial content to readers and reader attention to advertisers, in exchange for revenue from both

B) 'Free media' business model with publisher deriving revenues from advertisers alone

C) 'Premium media' business model with publisher deriving revenues from readers in exchange for editorial content (and no advertising)

D) 'Advertising as the content' business model with publisher deriving revenues from readers in exchange for extensive advertising

E) 'Demographic data as the value' business model with publisher deriving revenues from advertisers wanting access to consumers with given demographic characteristics

own favor. Specifically, they wanted to limit cannibalisation of the *Evening Standard* so they agreed that *Metro* would only be distributed from 6 to 10 in the morning – and then it would be removed. Apparently, disagreement remained in the upper management at Associated as to whether or not *Metro* was a spoiler newspaper for them or not.

Whether or not it was a spoiler for Associated in London might have been a matter for internal debate, but it didn't stop Associated from pushing ahead with the strategy elsewhere. They also launched free newspapers in Manchester, Liverpool, Glasgow, and Edinburgh and used cross-promotional efforts to lure marginal readers to their paid products. MTG responded by launching under the *Metro* name in Newcastle – only to land promptly in a legal battle over their name and to face the rival *Metro* just outside the subway doors.

When it was preparing for public listing, Metro itself recognized the lack of any real barriers to entry in its markets. In the Netherlands, for example, it had launched only to meet a responding volley from the Dutch publisher of *De Telegraaf*, a leading Dutch newspaper. Triggering such responses from competitors had two problems. The first was that the competitors generally had far greater resources. The second was that they were teaching old dogs new tricks. Once a traditional publisher had mastered this new business model there was no reason they shouldn't replicate it in other markets either preempting Metro or competing for its readership and ad revenues. The Dutch publisher rapidly acquired an independent publisher in Sweden that published a free newspaper in Stockholm. Metro also encountered strong competition in Helsinki and in Zurich.

In Toronto they were both countered by two local newspapers and constrained by the government to acquire a local partner. Metro's ill-fated *Everyday* was, in fact, launched in anticipation of a rival.

The increased competition and the heightened awareness of traditional publishers have put the Metro mode under severe stress. They have had to offer extremely deep discounts to advertisers. Running up to 90%, these discounts have left Metro significantly indebted, cash short, and shaken. Its goal of profitability by year three (on an annual basis) for each publication has in fact only been met by their original Stockholm paper. Their limited liquidity has left them vulnerable and unsure as to the availability of additional financing. The response of the market can also be seen in the volatility of the stock prices as shown in Figure 2. (Metro A shares have voting rights and Metro B shares do not.)

The ability to use the name and the distribution strategy has both come under pressure. The Newcastle newspaper is published under the *Morning News* name. The Zurich and Warsaw papers have not been able to use the Metro name either and are published under the *Metropol* name. And while Metro is proud of its global presence it is publishing

FIGURE 2   Metro International share price, 2000–01

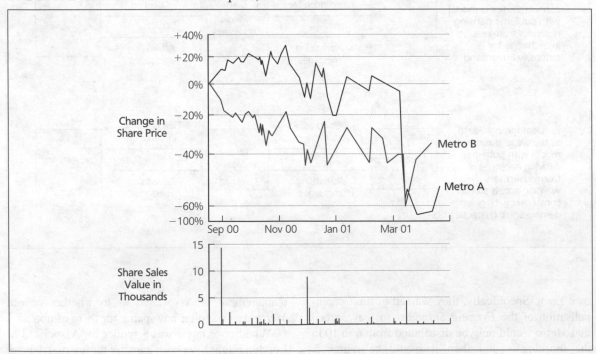

Source: Copyright 2001 Yahoo! Inc.; http://finance.yahoo.com.

its Santiago and Buenos Aires papers as *Publimetro*. The distribution strategy has been challenged in multiple cities (and most problematically in Philadelphia where they also encountered labor union resistance) and Metro has admitted that they have limited knowledge of other distribution methods although they are experimenting in different markets with other channels (see Figure 3).

So while, Pelle Törnberg could put a brave face on the closure of *Everyday*, the risks that Metro faced were multiple, known, and all too real. The question was whether Metro would be able to continue its seemingly unstoppable growth and whether it would be able to staunch its losses and become the profitable venture it was strategically committed to being. Metro planned to launch in other markets but the markets were more populous and Metro wondered if they had the management resources to manage such expansion and the knowledge to handle these larger markets.

FIGURE 3 Alternative distribution channels

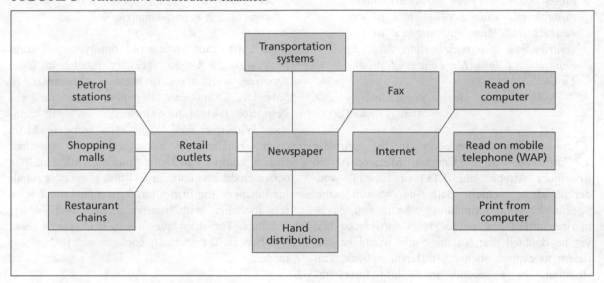

Grupo Elektra

By Luiz Felipe Monteiro, David Arnold and Gustavo Herrero[1]

We will continuously seek acquisition opportunities that provide upside potential for Grupo Elektra and our shareholders. We will continue to add new brands, products and services for distribution through our store network that fit our markets and have the potential to contribute to the bottom line. Most important, I look for continued profitable growth.

(Javier Sarro, Elektra's CEO,
Annual Report 2000)

Scuba diving 50-feet deep in the turquoise Caribbean Sea in Cancun, Mexico, Alvaro Rodriguez Arregui, the CFO of Elektra, wondered about which path he should take. Spectacular coral formations, colorful fish, caves, marine turtles, and unique reefs surrounded him yet he doubted that his air bottle would be sufficient to explore so many different options. This situation, for a second, made him forget the peaceful and silent underwater world and remember that a couple of hours later, above on the surface, he would face another crossroads. It was October 2001, and Rodriguez (HBS MBA '95) knew that in this year's Annual Convention in Cancun, he and the top management of Elektra would have the difficult task of choosing, among several promising opportunities, the options that would promote and maintain a sustainable and profitable growth of the company. Rodriguez reflected that:

We have been growing steadily in the last decade. In 1990, we just had the Elektra

chain format and only did business in Mexico with 225 chains. In 2000, our sales reached US$1.53 billion, we had 4 different chains – Elektra, Salinas y Rocha, Bodega de Remates and The One – almost 1,000 stores, and we were in 6 different countries.

In 2001, this 51-year-old family-owned company was the largest specialty retailer in Latin America, with stores in Mexico, Guatemala, El Salvador, Dominican Republic, Honduras and Peru. See Table 1 for information on these countries. With over 65% of its sales being made on credit, Elektra was also the largest consumer finance company in Latin America, with 2 million active credit accounts. In addition to its core retailing business, the firm offered its clients other services including wire transfer services and savings accounts. The main question in Rodriguez's mind was how far the company could stretch its business model:

In the early 1990s, we basically offered hard goods and credit. Then, we introduced international money transfers, and today we are the largest Western Union distributor in the world. Then, we started with the clothing business, initiated our international expansion, acquired a new chain of stores and provided our customers with other services such as domestic money transfers, extended warranties and savings accounts. But, how far does the Elektra model go? Our resources are limited and we are entering a period of slowdown: where do we go now?

[1]Source: © 2001 by the President and Fellows of Harvard College. Harvard Business School Case 9–502–039. This case was prepared by L.F. Monteiro, D. Arnold and G. Herrero as the basis for class discussion rather than to illustrate either effective or ineffective handling of an administrative situation. Reprinted by permission of Harvard Business School.

TABLE 1 Macroeconomic data of selected countries in Latin America, 2000

	Dominican Republic	El Salvador	Guatemala	Honduras	Mexico	Peru
GDP at market prices (US$billion)*	19.89	13.21	19.04	5.93	574.51	53.88
Population (million)*	8.55	6.27	11.38	6.48	97.96	25.66
Urban population, % of total**	65	47	40	53	74	73
GDP per capita (US$)**	2,320	2,130	1,670	898	5,800	2,083
Average interest rate charged by banks in local currency (%)**	26.8	13.9	20.9	26.8	18.2	27.9
Consumer prices % change per year**	9.01	4.28	5.06	10.10	8.95	3.73

*World Bank, available through http://sima-ext.worldbank.org/data-query/ (15 October 2001)
**Economist Intelligence Unit Country Data, 15 October 2001.

Tradition with vision

Elektra was founded in 1950 by Hugo Salinas Rocha, the grandfather of Ricardo Salinas Pliego, Elektra's chairman. Elektra was the first Mexican manufacturer of TV sets and during its first years the company sold its products directly from its manufacturing facilities to end consumers through door-to-door vendors.

Elektra's credit program had been initiated as early as 1954, and three years later the first store was inaugurated. During the following decades the company experienced alternating periods of marginal growth with moments of extreme difficulties. In 1976, after the first devaluation of the peso in 22 years, Elektra had to change its sales policy to cash only. In 1982, Elektra filed for bankruptcy protection (equivalent to Chapter XI in the United States).

The retirement of Hugo Salinas in 1987 and the appointment of his grandson Ricardo Salinas as Elektra's new CEO was a turning point in the company's history. After a couple of years heading the company, Ricardo realized that Elektra needed to be managed by a professional team (see Exhibit 1 for the biographical data on Elektra's main officers). Sarro recalled:

Ricardo was very conscious that the company had to get out of the family trap. His first major move in this direction was hiring Pedro Padilla, who was only 24 at that time, in 1989. Ricardo prepared him to be the new president of Elektra, culminating in his appointment as the company's CEO in 1993. Ricardo knew that he himself would add more value by being the chairman, and giving the management of Elektra to a group of talented and competent professional managers.

The early 1990s saw an unparalleled growth of Elektra. The company started a new credit program (*Credifacil*) and created *Dinero en Minutos*, money transfer service in partnership with Western Union.[2] In 1995, Elektra acquired Hecali, a clothing retailer, and increased its distribution network to more than 500 stores all over Mexico. Elektra also introduced a new set of services: *Dinero Express* (domestic wire transfer), *Milenia* (extended warranty program), *Fotofacil* (photo products and processing services) and *Guardadito* (savings accounts). See Exhibit 2 for a list of Elektra's services.

The organizational consequences of this diversification were reflected in Javier Sarro's description of Elektra in 2001:

[2]*Credifacil* translates as 'Easy Credit' and *Dinero en Minutos* as 'Money in Minutes'.

EXHIBIT 1 BIO OF ELEKTRA'S MAIN DIRECTORS AND OFFICERS

Ricardo Salinas, 45, has served as Elektra's President since 1989 and Chairman of the Board of Directors since 1993. Prior to joining Elektra in 1981 he worked for Arthur Andersen and The Brinkman Company. Mr. Salinas studied public accounting at the Instituto Technologico y de Estudios Superiores in Monterrey (ITESM) and graduated with honors in 1977. He received his Master's in Finance from University of Tulane and was the first foreigner to be recognized as a Distinguished Alumnus.

Pedro Padilla, 35, has served as a board member since 1993 and was Elektra's CEO from 1993 until 2000, and now serves as CEO of TV Azteca. Mr. Padilla has extensive experience in cross border financial and commodities transactions and holds a degree in Law from UNAM.

Javier Sarro, 40, was appointed Elektra's CEO in 2000. He originally joined Elektra in 1995 as the Vice President for Financial Services. He served as the first CEO of Unefon, building its management team, strategic supplier relations and financial structure. Mr. Sarro has an MBA from Instituto Panamericano de Alta Direccion de Empresas (IPADE) and completed under-graduate studies in Law at the Universidad Iberoamericana.

Alvaro Rodriguez, 34, has served as Elektra's Chief Financial Officer since 1999. He was appointed CFO of Unefon in 1997 and helped raise US$1 billion to start that company, estab-lishing its accounting, administration, budget, finance, legal and treasury departments. Before joining Unefon, he worked for several years as a banker in Latin America, Europe and the United States. Mr. Rodriguez holds a bachelor's degree from the Instituto Tecnologico Autonomo de Mexico (ITAM) and an MBA from the Harvard Business School.

Mario Gonzalez, 47, joined Elektra in 1999, as Vice President of Marketing. Prior to it, Mr. Gonzalez spent 23 years in marketing, marketing research, sales and operations in both local and international markets, and worked for companies including Nabisco, Gillette, PepsiCo and Casa Cuervo. He holds a degree in Business Administration and a Marketing specialization from Universidad Iberoamericana.

Filiberto Jimenez, 30, has served as the General Director of Store Operations since 2000. He joined Elektra in 1996 and oversaw the launch of the company's Latin American operations as one of his early job responsibilities. He served as the Director of Operations of Elektra and as the CEO of Salinas y Rocha. Mr. Jimenez holds a degree in Marketing and an MBA from the Instituto Tecnológico de Estudios Superiores de Monterrey (ITESM), with a major in International Business.

Mario Gordillo, 33, joined the Budgeting Department of Grupo Elektra 8 years ago. He has occupied several positions in the company within the departments of purchasing, financial services, distribution, Hecali and The One operations. In 2001, he was appointed head of Financial Services. Mr. Gordillo holds an undergraduate degree in Industrial Engineering and Systems from the Instituto de Estudios Superiores de Monterrey (ITESM), a Master's degree from the Instituto Panamericano de Alta Dirección Empresarial (IPADE) and a master of Finance degree from the ITESM in Mexico City, Mexico.

Source: Elektra

EXHIBIT 2 ELEKTRA'S SERVICES

Credimax

First financial service provided by Elektra, Credifacil (later Credimax) accounted for approximately 65% of Grupo Elektra's total sales. It had 2 million active accounts and an accumulated database of more than 4 million accounts. Credimax had more than 3,000 credit employees and Elektra had a recovery rate of over 97%.

Dinero en Minutos

As the first service to leverage Elektra's store network, Dinero en Minutos is a money transfer service in association with Western Union. Western Union has 27,000 branch offices in the United States, through which any of the 22 million Mexicans living there can send money back to their families in Mexico to be collected at any of the Grupo Elektra chains. Senders and receivers are current and potential customers and the business generates an important stream of U.S. dollar revenues.

Dinero Express

In February 1996, Elektra launched a second money transfer service and, in the process, created an entirely new market. Dinero Express was created for money transfers within Mexico and is an Elektra-owned service. From its launch in 1996 to December 2000, Dinero Express has exceeded the company's projections and has provided 4.3 million secure money transfers within Mexico so far.

Guardadito

Through a joint venture with Serfin Bank, Elektra created an innovative approach to savings that answers the needs of a large majority of the Mexican population to put some money aside for the future. Elektra used monthly raffles to motivate and reward Guardadito customers, and no commissions or fees are charged.

Milenia

Elektra began selling extended warranties in 1997 and it has had an outstanding record to date. Two, three and five-year warranties are offered in fourteen different product groups, with an emphasis on home electronics and white goods. Elektra believes that Milenia encourages the purchase of its products.

Fotofacil

Fotofacil kiosks offer film processing, inexpensive cameras, film, batteries, photo albums and portable electronics. The kiosks take up very little sales space and answer a great demand among Elektra's customers.

Source: Elektra

I see two cultures co-existing in Elektra: on the one hand, we have the traditional retailer mindset, results-oriented, tough culture. On the other, in the last decade there has been a renovation in the management of the company and we have forged a group of young managers with a strategic vision and creative ways of managing this company.

The best defense is attack

In 1996, an aggressive competitive move prompted Elektra to start its international expansion. The Dutch-owned chain La Curacao, which had already done business in Latin America for more than 10 years and had 400 stores in the region, decided to enter the Mexican market, opening 20 stores in the southeast of Mexico.

La Curacao belonged to Ceteco Holding NV, had a format similar to the Elektra chain, and also made a significant portion of its sales on credit. Feeling threatened in its home market, Elektra decided to attack the competition abroad. Filiberto Jimenez, Elektra's Store Operations General Director, then assistant to the company's CEO, was sent to El

Salvador to benchmark the competition, establish local partnerships, and look for potential locations where the Elektra stores could be built.

I was only 25, recently married and didn't know much about store operations. Nevertheless, the company decided that I should live in Central America and prepare the business plan for the international expansion. We decided to focus on Guatemala first, but at the time we judged that the risk of kidnapping was too high there, and so I actually moved to live in El Salvador in January 1997. I traveled extensively in Central and South America and it was not hard to realize that La Curacao was creaming the market. They were the kings of what was virtually a monopoly, enjoying extremely high margins due to the lack of competition. It became clear to us that if we cut-off its cash flow in those countries, we would force La Curacao to refocus its business and get out of Mexico.

In April 1997, the first Elektra store abroad was opened in Guatemala. In that same year, 43 other stores were inaugurated in El Salvador, Guatemala, the Dominican Republic and Honduras. The following year, Elektra decided to enter the Peruvian market, opening 20 stores in that country. Filiberto commented:

All our stores abroad were green fields; we started everything from scratch. For that purpose, I benefited from the help of a group of 15–20 of Elektra's Mexican managers. The only local partnerships we formed were with local business people of influence, who could represent us in dealing with local governments and other authorities. Working with influential local people is essential to doing business in this part of the world.

Elektra entered these markets with the same margin it had in Mexico, and as a result its prices were roughly 20% lower than those of La Curacao. 'The customers' reaction could not have been better for Elektra. They simply became mad at La Curacao because they realized they had been exploited for years,' declared Filiberto.

New store chains

In parallel with the international expansion, Elektra continued to grow the number of its stores in Mexico, and also started to operate new store formats. In 1995, Elektra created Bodega de Remates, a channel to retail refurbished and repossessed goods and discounted models, targeted at low-income customers of class E of the Mexican population. This new format enabled the company to compete with regional players without damaging the Elektra chain's brand whose target customers belonged to classes C and D. See Tables 2 and 3 for a description of the socio-economic levels in Mexico.

In 1999, Elektra acquired the Salinas y Rocha stores, a furniture and home appliances retail chain founded in 1906 by the great grandfather of Ricardo Salinas and one of his cousins. Salinas y Rocha had a brand with a very strong national recognition, and was targeted at higher income customers of classes C+ and B. In that same year, Elektra decided to transform the old Hecali stores into a new chain of clothing stores called The One. The US$6 billion clothing market in Mexico was very fragmented and Elektra considered that The One could suit the lifestyle of the majority of the Mexican people. See Exhibit 3 and Table 4 for detailed information on each store format.

Elektra in early 2001

The year 2000 was the best ever in Elektra's history. Grupo Elektra, comprising Elektra, Bodega de Remates, Salinas y Rocha and The One chain, posted sales of US$1.53 billion and an EBITDA of US$244 million, representing a growth of 15% and 16%, respectively, over the previous year. See Figure 1 and Table 5 for Elektra's financial performance.

Throughout the 1990s, the number of stores rocketed both in Mexico and abroad, and both the volume and the range of financial services grew significantly (see Table 6). With the four different chains, Elektra estimated that it covered 87% of the Mexican population.

TABLE 2 Socioeconomic levels in Mexico

Class	Description	Percentage of the Mexican population
A/B	■ Household income per month over US$7,000 ■ Checking account and more than two credit cards ■ Homes or apartments with more than three or four bedrooms, and two or three bathrooms ■ Two or more luxury automobiles, two telephone lines, two or more television sets and one computer	6%
C+	■ Household income per month between US$3,000 and US$7,000 ■ One or two credit cards ■ Homes or apartments with two or three bedrooms and one or two bathrooms ■ One or two cars, two telephone lines, two television sets and 20% of this segment has a computer	9%
C	■ Household income per month between US$1,000 and US$3,000 ■ ome have a credit card ■ Homes or apartments with two bedrooms and one bathroom ■ One basic automobile, one telephone line, two television sets and one radio	26%
D+	■ Household income per month between US$600 and US$1,000 ■ No credit cards ■ Homes or apartments with one or two bedrooms and one bathroom ■ No automobile, one telephone line and one radio	22%
D	■ Household income per month between US$200 and US$600 ■ No credit cards ■ Homes or apartments with one bedroom and one bathroom ■ No telephone, one television set and one radio	30%
E	■ Household income per month under US$200 ■ Small homes, a third of which have a bathroom, but most do not have a connection to a municipal sewage system ■ No telephone, most have only one television set and one radio	7%

Source: Elektra, 2000 Annual Report

TABLE 3   Socioeconomic profiles of Elektra's customers, October 2001

	Elektra	Salinas y Rocha	Bodegas de Remates	The One
Class (%)				
C+	19	28	13	20
C	25	29	23	35
D+	27	29	34	30
D	29	14	30	15
Age (%)				
18–25	18	8	21	45
26–35	32	21	35	35
36–45	27	28	27	15
46–55	23	43	17	5
Sex (%)				
Male	52	50	50	65
Female	48	50	50	35

Source: Elektra.

EXHIBIT 3 CHAINS

Elektra

- Most important chain of the Group
- More than 600 stores in Mexico and Latin America
- Attends market segments D, D+ and C
- Focus in electronics, white goods, home appliances and furniture
- Locations in strategic neighborhoods
- Average surface per store: 743m² (7998 sq. ft.)

Bodega de Remates

- More than 50 stores
- Attends market segments D, D+
- Focus in remanufactured and repossessed goods as well as discontinued models

- Excellent format to confront local competition
- Average surface per store: 574m² (6178 sq. ft.)

Salinas & Rocha

- More than 85 stores in Mexico
- Attends market segments C and C+
- Focus in furniture and Hi-Tech electronics
- Average surface per store: 968m² (10,419 sq. ft.)

The One

- More than 130 stores in Mexico
- Attends market segments D, D+ and C
- Focus in casual clothing and accessories
- Average surface per store: 376m² (4047 sq. ft.)

TABLE 4 Sales mix per store format, by type of product (as % of total)

	2000
Elektra Mexico	
Electronics	42.8
Appliances	28.7
Furniture	16.8
Small appliances	10.5
Telephones	1.2
Elektra Latin America	
Electronics	50.1
Appliances	23.7
Furniture	19.5
Small appliances	6.7
The One	
Men's clothes	50.5
Children's clothes	24.7
Ladies' clothes	22.4
Sport shoes	0.3
Telephones	2.1
Salinas y Rocha	
Electronics	33.0
Appliances	29.5
Furniture	27.6
Small appliances	9.3
Telephones	0.6

Source: Elektra.

Elektra had approximately 2 million active credit accounts, and a database of more than 4 million customers. Alvaro Rodriguez commented:

Our consumer credit portfolio is larger, in terms of number of customers, than that of any bank in Mexico. We have 2 million active customers who go every week to our stores to pay their installments. Citibank tried to provide consumer credit to the C and D socio-economic segment and has gotten only 30,000 accounts. In fact, investment analysts often have trouble categorizing us, and are unsure whether to rank us against a retailing multiple benchmark, or that of a financial services company. Our wire transfer businesses are also huge. We transfer US$700 million a year with Dinero en Minutos *and US$200 million with* Dinero Express. *We also made an agreement with Banco Serfin (a subsidiary of Banco Central Hispano from Spain) in Mexico to offer savings accounts in our stores, which we brand* Guardadito. *This requires a minimum deposit of only two dollars, with no opening fee, and at the end of 2000, we had 1.5 million accounts.*

FIGURE 1 Historic sales and EBITDA

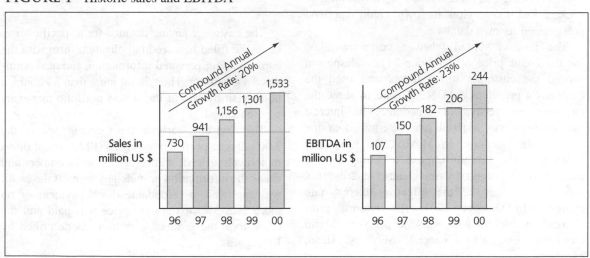

Source: Elektra.

TABLE 5   Financial performance in 2000, in US$ million

	Elektra Merchandise	S y R Merchandise	Credit	The One Merchandise	Money Transfer	Extended Warranties	Total
Revenues							
Sales	996.7	97.7		73.4	59.7	16.3	1,243.8
Credit income			313.9				313.9
Credit losses			(23.8)				(23.8)
Total revenues	996.7	97.7	290.1	73.4	59.7	16.3	1,533.9
Cost							
Cost of goods sold	685.9	66.2		44.0	1.4	4.9	802.4
Interest expense			32.0				32.0
Provisions			59.8				59.8
Credit gains			(15.5)				(15.5)
Total direct cost	685.9	66.2	76.4	44.0	1.4	4.9	878.8
Gross profit	310.8	31.5	213.7	29.4	58.3	11.4	655.1
Gross margin (%)	31	32	74	40	98	70	43
Percentage contribution	47	5	33	4	9	2	100

Credifacil

In 2001, roughly 65% of all sales of the Elektra group were on credit. See Tables 7 and 8 for the breakdown of credit and cash sales in each chain and in Elektra's subsidiaries abroad. The typical applicant for Elektra credit did not have access to consumer credit from the traditional financial institutions. Also, since there was no credit bureau in Mexico rating an individual's creditworthiness, Elektra had to develop its own credit approval process and its own database.

The process started when a customer asked for the credit price of a product. The salesperson invited the customer to sit down, and used the company's proprietary ADN software to show the customer the repayment schedule. The interest rate charged was a fixed rate determined at the time of the purchase. In Mexico, the Consumer Protection Act did not impose a ceiling on the interest rate charged by merchants, and did not require disclosure of the effective interest rate charged. In October 2001, flat interest rates charged by Elektra were 42.45% per year. Mario Gordillo, Elektra's Financial Services Head, explained:

Our customers are not concerned about the interest rates they are paying. All they want to know is the amount of the weekly installment. If they think they can afford it, they buy the product. Many people say that our interest rates are high. In fact, the rates are high but lower than those of many banks. Besides, it is important to bear in mind that providing this type of credit involves a very expensive operation.

The customer having decided for a specific term, he or she filled in a credit application form with the corresponding personal information, and also nominated a guarantor. Then, in no more than 24 hours, a home visit by one of the store's portfolio managers was scheduled.

The next day, early in the morning, one of the 3,000 Elektra portfolio managers (PMs) would ride a motorcycle to visit an average of 30 customers and check the information provided by them. If the credit was approved, a refundable down payment of no more than 5% of the case price was paid and the client took the product with him. As described by Rodriguez:

TABLE 6 Balance sheet in 2000, in US$ million

ASSETS	
Cash and Cash Equivalents	79.86
Customers	227.19
Accounts Receivable	61.08
Inventory	298.06
Other Current Assets	161.30
Total Current Assets	**827.49**
Investment in TVA	0.00
Investment in Other Shares	86.31
Deferred Taxes	4.76
Property Plant and Equipment (Net)	382.86
Goodwill	131.82
Other Assets	43.37
Total Assets	**1,476.61**
LIABILITIES AND EQUITY	
Bank Loans	150.03
Financial Leasing and Others	10.65
Current Liabilities with Cost	**160.7**
Suppliers	260.64
Other Current Liabilities	110.78
Current Liabilities without Cost	**371.4**
Total Current Liabilities	**532.1**
Long-Term Liabilities with Cost	289.951354
Long-Term Liabilities without Cost	8.39
Long-Term Liabilities	**298.3**
Total Liabilities	**830.4**
Deferred Income	77.0
Common Stock	229.254063
Retained Earnings	339.912917
Total Stockholders' Equity	**569.2**
Liabilities + Equity	**1,476.6**

Elektra's customers do not live in fancy neighborhoods, but rather in poor areas where access is quite complicated. The first challenge for our PMs is to find out where the customer actually lives. Here in Mexico we have hundreds of streets called Reforma, for instance, and there is no reliable zip code. Indeed, in many cases, there is no address, and the customer fills out Domicilio Conocido on the form.[3] So the first thing our PMs do is draw a map of the address of each customer, which turns out to be valuable information. We reach certain streets that not even the mail service gets to!

Elektra developed a unique internal credit rating system, as described by Mario Gordillo:

The system is both very simple and at the same time very sophisticated. The PM visiting the customer's home will try to build up a picture of the cash flow of the household, trying to identify the sources of income of the customer and family and also their expenses. Even if the customer does not have a formal statement of income, we have developed over the years our own income estimates for several jobs, such as a taxi driver or a taco salesman. This is the quantitative part, but what really makes the difference is the subjective assessment of our employees. They will pay attention to small details such as whether the customer's home is clean; how many appliances or electronic items the family has in the home; whether there seems to be a stable family set-up, and so on. Our PM will also knock on the doors of the customer neighbors to get some customer references. Finally, the PM will visit a couple of stores in the neighborhood, such as bakeries and grocery shops, to get more information on the prospect customer.

The maximum authorized loan amounts were approximately US$800 and US$1150 for a first time buyer and a repeat customer respectively. In both cases, the weekly installment could not

---

[3]*Domicilio Conocido* translates as 'known residence,' i.e. if the PM arrives in the neighborhood and asks around, he or she is directed to the home of the customer.

TABLE 7 Number of stores in December 2000

	Mexico	El Salvador	Guatemala	Honduras	Dominican Republic	Peru
Elektra	545	14	26	16	23	23
Salinas y Rocha	89	0	0	0	0	0
The One	161	0	0	0	0	0
Bodegas de Remates	53	0	0	0	0	0
Total	852	14	26	16	23	23

Source: Elektra 20-F, SEC filing, 2000, pp. 32, 38, 42 and 44

exceed 20% of the household income. A repeat customer did not have to make a down payment, but was still visited by the PM in what the company described as a 'courtesy visit,' conducted after the sale had been confirmed. See Table 9 for the repeat purchase rates of the 2000 Elektra credit customer base. In Mexico, at the end of 2000, the average loan was approximately US$251, with an average term of 44 weeks. The approval rate on credit applications was approximately 50%. Elektra had a credit portfolio of US$446 million (see Figure 2).

The same PM who visited the customer authorized the credit, and was also responsible for collection if the credit was past due. 'Each employee should be accountable for the whole process and compensated according to his or her performance,' explained Gordillo. The compensation of PMs was 10% fixed and 90% variable, depending on the performance of their portfolio. Each PM typically handled 650 accounts, and if more than 220 accounts were past due for more than 2 weeks, the ADN system automatically started to decrease the number of active accounts of the respective PM. If the PM's accounts started to be 13 weeks or more late, the PM's compensation had declined to the minimum wage level because of poor payment performance by his or her accounts, then the system automatically fired the PM. Gordillo commented, 'We have very rigid controls, and if the PM is not performing well, there will not be any excuse. The "system" will fire him or her.' Rodriquez added:

Giving loans is very easy; anyone with available funds can do it. It is the collection that is difficult, and I think this ability is in the blood of our employees. They can 'smell' whether or not a customer will pay a loan. . . . The secret is in the way you talk to people, the things you say and the questions you ask.

Elektra's credit process proved to be consistently profitable and efficient. Customers with past-due credits paid a penalty fee of 0.47% per day, but in 2000, its delinquency rate was only 2.7%, compared to the average of 15% of banks in Mexico (Figure 2).

TABLE 8 Cash and credit mixes per store format

	Percentage in September 2001
Elektra	
Cash	37
Credit	63
Salinas Y Rocha	
Cash	45
Credit	55
The One	
Cash	61
Credit	39
Bodegas de Remates	
Cash	46
Credit	54

Source: Elektra.

FIGURE 2 Elektra credit portfolio compared to Mexican Banks

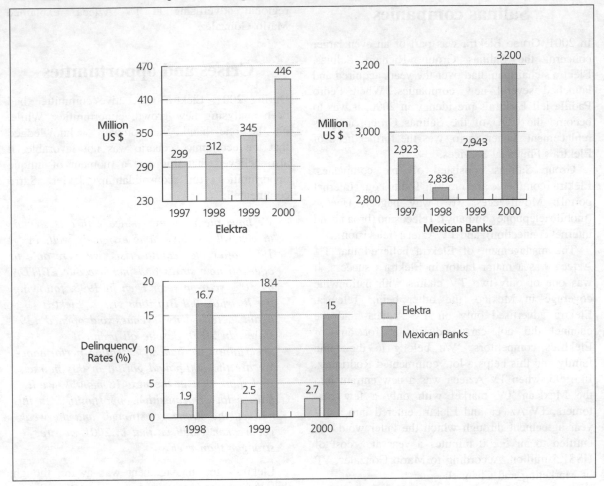

Source: Elektra.

TABLE 9 Number of purchases per customer, 2000

Number of purchases	Percentage
1	17
2–3	38
4–5	23
6–7	8
8–9	3
More than 10	3
Do not remember	8

Source: Elektra

Synergies with other Salinas companies

In 2001, Grupo Elektra was part of an even larger concern: the Salinas Group. Richard Salinas, Elektra's chairman, had over the years acquired and launched several new companies. When Pedro Padilla left Elektra's presidency in 2000, it was to become the COO of the Salinas Group, and his replacement, Javier Sarro, was the former head of Elektra's Financial Services.

Group Salinas consisted of five companies: Elektra (commerce and credit); Todito.com (Internet portal); Movil@ccess (two-way pager); Unefon (mobile telephone company); Telecosmo (broad band internet connection); and TV Azteca (television).

The management of Elektra believed that TV Azteca was a major factor in Elektra's success. It was one of only two TV chains with nationwide coverage in Mexico, the other being Televisa. Elektra advertised only on TV Azteca, and the channel did not carry advertising for any of Elektra's competitors. 'We belong to the same family and this helps a lot,' commented Rodriquez. In 1996, when TV Azteca was a new entrant into the Mexican TV market with only a few customers, TV Azteca and Elektra entered into a 10-year agreement through which the latter would be entitled to air 5,200 minutes a year at a cost of US$1.5 million. According to Mario Gonzalez, VP of Marketing and Channel:

> *We are the largest advertiser in Mexico, in terms of airtime, with roughly 14 minutes every day of the year. Our partnership with TV Azteca has helped us be very effective with our advertising efforts. Having the same controlling shareholders allows us to work better together.*

Elektra had a media budget of US$27 million per year and developed approximately 200 TV ads annually, most of them highlighting the brand values, the credit terms, and sometimes the cash price. Since October 2001, TV Azteca was able to air different ads for different regions in Mexico. 'We don't have nationwide competition but local competition from more than 7,000 moms-and-pops stores. That it why it's so important to have this regional advertising at TV Azteca,' explained Mario Gonzalez.

Crises and opportunities

During 2001, Elektra's executive committee had been analysing new growth opportunities. While, on the one hand, the company acknowledged that the economic scenario was not favorable, it also believed that this was a moment of unique opportunities for consolidation. Javier Sarro commented:

> *We have plenty of experience with crises, and in general we have done extremely well. In 1995, after the Tequila crisis, we were able to open 86 new stores and increase our EBITDA by 30% year-on-year. Then in 1998, following the Russian and Brazilian crises, Elektra again increased its revenues and opened 139 stores. In 2000, despite all political uncertainty, we had an exception performance. We are the 800-pound gorilla in this market, so I think that in the next 18 months, we'll have a lot of acquisition opportunities. In this market, the strong get stronger and the weak get weaker. I believe that in 2001 we are stronger than ever.*

Elektra's top management was aware, though, that the company had expanded on several new fronts in the last couple of years and that it was gong to be very challenging to continue to grow in all of them. Some investment analysts even considered that 'Elektra might have been overstretching itself by entering into new lines of businesses that may add only marginally to Elektra's bottom line.'[4]

The One

Rodriguez, as Elektra's CFO, knew better than anyone else that the company had to be very clear with its investors regarding each of its business lines. One of his major concerns was in relation to the clothing chain The One.

[4]Meredith Jensen, 'Elektra: Margin Pressures to Weigh on Market Leader,' J.P. Morgan Securities Inc. Equity Research, 24 September 2001.

The idea behind The One was that we are a basic needs retailer so let's explore the clothing business. Yet there is a lot of fashion in this business, and we might not have fashion in our DNA. We have had some problems with the supply chain, and have not always managed to turn lines over quickly enough, or to maintain the right stock levels in all colors and sizes. Today, I wonder if selling clothes is really fulfilling a basic need. There is a lot to be done to improve the performance of The One and we are working on it, changing the inventory management, relocating a lot of the stores to better sites, and analyzing the critical mass we need to make The One profitable.

North or Latin Americans?

In 2001, Elektra had 102 stores abroad, and the main goal of its international expansion had been achieved: La Curacao went bankrupt and had to sell its operations to local players in each of the Latin American countries in which it operated. In July 2001, Elektra acquired the 35 stores that La Curacao had in Mexico for US$5.4 million.

Yet, the performance of the international subsidiaries in financial rather than strategic terms was not so obviously successful. Indeed, Elektra was fac-ing serious problems in some countries (see Table 10). Rodriguez explained:

We thought we could replicate our model in other countries. In some of them, it worked well but in others, such as El Salvador and the Dominican Republic, the model simply did not work. There are many subtleties that make each country different. For instance, in the Dominican Republic, you can't charge a penalty fee; customers simply don't accept it. Thus, we decided to work the other way round: we told our customers that if they pay on time they would get a bonus. At the end of the day, economically speaking, it's the same thing but it takes time until you learn how to deal with each country's idiosyncrasies. In contrast, in Peru, we've been extremely successful. La Curacao and Carsa of Peru, which were our competitors, both went bankrupt and now we are the only one in the market. In Honduras and Guatemala, we are doing OK.

Entering the U.S. market was something that the management of Elektra had spent a lot of time discussing. Elektra's estimates were compelling: 75% of the U.S. Hispanic population lived in 15 cities; Los Angeles was the second largest city in number of

TABLE 10 Income statement, Elektra's subsidiaries in Latin America, December 2000, in US$ million

	Guatemala	El Salvador	Honduras	Dominican Republic	Peru	Total
Products and services revenues	20,806	5,744	11,492	12,546	20,263	69,851
Products and services cost	14,304	4,075	8,102	8,207	14,407	49,095
Products and services gross profit	6,502	1,669	3,389	3,339	5,856	20,755
Credit revenues	4,772	1,733	3,527	3,415	4,676	18,123
Credit cost	1,835	890	1,642	2,285	2,531	9,184
Credit gross profit	2,937	843	1,885	1,130	2,145	8,939
Total gross profit	9,439	2,512	5,274	4,468	8,001	29,694

Source: Elektra.

Mexicans after Mexico City; the U.S. Hispanics' spending was equivalent to 80% of Mexico's GNP. Besides, according to the U.S. Census of 2000, the Hispanic population living in the United States increased by more than 50% from 1990 to 2000, reaching 35 million people.[5] Elektra also expected that the U.S. Hispanic consumer spending would grow significantly in the following years. Mexicans were the largest Hispanic-origin group, accounting for 59% of the U.S. Hispanic population.[6] Elektra also believed it could replicate in the United States the successful association with TV Azteca, using its TV sister company to reach the Hispanic population. Sarro commented: 'Indeed, upon analyzing our international expansion, the first question we ask ourselves is whether we are a Latin or a North American company. I think we're a NAFTA company.'

Operating in the United States, though, was a completely different game, acknowledged Alvaro: 'We are in a low volume-high margin market while in the U.S. we would have to be high volume-low margin.' Filiberto Jimenez who was responsible for the launching of all of Elektra's stores abroad also had concerns about a possible expansion to the United States:

I'm very apprehensive about the U.S. regulations. It's something that we don't know well enough. If we are to enter the U.S. market, it should be through a joint venture or an acquisition and I want to spend some time as an assistant of the CEO of the company learning how the market works. I don't want to be sued and have Elektra liable for millions of dollars because one customer fell down in my store and broke a leg. In Latin America, we know how things work and how to fix them when something goes wrong. It's also important to bear in mind that operating in the United States would require different capabilities both in terms of operation and meeting the customers' needs. In addition, in Mexico we have the bargain power with our suppliers that

would not be true in the United States. But, all the same, it's definitely right to say that we have many opportunities in the United States. For instance, I love the idea of entering Puerto Rico: it's the typical Latin American country, yet it is part of the United States. I think it would be the perfect market for us.

Offering financial services to the U.S. Hispanics was also an option. According to a market survey done by Gallup, Telmex and Fundacion Solidariedad Mexicano Americano in July 2000, 50.4% of the U.S. Hispanics had never used any type of banking services and 56.8% had never had access to banking credit.[7] According to the same survey, only 41.7% of the U.S. Hispanics had a bank account and 7.4% a credit card.[8] Rodriguez commented:

Most Hispanics are Mexicans and Central Americans. We know them better than anyone else and they are very familiar with our brands. They seldom have access to credit in the U.S. and we would feel comfortable in providing them credit in the U.S. It's a huge market with a lot of upside potential.

Specialty (finance) retailer

One of the most successful businesses of Elektra had been financial services. Elektra's management considered that there was a huge avenue for providing new financial services such as mortgages, loans for used car purchase or home improvement projects, and even personal loans. Elektra was also considering using its retail network to install ATMs, a business that was not developed in Mexico. According to Alvaro:

We know that our financial services business is already a big business but we think it can grow even more. We have a database with 4,000,000 credit accounts. We could be the provider of every type of financial services to

---

[5]U.S. Census Bureau. Available through http://www.census.gov/statab/www/part1a.html (15 October 2001).

[6]U.S. Census Bureau. Available through http://www.census.gov/mso/www/rsf/hisorig/sld024.htm (15 October 2001).

[7]Gallup, Telmex and Fundacion Solidariedad Mexicano Amercia, 'Estudio de los Habitos de Consumo de la poblacion mexicana en los Estados Unidos,' July 2001, p. 18.

[8]Ibid, p. 19.

this segment of the population. We understand them and they feel at ease dealing with us. That does not happen when they go to a bank.

In 2001, Elektra created a new business unit for the credit business called Credimax. This unit consolidated the credit operations of Elektra, Salinas y Rocha, The One and Bodegas de Remates. Elektra expected a huge growth in this business based on the fact that, according to the company's estimates, the penetration of consumer loans in Mexico was only 1.5% of GDP while in the United States it reached 16%. The management of Elektra was also analyzing the possibility of transforming Credimax into an autonomous company or even into a bank (see Figures 3 and 4). Said Javier:

FIGURE 3   Number of savings accounts in Mexico, Elektra vs. Mexican banks

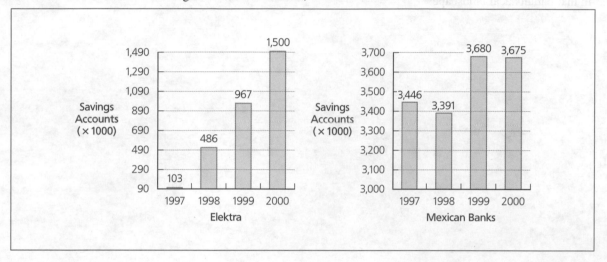

Source: Elektra.

FIGURE 4   Distribution network, Elektra vs. Mexican banks

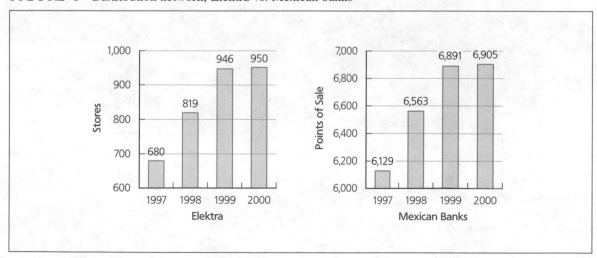

Source: Elektra.

To a certain extent, we could be considered a bank even though we don't have a license. We have credit operations, wire transfer services and even savings accounts. The only difference is that today we still have to outsource the back end process and we cannot tap on the interbank financial circuit.

With all those questions in mind, Alvaro could hardly realize that he had spent more than 20 minutes diving. It was time to get back to the surface and as Alvaro took off his mask he looked for inspiration in that paradisiacal landscape.

Where do we go now? Where should the company allocate its resources? Mexico, Latin America, the United States? In what kind of business: hard goods, clothing, financial services? These are tough questions that we have to answer now. I'm very optimistic but I don't underestimate the challenges we have ahead. We're pushing a lot of things through the same window. But, Alvaro wondered, how much is enough?

CASE

11

A new business in the Lego Group: Lego Mindstorms

By David Oliver, Johan Roos and Bart Victor[1]

Reading through his e-mail, Christian Majgaard, Lego's corporate executive vice president of new business development, pondered a business proposal he had received that morning from the Lego Mindstorms team. After a resoundingly successful launch and strong early sales figures, the Mindstorms strategic project unit (SPU) was proposing to set itself up as a separate business in the Lego Group. Majgaard knew that the fast-moving Mindstorms team often felt constrained by the more formal structures of the Lego core business. Providing the team with business unit status would release it to explore new ways of developing its exciting product. He then notices an e-mail message from Paul Edwards, a senior manager from the Lego core business in the US.

> *Christian: I am concerned that, six months after the launch of its product, the Mindstorms team is still operating like a separate 'strategic project.' As I have mentioned before, its high-flying operating style is highly disruptive to the 200 employees for whom I am responsible. Now that its product has been launched, I think the most cost effective thing to do would be to integrate its business systems with those of the core business. We are all selling creative products to kids – shouldn't we try to build up some synergies between our processes?*
> *Best regards,*
> *Paul*

Majgaard knew that a separate Mindstorms business unit would have to develop its own new sales force and other systems, making it unlikely to turn a profit for several years. Also, the successful core business – the backbone of the Lego organization – was in the process of merging many of its processes

to become more efficient and customer-focused. So, integrating Mindstorms into the core might also help spur these changes. He reflected on the two diametrically opposed alternatives for Mindstorms: which decision would be best for the Lego Group?

The Lego Group: Background

In 1999 Lego was the fifth largest toy manufacturer in the world and the biggest in Europe,[2] with revenues of US\$1.1 billion and nearly 10,000 employees in 30 countries. From its founding in 1932 in the village of Billund, Denmark, Lego had grown to become one of the best-known brands on the planet. An estimated 300 million children had played with Lego, and 64% of the US households and 74% of European households owned Lego toys. The company had always been family-run, with the founder's grandson Kjeld Kirk Kristiansen currently serving as president and CEO. Lego had grown at a controlled pace of between 10% to 18% annually throughout the 1980s and early 1990s, although the rate of sales growth had begun to slow in the late 1990s (see Table 1). Organizationally, the company was divided into two main parts: core and new businesses (see Figure 1).

Building a core business

Since the patented 'stud and tube' plastic brick had been introduced in 1958 – the patent expired in 1981 – Lego's core business had been built around plastic brick construction toys. In 1999 Lego's core business consisted of four basic age-related product lines: Lego Primo (for children aged between 6

---

[1]Source: © 2000 by IMD – International Institute for Management Development, Lausanne, Switzerland. All rights reserved. Not to be used or reproduced without permission from the IMD, Lausanne, Switzerland.
[2]Lego accounted for 10% to 15% share of the toy market in Europe, and 2% share in the United States (see Stogel, Chuck, *Brandweek*, New York, September 11, 2000, page 92).

TABLE 1 Revenue and profitability of the Lego Group (in DKK million)

	1998	1997	1996	1995	1994	1993
Net turnover	7,680	7,616	7,534	6,844	5,707	5,295
Profit (loss) after tax	(194)	62	470	431	471	516

On December 31, 1998, DKK 6.4 = US$1
Source: Lego Group.

FIGURE 1 Lego Group organization chart, 1998 (adapted)

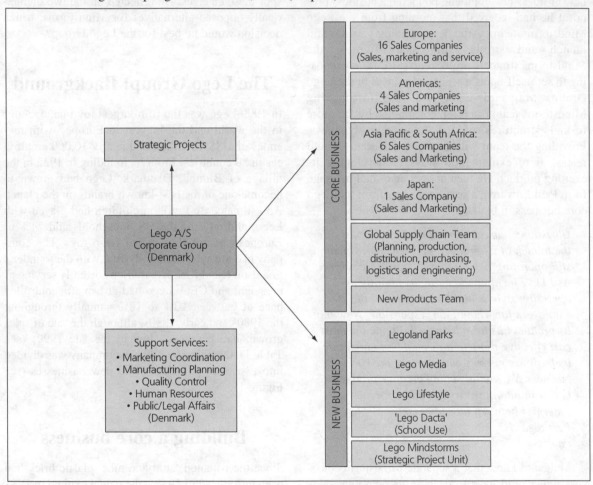

Source: Lego Group.

months and 2 years), Duplo (1½ to 5 years), System (5 to 12 years), and Technic (7 to 16 years). The company had also extended its product line to include a new line of doll-based toys called Lego Scala, targeted at girls. Lego toys had received many awards from child development specialists and toy surveys for their quality, design and play value.

The core business was organized into four strategic business units (SBUs): Europe, Americas, Asia-Pacific and South Africa, and Japan, as well as business units focused on the global supply chain (which handled planning, production, distribution, purchasing, logistics and engineering), and new product development. Each SBU arranged production and sales of Lego products in its region, and developed its own product plans and localized sales strategies. The SBUs had functional structures with largely standardized operating procedures and work routines that were designed to maximize efficiency in all stages of its internal business system. New product ideas – usually elaborate construction toy models – were developed in Lego's 250-employee R&D division in Billund, which then 'sold' the new product ideas to project managers from the SBUs. These project managers arranged for Lego's engineering department to design and build molds for the selected models. The toys were then manufactured in SBUs around the world, and finally distributed by Lego sales companies. All products were thoroughly tested, and the production group worked to exceptionally high quality and environmental standards, as Edwards described:

> Lego employees are guided by the motto adopted by our founder in 1932: 'Only the best is good enough.' To this day, Lego upholds this philosophy in every facet of its business.

Planning and production in the core

The company's development and production processes had been highly successful in dealing with predictable product life cycles, and emphasized continuous marginal improvement. The planning cycle began in April with Lego's annual 'Spring Meeting,' at which the heads of the SBUs and other business units met with Lego's executive management group. The agenda typically included a discussion of sales forecasts, cost trends, investment and the product program for the coming year. The objective was to ensure that all parties understood the company's expectations and challenges. The meeting also functioned as a precursor to the annual 'June agreements' between individual SBU heads and Lego management.

Each June agreement was a contract negotiated between an SBU manager and senior Lego management and stipulated budget figures for the following year. Signing such an agreement committed the SBU manager to attain the agreed-on financial targets, with an agreed-on deviation from plan – such as 2% difference in sales in either direction – for the subsequent year. As long as the managers met these targets, nobody from headquarters would intervene or raise any questions about their businesses. The agreements were intended to free SBU managers from day-to-day activities such as extensive budgeting, and give them more time and responsibility to focus on long-term, targeted overall strategies. Because their targets were negotiated six months in advance of the year in question, managers had time to make necessary preparations to meet them.

Sales companies

Lego's 27 sales companies were distributed throughout the four SBUs (see Figure 1).[3] Sales representatives had developed well-established relationships with buyers from large toy stores such as 'Toys R Us,' and rewards were established for sales representatives who met or surpassed their targets. The company focused its marketing and sales initiatives on specific accounts with promotional events such as nation-wide 'truck tours,' and developed award-winning television advertising. Edwards commented:

> With the exception of 1994, when we faced huge competition from brick imitators and alternative construction toys, the Americas division reported sales increases in every year since 1974. Sales even grew in 1998 when the Lego Group as a whole suffered a loss.

To ensure that its product remained fresh, the core business developed a steady stream of new products and line extensions. In 1999 the company's product range consisted of 503 retail items – 201 were new – sold in 130 countries. Among these new products were eight new Lego building sets based on Episode 4 of the *Star Wars* movie, developed through an alliance between the Lego Group and *Lucasfilm*.

The development of 'Compass Management'

In the 1990s some dark clouds began appearing on the horizon for the Lego core business. Competitors began appearing on the scene, some selling almost identical copies of Lego, while others such as K'NEX offered alternative systems with a technical quality approaching Lego's. In parallel, as the Internet and technology-oriented products took hold, children began outgrowing traditional building

---

[3]The Europe SBU included 16 sales companies; Americas had 4; Asia-Pacific and South Africa had 6; and Japan 1.

bricks at an earlier age. Within the Lego Group, there was thought to be a great deal of duplication in corporate structure, with each of the country operations handling local marketing and distribution. The company was also thinking about better ways to develop new product ideas, as few employees were willing to 'rock the boat' by making radical changes in such a successful formula.

In 1994 senior management announced the launch of the new Compass Management program for the core business. It was intended to address problems related to both the organizational structure and mindset. Many felt that Lego's traditional consensus orientation had become overdeveloped, and that some decisions were over-discussed in a long series of meetings. Edwards described the overall goal of the program:

Our objective is to improve responsiveness to market dynamics through dialogue and empowerment within a set of clear, agreed-on targets. We have to move away from the detailed control model to which we have become accustomed.

The program involved training 40 compass maritime 'pilots' to help introduce all the changes in Lego companies around the world. Through a six-module training program, Lego managers learned about how to move from a traditional hierarchical approach to a more decentralized structure of overlapping teams, where members' roles could vary depending on the task at hand.

In 1996 Lego worked to speed up Compass Management in order to achieve its stated corporate strategic intent of making the Lego brand 'the most powerful brand in the world among families with children by 2005.' At this time some white-collar staff were dismissed, and the company began identifying qualitative key success factors and quantitative key performance indicators. The group also sought advice from internal and external consultants on ways to improve efficiency. In June 1997 an Intranet named 'the Lego Web' was developed to facilitate cross-boundary information sharing. As Kristiansen explained: 'We have to share information and experience . . . we must think in terms of the whole and of cross-connections.'

In early 1999 the core business embarked on another efficiency improvement initiative referred to as the 'Fitness Program.' The Fitness Program was designed to make the company more customer-focused, reduce the number of organizational layers,

develop clearer areas of responsibility and reduce overlap. The project would reduce the number of sales companies from 27 down to 7 and ultimately lay off 1,000 staff worldwide.

Exploring new business ideas

Kristiansen believed that the Lego name should not be limited to specific objectives or goals, and should stand for more than just a product or even the company itself. Rather, he belived that the Lego name was a universal concept that should refer to '*idea*' (creativity, imagination, unlimited, discovery and 'constructionism'), '*exuberance*' (enthusiasm, spontaneity, self-expression and unrestrained), and '*values*' (quality, caring, development, innovation and consistency). From the beginning, the new business division operated in ways very different from the core business. For example, Majgaard explained how he recruited managers for what would become four new businesses:

I recruited each of the new business leaders from outside Lego, yet included some internal know-how. All were partly located near Billund and partly elsewhere, and all were given some freedom to be different while respecting the Lego brand vision.

The 'new business' division came to include:

1 *Legoland Theme Parks.* Building on the success of the first Legoland park, which had opened in Billund, Denmark in 1968, this business opened parks in Windsor (UK) in 1996, Carlsbad, California (US) in 1999, and a fourth scheduled for completion in 2003 in Gunzberg, Germany. The parks featured rides, Lego landscaping, and hands-on exhibits for children and adults. The theme parks were highly successful: each received an average of 1.5 million visitors per year.

2 *Lego Lifestyle.* Established in 1991, this business handled licensing agreements for the Lego name for a variety of children's products, such as activity books, clothing, footwear, bags, games, puzzles and watches. The group was headquartered in Windsor, and had 1998 consumer sales totaling $50 million.

3 *Lego Media.* Established in 1996 in London, this business focused on developing children's software, music, video, books and video development. The 90 employees in Lego Media

developed multimedia products such as 'Lego Racers,' which allowed users to assemble and race cars using a huge selection of virtual 'bricks' and other components.

4 *Lego Mindstorms.* Although included within Lego's new businesses in 1993, work on computerized building bricks had begun in 1984, with a collaborative effort between Lego and child learning expert Professor Seymour Papert from the MIT (Massachusetts Institute of Technology) Media Lab. In 1986 Lego launched a computerized building set for schools, but the low rate of household personal computer (PC) ownership at the time meant that the product was deemed premature for the consumer market. Development continued until 1993, when a programmable Lego brick (P-brick) was successfully tested at MIT and in Lego's central lab. Although Lego's core business believed the home market was still not ready for the P-brick at this time, Kristiansen himself intervened to ensure that the project was not dropped altogether. Believing that the concept was highly consistent with Lego's core values, he took it out of the core and added it to the new business group.

The development of Lego Mindstorms

In 1993 Majgaard set up a new project team to look into ways the P-brick could be used to develop a 'home learning' concept that would be exciting enough to compete with children's at-home alternatives such as video games (see Figure 2 for data on the changing toy market). By 1995 the rate of PC ownership and Internet use was skyrocketing, so Lego product manager Tormod Askildsen – who was familiar with the impact that digital computing was having on children's lives – joined the new team. Torben Sørensen, left his job in an information technology company in April 1996 to take over Lego's educational division (Dacta) and manage the home learning team – determined to bring the P-brick to market.

One of the first tasks the project team undertook was to commission a study of the potential market in the US for home learning products. The study confirmed that the home learning market was dominated by game-oriented 'edutainment' (*education* combined with *entertainment*) software, but it also identified a key market segment of parents they referred to as 'CCC' (conscious, caring and capable), which represented about 20% of all US households with children aged 6 to 12. These parents took an active interest in their children's learning processes, believing they should 'give their children every edge to succeed.' Valuing problem-solving skills over what Sørensen referred to as 'reflex training,' these parents were concerned with the low quality of school education. Their children were interested in solving problems in creative ways using complex

FIGURE 2   Video and PC games are changing the market for toys

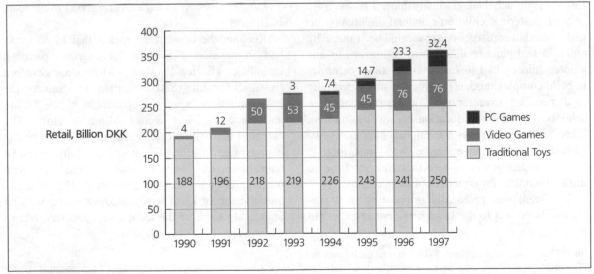

Source: Lego Group.

technology,[4] and even spent hours or days working on solutions to problems that excited their interest.

With the CCC target market in mind – and the basics of the P-brick in hand – the project team sat down with model builders, software and hardware experts for three days in July 1996 to iron out all the specifications of a new product that would, in March 1997, be named 'Lego Mindstorms.'[5]

Constructionism or instructionism?

Early on, the Lego Mindstorms team realized that its product was based on some learning assumptions that were different from many of the more recent model sets in Lego's core business. Lego had been founded on the principle that children could construct anything they could imagine from just a few pieces. However, the elaborately designed construction models Lego developed in the 1970s to 1990s included detailed instructions that children had to follow to complete the model pictured on the box. While such models sold well, and provided both long hours of play value and some development of the child's understanding of the world, the models – once completed – often ended up on a child's shelf. Lego toys were starting to resemble elaborate jigsaw puzzles, where the child was provided with both the process *and* the result.

MIT's Papert referred to this method of education as 'instructionism' – learning by following instructions – a method commonly used by teachers in the formal education system. The other basic form of education, 'constructionism,' drew on children's creativity and natural desire to learn through doing. Lego's approach had gradually moved away from one of fostering children's natural inclination to make original constructions that could be 'valued' by children and parents alike (constructionism) to one where children had to follow instructions carefully to build complex models (instructionism). According to Papert, an overemphasis on instructionism in schools was making education boring for children. Kids then turned to non-educational 'junk play' – so named for its addictive similarity to 'junk food' – such as video games, where they did not have to think about the consequences of their actions.

The team was given a huge boost when it presented its project to the Lego president and CEO in

February 1997. Kristiansen immediately noted that Lego Mindstorms strongly reinforced Lego's core constructionist values, and elevated the project to the status of strategic project unit (SPU), where it would report directly to executive management.

The Mindstorms team grows

Motivated by the link between its product and Lego's core values, the Mindstorms team began actively recruiting new members with competencies like computer programming and Internet website development. However, Sørensen quickly ran into problems when he tried to recruit employees from within the Lego organization to work for the fledgling team. He recalled: 'Many people didn't want to be too closely associated with Mindstorms . . . they wanted to maintain some distance in case it failed.' Those Lego employees who were enthusiastic about joining Sørensen's team often had difficulty receiving permission from their managers to work for Mindstorms. Consequently, it took a great effort for the team to acquire a project manager and public relations specialist from the core business.

In many cases, Sørensen had to resort to hiring external people rather than drawing on the knowledge inside Lego. In February 1997 he hired a US-based Internet specialist who worked out of his home to develop the project's Internet community. In May 1997 the team widened its international dimension by hiring Linda Dalton, a marketing director from an educational software company, and basing her in Lego's US office in Connecticut. As Dalton put it: 'We are not a Danish business: we want to be a *global* business with a lean, central part of the team in Billund.'

Keeping the center lean meant that Mindstorms had to develop a network of external partners, including Hewlett-Packard, Motorola, Stanford Research Institute (SRI), the Planetary Society, the public relations agency Department of the Future and the advertising agency Mintz & Hoke. The extent of these alliances meant the team even had to contemplate forming partnerships with possible competitors. On this point, disagreements arose with other parts of the Lego organization. For example, one division of Lego was already working with an arch rival of one of the team's new partners, and so

---

[4]In 1997 an estimated 8 million US children used the Internet daily.
[5]The project was named after Seymour Papert's 1980 book: *Mindstorms: Children, Computers, and Powerful Ideas*, Reading (USA): Basic Books.

it tried to persuade Mindstorms to end its budding alliance.

'If your dad understands it, it's probably outdated'

Tests revealed that children enjoyed showing off their competence to their parents, and the PC-orientation of Mindstorms was expected to make this competence appear all the more impressive. Kids would also be connected in a 'global community' focused around an Internet website: www.legomind-storms.com. In addition to answering questions from and supporting product buyers, the Web site would allow children to create personal home pages, to which they could upload programs and display pictures of their robotic creations. On-line tutorials would be made available to help kids master difficult programming and building tasks.

In addition to the website, a 'Lego League' was developed in cooperation with FIRST (For Inspiration and Recognition of Science and Technology)[6] to use Lego Mindstorms as the basis for a series of robotic team competitions. Community development was also expected to be stimulated through a series of 'Learning Centers,' the goal of which was to offer inspiration and a cooperative learning environment for children. In these centers children would form teams and engage in friendly competitions using Mindstorms to develop solutions to challenges. The first such center opened in late 1997, hosted by the Museum of Science and Industry in Chicago.

The finished product

By late 1997 the full product offering was almost ready. The centerpiece of Lego Mindstorms would be the 'RCX' programmable brick which used sensors to take information from its environment and signal output motors to turn on and off. Children could use the RCX along with other Lego pieces to build robots that could be programmed – using the simple yet powerful programming language named 'RCX code' – to follow lines, clear a table, or perform almost any task. The computer program could be downloaded from a PC to the RCX using a special infrared transmitter, after which the robot 'creation' could move around independent of the computer.

The Lego Mindstorms robotics invention system would include over 700 Lego pieces, including the RCX (each having its own personalized number), an infrared transmitter, light and touch sensors, motors, gears, and a 'Constructopedia' building guide. Twelve CD-ROM 'challenges' were included for which there was no single right answer or method. The challenges were designed to be difficult, yet enjoyable (so-called 'hard fun'), with help available when necessary to ensure a 'low threshold and high ceiling.' Unlike other Lego products, no picture of a finished product would appear on the box. The selling price of $200 to $219 was controversial among some executives from the rest of the Lego organization. 'We cannot sell a mass-market product that costs over $39.99,' remarked one Lego marketing executive.

The Mindstorms team planned largely to forgo traditional distribution channels in favor of consumer electronics stores, special chains for learning, direct sales through Lego clubs and other CCC communities, Lego Mindstorms learning centers, and the Internet. Although these new channels provided the team with access to previously untapped markets, some in the organization were skeptical about the notion that the cost of developing these new channels could ever make them profitable, and further believed that the channels could hurt relations with existing distributors. The team also faced an unfamiliar lineup of competitors; instead of Mattel and Hasbro, Mindstorms would compete with products from Microsoft, Sony, Nintendo and Sega.

The Mindstorms team's operating style: Staying in orbit

Early on, the Mindstorms team set out some operating principles that contrasted sharply with those of the core Lego organization. The team would meet regularly and make extensive use of external alliances – not just internal ones. Members would strive to run processes in parallel – for example, developing software and hardware at the same time – instead of sequentially, and across boundaries. More 'chaos' was permitted than in the core business. An enthusiastic 'can-do' attitude infused the fast-moving team, which knew it had to achieve results quickly in order

---

[6]FIRST's founder, Dean Kamen, was an entrepreneur whose goal was to inspire kids to pursue careers in science and engineering by showing them that science could be 'cool.'

to survive in and create its new category in an emerging industry. But the fast pace of the team sometimes took a toll on its members. Recalled Askildsen: 'I was getting exhausted from all our parallel processes – it never stopped. The excitement was energizing but it can wear you out.'

The team made other decisions that were slightly controversial in the core organization. For example, it based some of its R&D and marketing development in the US – closer to the target market – instead of in the head office in Denmark. Team meetings were highly informal, and despite the core business's 'go it alone' orientation, the Mindstorms team established tight and equal relations with its many alliance partners. But this very different operating style led to some tension between the team and the core business.

A common subject of debate was how Mindstorms should be connected to the rest of the organization. After spending a great deal of time and effort building contacts with managers in the core business, in August 1997 Sørensen designed a highly elaborate organization chart showing how his team 'fitted in' with the rest of Lego. However, the boxes and arrows of an organization chart seemed inadequate to describe the fundamental differences between the orderly core business that was servicing an existing market on the one hand, and the newer, more chaotic team trying to create a new market on the other. Majgaard began adopting a more metaphorical way of describing the linkage, referring to Mindstorms as a 'planet' orbiting around the core business. He emphasized that it was important for all new business development ventures to 'stay in orbit,' neither drifting too far into oblivion, nor getting too close and burning up. As could be expected, this balance was not always easy to maintain. Just months before the launch of Mindstorms, the core business's R&D division announced its intention to set up its own strategic project unit on robotics.

Given the robotics theme of Mindstorms, the team grew concerned that this new project could confuse customers. This initiative of the core business was subsequently dropped.

Launching Mindstorms

In January 1998 Lego Mindstorms conducted its global public relations launch. The event was covered by one-half of all US television stations, as well as CNN and the BBC, and was estimated to have reached more than one billion people around the globe. In September 1998 the product went on sale in the United States and the UK, and sales doubled projections – stores were sold-out by Christmas. By March 1999 more than 2 million consumers had visited the Internet website, and the Internet community's 22,000 members had already posted thousands of invention pictures.

What should be done with Mindstorms?

In 1998 Lego Mindstorms and the other three 'new' businesses had grown to account for 25% of total company revenues. In the core business, despite posting a 20% increase in consumer sales in North America in 1998, profitability had begun to fall, and by year end the Lego group reported its first-ever loss, equivalent to $31 million. But the 1999 *Star Wars* building sets exceeded all sales forecasts and contributed to a 25% increase in group sales in the first half of 1999.

Majgaard reflected on what to with Mindstorms given the recent sales increases in the Lego core business. Should he accept the proposal to establish a separate business unit for Mindstorms within the broader Lego Group, or should be begin to integrate it into the Lego core business?

CASE 12

Mining for synergies: Billiton's quest to be worldclass

By Bob de Wit, Richard Renner and Jaco Lok[1]

In less than ten years after buying the loss making mining company Billiton from RoyalDutch/Shell, Billiton chairman Brian Gilbertson had accomplished what the mighty Shell had failed to accomplish in their twenty three years as a Billiton parent. Through the merger with the Broken Hill Proprietary company (BHP) of Australia, Gilbertson had created the second largest mining and metals conglomerate in the world valued at around US\$ 30 billion. Despite a generally gloomy outlook for the industry as a whole, the prospects for BHPBilliton were good. The BHP–Billiton deal, code-named 'Bardot' because investments bankers considered it a beautiful thing, was seen as a 'sensational fit' spelling good news for both BHP and Billiton shareholders. However, only six months after appointing Mr Gilbertson as the new BHPBilliton CEO, the board forced Mr. Gilbertson to resign in January 2003 citing 'irreconcilable differences'. Is this a sign of trouble ahead for Billiton? In the context of an increasingly difficult economic environment and without its opportunistic, risk-taking leader will Billiton lose its momentum? Or are the synergies large enough to avoid slipping back to the days of underperformance?

Royal Dutch/Shell

The Royal Dutch/Shell Group of Companies originates from an alliance in 1907 between the Dutch N.V. Koninklijke Nederlandsche Petroleum Maatschappij (Royal Dutch Petroleum Company) and the British Shell Transport and Trading Company Ltd. The Group operates on a world-wide basis in oil, natural gas, and chemicals. Shell is well known for continuously striving to look beyond horizons. Their explicit strategic plans are well implemented and controlled, and have been rewarded by sustained high performance in the international oil industry. Shell invests pro-actively and creatively in the demanding and rapidly changing oil industry, and allocates significant resources to promising new activities on the basis of a long-term vision.

The 'Shell Group Planning System', the annual strategic planning cycle, is famous for using scenarios to formulate operating companies' visions since the 1970s. Although the strategic planning process pays attention to financial consequences of the new plans, it is not focused on detailed financial analyses. According to Shell an overly narrow focus on financial details distracts management attention from innovative strategic thinking. Only after the strategic planning process and after developing or adjusting a vision, do operating companies present investment proposals. In this phase detailed financial analyses are made in order to evaluate investment proposals on criteria of feasibility and minimum rates of return.

Each of Shell's *operating companies* concentrates on one or several of the following activities: exploration, exploitation, production, transport, and marketing and sales. The operating companies are accountable for their financial results, and for building up and maintaining activities. They may consult the group service companies or, through them, other group companies. These *service companies* bridge the group companies' activities by means of advice and attuning objectives and/or by financial means. They also connect the operating companies' investment plans and the holdings. In addition, service companies carry out all activities that are most efficiently executed centrally.

Shell's diversification plans in the 1970s

At the end of the 1960s the major oil companies showed a strong urge to diversify into remote

---

[1]Source: The case was compiled from publicly available sources. © 2003 by Bob de Wit.

activities like hotels and office furniture, and more or less related activities such as coal and metals. Between the Second World War and the end of the 1960s the major oil companies had experienced more than two decades of stable growth. Demand for oil products increased, and the international oil companies became enormous firms, in terms of size, number of activities and financial wealth. However, the 1970s ended the stability of the world energy markets. Oil demand dropped as prices rose, and governments as well as consumers realized that oil and gas reserves were finite.

Many oil companies focused on expansion into the mining and the metal industry, as these industries appeared to have similar characteristics to the oil industry: international dispersion, extensive projects with long lead times, economic and political risks, governmental involvement, and international trade and transport.[2] Consequently mining and metal companies became targets for most of the major oil companies. Shell was no exception. Shell believed that diversification would guarantee long-term sustainable growth. The metal sector was regarded as a potentially enduring and stable source of income. In addition, the future prospects for metals were favorable at the time. In the short-term the future of the oil- and gas industries looked strong, but Shell worried about some long-term issues such as increasing power of the OPEC-countries and the finite world oil- and gas reserves. Shell generally agreed that the strong growth rates of the oil industry could not continue.

Potential diversification projects had to meet two important criteria at Shell. Compared with the traditional activities the magnitude of the new activities had to be considerable, both in terms of potential turnover and required capital investments, and the new activities had to be related to the traditional ones. In 1984 the head of Shell's Non-Traditional Business, Mr. Van der Toorn, explained Shell's diversification philosophy[3]: '. . . one thing Shell still knows for sure is that we will one day run out of oil. At the moment Shell wants to substantially participate in new and profitable industries with growth potential . . . It is important that we search for opportunities in industries that closely relate to the group's strengths. We do this by selectively investing in a limited number of new activities.'

The rationale behind entering the metals business was formulated as follows: (1) Metals are – like oil, gas and chemical products – raw materials for a wide range of companies and industries: (2) The metals industry explores, exploits, processes, recycles, and sells non-ferrous metals, industrial minerals, and related products, which are exactly the same activities Shell employs in oil, gas and chemicals; (3) Shell strives for more intensive use of its geological know-how, drilling, and technological knowledge, in fields other than oil and gas.

Both industries employ geological and geophysical methods; both process the raw materials to products before they are ready to use; all products must be mass-shipped by especially constructed ships; marketing and sale of both industries often focus on the same clients; both industries require high capital investments; and both industries require excellent relations with governments of host countries and diplomacy skills. These similarities convinced Shell that metals, and more specifically 'non-ferrous metals', should become the fourth leg in Shell's business portfolio on a par with oil, gas, and chemicals.

The non-ferrous metal industry

The metal industry can be divided into the basic metal and metal processing industries. The most important basic metals are iron and steel, industries with strong (supra-national) government involvement. All other metals are categorized into the 'non-ferrous' metals industry. Aluminum is the world's most important non-ferrous metal. In terms of tons produced, aluminum comes third behind only iron and steel. Other important non-ferrous metals are copper, zinc, lead, nickel, tin, gold, silver, magnesium, titanium, and tungsten. The non-ferrous metal industry operates world-wide, and can be subdivided into exploration, mining and metallurgy, metal processing, and sales. The non-ferrous metal deposits are scattered around the globe, and per metal there are typically only few deposits. The buyers are primarily located in the industrial areas of North America, Europe, and Japan.

Ores and most metals (except for the very rare ones) are commodities, just like sugar and coffee.

---

[2]*Billiton Brief* (1982). 'De diversificatie van oliemaatschappijen in de mijnbouw' ('Diversification of oil companies in mining'), December.

[3]*Shell Venster* (1984), 'Activiteiten non-traditional business. Van der Toorn: Eens zal de olie op zijn' ('Activities non-traditional business. Van der Toorn: One day we will run out of oil', September.

Prices are set by forces of supply and demand and can fluctuate quite dramatically. On the wave of economic cycles the five dominant buyers of metals – construction, capital goods, durable consumer goods, packaging and transportation – change consumption patterns of metals greatly influencing market prices.

Vertically integrated firms that cover all activities from exploration to sales, like the integrated oil companies, have only emerged in aluminum. Crucial factors in the aluminum industry are large scale economies, high capital intensity, a need for cheap electricity and closely guarded technology. Six major international integrated firms originally dominated the aluminum industry for many years, from bauxite mining (the primary aluminum ore) to processing aluminum: Alcan, Alcoa, Kaiser, Reynolds, Pechiney, and Alusuisse. Limited competition and the inelastic price of aluminum characterized the period of market dominance by the 'Big Six'. The large integrated companies formed a *de facto* cartel and kept prices high and stable. High stable prices combined with rising demand gave favorable prospects for the aluminum industry, which led to an incredible investment boom in the 1970s.

Shell buys Billiton

After deciding to enter the world of metals, Shell began to develop some projects on an individual basis, such as exploiting magnesium reservoirs in the northern region of the Netherlands. Shell soon realized however, that an acquisition would be better and quicker than growing activities from scratch. The target firm was required to be internationally active in exploration and processing with a head-office in Western Europe.

Billiton was the preferred target. Billiton was a Dutch firm active in mining, metallurgy and non-ferrous metals on a world-wide basis. Billiton was founded in 1860 when a group of Dutch entrepreneurs obtained a concession to mine tin on the Indonesian island Billiton, now called Belitung. After having been active for 75 years in only the exploitation of tin ore and the production of tin, the company extended activities in 1935 into bauxite mining (aluminum ore) on Bintang, Indonesia and in 1939 in Surinam, another Dutch colony. After Indonesia nationalized all bauxite mining in 1958, bauxite from Surinam became Billiton's mainstay activity. During the 1960s Billiton diversified into more downstream activities, not only into related activities, but also into industrial and construction activities. The strategy was to create a fully integrated industry chain, to secure a stable demand and enable the contracting of turnkey projects.

At the end of the 1960s Billiton was active in over 80 participations. All activities were divided into three divisions: mining, metallurgy, and industry. Billiton's image in the Dutch financial world was close to that of a trader in unassorted goods. In most of the firm's industries Billiton was only at best a medium-sized company. Although financial results had been very good, financial institutions had major doubts as to whether the company would ever be able to escape its mediocre status. Billiton could not afford to invest in all of its activities at the same time and would have to change its structure soon.

Shell approached Billiton's management board, which was astonished by Shell's advances, to express its interest in a take-over. Shell said that it would only consider a friendly take-over and that it would withdraw its offer if Billiton rejected their proposal. Billiton accepted the take-over bid on the basis of two arguments:[4]

1 *Shell's financial strength and technological capabilities* would consolidate Billiton's position and strengthen economies of scale. Billiton realized that its intended further growth would require major financial resources and upgraded technological capabilities. In addition, as a result of increasing scale economies in the metal industry, the political risks and the consequences of a major mining project failure were getting too big to be carried by a firm of Billiton's size.

2 *Shell guaranteed independence and a key position within the Group.* It was agreed that Billiton would become the core firm for all mining and processing of ores and non-ferrous metals. Billiton would remain relatively independent as a

[4]Sources: (1) Shell Petroleum N.V. (1970), 'Bericht aan de aandeelhouders van Billiton en Singkep Tin' ('Announcement to the shareholders of Billiton and Singkep Tin'), The Hague. (2) a mutual press release of 27 May 1970: 'Shell doet bod op Billiton' ('Shell makes a bid for Billiton'), and (3) a mutual statement of the management boards of Shell and Billiton, including explanation, July–September 1970.

separate division within the Royal Dutch/Shell Group and was promised involvement in all important decisions.

Additional arguments of lesser importance were the projection of a stronger competitive position vis-à-vis the Big Six multinationals in aluminum, a stronger basis for R&D expenses, positive effects of mutual activities, increased political strength, especially important in developing economies, and entrance to Shell's world-wide contacts in business and finance.

On July 13, 1970 Shell bought Billiton for 423 million Dutch guilders. According to Shell, the benefits were significant. First, because of the significant size of Billiton, Shell entered the metal industry quickly. Billiton would be an excellent basis for rapidly forming a fourth leg within the Shell Group. Without this major acquisition it could have taken some forty years to develop a mining business and Shell did not have that patience. Second, the strong diversification of Billiton allowed Shell to quickly become an important producer of a variety of non-ferrous metals, particularly tin. Third, the vertically integrated structure of Billiton was a big advantage to Shell. In one swoop Shell bought competencies in exploration, exploitation, processing, marketing, sales, and research of ore and metals. And last but not least, both companies were Dutch (Shell 60%, Billiton 100%), which made cultural and language problems unlikely.

Absorption of Billiton into the Shell organization

After the merger Billiton was kept relatively independent, a sort of multinational within a multinational. The organizational structure became similar to Shell's. A small number of holdings controlled the many operating companies, and a service company, Billiton International Metals B.V. (BIM), provided centralized support. As with Shell, the management board of each Billiton operating company was held responsible for financial results and for the long-term planning of its activities. However, BIM played a very active role in central strategic planning and was strongly focused on realizing synergies.

The BIM Service Company provided advisors to operating companies in exploration, production, transport, processing, marketing, some applications of metals, and management of large metal projects. BIM also connected the Billiton operating companies and evaluated economic developments, plans, and investments. At Shell's Group level the Metals Panel a coordination committee for metals was established. In this committee future directions were set for Billiton's operating companies and other companies in the metal division. The BIM service company was responsible for realizing and monitoring Shell's corporate planning for the metal division, applying Shell's scenarios of possible economic, social, and political developments on a world-wide scale. On the basis of these scenarios corporate and division plans were worked out, and adapted by Billiton for specific metal issues. Medium-term plans were then prepared per metal and per operating company, to be approved by BIM, which also had a major role in the annual investment appraisals.

Prior to 1970, Billiton's head office mainly focused on financial and administrative support of the relatively independent operating companies. A deliberate strategic planning process across the different businesses for the development of activities and project evaluations did not exist. After 1970, Billiton was expected to design strategies on the basis of recent information and extensive prognoses. Billiton's management was handicapped by its inexperience in this kind of long-term strategic planning. This process soon led to decisions that hurt both Billiton and Shell. Many years after the take-over Billiton's Managing Director Mr. Slechte admitted for example that Billiton's large investments into aluminum should not have been made, and that a significant part of Billiton's losses could be blamed on the laborious cooperation between Shell and Billiton. He said:[5] 'Billiton's mining philosophy did not come about as expected. They just looked up at the new Shell-people. They thought: if they say so, who are we to argue to the contrary. Unjustified, because the Billiton-people possessed the professional knowledge on metals.'

Other differences between the Shell and Billiton organizations proved problematic as well. In the world of metals a well known saying goes: 'One can only talk metals after at least twenty years work.' For this reason most metal companies focus on one or

---

[5]*Het Financieele Dagblad* (1989). 'Billiton wacht op zeven vette jaren' (Billiton is waiting for seven fat years'), 4 March.

only a few metals. However, Shell's plan for Billiton was to become a geographical dispersed multi-metal group of companies with downstream and upstream activities. Shell introduced this distinction between upstream (exploration and exploitation) and downstream (processing, refining, transport, marketing and sales) activities at Billiton, because it was useful and accepted in the oil industry. However, the characteristics of upstream and downstream oil activities proved inapplicable to the metal industry. In the oil industry only a few dozen major oil firms perform significant upstream activities, in the metals industry many hundreds. The downstream oil sector generates well-defined products for well-defined markets (e.g. car fuels), while there are thousands of applications of metals for very diverse markets.

Another deviation from conventional metal-wisdom after the take-over was the introduction of job rotation at Billiton. In the metals business it takes a long time before someone really feels settled in a particular branch, and so job rotation is an exception. Billiton deviated from this practice after 1970, because Shell emphasized the advantages of job rotation. The Billiton employees were also restricted in gaining more in-depth experience in metals because of a large inflow of Shell-people during Billiton's fast growth period. The pool of Billiton employees was insufficient to fill higher management positions, so many new managers and specialists came from Shell. These people did not bring specific knowledge and experience in metals, and often returned to oil, gas, or chemicals after a number of years. The involvement of Billiton employees in new joint ventures was also limited. Although Billiton deliberately formed joint ventures to learn from the new activities in non-ferrous metal, few Billiton people got that chance.

Although mutual love was initially abundant, the newly weds clearly had to get used to each other. Company cultures, systems and processes differed in crucial areas. Shell's assumption of clear and important similarities between Billiton's and their own activities had to be counterbalanced with the realization that the differences were just as important. Fundamental differences showed up in applied technologies, competition, markets, and characteristics and applications of the products – differences that sometimes proved irreconcilable.

Billiton's aggressive growth strategy

Shell's intention was to rapidly develop the new Mining & Metallurgy division. Billiton would set up new projects, form joint ventures with several partners, and take over companies, in order to quickly become a diversified and substantial division. Shell gave Billiton 25 years to reach this goal, because it expected a severe downturn in the oil industry in the mid-nineties. Mr. Swart, Group Managing Director of Royal Dutch/Shell at the time, said: 'In 1990–1995 Shell should ask the question whether it has reached its goal of having a strong position in the metal industry, because then the oil industry has just sunk.'[6]

The new metal division had to grow until it counted for at least 10% of Shell's turnover. This meant that Billiton had to become a firm with an asset base of US$ 12 billion. In the context of the total metal industry turnover this was an extremely ambitious goal, a goal which in the eyes of some Billiton managers was clearly unrealistic. Billiton's activities in the metal industry at the time were of limited volume, with mining activities in only bauxite and tin. 40% of Billiton's turnover in 1970 was realized outside of the metal industry. Pressured by its new parent, this hotchpotch of unrelated subsidiaries was quickly cut back. Within a few years Billiton's activities were fully focused on mining, metallurgy, and trade of non-ferrous metals.

After this period of restructuring Billiton was ready for rapid expansion. The first plans included expansion of existing sectors, the development of an extensive world-wide exploration program to find ores and develop mines, and participation in many joint ventures. In the field of research new ideas were developed on ore processing and production of metals. Much of Billiton's early growth came from acquisitions. Through these acquisitions Billiton quickly became an internationally dispersed firm that covered the whole spectrum of non-ferrous metals. After the period of restructuring from 1970–1972, the total number of employees increased between 1973 and 1979 from 4100 to almost 6000 and turnover grew rapidly[7] (see Table 1).

Around 1977 Billiton started to invest heavily. Hundreds of millions of dollars were spent in

[6]*Shell Venster* (1985), 'Overneming Billiton 't best bewaarde geheim' ('Acquisition of Billiton the best kept secret'), October.
[7]*Shell Venster* (1979), 'De Toekomst van Billiton' ('The Future of Billiton'), April.

TABLE 1 Billiton turnover 1970–1979 (in £ million)

	1970	1971	1972	1973	1974	1975	1976	1977	1978	1979
Turnover	45	123	142	159	253	223	482	597	613	770

Source: Shell annual reports.

research, exploration, and promising new projects, even while the metal industry was in a deep crisis. At the center of Billiton's expansion was its aluminum-strategy, developed in the mid-1970s. Shell aimed at making Billiton one of the world's biggest six or seven aluminum companies. Billiton initially focused on mining only, but in 1975 the strategy changed to also include smelting and refining. Vertical integration was necessary to get control over all aluminum activities, from bauxite and alumina to the production of aluminum. Billiton invested in major joint ventures in Brazil, Australia, and Ireland, for a total amount of US$ 2.3 billion. The Surinam operations were expanded (bauxite and alumina), and in Guinea (Boké) it participated in a bauxite mine. The peaks in Billiton's investments in 1977–1978 and 1980–1984 are both related to expansion into the aluminum industry (see Table 2).

Growth remained the most important strategic driver for 13 years after the take-over. Despite a continuing crisis in the metal industry, Shell invested more money in Billiton in the few years after 1980 than in the whole previous decade since the take-over. Billiton was convinced that the new investments would prepare the company to benefit from the next economic recovery. Shell knew that Billiton's investments did not pay off as projected, but it preferred long-term growth to short-term gains. It understood that exploration, development, and research were expensive but necessary means to gain a strong position in the long-term.

The effects of a structural downturn in the industry

The 1970s marked an unexpected decline in growth in demand for metals. The first significant decline took place in 1973 during the first oil crisis. The second decline coincided with the second oil crisis in 1979. Despite these crises the total industry production capacity continued to expand at the same rate as in the post-World War period. Consequently huge overcapacity and unbalanced world metal market characterized most of the 1980s. During this period the non-ferrous metal industry fell into a depression. The industry was plagued by over capacity, weak demand, and severe price drops. This led to extensive world wide losses, cost reduction programs, and eventually closures of mines and plants. There was so much overcapacity on world markets that even when demand picked up, prices remained low.

Shell's expectations for the metals industry thus turned out to be much too optimistic. The depression in the aluminum industry, of central importance to Billiton's growth strategy, continued into the 1990s despite a brief recovery at the end of the 1980s. The collapse of aluminum demand was primarily related to shrinking worldwide industrial activity in the early 1980s. However, the high pricing policy of the aluminum cartel also contributed to the crisis as it led to increased substitution of plastics for aluminum, particularly in construction, packaging, and transportation. The impact of lower demand was

TABLE 2 Billiton investments 1970–1986 (in £ million)

	1970	1971	1972	1973	1974	1975	1976	1977	1978	1979	1980	1981	1982	1983	1984	1985	1986
Investments	7	24	25	37	26	35	20	70	63	34	126	316	504	310	176	66	55

Source: F. Hendriks (1987), *Shell: Energie, Metalen, Bosbouw en Zaaizaad* (Shell: Energy, Metals, Forestry, Sowing Seeds), Utrecht: Jan van Arkel, pp 286–287

aggravated by permanent oversupply of aluminum – a result of large investments in the 1970s. As many investments came from governments of developing countries whose primary interests were not always profits, the Big Six companies on the aluminum market slowly lost control of the industry. This was most clearly reflected in their inability to prevent quotation of aluminum prices on the London Metal Exchange in 1978 and the Commodity Exchange in New York in 1983. Until then, aluminum prices were set by the Big Six. Fluctuations of aluminum prices have since become as common as fluctuations of other commodities' prices.

The structural downturn in the metal industry severely affected Billiton, which continued to make losses throughout most of the 1980s (see Table 3). Economic growth at the end of the 1980s made a change, albeit for a short time, as after 1989 the world economy deteriorated again, prices for metals dropped, and losses returned to the industry. The subsequent years showed further worsening as demand continued to be low while supply continued to grow.

Given these poor financial results it was not surprising that Billiton's diversification policy was questioned and discussed more than once during the 1970s and 1980s. Billiton argued that broad diversification would spread risk as it became less dependent on a cyclical decline of one metal. For certain periods some of Billiton's activities were indeed remarkably profitable, but after 1980 prices for all non-ferrous metals were so low that no metal could compensate losses in others. Billiton's poor performance in investment projects was also striking. Time after time 'me-too' projects were developed after Billiton had analyzed markets and followed trends. This behavior of adaptation and imitation made Billiton a sure participant in projects at the brink of overcapacity and spoilt markets.[8]

Rationalization and strategic reorientation

During the 1980s Billiton slowly came to the conclusion that the market situation would deteriorate, and changed course. New activities were postponed, only running projects beyond the point of no return could proceed. It was decided to concentrate on bringing existing projects into operation and efficiently exploiting running installations and plants. Billiton's top manager Mr. Van der Graaf said in 1983:[9] 'Our policy is now to finish projects and bring them into operation. New investments will only be available for current and proven companies. We feel something is structurally changing in the West, as a result of which future developments are less predictable than before. We have to be careful with new expansion plans, because mistakes will never be compensated.'

In 1983 approximately 100 out of 430 employees of BIM were relocated. These were mainly people that generated new projects. The exploration program was also reduced. By 1984 consolidation, cost cutting, and disposal of unprofitable and marginally profitable activities had replaced Billiton's growth strategy. In that year Billiton took provisions to close or sell off cash demanding activities with poor prospects. Its ambition to become one of the world's leading upstream aluminum firms was put on hold. Although projects in Ireland, Australia, and Brazil had brought Billiton a firm basis of raw materials

TABLE 3 Turnover and profits of Billiton 1980–1992 (in £ million)

	1980	1981	1982	1983	1984	1985	1986	1987	1988	1989	1990	1991	1992
Turnover	720	617	641	733	995	961	772	862	1185	1662	1361	1287	1260
Profits	23	−39	−95	−91	−62	−187	−44	15	109	168	97	8	−41

Source: Shell annual reports.

[8]F. Hendriks (1987), *Shell: Energie, Metalen, Bosbouw en Zaaizaad* (Shell: Energy, Metals, Forestry, Sowing Seeds), Utrecht: Jan van Arkel.
[9]*Shell Venster* (1983), 'Billiton moet op adem komen' ('Billiton has to take a breath after a stormy growth period'), May.

bauxite and alumina, its melting capacity was still far lower than those of the Big Six.

After the appointment of Mr. Slechte as Coordinator Metals in 1986, Billiton's new 'mission' was to provide a positive contribution to the Royal Dutch/Shell Group. No later than by 1988 was Billiton to return to black figures. In order to become profitable quickly, Billiton aggressively cut costs, especially in its aluminum activities, which were the biggest loss-maker. Many other loss-making or marginally profitable activities were stopped or sold. The head office near The Hague was further reduced until only 125 employees were left. In 1983 Billiton counted 5800 employees worldwide, by 1986: 4600.

Billiton's strategic planning process was also changed. In the 'good old days' of expansion BIM had acted as a centralized strategic planning unit that was primarily responsible for deciding on investments in new projects and activities. According to Shell, this was not how a service company should operate. Shell made clear to BIM that its raison d'être was related to a demand for its services based on added value for the operating companies. It had to become less bureaucratic and truly act as an adviser and service company. BIM's formal hierarchical pyramid was replaced by a Shell-style matrix-organization and planning responsibilities returned to the operating companies that were closer to the subsequent markets. They knew better how to survive in their branch, and how to prosper in the future.

For the first time since 1980 Billiton returned to profitability in 1987. A modest profit of £15 million (2% ROI) was followed by £109 million in 1988, which represented a healthy 13% ROI. The objective to quickly return to profitability was reached. However, Mr. Slechte indicated that higher prices of metals were the primary reason for the financial improvements, and that the real proof of a structural change for the better would be given in a new recession. In the early 1990s the economic situation deteriorated again, and Billiton again faced overcapacity and plummeting metal prices, returning to losses in 1992. One of the key problems was the situation in the downstream sector. The performance was disappointing as most of the activities were loss-making. It had proven extremely difficult for Shell to find the synergies for which it had been looking for so long. The downstream activities were Billiton's only loss-maker in 1991, in 1992 they were the principal loss-maker. In 1992 Billiton announced withdrawal from the loss-making downstream sector. Within a few years Billiton would dispose of all down stream activities, which meant withdrawing the majority of its home country activities.

Shell sells Billiton

Despite its large investments in Billiton, the metal sector had remained a small part of the Royal Dutch/Shell Group of Companies. In 1992 it represented only approximately 2% of its US$ 80 billion turnover, and 3.5% of the Group's investments of over US$ 60 billion. In 23 years Billiton had become an international firm, but the main ambition to represent approximately 10% of the Group's turnover was not achieved by a long shot. Billiton had not become the group's cash cow Shell had planned for in the early 1970s. On the contrary, the metal industry turned out to be much less profitable than the oil industry and highly cyclical in nature.

The explosive growth that had been projected in the 1970s never materialized. Although Shell is well known for looking beyond horizons, it had not been able to 'read' the future of metals. It therefore did not come as a great surprise when on May 11, 1993, Royal Dutch/Shell announced Gencor's interest for Billiton's metal activities. Gencor was a South African mining company, and was primarily interested in Billiton's mining and aluminum activities and its market and trading activities. Gencor had thus far mainly been active in South Africa and the acquisition would make Gencor an international mining firm. Shell would withdraw from the metal market altogether, a move that would fit into its new strategy 'to concentrate on its core activities oil and gas'. Shell would be the last of the multinational oil firms to leave the metal industry.

Within Billiton people did not react negatively to the idea of transferring to Gencor. Billiton's way of thinking would possibly correspond better with Gencor's than with Shell's, whose dominant direction was now clearly oil and gas. In addition, Gencor would continue Billiton as a 'going concern', including its name, and as a core for a new international mining company. Gencor also promised not to change the management of the Billiton companies. Gencor expressed its confidence of a successful take-over, because of Billiton's low production costs in mining and aluminum, and high quality management. Moreover, the phrase in Gencor's mission statement: '. . . real long-term growth and an internationally leading position in mining and metals' sounded very familiar to Billiton, while the effect of the 'merger' was music to Billiton's ears: Gencor/Billiton would become one of the world's top-5 mining companies.

Gencor's core is ore

In the mid-1980s Gencor was known among investors as a bureaucratic conglomerate that performed badly. In 1986 institutional investors appointed Derk Keys as the new CEO. After five and a half years Derk Keys left a highly successful entrepreneurial and decentralized group, and became Minister of Economic Affairs. Investors were happy and Gencor's rating improved substantially. In 1993 Gencor decided to only focus on mining activities and unbundled its major industrial assets by distributing shares in Engen, Genbel, Sappi and Malbak to its shareholders. That left it to focus on its aim of becoming a major international mining group, instead of a huge conglomerate. 'Today, conglomerates are out of favor around the world,' Gencor chairman Brian Gilbertson contended. 'Investors like focused, pure-play businesses. The general public is suspicious of corporate giants.' This strategy created a mass of new energy among management, and became an enormous success. Stripped of its industrial interests, Gencor shrank by a full third, but the stock value of the new focused mining firm quickly rose higher than the former conglomerate's. Gencor invested almost a billion US dollars in the Columbus stainless steel project and started building one of the world's biggest aluminum smelters, Alusaf.

Gencor's activities were almost entirely concentrated in South Africa. It had to internationalize to compete with other, international, mining companies. For Gencor, Billiton presented an exceptional opportunity to acquire assets outside South Africa. In line with Gencor's new vision *'world-class ore is our core'*, Gencor thus paid Shell $1,144 billion for the Billiton base metals group in October 1994. The question was however whether Gencor's ambitions could be realized. The newly acquired Billiton could reveal itself again as the huge loss-maker it had been for the majority of 23 years as a Shell subsidiary. These losses didn't hurt Shell too much since Billiton accounted for only 2% of total revenues, but

for Gencor continued Billiton losses could jeopardize the future of the whole company. Despite these risks Gilbertson remained confident, and even Shell's President Mr. Herkströter admitted at a shareholder meeting that the new parent might bring Billiton back into the black figures: 'Maybe Gencor can do something Shell could not.'[10]

Billiton's 'miraculous' recovery under Gencor's transformation

The acquisition of Billiton was a bet on the aluminum industry, for this was Billiton's center of gravity. Including the Alusaf smelters the new Gencor would be the world's seventh aluminum firm in terms of size. The new Gencor generated 24% of turnover in aluminum and related metals, 18% chrome, manganese and stainless steel, 16% titanium minerals, 12% gold, 10% platina group-metals, 10% coal, and 2% nickel. In all activities except nickel Gencor would be a world top-10 firm. Since Gencor was relatively inexperienced in aluminum, it decided to change little at Billiton.

It wasn't long before the acquisition of Billiton helped Gencor record a 62.7% increase in attributable income for the year to end-June in 1995. Billiton's maiden contribution to income from operations represented 43% of the total. Excluding the contribution from Richards Bay Minerals – previously 50% owned by Gencor but now part of Billiton – Billiton's contribution was 27% of the total income. Analysts were obviously enthusiastic about the transformed Gencor, although they were quick to point out that the group was lucky with the timing of the Billiton deal and start-up of the Alusaf smelter. Both were completed just in time to benefit from a sharp rise in the aluminum price, which increased by more than a 100% from its low of US$ 1,109 on November 1 1993 to a high of US$ 2,147 on January 25 1995 (see Figure 1).

However, Gencor's initial success was not solely based on the rise of aluminum prices that greatly benefited Billiton. There were other important building blocks in Gencor's transformation. In South Africa it built some strong businesses; one through a significant platinum merger creating a new company of the same size as the leader Rustenburg Platinum, another by increasing its shareholding in the Richards Bay Minerals mineral sands business so

[10]*De Volkskrant* (1993), 'Met Billiton vertrekt een oud-koloniaal naar Zuid-Afrika' ('The once colonial Billiton moves to South Africa'), 15 May.

FIGURE 1   20 day average aluminum price, 1990–2002

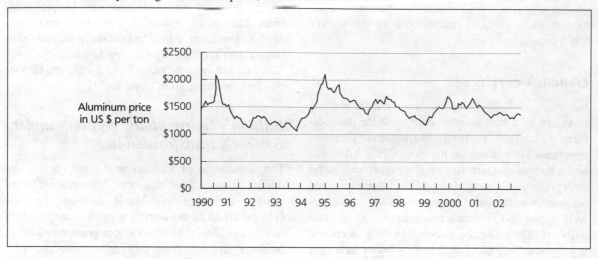

Source: London Metal Exchange.

that it was in 50-50 ownership with RTZ of the UK, and thirdly by merging Trans-Natal Coal with Rand Mines, two companies that made a perfect fit, to form Ingwe, a deal that leap-frogged Gencor to being world-class in the coal business.[11]

After this series of major deals Mr. Gilbertson focused on tidying up Gencor's portfolio, discarding any mineral assets that did not meet his definition of 'world-class'. In the meantime, Mr. Gilbertson introduced several new management practices. He encouraged his managers to be responsive to market opportunities and gave his managers more freedom to take risks. He slimmed down the head-office staff from 1,100 to 550 in five years and consolidated the maze of different companies, restructuring Gencor into seven global product businesses: 'one commodity, one brain'.[12] Gilbertson also encouraged 'opportunism', realizing that in a fluctuating market there were always opportunities for good take-over deals. Although some analysts expressed concerns that Gencor's small management team might be over-stretching itself, Gencor successfully managed to keep Billiton profitable until the end of the 1990s, despite a complete collapse of metal prices during 1997 and 1998 (see Table 4).

Gencor's subsequent demerger

In the mid-1990s Mr. Gilbertson decided that Gencor needed to address 'the difficulties that a South African company faces when it wishes to finance major international acquisitions'. He had become increasingly convinced of the difficulty of expanding and funding an international mining operation under South Africa's restrictive foreign exchange controls. He therefore decided to relocate the base metals business to a market with less strict exchange controls.

The best way to achieve this aim was to demerge the larger base metals business from the precious metals (gold and platinum) operations and list the base metals business on a stock exchange outside South Africa. Gencor subsequently sold to a new Billiton group all its interests in aluminum, coal, mineral sands, nickel, Samancor (which houses Gencor's manganese assets), chrome and stainless steel – equivalent to 80% of Gencor's net assets. To pay for them. Billiton made a share issue to Gencor that was redistributed to Gencor's shareholders, giving Billiton a listing in South Africa in addition to its international listing. To build a strong balance sheet, Billiton simultaneously made an offering of 375 million new shares to international investors. As

[11]*The Economist*, March 9, 1996.
[12]*Ibid.*

TABLE 4 Five years financial summary, in US$ million, except per share data

	1994*	1995**	1996	1997	1998
Net turnover	3063	9061	10841	5286	5446
Operating costs	−1314	−3933	−4526	−4658	−4808
Operating profit	1749	392	667	628	638
Attributable profit	177	261	433	537	481
– as % of turnover	10.5	5.5	7.7	9.2	7.9
Investments	1221	1585	1220	1059	632
Attributable net assets	1456	1791	1997	3014	4582

*10-month period only (September 1, 1993 to June 30, 1994).
**Years run from July 1 to June 30 of the given year (e.g. 1995 runs from July 1, 1994 to June 30, 1995).
Source: Billiton annual reports.

Billiton already had an office in London, the company chose the UK capital as its base. On September 22, 1997 Billiton entered the FTSE-100 index as the UK's 48th largest company, valued at US$ 7.5 billion.

As a result of the demerger, the number of employees at Gencor dropped to 5 by February 1998, from more than 100,000 people 10 years earlier. Thus, in the course of only 12 months, Gilbertson brought more than a century of development as a traditional mining finance house to an end. Gencor became an investment holding company with stakes in three of the world's finest mining companies: a 59% stake in Billiton (base metals), 47.9% in Gold Fields (gold) and 18.7% in Implats (platinum group metals). The holding company passed the receipts from the underlying investments directly to Gencor's shareholders.

Navigating Billiton into the 21st century

It wasn't long before the slump in the metals market caught up with the new Billiton, despite managing to remain profitable. A year after its listing in London at 220p per share, in which it raised US$ 1.5 billion in new equity, the Billiton share price dipped below 100p, and it decided to buy back 2.5 percent of the equity. Investors were very unhappy and accused Billiton of not spending the extra capital it had raised on profitable projects.

However as soon as the 1997 and 1998 crisis was over, Billiton started both buying up minority interests and investing in new projects. Its average capital expenditure at the end of the 1990s was US$ 1 billion a year, and Billiton's stock price quickly recovered in parallel to the rise in metals prices. Gilbertson continued to invest heavily, buying Alcoa's Worsley stake for US$ 1.5 billion making Billiton more than self-sufficient in alumina, and spending US$ 2 billion on Rio Algom (copper in Latin America). Especially after this last deal investors started to get worried and instead of accusing Billiton of doing too little with its money, they now accused Billiton of spending too lavishly. By the end of 2000 Billiton was beginning to be seriously constrained by its balance sheet, with gearing up to some 70 per cent. Despite a succession of deals, its market capitalization remained at less than US$ 8 billion, a value comparable to its value at its launch on the London Stock Exchange in 1997.

Mr. Gilbertson was critically asked how much he was driven by being big and how much by running an operation which is profitable for its shareholders. He replied that Billiton was not driven solely by size, but he had also made it clear earlier than he believed the future mining scene would be dominated by a small number of large international companies and that Billiton wanted to be one of them. Gilbertson was unhappy with the share price, but realized that Billiton was not large enough yet, still too dependent on aluminum prices, and too overstretched financially to be one of the few large dominant players of the future.

He thus set out to work on a deal with would surmount all of his previous deals, a deal that would launch Billiton straight into the major league of mining and metals companies. Gilbertson had long been interested in exploring the possibility of a merger with Broken Hill Proprietary Company (BHP), a large Australian mining, metals and oil conglomerate, which was undergoing major restructuring after its diversified growth strategy of the 1980s had failed miserably. Within weeks of Billiton's London debut, Billiton's bankers approached BHP at a conference in Edinburgh, followed by a meeting of executives of the two companies in early 1988. But BHP was in the midst of a major overhaul, and was not in the mood to talk.

Things changed after Mr. Anderson became CEO of BHP in December 1988. BHP had experienced Australia's biggest financial loss ever, after which it restructured and sold US$ 3.6 billion of assets. The BHP share price recovered, but the price was still half of where Mr. Anderson and his fellow American, Charles Goodyear, CFO, thought it needed to be to fund growth. The collapse of the Australian dollar made overseas deals expensive and BHP vulnerable to foreign predators. BHP became increasingly convinced that it needed to be on either the New York or London Stock Exchange to attract investor attention, win a re-rating and have access to deeper capital markets.

A third 'parent' for Billiton: BHP of Australia

Brian Gilbertson had already told Anderson in 1998 that a merger between their two companies was the best deal in the industry. But the critical meeting came in early 2001 in Johannesburg where Mr. Gilbertson and Mr. Anderson, in a couple of hours, sketched out the main elements of a deal that was subsequently billed as 'the largest in Australia's corporate history'. On June 29th 2001, after only four months of preparatory work, the deal was completed. The merger created a mining and metals powerhouse, second only in size to Alcan, the Canadian aluminum group. As the world's biggest exporter of metallurgical coal, its third largest producer of iron ore and its fourth of copper, BHPBilliton had annual sales of nearly US$ 19 billion and had US$ 8 billion to spend on capital projects over the next four years.[13]

In spite of BHP's pre-announced market capitalization of US$ 18.5 billion being almost double Billiton's, BHP agreed to a 58% stake in the merged entity and thus paid a significant premium. It was also agreed that within a year, the leadership of the combined group would pass to Billiton's management when Paul Anderson was to retire to make way for Brian Gilbertson. Headquarters would be based in Melbourne, and the company would retain its dual listing in Australia and in London.

Mr. Anderson considered the deal to be a 'sensational fit'. Billiton would give BHP a better understanding of business in Africa, a broader portfolio to ride out cyclical movements in the commodities markets and advantages of scale in shipping, marketing and purchasing. In return, Billiton would have access to cheaper financing for new projects and existing debt, greater liquidity and better protection from political risks. Billiton's proposed merger with BHP also removed the UK group's high exposure to African-based operations and a reliance on aluminum as a major earnings driver. The two groups clearly complemented each other's portfolios. BHP brought in iron ore, coal and its share in Chile's Escondida, known as the world's best copper mine, as well as a small but highly profitable oil and gas business. Billiton provided BHP with three new businesses – aluminum, nickel and titanium – all areas BHP had said it wanted to enter.[14] In addition, savings from the deal were set to reach US$ 270 million net of restructuring costs by 2003.[15]

Mr. Anderson dismissed criticism that the deal would leave BHPBilliton too diverse, with interests in base metals, oil and gas, coal, ferroalloys, iron ore, nickel and aluminum. He said:[16] 'Fund managers are schizophrenic: they say they want a $ 30 billion company but they want it to be focused. You could put all the copper in the world together and you wouldn't get a $ 30 billion company.' BHPBilliton was aware however that some activities did not fit its portfolio particularly well. As part of the deal it was therefore agreed that BHP would spin off its remaining steel assets, which represented about 5 per cent of the combined group's portfolio.

However, despite expectations that this signaled a concentration on its minerals business, the

[13] *Financial Times*, March 24, 2001.
[14] *Ibid.*
[15] *Ibid.*
[16] *Financial Times*, March 20, 2001.

BHPBilliton group did decide to hang on to its oil interests, which delivered 39% of its earnings. BHPBilliton Petroleum's president Phil Aiken confirmed the group's commitment to its petroleum business:[17] 'I have had no suggestion at all that there is anything but 100 per cent support for petroleum to be part of BHPBilliton for some time to come,' he said. 'I think it has very good growth opportunities with a number of brown(field) and greenfield projects to continue into the future and be an important part of the group.' He expected to boost output by 37% by the fiscal year 2006.

BHPBilliton's successful start

Shortly after the deal was completed BHPBilliton announced a record combined profit of US$ 2.189 billion before exceptional items for the year ending June 30, 2001. The result was up 26% from the companies' combined profit of US$ 1.743 billion in 1999/2000. BHPBilliton received a further boost when Standard & Poor's upgraded its long-term debt rating for BHPBilliton to 'A' Outlook Positive. The credit rating upgrade from Standard & Poor's was an endorsement of one of the elements of the strategic rationale for the merger and reflected the stronger financial position and more diversified risk structure of the combined Group.

After the merger BHPBilliton focused on sequencing the extensive pipeline of growth opportunities, streamlining the organization and realizing merger synergies. 'Reducing costs remains a prime area of focus for the management team,' said Deputy CEO Gilbertson.[18] 'Many commodity markets have deteriorated materially and several traded commodities, including copper, nickel and aluminum are trading at near record lows. If these conditions persist our earnings will not escape the impact. However, the quality, size and diversity of the BHPBilliton portfolio provide us with more options for responding to the slowdown than may be available to many of our competitors.' BHPBilliton made deep management staff cuts, involving up to a third of former Billiton head office staff in London. There were rumors that the company was internally targeting much bigger savings than the announced target of US$ 270 million.

The Group also remained focused on further growth, although Paul Anderson took a much more vigorous approach to capital expenditure than Gilbertson in his days at Billiton. The financial year 2002 saw the pipeline of growth opportunities expand further. Some long-time investors and observers of BHP drew parallels with BHP's early-1990s disastrous growth program and asked themselves if the same couldn't happen again. However, most shareholders were reasonably content with BHPBilliton's progress as its share price had significantly outperformed relevant indices since announcement of the merger (see Figure 2).

A Billiton future without its deal-making leader

In December 2001, only six months after completion of the merger deal, BHPBilliton claimed that that integration of the two companies was complete. Meanwhile Mr. Anderson was preparing the way for Brian Gilbertson to take over the CEO position in July 2002. 'In the interim, there will be a gradual transition, with more and more of the future direction of the company left to Brian,' Mr. Anderson said.[19] 'I will be more and more focused on putting together this financial year and wrapping up loose ends, like steel.' Throughout 2002 Mr. Gilbertson took on a greater role in shaping the future of the company. BHPBilliton managed to get through the year relatively well reporting a 7.2% drop in earnings, notwithstanding much weaker commodity prices. As agreed, at the end of the financial year 2002 Paul Anderson passed the baton to Brian Gilbertson, who was now CEO of one of the world's largest metals and mining companies.

As usual though, Gilbertson had his mind fixed on further aggressive growth. He drafted a 'hit list' of potential merger partners, including some of the biggest mining and oil groups in the world, and started work on a proposed secret deal, dubbed Project Six, which was rumored to be a 'very significant, single transaction' and was due to go to the board in February 2003.[20] There was speculation that Alcan Inc. may be involved, which was itself

---

[17]*Daily Telegraph*, November 27, 2001.
[18]*Ibid.*
[19]*The Asian Wall Street Journal*, December 24, 2001.
[20]*Reuters*, January 14, 2003.

FIGURE 2 Billiton's share price relative to the LSE Mining Index, 1998–2002

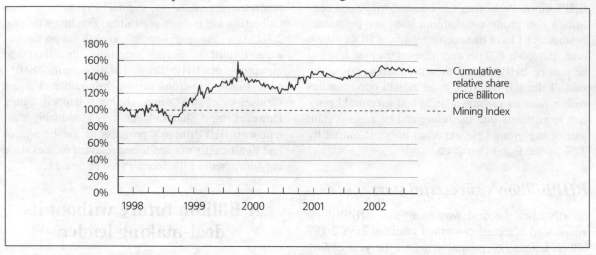

Source: Datastream.

rumored to have been planning a bid for Billiton within days of the BHP–Billiton merger. Media reports also suggested Mr. Gilbertson might have in his sights Australia's Woodside Petroleum Ltd., Canada's biggest oil producer Imperial Oil Ltd., and U.S.-listed oil exploration and production firm Kerr-McGee Corp.

Then, on January 6th 2003, BHPBilliton stunned investors by announcing the abrupt departure of Brian Gilbertson after less than six months in the CEO job. Mr. Gilbertson was replaced immediately by chief development officer Charles Goodyear, former CFO of BHP. BHPBilliton Chairman Don Argus, one of Australia's most important businessmen nicknamed 'Don't Argue', had moved against Gilbertson's expansion plans and forced his resignation.

Since the merger, the market had speculated that Mr. Gilbertson could not reconcile himself to working under the chairman of an independent board in a company known for its bureaucratic culture. Russell Skirrow, global head of metals and mining research at Merrill Lynch, said:[21] 'The two companies had very different cultures and styles. Brian Gilbertson was like a racing car. He could get you there very

quickly but there was always a chance of a crash on the way.' BHPBilliton cited unspecified 'irreconcilable differences' with the board as the reason for Mr. Gilbertson's sudden departure, but some observers argued that Don Argus fired Brian Gilbertson after it became clear that Gilbertson's proposed merger meant that Argus' chairmanship was at stake.

A BHP spokesman later said the differences between BHPBilliton's board and Mr. Gilbertson were 'related to matters of style and approach'. However, some London investors said they were unhappy with the group's explanation of Mr. Gilbertson's departure and were left wondering whether there had been a split between Gilbertson and Argus over strategy, not just management style. 'Gilbertson would have been looking at the possibility of a company-transforming type acquisition, and the board has seemingly decided that maybe the emphasis will be much more on the organic,' said Deutsche asset Management resources analyst Lawrence Grech.[22]

Mr. Argus emphasized that the installation of a new chief executive would not detract from the strategy unveiled by the company in 2002. This included the promise to cut costs by US$ 500 mil-

[21]*The Times*, January 7, 2003.
[22]*Reuters*, January 14, 2003.

lion a year by 2005 and to invest US$ 10 billion in new growth projects over the next few years. However, Mr. Gilbertson's departure did fuel speculation that the merger was unraveling. 'It has certainly changed the power balance,' said one insider.[23] 'If you look at the Billiton-ness of the company versus the BHP-ness, the power has shifted back the other way.' Other investors and analysts were less pessimistic and said that BHPBilliton still had a strong growth profile even without major acquisitions. They would not lose any sleep over Mr. Gilbertson's departure and the demise of his mysterious grand plan, Project Six.

Is Gilbertson's departure a sign of trouble ahead for BHPBilliton? In the context of an increasingly difficult economic environment and without its opportunistic, risk-taking leader, will the company lose its momentum? Or are the BHPBilliton synergies large enough to avoid slipping back to the days of underperformance?

[23]*The Australian*, January 7, 2003.

LoJack and the MicroLogic alliance

By David Wylie, Maxwell Morton and U. Srinivasa Rangan[1]

The LoJack Corporation, founded in 1978 and headquartered in Dedham, Massachusetts, developed and sold the LoJack 'Stolen Vehicle Recovery System', a unique patented system designed to assist law enforcement personnel in locating, tracking, and recovering stolen vehicles. Sales for the year ended February 28, 1998 were $74,502,000. 81% of revenues were derived from the sale of the LoJack System in the United States through a distribution network consisting primarily of new automobile dealers. International revenues were primarily derived from product sales and licensing revenues from unaffiliated distributors.

Joe Abely, president and chief operating officer of LoJack since 1996, had joined LoJack in October 1988 as senior vice president and chief financial officer. Prior to joining, he had been a partner in Deloitte Haskings & Sells. Along with Mike Daley, the CEO, Joe was the guiding light in casting the future direction of the company. He was committed to a strategy for LoJack of expansion into more metropolitan areas, states, and countries where the combination of population density, new car sales, and vehicle theft was highest. He realized, however, that the strong consumer confidence in the LoJack brand, the extensive network of distributors, sales and marketing expertise, and experience in the technology of tracking and position location opened up a world of opportunity for the company.

The company was also in an excellent financial position, with enough cash and treasury stock to support quite extensive expansion plans. Indeed, LoJack had repurchased $54 million in stock just since 1996 (see Table 1).

Abely and Senior Vice President Bill Duvall had recently met with senior managers from MicroLogic, LoJack's long standing strategic partner in the development and manufacture of the Stolen Vehicle Recovery System, to discuss joining with them in introducing a new monitoring and maintenance system for construction equipment. MicroLogic was already in the process of changing its strategy and was now committed to entering this new marketplace with its own product and service. Alternatively, Abely was exploring opportunities in the automatic vehicle location industry including trailer tracking, passenger car, and commercial fleet equipment and service.

History of LoJack

Bill Reagan, a former Navy pilot, was operating his own mergers and acquisitions company in 1977 while serving part-time as a selectman and police commissioner in the town of Medfield, Massachusetts. Hearing that several police officers in other departments had been shot while pulling over a car, he became deeply disturbed and considered how to prevent similar events in the future. Unable to sleep one night, he conceived of the LoJack concept while sitting at the kitchen table at 2:00 AM. He spent the rest of the night drafting an invention disclosure.

Lacking a background in this particular technology, he turned to Frank Massa, a friend who was president of a small electronics firm, to help complete the patent application. When the patent was issued in early December of 1979, Massa decided that his firm lacked the appropriate technical resources and time required to develop fully the LoJack technology. However, Reagan was able to find a small group of potential investors who had sufficient faith in his ability to 'pull this off' so that they were willing to provide preliminary funding of about $250,000 in exchange for 40% of the company's equity to start the company.

About the same time, Reagan was introduced to Sheldon Apsell, Founder and President of

TABLE 1 Financial statements, LoJack, Inc. 1992–1999

Assets (×1000)*	1999	1998	1997	1996	1995	1994	1993	1992
Cash & equivalents	10,230	6,898	16,272	31,631	21,666	8,417	1,404	2,277
Net receivables	9,679	8,074	7,430	5,874	4,259	2,662	2,408	1,908
Inventories	5,668	4,883	3,745	2,780	1,846	1,803	2,135	2,683
Other current assets	1,791	2,760	1,679	385	64	54	58	30
Total current assets	27,368	22,615	29,126	40,670	27,834	12,935	6,005	6,897
Other investments	–	–	–	–	–	–	160	160
Net PP&E	9,873	9,764	8,723	7,653	8,440	7,916	7,088	7,342
Other Assets[1]	237	282	316	355	420	525	306	376
Total Assets[2]	38,479	32,661	38,165	48,678	36,695	21,376	13,559	14,775

Liabilities (×1000)*	1999	1998	1997	1996	1995	1994	1993	1992
Accounts payable	3,438	2,578	2,842	2,563	2,549	2,782	2,577	1,788
St Debt & Cur Ltd	1,297	746	694	671	652	323	230	1,693
Accrued payroll	1,230	1,058	838	673	709	468	593	521
Income taxes payable	–	137	287	365	NA	NA	–	–
Other current liab	2,669	2,609	2,582	2,780	1,957	1,356	1,334	716
Total current liab	8,634	7,129	7,243	7,051	5,866	4,929	4,734	4,717
Capital lease oblig	1,373	793	782	644	899	618	1,884	2,222
Deferred income	3,114	2,676	2,150	1,657	1,164	667	–	–
Deferred taxes[3]	242	560	770	(4,401)	–	–	–	–
Other liabilities	–	–	–	–	–	–	753	–
Total liabilities	11,157	11,158	10,945	4,951	7,930	6,214	7,371	6,939
Preferred stock	–	–	–	–	–	15,561	14,345	13,128
Common stock/ord cap	224	223	220	219	213	151	128	128
Capital surplus[4]	60,330	59,494	57,540	56,872	53,046	23,961	17,456	18,791
Retained earnings	16,559	5,551	(4,336)	(12,516)	(24,494)	(24,510)	(25,740)	(23,998)
Treasury stock	52,232	43,765	26,204	848	–	–	–	213
Common shldrs equity	25,116	21,502	27,220	43,727	28,765	(398)	(8,156)	(5,292)
Total liabs & equity	38,479	32,661	38,165	48,678	36,695	21,376	13,559	14,775

Income statement (×1000)*	1999	1998	1997	1996	1995	1994	1993	1992
Net sales or revenue	83,210	74,502	61,665	52,516	41,658	30,219	23,346	17,535
Cost of goods sold	37,565	31,800	26,775	23,131	20,274	14,939	12,306	9,160
Gross income	45,645	39,924	32,464	26,655	18,524	12,928	8,849	6,160
Depreciation & amort		2,778	2,426	2,730	2,860	2,351	2,191	2,215
sell gen & admin exp	29,158	24,404	20,544	18,050	14,955	11,314	10,224	9,473
Operating income	16,486	15,520	11,920	8,605	3,568	1,614	(1,375)	(3,314)
Non oper int income[5]	428	788	1,572	1,526	817	171	14	101
Other inc/exp–net	300	108	66	82	91	–	–	–
Interest expense	265	211	154	167	344	313	381	1,425
Pretax income	18,049	16,205	13,404	10,047	4,133	1,472	(1,742)	(4,638)
Income taxes		6,318	5,224	(1,931)	295	79	–	–
Net income		9,887	8,180	11,978	3,412	177	(2,958)	(4,638)

*Years end on last day of February
[1] May include intangible assets and/or deferred charges. 1992 – includes deposits
[2] 1996 – adjusted to exclude deferred taxes
[3] 1996 – adjusted to include deferred tax debits
[4] 1994, 1993, 1992 – net of excess liquidation value on preferred stock
[5] 1994 – includes other income

MicroLogic, a ten-person product development firm which specialized in developing electronics products for others. They immediately hit it off. With only a hand-shake to consummate the deal, MicroLogic helped refine the product specifications (going so far as to interview convicted car thieves), designed the entire system, worked with various government agencies to obtain the appropriate approvals, and performed the required field work to prove to the FCC (Federal Communications Commission) that the assigned radio frequency would not interfere with that assigned to television's channel 7. By July 1986, the System became available in Massachusetts as a market experiment. Ultimately, in 1989, the FCC, satisfied with the test and success of the technology, allocated a police radio band for operation of a nationwide Stolen Vehicle Recovery Network. In return for its initial contribution, MicroLogic received a total of $350,000 and 90,000 shares of LoJack stock.

With everything in place, a contract was finally signed for MicroLogic to manufacture the police tracking computers. Motorola agreed to manufacture the transponders that were installed in each automobile.

To obtain financing for the rollout of the system in 1983, Reagan and his wife created their own road show to seek an investment bank to take them public. Armed with stubborn resolve and dogged determination, Reagan lived on his credit card for three weeks in New York City until he was able to find a firm that would agree to take LoJack public to raise $875,000. In 1985, he was able to obtain another round of financing of $4.5 million from Tucker-Anthony with the help of board member Mary Cunningham.

His good fortune, however, proved to be ephemeral. By July 1986, the company was in trouble. Most of the money had been spent, product development was not quite complete and the distribution system consisted mostly of two converted garages that served as retail outlets and a handful of new-car dealerships. Sales were about 100 units per month, but payroll had grown to almost $1 million per year. Reagan resigned and the board of directors asked Mike Daley, a board member himself and former real estate developer, to take over as temporary CEO until a permanent replacement could be found.

Daley immediately reduced staff by 40% and sought additional capital infusions. He was able to obtain it in small chunks of about $300,000 at a time

but had to provide a 25% discount. During 1987, the garage retail outlets were closed. In order to expand the marketing reach while conserving cash, a new franchising model was being tested in Florida. Anticipating strong initial sales and wanting to take advantage of volume discounts, LoJack ordered 34,000 units from Motorola at $120 per unit, but found itself unable to fund the purchase. Motorola executives were extremely helpful and supportive, working out a long-term payment plan. Indeed, LoJack executives still attribute this support as critical to the early survival of the company.

Sales began to grow, although only slowly at first. By late 1987, 450 units per month were being sold.

The LoJack Stolen Vehicle Recovery System

The concept behind the LoJack Stolen Vehicle Recovery System was quite straightforward, while the underlying technology was fairly complex. The components of the system included a 'LoJack Unit' which was installed in a car, a registration database which correlated unique Unit codes with each vehicle, a 'Sector Activation System' in the state computers that could activate a LoJack Unit, and 'Police Tracking Computers' that allowed police to locate the stolen car.

The LoJack system was available in the United States in areas where state and local police departments had agreed to support the system. LoJack had to maintain the registration database, tie in the Sector Activation System with the state-wide stolen vehicle reporting system, and install tracking computers in police cars and at strategic locations. LoJack donated these units to the various police agencies while retaining responsibility for their maintenance.

When buying new vehicles, customers usually purchased LoJack Units as a $595 option. Like other options, the LoJack Unit could usually be financed conveniently as a part of the purchase price of the vehicle. There were no recurring fees and the cost was often mitigated by an annual reduction of insurance rates of up to 35%. LoJack warranted that if a LoJack equipped vehicle were stolen within two years of installation and not recovered within 24 hours from the time that the theft was reported to the police, it would refund the full purchase price.

LoJack management also discovered that the majority of purchasers were buying mid-priced cars rather than expensive cars such as Mercedes or Jaguars. Indeed, installations were most frequent on the Honda Accord, also the most 'stolen' car in America. Perhaps this had more to do with the fact that car thieves were more attracted to more abundant cars which could be more easily sold on the 'gray' market or dismantled to sell as parts.

Specially trained and bonded LoJack employees traveled in vans between dealerships in each city to install the Units before customers took delivery. The Units were actually 'hidden' somewhere in the vehicle so that they could not be removed by prospective thieves. Thus LoJack maintained full responsibility for installation and warranty service of LoJack Units both for the convenience of dealers and to maintain a high degree of quality control and security over its technology.

When a LoJack owner reported to the police that a vehicle was stolen, the routine processing of a stolen vehicle automatically forwarded a message to the sector activation system. This in turn sent a unique radio signal to activate the LoJack Unit in the stolen vehicle to begin broadcasting a signal.

Police officers who detected the transmissions of an activated LoJack Unit called into the dispatcher for a description of the transmitting vehicle. Police tracking computers, sophisticated radio direction finders each consisting of a radio receiver with a directional antenna array, Doppler signal processor, computer, and a controllable display, then guided the police to the exact location of the stolen vehicle. While the police tracking computers were generally installed in police vehicles, modified designs had been developed for use in helicopters and fixed locations such as toll booths, radio towers, or police communication centers. Effective tracking ranged from about one mile to approximately five miles depending on topographical and climatic conditions. The activated LoJack Unit continued to broadcast until the police sent a properly coded report to the National Crime Information Center (NCIC) that the vehicle had been recovered. At that point, the NCIC computer automatically generated a signal to shut off the LoJack Unit.

The LoJack Vehicle Recovery System had a proven track record of recovering the stolen vehicle, usually within hours of being reported stolen. This speed tended to minimize damage to the vehicle and increase the chance of catching the thief.

Marketing and distribution

There were several stages in establishing distribution of the LoJack System in a new region in the United States. First the law enforcement agency (and often executive or legislative bodies) had to be persuaded to support the system. Since most government agencies required competitive bidding for all acquisitions of products and equipment, LoJack charged nothing for the Law Enforcement Components. In some jurisdictions this presented a problem since some government agencies had no mechanism to allow them to accept something without payment. Additionally, many government bureaucrats saw no reason to disturb the status quo.

Once the bureaucracy in each jurisdiction agreed to support a LoJack system, LoJack salespeople approached franchised new car dealers who would offer the LoJack Unit as an option on both new and used car sales. LoJack's sales force was comprised primarily of former new car salespeople who routinely visited franchised new car dealers to educate and train dealership personnel on the benefits of the LoJack System. The continued improvement of the sales force had been a major factor in the domestic growth. A formalized training program had been introduced for all of sales and management employees to bring more consistency into hiring, training and presentation practices.

For dealers, the system had proven to inspire high customer satisfaction ratings and provided a high margin add-on to any sale. A dealer could make several hundred dollars on each installation. Given that new car sales had razor thin margins, LoJack's pricing structure encouraged dealers to require that their salespeople try to sell LoJack. A commonly used method was to offer extra commissions to direct the customer to see the finance director in each dealership. It was then up to this individual to convince the customer that adding a LoJack was cost effective 'insurance.' LoJack also marketed vehicle alarms and devices to prevent vehicles from starting under the names 'LoJack Prevent' and 'LoJack Alert.' The market for these products was decreasing, however, since many automobile manufacturers were including these features as standard equipment.

LoJack's direct marketing efforts to dealers emphasized the benefits to the dealers and their customers of the LoJack Unit as a purchase option for new and used car buyers. LoJack used radio advertising targeting consumers to generate brand and product awareness and demand.

International operations

LoJack also licensed the use of its stolen vehicle recovery system technology in selected international markets. In connection with its efforts to expand outside of the United States, LoJack developed the CarSearch Stolen Vehicle Recovery System. Unlike the LoJack System used in the United States, CarSearch was not tied in with police computers or national crime prevention data banks. While the LoJack system could be customized to fit the needs and limitations of any jurisdiction, generally the LoJack Licensee had to activate the LoJack Unit with a specific radio command.

As of February 28, 1998, LoJack had licensees in the following countries: Argentina, Colombia, Czech Republic, Ecuador, Germany, Greece, Hong Kong, Kenya, Korea, Mexico, Nigeria, Panama, Russia, Slovak Republic, South Africa, Trinidad and Tobago, United Kingdom, and Venezuela. It had also entered into agreements in countries such as the Peoples' Republic of China, Poland, and Uruguay. However, not all the countries had as yet implemented the LoJack System.

Competition

Several competitors such as Teletrac, a unit of Pacific Bell were already in the market while other potential competitors had announced the development of products, including those which were GPS-based (Global Positioning System), that claimed to have stolen vehicle recovery features similar to those of the LoJack System. To the knowledge of LoJack management, none were compatible with the LoJack System, and none were operated or actively monitored by law enforcement agencies, as was the LoJack System. Most of these potential competitors also required consumers to pay recurring monthly fees.

In addition, some makers of auto theft prevention devices (as opposed to the auto recovery system which LoJack offered) positioned their products as competitive to the LoJack system.

By 1999, several vehicle manufacturers were installing on-board navigation systems such as the 'OnStar' as options or as standard equipment in higher priced vehicles. Dealers were promoting the stolen vehicle recovery capabilities of these systems.

The operation of such a feature, however, required a separate cellular phone connection with ongoing monthly fees, and suffered from the same limitations as other GPS based systems such as loss of signal when inside a building or on a street with many tall buildings. Consumer perceptions, however, were often shaped by automobile salespeople so that facts were clouded by false perceptions.

Strategy for the future

Despite decreases in stolen vehicles over the last several years, auto theft was still a significant problem, costing almost $8 billion in losses annually in the United States. The problem was at least as severe internationally. LoJack's broad strategy was to expand into those domestic and international markets where the combination of population density, new car sales, and vehicle theft was high. Its new mantra was to be a 'global mobile safety and security tracking company.' It was thus exploring new markets and technologies as opportunities for growth.

In the United States, LoJack intended to improve its sales and marketing efforts both in the media and by strengthening its sales force while expanding the new car dealer network in existing markets. It also sought to continue expansion into new markets to increase geographic coverage and to improve distribution into the fleet and commercial markets. LoJack was, at least partially,[2] already in 15 of the top 16 states in terms of population, new car sales, and auto theft. Entry into smaller, but growing urban markets such as San Francisco, Jacksonville, San Antonio, or New Orleans was under review as a next tier of opportunity.

With the combined strength of sales personnel and processes, improved sales materials, consistent advertising, and public relations initiatives, LoJack intended to increase both the number of new car dealers and the sales per dealer in existing dealers. While the percentage of dealers was high, the overall ratio of LoJack sales to new car sales in many of those outlets was still in need of improvement and represented a major opportunity. In a number of existing markets, LoJack was installed on about 10% to 15% of new vehicles, suggesting plenty of room for growth. The consolidation of the new car dealer

[2]For example: LoJack covered Dallas/Fort Worth but not San Antonio and many other parts of the state.

distribution network and the advent of large dealer groups also presented major long-term market opportunities. These new dealer networks also posed a potential threat because with their increased purchasing power they might well apply pressure to reduce LoJack's prices and margins.

International markets offered long term opportunities. With as many as 30 licenses negotiated, LoJack was actually in operation in eighteen countries. LoJack management thought that international sales could grow at a pace of 15% to 20% per year for the foreseeable future.

LoJack also planned to increase its efforts to market its products directly to operators of fleet and commercial vehicles. The Company had contracted with Motorola for development and redesign of the LoJack Unit that would accommodate additional applications, and meet the technical and economic constraints of the leasing and trucking industries. While car rental companies had at one point been considered to represent a significant opportunity, most such companies kept their cars for such a short time that the investment could not be justified.

The fleet and commercial market, however, represented approximately 30% of the new vehicles sold annually in the United States, and still offered an opportunity with the potential of adding 20–30% to existing business. Since most of the cost structure was already absorbed by current business, management thought that success in this area would be very profitable, even at a modest level of sales. However, there was a competitive threat from other companies, primarily new entrants, bringing new technology and capabilities associated with automatic vehicle location (AVL).

Private truck fleets with more than 100 trucks comprised the major market for AVL. Most of these were 'for hire' fleets which operated nationally. In 1998, AVL was installed on 430,000 trucks in the United States. Two companies dominated the industry: Qualcom boasted an installed base of 185,000 trucks, with Teletrac having a base of 71,000 trucks. The systems were both terrestrial and satellite based, although a trend was starting to emerge towards cellular. Equipment sales were about $131 million, while service revenues from recurring subscriptions were over £235 million. These were expected to grow to $396 million and $655 million respectively in the next five years as prices dropped from their current level of $1,000 per unit and monthly fees ranging from $20 to $50.

Meanwhile, LoJack was continuing to work on the development of its third generation LoJack Unit, or LoJack Unit III. Originally, MicroLogic and LoJack had entered into a joint venture to develop the LoJack Unit III as a low cost, small, separate, self-powered unit to be initially marketed to the fleet and commercial markets. However, MicroLogic had difficulty meeting some of the initial specifications of the product. Eventually the direction of this project was altered and Motorola was engaged to incorporate many of the improvements into a redesign of the present LoJack Unit to be ready for sale by August 1999. The redesign of this product was intended to change the appearance and size of the LoJack Unit and also to take advantage of improvements in technology, reduce the cost of the hardware, to improve the efficiency of the installation process. It would also include a self-contained power supply so that it could be installed in unpowered assets like trailers.

The success of the LoJack III units would allow LoJack to enter the highly competitive market for stolen vehicle recovery of the 13 million trailers in the United States. The cost of hardware and service had been dropping fast, encouraging new entrants which also offered total asset management capabilities. In the past, each unit could cost up to $2,400 and demand a $50 per month service fee. More recently it had dropped to around $1,000. LoJack management hoped that they could enter this market with its new unit that would be compatible for application in a non-powered environment at pricing attractive to the industry. LoJack was also exploring cellular and satellite technologies to enhance its opportunities in this market.

MicroLogic

While expansion of the LoJack System into new geographic areas and markets represented a logical growth strategy, Abely though that there might be even greater opportunities in leveraging LoJack's connections with law enforcement agencies, reputation, brand awareness, and distribution muscle. In particular, one opportunity with an old ally attracted his attention. MicroLogic had recently decided to enter the mobile asset management market starting with construction equipment management. MicroLogic needed cash to finance its expansion.

MicroLogic had been a significant ally and an instrumental partner in the success of LoJack. From the very early days, it had assumed the primary responsibility for technology development and much of the early implementation. Indeed, it still manufactured all of the police tracking computers. It indeed had been a trustworthy partner. However, things had changed over time. LoJack, with MicroLogic's help and concurrence, had been taking on more and more of MicroLogic's tasks. In fact, several years earlier LoJack had hired some MicroLogic staff with MicroLogic's blessing.

Sheldon Apsell, president of MicroLogic, thought that trust and good will were the absolute key to a successful alliance. He also thought that flexibility was also very critical since so much is unknown at the creation of an alliance. Indeed, early predictions can often be wrong, as was the case with the LoJack alliance. For example, allies must be prepared to deal with changes in markets, technology, competition and regulations. They had expected significant competition early on but it had still not materialized. They also thought that there would be a large retro-fit market with people buying LoJack units to protect the cars they already had. That proved to be wrong and people almost never bought to protect an existing car but only when they purchased a new car. Technically, they expected the next generation systems to be satellite based but it never made technical sense. Political opposition was, however, much greater than expected. They thought that State and Federal agencies would be much more supportive and much easier to get along with than they were, particularly once the system was working well in Massachusetts. The government bureaucracies were very difficult to deal with and adverse to anything new. Also, the decision making process in big government was far more difficult and time consuming than anticipated.

Apsell also thought that allies must understand that there will be 'hard times' and have faith in the product and 'stick it through'. True alliances, he thought, do not make sense in the short term and both parties should enter into it with the idea of both parties becoming more independent over time and benefiting from the independence. He thought that alliances must be beneficial to both sides, and that it is critical to let each partner do its job without much interference. In the LoJack alliance, for example, LoJack handled all marketing and sales, while MicroLogic was left to concentrate on technology.

Recently, while the relationship was still trusting, it had become much more 'business like' with more written documents and formal contracts, because there are more people involved. The MicroLogic role had also changed and the companies are far more independent. MicroLogic was no longer involved in all the technical decisions and LoJack had its own technical staff. However, MicroLogic was still involved in the long term technology strategy and there to pitch in when LoJack staff needed help.

MicroLogic was a privately held company, founded as a contract product development company in 1978 by Sheldon Apsell and Dan Crown. Apsell had earned his BS from MIT and a Ph.D in High Energy Physics from Brandeis University. Crown was an electrical engineer with a Bachelor's degree from Northeastern University. Crown and Apsell had worked together at several organizations before founding MicroLogic. Many of MicroLogic's clients were startup companies with insufficient engineering and manufacturing capabilities although they also had a fair number of larger clients. Micrologic often charged reduced fees for the development work in exchange for an equity position, a long term manufacturing contract, or royalties based on units sold. Over the years MicroLogic's clients had included the likes of LoJack, LifeLine, ADT, PepsiCo, Bell Atlantic, and a host of smaller or less well known companies.

By 1999, both founders were still involved in MicroLogic. Apsell owned more than 50% of the company and was still its CEO and President. Crown no longer an employee, but still was a member of the Board of Directors.

Until very recently MicroLogic had been, by design, a 'lifestyle company'. At its peak, employment was about 40 people but usually hovered around 20. One of its long-time employees described it as having a 'relaxed' atmosphere. Recently, however, MicroLogic had changed its strategic direction. Rather than continue to develop products for others as had been its focus over the past 20 years, Aspell decided that the company should develop and market its own products. After a number of false starts, his management team finally settled on an information service business which would initially provide information about the location and operating parameters (e.g.; run-hours, water or oil temperature or pressure, air filter condition) of expensive construction equipment. Other potential market segments to be attacked after construction equipment included other mobile high-value assets such as vehicle fleets, rail cars, and trailers. The system would produce standard reports or use sophisticated mapping software to produce easily understandable graphic information that could be communicated to personal computers.

Construction equipment market size and structure

Approximately 170,000 to 200,000 pieces of new construction equipment valued at over $10,000 each were produced in the United States each year with average growth at about 8% to 10% per year although the market could be quite cyclical. The US installed base of this equipment was about 1.5 million units with the total world market estimated to be about 4 times larger than the US. Growth outside the US was expected to be at about 30% per year once the current recession ended. The average life of a piece of equipment was between 5 to 8 years.

Equipment owners were generally large construction equipment rental companies such as Hertz Equipment Rental Corporation (HERC), US Rental, Prime Equipment. These companies each had over a hundred locations and owned tens of thousands of pieces of equipment which ranged in value from $5000 to over $100,000; there were also a host of medium sized and smaller rental companies. In fact, the same 'roll-up' phenomenon that was occurring in LoJack's automobile dealer world was also occurring in the construction equipment rental business. The top 5 US rental companies accounted for about 180,000 pieces of equipment over $10,000. Furthermore, equipment dealers (e.g.; Caterpillar etc.), who formerly only sold and serviced equipment from one or two specific manufacturers were also getting into the rental business and it was fast becoming very difficult to separate rental businesses from 'ordinary' dealerships.

Other categories of major construction equipment owners included large construction companies (e.g. Bechtel, Kiewet Construction Group, and Fluor), railroads, and large manufacturing companies (e.g., General Motors, US Steel). Of course, some of these also rented equipment from the large equipment rental companies. And, as in many other situations, outsourcing was becoming a major trend with large corporations such as GM or Burlington Northern which wanted to out-source the management of all their construction equipment to others – most notably the equipment rental companies.

Along with the consolidation and outsourcing trends came the need for companies to become more efficient and make better use of their assets. MicroLogic's new information product/service fit these new requirements perfectly since it helped customers increase equipment utilization, improved maintenance while reducing costs, improved billing capability for rental companies, discouraged unauthorized use, and helped in the recovery of stolen equipment.

Initial revenues for the new MicroLogic business would be derived from the sale of units to be located on the equipment (RF receivers and transmitters, a GPS unit, a sensor I/O device and controller and an antenna) which would be sold at break-even or a very small profit. Long term revenues and the majority of profits would result from a monthly fee for a 'standard' package of information (e.g., location and run hours) plus individual charges for special inquiries or alarms.

The initial system would rely on satellite communications technology so that equipment could be located anywhere in the world, but cellular or other terrestrial communications technologies would be incorporated as coverage widened.

Up to this point, MicroLogic had self-funded the product development, testing, and marketing for this new business while continuing to operate the traditional business. However, Apesell's decision to change the essence of the MicroLogic organization had brought marketing and sales of the original product development business to a halt. Cash flow would soon be inadequate to support further development and marketing. Thus, MicroLogic, in a bid for about $6 million in outside funding, was courting venture capitalists, private investors and potential corporate partners. Fortunately, MicroLogic had just obtained orders for the new product from two prestigious companies: a large construction company that was interested in testing the product's capabilities in a difficult pipeline laying project and one of the largest equipment rental companies in the country. In addition, MicroLogic was about to submit proposals to several other large equipment rental companies as well as another major construction company.

Meanwhile, the competitive landscape was changing as many more companies were entering the construction equipment asset management marketplace. Originally, MicroLogic's major competitor had been Caterpillar, the large construction equipment manufacturer. However, its product was only offered to Cat dealers, but many of these dealers were having some difficulty with the product. Some had already turned to another competitor – ATX

Technologies Inc., a San Antonio based company which was also involved in other location services, most notably for the railroads and shipping containers. ATX was offering a cellular based system that seemed to be working well, at least in demonstration programs. Another major competitor was the Enterprise Group of ORCOMM, the owner of the low earth orbit satellite communications system that MicroLogic used.

MicroLogic viewed this increased activity with mixed feelings. On the one hand, excitement in the industry about such a system validated the concept and educated potential customers. On the other hand, it narrowed the window of opportunity for capturing a large enough share of the market to make implementation worthwhile. Additional capital and marketing capability were essential if MicroLogic was going to be the market leader. LoJack was in a position to supply both.

A possible alliance

As Abely pondered the future of LoJack, he knew that expansion of the historically successful system into both domestic and international markets was important. Yet this expansion had to be methodical and perhaps slower than some of the company's investors would have liked. While the company was in an excellent cash position, he did not want accelerated growth to erode LoJack's key strengths: an excellent product, strong distribution, and an impeccable consumer franchise.

Mike Daley, CEO of LoJack, thought that it was critical in a successful alliance for personalities to be compatible. He thought that Sheldon Apsell had been an important contributor to the LoJack Board of Directors at the beginning of the alliance, although the importance of his role was diminishing. It had certainly been impressive to the Board that MicroLogic had embraced the initial idea and been willing to risk as much as LoJack. They had found the right personal characteristics and technical skill in Sheldon Apsell. He understood the concept and had the vision and courage to follow

through and push the envelope on the existing technology. Indeed, Apsell and Daley had always functioned as trusting and cooperative partners even in the face of occasional disagreements. There had been conflicts at the lower levels of the organizations, but because of the strong relationship at the top they were able to take corrective action before they got completely out of hand. MicroLogic had also been willing to work closely with LoJack's other partner – Motorola. Perhaps most important was the mutual realization that the alliance must be flexible and be able to adapt to changing circumstances as the company matured.

For many years MicroLogic had been the technical backbone of LoJack. As time progressed, LoJack had separated somewhat; they hired in-house people to do some of the work formerly handled by MicroLogic. In fact one of the first of these hires was a MicroLogic employee, Pete Johnson. LoJack hired Pete with the full knowledge and concurrence of MicroLogic. Sheldon Apsell's feeling was that LoJack should in fact take over the mundane, day to day tasks, as it was neither interesting for MicroLogic nor cost effective for LoJack to continue to have MicroLogic do 'standard' stuff. Today, LoJack does much of their own work with the exception of brand new design work or work on the base software that MicroLogic designed originally.

On one hand, joining forces with MicroLogic would continue what had been a very successful alliance and, more importantly, open up an entirely new market for LoJack. On the other hand, he wondered if such an alliance would leverage to the utmost LoJack's strengths and whether the alliance would continue to be as successful given MicroLogic's new strategy. In fact, some of LoJack's senior management questioned whether or not MicroLogic was still the right partner. Perhaps it was time to find a new partner and/or go it alone in the broader AVG/Telematics market. What might be the downside, Abely questioned of a failed thrust into this new arena? Finally, if the company did go ahead given all the potential risks and rewards of an alliance with MicroLogic, he wondered how to structure a relationship.

Proteome Systems

By Mona Ashiya and Jonathan West[1]

On July 11, 2001, Keith Williams, the CEO of Proteome Systems Limited (PSL), hurried around his office preparing for an important meeting with a prominent potential IT partner for the young company. Wearing a suit, Williams joked that he was in disguise for the day. For PSL, based in Sydney, Australia, this was a relationship that could propel it into the limelight and give it global exposure.

In the two and a half years since the company's founding, Williams and his team had quickly developed a range of products that spanned the length of the protein analysis chain. The current product range included instruments as well as kits and consumables. PSL had entered into an agreement with the Shimadzu Corporation to develop two proteomics instruments[2] and had met all milestones. Similarly, the company had established a number of other alliances to further its technology development efforts towards an integrated proteomics platform, as well as the marketing and distribution of its consumables. It had also recently established a US subsidiary in Boston to maintain closer contact with its largest market. PSL believed that its current and proposed product range would also help to fuel its in-house drug discovery projects.

The company, however, was not alone in the proteomics field. Proteomics had become the new buzzword on Wall Street in the post-genomic era and companies with far greater resources were moving into the field. Even in mid-2000, Williams had observed, 'six months ago, none of the proteomics companies had too much money to spend; there wasn't too much pressure. Now, virtually everyone

has upwards of $100 million. The pressure is enormous'.[3] And Williams recognized, 'the first proteomics group that shows they can deliver the goods as far as high throughput analysis of proteins will attract big pharma', and noted, 'now is the defining moment'.

With about 50 products in the production or development phase and with a staff of 80, the company was in the midst of a second private capital raising. Williams and his team were cautious about raising money and had guarded their equity thus far but their 'burn rate' was escalating. PSL did not intend to go broke but Williams had wondered, 'Do you raise piles of money and not own the business anymore?' As the company had grown, the task of managing resources as well as growing and moving to other markets had become more challenging. PSL was engaged in technology development, limited manufacturing as well as discovery. The company did not fall into any of the traditional buckets – PSL was neither just a 'tool box' company nor only a discovery company.

In the near future, to raise additional capital, they were considering a stock offering either in Australia or on the NASDAQ but how would Wall Street analysts who had only recently taken notice of the company perceive PSL's business plan going forward? Would they have to move out of Australia? How would Williams and his team decide which parts of the business to base in Australia and which in the US? How would things change as they rolled out their products and started interacting more with their customers who would largely be in the US, Europe and Japan?

[1]Source: Copyright © 2001 President and Fellows of Harvard College.

[2]The word 'proteome' originated in 1994 when Marc Wilkins, who became a lead scientist at PSL, coined the term to describe the set of all PROTEins expressed by a genOME. Proteomics, was the large-scale study of proteins in a cell or organism; in other words, the study of a proteome.

[3]'On the trail of the profitable proteins', *Biotechnology*, June 30, 2000.

The proteomics opportunity

On June 26, 2000, even as Craig Venter, the founder of Celera, and Francis Collins of the National Human Genome Research Institute, jointly announced the completion of the human genome project, both sides recognized that the real work was far from finished. While the sequencing efforts of the previous decade had delivered a wealth of information and commercial ventures had focused on uncovering genes responsible for various disease states, scientists recognized that mapping the genome was only the first step and far from the final one in addressing disease. The focus was shifting to proteins since, ultimately, it is these molecules that lie at the heart of all cellular function and thus form the molecular basis of disease (see Figure 1 for an overview on genes and proteins).

By focusing on proteins – the active agents within cells – the field of proteomics provided a link between genomics and combinatorial chemistry and offered the pharmaceutical and biotechnology industry a set of powerful tools to bring a host of novel and more effective drugs to market.[4] Specifically, proteomics allowed the study of the entire set of proteins in a cell as it responded to developmental signals, available nutrients, drugs, disease and more.

Efforts in proteomics ranged from the comparison of various diseased and normal cells to uncover the identity of rogue proteins in disease processes to the creation of maps displaying interactions between proteins to atlases of all proteins expressed by a particular cell type or organism. Venter noted that '[I]t's only by understanding protein function that we can truly understand and

FIGURE 1   Overview of genes and proteins

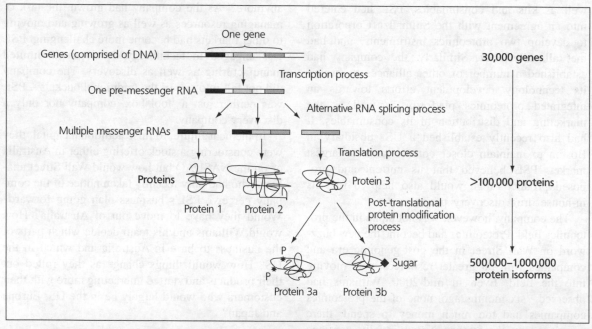

Note: Proteins outnumber genes considerably because multiple proteins can be generated from a single gene by processes such as alternative RNA splicing and post-translational protein modifications (for instance, addition of a sugar group to distinct amino acids). While it is possible in some cases to infer from the gene sequence what kind of RNA splicing and modification events will take place, to be sure one has to directly analyze the protein.

[4]Denis Hochstrasser and Keith L Williams. In *Proteome Research: New Frontiers in functional genomics*, pp. 232–234, Springer-Verlag. 1997.

predict medical outcomes' and added that 'more will happen in biology in the next 10 years than in the past 50'.[5] However, after big pharmaceutical companies had channeled considerable funds into genomics technologies that had not fulfilled their promise of speeding drug development, the proteomics field would have to demonstrate its value.

Overview of methods in proteomics

Mapping the human genome had become possible through a revolution in technology and instrumentation and a similar revolution was now required to enable high-throughput protein analysis. This, however, posed considerable challenges since techniques that had been developed for automated DNA sequencing and analysis could not be easily adapted to protein analysis. The chemical nature of proteins makes them fundamentally different from DNA. Unlike DNA that consists of a string of four chemically similar units (bases), the 20 units (amino acids) that make up proteins have vastly different chemical attributes and some of these units can be modified further, adding to the complexity. The substitution of a single unit in a protein with a different unit can, in some cases, substantially alter a protein's properties to require modifications in the analytical techniques required to study it. Hence, techniques had been tailored to study different classes of proteins. Furthermore, while the human genome contained roughly 30,000 genes, estimates of the average number of proteins present in a human cell stood at 500,000 to a million. Proteins also varied in abundance and key proteins that were often likely to be drug targets were available only in minute quantities and posed a special challenge for analysis. In addition, unlike the genome of an organism, a proteome was dynamic and changed in response to variations in the cellular environment.

Conventional techniques for protein analysis were laborious as the initial mapping of the human genome was being completed. The standard approach to studying proteins en masse started with the preparation of the sample for analysis. Samples such as that from a tissue or cell line had to first be appropriately solubilized. The separation of the proteins in the solubilized sample was then accomplished by a technique called 2-dimensional gel electrophoresis (2DE) where the proteins were first separated according to their electric charge and then by their size in polymer matrix. Once separated, the arrayed proteins could be seen as a pattern of spots on the polymer matrix (gel) with each spot representing a distinct protein. Individual protein spots then had to be treated by specific enzymes to fragment the protein into 'peptides' before mass spectrometry could be used for protein identification.

If proteins were to be studied in a high-throughput, automated fashion, many concerns would have to be addressed. Sample preparation would first have to be optimized since conventional approaches typically missed many proteins. Conventional 2DE was also considered to be more of a craft since the technique was non-standardized, labor intensive, slow, prone to contamination, and, as a result, did not easily generate reproducible data. Similarly, proteins that had extremes in charge or size were also problematic. For example, concerns revolved around the ability of the 2DE method to separate membrane proteins that were often key players in signal transmission between cells and hence candidate drug targets. However, 2DE was still the best technique for looking at all forms of a protein – that is, even proteins from the same gene that only differed by the attachment of a sugar group, for instance. For these reasons, the technique was considered by many to be a bottleneck in the pursuit of automated protein analysis.

It was also widely agreed that commercial information management systems would have to be developed in any proteomics automation effort and such systems were only in their infancy. Software would have to be developed to handle the onslaught of data from the mass spectrometers as well as to allow automated image analysis of the spots on 2DE gels – that is, to archive, compare and determine what differences existed between samples. Others felt that the bottleneck of protein identification and analysis lay at the mass spectrometry stage and large numbers of mass spectrometers would be key in automated analysis.

[5]Andy Coghlan, 'Land of Opportunity', *New Scientist*, November 4, 2000.

Market size and growth

The emerging proteomics market was seen to encompass laboratory instruments and supplies, laboratory services as well as informatics that included databases and software.[6] The global market for proteomics instruments and consumables was estimated to be $708 million in 1999 and projected to grow to $5.8 billion by 2005 at an average annual growth rate of about 40%.[7] Table 1 provides yearly projections for the global proteomics market. Other more conservative estimates suggested a $561-million market in 2001 that would increase five fold to a $2.8 billion market by 2005.[8] Nonetheless, it was clear that the proteomics market would be the next key growth driver for biotechnology and pharmaceutical companies.

In the emerging proteomics market, the instrument suppliers would be first to benefit and see increased revenue growth along with those companies that provided the tools required for sample preparation and handling prior to identification. Similarly, bioinformatics tools on the back end of

the mass spectrometry were expected to be in demand and some analysts thought that companies that integrated their instrument hardware with a bioinformatics software package would 'take home a large slice of the proteomics pie'.[9] Sales of 2D gel systems and mass spectrometry instruments represented over half of the proteomics tools market and the rest consisted of other protein separation tools such as high performance liquid chromatography, protein chips and bioinformatics tools.[10]

Company history

While the world focused on the human genome sequencing efforts in the 1990s, Williams and his team at Macquarie University in Sydney continued to build their expertise in protein analysis. In 1984, after three years as a professor at the Max Planck Institute for Biochemistry in Munich, Williams returned to Australia where he had accepted a chair at Macquarie University. A scientist, who cited his childhood in a farm near Melbourne with kindling his interest in biology, Williams was working on basic problems in developmental biology using the slime mold, *Dictyostelium*, as a model system.

Protein analysis was key in these projects and Williams recognized the power of high mass accuracy/high mass resolution mass spectrometers and thought that this ability to weigh molecules accurately was a powerful tool. He felt they had transformed protein science, glycobiology and were impacting molecular biology as well. Williams felt that Venter had made the most important contribution to the life sciences in the past 10 years by showing that an organism's complete genome could be sequenced and he now saw proteomics as the focus of the next phase.

Even while at the university, Williams was considered to be always walking, 'the finest line between what was expected of a professor and what was pushing the boundary [with respect to]

TABLE 1 Global proteomics market (revenue forecasts)

Year	Revenues (US$ million)	Revenue growth rate (%)
1999	708	–
2000	1001	41
2001	1528	53
2002	2264	48
2003	3237	43
2004	4383	35
2005	5810	33

Source: 'World Proteomics Markets,' Frost & Sullivan, 2000, pp. 1–3.

[6]Frost & Sullivan. World Proteomics Markets, 2000.

[7]Frost & Sullivan. World Proteomics Markets, 2000.

[8]'Proteomics Market seen quintupling to $2.8 billion by 2005', June 7, 2001. <www.genomeweb.com/ar...es/view-article.asp?Article=200167103559> accessed August 2, 2001.

[9]US Bancorp Piper Jaffray, 'Proteomics: Don't "Ms" the Boat', May 2001.

[10]Merrill Lynch, 'Proteomics: The new new thing', May 3, 2001.

entrepreneurial and commercial strategies'.[11] He had defined the early genetic maps of the slime mold and seeing commercial potential in some of his findings, had formed a company called Dictytech to hold intellectual property for making recombinant proteins in a cheap and efficient manner. In another instance, he had joined two other scientists who were working on a fungus that destroyed plant root systems and that was destroying the banana crop in the Philippines. Williams worked out a way to grow the fungus on a large scale and had built a little factory on the university campus. Williams half-joked that these experiences were his MBA.

Australian Protein Analysis Facility (APAF)

Over time, Williams and his group not only developed deep expertise in protein analysis but grew to have a technology focus as well. Having established the Macquarie University Centre for Analytical Biochemistry in 1992, Williams and his team had begun to work with corporations in Australia and overseas on scientific instrumentation. Williams explained, 'We saw what was happening in genomics and we realized that we needed to industrialize protein science, and in 1995 Paul Keating's[12] government had a competition for major national facilities and so through [19]96 we built that facility at Macquarie University'.[13] In 1995, Williams and his group had received a $7 million government grant to set up a proteomics facility at the university and they were then provided a $5.6 million R&D grant to develop new instrumentation for proteomics.

APAF was the first major national facility for the analysis and characterization of proteins and Williams recruited an old student of his, Andrew Gooley, to run the group. The R&D grant meant a commitment to the development of automation, robotics and integrated systems for proteomics. The team would develop instruments for protein sequencing and for automating the process of

cutting out protein spots from gels following 2DE among other projects. For instance, Ben Herbert, a student of Williams' at the time had built expertise in sample preparation and separation and had been developing considerable intellectual property in the area. Some of this was then licensed by the university to Bio-Rad, a US-based biotech instrumentation company, and Williams and his team worked with the company to develop equipment for improved 2DE as well as better methods for sample preparation. In 2000 Bio-Rad launched ProteomeWorks™, its protein separation and identification platform, and an outcome of its relationship with APAF.

Even at this time, Williams and his group had envisioned a 'proteomics platform' that would allow researchers to do fast, high-throughput protein analysis since their research had made clear what the gaps in the instrumentation and technology area were. Gooley, who had been working on protein analysis steps between 2DE and mass spectrometry, had come up with the idea for a chemical printer – an idea that would become central to the group's commercial efforts later. After seeing the chemical printer technique adapted for DNA printing on a chip, Gooley had scribbled his ideas down on a flight back home and the idea was filed as a provisional patent with Macquarie University holding the intellectual property rights to it. While Williams and Gooley made some efforts to commercialize the idea, the companies they spoke with considered the project too risky. Williams commented, '[It] was very similar to the ABI [Applied BioSystems][14] story. They approached 70 companies but in the end they had to set it up themselves'.[15]

However, while APAF was operating more like a service contract organization, working on small projects with commercial partners, the government funds that had created APAF did not pay for the salaries of the skilled scientists in the group. Increasingly, over the next two years, as APAF had built a critical mass of expertise, Williams saw that one of his biggest challenges

[11]Case writer interview with Andrew Gooley, Proteome Systems Limited.
[12]Paul Keating was the Prime Minister of Australia from 1991–1996.
[13]'Future of Biotechnology in Australia', ABC radio current affair special, January 2, 2001.
[14]Applied Biosystems was a company that became the dominant provider of DNA sequencing instruments.
[15]Case writer interview with Keith Williams, Proteome Systems Limited.

was keeping the scientists working in Australia despite tempting offers from overseas.

Creation of Proteome Systems Limited (PSL)

Over the course of 1997 and through 1998, as Williams saw the threat of his team being poached by corporations around the world for the expertise group members possessed, it became clear that the group would have to 'go corporate if it wanted to stay together'. Williams noted, 'Everyone was getting sensational job offers. We decided forming a company was the best way of keeping the team together'.[16] So, with the idea of the chemical printer technology, Herbert's technology for sample preparation and 2DE and at the heels of success with the Bio-Rad collaboration, Williams and Gooley entered into negotiations with the university with the intent of forming a commercial venture. Looking back on their days at APAF, Williams observed that Bio-Rad had thought the group had been running like a little company.

In their negotiations with the university starting in 1997, the scientists had legal and financial advice from John Martin, a lawyer at the prominent corporate legal firm Allen Allen and Hemsley while Bruce Hogan, a prominent Australian company director, helped with structure. Martin, a partner at the firm

later resigned his position to join Proteome Systems in 2001, while Hogan joined the board as chairman.

The protracted negotiations with the university lasted a year during which the group had also entered into a dialogue with Dow Agrosciences, a large agricultural biotechnology company, who wanted to start a project with the group. However, Dow was reluctant to begin the project while they were at the university fearing an academic group would lack the commercial focus. In the end, on Christmas Eve 1998, the dialogue with the university broke down. Williams and 13 key members of his group, handed their resignations to the university, spurred in part by Dow's reluctance to deal with APAF. For the scientists this constituted significant personal risk taking – Williams, for instance, had walked away from the security of a university pension plan.

Others who left the university with Williams and came to have key positions in the management of the new venture[17] included Herbert who would head the protein array technology group and Nicole Packer, an expert on protein modifications who would lead the glycoproteomics group. Marc Wilkins, who had coined the term 'proteomics' while a graduate student in Williams' lab in 1994 would head the bioinformatics group and Jenny Harry would lead the company's discovery programs. (Exhibit 1 provides more background on the

EXHIBIT 1 PSL'S MANAGEMENT TEAM

Keith L. Williams, Chief Executive Officer and Executive Director and founder of PSL. Williams was a Professor of Biological Sciences at Macquarie University in Sydney and Director of the Macquarie University Center for Analytical Biotechnology. Subsequently, he was the founder and Director of APAF from 1996–1998. He had 250 publications in the field of cell, molecular and developmental biology and was the co-editor of the first book published on proteomics. He had trained 30 PhD students and led a team of 25 scientists at the university.

John D. Martin. Deputy Chief Executive Officer and Executive Director. Martin was a former Executive partner of the corporate group of the Sydney based law firm, Allen Allen & Hemsley. He specialized in mergers and acquisitions, fundraising and advising high growth companies in emerging technologies. He worked with Williams on structuring PSL since its inception. He was also founder of Xcelerator Ltd.

[16]Peter Roberts, 'Companies and Markets: Best practice when better beans means genes', *Australian Financial Review*, February 19, 1999.
[17]Proteome Systems Limited was incorporated in October 1997.

Andrew Gooley, Director and Chief Scientific Officer. Gooley was Director of Protein Technology at APAF from 1996 till 1998. He had 15 years experi- ence in instrument and application development in proteomics with major corporations including Bio-Rad, Novo-Nordisk and Genentech. At PSL, he focused on the development of several motion control systems to automate many of the steps in proteomics. He was the project leader for the design and prototype devel-opment of two new instruments in collaboration with Shimadzu Corporation.

Bill Hunter, Chief Technology Officer. Hunter had more than 15 years experience in senior management and commercialization roles at other successful Australian organizations. An engineer, Hunter led a team at Vision Systems that developed sever histopathology instruments for Leica and then foundered his own product development group, Niche Innovation. Niche went on to have clients such as AstraZeneca, CSL, Fosters Brewing among others. Niche Innovation was acquired by PSL in June 2001 to lead development and commercialization of its integrated proteomics platform.

George Favotto, Chief Financial Officer. Favotto completed his training with the char-tered accounting firm, Deloitte Touche Tohmatsu and had subsequently worked for 7 years in a senior position for a major property developer where he managed large scale construction projects. Prior to joining Proteome Systems in a full time capacity in July 2000, Favotto also consulted with several start-up companies including Proteome Systems from its inception.

Bruce Hogan, Chairman. Hogan had 25 years experience in the financial industry including 15 years with Bankers Trust, Australia, retiring as joint Managing Director in 1994. He also served as non-executive director of several leading Australian corporations. He was also chairman of Xcelerator Ltd.

Ben Herbert, Executive Vice President and Head of Array Technology. Herbert was a student in Williams' laboratory and then a post-doctoral fellow at APAF. He was one of the key innovators in the use of 2DE for protein separation and had over 20 publications and several key patents in the area of separation science methods development. He played a key role in the development of the Bio-Rad ProteomeWorks package and in collaboration with Prof. Righetti of Verona, Italy, worked on new technology and instrumentation for sample fractionation.

Mark Wilkins, Executive Vice President and Head of Bioinformatics. Wilkins coined the term proteome and was senior post-doctoral fel-low in APAF prior to joining PSL. Prior to that he held a post-doctoral fellowship at the University of Geneva and had more than 6 years experience in developing bioinformatic tools and databases. He co-developed many of the protein analysis tools currently available and was co-editor of the first book on proteomics. At PSL, Wilkins was responsible for the planning and execution of a major research project with Dow Agrosciences and now coordinated PSL's integrated bioinformatics.

Nicole Packer, Executive Vice President and Head of Glycoproteomics. Packer had 20 years experience in protein modification and biochem-istry and was part of the team that established APAF. She collaborated with major corporations such as Beckman and Bio-Rad on methods development and was on the Editorial Board of the *Proteomic Journal*. She developed new methodologies for the analysis of a class of protein modifications and held several key patents in the area.

Jenny Harry, Executive Vice President and Head of Discovery Programs. Harry was responsible for the company's discovery programs and oversaw the implementation of PSL's proteomics discovery platform and was developing PSL's discovery initiatives and alliances in the area of human disease. Prior to joining PSL at its inception, Harry directed discovery programs at APAF during which she implemented the group's first commercial project with Chiron Corporation. Prior to joining APAF, Harry was a post-doctoral fellow at the University of Melbourne.

Bill Skea, Executive Vice President, General Manager US Operations (Boston-based). Skea was Vice President of Proteomics at Genomic Solutions prior to joining PSL. He also served as vice president of US operations for Oxford Glycosciences, vice president of development at PerSeptive Biosystems and Director of Life Science Corporate R&D at Millipore. He had more than 20 years experience in chromatography, analytical, 2DE as well as instrument design, development and manufacturing and consumable development and manufacturing.

Malcolm Pluskal, Executive Vice President of New Technology & Business Development (Boston-based). Pluskal had served as Director of BioSeparations and Production for Unisyn Technologies, as well as Director of Custom DNA & PNA Synthesis group at Millipore Corporation. He developed key technology for blotting proteins to membranes,

2DE hardware, as well as applications of membranes in mass spectrometry. His work had led to several successful products and he had also been the founder of a successful R&D and business development consulting business.

Mary Lopez, Executive Vice President, Proteomics Research & Development (Boston-based). Lopez had served as Vice President of Proteomics Research and Development at Genomic Solutions Inc. and previously as Director of Applications and Technical Support at Oxford Glycosciences. She had also held positions at PerSeptive BioSystems, Millipore and at ESA Inc. Lopez' area of expertise included proteomics, 2DE and computer image analysis of gels. She had also created a number of Proteomics consumables.

Ed Breen, Vice President and Head of Information Technology. Breen had more than 10 years experience in image analysis with Macquarie University and CSIRO Division of Information Sciences. He had also been a program leader on a number of industry projects where he designed and developed software solutions for a variety of image-related technologies.

Source: Proteome Systems Limited.

management team of the company.) Martin joined the team in 2001 as the new company's deputy chief executive officer while Hogan would serve as the chairman of the new entity. The company was 90% owned by the six original scientists who had worked together in Williams' group at Macquarie University since the late 1980s. Serendipitously, Gooley had found laboratory space for the new company close to the university in January 1999. This new space in North Ryde, a suburb north of

Sydney, was already fitted for laboratory use and perfectly suited the new company's needs.

The company was adamant about being based in Australia although they recognized that their market did not lie at home but largely in the US, Europe and Japan. Williams felt, 'Australia has traditionally been strong in protein science. What we are trying to do is turn that into an industry and keep the smarts here onshore'.[18] He noted, 'We are building a $1 billion global company that will stay in

[18]Peter Roberts, 'Companies and Markets: Best practice when better beans means genes', *Australian Financial Review*, February 19, 1999.

Australian hands' and added that 'you have got to dance with the big pharmas but you don't necessarily have to sell out to them'. Nonetheless, Williams acknowledged that the issue had always come up in conversations with investors and he always had to stress that PSL was going to be an Australia-based company. 'There's this concept that America is the only place a biotech company can be. It is a mantra and a huge issue for the country', said Williams. For PSL being based in Australia, meant a lower cost of developing new intellectual property. They were in Australia because they were Australians[19] and Williams and his team also felt that a move would have surely broken the team. Williams added, 'This concept of business having no connection with people's lives and making people tear up and move just doesn't make sense to me'.[20]

The Dow Agrosciences project

When Williams and his team left the university, they recognized that even though the university held the intellectual property they had created while at APAF, they did not need any of it to practice their proteomics craft in the proposed program with Dow. In February 1999, a month after PSL had settled into its new location, the company announced the signing of a multiyear agreement in the field of proteomics with Dow Agrosciences. Dow was investing what was thought to be a multi-million dollar figure in PSL to boost its efforts in pest management and the alteration of food plants.[21] PSL worked on three projects from Dow Agrosciences using its proteomics instruments and technologies. The aim of these projects was to identify new enzymes and novel pathways in the biosynthesis of plant products with the aim of producing plant products with improved nutrient content. Jim Petell, a researcher at Dow noted, 'Proteomics research will allow us to identify the functionality of genes more precisely at less cost

than traditional technologies currently used, in less time'.[22]

PSL surpassed expectations and easily met its milestones with Dow at the end of the first year. In February 2000 Dow extended the agreement for another year. PSL had performed the molecular characterization of an entirely new class of proteins being developed by Dow Agrosciences, had used its technologies to map diversity in particular protein families and had developed tools to elucidate novel biosynthetic pathways in plants. For Dow Agrosciences, the relationship with PSL was one of the few external programs they were happy with. However, in 1999 and 2000, following the worldwide public debate over GM-crops and negative public sentiment toward such products and technology, Dow decided to end the collaborative venture. PSL finally completed its discovery program with Dow Agrosciences in late 2000.

The business plan and its evolution

Williams and his group had always envisioned PSL to be a discovery company that would 'establish a long-term economic interest in [the] product pipelines of [its] collaborators'.[23] While they had the option of operating as they had at APAF where they had taken on small projects for commercial entities, Williams explained, 'We [didn't] want to be [a service contract organization] because it's mean and lean and it's a boring way to make a living'.[24]

Speaking of the discovery and technology arms of the company and its business model, Williams elaborated:

If you want [to do] real discovery stuff [and] have some real upside and ownership, [that] takes a long time and [it's] hard to see how you're going to have a sustainable business. So you can do what you do in the US, which is to raise $60 million and hope that by the time you

[19]Case writer interview with Nicole Packer, Proteome Systems Limited.
[20]Case writer interview with Keith Williams, Proteome Systems Limited.
[21]Peter Roberts, 'Companies and Markets: Best practice when better beans means genes', *Australian Financial Review*, February 19, 1999.
[22]Ibid.
[23]Proteome Systems Limited, 2001.
[24]Case writer interview with Keith Williams, Proteome Systems Limited.

get to the bottom of it, you have a business. Or you do what we've done. . . . We said – what are we good at? Where's the revenue and the revenue was in the picks and shovels[25] and we needed that stuff anyway to do our discovery. We looked at other business models. . .but when your investment in technology comes off your bottom line and [if] all it's doing is contributing to your discovery program, it's a hurtful spend. . . . We knew we couldn't do it ourselves so we set about defining a series of partnerships . . . We think the instruments and consumables is a very interesting emerging business and will provide us with substantial cash flow, which will help us fund some of our own discovery and informatics programs.[26]

The relationship with Dow Agrosciences was key for PSL in that it had enabled the company to be cash flow positive in its first year and had provided it with sufficient revenue to survive but it could only make dents in other areas. It had also become clear in the course of the Dow project that PSL had to continue to develop technology as it had at APAF with Bio-Rad. Williams and his team had the requisite expertise and saw the gaps in the existing technology and now, Williams observed, '[we had to] get serious and just build the stuff'.[27] However, the revenue the company was receiving from its project with Dow was insufficient to pursue such projects. Wilkins, who was handling the finances of the young company in addition to heading its bioinformatics program acknowledged that it was a difficult time for PSL where they had wondered, 'Are we going to be able to fund tech[nology] development and make it happen or is this company going down the discovery path?'.[28]

If the company could find commercial partners to fund its technology development efforts, PSL was confident that it would be in a position to generate near-term revenues from the sale of developed products. While others expressed concern that the company was undermining its discovery arm, Williams compared his company to big pharmaceutical companies, noting, 'We could give our systems to big pharma, but they won't win with them. We know much more about how to use them. It's like if you put me in a formula one racing car against professional race drivers, I'd still lose. They know how to use the full potential of the equipment; I don't.' Instead, the company valued the synergies between its two arms. As Herbert explained, 'Defining [the technology] at a level where you can sell it imposes rigor on the company and forces you to make equipment you can sell. So what you give your discovery team is very robust'.[29]

The company's products would include an integrated proteomics platform, ProteomeIQ™. Williams recognized that, '[the] lesson from genomics is that you make your money from consumables',[30] and that the revenue from kits was of a similar magnitude to the sale price of the instruments.[31] Therefore, PSL's instruments would come with customized kits and the company believed that a market existed for hundreds or even thousands of such platforms.[32]

On the discovery side of the business, the company knew it could generate revenue from collaborations with companies in the pharmaceutical and agricultural biotechnology industries in the form of R&D payments, milestone payments and royalties based on achievement of commercial outcomes.[33] The company would 'seek to share in the long-term value of products where [it] had assisted in product development through the retention of product rights including the right to manufacture and co-distribute, from royalty fees and the sale of products through [its] technologies'.[34] Medium and long-term revenue would be derived

[25]Enabling technologies involving instruments, software, kits and consumables.
[26]Case writer interview with Keith Williams, Proteome Systems Limited.
[27]Case writer interview with Keith Williams, Proteome Systems Limited.
[28]Case writer interview with Marc Wilkins, Proteome Systems Limited.
[29]Case writer interview with Ben Herbert, Proteome Systems Limited.
[30]Case writer interview with Keith Williams, Proteome Systems Limited.
[31]Proteome Systems Limited, Summary of information, 2001.
[32]Ibid.
[33]Proteome Systems Limited website. <www.proteomesystems.com/Company/strategy.asp> accessed August 2, 2001.
[34]Proteome Systems Limited, Summary of Information, 2001.

from 'the development of intellectual property leading to the sale of protein and protein-related database products developed independently or in collaboration with third parties in their specific areas of interest as well as the development of molecular markers, diagnostics and commercially important proteins for the pharmaceutical and agricultural biotechnology industries'.[35]

The company intended to target the university research market for its products and had not focused on the pharmaceutical industry in the first instance. Speaking of the pharmaceutical industry, Williams argued, 'People spent a lot of money on genomics but it wasn't well spent because they bought stuff that worked well for operation A but not much else. So in the end you have institutions spending millions of dollars with pretty average outcomes. This made them sceptical of the next technology. Universities were ready, so we chose them as our first targets'. PSL's approach was to pitch its flagship proteomics platform to the academic market for $2 million though Williams acknowledged, that after 15 years of not much innovation in the 2DE area for example, people were scared that the technology was too complex. To allay such fears, the company intended to set up its integrated platforms at 'friendly' academic sites and work with researchers to 'get them up to speed' – this way, such sites would serve as showcases for PSL's technology for the observing pharmaceutical and academic markets.

The company had not initially intended to do any manufacturing of instruments or consumables but over the course of their work on their first major technology development[36] undertaking, Gooley acknowledged that they realized, 'Hang on, we know what to do here... if we [are] defining [the] technology, then there must be some opportunity to leverage the technology component of business'.[37] Williams acknowledged that the manufacturing operations would likely be transferred to partners eventually, noting, 'Manufacturing is not [our]

future ... but [I'm] cautious of getting rid of it if it makes me a $100 million a year of fairly easy money'.[38] The company was unclear on how it would handle the manufacturing of the smaller equipment it was developing though Williams thought it likely they would find a partner for those products as well.

While the company knew its major market would be the United States, it did not underestimate the size of the Japanese market. With the Shimadzu partnership, the company felt it could access the Japanese market as an insider and hoped that this would allow it to forge partnerships with big pharmaceutical companies in Japan. Williams noted, 'Because of the way the Japanese industry works ... we (now) have the opportunity to get introductions to different groups in Japan through our Shimadzu connection'.[39] In addition to US, Europe and Japan, PSL also viewed Asia as an opportunity it was well positioned to take advantage of.

Financing

The company funded its operations through its corporate relationships in its first year, and had then considered a stock offering to raise capital. It had considered listing on the NASDAQ in 2000 rather than the Australian Stock Exchange (ASX) to gather much needed capital, since Williams and his team believed that US investors were more knowledgeable about biotechnology and better understood the attendant risks and rewards.

In September 2000, with an estimated value of A$160 million, the company completed a private capital raising of A$16.3 million.[40] Shareholders of the company included the Queensland Investment Corporation, the Challenger International Limited's pooled investment fund, BioTech Capital Limited, as well as venture capital funds and high net worth individuals. The investors also appeared to be comfortable with the company's plans of generating a

---

[35]Proteome Systems Limited website. <www.proteomesystems.com/Company/strategy.asp> accessed August 2, 2001.

[36]The Xcise instrument.

[37]Case writer interview with Andrew Gooley, Proteome Systems Limited.

[38]Case writer interview with Keith Williams, Proteome Systems Limited.

[39]'Q&A with Keith Williams, CEO of Proteome Systems', December 6, 2000. <www.genomeweb.com> accessed August 1, 2001.

[40]Approximately US$10 million with the exchange rate at that time.

near term revenue from the manufacturing and sales of their instruments and consumables rather than simply a long-term drug focus. The company felt that, had it been in the US, it 'would have been put on a very narrow rail at [this] early phase'.[41]

With the private capital raising, the company also received an A\$3.3 million grant from the Commonwealth Government of Australia's START Program to support an A\$12 million initiative by the company to develop instruments for proteomics research. Specifically, the grant would be used to support the development of three instruments the company was working on with its partners, Shimadzu and MicroFab technologies.

While the company continued to make its regular visits to the US and worked to create a 'feeding frenzy' among global investment banks by holding regular information sessions at its offices, Williams recognized that the decision to be based in Australia had made it harder to access capital. He acknowledged, 'We'd been told on many occasions I guess that, had we set up in San Francisco,

there would have been a line out the door and around the corner wanting to give us money and so it's clear that the environment that we lived in here was a little more lonely and now we are paying attention to some very substantial competition in the US and Europe where people have literally hundreds of millions to spend'.[42] Nonetheless, he noted, 'We are trying to generate a bit of tension about our company and its technology. I think it's possible that Australian high-tech companies like ours can get into the world and do it out of Sydney'.[43]

Now, in mid-2001, with its first instruments in production phase, the company anticipated revenues of $20 million for the year ending in June 30, 2002 (see Table 2 for the company's financial statements). It was also in the process of a second private capital raising and foresaw listing on the NASDAQ in the near future as an Australian company with a US subsidiary though Williams had not ruled out listing on the ASX instead.

TABLE 2   Summary of consolidated financial data (in thousands Aus $)

	12 months to June 30, 2000	12 months to June 30, 2001
Revenue	3399	6623
Operating expenses	2635	(14333)
Profit/(loss) from operations	764	(7710)
Interest income/(expense)	(10)	552
Net income (loss)	754	(7158)
Balance sheet data		
Cash and cash equivalents	597	6990
Total assets	2838	13362
Total liabilities	2606	4404
Net equity	31	8957

Source: Proteome Systems Limited.

[41]Case writer interview with Andrew Gooley, Proteome Systems Limited.

[42]'Future of Biotechnology in Australia', ABC radio current affair special, January 2, 2001.

[43]Tony Boyd, 'The Big Leap', *Australian Financial Review*, February 9, 2001.

Establishment of a US subsidiary

The US was the world's largest technology market and had the infrastructure and capital to nurture young companies. Companies realized that they could garner higher visibility and credibility by dealing with the US market if they had a ground presence in a US technology center. They would also realize good connections in this target market and gain a better understanding of US business culture.

PSL recognized that it needed a base in the US and in October 2000, announced the opening of a proteomics factory in Woburn, MA – a suburb of Boston. The company had been fortunate in being able to recruit the Boston-based proteomics team of Genomics Solutions, a competitor, to create PSL's 'beachhead' in the US. PSL's Woburn factory would allow the company to have a demonstration and training facility to showcase its proteomics technologies and the kits and consumables would be manufactured here because of shelf life issues. The company had originally intended to manufacture its instruments in the Boston facility as well but had then decided against it observing the cost differential. PSL now had 50,000 sq. feet at its Sydney facilities and 20,000 sq. feet at its Boston facility.

Technology and product development

Following the Dow project, technology development had quickly become the focus of the company's efforts. The company had over 50 products that it was either in the process of developing or had already developed. The products spanned the entire chain of steps in protein analysis from sample preparation to bioinformatics and protein chips. Williams and his team believed that for the technologies and consumables to be accepted by scientists, they had to be easy to use and the consumables had to be in kit form. Exhibit 2 provides information on the company's proteomics platform and the products it incorporated.

Sample preparation, separation and gel array technology

While there were alternative protein separation technologies, PSL firmly believed that 2DE technology was, 'the only way proteins [were] ever going to be separated to purity'. PSL had developed sample preparation kits called ProteoPrep that allowed better sample solubilization and which addressed the problems associated with 'difficult' proteins such as membrane proteins. The kits were designed by PSL but the company did not intend to market and distribute these products. So, in May 2001, PSL entered into an agreement with Sigma-Aldrich, a prominent distributor of biological and chemical reagents around the world and soon after, Sigma manufactured the first batch of these kits, which sold out almost immediately. The two companies also extended the relationship by including additional products manufactured by PSL in Boston and marketed by Sigma.

Image analysis

In July 2000, the company also started collaborating with the Commonwealth Scientific and Industrial Research Organization's (CSIRO) division of mathematics and informatics research team to develop software for protein spot identification, following the 2DE separation technique. Only after the position of a protein spot had been identified and recorded could it be treated with enzymes prior to identification in the mass spectrometer. Therefore, image analysis following 2DE was a crucial step in the process. The software developed by the company had graphical user interface designed for ease of use. Results and inputs could be stored in database format for ease of grouping and network access. This way, users could browse and access gel information using a network, compare gels within projects, experiments and samples and annotate them. While other competitor firms had also developed such software, PSL felt that its in-house discovery group was particularly valuable in 'road-testing' its prototype software and improving it as a result. For instance, PSL's software, like those of its competitors could be used to automatically pick spots on a 2-D gel, but the PSL product also allowed users to manually delete spots they didn't think were real.

CASE 34

EXHIBIT 2 PROTEOME IQ: THE INTEGRATED PROTEOMICS PLATFORM WITH PSL'S PRODUCTS INCLUDED

Sample preparation. In collaboration with Sigma-Aldrich, PSL developed a new generation of kits to make sample preparation simple and reproducible. These kits were commercially available. PSL intended to develop a broad range of specialty kits such as kits designed for fractionation targeted to specific classes of proteins.

Sample fractionation. The Multi-compartment Electrolyzer allowed pre-fractionation of protein samples. This enabled high sample loading on 2DE and resulted in high resolution separation of protein spots on narrow pH range gels.

Gel array technology. Multi-functional electrophoresis systems comprised an electroblotter, SDS-PAGE Gel Running System and IPG Running System for protein separation. This platform of integrated hardware allowed for running of standardized IPG strips and Gel Chips which PSL had developed and would OEM for distribution by Sigma-Aldrich.

Gel image analysis. Gel image analysis software and hardware would facilitate analysis of high-resolution images of the protein gels and blots. The fluorescent image would be captured by the Alphalnnotech Image 3300.

Gel to mass spectrometry. In collaboration with Shimadzu, PSL developed an integrated device (Xcise) to excise, digest and clean up the proteins from the gel, in preparation for delivery to the mass spectrometer for automated analysis. It also developed with Millipore, a MALDI Gel Digest kit to provide a fast, convenient and reproducible method to digest and purify up to 96 SDS-PAGE gel plugs simultaneously. Millipore would distribute these kits. Its second-generation platform would include the company's Chemical Printer instrument, eliminating the need for the Xcise. The company was also creating the Chemical Printer and the Peizo LC Instrument.

Mass spectrometry. PSL integrated Kratos Analytical's Axima-CFR MALDI-TOF mass spectrometer in the platform. It also proposed to integrate a liquid chromatograph-mass spectrometer (LC/MS) solution into the platform and was in discussion with a leading LC/MS manufacturer about a technology alliance.

Bioinformatics. BioinformatiqIQ was PSL's sophisticated informatics package integrated platform. It was a web-based platform for the storage, management and automation of proteome analysis.

Source: Proteome Systems Limited.

Gel to mass spectrometry (MS)

In March 2000, the company entered into its first major technology development alliance with the Kyoto-based Shimadzu Corporation. PSL had always envisioned creating a proteomics platform and while the company had expertise in many areas of protein analysis, it did not have access to a mass spectrometer manufacturer. Shimadzu owned Kratos Analytical, a Manchester, UK-based mass spectrometer manufacturer, and, therefore, fitted the bill. For its part, Shimadzu had recognized that proteomics was coming to the forefront in biotechnology and with PSL it could tap into this market.

The two companies first worked on the Xcise, an instrument that could excise spots from gels, do the liquid handling and have the samples on a molding plate for use in the mass spectrometer. The instrument would speed the protein identification process 10-fold over current equipment and the two partners would split the development costs equally. To assemble the prototype, PSL worked with Sydney-based Pneumatic Products, a company whose expertise lay in motion control technologies. PSL had also recruited Niche Innovation, a Melbourne-based product design and development group to help in the design of the instrument.

In addition to the Xcise, the two companies were also working on the Chemical Printer that Gooley had envisioned while at APAF. This instrument would do away with the need for the Xcise and could be incorporated into the company's second-generation platform. In November 2000, PSL had acquired the required 'matrix jet' technology from MicroFab Technologies of Plano, TX in an exclusive arrangement after Gooley, the company's chief scientific officer had found MicroFab in an Internet search for the word 'inkjet'.[44] The original patent Gooley and Williams had filed on the chemical printer idea, while at the university, had also reverted back to them. The key feature of the chemical printer was that it would, 'bring the chemistry to proteins immobilized on membranes, rather than the traditional art of moving proteins for analysis. [The] technology minimizes sample manipulation, maximizes sensitivity of the analysis and provides an ideal substrate for archiving the sample', explained Gooley.[45]

By January 2001, the company had achieved the second milestone in its collaboration with Shimadzu in the development of the Chemical Printer and by mid-2001, the Xcise was in early stage production. The company anticipated charging about US$240,000 for each Xcise instrument and US$2 million for each platform which would include the range of instruments allowing separation, mass spectrometry and subsequent analysis.[46] PSL had also acquired Niche Innovation in May 2001 to bring experience in developing instruments and establishing manufacturing operations in-house. PSL wanted its instruments to have a distinctive look and Williams noted, '[We're] not trying to be Wal-Mart – [we're] trying to be up-market'.[47] However, the company was trying to decide whether it should provide multiple versions of the platform that differed by various additional features or whether it should simply make two models – 'one fancy and one not [as] fancy'.[48]

Meanwhile, the partnership between the two companies had also deepened and Shimadzu chose to co-locate its biotechnology division within PSL's Boston branch in April 2001. PSL planned to establish proteomics facilities in Sydney and Boston (and soon after, in Kyoto) that would feature PSL's sample preparation products and instruments, its chemical printer as well as Kratos' mass spectrometry systems.

Aside from its collaboration with Shimadzu, PSL was also developing a third instrument with MicroFab Technologies called the PiezoLC. The instrument was similar to the chemical printer except it had a miniaturized chromatography system for preparing protein samples for mass spectrometry. The technology would also allow the company to enter the protein 'chip' market by 2002. In the process, in March 2001, the company had forged an alliance with the Millipore Corporation, a dominant player in the membrane field. Millipore had 'ZipTip' technology that allowed small volumes of samples to be purified and concentrated which PSL required for the PiezoLC instrument. PSL would adapt this technology for its platform and also develop kits to clean and concentrate protein samples prior to use in the mass spectrometer. While Millipore would be the sole distributor, PSL would have exclusive assembly rights for these kits and intended to assemble them in its Boston facility.

Bioinformatics

To support its integrated proteomics platform, ProteomeIQ, PSL had developed a set of informatics tools in-house. These were web-based, ran on PSL's intranet and were used on a daily basis by researchers within the discovery division of the company. Such 'road-testing' allowed the company to get rapid feedback on its prototypes and allowed it to incorporate features that were demanded by the end users of the software. Ultimately, using a web-based intranet application, researchers would be able to manage projects, visualize and compare data. Centralized information would include sample and experimental details, gel images and protein

[44]Case writer interview with Andrew Gooley, Proteome Systems Limited.

[45]PR Newswire, 'Proteome Systems achieves key technical milestone on chemical printer instrument', December 1, 2000.

[46]Proteome Systems Limited. Summary of information, 2001.

[47]Case writer interview with Keith Williams, Proteome Systems Limited.

[48]Ibid.

spot coordinates, mass spectra and peak information. The company was also working with its partners, Shimadzu to further automate and integrate Kratos' mass spectrometer in its proteomics platform.

In addition the company had also developed tools for large-scale analysis and visualization of proteomics data and for undertaking complex queries of public gene and protein databases such as GenBank and SWISS-PROT. The company had already developed a database product, GlycoSuiteDB that was useful in the characterization of proteins that were modified in a certain manner and in May 2000, the product was launched by GeneBio, a Geneva-based informatics company who would handle the distribution. In 2001, the company chose IBM as its hardware and middleware supplier.

Discovery program

Following the Dow project, the company had largely focused on technology development. Now, however, with its first instruments in the early production phase, the company could move faster on the discovery front. PSL had chosen to focus its discovery efforts in the areas of infectious disease, cancer and aging – areas where, the company believed, proteomics could have an impact relatively rapidly. The technology program at the company had benefited from its association with the discovery group and it was hoped that the discovery program would similarly benefit from early access to newly developed technologies.

In January 2001, PSL announced its second discovery collaboration since its founding. It would collaborate with researchers at the University of Columbia, Missouri, to determine why some tumor cells become resistant to cancer drugs with the hope of uncovering potential protein targets for therapeutic intervention. Similarly, the company had chosen to focus on ovarian cancer that had a high mortality rate and which usually generated few symptoms in patients till it was considerably advanced. Proteomics could enable early diagnosis and point the way to research on the therapeutic avenues.

In the infectious disease area, the company was focusing on tuberculosis with AP Clinical, a com-

pany it had an equity stake in and that had access to valuable clinical samples from China. PSL had also recently begun projects in the pain and aging areas. The Boston subsidiary had identified an academic partner focusing on the metabolic process in aging with the aim of relating this to the progression of disease states. Speaking of the company's approach to discovery, Harry explained:

[One approach] is to wait till people say we'll pay you $2 million to do this. If you do that, you tend to give [your partners] products to develop although you can share [the] intellectual property if you do co-funding [for a project]. Or there's the other [possibility] where Pfizer or Aventis is behind you and you go to list but one of the things you lose is control over how you develop your program. To have complete freedom – particularly in the beginning of a program is very valuable.[49]

For the future, depending on how the projects progressed, Harry envisioned the company narrowing its focus to fewer projects. In addition to relationships with prominent academic groups, the company also intended to establish a few select relationships with larger bio-pharmaceutical companies. The company had recently expanded its in-house mass spectrometry facility with the installation of six mass spectrometers manufactured by its partner, Kratos Analytical. The acquired instruments would allow them the increased capacity to carry out in-house high-throughput discovery programs.

The competitive field and emerging technologies

As proteomics was coming to the forefront of the life sciences, many companies had entered the race to develop new technologies for it. Celera and PE Biosystems – the companies that had dominated genome-sequencing efforts, had now turned their focus to proteomics and had initiated a large-scale effort. And companies such as Oxford Glycosciences, one of the earliest companies in the proteomics field, had, by 2001, already filed patent applications on 1,500 targets identified by proteomics.

[49]Case writer interview with Jenny Harry, Proteome Systems Limited.

Like PSL, some companies were focusing on developing integrated platforms that spanned the length of the protein analysis chain while others were focusing on specific stages of protein analysis. There was, however, no consensus on which stage of protein analysis needed greatest attention or which technology to focus on. While PSL had identified the sample preparation and data analysis steps was important bottlenecks that the industry had largely ignored, others viewed the mass spectrometry stage as a key block that could be overcome by the acquisition of tens or hundreds of mass spectrometers. Similarly, others cited the inability of the 2DE protein separation technique to allow adequate relative quantification of the protein levels between samples. These skeptics had developed alternative techniques such as Isotope Coded Affinity Tagging (ICAT) that allowed better relative quantification and concurrent identification. The ICAT technique, however, also suffered limitations since it did not address protein modifications, an area that PSL considered essential for comprehensive protein analysis. Some combined the two methods while Celera's proteomics efforts, for instance, planned to dispense completely with 2DE using liquid chromatography (LC) methods for protein separation instead.

Yet others such as Ciphergen had taken an entirely different approach and had developed technologies that allowed users to isolate proteins according to their chemical attributes using a range of 'chips' that could then be used in a 'chip-reader' that included a mass spectrometer. Some were banking on developing protein interaction maps that they felt would be key in uncovering critical pathways and therapeutic targets but most of these companies used recombinant proteins that PSL felt missed the point since they were not authentic. PSL also intended to address protein-protein interactions but stressed that their approach would be different in that it would focus on authentic proteins.

Genomics Solutions Inc., an Ann Arbor-based company that PSL's Boston team had sprung from, was also developing a proteomics platform but announced in October 2000 that it was designing its platform to integrate with mass spectrometers from all manufacturers. This, the company claimed, would give their customers increased flexibility and choice since users would no longer be constrained to buy from a single vendor.[50] PSL, however, was betting on tight integration of its systems with Kratos' MALDI mass spectrometer and Thermo Finnigan's LCQ LC/MS/MS instrument. The company saw its primary competitors to be Amersham Pharmacia Biotech, it's old partner, Bio-Rad, PE BioSystems as well as the smaller Genomics Solutions (Table 3 provides information on select proteomics companies). Finally, PSL was not alone in wanting to use its proteomics technologies to fuel its drug discovery programs. Companies with greater resources such as GeneProt and Oxford Glycosciences were already drawing attention from large pharmaceutical companies.

Xcelerator Ltd

In February 2000, Proteome Systems Limited and other private investors established Xcelerator Ltd., the first privately financed biotechnology incubator in Australia. Mark Bradley, an entrepreneurial scientist, was hired to run the incubator company and Bradley felt that with the right drivers in place, 'there [would be] no reason why Australia [couldn't] produce a biotech industry worth up to $10 billion annually within just a few years'.

The idea for the incubator company had come about when Williams was approached in 1999 by two scientists who were still at Macquarie University. They were seeking advice on how they might commercialize their testing system for microorganisms in water supplies. Williams and Martin quickly realized that there was a market for incubator firms in Australia – to provide startup companies with mentoring, access to contacts in the commercial world as well as facilities in an environment where university technology licensing organizations were only just learning the ropes. Proximity to know-how was critical and Williams and Martin felt that PSL could play a role in addressing this need.

By mid-2001, the two scientists who had initially approached Williams and established a company called Biotechnology Frontiers were in the middle of a capital raising and their company was

[50]Press Release Newswire, 'Genomic Solutions to collaborate with major mass spectrometer companies', October 6, 2000.

about to be the first to graduate from Xcelerator Ltd. The incubator was also helping AP Clinical, a company that had been started by one of Williams' students and that was working with PSL's discovery group, to get off the ground. In the future, Williams anticipated Xcelerator could even incubate a manufacturing operation that would produce the instruments that PSL intended to manufacture in Australia. In this scenario PSL would, however, maintain a 60% stake in such a company and 'watch them'.[51] That way, Williams explained, one could 'avoid VC sharks and get the business going'.[52]

Growth challenges

Williams thought that scientists could be good business managers, noting, 'If you can build and run a successful lab, you have acquired the skills needed to run a small business – juggling cash flow, people skills, project flows etc.' However, as the company had grown, Williams and his team had to quickly recognize areas where they 'were out of their depth'. As Gooley explained, 'we [had] to face and say this is not my area of expertise – [for instance], I have never manufactured anything before'.[53] And more so than other companies in the field, PSL had to 'juggle cash-flow'. The company had been focusing on technology development in the past year and, as a result, the informatics division and discovery programs had begun to feel under-resourced. The lean cash position also meant that the technology development division had to exercise strong discipline over its projects to avoid 'creeping features' – that is, the gradual inclusion of additional features to the company's prototype instruments that had the potential to slow development.

Following the rapid pace of events in the first year and half, the company had also realized that it needed an external evaluation of its management structure with an employee survey highlighting areas that required attention. PSL learned that as it had grown there had not been effective transfer of responsibility across different levels of the firm. While the management team had tried to maintain as non-hierarchical a structure as possible, it was clear that some structure was needed to maintain accountability. For instance, the top management would have a particular view of a project while employees down below were often not sure who they were directly accountable to. The company had also begun running workshops to educate and train its employees to recognize novel ideas and create new intellectual property for PSL.

In addition, the company was working to integrate its Boston-based subsidiary into the firm's culture. It was unusual for a biotechnology company to be based in Australia with a subsidiary in the US. The large time zone gap made communication difficult at times and, occasionally, there were situations where one group would be unaware of a decision the other had taken. Different cultural outlooks also became apparent, for instance, the company initiated its first advertising campaign, and each group had a different view of the ads proposed by the other.

By mid-2000, the company employed 80 people (65 in Sydney and 15 in Boston), over half of whom had PhDs. As testament to the atmosphere of the company, Gooley noted that, 'only three [had] left'. To infuse the company with the founders' informal culture, firm-wide meetings were held every Friday in a social setting with catered food and drinks.

Conclusion

While the company had made considerable progress in the two and a half years of its existence and was now on the verge of rolling out its first major product offerings and its flagship proteomics platform, Williams and his team also recognized that they were going to need a larger global presence. Specifically, Williams and his team knew they needed a branch on the West Coast of the US where a large number of biotechnology and pharmaceutical companies had based their R&D operations. Europe, however, was their biggest challenge since PSL had no presence in this market at all.

While Williams considered the company's growth and future, his conviction in PSL's tech-

---

[51]Case writer interview with Keith Williams, Proteome Systems Limited.
[52]Case writer interview with Keith Williams, Proteome Systems Limited.
[53]Case writer interview with Andrew Gooley, Proteome Systems Limited.

TABLE 3   Selection of companies in the proteomics field

Company (Symbol)	Location	Market capitalization ($ millions)	P/E ratio	Comments
Applied Biosystems (ABI)	Norwalk, CT	5,489	27	Instruments and consumables for genomics and proteomics
Amersham Pharmacia Biotech, unit of Nycomed Amersham (NYECF)	Buckinghamshire, UK	3,908	27	Instruments and consumables for genomics and proteomics
Bio-Rad (BIOa)	Hercules, CA	650.2	14.73	Instruments and consumables; alliance with Micromass to provide integrated proteomics tools
Celera Genomics (CRA)	Norwalk, CT	1,808	NM	Genomics company entering proteomics
Ciphergen (CIPH.O)	Fremont, CA	115.8	NM	Protein chips
Genomic Solutions (GNSL)	Ann Arbor, MI	62.4	NM	Instruments for proteomics and genomics
Oxford GlycoSciences (OGSIF)	Oxford, UK	580	NM	Combined proteomics platform development with drug development
Large Scale Biology Corporation (LSBC)	Vacaville, CA	111.6	NM	Focused on application of 2DE to determining changes in protein expression; intends to license databases
Geneva Proteomics (GeneProt)	Evanston, IL	431 (Private)	NA	Proteomics information based products; strategic alliance with Bruker Daltonics and with Compaq
MDS Proteomics – Subsidiary of MDS Inc. (MDZ)	Toronto, Canada	1,481	62.7	Focused on complete proteomics platform

NM = Not meaningful.
Source: Adapted from finance.yahoo.com (accessed August 14, 2001).

nology remained unflappable. The company appeared to relish being the underdog and even the company's chairman had acknowledged, 'We're miniscule by [the] US perspective – our type of companies have US$100 million in cash! But we're very focused and time is key. [We're] driven by great anxiety over who will beat the bottlenecks'.[54] There were biotechnology compa-

nies that had felt the pressure and had left Australia for the US or Europe. Williams, however, felt his nation was suffering from an inferiority complex. He had spent 30 years in the field and now, with PSL, he was going to try and prove them all wrong and, with Xcelerator Limited, help build a biotech sector in the process.

[54]Case writer interview with Bruce Hogan, Proteome Systems Limited.

Swatch: Coping with market changes

CASE 15

By Franz Weisbrod and Colin Gilligan[1]

In the spring of 1998, members of the management team of Swatch were reflecting on the success of their product and the challenges ahead. Developed 15 years previously, the Swatch watch had revolutionised the Swiss watch industry and, in doing this, had exceeded the most optimistic expectations both of its creator, Nicholas Hayek, and Ernst Thomke, the technological brain behind it.

What was seen initially by many to be a funny plastic watch, had been launched during the climax of the onslaught on the Swiss watch industry by Japanese and Hong Kong competitors. It was a meticulously planned response to the Far Eastern companies who had almost eliminated the Swiss presence in the high volume and relatively low price market segments that made up more than 80% of unit sales worldwide. Hayek had succeeded in creating an entirely new market segment, appealing to the hitherto largely unserved teenage market and people who were young at heart. The concept proved so successful that the brand sold more than 200 million units within the next decade and established a strong presence in all major markets. However, in 1998, Hayek and his team had reason to be thoughtful about the further development of their brand. The

changing watch market, changes in style and fashion, and strong competition had all conspired to put Swatch under pressure.

The situation in 1998

In 1998, Swatch was a global brand with subsidiaries or agencies in more than 70 countries. The global marketing strategy had resulted in very high levels of brand awareness, clear positioning, a universally appealing product range, a well formulated global pricing strategy, and a worldwide promotional strategy. The company's success was due largely to their first product, the *Standard*.

However, between 1990–94 *Standard* sales had remained relatively stable and had only increased by 30% since 1986. Despite more than 70 different models per season, and a high variety of limited editions, the novelty of Swatch appeared to have faded as it moved into the mature phase of the life cycle (see Figure 1).

For this reason, Swatch had launched numerous new product lines including *Chrono*, *Automatic*, *Scuba*, *Pop*, *MusiCall*, *The Beep*, *Aquachrono*, *Pop-up*, and most recently *Irony*, *Access*, and the

FIGURE 1   'Standard' production between 1983 and 1994

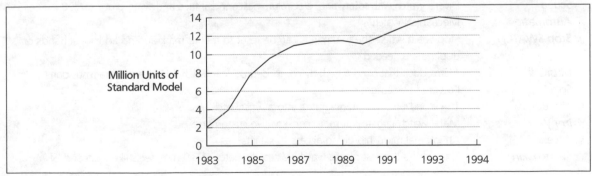

[1]Source: Franz Weisbrod is a senior manager with Compare (Germany). Colin Gilligan is Professor of Marketing, Sheffield Hallam University. Case reproduced with permission.

SwatchSkin (see Table 1). At the same time, the company also began a programme of diversification into textiles, clothing, and, initially with Volkswagen but subsequently with Mercedes-Benz, the *Smart* car (the reader should note that in November 1998, Swatch announced its withdrawal from the joint venture.)

Some of the new models such as *Chrono*, *Scuba* and *Irony* had proved to be very successful. Others, however, such as *MusiCall* and *Pop Swatch* were, on the face of it at least, less successful. The *Standard* had therefore maintained its position as the most popular Swatch product, even though sales declined slightly between 1993 and 1994. Overall, therefore, Swatch had managed to extend their life cycle through the launch of new products, even though the majority of the new lines failed to play more than a marginal role (see Figure 2).

Further analysis of sales figures revealed another worrying factor to Hayek's management team: the extension of Swatch's life cycle had been largely supported by two new lines, *Chrono* and *Scuba*. None of the other new lines had been nearly as successful and none had been able to repeat the performance of the *Standard*. However, the team's expectations of *Irony* were high, as the watch was more in line with the growing trend for metal watches.

The customer base

A detailed analysis of customers showed the team that lifestyles in their traditional European markets had changed. Due to the long and severe recession of the late 1980s and early 1990s, customers had become more price conscious. At the same time, attitudes towards materials had also changed. The plastic throw away mentality of the buoyant early to mid-1980s had been replaced by a new trend towards more solid, longer lasting products, a trend that had been led by a growing environmental awareness amongst consumers that rebelled against the excessive use of plastic in favour of the more easily recycled glass.

The other constraint to Swatch's future growth was proving to be a series of far-reaching demographic changes. Research[2] demonstrated to the team that the typical Swatch customer age group (between 15 and 29 years) would decline heavily over the next decade. The significance of this is illustrated by the way in which in 1993 Swatch had more than 80 million potential customers in the European Union. Market projections showed that by 2008 this market segment will have declined to 65 million consumers, a decrease of more than 20 percent (see Tables 2 and 3).

These problems were, in turn, being compounded by the way in which the market was becoming ever more competitive, with a greater number of compa-

TABLE 1 The Swatch product line in 1998

Product line	Features
Pop Swatch	Large flexible cotton wristband to fit over clothes
Chrono	Stopwatch for sprinters with intermediate and finishing times
Scuba	Diver's watch with rotary ring, electroluminescent dial face and waterproof to 200 metres
Automatic	Mechanical watch
Stop SWATCH	Stopwatch where the two hands can be reset to the 12 mark and no additional hands or displays are needed
MusiCall	Alarm clock that plays a melody composed by Jean Michel Jarre and other musicians
Solar	Powered by sunlight
The Beep	The world's first pager integrated into a wristwatch
Irony	Metal watch targeted at more conservative customers
Access	An internal microchip giving access to ski lifts
SwatchSkin	The world's thinnest plastic watch with a diameter of 3.9 mm; feels like a second 'Skin'

[2]Source: Euromonitor (1997), *European Marketing Data and Statistics*, 32nd Ed., London, p. 124.

FIGURE 2   Swatch production between 1983 and 1994

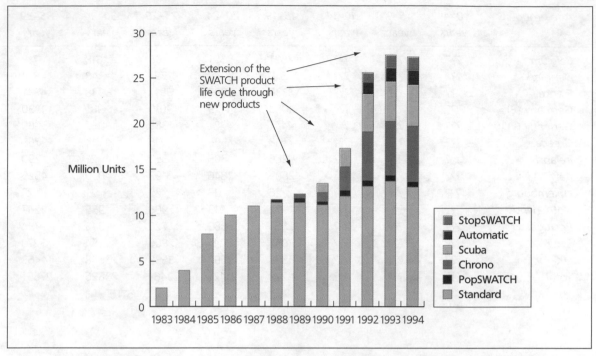

Source: Adapted from Miller, A. (1997) 'Nur an der Burse tickt die SMH nicht richtig' in *CASH*, ISS.32, No. 8, August, p.5.

TABLE 2   Demographic group sizes in the European Union in 1993 (×1000)

Age group	0–4 years	5–9 years	10–14 years	15–19 years	20–24 years	25–29 years	30–34 years	35–39 years
Belgium	621	591	618	618	713	791	804	760
Denmark	318	274	291	348	374	424	379	372
France	3738	3803	3917	3938	4341	4335	4323	4269
Germany (E)	1063	1129	1010	981	1230	1392	1261	1232
Germany (W)	4441	4421	4380	4161	5809	7166	6736	5912
Greece	518	595	716	714	768	812	766	712
Ireland	266	305	350	321	290	247	248	245
Italy	2809	2846	3193	4025	4525	4827	4339	3884
Luxembourg	26	23	22	21	27	34	34	32
Netherlands	972	913	906	955	1247	1308	1277	1183
Portugal	551	589	720	843	794	734	703	666
Spain	2054	2241	2800	3254	3270	3289	3038	2642
UK	3898	3692	3538	3648	4463	4795	4331	3830
Total	21273	21421	22461	23826	27851	30153	28239	25739

nies competing for the decreasing number of customers. The team also realised that the market was demanding more durable, solid and upmarket watches than ten years earlier. But most importantly, the watch's fashionable character made it vulnerable to changes in fashion and raised the fundamental question of whether the brand still had its novelty, unique appeal and symbolic character.

TABLE 3 Demographic group sizes in the European Union in 2008 (×1000)

Age group	0–4 years	5–9 years	10–14 years	15–19 years	20–24 years	25–29 years	30–34 years	35–39 years
Belgium	???	???	???	621	591	618	618	713
Denmark	???	???	???	318	274	291	348	374
France	???	???	???	3738	3803	3917	3938	4341
Germany (E)	???	???	???	1063	1129	1010	981	1230
Germany (W)	???	???	???	4441	4421	4380	4161	5809
Greece	???	???	???	518	595	716	714	768
Ireland	???	???	???	266	305	350	321	290
Italy	???	???	???	2809	2846	3193	4025	4525
Luxembourg	???	???	???	26	23	22	21	27
Netherlands	???	???	???	972	913	906	955	1247
Portugal	???	???	???	551	589	720	843	794
Spain	???	???	???	2054	2241	2800	3254	3270
UK	???	???	???	3898	3692	3538	3648	4463
Total	???	???	???	21273	21421	22461	23826	27851

The competition

Competition in Swatch's market segment had increased considerably throughout the late 1980s and into the 1990s (see Figure 3). When Swatch was launched in 1983, it created a completely new market. However, other companies quickly followed and launched their own brands that appealed to the newly created 'teeny segment'. Many of these companies copied Swatch's designs, positioning and pricing strategy. Although this made life difficult for the company, Swatch's clear branding, marketing creativity and aggression ensured that it was consistently far more successful than its rivals. This was illustrated by the fact that the company had sold its 200 millionth Swatch back in 1996. The market was, however, changing and other companies were becoming more innovative and successful. The trend away from plastic towards more robust metal sports watches was, for example, posing a serious threat. The launch of *Irony* had acknowledged this change, but at the beginning of 1998 the management team was being forced to consider whether the company had fully appreciated the nature and significance of the changing market.

Swatch's leading competitor today is Timex Corporation. In 1997 their market share in America, Swatch's major export market, was 11% compared with Swatch's share of 1–2%.[3] The majority of their sales are generated in Swatch's traditional market segments. By contrast with Swatch's strategy in which all watches have the Swatch logo, Timex watches are marketed under several leading names, including Indiglo, Benetton, Timberland, Joe Boxer, Burwood, and Guess. All are marketed as fashion accessories, but are positioned slightly differently in order to cover a wider market. The differentiated marketing strategy ranges from economical plastic watches (Benetton) to more upmarket metal watches with leather straps (Timberland). Timex's DataLink, was developed in conjunction with Microsoft and allows comprehensive databases to be downloaded straight from a computer.

Guess is Swatch's second strongest competitor in the US, with sales of 5.5 million units, and a turnover of US$75 million. Launched in 1984, the Guess strategy might loosely be labelled as a Swatch strategy in reverse in that the Guess brand was established in 1981 by a French group market-

[3]Source: Euromonitor (1996), p.54.

FIGURE 3   The development of the world watch market

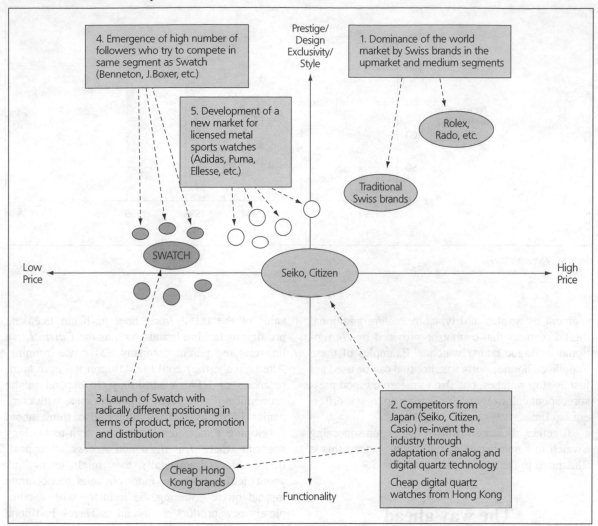

ing clothes and leather products. Having established the brand in that sector, the watch collection was then launched. By contrast Swatch established the watch brand first, and then tried to diversify into textiles and apparel. Today, Guess is part of the Timex Group.

Another strong competitor in Swatch's segment is Fossil. This American brand, produced in Hong Kong, has copied the Swatch marketing strategy, but has positioned the brand slightly further upmarket than Swatch. According to Fossil manager Tim Hale, 'The company does exactly the same as the Swiss [Swatch], just in a different [metal] segment'.[4] The

annual collection of metal watches is designed in the style of the 1950's, and is supplied in aluminium boxes. This is designed to emphasise the watch's solidity, robustness and greater 'value for money' than Swatch's plastic product and packaging. Having established themselves in the United States, Fossil began expanding into Europe. Within four years, sales soared from $50 million to more than $200 million. Fossil's growth is highlighted in Figure 4.

A further competitive threat was proposed by Casio who, when the market for digital quartz watches started declining, introduced analogue quartz watches. These are offered in the same price

[4]Willmanns, B.: 'Das jüngste Fossil der Zeitgeschichte', in: *Facts*, 25/1997, p.67.

FIGURE 4 Turnover of Fossil between 1992 and 1996

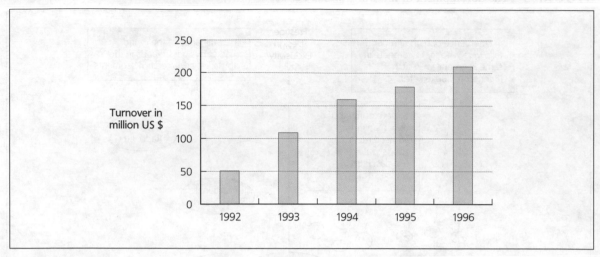

Source: Willmanns (1997)

segment as Swatch and typically feature additional digital features that cannot be provided by conventional analogue quartz watches. Examples of these include elaborate sports watches that can be used not just as stop watches, but also to measure blood pressure, spent calories, and for storing up to 100 different lap times.

Together, these competitors had begun squeezing Swatch in a number of its traditional sectors; this is illustrated in the market map in Figure 5.

The way ahead

Given the nature of these changes within its market, it was obvious to Swatch's management team that the company was faced with a number of major challenges. Critics were beginning to say Swatch had not really adapted to the new market conditions. If the company ignored these developments, its future would be under serious threat. So what alternatives did they have? In the watch market, there appeared to be a number of possibilities. They could fight to retain their current position, reposition the brand by moving upmarket through exten-

sions of the metal *Irony* line, or begin licensing prestigious fashion brands such as the *Calvin Klein* line that the parent company SMH was running. Alternatively, they could build upon the core competencies of ETA, a subsidiary, to expand in the economical digital segment and compete with companies like Casio. They might also think about developing a new market in the high-technology segment where *The Beep* and *Access* were positioned. More dramatically, they might even think about letting Swatch fade out and concentrate instead on re-inventing the industry with a completely new product and brand as Hayek had done 15 years previously. A major consideration in all of this was the scope that existed for capitalising upon possible synergies with SMH's other successful brands such as Tissot, Rado and Omega. At the same time, they needed to think about whether they should continue their activities in other industries like telecommunications or automobiles. At the heart of all of this was the question of what the company's *real* core competencies and organisational capabilities were that would help to defeat the competition once again.

FIGURE 5   Product positioning of Swatch in comparison to other major brands in its segment*

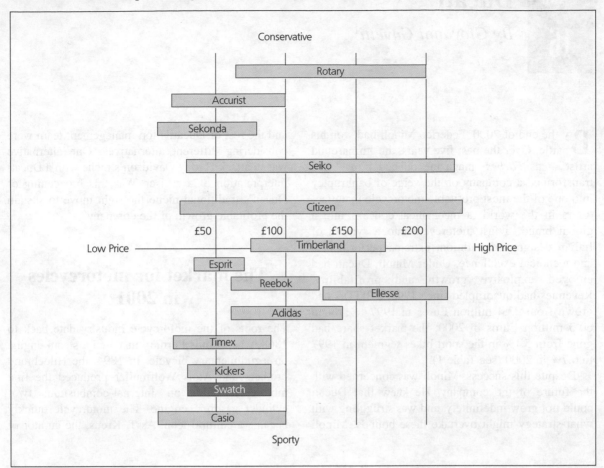

* This research was conducted by the authors in major UK catalogue shops (Argos, Index), retail chains (Goldsmiths, H. Samuel) and a major mail order company (Littlewoods) in August 1997. A very similar pattern emerged when German companies were researched. This survey included major mail order companies (Neckermann, Quelle, Wenz), as well as major retail chains (Christ and Gold Meister). N.B.: Several brands that are promoted in the UK are not marketed in Germany (Accurist, Rotary, Sekonda), but have been included in the map to demonstrate the high level of competition in the lower/medium segment.

Ducati

By Giovanni Gavetti[1]

By the end of 2000, Federico Minoli had won his battle. Over the past five years, the 'turnaround artist' – as *Forbes*[2] magazine dubbed him – had transformed a company on the verge of bankruptcy into one of the most profitable motorcycle manufacturers in the world; a mechanical concern into a global brand; a fast motorcycle into a symbol of Italian design and tradition, extreme performance, and technical excellence. Under Minoli, Ducati had enjoyed explosive growth and profitability. Revenues had quadrupled since 1996; EBITDA had grown from 33.4 million Euros in 1997 to around 60.0 million Euros in 2000; the market share had gone from 5.1% in the sport bikes segment in 1997 to 6.7% in 2000 (see Table 1).

Despite this success, Minoli was concerned with the future of the company. He knew that Ducati could not grow indefinitely, and was struggling with what strategy might overtake these bounds. Minoli and the rest of Ducati's top management team were considering different alternatives. One alternative was to attack Harley Davidson's niche with a Ducati interpretation of a cruiser. Was this broadening of Ducati's traditional niche the right move to sustain the profitable growth of the company?

The market for motorcycles in 2001

The roots of the motorcycle industry date back to 1868, when Louis Perraux installed a steam engine on a rudimentary bicycle. In 1894, the Hildebrand brothers and Alois Wolfmüller produced the first motorcycle with an internal-combustion, two-cylinder gasoline engine. The motorcycle quickly became a cultural icon. As T. Krens, the curator of

TABLE 1 Select financial data for Ducati (Euro millions): 1997–2001

	1997	*1998*	*1999*	*2000*	*2001*[a]
Total revenues	195.63	240.05	294.5	379.5	422.1
Gross profit	74.57	91.71	118	150.5	165.9
Other operating income	0.53	1.18	4.1	4.9	7.0
SG&A	41.7	52.4	71.3	95.4	103.0
EBITDA	33.4	46.49	50.8	60.03	69.9
D&A	16.67	19.17	24.4	29.6	32.8
EBIT	16.37	27.32	26.4	30.4	37.0
Net income	2.7	(1.24)	8.9	10.5	13.4
Market share[b]	5.1	6.2	6.0	6.7	7.0

Source: Company data.
[a]Analysts' estimates.
[b]Ducati Relevant Market.

[1]Source: © 2001 by the President and Fellows of Harvard College. Harvard Business School Case 9–701–132. This case was prepared by G. Gavetti as the basis for class discussion rather than to illustrate either effective or ineffective handling of an administrative situation. Reprinted by permission of Harvard Business School.
[2]*Forbes*, July 1999.

'The Art of the Motorcycle' exhibition at the Guggenheim Museum in New York, observed:

> *The motorcycle is a perfect metaphor for the twentieth century. Invented at the beginning of the industrial age, its evolution tracks the main currents of modernity. The object and its history represent the themes of technology, engineering, innovation, design, mobility, speed, rebellion, desire, freedom, love, sex, and death. Park the latest Ducati, Harley, Honda, or BMW on a street corner in any city or town in the world, and a crowd will gather.*[3]

Products

Approximately 1.6 million motorcycles were sold around the world in 2001 (see Figure 1). Industry experts divided the market for large-displacement motorcycles into four segments: off-road, cruisers, touring and sport bikes. The off-road segment typically included both motorcycles for purely off-road use, and motorcycles designed for both on-road and off-road use (dual purpose bikes). These motorcycles were characterized by an upright ergonomics, thickly padded seats, soft shocks, and superior sturdiness. The largest players within this segment were all of the Japanese manufacturers, KTM, BMW, and Huskvarna. Cruisers were big motorcycles with an upright riding position. Their design emphasized styling over comfort and speed, and was preferred by many American riders. Harley-Davidson dominated this segment, while Japanese companies such as Honda, Yamaha, Suzuki, and Kawasaki imitated the traditional Harley style. In 1997, BMW introduced its own interpretation of a cruiser, which enjoyed a stunning commercial success. Touring bikes were larger motorcycles equipped for longer rides and greater comfort. Within this segment, the three largest players were BMW, Harley-Davidson, and Honda. Sport bikes had lighter frames, a more forward seated position, and emphasized speed, acceleration, and minimal comfort. This niche, which Ducati identified as its relevant market (see Table 2), could be further disaggregated into four

FIGURE 1   The worldwide market for motorcycles

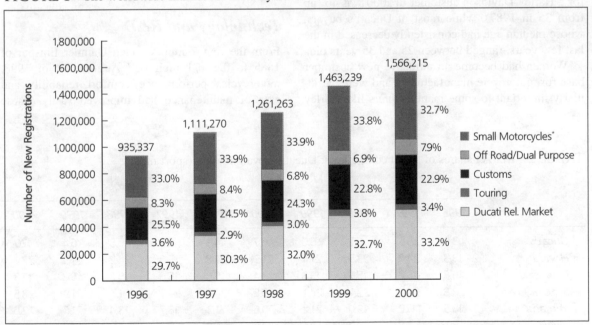

Source: Company estimates.

*The Small Motorcycles segment includes motorcycles with an engine displacement < 500 cc, and excludes scooters.

[3] *The Art of Motorcycle*, Guggenheim Museum Publications, 1998.

sub-segments: hyper-sport (extreme performance, closely derived from the racing world), super-sport (high performance, good handling and low weight), naked (good performance and urban riding) and sport touring (speed and handling, married with comfort for longer rides). Japanese companies dominated this niche, while European firms such as Ducati, BMW, and Triumph also vied for market share. Harley-Davidson entered the sport bike market by acquiring Buell Motorcycles in 1998. This segment was Ducati's reference market.

Customers

A wide variety of individuals, with equally different tastes, bought and rode motorcycles (Figure 2). 'Knee down', or racing aficionados, sought extreme performance and functionality (e.g., reliability and technical excellence). 'Easy-riders' lay at the other extreme, and associated the motorcycle with a particular lifestyle. 'Weekend riders' and 'highway lovers' were more interested in attributes like functionality and comfort, while a large portion of 'undecided bikers' preferred a more balanced and versatile bike. Each customer type differed by age, income, education and gender. For instance, the median age for a Harley-Davidson customer in 2000 was 46 (up from 35 in 1987), while most of Ducati's buyers, whose median age had consistently decreased in the last few years, ranged between 25 and 35 years old.

Women had become an attractive new customer base for motorcycle manufacturers, and were particularly important to some manufacturers like Harley and Ducati. Harley's proportion of female purchasers had increased from 2% in 1987 to 9% in 2000. Ducati claimed that women were attracted by the low seat height and weight of its motorcycles and accounted for 8% of sales of some models of its most popular bike, the Monster.

Specialized magazines, such as *Motorcycle Consumer News*, *Rider*, and *Cycle World*, catered to cycle buyers and educated them about the technical and stylistic characteristics of new products. They tested and ranked new motorcycles on several criteria, such as style, engine performance, handling, and overall comfort. Although the majority of the motorcycle companies advertised through specialized magazines, only some of them – typically the largest manufacturers – also advertised through the non-specialized press. Motorcycle firms also gained media coverage by participating in racing events. In addition, movies brought cachet to motorcycles. Motorcycles had been featured prominently in Hollywood movies, most notably the Triumph ridden by Marlon Brando in 'The Wild One' and the Harleys ridden by Peter Fonda, Dennis Hopper, and Jack Nicholson in 'Easy Rider.' Department stores like Bloomingdale's and Harrods sometimes used motorcycles in their window displays.

Technology and R&D

From the first 7 mph wooden Daimler Einspur of 1885 to the 171 mph MV Augusta F4 of 1998, motorcycles' performance, comfort, reliability, and ease of maintenance had improved vastly. These

TABLE 2   Market shares of select competitors: Ducati relevant market (sport niche)

	World					Europe				
	1996	1997	1998	1999	2000	1996	1997	1998	1999	2000
Ducati	3.9	5.1	6.2	6.0	6.7	4.3	5.2	6.5	6.4	7.0
Honda	23.3	24.7	23.5	21.4	21.5	23.8	25.8	24.2	21.5	22.7
Kawasaki	16.3	15.0	15.7	15.8	13.4	15.0	15.0	15.3	15.8	12.3
Suzuki	23.8	24.4	22.1	22.1	23.8	24.5	24.1	21.3	21.9	23.5
Yamaha	18.5	17.0	19.0	21.2	20.6	21.3	18.7	18.4	21.8	22.0
BMW	5.1	4.8	4.7	4.6	3.5	5.8	5.4	4.8	4.8	3.6
Harley-Davidson	5.8	4.8	3.8	3.3	3.3	1.5	1.2	1.2	1.0	1.0
Buell	0	0.2	1.2	1.3	1.6	0	0.3	0.5	0.6	0.5

Source: Company data.

FIGURE 2 A map of the market

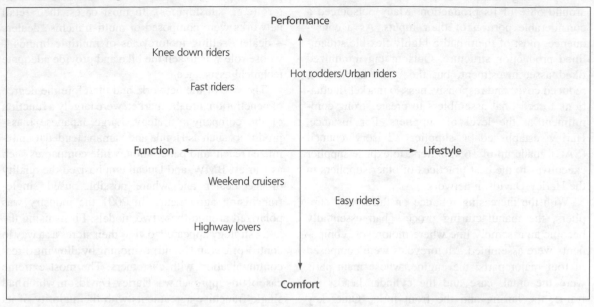

Source: Case-writer elaboration of company data.

advances ranged from significant innovations, which offered superior performance and distinguished companies' brands, to stylistic features introduced for little cost by combining modified components from old models. Kawasaki's 1984 world's first, 16-valve, liquid-cooled, 4-cylinder engine, Ducati's Desmodromic valve management system and L-Twin engine, or BMW's anti-lock braking system were examples of the former type of innovation. Nevertheless, improvements like paint, trim, chrome, and exhaust pipe shaping were also necessary to appeal to modern bikers, especially when deference to the company's styling tradition caused innovation to occur incrementally.

Starting in the mid-'70s, the most important trend had been the progressive introduction of electronic components. More recently, advances in materials science led companies to introduce composites, carbonium, titanium and magnesium to make their bikes lighter and more reliable. Industry experts estimated that in 2001 in-house R&D expenditure ranged between 2% and 5% of total revenues.

Motorcycles' technological improvements stemmed from different sources. Manufacturers concentrated on optimizing engine performance while decreasing motorcycles' weight, as well as improving their aerodynamics to lower fuel consumption and toxic emissions. They also pushed suppliers to improve quality and technology, thus enhancing

components like sophisticated 'air-assisted' forks, mono-shock rear suspensions, and front and rear disc brakes. Especially since the early '80s, some major companies like Honda, Kawasaki, Yamaha, and Ducati had also used racing competitions to develop technical solutions and test materials, and eventually transferred effective solutions to their production series. The racing circuit encompassed a number of different competitions, the most important of which were the Grand Prix (with the 125 cc, 250 cc, and 500 cc categories) and the Superbike Championship (with bikes ranging from 750 cc to 1,000 cc). Industry analysts agreed that a recent trend that can be generalized to the entire industry had been a stronger integration between R&D and marketing, which caused a larger number of technical improvements or innovations to derive from market surveys or customer feedback.

The pace of technological innovation was aided by the advent of CAD and CNC technologies, which greatly helped manufacturers' efforts in styling, prototyping and assessing product feasibility.

Manufacturing

Most motorcycle companies invested heavily to automate production lines and worked with parts suppliers to improve quality and delivery. Only a few firms, such as Triumph, increased their level of vertical integration. Triumph in 2000 outsourced around 58% of its production. Many outsourced a considerable portion of their inputs. As a consequence, most of them had a highly flexible streamlined production structure. Outsourcing minimized fixed asset investment, but the quest for quality, reduced costs, and responsiveness to market fluctuations forced final assemblers to create strong commitment at the level of suppliers. For instance, Harley established a supplier advisory council (SAC), made up of 16 suppliers, to expose supplier executives to the best practices of other suppliers in the Harley-Davidson network.

With the increasing reliance on third-party suppliers, the manufacturing process had essentially become an assembly line where motorcycle components were assembled. Motorcycles were composed of four major parts: the engine, whose main parts were the crank case and the cylinder heads, the frame, the fairing and the front forks. Other key components included the wheels, the braking system, the handlebars, the fuel tank, the headlights and the control instruments. The majority of the components were first tested, then assembled together as 'sub-groups,' and finally mounted on the vehicle, while others (such as the exhaust system) were individually fitted to the bike.

Leading motorcycle firms throughout the world also implemented Japanese manufacturing techniques, including Just-in-Time and Materials as Needed production in order to respond more readily to market fluctuations, optimize production levels, and improve quality. To make such programs work, these firms solicited the commitment and participation of all employees. At Triumph, for instance, yellow sheets stood out on bulletin boards everywhere, exhorting workers to write down ideas and suggestions that would increase efficiency and quality. They also changed job design and human resource management practices at the plant level, and emphasized group effort to solve problems.

Distribution

All the major motorcycle companies had some presence in the three major markets: United States, Europe, and Japan. Their typical distribution systems comprised two types of agents: wholesale distributors and retailers. They used wholesale distributors to build and manage the network of retail dealers in a geographic area. Depending on the strategic importance of this area, they used independent, partly, or totally owned wholesale distributors (e.g., subsidiaries). In most cases, their retail networks were composed of multi-franchise dealers – dealers selling motorcycles of multiple brands – whose role was to sell the bike and provide adequate technical assistance.

The size of the network, and therefore the degree of penetration into the market, were largely a function of the company's strategy. Large Japanese mass-producers such as Honda and Yamaha tended to maximize 'reach' and penetration, while companies such as Harley, BMW, and Ducati emphasized the quality of the dealer and where possible, used single-franchising agreements. In 2001 the industry was polarized around these two models. Firms using the latter strategy appeared to view their stores as a way to control prices and brand positioning by allowing direct communication with customers. The most extreme case of this approach was Harley-Davidson, which had single-franchise agreements with the majority of its dealers (a total of approximately 600 dealers in the United States) and had also launched the 'Genuine Deal' campaign to build dealership loyalty.

Competitors

Over the last century, the number of motorcycle manufacturers had decreased dramatically. As of 2001, there was one major American manufacturer, four Japanese manufacturers, and a handful of European firms (see Figure 3).

Harley-Davidson. Harley-Davidson was the major American motorcycle manufacturer, and dominated the U.S. heavyweight (>650cc) motorcycle market. In 2000, it achieved its fifteenth consecutive year of record revenue and net income, increasing the former by 18.5% to $2.2 billion and the latter by 30.1% from 1999. In 2000, Harley produced 204,500 motorcycles, a 15.5% increase over 1999, and Buell sold 10,200 with 2,400 additional unit shipments. Its Parts and Accessories and General Merchandise business made strong gains in 2000, with increases in revenues of 23.5% and 14% respectively, over 1999. Relative to the other major motorcycle producers, Harley had a more modest global presence. However, despite its strong focus on the American market (in 2000, 78% of Harleys were sold in the United States), it recently increased its presence in Europe by fine-tuning some bikes to fit European tastes (e.g., taking off chrome and accessories on popular European models such as the

FIGURE 3 Presence in different market segments

	Off Road/Dual Purpose	Cruiser	Touring	Sport			
				Hyper-Sport	Super-Sport	Sport-Touring	Naked
Ducati		■	■	■	■	■	■
Harley	■	■	■	■	■	■	■
BMW	■	■	■			■	■
Triumph	■		■		■	■	■
Honda	■	■	■		■	■	■
Kawasaki	■	■	■	■	■	■	■
Suzuki	■	■	■	■	■	■	■
Yamaha	■	■	■	■	■	■	■

Source: Case-writer elaboration.

Night Train). Since going public in 1986, its stockholders had realized a compound annual growth rate of over 40%.

Industry experts considered Harley-Davidson the prototypical example of a 'lifestyle' company. Particularly in the United States, Harley was a social and cultural phenomenon, representing the history of motorcycling – Harley was founded in 1903 – and symbolizing a set of values – freedom and rebelliousness above all – that were key attributes of the American biker culture. Harley's brand was among the strongest in the industry, and the Harley Owners Group (H.O.G.), founded in 1983, was the largest club of motorcycles owners in the world, with 640,000 members. Harley-Davidson competed in the touring and custom market segments, and with one model – the 883 – in the Naked sub-segment of the sport market. Buell competed in the Sport segment. In 2001 Harley-Davidson offered 23 models in four major families with U.S. prices ranging between $5,595 to $20,360. The U.S. average price was $14,350.

Honda. With 5.4 million bikes produced (including scooters and small displacement bikes), Honda was the world largest manufacturer of motorcycles. The company shared technology, engineering capabilities, marketing and distribution know-how with its automobile division. The Honda CB750 Four, first introduced in 1969, started the 'superbike' boom and represented a major shift in the motorcycle industry. Like the other Japanese manufacturers, Honda competed in all of the segments of the motorcycle industry, and had a strong reputation for reliability and technical excellence. With its capabilities in four-stroke technology, Honda also led the motorcycle industry in producing motorcycles and scooters utilizing low emission, fuel-efficient four-stroke engine designs. Honda entered the U.S. market in 1959. In 2001 Honda offered 23 models of >500cc motorcycles. U.S. prices ranged between $4,999 and $18,999. The U.S. average price was $9,300.

BMW. Bayerische Motoren Werke (BMW) was one of Europe's top automakers. Its automobiles accounted for nearly 60% of its sales. Its motorcycle division celebrated its seventy-fifth anniversary in 1998. BMW was the top European competitor in the United States. In 2000, with a network of 160 motorcycle retailers, the company posted record sales in the North American market of almost 12,000 units, an increase of nearly 20% over year-end sales figures for 1999. BMW bikes pioneered technical innovations like advanced suspension systems, fuel injection, and anti-lock brakes, thus giving the firm a reputation for exceptional quality, safety, reliability, and comfort. BMW entered the U.S. market in 1975. In 2001 BMW production was specialized in touring bikes accounting for a total of 11 models. The company also offered a cruiser and a performance bike. U.S. prices ranged from $8,100 to $19,600. The U.S. average price was $14,500.

Triumph. In 2001 Triumph produced approximately 30,000 motorcycles. The company started producing motorcycles in 1902. It was one of the world's most notable brands in the 1950s, thanks in part to its appearance in Marlon Brando's movie 'The Wild One.' Although forced to liquidate in 1983 due to financial problems, Triumph was turned around in 1991. By applying Japanese production techniques, Triumph had recently gained a reputation for making virtually unbreakable bikes. Triumph's customers were largely high-income middle-aged professionals. Its most popular model was a naked, the Thunderbird, which was similar to what it marketed in the 1960s. In 2001 it competed in the touring, sports and off-road/dual purpose segments for a total of 9 models with U.S. prices ranging between $7,000 and $12,000. The U.S. average price was $9,500.

Other Japanese manufacturers. In 2001 the other three Japanese competitors held a market share of 57% of Ducati relevant market. Yamaha, Suzuki, and Kawasaki entered the U.S. motorcycle market in the 1970s by selling small motorcycles. They then moved into the heavyweight segment. In Europe, Suzuki had a larger market share than Honda; in Asia, Kawasaki trailed only Harley and Honda. These companies competed on technological innovation and price, but were not as strong in the cruiser market, where Harley had a stronger appeal.

Best known for its motorcycles, which accounted for almost half of its sales, **Yamaha** Motor also made water vehicles, all-terrain vehicles, leisure and fishing boats, snowmobiles, and golf carts. It sold about 85% of its motorcycles outside Japan. In 2001 the average U.S. price of Yamaha motorcycles was $10,200. **Suzuki** was Japan's #1 minicar producer. Its non-vehicle products included generators, outboard marine engines, and prefabricated housing. It sold about half of its cars and nearly 75% of its motorcycles outside Japan, and partnered with General Motors, which owned 10% of Suzuki, and planned to double its stake. Suzuki sold motorcycles in the United States since 1963 and had a reputation for reliability. It offered bikes for road riding, motorcross, and everything in between. In 2001 the average U.S. price for Suzuki motorcycles was $7,600. **Kawasaki** Heavy Industries had many divisions, from industrial equipment, transportation, aerospace, and consumer products. Its consumer products (23% of sales) ranged from motorcycles to Jet Ski watercraft and all-terrain vehicles. After introducing 11 new models in 2000, it introduced four new models in 2001 and made significant changes to key models in its Vulcan™ cruiser line – which was named 'Cruiser of the Year' by *Motorcycle Tour & Cruiser* magazine. In 2001 the U.S. average price for Kawasaki was $8,450.

Honda and Yamaha recently agreed to jointly transport their motorcycles and spare parts with the hope of saving 30% on their delivery costs. Kawasaki and Suzuki planned to enter a similar alliance shortly.

The turnaround program

Ducati was founded on July 4, 1926, when Antonio Cavalieri Ducati and his three sons established one of the first Italian operations of radios and electrical components. In 1935 Ducati started production at a new factory in Borgo Panigale, just outside Bologna, at the heart of what later became the most extensive Italian mechanical district. Not until the post-war period did Ducati's first motorcycle appear. The bike, 'il Cucciolo,' soon became a blockbuster. The 1950s witnessed the introduction of a series of increasingly sophisticated and powerful bikes, and particularly the appearance of Ducati's technical signature: the Desmodromic valve distribution system. This innovation, developed by the celebrated Ducati engineer Fabio Taglioni, was a sophisticated mechanical system allowing the engine to achieve more revolutions per minute and greater 'usable' power. The Desmo system could still be found in 2001 on every motorcycle produced, representing the soul of all Ducatis; the deep intoxicating noise made by the desmo engine was music to the ears of purists.

Thanks to their technical superiority, Ducati motorcycles rapidly achieved success in the international racing circuit. This success fueled growth throughout the sixties and the seventies, and the development of a strong reputation in the performance segment of the motorcycle industry. In 1972, a Ducati 750 Super Sport prototype won a dramatic victory in the Imola 200cc race. This motorcycle, which was configured with an L-shape desmo engine (two cylinders mounted at a 90-degree angle) and a Formula Uno-derived tubular trestle frame, inspired the production of a new line of larger displacement motorcycles that represented the stylistic and technical foundation of modern Ducatis.

Despite the innovativeness and technical excellence of its product lines, Ducati's fortunes declined sharply in the early 1980s, primarily due to the decision of its major shareholder at that time (IRI, a State holding company) to refocus the company on products other than motorcycles. In 1985 IRI decided to sell its motorcycle assets, and Cagiva, an Italian manufacturing conglomerate and producer of small displacement motorcycles, acquired Ducati. Under Cagiva, Ducati suddenly recovered its reputation for on and off-track excellence. An impressive series of victories in the World Superbike Championship where, for the first time, a Ducati two-cylinder engine defeated a four-cylinder engine produced by Japanese competitors, was paralleled by the introduction of a new series of stunningly beautiful street performance bikes. However, towards the mid nineties, liquidity problems at the larger Cagiva group deprived Ducati of the necessary working capital funding, which, in turn, delayed its payment terms to some key suppliers, resulting in significant production delays.

Ducati was one step from going bankrupt when, in September 1996, a majority stake in the company was acquired by the Texas Pacific Group, an American private equity firm. Abel Halpern, HBS '93 and TPG partner was the driving force behind the deal. He had a passion for high-end, 'nichey' businesses, and was driven by the firm belief that Ducati had enormous potential that was largely unexploited due to poor management. For this reason, he needed a first-class, highly committed management team, and TPG appointed Halpern's friend and former colleague at Bain & Co., Federico Minoli, as CEO of Ducati.

Prologue

Federico Minoli began his career at Procter & Gamble, Italy, in 1974. It was a few years later at McKinsey that he became involved with, and fascinated by, problems of strategic change. He then moved to one of McKinsey's clients, Benetton, as CEO of the U.S. subsidiary, which he turned around in less than four years. Finally, before his experience in Ducati, he joined Bain & Co. in Boston, where he specialized in 'turnaround management'.

I was a University student between '68 and '72. It was a 'hot' period in Italy. I remember spending full nights discussing the meaning of revolution, of Marxism . . . we were all little revolutionaries, we wanted to change the world,

everything. Well, while these ideologies are well behind me, I can certainly say that this disposition towards change, the idea that everything should be continuously re-discussed is still the way I look at things. Any decision to change, even if well planned and analyzed, always leads to a new territory that needs to be discovered and charted. That's where I draw my professional satisfaction. I like the process of change, not success per se. I accepted [the chance] to run Ducati because I saw a company that, beyond its liquidity crisis, needed to be radically changed in order to fully exploit its enormous potential.[4]

Minoli moved to Ducati's Bologna headquarters in summer 1996 with two goals in mind: double-digit growth, and equaling Harley-Davidson's profit level, which was by far the highest in the industry, with an EBITDA margin of about 20%. In a few weeks, Minoli appointed a completely new top management team. He looked not only for 'talent,' but also for talented managers who could become passionate about Ducati. None of the new hires had previous experience with the motorcycle industry. At the very beginning of Minoli's tenure, Ducati was struggling to develop a clear strategic direction, functional divisions were largely absent, and the top management team operated in what Minoli terms 'a structured chaos.' He believed the lack of rigid internal boundaries, especially if coupled with clear leadership and managers who identified strongly with Ducati, would stimulate creative decision-making.

When Minoli arrived at Ducati, he found it had three things. First, Ducati had a good product. Although they were regarded as less efficient and reliable than Japanese bikes were, Ducatis were unique, beautiful performance motorcycles. Second, Ducati had a group of top-notch engineers – both in the R&D and in the racing divisions – whose main goal was to continue defeating the Japanese in the Superbike Championship (see Table 3). These people were the real soul of Ducati. According to Minoli, these were the people who ultimately ran the company:

The company was driven by its excellent engineers and designers. These people were all purists, 'knee down' riders, fanatics of the

[4]Interview with Federico Minoli at Ducati headquarters, Bologna, Italy, March 22, 2001.

TABLE 3 World Superbike Championship –
1990–2000 Hall of Fame

	Winner: Rider	Winner: Manufacturer
1990	Ducati	Honda
1991	Ducati	Ducati
1992	Ducati	Ducati
1993	Kawasaki	Ducati
1994	Ducati	Ducati
1995	Ducati	Ducati
1996	Ducati	Ducati
1997	Honda	Honda
1998	Ducati	Ducati
1999	Ducati	Ducati
2000	Honda	Ducati

Source: Case-writer elaboration.

motorcycle: speed, performance and innovation were the attributes defining their world. They had an extreme notion of what a Ducati and therefore a Ducati rider, a 'Duke,' should be. When I came here for the first time, I left with the clear impression that it was almost by chance and not by strategic choice that Ducati had a product that the public loved. The market and market research were unknown to them . . . this place had an incredibly strong engineering culture with a real passion for races . . . and don't forget that we are in the middle of Emilia, the region of Ferrari, Lamborghini, Maserati and many others, a place where you can almost breathe the passion for races and mechanics.[5]

Third, Minoli found a brand with strong potential. In major European markets, Ducati's brand loyalty ranked among the highest in the motorcycle industry, with about 55% of its small customer base expressing repeat purchase intentions.

Strategizing at Ducati

With these beliefs about Ducati's strengths in mind, the challenge for Minoli and his team was to define a turnaround program that would support the profitability goals he had set. With a production of 12,117 motorcycles in 1996, Ducati had a worldwide market share of 4% in the sport sub-segment of the >500cc Road Market. The objective was to bring the market share to 10%, although Ducati personnel were polarized around two alternatives. One involved continuity with the company's culture and dominant thinking: invest heavily in the product and rationalize production processes. Many of Ducati's engineers were convinced that a totally new engine – perhaps a standard non-desmodromic engine – was important to stay ahead of competitors, in particular Japanese manufacturers. Others, especially engineers in the racing division, were fascinated by the idea of entering the Grand Prix Championship, the prestigious competition from which Ducati was still absent. But Minoli disagreed. Despite acknowledging the possibility of efficiency improvements, he felt that the right strategy for Ducati was to develop a global brand that could appeal not only to 'extreme' riders, but also to a broader spectrum of customers. He believed that large segments of buyers were not attracted by the intrinsic attributes of the motorcycle, but by what the motorcycle evokes and represents. As Minoli put it:

Soon after my arrival I had 20 billion lire to invest. How to invest it? It was a difficult period. Our engineers were frustrated, and our workers were operating in difficult conditions. The roof of the factory was broken. It rained into the factory . . . and here we are in Bologna, the Italian communist stronghold . . . you can imagine the pressures from the unions. Well, in this situation, instead of fixing the roof, I decided to build the museum. It was a difficult decision, but it was an important one. It sent the right signal to the company. It symbolized the radicalness of the ideological change I was proposing: that Ducati is not only about beating Japanese bikes, that we have a powerful brand to preserve and develop, and ultimately that Ducati is not, or not only, a motorcycle company. We sell something more: a dream, passion, a piece of history, and the motorcycle is at its core. In one word, we were moving from the mechanical to entertainment.[6]

[5] Interview with Federico Minoli at Ducati headquarters, Bologna, Italy, March 22, 2001.
[6] Interview with Federico Minoli at Ducati headquarters, Bologna, Italy, March 22, 2001.

The core of Ducati's branding strategy was soon crystallized into what was dubbed 'The World of Ducati' (see Figure 4). The motorcycle was the center of this system. The satellites represented activities, some of them totally new, that were held together by the same goal of creating the intangible attributes that, according to Minoli, would have made Ducati something more than a unique motorcycle.

Products

In 1996 Ducati offered products in three categories of the sport segment of the large displacement (>500cc) motorcycle industry: hyper-sport, super-sport and naked (see Tables 4 and 5). One year later, it entered for the first time the Sport-Touring segment, a category with an older customer base. While 62% of the customers in the Hyper-sport category were between 18 and 30 years old, 73% of the customers in the Sport-touring category were over 30 (see Table 6). Since 1996 Ducati had also considerably widened the offering within each family. Typically, the introduction of new entry-level models (e.g. Monster Dark) was coupled to the introduction of new high-end models (e.g. Monster Cromo). One of the first challenges that Minoli and his team confronted was identifying the core attributes underly-ing the identity and uniqueness of Ducati motorcycles – elements to be universally associated with the brand. Five distinctive traits emerged, and all of the company's current production was characterized by these features: Desmodromic distribution system, L-twin engine, tubular trestle frame, Italian style, and Ducati's unique sound (which the company was attempting to patent). Thanks to a rigorous quality control system, since 1996 Ducatis also improved reliability and overall quality. Ducati motorcycles had longer lifespan than typical competitors' machines. For instance, the lifespan of the engine was typically 10 years, and the frame at least 5 years.

In 1997 Minoli decided to enter the business of accessories and apparel by acquiring a controlling stake in Gio.Ca.Moto, a company that was already producing a line of accessories for Ducati.

Hyper-Sport. These high-tech motorcycles were closely derived from the motorcycles competing in the World Superbike Championship, and were fitted with a performing 4-valve engine. The predecessor of the current production – the 916 – won four 'motorcycle of the year' awards from Motorcycle Consumer News (MCN), the leading British specialized magazine. Utan Guilfoyle, one of the curators of the 'Art of Motorcycles' Guggenheim Exhibition commented:

FIGURE 4 The 'World of Ducati'

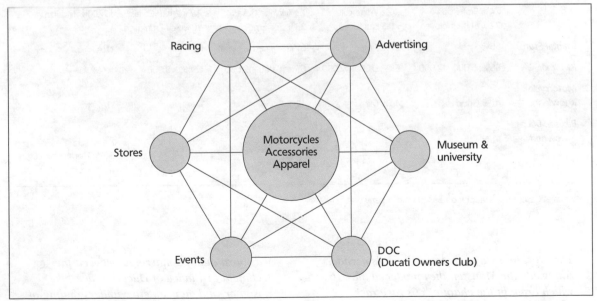

Source: Company document.

TABLE 4   Breakdown of motorcycle sales (in units sold)

Units	1996	1997	1998	1999	2000
Hyper-sport	4,780	8,263	8,299	9,207	12,289
Super-sport	2,900	4,160	5,139	4,254	4,058
Touring	0	3,517	2,649	2,893	3,081
Naked	4,959	8,271	11,994	16,770	19,659
Total	12,639	24,211	28,011	33,124	39,087

Source: Company data.

TABLE 5   The Product Line

	cc	HP	Number of models	U.S. Price	Competitors
Hyper-sport	748–996	97–135	6	$13,295–$21,895	Honda, Yamaha, Suzuki, Kawasaki
Super-sport	750–900	64–80	3	$7,895–$11,495	Japanese, BMW, Triumph
Naked	400–900	43–101	9	$6,195–$12,995	BMW, Triumph, Honda, Harley
Sport-touring	900	83–117	3	$12,295–$13,795	BMW, Triumph

Source: Case-writer elaboration.

TABLE 6   Customer profile

	Ducati Hyper-Sport	Ducati Super-Sport	Ducati Sport-Touring	Ducati Naked	Harley-Davidson
Sex	98% Male	99% Male	98% Male	96% Male	91% Male
Age Range	62%: 18–35	64%: 18–35	73%: 31–43	66%: 18–35	45.6 (Median)
Job	24% Professional 22% Self Employed	26% White collar 21% Blue Collar	23% White Collar 23% Self Employed	26% White Collar 20% Self Employed	$77,000 (Median)
Marital Status	56% Single	57% Single	51% Married	65% Single	N/A
KM/Year	65%: 5,000–12,000	61%: 5,000–12,000	65%: 5,000–12,000	65%: <8,000	N/A
Motorcycle Knowledge	41% Good	40% Fair	43% Good	47% Fair	N/A
Bikes>500cc owned	41%: >3	54%: <=2	49%: >3	69%: <=1	21%: <1 30%: From competitors 49%: From Harley

Source: Case-writer elaboration based on company data.

The '90s, in a way, has been Ducati's decade. Alongside the Monster, they produced the 916, which brought the chaotic '80s racetrack aesthetic to a sublime expression. This design was born out of a marriage between the technical brilliance of Ducati's race-bike designer, and an instinctive understanding of how a motorcycle could appeal to the rider now *ten years older than the young buck who first threw his leg over an '80s Japanese speedster. Aspirational and inspired, the 916 is the motorcycle for the would-be Ferrari driver: Italian, fast, and, of course, red.*[7]

In 2001, the company offered two basic models – the 996 and the 748 – each produced in three different versions. The 996S, Ducati's flagship motorcycle, sold for $21,895, allowing the company to charge the premium shown in Table 7, and contributed 43% to the total revenue generated by motorcycles. The key competitors were Honda, Yamaha and Suzuki.

Super-Sport. The company launched its first super-sport (SS) bike in 1973. For years, the SS had been the most popular Ducati on the road. In 1998 Ducati launched a radically new model, characterized by a futuristic design and good handling. These motorcycles were fitted with Ducati's traditional 2-valve engine, which, while not guaranteeing the same performance as the 4-valve engine, was popular for its smooth power delivery. The SS competed with all of the Japanese manufacturers, Triumph, and finally BMW, which recently entered the super-sport segment.

Naked. The Monster, Ducati's naked motorcycle, recently became its most popular bike. On the Monster, Utan Guilfoyle commented:

Ducati's designer Galluzzi got the idea to recreate these naked grunge guns in a production motorcycle, a notion that flew in the face of every contemporary motorcycle design rubic from Tokyo to Munich . . . the Monster is a brilliant piece of pop-culture interpretation, a bike for the streets, rather than the fantasy

racetrack that had inspired a previous generation of motorcycles.[8]

Since 1996, the number of models in this family had continuously increased, thanks to mainly exomorphic modifications. The monster was now offered in 9 different models, ranging from $6,150 to $13,000. The key competitors were BMW, Triumph and Honda.

Sport-Touring. These motorcycles offered a more comfortable riding position than the other Ducatis. After the launch of the ST2 in 1997, which was fitted with the 2-valve engine, a new model – the more performing ST4 – was introduced in 1998. Different from the other Ducati's families, the number of Sport-Touring models had not increased since 1998 (with the exception of the launch this year of the ST4S, a more performing version of the ST4, fitted with the championship-winning 996 engine). Both BMW and Triumph competed in this segment, as well as all of the Japanese manufacturers.

Limited editions. In 1999 Ducati launched the MH 900 Evolution, inspired by the 1974 Ducati MH 900. Created by Ducati's famous designer Pierre Terblanche, the MH 900 Evolution, of which only 2,000 were produced, was sold through Ducati's website for EURO 15,000. The 996R, another limited edition of 500, sold at the worldwide price of Euro 26,000.

Spare parts, accessories and apparel. Ducati recently outsourced both production and logistics of spare parts to two companies operating in the Emilian mechanical district. Greater availability of parts (the catalogue went from 10,000 items in 1997 to 15,000 items in 2000), improved distribution, and

TABLE 7 Price premium vs. comparable products (average % premium per family)

Year	Hyper-Sport	Super-Sport	Sport-Touring	Naked
1997	31.02%	8.03%	29.97%	13.27%
2001	31.4%	7.2%	20.4%	13.03%

Source: Case-writer elaboration based on company estimates.

[7]*The Art of Motorcycle*, Guggenheim Museum Publications, 1998.
[8]*The Art of Motorcycle*, Guggenheim Museum Publications, 1998.

revised pricing policy resulted in a considerable increase in the contribution of spare parts to total revenues.

The accessories and apparel business was comprised of three categories of products. First, custommade bike components to increase the performance and individuality of the motorcycle. Second, the company offered high-quality Ducati-branded riding gear (racing suits, jackets, helmets, gloves etc.). Ducati had a joint venture with Dainese – a worldwide leader in the production of technical gear for sport riders – to develop and manufacture riding equipment reflecting the exclusivity and racing character of the company. The third line of products included t-shirts, caps and memorabilia. The accessories and apparel business had grown consistently since Ducati entered it. Among motorcycle manufacturers, only Harley had a higher incidence of accessories and apparel (12% of revenue), about doubling what Ducati derived from these products.

Activities

Production. Although in 1996 almost 80% of production activities were already outsourced, since then Ducati had been implementing an aggressive outsourcing policy, maintaining in house only R&D, design, quality control, and the machining of two

key strategic components: crank cases and cylinder heads (Table 8 displays how the cost structure of Ducati had changed over time). As of 2001, outsourcing hd grown to approximately 87%, and the company planned to bring it to 90%, probably the highest in the industry (industry experts estimated that the average outsourcing level for the industry was lower than Ducati's). The majority of Ducati's suppliers belonged to the Emilian district, which was populated by a dense web of small and medium specialized mechanical manufacturers (the parts and components acquired by non-Italian suppliers accounted for around 15% of the total value acquired by third parties). This industrial district was comprised of a number of smaller clusters of firms, each of which specialized in particular classes of mechanical products (agro-mechanical, automobile/motorcycle components, machine tools etc.). The number of firms gravitating around the motorcycle industry (scooters and small displacement motorcycles as well as bigger motorcycles) in the proximity of Bologna had recently been estimated at around 2,400. Ducati was collaborating with a number of these firms (Ferrari, Maserati, Minarelli-Yamaha, Lombardini Motori etc.) to form the 'Engine Technology District,' a series of joint activities such as R&D, purchasing, suppliers' quality control, employee training etc. Despite its relatively low

TABLE 8   Cost structure (% of total revenues)[a]

	Ducati 2000	Ducati 1996	Harley-Davidson
1. Motorcycles Material	43.4	55.8	45.0
2. Related Products	6.9	2.2	8.0
3. Direct Personnel[b]	5	6	6.4
4. Indirect Personnel	3.7	4.2	4.5
COGS (1+2+3+4)	59	68.2	65.9
5. R&D[c]	1.1	0.1	2.0
6. Variable Sales Costs[d]	5.9	5.1	6.0
7. Fixed Sales Costs[e]	14.5	10.4	5.0
8. G&A	4.7	5.3	3.0
Total 5+6+7+8	26.2	20.9	16

Source: Case-writer estimates.
[a] Includes parts, accessories and apparel (16.6% of total revenues in 2000).
[b] Inbound logistics, quality management and operations.
[c] Part of Ducati's R&D costs are capitalized (approx. 2.7% of total revenues).
[d] Distribution, dealer bonus and warranties costs.
[e] Sales, Marketing and after sales department costs, advertising, events, racing costs, subsidiaries costs.

volumes, in 2001 Ducati was considered one of the most efficient manufacturers in the industry also thanks to the standardization of its products. In 1999, it produced all of its models using only two crank cases and three cylinder heads (see Table 9). The number of motorcycles produced per worker increased from 76 in 1997 to 87 in 2000.

Ducati also radically rationalized its network of suppliers through the adoption of more strict selection procedures and careful quality control procedures. Since 1996, the total number of suppliers had decreased from 200 to 130. The three most important suppliers were Brembo (for brakes, wheels rims and clutch), Magneti Marelli (for control units and fuel-injection systems), and the Japanese Showa Corporation (for forks and shock absorbers). With the exception of a small number of long-term supply contracts for components, Ducati had only short-term contracts with its suppliers. It typically identified at least two sources of supply for each component, and switched to the alternative supplier as the need arose. These arrangements ultimately increased the quality and reliability of Ducatis, which in 1996 were known for their mediocre reliability and high maintenance costs.

Finally, the company moved towards a platform approach to production: the motorcycle was divided into a relatively small number of components, which were in turn made of sub-components. One key supplier was responsible for the provision of a component, and managing the suppliers of the sub-components. Ducati already implemented platform production processes for a large number of components, and already identified other platform projects that it expected to implement in the next two years.

Distribution. In the past, Ducati distributed its motorcycles directly through multi-franchise retail dealers in Italy, and through a series of independent distributors covering specific geographic areas in the rest of the world, with the only exception of the United States, where the company owned a subsidiary. Each distributor was responsible for managing its network of retail dealers, the majority of which were multi-brand.

In 1997 Ducati started a new distribution strategy, which was designed to unfold in three phases. The first phase consisted of taking control of distribution and marketing in strategic markets by establishing totally owned sales and marketing subsidiaries. In the last four years, Ducati established subsidiaries in Japan, France, Germany, the United Kingdom and Holland. The second phase was centered around the re-organization of the network of dealers. Different from the majority of its competitors (with the exception of Harley), Ducati did not aim to increase geographical reach, but rather to improve the average quality of the dealers. This meant competent sales forces, good technical assistance, and an adequate physical space where Ducati motorcycles and apparel could be displayed. In this vein, the company greatly reduced the overall number of retailers throughout the world. For instance, in Italy the number of dealers decreased from 165 in 1996 to 65 in 2000. As a consequence, annual registrations per dealer went from 14 to around 150.

The third phase consisted of the creation of a chain of 'Ducati Stores' – mono-franchise dealers in select markets and cities around the world. These stores not only offered superior technical and service support, but also a unique retail environment emphasizing the distinctive traits of Ducati's brand: while a 'History Wall' displayed images of Ducati's racing heritage, an 'Engineering Wall' showed a large scale engineering drawing of the 916, Ducati's symbol. In addition to motorcycles, these stores presented merchandised areas dedicated to 'Ducati Performance'

TABLE 9 Product standardization in 1999

	Crank Cases	Cylinder Heads	Engines	Models	Segment/Families
Ducati	2	3	7	15	4
Harley-Davidson	3	3	5	21	4
BMW	5	5	7	15	4
Honda	12	12	20	26	6

Source: Company document.

accessories and apparel. In Italy, which represented the benchmark for the distribution strategy (see Figure 5), the company had 36 Ducati Stores. Outside Italy, Ducati Stores were launched in a number of major cities, from Manhattan to London, from Vienna to Sydney, and so on.

Product development and R&D. In the last few years the company invested heavily, especially in new design technologies, product development and human capital. R&D investments went from 3.2 million Euro in 1997 to 12.9 million Euro in 2000. Excluding research activities carried out in the racing division, in 2000 the company spent around 3.7% of its revenues in R&D activities. Although in the past Ducati employed an external design house (The Cagiva Research Center), it had recently established an internal design division (Ducati Design Center). As a consequence of these efforts, the company greatly reduced the 'time to market' for new product launches. In 1998, Ducati developed the new 900SSie in 15 months compared to over 36 months for previous model development. In 2001, Ducati's engineering team was reputed as one of the most expert and skilled in the industry. The product development and R&D department operated in close contact not only with the racing division, but also with the marketing department. Market research provided a fundamental input to both design and technological innovation.

With the exception of design activities, since 1996 the company's product development and R&D activities have evolved from being largely internal to a more 'open' structure, where Ducati coordinated a number of external sources of technical skills and innovations, typically located in the mechanical district of Bologna. For example, the company started cooperating with TWR, a major Formula One engine development center, and formed a joint venture named HPE (High Performance Engineering) with some local producers like Piero Ferrari of the Ferrari car company to develop advanced engine technology.

The World of Ducati

In addition to the 'Ducati Stores,' the 'World of Ducati' comprised a series of other activities that had been consistently developing in the past three years.

Racing. In contrast to competitors' teams, Ducati recently adopted what Minoli dubbed an 'open paddock' policy: members of Ducati Clubs could 'live' the racing event in close contact with the team, participating in dinners or social events during the days preceding the competition. In a recent study conducted for the U.S. market, the presence of Ducati in the Superbike competitions was indicated as the most important purchase factor by 27% of the people interviewed (all current Ducati customers). The second most important purchase factor was magazine tests (25%). Additionally, the sport orientation of the brand and its link to competition (together with Ducati's Italian style) ranked as the most prominent features of the brand in a recent large-scale

FIGURE 5 Distribution strategy

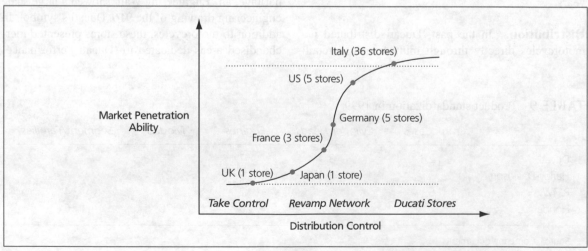

survey conducted through the company website (see Figure 6). The brand loyalty of Ducati's customers strongly improved since 1996 (see Figure 7).

In the last few years, revenues from sponsors and the sale of race engines and bikes greatly increased. In 1996, the racing division spent approximately 3.9 million Euro, with almost no revenue. In 2000 it spent around Euro 10.2 million, but revenues increased to Euro 7.9 million.

The racing team was also a sophisticated R&D laboratory: new features designed specifically for improving performance on the racetrack were

FIGURE 6 Central brand attributes

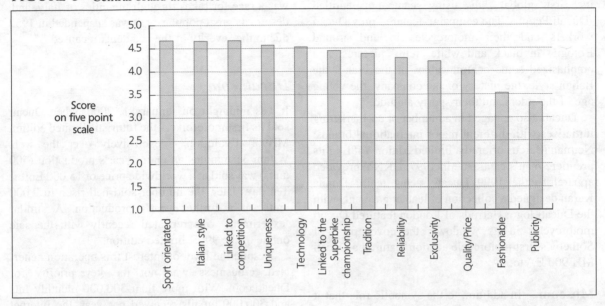

Source: Company document.

FIGURE 7 Repeat purchase intentions 1995–2000 (European data for major competitors)

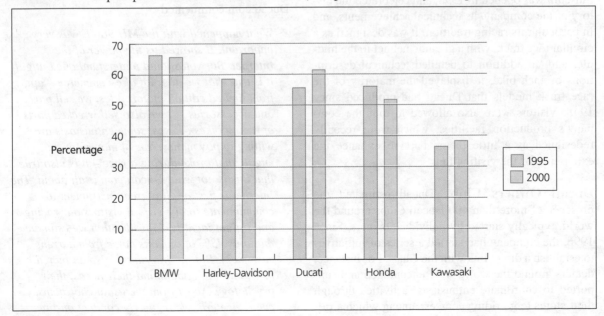

Source: Case-writer elaboration based on company data.

continuously created and tested. Some of them were later adapted and introduced in series road bikes, especially (but not only) in the Hyper-sport family. In fact, the racing team operated in close collaboration with Ducati's R&D and product development units.

Advertising. In contrast to many other motorcycle companies, Ducati advertised its products only through specialized magazines. In 1998 it launched its first global advertising campaign entitled 'Ducati/People.' The campaign featured only Ducati workers and their motorcycles in and around Bologna in black and white 'retro' pictures, and emphasized some central values of the brand: the Italian style, the history of the company, the young age of the riders and their sporty attitude.

Ducati also engaged in a number of co-marketing initiatives with different major international brands: Neiman Marcus offered a limited edition 748L in its premiere men's catalogue in 1997; DKNY provided apparel to the 1999 Ducati racing team; Donna Karan designed a collection of leather garments with the Ducati logo; Harrods of London featured Ducati motorcycles in its windows; the cover page of Sotheby's first motorcycle auction featured a Ducati MH 900 E, etc.

Museum. In addition to the symbolic role that it played in the context of Ducati's strategic transition, the museum, which was located in Ducati's headquarters, also attracted 10,000 visitors each year. The museum was opened in 1998, and celebrated the history of the company, its technical achievements, and in particular its racing tradition. It was designed as a circular race track, with a gigantic helmet in the middle, and, in addition to detailed technical descriptions of each bike, it displayed the majority of the race track models that Ducati had produced since 1948. Visitors were also allowed to tour the company's production facilities, which were recently redesigned as a little theme park to enhance the experience of the visiting fans.

Ducati Owners Club. Ducati estimated the presence of more than 400 Ducati Clubs around the world, typically started by individual owners. Since 1996, the company had started a series of initiatives to establish a direct link with the Clubs. For instance, dealers around the world were encouraged and supported to coordinate enthusiasts' activities through their stores (e.g., riding courses, among which a riding school for women, social events etc.).

Events. In 1998 the company organized the first World Ducati Weekend in Bologna, which had a great public success and was attended by approximately 10,000 Ducati enthusiasts from around the world. The same event was repeated in 2000 attracting 23,000 fans. In 2001 Ducati was organizing the revival for vintage motorcycles of the 'Motogiro d'Italia,' one of the oldest and most celebrated motorcycle competitions. The 'Motogiro d'Italia' was a race for bikes through the cities of Italy, and, despite its great popularity, it was suspended in 1957 due to the severity of the accidents it caused.

Ducati.com

It was midnight on January 1, 2000, when Ducati sold its first motorbike – the futuristic limited edition MH900 Evolution – exclusively over the web. Within 31 minutes an entire year's production (500 units) was sold at a worldwide price of 15,000 Euros. Ten days later, the number sold had risen to 2,000 units, or a further year's production. A similar 'experiment' was repeated recently with the sale online of the 996R limited edition.

Despite the level of interest this operation generated, e-business was not the key priority for Ducati.com. With more than 500,000 monthly hits and 300,000 emails received per year, the Internet was for the company a powerful interface with its customers. Cristiano Silei, Minoli's right arm in the turnaround program, and the mind behind Ducati.com commented:

What happened with the MH 900 E was very important. It showed us the power of the Internet. But you should understand one thing. If it is true that we do a lot of e-commerce – apart from limited edition motorcycles, we sell parts and accessories . . . we also sell wrecked parts of racing bikes . . . yes, some enthusiasts are willing to pay money, lots of money for an engine that broke during a race – it is also true that this is not what Ducati.com is all about. The Internet is first of all a great instrument to communicate to our virtual visitors our racing and Italian identity. Consider that we estimate that only 43% of our hits come from current customers. But the Internet is also an incredible mechanism to understand their needs, their psychology. Apart from the usual chatrooms, email etcetera, we regularly conduct on-line polls, market surveys. The response rate is always impressive. And we take them into account for our decisions. Finally, the Internet creates a community. These people talk to each other, they feel part of something. . . .[9]

Decisions

At the end of April 2001, Ducati had a market share of almost 7% of its relevant market, and industry analysts agreed that the company had excellent growth prospects for a few years to come. The goal of 10% market share was in sight. But Minoli was not satisfied:

I consider the turnaround practically over. The company has changed in all of the right areas. We are approaching Harley's profitability, and, while I think we can reach it, we should find new

sources of business to continue our profitable double-digit growth in the next decade.[10]

Minoli was, among other alternatives, considering entering Harley's niche, the cruiser market. With approximately 400,000 units sold in 2000, this was an extremely large segment in the large-displacement motorcycle industry. To develop a cruiser Ducati would need to make additional investments for Euro 17 million, and additional costs of approximately Euro 26 million. Minoli had in mind a Ducati interpretation of the cruiser, a cruiser fitted with Ducati's desmodromic L-twin engine, and also a motorcycle that could strike a frontal attack, at least in Europe, to the entire Harley-Davidson's line of cruisers. He therefore envisioned a line of bikes to be priced at Harley's levels: from $10,000 to approximately $20,000.

[9]Telephone interview with Cristiano Silei, April 21, 2001.
[10]Interview with Federico Minoli at Ducati headquarters, Bologna, Italy, March 22, 2001.

'A multiplicity of roles': The Chicago Museum of Contemporary Art search for a director

By Howard Husock[1]

When it began its work in late 1997, the Chicago Museum of Contemporary Art's 15-member search committee was nearly unanimous in its view about the type of museum director for whom it was looking. The museum, long housed in a small building on the city's near north side, had, two years before, climaxed a six-year campaign with the opening of a new $70 million home in a prominent location in the heart of Chicago's shopping and entertainment district. Implicit in the construction of the new building was the belief that the Chicago MCA could take its place among the small handful of major, big-city American contemporary art museums. It was with that expectation that the MCA's search committee believed it would almost undoubtedly find the museum's next director among the upper levels of curators and administrators of those other museums, or, perhaps, from the ranks of the directors of smaller but important regional art museums.

Six months after its search began, however, the committee found itself giving its most serious consideration to a distinctly untraditional candidate. After finding some candidates disappointing and others uninterested in the position, the committee began to consider someone who had never worked for any museum at all – and was best known, moreover, as the head of the Walt Disney theme park outside Paris, EuroDisney. Yet the candidate appeared to some on the committee, including MCA board chair Penny Pritzker, to offer the sort of entrepreneurial energy which the museum, facing attendance and financial challenges, needed. At the same time, both she and others on the committee were aware that hiring him would pose significant risks for a museum which wanted to be taken seriously at the highest levels of the art world and which needed an infusion of curatorial talent at its top staff level. It was in this context that the committee had to decide whether to offer the job to Robert Fitzpatrick, or to look elsewhere.

Background: Early years

The Chicago MCA was a relatively young museum, dating only to 1967. A number of its founders, themselves collectors of avant-garde and contemporary art, were still active on the 53-member board of directors and its 13-person executive committee, the inner circle which most closely oversaw the institution and was mainly comprised of the heads of its various committees. Throughout most of its history, the museum had been a small one, somewhat hidden away, not unlike the loft studios of many contemporary artists themselves. It had started out in a 2500-square foot former bakery building in Chicago's gallery district. Board members were dedicated enthusiasts, some of whom had donated significant work from their own private collections to the museum and who 'felt a proprietary interest in the institution, in the words of Marshall Front, vice-chairman of the museum board and chairman of the museum's Finance Committee. In its early years, board members might meet around a kitchen table or volunteer to answer questions at the museum's front entrance. 'The Museum of Contemporary Art', writes Eva Olson in a history published by the museum itself, 'started as the dream of a small group of postwar collectors with similar tastes; passionate individuals who remained the museum's spiritual parents for many years.'[2]

In those early years, board members and the small museum staff worked closely together in considering

[1]Source: This case was written by Howard Husock, Director, Case Program, John F. Kennedy School of Government, Harvard University, for Christine Letts, Rita E. Hauser Lecturer, John F. Kennedy School of Government, Harvard University. Support provided by the Museum Trustees Association and prepared for the conference 'Museum Governance in a New Age: Assembly 2001', October 4–7, 2001 (0801). Reprinted with permission of the Kennedy School of Government Case Program, Harvard University.
[2]*Collective Vision: Creating a Contemporary Art Museum*, 1996, Museum of Contemporary Art, Chicago, p. 3

what sorts of exhibitions the museum would mount and what sorts of works the museum would purchase. On occasions, the collections of board members were mounted as their own exhibitions. The museum director doubled as a curator and, even as the museum became established and its staff grew, directors continued to mount some, though by no means all, exhibitions, some much influenced by board member suggestions. At one point in the early 1980s, the board took on the executive role itself, in the absence of a director. Marshall Front observes that the relatively deep involvement of the board – compared with a 'corporate board' that would merely 'rubber stamp' staff decisions – led to its being known as a board that would 'micromanage'.

Life in the museum's Ontario Street location was characterized both by the strong commitment of the board and by relatively low overhead costs, a combination that allowed artistic concerns to take precedence over financial ones. The museum took risks, among them the 1969 decision to have its entire building 'wrapped' (with rope and tarpaulin) by the artist Christo. Other shows, too, tested the definition of art. Referring to an exhibit of 54 eight-foot fluorescent tubes entitled Dan Flavin: Ping and Gold, founding member Joseph Shapiro observed, 'People would come in, pay their admission fee, walk in and say, "Where's the exhibition?" And we'd say, "This is it." And they'd say, "I want my money back."'[3] Attendance often averaged fewer than 3000 visitors a month, a reflection of the fact, well-understood by board members, that contemporary art did not command the sort of mass audience which a Monet or Van Gogh show could draw to institutions like the Chicago Art Institute, by far the best-known arts institution in Chicago. As one MCA staff member puts it:

> *Contemporary art is less immediately accessible to people than the Impressionists, than medieval armor, than Egyptian antiquities. And it's less accessible because it is less familiar and because it frequently deals with things that are very much of the moment; attitudes towards sexuality, race, politics, contemporary society. It's posing questions, and a contemporary museum, by its nature covering present time as opposed to millennia, has a narrower base to appeal to.*

The challenge of expanding that base – and almost everything else about the museum – would, however, take center stage as a result of a momentous decision, whose roots lay in a 1984 study of the museum. The study concluded that the East Ontario Street building was far too limited for the institution's aspirations – so small that major new works would not be able to be shown there and that a declining fraction of the museum's permanent collection would ever be on view. The study sparked the museum to undertake what it called the Chicago Contemporary Campaign, a high-profile vehicle designed to raise funds for a new building. It was a campaign anchored by commitments of $37 million from the museum's trustees themselves. A 1989 deal with the state of Illinois provided the building site, allowing MCA to purchase (for a nominal price of but one dollar) a prime piece of downtown Chicago real estate. Instead of a 15,000 square foot building on a minor commercial street, the museum would be housed in a building of 130,000 square feet on the site of a former Illinois National Guard armory in the heart of Chicago's famed Gold Coast – bounded on one side by Lake Michigan, on the other by the city's main Michigan Avenue shopping district and by one of its oldest buildings and most prominent tourist sites, the Chicago Water Tower. The operating budget increased accordingly – from $3.2 million for fiscal year 1996 (the last in the old building) to $10.7 million for fiscal 1997, the first in the new one.

Says founding member Lew Manilow, himself one of the nation's leading contemporary art collectors, 'We went from being a minor player to being one of the big boys. The change was enormous.' The scale of gallery space was vastly expanded and complemented by auditorium space planned for theatrical and musical performance, as well as educational programs. Effectively, the Chicago MCA was bidding both to be a major cultural institution in America's third largest city but to take its place among a small handful of top contemporary art museums in the world. It wanted very much to avoid being seen as a 'regional' museum – one that brought some elements of its subject matter to a regional audience but would not be considered a major institution.

[3]*Collective Vision*, p. 6.

New building, new era

The search for a new executive director for the MCA began in earnest in late 1997, just over a year after the opening of the museum's new home. That opening had been viewed as a major civic event in Chicago. The new building, designed by the German architect Josef Kleiheus, was an imposing addition to the city and, in its first year, attracted legions of both art-lovers and the curious. Attendance topped 300,000, far outstripping previous records. Although the building itself was controversial – a little-used front plaza and steep front steps led some critics to brand it as austere and remote – board members were largely exuberant about their accomplishment. Says Lew Manilow: 'To me, it just seemed wonderful that we did it. Damn it, we did it. The dream came true. It's fabulous. How anybody wouldn't be upbeat about it, would be beyond me. I mean, there's a few battle scars left on people, I

suppose. Some people didn't like the German architect. Some people didn't like the building. OK. But the overriding fact is that we did it. We created the great new institution, which is an institution which will be here for 50 years at least, and it could be forever.'

As the ribbon-cutting receded in memory, however, it became more and more clear that the MCA faced a set of challenges every bit as difficult as financing, designing and constructing its new building. So big was the change in the size and scope of the museum that, as vice-chairman Marshall Front puts it, 'I would characterize us as being at an embryonic stage. We were basically starting over.'

Others are less neutral in describing the MCA's situation. 'As a business,' says Penny Pritzker, board chairman as the search for a new director got underway, and president of one arm of the Hyatt hotel and real estate empire, 'I would have to say we were dysfunctional. There was an enormous sense of

TABLE 1 Statement of activity, fiscal year 1995 (in US$)

	Operating Fund	New Museum Fund	Plant Fund	Endowment Funds/ Funds Functioning As Endowment	Permanent Collection Fund	Total
Support and Revenue						
Public Support	1,868,262	4,176	–	3,828,998	–	5,701,436
Earned Income	316,474	–	–	–	–	316,474
Investment Income	852,986	1,526,180		1,602,220	27,393	4,008,779
TOTAL	3,037,722	1,530,356	–	5,431,218	27,393	10,026,689
Expenses						
Program Expenses	1,276,573	–	–	–		1,276,573
Supporting Expenses	1,649,662	1,497,146	254,922	–		3,401,730
TOTAL	2,926,235	1,497,146	254,922	–		4,678,303
Surplus Before Interest	111,487	33,210	(254,922)	5,431,218	27,393	5,348,386
Interest Expense		(1,049,228)				(1,049,228)
After Interest Expense	111,487	(1,016,018)	(254,922)	5,431,218	27,393	4,299,158
Fund Balances	433,129	2,545,769	3,365,365	26,991,952	267,600	33,603,815
Donations for Buildings		8,105	17,550	25,000	118,150	168,805
Accessions of Art	–	–	–	–	(132,542)	(132,542)
De-accessions of Art		2,607,073	(1,067,277)			
Transfers	(104,723)			(1,435,073)		
End of Year Balances	439,893	4,144,929	2,060,716	31,013,097	280,601	37,939,236

TABLE 2 Statement of activity, fiscal year 1996 (in US$)

	Unrestricted	Temporarily Restricted	Permanently Restricted	Total
Public Support and Revenue				
Contributions	1,268,942	2,429,807	–	3,698,749
Campaign Contributions	–	7,333,420	94,394	7,427,814
Government Grants	87,600	50,000	–	137,600
Fundraising Events	3,006,858	–	–	3,006,858
Ancillary Services	524,564	–	–	524,564
Exhibitions, Collection, Education and Performance Programs	129,757	–	–	129,757
Membership and Admissions	284,132	–	–	284,132
Investment Income	3,278,592	168,663	–	3,447,255
Released from Restrictions	8,571,572	(8,571,572)	–	–
Total	17,152,017	1,410,318	94,394	18,656,729
Expenses				
Exhibitions, Collection, Education and Performance Programs	3,203,146	–	–	3,203,146
Marketing, Membership and Public Relations	1,407,458	–	–	1,407,458
Ancillary Services	675,739	–	–	675,739
General and Administration	2,287,379	–	–	2,287,379
Fundraising	2,406,514	–	–	2,406,514
Total	9,980,236	–	–	9,980,236
Excess Over Expenses	7,171,781	1,410,318	94,394	8,676,493
Other Changes in Net Assets				
Gain on Sale of Property	828,977			828,977
Earnings on Invested Bond Proceeds	586,691	–	–	586,691
Permanent Collection Funds, Released from Restrictions	109,820	(109,820)	–	–
Permanent Collection Acquisitions	(109,820)	–	–	(109,820)
Change in Net Assets	8,587,449	1,300,498	94,394	9,982,341
Net Assets, Beginning of Year	34,567,386	12,704,727	4,182,453	51,454,566
Net Assets, End of Year	43,154,835	14,005,225	4,276,847	61,436,907

TABLE 3 Statement of activity, fiscal year 1997 (in US $)

	Unrestricted	Temporarily Restricted	Permanently Restricted	Total
Public Support and Revenue				
Contributions	2,255,439	877,817	94,102	3,227,358
Campaign Contributions	–	596,101	–	596,101
Government Grants	10,000	–	–	10,000
Fundraising Events	551,075	–	–	551,075
Ancillary Services	2,536,204	–	–	2,536,204
Exhibitions, Collection, Education and Performance Programs	405,513	–	–	405,513
Membership and Admissions	1,641,713	–	–	1,641,713
Iinvestment Income	6,420,974	119,074	–	6,540,048
Released from Restrictions	4,375,651	(4,375,651)	–	–
Total	18,196,569	(2,782,659)	94,102	15,508,012
Expenses				
Exhibitions, Collection, Education and Performance Programs	6,184,193	–	–	6,184,193
Marketing, Membership and Public Relations	1,649,100	–	–	1,649,100
Ancillary Services	3,179,518	–	–	3,179,518
General Administration	3,426,602	–	–	3,426,602
Fundraising	1,271,038	–	–	1,271,038
Total	15,710,451	–	–	15,710,451
Excess Over Expenses	2,486,118	(2,782,659)	94,10	(202,439)
Other Changes in Net Assets				
Earnings on Invested Bond Proceeds	57,239	–	–	57,239
Collection Funds, Released from Restrictions	204,177	(204,177)	–	–
Collection Acquisitions	(204,177)	–	–	(204,177)
Change in Net Assets	2,543,357	(2,986,836)	94,102	(349,377)
Net Assets, Beginning of Year	43,154,835	14,005,225	4,276,847	61,436,907
Change in Donor Stipulation	(98,175)	(185,811)	283,986	–
Net Assets, End of Year	45,600,017	10,832,578	4,654,935	61,087,530

accomplishment felt by the entire board. But then there was also sense of exhaustion. The history of the MCA has really been about art, not about building, but we'd really gone through a phase of five, six, seven years, in which our energies were almost entirely focused on creating and funding a new building. And I'm not suggesting that the art content wasn't good. I'm just saying that the focus of meetings, the focus was raising money, the construction issues for the new building, and planning the opening. We gave a lot of thought to how to present and introduce the institution but not a lot of thought about life after we opened the building.'

A search consultant retained by the MCA viewed the situation as one requiring a sharp turnaround. 'When I took on this search', says Nancy Nichols, of the search firm Heidrich and Struggles (and herself an art historian), 'the MCA should have been one of the leading contemporary art museums in this country. It simply was not.'

The 15-member search committee convened by board chair Pritzker was deliberately designed to represent a wide range of interests, such that it would be aware of the range of challenges facing the museum. Says Pritzker: 'I drew from our trustees, both new and life (emeritus) trustees. I wanted to make sure I had a variety of points of view: some corporate representation, some of the great collectors. I wanted some of the money people, and some of our finance committee members who understood our financial picture. To run a museum, you have to be an orchestra leader and I wanted to make sure I had the expertise of all these constituencies.' The committee even included the former head of another major Chicago museum – the Field Museum of Natural History – so as to avoid what Pritzker calls too 'ingrown' a perspective.

Challenges

The problems which the search committee knew would face the next director were many and varied.

Attendance. After reaching 300,000 – its all-time high – during the first year the new building was open, attendance had begun to decline rapidly. The sharply higher fixed costs associated with a larger operation made the decline particularly problematic. But maintaining high attendance was a challenge, particularly given the relatively limited mass appeal of some MCA exhibitions. Observes Marshall Front: 'As is the case with all museums,

we're very heavily dependent on tourist trade. Well over half the people who come into the museum come from out of town. That's the nature of most museums. We, unfortunately, don't have in the Midwest, sophisticated European and Asian travelers coming to Chicago as frequently as some other cities. We've got Iowa, Indiana, Michigan, Kentucky, Tennessee. And the taste for contemporary art in Nashville isn't what it is in New York.' Observes Penny Pritzker: 'We are both in the business of producing scholarly academic shows and in the business of entertainment. We're competing for people's leisure time.' Tight budgets had, however, limited promotional efforts. Direct mailings designed to attract new members had been suspended and other forms of advertising were, says one museum staff member, 'limited'. There was, for instance, no advertising at the city's airports and train stations.

Headless. Not only was the MCA looking for a new director, it was doing so in the effective absence of a current director and top staff. The museum's previous director, who'd successfully overseen the construction and opening of the new building, had announced his intention to leave and was, in effect, on sabbatical. Moreover, three of the four top curator positions were vacant. As Penny Pritzker describes it, 'We were sitting there with no director, no senior curators and several vacancies in key management positions. We were headless from both the general management standpoint and the artistic standpoint.' A new director would thus have to recruit new senior curators – those who stage exhibitions and oversee the crucial process of developing exhibition catalogs.

Endowment. On paper, the MCA appeared to be well-endowed. At the end of fiscal 1995, for instance, endowment was listed at more than $37 million. But very little of those funds were actually providing income for the museum. In a complex financing arrangement, the museum had obtained favorable loan terms to finance its new construction in exchange for pledging the bulk of endowment income for construction loan repayment. The MCA thus had been able to avoid spending endowment principal outright – but it was now constrained in its use of endowment funds. 'It was always expected', says vice-chairman Marshall Front, 'that, within a few years of the opening of the new building, we'd have to undertake another serious fundraising effort.' In the mean time, there was already pressure on the museum's operating budget, forcing it to keep shows up, for instance, for up to six months – thus running the risk of an attendance drop-off as the museum's core enthusiasts lacked a reason to return.

'Co-Development'.   In recent years, the MCA had not developed the sort of major exhibitions that would go on to 'travel' – exhibitions often co-developed with other museums, which might share development costs. Co-development was considered important for reasons far beyond the financial. Traveling exhibitions brought the museum's name before a wider public, as well as, potentially bringing exhibitions to the attention of critics in the national press. Prominently-reviewed exhibitions could help stimulate the interest of donors. Exhibitions thus might lose money in the short-term (and typically would) but encourage significant gifts, either of money or art. 'A successful museum', observes MCA search consultant Nancy Nichols, 'is involved in a dialogue with the art world and with the public. The MCA had not been part of that dialogue.'

So it was that as the MCA search committee undertook its work, the list of qualities it sought in a new director was a long one. Says Penny Pritzker: 'The consensus was we needed vision. We needed personality. We needed social skills. We needed energy. And we needed someone that would be respected both in the international art community and within the Chicago community. Somebody who could sit at the dinner table with anyone in the city or around the world, and who you as trustee would feel proud to have that individual as your spokesperson.'

The first round

Over the first six months of the search process, Pritzker and the committee saw (as best they recall) a half dozen candidates. The large size of the search committee – which Pritzker believed was necessary to find a consensus choice – meant, however, that candidates were interviewed first by Pritzker and Nancy Nichols. Those whom they believed would interest the full committee would visit Chicago for a series of interviews with those committee members who were available. At its inception, the committee had stipulated that a successful candidate for the position would, in all probability, be someone on a career path whose next logical step would be a

museum director's position. Recalls Lew Manilow: 'We came to the conclusion about what it is we wanted to have in a new director and it was primarily that he or she had some significant experience in curating contemporary art, either as a director at a small institution, moving up to a larger one, or as a chief curator of a large institution who would like to become a director.' Manilow himself did not share this view. 'I objected. I said, I think you have to cast your net much wider. The job today is political, social. It is fundraising. It is all kinds of things. Yes, you have to have a passion for culture, especially a passion for art, and it would help if you had a passion for contemporary art, but that wasn't the most important part. In fact, if you get a really terrific guy or gal, who you know is going to lead you and raise the money and give you the inspiration and the vision and the drive and all the good things, and if he doesn't happen to have a contemporary art background, I'd take that guy any time, over someone who had the contemporary art background, but didn't have a vision, the drive, the managerial skills.'

In fact, a series of high-level curators and assistant directors failed to capture the imagination of the search committee. In part, this was seen as a reflection of a limited field of potential candidates and the fact that other museums – including the contemporary art museum in Los Angeles – were conducting searches at the same time. Reflects Penny Pritzker: 'There are fewer great contemporary art leaders than there are positions available in the world.' At least two candidates, however, did excite enthusiasm on the committee. Both, however, took themselves out of the running. One was a high-ranking staff member at the Smithsonian's Hirshorn Museum of modern art and sculpture in Washington, D.C., who'd previously worked at the Chicago Art Institute and was well-known and well-respected by the search committee. His withdrawal was thought to be linked to an interest in returning to the Art Institute. Another candidate, a gay woman, was concerned that Chicago – although cosmopolitan compared to the rest of the Midwest – might not be an 'open' enough community to accept her.

'Either they wouldn't fly or didn't want to fly', says Marshall Front of the field of 'traditional' candidates. Increasingly, given the leadership vacuum at the museum, the board felt under pressure to find a director quickly.

Says Penny Pritzker: 'We were on a precipice, we were at a pivotal point. The press was hammering us, saying we don't like the building, the museum's lost its way, the director's left, and you don't have any senior curators. It was a difficult position.'

Enter Fitzpatrick

It was at this point that search consultant Nancy Nichols threw an unconventional candidate into the search mix. Nichols had originally called Robert Fitzpatrick, dean of the school of the arts at Columbia University, in hopes he could suggest candidates for the position. It soon occurred to her, however, that Fitzpatrick himself might be a good candidate. Without doubt, however, he was an untraditional candidate.

Fitzpatrick had had a markedly diverse career (see Exhibit 1). He'd held dean's positions at two major universities – Johns Hopkins and Columbia – and had served for 12 years as the president of the California Institute for the Arts, a school for artists of many disciplines which was on the verge

of closing before he turned its fortunes around. He had served, too, during his tenure at CalArts, as director of an arts festival that was staged in conjunction with the 1984 Los Angeles Olympic games. His scholarly work, however, had not been in art or art history but in French; he'd once headed the modern languages department at a private secondary school in Baltimore. Nor had his career been exclusively focused on the arts. He had served as a member of the Baltimore City Council and, more recently, the chief executive office of the EuroDisney theme part, in France. He had never, moreover, worked for any sort of museum. Despite that, Fitzpatrick struck Penny Pritzker as someone filled both with energy and ideas, someone who might be able to fill what she called the 'multiplicity' of roles which the director's job combined. He was, after all, a seasoned professional who was both familiar with the art world but who had run for-profit and non-profit institutions, who knew the political process, who spoke French and had lived in Europe.

EXHIBIT 1 ROBERT FITZPATRICK

Curriculum Vitae

1940	Born May 18 in Toronto, Canada
1952–56	Brophy School, Phoenix, Arizona
1957	Price School, Amarillo, Texas
1962	U.S. Citizen
1963	Bachelor of Arts (magna cum laude) in French, Spring Hill College, Mobile, Alabama
1964	Master of Arts (magna cum laude) in Philosophy, Spring Hill College, Mobile, Alabama
1964–65	Woodrow Wilson Fellow in Romance Languages, Johns Hopkins University, Baltimore, Maryland
1965	Institut d'Etudes Francaises, Avignon, France; French Government Fellowship; Bryn Mawr College Fellowship for Study Abroad
1965–68	Assistant Professor of French, University of Maine
1966	Married to Sylvie M. Blondet, Paris, France; three children: Joel (1967), Michael (1970), Claire (1974)
1968	State Chairman, Maine, McCarthy for President Committee; Staff Member, McCarthy National Campaign Headquarters
1968–70	Course work completed for Ph.D. in French; Johns Hopkins University
1968–72	Chairman, Department of Modern Languages; Gilman School, Baltimore, Maryland
1970	Campaign Assistant to U.S. Senator Joseph D. Tydings; Staff assistant to Senator Joseph D. Tydings
1970–74	Member, Maryland Democratic State Central Committee
1971–75	Member, Baltimore City Council 2nd District; Chairman, Intergovernmental Relations Committee

1971–75   Member, Judiciary, Urban Affairs, Executive Nominations Committees Baltimore City Representative, Regional Planning Council; Chairman, Cultural Resources Committee

1972–75   Dean of Students, Johns Hopkins University, Baltimore, Maryland; Fiscal, administrative and planning responsibility for housing, residential life program, medical and psychiatric services, sports, placement and auxiliary services.

1975–87   President, California Institute of the Arts, Valencia, California. CalArts is a fully accredited, independent institution of higher education devoted exclusively to the visual and performing arts with schools of art, music, dance, theater and film/video.

1980–84   Vice President, Los Angeles Olympic Organizing Committee; Director, 1984 Olympic Arts Festival. Responsible for the artistic programming and financial management of the 10-week festival, which included 424 performances, exhibitions and events and 145 performing arts companies (1,500 artists) from 18 countries. The Festival presented 34 world, American and Los Angeles premiers. More than 300,000 tickets were sold for performing arts events (81% of capacity) and 200 performances sold out. Over 1 million guests attended the 400 performing arts events and 24 visual arts exhibitions. Among the highlights were Le Theatre du Soleil, Piccolo Teatro di Milano, the Royal Opera of Covent Garden, Pina Bausch and Sankai Juku. Visual arts exhibitions included *A Day in the Country: Impressionism and the French Landscape* and *The Automobile and Culture*.

1985–87   Founder/Director, Los Angeles Festival. This biennial Festival was created at the request of Mayor Tom Bradley in order to continue the success of the Olympic Arts Festival in attracting new audiences to the arts. The 25-day festival with 37 companies was opened with the American debut of Le Cirque du Soleil and Peter Brooks's *Mahabharatu*. Among other highlights were Maguy Marin, the Market Theatre Company, Michael Clark, La La La Human Steps, Muteki-sha, El Tricicle, and Bergman's Royal Dramatic Theatre Production of Strindberg's *Miss Julie*.

1987–92   President and CEO, EuroDisney S.A. As CEO, responsible for overseeing the creation of the $4 billion EuroDisney Resort, composed of a theme park, entertainment center, 6 hotels (5,200 rooms), a campground and golf course. The company grew from 2 employees to 10,000 (from 20 different countries) in 5 years.

1992–93   Chairman, EuroDisney S.A. As Chairman, responsible for the development of and transition to a European management team. EuroDisney (now Paris Disneyland) welcomed 11 million guests during its first year of operation.

1993–95   Managing Director, Robert Fitzpatrick Consultants. Clients included Schal Bovis (Japan, Osaka Universal Project), Sony Europe (Sony Center Berlin), Sama World Resort (Malaysia), Centre National de Dance et de l'Image (France), National Park Service (White House Renovation Project, USA), Leipziger Messe (Germany).

1995   Executive Producer, *It's My Party*, directed by Randall Kleiser, released by United Artists.

1995   Dean, School of the Arts, Columbia University, New York. The School of the Arts provides graduate education and professional training in writing, theater, film and the visual arts as well as undergraduate education in the arts for students of Columbia College New York. The School of the Arts is also responsible for the programming of Miller Theatre and its public presentations of music, dance, film, theater and the theater of ideas.

Community Activities		Honors	
Present	Trustee, American Center Foundation, Paris	1965–65	Woodrow Wilson Fellow, Johns Hopkins University
Past	Trustee PS 1 Contemporary Art Center Member, Tony Awards Nominating Committee; Trustee, American Hospital, Paris; Trustee, American Film Institute; Trustee, Bennington College; Trustee, Craft and Folk Art Museum; Board of Directors, Los Angeles Chamber Orchestra Society; Board of Directors, American Cinematheque; Chairman, Interdisciplinary Panel, National Endowment for the Arts	1974	Selected by *Time Magazine* as one of the 200 Americans under the age of 45 most capable of assuming leadership roles
		1984	*Officier dans l'Ordre des Arts et des Lettres*, French Minister of Culture; *Chevalier de l'Ordre National du Merite de la Republique Francaise*, President of France.
		1992	Man of the Year, MIPIM, France; Man of the Year, French-American Chamber of Commerce, New York;
		1993	Doctor of Humane Letters, *Honoris causa*, State University of New York.

I was in New York on business, and he and I met for breakfast. And clicked. We spent three hours talking, and I think it was a mutual click. I wasn't sure he was the right guy, but I thought this guy is intriguing to me and merits a lot more investigation and thought. He was a man who had led many different lives in one. And he struck me as someone of extremely high energy. He said he didn't believe in job longevity but in spurts of energy and focus and accomplishment. I said to him, look, I really think it's important we find someone who's willing to commit ten years to the institution. I think it's time we need to build the institution. We need to create stability. We need to think about another campaign. And I had kind of a long, slow architecture in my mind. He looked at me and said, first of all, I'm not prepared to make that kind of commitment. I don't believe in those kinds of commitments. I believe in commitments of intensity not of duration. That's what he said. And that was one of the things, among things that he said, that I thought a lot about.

Despite, or because of his unconventional background, Pritzker quickly concluded that Fitzpatrick should, if he was willing, go to Chicago to meet with members of the search committee. From the first, there was both enthusiasm and caution. At least one

member complained that Fitzpatrick did not fit the profile of the 'job description'. And there was widespread awareness that hiring someone who had been associated with Disney invited ridicule – and, worse yet, difficulty in convincing other museums to work with the MCA and in attracting curators. Nor was his tenure at EuroDisney considered a clear success. He was replaced as CEO after six years – although Marshall Front, a former high-level business consultant says, 'in situations like that it's never clear where responsibility actually lies.' His previous career, both in the private sector and high-level nonprofit positions, seemed to have had at least one incontrovertible effect, however: Fitzpatrick's salary history was at a level higher than that the museum had expected to pay.

As the interview process began, Fitzpatrick came to it with strong ideas about the MCA, based on his own evaluation of the museum. 'I'd spend a lot of time in and around museums and working on projects with museums, and it was very easy to pick up the phone and talk to a lot of colleagues who were either curators or running museums and say what's your take on this museum?' Fitzpatrick decided that the MCA was 'underfunded and unremarkable and had not lived up to expectations or its own aspirations.' He was sharply critical of the new building, which he characterized as 'a Masonic Temple without masons.' He felt the building as a whole 'was particularly unfriendly.' The interior, in his view, lacked 'attractive and informative signage. The security guards looked like they were guerrilla commanders in paramilitary uniforms, and were not particularly friendly or informative. The exterior was austere: no signs or banners that identified the museum and its exhibitions, nothing that said welcome.' He also felt that the fourth floor galleries, which housed the permanent collection, were flawed because a last-minute construction budget cut had led to carpeting being substituted for a terrazzo floor, with the result, in his view, that many sculptures simply 'blended into the floor.'

Fitzpatrick made clear that, were he to accept the position, he would expect that specific changes would be implemented. He envisioned a system of banners identifying both the museum and its exhibitions. He wanted the carpeting in the fourth-floor gallery replaced with terrazzo. Fitzpatrick regarded a pledge that such things would be changed as the

equivalent of a 'dowry' which he'd receive as the new director – and which would undoubtedly have budget implications for the MCA.

Says Marshall Front: 'He posed a number of risks. The risks were that he did not thoroughly understand the contemporary art scene' and that not all of 'his prior engagements had been altogether successful.' Says search committee chair Penny Pritzker:

> We could be criticized for hiring somebody who's expensive, who's never done this before, who has Disney attached to his name, who's unconventional. At the end of the day, you can have a great leader, but if you don't have product, then what are you? If we could not attract the kind of curatorial staff we needed, that would be a big problem.

However, she concluded: 'He had lived many lives. He understood how to run a business. He could communicate. He had ideas.'

Trilogy University

By Michael Paley and Thomas J. DeLong[1]

I would never vote to kill TU because that would be a vote to kill Trilogy's future.

(Joe Liemandt, Chairman and CEO,
Trilogy Software)

In February 2001, Joe Liemandt, chairman and CEO of Trilogy Software (Trilogy), sat in his office, preparing for a staff meeting with his executive leadership team. The team faced several critical decisions regarding the firm's corporate training program, Trilogy University (TU), which Liemandt believed had played a crucial role in the company's success to date. Since the program was introduced in 1995, TU had served a unique function within Trilogy by transforming recently recruited undergraduates into 'Trilogians'[2] – people who embraced the company's history, culture, and style, but who also were charged to have an impact within the organization and thereby change the company for the better. TU was also the breeding ground within Trilogy for new ideas, new products, and new approaches. As such, TU had become significant in helping the company preserve its innovative edge.

With the arrival of the new millennium Trilogy faced a slowdown in its business, a large number of unsuccessful customer deployments, and an overall weakening in the enterprise software market. In response to the situation, Liemandt decided to revamp the company's business model from one of providing broad software products to one in which the firm offered industry-specific solutions. This change in strategy was accompanied by an organizational restructuring. The company therefore embarked simultaneously on a major shift both in how it approached its business and customers and in how it was structured internally. Liemandt recognized that with these shifts, he and his senior management team would need to take a critical look at how TU supported or detracted from the company's new objectives.

How could TU be adapted so that it supported the strategic changes that were taking place throughout the organization? How would the company successfully implement the necessary changes to the training program at the same time as the corporate identity was being altered? Would TU, a program designed to drive innovation through chaos, be inconsistent with a corporate strategy that espoused predictability and more organization structure? Was the expensive program a luxury of the past that should be disbanded so that financial resources could be diverted to other more critical programs?

History of Trilogy

As an undergraduate student at Stanford University, Liemandt often became frustrated while working in the computer labs because new computer equipment would not work to fit his needs. Liemandt reasoned that he could not be alone in his experience and imagined the difficulties that established companies encountered as they attempted to successfully incorporate new technology into their existing operations with little margin for error. Liemandt believed that his disappointment in the new technology represented a business opportunity. Liemandt's idea was to create a software package that would help manufacturers of computer hardware and other process manufacturing equipment to accurately complete orders according to detailed customer specifications. In less than two years after he envisioned this new product, Liemandt, at the age of 21, dropped out of school and with the assistance of four classmates[3] founded Trilogy.

---

[1]Source: © 2002 by the President and Fellows of Harvard College. Harvard Business School Case 9–403–012. This case was prepared by M. Paley and T.J. DeLong as the basis for class discussion rather than to illustrate either effective or ineffective handling of an administrative situation. Reprinted by permission of Harvard Business School.
[2]Trilogy calls those who work at the company 'Trilogians.'
[3]John Lynch, Christina Jones, Chris Porch, and Seth Stratton joined Liemandt to found Trilogy.

The five founders spent three years developing the company's first software product called SalesBuilder™. SalesBuilder™ was a software product that enabled a client's salespeople to design detailed products for their customers.[4] A salesperson could sit down with a customer, discuss their detailed needs, and in real time translate those needs into a viable product specification with an accurate price quote.[5] For many companies this represented a timesaving of many weeks over their existing paper-based systems. The technology also dramatically reduced errors by providing an expert tool to sales reps who may not otherwise have been knowledgeable about all the options required to make a customer system a viable offering. Shortly after the new product was completed, the company's operations were relocated from Palo Alto to the current facility in Austin, Texas.

SalesBuilder™ fueled the early phases of growth at Trilogy. However, by the mid-90s the company faced still competition from large competitors such as SAP. To retain and to increase market share Trilogy sought to expand its product offerings to include broader sales and marketing functionality. By 1996, Trilogy introduced its second product, Selling Chain™, which was a set of software products that were aimed at helping companies to solve problems throughout their demand chain.[6] These products transformed Trilogy from a company with one software product to a company that offered a broad range of sales and marketing software applications. In conjunction with the addition of this product suite to its line-up, Trilogy adopted a horizontally focused business model similar to that of key competitors such as SAP, Oracle and PeopleSoft, thereby selling software to customers across a wide array of industries. The Selling Chain™ powered Trilogy's growth through the better part of the 1990s.

Joe Liemandt

To understand Trilogy, you must first understand Joe. This might be true in many start-up organizations as so much about the company's leader becomes embedded in the company itself – from its culture to its strategy to its recruiting practices. However, this has been especially true throughout (Trilogy's) 13-year existence.

(David Cushman, Director of TU)

Liemandt's interest in the business world developed while growing up in Pittsfield, a town in Western Massachusetts. Liemandt was one of three children. His mother, Diane, a homemaker, was active in charitable work, and his father, Gregory, was a general manager at General Electric's components and materials group. At GE, Gregory worked for a fast-rising star manager named Jack Welch. As a youth, Joe went to the same school and played hockey with Welch's children, and often vacationed with the entire Welch family. In Welch, Joe Liemandt found a mentor with whom he would consult many times throughout Trilogy's early years.

In 1983, Gregory Liemandt left GE and moved the family to Dallas to become CEO at UCCEL, a software development firm. His father's experience convinced Joe that he would start a software company some day. As a summer intern at UCCEL, 16-year-old Joe learned his first business lesson. He noticed that UCCEL's large development teams (anywhere from 50 to 100 developers) were too big to be managed effectively. He realized that project development teams needed to be small in order to be effective. He also learned that innovation could only happen when individuals felt they could have an impact – a lesson he carried with him to Trilogy. Both his father and Welch exposed Joe early on to professional management.[7]

---

[4]Sales configuration software enables a sales rep or a buyer to design the product to the buyer's specifications. The key difference between SalesBuilder™ and previous/other configuration applications was that SalesBuilder™ worked for more complex problems. Configuration complexity is in large part defined by the number of interdependent choices available for a given offering. Thus configuration of a high-end computer terminal/workstation in which a buyer wanted and was able to tweak all the components of the product, such as RAM, hard disk space, processor speed, and memory expansion capability, was much more complex than the configuration of a car in which a buyer chose between two types of stereos, both of which probably fit into the single predetermined slot in the dashboard, or six to eight colors, none of which affected the design of the vehicle.

[5]Noel Tichy, 'No Ordinary Boot Camp,' *Harvard Business Review*, Volume 70, Number 4 (2001): 63–70.

[6]The term demand chain refers to the set of product or service channels and business processes that exist between a company and its customers. Key demand chain activities include sales, marketing, and customer service.

[7]This section draws heavily from Josh McHugh, 'All or Nothing,' *Forbes*, June 1996, p. 128.

Liemandt entered Stanford University with the notion of starting a software company firmly in mind. Throughout his freshman and sophomore years, he worked as a part-time consultant for numerous software companies and spent countless hours researching the industry. Through his work, he discovered that a real and significant need existed for sales configuration software. Liemandt saw in this need his opportunity. Unfortunately, he recognized that he could not simultaneously study full-time and start his company. Liemandt realized that nine months (roughly the length of his senior year) was an eternity in the software industry. If he waited to develop his product, he believed someone would beat him to the punch. Despite his parents' objections (his father called him a 'moron'), Liemandt dropped out of Stanford and convinced John Lynch to drop out with him. Christina Jones, Chris Porch, and Seth Stratton remained in school and continued to work at the new company. And thus, Liemandt founded his software company.

Liemandt quickly learned that it was one thing to start a software company, but that to develop a product that customers wanted to buy represented a formidable challenge. Venture capitalists refused to back a 21-year-old kid and so, from 1989 to 1992, Liemandt 'financed' Trilogy using some 22 credit cards and income he earned from part-time consulting work. Over this three-year period, Trilogy never missed a payment. It was not until 1992, when Hewlett Packard paid Trilogy $3.5 million for its SalesBuilder™ product, that the Trilogy founders finally stopped worrying about incoming calls from creditors.

After their first major sale, Liemandt started to receive phone calls from investment bankers eagerly looking to take Trilogy public. Liemandt resisted these offers and resolved to keep Trilogy a privately held company. Money for Liemandt was not the end game – building software that solved real business problems was. Liemandt believed that if Trilogy were to become a public company preoccupied with 'making the numbers', he would have to compromise on his ideal. However, he quickly realized that everyone in his organization did not share his values and motivations. Faced with this reality, Liemandt decided he needed to find a way to 'teach' his staff about what Trilogy did, why it did it, and what Trilogy could do.

Trilogy University: The first class

It was early- to mid-1994 when Liemandt realized that not everyone at Trilogy shared his vision. Trilogy was growing rapidly. Customers had responded well to SalesBuilder; in fact, IBM had just signed an additional $25 million deal, the largest order Trilogy had yet received. Despite these early successes, Liemandt was worried that the company's success would be short-lived: 'I woke up in '94 and realized that this place sucked. We were out of alignment. I saw a group of very young kids with dollar signs in their eyes, kids who wondered when Trilogy would take its turn in the IPO boom that had recently begun.'

Liemandt worried not only about the 'alignment' of his recent hires, but also about their basic skills and capabilities. Liemandt called on John Price, vice president of marketing, for assistance. Price, who Liemandt affably described as Trilogy's 'main guy for demand creation', was one of the key people responsible for the company's recent customer growth. Liemandt challenged Price to focus exclusively on the recruitment of stellar new people. Price traveled to various college campuses around the country and presented Trilogy as an upstart company that empowered its employees. Through his efforts Price successfully recruited 42 recent graduates to join Trilogy in the summer of 1995. Among the recruits were the number-one-ranked computer science graduate from MIT and the number-one-ranked economics student from Stanford.

Liemandt was unsure what to do with this cohort of 42 impressive new recruits. First, Price had sold many recruits on the promise that Liemandt would train them. Second, the existing Trilogy staff was not prepared to absorb such a large group of extremely talented computer programmers into the existing operations. At this point Liemandt realized that Trilogy lacked capable management. 'If these new hires were placed right into the organization,' he explained, 'Trilogy's current management would 'screw them up'.' Therefore Liemandt decided to put aside many of his short-term responsibilities as CEO in order to personally run the first class of Trilogy University, 'TU95.'

Liemandt explained his decision, 'I wanted to train them, because I wanted to set the standard for what we can expect from these new employees and to see what they could deliver.' To make this point perfectly clear and to defend his new hires from the influences of the existing organization, Liemandt forbade the existing managers from entering the TU workspace. Many of Trilogy's managers who were responsible for engagements that were understaffed and in desperate need of people were frustrated by Liemandt's decision, which prevented them from adding additional resources to their teams.

When that first class filed into the building, nobody, including Liemandt, knew what the next steps in the training process would be: 'I was the first teacher of TU. I had no curriculum and no teaching plan. So I began by asking the kids what they knew.' Liemandt quickly realized that this group had so much talent that they could almost teach each other. Together the group developed a program of study that they would cover over the next two months.

A part of Liemandt's method involved impressing upon the new hires his edgy personality and aggressive style. This included placing a high degree of importance on taking risks in order to achieve breakthrough innovations, risks that were similar to the one he took in dropping out of Stanford to start the company. David Cushman described one of the most memorable aspects of the earlier TU years:

> One of the things Joe would do is take the entire TU class to Las Vegas. At some point in the evening, he'd get the house to corner off a roulette table and he'd ask for 35 TUers to step up to a game. Each of the players would place a $2,000 bet on one number on the wheel. Thirty seconds later, someone would be the big winner, and everyone else was out a major portion of his or her monthly paycheck. Though it was an expensive lesson (one that earned the nickname, 'L2k' for lose $2,000), it was effective in getting the point across that to win big you often have to be willing to lose big.

At the same time as the 42 new hires worked together to develop their course of study and teach it to one another, Liemandt focused on developing his overarching goals for the newly created TU program – and by extension, his company. Liemandt recognized that Trilogy needed a new product line – the company needed to move from just offering SalesBuilder to offering a more complete product suite. Looking around, Liemandt realized the talent with which he now had to work afforded him a

tremendous opportunity for product innovation. Working grueling hours,[8] the new Trilogians completed their course by developing precisely what their boss was looking for, a new product suite called Selling Chain. The new product suite quickly became a hit with customers and set Trilogy on a new growth trajectory.

Liemandt realized the business success of the TUers' work was only one element of what he sought to accomplish with TU. If TU were to be successful it also had to turn new recruits into employees that could succeed once they 'graduated' into the Trilogy organization. Liemandt articulated his three goals for TU as follows:

1 TU should serve as a cultural indoctrination process for new Trilogians. The staff at Trilogy views itself and its company as fundamentally different from other firms, and takes joy in that. New hires should understand this, and should do so quickly.

2 TU should allow its graduates to push the development of their technical skills and to learn the tricks and procedures necessary to effectively produce results in the Trilogy environment.

3 TU graduates should not only be taught that they could have a huge impact on an organization, but that they *must* have such an impact.

By accomplishing these objectives, Liemandt had created a program that dramatically changed the face of Trilogy. Liemandt proudly reflected, 'There is no doubt in my mind that it was TU95 that turned this company around.'

Evolution of TU

In the years that followed its founding, the leaders of TU tried to keep the program focused on the three aforementioned goals and to continue to enhance and enrich TU's structure and methodology. Liemandt continued to lead the new hires through the training program, but by 1998 the new class grew too large, and Liemandt saw a need and an opportunity to systematize the TU experience. Therefore, in 1998 smaller sections were created within TU so that TUers could not only continue to work together to learn and gather information about what was

---

[8]Liemandt set clear expectations that the normal schedule should include working from 8 a.m. to 12 midnight six days a week, with a 'relaxing' Sunday of work from noon to midnight.

expected of a Trilogian but also could collaborate in a small team environment to develop the next innovation for the company. Liemandt tapped existing employees to serve as stand-ins for him in the program, and committed seven of his best employees to serve as section leads.

Beginning with the introduction of sections, Liemandt and his staff continued to refine TU, all the while maintaining its focus on the three goals around which it was developed in 1995, and thereby progressively formalizing the TU process and structure. By 2001, a new recruit spent his or her first week in the organization going through an extensive orientation process. After the first week, TUers were expected to be familiar with Trilogy's history and value system, its customers, and what the organization expected of its people. During the subsequent three weeks, TUers were split into two parallel tracks, the section track and the technical track. The 'tech track' focused on teaching core skills, such as Java programming and software testing methodologies that were critical to developing enterprise software. Within 'section,' the section leads continued the indoctrination process by teaching the TUers more about the company and its approach to its customers.

Following this first month of training, students spent six weeks working in teams on new initiatives and innovations at Trilogy. Under the direction of Liemandt and various section leads, TUers were immediately expected to begin to develop innovative ideas that would eventually become the next generation of Trilogy software products. As Liemandt explained, 'They become Trilogy's main innovation engine.' In 1998 and 1999, the TUers were instructed to come up with ideas and solutions that would enable Trilogy to enter and compete in the fast growing worlds of e-commerce. In addition, they were asked to work toward the development of 'dot-com' enterprises. The TUers were divided into four-person teams (consistent with Liemandt's belief that smaller development teams were more productive) and given the responsibility for 'soup-to-nuts' business creation by developing: a product, technical demonstrations, a business plan, and the necessary marketing materials to launch and to support their new initiative. The objective was to convince Liemandt that their idea was worth Trilogy's investment and to obtain his approval to push forward with the idea. The leading project from TU98 was CarOrder.com, which ultimately became a distinct business that Trilogy spun off in 1999. The online car dealer won *PC Magazine*'s award for Best Car-Buying Site in

2000. In TU99, one of the best groups developed an online shopping agent and gift registry Web site, IveBeenGood.com. This technology was sold to another firm in 2000 in a deal that netted Trilogy $11 million in profit.

As Trilogy recognized the value of TU, the company sought to apply these processes to a broader set of employees. Originally designed to develop new hires that were recent college graduates into Trilogians, some senior managers at Trilogy began to believe that all new hires at Trilogy should go through some sort of training program in order to better understand the company, its culture, and its methods. In 1999, Trilogy began a TU for new hires who had previously worked at other firms in the industry. The program was called 'Industry TU' (ITU) and the company envisioned running it approximately six times a year. Similar to the college program, participants in ITU would participate in an orientation and rigorous section/technical tracks modeled after those in the traditional TU program. The difference between the two programs was that ITU spanned a shorter time frame and did not include the TU innovation projects. By early 2001 as Liemandt strove to reorganize the company, ITU had achieved a moderate level of success, but was no where near as successful at TU in terms of indoctrinating new hires and driving innovation for the company.

TU's role in the organization

Trilogy's outlook starkly contrasts those of other corporate training programs. Most boot camps reinforce that you can't effect change. I completely disagree. You have to engage every person in your team, be under their skin, so they end up knowing that they can, and must, have an impact.

(Joe Liemandt)

In the years that followed its founding, Trilogy continually shifted and refined its business focus; one year concentrating on a suite of products for a customer's sales processes, two years later working to incubate spin-off companies, and the next year targeting enterprise e-commerce solutions. With each change in direction, Liemandt looked towards TU to serve as the agent of innovation for the company.

Despite a successful run with SalesBuilder, in early 1995 Trilogy faced formidable threats from competitors such as SAP, Antalys, and Calico. The chief information officers from most of Trilogy's major customers were approaching Liemandt and his sales team, informing Trilogy that they were seriously considering replacing Trilogy's software with products from SAP. Liemandt realized that he needed new products, and he needed them quickly. Liemandt also looked in the mirror and realized that his own abilities were not sufficient to fix the problem: 'I wasn't good enough to get what I wanted out of Trilogy in 1994. Instead of fighting Trilogy, I realized I couldn't move the ship, so I used TU as the lever. For example, I attribute the development of the Selling Chain, a breakthrough product suite, to the fact that we successfully empowered the TUers.'

Because of the vital role that it served as agent of innovation in the company, TU had also become an attractive selling point to entice new recruits to join Trilogy. During the late 1990s, at the peak of Trilogy's campus hiring, the firm competed head-to-head with firms such as Microsoft for the top computer programming talent across the country. In fact, many of Trilogy's younger employees (the average age of employees was 26 when TU98 began) had turned down employment offers from Microsoft in order to join Trilogy. TU played a critical role in their decisions.

David Pratt, a senior programmer who joined the firm in 1999, had interned at Microsoft and was one of the people who turned down a Microsoft offer to come to Trilogy. Pratt commented, 'I would have given my kidney to get a chance to go through TU. Compared to opportunities in other organizations, ones in which technical programmers are expected to code, code, and code, the opportunity for computer science guys to have a real impact on the business is virtually unparalleled.'

Jeff Daniel, the company's recruiting director, saw the impact of a program like TU every time he visited college campuses. 'Along with the people at Trilogy, TU is the number one sales pitch that I give during each recruiting visit.' Jonathan Berkowitz, a senior consultant and former TU section lead, joined Trilogy because 'the culture of the company was absolutely fascinating. It's a young upstart. It combines 100% work, 100% fun, and 100% play all at the same time.'

However, the view that TU was the company's innovation agent and pride of the company created tension between TU and the rest of the organization. Employees throughout the company, some of them former TUers themselves, felt that after they gradu-ated from TU their efforts were minimized. Existing employees questioned their own significance in the organization. Some felt slighted, as if they were the forgotten soldiers. Jeff Daniel, a graduate of the first TU class, described the situation: 'People who had been at the company for a few years were busting their asses and felt like outsiders, as Joe took all the new hires to Vegas as part of the program. Some of them saw TU as Liemandt just wanting to surround himself with all the new, young guys. Some people worried that it was just an ego trip.'

As Trilogy's growth accelerated throughout the latter part of the 1990s, the size of the classes of new recruits also grew. The TU class of 1998 had 268 members, increasing the size of the company by more than 50%. Such a large group exacerbated the concerns of several existing employees.

By 2001, the tension was strongest among middle management at Trilogy. The percentage of middle managers who had experienced TU was smaller than that of individual contributors who were graduates of the program (see Table 1). Ajay Agarwal, a member of the executive leadership team and a seven-year Trilogy veteran, admitted that as long as TU continued to be an agent of change, tension would exist. Nevertheless, Agarwal described TU as 'one of those things that once you've been through it and witnessed its impact, you become a believer.' Many Trilogians, Liemandt included, wondered whether people who had not gone through the program fully understood it. Liemandt reflected: 'We need to make sure everyone, even those who have not gone through TU, appreciate it. If there is a sense of ill will towards TU, it is a sign of bad leadership – what am I doing wrong that people don't see how valuable it is?'

The bubble bursts

The overheated business environment of the late 1990s allowed Trilogy to spend considerable time and energy searching for breakthrough opportunities and it enabled the company to continually change its strategic focus without paying a penalty. Following years of rapid growth and the seemingly endless rise in the capital markets, Trilogy began to struggle in the first year of the new millennium. Liemandt and his sales force began to encounter difficulty selling new software (see Figure 1 for chart on the performance of the NASDAQ stock market). In response to the downturn, Liemandt felt the company could go

TABLE 1 Trilogy consulting organization by TU experience

Organization Level	TU Graduates	Total Employees	% with TU Experience
Vice President level	0	2	0
Director level	2	12	17
Sr. Manager & Manager levels	11	43	26
Sr. Associate level	47	74	64
Associate level	49	65	75
Support level	0	5	0
TOTAL	109	201	54

Source: Company documents.

in two directions. It could either attempt to sell its existing software to a broader set of clients by maximizing marketing and distribution, or it could try to strengthen its relationships within its current customer base and focus on delivering follow-on business value.

Since its inception Trilogy had developed a set of software products that provided generic solutions for businesses across a broad set of industries. This horizontal approach was standard among Trilogy's key competitors such as PeopleSoft, Oracle, and SAP. However, customers told Trilogy that its products were no longer sufficiently tailored to meet their specific business needs. The company discovered that an application that worked well for the firms in one industry often did not prove to be as effective for firms in other industries. The conclusion was that each industry required unique technology solutions for the unique business processes and challenges that the firms within the industry confronted.

Based on this information, Liemandt decided that efforts to broaden Trilogy's customer base would not solve the company's problems in the long run. Therefore he decided that Trilogy should retrench and focus on the needs of its existing customers such as Sun Microsystems, Ford Motor Company, and Prudential. In late 2000, Trilogy developed the first tangible strategic vision since the company's founding 11 years earlier: Delivering 100% customer success. To satisfy this newly found commitment, Trilogy sought to build a set of software applications that provided unique solutions for a specific industry ('business vertical' in Trilogy's nomenclature). In short, they sought to reinvent Trilogy as a company that provided vertical software solutions.

At the same time as they introduced the new vision, Trilogy's senior management also developed and articulated a clear strategy and a set of corporate values that all employees were expected to adopt. The four pillars of the strategy were:

FIGURE 1 Value of the NASDAQ stock market in the 1990s

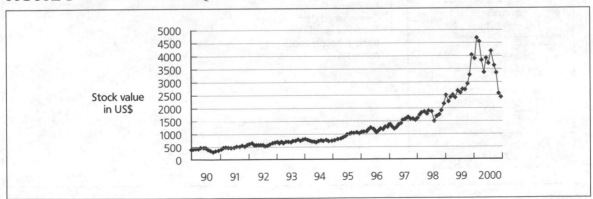

Source: Annual Report.

1 *Take The Hills*: solve an industry's toughest, and most valuable problems.

2 *Build Killer Apps*: be recognized for having gold standard technology.

3 *Make It Work*: make the solutions work technically and deliver the value sold.

4 *Develop All Star Teams*: have great players in every role and maintain a deep bench.

This strategic shift at the company was accompanied by substantial restructuring of the organization (see Figure 2). It was around this time that Jim Abolt joined Trilogy as vice president of human resources. Abolt's arrival represented the first big change in the new structure. As part of his duties, Abolt was responsible for TU, though he firmly believed that the program could only maintain its magic so long as Liemandt continued to believe in it. Additionally, in the new organization, the general managers of the five business units (such as automotive and telecommunications) focused directly on delivering customer success and growing the business. These executives partnered with a set of functional vice presidents (functions such as software development and professional services) who had responsibility for developing world-class processes and people that provided the organizational capability to deliver on the company's objectives. Abolt was the first of five new executives that Liemandt hired into these vice president level positions as he strove to acquire seasoned leaders to head up the new Trilogy.

In conjunction with the reorganization, Liemandt and CFO Pat Kelly established profit and loss statements for each of the business units. For the first time in the company's history, experienced general managers (GMs) who would and could be held

FIGURE 2 Trilogy Software: Corporate structure following reorganization

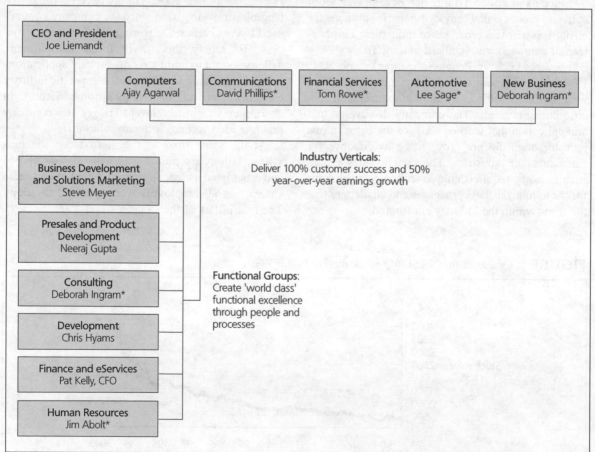

Source: Company documents.
*Hired by Joe Liemandt in late-2000 and early-2001 as part of the firm-wide reorganization.

accountable for unit performance managed the business units. One aspect of the new financial reporting structure was that business units were charged directly for the costs associated with recruiting and training those new hires that joined a particular GM's group.

With this change, the cost of running TU would become more apparent as managers were charged with both the infrastructure costs involved in running TU as well as the three to four months of salary and overhead expense for the time the new hires spent participating in TU. Not only would GMs be required to dedicate financial resources to TU, but also they would need to provide human resources to the program in the form of section leads. From the GMs' perspective, the training of section leads proved invaluable in enhancing that employee's ability to lead within the group and thereby strengthened the business unit as a whole. Furthermore, the constant interaction between TUers and section leads presented GMs with a opportunity to use the section leads that they committed to the program as a recruiting agent for their unit, the intent being to entice the best of the new hires to join their business unit.

The section lead program also aimed to help improve the management capabilities of top calibre, high potential people throughout the company. Trilogians viewed being chosen as a section lead as a prestigious honor and a great challenge. Joshua Koppelman, a former TU section lead, recognized the impact that the experience had on his career: 'Like TU, the whole [section leading] experience is incredibly intense. It is definitely the best thing that I will never do again.'

TU: Still vital to the new Trilogy?

Although history might suggest that the incoming TU class would be asked to radically challenge the direction of the company with innovative ideas for new businesses, aligning the company to the new strategy and direction was of paramount importance. Of added concern to Liemandt was to transform each of the company's unsuccessful engagements, of which there were many, to a successful engagement. Liemandt believed that TU could continue to address significant issues and drive important initiatives at the company. He stated, 'Even today, when I want to do something radical, I will use TU. In my mind, it is the path of least resistance, because I need people who will go out on a limb and be willing to get their head cut off to achieve the objective.' What remained unclear was whether TU could affect the obvious challenges at hand.

As he looked through his office window at Lake Austin, Liemandt considered TU's role in the context of the company's new strategy and organizational design. He knew that some of Trilogy's new leaders were wondering whether the program was still relevant or whether it detracted from the goal of delivering customer success. If Trilogy chose to maintain the training program, should it be restructured, and if so, how? How could TU be used to reinforce rather than detract from the new strategy? What level of resources should the company invest in TU given the tough economic climate both current and future? Liemandt knew that these were only some of the issues concerning TU that his company would have to address as they prepared for the incoming cohort of new hires.

As he watched a water skier fall in the distance, Liemandt reflected on the company he had created. He understood that the company's second decade would present an entirely new set of challenges that would be fundamentally different from those the company had confronted in its first 10 years of operation. In his heart, Liemandt believed that TU would continue to play a critical role in providing answers and solutions to current and future challenges. However, he realized that in order for TU and Trilogy to be successful, he believed that he should not force his views on the entire organization as he had sometimes done in the past. The decision about TU and more importantly how the corporate training program should be sponsored would need to come not only from him, but also from the members of his senior management team. Jim Abolt walked into Liemandt's office to help him prepare for the executive team meeting. He was excited to get the group focused on TU.

Cap Gemini Sogeti: Building a transnational organization

By Tom Elfring[1]

As the hundreds of group managers of Cap Gemini Sogeti (CGS) poured into the conference building in Prague on this nice summer day, June 25, 1992, the company's executive chairman, Serge Kampf, wondered what their ideas would be regarding the transformation of the organization. After all, he had not only called these managers together to present his own vision of what the future organizational form might look like, but also to get their input and to arrive at decisions that would be widely supported throughout the company. Kampf realized that restructuring the organization would be a difficult task, but he also knew that to continue the company's success it was imperative that CGS and the large number of recently acquired firms be molded into a coherent transnational company.

Although reorganizations are always difficult, CGS had quite a few factors making the task more easy. CGS was a growing firm in a growing industry – world-wide CGS held the fourth place in the 'big league' of information technology service companies, while in Europe CGS was by far number one. Internally, Kampf could also count on widespread support for his efforts to build CGS into a global company. During the four day Marrakesh Rencontre in June 1990, the 550 attending group managers had opted overwhelmingly for a strategy of globalization, with the intent of belonging to the top three information technology services corporations worldwide. This bottom-up decision had created a shared vision of the company's future and willingness throughout the organization to change.

However, Kampf and CGS were also faced with some daunting challenges. First, competition within the information technology services industry had grown increasingly intense since 1990 and the firm's net income had suffered as a consequence. Second, after the Marrakesh Rencontre, CGS had acquired a large number of companies that needed to be merged into the CGS organization. Finally, building an effective transnational organization would probably mean that the company's well-known strict decentralization policy would need to be adapted, either marginally or radically. Any further move away from the high level of local autonomy, however, would probably meet with some anxiety, if not resistance.

To Serge Kampf it was clear that the group managers' bold Marrakesh decision for a global push was a vote 'for a dream or a nightmare.' Since June 1990 he had brought together many of the building blocks for the envisioned global company, but now at this Prague Rencontre it was up to group managers to help realize the dream. The building blocks needed to be brought together to form an effective transnational company. Of course, the question was, how? What type of organizational setup and systems would suit the demands of a knowledge-intensive service firm operating on an international scale? To this pressing question the group managers – and Serge Kampf – needed to find an answer.

The company's history

The growth of Cap Gemini Sogeti had been built on its ability to 'make computer systems work' and meet the requirements of the client. The Cap Gemini Sogeti Group's official birthdate was January 1, 1975. In that year Gemini Computer System merged with the Cap/Sogeti Group. The latter group was the result of a merger between Cap, a computer services firm, and Sogeti, a business management and information-processing company. At that time Cap had 780 employees, Gemini employed about 320

[1]Source: © 1994 by Tom Elfring. This case was prepared by Tom Elfring, Rotterdam School of Management, Erasmus University, with the assistance of Saskia van Rijn. This case is intended for classroom discussion, not to illustrate the effective or ineffective handling of a managerial situation. Unless mentioned otherwise, all information was obtained with the kind assistance of Cap Gemini Sogeti. The author would like to thank Ron Meyer for his useful comments. Used with permission of the author.

people, and Sogeti was the smallest, with 250 workers on the payroll. Cap Gemini Sogeti started out with European subsidiaries in Great Britain, The Netherlands, Switzerland, and Germany, but most of its business was conducted in France. This new Cap Gemini Sogeti Group had a good start in life through powerful (French) government patronage and the national management tradition of contracting out services instead of performing these tasks themselves.

Cap Gemini Sogeti (CGS) grew from small autonomous groups of programmers-for-hire scattered around France, with a common policy of tight financial control and a thoroughly professional reputation. During the 1980s, CGS acquired a large number of mostly smaller firms in Europe and some in the United States. They improved their position in the market for professional information technology services, such as information technology (IT) consulting, customized software, and education and training. Their expansion in the 1980s was centered on these services, and CGS achieved an average annual growth rate of about 30 percent, of which roughly two-thirds was due to internal growth. The remaining one-third had been the result of friendly acquisitions and alliances. This seemed to be the only way to provide global coverage some of the clients required.

An important acquisition was that of Sesa (Société d'Études des Systèmes d'Automation) in 1987. It could be seen as a turning point, because Sesa was a distinguished French software house with a broader corporate culture than the narrowly based CGS, with its origins in 'body shopping,' hiring out computer specialists on a daily basis to work on customers' contracts. In the late eighties, CGS concentrated on the integration of the Sesa team and on consolidating and streamlining its organization, thereby improving its profitability.

CGS's current position

Cap Gemini Sogeti is now Europe's number one computer services and consulting company and one of the industry's leaders world-wide. Located in 15 European countries and the United States, the group specializes in software services, its goal being to assist its clients in drawing the greatest possible benefit from information technologies. Ever since its creation in 1975, the group has upheld a strong development policy, multiplying its revenues, profits, and size. In 1992, however, CGS incurred the first losses in its history. The net group loss of $14.9 million is partly due to $60 million worth of restructuring (see Figures 1 and 2.)

Cap Gemini has always had a certain gloss and sparkle (even by French standards). It is proud, elitist, almost arrogant and has a single-minded devotion to developing methods and tools for writing better, more accurate software. In France, especially in government circles, software skills are equated directly with pure intellectual effort and are much prized, which has resulted in substantial government backing and patronage. Much of Cap Gemini's success was said to be due to its simple management strategy; it concentrated on what it does best (professional software engineering) and wasted little time arguing about whether it should be selling computer hardware, applications packages, or

FIGURE 1 CGS revenue, 1980–1992

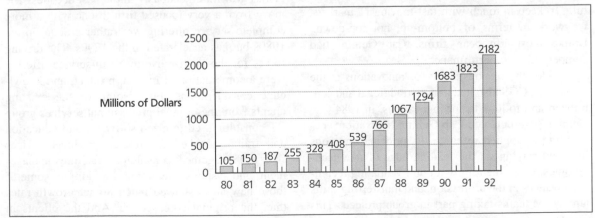

FIGURE 2   CGS net income, 1980–1992

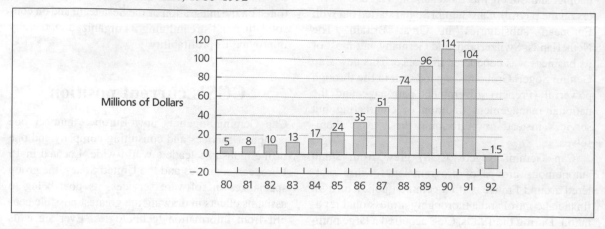

administrative services, all of which have diluted the effort of many other software houses. It articulated this philosophy to its employees continuously.

Michel Berty, general secretary of Cap Gemini Sogeti, described his satisfaction with people with well-developed minds. Two-thirds of Sogeti's employees have an advanced engineering degree. 'They are good,' he says. 'They have learned to work and to reason. Human qualities are also essential but are not always so well developed.'

One of Cap Gemini's formulas for success has been an inviolate decentralization policy that stipulates that when any of its branches – 250 in 1989 – reaches 150 staff, it splits in two, and a new manager is appointed to head the new branch. Eric Lutaud, a member of the corporate development team at Cap Gemini Sogeti, explains: 'We are so decentralized that at any point in time we have several people doing things that are not kosher.'

This highly decentralized style of organization, however, was subject to very strong financial controls. Cap Gemini believed local operations had to be in the hands of locally hired managers to be successful. 'To keep in touch with fast-moving IT markets, we work in terms of bottom-up, not top-down.' Unlike most European firms, Cap Gemini tied compensation to performance.

Besides the responsibility for innovations at the local level, CGS also had a more traditional and centralized unit to look to for innovations. In 1984 Cap Gemini Sogeti created Cap Gemini Innovation, specializing in applied research. Its principal missions included staying on the leading edge of new technologies, experimenting with and validating technical advances in the profession, and transferring skills among the teams taking part in group projects. This

research and development policy was carried out jointly at four research centers in France, Belgium, and The Netherlands, bringing together researchers and technicians from more than 10 countries. The sums invested in this activity have grown steadily since 1985, at which time they represented $20 million; at the end of 1991, the figure had climbed to $109 million.

Traditionally Cap Gemini Sogeti's business was the provision of general technical backup for customers' data-processing departments. But the most profitable and fastest-growing part of the business results from companies wanting Cap Gemini Sogeti to design and set up a specific project. For this you need staff with in-depth knowledge of the customer's sector (see Figure 3 and Table 1.)

From one to four related businesses

The number of different types of services related to IT has grown tremendously in the past decades. The move from a very focused firm to one with a more complete service offering was rather gradual in the 1980s but has accelerated in the 1990s. The driving forces for the swift move to a full-service offering were a combination of market, product, and knowledge considerations. First, some of the existing clients from the original professional services group (IT consulting, customized software, and education and training) asked for related products/services such as management consultancy, facilities management, and systems integration. In addition, some of those new areas showed much higher growth rates than the original core service. And the clients in

FIGURE 3 A comprehensive range of services

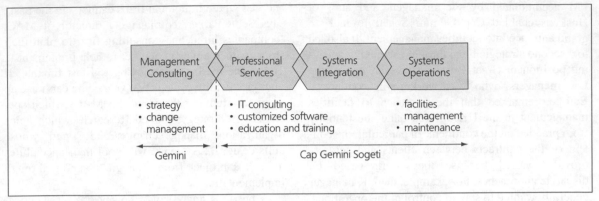

TABLE 1 Information technology services by CGS

Business	Description
Facilities Management	Taking over all or part of a client's IT resources (hardware, software, and staff) and running this operation for a given time period and with commitment to results.
Systems Integration	Providing a client with a complete IT solution integrating hardware and software, with a commitment to respect established costs and delivery times.
IT Consultancy	Involves analyzing an IT problem and developing solutions; designing, planning, and organizing information systems: implementing solutions either by developing customized software, or by adapting already-existing applications.
Management Consulting	Helping and assisting firms to transform their business by integrating disciplines such as strategy, operations, and information technology.

those new service categories were also potential clients for the professional services group. Second, the expansion by acquisitions and alliances had also been partly knowledge driven. The degree to which targeted firms were able to fill in the gaps in the CGS skills portfolio was a serious consideration. The takeover of Hoskyns was valuable in terms of its competencies in facilities management. Hoskyns' speciality is outsourcing, or running a customer's entire data-processing department, a business that was growing at 25 percent a year, nearly twice as fast as other computer services. Its other main lines of business were IT consultancy and systems integration. The development of the market for facilities management was more advanced in the UK than in continental Europe. CGS used the Hoskyns' competencies to expand its firm's operations in continental Europe.

Facilities management

Contemporary corporations expect their information systems to keep pace with competitiveness. That is the function of their IT departments, which must be able to accommodate growing technological complexity, be easily adaptable, make practical use of their experts' time and stay fully in control of quality and costs. In its response to each of these criteria, facilities management (FM) has proven its effectiveness as a powerful resource for helping companies implement their strategies and achieve their objectives, while allowing them to concentrate on their own business. The acquisition of Hoskyns marked the commitment of Cap Gemini to move into that market in a serious way.

Hoskyns brought to the Cap Gemini Sogeti group its expertise and market-leader position in the UK, and 3500 employees. The 25 years of experience in FM accumulated by the managers and staff of Hoskyns enabled Cap Gemini Sogeti to make a grand entrance into facilities management. It also led to a second strategic breakthrough: achieving a leading position in Great Britain. However, one of the UK managers, who was working in continental Europe, remarked that the approach to facilities management in the UK differed quite substantially from practice on the continent. In particular, the content of the contracts between clients and service-provider varied because they were based on disparate approaches. For example, the UK manager generally wanted to stay in control of the operations, while in the Scandinavian countries joint ventures with equal shares are often established to regulate facilities management contracts, and in The Netherlands quite a number of partnerships with minority shares are to be found.

CGS strengthened its position in the facilities management market and in the Scandinavian market simultaneously by an $88.3 million friendly bid for Programator, its Scandinavian competitor, in February 1992. In joining forces with Programator, Cap Gemini Sogeti confirmed its stated goal of becoming the number one computer services company and market leader in northern Europe. In acquiring Programator, which generated 40 percent of its turnover from facilities management, CGS mainly targeted the FM market in Scandinavia and thus pursued its FM development strategy. As a result of this operation, Cap Programator was the uncontested professional services leader in this region, unequalled in terms of number of locations, and able to handle all types of IT projects at both local and international levels. The acquisition of Programator should have enabled CGS to generate a turnover of more than $500 million in northern Europe in 1992.

Consultancy

When more and more of CGS's customers asked for collaboration on problems of major technology projects linked to their specific activity, Sogeti created a consulting group that was structurally and professionally independent of Cap Gemini Sogeti. Gemini Consulting was created by bringing together three leading consultancy firms: the MAC Group, United Research, and Gamma International. United Research, MAC Group and Sogeti are betting that the increased speed of corporate decision making

will mean that a linked network of consultants will succeed where individual firms cannot. 'In the past,' says Scott Parker, co-managing director of MAC, 'companies hired one consulting firm to plan their strategy, then engaged another to help implement it. Today, the markets are moving too fast for that. If your product life cycle is two years, you can't use up one year studying the issue. So MAC, which specializes in strategy; United Research, which helps organizations manage change; and Sogeti, whose units design IT systems, will pool their specialities to take a project from strategic planning through implementation.'

A business analyst was, however, a bit skeptical about the related diversification of CGS into other services. 'In particular, inclusion of consultancy in their integrated service offering looks nice in theory but might be difficult to implement. I hope they've learned from the problems encountered by Saatchi and Saatchi and also by Arthur Andersen in offering consultancy services as part of the package.'

In 1992 Gemini Consulting took a controlling interest in Gruber, Titze and Partner (GTP), Germany's third largest management consultancy firm. The skills of Gemini and GTP were complementary, and the combined operation (340 consultants in Germany) would boost Gemini's presence in Germany and become its largest subsidiary in Europe.

Gemini Consulting was legally, organizationally, and culturally separate from Cap Gemini Sogeti. The major reason was that the culture, the organization, and the internal management procedure at Gemini Consulting are integral to and inseparable from the firm's ability to deliver the results its partner-clients expect. And these were quite different from the Cap Gemini Sogeti way of doing business.

Systems integration

Systems integration involves submitting all-in-one bids to deliver working packages of hardware and software that, for instance, will automate a factory or computerize a billing process. The customers' primary focus is no longer on choosing what equipment to buy but on maximizing the contribution of IT to the enterprise's success and well-being. Systems Integration submits all-in-one bids to deliver working packages of hardware and software.

In the SI process, the integrator often selects technology, builds interfaces, and provides integration, installation, operation, training, and technology refreshment. Systems Integrators develop, implement, and manage for their customers all the technologies used to provide information as a strategic corporate asset. While they work in close partnership with their customers to address business needs, the customers ultimately control their business and the direction it is going in. The value of systems integrators and systems managers is their technical resources and in-depth understanding of their customers' markets. Cap Gemini Sogeti argued that they could be trusted more, as they were free from the pressure to peddle their own merchandise (see Table 2).

The four related businesses CGS did serve represented about 38 percent of the total market of IT services. However, there was still a huge part of the total IT services market in which CGS wasn't involved, like tax audit consulting, packaged software (systems products, applications products), turnkey systems and hardware sales, and processing and network services.

Increasingly, customers of IT-service firms, such as CGS, require that the service suppliers have prior knowledge about the industry from which the customer stems. An understanding of the particular industrial context is beneficial for the customer because no time is wasted by the supplier in investigating the industrial setting and introducing IT applications. As a result the service suppliers can judge relatively quickly and accurately what it takes to satisfy customers' demands. By showing in-depth knowledge of the clients' industrial context, service suppliers can more convincingly argue that they can indeed offer state-of-the-art IT solutions. In a number of cases the competitive context and demanding clients in a particular country forced the local Cap Gemini unit to find innovative solutions. These innovative solutions, being developed in one country, can be applied by other CGS units working in other countries.

One aspect of organizational capabilities concerns the creation of optimum conditions for pooling application expertise generated from completed projects. It becomes important as a skill for full-service suppliers, and CGS had developed some capabilities for the upgrading of organizational memory. The solutions implemented were aided by IT-based tools such as electronic bulletin boards and extensive electronic mail facilities (including voice mail). In addition, it appeared that these formal aspects of routines were complemented by the reliance on informal networks of professionals who cooperated in previous project-teams.

Information could also be acquired at competence centers, which provided line managers with skills

TABLE 2 Market for IT services, 1990

The 'Big League' in IT Services		1990 European Revenues, $ Millions		
	$ Millions		Country	Revenue
1. EDS (excluding GM revenue)	2,788	1. Cap Gemini Sogeti	France	1,464
2. IBM (about 3.3% of the total revenue)	2,280	2. Finsiel	Italy	875
3. Computer Sciences Corp (3/31/91)	1,738	3. EDS + SD Scicon	USA	300*
4. Cap Gemini Sogeti	1,683	4. IBM	USA	700
5. Andersen Consulting (about 75% of total)	1,420	5. Sema Group	France	559
		6. O.I.S (Olivetti)	Italy	667
		7. Sligos	France	532
		8. GSI	France	375
Next ones are far below:		9. Volmac	Holland	347
Finsiel (Italy)	875	10. CGI	France	325
Sema Group (France)	667	11. Axime	France	325
CSK (Japan)	618	12. Programator	Sweden	298
Olivetti (Italy)	559	13. Logica	UK	253
Sligos (France)	532	14. CISI	France	250
SD-Scicon (UK)	412			

*=estimated revenue in Europe.

related to a given technique or application. Development of project routines helped to structure project management. Organizing for cross-market opportunities was based on knowledge of the industry represented in reference databases developed by CGS that offered descriptions and information on activities.

Reconfiguration of the competitive context

Cap Gemini Sogeti's strategies were partly a response to the changes in the European competitive context. The acquisitions and alliances were necessary to gain market share and remain one of the top players in a fast-concentrating market. An industry analyst concluded that the industry had entered a Darwinian phase: those who failed to get stronger would be absorbed. One element of growth strategies is to increase geographical coverage. The need to be present in more countries was closely related to the internationalization of the business community and in particular to the fact that a rising number of clients throughout Europe wanted IT-system developers to create systems that worked across national boundaries.

The setup of the international support division was motivated by the need to offer solutions to multinational clients. This unit combines the commercial and technical support functions required by the operational groups. These ranged from providing assistance in technical developments, such as quality assurance and research and development (R&D) programs, to marketing developments. The latter focused on initiating and coordinating international projects and, if necessary, dealing with the top management of client companies.

The move from one to four related businesses can be seen as a result of the changes in the way business was done. Spotting business opportunities for each other became increasingly important. CGS was beaten in its home market by competitor Arthur Andersen when they were given a systems-integration contract for the Paris Stock Exchange after Andersen consulted for the French treasury ministry. Cooperation with the newly formed Gemini Consultants, however, had been similarly beneficial. A United Research (one of the partners in Gemini Consulting) contract with Mobil Oil Corporation in the United States led to a contract for

CGS to work on Mobil's European distribution network. CGS's new service offering matched the cross-marketing capabilities of competitors such as the large accountancy/consultancy firms.

A different but related aspect in these cross-marketing efforts was CGS's ability to achieve boardroom access. Cooperation with Gemini Consulting provided a direct link to the top management of client companies. That is important because, as a result of growing complexity and uncertainty, IT management had become an essential corporate function affecting large parts of the organization. Decisions concerning investments in information technology were very often made at the middle-management level, in particular by managers of the IT departments. Increasingly, however, because of the growing corporate importance and complexity of IT investments, it had become a concern of top management.

Besides the growing competition from the large accountancy conglomerates, the IT services market was also attractive for the large computer manufacturers. They were expanding their service activities to compensate for declining profit margins on hardware. CGS had a strong selling point in its objectivity and independence from the computer equipment vendors. The strategies of IBM could have a substantial influence on CGS performance, since about 60 percent of its clients were IBM users. Its relationship with the struggling US giant was a mixture of competition and collaboration.

Probably the most serious competitive threat came from Electronic Data Systems (EDS), the IT services firm owned by General Motors. EDS was boosting its European sales and trying to expand its non-GM business. Just as with CGS, EDS had been trying to grow in Europe as fast as possible. For example, SD-Scicon, one of the main European IT services firms in the 1980s, sold its German subsidiary (Scientific Control Systems, SCS) to CGS. To counter that move and the takeover of Hoskyns, EDS reacted in 1991 by buying, after a serious takeover fight, the UK part of SD-Scicon (see Table 3).

The Marrakesh Rencontre

At the Marrakesh meeting in June 1990, it was decided that the hallmarks of the group were to be a comprehensive service and a well-run organization staffed by highly motivated men and women.

TABLE 3 CGS's major acquisitions and alliances

Company (country, main business)	Year	Type
Sesa (France, software house)	1987	Takeover
SCS (Germany, computer services)	1990	Takeover
Hoskyns (United Kingdom, facilities management)	1990	Takeover
Daimler-Benz (Germany, industrial group)	1991	Alliance
Debis Systemhaus (Germany, software services)	1991	Merger
Programator (Sweden, facilities management)	1991	Takeover
MAC Group (US, management consultancy)	1991	Alliance
United Research (US, management consultancy)	1991	Alliance
Volmac (Netherlands, software house)	1992	Alliance
GTP (Germany, management consultancy)	1992	Takeover

These managers were presented with a choice between three different strategies: staying local but adding some new related services; expanding geographical coverage with the existing focus of service provision; or expanding the service offering in combination with achieving global presence. Each of these strategies was discussed intensively with regard to content and implications. When the results of the poll were announced, it became clear that the managers had opted overwhelmingly for the third strategy, global presence.

The current organizational structure

The director of the newly formed Cap Volmac in the Benelux remarked that internal coordination and cooperation in the world-wide operations of Cap Gemini Sogeti should improve quickly, because only then can CGS really profit from the trend of increasing client demand for IT services – showing that they can indeed offer the promised solutions.

CGS's alliance with Daimler-Benz in 1991 was a direct result of the decisions taken in the Marrakesh meeting and represented a response to the changes in competitive context as sketched above. CGS obtained financing of $585 million through this alliance, concluded after a year of negotiations in July 1991. It gave Germany's largest industrial group 34 percent of Sogeti, the holding company that owns 58 percent of Cap Gemini Sogeti (see Figure 4). Daimler-Benz also has the option of taking full control of Sogeti and Cap Gemini in February 1995. However, Serge Kampf, who controls Sogeti through another holding company, SKIP, has the option of buying back the 34 percent Daimler-Benz stake starting in 1994, before the German group can exercise its option.

In addition, CGS set up a joint venture with Debis Systemhaus, Daimler's software arm. In the joint venture, Sogeti's German activities and Daimler's informatics operations were brought together. Debis was a newcomer to the computer industry, it being established in 1990 as a 100 percent subsidiary of Daimler-Benz providing services internally as well as working with outside companies. The Systemhaus had a staff of 3600 people with revenue of over $400 million. The largest percentage of its business was in IT services, and it covered a wide range of services, from software packages to full-system implementation, and from consultancy and training to computer center, network, and telecommunications management.

One of the challenges for Cap Gemini Sogeti was to integrate the acquisitions and alliances of local companies and the local CGS units. The establishment of a new Cap Gemini Benelux, to be named Cap Volmac, an alliance of existing CGS units and Volmac was representative for challenges encountered by CGS in increasing geographical coverage. In February 1992, the alliance and shares exchange between CGS and Volmac, the leading Dutch IT services firm in which CGS already had a small stake, was made public. This move was in line with the attempts of CGS to increase its European market coverage and met the demand from multinational clients to handle IT services contracts spanning several countries. For CGS the strong market position of Volmac in facilities management, one of the new lines of business with above-average growth rates, was particularly attractive. CGS and Volmac would pool their activities in the new firm in the Benelux

FIGURE 4 Capital structure after alliance with Daimler-Benz

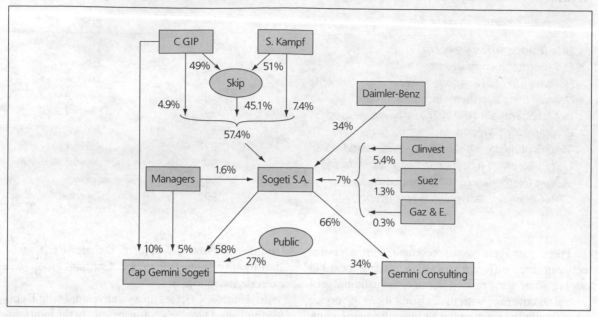

region. Sixty percent of Cap Volmac would be owned by a new holding group. The other 40 percent would be divided between Volmac's existing public shareholders, institutional investors and the World Software Group, which was Volmac's holding company. The new holding group would in turn be roughly two-thirds owned by CGS and one-third by the World Software Group. The new Cap Volmac had around 4,000 staff and annual sales of slightly under $500 million.

The Prague Rencontre

The main issues to be discussed by the participants of the Prague Rencontre on June 25, 1992, were the following:

- How can the existing organizations (such as Hoskyns, Programator, Volmac, and Debis) be integrated and 'welded' more cohesively into the group, as changes in demand increase?
- What should the organizational structure look like?
- How can expertise of acquired companies be retained when experts can leave so easily?
- How can a common company culture be created?
- How can cross-selling be made a success?
- What role can Gemini play in the restructuring?

With respect to these issues and the necessary changes, Serge Kampf remarked that important CGS values such as cooperation, teamwork, and manager mobility should be respected, and he emphasized that 'even though we want to rebuild a new house together, we cannot destroy the foundations of the old one.' What such a house should look like was the question he hoped the Prague Rencontre delegates would be able to resolve.

Cap Gemini Sogeti: Building a transnational organization

By Ron Meyer, Hervé Amoussou and Tom Elfring[1]

On January 10, 1995, Serge Kampf, chief executive officer of Cap Gemini Sogeti (CGS) and chairman of Sogeti, met with 35 executives of CGS and Gemini Consulting to rethink their joint future. Two and a half years had passed since the Prague Rencontre at which CGS had plotted a course towards becoming a transnational organization (see Case 19(A)). The goals agreed upon in Prague had been ambitious. A reorganization program called Genesis had been adopted, with the intent of meshing together the diverse companies that CGS had acquired, or had formed an alliance with, between 1990 and 1992. As a consequence of Genesis, the reborn CGS had come to share the same working procedures and services throughout the entire firm. Much had also been done to create a common culture and shared ambition among the 25,000 employees spread across 16 countries on two continents. This extensive change process had been guided by Gemini Consulting, specialists in 'Business Transformation™'.

Yet, despite the enormous efforts put into building a lean and mean organization, profits were still nowhere near the pre-integration level of 1991 (see Table 1). Of course, CGS was facing a number of very strong international competitors, such as EDS, IBM and Andersen Consulting. However, many analysts were wondering whether CGS had bitten off more than it could chew. Merging five large information technology service firms (Hoskyns, UK; Debis, Germany; Programator, Sweden; Volmac, The Netherlands; CGS, France) into a coherent transnational group was a Herculean task. The result, Kampf had predicted in 1990, would be 'a dream or a nightmare.' While the current reality was still somewhere in between, it was paramountly clear to Kampf and the assembled managers that a powerful impulse was needed for CGS to gain a strong competitive edge and for profitability to rebound.

For Gemini Consulting more or less the same was true. Gemini was the result of an alliance between the MAC Group (USA), United Research (USA) and Gamma International/Sogeti (France), formed in 1991. The next year GTP (Germany) was acquired, bringing to four the number of organizations that needed to be integrated into a coherent group. Much like CGS, Gemini was also confronted with a pack of strong international competitors, not intent on giving Gemini the luxury of sorting out its internal reorganization at its ease. Not surprisingly, Gemini's marketshare and profitability were also under pressure.

As Kampf and the upper echelons of CGS and Gemini Consulting started on their two-day meeting, they were determined that it should result in some breakthrough initiatives. The question was whether these initiatives should be sought in the existing strategic direction of the companies or whether a bold redirection was needed. Could a strong competitive position be obtained by 'debugging' and extending the current strategy or would the companies have to rewrite their strategic program?

The Prague Rencontre

The Prague Rencontre (June 24–27, 1992) was attended by 670 managers from all five parts of the company: Cap Gemini America, Cap Gemini Europe, Cap Sesa (the French entity), Hoskyns (the British entity) and Cap Gemini International Support. The first speech, by Robert Sywolski, chairman of Cap Gemini America, emphasized global change. He first spoke of his Czech origin and then showed a video tape that demonstrated how fast the world had changed during the last three years. Images of the Gulf War, the fall of the Berlin wall, the putsch against Gorbachev, the German

[1]Source: This case was prepared by Ron J.H. Meyer, in collaboration with Hervé Amoussou and Tom Elfring. The case is intended for classroom discussion, not to illustrate the effective or ineffective handling of a managerial situation. Unless mentioned otherwise, all information was obtained with the kind assistance of Cap Gemini. Copyright 1997 by Ron Meyer, Rotterdam School of Management, Erasmus University.

TABLE 1 CGS financial results 1989–1994

(in millions of French francs)	1989	1990	1991	1992	1993	1994
Consolidated revenue	7,055	9,172	10,028	11,884	11,028	10,176
Net income (loss) before amortization of goodwill	586	682	629	20	(330)	4
Net income (loss)	525	623	560	(72)	(429)	(94)
Dividends distributed	152	196	262	–	–	–
Net margin (%)	7.4	6.8	5.6	(0.6)	(3.9)	(0.9)
Number of shares*	25,251,046	27,939,313	37,472,775	41,964,338	42,431,755	53,068,478
Earnings per share (FF) before amortization of goodwill	23	24	18	0	(8)	0
Earnings per share (FF)	21	22	15	(2)	(10)	(2)
Average headcount** for the period	12,974	16,489	17,971	21,675	20,900	19,001
Total number of employees as of December 31	13,540	18,919	16,892	21,374	20,559	19,823
Professional staff	11,426	15,542	14,012	17,932	17,061	16,717

* Adjusted for share splits and bonus share issues
** In 1992 and 1993 49% of the headcount of Cap Debis was included

reunification, the outburst of rage in Yugoslavia and the release of Nelson Mandela plunged the whole assembly into a maelstrom of emotions about change. He described all these events as macro changes and explained that with the disintegration of the Soviet Union, business was winning over politics.

Then came Geoff Unwin, chairman of Hoskyns, who focused on changes in the data processing service sector. He stressed that powerful actors from the automotive industry, telecommunications, computer hardware, banking and auditing were entering the industry. He added that 40 percent of the world's software was already being produced in India. The third member of the management team to speak was Christer Ugander, chairman of Cap Gemini Europe, who presented a set of figures that demonstrated how profoundly CGS had changed between the Marrakech (1990) and the Prague Rencontre (see Table 2).

Finally, Serge Kampf introduced *Genesis* ('CGS *E*ntering a *N*ew *E*ra of *S*uccess, *I*nnovation and *S*ervice'), the process that was going to create a new CGS. The first step in this process was going to be the introduction of a new organizational structure. Kampf had been working on a proposal for a new structure with Gemini consulting for over a year. They had considered four structural alternatives:

■ A region-based organization. A structure along geographical lines was more or less the existing situation within CGS. However, this form held little scope for cross-border synergies and, therefore, was quickly rejected.

■ A sector-based organization. As CGS's services need to be tailored to customer needs, it would be logical to bring together CGS units with similar clients into the same division. Such a structure along industry sector lines (bank industry servicing division, automotive industry servicing division, etc.) was rejected due to four reasons. First, the differences in European corporate law were judged to be too large. Second, the differences between the US and Europe made cross-Atlantic integration particularly tricky. Third, some sectors, like the defense industry, absolutely required a regional organization. And last, but not least, the

TABLE 2 State of the group 1990–92

	Marrakesh, May 1990	Prague, June 1992
Number of Employees	14000	25000
Percentage in France	43	23
Percentage in the USA	24	10
Managers at the Meeting	550	670
Potential Market for Service	$57 billion	$87 billion
World Market Share	2.1%	3.2%
European Market Share	6.5%	8%
Employees/Million Inhabitants	100 for F, NL, CH	300 for NL, S
	25–50 for N, CH, DK	100 for F, SF
		50–100 for UK, N

transformation from a pure regional to a pure sector-based form was judged to be too difficult.

■ A matrix organization. This organizational form would be half way between the existing regional form and the industry sector organization. However, it was feared that conflicts between sector and region management would inhibit cooperation.

■ A dual organization. In this structure the regions would remain dominant, but each would also receive the responsibility for coordinating world-wide efforts within a certain sector.

Kampf proposed that the latter organizational structure be chosen. He sketched an organizational chart consisting of seven regions, to be called Strategic Business Areas (SBAs): the US, the UK, the Nordic countries, the Benelux, Germany, the Paris region, and a southern region made up of the French provinces, Spain, Italy, Switzerland and Austria. Each SBA would be split into approximately 7 'divisions', of approximately 3500 exployees each (see Figure 1 and Table 3).

Redrawing organizational charts was not enough, Kampf knew. Therefore, the second and third day of the Prague meeting were spent on discussing how to really transform the organization. The organizational structure was further hammered out, with an emphasis on improving service to clients and creating transnational sales and production teams. Importantly, while striving for cross-border integra-

tion and consistency, it was made clear that reducing reporting levels and respect for subsidiarity[2] should also be guiding principles in the organizational design.

It was also decided to strengthen the seven corporate values that CGS had already identified as central to their members' shared philosophy. An eighth value, client-oriented, was added to honesty, solidarity, liberty, boldness, trust, simplicity and fun, to signal the essence of the cultural transformation.

Finally, it was agreed that CGS could only function as a transnational organization if all parts of the company worked in roughly the same way. There would have to be a significant amount of cross-border unification of working methods if cross-border teams were to work together. Therefore, it was decided to find out where excellence existed within the company and to use these best practices as a standard for the entire company.

The initiation of Genesis (June–December 1992)

Following the Prague Rencontre, Michel Jalabert, CGS's former-president of Central Functions, was named General Manager of the Genesis Project and Francis Behr became Deputy General Manager. They set out to quickly execute the first phase of the Genesis Project, codenamed the *As-is phase*. The objective of this phase was to collect best practices

---

[2]CGS borrowed this concept from the European Community. It is the principle that only issues of supranational importance should be dealt with at the EC level. All other issues, and the associated powers, should be devolved to the national governments.

FIGURE 1   Cap Gemini Sogeti structure

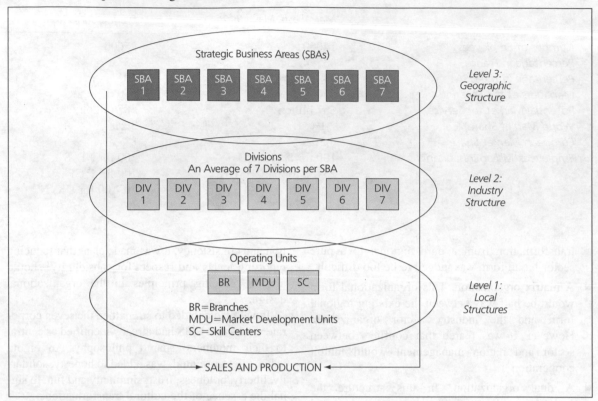

TABLE 3   Cap Gemini Sogeti's management team

Executive Chairman: Serge Kampf	Central Functions	Group Vice Presidents
Central Functions President:	Development	Eric Lutaud
Michel Jalabert	Finance	Vincent Grimond
Regions President: Geoff Unwin	Image & Communications	Jacques Collin
Sectors President:	Quality & Innovation	Wolfgang Schönfeld
Jaques Arnould	Human Resources	Adolfo Cefis
SBA	**Divisions**	
1. United States	Gas & Oil	Michel Berty/Robert J. Sywolski
2. United Kingdom	Financial Services	Tony Fisher/Tony Robinson
3. Nordic Countries	Utilities	Anders Skarin/Christer Ugander
4. The Benelux	Distribution	Chris van Breugel/Bernd Brix
5. Germany	Industry	Karl Heinz Achinger
6. Ile de France	Telecommunications	Alexandre Haeffner/Henri Sturtz
7. French Provinces, Spain, Italy, Switzerland, Austria	Space, Air Traffic Control, Railways	Alexandre Haeffner/Gennaro de Stasio

throughout the company, that could serve as the basis for unification. At Prague, Kampf had identified the three major areas where unification should be pursued:

- What do we sell? The service offering portfolio.
- How do we sell? The sales process.
- How do we produce what we sell? Project management.

Groups were formed to research each of these issues. In CGS jargon, their research projects were referred to as work streams. In each workstream a number of teams, usually consisting of an experienced local CS manager together with a Gemini consultant, set about conducting interviews with numerous CGS people. More than 500 interviews were carried out by these teams within a few weeks.

A fourth work stream was created to track the progress and success of Genesis. Futhermore, a number of support work streams were also established – communications, human resource management and management information systems – to facilitate the four primary work streams.

On September 1st, 1992, representatives of the four work streams assembled in Paris to present their conclusions on the current best practices, thereby completing the As-is phase. On the basis of these results, CGS top management decided to move to the second phase of Genesis, the *To-be phase*. In this phase the work streams would attempt to implement the best practices within one division of the organization, known as the pilot site. This trial division would later act as a model for the transformation of the entire organization.

In order to keep all employees informed of progress, it was also decided to establish a newspaper, edited by the communications work stream, and to develop a dictionary of new terms in the company. Furthermore, e-mail and a hot line were made available for questions.

The service offering portfolio work stream

While almost every project for a client is unique, it was believed that an explicit overview of the types of service offerings available within CGS was important. An explicit portfolio would provide the terminology for CGS people to communicate with one another. Moreover, a portfolio overview could be used to communicate a clear message of CGS's abilities to clients.

The analysis of 300 interviews with CGS marketing executives provided an outline of the portfolio (see Figure 2). All services were first divided into five groups of IT businesses, referred to as business

FIGURE 2   CGS's service offering portfolio

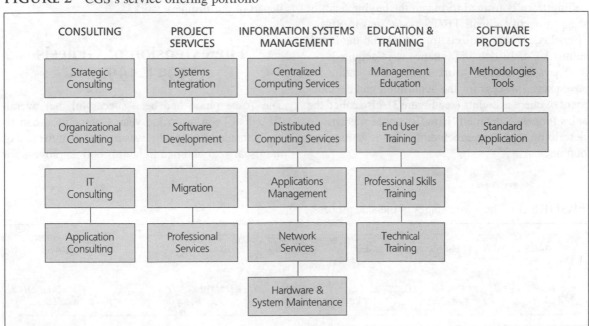

lines: Consulting, Project Services, Information Systems Management, Education & Training, and Software Products. Each business line was subsequently divided into sets of related services, referred to as service lines. Concrete service offers to clients combine elements from the service lines and tailor them to the particular client needs.

The sales process work stream

In the As-is phase, more than 500 sales people had been interviewed and over 1000 business proposals had been analyzed. These revealed a number of common reasons for failure of a business proposal: costs were often incorrectly evaluated, clients had not been contacted when they were ready to decide and the company's image had not been supportive enough. The research also revealed some critical success factors in the sales process: it was necessary to understand the client's needs, to establish contacts at the appropriate level in the client's organization, to propose high quality solutions and to realize that CGS was selling to groups of people, not to individuals.

Especially this latter point had not yet been fully recognized. Increasingly clients had come to understand that IT investments were of strategic importance. Consequently, the buying decision had become a long process involving a lot of specialists and decision makers. This insight led to the development of a new commercial approach, called Team Buying/Team Selling (TB/TS). In this approach a selling team is formed to match the buying team of the prospective client. TB/TS was tested in SBA 4 (Benelux), where projects for NATO and the Dutch ministries of Justice and Finance were acquired.

The sales process work stream also outlined a seven stage process for the acquisition and development of client accounts (see Figure 3), also called the sales funnel. A detailed 'How To' guide was written describing each stage, including a list of actions and outputs.

The project management work stream

Each national entity had its own project management methodology to ensure service quality, like LOGIC in Scandinavia, PRISM in the UK, SDM in the Netherlands and EXPERT in France. It was recognized by all that international customers and cross-border projects would require a common methodology. Therefore, the project management work stream designed a new system, PERFORM, integrating the best elements of the various national approaches into an international, open, and efficient tool. 'Built on CGS's 20 years of experience in methodologies, PERFORM is a modular system that can integrate foreign systems. This is a major advantage since some clients, like the armed forces, have their own systems,' explains Reinhard Degen, the manager later in charge of PERFORM implementation in SBA 5 (Germany). The greatest asset of PERFORM is its ability to fit the large, long-term projects that often characterize the international clients. PERFORM includes other features such as profitability tools and commercial support techniques, and complies with the ISO 9000 quality norm.

Sweden was selected as pilot site and the methodology was tested on 16 projects. By December 1992, more than 350 project leaders and engineers had attended PERFORM courses. According to the head of SBA (The Nordics), Anders Skarin, 'integration of PERFORM in our systems takes place smoothly. Our quality system, like the accounting procedures, is part of our ordinary work.'

The extension of Genesis (1993–1994)

The To-be phase had been successful, but overall 1992 had been a terrible year. Competition had so badly mauled CGS that it was in the red at the end of the fiscal year and had to lay off 600 employees for

FIGURE 3   The seven stages of the sale process

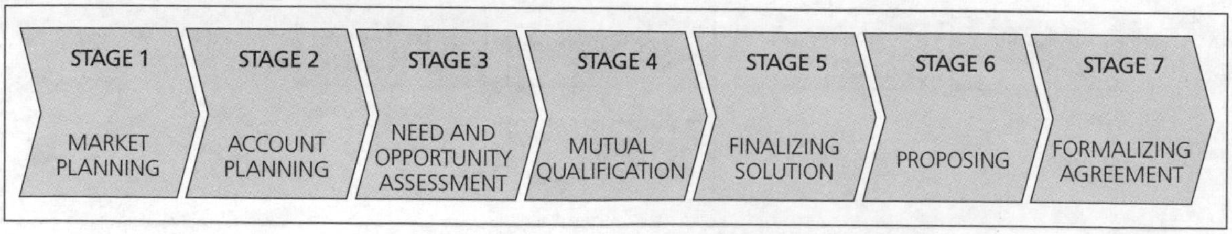

the first time in its 25 year history. It was under these circumstances that the top 80 managers of CGS met each other at the Béhoust castle in France on January 21, 1993. Michel Jalabert, head of the Genesis project, stated the intention of meeting: 'Last year, our partners and friends of Gemini Consulting helped us to develop the Service Offering Portfolio, the Team Buying/Team Selling process and so on. Now the initiative is ours.' CGS was ready to launch the full-scale transformation of the entire company.

The first step was to identify 81 Managers of Change (MOC), whose responsibility it would be to help people within their region to transform their working habits and to use the new tools, like PERFORM and the sales funnel. Fourteen MOC came from SBA 7 (Southern Europe), 12 each from SBA 4 (Benelux) and SBA 1 (US), 10 from both SBA 6 (Paris) and SBA 5 (Germany), eight from SBA 3 (Nordics) and SBA 2 (UK), and seven people from the Central Functions. The Managers of Change attended a two-week training program in February 1993 at the Béhoust castle, where they learnt about the new methods and how they could be implemented in the regions. The MOC from each region also established the current state of Genesis in each SBA – the Base Line – as a reference point to direct and measure change.

The second step taken by CGS top management was to outline seven Axis of Development, that would help to restore CGS's profitability. The axis of development were:

- Service Offering. To extend group-wide high growth and high profitability service offers.
- Sales. To become a partner of the client thanks to TB/TS.
- Project Management. To increase quality management of the projects.
- Structure. To promote transnational behavior.
- Sectors. To foster growth in each selected sector.
- Communication. To strengthen brand image.
- Benchmarking. To monitor performance after change implementation.

In each region seven so-called Champions were selected, each with the task of coordinating one of the axes of development in their SBA. Together the Managers of Change and Champions in each region worked to produce a development plan for their SBA, called the Business Case. This plan took the Base Line document as a starting point and detailed how the Axis of Development could be implemented in the region. By April 1993 these plans had been completed and each of the Group Vice Presidents in charge of an SBA knew the specific actions that had to be taken in his organization.

Realizing change

In September 1993, for the first time in the history of CGS, Kampf delegated the bulk of the company's operational activities. Geoff Unwin became Chief Operating Officer (COO), while Kampf, as Chief Executive Officer, remained responsible for image and communication, corporate development and shareholder relations. Pierre Hessler, formerly general manager Operations for IBM Europe, was named Deputy General Manager of CGS, second to Geoff Unwin.

Surveys indicated that an overwhelming number of managers endorsed Genesis, but Hessler still wondered about 'morale of the troops.' He organized a round of informal interviews in France, Sweden, Switzerland and the United States that revealed underlying skepticism. Francis Behr therefore organized a second round of formal interviews, with the topics: Knowledge of the group's strategy, labor environment, communication, and perception of Genesis. The outcome of these interviews was worrying. While managers throughout the group where satisfied with the level of written communication, some were confused about CGS's strategy. Moreover, Genesis was widely perceived as a marketing tool. As for morale, job satisfaction and anxiety were both wide-spread.

Hessler decided to accelerate the change process by launching Genesis 2. The new program aimed to foster the effects of Genesis by putting emphasis on human resource management and communication. A monthly distinction, the Profitable Growth Award, was introduced to congratulate the employees whose contribution to growth and profit had been outstanding. He also launched the company's first international advertising campaign, to improve the company's image and morale. The advertising slogan 'Total Respect. That's what Business needs today' was chosen for this campaign.

It was clear, however, that pushing through real changes would be a long and arduous task. As Michel Jalabert put it, 'Five years will not be superfluous to transform a group of more than 20,000 employees across two continents.'

The new challenge

While five years might be needed to transform CGS, it was doubtful whether CGS's competitors and shareholders were willing to give the company that much time. As Serge Kampf met with the 35 top executives of CGS and Gemini Consulting on January 10th, 1995, to discuss the future strategy of the two companies, all participants felt the intense pressure to improve performance. In 1994 their combined European market share had fallen from 9 percent to 8.2 percent, according to Dataquest, while EDS and Andersen Consulting had been able to increase their slice of the market. The company's financial performance had not been very much better (see Table 1).

As a consequence, shareholders were becoming restless, seeking prompt and decisive action. One shareholder was of particular importance to CGS and Gemini, namely Daimler-Benz. Through its computer services subsidiary, Debis, Daimler-Benz had a 34 percent stake in the Sogeti holding company (see Figure 4 in Case 19(A)). Kampf had not exercised his right to buy back these shares in 1994 through another holding company, SKIP. Under these circumstances Daimler-Benz now had the option of buying a controlling stake of the Sogeti holding before January 1st, 1996. It did not seem as if Daimler-Benz was particularly interested in tying up even more capital in Sogeti, especially given Daimler's stretched financial resources after years of large-scale diversification. However, Daimler-Benz did feel that its 34 percent stake, that had cost it $585 million in 1991, brought it almost no influence in the management of the company. Given the worrying state of affairs at CGS, influence was something that Daimler-Benz definitely did wish to obtain.

As Kampf and the assembled managers discussed these pressures, a number of key questions continually surfaced. How could CGS and Gemini accelerate their integration processes? How could both companies use their internal diversity as an advantage instead of experience it as a disadvantage? How could CGS and Gemini add value to each other in search of a competitive edge? And what stance should the company take *vis-à-vis* Daimler-Benz? Before the meeting was over, these questions would have to be answered.

CASE 20

Kentucky Fried Chicken and the global fast-food industry

By Jeffrey A. Krug[1]

Kentucky Fried Chicken Corporation (KFC) was the world's largest chicken restaurant chain and third largest fast-food chain in 2001. KFC held more than 55 percent of the US market in terms of sales and operated more than 10,800 restaurants in 85 countries. KFC was one of the first fast-food chains to go international in the late 1950s and was one of the world's most recognizable brands. KFC's early international strategy was to grow its company and franchise restaurant base throughout the world. By early 2000, however, KFC had refocused its international strategy on several high growth markets, including Canada, Australia, the United Kingdom, China, Korea, Thailand, Puerto Rico, and Mexico. KFC planned to base much of its growth in these markets on company-owned restaurants, which gave KFC greater control over product quality, service, and restaurant cleanliness. In other international markets, KFC planned to grow primarily through franchises, which were operated by local business people who understood the local market better than KFC. Franchises enabled KFC to more rapidly expand into smaller countries that could only support a small number of restaurants. KFC planned to more aggressively expand its company-owned restaurants into other major international markets in Europe and Latin America in the future. Latin America was an appealing area for investment because of the size of its markets, its common language and culture, and its geographical proximity to the United States. Mexico was of particular interest because of the North American Free Trade Agreement (NAFTA), a free trade zone between Canada, the United States, and Mexico that went into effect in 1994. However, other fast-food chains such as McDonald's, Burger King and Wendy's were rapidly expanding into other countries in Latin America such as Venezuela, Brazil, Argentina, and Chile. KFC's task in Latin America was to select the proper countries for future investment and to devise an appropriate strategy for penetrating the Latin American market.

Company history

In 1952, fast-food franchising was still in its infancy when Harland Sanders began his travels across the United States to speak with prospective franchisees about his 'Colonel Sanders Recipe Kentucky Fried Chicken.' By 1960, 'Colonel' Sanders had granted KFC franchises to more than 200 take-home retail outlets and restaurants across the United States. He had also established a number of franchises in Canada. By 1963, the number of KFC franchises had risen to more than 300 and revenues topped $500 million. The Colonel celebrated his 74th birthday the following year and was eager to lessen the load of running the day-to-day operations of his business. Thus, he looked for potential buyers and sold his business to two Louisville businessmen – Jack Massey and John Young Brown Jr. – for $2 million. The Colonel stayed on as a public relations man and goodwill ambassador for the company. During the next five years, Massey and Brown concentrated on growing KFC's franchise system across the United States. In 1966, they took KFC public and the company was listed on the New York Stock Exchange. By the late 1960s, a strong foothold had been established in the United States, and Massey and Brown turned their attention to international markets. In 1969, a joint venture was signed with Mitsuoishi Shoji Kaisha Ltd in Japan and the rights to operate franchises in England were acquired. Subsidiaries were later established in Hong Kong, South Africa, Australia, New Zealand, and Mexico. By 1971, KFC had established 2,450 franchises and 600 company-owned restaurants in 48 countries.

[1]Source: Reprinted by permission of Jeffrey A. Krug.

Heublein, Inc.

In 1971, KFC entered into negotiations with Heublein, Inc. to discuss a possible merger. The decision to pursue a merger was partially driven by Brown's desire to pursue other interests that included a political career (Brown was elected Governor of Kentucky in 1977). Several months later, Hueblein acquired KFC. Heublein was in the business of producing vodka, mixed cocktails, dry gin, cordials, beer, and other alcoholic beverages; however, it had little experience in the restaurant business. Conflicts quickly erupted between Colonel Sanders and Heublein management. In particular, Colonel Sanders became increasingly distraught over quality control issues and restaurant cleanliness. By 1977, new restaurant openings had slowed to only twenty a year, few restaurants were being remodeled, and service quality had declined. To combat these problems, Heublein sent in a new management team to redirect KFC's strategy. A 'back-to-the-basics' strategy was implemented and new restaurant construction was halted until existing restaurants could be upgraded and operating problems eliminated. A program for remodeling existing restaurants was implemented, an emphasis was placed on cleanliness and service, marginal products were eliminated, and product consistency was re-established. This strategy enabled KFC to gain better control of its operations and it was soon again aggressively building new restaurants.

R.J. Reynolds Industries, Inc.

In 1982, R.J. Reynolds Industries, Inc. (RJR) acquired Heublein and merged it into a wholly owned subsidiary. The acquisition of Heublein was part of RJR's corporate strategy of diversifying into unrelated businesses such as energy, transportation, food, and restaurants to reduce its dependence on the tobacco industry. Tobacco had driven RJR's sales since its founding in North Carolina in 1875; however, sales of cigarettes and tobacco products, while profitable, were declining because of reduced consumption in the United States. Reduce consumption was primarily the result of an increased awareness among Americans of the negative health consequences of smoking.

RJR, however, had little more experience in the restaurant business than did Heublein when it acquired KFC eleven years earlier. In contrast to Heublein, which tried to actively manage KFC using its own managers, RJR allowed KFC to operate autonomously. RJR believed that KFC's executives were better qualified to operate the business than its own managers, therefore, KFC's top management team was left largely intact. By doing so, RJR avoided many of the operating problems that plagued Heublein during its ownership of KFC.

In 1985, RJR acquired Nabisco Corporation for $4.9 billion. The acquisition of Nabisco was an attempt to redefine RJR as a world leader in the consumer foods industry. Nabisco sold a variety of well-known cookies, crackers, and other grocery products, including Oreo cookies, Ritz crackers, Planters peanuts, Lifesavers, and Milk-Bone dog biscuits. RJR subsequently divested many of its non-consumer food businesses. It sold KFC to PepsiCo, Inc. one year later.

PepsiCo, Inc.

PepsiCo, Inc. was formed in 1965 with the merger of the Pepsi-Cola Co. and Frito-Lay Inc. The merger created one of the largest consumer products companies in the United States. Pepsi-Cola's traditional business was the sale of soft drink concentrates to licensed independent and company-owned bottlers that manufactured, sold, and distributed Pepsi-Cola soft drinks. Pepsi-Cola's best known trademarks were Pepsi-Cola, Diet Pepsi, and Mountain Dew. Frito-Lay manufactured and sold a variety of leading snack foods that included Lay's Potato Chips, Doritos Tortilla Chips, Tostitos Tortilla Chips, and Ruffles Potato Chips. Soon after the merger, PepsiCo initiated an aggressive acquisition program, buying a number of companies in areas unrelated to its major business such as North American Van Lines, Wilson Sporting Goods, and Lee Way Motor Freight. However, PepsiCo lacked the management skills required to operate these businesses and performance failed to live up to expectations. In 1984, chairman and chief executive officer Don Kendall restructured PepsiCo's operations. Businesses that did not support PepsiCo's consumer product orientation (including North American Van Lines, Wilson Sporting Goods, and Lee Way Motor Freight) were divested. PepsiCo's foreign bottling operations were then sold to local business people who better understood their country's culture and business practices. Last, PepsiCo was organized into three divisions: soft drinks, snack foods, and restaurants.

Restaurant business and acquisition of KFC

PepsiCo believed that the restaurant business complemented its consumer product orientation. The marketing of fast-food followed many of the same patterns as the marketing of soft drinks and snack foods. Pepsi-Cola soft drinks and fast-food products could be marketed together in the same television and radio segments, thereby providing higher returns for each advertising dollar. Restaurant chains also provided an additional outlet for the sale of Pepsi soft drinks. Thus, PepsiCo believed it could take advantage of numerous synergies by operating the three businesses under the same corporate umbrella. PepsiCo also believed that its management skills could be transferred among the three businesses. This practice was compatible with PepsiCo's policy of frequently moving managers among its business units as a means of developing future executives. PepsiCo first entered the restaurant business in 1977 when it acquired Pizza Hut. Taco Bell was acquired one year later. To complete its diversification into the restaurant industry, PepsiCo acquired KFC in 1986. The acquisition of KFC gave PepsiCo the leading market share in the chicken (KFC), pizza (Pizza Hut), and Mexican food (Taco Bell) segments of the fast-food industry.

Management

Following its acquisition of KFC, PepsiCo initiated sweeping changes. It announced that the franchise contract would be changed to give PepsiCo greater control over KFC franchises and to make it easier to close poorly performing restaurants. Staff at KFC was reduced in order to cut costs and many KFC managers were replaced with PepsiCo managers. Soon after the acquisition, KFC's new personnel manager, who had just relocated from PepsiCo's New York headquarters, was overheard in the KFC cafeteria saying 'There will be no more home grown tomatoes in this organization.'

Rumors spread quickly among KFC employees about their opportunities for advancement within KFC and PepsiCo. Harsh comments by PepsiCo managers about KFC, its people, and its traditions, several restructurings that led to layoffs throughout

KFC, the replacement of KFC managers with PepsiCo managers, and conflicts between KFC and PepsiCo's corporate cultures created a morale problem within KFC. KFC's culture was built largely on Colonel Sanders' laid-back approach to management. Employees enjoyed good job security and stability. A strong loyalty had been created among KFC employees over the years as a result of the Colonel's efforts to provide for his employees' benefits, pension, and other non-income needs. In addition, the Southern environment in Louisville resulted in a friendly, relaxed atmosphere at KFC's corporate offices. This corporate culture was left essentially unchanged during the Heublein and RJR years.

In contrast to KFC, PepsiCo's culture was characterized by a much stronger emphasis on performance. Top performers expected to move up through the ranks quickly. PepsiCo used its KFC, Pizza Hut, Taco Bell, Frito Lay, and Pepsi-Cola divisions as training grounds for its executives, rotating its best managers through the five divisions on average every two years. This practice created immense pressure on managers to demonstrate their management skills within short periods in order to maximize their potential for promotion. This practice also reinforced the feelings of KFC managers that they had few opportunities for promotion within the new company. One PepsiCo manager commented that 'You may have performed well last year, but if you don't perform well this year, you're gone, and there are 100 ambitious guys with Ivy League MBAs at PepsiCo's headquarters in New York who would love to have your job.' An unwanted effect of this performance driven culture was that employee loyalty was often lost and turnover was higher than in other companies.

Kyle Craig, president of KFC's US operations, commented on KFC's relationship with its corporate parent:

The KFC culture is an interesting one because it was dominated by a lot of KFC folks, many of whom have been around since the days of the Colonel. Many of those people were very intimidated by the PepsiCo culture, which is a very high performance, high accountability, highly driven culture. People were concerned about whether they would succeed in the new culture. Like many companies, we have had a couple of downsizings which further made people nervous. Today, there are fewer old KFC people around and I think to some degree people have seen that the PepsiCo culture can drive some pretty positive results. I also think the PepsiCo people who have worked with KFC have modified their cultural values somewhat and they can see that there were a lot of benefits in the old KFC culture.

PepsiCo pushes their companies to perform strongly, but whenever there is a slip in performance, it increases the culture gap between PepsiCo and KFC. I have been involved in two downsizings over which I have been the chief architect. They have been probably the two most gut-wrenching experiences of my career. Because you know you're dealing with peoples' lives and their families, these changes can be emotional if you care about the people in your organization. However, I do fundamentally believe that your first obligation is to the entire organization.

A second problem for PepsiCo was its poor relationship with KFC franchises. A month after becoming president and chief executive officer in 1989, John Cranor addressed KFC's franchises in Louisville in order to explain the details of the new franchise contract. This was the first contract change in thirteen years. It gave PepsiCo greater power to take over weak franchises, relocate restaurants, and make changes in existing restaurants. In addition, restaurants would no longer be protected from competition from new KFC units and PepsiCo would have the right to raise royalty fees on existing restaurants as contracts came up for renewal. After Cranor finished his address, there was an uproar among the attending franchisees who jumped to their feet to protest the changes. KFC's franchise association center sued PepsiCo over the new contract. The contract remained unresolved until 1996, when the most objectionable parts of the contract were removed by KFC's new president and CEO, David Novak. A new contract was ratified by KFC's franchisees in 1997.

PepsiCo's divestiture of KFC, Pizza Hut, and Taco Bell

PepsiCo's strategy of diversifying into three distinct but related markets – soft drinks, snack foods, and fast-food restaurants – created one of the world's largest consumer product companies and a portfolio of some of the world's most recognizable brands. Between 1990 and 1996, PepsiCo's sales grew at an annual rate of more than 10 percent, surpassing $31

billion in 1996. PepsiCo's growth, however, masked troubles in its fast-food businesses. Operating margins (profit after tax as a percent of sales) at Pepsi-Cola and Frito Lay averaged 12 and 17 percent between 1990 and 1996, respectively. During the same period, margins at KFC, Pizza Hut, and Taco Bell fell from an average of more than 8 percent in 1990 to a little more than 4 percent in 1996. Declining margins in the fast-food chains reflected increasing maturity in the US fast-food industry, more intense competition, and the aging of KFC and Pizza Hut's restaurant bases. As a result, PepsiCo's restaurant chains absorbed nearly one-half of PepsiCo's annual capital spending during the 1990s, but they generated less than one-third of PepsiCo's cash flows. This meant that cash had to be diverted from PepsiCo's soft drink and snack food businesses to its restaurant businesses. This reduced PepsiCo's corporate return on assets, made it more difficult to compete effectively with Coca-Cola, and hurt its stock price. In 1997, PepsiCo decided to spin off its restaurant businesses into a new company called Tricon Global Restaurants, Inc. The new company would be based in KFC's headquarters in Louisville, Kentucky (see Figure 1).

PepsiCo's objective was to reposition itself as a beverage and snack food company, strengthen its balance sheet, and create more consistent earning growth. PepsiCo received a one-time distribution from Tricon of $4.7 billion, $3.7 billion of which was used to pay off short-term debt. The balance was earmarked for stock repurchases. In 1998, PepsiCo acquired Tropicana Products, which controlled more than 40 percent of the US chilled orange juice market. Because of the divestiture of KFC, Pizza Hut, and Taco Bell, PepsiCo sales fell by $11.3 billion and assets fell by $7.0 billion between 1997 and 1999. Profitability, however, soared. Operating margins rose from 11 percent in 1997 to 16 percent in 1999. By focusing on high cash flow market leaders, PepsiCo raised profitability while decreasing its asset base.

Fast-Food Industry

According to the National Restaurant Association (NRA), food service sales increased by 5.4 percent to $258 billion in 1999. More than 800,000 restaurants and food outlets made up the US restaurant industry, which employed 11 million people. Sales were highest in the full-service, sit-down sector, which grew 7 percent to $121 billion. Fast-food sales

FIGURE 1 Tricon Global Restaurants Inc. organizational chart (2001)

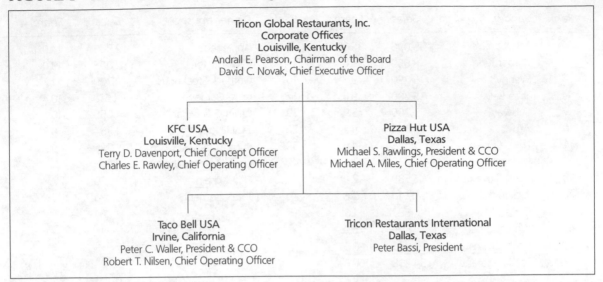

grew at a slower rate, rising about 5 percent to $110 billion. Fast-food sales surpassed the full-service sector during the mid-1990s; however, maturation of the fast-food sector and rising incomes among many Americans helped full-service restaurants again overtake fast-food as the largest sector in the restaurant industry.

Major fast-food segments

Eight major segments made up the fast-food segment of the restaurant industry: sandwich chains, pizza chains, family restaurants, grill buffet chains, dinner houses, chicken chains, non-dinner concepts, and other chains. Sales data for the leading restaurant chains in each segment are shown in Table 1. Most striking is the dominance of McDonald's, which had sales of more than $19 billion in 1999. McDonald's accounted for 15 percent of the sales of the nation's top 100 restaurant chains. To put McDonald's dominance into perspective, the second largest chain – Burger King – held less than 7 percent of the market. The full-service and fast-food segments were expected to make up about 65 percent of total food service industry sales in 2000.

Sandwich chains made up the largest segment of the fast-food market. McDonald's controlled 35 percent of the sandwich segment, while Burger King ran a distant second with a 16 percent market share. Despite continued success by some chains like McDonald's, Carl's Jr., Jack in the Box, Wendy's, and White Castle, other chains like Hardee's, Burger King, Taco Bell, and Checker's were struggling. McDonald's generated the greatest per store sales of about $1.5 million per year. The average US chain generated $800,000 in sales per store. Per store sales at Burger King remained flat and Hardee's per store sales declined by 10 percent. Franchisees at Burger King complained of leadership problems within the corporate parent (London-based Diageo PLC), an impending increase in royalties and franchise fees, and poor advertising. Hardee's corporate parent (CKE Enterprises), which also owned Carl's Jr. and Taco Bueno, planned to franchise many of its company-owned Hardee's restaurants and to allow the system to shrink as low performing units were closed. It also planned to refocus Hardee's strategy in the southeastern part of the United States, where brand loyalty remained strong.

Dinner houses made up the second largest and fastest growing fast-food segment. Sales of dinner houses increased by more than 13 percent during the year, surpassing the average increase of six percent among all fast-food chains. Much of the growth in dinner houses came from new unit construction, a marked contrast with other fast-food chains, which had already slowed US construction because of market saturation. Much of the new unit construction took place in new suburban markets and small towns. Applebee's and Red Lobster dominated the dinner house segment. Each chain generated more than $2 billion in sales in 1999. The fastest growing dinner houses, however, were chains generating less than $500 million in sales such as On The Border,

TABLE 1   Top 50 US fast-food restaurants (ranked by 1999 sales, $000s)

Rank	Sandwich chains	Sales	Share		Rank	Dinner houses	Sales	Share
1	McDonald's	19,006	35.0%		9	Applebee's	2,305	14.9%
2	Burger King	8,659	16.0		15	Red Lobster	2,005	13.0
3	Wendy's	5,250	9.7		16	Outback Steakhouse	1,729	11.2
4	Taco Bell	5,200	9.6		17	Olive Garden	1,610	10.4
7	Subway	3,200	5.9		19	Chili's Grill & Bar	1,555	10.1
10	Arby's	2,260	4.2		22	T.G.I. Friday's	1,364	8.8
11	Dairy Queen	2,145	4.0		30	Ruby Tuesday	920	5.9
12	Hardee's	2,139	3.9		49	Lone Star Steakhouse	468	3.0
18	Sonic Drive-In	1,589	2.9			Other chains	3,520	22.7
20	Jack in the Box	1,510	2.8			Total segment	15,476	100.0%
32	Carl's Jr.	887	1.6					
46	Whataburger	503	0.9					
	Other chains	1,890	3.5					
	Total segment	54,238	100.0%					

Rank	Pizza chains	Sales	Share		Rank	Chicken chains	Sales	Share
5	Pizza Hut	5,000	44.0%		6	KFC	4,378	55.2%
8	Domino's	2,560	22.5		28	Popeyes	986	12.7
21	Papa John's	1,426	12.6		29	Chick-fil-A	946	12.1
23	Little Caesars	1,200	10.6		34	Boston Market	855	11.0
50	Sbarro	466	4.1		38	Church's	705	9.0
	Other chains	703	6.2			Total segment	7,870	100.0%
	Total segment	11,355	100.0%					

Rank	Family restaurants	Sales	Share		Rank	Other dinner chains	Sales	Share
13	Denny's	2,079	22.7%		37	Long John Silver's	716	15.7%
24	Cracker Barrel	1,163	12.7		41	Walt Disney Co.	666	14.7
26	IHOP	1,077	11.8		43	Old Country Buffet	589	13.0
33	Shoney's	869	9.5		47	Luby's Cafeteria	502	11.0
35	Perkins	790	8.6		48	Captain D's Seafood	499	11.0
36	Bob Evans	727	8.0			Other chains	1,574	34.6
40	Friendly's	671	7.3			Total segment	4,546	100.0%
42	Waffle House	620	6.8					
	Other chains	1,144	12.6					
	Total segment	9,140	100.0%					

Rank	Grill buffet chains	Sales	Share		Rank	Non-dinner concepts	Sales	Share
31	Golden Corral	899	32.3%		14	Dunkin' Donuts	2,007	42.9%
39	Ryan's	704	25.3		25	7-Eleven	1,117	23.8
45	Ponderosa	560	20.1		27	Starbucks	987	21.1
	Other chains	621	22.3		44	Baskin-Robbins	573	12.2
	Total segment	2,784	100.0%			Total segment	4,684	100.0%

Source: *Nation's Restaurant News.*

The Cheesecake Factory, O'Charley's, Romano's Macaroni Grill, and Hooters. Each of these chains increased sales by more than 20 percent.

Increased growth among dinner houses came at the expense of slower growth among sandwich chains, pizza chains, grilled buffet chains, and family restaurants. 'Too many restaurants chasing the same customers' was responsible for much of the slower growth in these other fast-food categories. However, sales growth within each segment differed from one chain to another. In the family segment, for example, Friendly's and Shoney's were forced to shut down restaurants because of declining profits, but Steak 'n Shake and Cracker Barrel expanded their restaurant base by more than 10 percent. Within the pizza segment, Pizza Hut and Little Caesars closed underperforming restaurants, but Papa John's and Chuck E. Cheese's continued to aggressively grow their US restaurant bases. The hardest hit segment was grilled buffet chains, which generated the lowest increase in sales of less than 4 percent. Dinner houses, because of their more upscale atmosphere and higher ticket items, were better positioned to take advantage of the aging and wealthier US population, which increasingly demanded higher quality food in more upscale settings. Even dinner houses, however, faced the prospect of market saturation and increased competition in the near future.

Chicken segment

KFC continued to dominate the chicken segment with sales of $4.4 billion in 1999 (see Table 2). Its nearest competitor, Popcyes, ran a distant second with sales of $1.0 billion. KFC's leadership in the US market was so extensive that it had fewer opportunities to expand its US restaurant base, which was only growing at about 1 percent per year. Despite its dominance, KFC was slowly losing market share as other chicken chains increased sales at a faster rate. KFC's share of chicken segment sales fell from 71 percent in 1989 to less than 56 percent in 1999, a ten-year drop of 15 percent. During the same period, Chick-fil-A and Boston Market increased their combined market share by 17 percent (see Table 3). In the early 1990s, many industry analysts predicted that Boston Market would challenge KFC for market leadership. Boston Market was a new restaurant chain that emphasized roasted rather than fried chicken. It successfully created the image of an upscale deli offering healthy, 'home-style' alternatives to fried chicken and other fast food. In order to

distinguish itself from more traditional fast-food concepts, it refused to construct drive-thrus and it established most of its units outside of shopping malls rather than at major city intersections.

On the surface, it appeared that Boston Market and Chick-fil-A's market share gains were achieved primarily by taking customers away from KFC. Another look at the data, however, reveals that KFC's sales grew at a stable rate over the last ten years. Boston Market, rather than drawing customers away from KFC, appealed primarily to consumers who did not regularly frequent KFC and wanted healthy, non-fried chicken alternatives. Boston Market was able to expand the chicken segment beyond its traditional emphasis on fried chicken by offering non-fried chicken products that appealed to this new consumer group. After aggressively growing its restaurant base through 1997, however, Boston Market fell on hard times as it was unable to handle mounting debt problems. It soon entered bankruptcy proceedings. McDonald's acquired Boston Market in 2000. It had acquired Denver-based Chipotle Mexican Grill in 1998 and Columbus, Ohio-based Donatos Pizza in 1999. McDonald's hoped the acquisitions would help it expand its US restaurant base, since fewer opportunities existed to expand the McDonald's concept. Chick-fil-A's success came primarily from its aggressive shopping mall strategy that leveraged the trend toward large food courts in shopping malls. Despite gains by Boston Market and Chick-fil-A, KFC's customer base remained loyal to the KFC brand because of its unique taste. KFC also continued to dominate the dinner and takeout segments of the industry.

Popeyes replaced Boston Market as the second largest chicken chain in 1999. Popeyes and Church's had traditionally followed similar strategies – to compete head-on with other 'fried chicken' chains. Popeyes, however, was in the process of shifting its focus to Cajun fast-food, after it successfully launched its Louisiana Legends One-Pot Cajun Meals of jambalaya, gumbo, shrimp, and crawfish étoufée. Church's was determined to distinguish itself by placing a heavier emphasis on its 'made-from-scratch,' Southern image. In 1999, it broadened its menu to include buffalo chicken wings, macaroni and cheese, beans and rice, and collard greens. Chick-fil-A focused on pressure-cooked and char-grilled skinless chicken breast sandwiches, which it had traditionally sold to customers in sit-down restaurants in shopping malls. As more malls added

TABLE 2 Top US chicken chains

	1994	1995	1996	1997	1998	1999	Growth Rate
Sales ($ Millions)							
KFC	3,587	3,740	3,935	4,002	4,171	4,378	4%
Popeyes	614	660	677	720	843	986	10%
Chick-fil-A	451	502	570	643	767	946	16%
Boston Market	371	754	1,100	1,197	929	855	18%
Church's	465	501	526	574	620	705	9%
Total	5,488	6,157	6,808	7,136	7,330	7,870	7%
US restaurants							
KFC	5,081	5,103	5,078	5,092	5,105	5,231	1%
Popeyes	853	889	894	945	1,066	1,165	6%
Chick-fil-A	534	825	717	749	812	897	11%
Boston Market	534	829	1,087	1,166	889	858	10%
Church's	937	953	989	1,070	1,105	1,178	5%
Total	7,939	8,599	8,765	9,022	8,977	9,329	3%
Sales per unit ($ 000s)							
KFC	706	733	775	786	817	837	3%
Popeyes	720	742	757	762	790	847	3%
Chick-fil-A	845	608	795	859	945	1,055	5%
Boston Market	695	910	1,012	1,027	1,045	997	7%
Church's	496	526	532	536	561	598	4%
Total	691	716	777	791	816	844	4%

Source: Tricon Global Restaurants, Inc., *1999 Annual Report*; Chick-fil-A, corporate headquarters, Atlanta, Boston Chicken, Inc., *1999 Annual Report, Nation's Restaurant News*, 2000.

TABLE 3 Top US chicken chains – market share (%, based on annual sales)

	KFC	Popeyes	Chick-fil-A	Boston Market	Church's
1989	70.8	12.0	6.2	0.0	11.0
1990	71.3	12.3	6.6	0.0	9.8
1991	72.7	11.4	7.0	0.0	8.9
1992	71.5	11.4	7.5	0.9	8.7
1993	68.7	11.4	8.0	3.0	8.9
1994	65.4	11.2	8.2	6.7	8.5
1995	60.7	10.7	8.2	12.3	8.1
1996	57.8	9.9	8.4	16.2	7.7
1997	56.1	10.1	9.0	16.8	8.0
1998	56.9	11.5	10.5	12.7	8.4
1999	55.6	12.5	12.0	10.9	9.0
5-Year Change (%)	−9.8	1.3	3.8	4.2	0.5
10-Year Change (%)	−15.2	0.5	5.8	10.9	−2.0

food courts, however, malls became less enthusiastic about allocating separate store space to restaurants. Therefore, Chick-fil-A began to open smaller units in shopping mall food courts, hospitals, and colleges as a way of complementing its existing sit-down restaurants.

Demographic trends

A number of demographic and societal trends influenced the demand for food eaten outside of the home. During the last two decades, rising incomes, greater affluence among a greater percentage of American households, higher divorce rates, and the fact that people married later in life contributed to the rising number of single households and the demand for fast-food. More than 50 percent of women worked outside of the home, a dramatic increase since 1970. This number was expected to rise to 65 percent by 2010. Double-income households contributed to rising household incomes and increased the number of times families eat out. Less time to prepare meals inside the home added to this trend. Countering these trends, however, was a slower growth rate of the US population and an overpopulation of fast-food chains that increased consumer alternatives and intensified competition.

Baby Boomers aged 35 to 50 years of age constituted the largest consumer group for fast-food restaurants. Generation X'ers (ages 25 to 34) and the 'Mature' category (ages 51 to 64) made up the second and third largest groups. As consumers aged, they became less enamored with fast-food and were more likely to trade up to more expensive restaurants such as dinner houses and full-service restaurants. Sales of many Mexican restaurants, which were extremely popular during the 1980s, began to slow and Japanese, Indian, and Vietnamese restaurants became more fashionable. Ethnic foods in general were rising in popularity as US immigrants which constituted 10 percent of the US population in 2000, looked for establishments that sold their native foods.

The greatest concern for fast-food operators was the shortage of employees in the 16 to 24 age category. Most Americans in this age category had never experienced a recession or economic downturn. During the 1970s, Americans experienced double-digit inflation, high interest rates, and high unemployment, as well as two major oil crises that resulted in gas shortages. The US economy began to expand again during the early 1980s and continued to expand almost unabated through 2000. Unemployment was at its lowest point in more than two decades and many high school and college graduates, especially those in business and engineering, enjoyed a robust job market that made it more difficult for fast-food operators to find capable employees.

Labor costs made up about 30 percent of the fast-food chain's total costs, second only to food and beverage costs. Intense competition, however, made it difficult for restaurants to increase their prices sufficiently to cover the increased cost of labor. Consumers made decisions about where to eat partially based on price. Therefore, profit margins were squeezed. In order to reduce costs, restaurants eliminated low-margin food items, increased portion sizes, and improved product value to offset price increases. Restaurants also attempted to increase consumer traffic through discounting, by accepting coupons from competitors, by offering two-for-one specials, and by making limited-time offerings.

Costs could also be lowered and operations made more efficient by increasing the use of technology. According to the National Restaurant Association, most restaurant operators viewed computers as their number one tool for improving efficiencies. Computers could be used to improve labor scheduling, accounting, payroll, sales analysis, and inventory control. Most restaurant chains were also using point-of-sale systems that recorded the selected menu items and gave the cashier a breakdown of food items and the ticket price. These systems increased serving times and cashier accuracy. Other chains like McDonald's and Carl's Jr. converted to new food preparation systems that allowed them to prepare food more accurately and to prepare a great variety of sandwiches using the same process.

Higher costs and poor availability of prime real estate was another trend that negatively affected profitability. A plot of land suitable for a normal sized freestanding restaurant cost between $1.5 and $2.5 million. Leasing was a less costly alternative to buying. Nevertheless, market saturation decreased per store sales as newer units cannibalized sales from existing units. As a result, most food chains began to expand their US restaurant bases into alternative distribution channels in hospitals, airports, colleges, highway rest areas, gas stations, shopping mall food courts, and large retail stores or by dual branding with other fast-food concepts.

While the new media touted the benefits of low-fat diets during the 1970s and 1980s, consumer demand for beef began to increase again during the 1990s. The US Department of Agriculture estimated that Americans ate an average of 64 pounds of red meat each year. The growing demand for steak and prime rib helped fuel the growth in dinner houses that continued into 2000. According to the NRA, other food items that were growing in popularity included chicken, hot and spicy foods, smoothies, wraps and pitas, salads, and espresso and specialty coffees. Starbucks, the Seattle-based coffee retailer, capitalized on the popularity of specialty coffees by aggressively expanding its coffee shop concept into shopping malls, commercial buildings, and bookstores such as Barnes & Noble. Starbucks increased its store base by 28 percent in 1999, the greatest increase of any major restaurant chain.

International fast-food market

As the US market matured, many restaurants expanded into international markets as a strategy for growing sales. Foreign markets were attractive because of their large customer bases and comparatively little competition. McDonald's, for example, operated 46 restaurants for every one million US residents. Outside of the United States, it operated only one restaurant for every three million residents. McDonald's, KFC, Burger King, and Pizza Hut were the earliest and most aggressive chains to expand abroad beginning in the late 1950s. By 2001, at least 35 chains had expanded into at least one foreign country. McDonald's operated the largest number of restaurants (more than 12,000 US units and 14,000 foreign units) in the most countries (119). In comparison, Tricon Global Restaurants operated more than 20,000 US and close to 30,000 non-US KFC, Pizza Hut, and Taco Bell restaurants in 85 countries. Because of their early expansion abroad, McDonald's, KFC, Burger King, and Pizza Hut had all developed strong brand names and managerial expertise operating in international markets. This made them formidable competitors for fast-food chains investing abroad for the first time.

Table 4 lists the world's thirty-five largest restaurant chains in 2000. The global fast-food industry had a distinctly American flavor. Twenty-eight chains (80 percent of the total) were headquartered in the United States. US chains had the advantage of a large domestic market and ready acceptance by the American consumer. European firms had less success developing the fast-food concept, because Europeans were more inclined to frequent more mid-scale restaurants, where they spent several hours enjoying multi-course meals in a formal setting. KFC had trouble breaking into the German market during the 1970s and 1980s, because Germans were not accustomed to buying take-out or ordering food over the counter. McDonald's had greater success penetrating the German market, because it made a number of changes to its menu and operating procedures to appeal to German tastes. German beer, for example, was served in all of McDonald's restaurants in Germany. In France, McDonald's used a different sauce on its Big Mac sandwich that appealed to the French palate. KFC had more success in Asia and Latin America, where chicken was a traditional dish.

Aside from cultural factors, international business carried risks not present in the domestic market. Long distances between headquarters and foreign franchises made it more difficult to control the quality of individual restaurants. Large distances also caused servicing and support problems. Transportation and other resource costs were higher than in the domestic market. In addition, time, cultural, and language differences increased communication and operational problems. As a result, most restaurant chains limited expansion to their domestic market as long as they were able to achieve corporate profit and growth objectives. As companies gained greater expertise abroad, they turned to profitable international markets as a means of expanding restaurant bases and increasing sales, profits, and market share. Worldwide demand for fast-food was expected to grow rapidly during the next two decades, because rising per capita incomes worldwide made eating out more affordable for greater numbers of consumers. In addition, the development of the Internet was quickly breaking down communication and language barriers. Greater numbers of children were growing up with computers in their homes and schools. As a result, teenagers in Germany, Brazil, Japan, and the United States were equally likely to be able to converse about the Internet. The Internet also exposed some teenagers to the same companies and products, which enabled firms to more quickly develop global brands and a worldwide consumer base.

TABLE 4 The world's 35 largest fast-food chains (2000)

Rank	Franchise	Operational Headquarters	Parent Country	Countries
1.	McDonald's	Oakbrook, Illinois	U.S.A.	119
2.	Pizza Hut	Dallas, Texas	U.S.A.	88
3.	KFC	Louisville, Kentucky	U.S.A.	85
4.	Subway Sandwiches	Milford, Connecticut	U.S.A.	73
5.	TCBY	Little Rock, Arkansas	U.S.A.	68
6.	Domino's Pizza	Ann Arbor, Michigan	U.S.A.	64
7.	Burger King	Miami, Florida	U.K	58
8.	T.G.I. Friday's	Dallas, Texas	U.S.A.	53
9.	Baskin Robbins	Glendale, California	U.S.A.	52
10.	Dunkin' Donuts	Randolph, Massachusetts	U.S.A.	41
11.	Wendy's	Dublin, Ohio	U.S.A.	29
12.	Sizzler	Los Angeles, California	U.S.A.	22
13.	A&W Restaurants	Livonia, Michigan	U.S.A.	21
14.	Popeyes	Atlanta, Georgia	U.S.A.	21
15.	Chili's Grill & Bar	Dallas, Texas	U.S.A.	20
16.	Little Caesar's Pizza	Detroit, Michigan	U.S.A.	19
17.	Dairy Queen	Edina, Minnesota	U.S.A.	18
18.	Taco Bell	Irvine, California	U.S.A.	15
19.	Carl's Jr.	Anaheim, California	U.S.A.	15
20.	Outback Steakhouse	Tampa, Florida	U.S.A.	13
21.	Hardee's	Rocky Mt., North Carolina	U.S.A.	11
22.	Applebee's	Overland Park, Kansas	U.S.A.	10
23.	Arby's	Ft. Lauderdale, Florida	U.S.A.	10
24.	Church's Chicken	Atlanta, Georgia	U.S.A.	9
25.	PizzaExpress	London, England	U.K.	9
26.	Denny's	Spartanburg, South Carolina	U.S.A.	6
27.	Mos Burger	Tokyo	Japan	6
28.	Taco Time	Eugene, Oregon	U.S.A.	5
29.	Yoshinoya	Tokyo	Japan	5
30.	Loterria	Tokyo	Japan	4
31.	Orange Julius	Edina, Minnesota	U.S.A.	4
32.	Quick Restaurants	Brussels	Belgium	4
33.	Skylark	Tokyo	Japan	4
34.	IHOP	Glendale, California	U.S.A.	3
35.	Red Lobster	Orlando, Florida	U.S.A.	3

Kentucky Fried Chicken Corporation

Marketing strategy

Many of KFC's problems during the 1980s and 1990s surrounded its limited menu and inability to quickly bring new products to market. The popularity of its Original Recipe Chicken allowed KFC to expand through the 1980s without significant competition from other chicken chains. As a result, new product introductions were not a critical part of KFC's overall business strategy. KFC suffered one of its most serious setbacks in 1989 as it prepared to introduce a chicken sandwich to its menu. KFC still experimented with the chicken sandwich concept when McDonald's test-marketed its McChicken sandwich in the Louisville market. Shortly after, McDonald's rolled out the McChicken sandwich nationally. By beating KFC to the market, McDonald's developed strong consumer awareness for its sandwich. This significantly increased KFC's cost of developing awareness for its own sandwich, which KFC introduced several months later. KFC eventually withdrew the sandwich because of low sales. Today, about 95 percent of chicken sandwiches are sold through traditional hamburger chains.

By the late 1990s, KFC had refocused its strategy. The cornerstone of its new strategy was to increase sales in individual KFC restaurants by introducing a variety of new products and menu items that appealed to a greater number of customers. After extensive testing, KFC settled on three types of chicken: Original Recipe (pressure cooked), Extra Crispy (fried), and Tender Roast (roasted). It also rolled out a buffet that included some 30 dinner, salad, and dessert items. The buffet was particularly successful in rural locations and suburbs. It was less successful in urban locations because of space considerations. KFC then introduced its Colonel's Crispy Strips and five new chicken sandwiches to appeal to customers who preferred non chicken-on-the-bone products. KFC estimated that its Crispy Strips and chicken sandwiches accounted for $250,000 (30 percent) of KFC per restaurant sales, which averaged $837,000 per year. One of the problems with these items, however, was that they cannibalized sales of its chicken items; they were less expensive and easier to handle. The latter was especially appealing to drive-thru customers.

Overcapacity in the US market made it more difficult to justify the construction of new free-standing restaurants. Fewer sites were available for new construction and those sites, because of their increased cost, drove profit margins down. KFC initiated a three-pronged distribution strategy that helped beef up sales. First, it focused on building smaller restaurants in non-traditional outlets such as airports, shopping malls, universities, and hospitals. It also experimented with units with drive-thru and carry-out service only, snack shops in cafeterias, scaled-down outlets for supermarkets, and mobile units that could be transported to out-door concerts and fairs. Second, KFC continued to experiment with home delivery, which was already firmly established in the Louisville, Las Vegas, and Los Angeles markets. Third, KFC established '2-n-1' units that sold both KFC and Taco Bell (KFC/Taco Bell Express) or KFC and Pizza Hut (KFC/Pizza Hut Express) products. By early 2000, Tricon Global Restaurants was operating 700 multi-branded restaurants that simultaneously sold products from two of the three chains. It was also testing '3-n-1' units that sold all three brands.

Refranchising strategy

When Colonel Sanders began to expand the Kentucky Fried Chicken system in the late 1950s, he established KFC as a system of independent franchisees. This strategy helped the Colonel minimize his involvement in the operations of individual restaurants and to concentrate on the things he enjoyed the most – cooking, product development, and public relations. The franchise system resulted in a fiercely loyal and independent group of KFC franchises. When PepsiCo acquired KFC in 1986, a primary objective was to integrate KFC's operations into the PepsiCo system to take advantage of operational, financial, and marketing synergies. This strategy, however, led to greater interference by PepsiCo management in franchise menu offerings, financing, marketing, and operations. This interference was met by resistance by KFC franchises. PepsiCo attempted to decrease these problems by expanding KFC's restaurant base through company-owned restaurants rather than through franchising. It also used its strong cash flows to buy back unprofitable franchises. Many of these restaurants were converted into company-owned restaurants. By 1993, company-owned restaurants accounted for 40 percent of KFC's worldwide system. When PepsiCo spun off its restaurants into Tricon Global Restaurants in 1994, Tricon's new top management team began to sell company-owned restaurants back to franchises they believed knew the business better than they. By 2000, company-owned restaurants had fallen to about 27 percent of the total KFC system.

International operations

KFC's early experiences operating abroad put it in a strong position to take advantage of the growing trend toward international expansion. By 2001, more than 50 percent of KFC's restaurants were located outside of the United States. Historically, franchises made up a large portion of KFC's international restaurant base, because franchises were owned and operated by local entrepreneurs who had a deeper understanding of local language, culture, customs, law, financial markets, and marketing characteristics. Franchising was also a good strategy for establishing a presence in smaller countries like Grenada, Bermuda, and Suriname, which could only support a single restaurant. The costs of operating company-owned restaurants were prohibitively high in these smaller markets. Of the 5,595 KFC restaurants located outside of the United States in 1999, 69 percent were franchised, while 21 percent were company-owned and 10 percent were licensed restaurants or joint ventures. In larger markets such as Mexico, China, Canada, Australia, Puerto Rico, Korea, Thailand, and the United Kingdom, there was a stronger emphasis on building company-owned restaurants. By coordinating purchasing, recruiting and training, financing, and advertising, fixed costs could be spread over a larger number of restaurants. Increased bargaining power also enabled KFC to negotiate lower prices from suppliers. KFC was also better able to control product and service quality.

Latin American strategy

KFC operated 438 restaurants in Latin America in 2000 (Table 5). Its primary presence was in Mexico, Puerto Rico, and the Caribbean. KFC established subsidiaries in Mexico and Puerto Rico beginning in the late 1960s and expanded through company-owned restaurants. Franchises were used to penetrate other countries in the Caribbean whose market size prevented KFC from profitably operating company-owned restaurants. Subsidiaries were later established in the Virgin Islands, Venezuela, and Brazil. KFC had planned to expand into these regions using company-owned restaurants. The Venezuelan subsidiary, however, was later closed because of the high costs of operating the small subsidiary. KFC had opened eight restaurants in Brazil but decided to close them in 1999 because it lacked the cash flow needed to support an expansion program in that market. Franchises were opened in other markets that had good growth potential such as Chile, Ecuador, Peru, and Colombia.

KFC's early entry into Latin America gave it a leadership position over McDonald's in Mexico and the Caribbean. It also had an edge in Ecuador and Peru. KFC's Latin America strategy represented a classic internationalization strategy. It first expanded into Mexico and Puerto Rico because of their geographic proximity, as well as political and economic ties, to the United States. From these regions, KFC expanded its franchise system throughout the Caribbean, gradually moving away from its US base as its experience in Latin America grew. Only after it had established a leadership position in Mexico and the Caribbean did it venture into South America. McDonald's pursued a different strategy. It was late to expand into the region. Despite a rapid restaurant construction program in Mexico during the 1990s, McDonald's still lagged behind KFC. Therefore, McDonald's initiated a first mover strategy in Brazil and Argentina, large markets where KFC had no presence. By early 2000, more than 63 percent of McDonald's restaurants in Latin America were located in the two countries. Wendy's pursued a slightly different strategy. It first expanded into Puerto Rico, the Caribbean Islands, and Central America because of their geographical proximity to the United States. The shorter distance to the United States made these restaurants easier to manage. Wendy's late entry into Latin America, however, made it more difficult to penetrate the Mexican market, where KFC, McDonald's, and Burger King had already established a strong presence. Wendy's announced plans to build 100 Wendy's restaurants in Mexico by 2010; however, its primary objective was to establish strong positions in Venezuela and Argentina, where most US fast-food chains had not yet been established.

Country risk assessment in Latin America

Latin America comprised some 50 countries, island nations, and principalities that were settled primarily by the Spanish, Portuguese, French, Dutch, and British during the 1500s and 1600s. Spanish was spoken in most countries, the most notable exception being Brazil, whose official language was Portuguese. Catholicism was the major religion, though Methodist missionaries successfully exported Protestantism into many regions of Latin America in the 1800s, most notably on the coast of Brazil. Despite commonalities in language, religion, and history, however, political and economic policies often differed significantly from one country to another. Historically, frequent changes in governments and economic instability increased the uncertainty of doing business in the region.

TABLE 5   Latin American restaurant count – McDonald's, Burger King, KFC, and Wendy's

	McDonald's	Burger King	KFC	Wendy's
Mexico	170	108	157	7
Puerto Rico	121	148	67	30
Caribbean Islands	59	57	91	23
Central America	80	85	26	26
Subtotal	430	398	341	86
% Total	24	80	78	60
Colombia	21	0	19	3
Ecuador	7	12	18	0
Peru	10	10	17	0
Venezuela	83	13	6	33
Other Andean	6	7	0	0
Andean Region	127	42	60	36
% Total	7	9	14	25
Argentina	205	25	0	21
Brazil	921	0	8	0
Chile	61	25	29	0
Paraguay + Uruguay	32	5	0	0
Southern Cone	1,219	55	37	21
% Total	69	11	8	15
Latin America	1,776	495	438	143
% Total	100	100	100	100

Note: Restaurant data obtained from corporate offices at McDonald's Corp (as of 12/99), Burger King Corp (as of 6/30/00), Tricon Global Restaurants (as of 6/30/00) and Wendy's International (as of 5/15/00).

Most US and Canadian companies were beginning to realize, however, that they could not overlook the region. Geographic proximity made communications and travel easier and quicker between countries and the North American Trade Agreement (NAFTA) had eliminated tariffs on goods shipped between Canada, Mexico, and the United States. A customs union agreement signed in 1991 (Mercosur) between Argentina, Paraguay, Uruguay, and Brazil eliminated tariffs on trade among those four countries. Many countries such as Chile and Argentina had also established free trade policies that were beginning to stimulate growth. These factors made Latin America an attractive location for investment. The primary task for companies investing in the region was to accurately assess the different risks of doing business in Latin America and to select the proper countries for investment.

Miller (1992) developed a framework for analyzing country risk that was a useful tool for analyzing the attractiveness of a country for future investment. He argued that firms must examine country, industry, and firm factors in order to fully assess country risk. *Country factors* addressed the risks associated with changes in the country's political and economic environment that potentially affected the firm's ability to conduct business. They included the following:

1 Political risk (e.g., war, revolution, changes in government, price controls, tariffs and other trade restrictions, appropriations of assets, government regulations, and restrictions on the repatriation of profits).

2 Economic risk (e.g., inflation, high interest rates, foreign exchange rate volatility, balance of trade movements, social unrest, riots, and terrorism).

3 Natural risk (e.g., rainfall, hurricanes, earthquakes, and volcanic activity).

Industry factors addressed changes in the structure of the industry that inhibited the firm's ability to successfully compete in its industry. They included the following:

1 Supplier risk (e.g. changes in quality, shifts in supply, and changes in supplier power).

2 Product market risk (e.g., changes in consumer tastes and availability of substitute products).

3 Competitive risk (e.g., rivalry among competitors, new market entrants, and new product innovations).

Firm factors examined the firm's ability to control its internal operations. They included the following:

1 Labor risk (e.g., labor unrest, absenteeism, employee turnover, and labor strikes).

2 Supplier risk (e.g., raw material shortages and unpredictable price changes).

3 Trade secret risk (e.g., protection of trade secrets and intangible assets).

4 Credit risk (e.g., problems collecting receivables).

5 Behavioral risk (e.g., control over franchise operations, product quality and consistency, service quality, and restaurant cleanliness).

Many US companies believed that Mexico was an attractive country for investment. Its population of 103 million was more than one-third as large as the US population and represented a large market for US goods and services. In comparison, Canada's population of 31 million was only one-third as large as Mexico's. Mexico's close proximity to the United States meant that transportation costs between the United States and Mexico were significantly lower than to Europe or Asia. This increased the competitiveness of US goods in comparison with European and Asian goods, which had to be transported to Mexico across the Atlantic or Pacific Ocean at significantly greater cost. The United States was in fact Mexico's largest trading partner. More than 80 percent of Mexico's total trade was with the United States. Many US firms also invested in Mexico to take advantage of lower wage rates. By producing goods in Mexico, US goods could be shipped back to the United States for sale or shipped to third markets at lower cost.

Despite the advantages of doing business in Mexico, Mexico only accounted for about 20 percent of the United States' total trade. Beginning in the early 1900s, the percentage of total US exports going to Latin America has declined as exports to other regions of the world such as Canada and Asia have increased. The growth in economic wealth and consumer demand in Canada and Asia has generally outpaced Mexico for most of the last century. However, the volume of trade between the United States and Mexico has increased significantly since the North American Trade Agreement went into effect in 1994.

A commonly held perception among many Americans was that Japan was the United States' largest trading partner. In reality, Canada was the United States' largest trading partner by a wide margin. Canada bought more than 22 percent ($154 billion) of all US exports in 1998; Japan bought less than 9 percent ($58 billion). Canada accounted for about 19 percent of all goods imported into the United States ($178 billion); Japan accounted for 13 percent ($125 billion). The perception that Japan was the largest US trading partner resulted primarily from extensive media coverage of the long-running US trade deficit with Japan. Less known to many Americans was the fact that the United States was running a balance of trade deficit with China that almost equaled the deficit with Japan. China was positioned to welcome the United States' largest trading partner in Asia within the next few years.

The lack of US investment in and trade with Mexico during the 20th century was mainly the result of Mexico's long history of restricting foreign trade and investment. The Institutional Revolutionary Party (PRI), which came to power in Mexico during the 1920s, had a history of promoting protectionist economic policies to shield Mexico's economy from foreign competition. Many industries were government owned or controlled and many Mexican companies focused on producing goods for the domestic market without much attention to building exports. High tariffs and other trade barriers restricted imports into Mexico and foreign ownership of assets in Mexico was largely prohibited or heavily restricted.

A dictatorial and entrenched government bureaucracy, corrupt labor unions, and a long tradition of anti-Americanism among government officials and intellectuals also reduced the motivation of US firms to invest in Mexico. The nationalization of Mexico's banks in 1982 led to higher real interest rates and lower investor confidence. This forced the Mexican government to battle high inflation, high interest rates, labor unrest, and lower consumer purchasing power during the early to mid-1980s. Investor confidence in Mexico, however, improved after 1988, when Carlos Salinas de Gortari was elected president. Salinas embarked on an ambitious restructuring of the Mexican economy. He initiated policies to strengthen the free market components of the economy, lowered top marginal tax rates and eliminated many restrictions on foreign investment.

The privatization of government owned companies came to symbolize the restructuring of Mexico's economy. In 1990, legislation was passed to privatize all government run banks. By the end of 1992, more than 800 to 1,200 government-owned companies had been sold, including Mexicana and AeroMexico, the two largest airline companies in Mexico, and Mexico's 18 major banks. More than 350 companies, however, remained under government ownership. These represented a significant portion of the assets owned by the state at the start of 1988. Therefore, the sale of government-owned companies in terms of asset value was still modest. A large portion of the remaining government-owned assets was controlled by government-run companies in certain strategic industries such as steel, electricity, and petroleum. These industries had long been protected by government ownership. However, President Salinas opened up the electricity sector to independent power producers in 1993 and Petroleos Mexicanos (Pemex), the state-run petrochemical monopoly, initiated a program to sell off many of its non-strategic assets to private and foreign buyers.

North American Free Trade Agreement (NAFTA)

Prior to 1989, Mexico levied high tariffs on most imported goods. In addition, many other goods were subjected to quotas, licensing requirements, and other non-tariff trade barriers. In 1986, Mexico joined the General Agreement on Tariffs and Trade (GATT), a world trade organization designed to eliminate barriers to trade among member nations. As a member of GATT, Mexico was required to apply its system of tariffs to all member nations equally. Mexico subsequently dropped tariff rates on a variety of imported goods. In addition, import license requirements were dropped for all but 300 imported items. During President Salinas's administration, tariffs were reduced from an average of 100 percent on most items to an average of 11 percent.

On January 1, 1994, the North American Free Trade Agreement (NAFTA) went into effect. The passage of NAFTA created a trading bloc with a larger population and gross domestic product than the European Union. All tariffs on goods traded between the United States, Canada, and Mexico were eventually phased out. NAFTA was expected to benefit Mexican exporters, since reduced tariffs made their goods more competitive compared to goods exported to the United States from other countries. In 1995, one year after NAFTA went into effect, Mexico posted its first balance of trade surplus in six years. A large part of this surplus was attributed to greater exports to the United States.

Despite its supporters, NAFTA was strongly opposed by farmers and unskilled workers. The day after NAFTA went into effect, rebels rioted in the southern Mexican province of Chiapas on the Guatemalan border. After four days of fighting, Mexican troops drove the rebels out of several towns the rebels had earlier seized. Around 150 people – mostly rebels – were killed. Later in the year, 30 to 40 masked men attacked a McDonald's restaurant in the tourist section of Mexico City. The men threw cash registers to the floor, smashed windows, overturned tables, and spray-painted 'No to Fascism' and 'Yankee Go Home' on the walls. Such protests continued through 2000, when Mexican farmers dumped gallons of spoiled milk in the streets to protest low tariffs on imported farm products. Farmers also protested the Mexican government's practice of allowing imports of milk powder, corn, and wheat from the United States and Canada above the quotas established as part of the NAFTA agreement. The continued opposition of Mexican farmers, unskilled workers, and nationalists posed a constant threat to the stability of the NAFTA agreement.

Another problem was Mexico's failure to reduce restrictions on US and Canadian investment in a timely fashion. Many US firms experienced problems getting required approvals for new ventures from the Mexican government. A good example was United Parcel Service (UPS), which sought government approval to use large trucks for deliveries in Mexico. Approvals were delayed, forcing UPS to use smaller trucks. This gave UPS a competitive disadvantage vis-à-vis Mexican companies. In many cases, UPS was forced to subcontract delivery work to Mexican companies that were allowed to use larger, more cost-efficient trucks. Other US companies such as Bell Atlantic and TRW faced similar problems. TRW, which signed a joint venture agreement with a Mexican partner, had to wait 15 months longer than expected before the Mexican government released rules on how it could receive credit data from banks. TRW claimed that the Mexican government had slowed the approval process to placate several large Mexican banks.

Foreign exchange and the Mexican peso crisis of 1995

Between 1982 and 1991, a two-tiered exchange rate system was in force in Mexico. The system consisted of a controlled rate and a free market rate. A controlled rate was used for imports, foreign debt payments, and conversion of export proceeds. An estimated 70 percent of all foreign transactions were covered by the controlled rate. A free market rate was used for other transactions. In 1989, President Salinas instituted a policy of allowing the peso to depreciate by one peso per day against the dollar. In 1991, the controlled rate was abolished and replaced with an official free rate. The peso was thereafter allowed to depreciate by 0.20 pesos per day against the dollar. When Ernesto Zedillo became Mexico's president in December 1994, one of his objectives was to continue the stability of prices, wages, and exchange rates achieved by ex-president Carlos Salinas during his tenure as president. This stability, however, was achieved primarily on the basis of price, wage, and foreign exchange controls. While giving the appearance of stability, an over-valued peso continued to encourage imports that exacer-

bated Mexico's balance of trade deficit. At the same time, Mexican exports became less competitive on world markets.

Anticipating a devaluation of the peso, investors began to move capital into US dollar investments. On December 19, 1994, Zedillo announced that the peso would be allowed to depreciate by an additional 15 percent per year against the dollar. The maximum allowable depreciation at the time was 4 percent per year. Within two days, continued pressure on the peso forced Zedillo to allow the peso to float freely against the dollar. By mid-January 1995, the peso had lost 35 percent of its value against the dollar and the Mexican stock market plunged 20 percent. By the end of the year, the peso had depreciated from 3.1 pesos per dollar to 7.6 pesos per dollar. In order to thwart a possible default by Mexico, the US government, International Monetary Fund, and World Bank pledged $25 billion in emergency loans. Shortly thereafter, Zedillo announced an emergency economic package called the 'pacto' that included reduced government spending, increased sales of government-run businesses, and a freeze on wage increases.

By 2000, there were signs that Mexico's economy had stabilized. Gross domestic product was increasing at an average rate of 24 percent and unemployment was low at slightly more than 2 percent (see Table 6). Interest rates and inflation were also low by historical standards (24 and 17 percent in 1999), far below their highs of 61 and 35 percent in 1995. Interest rates and inflation were, however, still considerably higher than in the United States. Higher

TABLE 6 Mexico: Selected economic data (annual growth rates)

	1994	1995	1996	1997	1998	1999	Annual Growth Rate
Population (millions)	93	91	97	96	100	102	2%
Gross domestic product	13%	29%	36%	27%	19%	21%	24%
Money supply (M1)	4%	5%	43%	33%	19%	26%	22%
Inflation (CPI)	7%	35%	34%	21%	16%	17%	22%
Money market rate	17%	61%	34%	22%	27%	24%	31%
Peso devaluation against $US	71%	44%	3%	3%	22%	−4%	23%
Unemployment rate	3.6%	4.7%	3.7%	2.6%	2.3%	n/a	

Source: International Monetary Fund; *International Financial Statistics*, 2000

relative interest rates and inflation put continued pressure on the peso to depreciate against the dollar. This led to higher import prices and contributed to inflation.

A number of social concerns also plagued President Zedillo's government. These included a lack of success in controlling organized crime surrounding the drug trade, high profile political murders (e.g., the murder of a Roman Catholic Cardinal at the Guadalajara airport in 1993), and a high poverty rate, particularly in southern Mexico. These social problems, and voters' disenchantment over allegations of continued political corruption, led to strong opposition to the ruling PRI. In 2000, the PRI lost its first presidential election in five decades when Vicente Fox, leader of the opposition National Action Party, was elected president. Fox took office on December 1, 2000.

Risks and opportunities

KFC faced a variety of risks and opportunities in Mexico. It had eliminated all of its franchises in Mexico and operated only company-owned restaurants that enabled it to better control quality, service, and restaurant cleanliness. Company-owned restaurants, however, required more capital than franchises. This meant that KFC would not be able to expand as quickly as it could using a franchised restaurant base. KFC still had the largest number of restaurants in Mexico of any fast-food chain. However, McDonald's was growing its restaurant base rapidly and was beating KFC in terms of sales. KFC's other major competitors included Burger King and El Pollo Loco ('The Crazy Chicken'). Wendy's had also announced plans to open 100 restaurants in Mexico by 2010, though Wendy's emphasis in Latin America continued to be in Venezuela and Argentina. Another threat came from Habib's, Brazil's second largest fast-food chain, which opened its first restaurant in Mexico in 2000. Habib's served traditional Middle Eastern dishes such as falafel, hummus, kafka, and tabbouleh at prices below KFC or McDonald's. It planned to open 400 units in Mexico between 2000 and 2005.

Another concern was the long-term value of the peso, which had depreciated at an average annual rate of 23 percent against the US dollar since NAFTA went into effect. This translation risk lowered Tricon Global's reported profits when peso profits were translated into dollars. It also damaged

Tricon Global's stock price. From an operational point of view, however, KFC's Mexico operations were largely insulated from currency fluctuations, because it supplied most of its needs using Mexican sources. KFC purchased chicken primarily from Tyson Foods, which operated two chicken processing plants in Mexico. Tyson was also the primary supplier of chicken to McDonald's, Burger King, Applebee's and Wal-Mart in Mexico.

KFC faced difficult decisions surrounding the design and implementation of an effective Latin American strategy over the next twenty years. It wanted to sustain its leadership position in Mexico and the Caribbean, but it also hoped to strengthen its position in other regions in South America. Limited resources and cash flow, however, limited KFC's ability to aggressively expand in all countries simultaneously. What should KFC's Latin American strategy be? KFC's strategy in 2001 focused on sustaining its position in Mexico and the Caribbean, but postponed plans to expand into other large markets like Venezuela, Brazil, and Argentina. This strategy carried significant risk, since McDonald's and Wendy's were already building first mover advantages there. A second strategy was to invest more capital in these large markets to challenge existing competitors, but such a strategy might risk KFC's leadership position in Mexico and the Caribbean. Another strategy was to focus on building a franchise base throughout Latin America, in order to build KFC's brand image and prevent competitors from establishing first mover advantages. This strategy, however, was less effective in building a significant market share in individual countries, since market leadership often required a country subsidiary that actively managed both franchised and company owned restaurants and took advantage of synergies in purchasing, operations, and advertising. A country subsidiary could only be justified if KFC had a large restaurant base in the targeted country. KFC's Latin American strategy required considerable analysis and thought about how to most efficiently use its resources. It also required an in-depth analysis of country risk and selection of the right country portfolio.

References

General references

Direction of Trade Statistics, International Monetary Fund, Washington, DC.

International Financial Statistics, International Monetary Fund, Washington, DC.

Miller, Kent D., 'A Framework for Integrated Risk Management in International Business,' Journal of International Business Studies, vol. 23, no. 2, pages 311–331, 1992.

Standard & Poor's Industry Surveys, Standard & Poor's Corporation, New York, NY.

Quickservice Restaurant Trends, National Restaurant Association, Washington, DC.

Periodicals

FIU Hospitality Review, FIU Hospitality Review, Inc., Miami, FL.

IFMA Word, International Foodservice Manufacturers Association, Chicago, IL.

Independent Restaurant, EIP, Madison, WI.

Journal of Nutrition in Recipe & Menu Development, Food Product Press, Binghamton, NY.

Nation's Restaurant News, Lebhar-Friedman, Inc., New York, NY (http://www.nrn.com).

Restaurant Business, Bill Communications Inc., New York, NY (http://www.restaurant.biz.com).

Restaurants & Institutions, Cahners Publishing Co., New York, NY (http://www.restaurantsandinstitutions.com).

Restaurants USA, National Restaurant Association, Washington, DC (http://www.restaurant.org).

Associations

National Restaurant Association, 1200 17th St. NW, Washington, D.C. 20036-3097, (202) 331-5900, http://www.restaurant.org.

International Franchise Association, 1350 New York Ave. NW, Suite 900, Washington, DC. 20005-4709, (202) 628-8000, http://www.franchise.org.

Books

Dave's Way: A New Approach to Old-Fashioned Success, by R. David Thomas (founder of Wendy's), Berkley Publishing Group, 1992.

Golden Arches East: McDonald's in East Asia, by James L. Watson (ed.), Stanford University Press, Palo Alto, CA, 1998.

Grinding It Out: The Making of McDonald's, by Ray Kroc (founder of McDonald's) and Robert Anderson, St. Martins, 1990.

I'd Like the World to Buy a Coke: The Life and Leadership of Roberto Goizueta, by David Greisling, John Wiley & Sons, 1999.

It's Easier to Succeed than to Fail, by S. Truett Cathy (founder of Chick-fil-A), Oliver-Nelson Books, Nashville, TN, 1989.

Kentucky Fried Chicken Japan Ltd.: International Competitive Benchmarks and Financial Gap Analysis, by Icon Group Ltd., 2000.

Kentucky Fried Chicken Japan Ltd.: Labor Productivity Benchmarks and International Gap Analysis, by Icon Group Ltd., 2000.

McDonaldization Revisited, by Mark Alfino, John S. Caputo, and Robin Wynyard (eds.), Greenwood Publishing Group, 1998.

McDonald's Behind the Arches, by John F. Love, Bantam Books, 1986, 1995, 1999.

Selling 'Em by the Sack: White Castle and the Creation of American Food, by David Gerard Hogan, New York University Press, 1999.

Taco Titan: The Glen Bell Story, by Debra Lee Baldwin, Summit Publishing Group, 1999.

The Globalization Reader, by Frank Lechner and John Boli (eds.), Blackwell Publishing, 2000.

The McDonald's Thesis: Explorations and Extensions, by George Ritzer, Sage Publications, 1998.

The McDonaldization of Society: An Investigation into the Changing Character of Contemporary Social Life, by George Ritzer, Pine Forge Press, 1995.

Web pages

Boston Market Corporation (http:www.bostonmarket.com).

Burger King Corporation (http:www.burgerking.com).

Chick-fil-A (http://www.chickfila.com).

Church's Chicken (http://www.churchs.com).

McDonald's Corporation (http://www.mcdonalds.com).

Popeyes Chicken & Biscuits (http://www.popeyes.com).

Tricon Global Restaurants, Inc. (http://www.triconglobal.com).

Wendy's International Incorporated (http://www.wendys.com).

Even a clown can do it: Cirque du Soleil recreates live entertainment

By Matt Williamson, W. Chan Kim, Renée Mauborgne and Ben M. Bensaou[1]

Cirque du Soleil began with a very simple dream. A group of young entertainers got together to amuse audiences, see the world, and have fun doing it. Every year, the audience becomes bigger, we continue to discover new places and ideas and we're still having fun. We also dream of suffusing our new projects with the energy and inspiration, that are the essence of our shows. And we want to help young people express their dreams . . . and make them come true.

(Guy Laliberté, President and Chief Executive Officer, Cirque du Soleil)

In 1984, a determined Guy Laliberté set out to reinvent the circus industry. This was no small challenge given that the very core of the product was delivering spectacles and surprise on a daily basis. As with many other industries, this one had its share of white elephants and dogs. It was rife with promoters, hustlers and fire-breathers of all sorts, but had its impassive iron-men as well. An amalgam of both strong traditions and quest for novelty, it was a circus.

From its original incarnation as a troupe called 'Le Club des Hauts Talons', so named because of its host of stilt-walkers, Laliberté's Cirque du Soleil rapidly evolved from a pack of under-employed kids into one of the largest Canadian cultural exports. Almost 30 million people saw one of the troupe's productions between 1984 and 2000. In that last year alone, approximately 50,000 people took in the Soleil experience, as productions appeared in 120 cities around the world. From a production which put on its show in an 800 people tent purchased with an Arts grant from the Quebec government, the show now boasts three separate traveling productions housed in 2,500 people tents and four permanent shows in purpose built theaters in Orlando, Biloxi (Mississippi) and Las Vegas.[2]

The origins of Cirque du Soleil

Cirque du Soleil was created in 1984 by a group of young street performers who had pooled their talents and formed the 'Club des Talons Hauts' two years earlier. Initially formed as part of the celebration of the 450th anniversary of Jacques Cartier's arrival in Quebec, the brainchild of Guy Laliberté was based on a totally new concept: a mix of the circus arts and street entertainment, featuring wild costumes, staged under 'magical' lighting and set to original music. As such, Cirque du Soleil was part of a movement that many call the New American Circus.

Cirque du Soleil scrambled the existing traditions of the circus and the performing arts, and reinvented the wheel. The resulting dream world, populated by operatic, choreographed and acrobatic sprites is like no other place on earth; a reflection of the arts which inspired it. Sharing elements of dance, circus and opera, Soleil competes with them all but remains utterly unique. Nor has Soleil failed to draw attention to its novel position as a non-circus; early shows, *We Reinvent the Circus* and *Nouvelle Expérience* forewarned the audience that the show would be unlike anything they had ever seen before, under the Big Top or anywhere else.

It was not, however, the first to take this new route. Paul Binder and Michael Christiansen founders of the Big Apple Circus in 1979, and Larry Pisoni, founder of the Pickle Family Circus, brought the more classical one-ring circus back to America after over a hundred years, when even the smallest circus spread their shows over three rings.[3] Also in 1979, Guy Caron established the circus school that

---

[1]Source: © 2002 INSEAD-EAC, Fontainebleau, France. All rights reserved.
[2]Cirque du Soleil is based in Montreal, Quebec and runs shows around the world. Nevertheless, the majority of its performances take place in the United States.
[3]Ernest Albrecht, *The New American Circus* (Gainesville, FL: University Press of Florida), p2.

would eventually become the Ecole Nationale du Cirque and train a significant number of the original performers in Cirque du Soleil's initial thirteen-week tour. Each of these key players were outsiders in the tradition bound world of the circus, having roots more akin to the hippie counter-culture than anything else. In contrast to the consciously intimate scale and deference to skill and artistry above commercialism of the Pickle Family Circus and Big Apple Circus, Cirque du Soleil has never hesitated to make theirs a commercial enterprise.

With a US$1.7 million contract from the provincial government of Quebec, the show traveled the province and produced some powerful fans that it would later need. Ending the first season with a surplus of US$50,000, Laliberté decided to promote his new show, and invested heavily in a new tent and other equipment. Ending 1985 to critical acclaim, Cirque du Soleil was nevertheless US$750,000 in debt from its investments in equipment despite extending the run several cities beyond the initial route. Rene Levesque, then the Prime Minister of Quebec, and an avid fan from the 1984 opening show, saw the cultural value in supporting the enterprise and refinanced the debt.[4]

The troupe made another huge gamble in spending all its remaining funds after the 1986 season to join the Los Angeles Arts festival in 1987, its first serious foray outside of the Quebec region. This time the gamble paid off. Cirque du Soleil was a big success and almost immediately sold out its later shows. Patronage of celebrities like Steve Martin, David Bowie, Madonna, Elton John and Francis Ford Coppola helped the troupe seal its identity as a sophisticated and new form of entertainment.

The content and style of Cirque du Soleil

Cirque du Soleil has a unique approach to developing its shows, setting it apart from most other circuses. 'A Cirque du Soleil performance is like no other circus ever seen in the United States or anywhere else. It is relentless in its drive to be nothing short of spellbinding.' A thematic line, though frequently rather vague and intentionally so, is mani-

fested throughout the show in costumes, music, the types of acts performed. While not rising to the level of storylines, the themes bring harmony and an intellectual component to the show, without introducing limits on the potential for acts. Rather than taking acts as they exist and compiling them into a show, Guy Caron, Franco Dragone and the creative teams at Cirque du Soleil who have followed them, begin with the theme, such as Saltimbanco or Quidam and build a show to suit. The result is a seamless entertainment experience for the audience rather than a punctuated series of acts. Moreover, unlike traditional circus, the company has multiple productions where shows have distinctive themes that allow the possibility for the same buyer to visit Le Cirque multiple times.

In creating the performance that rocked the Los Angeles Arts Festival, Caron took his team on a weeklong retreat to focus simply on developing the theme and how it would be conveyed through each component of the show. That theme rather than simply being a new edition of the circus, each time is a performance and an experience in itself. It serves as the audience's guarantee for a high quality and exotic experience.

The most important element of this thematic drive, and the starting point from which the creative team begins, is an original score. Since the inception of Cirque du Soleil, Rene Dupere has taken the creative director's expression of the theme and transformed it into a full-length original score. The music for a Soleil show drives the selection of the visual performance, lighting and timing of the acts, rather than the reverse.[5] Says Caron, 'In the movement you see the music and in the music you hear the movement.'[6]

In more than just the theme sequencing of production, Cirque du Soleil represents a true mixture of performance arts. It is not quite a circus and not quite an opera or theater either, but takes elements from them all. While the signature blue and yellow tent and the circus acrobatics and clowns that form much of the show's content are clearly circus, the show takes place on a stage without a ring and seating on three sides.

In constructing the physical dimensions of the show, the creative team draws heavily upon the

[4]Albrecht, p75.
[5]Albrecht, p77.
[6]Guy Caron in Albrecht, p77.

circus arts, featuring jugglers, trampolinists, trapeze artists, teeterboard virtuosos and, of course, clowns. Nevertheless, each act, even each movement, has a purpose within the show and contributes to the development of the thematic element. Because of this singularity of purpose, big name acts have no place in Cirque du Soleil. The presence of Gunther Gebel-Williams and 40 wild cats or a drum roll leading into a Gaona quadruple somersault would undercut the dreamlike development of the theme.

Performers in Cirque du Soleil, while very accomplished in their own right, play roles within the larger show. In part because of the outlandish costumes, but also because of the lack of a ringmaster announcing the acts and a program which buries the names of the individual performers in a cast list at the back, individual performers are in essence anonymous to the audience. This was not lost on the initial cast of Cirque du Soleil and many were dismayed to learn that Laliberté might not always include them in future productions.

A final striking detail of the Cirque du Soleil experience, which sets it apart from most traditional circuses, is the complete absence of performing animals. There are none. This is a dramatic departure for a medium that originated in a horse ring and has been synonymous with elephant shows and wild animal trainers. Leaving animal acts behind, Laliberté has created something new and different, not quite circus, but not quite anything else. Circus historian Fred Pfening notes, 'there's one question that always annoys me: "But is it circus?" That's utterly irrelevant. It is what the audience thinks it is. It is Soleil.'[7]

The business of Cirque du Soleil

Certainly, the initial vision that drove the founders of the various New American circuses were much more artistic than commercial. The family nature of both the Pickle Family Circus and the Big Apple Circus were much more reminiscent of a hippie commune than a typical start-up. Somewhat in contrast, Cirque du Soleil took little time to become immensely profitable after its success at the Los Angeles Arts Festival. Unlike the others, Soleil pursued the dual goals of artistry and profit, exemplified in the initial

agreement between Caron and Laliberté to lead these two components separately.

Over time, Soleil has come up with a lifecycle strategy that features an opening in Montreal followed by a North American tour, stretching over several years. The show then remains on tour for up to 4 more years, traveling first through Europe usually followed by a jaunt through Asia. Instead of traveling to audiences, three permanent shows tap into the continuous flow of potential viewers through such places as Las Vegas and Disney World. Mystere, La Nouba and 'O' have run in such permanent installations from the beginning, while Alegria, one of Soleil's older touring shows, has performed in the riverboat gambling casinos of Biloxi, Mississippi for what was to be a permanent engagement, only to begin touring anew two years later in the spring of 2001. Surprisingly, not since Nouvelle Experience has a Soleil show stopped touring.

Quidam is exemplary of the typical touring Cirque du Soleil show. The show was produced for approximately US$5.9 million and first staged in Montreal in April 1996. Following a three-year tour of North America, the show has traveled throughout Europe. Expected annual gross revenue at initiation of the tour was US$14.6 million, a number that has been exceeded year after year by a significant amount, according to Soleil staff.

Cirque du Soleil draws its revenue in significantly different fashion from the traditional circus and other shows which take place in civic arenas and sports stadiums. The show derives the great majority of revenues from ticket sales, though sponsor partners and concession sales contribute to the margins.

Soleil's focus on providing sophisticated entertainment enables a different approach to ticket pricing. Rather than a family event with free or discounted tickets for children or certain family members, Soleil seats are generally sold at full face value. 'Sure there are a couple of kids at a Soleil performance, but children make up a much smaller share of the audience. With the Ringling Brothers and Barnum & Bailey's circus (hereafter referred to as the Ringling Brothers & Co.) the audience is almost all families or kids.'[8] Reflecting the adult market for live entertainment, Soleil tickets are available at a substantially higher price, in keeping with a major theater or opera ticket. Tickets for

---

[7]Author's interview with circus historian Fred Pfening, May 15, 2001.
[8]Author's interview with circus historian Fred Pfening, May 15, 2001.

Dralion's 2001 New York engagement sold at US$65 to US$85. VIP packages including food offered in a separate pre-show gathering tent sell at up to US$230 per seat. Meanwhile, 'O' sported the most expensive seat for Vegas based productions after boosting the price to US$110 per seat in November 2000. It remains one of the hardest tickets to find. Its shows are also regularly sold out and boast the highest seat occupancy in the industry, consistently approaching 85–95%.

Soleil holds a traditionally large source of circus revenues, i.e., the concessions, at arm's length. Not surprisingly, less than 10% of revenues come from concessions at a Soleil show. In keeping with the performance-centered ethic of the troupe, nothing is sold during the performance or inside the tent. For the Ringling Brothers & Co. shows, this number may be dramatically higher, closer to 20%, as the sales effort is substantially stronger. The Ringling Brothers & Co. circus has hawkers who travel amongst the seated audience selling food and toys; concession stands are also packed tightly outside the performance space.

Sponsorships are a low-key but significant source of revenue for Soleil. Originally a key revenue earner from the days when the show operated as non-profit, many of the traveling shows have a primary sponsor, usually associated with the VIP tent. Lincoln Automobiles is the primary sponsor of Dralion, with 5 other corporations taking minor sponsorship roles entitling them to discreet mention in the playbill, advertising and banners around the tent.[9] For a typical 'shrine' circus or even a larger show such as the Big Apple Circus, a main sponsor guarantees a gate to the circus and sells the tickets independently. Sponsors in this vein are normally powerful local non-profit organizations who use the event as a major fundraising opportunity. They view it as a chance to associate themselves with the panache of Soleil and the upscale consumers attending the show. The arrangement is much more like a sponsor at a sporting event such as the Masters or the US Open.

Using its fantastic creative team and seeking to build on the brand the live shows have created, in recent years Soleil has somersaulted into film and other ventures. Beginning with videos of live performances and behind the scenes documentaries, the troupe graduated to film, creating *Journey of Man* in the IMAX format. Pieced together using performers from several of the different productions, the film creates a dreamlike vision of the trajectory of one man's life using the brushstrokes of Soleil's signature costuming and circus arts. Though the IMAX format limits the potential box office take – both the projection equipment and special dimension screens are extremely expensive and limited in numbers – longer term engagements at the science museums that often host these films enable Soleil to bridge the film barrier by adding a physical dimension of rides and interactive displays that would not be available at a normal cinema. At the Franklin Institute in Philadelphia, for instance, movie-goers willing to pay an additional US$2, can bicycle on a high-wire 10 meters above the heads of other patrons standing on the ticket line.[10]

Finale

One might think that in the performing arts and the circus, the need for innovation is obvious. Yet, even in such an innovation friendly environment, the circus industry had become stagnant, generating new acts by dressing up what already existed. Circus families and individual artists created highly developed and ever more challenging variants on the same formula of trained animals and 'death-defying' stunts that had been popular in the past century. Irving Feld was well known for pressing performers to add yet another somersault off the flying trapeze or add one more tiger to a simultaneous roll over act. Yet, added difficulty and danger faced by the performers was all but lost on the vast majority of the audience. This was novelty but not innovation, adding little value to the audience's experience, yet requiring significant expenditures by the circus company. By reinventing the circus industry, Cirque du Soleil created a phenomenon that has inspired and amazed millions of fans. In the process, it has generated revenues and an exciting line of shows that has attracted millions of people. This would have made P.T. Barnum blush (see Figures 1 and 2).

[9]Author's personal observation, May 30, 2001.
[10]Author's personal observation, May 5, 2001.

FIGURE 1 Major circus revenues

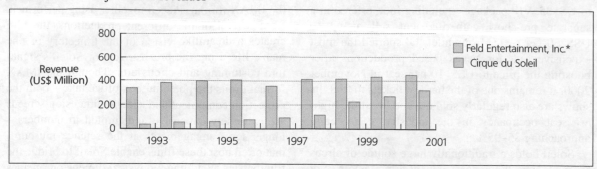

*Estimates based on the data of Hoovers Online. Note: RBB&B is a major division of Feld.

FIGURE 2 Cirque du Soleil attendance*

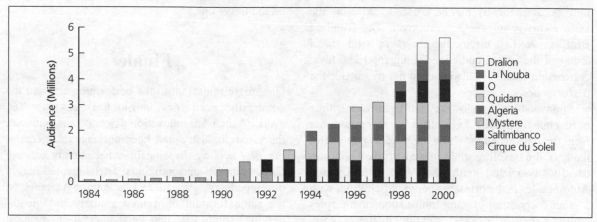

*Estimates based on available company information.

Nike's dispute with the University of Oregon

CASE 22

By *Rebecca J. Morris* and *Anne T. Lawrence*[1]

On April 24, 2000, Philip H. Knight, CEO of athletic shoe and apparel maker Nike Inc., publicly announced that he would no longer donate money to the University of Oregon (UO). It was a dramatic and unexpected move for the high-profile executive. A former UO track and field star, Knight had founded Nike's predecessor in 1963 with his former coach and mentor, Bill Bowerman. Over the years, Knight had maintained close ties with his alma mater, giving more than $50 million of his personal fortune to the school over a quarter century. In 2000, he was in active discussion with school officials about his biggest donation yet – millions for renovating the football stadium. But, suddenly, it was all called off. Said Knight in his statement: '[F]or me personally, there will be no further donations of any kind to the University of Oregon. At this time, this is not a situation that can be resolved. The bonds of trust, which allowed me to give at a high level, have been shredded.'

At issue was the University of Oregon's intention, announced April 14, 2000, to join the Worker Rights Consortium (WRC). Like many universities, UO was engaged in an internal debate over the ethical responsibilities associated with its role as a purchaser of goods manufactured overseas. Over a period of several months, UO administrators, faculty, and students had been discussing what steps they could take to ensure that products sold in the campus store, especially university-logo apparel, were not manufactured under sweatshop conditions. The University had considered joining two organizations, both of which purported to certify goods as 'no sweat.' The first, the Fair Labor Association (FLA), had grown out of President Clinton's Apparel Industry Partnership (AIP) initiative and was vigorously backed by Nike, as well as several other leading apparel makers. The second, the Workers Rights Consortium, was supported by student activists and several U.S.-based labor unions that had broken from the AIP after charging it did not go far enough to protect workers. Knight clearly felt that his alma mater had made the wrong choice. '[The] University [has] inserted itself into the new global economy where I make my living,' he charged. 'And inserted itself on the wrong side, fumbling a teachable moment.'

The dispute between Phil Knight and the University of Oregon captured much of the furor swirling about the issue of the role of multinational corporations in the global economy and the effects of the far-flung operations on their many thousands of workers, communities, and other stakeholders. In part because of its high-profile brand name, Nike had become a lightening rod for activists concerned about worker rights abroad. Like many U.S.-based shoe and apparel makers, Nike had located its manufacturing operations overseas, mainly in Southeast Asia, in search of low wages. Almost all production was carried out by subcontractors, rather than by Nike directly. Nike's employees in the United States, by contrast, directed their efforts to the high-end work of research and development, marketing, and retailing. In the context of this global division of

[1]Source: Reprinted by permission from the *Case Research Journal*, Volume 21, Issue 3. © 2001 by Anne T. Lawrence and Rebecca Morris and the North American Case Research Association. All rights reserved. Sources include articles appearing in the *New York Times*, *The Oregonian*, *Washington Post*, and other daily newspapers and material provided by Nike at its Web site www.nikebiz.com. Book sources include J. B. Strasser and L. Becklund, *Swoosh: The Unauthorized Story of Nike and the Men Who Played There* (New York: HarperCollins, 1993); D. R. Katz, *Just Do It: The Nike Spirit in the Corporate World* (Holbrook, Mass.: Adams Media Corporation, 1995); T. Vanderbilt, *The Sneaker Book* (New York: The New Press, 1998). Web sites for the Fair Labor Association and the Worker Rights Consortium may be found, respectively, at: www.fairlabor.org and www.workersrights.org. Ernst & Young's audit of Nike's subcontractor factories in Vietnam is available at: www.corpwatch.org/trac/nike/ernst. Coverage of Nike and the WRC decision in the University of Oregon student newspaper is available at: www.dailyemerald.com. A U.S. Department of Labor study of wages and benefits in the footwear industry in selected countries is available at: www.dol.gov/dol/ilab/public/media/reports/oiea/wagestudy. A full set of footnotes is available in the *Case Research Journal* version.

labor, what responsibility, if any, did Nike have to ensure adequate working conditions and living standards for the hundreds of thousands of workers, mostly young Asian women, who made its shoes and apparel? If this was not Nike's responsibility, then whose was it? Did organizations like the University of Oregon have any business pressuring companies through their purchasing practices? If so, how should they best do so? In short, what were the lessons of this 'teachable moment?'

Nike, Inc.

In 2000, Nike, Inc., was the leading designer and marketer of athletic footwear, apparel, and equipment in the world. Based in Beaverton, Oregon, the company's 'swoosh' logo, its 'Just Do It!' slogan and its spokespersons Michael Jordan, Mia Hamm, and Tiger Woods were universally recognized. Nike employed around 20,000 people directly, and *half a million* indirectly in 565 contract factories in 46 countries around the world. Wholly owned subsidiaries included Bauer Nike Hockey Inc. (hockey equipment), Cole Haan (dress and casual shoes), and Nike Team Sports (licensed team products). Revenues for the 12 months ending November 1999 were almost $9 billion, and the company enjoyed a 45 percent global market share. Knight owned 34 percent of the company's stock and was believed to be the sixth-richest individual in the United States.

Knight had launched this far-flung global empire shortly after completing his MBA degree at Stanford University in the early 1960s. Drawing on his first-hand knowledge of track and field, he decided to import low-priced track shoes from Japan in partnership with his former college coach. Bowerman would provide design ideas, test the shoes in competition, and endorse the shoes with other coaches; Knight would handle all financial and day-to-day operations of the business. Neither man had much money to offer, so for $500 a piece and a handshake, the company (then called Blue Ribbon Sports) was officially founded in 1963. The company took the name Nike in 1978; two years later, with revenues topping $269 million and 2,700 employees, Nike became a publicly traded company.

From the beginning, marketing had been a critical part of Knight's vision. The founder defined Nike as a 'marketing-oriented company.' During the 1980s and early 1990s, Nike aggressively sought out endorsements by celebrity athletes to increase brand awareness and foster consumer loyalty. Early Nike endorsers included Olympic gold medallist Carl Lewis, Wimbledon champion Andre Agassi, and six members of the 1992 Olympic basketball 'Dream Team.' Later endorsers included tennis aces Pete Sampras and Monica Seles, basketball great Michael Jordan, and golf superstar Tiger Woods.

An important element in Nike's success was its ability to develop cutting-edge products that met the needs of serious athletes, as well as set fashion trends. Research specialists in Nike's Sports Research Labs conducted extensive research and testing to develop new technologies to improve the performance of Nike shoes in a variety of sports. For example, research specialists studied the causes of ankle injuries in basketball players to develop shoes that would physically prevent injuries, as well as signal information to the user to help him or her resist turning the ankle while in the air. Other specialists developed polymer materials that would make the shoes lighter, more aerodynamic, or more resistant to the abrasions incurred during normal athletic use. Findings from the Sports Research Labs were then passed on to design teams that developed the look and styling of the shoes.

Although it was the leading athletic footwear company in the world, Nike never manufactured shoes in any significant number. Rather, from its inception, the company had outsourced production to subcontractors in Asia, with the company shifting production locations within the region when prevailing wage rates became too high. In the early years, it had imported shoes form Japan. It later shifted production to South Korea and Taiwan, then to Indonesia and Thailand, and later yet to Vietnam and China.

The reasons for locating shoe production mainly in Southeast Asia were several, but the most important was the cost of labor. Modern athletic shoes were composed of mesh, leather, and nylon uppers that were hand-assembled, sewn and glued to composite soles. Mechanization had not been considered effective for shoe manufacturing due to the fragile materials used and the short life spans of styles of athletic shoes. Therefore, shoe production was highly labor-intensive. Developing countries, primarily in Southeast Asia, offered the distinct advantage of considerably lower wage rates. For example, in the early 1990s, when Nike shifted much of its shoe production to Indonesia, daily wages there hovered around $1 a day (compared to wages in the U.S. shoe industry at that time of around $8 an hour).

Along with lower labor costs, Asia provided the additional advantage of access to raw material suppliers. Very few rubber firms in the United States, for example, produced the sophisticated composite soles demanded in modern athletic shoe designs. Satellite industries necessary for modern shoe production, plentiful in Asia, included tanneries, textiles, and plastic and ironwork moldings. A final factor in determining where to locate production was differential tariff rates. In general, canvas sneakers were assessed higher tariffs than leather molded footwear, such as basketball or running shoes. As a result, shoe companies had an incentive to outsource high-tech athletic shoes overseas, because tariffs on them were relatively low.

Many of Nike's factories in Asia were operated by a small number of Taiwanese and South Korea firms that specialized in shoe manufacturing, many owned by some of the wealthiest families in the region. When Nike moved from one location to another, often these companies followed, bringing their managerial expertise with them.

Nike's subcontractor factories

In 2000, Nike contracted with over 500 different footwear and apparel factories around the world to produce its shoes and apparel. Although there was no such thing as a typical Nike plant, a factory operated by the South Korean subcontractor Tae Kwang Vina (TKV) in the Bien Hoa City industrial zone near Ho Chi Minh City in Vietnam provided a glimpse into the setting in which many Nike shoes were made.

TKV employed approximately 10,000 workers in Bien Hoa City factory. The workforce consisted of 200 clerical workers, 355 supervisors, and 9,465 production workers, all making athletic shoes for Nike. Ninety percent of the workers were women between the ages of 18 to 24. Production workers were employed in one of three major areas within the factory: the chemical, stitching, and assembly sections. Production levels at the Bien Hoa City factory reached 400,000 pairs of shoes per month; Nike shoes made at this and other factories made up fully 5 percent of Vietnam's total exports.

Workers in the chemical division were responsible for producing the high-technology outsoles. Production steps involved stretching and flattening huge blobs of raw rubber on heavy duty rollers and baking chemical compounds in steel molds to form the innovative three-dimensional outsoles. The chemical composition of the soles changed constantly in response to the cutting-edge formulations developed by the U.S. design teams, requiring frequent changes in the production process. The smell of complex polymers, the hot ovens, and the clanging of the steel molds resulted in a work environment that was loud and hot and had high concentrations of chemical fumes. Chemicals used in the section were known to cause eye, skin, and throat irritations; damage to liver and kidneys; nausea; anorexia; and reproductive health hazards through inhalation or in some cases through absorption through the skin. Workers in the chemical section were thought to have high rates of respiratory illnesses, although records kept at the TKV operations did not permit the tracking of illnesses by factory section. Workers in the chemical section were issued gloves and surgical-style masks. However, they often discarded the protective gear, complaining that it was too hot and humid to wear them in the plant.

In the stitching section, row after row of sewing machines operated by young women hummed and clattered in a space the size of three football fields. One thousand stitchers worked on a single floor of the TKV factory, sewing together nylon, leather, and other fabrics to make the uppers. Other floors of the factory were filled with thousands of additional sewing machines producing different shoe models. The stitching job required precision and speed. Workers who did not meet the aggressive production goals did not receive a bonus. Failing to meet production goals three times resulted in the worker's dismissal. Workers were sometimes permitted to work additional hours without pay to meet production quotas. Supervisors were strict, chastising workers for excessive talking or spending too much time in the restrooms. Korean supervisors, often hampered by language and cultural barriers, sometimes resorted to hard-nose management tactics, hitting or slapping slower workers. Other workers in need of discipline were forced to stand outside the factory for long periods in the tropical sun. The Vietnamese term for this practice was *phoi nang*, or sun-drying.

In the assembly section, women worked side by side along a moving line to join the uppers to the outersoles through the rapid manipulation of sharp knives, skivers, routers, and glue-coated brushes. Women were thought to be better suited for the assembly jobs because their hands were smaller and more capable of the manual dexterity needed to fit the shoe components together precisely. During the assembly process, some 120 pairs of hands touched a single shoe. A strong, sweet solvent smell was prominent in the assembly area. Ceiling-mounted ventilation fans were ineffective since the heavy fumes settled to the floor. Assembly workers wore cotton surgical masks to protect themselves from the fumes; however, many workers pulled the masks below their noses, saying they were more comfortable that way. Rows and rows of shoes passed along a conveyor before the sharp eyes of the quality control inspectors. The inspectors examined each of the thousands of shoes produced daily for poor stitching or crooked connections between soles. Defective shoes were discarded. Approved shoes continued on the conveyor to stations where they were laced by assembly workers and finally put into Nike shoeboxes for shipment to the United States.

Despite the dirty, dangerous, and difficult nature of the work inside the Bien Hoa factory, there was no shortage of applicants for positions. Although entry level wages averaged only $1.50 per day (the lowest of all countries where Nike manufactured), many other workers viewed factory jobs as better than their other options, such as working in the rice paddies or pedaling a pedicab along the streets of Ho Chi Minh City (formerly Saigon). With overtime pay at one and a half times the regular rate, workers could double their salaries – generating enough income to purchase a motorscooter or to send money home to impoverished rural relatives. These wages were well above national norms. An independent study by researchers from Dartmouth University showed that the average annual income for workers at two Nike subcontract factories in Vietnam was between $545 and $566, compared to the national average of between $250 and $300. Additionally, workers were provided free room and board and access to on-site health care facilities. Many Vietnamese workers viewed positions in the shoe factory as transitional jobs – a way to earn money for a dowry or to experience living in a larger city. Many returned to their homes after working for Nike for two or three years to marry and begin the next phase of their lives.

The campaigns against Nike

In the early 1990s, criticism of Nike's global labor practices began to gather steam. *Harper's Magazine*, for example, published the pay stub of an Indonesian worker, showing that the Nike subcontractor had paid the woman just under 14 cents per hour, and contrasted this with the high retail price of the shoes

and high salaries paid to the company's celebrity endorsers. The Made in the U.S.A. Foundation, a group backed by American unions, used a million dollar ad budget to urge consumers to send their 'old, dirty, smelly, worn-out Nikes' to Phil Knight in protest of Nike's Asian manufacturing practices. Human rights groups and Christian organizations joined the labor unions in targeting the labor practices of the athletic shoes firm. Many felt that Nike's anti-authority corporate image ('Just Do It!') and message of social betterment through fitness were incompatible with press photos of slight Asian women hunched over sewing machines 70 hours a week, earning just pennies an hour.

By mid-1993, Nike was being regularly pilloried in the press as an imperialist profiteer. A CBS news segment airing on July 2, 1993, opened with images of Michael Jordan and Andre Agassi, two athletes who had multi-million-dollar promotion contracts with Nike. Viewers were told to contrast the athletes' pay checks with those of the Chinese and Indonesian workers who made 'pennies' so that Nike could 'Just Do It.'

In 1995, the *Washington Post* reported that a pair of Nike Air Pegasus shoes that retailed for $70 cost Nike only $2.75 in labor costs, or 4 percent of the price paid by consumers. Nike's operating profit on the same pair of shoes was $6.25, while the retailer pocketed $9.00 in operating profits. Also that year, shareholder activists organized by the Interfaith Center on Corporate Responsibility submitted a shareholder proposal at Nike's annual meeting, calling on the company to review labor practices by its subcontractors; the proposal gathered 3 percent of the shareholder vote.

A story in *Life* magazine documented the use of child labor in Pakistan to produce soccer balls for Nike, Adidas, and other companies. The publicity fallout was intense. The public could not ignore the photographs of small children sitting in the dirt, carefully stitching together the panels of a soccer ball that would become the plaything of some American child the same age. Nike moved quickly to work with its Pakistani subcontractor to eliminate the use of child labor, but damage to Nike's image had been done.

In October 1996, CBS News *48 Hours* broadcast a scathing report on Nike's factories in Vietnam. CBS reporter Roberta Baskin focused on low wage rates, extensive overtime, and physical abuse of workers. Several young workers told Baskin how a Korean supervisor had beaten them with a part of a shoe because of problems with production. A journalist in Vietnam told the reporter that the phrase 'to Nike someone' was part of the Vietnamese vernacular. It meant to 'take out one's frustration on a fellow worker.' Vietnamese plant managers refused to be interviewed, covering their faces as they ran inside the factory. CBS news anchor Dan Rather concluded the damaging report by saying, 'Nike now says it plans to hire outside observers to talk to employees and examine working conditions in its Vietnam factories, but the company just won't say when that might happen.'

The negative publicity was having an effect. In 1996, a marketing research study authorized by Nike reported the perceptions of young people aged 13 to 25 of Nike as a company. The top three perceptions, in the order of their response frequency, were athletics, cool, and bad labor practices. Although Nike maintained that its sales were never affected, company executives were clearly concerned about the effect of criticism of its global labor practices on the reputation of the brand they had worked so hard to build.

The evolution of Nike's global labor practices

In its early years, Nike had maintained that the labor practices of its foreign subcontractors, like TKV, were simply not its responsibility. 'When we started Nike,' Knight later commented, '. . . it never occurred to us that we should dictate what their factor[ies] should look like.' The subcontractors, not Nike, were responsible for wages and working conditions. Dave Taylor, Nike's vice president of production, explained the company's position: 'We don't pay anybody at the factories and we don't set policy within the factories; it is their business to run.'

When negative articles first began appearing in the early 1990s, however, Nike managers realized that they needed to take some action to avoid further bad publicity. In 1992, the company drafted its first Code of Conduct, which required every subcontractor and supplier in the Nike network to honor all applicable local government labor and environmental regulations, or Nike would terminate the relationship. The subcontractors were also required to allow plant inspectors and complete all necessary paperwork. Despite the compliance reports the factories filed every six months, Nike insiders acknowledged that the code of conduct system might not catch all

violations. Tony Nava, Nike's country coordinator for Indonesia, told a *Chicago Tribune* reporter, 'We can't know if they're actually complying with what they put down on paper.'

In 1994, Nike tried to address this problem by hiring Ernst & Young, the accounting firm, to independently monitor worker abuse allegations in Nike's Indonesian factories. Later, Ernst & Young also audited Nike's factories in Thailand and Vietnam. A copy of the Vietnam audit leaked to the press showed that workers were often unaware of the toxicity of the compounds they were using and ignorant of the need for safety precautions. In 1998, Nike implemented important changes in its Vietnamese plants to reduce exposure to toxics, substituting less harmful chemicals, installing ventilation systems, and training personnel in occupational health and safety issues.

In 1996, Nike established a new Labor Practices Department, headed by Dusty Kidd, formerly a public relations executive for the company. Later that year, Nike hired GoodWorks International, headed by former U.S. ambassador to the United Nations Andrew Young, to investigate conditions in its overseas factories. In January 1997, GoodWorks issued a glossy report, stating that 'Nike is doing a good job in the application of its Code of Conduct. But Nike can and should do better.' The report was criticized by activists for its failure to look at the issue of wages. Young demurred, saying he did not have expertise in conducting wage surveys. Said one critic, 'This was a pubic relations problem, and the world's largest sneaker company did what it does best: it purchased a celebrity endorsement.'

Over the next few years, Nike continued to work to improve labor practices in its overseas subcontractor factories, as well as the public perception of them. In January 1998, Nike formed a Corporate Responsibility Division under the leadership of former Microsoft executive Maria S. Eitel. Nike subsequently doubled the staff of this division. In May of that year, Knight gave a speech at the National Press Club, at which he announced several new initiatives. At that time, he committed Nike to raise the minimum age for employment in its shoe factories to 18 and in its apparel factories to 16. He also promised to achieve OSHA standards for indoor air quality in all its factories by the end of the year, mainly by eliminating the use of the solvent toluene; to expand educational programs for workers and in its microenterprise loan program; and to fund university research on responsible business practices. Nike also continued its use of external monitors, hiring PricewaterhouseCoopers to join Ernst & Young in a comprehensive program of factory audits, checking them against Nike's code.

Apparel Industry Partnership

One of Nike's most ambitious social responsibility initiatives was its participation in the Apparel Industry Partnership. It was this involvement that would lead, eventually, to Knight's break with the University of Oregon.

In August 1996, President Clinton launched the White House Apparel Industry Partnership on Workplace Standards (AIP). The initial group was comprised of 18 organizations. Participants included several leading manufacturers, such as Nike, Reebok, and Liz Claiborne. Also in the group were several labor unions, including the Union of Needletrades, Industrial, and Textile Employees (UNITE) and the Retail, Wholesale and Department Store Union; and several human rights, consumer, and shareholder organizations, including Business for Social Responsibility, the Interfaith Center on Corporate Responsibility, and the National Consumer League. The goal of the AIP was to develop a set of standards to ensure that apparel and footwear were not made under sweatshop conditions. For companies, it held out the promise of certifying to their customers that their products were 'no sweat.' For labor and human rights groups, it held out the promise of improving working conditions in overseas factories.

In April 1997, after months of often-fractious meetings, the AIP announced that it had agreed on a Workplace Code of Conduct that sought to define decent and humane working conditions. Companies agreeing to the Code would have to pledge not to use forced labor, that is, prisoners or bonded or indentured workers. They could not required more than 60 hours of work a week, including overtime. They could not employ children younger than 15 years old or the age for completing compulsory schooling, whichever was older – except they could hire 14-year-olds if local law allowed. The code also called on signatory companies to treat all workers with respect and dignity; to refrain from discrimination on the basis of gender, race, religion, age, disability, sexual orientation, nationality, political opinion, or social or ethnic origin; and to provide a safe and healthy workplace. Employees'

rights to organize and bargain collectively would be respected. In a key provision, the Code also required companies to pay at least the local legal minimum wage or the prevailing industry wage, whichever was higher. All standards would apply not only to a company's own facilities but also to their subcontractors or suppliers.

Knight, who prominently joined President Clinton and others at a White House ceremony announcing the code, issued the following statement:

Nike agreed to participate in this Partnership because it was the first credible attempt, by a diverse group of interests, to address the important issue of improving factories worldwide. It was worth the effort and hard work. The agreement will prove important for several reasons. Not only is our industry stepping up to the plate and taking a giant swing at improving factory conditions, but equally important, we are finally providing consumers some guidance to counter all of the misinformation that has surrounded this issue for far too long.

The Fair Labor Association

But this was not the end of the AIP's work; it also had to agree on a process for monitoring compliance with the Code. Although the group hoped to complete its work in six months, over a year later it was still deeply divided on several key matters. Internal documents leaked to the *New York Times* in July 1998 showed that industry representatives had opposed proposals, circulated by labor and human rights members, calling for the monitoring of 30 percent of plants annually by independent auditors. The companies also opposed proposals that would require them to support workers' rights to organize independent unions and to bargain collectively, even in countries like China where workers did not have such rights by law. Said one nonindustry member, 'We're teetering on the edge of collapse.'

Finally, a subgroup of nine centrist participants, including Nike, began meeting separately in an attempt to move forward. In November 1998, this subgroup announced that it had come to agreement on a monitoring system for overseas factories of U.S.-based companies. The AIP would establish a new organization, the Fair Labor Association (FLA), to oversee compliance with its Workplace Code of

Conduct. Companies would be required to monitor their own factories, and those of their subcontractors, for compliance; all would have to be checked within the first two years. In addition, the FLA would select and certify independent external monitors, who would inspect 10 percent of each firm's factories each year. Most of these monitors were expected to be accounting firms, which had expertise in conducting audits. The monitors' reports would be kept private. If a company were found to be out of compliance, it would be given a chance to correct the problem. Eventually, if it did not, the company would be dropped from the FLA and its termination announced to the public. Companies would pay for most of their own monitoring. The Clinton administration quickly endorsed the plan.

Both manufacturers and institutional buyers stood to benefit from participation in the Fair Labor Association. Companies, once certified for three years, could place an FLA service mark on their brands, signaling both to individual consumers and institutional buyers that their products were 'sweatshop-free.' It was expected that the FLA would also serve the needs of institutional buyers, particularly universities. By joining the FLA and agreeing to contract only with certified companies, universities could warrant to their student and others that their logo apparel and athletic gear were manufactured under conditions conforming with an established code of fair labor standards. Both parties would pay for these benefits. The FLA was to be funded by dues from participating companies ($5,000 to $100,000 annually, depending on revenue) and by payments from affiliated colleges and universities (based on 1 percent of their licensing income from logo products, up to a $50,000 annual cap).

Although many welcomed the agreement – and some new companies signed on with the FLA soon after it was announced – others did not. Warnaco, a leading apparel maker that had participated in the Partnership, quit, saying that the monitoring process would require it to turn over competitive information to outsiders. The American Apparel Manufacturing Association (AAMA), an industry group representing 350 companies, scoffed at the whole idea of monitoring. 'Who is going to do the monitoring?' asked a spokesperson for the AAMA, apparently sarcastically. 'Accountants or Jesuit priests?' Others argued that companies simply could not be relied upon to monitor themselves objectively. Said Jay Mazur, president of UNITE, 'The fox cannot watch the chickens . . . if they want the monitoring to be independent, it can't be controlled by the companies.' A visit from an external monitor once ever 10 years would not prevent abuses. And in any case, as a practical matter, most monitors would be drawn from the major accounting firms that did business with the companies they were monitoring and were therefore unlikely to seek out lapses. Companies would not be required to publish a list of their factories, and any problems uncovered by the monitoring process would be kept from the public under the rules governing nondisclosure of proprietary information.

One of the issues most troubling to critics was the code's position on wages. The code called on companies to pay the minimum wage or prevailing wage, whichever was higher. But in many of the countries of Southeast Asia, these wages fell well below the minimum considered necessary for a decent standard of living for an individual or family. For example, the *Economist* reported that Indonesia's average minimum wage, paid by Nike subcontractors, was only two-thirds of what a person needed for basic subsistence. An alternative view was that a code of conduct should require that companies pay a *living wage*, that is, compensation for a normal workweek adequate to provide for the basic needs of an average family, adjusted for the average number of adult wage earners per family. One problem with this approach, however, was that many countries did not systematically study the cost of living, relative to wages, so defining a living wage was difficult. The Partnership asked the U.S. Department of Labor to conduct a preliminary study of these issues; the results were published in 2000.

The code also called on companies to respect workers' rights to organize and bargain collectively. Yet a number of FLA companies outsourced production to nondemocractic countries, such as China and Vietnam, where workers had no such rights. Finally, some criticized the agreement on the grounds it provided companies, as one put it, 'a piece of paper to use as a fig leaf.' Commented a representative of the needle trades unions, 'The problem with the partnership plan is that it tinkers at the margins of the sweatshop system but creates the impression that it is doing much more. This is potentially helpful to companies stung by public condemnation of their labor practices, but it hurts millions of workers and undermines the growing antisweatshop movement.'

The Worker Rights Consortium

Some activists in the antisweatshop movement decided to chart their own course, independent of the FLA. On October 20, 1999, students from more than 100 colleges held a press conference to announce formation of the Workers Rights Consortium (WRC) and called on their schools to withdraw from or not to join the FLA. The organization would be formally launched at a founding convention in April 2000.

The Worker Rights Consortium differed radically in its approach to eliminating sweatshops. First, the WRC did not permit corporations to join; it was comprised exclusively of universities and colleges, with unions and human rights organizations playing an advisory role. In joining the WRC, universities would agree to 'require decent working conditions in factories producing their licensed products.' Unlike the FLA, the WRC did not endorse a single, comprehensive set of fair labor standards. Rather, it called on its affiliated universities to develop their own codes. However, it did establish minimum standards that such codes should meet – ones that were, in some respects, stricter than the FLA's. Perhaps most significantly, companies would have to pay a living wage. Companies were also required to publish the names and addresses of all of their manufacturing facilities, in contrast to FLA rules. Universities could refuse to license goods made in countries where compliance with fair labor standards was 'deemed impossible,' whatever efforts companies had made to enforce their own codes in factories there.

By contrast with the FLA, monitoring would be carried out by 'a network of local organizations in regions where licensed goods are produced,' generally non-governmental organizations, independent human rights groups, and unions. These organizations would conduct unannounced 'spot investigations,' usually in response to worker complaints; WRC organizers called this the 'fire alarm' method of uncovering code violations. Systematic monitoring would not be attempted. The consortium's governance structure reflected its mission of being an organization by and for colleges and universities; its 12-person board was composed of students, university administrators and human rights experts, with no seats for industry representatives. The group would be financed by 1 percent of licensing revenue from participating universities, as well as foundation grants.

Over the course of the spring semester 2000, student protests were held on a number of campuses, including the University of Oregon, to demand that their schools join the WRC. By April, around 45 schools had done so. At UO, the administration encouraged an open debate on the issue so that all sides could be heard on how to ensure that UO products were made under humane conditions. Over a period of several months, the Academic Senate, the student body, and a committee of faculty, students, administrators, and alumni appointed by the president all voted to join the Consortium. Finally, after concluding that all constituents had had an opportunity to be heard, on April 12, 2000, University of Oregon President David Frohnmayer announced that UO would join the WRC for one year. Its membership would be conditional, he said, on the consortium's agreement to give companies a voice in its operations and universities more power in governance. Shortly after the University's decision was announced in the press, Phil Knight withdrew his philanthropic contribution. In his public announcement, he stated this main disagreements with the Workers Rights Consortium:

Frankly, we are frustrated that factory monitoring is badly misconstructed. For us one of the great hurdles and real handicaps in the dialogue has been the complexity of the issue. For real progress to be made, all key participants have to be at the table. That's why the FLA has taken so long to get going. The WRC is supported by the AFL-CIO and its affiliated apparel workers' union, UNITE. Their main aim, logically and understandably, however misguided, is to bring apparel jobs back to the U.S. Among WRC rules, no company can participate in setting standards, or monitoring. It has an unrealistic living wage provision. And its 'gotcha' approach to monitoring doesn't do what monitoring should – measure conditions and make improvements.

INDEX

bs
11.1.07

DEVELOPING MANAGEMENT SKILLS

SEVENTH EDITION

David A. Whetten
BRIGHAM YOUNG UNIVERSITY

Kim S. Cameron
UNIVERSITY OF MICHIGAN

Prentice
Hall

Upper Saddle River, NJ 07458

Library of Congress Cataloging-in-Publication Data

Whetten, David A. (David Allred)
   Developing management skills / David A. Whetten, Kim S. Cameron. —7th ed.
      p. cm.
   Includes bibliographical references and index.
   ISBN-13: 978-0-13-174742-5
      1. Management—Study and teaching.   2. Management—Problems, exercises, etc.
I. Cameron, Kim S.   II. Title.
HD30.4.W46 2007
658.40071'173—dc22

2006025223

Senior Acquisitions Editor: David Parker
VP/Editorial Director: Jeff Shelstad
Product Development Manager:
Ashley Santora
Marketing Manager: Anne Howard
Marketing Assistant: Susan Osterlitz
Associate Director, Production Editorial:
Judy Leale
Managing Editor: Renata Butera
Production Editor: Marcela Boos
Permissions Coordinator: Charles Morris
Associate Director, Manufacturing:
Vinnie Scelta
Manufacturing Buyer: Michelle Klein

Manager, Creative Services:
Christy Mahon
Composition Liaison: Suzanne Duda
Interior Design: Suzanne Duda and
Michael J. Fruhbeis
Cover Design: Suzanne Duda
Cover Illustration: Jim Frazier
Composition: TexTech
Full-Service Project Management:
Stratford Publishing Services
Printer/Binder: Von Hoffmann Press
Cover Printer: Phoenix Color Corp.
Typeface: 10/12 Weidemann-Book

Pearson Education LTD.
Pearson Education Singapore, Pte. Ltd.
Pearson Education Canada, Ltd.
Pearson Education–Japan

Pearson Education Australia PTY, Limited.
Pearson Education North Asia, Ltd.
Pearson Educación de Mexico, S.A. de C.V.
Pearson Education Malaysia, Pte. Ltd.

10 9 8 7 6 5 4 3 2 1
ISBN: 0-13-174742-8